CAMBRIDGE STUDIES IN LAW AND SOCIETY

Founded in 1997, Cambridge Studies in Law and Society is a hub for leading scholarship in socio-legal studies. Located at the intersection of law, the humanities, and the social sciences, it publishes empirically innovative and theoretically sophisticated work on law's manifestations in everyday life: from discourses to practices, and from institutions to cultures. The series editors have longstanding expertise in the interdisciplinary study of law, and welcome contributions that place legal phenomena in national, comparative, or international perspective. Series authors come from a range of disciplines, including anthropology, history, law, literature, political science, and sociology.

Series Editors

Mark Fathi Massoud, *University of California, Santa Cruz*
Jens Meierhenrich, *London School of Economics and Political Science*
Rachel E. Stern, *University of California, Berkeley*

A list of books in the series can be found at the back of this book.

LAW'S WARS

The Fate of the Rule of Law in the US "War on Terror"

Richard L. Abel
UCLA

CAMBRIDGE
UNIVERSITY PRESS

CAMBRIDGE
UNIVERSITY PRESS

University Printing House, Cambridge CB2 8BS, United Kingdom

One Liberty Plaza, 20th Floor, New York, NY 10006, USA

477 Williamstown Road, Port Melbourne, VIC 3207, Australia

314–321, 3rd Floor, Plot 3, Splendor Forum, Jasola District Centre, New Delhi – 110025, India

79 Anson Road, #06-04/06, Singapore 079906

Cambridge University Press is part of the University of Cambridge.

It furthers the University's mission by disseminating knowledge in the pursuit of education, learning, and research at the highest international levels of excellence.

www.cambridge.org
Information on this title: www.cambridge.org/9781108429818
DOI: 10.1017/9781108555302

First published 2018

Printed in the United States of America by Sheridan Books, Inc.

A catalogue record for this publication is available from the British Library.

Library of Congress Cataloging-in-Publication Data
Names: Abel, Richard L., author.
Title: Law's wars : the fate of the rule of law in the US "War on Terror" / Richard L. Abel.
Description: Cambridge [UK]; New York, NY: Cambridge University Press, 2018. | Series: Cambridge studies in law and society | Includes bibliographical references and index.
Identifiers: LCCN 2018007065 | ISBN 9781108429818 (hardback)
Subjects: LCSH: Rule of law – United States. | Terrorism – Prevention – Law and legislation – United States. | War on Terrorism, 2001–2009.
Classification: LCC KF382.A75 2018 | DDC 340/.11–dc23
LC record available at https://lccn.loc.gov/2018007065

ISBN 978-1-108-42981-8 Hardback

CONTENTS

TABLES

FOREWORD

The terrorist attacks of September 11, 2001, left a long trail. Some insisted that the world changed that day. The terrorists showed that a small group of individuals could – and would – inflict unthinkable damage on innocent civilians for political ends. They raised security fears in the United States and elsewhere, and ushered in what President George W. Bush labeled the "war on terror." That "war" (really a series of discrete, ever-morphing armed conflicts) in turn led to the loss of countless lives, as the United States in particular invested massive resources into surveilling, tracking down, detaining, and killing the ever-shifting "enemy." The "war on terror" also placed tremendous stress on some of the nation's – and the world's – most fundamental values, including the rule of law itself. The United States took to abducting suspects all over the world, detaining them in secret prisons, subjecting them to unconscionable and illegal treatment, and delivering them to third parties that US officials knew would torture them. That's the bad news. The good news is that significant voices reacted, stood up for basic human rights, and resisted the assault on the rule of law. They included line officers in the military, federal officials willing to say no, human rights organizations and journalists who brought the abuses to light, and lawyers who sought to hold the United States in check through litigation and public advocacy. The story is a complicated one, richly deserving careful and nuanced study. And that's precisely what Richard Abel has provided in this volume. Law is most tested when we have the most to fear. In the pages that follow, readers can assess how law measured up to that test.

David Cole[+]

[+] National Legal Director, ACLU, and author of *Engines of Liberty: How Citizen Movements Succeed* and *Enemy Aliens: Double Standards and Constitutional Rights in the War on Terror.*

FOREWORD

On January 11, 2009, Barack Obama was asked by *This Week* host George Stephanopoulos whether he would, as president, appoint a special prosecutor to "independently investigate the gravest crimes of the Bush Administration, including torture and warrantless wiretapping." The question came at a pivotal moment in the post-9/11 period. It was the last nine days of George W. Bush's presidency, the eighth anniversary of the day Bush sent the first 20 men to the prison at Guantánamo and 12 days before Obama would sign an executive order to close it. Obama's response was that "we need to look forward as opposed to looking backwards," implying that the focus of his administration would not include the question of investigation of and accountability for Bush administration crimes. With respect to the CIA, Obama told Stephanopoulos that he didn't want the Agency "to suddenly feel that they've got to spend their time looking over their shoulders and lawyering up." He concluded by saying that his "general belief is that when it comes to national security, what we have to focus on is getting things right in the future as opposed to what we got wrong in the past."

Obama's response to the question likely generated as much of a sigh of relief for Bush officials as it did a groan of resignation for human rights groups pushing for accountability, like my own – the Center for Constitutional Rights. But beyond that, it raised the question of how a society responds when the rule of law is applied through a political lens that seeks to carve out a series of bold exceptions to firmly accepted, internationally agreed-upon norms such as the prohibition of indefinite detention, war crimes, and torture. *Law's Wars* takes this question head on from a unique vantage point that examines the vital signs of the rule of law as it was exposed to the scourge of terrorism – and the steroidal responses to it – over the 16 years of the Bush and Obama administrations. The book provides a critical examination of a full array of unfolding events and how the various branches of government, the media, and civil society grappled with the question of whether the rule of law is, in the end, a dangerously limiting principle in the current era (as the government continues to contend) or a generative one from which we define our national ethos in the future.

Law's Wars approaches with great dexterity what President Obama declined to in January 2009. It looks backward at the complex set of narratives, rules, decisions, and policies that shape the current landscape of the USA's national security policy. It is an important contribution to the dialogue, especially for those of us who care about or have worked tirelessly to defend the rule of law during those years. The Center for Constitutional Rights had prominent roles in litigating the very issues examined in *Law's Wars*, being the first group to challenge in court detentions at Guantánamo and a leader in litigating to end torture, secret CIA black sites, abuses at Abu Ghraib, unlawful use of drones and warrantless surveillance. Most of that litigation continues today. *Law's Wars* stands not only as an in-depth chronicle of the important work we did at the time, but also as a compelling vista of the many legal trenches in which many NGOs were doing battle – a perspective that is otherwise impossible to see without Professor Abel's keen eye to guide us as we recount how we got to this point.

When it comes to the rule of law, looking forward is often the province of politicians, while looking back is the province of prosecutors and human rights lawyers. But *Law's Wars* also helps us look forward in ways that we couldn't at the midpoint in 2009. This work sheds as much light on how the Obama presidency would ultimately deal with accountability for lawlessness in the Bush years as it does on much of the polity's lack of appetite for engaging deeply in the serious moral and legal questions raised by both administrations' actions.

In May 2009 I met with President Obama and his advisers at the White House at a high-level human rights meeting that had only two topics on its agenda: the closing of Guantánamo Bay Prison and whether or not to release the second set of pictures taken at the infamous Abu Ghraib hard site prison in Afghanistan. President Obama pointed out of the Cabinet Room window, in the direction of Congress, and said that he had to be accountable to members of that body, who by then had mounted a comprehensive effort to block his efforts to close Guantánamo. It was how our democracy works, he said. And he was right. However, the very next day in a speech in which he stood in front of the US Constitution, Obama rolled out a new policy categorization for detainees at Guantánamo that essentially locked in Bush's indefinite detention regime for the next eight years. So, while it is true that no president should ever be above the law, the May meeting and subsequent speech raised questions of what civil society – particularly human rights organizations – should do in a legal system that must address one administration that clearly situates itself as above the law, and a subsequent one that is perhaps positioned differently, but nonetheless swims in a sea of legally sanctioned lawlessness. Many good answers to those questions are found in the pages of *Law's Wars*.

Vincent Warren[+]

[+] Executive Director, Center for Constitutional Rights.

PREFACE

On Sunday morning, May 2, 2004, I drove home to Santa Monica from hiking in the Grand Canyon. It's eight hours, mostly a straight shot on I-10 through the desert. That can be tedious, but I had NPR's "Weekend Edition" for company. It featured Seymour Hersh's exposé of Gen. Antonio Taguba's devastating report on Abu Ghraib. The story riveted millions in the USA and abroad. However, I had a personal interest for two reasons. First, Sy is my brother-in-law. I vividly remembered how, 35 years earlier, he had broken the news about Lt. William Calley's role in the My Lai massacre – reporting that contributed to ending the Vietnam War. Second, between 1989 and 1991 I studied the role of South African law and lawyers in the struggle against apartheid for my 1995 book *Politics by Other Means*. Abu Ghraib seemed to present a threat to the rule of law similar in magnitude to those I had studied in South Africa. I knew I had to explore the fate of the rule of law during the "war on terror," which the USA unleashed in response to the 9/11 attacks. I have spent the last 13 years doing so. (I use scare quotes because I agree with many others that one cannot wage a war against a noun.)

In the more than two centuries since the USA was founded, the rule of law has been tested and compromised in numerous ways: the oppression of Native Americans, slavery, Jim Crow, labor struggles, the treatment of German Americans in World War I, Japanese Americans in World War II, and radicals after both wars, the civil rights movement, protests against the Vietnam War, and more recently the distortion of the electoral process by money, gerrymandering, and disenfranchisement, and police responses to the Occupy movement and killings of young black men documented by Black Lives Matter. The "war on terror" has posed at least as great a danger.

I fully acknowledge that the "war on terror" has inflicted harms far more grievous than those suffered by the rule of law. It has killed hundreds of thousands and wounded many more, displaced millions of refugees, and caused untold amounts of property damage. The USA has squandered more than a trillion dollars on a "war" that cannot be won.

It has destabilized entire nations so severely that, like Humpty Dumpty, they may never recover: Afghanistan, Iraq, Syria, Yemen, Somalia, Libya. Iran has greatly increased its influence in Iraq, Syria, and Yemen. The "war on terror" spawned ISIS, which continues to export terrorists throughout the world and inspire imitators.

Nevertheless, I have focused on the rule of law for several reasons. It is an indispensable foundation of liberal democracy. It enjoys support (or at least elicits lip service) across the political spectrum, unlike geopolitics, which is fiercely debated. And it is what I know as a law professor. In Chapter 1, I offer a definition of the rule of law (one that would garner a broad consensus), explain why it is essential, and draw on studies of its fate at other times and places to construct the research questions I seek to answer.

For many reasons, I expected the rule of law to prove more resilient in the USA than it had in South Africa. The USA has had a written constitution and judicial review of legislative and executive action for more than two centuries; South Africa had neither. The two major American parties contest elections every two years and peacefully transfer power; the National Party had dominated South Africa since 1948, black people were disenfranchised, and for 13 years Helen Suzman was the sole opposition voice in parliament. US federal judges have been appointed by both parties; the National Party appointed all South African judges, almost none of whom was critical of the regime. The US legal profession is large, well-endowed, and increasingly (if imperfectly) representative of the population it serves; professional associations and many lawyers have courageously defended the rule of law. Almost all South African lawyers were white (even though 87 percent of the population was black), and few openly opposed apartheid. The USA has a rich civil society with many well-funded NGOs; South Africa had outlawed the ANC and aggressively sought to control or undermine the relatively few legal anti-apartheid organizations. US media are vibrant and aggressive; the South African government controlled all radio and television, and only a few small newspapers opposed the regime (some suffering closure for doing so). Finally, the South African government terrified white people with the specter of the *swaart gevaar* and *rooi gevaar* (black and red threats), convincing most that their very existence was at stake. Republicans in the USA tried to do the same by waging a "war on terror." But critics argued that the criminal justice system was a more appropriate response; and Obama insisted that terrorists, however evil, could never pose an existential threat to the USA.

Just as studying South Africa colored my expectations about the "war on terror," so it initially shaped my methodology when researching this book. I began by approaching the Center for Constitutional Rights, which generously let me study their ongoing litigation on behalf of Arab and Muslim men rounded up after 9/11 and harshly mistreated in federal prisons before being deported. (It is illuminating – and profoundly depressing – that one of those cases, *Ziglar v. Abbasi*, is still unresolved.) But I gradually realized that efforts to defend the rule of law in the US "war on terror" were very different from the anti-apartheid struggle of the 1980s. South Africa had just two principal legal organizations challenging apartheid: the Legal Resources Centres and the University of Witwatersrand's Centre for Applied Legal Studies (with its associated law firm of Cheadle, Thompson & Haysom). The 12 cases I analyzed in my earlier book represented a large proportion of all the legal challenges. In the USA, by contrast, thousands of lawyers from organizations like CCR, the ACLU, and Human Rights First joined private lawyers working pro bono and public defenders to defend the rule of law. And they litigated thousands of cases.

Although no book could encompass the entire universe, this book and its companion, *Law's Trials*, include 14 challenges to electronic surveillance, 20 criminal prosecutions, seven courts-martial, five reviews of military commissions, 37 civil damage actions, 33 civil liberties cases, and about a hundred habeas corpus petitions (many of which went up and down the appellate hierarchy, some several times). And both books necessarily emphasize the outsized roles played by NGOs, the media, and the political process.

My two volumes complement each other; but each can be read independently. The present volume discusses five terrains of contestation: Abu Ghraib (which exposed "war on terror" tactics, sparking the public debate), Guantánamo Bay (whose shackled men in orange smocks kneeling in front of razor wire beneath a blazing sun became the enduring image of the "war on terror"), interrogation (and the Bush administration's efforts to create a legal framework for and justify torture), electronic surveillance (uncovered first by the *New York Times* and then by Edward Snowden, and affecting virtually all Americans, as well as foreign governments and IT companies), and law of war violations (on battlefields in Afghanistan, Iraq, Pakistan, and Yemen, by drones, bombs and night raids; and in secret prisons and extraordinary renditions). *Law's Trials* deals with the legal processes in which the rule of law was tested: criminal prosecutions of alleged terrorists, courts-martial for law of war crimes, military commissions for so-called high-value detainees, habeas corpus petitions by those detained in Guantánamo (and elsewhere), civil damages actions by victims of both the "war on terror" and terrorism, and civil liberties violations and Islamophobia. Although there is inevitable overlap (e.g., CSRTs in Guantánamo and habeas petitions, extraordinary renditions and claims for civil damages), there is virtually no repetition.

I began this project to understand what happened to the rule of law during Bush's "war on terror," because his administration initiated the wars in Afghanistan and Iraq, extended them to Pakistan and Yemen, and bears responsibility for the law of war violations there as well as in Abu Ghraib and Guantánamo, and for the OLC memos, torture, secret prisons, extraordinary renditions, electronic surveillance, and military commissions. But I felt compelled to extend my research through the Obama administration. Obama immediately made several dramatic course corrections by closing secret prisons and repudiating torture. But he perpetuated other practices implicating the rule of law: electronic surveillance, criminal prosecutions, courts-martial, military commissions, and resistance to habeas petitions and civil damages actions. Congress frustrated his efforts to close Guantánamo. And he intensified the controversial use of drones, killing hundreds, including US citizens. I completed the books as Trump was elected and have not tried to cover his administration for two reasons. First, it is early days. More importantly, his utter contempt for the rule of law – calling for the imprisonment of Hillary Clinton, issuing the Muslim ban, personally attacking judges who opposed his actions, firing FBI Director James Comey, threatening Special Counsel Mueller's investigation, encouraging police brutality, and refusing to condemn racist violence – represent an extreme rupture of American traditions, which will require its own book (by someone else). Nevertheless, where appropriate I indicate some of the ways the Trump administration departs from its predecessors.

Although hundreds of books have been written about the "war on terror," the present volumes are distinctive in several ways. First, they address all 16 years of the Bush and Obama administrations, allowing comparisons between them. Second, they cover the entire gamut of rule of law violations, facilitating comparisons within each volume – did reactions to interrogation differ from those to surveillance, did the "war on terror" differently deform criminal prosecutions and civil damages actions – as well as across the volumes: did the Abu Ghraib courts-martial differ from those for battleground atrocities, did efforts to end torture differ from those to compensate victims?

Third, whereas many books expose how the Bush and Obama administrations *violated* the rule of law – offering indispensable critiques of OLC opinions, executive actions, legislation, and judicial opinions – I am concerned with efforts to *defend* it. For that reason, I do not focus on explicating or criticizing legal doctrine (though I present enough of the legal framework to make the defenders' actions comprehensible). Instead, I take a sociolegal approach, seeking to identify who responded to rule of law violations, how they did so, and with what consequences. And I look at the entire range of responses, both within the state (executive, legislative, judicial, electoral) and outside (victims of rule of law violations, lawyers, media, NGOs, foreign governments, and businesses). My ultimate objective in writing these books is to learn what works – and what doesn't. The "war on terror" appears to have no end. Rule of law defenders possess limited capital: political, cultural, and material. They must use it wisely.

Many individuals and institutions provided invaluable help over the last 13 years. UCLA Law School gave me an office after I retired in 2008, essential for housing the thousands of pages of documents I accumulated. Its Law Library found obscure sources and, through Linda O'Connor, assigned me dedicated law student Research Assistants: Robert Hurwitz, Matthew Sgnilek, Michelle Alig, Jennifer Roche, Matthew Meyer, Daniel Cha, Kyle Jones, Keri Livingston, Brian Maucotel, Cesar Rivera, and Maggie Yates. Benjamin Nyblade performed the statistical analysis of the tables of cases I constructed. The UCLA Academic Senate's Council on Research supported my research on NGOs in New York, whose important role in defending the rule of law will be apparent in list of references. At CCR, Michael Ratner (its director, who was several years behind me at Columbia Law School) and Rachel Meeropol (who litigated *Abbasi*) were especially hospitable. My debt to the investigative journalists who indefatigably uncovered rule of law violations is visible in almost every one of the thousands of footnotes. Three blogs augmented the newspapers I read – Lawfare, Center on National Security at Fordham Law School, Just Security – together with Robert Chesney's national security law listserv. Finally, the Torture listserv, which Kim Scheppele founded at Princeton University early in the "war on terror" became an indispensable source of insight and discussion, conducted according to the highest standards of collegiality.

In his 1890 *Principles of Psychology*, William James famously (if perhaps inaccurately) said the world presented itself to babies "as one great blooming, buzzing confusion." That was how the "war on terror" looked to me when I began to study it. David Foster Wallace perfectly captured my predicament:

> [N]on-fiction's abyss is Total Noise, the seething static of every particular thing and experience, and one's total freedom of choice about what to choose to attend to and represent and connect and how and why; & c.[1]

Readers will judge if I have chosen well.

This book is dedicated to the victims of the US "war on terror" and those who fought to defend the rule of law, in the hope of encouraging and informing their ongoing struggle.

ABBREVIATIONS

1st Lt.	First Lieutanant
1st Sgt.	First Sergeant
AAU	Association of American Universities
AAUP	American Association of University Professors
ABA	American Bar Association
ABCNY	Association of the Bar of the City of New York
ACLU	American Civil Liberties Union
ADMAX	Administrative Maximum Facility
AG	Attorney General
AI	Amnesty International
AIHRC	Afghan Independent Human Rights Commission
AK-47	Kalashnikov assault rifle
AMA	American Medical Association
ANA	Afghan National Army
AP	Associated Press
AQAP	Al Qaeda in the Arabian Peninsula
ARB	Administrative Review Board
Art. 32	Military equivalent of civilian court arraignment or grand jury indictment
ASEAN	Association of Southeast Asian Nations
ASIL	American Society of International Law
AUMF	Authorization for Use of Military Force
AUSA	Assistant US Attorney
BDS	Bureau of Diplomatic Security
BGen.	Brigadier General
BIJ	Bureau of Investigative Journalism
BMJ	Bundesministerium für Justiz (German Federal Justice Ministry)
BND	Bundesnachrichtendienst (German Federal Intelligence Agency)
BSA	Bilateral Security Agreement
CAIR	Council on American–Islamic Relations

Capt.	Captain
CAT	Convention Against Torture
CBS	Columbia Broadcasting System
CCR	Center for Constitutional Rights
CE	Council of Europe
CELS	El Centro de Estudios Legales y Sociales (Argentina)
CENTCOM	Central Command (Army)
CEO	Chief Executive Officer
CHRGJ	Center for Human Rights and Global Justice (NYU)
CIA	Central Intelligence Agency
CIC or CID	Criminal Investigation Command (Army) (both abbreviations used interchangeably)
CITF	Criminal Investigation Task Force
CJTF	Combined Joint Task Force
CNSD	Committee on National Security and Defense (Lithuanian Parliament)
COINTELPRO	Counterintelligence Program (FBI eavesdropping and infiltrating)
CPA	Coalition Provisional Authority
CPAC	Conservative Political Action Committee
CPJ	Committee to Protect Journalists
Cpl.	Corporal
CRRB	Combined Review and Release Board
CRS	Congressional Research Service
CSIS	Center for Strategic and International Studies
CSRT	Combatant Status Review Tribunal
CUNY	City University of New York
CYA	Cover your ass
D Colo	US District Court for the District of Colorado
D Id	US District Court for the District of Idaho
D Mass	US District Court for the District of Massachusetts
D Md	US District Court for the District of Maryland
DAB	Detainee Assessment Branch
DC	District of Columbia
DCI	Director of Central Intelligence
DDC	US District Court for the District of Columbia
DEA	Drug Enforcement Administration

DGSE	Direction générale de la sécurité extérieure (General Directorate for External Security) (France)
DHS	Department of Homeland Security
DIA	Defense Intelligence Agency
DIGOS	Divisione Investigazioni General e Operazioni Speciali (General Investigation and Special Operations Division) (Italy)
DNC	Democratic National Committee
DNI	Director of National Intelligence
DoD	Department of Defense
DoJ	Department of Justice
DoS	Department of State
DTA	Detainee Treatment Act 2005
EADS	European Aeronautic Defence and Space Company NV
EC	enemy combatant
ECOWAS	Economic Community of West African States
ECJ	European Court of Justice
ECHR	European Court of Human Rights
ED Mich	US District Court for the Eastern District of Michigan
EDNY	US District Court for the Eastern District of New York
ED Pa	US District Court for the Eastern District of Pennsylvania
ED Va	Eastern District of Virginia (District Court, Judge or U.S. Attorney)
EFF	Electronic Frontier Foundation
EIT	enhanced interrogation technique
EO	Executive Order
EP	European Parliament
ERF	Emergency (or Extreme) Response Force
EU	European Union
FAA	FISA Amendment Act 2008
FATA	Federally Administered Tribal Areas (Pakistan)
FBI	Federal Bureau of Investigation
FCC	Federal Communications Commission
FDR	Franklin D. Roosevelt

FIDH	Fédération internationale des ligues des droits de l'homme/International Federation for Human Rights
FISA	Foreign Intelligence Surveillance Act
FISC	Foreign Intelligence Surveillance Court
FISCR	Foreign Intelligence Surveillance Court of Review
FIU	Force Investigation Unit
FLN	Front de Libération Nationale (Algerian National Liberation Front)
FOB	Forward Operating Base
FOIA	Freedom of Information Act
GAO	General Accountability Office
GB	Guantánamo Bay
GCHQ	Government Communications Headquarters (UK)
Gen.	General
Gitmo	Guantánamo Bay detention camp
GNP	gross national product
GOP	Grand Old Party (the Republican Party)
GTMO	Guantánamo Bay detention camp
HASC	House Armed Services Committee
HJC	House Judiciary Committee
HPSCI	House Permanent Select Committee on Intelligence
HRF	Human Rights First
HRW	Human Rights Watch
HUAC	House Committee on Un-American Activities
HVD	High-Value Detainee
IACHR	Inter-American Commission on Human Rights
IADL	International Association of Democratic Lawyers
ICC	International Criminal Court
ICCPR	International Covenant on Civil and Political Rights
ICE	Immigration and Customs Enforcement
ICG	International Crisis Group
ICJ	International Commission of Jurists
ICRC	International Committee of the Red Cross
IED	improvised explosive device
IG	Inspector General
IMF	International Monetary Fund
IMN	Iraqi Media Network

IP	Internet Protocol
IRA	Irish Republican Army
IRF	Immediate Response Force (also known as Initial (or Internal) Reaction Force)
IROE	Interrogation Rules of Engagement
IRS	Internal Revenue Service
IS	Islamic State
ISAF	International Security Assistance Force
ISI	Inter-Services Intelligence (Pakistan)
ISIL	Islamic State of Iraq and the Levant
ISIS	Islamic State of Iraq and Syria
ISP	Internet Service Provider
JAG	Judge Advocate General
JCS	Joint Chiefs of Staff
JFK	John F. Kennedy Airport
JIDC	Joint Interrogation and Detention Center (Abu Ghraib)
JPRA	Joint Personnel Recovery Agency
JSOC	Joint Special Operations Command
JTF	Joint Task Force
JTF-GTMO	Joint Task Force-Guantánamo
KKA	Afghan Army Special Operations Force
KSM	Khalid Sheikh Mohammed
LAT	*Los Angeles Times*
LHRS	Libya Human Rights Solidarity
LOAC	Law of Armed Conflict
Lt.	Lieutenant
LtCdr.	Lieutenant Commander
LtCol.	Lieutenant Colonel
LtGen.	Lieutenant General
Maj.	Major
MAM	military age male
MC	Military Commission
MCA	Military Commissions Act 2006
MEJA	Military Extraterritorial Jurisdiction Act
MEP	Member of the European Parliament
MGen.	Major General
MI	Military Intelligence
MOU	memorandum of understanding
MP	Military Police

MSF	Médecins sans frontières (Doctors without Borders)
NAACP	National Association for the Advancement of Colored People
NATO	North Atlantic Treaty Organization
NCIS	Naval Criminal Investigation Service
ND Cal	US District Court for the Northern District of California
ND Ill	US District Court for the Northern District of Illinois
ND Oh	US District Court for the Northern District of Oklahma
NDAA	National Defense Authorization Act
NDS	National Directorate of Security (Afghanistan)
NFL	National Football League
NGO	nongovernmental organization
NKVD	People's Commisariat for Internal Affairs (Soviet secret police)
NLEC	No Longer Enemy Combatant
NPR	National Public Radio
NRCAT	National Religious Campaign Against Torture
NSA	National Security Agency
NSC	National Security Council
NSLs	National Security Letters
NYPD	New York Police Department
NYU	New York University
OARDEC	Office for the Administrative Review of the Detention of Enemy Combatants
OAS	Organization of American States
ODNI	Office of the Director of National Intelligence
OFAC	Office of Foreign Assets Control (Treasury Department)
OGA	Other Government Agency (euphemism for CIA)
OIG	Office of the Inspector General
OLC	Office of Legal Counsel, Department of Justice
OMB	Office of Management and Budget
OPR	Office of Professional Responsibility (DoJ)
OSCE	Organization for Security and Co-operation in Europe

OSI	Open Society Institute
PAA	Protect America Act 2007
PBS	Public Broadcasting Service
PCLOB	Privacy and Civil Liberties Oversight Board
PHR	Physicians for Human Rights
POC	Prisoner of Conscience
POW	prisoner of war
PSP	President's Surveillance Program
PTI	Pakistan Tehreek-e-Insaf (Pakistan political party)
PUC	person under control
RAdm.	Rear Admiral
Ret.	retired
RNC	Republican National Committee
ROE	rules of engagement
RPG	rocket-propelled grenade
SASC	Senate Armed Services Committee
SCIF	Secure Compartmented Information Facility
SDNY	US District Court for the Southern District of New York
SEC	Securities and Exchange Commission
SecDef	US Secretary of Defense
SERE	Survival, Evasion, Resistance, Escape
SFC	Sergeant First Class
Sgt.	Sergeant
SISMI	Servizio per le Informazioni e la Sicurezza Militare (Italian military intelligence)
SJA	Staff Judge Advocate
SJC	Senate Judiciary Committee
SNCC	Student Non-Violent Coordinating Committee
SOFA	Status of Forces Agreement
SOHR	Syrian Observatory for Human Rights
SOP	Standard Operation Procedure
SOUTHCOM	Southern Command (Army)
SPC	Specialist
SSCI	Senate Select Committee on Intelligence
SSgt.	Staff Sergeant
SSP	state secrets privilege
SUV	sport utility vehicle
SWIFT	Society for Worldwide Interbank Financial Telecommunication

TDIP	Temporary Committee on the Alleged Use of European Countries by the CIA for the Transport and Illegal Detention of Prisoners (EU)
TJAG	The Judge Advocate General
TRO	temporary restraining order
TSP	Terrorist Surveillance Program
UAE	United Arab Emirates
UC	University of California
UCI	University of California, Irvine
UCMJ	Uniform Code of Military Justice
UN	United Nations
UNAMA	United Nations Assistance Mission in Afghanistan
UNHRC	United Nations Human Rights Commission (later Council)
URG	Unity Resources Group
USAID	US Agency for International Development
USMC	US Marine Corps
VBNS	Verizon Business Network Services
WMDs	weapons of mass destruction
WSJ	*Wall Street Journal*

CHAPTER ONE

DEFENDING THE RULE OF LAW

The response of the United States to the 9/11 terrorist attack profoundly compromised the rule of law.[1] This book chronicles and evaluates the broad spectrum of efforts to *defend* those foundational principles. In this chapter I define the rule of law, explain why it is indispensable, and offer a framework for analyzing the successes and failures of its defense.

WHAT IS THE RULE OF LAW?

Although lawyers and philosophers have debated the meaning of the rule of law for centuries, there is a broad consensus about its core. Because its content has accreted gradually (and irreversibly), history is a powerful guide.[2] Eight centuries ago rebellious English barons extracted from King John the promises enshrined in Magna Carta:

> [N]o free man shall be seized or imprisoned or stripped of his rights or possessions, or outlawed or exiled, or deprived of his standing in any other way, nor will we proceed with force against him, or send others to do so, except by lawful judgment of his equals or by the law of the land.

The Petition of Right reaffirmed this in 1648.[3] About the same time John Lilburne asserted the right against self-incrimination before the Star Chamber; and William Penn insisted that the charges against him be public, comprehensible, and based on law.[4] In 1679 Parliament stopped the king from evading the writ of habeas corpus by sending prisoners outside the jurisdiction of courts; ten years later the Bill of Rights established that all state actors were subject to law.[5] English common law prohibited torture as early as the fifteenth century; other European nations followed in the eighteenth century.[6] English accused won the right to a speedy public trial before an independent judge and a jury of their peers, and not to suffer cruel or unusual punishment. The French Declaration of the Rights of Man and the Citizen (1789) and the first ten amendments to the US Constitution (1791) recognized these rights and others: freedom from unreasonable search and seizure, protection against double jeopardy, reasonable bail, representation by counsel of the accused's choice, indictment by a grand jury in serious crimes, confrontation of witnesses, deprivation of property only through due process of law, and freedoms of speech, assembly, association, the press, and religion. Centuries of struggle abolished slavery, whose domination of man by man is the antithesis of the rule of law.[7]

Although international human rights rarely were mentioned before World War II, President Roosevelt's 1941 State of the Union message embraced the "Four Freedoms": speech, expression and worship, and freedom from want and fear.[8] The postwar revision and expansion of the Geneva Conventions strengthened the rights of prisoners of war. Latin American nations incorporated basic rule of law concepts in the 1948 American Declaration on the Rights and Duties of Man; Europe did so in the 1950 European Convention on Human Rights. The Universal Declaration of Human Rights came into force in 1976 and was expanded by the International Convention on Civil and Political Rights and the Convention against Torture. The rule of law was embodied in the postwar constitutions of nations (Germany, Canada, the UK, South Africa, Spain, Switzerland, and the former socialist countries) and supranational unions (the European Union Treaty and the Preamble to its Charter of Fundamental Rights).[9] International bodies repeatedly reaffirm its principles: UN Secretary General Kofi Annan in 2004, a Helsinki Ministerial Council Decision in 2008.[10]

The rule of law also can be approached ontologically. A logical starting point is the Roman law maxim *nulla poena sine lege*, on which civil law regimes have built their ideals of *Rechtsstaat* and *état du droit*. A.V. Dicey paraphrased this: "no man is punishable or can lawfully be made to suffer in body or goods except for a distinct breach of law established in the ordinary legal manner before the ordinary courts of the land."[11] The rule of law also is defined by its opposite – the state of exception – grounded on other Roman law maxims: *necessitas legem non habet* (necessity follows no law) and *salus populi suprema lex* (the people's safety is the highest law), now often invoked as *raison d'état*.[12]

Karl Schmidt, its influential German theorist (and advocate), defined the sovereign as "he who decides on the exception," which "defies general codification."[13] Schmitt warned that the rule of law condemned the liberal state to suicide,[14] a view shared by Justice Jackson.[15] Clinton Rossiter agreed that "in time of crisis a democratic constitutional government must temporarily be altered to whatever degree is necessary to overcome the peril and restore normal conditions."[16] States of exception have been invoked by colonial regimes,[17] during the Cold War, in the "war on crime" – by both the state and vigilantes[18] – and during the present "war on terror." Although some characterize it as pure lawlessness,[19] others see a hyperlegality that perversely empowers the state.[20]

English philosophers conceptualized the rule of law as negative liberty: "a power to do or not to do" (Locke), "the absence of opposition" (Hobbes).[21] Their descendants concur: freedom is "not being interfered with by others" (Isaiah Berlin), "simply to be unconstrained from pursuing whatever goals we may happen to set ourselves" (Quentin Skinner).[22] The horrors of Nazism shaped German scholars. Franz Neumann insisted on "the generality and the abstractness of law together with the independence of the judge."[23] Otto Kirchheimer agreed that "the security of the individual is better served when specific claims can be addressed in institutions counting rules and permanency among their stock-in-trade rather than by reliance on transitory personal relations and situations."[24] The Holocaust convinced Isaiah Berlin of the imperative of human rights.[25] Communism provoked Martin Krygier to champion "opposition to arbitrary exercise of power," which "threatens the dignity of all who find themselves mere objects of power exercisable at the whim or caprice of another."[26] Memories of fascism may have influenced Gianluigi Palombella to argue that the purpose of the rule of law is "to prevent the law from turning into a sheer tool of domination, a manageable servant to political monopoly and instrumentalism."[27] Even without direct experience of oppression, American theorists arrived at similar concepts: "the sense of injustice" (Edmond Cahn), "the liberalism of fear" (Judith Shklar), "freedom from abuse, oppression, and cruelty" (Amy Guttmann), "law is not brutal in its operation; law is not savage; law does not rule through abject fear and terror, or by breaking the will of those whom it confronts" (Jeremy Waldron).[28]

Recently, some philosophers have based the rule of law on a Kantian respect for human dignity and autonomy.[29] The "most essential message of human rights" for Michael Ignatieff was "that there are no excuses for the inhuman use of human beings."[30] Human rights "help people to help themselves. They protect their agency." Kant's categorical imperative embodies "the idea of moral reciprocity: that we judge human actions by the simple test of whether we would wish to be on the receiving end." Martin Krygier warned that the "arbitrary exercise of power ... threatens the dignity of all who find themselves mere objects of power exercisable at the whim or caprice of another."[31] Jeremy Waldron sees law itself as "a mode of governing people that treats them with respect, as though they had a view or perspective of their own to present on the application of the norm to their conduct and situation."[32] Repudiating Nazism, the first, unamendable, article of the postwar German constitution declares: "Human dignity shall be inviolable. To respect and protect it shall be the duty of all state authority."[33]

Many lawyers and philosophers have embraced a procedural concept of the rule of law, partly because it elicits the broadest consensus. Justice Felix Frankfurter wrote in a 1943 opinion: "The history of liberty has largely been the history of observance of procedural safeguards."[34] Justice Robert Jackson stressed the centrality of procedure by asserting – paradoxically – that he "would rather live under Soviet law enforced by American procedure than American law enforced by Soviet procedure."[35] Lon Fuller advocated a "thin" version of the rule of law based on eight principles: the state should act through general rules that are publicly available, prospective, comprehensible, consistent, capable of performance, sufficiently clear and stable to let citizens orient their actions conformably, and administered in ways congruent with their terms.[36] Ronald Cass insisted on "fidelity to rules" that "tell officials how, to what ends, and within what limits they may exercise power."[37] Neil MacCormick places argumentation at the core of law.[38] Waldron takes a similar approach in his list of procedural protections:

A. A hearing by an impartial tribunal that is required to act on the basis of evidence and arguments presented formally before it in relation to legal norms that govern the imposition of penalty, stigma, loss, and so forth;
B. A legally trained judicial officer, whose independence of other agencies of government is ensured;
C. A right to be represented by counsel and to the time and opportunity required to prepare a case;
D. A right to be present at all critical stages of the proceeding;
E. A right to confront witnesses against the detainee;

F. A right to an assurance that the evidence presented by the government has been gathered in a properly supervised way;
G. A right to present evidence in one's own behalf;
H. A right to make legal arguments about the bearing of the evidence and about the bearing of the various legal norms relevant to the case;
I. A right to hear reasons from the tribunal when it reaches its decision that are responsive to the evidence and arguments presented before it; and
J. Some right of appeal to a higher tribunal of a similar character. [39]

The rule of law thus is the philosophical foundation on which nations have constructed civil rights and liberties and the global community has concluded treaties incorporating international human rights. In what follows I will often use those concepts interchangeably.

WHY IS THE RULE OF LAW IMPORTANT?

At the end of *Whigs and Hunters*, E.P. Thompson acknowledged that "concern with the rights and wrongs at law of a few men in 1723 is concern with trivia" compared to contemporaneous evils, like the slave trade and colonialism, or those of his own twentieth century, such as Nazism and liquidation of the *kulaks*.[40] The same criticism might be made of this book: even the worst American rule of law violations since 9/11 – extraordinary rendition, torture, targeted killing, electronic surveillance, civilian casualties, indefinite detention without trial, civil liberties abuses, and distortions of the criminal process (entrapment, military commissions) – seem insignificant next to the costs of America's wars in Iraq and Afghanistan, the shame of its prisons, climate change and other environmental threats, worsening inequality, and mistreatment of immigrants, Native Americans, African Americans, and other minorities.

But Thompson defended his chosen topic. "What is remarkable … is not that the laws were bent but the fact that there was, anywhere in the eighteenth century, a rule of law at all." While acknowledging law's "class-bound and mystifying functions," Thompson showed that the "ruled" "would actually fight for their rights by means of law" and "could actually win a case."

> It is inherent in the especial character of law, as a body of rules and procedures, that it shall apply logical criteria with reference to standards

> of universality and equality. It is true that certain categories of person may be excluded from this logic … But if too much of this is true, then the consequences are plainly counterproductive … The essential precondition for the effectiveness of law, in its function as ideology, is that it shall display an independence from gross manipulation and shall seem to be just. It cannot seem to be so without upholding its own logic and criteria of equity; indeed, on occasion, by actually *being* just … In the case of an ancient historical formation like the law, a discipline which requires years of exacting study to master, there will always be some men who actively believe in their own procedures and in the logic of justice … the rulers were, in serious senses, whether willingly or unwillingly, the prisoners of their own rhetoric; they played the games of power according to rules which suited them, but they could not break those rules or the whole game would be thrown away … There were even occasions … when the Government itself retired from the court defeated. Such occasions served, paradoxically, to consolidate power, to enhance its legitimacy, and to inhibit revolutionary movements. But, to turn the paradox around, these same occasions served to bring power even further within constitutional controls [original emphasis].

Breaking with fellow Marxists who cynically dismissed law as an epiphenomenal instrument of class domination,[41] Thompson concluded:

> [T]he inhibitions upon power imposed by law seem to me a legacy as substantial as any handed down from the struggles of the seventeenth century to the eighteenth … the notion of the regulation and reconciliation of conflicts through the rule of law – and the elaboration of rules and procedures which, on occasion, made some approximate approach towards the ideal – seems to me a cultural achievement of universal significance … an unqualified human good.

The philosopher Michael Oakeshott called the rule of law "the single greatest condition of our freedom."[42]

South Africans who fought against apartheid for nearly half a century appealed to the rule of law. Alan Paton, who published *Cry the Beloved Country* when the National Party first took power, praised the rule of law as "one of the noblest achievements of sinful man … protecting himself against his own cruelty and selfishness."[43] Nobel Prize Winner Nadine Gordimer called the Universal Declaration of Human Rights "the essential document, the touchstone, the creed of humanity."[44] Two leading human rights lawyers concurred. John Dugard found "opportunities for relief" in legal rules; Geoffrey Budlender noted that because "repression and discrimination were, for the most part, carried out through the mechanism of law," it could be a means of resistance.[45] Elie Wiesel, who survived the Holocaust to devote his life to fighting genocide, called the rule of law the sacred text of a "world-wide secular religion."[46] Michael Ignatieff saw human rights as "the lingua franca of global moral thought."[47] UN Secretary General Kofi Annan viewed them as the "yardstick by which we measure human progress."[48] The conservative British historian Paul Johnson pronounced them "the most important political development of the second millennium."[49]

Even unlikely heads of state feel compelled to pay lip service to the rule of law: Vladimir Putin (Russia), Jiang Zemin and Hu Jintao (China), Robert Mugabe (Zimbabwe), Mohammed Khatami (Iran), Abdurrahman Wahid (Indonesia), Burmese military rulers, Vicente Fox Quesada (Mexico), and Abdul Rashid Dostum (an Afghan warlord).[50] Apartheid South Africa repeatedly proclaimed its respect for law. In 1985 a Nationalist MP claimed that "even South Africa's severest critics readily concede that the standard of the administration of justice in South Africa is of the highest order."[51] Opening parliament the next year, Prime Minister Botha asserted: "We believe in the sanctity and indivisibility of law and the just application thereof." Chinese President Xi Jinping recently called his country's Constitution a "fundamental law," declaring that to "govern the nation by law means to govern in accordance with the Constitution."[52] China subsequently halved its imposition of the death penalty and adopted a new Criminal Procedure Law. The Chief Justice of the Supreme People's Court promised increased judicial independence, transparency, fairness, and professionalism. (But two years later he radically backtracked: "We should resolutely resist erroneous influence from the West: 'constitutional democracy,' 'separation of powers' and 'independence of the judiciary.'") In response to a damning report and resolution by the UN Human Rights Council, North Korea maintained that its citizens enjoyed robust human rights, including freedom of speech and religion and protection from slavery and torture.[53] It introduced a UN resolution praising its own human rights record and insisting it had "nothing to hide."[54] Its envoy claimed that alleged prison camps photographed by the UN were "normal" "reformatories" and "we don't even know the term 'political prisoners.'"[55] With no apparent sense of irony, Turkish President Erdogan justified his declaration of a state of emergency in July 2016 after the attempted coup: "The aim is to rapidly and effectively take all steps needed to eliminate the threat against democracy, the rule of law and the people's rights and freedoms."[56]

Although such rhetoric is intended as public relations, it makes promises that cannot be entirely ignored.[57] Therefore, when international relations realists assert that nations are motivated solely by self-interest,[58] constructivists reply that rule of law and human rights norms shape conceptions of self-interest.[59] Australia, for instance, enacted its first national anti-discrimination law in 1975 after signing the International Convention on the Elimination of All Forms of Racial Discrimination.[60] That UN Security Council resolutions rarely mentioned the rule of law during the Cold War but featured it 69 times between 1998 and 2006 argues for its increasing salience.[61]

Advocates make a variety of claims for the rule of law. For Michael Barkun and Friedrich Kratochwil, it offers the hope of a "third party" outside the state.[62] Michael Ignatieff elaborates:

> Human beings are at risk of their lives if they lack a basic measure of free agency; that agency itself requires protection through internationally agreed standards ... when all other remedies have been exhausted, these individuals have the right to appeal to other peoples, nations, and international organizations for assistance in defending their rights.[63]

A human rights lawyer visiting a refugee camp after the 2000 coup in Fiji said the Universal Declaration of Human Rights – prominently displayed and taught to residents – "was having a powerful effect on these people, many of whom were at the lowest point in their lives. As a set of ideals and statement of their rights as human beings, it helped these refugees gain courage and retain their sense of dignity and self-worth."[64]

Arguments for its value transcend political orientation. The libertarian Friedrich Hayek believed that a government "bound by rules fixed and announced beforehand" made it "possible to foresee with fair certainty how the authority will use its coercive powers in given circumstances, and to plan one's individual affairs on the basis of this knowledge."[65] Contemporary neoliberal policymakers contend that the predictability ensured by the rule of law is essential for economic growth.[66] Legal mechanisms redress wrongs that might provoke violence, even revolution, if allowed to fester. Especially at moments of crisis, legal remedies function as a residual glue, embodying values and binding factions that might otherwise rupture. Freedoms of speech, association, and assembly are both prerequisites for democracy and checks on the majoritarian tyranny to which democracy is susceptible. Justices Holmes and Brandeis, on the Supreme Court's liberal wing, saw those freedoms as the only path toward an otherwise unknowable political truth. Justice Sutherland, a conservative, embraced the same freedoms as a necessary corrective for governmental error.

Others advance utilitarian arguments. Violating the rule of law endangers a country's moral standing to insist that other nations conform, thereby endangering its own citizens, especially those who risk their lives in its defense. Henry Shue warned of torture's "metastatic tendencies," which Darius Rejali documented in excruciating detail.[67] Jeremy Waldron agreed: "if we mess with the prohibition on torture, we may find it harder to defend some arguably less important" prohibitions, such as those against flogging, coerced confessions, the stomach pump, and police brutality.[68] Cesare Beccaria, the eighteenth-century founder of criminology, argued that torture was more likely to produce falsehood than truth.[69] Tom Tyler demonstrated empirically that American disputants' obedience to law is grounded in their beliefs that they have been heard and the decision-maker's procedures are fair, based on disputants' own evaluations of "representation, neutrality, bias, honesty, quality of decision, and consistency."[70] Carroll Seron and her colleagues found that respect for the police depended on New Yorkers' belief that the New York Police Department (NYPD) behaved professionally by not abusing its authority, exerting unnecessary force, indulging in offensive language, or being discourteous.[71]

In response to assertions that we must sacrifice liberty to preserve security, rule-of-law defenders argue that the relative costs and benefits are indeterminable.[72] The notorious "ticking-bomb" hypothetical, constantly invoked to justify torturing one person to save many, presupposes unattainable knowledge about the probability of the threat, the efficacy of torture in eliciting truth, and the impossibility of interdicting the threat by other means.[73] Cost–benefit arguments also tend to obscure the fact that the alleged collective good (security for all) is sought at the expense of individual burdens (loss of liberty or worse) inflicted on a few, who often are targeted because of their beliefs (communism), ethnicity (African American, Japanese American, Arab), or religion (Islam). The rhetorical power of utilitarian arguments (despite their flawed empirical foundation) leads some to respond with deontological claims that rights trump utility and the rule of law is essential to human dignity.[74]

The rule of law has been attacked on several grounds. Critics disparage it as historically and culturally specific, even imperialistic.[75] Some formulations are certainly guilty. Dicey identified the rule of law with the common law's preference for judicial decisions over the civil law's comprehensive codes.[76] Almost a century later Thibaut and Walker displayed an equally parochial conviction about the superiority of common law accusatorial process to civilian inquisitorial procedure.[77] But the German ideal of the *Rechtsstaat* antedates the common law conception of the rule of law and arguably is more coherent (even if it never attains the pandectist ideal). Apologists for authoritarian regimes reject the rule of law in the name of uniquely "eastern" or "nonwestern" conceptions of justice. The Central Committee of the Chinese Communist Party declared that "socialist rule of law must uphold the party's leadership."[78] Similar claims are made by some religions, especially fundamentalist Islam. Arguments for cultural relativism may be more persuasive in the rule of law's contested penumbra: issues such as abortion or marriage equality regardless of sexual orientation. But there is strong historical evidence that, given a choice, the subjects of authoritarian regimes would prefer core rule-of-law values: witness the aftermath of the 1989 fall of the Berlin Wall (including the later "color" revolutions), the Arab spring (especially Tahrir Square), the 2014 demonstrations in Hong Kong (not to mention Tiananmen Square a quarter-century earlier), and the millions of migrants voting with their feet. Communist and many developing nations prioritize economic and social rights over political and civil rights; but those categories are not inherently incompatible.

Nevertheless, two criticisms must be taken seriously by rule of law advocates. First, the powerful can use it as a weapon to preserve their prerogatives. For decades American courts invoked substantive due process to nullify laws protecting workers and strike down the New Deal response to the Great Depression. They applied antitrust law to prevent workers from organizing and deployed the labor injunction against strikes. Herbert Wechsler's critique of *Brown* v. *Board of Education* in the name of "neutral principles" anticipated (and legitimated) the numerous attacks on affirmative action.[79] The Supreme Court has used the Fifth Amendment's "takings" clause to abrogate local land use regulation.[80] The Second Amendment has frustrated efforts at gun control, contributing to untold numbers of deaths. Corporations have interposed the Fourth Amendment against enforcement of regulations promoting worker health and safety and protecting the environment. Most notoriously, the Court has extended First Amendment protections from individuals to corporations and from speech to money, striking down campaign contribution laws that seek to level the electoral playing field[81] and letting closely held for-profit corporations deny employees access to contraception because of the owners' religious beliefs.[82] If all these criticisms show how private power can exploit the rule of law to produce perverse results, other critics argue it is too constrained. Addressing only state power can obscure the harms inflicted by private actors: employers, manufacturers, financiers, sellers, polluters, common carriers, and landowners. But even if the rule of law has some unfortunate consequences and cannot remedy all forms of injustice, I remain convinced by Thompson's eloquent argument that its transcendent values must be defended.

WHAT PROTECTS THE RULE OF LAW?

Most writing about the rule of law seeks to define or justify it.[83] My concern (to paraphrase Marx)[84] is how to defend it in time of war, when it is most vulnerable. Max Weber argued that the modern state's authority rests not on tradition or charisma but rationality, especially as embodied in law. Philip Selznick predicted a half-century ago that "the quality of legality, and gradations in it, will be a primary preoccupation of the sociology of law in the future."[85] Because that promise was not fulfilled, the rest of this chapter develops an analytic framework by drawing eclectically on literature concerning the articulation and enforcement of international human rights, the roles of NGOs, professions, whistleblowers, and the media, and the record of the three branches of government in abridging or protecting fundamental rights.[86] At the end of each section I derive research questions to guide my analysis of the fate of the rule of law in the United States since 9/11.

Promulgating and Enforcing International Human Rights

Since World War II (and partly because of it), treaties have become an increasingly important source of human rights norms.[87] States are naturally reluctant to accept limitations on their sovereignty. The Soviet Union abstained from voting on the Universal Declaration of Human Rights because rights "could not be conceived outside the state."[88] Contemporaneously, the American Bar Association (ABA) president denounced treaties, especially the UN's "so-called human rights" instruments, as "the greatest threat to human freedom." The ABA led US opposition to signing the Genocide Convention, warning that this might prompt investigations of lynchings.[89] Sen. John W. Bricker (R-Oh) proposed several constitutional amendments to limit the ratification and effect of treaties.

Yet nations do sign treaties for various reasons. Countries may emulate each other: after French revolutionaries abolished torture, Switzerland, the Netherlands, and Spain followed suit.[90] The horrors of World War II may have inspired the prohibitions on torture in the African (Banjul) Charter on Humanity and People's Rights (1981), the Inter-American Convention to Prevent and Punish Torture (1985), and the European Convention for the Prevention of Torture and Inhuman and Degrading Treatment or Punishment (1989).[91] Mature democracies have been less likely (and new democracies more likely) to ratify the Convention Against Torture (CAT) or agree to enforcement. Richer countries and those that already embrace the rule of law are (paradoxically) more likely to add reservations to treaties. Common law countries are less likely than civil law countries to ratify treaties and more likely to add reservations (perhaps because their judges are more resistant to constraint). Even an authoritarian ruler may embrace a treaty for political reasons: Chile finally ratified the CAT because Pinochet hoped (unsuccessfully) to win a plebiscite. Communist nations agreed to respect basic human rights in exchange for recognition of their postwar boundaries by the Helsinki Final Act of the Conference on Security and Cooperation in Europe.

International relations "realists" dismiss treaties as mere "expressive" acts or "empty promises."[92] But "constructivists" contend that "states are embedded in dense networks of transnational and international social relations that shape their perceptions of the world and their role in that world. States are *socialized* to want certain things by the international society in which they and the people in them live" [original emphasis].[93] Thomas Jefferson advanced "a just regard for the opinion of mankind" as one reason for the American Declaration of Independence. Beth Simmons argues that treaties "help define the size of the *expectations gap* when governments fail to live up to their provisions" [original emphasis].[94] They can shape government agendas, invite litigation, encourage political mobilization, and enhance the size, resources and strategies of those seeking enforcement. Ratification of the CAT may reduce the severity of torture. Compared with stable democracies or autocracies, the human rights records of partially democratic countries display greater improvement after ratification. Stable democracies and autocracies that ratify the International Covenant on Civil and Political Rights (ICCPR) are more likely to abolish the death penalty. Partial democracies are more likely to conduct fair trials if they ratify the ICCPR and less likely to engage in torture if they ratify the CAT.

Ratification of the Convention on the Rights of the Child is associated with a reduction in child labor. Concern for reputation appears to be greater with respect to treaties involving trade or security than those involving the environment or human rights.[95]

Mary Dudziak has shown that competition with the Soviet Union for the allegiance of developing countries helped motivate the USA to abolish Jim Crow laws and practices enforcing racial segregation in the southern states.[96] In 1947 Eleanor Roosevelt threatened to resign from the board of the National Association for the Advancement of Colored People (NAACP) if it gave the Soviet Union a propaganda coup by appealing to the UN.[97] As US representative to the UN, she urged its Human Rights Commission not to hear a complaint about South Africa for fear this might encourage investigation of the conditions of "negroes in Alabama."[98] Several decades later, by contrast, Arthur Goldberg (her successor) supported sanctions against Southern Rhodesia because it would be a "double standard" for the USA to ignore racial inequality abroad while seeking to end segregation at home.[99] States with good human rights records – such as the Scandinavian countries, Netherlands, Switzerland, and Canada – tend to take the lead in enforcement, as they did against the Greek junta.

Based on paired comparisons of countries in which human rights struggles have succeeded (Chile, South Africa, the Philippines, Poland, Czechoslovakia) and failed (Guatemala, Kenya, Uganda, Morocco, Tunisia, and Indonesia), Thomas Risse and his collaborators found an upward spiral in which states that have responded to opposition challenges with repression feel compelled to deny that human rights abuses are occurring, then make tactical concessions, then begin to use human rights norms to justify their own behavior, and finally conform their behavior to those norms.[100]

Kathryn Sikkink has described a "justice cascade," in which enforcement of human rights in one country diffuses through individuals and networks to neighbors that are geographically proximate and culturally similar.[101] The South African Truth and Reconciliation Commission influenced other African nations; Argentina's redress of abuses encouraged similar action in Chile. Prosecutions of high-level officials are particularly effective. Exiles and expatriates mobilize support in their host countries to address the abuses from which they fled. Countries may be impelled to act by mistreatment of their citizens abroad: Sweden responded to disappearances in Argentina; Britain, France, Australia, Canada, Germany, Afghanistan, and Kuwait (among others) sought the return of Guantánamo detainees. A state's response to pressure may depend on whether it is centralized or fragmented, weak or strong, consensual or polarized.[102]

Treaties traditionally were enforced by one state approaching another, usually in secret. Many postwar treaties authorized states to complain to UN bodies; optional protocols allowed individuals to complain under the ICCPR and CAT. Global and regional courts – the International Court of Justice, the European, Inter-American and African Courts for Human Rights and the Association of Southeast Asian Nations (ASEAN) Intergovernmental Commission on Human Rights – have limited enforcement powers but may be willing to use publicity.[103] Beginning in the 1980s, the UN Human Rights Commission (UNHRC) appointed special rapporteurs on issues like executions and torture and exposed notorious violators (e.g., Myanmar, Somalia).[104] In 2011 its successor Council sent more than 600 communications about abuses to 131 countries (but only 35 percent of special rapporteurs' communications in 2010 received any reply). By 2012 more than ninety countries had issued "standing invitations" to Council investigations.

Such interventions seem to make a difference. Actions by special rapporteurs led Indonesia and Malaysia to revoke a secret agreement restricting migrants, Cambodia to release two journalists, Afghanistan to free hundreds of prisoners, Turkey to improve its treatment of internally displaced persons, and Spain to videotape police interrogations. After the special rapporteur on extrajudicial executions visited and reported on the Philippines, killings declined by more than 60 percent.[105] After the special rapporteurs on adequate housing and on contemporary forms of racism investigated the plight of Quilombos (descendants of African slaves) in Brazil, the government passed a statute codifying their property rights. After the special rapporteur on torture reported on Jordan, it closed its notorious al-Jafr prison. Country visits by special rapporteurs are the Human Rights Council's most effective tool, but their influence varies with the quality and specificity of their reports and the ability of local media to publicize them. Of the 120 states that declined to issue standing invitations, 44 had never been visited (19 of whom rebuffed 41 requests). States accepted 40 percent of requests for cooperation by other member states but only 18 percent of UN written communications.

Individual states can seek to correct foreign human rights abuses.[106] After the *New York Times* published a lengthy excerpt from a European Commission on Human Rights report on torture in Greece, Rep.

Benjamin Rosenthal (D-NY) persuaded the House to ban military aid to the junta. Sen. Henry M. "Scoop" Jackson (D-Wa) embraced the cause of Soviet Jewry, attracting bipartisan support from Rep. Donald Rumsfeld (R-Ill) (yes, *that* Donald Rumsfeld), who sought to enlist all "those who believe that the protection of human rights and fundamental freedoms is basic to the cause of peace." With encouragement from Sen. Jacob Javits (D-NY), the Jackson–Vanik amendment linked US trade to emigration by Soviet Jews. Revulsion at torture in Brazil prompted an amendment to the Foreign Assistance Act of 1973 withholding military and economic aid to any country practicing "the internment or imprisonment of that country's citizens for political purposes." Congress terminated or curtailed aid to authoritarian governments in Chile, South Korea, and Uruguay, mandated annual Department of State (DoS) country reports, and predicated aid on countries' willingness to permit NGO investigations. Former President Jimmy Carter recalled that when human rights became "the central theme of our foreign policy ... a spark had been ignited, and I had no inclination to douse the growing flames."

States also can address their own abuses, although scholars disagree about whether that advances human rights.[107] Sikkink found evidence that prosecutions correlated negatively with torture, summary executions, disappearances, political imprisonment, and military involvement in government, and positively with law and order and more stable transitions; she found no evidence that they led to coups or undermined democracy.[108]

RESEARCH QUESTIONS

Which human rights treaties has the USA ratified and with what reservations?
Does the USA feel an obligation to comply with the treaties it ratifies, or does it seek to minimize compliance or evade?
How do geopolitics and history influence compliance? The views or actions of other nations?
How is the USA influenced by threats to the human rights of its own citizens or the prospect of reciprocity?
How is the USA influenced by international or regional bodies?

Civil Society: Nongovernmental Organizations and Professions

Nongovernmental organizations (NGOs) play a pivotal role in protecting human rights.[109] Their nineteenth-century antecedents include the British Anti-Slavery Society and French protests over the Dreyfus affair (which generated La Ligue internationale des droits de l'homme, succeeded by La Fédération international des ligues des droits de l'homme, FIDH). The International Committee of the Red Cross (ICRC) also originated in the mid-nineteenth century, in part to monitor compliance with the first Geneva Convention "for the Amelioration of the Condition of the Wounded Armies in the Field" following the Franco-Austrian War. The fewer than three dozen international human rights NGOs in the 1970s multiplied to 168 in 1993.[110] Domestic human rights organizations proliferated even more rapidly in Latin America, from 22 to 550 in the 1980s. Although there was almost no foundation funding before 1975, human rights NGOs were receiving $23 million by 1993.

The American Civil Liberties Union (ACLU) emerged to defend critics of American participation in World War I.[111] Many of its earliest members were outsiders: Quakers, Jews, Irish, African Americans, socialists, and labor lawyers. On July 4, 1917, the *New York Times* patriotically dismissed the ACLU's precursor as a "little group of malcontents," "troublesome folk," an "unimportant and minute minority" for whom "jails are waiting." But by the ACLU's 25th anniversary immediately after the end of World War II, President Truman saluted its "outstanding service to the cause of true freedom," and New York Governor Thomas Dewey called it "an essential part of American life" in the "endless" "war for freedom." President Johnson sent his "warmest greetings" in 1964 and declared two years later that "all fair-minded Americans stand in your debt" (before assailing it for defending protesters against the Vietnam War). The media can be allies or enemies. The *Wall Street Journal* – which now regularly vilifies the ACLU – in 1938 urged citizens "to keep unsleeping watch on civil liberty" and "demand, most of all, Justice Holmes's 'tolerance for the thought we hate.'"[112] By contrast, the *New York Times* and the *Washington Post* – now generally supportive of civil liberties – applauded the Smith Act convictions in the 1950s.

The International Commission of Jurists (ICJ) was established in 1952 by Western lawyers as an alternative to the International Association of Democratic Lawyers (IADL), founded four years earlier and initially aligned with communist-bloc countries.[113] Amnesty International (AI) began in 1961 with an appeal in *The Observer*, quickly republished by newspapers in the USA, Germany, Switzerland, Denmark, Sweden, the Netherlands, Italy, South Africa, Belgium, Ireland, and India.[114] American membership leaped from 3,000 to 50,000 between 1974 and 1976. The Nobel Peace Prize award to human rights campaigners – Sean MacBride (1974), Andrei Sakharov (1975) and AI (1977) – greatly enhanced the movement's legitimacy and resources.[115] (Five years after receiving the award, AI membership had tripled to more than 500,000 in 160 countries.) The (US-based) Lawyers Committee for Human Rights, formed in 1978 (on the model of the Lawyers Committee for Civil Rights under Law), became Human Rights First (HRF) in 2003.[116] Helsinki Watch, founded in 1978 to monitor Communist countries under the Helsinki Final Accords, spawned similar groups for the Americas, Asia, and the Middle East, all of which merged into Human Rights Watch (HRW) in 1988.[117] Médecins sans frontières was established in 1971 following the Biafran war, the Committee to Protect Journalists in 1981, and Physicians for Human Rights in 1985.

International NGOs vary in composition (only AI has a mass membership), governance (democratic or centralized), and funding (by members, foundations, or governments). Human rights abuses increase public support. ACLU membership tripled during the McCarthy era, had doubled again by 1960, and then had increased fourfold by 1974 (from 10,000 to 275,000 over two decades).[118] Membership increased by 35,000 in 1981 after President Reagan embraced its hostility as a "badge of honor" and his Attorney General reviled it as the "criminal's lobby"; it grew by another 70,000 during the 1988 presidential campaign after George H.W. Bush attacked Michael Dukakis as a "card-carrying member" of the ACLU, whose values fell outside the "mainstream." (Bush's cavalier attitude toward civil liberties sadly presaged his son's actions as president.) Similar growth followed George W. Bush's response to the 9/11 attack; and the ACLU received more than $7 million from 120,000 donors in the five days after Trump's election (compared to less than $28,000 from 354 donors after Obama's 2012 victory).[119] But controversial positions can provoke defections (representing neo-Nazis seeking to march in Skokie) and splits (representing both sides in racial fighting among Camp Pendleton marines; supporting Supreme Court decisions extending First Amendment protections to corporate campaign contributions).[120] AI UK lost many members after it publicized British abuses in Northern Ireland, provoking Thatcher to call members "IRA apologists."[121]

NGOs define their missions differently. AI began with a single goal: freeing nonviolent Prisoners of Conscience (POCs), whose imprisonment was a human rights violation. (It adopted 47,000 prisoners in its first 40 years, but excluded Nelson Mandela and declined to take a "political" position on apartheid.)[122] This focus motivated people to join and contribute money, giving them a concrete task to perform (letter writing) and offering enormous satisfaction when prisoners were released. AI initially resisted adding extrajudicial executions because force was sometimes justified and deaths more difficult to investigate.[123] After launching a Campaign for the Abolition of Torture in 1972, AI acknowledged the need for speed by creating an Urgent Action network (unfortunately limiting membership participation).[124] Even when it embraced equal rights regardless of sexual orientation in 1978 (simultaneously increasing advocacy for Palestinians as part of an internal political compromise), AI refused to represent those accused of sexual offenses until 1991. The ACLU similarly debated whether to act for protesters who committed civil disobedience (as in lunch counter sit-ins). Although it declared in 1957 that it was "not within the province of the Union to evaluate the social validity of laws" criminalizing homosexuality, it endorsed gay rights seven years later.[125]

Although some NGOs (like the NAACP) align with causes, others maintain strict neutrality, defending the rights of all regardless of their political positions.[126] The ICRC protects prisoners of war (POWs) under all circumstances and in all countries. Zechariah Chafee began his seminal book *Freedom of Speech* by declaring: "I am not an atheist, neither am I a pacifist or an anarchist, or a Socialist or a Bolshevik. I have no sympathy myself with the views of most of the men who have been imprisoned since the war began for speaking out."[127] Although the ACLU was inspired by solidarity with labor and opposition to US involvement in World War I, it soon demonstrated its political neutrality by defending what Justice Holmes called speech by those "we hate," including communists, racists, neo-Nazis, anti-abortion activists, and terrorists.[128] In this it differs from the National Lawyers Guild and the National Emergency Civil Liberties Committee. Although Helsinki Watch focused on the communist countries bound by the Final Accord, it soon launched Americas Watch (exposing US complicity with torture) and then globalized into Human Rights Watch, partly to be more even-handed. For the same reason, its country reports document human rights violations on both sides of internal conflicts.

AI also insists on neutrality, refusing government funding and relying almost entirely on small contributions from its mass membership. Its POC campaigns and prison investigations always included three countries: communist, anti-communist, and unaligned. (It reaffirmed this "policy of political impartiality" in 1978 and 1988.) It prohibited "work on own country" to deflect charges of bias (and protect letter-writers from retaliation). Concern to preserve its moral authority led AI to decline to address the genocide in Bosnia or Rwanda in the 1990s because (according to its then director) "we didn't react to crises."[129] Researchers "were expected to take their time. And to get things right" (as they failed to do when publicizing the false charge by the daughter of the Kuwaiti ambassador to the USA during the first Gulf War that Iraqi soldiers had killed more than 300 neonates by dumping them out of incubators). This concern for accuracy created tension between AI's professional researchers and the mass membership of amateur letter-writers. AI insisted on the "one voice principle," before modifying that in 1987 to "one movement, one message, many voices" in order to increase involvement from Africa, Asia, the Americas, and the Middle East.

Rather than confront substantive wrongs (about which there may be political disagreement), NGOs seek to expose procedural injustices (which elicit a broader consensus). The ACLU challenged the process by which the USA interned Japanese Americans during World War II rather than the constitutionality of internment, the mechanism for placing groups on the Attorney General's list rather than the list itself, the practices of the House Committee on Un-American Activities rather than its mission. Instead of attacking the draft, it helped men qualify as conscientious objectors in World War I and used the Selective Service Act's procedural complexity when representing draft resisters in the Vietnam War.

In order to maximize access, the ICRC only reports secretly to the countries it investigates (and therefore never published what it knew about German concentration camps).[130] Even so, the ICRC was barred by Britain from Kenya during the Mau Mau uprising, by Nigeria during the Biafran war, by Chile after Pinochet's coup, and by North Korea and China (not then signatories to the Geneva Conventions) during the Korean War. Although the Front de Libération Nationale (FLN) denied the ICRC access to most prisoners during the Algerian War, *Le Monde*'s publication of ICRC reports on French prisoners produced "perhaps the greatest impact of ICRC activity on any war." Acknowledging that the Vietnam War was an international armed conflict, the USA granted access to its prisoners; but the ICRC suspended prison visits in South Vietnam, which restricted access. Beyond the prophylactic effect of such visits, ICRC reports may correct ongoing abuses: Portugal ended mistreatment in Mozambique, and the Greek junta temporarily suspended torture. The ICJ, by contrast, publicizes its requests to observe trials, any denials, and its subsequent diplomatic protests.[131] Some national sections have responded by refusing to assist investigations of their own governments and have even quit (as Libre Justice did over the ICJ inquiry into French actions in Tunisia).

NGOs deploy a range of tactics: gathering, evaluating, and disseminating information;[132] advocating for individuals in court, providing legal representation, and observing trials; displaying solidarity with local movements and internationalizing their concerns; voicing moral condemnation and praise;[133] and lobbying governments and international bodies.[134] NGOs typically refrain from mass action and electoral politics (sometimes because of tax laws). But Las Madres y Abuelas de la Plaza de Mayo not only demonstrated weekly in Buenos Aires for decades but also inspired others to bear witness in Latin America and Israel.[135] NGOs make principled or strategic choices about cooperating: the ACLU collaborated widely during the Popular Front period; by contrast, the Lawyers Committee for Civil Rights under Law and the Lawyers Constitutional Defense Committee (created by the ACLU, NAACP, and others) shunned the National Lawyers Guild in Mississippi in the 1960s.[136]

Information politics seeks to construct rhetorically persuasive cognitive frames, for instance by transforming Brazilian land rights from a seemingly parochial issue of social justice specific to indigenous peoples into a universal problem of environmental degradation, or renaming female circumcision (which sounds like the religiously prescribed and widely accepted practice of male circumcision) as what it really is: genital mutilation.[137] NGOs seek to demonstrate a short, clear, causal nexus between culpable actors and harms to vulnerable individuals or violations of universal legal rights (such as equal opportunity).[138] NGOs construct indices to measure and (invidiously) compare nations' human rights records.

Symbolic politics dramatizes abuses, for instance by disseminating videos of the burning of Brazilian rainforest, or exposing violence against women. As late as 1966, the Anti-Slavery Society declined to publicize slavery "in the hope of securing governmental and international co-operation" to end it. Now, however, publicity has become the preferred strategy for many NGOs. Such moral suasion may be more effective against states seeking to improve their international status.

Leverage politics uses the dependence of states or private elites on foreign money or trade (a strategy facilitated by US statutes that started tying foreign assistance to human rights in the 1970s).[139]

Accountability politics increases pressure on states to fulfill their international commitments, like those that communist regimes made in the Helsinki Final Accord. Campaigns learn from each other.[140] The refusal of the 1840 World Anti-Slavery Conference in London to seat women delegates led to the first women's rights convention in Seneca Falls, New York, eight years later. The Second Socialist International passed the first women's suffrage resolution in 1900.

Some NGOs seek insulation from political pressure by focusing on foreign countries, but then must overcome distance and disengagement.[141] Just as charities seek to personalize their causes – consider Operation Smile's heartrending pictures of children with cleft palates[142] – so iconic news photographs epitomize larger evils: a terrified Viennese child after the Anschluss, a starving albino boy in the Biafran war, Southern whites spitting at black children integrating schools, civil rights demonstrators threatened with fire hoses and snarling dogs, a naked Vietnamese girl napalmed by South Vietnamese warplanes, emaciated Bosnian prisoners reviving memories of the liberation of Nazi concentration camps, and most recently the hooded prisoners of Guantánamo Bay and Abu Ghraib.[143] (Yet a 1966 International Council Meeting resolved that AI literature should "avoid emotive or abusive expressions."[144]) Studies of responses to famine and war have found that viewers were more sympathetic to women and children than men and to suffering rather than dying.[145] The "Kony 2012" YouTube video by Invisible Children, which attracted nearly a hundred million hits, may have influenced the USA to commit Special Forces to search for him in the Central African Republic.[146] Participant Media is developing an index measuring the impact of documentary films based on the number of viewers and their emotional response and engagement.[147]

NGOs must counter compassion fatigue.[148] In its 1991 campaign "We Believe in Life Before Death," Christian Aid displayed images of world poverty, admonishing readers: "If you don't feel guilty about this, there must be something wrong with you. If you do feel guilty but don't act, your guilt can't be real." Stanley Cohen sought to explain the "consistent minority" who overcame cognitive, emotional, and practical obstacles to risk their own security in the service of others. Those who rescued Jews from the Nazis exhibited "extensivity: acting inclusively toward a wide range of people, attaching themselves to some, and assuming responsibility."[149] Rescuers felt they were "part of a common humanity ... rather than tied to specific interests of family, community or country."

NGO interventions succeed or fail for a variety of reasons.[150] A campaign against foot binding – initiated by foreign women but paradoxically embraced by the Chinese as an anti-European, anti-Christian protest – abolished the thousand-year-old practice in just over a generation.[151] By contrast, Kenyan freedom fighters invoked tradition to resist a campaign against female genital mutilation. Archbishop Josef Beran was freed from prison 18 months after AI's Sean MacBride contacted the Czech Foreign Minister. President Nkrumah released 152 political prisoners five months after AI founder Louis Blom-Cooper visited Ghana. Heinz Brandt, a trade unionist kidnapped in West Germany, was freed after two British clerics visited East Germany and Bertrand Russell threatened to return his Ossietsky Medal. Director Kenneth Roth claimed that HRW had "significant influence" on Yemen raising the age of marriage, Burma delaying anti-Muslim legislation, Syria feeling pressure to end use of chemical weapons, and enactment of a treaty on forced labor. He attributed this to HRW's ability "to shame and pressure governments that fall short of public expectations for their conduct." The global media cited it dozens of times a day, and more than two million people visited its website and viewed its YouTube, Twitter, and Facebook postings.[152]

Although most POC appeals go unanswered and some countries retaliate against prisoners, half of those AI adopted were ultimately released.[153] Acknowledging the difficulty of evaluating the effect of its interventions, AI declared in 1982 that it "does not claim credit" for freeing prisoners. Yet it publicizes successes, e.g., the release of Julio de Peña Valdéz after the Dominican Republic President received 3,000 letters on his behalf.[154] And fundraising campaigns proclaim the efficacy of letter-writers. In one AI USA appeal, a former Greek political prisoner buttonholed donors: "You cannot imagine, until it happens, the emotions you will experience when you can say to yourself, 'Because of me, he lives.' And this *will* happen. I can promise you that." Another appeal urged readers to "become part of a movement that last year got 1,600 prisoners of conscience out of jail." AI USA claimed "We have freed over 10,000 men and women." A British solicitation boasted: "A woman presses 'send' in Leeds ... and a stoning is stopped in Iran." "A man texts from Oxford ... and a torture cell in Bahrain closes forever."[155]

Avaaz.org claimed credit for international sanctions against Syria and US intervention in Libya, as well as frustrating both homophobic legislation in Uganda and American attempts to insert loopholes in the cluster bomb ban.

It is often difficult to unravel causality, given the complex interactions among NGOs, international organizations, and foreign nations, and the wide variety of strategies they deploy. After investigating the killing of students in the Central African Republic, AI protested to President Bokassa about the imprisonment of teachers.[156] Claiming to have released them, he invited AI to visit. Instead, it publicized the abduction of children just before the French President met Francophone African heads of state, who sent five African jurists to investigate. Their report contributed to France's decision to depose Bokassa. But AI's report on human rights abuses in Togo before a visit by the French President prompted the Togolese government to arrest one AI worker and bar three others, including the African-born Secretary General, who was threatened with contempt of court.

After the UN created the Special Court for Sierra Leone in 1996 to try war crimes, Nigeria granted asylum to Liberian President Charles Taylor.[157] Unable to persuade the Nigerian government to reconsider, the Open Society Institute (OSI) helped two Nigerians tortured in Liberia to sue their government. When Nigeria appealed a High Court ruling giving the plaintiffs standing, OSI and AI launched a Campaign Against Impunity, enlisting more than 300 NGOs from 17 African countries, as well as others. The UN High Commissioner for Human Rights urged Nigeria to extradite Taylor, whom the leaders of Liberia, Sierra Leone, and Guinea accused of continuing to support fighting in Liberia. HRW and journalists confronted Nigerian President Obasanjo. The Campaign plastered 10,000 "Charles Taylor Wanted" posters throughout Nigeria. A July 2005 UN Security Council resolution reaffirmed the importance of trying war criminals. The new Liberian Minister of Labor (a former human rights activist) demanded that Taylor be tried, as did the European Parliament. Just before Obasanjo was to meet President Bush, the US House of Representatives urged Nigeria to extradite Taylor; the Senate concurred. Congress approved $50 million in aid to Liberia after President Sirleaf asked Nigeria to extradite Taylor. Obasanjo said (for the first time) that ECOWAS (Economic Community of West African States) and the African Union had to approve extradition. But when NGOs tried to block his next meeting with Bush, Obasanjo told Sirleaf to take Taylor. After Taylor "escaped," Congress urged Bush to cancel the meeting, prompting Nigeria to "recapture" and extradite Taylor. He was convicted of war crimes in April 2012.

In response to AI criticism of disappearances during the dirty war, Argentina invited it to investigate in 1976.[158] The following year Las Madres de la Plaza de Mayo began demonstrating, soon joined by Las Abuelas and other human rights groups. (Tens of thousands were participating by 1981.) Although the Roman Catholic Church was complacent or complicit, other religious groups were active. La Liga Argentina por los Derechos del Hombre (communist) filed most of the legal actions; La Asamblea Permanente por los Derechos Humanos (noncommunist left and Christian Democrats) documented disappearances. AI reported that Argentina held 6,000 political prisoners, and more were presumed dead. The Carter administration denounced the country, terminating military aid; Secretary of State Vance presented the government with a list of the disappeared, as prepared by NGOs. Argentina released Jacobo Timerman, whose case had been championed by American Jews and journalists. To obtain desperately needed Export-Import Bank funds, Argentina invited an investigation by the Inter-American Commission on Human Rights (IACHR), which issued a lengthy critical report in 1980. When Argentina and the Soviet Union blocked action by the UNHRC, it created a Working Group on Disappearances, which they could not obstruct. The worst abuses ended by 1980 (the year Adolfo Pérez Esquivel, Servicio Paz y Justicia director, won the Nobel Peace Prize). The disastrous Malvinas War accelerated the transition to democracy. Human rights groups demanded "Trials and Punishment for All the Guilty." The 1983 presidential campaign debated the military's self-arrogated amnesty, which President Alfonsín revoked after winning. The legislature refused to let him prosecute offenders in military courts, which made the presumed obedience to apparently legitimate orders a defense. The government created La Comissión Nacional sobre la Desparición de Personas, which documented almost 9,000 disappearances and issued the report *Nunca Más*, inspiring 70,000 people to march.

The seven-month criminal trial transfixed a large audience, compiled a massive historical record, and convicted five of the nine high officials, imposing life sentences on former President Videla and Admiral Massera. Victims then brought private prosecutions against lower officials. But fears of a coup led to a new amnesty and laws limiting future trials to kidnapping; President Menem pardoned all those convicted or still on trial. In response to a lawsuit by El Centro de Estudios Legales y Sociales (CELS), the IACHR found that the amnesty and pardons violated the American Convention on Human Rights. Las Abuelas convinced Argentine courts that the amnesty did not cover kidnapping; and CELS persuaded the courts hearing the kidnapping prosecutions of Videla and Massera that it would be illogical to grant amnesty for worse crimes. The new Kirchner administration abrogated the amnesty; the Supreme Court found that it was unconstitutional, and that kidnapping and disappearance were crimes against humanity with no statute of limitations. A quarter century after the "dirty war" began, Las Madres ended their vigil.

Conditions sometimes worsen before they improve. In 1979 AI conducted a year-long campaign against human rights abuses in Guatemala, asking the Organization of American States (OAS) and IACHR to investigate.[159] Vice President Kramer resigned when his government refused to agree. AI's reports helped convince the US Congress to cut off aid and blocked the Reagan administration's efforts to resume it. This limited the Guatemalan government's ability to obtain loans, contributing to the 1982 coup by Gen. Ríos Montt, who was later deposed by subordinates. Abuses declined only when Guatemala returned to civilian rule. AI's 1968 report on the "Situation in Greece" prompted Scandinavian countries and the Netherlands to add torture to their accusation before the Council of Europe that the Greek junta had failed to justify its state of siege.[160] This report and another on torture were cited at a European Court of Human Rights (ECHR) hearing, at which AI investigators testified. When ECHR found numerous human rights violations, Greece withdrew from the Council to avoid expulsion. Only after civilian rule was restored did trials of human rights violations finally lead to convictions and harsh sentences.

Government forces killed many detainees during a 1996 riot in Libya's Abu Salim prison.[161] Although the government released more than 500 prisoners five years later, relatives sought news of the missing. As part of his 2004 opening to the West, Gaddafi acknowledged their right to that information. In May relatives complained to the UNHRC, which issued its findings in 2007 (having received no response from the government). That year several families sued in the North Benghazi court, represented by Fathi Terbil. After an appeals court overruled the lower court's dismissal, the latter found for the families in June 2008 and ordered the government to tell them about their relatives. Hearing nothing, they formed the Coordination Committee of the Families of the Victims, which held Libya's first public demonstration since 1976, repeating it weekly. Terbil and three Committee members were arrested but released at the behest of Gaddafi's son Saif, and the government offered to compensate those agreeing to take no further legal action. But many refused, and some who accepted the offer continued demonstrating. Several hundred Committee members marched on the 13th anniversary of the massacre. In November 2009 Saif's foundation invited families to speak at an open forum, which urged investigation of the massacre. Libya Human Rights Solidarity (LHRS) appealed to the UN Working Group on Enforced and Involuntary Disappearances, which accepted the case. LHRS, AI, and HRW published reports. Terbil and two other Committee members were arrested during the 2011 Arab Spring, sparking a protest by a few dozen women, soon joined by more than 2,000 Benghazi residents. The government killed at least 200. Terbil began an online video broadcast from the Benghazi courthouse roof. Tens of thousands of demonstrators seized Benghazi, creating a Transitional National Council (including Terbil). The 2,500 prisoners in Abu Salim rioted and escaped. Efforts to address the massacre continued after Gaddafi's overthrow.

Failures can also be illuminating. When tens of thousands died during the violent denouement of the Liberation Tigers of Tamil Eelam's 35-year war against Sri Lanka in 2009, AI and HRW each issued more than twenty press releases, and the International Crisis Group (ICG) wrote op eds in leading newspapers.[162] But NGOs failed to secure enough votes to put the war on the UN Security Council agenda, and UNHRC perversely adopted a Sri Lankan initiative welcoming "efforts by the Government to ensure safety and security for all Sri Lankans and bringing permanent peace to the country." Instead of using its financial leverage to press for an inquiry, the International Monetary Fund (IMF) approved the loan Sri Lanka needed to avoid bankruptcy. Although UN Secretary General Ban Ki-moon and Sri Lankan President Rajapaksa issued a joint communique committing the government to "take measures to address allegations related to violations of international humanitarian and human rights law," nothing happened. The US DoS, the ICG, and a UN panel of experts each produced reports detailing war crimes, while a British Channel 4 exposé was broadcast widely. But Sri Lanka barred international investigations and blocked any internal inquiry.

Professions also have played an important role in defending human rights. Religious groups were essential to the anti-slavery campaign, anti-war movements, opposition to the internment of Japanese Americans, civil rights struggle, immigrant and labor rights, and environmentalism. Doctors have examined torture victims, conducted autopsies after killings, opposed the death penalty, and advocated for access to health care. In 1988 the American Library Association denounced the FBI's Library Awareness Program, which snooped on borrowers.[163] New York City Bar committees prepared numerous reports questioning the legality of the Bush administration's actions in the "war on terror."[164]

Academics have a mixed record. Although the American Association of University Professors (AAUP) paid lip service to the concept of academic freedom, it advised faculty to accept "the necessities of the grave and perilous business" following America's entry to World War I, warning that teachers opposing conscription could be fired for "propaganda" and urging those of "Teutonic origin" to refrain from discussing the war.[165] John Dewey declared that "some surrenders and abandonments of the liberties of peace time are inevitable."[166] Northwestern University Law School Dean John Wigmore failed by a single vote to get the Harvard Board of Overseers to fire Zechariah Chafee for criticizing Justice Holmes's opinion upholding the conviction of Schenck[167] for encouraging draft resistance. When Holmes reversed course in *Abrams*,[168] Wigmore denounced the opinion as "obtuse" and "blind to the crisis."[169] Then during the 1930s Popular Front, the AAUP joined the Association of American Universities (AAU) in a statement affirming academic freedom.[170] As late as 1947 the AAUP declared that Communist Party affiliation "should not be regarded as a justifiable reason for exclusion from the academic profession." But the AAU and National Education Association, as well as most of their members, succumbed to the anti-communist hysteria of the 1950s.[171] The University of California Berkeley Academic Senate declared that "proved members of the Communist Party … are not acceptable as members of the faculty." And after more than a hundred professors were fired for their political views, the AAUP conducted just one investigation and issued no reports.

Of all professions, lawyers obviously have the strongest bonds to the rule of law.[172] Sadly, they do not always support it. During World War I the Illinois Bar Association declared it would be unpatriotic and unprofessional for a lawyer to defend those accused of draft evasion (even though the "hired gun" theory purports to immunize lawyers from moral taint by their clients).[173] Pennsylvania and Texas disbarred lawyers for associating with radicals.[174] The ABA unanimously endorsed a resolution by Elihu Root condemning "all attempts in Congress and out of it to hinder and embarrass the government of the United States in carrying on the war with vigor and effectiveness." Such actions were "in spirit pro-German and in effect giving aid and comfort to the enemy." After the war, however, a group of prominent lawyers and law professors (led by Ernst Freund, Felix Frankfurter, and Roscoe Pound) published a critical "Report upon the Illegal Practices of the United States Department of Justice."[175] The National Lawyers Guild was founded in part because the ABA excluded black lawyers and attacked the New Deal.[176] During the McCarthy era, Attorney General Tom Clark cautioned lawyers against representing those who "act like Communists." The ABA called for the expulsion of Communist Party members and urged states to disbar them, making it almost impossible for those accused of disloyalty to find a lawyer. Even the ACLU voted to bar new members who refused to sign an anti-communist oath; and in every brief filed after 1948 it felt compelled to declare it was "opposed to any governmental or economic system which denies fundamental civil liberties and human rights ... whether fascist [or] Communist."[177] By contrast with such timidity, professional associations in countries where lawyers' status is less secure – e.g., Ghana, Malaysia, Pakistan, and Hong Kong – have displayed far greater courage, demonstrating and even striking in support of the rule of law.[178]

RESEARCH QUESTIONS

How does each NGO define its purpose? Which individuals, groups, or causes does it represent? How do those choices shape its actions?

Does it identify with those it represents or does it assert apolitical neutrality? How does it acquire and preserve moral capital? How do those choices influence its membership, actions, and efficacy?

How do its size, structure, and funding affect its capacity to protect human rights and choice of causes? How do attacks on the rule of law and NGO responses affect membership and support?

What affects its size and reputation? Do efforts to enroll members and preserve its reputation influence its actions?

What alliances does it make?

Which victims take action? Individually or collectively? When do they bear witness or demonstrate? With what effect?

How does an NGO use information, symbols, leverage, and shame? Which other strategies does it use (e.g., information gathering and dissemination, issue framing, personalizing wrongs, advocacy, legal representation, direct action, mass mobilization, publicity, shaming)? Why? How does it balance access (which may require secrecy) and publicity (as a means of leverage)? When and why do states grant or deny access to NGOs? When do NGOs use courts, and with what consequences?

How do strategies differ in efficacy?

What explains individual responses to human rights violations? What encourages some to become involved by contributing money or taking action? Why do some insiders take risks by whistle-blowing or helping victims?

What are the consequences of NGO actions? How do NGOs interact with each other and with states (and their component parts), supranational bodies and the media? How do human rights NGOs interact with religious groups, trade unions, and political parties? When do NGOs succeed in mobilizing economic sanctions and with what effect?

What is the consequence of concessions by the regime?

Are NGOs more successful in preventing ongoing or future abuses or in redressing past abuses?

How does redress of human rights abuses relate to electoral political or regime change? Under what circumstances do regimes investigate and acknowledge abuses?

Which regimes are most vulnerable to NGO influence? Why do some regimes refuse to make any concessions, quitting international bodies that threaten to sanction them?

How have professions (e.g., clergy, doctors, academics) responded to human rights abuses? How have lawyers performed their pivotal role in preserving the rule of law?

Whistle-Blowers and the Media

Whistle-blowers and the media interact symbiotically in exposing government (and private) misconduct.[179] Four decades before Chelsea Manning and Edward Snowden, whistle-blowing changed history. Ronald Ridenhour, a helicopter gunner, gathered accounts of the My Lai massacre from participants and eyewitnesses, sending them to members of Congress and the DoD. Daniel Ellsberg, a RAND Corporation analyst, photocopied the Pentagon Papers, which documented the lies used to justify the Vietnam War and its secret escalation. When Henry Kissinger (Nixon's National Security Adviser) and Sens. William

Fulbright and George McGovern showed no interest, Ellsberg offered them to the *New York Times*, which deliberated three months before publishing the first installment.[180] After Attorney General Mitchell demanded it desist, the *Times* published the next installment, as well as Mitchell's threat. When SDNY Judge Murray Gurfein (a Nixon appointee) enjoined the *Times* (the first time a federal court ever engaged in prior restraint of speech), Ellsberg took the Papers to the *Washington Post*. Assistant Attorney General Rehnquist threatened the *Post*. But DDC Judge Gerhard Gesell (a Johnson appointee and former reporter) denied an injunction, after which Gurfein lifted his. Gesell threatened to dismiss the case when the government sought to present secret evidence. The DC and Second Circuits found for the newspapers.

Solicitor General Erwin Griswold warned the Supreme Court that publication would pose a "grave and immediate danger to the security of the United States." (In 1984 he admitted it would have taken him seven weeks to read the papers, so he asked three subordinates to identify "really bad" things and chose 11 of their 42 suggestions. In 1989 he admitted in a *Washington Post* op ed that there had been "massive overclassification" and he had "never seen any trace of a threat to the national security from the publication.") In nine separate opinions, six Justices found that the government had not met its burden for prior restraint. Justice Black wrote that "the word 'security' is a broad, vague generality whose contours should not be invoked to abrogate the fundamental liberties embodied in the First Amendment," which empowered the press to "bare the secrets of government and inform the people." "[P]aramount among the responsibilities of a free press is the duty to prevent any part of the government from deceiving the people and sending them off to distant lands to die of foreign fevers and foreign shot and shell." Because the other two branches tended to defer to the president in matters of national security, Justice Stewart warned, "the only effective restraint upon executive policy and power … may lie in an enlightened citizenry – in an informed and critical public opinion. For this reason, it is perhaps here that a press that is alert, aware, and free most vitally serves the purpose of the First Amendment." After publication Ellsberg surrendered and was indicted on a dozen felony charges, carrying up to 125 years in prison. Nixon told Charles Colson (his special counsel) to smear Ellsberg as a communist, hoping the House Committee on Un-American Activities (HUAC) would investigate. "Jesus Christ, [the audience will] be hanging from the rafters … Going after all these Jews." (Like other anti-Semites, Nixon conveniently forgot Jesus was Jewish.) But FBI Director Hoover refused to investigate, presciently warning Nixon: "I think we ought to be *awful careful* what we do in this case of this man Ellsberg. Because … they're going to make a martyr out of him … And in view of what the Supreme Court has now said, I doubt whether we're going to be able to get a conviction out of him" [original emphasis]. Instead, acting on White House orders, the "Plumbers" (a covert White House Special Investigation Unit) broke into Ellsberg's psychiatrist's office, provoking Judge Matthew Byrne to dismiss the prosecution.

In March 1971 the Citizens Commission to Investigate the FBI stole over a thousand classified documents from the Bureau's Media, Pennsylvania office, sending them anonymously to members of Congress and the press.[181] Defying Nixon administration pressure, the *Washington Post* and *New York Times* competed to expose COINTELPRO, which had illegally surveilled, infiltrated, and tried to discredit domestic political groups. The government ended the program and ultimately had to compensate many targets. The Senate Judiciary Committee's Subcommittee on Constitutional Rights investigated the army's domestic surveillance, forcing it to end. After Nixon resigned, President Ford appointed a new Bureau director, who apologized for Hoover's abuses. Ford's Attorney General, Edward Levi (a former University of Chicago president and law professor), limited FBI investigation, and Ford prohibited the CIA from conducting domestic surveillance and the National Security Agency (NSA) from intercepting domestic communications.

These examples illustrate the media's central role in disseminating whistle-blower revelations, increasing pressure on government to stop violating civil liberties and remedy past abuses. The media also can be a powerful force on its own. Radio and television transmission of the Army–McCarthy hearings (see below) and Edward R. Murrow's 1954 *See It Now* program contributed to McCarthy's downfall.[182] The media's investigative tools were greatly expanded by the 1966 Freedom of Information Act (FOIA), drafted by a conservative Republican senator hoping to use it to attack President Johnson's Great Society programs.[183] Half its sponsors were Republicans, including Donald Rumsfeld, who declared that all information "is in the public interest." Then House Minority Leader Gerald Ford decried the "mushrooming growth of Government secrecy." It was Nixon's obstruction of Congress's Watergate investigation that led Sens. Sam Ervin and William Moorhead to assemble a bipartisan coalition (including Barry

Goldwater) to strengthen FOIA, requiring the government to answer requests promptly and justify refusals. Although Ford (now president) vetoed the bill, Congress overrode him three days after Attorney General Saxbe (the first permanent replacement after the Saturday Night Massacre – see below) released the COINTELPRO documents. Once information is in the public domain, government has great difficulty suppressing it, as shown by the abortive efforts to stop publication of technical details about the hydrogen bomb and, more recently, the UK's absurd destruction of *Guardian* computer hard drives containing the documents disseminated by Edward Snowden (which were stored elsewhere).[184]

Some of the most dramatic evidence for the power of the press emerges, perversely, in government efforts to muzzle it. Vice President Spiro Agnew said that because television enjoyed "a monopoly sanctioned and licensed by the government," it should be "made more responsive to the views of the nation."[185] Nixon's communications director warned the media that their failure to eliminate "bias" would "invite the government to come in." After holding "off-the-record" meetings with the CEOs of major networks, White House special counsel Charles Colson boasted to Chief of Staff H.R. "Bob" Haldeman that "they are damned nervous and scared and we should continue to take a very tough line."

RESEARCH QUESTIONS

What moves whistle-blowers to act? What risks do they run? What consequences do they face? When does the press publish the information? What are the effects of disclosure? How do the courts, legislature, and executive respond? When does the government terminate illegality? When does it redress civil liberties violations?

When do the media take the initiative to investigate and expose government illegality? What are the consequences of such exposure?

Executive

All three branches of government may protect or violate the rule of law in response to perceived national security threats. Courts and legislatures usually defer to the superior knowledge and speed of the executive, which often overreacts (and may be misinformed).[186] During the Civil War, President Lincoln (a lawyer) suspended habeas corpus and authorized his Secretary of State to arrest anyone suspected of disloyalty.[187] Justifying one imprisonment, Lincoln declared: "the

Constitution is not, in its application, in all respects the same, in cases of rebellion or invasion involving the public safety, as it is in time of profound peace and public security." He had acted out of "public necessity," whether or not it was "strictly legal." Denouncing the Supreme Court's grant of habeas to John Merryman, Lincoln warned that its interpretation of the Constitution would allow "all the laws, *but* one, to go unexecuted, and the government itself to go to pieces, lest that one be violated."

In 1908 Woodrow Wilson (another lawyer, then president of Princeton) championed free speech: "it is pent-up feelings that are dangerous, whispered purposes that are revolutionary, covert follies that warp and poison the mind … the wisest thing to do with a fool is to encourage him to hire a hall and discourse to his fellow citizens."[188] But as US president a decade later he assailed those who "inject the poison of disloyalty into our most critical affairs." Proposing the Espionage Act of 1917, Wilson declared that the disloyal "had sacrificed their right to civil liberties."[189] After World War I his Attorney General, A. Mitchell Palmer, established the General Intelligence Division within the Bureau of Investigation (the FBI's precursor), assembling a list of more than 200,000 suspects, promptly rounding up 650 and deporting 249, and then detaining another 4,000, deporting the aliens, and handing over citizens to state authorities for prosecution under syndicalist laws.

When Franklin Roosevelt's (FDR's) Solicitor General, Robert Jackson, suspended wiretapping, FBI Director Hoover enlisted the support of Treasury Secretary Henry Morgenthau, who appealed to FDR's personal secretary. The latter reported that "the president said, tell Bob Jackson to send off J. Edgar Hoover and order him" to resume wiretapping.[190] Roosevelt (who had dropped out of Columbia Law School after passing the bar) secretly wrote Jackson the next day, declaring "to hell with the Supreme Court." The president sent Hoover the names of hundreds of critics, ordering him to investigate those opposing his lend-lease policy.[191] Jackson said that because the president (whom he knew well) "thought that his [own] motives were always good for things that he wanted to do, he found difficulty in thinking that there could be legal limitations on them."[192] Francis Biddle (Jackson's successor) observed that Roosevelt was "not much concerned with the gravity or implications" of Japanese American internment, believing that "what must be done to defend the country must be done." Biddle concluded cynically that "the Constitution has never greatly bothered any wartime president."

Fearing renewed McCarthyism during the Vietnam War, President Johnson told his Cabinet: "I don't want us to get into that dangerous situation. I love this system."[193] But rapidly convinced that criticism was a communist conspiracy, he encouraged the CIA to expand domestic intelligence. When CBS screened an anti-war documentary, Johnson screamed at station head Frank Stanton: "Frank, are you trying to fuck me? Frank, this is your president and yesterday your boys shat on the American flag." When Director of Central Intelligence (DCI) Helms told Johnson there was "no significant evidence that would prove Communist control or direction of the U.S. peace movement or its leaders," the White House suppressed his report.[194]

Nixon has become notorious for invoking national security to defend his abuses of power: the "enemies" list, Internal Revenue Service (IRS) audits, surveillance of phone calls and letters, the "Plumbers" breaking into Ellsberg's psychiatrist's office and the headquarters of the Democratic National Committee (DNC) in the Watergate complex, and the subsequent cover-ups. But Nixon was hardly unique. After exposure of al-Qaeda's Bojinka plot to bomb American flights over the Pacific, Congress authorized Clinton to "disrupt, dismantle and destroy international infrastructures used by international terrorists."[195] Under his Executive Order (EO) declaring extraordinary rendition a "matter of the highest priority," 87 men were imprisoned in Albania, Bulgaria, Azerbaijan, and the United Arab Emirates (UAE), some of whom were sent to Egypt and tortured.

The CIA has flagrantly violated civil liberties under many presidents and directors.[196] In 1951 it operated secret prisons in Germany, Japan, and the Panama Canal Zone. In 1952 it began opening international mail. That year its Guatemala office identified 58 people targeted for assassination. It seriously considered and may have attempted assassinating several heads of state, including Sukarno (Indonesia), Castro (Cuba), Lumumba (Congo), and Trujillo (Dominican Republic). For six years DCI Helms hid the report of his Inspector General (IG) on these plots. The CIA infiltrated the 1967 anti-war demonstration in Washington and spied on the peace movement for the next seven years. The Agency was implicated in Pinochet's coup in Chile and assassination of Orlando Letelier (who had sought refuge in the USA). And of course it covered up everything. Former DCI Porter Goss said at a 2006 college commencement: "If this were a graduating class of CIA case officers, my advice would be short and to the point. Admit nothing, deny everything, and make counteraccusations."

But the executive also can defend the rule of law and restrain overzealous subordinates. President Jefferson pardoned all his fellow Republicans convicted under the Sedition Act of 1798, declaring "the law to be a nullity, as absolute and palpable as if Congress had ordered us to fall down and worship a golden image."[197] Lincoln prohibited the military from arresting an estimated 13,000–38,000 people suspected of disloyalty.[198]

And executive overreaching can provoke backlash.[199] After the 1920 Palmer raids, the US Attorney in Philadelphia sent President Wilson an open letter of resignation. The US Attorney for Montana persuaded a grand jury *not* to indict 48 men for sedition, drafting their finding that "in many cases reports of so-called 'seditious utterances' and 'disloyal statements' were highly colored and greatly exaggerated." Louis F. Post, Assistant Secretary of Labor, convinced his superior that it was not a deportable offense to belong to the Communist Labor Party (which did not advocate violence) or Communist Party (which did, but it padded its membership rolls). Post granted those arrested a right to counsel and to confront witnesses, refused to hear illegally obtained evidence, and dismissed warrants in 2,000–6,000 deportation cases. Summoned before a hostile House Rules Committee, he declared: "when the executive department of the Government is the absolute judge of whether a man shall remain in this country or not, and the courts will not interfere, we should see to it that no injustice is done to the man." He took "from the criminal law its humane, its just, its American, its constitutional principles of protection to the liberty of the citizen." The Committee vindicated him.

Before leaving office, Attorney General Thomas Gregory urged President Wilson to release or commute the sentences of the 200 jailed under the Espionage or Sedition Acts.[200] Wilson pardoned all but Debs (later pardoned by President Harding). Harlan Fiske Stone, Coolidge's Attorney General (and former Columbia Law School dean), fired the Bureau of Investigation director, declaring:

> [A] secret police system may become a menace to free government and free institutions because it carries with it the possibility of abuses of power which are not always quickly comprehended or understood … The Bureau of Investigation is not concerned with political or other opinions of individuals. It is only concerned with their conduct and then only with such conduct as is forbidden by the laws of the United States. When a police system passes beyond these limits, it is dangerous to the proper administration of justice and to human liberty, which should be our first concern to cherish.

In 1938 Attorney General Frank Murphy created the Department of Justice (DoJ) Civil Liberties Unit, declaring: "in a democracy, an important function of the law enforcement branch of the government is the aggressive protection of the fundamental rights inherent in a free people."[201] After war began in Europe, he said: "I do not believe that a democracy must necessarily become something other than a democracy to protect its national interests ... We *can* prevent and punish the abuse of liberty by sabotage, disorder and violence without destroying liberty itself." "In the name of justice," the government should avoid the "inhuman and cruel things" it had done during World War I. "We need, and we earnestly ask, from every citizen and every government an unswerving resolve that for as long as this crisis endures, we will keep our heads – that we will not abandon the Bill of Rights." Robert Jackson (Murphy's successor) ordered charges dismissed against 16 members of the Abraham Lincoln Brigade (who had fought Franco in Spain), warning US Attorneys against calls for the scalps of dissenters in "times of fear or hysteria." Even after Pearl Harbor, Attorney General Francis Biddle cautioned against repeating the "periods of gross abuse" during the previous war, "when hysteria and fear and hate ran high, and minorities were unlawfully and cruelly abused."[202] He exhorted everyone "who cares about freedom" to "fight for the *other* man with whom he disagrees" (a close paraphrase of the defense of "freedom for the thought that we hate" in the *Schwimmer* dissent by Holmes, for whom Biddle had clerked). He directed US Attorneys that prosecution for "alleged seditious utterances must not be undertaken unless consent is first obtained from the Department of Justice"; and he created the Special War Policies Unit to ensure FBI compliance with the law. He dismissed charges against men arrested for praising Hitler and Japan and resisted Roosevelt's pressure for a grand jury investigation of the antiwar America First Committee. He initially opposed Japanese American internment (whose constitutionality Secretary of War Stimson doubted and whose necessity senior military officials denied). Although the FBI arrested over 16,000 aliens during the first 19 months after Pearl Harbor, civilian panels released about 10,000.

Discovering that Hoover had created a list of citizens designated for military internment as alleged fascists or communists, Biddle wrote him:

> [T]his classification system is inherently unreliable. The evidence used for the purpose of making the classifications were [*sic*] defective; and finally, the notion that it is possible to make a valid determination as to

> how dangerous a person is in the abstract and without reference to time, environment, and other relevant circumstances, is impractical, unwise, and dangerous.

Hoover merely renamed his list the Security Index, adding thousands during the war (mostly suspected communists) but shelving the plan when Truman won the 1948 election. DoJ declined to prosecute some suspected communists under the Alien Registration Law (Smith Act), even those named by the House Committee on Un-American Activities (Dies Committee), because Attorneys General Murphy, Jackson, and Biddle opposed the law.[203] Invoking his duty not to violate "the fundamental rights and privileges of free assembly, free opinion, and free speech," Murphy refused to prosecute the 563 federal employees Dies exposed as members of the American League for Peace and Democracy. Although Biddle reluctantly charged 29 Socialist Workers Party leaders, only 18 were convicted. He later admitted they had been guilty of nothing more than "time-honored Marxist lingo" and claimed he had expected the Supreme Court to invalidate the law.

During the postwar anti-communist hysteria Truman vetoed the Internal Security Act of 1950 (although Congress easily overrode him).[204] Administrative proceedings exonerated almost all those charged with disloyalty, although the process was long and painful.[205] The more than 4.7 million loyalty checks between 1947 and 1953 led to only 40,000 FBI investigations; departmental or agency loyalty boards cleared 90 percent of the 8,000 charged; and a third of the 500 employees ordered discharged won their appeals.

President Johnson's Attorney General Nicholas deBelleville Katzenbach (a former law professor at Rutgers, Yale, and Chicago) directed the FBI to report about wiretapping (although it revealed only about a fifth of its bugs).[206] Solicitor General Thurgood Marshall (who, as NAACP General Counsel, had been surveilled by the FBI) informed the Supreme Court that an appellant had been wiretapped, leading to reversal of his conviction. Six days later Hoover banned black bag jobs and break-ins, and stopped opening first-class mail. By 1970 he refused to authorize illegal actions without the president's written approval: "I'm not going to accept the responsibility myself anymore … it is becoming more and more dangerous and we are apt to get caught."

Hoover's newfound caution led the Nixon White House to create the "Plumbers" to break into the DNC headquarters in Watergate.[207] After they were arrested by District of Columbia police, FBI supervisory agent

Daniel Bledsoe opened a case under the wiretapping statute, prompting a furious phone call from John Erlichman (Nixon's Chief Domestic Adviser): "I have a mandate from the president of the United States. The FBI is to terminate the investigation of the break-in. Did you hear what I said? Are you going to terminate the investigation?"

Bledsoe's reply that the FBI had a constitutional obligation to determine whether there had been an illegal act provoked Erlichman to explode: "Do you know that you are saying 'no' to the President of the United States? … Your career is doomed." The next day the FBI's Criminal Investigative Division chief warned colleagues that the Bureau's "reputation was at stake … the investigation should be completely impartial, thorough and complete." Nixon then ordered the new CIA deputy director to tell FBI Director Patrick Gray to back off. When Gray resisted, Erlichman surrendered the files incriminating the White House, which Gray destroyed six months later. Months after that, Mark Felt (Gray's deputy) shared information about Watergate with four other FBI employees, who leaked it to the *Washington Post*. Under White House pressure Attorney General Richard Kleindienst instructed Gray five times to fire Felt. Nixon himself warned Gray: "I am certainly going to have to ask the Director of the Bureau at times to do things that are going to protect the security of this country." Kleindienst and Gray resigned rather than capitulate. When independent prosecutor Archibald Cox (a former Harvard Law School professor) subpoenaed the Watergate documents and tapes, Nixon told his new Attorney General, Elliott Richardson, to fire Cox and then fired Richardson for refusing. His replacement, Deputy Attorney General William Ruckelshaus, resigned rather than comply. His successor – Solicitor General Robert Bork – ultimately executed Nixon's order to fire Cox.

After Clarence M. Kelley, the new FBI Director, ordered agents to abstain from "investigative activity that could abridge in any way the rights guaranteed citizens by the Constitution," the Bureau terminated 94 percent of its domestic intelligence investigations, erased 9,000 open cases, transferred national security cases to the Criminal Investigative Division, reassigned at least 645 agents from national security to ordinary crime, and abolished the powers of the Intelligence Division. Attorney General Levi promulgated the first guidelines for FBI intelligence operations. On his orders, Kelley ordered agents to report illegal activity during the previous decade. Although none did, the DoJ Civil Rights Division launched investigations of 53 agents. Accusing high

FBI officials of lying to him, Kelley created a new task force for internal investigations, and the FBI raided its own headquarters and New York office, uncovering secret documents, including Hoover's file of black bag jobs.

DCI Helms refused Nixon's request for $1 million from the Agency's secret funds to buy the silence of the Watergate burglars.[208] James Schlesinger, Helms's successor, ordered "all senior operating officials of this Agency to report to me immediately on any activities now going on, or that have gone on in the past, which might be construed to be outside the legislative charter of this Agency." Although his successor (William Colby) hid the damning report, Acting Attorney General Laurence Silberman (a staunch conservative) transmitted its contents to President Ford, who appointed the Rockefeller Commission to investigate the CIA's domestic activities. President Carter's DCI, Stanisfield Turner, refused to authorize an agent to conduct an assassination to prove his bona fides to the terrorist organization he sought to infiltrate. "I thought that was not the right way to play the game." Deputy Director Bobby Inman (a retired admiral) resigned when he caught Reagan's DCI Casey "lying to me in a number of cases." Shown a draft secret executive order to assassinate alleged terrorists, Deputy Director McMahon "told our folks to send it back and tell them: 'when the President revokes the executive order which precludes CIA from assassinations, then we'll take this on.'"

Independent counsel Lawrence Walsh, though a lifelong Republican and early Reagan supporter, found that the president, Secretary of Defense Weinberger, DCI Casey, and subordinates illegally sold arms to Iran to fund the Nicaraguan Contras.[209] But a Court of Appeals overturned two convictions (Oliver North and John Poindexter), finding them tainted by Congressional testimony; and President George H.W. Bush pardoned the other six. Walsh wrote later: "What set Iran–Contra apart from previous political scandals was that a cover-up engineered in the White House of one president and completed by his successor prevented the rule of law being applied to perpetrators of criminal activity of constitutional dimensions."

RESEARCH QUESTIONS

When do presidents abridge civil liberties? How do they justify such actions?
How do executive officials violate civil liberties through surveillance, interrogation, detention, prosecution, rendition, deportation, and assassination?

Do they compile lists of those suspected of disloyalty? Do they tolerate freedom of association, media criticism, and demonstrations? When do they suppress information? Cover up their misconduct? When do subordinates resist superiors' orders to abridge civil liberties? To respect civil liberties? With what consequences for both the subordinates and civil liberties?

When do executive officials use their power to defend the rule of law? Decline to prosecute those wrongly arrested or charged? Resign rather than engage in unlawful acts? Which civil liberties do they protect? What lessons do they learn from previous abuses? What happens to those who blow the whistle or oppose superiors?

When does executive overreaching produce a backlash?

What happens when the national security threat diminishes?

Does fear of liability restrain executive officials from engaging in illegal conduct? When are executive officials held liable for violating the rule of law? How do new leaders uncover past illegal acts? Do they punish them? How do they change those policies? How effective are internal checks like Inspectors General?

How do the biographies and characters of executive officials shape their attitudes and actions with respect to the rule of law? How do views change when people ascend to higher executive offices?

Legislature

Congress and its state counterparts construct the legal framework within which the executive protects or infringes civil liberties.[210] Legislatures tend to rubber-stamp whatever the executive proposes. In 1723, in the space of less than a month, without debate or serious division, the English parliament passed the Waltham Black Act, drafted by the Attorney General and Solicitors-General, creating some fifty new capital offenses, presuming the guilt of those who failed to surrender, and subjecting accused to trial in any county.[211] But after prosecutors had routinely used the law for several decades, they became reluctant to charge under it and courts began to construe it narrowly; and a century after its enactment, it was repealed. In the first decades after American independence, Federalists passed the Alien and Sedition Acts of 1798 (discussed below), publicly justified by fear of a French invasion but actually directed at Republican opponents. However, the Virginia legislature resolved that the Sedition Act was "leveled against the right of freely examining public characters and measures, and of free communication among the people thereon, which has ever been justly deemed the only effectual guardian of every other right."[212] And the laws expired at the end of the Adams administration, just two years after their passage. Congress ratified Lincoln's suspension of habeas corpus (albeit a year after the fact).[213] Soon after the outbreak of the Korean War and the indictment of the Rosenbergs, Congress passed the Internal Security Act, broadening the definitions of espionage and sabotage, and ordering communist and communist-front organizations to register with the Subversive Activities Control Board.[214] Legislation also may strip courts of jurisdiction to hear challenges to executive power, as the South African Parliament did after declaring the 1980s Emergency.[215]

Investigations by committees of Congress (and state legislatures, especially during the civil rights struggle) can abridge civil liberties. Rep. Hamilton Fish (R-NY), who created and chaired the Special Committee to Investigate Communist Activities, declared in 1930 that the ACLU was "closely affiliated with the Communist movement in the United States, and fully 90 per cent of its efforts are on behalf of communists."[216] Although HUAC, created by Rep. Martin Dies (D-Tex) in 1938, could not "definitely state whether or not the ACLU was a Communist organization," it maligned as "communistic" 240 other groups (including the Boy Scouts and Camp Fire Girls), 483 newspapers, and 280 labor organizations.[217] After HUAC identified 38 federal employees as subversives, the House voted overwhelmingly to withhold the salaries of three, although the Senate initially demurred.

State legislatures can be even more contemptuous of constitutional rights. During the post-World War I Red Scare, 32 states passed laws prohibiting displays of the Red flag; in 1919–20, at least 1,400 people were arrested under such legislation and at least 300 convicted, some sentenced to 20 years.[218] In 1920 the New York State Legislature voted almost unanimously to suspend the five Socialists just elected.[219] Charles Evans Hughes (who had been Governor of New York, Chief Justice of the US Supreme Court, and unsuccessful Republican candidate for president) persuaded the Association of the Bar of the City of New York and the New York State Bar to support calls for reinstatement. A half century later the Supreme Court unanimously overturned a Georgia House of Representatives decision to exclude Julian Bond for endorsing a statement by the Student Non-Violent Coordinating Committee (SNCC) that "we are in sympathy with, and support, the men in this country who are unwilling to respond to a military draft."[220]

If Congress usually does the executive's bidding, it sometimes defends civil liberties. Congress declined to expel Matthew Lyon after he was jailed under the Sedition Act of 1798.[221] In passing the Espionage Act of 1918, it refused to ban publication of information that the president found "is or might be useful to the enemy."[222] It repealed the Sedition Act of 1918 just two years after passage. Although the Supreme Court ruled in 1928 that wiretapping did not violate the Fourth Amendment, the Communications Act 1934 barred the interception of phone calls and disclosure of their contents.[223] The following year, despite rising concern about Nazism, the House rejected legislation forbidding groups like the German American Bund to incite disaffection.[224] Exposure of CIA involvement in Pinochet's coup in Chile led Congress to amend the Foreign Assistance Act, increasing its oversight of the Agency and requiring the president to brief Congressional committees before any covert action. Congress denied President Clinton some of the increased powers he sought after disclosure of the Bojinka plot.

Congress may investigate executive illegality. NSA refused to cooperate with the Senate Select Committee to Study Governmental Operations with Respect to Intelligence Activities (chaired by Frank Church) until the *New York Times* reported that the Agency had eavesdropped on American citizens.[225] After the Church Committee disclosed that NSA had monitored all international telegrams since 1945, it terminated the program. The committee's exposé of FBI and CIA misconduct contributed to passage of the Foreign Intelligence Surveillance Act, which limited (but also legalized) wiretapping. The discovery that Rep. Robert Drinan SJ had been wiretapped stimulated the Senate to explore similar abuses. Efforts by the Senate Select Committee on Presidential Campaign Activities (chaired by Sam Ervin) to obtain Nixon's White House tapes concerning Watergate prompted the Saturday Night Massacre (the cascade of DoJ resignations), a Supreme Court order to surrender the tapes, and Nixon's resignation to avoid almost certain impeachment – the ultimate check on presidential misconduct. Watergate also led Congress to strengthen FOIA (over the opposition of President Ford, who had supported it as a member of Congress). But Congressional investigations can also compromise criminal prosecutions for civil liberties violations. And the executive may oppose Congressional investigations for endangering intelligence agents, pointing to the assassination of the CIA's Athens station chief.

Congress can restrain overzealous members. In February 1950 the Senate adopted the report of a committee chaired by Sen. Millard Tydings (D-Md), calling for investigation of Sen. Joseph McCarthy's claims of communists in government.[226] Sen. William

Benton (D-Ct) urged the Senate to expel McCarthy but then lost his own re-election bid. At a May 1954 hearing of the Senate Internal Security Subcommittee, McCarthy produced a letter from Hoover alleging there were 35 suspected subversives at the Army's Fort Monmouth. At the behest of Hoover and President Eisenhower, who thought McCarthy had gone too far, Attorney General Brownell ruled that possession of the letter was unauthorized use of classified information, a federal crime. McCarthy (who chaired the Senate Committee on Government Operations' Permanent Subcommittee on Investigations) retaliated by asking all two million government employees to communicate with him secretly. Invoking executive privilege, Eisenhower forbade executive branch employees to testify. The Army–McCarthy hearings (televised at the insistence of Senate Majority Leader Lyndon Johnson) publicized McCarthy's abhorrent tactics. A Senate investigation of his Subcommittee's hearings found that its counsel, Roy Cohen, had abused his authority by intervening (with McCarthy's permission) in the military's treatment of fellow staffer David Shine. Sen. Ralph Flanders (R-Vt) defied his party's leadership by introducing a censure resolution. A six-member bipartisan committee responded by unanimously recommending "condemnation," which the Senate adopted 67–22, effectively ending McCarthy's crusade. (This may be a common trajectory: the Salem witch trials ended soon after they targeted community leaders.[227]) McCarthy died less than three years later.

RESEARCH QUESTIONS

When do legislatures accept or reject executive proposals to abridge civil liberties? When do they deprive courts of jurisdiction to hear challenges to executive action? When do they pass laws limiting executive abridgements of civil liberties?

When do prosecutors use or abjure laws abridging civil liberties?

When do legislative committees use or abuse their investigative powers to abridge civil liberties? When do they use their investigative powers to curtail executive violations of civil liberties?

When do legislatures curb overreaching by their own members?

When does the executive curtail legislative investigations and with what justification?

When does the threat of impeachment restrain executive misconduct or prompt a resignation?

CONCLUSION

The history of the rule of law in times of stress reveals the pressures to which it has been subjected and the resources mobilized in its defense. Like all ideals, the rule of law is never fully realized but also never entirely extinguished. Context is all: advocates in one struggle may be antagonists in another; strategies that work in one time and place may be ineffective in another. The examples discussed above generate questions that will guide my analysis of the relative success or failure of efforts to preserve the rule of law in the United States since 9/11. (The judiciary is the subject of the companion volume *Law's Trials*.)

CHAPTER TWO

ABU GHRAIB

Although investigative reporters had exposed US abuses of prisoners in Afghanistan as early as March 2003,[1] it took the revelations about Abu Ghraib to generate widespread debate on the treatment of detainees. Many have described the egregious misconduct by members of the military, CIA agents, and civilian contractors, and the responsibility of those who crafted orders and legal justifications.[2] This chapter focuses on the response, which mobilized most of the remedial mechanisms discussed in these volumes, raising the following questions: Who blew the whistle, why, and with what consequences? How did the media expose and judge the behavior? How did the photographs of sexualized behavior shape responses? When and how did the military learn, and what did it do? What was disclosed, and what remained secret? How did the military explain the behavior? Whom did it hold responsible? Which military personnel were investigated, who was found guilty, and how were they punished? What corrective actions were taken? How did other governmental bodies react? How did the executive respond? How effective was Congressional oversight, and how was it influenced by party politics? What does this sordid episode tell us about the capacity of the rule of law to correct violations?

Just before midnight on January 13, 2004 in Abu Ghraib, Sgt. Joseph Darby gave Army CID a disc of photos lent him six weeks earlier by Cpl. Charles A. Graner Jr., with a cover note:[3]

> I am writing this letter as a matter of moral ethics ... [I have] seen some very disturbing photos of inmates in the hard site prison, Tier 1A to be specific. I had heard stories in the company about the incidents that were taking place but I did not believe them till I was given these photos.

Although "kind of shocked" and "bewildered," he took no action because Graner had been transferred out of Abu Ghraib. But when Darby heard that Graner – "the most charismatic, most manipulative person you will meet" – was about to return, "I knew I had to turn [the photos] in now and not wait. Because I was concerned [that the behavior] was going to start again." In addition to Graner, the ringleader, he identified others in the photos: Ivan L. "Chip" Frederick, Lynndie England, Sabrina Harman, Megan M. Ambuhl, and Jeremy C. Sivits. "I am writing this to try to right the wrongs that I have seen in these photos and video clips. Since no one will come forward ... I feel something must be done. So I am giving this disc to you. Do with it as you wish."

Darby later said he initially thought the photos were "pretty funny." "I'm not a Boy Scout. To me, that pyramid of naked Iraqis, when you first saw it, is hilarious." (Graner felt the photos were so innocuous that he gave them to his own parents!) Darby's Military Police (MP) unit had seen detainees wearing women's underwear and had handled "ghost prisoners" for OGA (Other Government Agency – a euphemism for the CIA) when they first replaced the 72nd MP Brigade in October 2003. But pictures of "prisoners being beaten, or the one with a naked Iraqi sitting on his knees in front of another naked Iraqi ... just didn't sit right with me." A roommate and a sergeant whom he viewed as a mentor both advised him to report the photos. It was "a hard decision to do something that puts your friends in prison," but their behavior "violates everything I believe in, violates the very rules of law." (Others accused him of hoping for a promotion or seeking revenge against Frederick and Graner for mocking his weight.) Soon after testifying in the Art. 32 hearings for those named above, he was placed in protective custody following death threats. Because neighbors and even family members viewed him as a "traitor" and stopped talking to him, he never returned to his small western Maryland town. "People there don't look at the fact that I knew right from wrong. They look at the fact that I put an Iraqi before an American ... But I don't regret any of it." He received the John F. Kennedy Profile in Courage Award for his actions.

The Army Criminal Investigation Command (CID) arrested and searched the suspects on January 14, 2004.[4] Two days later Col. Thomas Pappas (commander of the 205th Military Intelligence (MI) Brigade) banned cameras and the "creation or display of any pornographic or sexually explicit photographs." That night "there was a big fire" with "a lot of porn being burned," and soldiers scrubbed their computer photo folders. Three days after that LtGen. Ricardo S. Sanchez, commander of US forces in Iraq, ordered an investigation. MGen. Antonio M. Taguba, appointed to conduct it on January 31, submitted his report on February 26. On January 23 Sanchez summoned BGen. Janis Karpinski (commander of the 800th MP Brigade in Abu Ghraib), gave her an admonishment (dated a week earlier) for "poor leadership," and suspended the platoon leader and company and battalion commanders.[5] She called the process "a joke."

Warned that the media were about to break the story, on April 24 the Department of Defense (DoD) ordered MGen. George R. Fay (incoming deputy commander of intelligence) to examine MI interrogation at Abu Ghraib. Four days later Dan Rather showed some of the shocking photographs on CBS's *60 Minutes II*. (An MP had sent them to his uncle to pass on to a retired Army colonel writing for *Newsweek*.) Although CBS had delayed broadcasting at the request of Joint Chiefs of Staff (JCS) chairman Gen. Richard B. Myers, it acted now because "other journalists" were "about to publish."[6] Indeed, two days later *The New Yorker* posted on its website Seymour M. Hersh's account based on Taguba's secret report, publishing three articles by Hersh in quick succession.[7]

Concurring with the conclusion of the (still secret) November 2003 report by MGen. Donald J. Ryder (Army Provost General) that MPs should "not participate in military intelligence supervised interrogation sessions," Taguba described "numerous incidents of sadistic, blatant, and wanton criminal abuses intentionally perpetrated" by MPs, MI, and the Joint Interrogation and Detention Center (JIDC).[8] He urged a criminal investigation of MI Because its interrogators "actively requested that MP guards set physical and mental conditions for favorable interrogation of witnesses." He found that MPs were insufficiently trained and understaffed, and tension between Karpinski and Pappas was exacerbated when Sanchez made Pappas "responsible for MP units conducting detainee operations." Taguba recommended reprimands for Karpinski, Pappas, LtCol. Jerry L. Phillabaum, LtCol. Steven L. Jordan, Maj. David W. DiNenna, Capt. Donald J. Reese, 1st Lt. Lewis C. Raeder, and others.

Appearing on three talk shows the Sunday after these disclosures, Gen. Myers dismissed the abuses as the actions of "just a handful of soldiers," but admitted he had not read the Taguba report.[9] The next day Senate Armed Services Committee (SASC) chairman Warner asked DoD officials to testify. Sen. McCain (R-Az) called for a public hearing "as soon as possible." Sen. Levin (D-Mich) (SASC's ranking minority member) warned that the effects of the abuses would extend "beyond what we can imagine today on our troops and our nation's security." A day later Donald Rumsfeld condemned the conduct as "totally unacceptable and un-American," but added it was just "abuse, which I believe technically is different from torture … And therefore I'm not going to address the 'torture' word."[10] The military's six reviews showed "the system works." DoD would "continue to take whatever steps are necessary to hold accountable those that may have violated the code of military conduct and betrayed the trust placed in them by the American people."

MGen. Geoffrey Miller (who had become commander of US military prisons in Iraq after the abuses) responded by promising to cut the Abu Ghraib prison population by more than half and forbidding physical contact with or threats against detainees.[11] "We follow the tenets of the Geneva Convention" and "do not use stress positions … [or] sleep deprivation, unless that is approved at the general-officer level." His staff was "a little bit embarrassed because some people who came before them didn't follow the standards." He was "absolutely confident" his recommendations for MP involvement in interrogations, made when visiting Abu Ghraib in September 2003 as Guantánamo commander, were "not only appropriate but did and would have made this operation more effective and efficient." MPs "understand what the detainees' life is … [whom] they spoke with … their mental attitude. That information should be collected and provided to the interrogation teams to better prepare … to assist the interrogation of each detainee."

A week after the abuses were exposed, President Bush rebuked Rumsfeld for not alerting him to the photographs and spoke to two Arabic-language television channels:[12] "People in Iraq must understand that I view those practices as abhorrent. They must also understand that what took place in that prison does not represent [the] America that I know." He promised that the inquiry "will be transparent, it will be open and people will see the results." At a press conference the next day Bush told Jordan's King Abdullah II:

> I was sorry for the humiliation suffered by the Iraqi prisoners, and the humiliation suffered by their families. I told him I was equally sorry that people who have been seeing those pictures didn't understand the true nature and heart of America. I assured him Americans, like me, didn't appreciate what we saw, that it made us sick to our stomachs.

Prominent Democrats, such as Sens. Biden (D-De) and Harkin (D-Ia), called for Rumsfeld's resignation. Sen. Kerry (D-Mass) said he had done so "months ago over Iraq. This is the frosting." Sen. Leahy (D-Vt) asserted that Rumsfeld and Deputy Defense Secretary Paul Wolfowitz "bear ultimate responsibility" for "a colossal failure of leadership." Rep. Pelosi (D-Ca) (House Minority Leader) accused Rumsfeld of misleading lawmakers during an April 28 closed-door briefing: "Mr. Rumsfeld has been engaged in a cover-up from the start on this issue and continues to be so." But Bush called him "a really good Secretary of Defense" who had "served our nation well."

The same day the *Wall Street Journal* published the ICRC's confidential February 2004 finding that "the use of ill-treatment against persons deprived of their liberty" in Abu Ghraib "went beyond exceptional cases and might be considered a practice tolerated by" coalition forces.[13] ICRC President Jakob Kellenberger was "unhappy" the *Wall Street Journal* had acted without ICRC consent because "confidentiality is an element vital to obtaining access to prisoners world-wide." But now that the leak had occurred, an ICRC spokesman said that between May 2003 and February 2004 it had sent senior Bush administration officials "very extensive and detailed" accounts, "with clear descriptions of the treatment of prisoners." ICRC Operations Director Pierre Kraehenbuehl had found "a broad system" of "incidents of degrading and inhuman behavior," which were "tantamount to torture" and not "isolated acts." Christophe Girod, chief ICRC delegate in Washington, said "we had regular meetings with the Pentagon, the State Department and the White House to discuss these prison conditions." Kellenberger had reported the abuses to Secretary of State Powell on January 15. DoS now acknowledged that Powell and Coalition Provisional Authority head J. Paul Bremer III had often raised the issue with the Pentagon.

Karpinski admitted having seen the ICRC's November 6, 2003 Working Paper, although not until about two weeks later.[14] Had she been alerted earlier, she would have said "Hold on a second, because not in my facility you don't." Col. Marc Warren (Sanchez's senior legal adviser) helped draft the December 24 response to the ICRC, which was discussed with Sanchez's top deputy, MGen. Walter Wojdakowski. (Sanchez claimed not to have seen the ICRC report until January 2004.) Warren confirmed that the ICRC Working Paper had been distributed throughout Army headquarters in Baghdad. He later told a CID investigator: "When I saw the ICRC report ... I couldn't believe it. I spoke to Judge Advocates and MI officers who were familiar with the conditions at Abu Ghraib and the uniform reaction was that these reports could not be credible … the report had to be exaggerated … the allegations were crazy."

At the meeting to discuss the response, officers proposed limiting further ICRC access. Karpinski said the military "wanted the I.C.R.C. to schedule visits for those particular cellblocks, because it could interrupt any of the military intelligence. The position that they were taking was that the I.C.R.C. could not have unrestricted access to those particular cellblocks."

White House General Counsel Alberto R. Gonzales admitted having had "concerns" about ICRC inspections. "Part of the concerns is [*sic*] whether or not there were interrogations that might be interrupted under a spot check." The response also claimed that "security detainees" could be treated differently from POWs. (Art. 5 of the Fourth Geneva Convention states that in the name of "absolute military security" prisoners "under definite suspicion of activity hostile to the security of the Occupying Power" could be held incommunicado indefinitely, but still had to be treated with humanity. Coalition Provisional Authority (CPA) Administrator Bremer issued Memorandum Number Three defining *everyone* in military custody not charged under Iraqi law as a "security detainee.") LtGen. Lance Smith (CENTCOM (Central Command) deputy commander) confirmed that before Darby delivered the photos, "there were reports that there was trouble in those places, but not of the character we're talking about." After the ICRC visit on January 4–8, "the indication from there was that there were improvements."

The day after the ICRC reports were disclosed, Rumsfeld told SASC he took:[15]

> full responsibility … to evaluate what happened, to make sure that those who have committed wrongdoing are brought to justice, and to make changes as needed to see that it doesn't happen again. I feel terrible about what happened to these Iraqi detainees. They are human beings. They were in U.S. custody. Our country had an obligation to treat them right. We didn't, and that was wrong.
>
> So to those Iraqis who were mistreated by members of the U.S. armed forces, I offer my deepest apology. It was inconsistent with the values of our nation. It was inconsistent with the teachings of the military, to the men and women of the armed forces. And it was certainly fundamentally un-American.
>
> Further, I deeply regret the damage that has been done.

> First, to the reputation of the honorable men and women of the armed forces, who are courageously and responsibly and professionally defending our freedoms across the globe …
>
> Second, to the president, the Congress and the American people, I wish I had been able to convey to them the gravity of this before we saw it in the media.
>
> And finally to the reputation of our country …
>
> It's important for the American people and the world to know that while these terrible acts were perpetrated by a small number of U.S. military, they were also brought to light by the honorable and responsible actions of other military personnel … [like] Spc. Joseph Darby, who alerted the appropriate authorities that abuses were occurring …
>
> Let me be clear: I failed to recognize how important it was to elevate a matter of such gravity to the highest levels, including the president and the members of Congress …
>
> I'm seeking a way to provide appropriate compensation to those detainees who suffered such grievous and brutal abuse and cruelty at the hands of a few members of the United States armed forces. It's the right thing to do.
>
> I wish we had known more sooner and been able to tell you more sooner, but we didn't.

(In fact, two days after Darby delivered the photos, Rumsfeld's senior military adviser and the JCS chair were emailed a summary of the alleged abuses.)[16] Rumsfeld continued:

> there are other photos that depict incidents of physical violence toward prisoners, acts that can only be described as blatantly sadistic, cruel and inhuman … Congress and the American people and the rest of the world need to know this …
>
> However terrible the setback, this is also an occasion to demonstrate to the world the difference between those who believe in democracy and in human rights, and those who believe in rule by terrorist code … part of what we believe in, is making sure that when wrongdoings or scandal do occur, that they're not covered up, but they're exposed, they're investigated, and the guilty are brought to justice.
>
> Mr. Chairman, I know you join me today in saying to the world, judge us by our actions, watch how Americans, watch how a democracy deals with the wrongdoing and with scandal and the pain of acknowledging and correcting our own mistakes and our own weaknesses.

Rumsfeld maintained that as early as January 16 "the Central Command public affairs people went out and told the world. They told everyone in the world that there were allegations of abuse and they were being investigated."[17] But the world learned little, since the entire press release read:

> An investigation has been initiated into reported incidents of detainee abuse at a Coalition Forces detention facility. The release of specific information concerning the incidents could hinder the investigation, which is in its early stages. The investigation will be conducted in a thorough and professional manner. The Coalition is committed to treating all persons under its control with dignity, respect and humanity. Lt Gen. Ricardo S. Sanchez, the Commanding General, has reiterated this requirement to all members of CJTF-7 [Combined Joint Task Force 7].

Stephen A. Cambone (Under Secretary of Defense for Intelligence) told SASC he had sent Miller to Iraq to improve intelligence from people "captured on the battlefield" for "force-protection purposes."[18] Miller recommended that "the detention operations function must act as an enabler for interrogation" by "setting the conditions for successful exploitation of the internees. Joint strategic interrogation operations are hampered by lack of active control of the internees within the detention environment," which required "synergy between MP and MI resources and an integrated, synchronized and focused strategic interrogation effort." But in response to Sen. Reed (D-RI) (a former Army officer), Cambone denied "encouraging a policy that had military police officers enabling interrogation." Sen. Levin called the abuses a "willful determination to use these techniques as part of an interrogation process."

After Rumsfeld privately submitted two letters of resignation, Bush went to the Pentagon to declare to his Defense Secretary in front of the media: "You are courageously leading our nation in the war against terror. You are doing a superb job. You are a strong secretary of defense, and our nation owes you a debt of gratitude."[19]

Karpinski now complained that the military treated her as a "disposable" "leper" because she was a reservist.[20] Taguba's report was "flawed." The military had been "setting me up over time." She wondered why Sanchez, who had "divisions all over Iraq," just happened to visit Abu Ghraib three times in October 2003. "Did he know that something was going on?" Was he "starting a campaign to stay out of the fray and blame the 800th [MP Brigade]?" Miller's August–September 2003 visit "gave them plans, told them what they were succeeding with in Gitmo." "MI people were in this all the way." "I don't believe that the MPs, two weeks onto the job, would have been such willing participants, even with instructions, unless someone had told them it was all okay."

The *New York Times* said Taguba's testimony and the ICRC report "made it plain that the abuse of prisoners by the American military and intelligence agencies was systemic."[21] It accused Republicans of seeking to deflect attention by focusing responsibility "onto officers in the battlefield, far away from President Bush and his political team," and complaining that Democrats and the media were "overreacting." Sen. Inhofe (R-Ok) was "more outraged by the outrage" than by the treatment of prisoners who were probably guilty of something.

Rumsfeld told SASC that Sanchez's "Interrogation Rules of Engagement" were "deemed to be consistent with the Geneva Conventions."[22] Army lawyers had concluded that 45 minutes of stress positions and 72 hours without sleep did not violate the Army Field Manual or the Geneva Conventions. Shown photos and videos that were still secret, Sen. Campbell (R-SC) wondered "how the hell these people got into our Army," and Rep. Harman (D-Ca) said they depicted "cruel and sadistic torture."

The next day Rumsfeld made a one-day surprise trip to Abu Ghraib, declaring: "In recent months, we've seen abuses here, under our responsibility, and it's been a body blow for all of us. The people who engaged in abuses will be brought to justice. The world will see how a free system, a democratic system, functions and operates transparently, with no cover-up." [23] He told MPs the abuse "doesn't represent America." "The United States government is going to take care of the people who end up being convicted of some wrongdoing. The justice system of the United States is serious, professional, and it's under way." Myers, who accompanied Rumsfeld, explained that still-secret photos and videos of abuses would be withheld to avoid compromising prosecutions. Miller was transferring all prisoners the USA held in Abu Ghraib to the hopefully named Camp Redemption. In fact, about 2,000 prisoners were released between May 21 and June 6.[24]

A few days later SASC chairman Warner promised that his committee would look "up and down and sideways in the chain of command and get to the bottom" of "the mistreatment of Iraqi prisoners by a small – hopefully a very small – number of personnel."[25] "We must not allow these acts of a few to tarnish the honor of the many dedicated men and women in uniform, 99.99 percent." "A very brave enlisted man sought to bring to the attention of his superiors a problem which, frankly, in his guts he knew was wrong." "I'm proud of the manner in which the armed forces of the United States ... have promptly reacted to the allegations, undertaken an appropriate investigation, and begun disciplinary action." The "really distressing thing is watching the families ... of the soldiers who are under the uniform code now being examined." Hersh's third article claimed that Rumsfeld had secretly approved harsh interrogation of Iraqi prisoners. *Newsweek* revealed that a January 2002 memo by White House counsel Gonzales declared that the Geneva Conventions were "obsolete" and dismissed some provisions as "quaint." Sen. McCain responded: "We need to take this up as far as it goes, and we need to do it quickly." Sen. Levin decried the fact that "all the focus has been on the few at the bottom that we've seen pictures of. It goes way further up than that, both on the military and the civilian side." "The inquiry is not just about the behavior of a few soldiers ... but also those who are responsible for encouraging, condoning or tolerating such behavior." Sen. Biden warned that any "morphing of the rules of treatment" was "a dangerous slope."

Colin Powell did not remember the Gonzales memo but had "always said that the Geneva Accord is an important standard in international law and we have to comply with it." The White House equivocated: "We are a nation at war and we are a nation of laws. Our most important responsibility is to protect the American people, and we act in an appropriate manner to protect that responsibility." National Security Adviser Condoleezza Rice said "there's really nothing" to Hersh's story. DoD called it "a tapestry of nonsense." "No responsible official of the Department of Defense approved any program that could conceivably have been intended to result in such abuses as witnessed in the recent photos and videos." The next day DoS issued its annual human rights report, delayed two weeks by the Abu Ghraib scandal, which the Assistant Secretary of State for Human Rights acknowledged was "a cloud that was obscuring what we were trying to do." Some governments criticized for human rights violations retorted by citing those abuses.

Warner called Rumsfeld as the first witness and ordered him sworn in, "a breach of common practice that infuriated the Defense Secretary." Sen. Stevens (R-Ark) angrily confronted Warner afterwards, demanding "no more hearings." All SASC Republicans except McCain, Graham, and Collins threatened not to support Warner's chairmanship if he continued the hearings. He persisted but focused on the future rather than past abuses. Before one hearing Sen. Roberts (R-Kan) told CENTCOM Commander Gen. John P. Abizaid: "the press accounts are just unreal. It's been a landslide of criticism." He promised to "throw you a couple of softballs" and did just that. Abizaid characterized the misconduct as "isolated incidents," the "failures of a few." There was no "culture of abuse." The "criminal misconduct is not the subject of any order or policy" but rather a "doctrinal problem of understanding … what do the M.P.'s do, what do the military intelligence guys do." "[T]here is great confusion in a combat zone all the time, almost as much as there is here in Washington." "We emphasize to them all the time that they need to treat people right." In February 2004 the Army IG had found no "pattern of abuse of prisoners." Claiming that the ICRC's November 2003 report did not reach senior commanders for months, he acknowledged "a real problem with ICRC reports and the way that they're handled." Asked why Gen. Ryder had not seen any abuse during his October–November 2003 visit, Abizaid said "as I travel around, I don't always get the whole truth."

It later emerged that interrogation policy at the time had been unclear and in constant flux.[26] On December 2, 2002, Rumsfeld had approved for Guantánamo the use of the enhanced interrogation techniques (EITs) of yelling, deception, false flag (the deception that the interrogator was from a country that treated detainees harshly), stress positions, isolation, sensory and sleep deprivation, hooding, removal of comfort items, dietary limits, nudity, forced grooming, exploitation of phobias like fear of dogs, and grabbing, poking, or pushing. After January 15, 2003 he had to approve requests for those techniques. On April 4 Air Force General Counsel Mary Walker urged approval of 26 techniques, including Fear Up Harsh, Pride and Ego Down, poking and grabbing, dietary and environmental manipulation, false flag, and threat of transfer, and recommended that another nine techniques require individual approval: isolation, interrogation for 20 hours a day, forced grooming, stress positions, sleep deprivation, physical training (PT), face or stomach slap, nudity, and creating anxiety, e.g., by using dogs. On April 16 Rumsfeld approved 24 techniques, including Fear Up Harsh, Pride and Ego Down, dietary and environmental manipulation, and isolation.

On September 10 Warren circulated in Iraq an unsigned "Interrogation and Counter-Resistance Policy," largely reproducing Miller's Guantánamo rules but adding techniques Capt. Wood had authorized for interrogation at Bagram Air Base in Afghanistan (isolation up to 30 days, nudity, shackling in stress positions, sleep sensory deprivation, and barking dogs) as well as yelling, loud music, light control, and deception by false statements.[27] Wood testified elsewhere that "I increasingly felt the need to draw on my experience in Afghanistan," where she "had used 'sleep adjustment' and 'stress positions' as effective techniques." Sanchez's approval was required for use of these techniques on POWs (but there were none at Abu Ghraib). A September 14 draft signed by Sanchez eliminated sleep deprivation and required his approval for dogs, stress positions, and noise and light control. Two weeks later a new list eliminated changes of scenery, dietary and environmental manipulation, sleep adjustment, false flag, dogs, sensory deprivation, loud noise and light control, deception and stress positions. On October 12 a new list of permitted practices excluded all the harsh techniques. Capt. Wood produced a slide of "Interrogation Rules of Engagement" (IROE), with a left column of permitted practices and a right column of harsher ones, which could be approved by Sanchez. In a sworn statement to CID on May 14, 2003 Pappas said the IROE "was a JIDC published poster based on the 12 October policy so soldiers and civilians working in the JIDC could have an easy to follow set of rules. It was meant to provide an unclassified reminder that emphasized approved approaches," because all the official interrogation policies were secret documents. "The IROE was never intended to be, nor was it in fact an approved CJTF-7 policy."

At the SASC inquiry Warren testified that the rules concerning detainee treatment were so confusing that low-level officers made up their own. Asked how harsh interrogation techniques could be reconciled with the Fourth Geneva Convention's prohibition of "physical or moral coercion," he said sensory deprivation and 72 hours of sleep management could be applied to "security detainees" under Art. 31. "You have to look at it on a case-by-case basis." Capt. Wood's IROE were posted on the JIDC wall "to be a profilacis [*sic*]." "The intent … was to ensure that interrogators understood that those measures on the left hand column … were authorized, but that any other measures [in the right hand column] were not [allowed] without commanding general approval." The reason that "the so-called harsh methods appear on the right … is because … the legal community and the military intelligence community took every doctrinal approach that was authorized" or "that was contained in any document we could find and we put that in a policy so as to regulate it." "[T]here were three requests for stress positions which were submitted and … denied at the brigade commander level." But he agreed that "the optics are bad on that chart," using "a term I've learned in the past week in Washington."

BGen. Sanchez was "horrified at the abusive behavior." "As senior commander in Iraq, I accept responsibility for what happened at Abu Ghraib, and I accept as a solemn obligation the responsibility to ensure that it does not happen again." In September 2003 he had ordered soldiers to conduct all interrogations in a "lawful and humane manner with command oversight." "I have never approved the use of any of those [harsh] methods within CJTF-7 in the 12.5 months that I've been in Iraq." "[M]y understanding is that" the IROE slide "was produced at the company commander level." He saw it for the first time at a SASC hearing. "The only approvals that I ever had at my desk was [*sic*] for continued segregation beyond 30 days." He had distributed a memo on "Proper Treatment of Iraqi People During Combat Operations" in October 2003, reissued it on January 16, 2004, and later emphasized that all Iraqis should be treated with dignity. On November 19, 2003 he had put Pappas in charge of the prison "for forward operating base protection and for security of detainees." "All of the other responsibilities for continuing to run the prison for logistics, training, discipline and the conduct of prison operations remained with" Karpinski. MP duties did not include "conducting detainee interrogations." Sanchez never saw Pappas's November 30, 2003 request to interrogate a prisoner by throwing chairs and tables to "invade his personal space," hood and expose him to barking dogs, and use loud music to keep him awake for three days. A week before the hearing Sanchez had prohibited MPs from seeking permission to use any coercive method except isolation.

Miller "categorically" denied having developed "a 72-point matrix for stress and duress" at Guantánamo, including "heat or cold, withholding food, hooding for days at a time, naked isolation, and cold, dark cells." "I read the Geneva Convention … in great depth, my lawyer probably spent one to two hours a day with me." He had briefed MP battalion commanders and MI company commanders in Iraq, but "no methods contrary to the Geneva Convention were presented at any time." He did not believe his instructions "may have been misinterpreted." Rather, there was "a breakdown in leadership on how that [*sic*] the follow-on actions may have occurred." He had recommended that MPs "conduct passive intelligence gathering," which "meant to observe the detainees … see who they would speak with and then report that to the interrogators." "I did not tell General Karpinski I was going to Gitmo-ize Abu Ghraib." Miller later told a CID investigator he had explained to Pappas "that the working dogs were used in GTMO to help the MPs with the custody and control issue and that it was very effective." "We have never used the dogs for interrogations at GTMO and I did not discuss this with them because I did not have the concept." "We had received SecDef [US Secretary of Defense] authority to use the removal of clothing as a technique for about a six-week period between Dec 02 and Jan 03 but that was never done at GTMO." But Pappas had told Taguba on February 12, 2004 that a list of about twenty approved interrogation techniques vetted by his Staff Judge Advocate (SJA) had included the use of dogs:

> I did not personally look at that with regard to the Geneva Convention. It was a technique that I had discussed with General Miller … In the execution of interrogations … we are trying to get information from people. We have to … assert control and get detainees into a position where they're willing to talk to us … [Miller] said that they used military working dogs, and that they were effective in setting the atmosphere for which … you could get information. Certainly using the dogs, okay, in the booth with or without a muzzle, they would have been leashed … [The IROE said] "Presence of military working dogs require [*sic*] CG's [Commanding General] approval." It didn't say where. It didn't say "muzzled."

Sen. Byrd (R-WV) declared that "this travesty of justice … the Iraqi prisoner scandal has dealt a body blow to the heroic efforts of scores of American military troops and civilian workers in Iraq to win the hearts and minds of the Iraqi people." Sen. Dayton (D-Mn) deplored that: "We've now had 15 of the highest-level officials involved in this entire operation, from the secretary of defense to the generals in command, and nobody knew that anything was amiss, no one approved anything amiss, nobody did anything amiss. We have a general acceptance of responsibility, but there's no one to blame, except for the people down at the very bottom of one prison." Sen. Graham (R-SC) had "never seen a more dysfunctional command relationship in the history of me looking at the military like that jail." "I'm just not convinced that it's six or seven M.P.s doing this by themselves." "We know that military intelligence analysts and maybe interrogators are present at abuse situations." But he did not blame Miller: "People didn't misunderstand what you said. They just totally ignored it."

Other Republicans defended the military. Sen. Allard (R-Co) said "the real travesty of justice is on the other side," i.e. the investigations. Sen. Sessions (R-Ala) deplored that "in this city, people get preoccupied with failure and error." Sen. Inhofe believed that concern about Abu Ghraib was "so press driven that it's – this is out of control." "Quite frankly, I'm sorry that you guys are here." He told the officers testifying: "I just think that we need to talk about the good things that have been happening and get you back in the battle where you belong." Sen. Cornyn (R-Tex) was "not troubled by the fact that some person who's trying to kill Americans is deprived of a good night's sleep in order to elicit information consistent with the Geneva Convention and our laws and humanity – information that might save American lives."

House Armed Services Committee (HASC) chairman Hunter assailed Warner for summoning senior commanders from the field to testify before SASC.[28] It was "sad" that "the Senate has become mesmerized by cameras." HASC had held just one public and one closed-door hearing, whereas SASC had conducted two public hearings and had scheduled a third. House Majority Leader DeLay was "pleased with the way that the House committee has handled this ... I would rather them do the work than be on television." Sen. Cornyn sympathized with Rumsfeld's complaint that "essentially all of his time is being taken up in addressing the need to produce testimony and witnesses." But another HASC member, Heather A. Wilson, replied that "Congress must not only ask tough questions, we must be seen by the world and by Americans to be doing so." (She was a former Air Force officer who had served on the National Security Council staff and written a book based on her Oxford D. Phil dissertation, which had won the ICRC prize for international humanitarian law.) And House Minority Whip Hoyer said "this shocking episode demands a full, open inquiry." Finding it "hard to believe that the military's own investigations will yield much" and "not likely that the Senate hearings will produce the answers the public deserves," the *New York Times* called for an independent investigation.

Abu Ghraib led to disclosure of several secret memos authorizing harsh interrogation.[29] DoJ Office of Legal Counsel (OLC) lawyers Robert Delahunty and John Yoo and White House counsel Gonzales had advanced legal rationalizations in January 2002. An October 2003 JIDC "memorandum for the record" approved the use of working dogs following authorization by the interrogation officer in charge. A secret annex to Taguba's report contained Pappas's November 30, 2003 request for harsh interrogation techniques. Pappas's December 12, 2003 situation update said "sleep management, sensory isolation longer than 30 days, [and] dogs" could be used only with Sanchez's approval.

Bush declared that as "a fitting symbol of Iraq's new beginning," the USA would demolish Abu Ghraib, which had become "a symbol of disgraceful conduct by a few American troops who dishonored our country and disgraced our values."[30] DoD simultaneously announced it would replace Sanchez. (Although it denied this was related to Abu Ghraib, Gen. Abizaid had said in January 2004 that Sanchez would remain.) The same day Karpinski learned she had been suspended. She claimed that because, by December 2003, the prison was being run by MI, it was she who had been ordered to sign the response to the ICRC Working Paper (which she was not shown), declaring that detainees were getting the best possible treatment, "improvements are continually being made," and "all internees are guaranteed humane treatment as a minimum standard."

Now that confidentiality had been breached, ICRC investigator Martin Damary described what he had observed in Abu Ghraib.[31] Presented with an unclothed detainee on his first visit on October 9, 2003, he told Karpinski: "Sorry, I can't talk to people when they're naked." Guards tried to stop him from seeing cellblock 1A (where the worst abuses occurred). The ICRC's November 6, 2003 Working Paper complained about nudity, lack of access, verbal abuse, sleep deprivation, stress positions, and scars from tight handcuffing. Prisoners displayed "concentration difficulties, memory problems, verbal expression difficulties, incoherent speech, acute anxiety reactions, abnormal behavior and suicidal ideas." Capt. Reese (372nd MP Brigade commander and Tier 1A warden) told CID on January 18, 2004: "it was not uncommon to see people without clothing." "I was told the 'whole nudity thing' was an interrogation procedure used by military intelligence, and never thought much of it." Nudity had ceased by the ICRC's second visit in January 2004.

Two memos on Abu Ghraib surfaced at the end of May 2004, one written on January 12, 2004 and the other earlier, abolishing (and thereby acknowledging) the CIA practice of concealing "ghost detainees" from the ICRC.[32] More evidence emerged of the abuses' antecedents. A 205th MI Brigade interrogator said that after visiting Iraq in August–September 2003, Miller sent about 15 interrogators, analysts, and specialists "to set up a Gitmo-style prison" in Abu Ghraib. A member of the 372nd MP Brigade explained they had been told in Afghanistan that prisoners were "enemy combatants," unprotected by the Geneva Conventions. Detainee treatment "was based on racism, really. We called them hajis, and that psychology was really important."

At the end of May 2004 the *New York Times* leaked the November 5, 2003 report by Army Provost Marshal Ryder, who criticized the process for deciding whom to detain, the absence of any "trained professional correctional force," and the "lack of policy and standard operating procedures," but said nothing about the abuses.[33] The Army now replied that no prisoners had been released after being found innocent or serving their time. All had been "determined to be security threats" and went before a review board "far more frequently than required by the Geneva Conventions." But the February 2004 ICRC report said that although MI estimated that 70–90 percent of the detainees had been "arrested by mistake" and only 2 of the 57 detained in September 2003 had intelligence value, a general ordered all of them held.

The Art. 32 proceedings initiated against seven MPs in April were leaked at the end of May 2004.[34] Guy Womack, a former Marine Corps officer representing Graner, said his client had been following orders "by his superiors in a military police chain of command." "The photos proved that MI had directed the abuses." "Only the intelligence officers who study the psyche of the prisoners know that there are certain poses and ways to stage them." Graner testified that he had been sleeping only 3–5 hours a night when the abuses occurred. "Several of our platoon had taken fire … both of my roommates had been injured in an IED [improvised explosive device]. Many times we went out without armor, a few times we went out without doors" on the vehicles.

Sgt. Samuel Provance III testified in SPC Ambuhl's hearing that MI SPC Armin Cruz "was known to bang on the table, yell, scream and maybe assaulted [*sic*] detainees during interrogations in the booth." Her lawyer, Harvey J. Volzer, said "everybody knew what was going on at the prison and nobody reported it because everybody thought there was authorization for what was going on." The hearing judge recommended dismissal of the charges of maltreating prisoners and indecent acts because Ambuhl, though present, had not "carried out any act of cruelty or maltreatment."

The *Washington Post* published a July 2003 memo to ALLCON (all concerned) by Capt. William Ponce Jr., an MI officer at Baghdad headquarters: "The gloves are coming off, gentlemen, regarding these detainees. Col. [Steven] Boltz [MI chief in Baghdad] has made it clear that we want these individuals broken. Casualties are mounting, and we need to start gathering info to help protect our fellow soldiers from any further attacks."

But Army CIC concluded that the MPs were a rogue band "just having some fun with the prisoners" after "the chain-of-command shifts had gone home." It found no evidence that any of the 25 MI interrogators had encouraged abuse. Only one acknowledged seeing any of the photos or videos, and just seven had witnessed mistreatment, mostly minor and outside the prison. They had suggested sleep deprivation but not physical abuse or sexual humiliation. Many victims were not even scheduled for questioning.

Paul Bergrin, representing Sgt. Javal S. Davis, said MPs had orders to use dogs, nudity, isolation, and other methods employed at Guantánamo. MPs "were told consistently, 'Soften them up; loosen them up. Look what's happening in the field. Soldiers are dying in droves. We need more intelligence.'" When Davis asked "Should we be following these orders?," Sgt. Frederick replied "Absolutely. We're saving American lives." Frederick's military lawyer said Capt. Reese was prepared to testify that Sanchez had observed some of the abuses, and that Capt. Wood "condoned some of the activities and stressed that that was standard procedure." 1st Sgt. Brian G. Lipinski would testify that MI had told him that abusing detainees was "the right thing to do."

In early June 2004 SPC Sivits pleaded guilty, agreeing to testify against the other six in exchange for a one-year sentence and demotion.[35] He photographed an abused detainee because "I was just trying to be nice to everybody," and had not reported the abuse after Frederick warned: "you didn't see" anything.

A week later Sgt. Provance talked to the media, defying an order not to do so even though unprotected by the whistle-blower statute.[36] He had testified against the MPs after others had begun speaking because, having attended a fundamentalist seminary before joining the military, "I started getting bothered because innocent people were being held and they were getting lost in the system, and the military wanted to keep it secret." Sen. Graham had assured Provance that "he was doing his legal duty" by testifying.

Some of the evidence submitted to MGen. Fay's investigation was leaked at the beginning of June.[37] An interrogator said that LtCol. Stephen L. Jordan (JIDC director and the second highest MI officer after Capt. Wood) concealed 5–6 prisoners from the ICRC. Jordan confirmed this: "The O.G.A. folks wanted to be able to pull somebody in 24, 48, 72 hours if they had to get 'em to Gitmo." Pappas had wanted a written agreement about this, declaring "if I go down, I'm not going down alone. The guys from Langley are going down with me." When two MI interrogators paraded a detainee naked in the cold before other detainees, Jordan only had them transferred. A leak of classified portions of Taguba's report revealed that Jordan told him: "I've no training on the military side of what constitutes interrogation operations." "[S]ince

I rated nobody, since I had no input or evaluations, had no responsibilities or resources, Colonel Pappas was the [effective] commander of the J.I.D.C." But Reese said his MPs viewed Jordan's constant presence on the prison tiers as evidence they were behaving properly. When Reese complained about nudity, Jordan replied: "that's an interrogation method that we use."

Five ranking House Democrats (Waxman, Skelton, Harman, Lantos, and Obey) asked Bush and Rumsfeld for ICRC reports, interrogation guidelines, and autopsies.[38] Waxman complained of "a pattern of Republicans refusing to hold oversight hearings on any issue where the administration might be embarrassed." But House Speaker Hastert accused the Democrats of an election-year "political witch hunt." The White House stonewalled, claiming that Congressional inquiries could jeopardize ongoing investigations. When Waxman sought to create a special panel to investigate prisoner abuse, HASC chairman Hunter asked sarcastically if Waxman wanted "another 15 hearings? Maybe we should cancel every piece of congressional business for the entire year so that the issue of Abu Ghraib can be milked until the election." Republicans like Sen. Graham and Rep. Wilson (R-Az) reiterated their concerns. And DoD insisted: "we're going to go wide, we're going to go deep, we're going to look under every rock and find out just how far this went." But Tillie K. Fowler (a former Republican Congresswoman appointed to the military inquiry led by James R. Schlesinger) had already concluded that Rumsfeld "is an honest, decent, honorable man, who'd never done this type of activity."

Several MI interrogators spoke to the press.[39] SPC Israel Rivera saw detainees stripped naked, made to crawl on their stomachs, and chained into a pile, while MPs shouted homosexual slurs in Arabic to get them to admit a rape. "Anyone who says this was condoned by MI – no, absolutely not." He had assured Cruz he would not report it but told SPC Schlegel, who did so. Although he had previously refused to testify, he was speaking now out of "a big sense of guilt." SPC Roman Krol denied Rivera's allegations that he had dumped water on detainees and thrown a foam football at them, but admitted witnessing these actions. He had not reported the incident because he "didn't care" and did not "know the rules of engagement of MPs."

The *New York Times* disclosed Walker's March 6, 2003 memo to Rumsfeld advancing a necessity defense for *any* treatment of Guantánamo detainees and recommending 35 interrogation procedures

(18 new), including forced nudity to create "a feeling of helplessness and dependence" and "a quick glancing slap to the fleshy part of the cheek or stomach."[40] Gen. Hill (who replaced Miller as Guantánamo commander) claimed Walker's group "wanted to do what is humane and what is legal consistent not only with" the Geneva Conventions but also with "what is right for our soldiers." Lawrence Di Rita, DoD chief spokesman, bizarrely maintained that Walker's memo "was not a legal analysis" and insisted that the 24 interrogation techniques Rumsfeld authorized did not constitute torture and complied with international treaties. The day after Walker's memo was published, Attorney General John Ashcroft told the SJC that Bush had "made no order that would require or direct the violation" of international treaties or domestic laws prohibiting torture. Confronted with the Abu Ghraib photos by Sen. Kennedy (D-Mass), Ashcroft insisted "this administration opposes torture" and "atrocities" were being prosecuted. He accused critics of ignoring the fact that the USA was at war, and refused to provide the OLC opinions (on which Walker's memo was based) because they were confidential legal advice to the president and it was not good policy to debate the president's legal powers during wartime. Asked by Biden if torture ever was justified, Ashcroft refused to answer.

The media intensified its criticism.[41] The *Los Angeles Times* condemned "out-of-control government servants willing to discard the most fundamental values of this nation." The *New York Times* declared that "the inhumanity at Abu Ghraib grew out of a morally dubious culture of legal expediency and disregard for normal behavior fostered at the top of this administration." It might be "necessary for Congress to form an investigative panel with subpoena powers" to determine "how high up in the chain of command the specific sanction for abusing prisoners was given." It also published two op eds. A senior foreign affairs editor warned that American officials "could find themselves in serious jeopardy under international law" and "the United States will find it difficult to prosecute foreign war criminals if it refuses to accept for itself the legal standards it accuses them of breaking." Donald P. Gregg, a 30-year CIA veteran who had been National Security Adviser to Bush's father, could "think of nothing that can more devastatingly undercut America's standing in the world" than legal memos that "push aside longstanding prohibitions on the use of torture by Americans." While interrogating Vietnamese in 1970–72, Gregg had learned that "by treating prisoners humanely we frequently … gained valuable intelligence from them." As Seoul station chief he had ended torture by the

South Korean intelligence agency by reporting it to President Park's chief bodyguard in defiance of his own superiors' orders. But Sen. Lott (R-Miss) retorted that "interrogation is not a Sunday-school class." He saw nothing wrong with threatening prisoners with dogs as long as they did not actually bite. An ABC News/*Washington Post* poll found that 46 percent of Americans believed torture was "sometimes acceptable."

Acknowledging that it had to expand Fay's investigation to include Sanchez, DoD added LtGen. Anthony R. Jones to the inquiry.[42] The *Washington Post* published the "interrogation and Counter-Resistance Policy" Sanchez promulgated on September 10, 2003 (the day after Miller left Iraq), authorizing yelling, loud music, heat and cold, dietary manipulation, and stress positions for up to 45 minutes every four hours. A month later (after a CENTCOM lawyer had disagreed with Warren's legal advice) Sanchez prohibited the denial of religious items or light, Pride and Ego Down, and false flag. But interrogators could still manipulate diet, isolate detainees for long periods, and use military dogs to frighten prisoners.

Some interrogators complained that the rules provided inadequate guidance. SPC Luciana Spencer, removed from interrogation for making a detainee walk naked to his cell, said MPs told her "they had no SOP [standard operating procedure]" for detainee treatment. Adel Nakhla (a contract interpreter) was given the rules only after participating in abuses. Even after yelling was banned in October 2003, SPC Krol said he and other MI interrogators sometimes asked MPs to "randomly yell at the detainee." Steven Stefanowicz, a contract interrogator, said MPs were "allowed to do what is necessary to keep the detainee awake" and force a detainee to shower daily and shave.

The military's claim that it first learned about the abuses on January 13, 2004 was belied by the fact that in November 2003 not only had the ICRC reported them but the Abu Ghraib Detainee Assessment Branch (which screened prisoners for release) began documenting abuses in its weekly reports to the Review and Appeal Board.[43] An MI soldier said he had disclosed abuse because "we didn't want people to know that we knew about it and didn't report it."

Sen. Kerry (the presumptive Democratic presidential nominee) said the abuse was not confined to "just a few people, and there are serious questions about how high it goes."[44] Compliance with the Geneva Conventions was essential to "protect our soldiers." As president, he would have directed an investigation by someone like McCain to "restore people's faith in getting to the bottom" of the scandal. The

Senate passed the Defense Authorization Act with an amendment by Sen. Durbin (D-Ill) reaffirming the US commitment not to torture and requiring Rumsfeld to issue guidelines and report violations to Congress. Ashcroft refused a request by Senate Judiciary Committee (SJC) Democrats for classified documents on detainee treatment, and Republicans defeated a motion to subpoena them. Rep. Conyers (D-Mich) introduced a resolution directing Ashcroft to give Congress those documents; Rep. Hunter (D-Ca) responded with a resolution declaring that the apprehension, detention, and interrogations of terrorists were essential to the successful prosecution of the Global War on Terror.

Because some of their contents had been leaked, the White House released Bush's February 2002 directive and Jay Bybee's August 2002 OLC memo, prompting new efforts at damage control.[45] Daniel J. Dell'Orto, DoD chief deputy general counsel, said that even though interrogators were in "uncharted waters" at Guantánamo, "less than a handful" of detainees had been subjected to EITs, and the administration had directed that the treatment of Iraqi prisoners would be "all Geneva, all the time." Gonzales said the OLC memos demonstrated the "thorough and deliberative process the administration used to make policy decision [*sic*]." They were merely "exploring the boundaries as an abstract matter" and were never sent to "soldiers in the field, nor to the president." "All interrogation techniques actually authorized have been carefully vetted, are lawful and do not constitute torture." "We categorically reject any connection" between the memos and Abu Ghraib. But DoJ now said Bybee's "overbroad and irrelevant" memo was being rewritten. Sen. Leahy said "much more remains held back and hidden away from public view." Asked about the memos, Bush declared: "I have never ordered torture. I will never order torture. The values of this country are such that torture is not part of our soul or our being." The *New York Times* said: "the document dump only reaffirms the need for a more robust Congressional response to this mess."

In her Art. 32 proceeding, SPC Sabrina Harman claimed to have been obeying MI officers.[46] Capt. Reese testified that on Tier 1A, which was "run by the MI folks," Col. Pappas directed the use of sleep deprivation and other techniques to "soften" detainees for interrogation. Pappas, Jordan, a female major, and "some OGA guys" conducted an interrogation in which Manadel al-Jamadi died. "I heard Col. Pappas say, 'I'm not going to go down alone for this.'" Pappas ordered an officer "to get some ice out of the chow hall" to chill the corpse. The next day guards inserted an intravenous tube in the corpse so inmates would not "get upset he had passed during the interrogation." SPC Rivera testified that Graner had guards drag naked detainees so their genitals scraped the floor. Harman was also "instigating it, giving the orders, telling them to keep going." Her civilian lawyer, Frank Spinner, ridiculed the notion that a woman who "sells, makes and delivers pizza for a living, is supposed to come in and challenge" her superiors. But SPC Matthew Wisdom testified that he obtained a transfer out of Abu Ghraib after reporting the abuses he saw on November 8, 2003.

Sen. Graham called Abu Ghraib "the biggest breakdown of command I've ever seen in my 20 years as a military lawyer."[47] "What are we fighting for? To be like Saddam Hussein?" "The people who want this fixed the most are the men and women in uniform. It's their honor that's been stained." When Vice President Cheney urged Rumsfeld's critics to "let him do his job," Graham retorted: "We're doing our job." The *New York Times* accused the administration of having "spent nearly two months obstructing investigations."[48] "The Pentagon has still not accounted for the 2,000 pages missing" from Taguba's 6,000-page report. Rumsfeld's refusal to produce the ICRC reports "is the most outrageous example of the administration's bad faith on the prison scandal."

The capture of Saddam Hussein on December 13, 2003 had provoked harsh interrogation in Abu Ghraib of more than a dozen bodyguards and other loyalists.[49] One MI analyst was told: "Do whatever you have to do, find out where they are and let's get 'em fast." Another said Pappas claimed to have just gotten off a conference call with Sanchez and Rumsfeld, who told them: "We want this info. Do what you have to do to get it." "Just having [unmuzzled] dogs in the room worked pretty effectively." A contract interrogator said Pappas told them: "We got a chance to break this unlawful insurgency, and the people in an unlawful insurgency have no protection under the Geneva Conventions." The military chief of public affairs in Iraq confirmed that "we prioritized the interrogation of these personnel."

Rep. Waxman (D–Ca) decried that House Republicans "took more than 140 hours of testimony to investigate whether the Clinton White House misused its holiday card database but less than five hours of testimony regarding how the Bush administration treated Iraqi detainees."[50] A Republican chairman promptly furnished evidence for Waxman's complaint by declaring: "the last thing our nation needs now is for others to enflame this hatred by providing fodder and sound bites for our enemies." In early July 2004 the *Washington Post* criticized Warner's failure to hold any public hearings since May. "The accountability" of Sanchez and Miller "for the illegal procedures adopted at Abu Ghraib must be fully investigated and publicly clarified." If DCI "Tenet and Mr. Rumsfeld conspired to violate the Geneva Conventions" by hiding prisoners from the ICRC, "they should be held accountable – just like the lowly reservists whom the Pentagon now prosecutes."

When DoD finally gave HASC nearly two dozen confidential ICRC reports, Rep. Tauscher (D-Ca) said: "there was contemporaneous reporting by the ICRC to the chain of command … of deep concerns on their part on treatment issues of detainees," which were "a pattern and practice."[51] Rep. Cooper (D-Tn) said "Lots of problems were raised. They would have known about them if they can read English."

Reese and Pappas had made conflicting statements to Taguba.[52] Reese claimed to have been told that nudity "was an MI tactic that was used to make detainees uncomfortable. Pappas's MI soldiers were in charge and urged MPs to soften up detainees. There were many people way above my pay grade that walk through that wing and nothing was ever said about it." He also blamed subordinates: Graner "constantly challenges orders and requests from the leadership." Had he known Graner's "long history" as an abusive prison guard in civilian life, "I wouldn't have put him on a night shift in charge of a wing." But Reese was "ashamed of what my soldiers did." Maj. DiNenna (the top MP operations officer at Abu Ghraib) and another MP said MI officers kept telling guards to deprive detainees of sleep, play loud music, and limit food. By contrast, Pappas claimed he had declared nudity "inappropriate" and ordered Reese's MPs to "have the detainees put their clothes back on." Pappas blamed Miller for encouraging the use of dogs "with or without a muzzle."

Graner had been "disciplined" once the previous fall.[53] On November 14, 2003 LtCol. Jordan directed him to "PT" six prisoners accused of trying to riot: "naked and ups and downs with the sandbags on their heads." When one resisted, Graner "bashed him against the wall," inflicting a 1.5-inch gash on his chin that required stitches (which Graner helped administer). Because a Marine JAG saw and reported this, Graner's platoon leader, Capt. Christopher Brinson, presented Graner with a Developmental Counseling Form. But instead of offering criticism, Brinson wrote that Graner was "doing a fine job in Tier 1" and had "received many accolades from the MI units here and specifically from LtCol. Jordan." "Continue to perform at this level and it will help us succeed at our overall mission." Declaring "first and foremost, you have an inherent right to self-defense that cannot be taken away from you," Brinson said he "accept[ed] your version of events."

LtGen. Paul T. Mikolashek (Army IG), who had been directed to investigate on February 10, issued the third military report on July 21, 2004. "[U]nable to identify system failures," he attributed the 94 abuses he found (out of more than 50,000 detentions) to "unauthorized actions taken by a few individuals" who "failed to adhere to basic standards of discipline, training or Army values ... coupled with the failure of a few leaders to provide adequate monitoring, supervision and leadership of those soldiers."[54] Nearly half of the abuses had occurred at the point of capture. "No confirmed instance of detainee abuse was caused by the approved policies." But "established policies were not clear and contained ambiguity." Although he blamed a shortage of trained interrogators, he conceded that "a command climate that encourages behavior at the harsher end of the acceptable range of behavior towards detainees may unintentionally increase the likelihood of abuse."

Sen. Talent (R-Mo) praised the report for "vindicating our leaders and our soldiers." Sen. Sessions said: "we want our soldiers right up to the limit of what they legally can do to obtain good intelligence to help save lives." Gen. Peter J. Schoomaker (Army Chief of Staff) warned against "overreacting in a way that is removing lawful tools or setting conditions that would cause people to be hesitant." But Sen. Reed called the report "pretty murky." At the SASC hearing he accused Mikolashek of "reinforcing the conclusion that there are five or six aberrant soldiers." Sen. Levin found it "difficult to believe that there were not systemic problems." And Sen. McCain said that though it was not a whitewash, "there are certainly questions" remaining. The *New York Times* insisted that Abu Ghraib had been "whitewashed." "Mr. Rumsfeld's team may be turning over stones, but it's not looking under them." It renewed its call for "a formal Congressional inquiry, with subpoena power."

More than fifty media outlets covered SPC Lynndie England's Art. 32 hearing.[55] She had told a CID agent "they were joking around ... it was just for fun." She claimed MI allowed MPs to pressure detainees to talk by taking photos and threatening to show them to others; but only about a quarter of the more than 1,000 photos depicted detainees. Others were exhibitionist: England engaging in oral sodomy with a soldier, waving her breasts in a sleeping soldier's face, and posing nude. Another CID agent said England claimed MI and CIA "would tell us we were doing a good job and to keep it up, but she could not identify anyone." She admitted stepping on detainees and posing in front of naked detainees to humiliate them. Sgt. Sivits testified that she was a willing participant in building the human pyramid of naked detainees. She claimed MI had given permission to "rough up" two rape suspects but could not say who gave the order; and eight other members of the 372nd MP Company denied having abused prisoners.

SPC Wisdom described escorting seven hooded detainees to Tier 1A after they allegedly started a riot. Graner, Frederick, and Davis "would run them into walls and things" and beat and kick them on the ground. "Sgt. Frederick said to me, 'Wisdom, you need to get some of this,' as if I should hit them too." After quitting the hard site to report this, he returned to find a naked Iraqi masturbating onto another. Frederick sneered: "Look at what these animals do when we leave them alone for two seconds." England exclaimed "he's getting hard" in a "sarcastic this-is-fun tone of voice." Wisdom was transferred out of the prison after complaining again. An MI analyst said MPs kept prisoners naked to establish dominance; she and other MIs asked for sheets to cover those they interrogated, but accepted MPs' assurances that it was being "taken care of." But another MP testified that he objected when two MIs handcuffed naked detainees to bars in an embrace while accusing them of raping a boy in prison, only to be told: "We know what we are doing." When Frederick brought a third detainee, the two MIs flooded the cell, ordered the naked detainees to crawl across it on their elbows, and trampled on those trying to avoid rubbing their genitals on the floor.

Richard Hernandez, England's lawyer, said the 21-year-old's "very personal" nude photos – the kind "you'd see at Mardi Gras or spring break" – had "absolutely nothing to do with Abu Ghraib" but were "very indicative of her following orders," especially from Graner, who was 15 years older. Hernandez reiterated that MI had directed MPs to "loosen up" detainees. But Capt. Wood testified that Miller had directed guards only to gather information about detainees' social interaction. "Words cannot describe my reaction" to the photos. "I was shocked … outraged." Capt. Reese also denied encouraging MPs to abuse detainees. But SFC Shannon Snider said: "we got … in writing from the commander, Col. Thomas Pappas, that military police should 'set the conditions' for MI interrogators." The investigating officer recommended a court-martial but noted that England was "one of the younger participants" and "the kind of person who was easily led."

Continuing to speak out, Karpinski claimed that soon after arriving in Iraq, Miller got daily reports on Abu Ghraib interrogations from

Pappas, who was "under tremendous pressure," which "intensified immediately following" the visit. Miller also "was giving Gen. [Barbara] Fast instructions."[56] Frederick said he "accepted responsibility," would plead guilty, and hoped others would "come forward and accept responsibility" and not retaliate against SPC Darby.[57]

At Sgt. Davis's Art. 32 hearing, his lawyer, Bergrin, read the Ponce memo (mentioned previously) asking interrogators for a "wish list" of "what techniques would be effective."[58] Bergrin called this "a smoking gun," which "corroborate[s] our position ... that very aggressive interrogation techniques were being employed at Abu Ghraib prison and those techniques were called for at the highest levels." MGen. Fast's denial she had seen the memo was "incredible." Two members of the 205th MI Brigade testified that MI had told MPs they expected detainees to be "softened up" for interrogation by abuses and threats to imprison their children, exposing them to rape.

DoD released its fourth report, by former Defense Secretaries James R. Schlesinger and Harold Brown, former Republican Rep. Tillie K. Fowler (R-Fla), and Gen. Charles A Horner, finding that the "acts of brutality and purposeless sadism ... were not part of authorized interrogations nor were they even directed at intelligence targets."[59] Although 50,000 people had been detained, the investigation of 155 alleged abuses substantiated just 66, a third at the point of capture. "No approved procedures called for or allowed the kinds of abuse that in fact occurred. There is no evidence of a policy of abuse promulgated by senior officials or military authorities." Abu Ghraib was "seriously overcrowded, under-resourced, and under continual attack." It had 75 prisoners per guard, compared to Guantánamo's 1:1 ratio. Karpinski and Pappas exhibited "weak and ineffectual leadership"; they and MI should be disciplined; but there was "no evidence that organizations above" them "were directly involved." Bush's February 2002 memo concluding that the Geneva Conventions did not apply to al-Qaeda or the Taliban led Sanchez to believe that "additional, tough measures were warranted" in Iraq. Techniques Rumsfeld approved for Guantánamo "migrated" to Afghanistan, where the 519th MI Brigade supported Special Operations Forces, and then were brought by the brigade to Iraq, "where they were neither limited nor safeguarded." MI "personnel share responsibility for the abuses at Abu Ghraib." Changes in DoD detainee policy between December 2002 and April 2003 should have been informed by a "wider range of legal opinions and a more robust debate." Visiting Abu Ghraib in August–September 2003, Miller had called for "strong, command-wide interrogation policies." Although CENTCOM found the new techniques Sanchez authorized "unacceptably aggressive," it "did not adequately set forth the limits." "The existence of confusing and inconsistent interrogation technique policies contributed to the belief that additional interrogation techniques were condoned."

The "unique" "brutality and purposeless sadism" of the Tier 1A abuses were "fostered by the predilections of the noncommissioned officers in charge." "They were not part of authorized interrogations, nor were they even directed at intelligence targets," although other "egregious abuses" occurred during interrogation. Still, there was "both institutional and personal responsibility at higher levels." Sanchez failed to deal with command and resource problems. Wojdakowski and the Baghdad headquarters "should have seen that urgent demands were placed to higher headquarters" for more prison staff. Senior DoD officials should have noticed that aggressive interrogation in Afghanistan was echoed in Iraq. Although Gen. Myers saw the Abu Ghraib photos in January, their impact was not "appreciated," and "the highest levels of command and leadership … were not adequately informed." The report rejected calls for Rumsfeld's resignation, which would "be a boon to all of America's enemies."

At the press conference Fowler acknowledged "fundamental failures throughout all levels of command."[60] Schlesinger agreed that "personal and institutional responsibility" went "right up the chain of command." But he worried about the "chilling effect on interrogation operations. It is essential in the war on terror that we have adequate intelligence." Brown warned that "if a head of a department had to resign every time someone below him did something wrong, it'd be a very empty cabinet table." A few days later he praised Rumsfeld for having "behaved very carefully and very effectively" after Bush decided that al-Qaeda and the Taliban were unprotected by the Geneva Conventions. Unapproved interrogation techniques "migrated" to Afghanistan and then Iraq. Some abusers "said they did it for fun." There had been no torture. "[P]eople can define torture the way they want … the International Committee of the Red Cross defines interrogation of prisoners as torture – and I think that's rather excessive."

Some abuses "took place on the battlefield where … the situation is perhaps most fraught." Even these were punished. Sen. Kerry's national security adviser disagreed: "This report makes clear that the failures at Abu Ghraib and elsewhere start at the top."

The Army released only a small fraction of the fifth report, by Gens. Jones and Fay, who identified the "primary causes" of the abuse as: "misconduct (ranging from inhumane to sadistic) by a small group of morally corrupt Soldiers and civilians, a lack of discipline on the part of the leaders and soldiers of the 205th MI BDE and a failure or lack of leadership by multiple echelons within CJTF-7."[61]

MI personnel "requested, encouraged, condoned or solicited Military Police (MP) personnel to abuse detainees and/or participated in detainee abuse." "The delineation of responsibilities seems to have been blurred when military police Soldiers, untrained in interrogation operations, were used to enable interrogations." "Most, though not all, of the violent or sexual abuses occurred separately from scheduled interrogations." They were "not the result of any doctrine, training or policy failures, but violations of the law." Nudity, forced grooming, hooding, yelling, loud music, and light control were not interrogation techniques. The 29 MI soldiers and 6 contractors implicated "knew right from wrong and that they were supposed to treat people humanely, but they didn't do it." MI conspired to conceal at least eight detainees from the ICRC. MP claims to have followed MI directions were "self-serving" but did "have some basis in fact." Miller had recommended the use of dogs, which Pappas approved, and handlers then terrorized prisoners into urinating and defecating. Jordan was assigned to supervise the JIDC just four days after arriving in Iraq. But though believed by Pappas to be supervising interrogation, Jordan actually focused on staff living conditions. When it quickly became clear he was unsuited for his duties, Pappas made a "critical error" by failing to remove Jordan. After a detainee wounded one soldier and shot at others on November 24, 2003, suspects were strip-searched in front of women soldiers, interrogated naked for hours, and threatened with military dogs. Soldiers' belief that Jordan tacitly approved those actions "set the stage" for subsequent abuses. Still, there were "very few instances" of torture. Sanchez was "responsible" but not "culpable." Echoing the Schlesinger report, Jones and Fay blamed "inadequate interrogation doctrine and training, an acute shortage of M.P. and M.I. soldiers, the lack of clear lines of responsibility between the M.P. and M.I. chains of command, the lack of a clear interrogation policy for the Iraq campaign, and intense pressure felt by the personnel on the ground to produce actionable intelligence from detainees." By operating "outside the established local rules and procedures," the CIA "eroded the necessity in the minds of soldiers and civilians … to follow Army rules." Fascinated by "OGA," Jordan waived the rule requiring military officers to monitor CIA interrogations. The report recommended that Jordan and Pappas be punished.

Promising to make the abuses a campaign issue, Sen. Kerry reiterated his call for Rumsfeld's resignation: "it's not just the little person at the bottom who ought to pay the price of responsibility. The buck doesn't stop at the Pentagon." Sen. Graham agreed that the two reports contained a "clear message … that the system failed in a widespread manner." Sen. Warner (D-Va) concluded Rumsfeld should not resign because he had no "actual knowledge of these horrific incidents," which were attributable to the "lack of training, lack of supervision by the immediate command." The reports showed that the military "can investigate itself."

The *New York Times* disagreed. The Schlesinger report "did an enormous disservice" by failing to connect the dots "from President Bush's decision to declare Iraq a front in the war against terror, to government lawyers finding ways to circumvent the Geneva Conventions, to Mr. Rumsfeld's bungled planning of the occupation and understaffing of the ground forces in Iraq, to the hideous events at Abu Ghraib prison." The failure to offer "even the mildest reprimand for Mr. Rumsfeld" should "not be all that surprising from a commission appointed by the secretary of defense and run by two former secretaries of defense." The *Times* criticized Warner for failing "to produce any satisfying answers for the public about Abu Ghraib before the election." The *Los Angeles Times* concurred that the Schlesinger panel "traced some of the blame all the way" to Rumsfeld and "should force the resignation or firing of top officials, military and civilian."

The *New York Times* also disclosed classified sections of the Fay–Jones report showing that the 519th MI Battalion adopted "almost verbatim" the July 15, 2003 interrogation policy drafted by the Special Operations and CIA Joint Task Force searching for former Iraqi government officials.[62] Furthermore, Sanchez's September 14, 2003 memorandum authorized use of Fear Up Harsh, dietary and environmental manipulation, sleep management, isolation, and (with his permission) Pride and Ego Down, military working dogs, and stress positions. The CENTCOM revision a month later still exceeded what the Geneva Conventions permitted and (according to Fay–Jones) "confused doctrine and policy even further." For instance, interrogators did not understand it to limit the "approved" techniques, and Pappas believed *he* could approve the use of dogs. The *Washington Post* claimed to have seen a classified cable from Sanchez directing interrogators to "exploit Arab fear of dogs."

England's lawyer said the reports showed that she and the other accused were not "rogue soldiers" because "they were getting orders from M.I."[63] Frederick's lawyer called the trials "essentially political" and predicted "the court martial of at least one senior officer." Rumsfeld declared that neither report found detainees "were abused … for interrogation purposes." A few hours later he asserted that any claim "to link the abuse that took place to interrogation techniques in Iraq has not yet been demonstrated." But slipped a note by an aide, he conceded that Fay–Jones found "two or three" cases of abuse during interrogation. (They actually found that abuse occurred during interrogation in 13 out of 44 instances.) Rumsfeld added: "if you are in Washington, D.C., you can't know what's going on [during] the midnight shift in one of those many prisons around the world." (Earlier he had said CENTCOM had "told the world" about the abuses on January 16, 2003.)

Miller reiterated that his September 2003 recommendation that MPs help set "conditions for successful exploitation" of detainees had contemplated only "passive intelligence gathering."[64] Pappas had misinterpreted Miller's suggestion – that military dogs guard the prison perimeter and control prisoners – to authorize the use of dogs during interrogation as well. In response to the Schlesinger report finding that Karpinski's leadership failures "helped set the conditions at the prison which led to the abuses" and its recommendation that she be relieved of her command and given a letter of reprimand, Karpinski said there had been "a conspiracy all along. Sanchez and Miller and likely Fast had fallback plans and people to blame if anything came unglued."

HRF and eight retired generals and admirals urged Bush to create an independent commission to investigate the mistreatment.[65] Sen. Reed agreed that "the persistent drumbeat that this is just a few corrupt soldiers … doesn't really fit when you're talking about 'ghost' detainees." McCain said Abu Ghraib was "beginning to look like a bad movie." Levin found it "totally unacceptable that the documents that are requested from the CIA have not been forthcoming." The CIA replied that its IG had been conducting his own review. Gen. Kern said the army had an obligation to treat the nearly 100 "ghost detainees" "by our rules, not someone else's rules." The Director of the Defense Intelligence Agency (DIA) had prohibited the CIA from questioning detainees at a military facility near Baghdad airport unless military personnel were present. The CIA retorted that its Baghdad station had reported it "was not happy that the military was using certain interrogation techniques."

At the HASC hearing following the reports, Schlesinger and Brown repeated that Rumsfeld had behaved responsibly but criticized two DoD undersecretaries and the general counsel. Schlesinger described Sanchez's likely inability to get a fourth star as a "comment on failed responsibility." Rep. Hunter insisted that only a tiny minority were responsible for the abuses. But Skelton (the ranking Democrat) denied this was "the work of just a few bad apples." And Kline (a former Marine colonel) condemned the "gigantic failure of leadership." Noting that 11 naval officers had been removed for misconduct in 2004, Sen. Kennedy asked "who is accountable" for the Army's failures: Sanchez, Abizaid, Myers, Wolfowitz, Rumsfeld, the president? The *New York Times* assigned blame broadly: Bush's memo declaring that the USA could suspend the Geneva Conventions, which did not protect "unlawful combatants"; Rumsfeld's authorization of "brutal interrogation techniques" in Guantánamo; Miller's visit to Iraq; and Sanchez's use of Miller's "brief" and Bush's memo "to authorize the use of dogs and other illegal interrogation methods."

SPC Cruz pleaded guilty to conspiracy and maltreatment of prisoners and was sentenced to eight months, demoted to private, and given a bad-conduct discharge.[66] He said in mitigation that a month before the abuse a mortar attack had killed his sergeant and another solider and injured him, and that he had reported the abuse to superiors the day after it occurred.

In mid-October 2004 the *Washington Post* noted the "remarkable omission" of Abu Ghraib from the presidential campaign.[67] Kerry had not said "whether he accepts or rejects the policy decisions that led to" the abuses or, "most importantly, Mr. Bush's contention that some detainees captured abroad should not be treated according to the standards of the Geneva Conventions." And there had been no Congressional hearings about ghost detainees in more than a month. DoD replied that the Schlesinger report had found "no policy of abuse" and repeated the half-truth that "the U.S. military – not journalists – first publicized the facts of the abuses at Abu Ghraib in January." Brown had praised Rumsfeld for being "extremely careful about the issue of treatment of prisoners during interrogation." Indeed, the one thing "to be commended on this whole operation," according to Horner, was "the way the Secretary of Defense has approached the investigations."

Sgt. Frederick pleaded guilty to 8 of 12 counts.[68] During the penalty phase he claimed there had been no manuals on operating procedures. When he first entered Abu Ghraib he saw naked men handcuffed to cell doors and others wearing women's underwear "to humiliate and degrade them." "It was very embarrassing for an Arabic [*sic*] male to be seen nude by another." Hoping to locate the remains of American soldiers, an Army investigator directed him to "stress[] out" a prisoner using any means "as long as you don't kill him." Stefanowicz said: "Treat them like shit. Put the dong on this one if you can." Both MI and civilian interrogators "would tell us what conditions to set" for detainees. When a detainee was identified as a ringleader who had hit a female soldier in the face with a rock, Frederick punched him so hard he needed medical attention. Another detainee whom Frederick had forced to masturbate in front of men and women and then sleep naked in a cell flooded with water said: "I felt humiliated but I had nothing to kill myself [with]." Frederick admitted: "I knew it was wrong at the time because it was a form of abuse" and "makes the Army look bad." His lawyer called him "a good person. A good father and a good man" whom "aiders and abettors [had] … got[ten] … to that point." Although Frederick had faced up to 18 years on all counts, the negotiated plea entitled him to 8 years, demotion to private, and a dishonorable discharge. Two weeks later he made a 119-page sworn statement implicating others. He served only three years.

The *Washington Post* published the 372nd MP Company logbook showing MI influence on MP behavior.[69] Graner wrote that he had received "verbal instructions" to let CIA detainees sleep only four hours a day, but "until this is put down on paper, the sleep plan is stopping at this point." Another entry stated: "MI handlers will be turning on heat" to a detainee who later alleged having been beaten, stripped, and shackled to his bed naked. After Darby disclosed the photos, a series of entries modified or terminated sleep deprivation programs and said all ghost detainees would be "taken out of their cells, processed, and given numbers."

SPC Ambuhl pleaded guilty to a single charge of dereliction of duty (three other counts were dismissed) and agreed to testify against others in exchange for reduction in rank to private and forfeiture of half a month's salary.[70] During her initial tour at Abu Ghraib she "saw detainees wearing underwear on their heads" and "just thought it was standard." When "nothing was working" with a naked prisoner who had been ripping his clothes and seemed to have "mental problems …

someone put the leash on and got him out" of the cell. (Ambuhl later said that though the detainee was "uncooperative," "you're not going to touch him" because he had "sores and stuff.") She assumed MI officers approved because they did not intervene. Her lawyer said "since the orders came down from the White House, someone has to bear responsibility for it."

A year after Darby exposed the abuses, Graner went on trial.[71] Walking into court, he joked with reporters: "We're going to find out what kind of a monster I am today." The prosecutor introduced an email in which Graner boasted to family and friends that beating a detainee was "a real upper body workout." He captioned a photograph of a shackled naked detainee howling with pain from bleeding legs "just another dull night at work" and wrote: "the guys give me hell for not getting any pictures while I was fighting this guy." Responding to a message from his wife about "Take Your Children to Work Day," he sent a photo of a detainee's head bloodied beyond recognition, captioned: "how about send a bastard to hell day?" He labeled a photo of himself stitching the wound over a detainee's eye "things may have gotten a bit bad when we were asking him a couple of questions. O well," and wrote in the email: "not only was I the healer, I was the hunter." A video showed SPC Sivits cutting cuffs off a detainee he thought "was going to lose his hands" because Graner had made them so tight. Sivits said Graner made an inmate weep by repeatedly hitting his gunshot wound with a nightstick. Graner had laughingly called photos of detainees masturbating "a present for our birthday." Prosecutors introduced Graner's copy of the Army Code of Conduct with notations showing he had read it and a notebook with comments on "how to hit someone and not leave a mark."

An Abu Ghraib inmate testified by video that Graner, "the primary torturer," forced inmates to eat from a toilet and threatened them with dogs. Soldiers "took off my clothes. They said certain things about my wife, my religion. They hit me in the back, my head. They took me into the bathroom and made me take a shower and one told me he was going to rape me … [Graner] laughed. He was whistling. He was singing. Graner hit me and made me say something against my religion … 'Thank Jesus because he gave you life'." Another detainee said Graner threw pepper in his eyes and beat him until the stick broke.

Womack argued that "even if an order is unlawful, it is an absolute defense in this case if Spc. Graner did not know that the order was unlawful." "[T]his is a much bigger deal than a few low-ranking military police." Building a pyramid of naked detainees was no different from what cheerleaders do at football games "all over America." Putting naked detainees on leashes resembled what parents did with toddlers in airports. "They're not being abused; they're being kept in control." The photos were integral to the interrogation and "showed that [Graner] followed orders."

Frederick testified that Graner was told by superiors to cuff detainees to a railing when MI asked for "sleep management." He named three interrogators who told them to rough up detainees. MI "would tell us we were doing a good job, to keep up the good work." Ambuhl concurred: "MIs would come down and let us know what they wanted us to do with the detainees." They told her to watch prisoners take showers and "point and laugh" at them. "They told us we were doing a good job in breaking down al-Qaeda. That we were saving a lot of lives." But she admitted MI never told her to pile naked prisoners into a pyramid or force them to masturbate or simulate oral sex. Like England, she had a "romantic relationship" with Graner. Sgt. Davis testified that when he found Graner and MI handcuffing two naked detainees together in an embrace, an MI declared: "we know what we're doing." But Davis admitted that the MI ranked below Graner and the detainees were not being interrogated. The next day he complained about this to his platoon leader, 1st Lt. Lewis Raeder, who said Frederick had no business on the hard site: "Stay out of MI's way and let them do their job."

Under cross-examination all but one defense witness conceded Graner had gratuitously abused detainees and had been reprimanded repeatedly for disobeying orders. The dissenter, Master Sgt. Brian Lipinski, said that two weeks after Graner took the notorious photos, MI told him "you are doing a good job." But on cross-examination, Lipinski admitted that the MI report was a response to his own discovery of blood on a wall and a detainee bleeding from four wounds inflicted by Graner, who first claimed the detainee tripped but then admitted slamming his head into the wall. The report formally admonished Graner, directing him to learn to handle stress, follow orders, and re-read the Army Rules of Engagement (ROEs). He had failed to follow "simple basic instructions" and ignored orders to keep away from England.

Graner said that when he complained about MI, a superior replied: "If M.I. is asking you to do this, it needs to be done. They're in charge, follow their orders." His broad smiles and thumbs up in photos of piles of bound detainees were just gallows humor. "There were a lot of things that we did that were so screwed up that if you didn't look at them as [if] they were funny, you couldn't deal with them." "I didn't enjoy anything

I did there … A lot of it was wrong. A lot of it was criminal." "I can see to a layperson, a lot of things happen in prison that may look wrong … But you can have a use of force that looks bad that can be justified." He claimed to have been following instructions from Jordan, Pappas, Reese, Raeder, and Brinson. "Like all good little soldiers, or bad little soldiers, I said, 'Right on, sir.'" Although Jordan had seen many of the abuse photos, he never told Graner to stop. "I know the Geneva Conventions better than anyone else in my company, and we were called upon to violate the Geneva Conventions." He could not be cross-examined because he did not testify under oath.

Womack asked the jury: "Where are the officers? Where are the senior enlisted?" "In Nuremberg, it was the generals being prosecuted." "We were looking very hard" for Saddam Hussein; "the more aggressive you are, the better intelligence results you get." MPs did not know they were humiliating detainees because they were not "experts" but just "implements and tools of the MIs." One prisoner had cut Graner's leg. After deliberating five hours, the jury found Graner guilty of 17 of the 25 charges. Facing 15 years, he received 10, demotion to private, and dishonorable discharge. After being granted immunity from further prosecution, he implicated many others, but continued to claim he had been following MI orders. "I was to manhandle [detainees] and treat them rough … smack them around a little or use cold water … use the sandbags as hoods always … yell and scream … cuff them in different standing positions … utilize loud music in the middle of the night … use the isolation cell." He made "Taxi Driver" wear women's underpants on his head. He married Ambuhl while in prison (but denied contact with her) and was paroled after 6.5 years (with more than two spent in solitary confinement).

Shortly after Graner's conviction, Sgt. Davis pleaded guilty to three minor counts on condition that he serve no more than 15 months of the 78 he faced for aggravated assault, conspiracy, and maltreatment.[72] At the sentencing hearing the prosecutor said Davis had threatened an Air Force major, assaulted an Iraqi, and sexually taunted prisoners. His battalion leader testified in mitigation that Abu Ghraib had been attacked by mortars and was "filthy, with rodents, rats, wild dogs and trash and an overpopulation" of rebellious prisoners. A psychologist attributed Davis's actions to the violent atmosphere and lack of discipline. He got six months and a bad-conduct discharge. A few days later SPC Krol got 10 months after admitting he had poured water on naked detainees, forced them to crawl, and threw a foam football at handcuffed detainees.

In March 2005 Vice Admiral Albert T. Church (Navy IG) released a 21-page summary of his 368-page report.[73] Little more than a third of the 187 incidents he investigated involved abuses, a majority of those were "simple assaults, punching, kicking and slapping detainees," and a third occurred at "point of capture," where "passions often run high." (Another 130 investigations were incomplete.) Authorized interrogation techniques had not been "a casual factor in detainee abuse." Church regretted the "missed opportunit[y]" to give interrogators clear guidelines, but added: "I don't know who you would have assigned responsibility necessarily to do that." He deplored that interrogation techniques had been employed at Guantánamo over senior military lawyers' objections and then used in Afghanistan, and confirmed that about thirty ghost detainees had been kept off the books on the CIA's instructions by soldiers who received no guidelines for dealing with the Agency. "[C]lear ... warning signs were present at Abu Ghraib, in the form of communiques to local commanders, that should have prompted those commanders to put in place more specific procedures and direct guidance to prevent further abuse." Indeed, a few weeks earlier Gen. George W. Casey Jr. (who had replaced Sanchez as senior coalition commander in Iraq) prohibited the use of dogs, specified how long field units could hold prisoners, and clarified command responsibilities.

The report elicited widespread criticism. HRF's Michael Posner accused the "civilian leadership of the military" of showing "an ongoing unwillingness ... to examine the full scope of the problem." The ACLU's Anthony Romero said: "the military can only look down the chain of command, not up, when it comes to holding people accountable." At the SASC hearing on the report, Levin said: "this failure of accountability of senior leaders sends the wrong signal to our troops and to the American people." The *New York Times* deplored that Abu Ghraib had been "whitewashed again." Like the other reports, Church had concluded "that only the lowest-ranking soldiers are to be held accountable, not their commanders or their civilian overseers." "[S]exual humiliation of prisoners ... happened so pervasively that it clearly was not just the perverted antics of one night shift in one cellblock at Abu Ghraib." Congress was "issuing subpoenas on steroid use by baseball players" but had "shown no interest" in "a serious investigation" of these abuses.

LtGen. Stanley E. Green (Army IG) issued a report clearing Sanchez, Wojdakowski, Fast, Warren, and eight others, even though the Schlesinger and Fay–Jones reports had found misconduct by the first two.[74] Sen. Warner again called it "absolutely essential to determine what went wrong, up and down the chain of command." Fast was promoted to head the Fort Huachuca, Arizona Intelligence Center and approved a new manual on Human Intelligence Collector Operations (the first revision in 13 years), prohibiting ghost detainees and excluding MPs from interrogation. Publishing Sanchez's September 2003 interrogation memo (which it had obtained through FOIA), the ACLU asked Atorney General (AG) Gonzales to open a perjury investigation because Sanchez had testified under oath before SASC: "I never approved any of those measures to be used within CJTF-7 at any time in the last year."

Lynndie England pleaded guilty to seven of the nine charges.[75] In the penalty phase her lawyers planned to claim she had mental health problems and learning disabilities, having married at 19 on a whim. She had been dominated by Graner, who made her pose for photos holding a leash around the neck of a naked crawling detainee, which he mailed home with the message: "Look what I made Lynndie do." The photos of detainees masturbating were his birthday gift to her. He videotaped the two of them having sex. He had been sleeping with Ambuhl and England at the same time, broke up with England, returned when she got pregnant, but then married Ambuhl, which England learned only days before being charged. She told Col. Pohl (the judge): "I had a choice, but I chose to do what my friends wanted me to do. They were being very persistent and bugging me, and I was like, OK, whatever." But when Graner contradicted her admission of guilt for the leash incident by stating "I was asking her as the senior person at that extraction," Pohl rejected her plea and declared a mistrial. After expert witnesses testified that England tried to please people in authority and did not understand complex language, Pohl excluded her incriminatory statements on retrial.

Karpinski received an administrative penalty of demotion to colonel.[76] The Army found she had failed to report either the Abu Ghraib abuse or an earlier conviction for shoplifting a $22 bottle of perfume. (Karpinski claimed she had been falsely accused of the latter and never even charged.) Col. Pappas also received an administrative penalty of reprimand and an $8,000 fine for failing to train and supervise interrogators and authorizing unapproved techniques, such as military dogs. Other officers fared better. Wojdakowski was appointed to head the Army infantry training school at Fort Benning, Georgia. Warren was promoted to Brigadier General. Calling him a "hero" and "straight shooter," Gen. Horner said Warren deserved this for acknowledging his mistakes. Although Sen. Collins (R-Me) said SASC "should give close scrutiny to any recommendations for promotions of military officers" criticized in the Schlesinger report, Sen. Warner said there was "no actionable item" before the committee that would delay the promotion. Sanchez, who became commander of V Corps in Heidelberg, said as graduation speaker at Texas A&M that "the great leader is one who is willing to 'lead under fire.'" "[O]ur ethics mandate it and our subordinates expect it." But after failing to be nominated for a fourth star, he retired on November 1, 2006. In a memoir two years later, he accused Rumsfeld of "covering his rear" by pretending not to have known that "CJTF-7 was never adequately manned."

Karpinski justified herself in three interviews and a memoir, claiming she suffered discrimination as a Reservist and a woman.[77] She complained of shortages of staff, equipment, and training. MP responsibilities were shifted from POWs to "security detainees," whose numbers increased from 1,200 at the end of August 2003 to 7,000 later that fall. When Miller visited Iraq, he told her: "the first you have to do is treat these prisoners like dogs." "He gave the MI interrogators the idea of having MPs soften up the detainees between interrogations." "The plan was to use these photographs to show newly-arriving prisoners: hey, start to talk or tomorrow you're on the bottom" of the pyramid of naked detainees. Even before Miller left, Pappas sought and obtained "full control" of Cellblocks 1-A and 1-B. The IROE authorizing EITs had Rumsfeld's handwritten note ordering "Make sure this happens!!" In his plea bargain, Capt. Reese said Pappas told him not to report this to his chain of command. "This is about instructions delivered with full authority and knowledge of the Secretary of Defense and probably Cheney." "For the rest of my days I will believe that, at Abu Ghraib, these soldiers … were following orders when they humiliated and abused detainees."

SPC Harman's court-martial saw the notorious photo of a hooded detainee (whom MPs had named "Gilligan") standing on a box holding wires in his hands.[78] The prosecutor alleged she had threatened him with electrocution if he fell off. She photographed prisoners forced to masturbate and was photographed near naked Iraqi prisoners and writing "rapeist" on one's thigh. Her lawyer, Frank Spinner, argued that she was the lowest-ranking soldier, poorly trained, and repulsed by the abuses, which she photographed only to report them to superiors. (In fact,

Harman admitted being obsessed with photographing death, injury, and degradation. "Even if somebody is hurt, the first thing I think about is taking photos of that injury." She photographed herself with corpses at the Al Hillah morgue. Once she saw the detainee they called "Taxi Driver" "handcuffed backwards to his window naked with his underwear over his head and face," looking "like Jesus Christ. At first I had to laugh so I went on and grabbed the camera and took a picture … then it hit me, that's a form of molestation. You can't do that. I took more pictures now to 'record' what is going on.")

Spinner said the inmate on whom Harman scrawled "rapeist" could not read English. He claimed that the photo of the hooded prisoner, with whom Harman had a friendly relationship, was a joke; but she had told an investigator that Graner said MI wanted "Gilligan" kept awake before interrogation. Frederick testified it was he who had made "Gilligan" stand on the box because MI said the detainee might have information about four missing American soldiers. He had not seen Harman there either then or when MPs forced prisoners to masturbate. But Cruz testified that after three prisoners suspected of raping a teenage boy prisoner had been stripped and forced to roll around on the cold floor, Harman helped handcuff them in an embrace. Convicted of six of the seven charges, she said at sentencing:

> I wish to apologize to any and all detainees. I failed in my duties. I failed my mission. Not only did I let down the people in Iraq, I let down every single soldier that serves today. My actions potentially caused an increased hatred and insurgency towards the United States, putting soldiers and civilians at greater risk. I take full responsibility for my actions. The decisions I made were mine and mine alone.

Although she faced 5.5 years and the prosecution sought 3, she received 6 months (with credit for 51 days served) and a bad conduct discharge.

At their Art. 32 hearing, Sgts. Santos A. Cardona and Michael Smith were charged with using unmuzzled dogs to "threaten and harass detainees."[79] Maj. DiNenna said MPs understood that Gen. Miller "was sent over by the Secretary of Defense to take their interrogation techniques they used at Guantánamo Bay and incorporate them into Iraq." DiNenna heard Miller boast to Karpinski and Pappas about how "effective" dogs had been at Guantánamo and ask "why we didn't have working dogs. He was going to talk to Sanchez and get us the resources we needed." A soldier testified that MI regularly instructed dog handlers and MPs to "scare up" detainees and Pappas approved using dogs for interrogation. SSgt. Christopher Aston, who oversaw a team of interrogators questioning three detainees captured at the same time as Saddam Hussein, sought to threaten one with dogs. Pappas gave permission (without asking Sanchez) but said they had to be muzzled in the interrogation booth. Frederick testified that Stefanowicz identified cells that dog handlers should visit to "intimidate inmates." The handlers were "laughing" and playing a "game" to see "who could get the most inmates to urinate on themselves." An interrogator said dogs were used to frighten two juveniles, aged 10 and 14, who screamed in fear; but he could not identify the handlers. Prosecutors introduced a photo of the accused cornering a naked detainee and letting dogs bite him on both thighs.

After serving his sentence, Javal Davis reiterated he was just following orders: "I was left with an open door to pretty much almost do whatever I want, you know like, 'hey, make sure this guy has a bad night you know' or 'make sure this guy gets the treatment.' "[80] He asked superiors to put the orders in writing, but they never did.

In England's retrial the prosecutor said photos showed her "smoking and smiling derisively and pointing in a humiliating and mocking way at the detainees," indulging "her own sick humor."[81] Her military lawyer, Capt. Jonathan Crisp, said she had a history of depression, had not been able to speak normally until she was eight, and continued having "language processing" problems even after being moved out of special education class in eighth grade. The military had classified her as a file clerk and should not have assigned her to handle prisoners. A psychologist described her "overly compliant" personality, incapacity to make independent judgments, and abusive relationship with Graner. Although the jury asked the judge about what her superiors had directed, they deliberated only two hours before convicting her of six counts. Gen. Myers expressed satisfaction: "We had a problem, and we dealt with the problem … in an appropriate way."

At the sentencing hearing the prosecution sought 4–6 years instead of the maximum 10. Graner testified that MIs encouraged MPs to mistreat detainees: he nearly beat a detainee to death with MI watching. But he admitted that MI had not been present the night England had abused detainees. Stjepan Mestrovic, a Texas A&M sociologist, testified that officers were responsible. England "was caught up in this chaotic situation that was going on around her, so the abuse was inevitable." England testified that:

> I was used by Private Graner. I didn't realize it at the time … He was very charming, funny and at the time it looked to me like he was interested in the same things I was. Now I know it was all an act to lure me in, I guess … After the photos were released, I've heard that attacks were made on U.S. armed forces because of them … I apologize to coalition forces and all the families.

She also apologized to the detainees. She was sentenced to three years and dishonorably discharged. Days later she said on television that commanders knew that "worse things" happened at Abu Ghraib. She was paroled after serving 521 days. Five years later she was unrepentant. The prisoners she abused "got the better end of the deal." All of them "had killed coalition forces or they were planning to." "[Y]ou want me to apologize to them? It's like saying sorry to the enemy." But she expressed anguish that the photos could have caused American casualties. "I think about it all the time."

In a lengthy radio interview Karpinski repeated that the blame "goes all the way to the top": Fast, Sanchez, Cambone, Rumsfeld, and Gonazles.[82] Miller had told her "he was going to 'Gitmo-ize'" Abu Ghraib and use MPs – who "were not being aggressive enough" – to "assist the interrogators." At Guantánamo prisoners were escorted everywhere in "belly chains, leg irons, hand irons." "You have to treat them like dogs." This was "consistent with" MPs' use of the "dog collar, the dog leash and un-muzzled dogs." The photos were "staged … at the direction of contract interrogators … for the use in future interrogations." Only when Karpinski saw the ICRC report in December 2003 did she learn about abuses beginning two months earlier. Warren said she had not seen it earlier because it had been routed incorrectly, but admitted that Karpinski's JAG officer also had not seen it; Karpinski believed it had been kept from her deliberately. When she resisted signing the response because Pappas was now in charge of the prison, Warren said: "we don't want to call attention to the fact that we have transferred the prison to the M.I."

She admitted holding "ghost detainees" on instructions from CJTF-7 "through General Fast or General Sanchez." When one of the notorious "deck of cards" detainees[83] was delivered to Abu Ghraib, "we were told specifically … by order from Secretary Rumsfeld, to not enter his name on any database," refer to him as "Triple X," and segregate him "in solitary confinement." When she complained to Warren that "this is a violation," he replied: "we'll try to get clarification, but this is from Rumsfeld's office." She told Warren to "take control of [Triple X]. If you want to violate a Geneva Convention, that's up to you, but I don't want to keep him in one of our camps this way." During Rumsfeld's visit she warned that overcrowding forced them to keep prisoners outdoors when it was "120 degrees, 140 degrees by noontime." "I spoke directly to Ambassador Bremer nearly every week. I spoke to General Sanchez at least once every week, reported it in the updates and the night time briefings to Gen. Wojdakowski." But she first heard about torture and nudity from the CID commander the night Darby left the photos. When she rushed to the prison, a sergeant pointed out Rumsfeld's interrogation memo posted inside the cellblock, which was unusual "because interrogations were not conducted in the cell block."

When Pappas accepted immunity and was ordered to testify at Cardona's court-martial, Miller took the very unusual step of refusing to testify under Art. 31 (the Uniform Code of Military Justice (UCMJ) equivalent of the Fifth Amendment), while also announcing his retirement (so he could not be ordered to attend).[84] Interviewed by defense lawyers in August 2004, Miller had insisted he never talked to Pappas about using dogs in interrogations. The *Washington Post* said Miller's refusal "added to his dishonor." Army CID recommended that Jordan be charged with dereliction of duty and false statements. Pappas's immunity would extend to testifying against Jordan.

Campaigning for the release of Graner, whom she still loved, Ambuhl told a newspaper that the first time she entered Abu Ghraib, an enlisted officer showed her naked men in cells and prisoners wearing women's underwear or hooded and shackled to cell bars.[85] She was assured this was an MI tactic "to break the detainees that were being interrogated." Some of the practices in the notorious photos were daily occurrences, known to "a whole slew of people." "We didn't know any different. Maybe that's why they sent a combat support unit to do it. We wouldn't know how it was supposed to work, and we wouldn't question it." She had not been trained to deal with POWs, taught the Geneva Conventions, or even given SOPs. A "roster board" specified which "treatment" to give each detainee. Guantánamo trainers taught MPs stress positions, and MIs told MPs to keep detainees naked, embarrass them, and exercise them to the point of exhaustion. Two OGAs asked her to move a man after interrogation, saying "it would be funny if I burned him with my cigarette."

SASC decided to investigate Miller, who had testified that dogs were restricted to perimeter security but was said to have told Pappas they could be used in interrogation.[86] He denied briefing Rumsfeld or his top aides after visiting Iraq, but then claimed he had briefed Wolfowitz and Cambone. Sen. Graham said: "shame on us if we allow a story to go forward that is not true and the two dog handlers are paying the price." Levin agreed that those accused should "have access to all the information which can help their case." The "lack of accountability for those above the enlisted levels here has been stunning, unacceptable." Warner and Levin urged the Army to delay Miller's retirement until after the dog handlers' trial.

Two years after Darby disclosed the photos, Australian media published another five dozen.[87] One showed a naked mentally ill man, who had become a "plaything" for the guards, smeared with his own feces, and hanging upside down from a top bunk. The DVD from the Army CIC investigation contained more than a thousand photos, videos, and supporting documents dated between October 18 and December 30, 2003. Some were rebroadcast by American television and al Arabiya and Al Jazeera; Salon published 279 photos and 19 videos, with a 30-page analysis. A June 2004 CID report had found:

> a total of 1,325 images of suspected detainee abuse, 93 video files of suspected detainee abuse, 660 images of adult pornography, 546 images of suspected dead Iraqi detainees, 29 images of soldiers in simulated sexual acts, 20 images of a soldier with a swastika drawn between his eyes, 37 images of military working dogs being used to abuse detainees and 125 images of questionable acts.

Rumsfeld said these were "nothing more than the same things that came out before ... That behavior's been punished." The White House concurred. DoS legal adviser John B. Bellinger III said that because there had been prosecutions and investigations, it was "unfortunate" that "these photos are coming out further and fanning the flames." The Iraqi response echoed the American one: "These are violations against proper procedure that were rejected by the American and Iraqi government. These were spontaneous actions committed without any official involvement, and we trust there was a fair investigation into these matters." (At the date of writing the ACLU was still litigating its FOIA request to release the photos.[88])

Prosecutors called 18 witnesses at Sgt. Smith's court-martial and introduced a photo of him holding a dog close to the face of Ashraf

Abdullah Ahsy al-Juhayshi, who was interrogated 63 times, subjected to stress positions, and threatened with rendition to Saudi Arabia, Israel, or Guantánamo.[89] An MP said: "OGA and MI were paying a lot of attention to him." Pappas admitted approving the use of dogs because Miller had told him about "Arab fear of dogs." Sanchez authorized their use in September 2003 (although he withdrew that in October). Sanchez expressed "some concerns to me about the intelligence we were obtaining and not using the full spectrum of tools and authority, but never did he say use dogs on any particular person or time." "[I]t turned out I was wrong. I misinterpreted the language." Interrogator notes seemed to show that Pappas and a senior interrogator had approved the use of dogs, and Pappas could not explain why his name was on the documents. But he claimed to have been unaware that soldiers were unmuzzling dogs and using them outside interrogation booths.

Smith testified that "they use us for interrogations [*sic*] purposes." Frederick said Smith and Cardona told him Pappas approved using muzzled dogs for interrogation. Declaring that Ahsy was al-Qaeda, Stefanowicz told Frederick: "any chance you get, put the dogs on." Stefanowicz "would come down in between and we would pull the dogs off and he would go in and talk to" Ahsy. Shown the photo described above, Frederick said Stefanowicz had told Smith to do that. Pappas testified that Stefanowicz had "overstepped his bounds and I reported that to my staff." Another contract interrogator said that after Saddam's capture interrogation teams were given more freedom to use dogs. An MI interrogator reported following screams to a cell where Smith's dog was straining at his leash and barking at two cowering teenage boys. Smith later said with a laugh that Cardona "and I are having a contest to see if we can get them to shit themselves because we've already had some piss themselves." But one dog handler left an interrogation when he realized dogs were being used to threaten detainees, and another testified "it's a wrong thing to do."

After deliberating 18 hours over 3 days, the jury found Smith guilty of maltreating detainees, conspiring to terrify two juvenile detainees into soiling themselves, and allowing a dog to lick peanut butter from a male soldier's penis and a female soldier's breast while another soldier videotaped it. DoD claimed the verdict showed it was committed to "a very broad and a very deep review of its detention operations across the board." Declaring defiantly at his sentencing that "soldiers are not supposed to be soft and cuddly," Smith only regretted not seeking orders in writing. He faced 8.5 years, but the prosecution asked for 3, and he got just 6 months, demotion to private, a $2,250 fine, and a bad conduct discharge. The *New York Times* deplored that the same day "President Bush said once again that Defense Secretary Donald Rumsfeld, whose benighted policies and managerial incompetence led to the prisoner abuse scandal, was doing a 'fine job' and should stay at his post."

Although DoD referred abuse cases against 19 military contractors to DoJ, the US Attorney for the Eastern District of Virginia concluded that the evidence was insufficient to prosecute Daniel Johnson, a CACI employee shown in a November 24, 2003 photo using an "unauthorized stress position" to interrogate an Iraqi prisoner suspected of having smuggled in a gun used by another prisoner to shoot American soldiers.[90] Frederick told an Army investigator there was agreement that when a detainee would not answer Johnson's questions, Frederick would "stomp in" the interrogation room, "get real close" to the suspect, "breathe real hard," and "slap[] the wall or bed real hard just to make a commotion." Twice at Johnson's signal "I would put my hand over [the detainee's] mouth and pinch his nose" so he could not breathe. Frederick also used pressure points around the suspect's cheek, nose, chin, ear, and wrist. Johnson "yelled and screamed a lot. He walked around like he was the man … and would pull [out] all the stops if he had to." When Graner "roughed up" a suspect, splitting open his forehead during an interrogation, Johnson refused to let a medic suture him, so Graner did so. Sen. Durbin later said this case "would have been on the table" had he known about it when the SJC voted to confirm Paul McNulty as US Attorney for ED Va.

The judge trying Sgt. Cardona (the other dog handler) ordered Miller to testify despite his invocation of Art. 31 (but rejected a defense request that Rumsfeld testify).[91] Although the prosecutor argued that Guantánamo and Abu Ghraib were "separate things," the judge ruled that Miller's September 2003 visit could be relevant to what followed. In July 2005 Sanchez told Army investigators that Rumsfeld had asked him in spring 2003: "why can't we figure this enemy out?" "There was intense pressure" for intelligence from "different levels of command." Sanchez resolved to "push our authorities to the limit without ever violating the Geneva Conventions." In September 2003, on Warren's advice, he authorized interrogators to "exploit Arab fear of dogs." Pappas told Army investigators in April 2006 that Miller's visit explained the belief dogs "were effective in doing interrogations with Arabs." "The tenor of the discussions was that we had to get tougher with detainees." In an email summarizing the visit, Capt. Wood wrote that Miller's team said "working dogs are highly effective and useful." Miller subsequently briefed Washington officials about his mission. Col. Boltz told investigators in May 2004 that "there was pressure from higher to provide actionable intelligence." The same month the DIA officer overseeing Iraq interrogations told investigators that interrogators were encouraged "to go to the outer limits to get information."

Miller admitted he had found dogs "very effective in assisting detention staff in maintaining custody and control" in Guantánamo because of a "fear of dogs in Arab culture," but insisted he had never urged their use in interrogation. Rumsfeld's authorization for Guantánamo interrogation techniques, which Miller had imported to Abu Ghraib, was just a "baseline, a framework." MPs' function was to "conduct custody and control" and "provide assistance to the intelligence function that can be translated to the intelligence booth." But they were only supposed to collect "passive intelligence," such as "who the detainee interacted with." Although Pappas had told Taguba that Miller said working dogs "were effective in setting the atmosphere for which, you could get information," now he testified he only had a "general discussion" with Miller about working dogs "being an effective tool at Guantánamo because of the Arab fear of dogs." The 320th MP Battalion commander said Miller "encouraged the use of dogs as much as possible." Maj. DiNenna testified that Miller said "dogs were extremely effective" and promised to request more. Capt. Wood remembered recommending to superiors that interrogators use ROEs developed by a Special Operations Task Force, but never got a response. A contract interrogator said he was told by MI that Rumsfeld and Wolfowitz received "nightly briefings." An MI corroborated this, claiming that Boltz frequently boasted that Rumsfeld and Wolfowitz had called and were "waiting for reports."

Cardona was convicted of dereliction of duty and aggravated assault for letting a dog bark inches from a prisoner's face, but was acquitted of unlawfully having a dog bite an inmate and conspiring with Smith to frighten prisoners into soiling themselves. Although he faced up to 3.5 years he got 90 days "hard labor," reduction in rank to specialist, and loss of security clearance.

At Jordan's Art. 32 hearing the prosecutor said he would argue that Jordan's command exhibited "breakdown and negligence."[92] The defense replied that Jordan was just the MI liaison, but MGen. Fay said: "that role didn't make any sense at that time." His report had "established" that Jordan was "in charge" of the JIDC and failed to stop sexual and physical abuse. On cross-examination, Fay acknowledged that Jordan had been wounded in a September 2003 mortar attack, which killed two subordinates, and was "still traumatized" six months later. After playing a central role in the gun smuggling incident, Jordan rounded up Iraqi prison guards and, without seeking Sanchez's permission, ordered a Navy dog handler to assist their interrogation. An investigator testified that others said Jordan was in charge of interrogation, but admitted on cross-examination he had not seen the defendant's name on any interrogation orders. Maj. DiNenna emphasized Abu Ghraib's bad conditions: "odor, sewage, rodents, trash, mortars, small arms fire." Jordan said there was "chaos" and "confusion" and insisted he "did not see or participate in any of the abuses." But Capt. Reese claimed to have seen Jordan at Tier 1A "every day." Jordan knew that detainees were stripped for interrogation. When Reese asked "why didn't anybody have any clothes on?," Jordan replied: "It's an interrogation tactic that we use," but also blamed nudity on a "lack of clothing." Sgt. Hydrue Joyner (an MP) said some "mental cases … chose not to wear anything." "The jumpsuits were deteriorating … so some wrapped themselves as best they could or didn't have anything."

The defense argued that it was Pappas who was actually in charge of the JIDC. A contract interrogator who reported to Wood and Pappas said Jordan "was never anyone I went to or through regarding interrogations" but rather "seemed to have some kind of support role." SSgt. Jeff Day agreed that Jordan spent most of his time improving troop living conditions and did not seem to be in charge of interrogations. Chief Warrant Officer Edward J. Rivas asked Pappas rather than Jordan about interrogation, but admitted that the organizational chart identified Jordan as JIDC chief. Maj. Michael D. Thompson (who reported to Pappas) testified that after the mortar attack "Col. Pappas came in and spoke to [the guards] to try to lift their spirits." Pappas had quarters in the prison between September 20 and October 31, 2003, although he did not stay there every night. Maj. Maurice Williams told Thompson that Pappas was in charge, a fact about which Thompson had "no doubt whatsoever." LtCol. Jeff Hamerick, who arrived on October 17, called JIDC leadership "nebulous," "absolutely broken." Pappas testified it was "in transition" until he took control in late November. Soon after arriving he began doubting the fitness of Jordan, who admitted he was not a "formal interrogator." Pappas had wanted to staff the JIDC with his own people, but Sanchez insisted on having at least a lieutenant colonel in charge. Col. Boltz explained that he chose Jordan for his skills and made him "responsible for the overseeing of interrogations and unit operations." Pappas (whose brigade was already conducting interrogations) felt that Jordan should focus on quality of life rather than intelligence. Growing more concerned when Jordan did not promptly inform him about the ICRC objections to nudity following its October inspection, Pappas increased his Abu Ghraib visits from biweekly to 2–3 times a week and then moved his headquarters there on November 19 because Sanchez was "not happy" and wanted more "rapid exploitation of information." At the time Pappas thought "sleep management" and muzzled dogs were appropriate interrogation techniques. "I don't recall seeing any nudity." Although the Art. 32 hearing recommended an administrative disposition "to preclude continued disgrace for our armed forces in this matter and execute justice in this particular case," two commanding generals referred Jordan for court-martial on eight charges.

Before the court-martial was held, Jordan maintained in a lengthy newspaper interview that "I was involved in no interrogations, ever." Before arriving at Abu Ghraib he was told: "I was going to the wild, wild west, that it was a dangerous area. That's all the guidance I got." He lived in a former bathroom reeking of urine. Although titular JIDC director, he focused on soldiers' needs. He claimed to have reported abuse but was "shocked" by the photos. An MI who conducted 100 interrogations at Abu Ghraib in late 2003 said Jordan was not involved in any of them. Another MI who interrogated there for three months in late 2003 and early 2004 agreed Jordan was not in charge.

The government dropped the two most serious counts (making a false official statement and obstruction of justice) because Fay had failed to read Jordan his rights.[93] The prosecution then narrowed the charge of cruelty and maltreatment of detainees from three months to a single day. Jordan was convicted of disobeying Fay's order but acquitted of all other charges. Although exposed to five years, he was got only a reprimand, the most lenient sentence. BGen. Louis Weber, president of the jury, called him "a superb leader and officer." Jordan pronounced the outcome "a vindication for my family, myself, and all the professional soldiers and civilians at Abu Ghraib that did outstanding duty in such an austere environment." Because even the conviction could block promotion, he sought clemency from his commanding officer, who erased it. Courts denied appeals by Sabrina Harman and Michael Smith.[94]

ANALYSIS

The Abu Ghraib abuses might never have been exposed had Darby not given Graner's CD to CIC. The photos had a shock value no words could equal – for Darby, the military, the executive, Congress, and ultimately the public, both American and global.[95] Some immediately became iconic. Competition for a scoop between CBS and *The New Yorker* ensured rapid publication of both the photos and Taguba report excerpts, encouraging other outlets to get and disseminate related documents: ICRC reports by the *Wall Street Journal*, Art. 32 proceedings by the *Washington Post* and *Los Angeles Times*, the 372nd MP Company logbook by the *Washington Post*, paraphrases of the OLC memos by the *New York Times*, and even more disturbing photos by Australian media and Salon (which is why the Bush and Obama administrations successfully obstructed release of the remaining photos). When the military issued sanitized summaries of its investigations, the media exposed at least some of the secret portions. The media also repeatedly demanded accountability at the highest levels, deploring administration and military efforts to blame foot soldiers and insisting the problem was systemic. As other remedial mechanisms ignored the root causes, Congressional Democrats and the *New York Times* kept calling (unsuccessfully) for an independent commission.

Because the photos made it impossible to deny that soldiers had committed terrible abuses, attention focused on why, the implications for responsibility, and remedies. Within days of the exposé, JCS chair Myers attributed the scandal to a few bad apples. Rumsfeld reiterated that the actions constituted "cruelty at the hands of a few" and had been "perpetrated by a small number." Bush, Warner, Abizaid, and Mikolashek echoed this view. Several emphasized that 50,000 detainees had *not* been abused. The military acknowledged that in the rush to call up reserves and expand the volunteer army to wage the Iraq war, it had relaxed recruitment standards. Rumsfeld denounced the "blatantly sadistic, cruel and inhuman" offenses, perhaps because their very heinousness reinforced this narrative. That the misconduct was flagrantly sexualized seemed to let superiors off the hook since they could not have ordered it.

Graner was the archetypal misfit. As a civilian, he had abused prisoners as well as his ex-wife, even bragging he had almost killed her. He photographed his sexual exhibitionism with other soldiers before deployment. In Abu Ghraib he was simultaneously sleeping with England (whom he impregnated and abandoned) and Ambuhl (whom he married while in prison) while bullying many male MPs. He continued to abuse prisoners and sleep with England after a formal rebuke. Other perpetrators refused to take their misconduct seriously. England said they were just having fun. Graner joked just before his court-martial: "we're going to find out what kind of a monster I am today." Even Darby (the whistle-blower) thought the pyramid was funny. Harman compulsively photographed abuses, injuries, and deaths. The two dog handlers seemed to join the fun, competing in terrifying detainees into soiling themselves and ordering dogs to lick peanut butter off one MP's penis and another's breast.

The bad apples quickly contaminated the rest of the barrel.[96] Several soldiers initially shocked by seeing naked detainees held in cells or paraded through prison corridors said they accepted this as an MI interrogation tactic when superiors observed it and did nothing. Many MPs knew first hand or from others that OGA was committing worse abuses with impunity. Yet ringleader warnings not to report this behavior suggest an awareness of its wrongfulness.

Some of the worst abuses were provoked by threatening or harmful events: rocket attacks on the prison, smuggled arms used to attack guards, an alleged rape of young Iraqi boys. Some abusers had suffered personally or lost colleagues in these attacks. (Other US military abuses in Afghanistan and Iraq followed American casualties.) The capture of Saddam Hussein intensified pressure for intelligence about his associates and supporters.

Even before military investigations were complete, the top brass settled on a convenient account. There was no "pattern of abuse." "[I]solated incidents" were attributable to multiple factors. The failure to anticipate the Sunni uprising in response to Saddam Hussein's overthrow led to chaos. The military had committed insufficient resources to the prison. Abu Ghraib living conditions were very difficult. Soldiers lacked training for assigned tasks and received no ROEs. Organization and supervision were inadequate. Sanchez issued one memo on September 14, 2003 and an inconsistent one the next month, leaving MPs uncertain about what they could do. A DoD directive the previous May distinguished POWs who were protected by the Geneva Conventions from "unlawful combatants" who were not. DoD later claimed (bizarrely) that this was not a legal analysis and OLC memos were merely "exploring the boundaries as an abstract matter," part of a healthy "deliberative process." John Yoo was eager to shift attention from his responsibility as author of the OLC memos to the inexcusable behavior at Abu Ghraib.

The administration deployed various strategies to deflect the avalanche of criticism. Rumsfeld and Myers seemed almost to welcome those (like the ICRC) who called the abuses torture, creating an opportunity to reiterate the meaningless mantra that "we do not torture," thereby claiming carte blanche for all other behavior. Officials from Bush through Rumsfeld, Sanchez, and Wood expressed horror at learning about the abuses, as though their noble sentiments demonstrated lack of complicity. But the claim uncomfortably resembled Capt. Renault's hypocritical protest that he was "shocked, shocked" to find gambling at Rick's Bar in *Casablanca*. And Bush declared himself "equally" upset by the abuses and the unjustified condemnation of America.

In an early public statement Rumsfeld took "responsibility" but could not hide his true feelings. He regretted "the damage that has been done. First, to the reputation" of the military. He apologized to the public for not being "able to convey the gravity of all this before we saw it in the media." (He had been perfectly capable of doing so.) He told SASC: "I wish we had known more sooner and been able to tell you more sooner, but we didn't." (DoD did.) He even presumed to take credit for Darby's whistle-blowing. In fact, DoD deliberately kept the public in the dark by investigating in secret and withholding the Taguba report. Rumsfeld's third (and perhaps only genuine) regret was for the damage "to the reputation of our country." Only as an afterthought did he claim to be seeking ways to compensate abused Iraqis. (He never found them.) Bush loyally defended Rumsfeld against Democratic demands for his resignation, and DoD claimed the Schlesinger report vindicated him. It was not until his memoir seven years later that Rumsfeld conceded he should have resigned.[97] Sanchez insisted his September 14, 2003 order directed "lawful and humane treatment" – even though CENTCOM made him modify it less than a month later. He was so convinced of his own rectitude that he gave a speech claiming to have been a great leader under pressure. Miller denied responsibility just as adamantly.

Rumsfeld and other high DoD, DoS, and the White House officials repeatedly maintained that the military investigations and courts-martial proved "the system worked." From their viewpoint it did: every report whitewashed the military except for Taguba's – which was supposed to remain secret. Rumsfeld urged the world to "watch how a democracy deals with the wrongdoing and with scandal and the pain of acknowledging and correcting our own mistakes," but then stage-managed the deceptive charade. He claimed, hypocritically, that DoD's January 16, 2004 press release "told everyone in the world that there were allegations of abuse and they were being investigated." But the release said nothing about the abuses, justifying its silence by reference to ongoing criminal investigations – which themselves would have remained secret but for the media exposés. Myers warned that publicity might lead to "the worst possible outcome ... that they get off." Many did – but not because of publicity.

Indeed, most of the remedial mechanisms demanded secrecy: the reports by the ICRC and Taguba, other military reports, CIC investigations and early Art. 32 hearings, administrative penalties, even Congressional briefings and hearings. After Darby exposed the photos Pappas banned cameras and pornography (as though they were the cause), with the predictable result that MPs destroyed potentially incriminating evidence. Military officials in Iraq responded to the ICRC's critical reports by obstructing access to detainees. DoD resisted disclosure of the ICRC reports, falsely claiming that confidentiality was meant to benefit the Committee rather than result in the state being investigated. Military officials used pending criminal investigations as a reason for withholding information from Congress and were supported by sympathetic Republicans. Members of the military were forbidden to speak outside the chain of command; Karpinski did so only after accepting that her military career was over – and was promptly suspended. DoD classified many of the reports it commissioned (although portions were leaked). It strenuously (and successfully) resisted FOIA requests for the other photos and videos of abuses. The administration withheld the OLC memos, arguing that the president's legal powers should not be debated during wartime, and still has not released some.

But secrecy always is imperfect and transitory. Disclosure of some DoD investigations and OLC memos intensified pressure to release others. The Detainee Assessment Branch (DAB) naively asked detainees how they had been treated and then reported the disturbing findings to the Review and Appeal Board – perhaps to protect the DAB against charges of cover-up. Attempts to conceal abuses often are harder to defend than the misconduct itself.

Administration efforts to present a united front in damage control were complicated by internal divisions. DoS acknowledged having known about some abuses and claimed to have reported them to DoD, perhaps to ensure the Pentagon was held responsible. Given its mission, DoS also was much more concerned than DoD about Abu Ghraib's effect on the nation's reputation and credibility when invoking international law against other offenders. Mistrusting each other, the CIA and DoD jealously guarded their prerogatives, especially control of prisoners. The CIA and FBI had been rivals since their founding. Even within the military there were tensions between the regular army, Reserves, and Special Operations; officers and enlisted soldiers; and MI and MPs.

The administration also responded to criticism by promising changes. Bush called for the closure of Abu Ghraib (treating it like a deodand, as though the building rather than the soldiers inflicted the abuses). Miller echoed this, proposing to transfer prisoners to the hopefully named Camp Redemption. He also said interrogation rules had been changed to prevent a recurrence of the abuse (while continuing to deny that those rules he introduced at Guantánamo and brought to Abu Ghraib had encouraged the abuses). The Army issued a new interrogation Field Manual but refused to disclose a lengthy appendix illustrating permissible practices; and the Manual did not bind the CIA. Pappas terminated the practice of "ghost prisoners" once they became visible. In anticipation of testifying before SASC, Sanchez forbade MPs to seek permission for any coercive interrogation method except isolation. But each reform contained the negative pregnant of acknowledging the evils it purported to correct.

The ICRC played a crucial but circumscribed role. Governments let it interview prisoners on condition that it report exclusively to them. The administration tried to disguise its own responsibility for secrecy by hypocritically blaming the ICRC (although DoD ultimately felt compelled to give HASC the ICRC reports). Despite this limitation, however, ICRC reports can influence governmental behavior – and not just through appeals to conscience. The investigations themselves can embarrass officials: Demary told Karpinski he could not interview naked prisoners. Fear of what the ICRC would see and report led military officials to obstruct its investigators, hide "ghost" detainees, and fabricate justifications for doing so (e.g., military necessity, "security detainees"). ICRC reports documented *when* officials learned of the abuses, undermining deniability: Warren said the ICRC November 6, 2003 Working Paper was widely distributed throughout Army headquarters in Baghdad, thereby contradicting Rumsfeld's claim that DoD learned of the abuses only after media exposés. Furthermore, the ICRC called the abuses torture and insisted they were systemic, not isolated. The reports generated an obligation to respond: witness the contortions in Abu Ghraib at the end of 2003 to make Karpinski appear responsible (thereby concealing the transfer of prison administration from MPs to MI). And, of course, reports create a risk that they will be leaked by disaffected administration officials.

Despite Republican control of both Houses, the initial Congressional response raised hopes of bipartisanship. SASC chair Warner condemned the abuses and promised an investigation. McCain called for accountability at the highest level. Graham wanted to know whether the problem was systemic. Reps. Heather Wilson (R-Az) and John Kline (R-Mn) agreed with them. It is noteworthy that all these Republican legislators had extensive military experience; and only they advanced the non-consequentialist argument that the abuses betrayed core American values. But the inevitable Republican backlash was almost as rapid. HASC chair Hunter attacked Warner for summoning senior commanders to testify and was supported by Sen. Cornyn. House Majority Leader DeLay and Minority Whip Hoyer split along party lines. Republicans uncritically backed EITs. Democrats, by contrast, blamed senior military and civilian officials and decried the scapegoating of MPs. Sen. Durbin and Rep. Conyers introduced legislation requiring the military to report abuses and respect international law. But Republicans blocked all these initiatives. Sen. Kerry – effectively the Democratic presidential nominee (and another decorated veteran) – declared that the legal memos raised questions about responsibility at the highest level and insisted, after the first military reports, that he would make the abuses a campaign issue. But when Republicans predictably denounced this as election-year politics, Kerry backed down. Although Warner kept reiterating his determination to investigate, years of SASC hearings produced little public information about ultimate responsibility for the abuses.

DoD launched a dozen investigations, constantly cited them as demonstrating its commitment to accountability, and then claimed the reports exculpated all higher officials. Ryder's report – the first – prefigured later whitewashes. DoD said it showed that *all* Abu Ghraib detainees were security threats (a ludicrous claim). Rumsfeld cynically stacked the committee assigned to investigate him with two former Defense Secretaries, a general, and a former Republican Congresswoman who declared at the outset that Rumsfeld could have "never done this type of activity." The Schlesinger report did not disappoint, characterizing the abuses as "purposeless sadism" unrelated to interrogation and blaming them on prison conditions. (Who was responsible for those?) Although it found that Miller and Sanchez had urged or authorized harsh techniques at Guantánamo and Abu Ghraib, Schlesinger (one of the former Defense Secretaries) warned that excessive criticism or restraint could impede intelligence gathering; and Brown (the other) ridiculed the ICRC definition of torture as overinclusive, claimed that even torture could be justified by circumstances, and defended Rumsfeld, especially against calls for him to resign. Although hinting that superiors might have encouraged "behavior at the harsher end of the acceptable range," Mikolashek also embraced the bad apple theory, calling for better monitoring, supervision, and training. Fay/Jones straddled the fence: Sanchez was culpable but not responsible (whatever that meant). Indeed, there were no human agents: interrogation techniques just "migrated" from Guantánamo to Afghanistan and Abu Ghraib, like birds following their instincts. Failures of doctrine, training, and policy could not have caused the abuses because the EITs employed were not on the approved list. Instead, the report blamed inadequate staffing and lack of cohesion. MPs were the most culpable but may have been acting at MI's behest and aping the CIA. Some abuses were understandable reactions to security threats. The report on Reservists ordered by LtGen. Helmly blamed training. The Church Report minimized the abuses: many were unsubstantiated, occurred at the point of capture, or were simple assaults. The rest were unrelated to interrogation and attributable to the difficult environment and lack of clear guidelines, good order, and discipline.

Despite (or perhaps because of) the enormous resources the military devoted to these investigations, they failed to answer the central question of ultimate responsibility. Every officer played the blame game, pointing a finger at others, generating a perfect storm of bureaucratic excuses. As commander of US prisons in Iraq (and perhaps not incidentally a female Reservist), Karpinski presented an obvious scapegoat. But she claimed to have been ignorant of the abuses until Darby blew the whistle. She signed the response to the ICRC without being allowed to offer any input or even see its report. Indeed, superiors insisted she sign it to distract attention from MI control of the hard site. She blamed Miller (who denied bringing his Guantánamo techniques to Abu Ghraib) and Sanchez (who insisted his two interrogation memos did not authorize the abuses – especially not the misuse of working dogs). Jordan, though formally responsible for interrogation, claimed he left it to Pappas, concentrating instead on improving staff living conditions. Reese said MIs in charge of the prison directed his MPs to soften up detainees for interrogation. Reese alleged that Jordan observed (and thereby condoned) interrogations and abuses, and blamed Pappas, whose disavowal of control over daily operations was backed by Sanchez. Pappas claimed Miller had said MPs should "support interrogations" and introduced the idea of exploiting Arab fear of dogs for interrogations. Miller's report said the MP "must act as an enabler for interrogation" and "be actively engaged in setting the conditions for successful exploitation of the internees." Cambone confirmed that Miller had been sent to Abu Ghraib to improve intelligence gathering, including the "coordination" of detention and interrogation. Indeed, after visiting Abu Ghraib, Miller dispatched 15 interrogators from Guantánamo.

Enlisted soldiers also blamed each other. MI claimed they ignored MP misconduct because it was not the business of interrogators, who did not know the ROEs. Far from ordering or encouraging MPs to mistreat detainees, MI sometimes intervened to stop abuses, including nudity. But some MI acknowledged telling MPs to "soften up" detainees for interrogation by abusing them. Provance said: "military intelligence was in control." The ICRC's February 2004 report found that "methods of physical and psychological coercion were used by the military intelligence in a systematic way," which one MI said was "part of the process."[98] MPs said they took MI's tacit observation as encouragement, approval, or at least condonation, and insisted some MI engaged in sexual abuse. MPs may have envied MI's more significant role. The numerous military reports never resolved these conflicting accounts.

Soldiers constantly claimed to have been following orders. Javal Davis repeated this justification even after serving his sentence. But the few written documents were ambiguous (perhaps deliberately so): Rumsfeld's statement that detainees were "unlawful enemy combatants" to whom the Geneva Conventions did not apply, Sanchez's inconsistent September 14 and October 6, 2003 memos on interrogation techniques, and Boltz's warning that the gloves were coming off. Otherwise, officers carefully avoided putting orders in writing, and enlisted soldiers rarely insisted they do so (Graner being a surprising exception, perhaps because of his civilian experience as a prison guard). Consequently, such claims devolved into a (less credible) enlisted soldier's word against a (more credible) officer's. (The military unsurprisingly refused most accused soldiers' requests to grant officers immunity to testify about their orders.) Wood's IROE, posted in the JIDC, may not have accurately captured Sanchez's orders; but it was the *only* visible document because all the official memos were classified. The alleged orders often were vague or even perverse. Wood claimed Miller told her to have MPs observe social interaction among detainees because MPs were "privy to some very valuable information." But many detainees were isolated in single cells, MPs knew no Arabic, and most abuses occurred at night, when detainees were trying to sleep. Pappas said that under intense pressure from Sanchez and after talking to Miller he had directed the use of dogs (which Sanchez had authorized in September 2003 before countermanding that in October). But Miller contradicted this, insisting he had told Pappas to use dogs only to guard perimeters and control prisoners, not to interrogate. Of course, orders could not have justified illegal acts.

Although soldiers also claimed they reported abuses to superiors, few did so. Darby, the poster child, was the exception. The ostracism and death threats he suffered may explain why disclosure was so rare. Matthew Wisdom declined to participate in the abuses on Tier 1A and was promptly transferred elsewhere. Furthermore, his objection forced Frederick to admit his behavior was wrong. Kimbro refused to use his dogs to threaten detainees. Some, like Reese and Karpinski, were dilatory in protesting. Others, like Graner and Stefanowicz, claimed to have objected while also participating in abuses. Although objections effectively extricated the speaker from involvement and sometimes ended the abuse, almost nobody blew the whistle, perhaps because most succumbed to (and enjoyed) the bacchanalian culture, feared being labeled a party-pooper or worse – a snitch – or worried they would be seen as complicit (at least for not reporting earlier).

Congressional hearings and military investigations were extraordinary responses to an unprecedented event. Courts-martial, by contrast, are routine. How did they handle these cases? Like other forms of self-regulation by lawyers, doctors, clergy, police, legislators, and athletes, courts-martial are very solicitous of the accused's rights – arguably more so than civilian criminal prosecutions (one reason the administration rejected the latter for trying alleged terrorists). Despite the heinousness of the acts and the administration's deep embarrassment by the tidal wave of adverse publicity, the military exhibited just that solicitude toward those implicated in Abu Ghraib. Many accused – especially officers – received administrative hearings, not only protecting their military careers but also depriving the public of information about the charges, findings, outcomes, and penalties imposed. Col. Pohl (later assigned to try High-Value Detainees (HVDs) in the Guantánamo military commissions) was tough on prosecutors, ordering them to accelerate their review of the evidence and disclose all exculpatory material. He threatened to grant Pappas and Jordan immunity unless the government promptly charged them. He took the extraordinary step of overturning England's guilty plea *sua sponte* after Graner claimed to have ordered her misconduct (a potential defense), and excluded her incriminatory statements on retrial because she had not fully understood the consequences when waiving her rights. Ambuhl's Art. 32 hearing officer recommended dismissal of some charges. Miller invoked the rarely used Art. 31 right not to incriminate himself (although a judge ordered Cardona to testify after he invoked that right). Perhaps most stunning of all, a judge dismissed Jordan's charges because Fay and Taguba had not read him his rights, although the accused must have known them. The few who went to trial – England, Graner, Harman, Smith, Cardona, and Jordan – received fair, thorough hearings.

As in the civilian criminal justice system, most accused, starting with Sivits, pleaded guilty and agreed to testify, earning lenience by helping prosecutors convict others. But even though the photographs constituted incontrovertible evidence of egregious misconduct, trials would have performed the indispensable function of exposing and preserving accounts of what happened and why. Guilty pleas foreclosed that opportunity.

Even after pleading or being adjudged guilty, accused used the penalty phase to justify their behavior. They offered a wide range of explanations: they or their close colleagues suffered attacks, injuries, and even deaths in the prison; they were under pressure (from MI and higher ranks) to generate intelligence (because of rising casualties from the Sunni uprising and in the wake of Saddam Hussein's capture); abuses antedated their arrival, were committed with impunity by OGA, and were pervasive and universally condoned (even by superiors); the accused were following orders; they reported abuses to superiors; living conditions were appalling; no one was in charge; training was inadequate. Yet soldiers in combat, under far greater stress and danger, in more ambiguous circumstances, with equally unclear chains of command, suffering much higher casualties, and enduring far worse living conditions, did not commit similar offenses. Some defense arguments blatantly failed the laugh test: detainees were naked because there was not enough clothing; the pyramid of naked detainees resembled the gymnastic feats of football cheerleaders; a woman leading a naked male prisoner on a leash was just like a mother controlling a toddler in a busy airport; the photographs were taken to assist interrogation – or to document the abuses; the detainee on whom Harman had written "rapeist" could not read English. Defendants objected to the proceedings on the ground that officers were not being held accountable (a selective prosecution argument that almost never prevails in civilian trials). Defendants apologized – but more often for having "embarrassed the country and the army that I love" and endangering American soldiers, not for abusing detainees. Finally, defendants pleaded for mercy. Graner, the ringleader, claimed he had not enjoyed himself (although his contemporaneous oral statements and emails showed him having the time of his life). He admitted knowing that "a lot" was "wrong," even "criminal," but evinced little remorse, joking at the outset of the trial: "We're going to find out what kind of a monster I am today."

Given the egregiousness of the behavior, lack of any credible justification, and seriousness of the consequences (for detainees, the image of the United States, and the recruitment of jihadis), the penalties seem exceptionally mild. Graner and Frederick were sentenced to 10 and 8 years respectively but served just 6.5 and 3. England faced 10 years, but the prosecution sought only 4–6, and she got just 3 and served less than 1.5. The others received even shorter jail terms: Sivits a year (perhaps because he was the first), Krol 10 months, Cruz 8, Smith and Davis 6, Cardona 3, and Capt. Martin 1.5. Ambuhl, Karpinski, and Jordan lost pay but spent no time in the brig. Indeed, Jordan's conviction was overturned by his commanding officer, who gave him just an administrative reprimand, thereby saving his career. Schlesinger said Sanchez's failure to earn a fourth star was more than enough punishment (do we punish thieves by denying them their spoils?). Others high up in the chain of command actually seem to have been rewarded: Wojdakowski became special assistant to the commanding general of Army European operations and then head of the Army infantry training school at Fort Benning, Georgia (a peculiar assignment, given the military's determination to blame Abu Ghraib on poor training). Fast was promoted to head the Army's Intelligence Center at Fort Huachuca, Arizona (conveying approval of the EITs she had authorized). Warren moved to Army headquarters in Washington and was promoted to brigadier general. Only Sanchez (denied his fourth star) and Karpinski (demoted to colonel) suffered meaningful punishment that ended their military careers. Civilian contractors enjoyed even greater impunity. Neither

Nakhla nor Stefanowicz was punished, and the government took no action against Titan or CACI.

Abu Ghraib – the first widely publicized abuse in the "war on terror" – elicited universal opprobrium. The most effective actors in correcting misconduct were the media, which ripped away the veil of secrecy, persisted in revealing incriminating evidence, and kept demanding accountability at the highest levels. Such exposure ensured that these specific abuses would not recur. By contrast, both the civilian administration and the military quickly bought the line that the problem was limited to a few bad apples, emphasizing the gratuitous, sadistic, and sexualized behavior to drive home that view. All remedial mechanisms displayed serious, potentially fatal, flaws. ICRC inspectors wrote vigorous denunciations of the abuses; but secrecy restricted their influence to pangs of a conscience most members of the military lacked. Republican obstructionism paralyzed Congressional Democrats; and the few Republicans whose military service moved them to outrage failed to follow through on their early rhetoric. Except for Taguba's investigation – which the military tried to keep secret – all others were whitewashes, refusing to pursue responsibility up the chain of command. The paper record of military orders was incomplete and ambiguous, perhaps deliberately so, making it impossible for MPs to prove their defenses. Aside from Darby, almost none of the many soldiers who witnessed abuses blew the whistle, even though the few who dared suffered no official retaliation. Most of the CIC investigations were disposed of administratively, producing neither a public record nor significant punishment. Most of those prosecuted pleaded guilty, thereby depriving the public of an accounting. Only three foot-soldiers were singled out for significant punishment: Graner, Frederick, and England. The rest were punished lightly – officers hardly at all. This first, highly visible, test of America's willingness and ability to correct unambiguous violations of the rule of law during its "war on terror" was an abject failure.

CHAPTER THREE

GUANTÁNAMO BAY

Indefinite detention without trial of nearly 800 men at Guantánamo Bay (GB) was the most prominent and constant US violation of the rule of law after 9/11.[1] Iconic photographs of hooded, shackled detainees in orange jumpsuits kneeling behind barbed wire provoked protesters around the world to don similar garb. Other rule-of-law violations, by contrast, were limited in time (Abu Ghraib), less visible (secret prisons, interrogation, NSA surveillance), or distant (targeted killing). Assured by OLC memos commissioned by the White House, the Bush administration deliberately chose Guantánamo to minimize scrutiny and legal constraint. This chapter examines the multiple forms of resistance to Guantánamo during the Bush and Obama administrations[2] (I discuss habeas corpus in the companion volume *Law's Trials*). It poses the following questions. How did the administration seek to preserve secrecy, how was it breached, and with what consequences? What were the effects of direct action: demonstrations at home and abroad, inmate hunger strikes, and suicides (attempted and successful)? Which nations secured the return of their nationals? Which nations agreed to accept the transfer of non-national detainees? What was the effect of investigations and reports by NGOs and international bodies? How did the different procedures for assessing detainees for release – Combatant Status Review Tribunals (CSRTs), Administrative Review Boards (ARBs), Obama Task Force, Periodic Review Boards (PRBs), and District Courts – compare with each other and the rule of law? How persuasive were the arguments for and against closure? Why did the Bush administration latterly express a willingness to close Guantánamo but fail to do so? Why did Obama fail to fulfill his promise to close the prison?

THE BUSH ADMINISTRATION

On December 28, 2001, the OLC issued a secret memo declaring that Guantánamo Bay was not subject to the jurisdiction of US law or courts.[3] The military promptly sent three men there – Shafiq Rasul and Asif Iqbal (British citizens) and David Hicks (Australian) – soon followed by 20 others. They and hundreds more remained largely invisible for three-and-a-half years. But in the wake of the Supreme Court's June 28, 2004 decision in *Rasul*[4] holding that Guantánamo detainees could seek habeas corpus, DoD initiated CSRTs: panels of three military officers who would secretly hear detainees and their representatives (nonlawyer military officers with access only to nonclassified evidence).[5] Although 465 of the first 487 CSRTs found the detainees were enemy combatants (ECs), 65 were soon transferred, and only a few more were sent to Guantánamo.[6] Indeed, seeking to obviate habeas petitions, Donald Rumsfeld asked DoS and other agencies in February 2005 to halve the number of detainees by returning citizens to Afghanistan, Saudi Arabia, and Yemen (each of which was the country of origin of over a hundred prisoners). A DoD report on interrogations showed that MI no longer sought to extract "actionable intelligence" from most prisoners.

Publicizing Abuse

Although the military blocked access to the island, it could not silence those released. After being freed on March 25, 2003, 18 Afghan men accused guards of sitting on the Koran and throwing one in a toilet.[7] Five months after the UK successfully repatriated five citizens, the Tipton Three wrote a detailed account of their abuse in Afghanistan and Guantánamo: stripped, beaten, deprived of sleep, placed in stress positions, threatened with death, shown videotapes of prisoners sodomizing each other, forcibly shaved, and watching their Korans being desecrated.[8] Under this torture Rasul "confessed" to having met bin Laden and 9/11 conspirator Mohammed Atta in Afghanistan in 2000 – even though he was working in England at the time. (*The Road to Abu Ghraib*, Michael Winterbottom's documentary on the Tipton Three, won the Silver Bear Award for direction at the Berlin Film Festival and was shown on BBC 4 in March 2006.) After being released to Kuwait in 2005, Nasser Nijer Naser al-Mutairi said he had suffered beatings, seen Korans defiled, and witnessed three major hunger strikes (over indefinite detention, sexual abuse, and Koran desecration). Two detainees returned to Bahrain told NPR about being exposed to heat and cold, shackled for up to ten hours, pepper-sprayed, forbidden to pray, and forced to witness desecration of the Koran. Back in Saudi Arabia, Adel al-Nusairi described being injected with drugs, deprived of sleep, and subjected to cold before signing a forced confession. In France, Mourad Benchellali said he suffered headaches, nausea, and drowsiness after being given what he was told were antibiotics or vitamins. Jumah al Dossari, freed in Saudi Arabia, wrote in a *Washington Post* op ed that "several soldiers once beat me so badly that I spent three days in intensive care." Other interrogators "slammed my head against the table" and shackled him to the floor for hours. After attempting suicide, he was kept in solitary for several months, clothed only in a pair of shorts, sleeping on a mat in a freezing room and drinking from the toilet.

Gen. James T. Hill (GB commander) acknowledged only seven "major accusations." A female Army interrogator who removed her blouse, "sat in the detainee's lap and ran her fingers through his hair," was reprimanded and suspended for 30 days but then promoted and returned to interrogations because she was so effective. Army specialists who hosed one prisoner and hit another with a radio were reduced in rank and given extra duty. A staff sergeant accused of improperly using pepper spray demanded a court-martial and was acquitted. Hill did not "have a clue" about the "incredibly ludicrous" allegations of sexual abuse made by a detainee released to Sweden. There was "no such place" as a "cold room." The disciplinary maximum security unit "has to be air-conditioned" because "otherwise, you'd bake them." He insisted they had "never used dogs at Guantánamo Bay" (although BGen. Miller, his predecessor, had used them and had them brought to Abu Ghraib). Hill declared that "the use of medication to manipulate a detainee has never been an approved DoD interrogation technique" (but a 2009 DoD Deputy IG report found that detainees were interrogated while drugged with powerful antipsychotics, subjected to "chemical restraints," and hydrated intravenously while being interrogated).

In February 2005 the Senate Committee on Homeland Security and Government Affairs considered Michael Chertoff's nomination as Secretary of the Department of Homeland Security (DHS).[9] Sen. Levin (D-Mich) asked about FBI emails describing weekly meetings with the DoJ Criminal Division (which Chertoff headed), where "all agreed DoD tactics were going to be an issue" if the government tried to prosecute those interrogated. Chertoff claimed: "I do not know what the meetings being referred to are" and called interrogation techniques "plain vanilla." But soon after his confirmation Levin obtained an unredacted version of the emails, documenting the participation of Chertoff's top deputy and his counsel. A few months later newspapers reported a leaked version of the Schmidt–Furlow investigation, launched at the end of 2004 after disclosures that the FBI had complained about prisoner mistreatment. A week after that a DoS report confirmed that 11 soldiers had been punished for abuse, including a female interrogator who wiped a detainee's shirt with what she said was menstrual blood (actually red dye) and a man who duct-taped shut the mouth of a prisoner who recited the Koran.

The following week a *Newsweek* report that Guantánamo interrogators "had placed Qurans on toilets, and in at least one case flushed a holy book down the toilet" sparked violent protests in Afghanistan that killed 16 and injured over a hundred, and which then spread to Pakistan, India, Indonesia, and Gaza.[10] Afghan President Karzai urged the USA to punish the perpetrators. Lebanon's senior Shiite cleric called the desecration a "brutal" form of torture. Pakistan's parliament unanimously condemned the incident "in the strongest possible terms," and its President and Prime Minister demanded an investigation. The 22-member Arab League called for an apology. The White House, DoD, and DoS denied the allegations. Claiming that a "knowledgeable government source" had seen these accounts, *Newsweek* expressed "regret that we got any part of our story wrong," but defiantly declared: "we're not retracting anything." A day later, however, it formally withdrew the story. An Afghan government spokesman asked *Newsweek* to pay for the damage caused by the demonstrations.

The *Los Angeles Times* reported earlier desecration allegations by detainees returned to Morocco and the UK, but the DoD dismissed them as fabrications by "members of Al Qaeda ... trained to allege abuse and torture."[11] The ACLU released FBI reports of desecration in 2002, but the DoD said the complainant "did not corroborate it" when reinterviewed. BGen. Hood (GB commander) said an investigation of *Newsweek's* 13 allegations rejected 8 but found that a soldier deliberately kicked a Koran, guards hit it with a water balloon, a guard splashed it with urine, a two-word English obscenity was written in it, and an interrogator stepped on it. Detainees desecrated a Koran 15 times, tossing it in the toilet, urinating on it, using it as a pillow, and ripping out pages. Nevertheless, demonstrations resumed in Pakistan, Bangladesh, Egypt, Indonesia, Malaysia, and the Middle East. In his *New York Times* column, Thomas Friedman pleaded with the government to "just shut [Guantánamo] down." It "has become worse than an embarrassment." In January 2007 the ACLU disclosed a 2004 FBI survey of nearly 500 employees, who reported more than 24 instances of abuse, including squatting over the Koran, female guards handling detainees' genitals and touching their faces while they prayed, and an interrogator forcing a detainee to listen to "satanic black metal music for hours" before dressing as a Catholic priest and "baptizing" him. Dismissing the allegations as "not new," DoD said 12 reviews had cleared the military.

Director Irene Khan wrote in AI's annual report in May 2005 that "Guantánamo has become the gulag [of] our times, entrenching the notion that people can be detained without any recourse to the law" and evoking "images of Soviet repression."[12] It was "ironic" that "incidents of religious humiliation of detainees in US custody … should happen as we mark the 60th anniversary of the liberation of Auschwitz." The White House called the allegations "ridiculous, and unsupported by the facts." Bush said they were "absurd," based on the word of "people who hate America, people that had been trained in some instances to disassemble [*sic*] that means not tell the truth." Rumsfeld harrumphed that the "reprehensible" phrase "gulag of our time" "cannot be excused." An "offended" Dick Cheney refused to take AI "seriously." But AI expressed no regret; Khan's words had increased memberships, donations, and volunteers. The *New York Times* said that whether or not Guantánamo's "harsh, indefinite detention without formal charges or legal recourse" resembled "the Soviet Union's sprawling network of Stalinist penal colonies," the metaphor was apt because "Guantánamo is merely one of a chain of shadowy detention camps." The *Times* agreed with Thomas Friedman that Guantánamo was "a propaganda gift to America's enemies; an embarrassment to our allies; a damaging repudiation of the American justice system; and a highly effective recruiting tool for Islamic radicals." Sen. Biden (D-De) and former president Carter concurred. When Sen. Durbin (D-Ill) compared Guantánamo to the Nazis and the Khmer Rouge, SASC chair Warner called the analogy "insulting to our men and women in uniform." Majority Leader Frist and five other Republican Senators complained to Minority Leader Reid that the statements were "hyperbolic, insensitive and inaccurate." House Majority Leader DeLay called it "a premeditated and monstrous attack." Even after Durbin apologized on the Senate floor, Sen. Lott (R-Miss) wanted the remark expunged.

Displaying unusual sensitivity to criticism, Bush did not rule out closing Guantánamo, saying: "we're exploring all alternatives."[13] House Leader Pelosi agreed with Sen. Biden that "we need a fresh start." Hours after Bush spoke, Rumsfeld insisted "no one in the … executive branch … is considering closing Guantánamo." But the next day he told a NATO defense ministers' conference: "Our goal is to have [detainees] in the hands of the countries of origin, for the most part." He was waiting until Iraq and Afghanistan could cope with dangerous prisoners. The *Washington Post* said the Democratic proposal to close the facility "is worth considering, mainly because Guantánamo has become a global symbol for U.S. abuse of prisoners." But closure "might lead prisoners to be housed under poorer conditions," and "it may be necessary for the United States to detain enemy combatants for many years in the future."

Days later Cheney said: "if we didn't have that facility at Guantánamo … we'd have to have it someplace else." Releasing detainees would put "a lot of bad guys back on the street to do exactly what they started to do in the first place." At least one of the 200 men released had resumed fighting. Describing meals served there, HASC chair Hunter said detainees had "never eaten better," "been treated better," or "been more comfortable." "We supply every one of them with the Quran. We supply them with oil. We supply them with prayer beads" and "do the call to prayer" five times a day "with arrows pointing in the direction of Mecca." Frist said "to cut and run because of image problems is the wrong, wrong thing to do." Acknowledging Guantánamo's "image … as a place where there's a lack of rule," Sen. Graham (R-SC) said: "reform it, don't close it." But reading from FBI reports on Guantánamo, SJC chair Specter (R-Pa) compared those "torture techniques" to the "shameful" Japanese American internment and promised hearings. Sen. Reid (D–Utah) said administration policies had "caused tremendous damage to American credibility around the world and placed our troops at greater risk." And Sen. Levin said a "cloud will remain" without an independent investigation.

The administration reacted vociferously.[14] Cheney said detainees were treated better than they would be "by virtually any other government on the face of the earth." One detainee released to Afghanistan had become a Taliban commander, another had organized a jail break (both were killed subsequently). Denouncing the "myth" of torture, Rep. Hunter (R-Ca) said the alleged "20th hijacker" (al-Qahtani) "is going to dine tomorrow on lemon fish with two types of vegetables, two types of fruit, and then he will be afforded his taxpayer-funded Koran … so he can pray, presumably to kill more Americans." Rumsfeld did not "know any place where we have infrastructure that's appropriate for that sizable group of people" who were "believed to be determined killers." White House Press Secretary McClellan said detainees "are being provided meals, clothing, medical care; they are being treated very humanely." Claiming that "there's 24 hour inspections by the International Red Cross," Bush urged members of the press corps "to go down to Guantánamo and see how they're treated … in accord with the Geneva Convention." Some of those released "went on to the battlefield again," proving that detainees were "dangerous people." But the *New York Times* reiterated its call to "shut down the Guantánamo prison."

Soon thereafter *Time* magazine published the government's own account of al-Qahtani's interrogation extending over 50 days (some sessions lasting 20 hours).[15] He resisted by staging a hunger strike, repeatedly ripping out his IV until he was strapped down. After being forcibly hydrated with 3.5 bags, he agreed to talk if allowed to urinate, but interrogators dismissed his answers as inadequate and made him wet his pants. When he refused to drink during the Ramadan fast, he was forbidden to pray. After Rumsfeld authorized 16 EITs, al-Qahtani was subjected to sleep deprivation and "invasion of space by a female," forcibly shaved, and threatened by a dog. Dehydration lowered his pulse to 35 beats/minute. He was made to stand nude and bark like a dog and had photos of scantily clad women hung around his neck. Anthony Lewis wrote in the *New York Times* that such treatment was "an exercise in degradation and humiliation … forbidden by three sources of law that the United States respected for decades."

When it was released, the Schmidt–Furlow report recommended that MGen. Miller be reprimanded for failing to supervise al-Qahtani's harsh interrogation. But SOUTHCOM commander Gen. Craddock just referred it to the Army IG, commenting that "the hype, the concern about this technique or that technique is over. It was done for a specific purpose and it was effective."[16] Sen. Reed (D-RI) criticized Craddock for having "taken an investigation which was sincere and detailed and turned it into a justification and exoneration for a senior officer." Sen. McCain (R-Az) asked why the military put "somebody in charge" like Miller, "who had no experience." But Sen. Inhofe (R-Ok) said: "we have nothing to be ashamed of." There were so few abuses "it makes me wonder if we're really getting the most out of these detainees." The *New York Times* urged even "die-hard supporters of President Bush" to condemn "the exploitation and debasement" of the women interrogators, which resulted from engaging in lap dancing and smearing fake menstrual blood.

Sen. Graham drafted a bill to investigate Guantánamo abuse "to prove to the world that we are a rule-of-law nation."[17] Democrats in both houses sought to attach it to the National Defense Authorization Act (NDAA). But SASC chair Warner rebuffed a request for an investigation by Sen. Levin (the senior Democrat). A week later DoD took a bipartisan group of senators to Guantánamo. (A Guantánamo spokesman explained that visiting lawmakers were forbidden to speak to detainees because "we don't want them to act up or yell.") Republicans extolled conditions: Bunning said they "even have air-conditioning and semiprivate showers"; Crapo complained that guards "get more abuse from the detainees than they give to the detainees." Even Democrats Wyden and Nelson praised the detainees' treatment. HASC chair Hunter led a 15-member House delegation, finding no "gulag of our times" but rather "a world-class detention facility where detainees … are well fed, given access to topnotch medical facilities and provided an opportunity to obtain legal representation." "We have been too liberal in releasing people who have ended up shooting at our soldiers on the battlefield." His fellow Republicans agreed: Porter claimed that "many of [the detainees] are happy to be there"; Hefley said "if you're going to be in prison, this sounds like the one to be in." Democrats concurred. Ranking member Skelton thought Guantánamo was better than state or federal prisons. Tauscher said it "meets the standards of a maximum-security prison in the United States." Reyes praised it as "the only place in Cuba where religious freedom is allowed." Butterfield called "reports of abuse at Guantánamo Bay … absolutely false." BGen. Hood said the vast majority of detainees were "dangerous men committed to harming Americans." After refusing to talk for two years, some had begun telling interrogators "where they were and what their activities were." RAdm. Harris (Hood's successor) said about a quarter of detainees were being "actively" interrogated, producing intelligence that "is not perishable" about safe houses, "terrorist tactics, techniques and procedures: how money flows. How they flow between their countries." (Of course, he conceded by implication that three-quarters were not being interrogated.)

Cheney said detainees posed "serious, deadly threats" and would "go back to trying to kill Americans" if released. "They're living in the tropics. They're well fed. They've got everything they could possibly want." Bush told German television "I would like to close the camp and put the prisoners on trial," but claimed he had to wait for the Supreme Court decision in *Hamdan*. A DoD spokesman immediately undercut the president: "U.S. policy for detention operations has not changed." The *Los Angeles Times* correctly observed that "Hamdan's lawsuit doesn't prevent the administration from closing Guantánamo." The chair of the UN Working Group on Arbitrary Detention and six Special Rapporteurs issued a highly critical report on Guantánamo. Several months later the UN Human Rights Committee subjected the US delegation to a hostile grilling.

Political Resistance

Taking control of Congress on the fifth anniversary of the opening of Guantánamo, Democrats vowed to shut it.[18] Weeks after being confirmed as Defense Secretary in December 2006, Robert Gates also called for closure and successfully blocked a new $100 million courthouse and detention complex, cutting the cost to $10 million. But his deputy, Gordon England, called Guantánamo "an international problem … not a U.S. problem." The *New York Times* regretted that Bush ignored Gates, as he had Rice and Powell, members of Congress, and allied heads of state listening instead to Cheney and Gonzales. "The [CSRTs] are kangaroo courts, admitting evidence that was coerced or obtained through abuse or outright torture. They are intended to confirm a decision that was already made … The omissions from the record of [KSM's] hearing were chilling. The United States government deleted his claims to have been tortured during years of illegal detention." The *Los Angeles Times* agreed that Guantánamo "is an embarrassment to the United States."

At the end of April 2007 Sen. Feinstein (D-Ca) introduced a bill requiring the administration to close Guantánamo within a year, transferring all detainees to a military or civilian facility in the USA and either trying them in an Article III court or military legal proceeding "before a regularly-constituted court," transferring them to an international tribunal or a country that gave assurances against torture or cruel, inhuman, or degrading treatment, or detaining them without trial as enemy combatants.[19] By a 220–208 vote, the House passed an amendment to the NDAA (proposed by James Moran, D-Va) requiring the administration to report on plans to try, transfer, or release detainees. Minority Leader Boehner warned that Democrats "are leading us down the road to importing dangerous terrorists into our local communities." The White House threatened to veto any law limiting its ability to detain enemy combatants. Former Secretary of State Powell said he would immediately close Guantánamo, which had become a major problem in "the way the world perceives Americans," and "simply move [detainees] to the United States and put them into our federal legal system," where they would be no burden because "America, unfortunately, has 2 million people in jail, all of whom had lawyers and access to writs of habeas corpus." Authoritarian leaders in other countries invoked Guantánamo to "hide their own misdeeds." The *Los Angeles Times* agreed that closing Guantánamo "is long overdue."

Presidential candidates Obama, Clinton, and McCain all wanted to close Guantánamo but did not support any of the concrete proposals.[20] Huckabee dismissed closure as "more symbolic than it is a substantive issue." At a Republican debate in May, Romney called for doubling the size of Guantánamo, "where they don't get the access to lawyers they get when they're on our soil." At the September debate Giuliani compared those advocating closure to judges who "would release criminals into the street." Graham said detainees in the USA "would be magnets" for terrorist attacks. Thomas Friedman wrote in his *New York Times* column: "I will not vote for any candidate who is not committed to dismantling Guantánamo Bay … the anti-Statue of Liberty." In December Huckabee complained that military meals at Guantánamo cost an average of $1.60 but detainees' halal meals cost more than $4. "The inmates there were getting a whole lot better treatment than my prisoners in Arkansas … If anything, it's too nice."

The *Washington Post* said Guantánamo "has been a disaster and must be shut down," thereby "depriv[ing] U.S. adversaries … of a powerful symbol they use to besmirch America and justify their own abuses."[21] "[S]imply closing Guantánamo and transferring its prisoners to their home countries or to prisons in the United States," however, "would create another legal quagmire," and granting them habeas corpus would result in "years of litigation." Still, "they should have lawyers and be allowed to call witnesses and challenge evidence" before "full-fledged judges whose decisions can be appealed." But Morris Davis, chief military commissions prosecutor, wrote in a *New York Times* op ed:

> [R]eality for Guantánamo Bay is the daily professionalism of its staff, the humanity of its detention centers … Most of the detainees are housed in new buildings modeled after civilian prisons in Indiana and

> Michigan. Detainees received three culturally appropriate meals a day. Each has a copy of the Koran. Guards maintain respectful silence during Islam's five daily prayer periods, and medical care is provided by the same practitioners who treat American service members. Detainees are offered at least two hours of outdoor recreation each day, double that allowed inmates, including convicted terrorists, at the "supermax" federal penitentiary in Florence, Colorado.

This provoked angry retorts. HRW's Jennifer Daskal said Davis ignored the "virtually total and continuous isolation in tiny windowless cells." Marc Falkoff's 16 Yemeni clients were beginning their sixth year of incarceration:

> Because they are unlikely to ever face trial, they will never have the opportunity to see the secret evidence against them. They will never have a chance to refute the coerced hearsay statements that have so far justified their detention ... Many have been punished for disciplinary infractions by having their beards shaved. Most have been stripped of their trousers so that they cannot pray while modestly dressed. Some have been interrogated at gunpoint and threatened with rendition.

J. Wells Dixon and Gitanjali Gutierrez, of the Center for Constitutional Rights (CCR), said: "hundreds of men waste away in isolation in small metal cells that any regularly constituted court would reject as a violation of United States and international law." HRF's Priti Patel wrote that the DoD's "own investigations document that detainees have been kept awake all night, subject to loud music and extreme hot and cold temperatures, and beaten."

A day after the media reported that Bush's national security and legal advisers would meet to consider closing Guantánamo by transferring detainees to Fort Leavenworth or the Charleston Naval Brig, the White House canceled the meeting, saying "the president has long expressed a desire to close the Guantánamo Bay detention facility," but "a number of steps need to take place" first, including "the repatriation to their home countries of detainees who have been cleared for release."[22] DHS opposed bringing any to the USA. DoD claimed that 22–50 ex-detainees had returned to the battlefield. Rep. Hastings (D-Fl) and Sen. Cardin (D-Md) told the UN Human Rights Commission that Guantánamo should be closed. House Majority Leader Hoyer told the US Helsinki Commission that Guantánamo was "an international disgrace that every day continues to sully this great nation's good reputation." But DoS Legal Adviser Bellinger told the

Commission that foreign and domestic critics "have not offered any credible alternatives." Bush's wife and mother and the Undersecretary of State for Public Diplomacy all urged closure. A week later it was reported that the White House and Congress were talking about dividing detainees into three categories: 25–50 high level detainees would remain indefinitely in a military brig; some would be tried by a revised military commission; and most would be released. But J. Alan Liotta, principal director of the DoD Office of Detainee Affairs, had warned in an invitation-only conference call that "detainees that come to the United States could have the full panoply of U.S. constitutional protections, which means you'd have to have a judicial hearing on them in a certain amount of time" or release them. Four months later, asked why the DoD had not given Congress a plan to close Guantánamo, Defense Secretary Gates replied: "I've run into some obstacles from a variety of lawyers" (presumably Addington). The administration's plan allegedly included giving detainees legal representation at CSRTs and letting a new specialized federal court review those decisions. Officials were considering transferring 130, trying 80 in military commissions, and holding 120 indefinitely. Attorney General Mukasey told the SJC he was seeking ideas "with the goal of closing down [Guantánamo] because it's hurt us."

Soon after the sixth anniversary of Guantánamo's opening, JCS chairman Adm. Mullen said: "I'd like to see it shut down. I believe that from the standpoint of how it reflects on us that it's been pretty damaging." But subordinates disagreed. RAdm. Buzby (GB commander) said: "We have everyone from the higher-ups to the trigger-pullers, and everybody in between. Basically, I have a rebuilt al-Qaeda cell inside my camp."[23] "For a Subway BLT, they will talk a whole lot," providing useful intelligence. There was one doctor for every three detainees, so "people who question the level of care don't know what the hell they are talking about." They had individual cells and two hours of recreation a day. About a hundred were scheduled for trials, and prosecutors were developing cases for others. A month after leaving Guantánamo, Buzby wrote in a *Wall Street Journal* op ed that the 20 percent of prisoners who were compliant "enjoy a communal, barracks-style environment, with movie nights, classes in Pashtu [*sic*], Arabic and English, shared meals and prayers, and up to 12 hours of recreation per day." Even the noncompliant detainees who engaged in "head-butting, kicking, biting, splashing young soldiers and sailors with feces and urine 'cocktails'" were in "modern, climate-controlled facilities" housed in "single-occupancy cells where they communicate with other detainees" and enjoyed a minimum of "two, soon to be three, hours of outdoor recreation per day adjacent to three to five other detainees." They sent and received "more than 27,000 pieces of mail last year" and got an annual phone call to their families. Given the more than 1,200 attorney visits the previous year, "suggestions that detainees are being held 'incommunicado' are simply not true." Medical care was "frankly better than what most Americans enjoy." Buzby's successor, RAdm. Thomas, repeated these claims.

In April 2008 both presumptive presidential candidates repudiated Guantánamo.[24] A McCain aide said the Bush administration "can be down in the weeds burrowed in the bureaucracy, coming up with all the reasons why it can't happen. But the fact is, their Commander-in-Chief and [Defense] Secretary have said they would like to close Guantánamo." An Obama adviser urged the government to return some detainees and prosecute others. "I hope we would not take the historically unprecedented step of creating a detention-without-trial regime until we exhausted every other possibility." AI Director Larry Cox responded that the next president "must not transfer the violations to other locations. Detainees should be charged with a recognizable criminal offense, brought to full and fair trial or released." ACLU Director Anthony D. Romero urged "that the Guantánamo prison camp be closed … and a real system of justice, based on the Constitution, be used to determine the guilt or innocence of those held there." HRW Director Kenneth Roth wrote that detaining prisoners "endlessly without trial has marred America's reputation, providing a boon to terrorist recruiters and discouraging cooperation with international law-enforcement efforts" and had "allowed the detainees to glorify themselves as combatants rather than bear the opprobrium of being labeled convicted criminals."

Hunger Strikes and Suicides

Detainees repeatedly resorted to the only resistance available to the powerless: control over their own bodies.[25] Mishal al-Harbi, released to Saudi Arabia in July 2005, had slurred speech and no control over his limbs or head.[26] The USA claimed he had tried to hang himself in January 2003, but his family insisted he had been beaten because Islam does not allow suicide. Saad al Azmi, another ex-detainee, said al-Harbi had sustained his injuries after detainees responded furiously to rumors of Koran desecration.

In July 2005 two Afghan ex-detainees reported that 180 prisoners had been on hunger strike for more than two weeks to complain about their treatment and silence about their cases.[27] DoD acknowledged the strike but claimed ignorance of the cause. A lawyer said "guards laughed at prisoners when they are praying and disrespect the Koran when they go into a cell to [restrain] a prisoner." The strike ended when the administration promised books and bottled water, turned off loud industrial fans during prayer, and stopped clothing prisoners in graded uniforms. But a month later Clive Stafford Smith (a lawyer for detainees) reported that 89 had resumed the strike (including his client Binyam Mohamed) in response to rumors of a violent interrogation, two rough cell extractions by the Immediate Response Force (IRF), and Koran desecration. Seven had been hospitalized. Three weeks later DoD said 128 were on strike and 18 hospitalized (13 force-fed through nasal tubes); lawyers claimed 200 were striking. A week after that the military insisted only 36 were still striking and then said in mid-October there were just 24 (with 7 being force-fed). Observing that "it can hardly serve either the national security interests of this country or enhance its image throughout the world to contribute in any way to the death of a detainee in custody," US District Judge Kessler ordered the DoD to tell lawyers within 24 hours if clients were force-fed and provide weekly medical records on hunger strikers. About the same time Joshua Colangelo-Bryan reported that his client, Jumah al Dossari, had attempted suicide after suffering solitary confinement for nearly two years, and alleging that interrogators wrapped him in US and Israeli flags and threatened to render him to countries that tortured. A month later he made his ninth attempt. Although the military claimed al Dossari "was allowed communication with other detainees on the block" when the narrow food tray slot in his door was left open, it moved him days after his twelfth attempt, just before US District Judge Walton was to hear his case. (On July 16, 2007 the DoD transferred him and 15 others to Saudi Arabia.)[28]

A Guantánamo spokesman said 22 detainees had made 36 suicide attempts. DoD dismissed 21 of the 23 in August 2003 (10 on a single day) as "self-injurious behavior incidents" motivated by "al Qaeda training" and "detainees' attempts to elicit media attention." Thomas Wilner filed an emergency motion to evacuate his client, Fawzi al Odah, who had been force-fed for more than two months, but US District Judge Kollar-Kotelly denied it based on a Guantánamo doctor's report, rejecting the opinions of two independent doctors that al Odah was suffering organ damage.

On Christmas Day, 46 joined the hunger strike, bringing the total to 84 at the end of 2005.[29] But a month later DoD claimed there were just four, a decline Wilner attributed to force-feeding assisted by IRF teams, frigid air conditioning, and denial of comfort items like blankets and books. Detainees reported that inserting and removing feeding tubes caused hunger strikers to scream with pain; some urinated and defecated in restraint chairs. Gen. Craddock explained that, since "some of these hard-core guys were getting worse" because they vomited after feeding, "you have to make sure that purging doesn't happen" by using restraint chairs. Although the practice was not inhumane, "pretty soon it wasn't convenient, and they decided it wasn't worth it." Navy Capt. Edmondson (GB's chief medical officer) insisted he was not force-feeding but "providing nutritional supplementation on a voluntary basis." A lawyer representing Mohammed Bawazir asked Judge Kessler to enjoin his forced feeding. Kessler said the allegations, if proven, "describe disgusting treatment … that is cruel, profoundly disturbing and violative of U.S. law and treaties." But Gen. Hood called Bawazir's claim "patently false," and the government argued that the 2005 Detainee Treatment Act ousted federal courts of jurisdiction. Noting that that the military made only general claims about all detainees in opposing of Bawazir's detailed petition, Judge Kessler commented: "it's a sad day when a federal judge has to ask a DoJ attorney this, but I'm asking you – why should I believe them?" More than 260 doctors signed a letter to *The Lancet* opposing force-feeding, but Judge Kessler denied the motion.

On May 18, 2006 four detainees attempted suicide.[30] At Camp 4 (for the most compliant) one tried to hang himself while 10 others attacked guards and another 50 demolished their quarters to forge weapons. Three at Camp 1 took anti-anxiety drugs they had hoarded. Col. Bumgarner (chief of detention operations) said inmates believed three had to die to create a backlash that would free them. RAdm. Harris, the new commander, said: "we trained for the possibility that a suicide attempt may be used by the detainees to create an opportunity to conduct an assault, take a hostage or kill the guards. In fact, that was exactly what was going on last night."

At the end of May, 75 prisoners went on hunger strike, joining three who had been force-fed since the previous August.[31] A Guantánamo spokesman believed they were responding to the suicide attempts or the forthcoming military commission hearings, which would bring lawyers to the base. The "technique" was "consistent with al Qaeda practice and reflects detainee attempts to elicit media attention to bring international pressure on the United States to release them back to the battlefield." Within days 89 were refusing to eat (with 6 being force-fed). Dr. Winkenwerder, Assistant Secretary of Defense for Health Affairs, promulgated new "humane" rules for force-feeding.

On June 10 three hunger strikers – two Saudis (Mani Shaman al-Utaybi and Yasser Talal al Zahrani) and one Yemeni (Ali Abdullah Ahmed) – hanged themselves.[32] Because their ARBs had been completed, they believed they were consigned to Guantánamo for at least another year. In fact, al-Utaybi had been approved for transfer to Saudi Arabia; but because his lawyer had learned this from a sealed court filing, he could not tell his client. Ahmed also did not know that a lawyer had filed a habeas petition for him. Human rights groups and the dead men's relatives questioned whether they had committed suicide. Al Zahrani's father said nothing in his son's last letter "suggested that he would commit suicide." His sister questioned how such "a strong believer" could "take his own life and spend eternity in hell."

Two years later the *Washington Post* reported that 3,000 pages of documents obtained through FOIA revealed the June 2006 suicides had been carefully planned. Detainees had been allowed to hang up clothes, towels, and blankets to dry, preventing guards from observing their cells. Al-Sulaimi left a note: "I gave away the precious thing that I have in which it became very cheap, which is my own self, to lift up the oppression that is upon us through the American government." Other writing indicated that more suicides were to follow. Detainees chanted songs that night to celebrate the suicides. Rear Adm. Harris denounced the "coordinated attempt": "They are smart, they are creative, they are committed. They have no regard for life, neither ours nor their own. I believe this was not an act of desperation, but an act of asymmetrical warfare waged against us." SOUTHCOM Commander Gen. Craddock agreed: this "determined, intelligent and committed element … will continue to do everything they can … to become martyrs in the jihad." Colleen Graffy, Deputy Assistant Secretary of State for Public Diplomacy, disparaged the suicides as "a good PR move to draw attention … part of a strategy in that they don't value their own life and they certainly don't value ours and they use suicide bombings as a tactic to further their jihadi cause." "They had ample means of protesting through their lawyers and families."

Deputy Assistant Secretary of Defense for Detainee Affairs Charles "Cully" Stimson "wouldn't characterize it as a good PR move … we are always concerned when someone takes his own life." But he also defended the military.[33]

> We're proud of the care and treatment we provide detainees at Guantánamo. They get three square meals a day, culturally sensitive meals, blessed by an imam. They have a menu … they get to order from every couple weeks … They practice call to prayer five times a day. There are arrows pointing toward Mecca … They get first class medical care, dental care … during some interrogations, which are no different than you or I sitting across from each other today, some of them ask for McDonald's … This country is entitled to detain enemies against it. We don't have any obligation to give them a quarter so they can call a lawyer. We don't have any obligation when we had 400,000 Nazis here in this country at the beginning of World War II, to give them a trial [*sic*].

(The USA treated the 425,000 German POWs captured on the battlefield according to the Geneva Conventions, paying them US military wages, letting them earn additional money by working, and releasing them after the war.)

Within hours the administration had contacted Congress, the UN, ICRC, European Union (EU), most European nations, and US embassies in the Middle East. Calling the suicides "not completely unexpected," the UN High Commissioner for Human Rights said: "the focus of attention should be on closing Guantánamo." The EU External Relations Commissioner told a meeting of foreign ministers that the suicides were "an occasion to reiterate" that "Guantánamo should be closed." Mourad Benchellali (released to France two years earlier) said: "the worst aspect of being at the camp was the despair, the feeling that whatever you say, it will never make a difference." "There is unlimited cruelty in a system that seems to be unable to free the innocent and unable to punish the guilty." The *New York Times* said the news "should not have surprised anyone." "It was the inevitable result of creating a netherworld of despair beyond the laws of civilized nations, where men were to be held without any hope of decent treatment, impartial justice or, in so many cases, even eventual release." "Admiral Harris's response was as appalling as the suicides." *Le Monde* said the remarks by Harris and Graffey illustrate "the gulf that separates the American authorities from the rest of the world." It urged European leaders to emulate Angela Merkel's refusal "to meet with the Americans at the highest level without demanding the close of Guantánamo."

The military's solution was to collect bed linen each morning (because the men had hung themselves with sheets) and withhold toiletries. Col. Bumgarner told guards to "acknowledge nothing" about the suicides. "Tell [detainees] it's none of their business." "If any brother says he's going to kill himself or says the death chant … that brother will immediately go to a suicide blanket and smocks." "There is not a trustworthy son of a bitch in the entire bunch." "They're nothing short of a damn animal that can't be trusted." At a dinner after the suicides he ate a massive fried pork chop between two pieces of bread "in honor of our three dead brothers." After the *Charlotte Observer* published this interview, Guantánamo expelled its reporters and all others. A military spokesman complained that "detainees' lawyers seized on [the suicides] and used them for a P.R. campaign in Europe to say their clients are being mistreated." Allowing the *Observer* reporter to attend staff meetings "adds to an already complex and difficult situation." "Transparency's good, but you have to maintain situational awareness." The *Observer* had just been "doing a home-towner" on Bumgarner, which "takes one day." "We are not into content management. The issue was that other media were threatening to take us to court." RAdm. Harris called for an investigation "to determine if classified and/or unclassified sensitive information about detention operations with respect to recent detainee suicides was disclosed to the public." The *Observer* commented that "higher-ups … got queasy and reacted as queasy higher-ups do all over the world." "When higher-ups withhold the truth about the fight because they think citizens can't handle it, they should expect to lose the public's trust." The *Los Angeles Times* (LAT)'s managing editor condemned this "stone age attitude that only feeds suspicions about what is going on at Guantánamo." Carol Williams (the LAT reporter expelled) wrote: "In the best of times, covering Guantánamo means wrangling with a Kafkaesque bureaucracy, with logistics so nonsensical that they turn two hours of reporting into an 18-hour day, with hostile escorts who seem to think you're in league with al Qaeda, and with the dispiriting reality that you're sure to encounter more iguanas than war-on-terror suspects."

Days after the suicides Bush told a press conference: "I'd like to close Guantánamo. No question. Guantánamo sends a signal to some of our friends – provides an excuse, for example, to say the United States is not upholding the values that they're trying to encourage other countries to adhere to."[34]

The Washington Post editorialized:

> Nearly five years into a war between the United States and Islamic extremists, U.S. policies and practices for arresting, holding, interrogating and trying enemy militants are in a state of disarray unprecedented in American history. They shame the nation and violate its values ... Guantánamo Bay has become a toxic symbol around the world of U.S. human rights violations, a status magnified by recent suicides ... the administration seems to have no plan for how and where it will hold long-term detainees, or those convicted of crimes. The Bush administration has set aside or evaded the rules for prisoner treatment contained in the Geneva Conventions and the CAT.

The *Post* returned to the issue the next day: "The administration's insistence on treating them as enemy combatants – subject to detention with little review for the duration of the conflict – is unsustainable." The DoD should repatriate Afghans, Saudis, and Yemenis and try "numerous other inmates." Congress should pass an administrative detention law to provide "a prompt, substantial military hearing to establish that an inmate is actively engaged in terrorist activity," subject to review by federal courts. In a full-page *New York Times* advertisement, AI said: "there is a government in Cuba that imprisons people for years *without charge or trial.* Unfortunately, it's ours" [original emphasis]. "[T]he only way to achieve real security for our country is to return America to its founding principles of adherence to the law and justice for all." The *Washington Post* "reluctantly" agreed that "Guantánamo will have to be shuttered" but called "the international campaign against the camp ... more than a little perverse." It was "wrongheaded" and "hypocritical" to demand that all detainees be tried or released.

Two weeks later Harris again denounced the suicides as "asymmetrical warfare ... less about the length of their detention than about the effect they think they'll have." The 20 detainees considered most at risk were put in suicide smocks. Declaring the suicides "part of a larger plan," Harris accused lawyers of complicity and had the military seize more than a thousand pages of documents. He wanted the Naval Criminal Investigation Service (NCIS) to search them, but the lawyers resisted, claiming some were privileged. The DoD spokesman found it "curious that habeas attorneys may have been involved in the deaths." The military had reviewed the papers of 155 detainees before asking the court to appoint a filter team to read the rest. US District Judge Leon refused, warning that any further review of privileged material by government officials comes "at their own peril."

The military moved 145 detainees out of Camp 4, where the riots had occurred, leaving just 30 Afghans who did not take part (the *only* detainees not in solitary), and shut down Camp 1 (the least restrictive). In Camp 6 (about to open) the common room intended for meals, games, and conversation was converted into individual 10 foot by 30 foot exercise pens, forcing prisoners to eat in their cells and be shackled whenever they left their cells. Harris said: "we had to think about whether there is such a thing as a medium-security terrorist." The warden feared it would "facilitate" "self-harm" to "let them live in a communal-type environment." At the end of May 2007 Abdul Rahman Ma'ath Thafir al-Amri, a persistent hunger striker whose weight had fallen from 150 pounds to 88.5 pounds, committed suicide; but this received scant media coverage.

AI published a report in April 2007.[35] Warning that some detainees "are dangerously close to full-blown mental and physical breakdown," the UK director urged the USA to end "extreme isolation" and "allow proper access for independent medical experts and human rights groups." In response to the transfer of about 160 prisoners into a new maximum security complex, 20–42 went on hunger strike and were force-fed. Majid al-Joudi, hospitalized on February 10 after losing 15 percent of his body weight during a month-long fast, told a military doctor: "we don't have any rights here, even after your Supreme Court said we had rights. If the policy does not change, you will see a big increase in fasting." (He was subsequently returned to Saudi Arabia.) A military spokesman dismissed complaints as "propaganda." The new cells in Camp 6 were 27 square feet larger than the old cells, with nicer toilets and sinks, a small desk, and air conditioning. But the men were confined there for at least 22 hours a day and could talk to other prisoners only by shouting through food slots in the steel doors. Previously they had been in cells of ten and could communicate with other cells through mesh fencing. In December it was revealed that an unidentified detainee had tried to commit suicide by slashing his throat with a sharpened fingernail.

For the first time, US District Judge Sullivan ordered a medical examination to determine if Ahmed Zaid Salim Zuhair could "meaningfully participate" in his habeas petition.[36] After 3.5 years on hunger strike his weight had dropped from 147 pounds to 111 pounds despite force-feeding. Declaring that "I don't want this man to dwindle down to the point where he is further damaged," Sullivan ordered the government to give Zuhair's lawyers his medical records but refused to end forcible restraint during force-feeding. Two weeks earlier Sullivan had told the government to give Ramzi bin al-Shibh's lawyers his medical records. A month earlier US District Judge Roberts had made a similar order concerning abu Zubaydah. But US District Judge Hogan denied a request for Adnan Latif because the Military Commissions Act (MCA) stripped him of jurisdiction.

David Remes reported that some of his 17 Yemeni clients launched a hunger strike after Salim Hamdan was released in November.[37] "They've actually gone ballistic at the fact that Hamdan, who was convicted of supporting terrorism, was released and they, who have been charged with nothing, continue to languish there." By early January, 30 of the 250 detainees were on strike, 25 being force-fed.

A DoD report found that the deaths of Abdul Rahman al-Amri in May 2007 and Mohammad Ahmed Abdullah Saleh al-Hanashi in June 2009 were suicides.[38] But skeptics noted that al-Amri was found hanging with his hands tied behind his back; and al-Hanashi, alleged to have hung himself using undergarments, had made five suicide attempts in the preceding four weeks, raising questions about why he was not in a suicide smock. Both were supposed to be under constant video surveillance and checked in person every 3–5 minutes.

Adnan Latif was found dead in his cell in September 2012, the ninth Guantánamo death.[39] He had been on hunger strike until June and was in Camp 5 in "disciplinary status" for splashing a guard with bodily fluid. Because Latif engaged in "indecent behavior," guards took turns watching him, leaving gaps in coverage. He had been granted habeas in July 2010; but the DC Circuit reversed, and the Supreme Court had recently denied review. In a *Los Angeles Times* op ed, Marc Falkoff, one of Latif's lawyers, said his death "should prompt all of us to reconsider our decision to continue the operation of our infamous offshore prison camp." In December NCIS was still investigating how he had gotten enough pills to kill himself and why, given acute pneumonia, he was in a solitary cell. Documentary filmmaker Laura Poitras wrote in a *New York Times* op ed that the suicide claim was "hard to take at face value." Nine months later Jason Leopold disclosed that NCIS concluded that Latif had swallowed two dozen Invega capsules he had hoarded, and his body contained traces of codeine, oxycodone, lorazepam, and six other narcotics. A day before his death a guard recorded that Latif had written his lawyer that "to die is better than to live."

International Pressure

Guantánamo provoked a stream of international criticism. In February 2006 the UN Human Rights Commission (UNHRC) severely criticized the USA, urging it to close the prison immediately, end force-feeding and "all special interrogation techniques," and prosecute "all perpetrators up to the highest level of military and political command."[40] Secretary General Kofi Annan made "the basic point that one cannot detain individuals in perpetuity." The US Ambassador to the UN in Geneva dismissed the report as "largely without merit and not based clearly on facts." But the *Los Angeles Times* and the *New York Times* seconded it. Even Tony Blair, Bush's loyal ally, repeated his previous year's statement that Guantánamo was "an anomaly and sooner or later has got to be dealt with." Lord Goldsmith, his Attorney General, called for a "fair trial" for detainees. Peter Hain, Secretary for Northern Ireland, said he "would prefer it closed." The House of Commons Foreign Affairs Committee called on Blair to push for closure. But Foreign Secretary Jack Straw hedged: "I am absolutely clear the U.S. has no intention of maintaining a gulag in Guantánamo Bay … I'm not going to second-guess the decisions they make."

Archbishop Tutu said on British radio: "I never imagined I would live to see the day when the United States and its satellites would use precisely the same arguments that the apartheid government used for detention without trial. It is disgraceful. One cannot find strong enough words to condemn what Britain and the United States and some of their allies have accepted." Dr. John Sentamu, Archbishop of York (and a former Ugandan High Court judge), said Guantánamo was no "anomaly." Idi Amin "did something similar," creating "special places to keep" prisoners where the law would not apply. Eighteen prominent scientists (including four Nobel Prize winners) wrote the *New York Times* that "the United States has crossed the limits of acceptable practices in the treatment of prisoners at Guantánamo." "Although this is not a scientific issue in the usual sense, we feel that to ignore it would be to abdicate our responsibility to the truth." Seventy-six leading Australian lawyers (including four former federal and Supreme Court judges) urged Prime Minister Howard to secure the return of David Hicks, whose imprisonment and trial were "an affront to international legal standards, indeed all civilised legal standards." The Council of Australian Law Deans concurred. Spanish Judge Baltasar Garzón called Guantánamo "an insult to countries that respect laws."

Sami al-Haj, a Sudanese journalist for Al Jazeera, was brought to Guantánamo in June 2002.[41] The Committee to Protect Journalists (CPJ) asked Rumsfeld that September why al-Haj had been detained, but received no reply. At his 2005 ARB he was accused of having "interviewed several Taliban officials"; most of his 130 interrogations concerned Al Jazeera. He claimed to have been offered release if he informed on it and warned that backing out "would endanger your child." Al Jazeera televised an hour-long documentary on him in 2006. The CPJ published a report on him in October 2006. In a column on him, Nicholas Kristof wrote that Guantánamo "will be remembered mostly as a national disgrace." Al-Haj was repatriated in May 2008, after 16 months on hunger strike.[42] When he said in Khartoum that "conditions in Guantánamo are very, very bad," DoD called him "a manipulator and a propagandist." He wrote a six-part series on Guantánamo for Al Jazeera, detailing his mistreatment, and co-founded the Guantánamo Justice Center to represent former detainees suing the USA. Kristof commented that "most of the inmates were probably innocent all along" and "torture was routine, especially early on." "It would take an exceptional enemy to damage America's image and interests as much as President Bush and Mr. Cheney already have done with Guantánamo."

Transfers and Releases

The Bush administration released 532 detainees. But the Uighurs posed special problems.[43] Responding to their habeas petition, US District Judge Robertson expressed frustration at the government's failure to transfer those it had cleared. The Washington-based International Uyghur Human Rights and Democracy Foundation offered to house them. But though Robertson declared that "this indefinite imprisonment at Guantánamo Bay is unlawful," he found in December 2005 that "a federal court has no relief to offer." The weekend before the DC Circuit was to hear the Uighurs' appeal (and possibly order them transferred to the USA), DoD sent five to Albania. DoS praised this "important humanitarian gesture," but the real motive surfaced two days later when Albanian Prime Minister Berisha met Cheney, who promptly endorsed Albania's NATO application.

After DoD reclassified the remaining 17 Uighurs as No Longer Enemy Combatants (NLECs) but nearly a hundred countries declined to take them for fear of angering China, their lawyers asked US District Judge Urbina to order their release.[44] He said at an August 2008 hearing: "I don't understand why" releasing them in the USA "would not be a viable option." DoJ objected that courts could not review this purely executive decision. On October 7 Urbina ordered them brought to his courtroom by the end of the week for a hearing on conditions for their release.

> After detaining 17 Uighurs ... for almost seven years exempt from judicial oversight, the moment has arrived to shine the light of constitutionality ... the unilateral, carte blanche authority the political branches purportedly wield over the Uighurs is not in keeping with our system of government ... Because the Constitution prohibits indefinite detention without cause, the government's continued detention of the [detainees] is unlawful. Because separation-of-powers concerns do not trump the very principle upon which this nation was founded – the unalienable right to liberty – the court orders the government to release the [petitioners] into the United States.

He chastised the DoJ lawyer for suggesting that immigration officials might have to arrest the Uighurs for alleged terrorist ties. "I would not take that kindly." "I do not expect these Uighurs will be molested by any member of the United States government. I'm a federal judge, and I've issued an order." He directed immigration officials not to act until he heard testimony about monitoring the Uighurs and rejected the government's motion for a stay while it appealed: "all of this means more delay, and delay is the name of the game up until this point." "I want to see the individuals." Several religious and social groups offered to take responsibility for them. Rep. Rohrabacher (R-Ca), who had been working for their release with Rep. Delahunt (D-Mass), said Urbina "made the morally right decision. We should offer the Uighurs an apology." But the DC Circuit issued an emergency stay.

Although the *Washington Post* said the men should have been freed years earlier, it approved the stay because of the "stark disagreement" about Urbina's power.[45] The *Los Angeles Times* used this controversy and others to denounce Guantánamo as one of Bush's "most ignoble legacies," which "has eroded America's reputation, embarrassed its allies and embittered its enemies." Those who established it had been "drunk on executive power, disdainful of due process and indifferent to international opinion." Urging the DC Circuit to affirm, the *New York Times* called Urbina's decision "an important blow for the rule of law." The Uighurs:

> are not enemy combatants, legal or illegal, nor are they terrorists. Their detention – along with the detention of others held at Guantánamo

> without charges or real hearings – has gravely injured the nation's tradition of due process and its international standing ... The administration is not afraid the Uighurs will take to the streets against the United States government. It is afraid they will take to the microphones.

Even DoS told the Circuit Court that DoJ opposition to bringing the Uighurs to the USA had obstructed government efforts to find a country to take them. Clint Williamson, US Ambassador at Large for War Crimes Issues, had to cancel a planned trip to negotiate with other countries. But in February 2009 the DC Circuit reversed. (I discuss the litigation in Chapter 5 on habeas corpus of the companion volume *Law's Trials*.) The *Washington Post* said the decision "places the Obama administration in a position of strength. The president should use his authority to bring a measure of justice to the 17 detainees" by granting them asylum "with all deliberate speed" (an unfortunate phrase). "Such a move could go a long way toward persuading other countries to open their doors, too, to these and other Guantánamo Bay detainees." The *Los Angeles Times* accused the DC Circuit of "abetting the unfairness" of Guantánamo. "President Obama, who has been adamant about ending abuses at Guantánamo, can order Homeland Security Secretary Janet Napolitano and Attorney General Eric H. Holder Jr. to grant political asylum."

At an April 2009 White House meeting, senior national security officials agreed that eight Uighurs would be resettled in the USA, two English-speakers immediately.[46] But Rep. Wolf (R-Va) (in whose district they would live) wrote a furious letter to the administration and released it to the media. The "American people cannot afford to simply take your word that these detainees, who were captured training in terrorist camps, are not a threat if released into our communities." The White House promptly capitulated.

Countries differed in their readiness to accept detainees. An Afghan delegation to Guantánamo sought the release of their 94 detainees, stating that about half were not guilty of serious crimes.[47] Algeria rejected its two dozen citizens. Yemen initially refused to accept its 106 nationals, questioning their citizenship. DoS legal adviser John Bellinger said "most countries ... think they didn't contribute to Guantánamo and therefore they don't have to be part of the solution." "It often takes us months and months, or even years, to negotiate the human rights assurances that we are comfortable with before we will transfer someone to another country." Sandra Hodkinson, Deputy

Assistant Secretary of Defense for Detainee Affairs, blamed other countries for the US failure to close Guantánamo. "Many countries just are not moving very quickly" and some "don't want them back."

In May 2006 a British court ruled that the government had no obligation to intervene on behalf of three residents: Bisher al-Rawi, Jamil el Banna, and Omar Deghayes; nevertheless, the Foreign Office made a "security-related request" for al-Rawi, who had assisted British intelligence.[48] In August 2007 Britain sought the return of the other two as well as Shaker Aamer, Binyam Mohamed, and Abdenour Sameur. Although DoD said the UK had to guarantee it would "take steps to mitigate the threat that these individuals pose," the Foreign Office said they would be subject only to the security restrictions that "apply to any other foreign national in this country." Deghayes's family released a detailed dossier about his alleged torture. Soon after Gordon Brown became prime minister in August he asked the USA to release the five. Four months later the USA decided to release el Banna, Deghayes, and Sameur, but not the others.

Some detainees feared repatriation. In March 2007 HRW released a report finding that the seven Russians returned in 2004 had been tortured. (Three fled the country, and one was killed by police near Chechnya.)[49] Abdul Ra'ouf Omar Mohammed abu al-Qassim resisted return to Libya, where he feared torture for having opposed Gaddafi. Rep. Markey (D-Mass) wrote DoS opposing the transfer. After Britain refused to accept Ahmed Belbacha, he asked the federal courts to block his transfer to Algeria. Abu Abdul Rauf Zalita sought to block his transfer to Libya. Sens. Durbin, Kennedy (D-Mass), Obama (D-Ill), Leahy (D-Vt), Feingold (D-Wi), and Whitehouse (D-RI) wrote Secretary of State Rice expressing "grave concern" that detainees would be sent home to torture in countries like Libya and Tunisia. CCR warned that Abdullah bin Omar risked torture in Tunisia, where he had been tried in absentia and sentenced to 23 years for membership in Ennahadha, a moderate Islamist party. On his return he was beaten and he and his wife were threatened with rape. Reps. Markey (D-Mass) and Schakowsky (D-Ill) asked Rice to clarify DoS policy concerning transfer and expressed concern about Omar and Lufti bin Swei Lagha, another former Guantánamo jailed on return to Tunisia. US District Judge Kesssler enjoined the transfer of Mohammed Rahman to Tunisia, which "would be a profound miscarriage of justice" because he had been sentenced to 20 years after being convicted in absentia.

Reports of "recidivism" became a numbers game (rarely with any evidence that those who allegedly fought after release had done so before capture).[50] DoD said about 15 of the 340 released had returned to the battlefield; RAdm. Harris claimed that 50 of 300 had done so, but could identify only one. After Mark P. Denbeaux and Joshua Denbeaux testified before a Senate Judiciary subcommittee, challenging the claim that 30 released detainees had returned to the battlefield, DoD replied: "it doesn't matter if it's seven, 14, 30 or 50. The point we're trying to make is that we assume some risk in this. Even one is too many." Defense Secretary Gates claimed a recidivism rate of 5–10 percent based on 12–36 known instances.

CSRTs and ARBs

In anticipation of the Supreme Court's decision in *Rasul*, DoD initiated the CSRTs and followed up with periodic ARBs. In June 2006 the *Boston Globe* exposed their failure to hear a single witness.[51] CSRTs agreed with 34 detainees that 64 witnesses were relevant but claimed none could be found, even though one was the Afghan Minister of Energy (who frequently met American diplomats) and another an American prisoner at Bagram. After Abdullah Mujahid's CSRT said it could not find the Afghan witnesses he named, the *Globe* located them in three days by internet and phone: one working for President Karzai, one teaching at a leading American college, and a third living in Kabul. Although Mujahid was alleged to have been fired as a police chief on suspicion of collaborating with anti-government forces, actually he had been promoted.

A baffled CSRT told Hadj Boudella (one of six Algerians seized by the USA in Bosnia): "at this point, we don't know why you are being accused of being a member of the Armed Islamic Group of Algeria. Do you have any idea?"[52] Boudella said no: "I've been here for three years and these accusations were just told to me." He had been arrested on suspicion of planning to attack the US Embassy but released by the Bosnian Supreme Court and awarded $6,000 damages by the Bosnian Human Rights Court. When he sought to introduce those rulings, however, the USA claimed the documents were "unable to be located" – even though all were available on the internet and in DDC papers. He was accused of fighting in Tora Bora while imprisoned in Sarajevo. The CSRT declared him an enemy combatant. At his ARB a year later he was accused of wearing a ring "similar to those that identified the Red Rose group members of Hamas." But his wife said it was an anniversary band worn by thousands of Bosnian Muslims and submitted an affidavit from the Sarajevo jeweler where he had bought it. In February 2005 Bosnian Prime Minister Adnan Terzic wrote Secretary of State Rice seeking the return of all six Algerians. She refused because "they still possess important intelligence data" and threatened US security. Four months later DoS said they could not be released because Bosnia "has not indicated that it is prepared or willing to accept responsibility for them upon transfer." Bosnia said it had never been asked.

Rumsfeld had asserted in June 2005 that "all" detainees had been "captured on a battlefield. They're terrorists, trainers, bomb makers, recruiters, financiers, [bin Laden's] bodyguards, would-be-suicide bombers, probably the 20th 9/11 hijacker."[53] After reviewing the 132 habeas petitions and 314 redacted CSRT transcripts, however, the *National Journal* said "most … were innocent of any terrorist activity … some, perhaps many, are guilty only of being foreigners in Afghanistan or Pakistan at the wrong time." One detainee falsely placed 60 detainees in an Afghan training camp at a time when none was in that country. The military accused ten detainees of being ECs partly because they owned a Casio watch al-Qaeda allegedly used for making bombs; but millions wore it. After a detainee slammed his hands on the table during a long interrogation and yelled in exasperation: "fine, you got me; I'm a terrorist," the government relied on that statement over the interrogator's own objections. When a detainee accused of being bin Laden's bodyguard exclaimed in disgust "OK, I saw bin Laden five times: three times on al Jazeera and twice on Yemeni News," the CSRT found that "detainee admitted to knowing Osama bin Laden." An *Arabic-speaking Iraqi Shiite* was accused of being regional intelligence director for the *Pashto-speaking Afghan Sunni* Taliban. Mark Jacobson (who had been Assistant Secretary of Defense for Detainee Policy November 2002 to August 2003) admitted that "the standards for sending someone to Guantánamo" during that period "were not as high as they should have been." The CSRTs' own legal adviser objected to the "double standard" allowing the government but not the detainee to present hearsay evidence.

The government strenuously resisted FOIA applications for the full CSRT transcripts, hypocritically invoking detainee privacy.[54] Accusing DoD of offering only "thin and conclusory speculation" to support fears that terrorist groups might attack detainees or their families, US District Judge Rakoff ordered the government to release the 5,000 pages of uncensored transcripts, which it did in March 2006, followed by 2,600 pages of ARB hearing transcripts. Many detainees retracted "confessions" they claimed had been made under torture. Abdur Sayed Rahman, a Pakistani villager, said he had been mistaken for Abdur Zahid Rahman, the Taliban deputy foreign minister. The *New York Times* commented that such "a case of mistaken identity" was "our nightmare since the Bush administration began stashing prisoners it did not want to account for in Guantánamo Bay." "Far too many show no signs of being a threat to American national security. Some, it appears, did nothing at all." CSRTs "were conducted under rules that mock any notion of democratic justice. Prisoners do not see the evidence against them and barely have access to legal counsel."

When CSRTs began, detainees were represented by laypersons out of concern that the role's constraints would expose lawyers to professional discipline.[55] To discourage lawsuits, tribunals were told to place exonerated detainees in the Orwellian category of "no longer enemy combatant" (NLEC) rather than calling them "not enemy combatant." Vice Adm. Moore (Ret.), who instituted the process, said "it was sort of a mantra in the system: 'you have got to make sure that you don't release any of the wrong people.'" When early hearings categorized a surprisingly large number of detainees as NLECs, DIA, CIA, and Special Operations accused hearing officers of misunderstanding the intelligence and subjected them to further training. A detainee who asked why he was being held was told: "that question is outside the limits of what this board is permitted to consider." DoD ordered repeats of CSRTs that found detainees to be NLECs. Although all 18 Uighurs told very similar stories, five were found to be NLECs and 13 to be ECs (several on a rehearing). The lawyers who presented the government's case in CSRTs were replaced by officers with an MI background in ARBs. Capt. Waddingham, who oversaw the panels, said they followed MI recommendations of continued detention 95 percent of the time. Deputy Secretary of Defense England overruled panels in more than 15 percent of the 237 cases he heard, almost always changing an EC finding to NLEC. But prisoners had become so disillusioned by the procedure that only 18 percent attended the 2007 round of ARBs. Documents obtained by the Associated Press (AP) revealed that in 2006 DoD cleared 55 detainees for transfer, including 24 whom CSRTs and ARBs had found were ECs, as well as dozens more who did not participate in those hearings.

A November 2006 report by Seton Hall Law School revealed that DoD had ordered rehearings of CSRTs, changing the outcomes in three cases, and detainees' lawyers found additional instances.[56] DoD retorted that "more process has been afforded to the detainees than ever provided to enemy combatants in the history of armed conflict." A few weeks later the *New York Times* denounced CSRTs as "kangaroo courts that give inmates no chance to defend themselves, allow evidence that was obtained through torture and can be repeated until one produces the answer the Pentagon wants." It urged Congress to repeal the MCA and "start anew on a just system for determining whether prisoners are unlawful combatants ... evidence obtained through coercion and torture should be banned."

In June 2007 LtCol. Stephen Abraham offered an insider critique of CSRTs.[57] The California lawyer and 26-year Army Reserve veteran had served in military intelligence and had been decorated for counterespionage and counterterrorism; a conservative, he had cried when Nixon resigned. While working in the Office for the Administrative Review of the Detention of Enemy Combatants (OARDEC) in Guantánamo, he had complained to the director, RAdm. McGarrah, and other superiors that the evidence presented to CSRTs lacked specificity and exculpatory information was unavailable, possibly withheld. Government hearsay was like "a game of telephone." In December 2004 he had asked to be relieved because participation "may be in conflict with my obligations as an attorney," but got no response. After his tour ended in March 2005, Abraham was asked by David Cynamon (representing Fawzi al Odah seeking judicial review of his CSRT) to look at McGarrah's affidavit calling the tribunals a diligent effort to gather all the evidence and consider it thoroughly.

Outraged, Abraham wrote an affidavit for al Odah. As liaison between the intelligence agencies and those preparing the government's case, he had seen the evidence on many detainees. CSRTs operated with a presumption of guilt; some people gathering evidence were insufficiently trained; unclassified evidence lacked solid corroboration; "classified information was stripped down, watered down, removed of context, incomplete and missing essential information." "As an intellagent, I would have written 'junk statement' across" the many general accusations that detainees were jihadists. He had asked to serve on one panel, which unanimously found Abdul Hamid al Ghizzawi, a Libyan meteorologist, NLEC and reaffirmed that finding after being directed to reconsider. A second CSRT held in Washington without the detainee's knowledge or any new evidence produced the government's desired result. Abraham was never placed on another panel. "Anything that resulted in a 'not enemy combatant' would just send ripples through the entire process. The interpretation is, 'you got the wrong result. Do it again.'" "The hearings amounted to a superficial summary of information, the quality of which would not have withstood scrutiny in any serious law enforcement or intelligence investigation." "There were too many assumptions, too many presumptions." DoD responded that Abraham "would not be in a position to comment" given his "limited experience." A month later he told a HASC hearing he had "expected to see … a fundamentally fair process" but found something "entirely different." McGarrah testified that because Abraham spent most of his six months "helping us build the database" for the CSRTs, "his view was of a very narrow piece of the process."

In October 2007 Capt. Fessel, the new OARDEC director, said it would review all cases.[58] "With all the outside eyes looking in at the process, it's forcing us to say, 'OK, did we take everything into consideration when we did the CSRTs?'" "It's an acknowledgement that if there is new evidence or a new thing to take into bearing, in the spirit of being an open and fair process, we have to take that into consideration." Abraham said this "repudiates every prior assertion that the original CSRTs were valid acts." A week earlier an Army major who had served on 49 tribunals said in an affidavit that they favored the government and, when they declared a detainee NLEC, OARDEC appointed a new panel, which sometimes reached the opposite conclusion without hearing more evidence.

In March 2007 CSRTs for the 14 HVDs excluded observers – the first time they were closed.[59] When transcripts were released, Khalid Sheikh Mohammed (KSM) had confessed many terrorist acts (even boasting he had beheaded Daniel Pearl), but also described his torture. Majid Khan said he had been "mentally tortured" at Guantánamo to the point where he twice attempted suicide by chewing through his own arteries. Sens. Graham and Levin (who had observed the hearing) called for an investigation of the abuses. Several readers wrote the *New York Times* voicing suspicions that the confessions had been made under torture. The CSRTs found all 14 HVDs to be ECs.

In the first challenge to the CSRTs, a unanimous DC Circuit panel ordered the government to give detainees' lawyers virtually all the information it had.[60] Judge Ginsburg wrote: "the court cannot, as the DTA [Detainee Treatment Act] charges us, consider whether a preponderance of the evidence supports the tribunal's status determination without seeing all the evidence, any more than one can tell whether a fraction is more or less than half by looking only at the numerator and not the denominator." But the government could provide only what was "reasonably available," ask the court to review the evidence before releasing it to detainees' lawyers, limit what they could discuss with their clients, and read lawyer–client correspondence. In a petition for rehearing, the directors of the CIA, FBI, and NSA, and the Director of National Intelligence (DNI) and Deputy Secretary of Defense objected to disclosure; DCI Hayden and NSA Director Alexander filed secret declarations. Hayden said disclosure would reveal "information about virtually every weapon in the C.I.A.'s arsenal … exceptionally grave damage can be expected to result." The panel refused to reconsider but said the DoD could "convene a new C.S.R.T., taking care this time to retain all the government information."

In the first substantive review, another DC Circuit panel invalidated the EC designation of Huzaifa Parhat, a Uighur.[61] "The evidence the government submitted to Parhat's Tribunal did not permit the Tribunal to make the necessary assessment, and … the record on review does not permit this court to do so." "To affirm the Tribunal's determination under such circumstances would be to place a judicial imprimatur on an act of essentially unreviewable executive discretion." Rejecting the government contention that its accusations should be accepted as true because they had been repeated in at least three secret documents, Judge Garland derisively quoted Lewis Carroll's *The Hunting of the Snark*: "I have said it thrice: What I tell you three times is true." The government asked the court to clarify that it had not authorized the transfer of detainees to the USA, but said it would no longer try to hold Uighurs as ECs. The *New York Times* called it "a rebuke to the lawless policies of the Bush administration." The *Washington Post* said: "President Bush must do right by Mr. Parhat even while working to keep off the books a judicial determination that could force future administrations to take in detainees who are far less sympathetic and even potentially dangerous." He should use his commander-in-chief powers to grant Parhat asylum.

In December 2007 the *Washington Post* published a redacted version of US District Judge Green's January 2005 decision harshly criticizing the 2004 CSRT, which found Murat Kurnaz (a Turkish resident of Germany) was an EC.[62] Soon after he arrived at Guantánamo in 2002, a German intelligence officer wrote: "USA considers Murat Kurnaz's innocence to be proven. He is to be released in approximately six to eight weeks." German and US intelligence jointly concluded in September 2002 he should be freed: there was nothing linking him to terrorism – he had simply chosen a bad time (soon after 9/11) to visit religious sites in Pakistan. A May 2003 memo by the Criminal Investigation Task Force (CITF) commander said it "is not aware of any evidence that Kurnaz may have aided or abetted or conspired to commit acts of terrorism." Judge Green found that the CSRT ignored "conflicting exculpatory evidence in at least three separate documents." She criticized the tribunal's reliance on an unsubstantiated June 2004 memo by BGen. Lacquement (head of the SOUTHCOM intelligence unit), which stated that Kurnaz's question about the height of the prison yard basketball rim meant he wanted to escape, and finding it suspicious that he prayed during the US national anthem and displayed interest in detainee transfers and guards' work schedules. Green wanted to know what inculpatory evidence had been discovered between May 2003 and June 2004. "However the record in Kurnaz is interpreted, it definitively establishes that the detainee was not provided with a fair opportunity to contest the material allegations against him." The January 2006 ARB found he was still "a danger," but ignored evidence his lawyer had submitted. In May the FBI said it had "no investigative interest in this detainee" and "there is no information that Kurnaz received any military training or is associated with the Taliban or al-Qaeda." After protests in Germany and pressure on Bush from Merkel, a second ARB in July found Kurnaz an NLEC, and he was released the following month.

Apparently in response to the Supreme Court's June 2008 *Boumediene* decision (discussed in Chapter 5 of the companion volume *Law's Trials*), Attorney General Mukasey urged Congress to pass legislation limiting detainees' access to evidence and denying them the right to attend the hearing.[63] He asserted (falsely) that "all of these people, every single one of them, are aliens captured abroad in essentially battlefield conditions who have absolutely no right to be here," and expressed the fear that courts could "release into our communities people who could pose a significant danger." The *New York Times* wrote that the administration fears "that hearings for any prisoner will reveal how much abuse has been meted out by American interrogators and how thin and tainted the evidence is against most of the Guantánamo prisoners." "There has been too much injustice already."

In April 2011 WikiLeaks published secret files revealing that eight detainees had incriminated at least 235 others.[64] A 2008 intelligence assessment of Mohammed Basardah, a Yemeni who gave evidence against at least 131 other people, said his "first-hand knowledge in reporting remains in question." Questioning Basardhah's allegations, US District Judge Urbina ordered the release of Saaed Mohammed Saleh Hatim, and US District Judge Kessler ordered the release of Alla Ali bin Ali Ahmed. Abdul Rahim Abdul Razak al-Janko (Syria) gave evidence against 20 others, but his file said: "there are so many variations and deviations in his reporting, as a result of detainee trying to please his interrogators, that it is difficult to determine what is factual." Mohammed al-Qahtani (Saudi Arabia) gave evidence against 31 others after being waterboarded, but then retracted his statements. Ibn al Shayk al Libi (Libya) gave evidence against 38 others, but said he exaggerated. Mohammed Hashim (Afghan) gave evidence against 21 others, but an analyst said he was "of an undetermined reliability and is considered only partially truthful." Abu Zubaydah gave evidence in 12 cases but had been waterboarded 83 times. Fawaz Naman Hamoud Abdullah Mahdi (Yemen) gave evidence against six others, but his file said his "severe psychological disorder and deteriorating attention span" meant that "the reliability and accuracy of the information … will forever remain questionable." The White House "strongly condemn[ed] the leaking of this sensitive information," but the *New York Times* said the documents were "a chilling reminder of the legal and moral disaster that President George W. Bush created" at Guantánamo, revealing "the chaos, lawlessness and incompetence" of the "system for deciding detainees' guilt or innocence and assessing whether they would be a threat if released." "Some assessments relied on innuendo, gossip or information supplied by individuals whose motives were untrustworthy and whose information later proved false." "The administration is wrong to insist on secrecy." "The administration should make its assessments of the remaining Guantánamo detainees public to the extent possible and free lawyers for detainees to fully communicate their clients' side of the story."

Restrictions on Lawyers and Journalists

Because lawyers and journalists were virtually the only independent source of information about Guantánamo, the military sought to control or silence them.[65] When an Afghan American recent college graduate translating for habeas lawyers wrote a *Washington Post* op ed about detainee abuses, the DoD denied her further access to Guantánamo, claiming that the article posed a "security risk" and possibly violated a protective order.

LtCdr. Matthew Diaz served as an SJA in the Guantánamo military command from July 2004 to January 2005.[66] In late 2004 DoD rejected

CCR's request for the names, nationalities, next of kin, and countries of residence of the detainees for whom it sought to file habeas petitions. Knowing this, Diaz logged onto the classified military network and printed the names and nationalities of 551 detainees with codes indicating who had disclosed intelligence and their interrogators' identities. Just before the end of his tour he sent this to a CCR lawyer, who notified the DoJ. Diaz was court-martialed in May 2007 (long after the government had released the detainees' names in response to a FOIA action), convicted of disclosing classified information, sentenced to six months in the brig and discharge, and disbarred by Kansas. He explained:

> I had observed the stonewalling, the obstacles we continued to place in the way of the attorneys … My oath as a commissioned officer is to the Constitution of the United States … I made a stupid decision, I know, but I felt it was the right decision, the moral decision, the decision that was required by international law. No matter how the conflict was identified, we were to treat them in accordance with Geneva, and it just wasn't being done.

During a DC Circuit review of a CSRT decision, the government moved to limit lawyers to three visits per detainee because they "cause unrest on the base," including hunger strikes.[67] Barry M. Kamins, president of the New York City Bar, wrote Attorney General Gonzales challenging this "astonishing and disingenuous assertion. Blaming counsel for the hunger strikes and other unrest is a continuation of a disreputable and unwarranted smear campaign against counsel" (a reference to Charles "Cully" Stimson's attack on habeas lawyers, discussed in Chapter 5 of the companion volume *Law's Trials*).

> Many Guantánamo detainees have been held for over five years without trial, many have been held in solitary confinement for prolonged periods. Many have lost hope of a fair hearing to demonstrate their innocence – let alone of seeing family again. It is these extraordinary conditions, in our view, which have precipitated unrest … Over the course of the last four years, Guantánamo has developed into a symbol of abuse, mistreatment and injustice in the eyes of the entire world.

The proposed rules "would constrain attorney access so as to make effective representation virtually impossible." "The CSRTs do not provide adequate fact-finding mechanisms for reasons that Judge Joyce Hens Green explained" (discussed above).

The *New York Times* said:

> the administration offered no evidence for these charges, probably because there is none. This is an assault on the integrity of the lawyers …

> It's obvious why the administration is attacking the lawyers. It does not want the world to know more than it already does about this immoral detention camp. And brave lawyers have helped expose abuse and torture there, as well as detentions of innocent men – who are a large portion, if not a majority, of the inmates at Guantánamo Bay … Perhaps the most outrageous of the Justice Department's proposals would allow government officials – on their own authority – to deny lawyers access to the evidence used to decide whether an inmate is an illegal enemy combatant.

The *Washington Post* condemned the Bush administration for "ruthlessly exploiting" the MCA "as an excuse to curtail the prisoners' access to the civilian lawyers who have been representing them."

> The military authorities at Guantánamo have developed a deep antagonism, tinged with paranoia, toward the lawyers …
>
> Their lawsuits have forced the few reforms that have taken place at the prison. They have rightly reported publicly on hunger strikes, suicide attempts and abusive treatment. Their investigations have made clear that many of those held at Guantánamo are not dangerous terrorists but Afghans forced into cannon-fodder service by the Taliban, or Arabs who were swept up and sold by Pakistani bounty hunters to the CIA.

The *Los Angeles Times* agreed with Kamins that "Guantánamo is still a legal black hole."

The government backed down, withdrawing its proposed three-visit limit but continuing to screen mail sent by lawyers, deny them access to secret evidence, and threaten to bar future visits for breach of any rule. Kamins objected that this "barely begins to address the egregious violations of the attorney–client relationship." In September 2007, DoJ barred lawyers for at least 40 detainees from visiting or writing their clients after US District Judge Urbina dismissed their habeas cases because the MCA stripped the courts of jurisdiction.

DoD erected other obstacles to effective representation, rescinding security clearance for two Arabic interpreters without giving a reason (leaving just over a dozen who met the criteria of citizenship and security clearance, some of whom were booked three months in advance and who charged $1,400/day), restricting contact with clients to six hours a day during visits, and prohibiting phone calls.[68] It required that lawyers meet clients in Camp Echo instead of Camps 5 and 6 where they were housed, and clients endure groin searches before and after each visit. US District Judge Lamberth enjoined these rules, but the DC Circuit reversed. Sometimes obstructionism deteriorated into farce. A Guantánamo commander accused Clive Stafford Smith and Zachary Katznelson (English solicitors at Reprieve) of smuggling Speedo swimsuits and UnderArmour briefs to their clients. Calling the charges "patently absurd," Stafford Smith wrote in a *Washington Post* op ed that "I take accusations that I may have committed a criminal act very seriously." He wrote in a *Los Angeles Times* op ed that he was not even allowed to talk about Speedos. He always carried lozenges to soothe the throats of force-fed hunger strikers. "By my next visit, the list of 'contraband' had expanded to bar this insignificant salve."

Even without explicit government restrictions, lawyers had difficulty securing and sustaining client trust.[69] After his toothpaste was confiscated, a detainee asked his lawyer: "what good are you? You can't even get me toothpaste." Another told his lawyer: "we all know that everything we say in these rooms [where they met lawyers] is being monitored by them." Interrogators told detainees their lawyers were Jewish or gay and warned that those with lawyers were less likely to be released. Some interrogators even posed as detainees' lawyers. Philadelphia lawyers honored for representing Guantánamo detainees described their frustrations. It took one 18 months to meet his client because he could not visit without a signed retainer, which he could not get without a visit (a perfect Catch-22); another was refused the photo his client needed to apply for asylum. A lawyer was prevented from bringing a client cigarettes. A lawyer who received notification that a client was eligible for release replied immediately but got no response for ten months.

THE OBAMA ADMINISTRATION

A week after Obama was elected, the ACLU took a full-page ad in the *New York Times* quoting him declaring in September 2007: "As president, I will close Guantánamo, reject the Military Commissions Act and adhere to the Geneva Conventions."[70] The ACLU exhorted: "On day one, with the stroke of a pen, you can restore America's moral leadership in the world." The same day Harvard law professor Lawrence Tribe, who had advised Obama during the campaign, said Guantánamo would be a top priority of the new administration. "I think the answer is going to be, [detainees] can be as securely guarded on U.S. soil as anywhere else. We can't put people in a dungeon forever without processing whether they deserve to be there." A campaign advisory group (since disbanded) had been sympathetic to a "try or release" proposal by HRF and the Center for Strategic and International Studies (CSIS). But Charles Stimson (Bush's Deputy Assistant Secretary of Defense for Detainee Affairs) said there still was a need for preventive detention for one or two dozen tough cases. And Benjamin Wittes of the Brookings Institution warned "there will be a sobering moment for enthusiasts of a 'try and release' regime when people start looking at the contents of those detainee files."

CCR, AI, HRW, Reprieve, and FIDH urged European governments to work with the new administration to close Guantánamo and mobilized 77 Members of the European Parliament to persuade member states to offer relocation.[71] Manfred Nowak, UN special rapporteur on torture, called European engagement "essential." Thomas Hammerberg, Council of Europe Human Rights Commissioner, encouraged European governments "to open their doors." Anne-Marie Lizin, Parliamentary Assembly Vice President of the Organization for Security and Co-operation in Europe (OSCE), did the same. The Portuguese Foreign Minister said his country would take some detainees and hoped the EU would accept others. John Bellinger called this "highly significant," the first time a European country had expressed willingness. Germany strongly supported closure and said it might take some detainees; but it and France wanted a common EU policy. Denmark's Foreign Minister categorically refused: "none of these detainees have anything to do with Denmark." The Austrian Foreign Ministry dismissed the discussion as "hypothetical." And the Australian Acting Prime Minister said her country was "unlikely" to accept any.

A public opinion poll immediately after Obama's election found that 44 percent favored keeping Guantánamo open and only 29 percent wanted it closed; even the majority of Democrats favoring closure preferred to wait. Jack Cloonan (a former FBI special agent) and Sarah Mendelson (CSIS) wrote in a *Washington Post* op ed that "to propose a new scheme of detention as part of the policy solution to closing Guantánamo would perpetuate one of the most delegitimizing aspects of the facility." Defense Secretary Gates said: "I think it is possible to close it. It should be a high priority." But "the biggest challenge is finding a statutory basis for holding prisoners who should never be released and who may or may not be able to be put on trial." He ordered the DoD to have a plan ready if Obama ordered closure. Thomas Wilner, a habeas lawyer, wrote in a *Wall Street Journal* op ed that closing Guantánamo was "not so complicated." The fewer than 40 of those accused of being al-Qaeda fighters could be tried in civilian criminal courts; many of the 200 others "never fought anyone." A file review to "weed out the many baseless cases … could be completed within a few weeks." "[W]e should take a hard look at the likelihood that any" of the "small number" who "may be found to have participated in hostilities" would "return to the battlefield" after "almost seven years." Yemen's Washington Embassy said the country was "ready to receive all" 101 detainees. But a forthcoming report by the West Point Combating Terrorism Center said "the remaining 97 are an eclectic group of intentional unrepentant combatants and accidental warriors," and "separating the detainees into two groups … is a nearly impossible task." Furthermore, Yemen's previous rehabilitation program "now appears to be a failure."

A week before his inauguration Obama said on ABC's *This Week* that closing Guantánamo was:[72]

> a challenge. I think it's going to take some time and our legal teams are working in consultation with our national security apparatus as we speak to help design exactly what we need to do. But I don't want to be ambiguous about this. We are going to close Guantánamo and we are going to make sure that the procedures we set up are ones that abide by our Constitution.

A transition spokeswoman said Obama "shares the broad bipartisan belief that Guantánamo should be closed." But the ACLU's Anthony Romero demanded "specifics about … the release or charging of detainees … An executive order lacking such detail, especially after the transition team has had months to develop a comprehensive plan on an issue this important, would be insufficient." HRF and HRW urged Obama to encourage European countries to take detainees by accepting some into the USA.

Rumors that DoD was exploring Fort Leavenworth, Kansas and Camp Pendleton, California, as well as federal civilian prisons, sparked immediate resistance.[73] Sen. Brownback (R-Kan) said: "under our laws, you can't mix military and foreign detainees together." Furthermore, Leavenworth "doesn't have an exterior fence" and was bisected by a train, so "it could be easily breached by someone bringing in a bomb or something like that." The Leavenworth mayor claimed detainees were "possibly a little more dangerous than our prisoners." Rep. Bilbray (R-Ca) said the area around Pendleton was one of the most populated places in the country. (Actually, the immediate vicinity is unpopulated.) "Once you move them onto U.S. soil, it opens up a Pandora's box of appeals." Rep. Hunter said putting detainees on a military base would be "an insult to military personnel serving in Afghanistan and Iraq."

The *New York Times* rebuked Bush and Cheney for "a long series of valedictory speeches … crowing about Guantánamo Bay."[74] "[T]he real nature of Mr. Bush's grotesque legacy" was "abuse and torture at an outlaw prison where hundreds of men – many of whom did nothing – have been held for years without real evidence or charges." "Guantánamo is the place to begin … We hope [Obama] sets a target date." "There is one unacceptable choice: creating a new detentions law that would allow [detainees to be] held without trial."

Obama's January 22, 2009 Executive Order declared that Guantánamo would be closed "as soon as practicable, and no later than 1 year" from now.[75] The AG, Secretaries of Defense, State, and Homeland Security, DNI, and JCS chairman would create a group to review the files and select detainees for transfer, prosecution, or continued detention in the USA. Until then the Secretary of Defense would ensure that conditions of confinement complied with all laws, including the Geneva Conventions.

John Bellinger said: "although the Gitmo order is primarily symbolic, it is very important. It accomplishes what we could never accomplish during the Bush administration."[76] But House Minority Leader Boehner warned that "the key question is where do you put these terrorists … most communities around America don't want dangerous terrorists imported into their neighborhoods, and I can't blame them." And Rep. Pete Hoekstra (R-Mich) said the decision "places hope ahead of reality – it sets an objective without a plan to get there." Administration officials "could not answer questions as to what they will do with any new jihadists or enemy combatants that we capture." Local residents were "going to say, 'no, why would we want them here and put them in a general prison population and make our hometowns a target for terrorists?'" When Sen. Bond (R–Mo) (ranking minority member of the Senate Select Committee on Intelligence (SSCI)) provocatively proposed moving detainees to Alcatraz, a spokesman for Sen. Feinstein (SSCI chair) replied it was a "national park and tourist attraction, not a functioning prison" or "a suitable place to house detainees." But she believed they could be moved to civilian or military prisons. Sen. Levin agreed. Rep. Murtha (D-Pa) thought detainees were no more dangerous in a secure prison than in Guantánamo (but his district had no Supermax facility). Sen. McCain said he would not have announced the closure without first deciding what to do with the detainees. Obama met with a group of 9/11 families, securing their tentative support for his decision. But Military Families United, which claimed 60,000 members, sought to persuade legislators to oppose jailing any detainees in their districts. The *Washington Post* praised Obama's "appropriate prudence in taking things slowly," but urged him to "be mindful not to delay too much."

> [M]any detainees have been held for years without a meaningful review of their cases. They have been denied the opportunity to scrutinize the evidence against them or to gather and present information that could exonerate them ... If there are dangerous detainees who cannot be tried ... the president should consider the creation of a specialized court, akin to the FISC [Foreign Intelligence Surveillance Court], in which such detainees would be guaranteed periodic review of their detentions by a federal judge empowered to order their release.

A public opinion poll just before the inauguration showed that 55 percent wanted Guantánamo closed, while 42 percent wanted it kept open.

Obama's pledge was welcomed in Saudi Arabia.[77] UN Human Rights Commissioner Navi Pillay lauded him for "the extremely important step he has taken, and for doing it so swiftly upon taking office." The Italian Foreign Minister called it "a good decision," which might persuade European countries to accept some detainees. Twenty-seven EU Foreign Ministers offered to take up to sixty detainees. But though the German Foreign Minister said Obama's decision raised "a question of our credibility," a Merkel spokesman thought it "premature" to announce Germany's response. France's Foreign Minister said it would take detainees "under extreme, precise conditions only." Italy and Spain would participate only under an EU plan. The UK, Netherlands, Austria, and Denmark rejected the idea.

Just after the inauguration it was reported that Ali al-Shihri, who had gone through Saudi Arabia's rehabilitation program following his November 2007 release, had become deputy leader of Al Qaeda in the Arabian Peninsula (AQAP) in Yemen and had directed a September 2008 car bombing outside the US Embassy.[78] He declared in a video: "By God, our imprisonment only increased our perseverance in the principles for which we went out, did jihad for, and were imprisoned for." DoD said two detainees returning to fighting would not change the policy of transferring the other 22 Saudis.

Obama administration officials found no comprehensive case files on many detainees.[79] Charles Stimson said he often had had to threaten to recommend release or transfer to get the CIA to "cough up a sentence or two." A DoD spokesman admitted that "not all the documents are physically located in one place." Opposing a habeas petition, DoJ said the record "is not simply a collection of papers sitting in a box at the Defense Department. It is a massive undertaking just to produce the record in this one case." In a January 2009 court filing Darrel Vandeveld (a military commission prosecutor) said evidence was "strewn throughout the prosecutor's offices in desk drawers, bookcases packed with vaguely-labeled plastic containers, or even simply piled on the tops of desks." He accidentally found "crucial physical evidence" that "had been tossed in a locker located at Guantánamo and promptly forgotten." Case files contained contradictory or ambiguous information: Mohammed Sulaymon Barre was in Sudan and Pakistan at the same time; Abdul al Rahman al Zahri trained in Afghanistan to fight Russian forces in Chechnya but condemned bin Laden as a heretic; Oybek Jabbarov fled Uzbekistan for Tajikistan, which sent him to Afghanistan, where local fighters turned him over to the USA.

In response to Obama's directive to report on conditions at Guantánamo in 30 days, DoD sent the Navy's number two officer, Adm. Walsh.[80] Human rights NGOs complained they had just 24 hours to submit information, defense attorneys were prevented from participating, and Walsh did not speak with detainees. Just before Holder's own visit, Walsh found that conditions satisfied the Geneva Conventions. About 40 detainees were on hunger strike, some of them being force-fed. Detainees were not in solitary confinement, just "single-occupancy cells." (CCR reported that a majority of detainees – those in Camps 5 and 6 and Camp Echo – were in solitary confinement.) Walsh recommended that the HVDs in Camp 7 be allowed to pray and gather for recess in rotating groups of at least three.

Ahmed Ghappour of Reprieve said that, soon after Obama's election, prison guards started to "get their kicks in" before Guantánamo closed, removing their IDs and beating detainees, dislocating a detainee's knee, shoulder, and thumb, pepper-spraying cells and toilet paper, and interrupting prayers.[81] Adm. Walsh acknowledged "substantiated evidence where guards had [committed] misconduct," including "gestures, comments, disrespect" and "preemptive use of pepper spray." Mohamad al-Qurani (a Chadian detainee who managed to speak to Al Jazeera by phone) said the mistreatment started about 20 days before the inauguration and continued daily. An IRF team had beaten him, breaking a tooth.

DoD had "no record of authenticity" for this "alleged phone transcript." Yasin Ismail complained to his lawyer of being beaten, but RAdm. Thomas, GB commander, said it was "a complete and total fabrication."

After Binyam Mohamed's military lawyer warned that he was in critical condition from his hunger strike, the UK sent a medical team to evaluate his ability to fly home.[82] Foreign Secretary Miliband said the USA had agreed to treat his case as "a priority." When Mohamed was transferred in February 2009, Britain refused to impose conditions on his release, which would violate British and EU law. Miliband saw the return "as the first step towards that shared goal" of closing Guantánamo.

Sen. McConnell (R-Ky) (Minority Leader) wrote a *Washington Post* op ed opposing closure.[83] Just as Holder had said after visiting Guantánamo that "the prisoners were being treated well," McConnell found detainees "well cared for" after his own visit. "They receive three meals a day. They are free to worship five times daily and provided with prayer beads, rugs and copies of the Koran in their native languages. They send and receive mail. The prison library offers more than 12,000 items in 19 languages … Medical care is said to be excellent." "[N]o acceptable alternatives exist." DoD reported that released detainees "appear to be reengaging in terrorism at higher rates." "As the pool of inmates has shrunk, those who remain are simply more dangerous."

In March 2009 Secretary of State Clinton appointed Daniel Fried (former Assistant Secretary of State for European Affairs) to negotiate with countries to accept detainees.[84] Although Clinton was "quite encouraged at the positive responses we've been getting," Spain's Deputy Prime Minister said "we'd have to study concrete cases," and an anonymous French official said "it would be easier if the U.S. administration is willing to take some detainees."[85] German Interior Minister Schäuble asked why the USA did not take any detainees if they posed no security risk. The EU Vice President said member countries needed complete information on the detainees, "otherwise we cannot accept that responsibility."

But Holder was "pleasantly surprised" by European willingness to accept detainees and planned to make requests within "weeks, not months."[86] He said at the American Academy in Berlin:

> Nothing symbolizes our new course more than our decision to close the prison at Guantánamo Bay … I can confidently report that the prison is

> now run in an efficient, professional manner ... But President Obama believes, and I strongly agree with him, that Guantánamo has come to represent a time and an approach that we want to put behind us: a disregard for our centuries-long respect for the rule of law and a go-it-alone approach that alienated our allies, incited our adversaries and ultimately weakened our fight against terrorism.

British Foreign Minister Straw said "we will do our best to help," although his government had previously said it would take only Shaker Aamer, whom the USA refused to release. France agreed to take only one detainee, soon thereafter accepting Lakhdar Boumediene. The administration had cleared 30 for release.

RAdm. Buzby (GB commander) said three-quarters of all detainees in Camps 5 and 6 "get at least two hours of outdoor recreation with other people every day" and "a shower every single day," while the "highly compliant" remainder in Camp 4 lived six to a room, with "access to recreation about 22 hours a day." "We don't have any solitary confinement," just "single cells ... right next to each other." They "can talk all day long, and they do" (through the small food-tray slots in the sheet-metal doors). The 17 percent receiving behavioral health services was half the rate in civilian prisons. "I do not see – significant mental breakdown issues." But he acknowledged "a vast spike" in disobedience: "feces-smearing ... dirty protests ... hunger striking."

Two April 2009 polls found that a higher percentage of Americans wanted to keep Guantánamo open than close it: 46–36 (Rasumussen) and 47–44 (CBS News/NYT).[87]

Telling the Senate Appropriations Committee there were "50 to 100 ... we cannot release and cannot try," Defense Secretary Gates sought $50 million in supplemental financing if the administration chose to transfer detainees to a US military facility.[88] Sen. Brownback said "please not at Leavenworth." Sen. McConnell warned that "by releasing trained terrorists into civilian communities in the United States, the administration will, by definition, endanger the American people." Montana's Congressional delegation denounced a town's offer of its empty prison. The Stafford County (Virginia) Board of Supervisors opposed transfers to the Quantico Marine base; California officials passed a similar resolution concerning Camp Pendleton. House Minority Leader Boehner produced a web video with images of the 9/11 attacks, asking "Just what is the administration's overarching plan to take on the terrorist threat and to keep America safe?"

Asked by Sen. Shelby (R-Ala) if "you know of any community that would welcome terrorists," Holder told the Senate Subcommittee on Commerce, Justice, and Science that any transfer to the USA would be "done in a way that will not have any impact on the safety of the place that will receive them."[89] When Sen. Mikulski (D-Md) demanded consultation before a decision, Holder promised to make sure "surprises do not occur." Rep. Smith (R-Tex) warned of the "clear and present danger to American lives." Sen. Nelson (D-Neb) declared: "I wouldn't want them, and I wouldn't take them." Republicans introduced the Keep Terrorists Out of America Act, requiring a state's governor and legislature to approve any transfer. Democrats on the House Appropriations Committee defeated an amendment to ban any funding to transfer prisoners to the USA, but the Committee passed a resolution directing the administration to produce a detailed plan by October. Senate Democrats introduced a bill to fund the closure of Guantánamo, but to bar any transfers to the USA. Sen. McConnell made speeches daily about the dangers of closure. FBI Director Mueller told Congress that detainees could pose a risk in US prisons by radicalizing other inmates and orchestrating crimes from inside (like gang leaders). At his first oversight hearing Holder assured the House Judiciary Committee that "we're not going to do anything, anything that would put the American people at risk – nothing."

After the Senate voted 90–6 to block the $80 million Obama sought to close Guantánamo, Majority Leader Reid said: "Guantánamo makes us less safe. However, this is neither the time nor the bill to deal with this. Democrats under no circumstances will move forward without a comprehensive, responsible plan from the president. We will never allow terrorists to be released into the United States." Sen. Durbin complained that "we were being asked to defend a plan that hasn't been announced." Sen. Boxer (D-Ca) pleaded: "Mr. President, give us a plan." Sen. Graham (one of the few Republicans favoring closure) said Obama "needs to convince people that he's got a game plan that will protect us as well as be fair to the detainees." But the DoD spokesman still expected the administration to meet its deadline, and the White House said Obama "intends to keep that promise."

In his May 21 National Archives speech Obama declared that "my single most important responsibility as President is to keep the American people safe."[90] "[C]andidates for President from both major parties ... recognized the imperative of closing the prison at

Guantánamo Bay." "There is … no question that Guantánamo set back the moral authority that is America's strongest currency in the world." "[P]art of the rationale for establishing Guantánamo in the first place was the misplaced notion that a prison there would be beyond the law." The status quo was "unsustainable." "As President, I refuse to allow this problem to fester. I refuse to pass it on to somebody else." He deplored the "return to politicization of these issues." Americans were "ill-served by some of the fear-mongering," including "words that, frankly, are calculated to scare people rather than educate them." "We are not going to release anyone if it would endanger our national security, nor will we release detainees within the United States who endanger the American people." "[N]obody has ever escaped from one of our federal supermax prisons." Detainees would be divided into five categories. The first priority would be to try them in civilian courts, the second to try them in military commissions. He would release the 21 whom courts "have found … no legitimate reason to hold." The review team had already identified 50 eligible for transfer to other countries. The rest would be detained indefinitely after being identified by "fair procedures," according to "clear, defensible, and lawful standards," subject to periodic review and "judicial and congressional oversight."

A day earlier the *New York Times* revealed a leaked DoD report claiming that one out of seven former detainees (74/534) had returned to terrorism (but naming only 29 and verifying terrorism by only a few).[91] Cheney (in a speech designed to preempt Obama) pronounced that "one in seven cut a straight path back to their prior line of work and have conducted murderous attacks in the Middle East." HRW noted that at least one of those named had been tortured in Russia before confessing to terrorism. Mark Denbeaux compared the DoD figures with the 68 *percent* three-year recidivism rate for those released from US prisons. The report, issued a week later, said 5 percent had returned to terrorism and 9 percent were suspected of having done so, acknowledging that the latter could be based on "unverified or single-source, but plausible, reporting." New America Foundation researchers said 14 of the 29 named were just "suspected" of terrorism, 9 had not targeted the USA or its immediate allies, 5 had been killed, and 3 had been recaptured. In 2007 the DoD had listed the Tipton Three as recidivists because they participated in Michael Winterbottom's documentary on their release from Guantánamo to the UK. In a *Los Angeles Times* op ed, Laurel Fletcher and Eric Stover of UC Berkeley Law School said most of the 62 ex-detainees they interviewed just wanted to resume their former lives.

EU Interior Ministers urged the Obama administration to issue a joint declaration committing the USA to accepting some prisoners.[92] After the USA had asked Germany to take nine Uighurs, Munich (which already had about 500 in its population) passed a resolution welcoming them. But when the USA refused to accept any, a German Interior Ministry official said "if the U.S. says they should come here, but they cannot travel to the U.S., we would have to ask why not?" When Rep. Wolf heard that a plane was ready to bring 2–5 Uighurs to his district (where others lived), he asked Obama to "declassify all intelligence regarding their capture, detention, and your administration's assessment of the threat they may pose to Americans, prior to any decision to release them." The White House accused Wolf of playing politics. Claiming the DoJ had promised not to carry out any resettlements without consulting Congress, Wolf wrote Holder that Uighurs were "trained terrorists" and members of an al-Qaeda affiliate, but got no response.

After chairing a meeting of the 27 EU Interior Ministers, Martin Pecina (Czech Republic) reiterated that their countries were likely to take "several dozen" detainees. The *Los Angeles Times* said "the best incentive for European cooperation is a willingness by the United States to do its part." "Obama must overrule advisors who are telling him to capitulate to a cowardly Congress and abandon plans to settle (or imprison) some detainees in the United States." Prime Minister Berlusconi promised that Italy would take three. Dropping its condition that the USA accept detainees first, the EU issued a joint statement with the USA that some member states "have expressed their readiness to assist with the reception of certain former Guantánamo detainees, on a case-by-case basis."

On June 2 Mohammad Ahmad Abdallah Saleh al-Hanashi was found dead in his cell.[93] The 31-year-old Yemeni, who had been in Guantánamo since February 2002, had never seen a lawyer; a hunger strike had reduced his weight from 124 pounds to 86 pounds. In a *Washington Post* op ed, Binyam Mohamed described the trauma of being force-fed with al-Hanashi and was "amazed that the U.S. government has the audacity to described [the] death categorically as an 'apparent suicide'" because he had been moved to the behavioral health unit designed to prevent suicide attempts.

A June poll found an even split (47–47) between those favoring or opposing closure.[94] Other polls were consistent: 46/39 (February 2), 51/38 (April 21), 45/46 (June 14), 46/50 (June 21).

After a visit by Daniel Fried, Palau President Johnson Toribiong agreed to accept the 17 Uighurs.[95] The Obama administration had just renegotiated its compact with Palau, offering $200 million to a country with a GNP of $157 million (a later article denied the offer). Palau did not recognize China, making it less vulnerable to threats. Although the Uighurs initially balked because Palau had virtually no Muslims, six went there at the end of October. DoD also released four Uighurs to Bermuda (which, as a British overseas territory, did not have diplomatic relations with China). The *Washington Post* was pleased the Uighurs "will finally get a chance to start their lives again," but found it maddening that "U.S. administrations and lawmakers of both parties did not act with cooler heads and good faith to welcome at least some of these men into this country." It urged the Supreme Court to hear the appeal from the DC Circuit decision blocking release of the Uighurs to the USA, fearing that two brothers "could face indefinite detention" – an "unconscionable" prospect. German news media said their country had rejected a request to take a Syrian and a Tunisian. Although only 15 Yemenis had been sent home, 26 of the remaining 97 had been cleared to return. The USA wanted them to go through the Saudi rehabilitation program, but the Saudis feared it would not work without family support. Of the 108 former Saudi detainees who had undergone it, 80 percent remained active participants, but nearly 20 percent had escaped abroad, disappeared, or been arrested.

As president, Bush had favored closing Guantánamo, and he had promised not to criticize his successor. But in June he warned: "there are people at Gitmo who will kill Americans at the drop of a hat. Persuasion isn't going to work. Therapy isn't going to change their mind."[96] The same day the Senate (spooked by rumors of an imminent transfer of Uighurs to Virginia) voted 90–6 for an emergency defense appropriations bill forbidding release of detainees in the USA and containing no funds to close Guantánamo. The *Washington Post* condemned "hypocrisy on the Hill." Although Democrats for years had "clamored for the closing" of Guantánamo, "now lawmakers are making it nearly impossible." It was "easy to understand" why Obama was considering an executive order. But the *Post* urged him to open "discussions with Congress on fashioning a preventive detention regime that will ensure due process and humane treatment of detainees." Having screened only half the 239 detainees by July, Obama's Task Force missed the six-month deadline to report and got another six months. The *Los Angeles Times* warned that "procrastination from the White House is making it easier for Congressional critics to frustrate a step vital to restoring American legitimacy." Public opposition to transfers had "been fed by nonsensical claims that Obama would free dangerous terrorists to run loose in the streets." After Democrats blocked Sen. Inhofe's amendment to keep Guantánamo open and prohibit transfers to the USA, Sen. Roberts (R-Kan) threatened to "shut down the Senate" unless it was enacted.

In September the administration decided to rely on the Authorization for Use of Military Force (AUMF), rather than seek to legislate indefinite detention. The *Los Angeles Times* shared critics' concern that legislation "would institutionalize a two-tier system of justice that never would be repealed," but hoped "Obama will find other ways to ensure that anyone he proposes to hold indefinitely has meaningful recourse to the federal courts." The *Washington Post* accused Obama of having "chosen the politically expedient and intellectually dishonest route." "Without question, judicial review is infinitely better than the deeply flawed tribunals that served as rubber stamps for the administration's detention decisions. But because there are no legislatively mandated legal standards in place, judges are essentially making up the rules as they go along."

In late September Obama replaced White House Counsel Gregory Craig (who strongly supported closure) with Pete Rouse. The White House said: "we're not focused on whether or not the deadline will or won't be met." Weeks later Holder said "it's going to be difficult" to meet it. "[W]e are going to have to ... come up with a facility here in the U.S. to house people for trial." The Senate voted overwhelmingly to bar the use of federal funds to bring detainees to the USA, even for prosecution; the House had approved a similar measure. The *Washington Post* accused Congress of "irrational and damaging bluster." "The U.S. refusal to allow even one cleared detainee into the country – coupled with the rantings from Capitol Hill – have made it that much more difficult to persuade allies to take in those who have been ordered released." The House passed a DHS appropriation allowing transfer of detainees to the USA to stand trial; Republicans failed to defeat the proposal even though 25 Democrats joined them. After Holder announced his decision to try the five HVDs in the SDNY (discussed in Chapter 2 on criminal prosecutions in the companion volume *Law's Trials*), he promised the SJC: "we will not release anyone into the United States if doing so would endanger national security or the American people … [or] move any detainees into the United States unless and until we are convinced that the detainees will be held safely and securely in a facility that satisfied all of our security concerns."

Illinois's Democratic Gov. Quinn and Sen. Durbin endorsed a proposal by the president of Thomson Village (150 miles west of Chicago) to use the state's unoccupied Thomson Correction Center. But two Republican Representatives – Manzullo (whose district included the prison) and Kirk (seeking Obama's former Senate seat) – opposed this invitation to "al Qaeda to make Illinois its No. 1 target." Kirk introduced a bill to study alleged safety issues. He and six Republican colleagues wrote Obama that "our state and the Chicago metropolitan area will become ground zero for jihadist terrorist plots, recruitment and radicalization." But two prominent conservatives – Grover Norquist (Americans for Tax Reform) and David Keene (American Conservative Union) – said the plan would create jobs. "The scaremongering about these issues should stop." Federal officials spent two hours briefing more than a dozen members of the Illinois Congressional delegation in Durbin's office. The White House suggested the plan could generate 3,000 jobs. Rep. Schakowsky, a supporter, called Republican opposition "politics at its worst." State Sen. Schoenberg (D) said several local communities had voted resolutions in support. "For those who live in that job-starved portion of the state, this is undoubtedly very welcome news." Gov. Quinn's office said he could sell the prison to the federal government once the Illinois Commission on Government Forecasting and Accountability made a (nonbinding) recommendation. But Sen. McConnell renewed his opposition; and Rep. Boehner (R-Oh) declared he would not vote to "spend one dime to move those prisoners to the U.S." and would "seek every remedy at our disposal to stop this dangerous plan." Sen. Cornyn (R-Tex) said "this move will put our citizens in unnecessary danger." Obama, Clinton, Gates, Blair, and Holder assured Quinn the federal government would build a second secure perimeter, there would be no visits by family or friends, and detainees would be guarded by military personnel and not mix with other federal prisoners.

The *New York Times* praised the administration for defying "all the chest pounding" and taking this "indispensable step," but criticized Obama for not "forswear[ing] the idea of indefinite detention without charges, as he vowed to do while running for president." "The *Washington Post* endorsed the proposal but said Congress "should establish clear legal guidelines that require periodic judicial review, set out clear rules of evidence and guarantee each detainee has an attorney." Federal officials said Thomson would host military commissions for those accused of bombing the *USS Cole* and house the five HVDs if they were convicted in the SDNY. The Illinois Commission held a six-hour hearing in late December, attended by dozens of demonstrators. One speaker warned that "terrorists would want to hit us to make a point, here in the Midwest, in the American heartland. Is a little economic gain worth the risk?" Support for the proposal provoked boos and jeers. But Congressional Democratic leaders refused the administration's $200 million request for the project, and there would be no opportunity to appropriate the money for nearly a year. Rep. Skelton (D-Mo), HASC chair, privately expressed doubts about the plan. Rep. Loretta Sanchez (D-Ca) raised concerns about security. Sen. Webb (D-Va) said terrorism suspects "do not belong in our country, they do not belong in our courts, and they do not belong in our prisons." The *Los Angeles Times* was "disappointed that Obama hasn't fulfilled his promise" to close Guantánamo in a year, but encouraged by "two important steps": the Thomson prison and the repatriation of 12 detainees, 6 to Yemen. "Obama must be prepared to expend political capital opposing inevitable attempts in Congress to block or micromanage the transfer of detainees to the U.S."

The Christmas Day bombing attempt by Umar Farouk Abdulmutallab, who had been trained in Yemen, intensified criticism of transfers.[97] Warning that sending "any people back – to Yemen right now is a really bad idea," Rep. Hoekstra accused Obama of spending "more time and energy on closing Guantánamo than on any of the other issues." Rep. King (R-NY) called releases to Yemen "a major mistake." Rep. Wolf "implore[d]" Obama to halt releases to Yemen –"a very dangerous policy that threatens the safety and security of the U.S. people." Rep. Thompson (D-Miss), chair of the House Homeland Security Committee, said sending any more to Yemen "would be a bit of a reach." Lawyers for Yemeni detainees had expected another 40 to be transferred. The *Washington Post* said: "considering that a number of al-Qaeda operatives previously escaped from a Yemeni prison, and two leaders of AQAP are former Guantánamo detainees," any further releases would be "an alarming prospect." Sens. McCain, Graham, and Lieberman (Independent D-Ct) had written Obama opposing the court-ordered release of six Yemenis – after the fact. House Minority Leader Boehner said: "turning these terrorists over to other countries is not working, and we shouldn't import them into the United States." But Obama's counterterrorism adviser John Brennan called Abdulmutallab's attempt a "unique incident." The USA was working with Yemen to make sure "the situation on the ground is taken into account." And Obama vowed to continue trying to close Guantánamo, which "has damaged our national security interests and become a tremendous recruiting tool for al Qaeda. In fact, that was an explicit rationale for the formation of al-Qaeda in the Arabian Peninsula."

A classified DoD report found that recidivism among ex-detainees had increased from 14 percent in April 2009 to 20 percent in January 2010. Sen. Feinstein said: "at least 24 or 28 are confirmed returns to the battlefield in Yemen ... [t]hey come out of Gitmo and they are heroes in this world." She agreed "we ought to be very, very careful about releasing anybody right now." Weeks later, however, Brennan said the 20 percent figure (half just suspected) applied to the Bush administration's 540 releases; *none* of Obama's 48 releases had recidivated. "We believe that significant improvements to the detainee review process have contributed to significant improvements in the results." There was "no basis" for Rep. Wolf's claim that Ayman Batarfi, returned to Yemen in December 2009, had once been involved with weapons of mass destruction. In June 2010 it was reported that 25 of the 120 ex-detainees who had gone through the Saudi rehabilitation program had returned to terrorism.

Obama responded with a "temporary" freeze on repatriations to Yemen. On January 7, 2010 Sens. McCain and Graham urged him to extend that to other countries with a "significant" al-Qaeda presence: Afghanistan, Pakistan, Saudi Arabia, Somalia, Algeria, and Sudan. The *Washington Post* opposed adding any country other than Somalia. The proposal "all but ignores the administration's moral and legal responsibility to release those who should never have been detained in the first place." Such a ban could include Germany and the UK and increase "the risk that a federal judge will order releases into the United States."

Prevented from buying Thomson, the administration was considering alternatives.[98] Kansas's two Republican Senators opposed using Leavenworth and put a hold on the nomination of Rep. John McHugh (a Republican) as Secretary of the Army to block its use. The *New York Times* called their arguments "ludicrous." "The prison in Guantánamo Bay, Cuba, and the abuses committed there, are a searing symbol of shame and a rallying point for international fury." By contrast, Michigan Republicans, including former Gov. Engler, proposed the state's maximum security prison in Standish. A spokeswoman said Sen. Levin "believes the idea should be considered." Rep. Rogers (R-Mich) was opposed. When a dozen state officials joined 18 federal officials to tour Standish, more than 200 people demonstrated in opposition; their organizer had been convinced by Rep. Hoekstra that detainees "would have rights, visitors and friends would come who could be jihadists." State Sen. Barcia (D) complained that opponents were recruited from around the state by the anti-Islamist group Act! For America. Debra Burlingame, founder of 9/11 Families for a Safe & Strong America, warned that detainees would plan attacks on tourists (to Standish?) and attract suicide bombers. A spokesman said Gov. Granholm (R) "has concerns that have not been addressed." The *Los Angeles Times* condemned "the hysterical opposition in Congress to transferring some inmates to the United States" and praised the "commonsense comments" of Sen. Feinstein, who noted that no one escaped from maximum security prisons and raised no objections to California housing some detainees. "Shuttering Guantánamo is essential to restoring the United States's image abroad. But … if this country doesn't take its share of detainees, how can it lecture other countries about their responsibility to help?" Defense Secretary Gates told a Congressional hearing that DoD was ready to transfer 116 of the remaining 211 detainees, but "the logistics of it have proven to be more complicated" than expected.

On the day Obama had promised to close Guantánamo his Task Force recommended prosecuting 35 detainees in federal court, transferring at least 110, and indefinitely detaining 47 (mostly from Yemen and Afghanistan) under the AUMF, with the right to seek habeas corpus.[99] Of the 110 cleared for release, about 80 (including 30 Yemenis) were eligible for immediate repatriation or resettlement in third countries; the other 30 (some also from Yemen) could be released only when conditions in their home countries stabilized. The administration believed 20 could be repatriated by summer and had commitments from countries to settle another 25. The ACLU strongly opposed indefinite detention. The *Washington Post* urged Congress and the White House to "work together to create a national security court that would give detainees robust adversarial rights and give the judiciary the authority to oversee such continued detentions."

Faced with mounting opposition, Holder abandoned criminal prosecutions of the HVDs in New York (discussed in the companion volume *Law's Trials*). Obama reiterated that "by closing Guantánamo, we can regain the moral high ground in the battle against these terrorist organizations." "There's been no bigger propaganda weapon for many of these extremists than pointing to Guantánamo and saying that we don't live up to our own ideals." Daniel Fried was "confident [Guantánamo] will be closed under President Obama's first term." Sen. Graham said the administration was considering his indefinite detention statute. Obama favored habeas petitions but opposed a national security court, which, the *New York Times* warned, "would permanently embed in law detention powers that a president properly has only in time of war." But DDC judges expressed unhappiness about reviewing detention. Judge Urbina had said: "[I]t's an honor to have the responsibility of blazing the trail in determining how justice should be administered in these cases. By the same token, it's also at times frustrating when not all the rules are clear and not all the specifics of how a matter should be dealt with are before us."

Judge Hogan had called it "unfortunate ... that the legislative branch ... and the executive ... have not moved more strongly to provide uniform, clear rules and laws for handling these cases." At an SJC hearing Holder was vague about how the administration would close Guantánamo, but "certainly" thought he would have a proposal that year. Accusing the administration of "a lot of inertia," Sen. Levin said it was "not putting a lot of energy behind their position." Sen. Graham agreed that the effort to close Guantánamo was "on life support."

Mullah Abdul Qayyum Zakir, a former detainee, was made top deputy to Taliban leader Mullah Omar.[100] Fox News repeated the inaccurate claim that more than a hundred ex-detainees (20 percent of the 560) had returned to terrorism, including Abdul Hafiz, released in December 2009.[101] A March 2010 poll found that 60 percent wanted to keep Guantánamo open, up from 47 percent two months earlier.[102]

In May HASC unanimously approved the 2011 NDAA, which banned spending money to build or modify any US facility for Guantánamo detainees.[103] A week later SASC concurred. But the administration still planned to buy the Thomson facility. At the end of the month the Guantánamo Review Task Force issued its final report, finding that about 10 percent of the 240 detainees in the prison when Obama took office were "leaders, operatives and facilitators involved in plots against the United States," but most at a low level. Although seven Republicans on the House Appropriations Committee had asked National Security Adviser Gen. Jones to recommend against any transfers, he refused to do so. The *Washington Post* again criticized the administration's "missteps" and Congress's "crass politicization of the issue." A month later the *Post* accused the Obama administration of erecting a "shameless smokescreen" while "embrac[ing] the Bush administration's approach." It published an op ed by Jack Goldsmith urging the administration to "give up on closing the Guantánamo Bay facility" and "acknowledge that military detention will remain the primary basis for holding terrorists." But the *Post* also reported that it had cost nearly $2 billion to build and operate Guantánamo, including football and baseball fields, volleyball courts, a running track, a skate park, an outdoor roller hockey rink, batting cages, a go-kart track, a soccer cage, and playgrounds.

The day after Republicans won control of the House, Rep. Smith, who was expected to chair the Judiciary Committee, said: "we should not close the terrorist detention center at Guantánamo Bay."[104] In December the Office of the Director of National Intellligence (ODNI) reported that two detainees released by the Obama administration had returned to terrorism and another three were suspected of doing so. Of the 532 released by the Bush administration, 79 were confirmed to have engaged in terrorist or insurgent activities and 66 were suspected. Sen. Bond said: "these latest numbers make clear that fulfilling a campaign promise to close Guantánamo Bay is overriding what should be the administration's first priority: protecting Americans from terrorism." Further transfers were "unacceptable."

A spending bill passed by House *Democrats* banned the use of federal money to bring detainees to the USA for *any* purpose before the fiscal year ended (September 1, 2011).[105] Holder denounced this for going "well beyond existing law" and "unwisely restrict[ing] the ability of the executive branch" to prosecute or incarcerate detainees. The *Washington Post* said the House was "irresponsibly filling a vacuum created because the Obama administration failed to lead." The *Los Angeles Times* urged the Senate not to "go along with the House in complicating President Obama's plan to close the detention center at Guantánamo Bay" but blamed him for not making closure a priority. The administration responded with a draft executive order creating a PRB to review detainees (Obama had suspended the ARBs). On its last day, Congress passed the NDAA, banning the transfer of detainees to the USA for any purpose or the expenditure of money to buy or construct a prison for them in the USA, and requiring the Defense Secretary to certify the safety of transfers to other countries.

The *Washington Post* praised the PRBs but criticized the administration for saying nothing about future detainees. The *New York Times* also endorsed this "realistic legal process." The *Post* published an op ed by HRW legislative director Tom Malinowski warning that the proposed executive order "could transform the Guantánamo system from an unfortunate, improvised response to Sept. 11 into a permanent feature of our legal landscape." The *Wall Street Journal* said "it's time for Mr. Obama to accept that Mr. Bush mostly got it right," since "about 150" of the 600 ex-detainees "have returned to jihad." It published an op ed by John Yoo and Robert Delahunty (who wrote the OLC memos) claiming (without evidence) that "even that 25% recidivism rate is likely too low" and "those freed by this administration are likely more dangerous" than those freed by the Bush administration. "If Americans die at the hands of released detainees, we will know who is to blame." The *Los Angeles Times* criticized the proposal "both because the right to a trial is central to American notions of due process and because the administration's criteria for indefinite detention are too broad." The executive order was "an improvement," but "falls short of affording inmates the protections they would enjoy in a trial." The newspaper favored a "special court to determine whether a prisoner at Guantánamo continued to pose a danger to this country." The criterion for indefinite detention should be "past involvement in violence and terrorism" not, as the administration proposed, "a history of association with extremist activity" or "strong ties (either directly or through family members) to extremist organizations." The paper published a New Year's wish list that Obama would "finally make good on his promises to close the Guantánamo Bay detention center and put accused terrorists on trial in civilian courts," and an op ed by Amos Guiora and Laurie Blank (law professors at Utah and Emory) asserting that "the idea that every person deserves his or her 'day in court' is a fundamental principle in the United States and many countries worldwide."

In his NDAA signing statement, Obama criticized the Guantánamo provisions, promising to seek their repeal. Sen. McConnell said: "the American people strongly oppose the president's goal of transferring these terrorists to the United States for trial and detention." The *New York Times* said that "as wrongheaded as this prohibition is, the president was right not to declare his intention to defy it," but he "could have pushed harder on this issue." The *Washington Post* agreed Obama "showed appropriate restraint" in his signing statement but "too much restraint in opposing the provisions"; he should have vetoed the bill.

The *Los Angeles Times* also said Obama "has received, and deserves, criticism for not working harder to make good on his pledge to close the detention center at Guantánamo Bay, Cuba." He was right not to declare the law invalid, but a veto "would have pressured Congress to submit an authorization bill without the Guantánamo language."

When Obama issued the executive orders in March 2011, HRF denounced them as "a step down the road toward institutionalizing a preventive-detention regime."[106] The ACLU said: "it is virtually impossible to imagine how one closes Guantánamo in light of this executive order." John Brennan denounced the transfer ban as an "unprecedented encroachment" on presidential powers. Closing Guantánamo was an "essential national security objective"; its continued operation was "preventing other countries from handing over terrorism suspects to the United States." Rep. King commended the executive order, which "affirms the Bush administration policy." Rep. Smith called on Obama to "abandon the ill-advised campaign promise to close Guantánamo Bay." Rep. Rogers was "disappointed the White House chose to put another Band-Aid on this problem, rather than working with Congress to develop the comprehensive and long-term legislative framework we need." Sen. Leahy said PRB reviews would fall "far short of core constitutional values" and "do little to bring us closer to closing the prison." The *New York Times* said Obama's promise to close Guantánamo –"the embodiment of Bush-era arrogance and lawlessness" – had just "crumbled, the victim of congressional spinelessness." The transfer ban was "an act of notable political cowardice," which "also makes it virtually impossible to release prisoners to other countries willing to take them." Although PRBs offered "improvements," the "Obama administration has still chosen to accept the concept of indefinite detention without trial, which represents a stain on American justice." The *Washington Post* called the orders "both an admission of failure and a step in the right direction." Closure was impossible "thanks largely to unconscionable Congressional restrictions." But "Mr. Obama shares in the blame for not fighting aggressively to reverse this regrettable intrusion." PRBs "should allay some of the concerns involving detention without trial. But review by executive branch panels is no substitute for truly independent evaluations by the courts." The *Los Angeles Times* accused Obama of "largely perpetuating the status quo." "Having made these concessions, Obama will find it hard to argue that he really wants Guantánamo to be closed."

The orders did nothing to end debate.[107] Former federal judges Abner Mikva, William Sessions, and John Gibbons wrote a *Chicago Tribune* op ed denouncing the Military Detention Procedures Improvement Act of 2011, which "would codify methods such as indefinite detention without charge." After the measure failed, the *New York Times* condemned "the usual gang of fearmongerers [*sic*]" who voted for it: 47 Republican senators, including McCain, Graham, Ayotte, and Lieberman, as well as "so-called Republican moderates like Susan Collins and Olympia Snowe." To defeat it, Sen. Levin made a deal with Sen. McCain (§1031 of the NDAA 2012), which the *Times* called "a step toward making permanent the Guantánamo prison, a blot on America's reputation and an increased danger to any soldier captured in battle." It authorized indefinite detention of "unprivileged enemy belligerents" (including US citizens), mandated detention of members of al-Qaeda or its affiliates, sharply limited transfers to other countries, and prohibited the closure of Guantánamo. "There is no provision for judicial review of the decision to send a prisoner to military detention," even though "the government has mistakenly detained hundreds of men." The *Washington Post* said the most "obnoxious" of the "several objectionable proposals" required "that terrorism suspects who are not U.S. nationals be held in military custody." The law also renewed the ban on using DoD funds to build or adapt a US prison for detainees, which was "little more than fear-mongering." The *Boston Globe* said: "this whole debate seems contoured mainly for political purposes."

The White House expressed "serious concerns"; senior advisers recommended a veto. McCain replied that SASC had endorsed it 26-0. The *Washington Post* urged a veto: "The new proposals are as problematic as the old and should be scrapped." The transfer provisions required the Secretary of Defense to "guarantee[] the impossible: that no released detainee will ever return to the fight." Sens. Levin and McCain wrote a *Washington Post* op ed calling the bill "a careful, bipartisan effort to provide the executive branch the clear authority, tools and flexibility of action it needs to defend us against the threat posed by al-Qaeda." Sen. Udall (D-NM) replied in a *Post* op ed that the "deeply flawed" bill "would require the military to take on a new responsibility as police, jailors and judges – jobs for which it is not equipped and which it does not want." DNI Clapper, Assistant Attorney General for National Security Monaco, and FBI Director Mueller added their criticisms. But the Senate approved the bill 61–37 (17 Democrats joining all the Republicans except Kirk and Paul), and defeated a Udall amendment (38–60) and a Feinstein proposal exempting citizens from detention (45–55). After vigorous debate, the Senate voted 99–1 to declare (confusingly) that the bill did not affect "existing law" governing arrests inside the USA. Graham argued against any exceptions for citizens since anyone suspected of joining al-Qaeda thereby exposed himself to "imprisonment and death." "And when they say, 'I want my lawyer,' you tell them: 'shut up. You don't get a lawyer. You are an enemy combatant, and we are going to talk to you about why you joined al Qaeda.'" Levin and he claimed the Supreme Court had authorized detention of citizens arrested in the USA; Feinstein and Durbin disagreed (each side citing different passages in *Hamdi*). The Senate passed the bill 93–7.

The White House reiterated its objections and veto warning. The *Philadelphia Inquirer* criticized Congress for charting a "reckless course," which "would threaten fundamental American freedoms." "Other countries might be reluctant to share counterterrorism intelligence if it could be used to lock suspects away for years without charging them with a crime." Matthew Waxman and John Bellinger said the Bush administration (in which both had served) probably would have "strongly opposed" the bill. Charles Stimson (another former Bush official) agreed that "to win this long war against terrorists, the president must have the maximum flexibility to use all tools of national power." The *New York Times* said the new rules "would harm the justice system and national security. They would hinder intelligence-gathering, make it harder to track down terrorists and make other countries less likely to cooperate." *Bloomberg News* urged a veto for the same reasons, adding: "We would like to see President Obama close" Guantánamo. Sens. Levin and McCain and Rep. Smith said they had modified the bill to eliminate the administration's concerns that it interfered with the FBI and civilian law enforcement. Calling the bill "improved ... but not enough," the *Washington Post* again recommended a veto. It was "inexcusable" to stop DoD from bringing detainees to the USA or improving detention facilities there. More than 40 Muslim, South Asian, and Arab American community organizations and bar associations urged Obama to veto the measure. But the White House said he would not do so, and Congress passed it by veto-proof majorities: 283–136 in the House and 86–13 in the Senate.

In his *New York Times* column Andrew Rosenthal called it "stunning" that Obama signed "a bill that might effectively turn the right of habeas corpus into a mere privilege." "As long as [executive authority is] secure, he simply does not seem to care about technicalities like the Constitution." The *Los Angeles Times* said the bill had made "all the wrong choices" and Obama "should have had the courage of his convictions." The *New York Times* criticized Obama for having "fallen far short" of "his dedication to the rule of law and to reversing the Bush-era policies." The "terrible new measures" would "make indefinite detention ... a permanent part of American law" and give "future presidents the authority to throw American citizens into prison for life without charges or trial." This "complete political cave-in ... reinforces the impression of a fumbling presidency." "It will make it impossible to shut the prison in Guantánamo Bay." In his signing statement, Obama voiced "well-founded constitutional objections" to the transfer restrictions, which he would apply without infringing his powers. He would "not authorize the indefinite detention without trial of American citizens." ACLU director Romero called the bill "a blight on his legacy because he will forever be known as the president who signed indefinite detention without charge or trial into law." The *Chicago Tribune* denounced the "abdication of responsibility by Congress and the president." DoD transferred no one between January and November 2011 because the NDAA required the Defense Secretary to "ensure" that the "individual cannot engage or re-engage in any terrorist activity," a provision DoD General Counsel Jeh Johnson called "onerous and nearly impossible to satisfy."

The *New York Times* published two ex-detainees' accounts of abuse.[108] Lakhdar Boumediene wrote: "I was kept awake for many days straight. I was forced to remain in painful positions for hours at a time ... I went on a hunger strike for two years because no one would tell me why I was being imprisoned ... [Force-feeding] was excruciating." Murat Kurnaz suffered "beatings, endless solitary confinement, freezing temperatures and extreme heat, days of forced sleeplessness" and was "punished with 30 days in isolation and darkness" for feeding iguanas.

The USA offered to release five Taliban detainees to Qatar in exchange for the Taliban opening an office there to negotiate a peace agreement with Afghanistan.[109] The *Washington Post* called this "a huge and unjustified gift to a group that is weaker than it has been in years." The *New York Times* urged "careful vetting" of the detainees and "vigilant monitoring to ensure that the prisoners don't go back to the battlefield." Mitt Romney (the likely Republican presidential candidate) pronounced: "we do not negotiate with terrorists." HRW questioned the transfer, noting that Mullah Mohammad Fazl, the Taliban's Deputy Defense Minister, was suspected of involvement in the summary execution of 170 Hazaras in January 2001. Although the administration repeatedly denied any such plan, DCI Petraeus told SSCI the administration had asked for further risk assessments. DNI Clapper said this was "very, very preliminary," but the transfer could build confidence. Sen. Chambliss (R-Ga)(ranking SSCI minority member) said the Task Force had determined in 2009 that these men –"five of the meanest, nastiest killers in the world" – were "too dangerous to transfer," and the USA would get nothing in return. There was "every reason to believe" some had been involved in the death of CIA officer Johnny Michael Spann; the administration denied there was any evidence of this. Sen. McCain found it "bizarre" that detainees, who had been "in positions of authority," might be transferred "in exchange for a statement by the Taliban." SASC chairman Levin said "we're not releasing them. They are going to … be imprisoned in Qatar." But the administration backed down.

The tenth anniversary of opening the prison sparked demonstrations in Guantánamo, Washington, and other North American and European cities.[110] The *Washington Post* published dueling op eds by the Brookings Institution's Benjamin Wittes and George Washington University law professor Jonathan Turley. Sen. Rand Paul (R-Ky) took a full-page advertisement in the *New York Times* listing "countries with indefinite detention … Hitler's Germany, Stalin's Russia, North Korea, Myanmar, Cuba, United States of America," and introduced a bill to repeal part of the NDAA. Mitt Romney, by contrast, said he would have signed it. Fifteen retired generals and admirals reminded Obama that three years earlier many had stood behind him in the Oval Office as he signed the executive order calling for closure in a year. "[W]e are asking you to act within the discretion available to you to move our nation forward in closing Guantánamo once and for all." Navi Pillay, UN Commissioner for Human Rights, said: "the facility continues to exist and individuals remain arbitrarily detained – indefinitely – in clear breach of international law."

HASC's Republican majority published a 93-page report claiming that "domestic political pressures" and "desire to earn good will abroad" had led to reckless releases and calling for further restrictions.[111] A Democratic dissent criticized the report for failing "to analyze in depth the strategic issues and concerns that resulted in each administration separately reaching the same conclusion: that it is in the strategic and national security interest of the United States to transfer low-risk detainees" as part of the process of closing Guantánamo. Both sides invoked recidivism statistics. In March ODNI said that of the 600 released, 95 were confirmed to have re-offended and another 72 were suspected of having done so.

A provision in the NDAA 2013 added by Reps. Smith (D-Wa) and Amash (a Tea Party freshman from Michigan) would prohibit the president from ordering the military to detain anyone in the USA indefinitely without charge or trial.[112] Opposing it, Rep. Thornberry (R-Tex) said: "the vast majority of people in this body and around the country do not think telling [suspected terrorists] they have the right to remain silent as the first thing they hear is a wise thing." Former Attorneys General Meese and Mukasey and other former Bush administration lawyers warned that "rewarding terrorists with greater rights for making it to the United States would actually incentivize them to come to our shores." Although 27 retired admirals and generals supported the Smith–Amash amendment, the House rejected it 182–238. Finding it "hard to believe there was an argument" about "something so basic … [as] a formal charge and trial for anyone arrested in the United States," the *New York Times* urged the Senate "to restore the due-process rights found in the Constitution."

In a case brought by journalist Chris Hedges and others challenging the NDAA provisions authorizing indefinite military detention of US citizens, newly appointed SDNY Judge Forrest ruled that they violated the First and Fifth Amendments, issuing a preliminary injunction in May 2012 and making it permanent in September.[113] The government immediately appealed; Forrest denied a stay, but the Second Circuit granted it. The *Washington Post* said: "her uncritical acceptance of the plaintiffs' claims – and equally summary dismissal of the administration's protestations of good faith – smack of judicial activism." The *Wall Street Journal* said her decision "stretches the definition of judicial overreach." The *New York Daily News* called it "judicial looniness of the arrogant variety." Sens. McCain, Graham, and Ayotte filed an amicus brief on behalf of the government. In July 2013 the Second Circuit reversed, dismissing the case for lack of standing.

The 2012 Democratic Platform retreated from the 2008 promise to "close the detention camp in Guantánamo Bay, the location of so many of the worst constitutional abuses in recent years," now saying: "we remain committed to working with all branches of government to close the prison."[114] The Government Accountability Office issued a report describing how detainees could be relocated to US prisons. A week after Obama's re-election the ACLU took a full-page ad in the *New York Times* entitled "Yes, You Can Create an America We Can Believe In," urging him to: "Close Guantánamo Prison. Guantánamo represents one of the greatest stains on American civil liberties in our history. It is long past time this shameful episode was brought to a close and for you to keep the first promise you made as president." The *New York Times* regretted that Obama's "self-imposed one-year deadline for closing Guantánamo passed, along with the initial boldness and inspiration." But it also blamed Congress for imposing "outrageous limits" on transfers. The recent suicide of Adnan Latif (described above) "was the kind of price a nation pays when it creates prisons like Guantánamo, beyond the reach of law and decency, a tragic reminder of the stain on American justice." Having reaffirmed in his campaign that "I still want to close Guantánamo," Obama had to "become more engaged this time around and be willing to spend political capital." The *Times* agreed with civil liberties and religious groups that Obama should veto the NDAA 2013 if it retained the transfer restrictions.

The bill did preserve the prohibition on building or modifying US prisons for detainees or transferring them abroad unless DoD made difficult certifications.[115] The White House "strongly object[ed]." Feinstein and seven other senators introduced an amendment (which passed 67–29) declaring that the AUMF did not authorize indefinite detention of citizens or lawful permanent residents. The Senate passed the NDAA 98–0 (the second time in 5 years it had passed unanimously). Urging Obama to veto it, Feinstein released a General Accountability Office (GAO) report (commissioned in 2008 but just completed), which "demonstrates that if the political will exists, we could finally close Guantánamo without imperiling our national security." "There hasn't been a single security problem" with the 373 convicted terrorists held in 98 federal prisons.

Echoing the ICRC rebuke that the military had not held a single PRB in the 21 months since Obama's executive order, the *Washington Post* deplored that "there is less due process at Guantánamo now than there was during the last years of the George W. Bush administration."[116] It urged Obama to veto the NDAA. But while criticizing the "unwarranted and burdensome restrictions," he signed with the bland statement that he would interpret the law so as not to violate "constitutional separation of powers principles." The *Los Angeles Times* called this "a hollow threat," condemning yet "another recent failure of statesmanship by both of those branches of government." HRW lawyer Jennifer Daskal, however, wrote in a *New York Times* op ed that she "now believe[d] that Guantánamo should stay open." "Thanks to the spotlight placed on the facility by human rights groups, international observers and detainees' lawyers, there has been a significant, if not uniform, improvement in conditions." Many detainees in group cells in Guantánamo would suffer solitary confinement in the USA. Indefinite detention in the USA would "set[] a precedent and creat[e] a facility readily available to future presidents wanting to rid themselves of a range of potentially dangerous actors." "With the end of the conflict, the legal justification for the detentions will finally disappear." Dan Coquillette, a Boston College law professor, responded that "it is a keystone of the rule of law that no one be indefinitely detained without indictment and conviction in a regular court." And David Kaye, a UCI law professor, warned that the government had no incentive to declare the war's end and probably would not release detainees even then. Obama's second term began with evidence of diminished political will when Daniel Fried, who had worked tirelessly to transfer detainees, was reassigned and his duties absorbed by the office of the DoS Legal Adviser.

On March 4, 2013 CCR informed the Guantánamo commander that almost all detainees were on hunger strike, which started three weeks earlier when guards confiscated "comfort items" (including family letters and photos and legal correspondence) and restricted exercise and Arabic interpreters searched Korans.[117] (The military later claimed detainees had hidden "improvised weapons, unauthorized food and medicine" in Korans.) DoD replied that only 6 had missed enough consecutive meals to be considered hunger strikers (5 were being force-fed), increasing that to 14 and 6 respectively two weeks later. But a client told David Remes on March 11 that 104 were on strike. Lawyers and human rights advocates wrote DoD that some men had lost 20–30 pounds and at least two dozen had lost consciousness. DoD was dismissive: detainees "have sort of fallen out of public view ... If you want to burst back into the media then you have to start complaining about either Quran abuse or detainee abuse or deteriorating conditions." Gen. Kelley, SOUTHCOM commander, told HASC that detainees were "devastated" that the administration no longer believed it could close the base, which "has caused them to become frustrated, and they want to ... turn the heat back up, get it back in the media." By March 21 at least 25 were on strike, 8 were being force-fed, and 2 had been hospitalized for dehydration. Three days later DoD reported 28 on strike and 10 being force-fed, but habeas lawyers said the overwhelming majority of detainees in Camps 5 and 6 had been striking for weeks. After advancing a planned visit, the ICRC said tensions were "the direct result of the uncertainty faced by detainees." Demonstrators held solidarity vigils in American cities. DoD increased its numbers to 37 and 11, but lawyers insisted a majority of the 130 Camp 6 prisoners were on strike and, days later, that virtually all were. The *New York Times* said this "collective act of despair" was "again exposing the lawlessness of the system." The USA "surely can find countries to take detainees who cannot be returned home." The cases of the nearly fifty in indefinite detention "must be reviewed and resolved according to the rule of law." UN Human Rights Commissioner Pillay said the indefinite detention was a "clear breach of international law." "It is scarcely surprising that people's frustrations boil over and they resort to such desperate measures."

Acknowledging that 43 were on strike, DoD replaced the Guantánamo commander. A day later – during a media blackout hours after the ICRC left the base – troops conducted a five-hour predawn raid, firing rubber bullets to drive striking detainees out of the communal cellblocks, ending the three-month protest. It acted "to transition detainees into single cells, remove obstructions to cameras … and to assess the medical condition of each detainee." Col. Bogdan (in charge of the guard force) said: "we hit the point where we were accepting too much risk and it was time to take action." One detainee attempted to hang himself the night before the raid, and another tried the day after. The *New York Times* published an op ed about the strike by Samir Naji al Hasan Moqbel, who had lost "well over 30 pounds" but vowed not to eat "until they restore my dignity." Two other hunger strikers weighed 98 and 77 pounds. When Moqbel was on hunger strike in the hospital, an Emergency Response Force (ERF) squad of eight MPs in riot gear:

> burst in. They tied my hands and feet to the bed. They forcibly inserted an IV into my hand. I spent 26 hours in this state, tied to the bed. During this time, I was not permitted to go to the toilet. They inserted a catheter, which was painful, degrading and unnecessary. I was not even permitted to pray. I will never forget the first time they passed the feeding tube up my nose. I can't describe how painful it is to be force-fed this way … When they come to force me into the chair, if I refuse to be tied up, they call the E.R.F. team. So I have a choice. Either I can exercise my right to protest my detention, and be beaten up, or I can submit to painful force-feeding.

On April 11, 25 human rights organizations urged Obama to take immediate steps to close Guantánamo by replacing Fried and directing Defense Secretary Hagel to issue waivers for transfers. A day after meeting Obama, the ICRC president issued a rare public statement declaring "a discrepancy between the position of the United States and the ICRC." On April 14, a day after the raid, the military said the number of hunger strikers had risen from 45 to 52 (15 being force-fed); a week later it acknowledged 63 and a day after that 77 (17 being force-fed). At the opening of the George W. Bush Library and Museum, the *New York Times* said Guantánamo "symbolizes Mr. Bush's legacy in a darker, truer way." It was "the embodiment of his dangerous expansion of executive power." The hunger strike was the "inevitable" result of this "purgatory of isolation." "Just as hunger strikes at the infamous Maze prison in Northern Ireland indelibly stained Britain's human rights record, so Guantánamo stains America's." By April 26 there were 97 strikers (19 being force-fed). Sen. Feinstein asked the White House to review the 86 detainees cleared for transfer, adding that "it would be prudent to revisit the decision to halt transfers to Yemen." By the end of April *Democracy Now!* reported more than 130 on strike, and even DoD acknowledged 100. In his *New York Times* column Joe Nocera asked "is there any wonder" that the detainees were on strike when the DC Circuit had "made a mockery" of habeas corpus? The AMA wrote Hagel that force-feeding violated medical ethics.

Obama said at a press conference:

> [I]t's not sustainable. The notion that we're going to keep 100 individuals in a no man's land in perpetuity … the idea that we would still maintain forever a group of individuals who have not been tried, that is contrary to who we are, contrary to our interests, and it needs to stop … this is a lingering problem that is not going to get better. It's going to get worse. It's going to fester … I don't want these individuals to die.

He had ordered a review of "everything that we can do administratively," but cautioned that transfers were "a hard case to make" because "it's easy to demagogue the issue." HASC chairman McKeon replied that "for the past two years, our committee has worked with our Senate counterparts to ensure that the certifications necessary to transfer detainees overseas are reasonable. The administration has never certified a single transfer." A National Security Council (NSC) spokesperson said Obama was considering "reappointing a senior official at the State Department to renew our focus on repatriating or transferring," and acknowledged that the PRB process "has not moved forward quickly enough."

The *New York Times* agreed with the president that Guantánamo "is a blight on the nation's reputation. It mocks American standards of justice by keeping people imprisoned without charges. It has actually hindered the prosecution and imprisonment of dangerous terrorists." Obama's renewed promise to close it "was tempered by the fact that he has failed to do so for five years and that he has not taken steps within his executive power to transfer prisoners long ago cleared for release." His "plans to try to talk Congress into removing obstacles to closing the prison do not reflect the urgency of the crisis facing him now." The *Washington Post* said Obama was "justified in blaming Congress" but "disingenuous in failing to acknowledge that his own actions – or his own inaction – have substantially contributed to an impasse that has prompted more than half of Guantánamo's inmates to undertake a hunger strike." He should transfer the 27 non-Yemeni detainees already cleared and work with Yemen to transfer the others. "What is needed above all is genuine political commitment from Mr. Obama." The *Los Angeles Times* also felt "Obama has contributed to the crisis by acquiescing in Congressional obstruction" by refusing "to expend political capital on closing Guantánamo." The *Chicago Tribune* said it was time to lift the Yemen moratorium and negotiate with other countries to accept detainees. On May 1 the IACHR, the UN's Working Group on Arbitrary Detention, and its special rapporteurs for the protection of human rights while countering terrorism, on torture and cruel, inhuman, or degrading treatment, and on physical and mental health, all called on the USA to close Guantánamo. President Karzai said he had "from the very beginning been a very strong supporter for the closing down of the Guantánamo prison." The New York City Bar President wrote Obama, urging closure.

Detainees' lawyers said 130 were on hunger strike. In a declassified affidavit filed in federal court Obaidullah, whose weight had fallen from 167 pounds to 112 pounds, described force-feeding and "men coughing up blood, being hospitalized, losing consciousness, becoming weak and fatigued." Albert J. Shimkus Jr., a Naval War College professor who had been commanding officer and chief surgeon at the Guantánamo naval hospital, wrote in a *Miami Herald* op ed that "the individual human rights of a rational detainee, including the right to die if he so chooses, should not be subordinated to the interests of the state." But the senior officer of the Guantánamo Joint Medical Group said: "if a patient is threatening to hurt themselves or kill themselves we're not going to stand by and watch that happen." Detainees "almost unanimously" requested medical intervention to keep them alive, asking "to come to the detention hospital to be [force-fed] because they're not allowed to eat on the blocks." The registered nurse in charge of the hospital claimed that "nobody has expressed to me" that force-feeding "hurts." But the ACLU, CCR, HRW, HRF, Physicians for Human Rights (PHR), and other groups exhorted Hagel to end forced feeding.

Sen. Levin urged Obama to appoint a White House official "to spearhead an interagency effort to determine which of the more than eighty detainees who have already been cleared for transfer ... meet the certification (and waiver) requirements" and seek their transfer. Defense counsel for 8 of the 15 HVDs wrote DoD condemning "recent command actions that defy justification, such as placing hunger-striking prisoners in solitary confinement, camp-wide temperature modifications, and guard disruptions during attempted prayers."

In an hour-long speech to the National Defense University on May 23, Obama lifted the moratorium on transfers to Yemen, promised to appoint a new senior envoy for transfers, and urged Congress to lift restrictions.[118]

> GTMO has become a symbol around the world for an America that flouts the rule of law. Our allies won't cooperate with us if they think a terrorist will end up at GTMO. During a time of budget cuts, we spend $150 million each year to imprison 166 people ... there is no justification beyond politics for Congress to prevent us from closing a facility that should never have been opened ... Imagine a future – ten years from now, or twenty years from now – when the United States of America is still holding people who have been charged with no crime on a piece of land that is not a part of our country. Look at the current situation, where we are force-feeding detainees who are holding a hunger strike. Is that who we are?

But he warned that even if all those cleared were transferred, there would be dangerous men "who cannot be prosecuted." In response to repeated interruptions by Medea Benjamin of Code Pink demanding immediate release of the 86 already cleared, Obama said: "the voice of that woman is worth paying attention to." A *New York Times* ad urging closure was signed by 1,300 activists.

Sen. Chambliss said the speech would be "viewed by terrorists as victory." It "sends the message to Guantánamo detainees that if they harass the dedicated military personnel there enough, we will give in and send them home, even to Yemen." Sen. Graham warned that releases would create "a national security problem for our soldiers and our diplomats." Sen. McCain asserted that "about 20 percent of [ex-detainees] went back into the fight." Sen. Inhofe said it would be "shameful" not to use an "extremely valuable" asset like Guantánamo "just because a certain element of the liberal constituency" was opposed. In his *New York Times* column Joe Nocera defended hunger striking as "a form of speech for prisoners who have no other way to communicate their concerns." "Put simply, force-feeding violates international law." "Obama could stop that in a heartbeat, with one call to the Pentagon." Yemen's Foreign Minister urged Obama "to really put his words into actions." A week after the speech Rep. McKeon (R-Ca) added a section to the NDAA 2014 barring all transfers to the USA or any other country, while Rep. Smith denounced the $250 million in the NDAA to replace temporary facilities at Guantánamo as a "ridiculous waste of money."

Gen. Kelly, SOUTHCOM commander, said the protest would continue "until [detainees] get tired of doing what they're doing." The power to end the strike was "entirely in their hands." He disparaged it as "hunger strike lite" because "they're all eating something." "We don't force-feed right now at Gitmo" but only engage in "enterally [*sic*] feeding." All but 14–15 detainees were in single-cell lockdown most of the day for "acting up" and "trying to harm themselves." Obama received a letter from 150 doctors and other medical professionals offering to treat the hunger strikers.

A group of retired military officers, many of whom had stood behind Obama when he signed the executive order pledging to close Guantánamo, met with NSC officials to press for closure. RAdm. Hutson claimed there was "a real sense of urgency" in the White House. "The boss has taken a stand and they want to move ahead." But the House defeated Rep. Moran's (D-Pa) proposals to eliminate both the ban on constructing or renovating a US prison for detainees (170–254) and the prohibition on releases or transfers (175–247). After the White House threatened to veto the 2014 NDAA, the House added a ban on using any funds to transfer prisoners to Yemen (236–188), defeated amendments to end indefinite detention (200–226) or close Guantánamo (174–249), and passed the NDAA (315–108). The Defense Secretary would need to certify that any country receiving a detainee had taken steps to mitigate the risk of engagement in terrorism and that the transfer served the interests of national security. The law exempted transfers after an acquittal or completion of a sentence or following a PRB decision approving release; but it banned all transfers to the USA. Obama named Cliff Sloan to replace Fried. A FOIA action elicited a list of indefinite detainees: Yemen 26, Afghanistan 12, Saudi Arabia 3, Kuwait 2, Libya 2, Kenya 1, Morocco 1, Somalia 1.

Sen. Feinstein urged Hagel to end force-feeding. Shaker Aamer said the military was seeking to break the hunger strike by keeping cells "freezing cold" and using "metal-tipped" feeding tubes, making detainees vomit. A detainee was hospitalized coughing up blood after a nurse pushed a tube into his lungs. Abdelhadi Faraj wrote in the *Huffington Post* that guards "have beaten us and used rubber-coated bullets and tear gas against us. They have confiscated everything from our cells ... They have confined us to cold, windowless cells ... It isn't unusual for prison guards to search prisoners' genital parts and their rectum [*sic*] ten times in a single day." He described the pain and indignity of force-feeding and the threat to force food up his rectum if he resisted (a practice later confirmed by the SSCI report). At the beginning of July, 106 were on strike, 45 were being force-fed, and 3 were in hospital. Sens. Feinstein and Durbin asked Obama to end force-feeding unless "medically necessary to save a detainee's life," invoking Judge Kessler's opinion calling it "a painful, humiliating, and degrading process." The *Los Angeles Times* denounced force-feeding as "a disgrace," which had "fueled anti-American opinion abroad" and "appears to be a violation of prohibitions in international law."

For Ramadan DoD let the 75 detainees locked down in Camp 6 pray and eat in groups. By mid-July 81 had ended their strike, and at least 99 had eaten a hot meal. A lawyer said they were doing so "because they have been threatened with deprivation of the right to perform special communal Ramadan prayers if they don't eat." Joe Nocera wrote in the *New York Times* that Obama "could stop the military from force-feeding the detainees." "Yet despite decrying the Guantánamo prison, the president has refused to do anything but stand by and watch the military inflict needless pain and suffering, much of it on men who simply shouldn't be there." There were 66 still on strike at the end of July.

Sen. Durbin called for ending this "sad chapter" by transferring most detainees to foreign countries and trying or holding the rest in the USA, which had spent more than $5 billion on Guantánamo: $2.7 million a year per prisoner, compared to the $78,000 it would cost at the Florence ADMAX (Administrative Maxium Facility). William Lietzau (stepping down as Deputy Assistant Secretary of Defense for Detainee Affairs) said he would have advised Bush to bring detainees to the USA as POWs.

SASC approved Levin's proposal to give the administration more flexibility in transfers and move some detainees to the USA for medical care, prosecution, or detention. Obama met with Yemeni President Hadi, who was instituting an "extremist rehabilitation program." But Sen. Chambliss did not see "how the president can honestly say any detainee should be transferred to Yemen" and accused him of taking a risk "just to satisfy a political promise." Sen. Cruz (R-Tex) assailed the administration for "apologizing for the existence of Guantánamo … for our detaining terrorists and standing up to defend ourselves."

Sens. Feinstein and Durbin wrote a *Los Angeles Times* op ed urging closure of the "abomination."

> If the pace of … transfers does not dramatically increase, by the end of President Obama's second term, the majority of Guantánamo detainees there will have been held without trial for almost 15 years. Guantánamo has devastated our reputation as a champion of human rights, weakened our international partnerships and remains a powerful recruiting tool for terrorists …
>
> [The] large-scale force-feeding violates international norms and medical ethics.

By late August there were still 46 on hunger strike, with 35 being force-fed. When the number dropped to 19 a month later, DoD declared the strike over (though 14 were still being force-fed in early November). More than thirty-five prominent doctors and health professionals – including a former Surgeon General, six Nobel prize winners, and 18 current and former public health and medical school deans – urged Obama to end force-feeding. When the number of strikers rose to 15 at the beginning of December, the DoD said it would "not further their protests by reporting the numbers to the public." The strikers sought "to draw attention to themselves, and so we're not going to help them do that." "Everyone is saying, 'you're trying to shut down reporting on this.' That's not true."

DoD decided not to spend nearly $200 million intended for "overseas contingency" matters to improve Guantánamo. (But in May 2014 HASC appropriated over $90 million, including $69 million for a new secret prison.) In October DoD appointed Paul M. Lewis to replace Lietzau. Obama met with Sloan and Lewis for the first time in November. The Senate defeated (43–55) an amendment by Sen. Ayotte (R-NH) to block all transfers, even after Sen. Chambliss claimed: "the recidivism rate is nearly 29 percent and has been climbing steadily since detainees began being released from Guantánamo. This includes nearly 10 percent of detainees who have returned to the fight after being transferred by the current administration." (In fact, the recidivism rate was much lower under Obama than under Bush.) The *New York Times* "applaud[ed] the Senate's good sense," and the *Washington Post* said its "action made eminent sense."

At the beginning of December DoD repatriated two Algerians over their objections. The *New York Times* denounced this "perverse move." Obama rightly acknowledged that Guantánamo "has become a symbol around the world for an America that flouts the rule of law," but "he does not help matters by forcibly returning detainees to countries where they reasonably fear for their safety." The UN special rapporteurs on torture and on human rights and counterterrorism criticized the transfers. But Algeria released the two within weeks.

A SASC–HASC conference committee rejected Obama's proposal to lift the prohibition on transfers and the use and construction of US prisons but approved Levin's proposal to allow transfers after a PRB determination or court order, or if the Defense Secretary determined it was in the interest of national security and steps had been taken to mitigate the risk. In mid-December DoD sent Ibrahim Otham Ibrahim Idris to Sudan; a judge had granted his habeas petition, which the USA did not resist because he posed no threat, given his "severe long-term mental illness and physical illness." Hours after arriving home, Idris said jailers had "systematically tortured" him and "doubled" the punishment of those on hunger strike.

Obama signed the NDAA 2014, calling it "an improvement over current law" and "a welcome step toward closing the facility," whose "continued operation … weakens our national security by draining resources, damaging our relations with key allies and partners and emboldening violent extremists." But he criticized it for retaining "unwarranted limitations on foreign transfer" and violating "constitutional separation of powers principles."

DoD sent the last three Uighurs to Slovakia at the end of December 2013, leaving 155 detainees in Guantánamo. Retired Judge Urbina, who had ordered the release of all the Uighurs into the United States, was "not sure that this outcome is real compensation for what happened." "[O]nce the U.S. government satisfied itself that we were not at risk and therefore recognized that these people were … wrongfully detained, it seems to me that steps should have been taken more affirmatively to take these people back to a position that would have compensated them for their loss." He had been disappointed by the DC Circuit reversal and wished it had been reviewed by the Supreme Court, which:

> had already decided that individuals who were detained at Guantánamo did have a right to petition the courts for a writ of habeas corpus. It seems to me incongruent that the Supreme Court would recognize a right but there was no remedy … they certainly were not "enemy combatants." And there was not a shred of evidence that they were disliked by anyone – anyone but the Chinese government.

His courtroom had been full of Christian and Muslim organizations "willing to step forward with jobs and houses and resources to make sure those people were not up to mischief." DHS, DoJ and Immigration and Customs Enforcement (ICE) had declined his invitation to raise any concerns.

DoD informed lawyers that 71 detainees (46 "indefinite detainees" and 25 candidates for military commissions) would go before new PRBs to "assess whether continued law of war detention is necessary to protect against a continuing significant threat to the security of the United States."[119] Unlike CSRTs, these PRBs would be secret, though a redacted transcript would be released later. Each panel would include a senior official from DoD, DHS, DoJ, DoS, JCS, and ODNI. Panels that were not unanimous would be reviewed by a committee of the Secretaries of State, Defense, and Homeland Security, and the Attorney General, DNI, and JCS chairman. The detainee's personal representative would get most of the information. There would be full reviews every three years and file reviews every six months.

Most efforts to persuade judges to oversee conditions at Guantánamo failed. When a lawyer for Mus'ab Omar al-Madhwani claimed guards were denying hunger strikers access to potable water and lowering the cell temperature, US District Judge Hogan said the MCA had stripped him of jurisdiction.[120] He refused to hear allegations that others had been abused because "this is not a class-action." When lawyers offered medical evidence that al-Madhwani's "life may be in imminent danger," Hogan replied that the petitioner had "self-manufactured" his health problems, and DoJ said no detainee had ever died from a hunger strike. In June 2013 US District Judge Lee dismissed Mammar Ameur's claim for damages for mistreatment in Guantánamo because the MCA divested the court of jurisdiction and the government enjoyed sovereign immunity with respect to the non-constitutional claims. US District Judge Collyer rejected Shaker Aamer's constitutional arguments against force-feeding and agreed that the MCA deprived her of jurisdiction. In February 2014 the DC Circuit allowed detainees to challenge conditions of confinement, but refused to enjoin force-feeding and remanded for fact-finding.[121] Judge Tatel warned that if the military disregarded an order to stop treating a detainee in an "unlawful manner," the judge could "simply order the prisoner released." Judge Williams rejected this "bravura reading" of the statute, asserting that the MCA "unmistakably sought to prevent the federal courts from entertaining claims based on detainees' conditions of confinement." A detainee's lawyer said 25 were still on hunger strike, with 16 being force-fed.

In a case brought by Jihad Dhiab, US District Judge Kessler ordered the government in May 2014 to produce 34 videotapes of forcible cell extractions and force-feeding, urging the administration to find a compromise that would spare him "the agony of having the feeding tubes inserted and removed for each feeding" and "the pain and discomfort of the restraint chair."[122]

> The court is now faced with an anguishing Hobson's choice: reissue another temporary restraining order [against force-feeding] despite the very real probability that Mr. Dhiab will die, because he has indicated a continuing desire to refuse to eat and/or drink liquids, or refuse to issue the TRO and allow the medical personnel on the scene to take the medical actions to keep Mr. Dhiab alive, but at the possible cost of great pain and suffering.

She chose the latter because "the court simply cannot let Mr. Dhiab die." After learning that the military had stopped videotaping force-feeding, lawyers sought to compel its resumption. Judge Kessler ordered the DoJ to produce four more tapes. The *New York Times* said Guantánamo "remains a grave embarrassment to American justice." "The hunger strike and force-feedings are a sorry chapter in the long-running travesty of justice that festers in Guantánamo." A Navy nurse who refused to participate in force-feeding Dhiab was sent home but was not disciplined. The American Nurses Association wrote Hagel supporting "the ethical right of a professional nurse to make an independent judgment about whether" to participate in force-feeding. (The DoD Health Board later ruled that military healthcare workers could refuse to perform procedures violating professional ethics or religious or moral beliefs.)

In August Judge Kessler ordered an examination by a doctor chosen by Dhiab's lawyer, told the military to explain why it had denied Dhiab a wheelchair to go to his force-feedings, and directed its medical professionals to state whether those feedings were "painful" and if it was "generally safe" to keep the "nasogastric feeding tube in place for three days at a time." She refused to close court hearings on force-feeding and ordered release of the 28 videotapes to 16 news organizations. Two medical experts testified for Dhiab. Dr. Sondra Crosby said civilian hospitals leave a feeding tube in place for several weeks rather than re-inserting it twice a day. The military replied that Dhiab could use the tube to strangle himself or fashion "a whip-like weapon." Dr. Stephen Miles said the military ordered unnecessary feedings and expressed "astonish[ment]" that it used olive oil as a lubricant. Nevertheless, Judge Kessler allowed Dhiab to be force-fed. "There is evidence … that he often tolerates the procedure without complaints of pain or significant discomfort" and "simply no evidence" that the restraint chair was used "to deliberately cause him pain or suffering." But she added: "It is hard for those of us in the continental United States to fully understand [Dhiab's] situation and the atmosphere at Guantánamo Bay. He has been cleared for release since 2009 and one can only hope that that release will take place shortly."

In October she again ordered the government to produce the videotapes. "It strains credulity to conclude that release of these videos has a substantial probability of causing the harm the government predicts." Two months later the government appealed because of "prior experience from the release of certain provocative photographs and information" (presumably the scandal of Abu Ghraib). The *New York Times* observed that Guantánamo had been operating as "a legal black hole" for 13 years. The "graphic" videotapes raise the "larger question" of "why Guantánamo officials continue to make imprisonment as inhumane as possible." "Americans … should be able to decide for themselves how to define, and protect," human dignity. In May 2015 the DC Circuit held it lacked jurisdiction to review. In July, assailing the administration's objections to the release as "the most frivolous I'd ever seen," Kessler ordered it to complete redactions within two months, which it did at the end of August (15 months after the original request). In October she again ordered release of the videos, criticizing the government's supplemental declarations as "repetitive, speculative, and extremely vague."

On May 24, 2014 (before the Bergdahl transfer discussed below) National Security Adviser Rice directed Hagel to "provide an update on progress on detainee transfers every two weeks until further notice" and interpret the NDAA to advance closure.[123] "As is the case with all decisions to return persons detained in an armed conflict, this is not a 'zero risk' standard, and this standard reflects in part the increased harm to national security caused by continued operation of the facility." The requirement that the host country "substantially mitigate" risk meant that "steps have been or will be taken that would materially lessen the risk that detainee, post transfer, will engage or re-engage in any terrorist or other hostile activity that specifically threatens the United States or U.S. persons or interests." Obama told NPR on May 27: "we cannot in good conscience maintain a system of indefinite detention in which individuals who have not been tried and convicted are held permanently in this legal limbo outside of this country." Lisa Monaco, his counterterrorism adviser, said Obama raised the transfers with Hagel "every week." Hagel explained he had developed a system "to look at every element, first of all complying with the law, risks, mitigation of risk. Does it hit the thresholds of the legalities required? Can I ensure compliance with all those requirements? There is a risk in everything." "My name is going on that document" (for the transfers to Uruguay discussed below). "That's a big responsibility ... I am taking my time." Although DoS concluded agreements to repatriate four Afghans and one Mauritanian in March, Hagel did not notify Congress.

In February 2014 the USA revived its proposal to transfer five Taliban members to Qatar, now in exchange for Sgt. Bowe Bergdahl (seized nearly five years earlier).[124] When this transpired at the end of May, Obama said: "the Qatari government has given us assurances that it will put in place measures to protect our national security." The five were strictly banned from incitement or fundraising, and were forbidden to travel for a year. Hagel did not notify Congress in advance because "we needed to get [Bergdahl] out of there essentially to save his life." But the deputy national security adviser apologized to Sens. Feinstein and Chambliss, explaining that the administration feared advance notification would undermine negotiations. An NSC spokesperson said no notice was required "given the credible reports regarding the risk of grave harm to Sergeant Bergdahl and the rapidly unfolding events surround his recovery." A videotape months earlier had shown him weak and dazed, and Qatari middlemen warned he was in imminent danger. Secretary of State Kerry said it would have been "offensive and incomprehensible" to leave Bergdahl in the hands of people who might torture him or "cut off his head."

Rep. McKeon and Sen. Inhofe (on HASC and SASC) said the release "clearly violated laws." McKeon planned to hold HASC hearings, and Rep. Rogers called for them in the House Intelligence Committee, on which he sat. "I have little confidence in the security assurances regarding the movement and activities of the now-released Taliban leaders and I have even less confidence in this administration's willingness to ensure they are enforced." Sen. McCain found it "disturbing that these individuals would have the ability to re-enter the fight." Sen. Graham warned: "it's going to be impossible for them to flow prisoners out of Gitmo now without a huge backlash. There will be people on our side calling for [Obama's] impeachment if he did that."

Obama retorted: "I write too many letters to folks who, unfortunately, don't see their children again after fighting a war. I make absolutely no apologies for making sure we get back a young man to his parents." The *Wall Street Journal* warned that the deal would encourage more hostage-taking, but conceded it did not violate the NDAA. The *Washington Post* said Obama "appears to have sidestepped a law," but "probably the president's lawyers are correct in saying that the Constitution gives Mr. Obama the authority to carry out such exchanges." The *New York Times* noted that McCain had said four months earlier: "I would support ways of bringing [Bergdahl] home, and if exchange was one of them, I think that would be something we should seriously consider." Now he called it "a mistake." The *Times* commented that "Mr. McCain, as he has so often in the past, switched positions for maximum political advantage."

Rep. Nugent (R-Fla) had championed Bergdahl, speaking on the House floor, sponsoring two resolutions, and telling a February rally the USA should "do everything possible not to leave any members of the armed forces behind." Now, however, he said "doing 'everything possible' in my mind does not include breaking the law and jeopardizing national security." Feinstein worried "about [the Taliban] in Doha. And we have no information on how the United States is actually going to" monitor them. Sen. Sessions (R-Ala) said: "it's got to be demoralizing for our allies" and "our soldiers" and would "embolden the people we're fighting against." Sen. Levin replied that when the JCS chair and vice chair tell "me as chairman of the Armed Services Committee … that they very much supported this deal … that has a big impact on me." But Sen. Manchin (D-WV) called it "still a bad deal." (In December HASC's Republican staff issued a report claiming that senior intelligence officials had told Congress the five were likely to "return" to fighting.)

In June the House Appropriations Committee voted 33–13 (six Democrats joining the Republicans) to bar federal money for any transfers. Sen. Cruz had drafted similar legislation. Sen. Sessions said "it's already clear" that the five Taliban were "under the most minimal of control." Two polls found that 43–45 percent disapproved of the release and 34–37 percent approved. House Leader Boehner said it violated "the policy that the United States has had for many, many years, that we don't negotiate with terrorists." Republican Senators introduced a resolution demanding an investigation into whether the trade had damaged national security. But noting that both houses had held hearings, Sen. Feinstein said "enough is enough." Rep. Hoyer (D-Md) called "the 30-day notice requirement … inconsistent with the Constitution." But Rep. Smith (HASC's senior Democrat) said "the law is the law." "If it wasn't right for President Bush" to rely on signing statements, "it's not right for President Obama to do it." In his first testimony before Congress, Hagel defended the exchange as a "military operation." But though he said the five had not been implicated in any attacks on the United States, he admitted they had been involved in "planning" Taliban operations. DoD General Counsel Preston told HASC that the OLC had said by email (not a formal written opinion) that the notice requirement was unconstitutional in the "extraordinary set of circumstances in which the President was seeking to repatriate a service member who was in captivity and in peril."

Rep. Franks (R-Az) said "for the last five years, the American people and terrorists themselves have watched in astonishment and disbelief as this administration has handed back blood-bought gains to our enemies." Rep. Wilson (R-SC) called the release "incredible" because "the terrorists have a goal in mind … death to America, death to Israel." But the *New York Times* noted that "the Republicans were not troubled by … the more than 400 [releases] that occurred during the Bush administration – because they were not then blinded by hatred of the White House occupant." The *Times* criticized the White House for ignoring the 30-day notice requirement, finding the administration's justifications "less than persuasive. But it is disingenuous for Republicans to act as though Mr. Obama is putting the nation at greater risk than his predecessor did." Republican Reps. Blackburn (Tn) and Wolf (Va) introduced a bill to impose criminal penalties on anyone transferring Guantánamo detainees. "Housing terrorists on American soil would put communities at risk and cost hard working taxpayers hundreds of millions of dollars."

Army BGen. Martins, the chief prosecutor, said the five could not have been successfully prosecuted in military commissions.

The House passed (230–184) an NDAA amendment by Rep. Cotton (R-Ark) banning all transfers and defeated (163–249) an amendment by Rep. Moran eliminating transfer barriers. It adopted (239–184) an amendment prohibiting transfers to Yemen and defeated (62–355) an amendment by Rep. Grayson (D-Fl) to ban funds for detentions at Guantánamo lasting more than 15 years. In July the entire JCS supported the Bergdahl exchange. Chairman Dempsey said Obama and Hagel had sought his opinion in advance, and he concluded that "the risk posed by the detainees' future activity would be less grave than breaking our faith with our forces in combat" that "America does not leave its troops behind."

HASC voted 34–25 (two Democrats joining the Republicans) for a nonbinding resolution disapproving the Bergdahl exchange and criticizing the failure to notify Congress. The Government Accountability Office concluded that DoD violated the notification requirement and used funds in violation of the Anti-deficiency Act. The House passed the resolution (22 Democrats joining the Republicans). At the end of January 2015 an official reported that one of the five transferees had engaged in militant activities. In May all House Intelligence Committee Republicans asked Obama to ensure that the five were not allowed to leave Qatar after the expiration of the travel ban.

In March 2014 ODNI reported that only 3 of the 71 men released under Obama were confirmed to have recidivated, with two more suspected to have done so (7 percent); two more were suspected of recidivism in July, raising the rate to 10 percent.[125] Nevertheless, the pace of PRBs and transfers increased in 2014.[126]

Uruguayan President Mujica, a former Tupamaro guerrilla who had been imprisoned for 14 years, offered to accept up to five detainees.[127] After Secretary of State Kerry thanked him and confirmed an invitation to visit the White House, Mujica increased his offer to 6 and then 12. "When the president that we criticize and bash every day for having them locked in decides to reverse the situation, it is our moral obligation to help him." In July Hagel secretly notified Congress of the transfer, which had been stalled by Republican outrage at the Bergdahl deal. The six included Dhiab, mooting his challenge to force-feeding. Praising the action, the *New York Times* called force-feeding "one of the many contemptible aspects of the prison." In May Emad Hassan said he was one of 17 detainees still on hunger strike and being force-fed. In September the military reported 68 on hunger strike, 44 being force-fed.

The government produced the report on Guantánamo required by the NDAA 2013, finding it unlikely that a federal court would release detainees relocated to a US prison.[128] Sen. Leahy said this "lends further support for lifting the Congressional ban on transferring Guantánamo detainees to the United States ... and should end any speculation that doing so would somehow endanger our nation." But HASC chair McKeon "remained concerned we would wind up with terrorists released and taking up residence in the United States." SASC approved the NDAA 2015 with an amendment authorizing transfer to the USA "once the president has submitted a plan to Congress for closing Guantánamo and Congress has had an opportunity to vote to disapprove that plan under expedited procedures." Sen. Levin praised this "path to close Guantánamo." But Sen. Inhofe hoped that "anything that comes" from Obama "can be slow-walked till he's out of office." Sen. Ayotte said the proposal "defies common sense, represents a serious national security risk, and prevents us from collecting the intelligence we need to prevent future terrorist attacks and save American lives." Sen. Graham won a requirement that any plan be subject to a joint resolution of Congress. Rep. Smith's amendment to close Guantánamo failed (177–247), as did Rep. Moran's to allow transfers (169–230). The White House threatened to veto NDAA 2015 if it contained "unwarranted restrictions regarding Guantánamo detainees." A May 2014 public opinion poll found that 54 percent opposed closing Guantánamo and less than 27 percent favored doing so.

In September the *New York Times* deplored that detainees "remain adrift in a limbo of justice denied ... trapped as much by the tooth-and-claw politics of Washington as by the legal dilemmas rooted in bungled government policy." "Congress remains determined to keep the prison open, if only as a symbol of vengeance." "It endures now as a symbol of injustice." The next month HASC chair McKeon wrote Hagel "to express my grave concerns regarding the administration's efforts to continue to transfer Guantánamo detainees despite unprecedented threats to our national security." "Many" DoD notifications of proposed transfers "contain troubling details." "The re-engagement rate of former Guantánamo detainees is ever-increasing and there are public reports that detainees are specifically rejoining the fight alongside ISIL [Islamic State of Iraq and the Levant]" – 20–30 according to *Fox News*. But after learning that ODNI said no more than two of the

22 detainees released since January 2011 had "re-engaged," Fox revised its story to say that "some" had done so. Rep. Westmoreland (R-Ga), a member of the House Intelligence Committee, said "releasing terrorists from Guantánamo Bay endangers our soldiers abroad and our security at home." At the end of November Hagel resigned under pressure, provoked partly by his resistance to transfers. Campaigning for re-election, Sen. Roberts produced a television ad entitled "Pat Roberts promises to keep terrorists out of Kansas." On camera he declaimed "Not. On. My. Watch!" and boasted at Republican state headquarters: "I stopped [Obama] once from trying to send the Gitmo terrorists to Leavenworth … I shall do it again, and if he tries it, I will shut down the Senate." Sen. McCain said "I am prepared to" close Guantánamo "and I think it can be done." "If I went to the members of [SASC] today and said, 'look they are going to be moved to a maximum security prison … and we have a plan for that transfer,' I think most of them would be perfectly happy about that." But he criticized the recent transfers to Uruguay, which were not "trustworthy."

Obama said at the end of 2014: "I'm going to do everything I can to close" Guantánamo, which "continues to inspire jihadists and extremists around the world … is contrary to our values and … is wildly expensive." Signing the NDAA two days earlier, he had warned that "under certain circumstances" it would "violate constitutional separation of powers principles." The same day Cliff Sloan resigned as Guantánamo envoy, declaring he had intended to stay only 18 months and denying he was leaving out of frustration with the pace of transfers. He wrote in a *New York Times* op ed that "the government must continue and accelerate the transfers" and expedite reviews of those not approved. An ally's high-ranking security official had told him that "the greatest single action the United States can take to fight terrorism is to close Guantánamo." Many detainees were "not 'the worst of the worst,' but rather people with the worst luck." The alleged 30 percent recidivism rate was "deeply flawed." Less than 7 percent of those released by the Obama administration were confirmed recidivists. JCS chairman Dempsey also called Guantánamo a "psychological scar." Paul Lewis, DoD special envoy for Guantánamo, said the USA was talking with countries to accept all 64 detainees approved for transfer. Obama "does not want to leave this to his successor." But McCain just repeated the discredited recidivism figure: "I don't want to see a situation [where] 30 percent of those released re-entered the fight." And Sen. Graham dismissed the cost of Guantánamo: "whatever money we spend to keep a terrorist off the battlefield is money well spent."

Republican Senators responded to the January 2015 attacks on staff of the French satirical newspaper *Charlie Hebdo* by demanding that Guantánamo remain open.[129] Introducing legislation to bar transfers of high- or medium-risk suspects for two years and to permanently ban any transfers to Yemen or countries with a confirmed recidivist, Sen. Ayotte said: "now is not the time to be emptying Guantánamo." SASC chair Burr claimed that "anybody at Guantánamo is a legitimate source to go to" for intelligence. Graham said detainees should not be released "to plan another 9/11." McCain, Ayotte, and Graham called on the administration to "provide the unclassified details ... for the 32 detainees whom the administration has transferred since May." The *New York Times* condemned Ayotte for "opportunistically" invoking the Paris massacre and not acknowledging that the recidivism rate declined from 33 percent under Bush to 6 percent under Obama. Siding with Ayotte "represented a striking turnaround" for McCain, "a former POW who has championed closing the prison." Graham's view that we were "just starting" a "war without end" was a "travesty." Obama told Congress that Guantánamo was "not who we are." "As Americans, we have a profound commitment to justice – so it makes no sense to spend $3 million per prisoner to keep open a prison that the world condemns and terrorists use to recruit ... now it's time to finish the job. And I will not relent in my determination to shut it down."

At a SASC hearing in February, Sen. Cotton (R-Ark) said:

> In my opinion the only problem with Guantánamo Bay is there are too many empty beds and cells there right now. We should be sending more terrorists there for further interrogation to keep this country safe. As far as I'm concerned every last one of them can rot in Hell, but as long as they don't do that they can rot in Guantánamo Bay.

He added later: "We should be proud of the way we treated these savages at Guantánamo Bay ... There's not one there who is not a hardened terrorist." Sen. Ayotte claimed that "one of the Taliban commanders on the ground in Helmand Province" said the transfer to Qatar of the former Taliban Deputy Defense Minister was "the best news he had heard in 12 years." It was "like pouring 10,000 Taliban fighters into the battle on the side of the jihad. Now the Taliban have the right lion to lead them in the final moment before victory in Afghanistan." But

Brian McKeon, Principal Deputy Undersecretary of Defense for Policy, denied that any of the five had "returned to battlefield." A week later Ayotte reiterated her claim that Abdul Rauf (another ex-detainee) "was acting as a recruiter for IS [Islamic State] in Afghanistan." SASC voted 14–12 for a bill sponsored by Ayotte, McCain, Graham, and Burr to block all transfers. Graham said it was "common sense" that detainees should remain there. "If you're still in Guantánamo Bay after all these years, you're probably a high risk." Obama threatened a veto. Campaigning for the Republican presidential nomination, Sen. Rubio (R-Fla) promised to reopen Guantánamo if Obama closed it.

In April 2015 DoD said it planned to transfer up to ten detainees in June and hoped all 57 approved for transfer would be resettled by the end of 2015.[130] HASC chair Thornberry's draft NDAA would prohibit closing Guantánamo and reinstate the previous certification requirement for transfers, forbidding them to the United States or any "combat zone" or country with a confirmed instance of recidivism. The House rejected Rep. Smith's bill to close Guantánamo. An amendment by Rep. Nadler (D-NY) to ease transfers lost (170–256). As passed by the Senate (71–25), NDAA required DoD to certify that recipient countries would ensure that former detainees "cannot engage or reengage in any terrorist activity," but allowed transfers to the USA for trial or detention after Congress approved an administration plan to close Guantánamo. McCain said Carter had promised such a plan. White House Press Secretary Earnest confirmed that "the administration is in fact in the final stages of drafting a plan." But noting that Greg Craig had made a similar promise in 2009, McCain said: "I have not been holding my breath." The White House had delayed the plan for fear of jeopardizing the vote on the nuclear arms deal with Iran. National Security Adviser Rice sent Carter an unsigned NSC memo giving him 30 days to decide on proposed transfers, but Carter did not commit to doing so. Counterterrorism adviser Monaco said: "we are going to whittle down this group to what I refer to as the irreducible minimum [of 64], who would have to be brought here to a secure location, held under the laws of war." The *New York Times* said Obama could accelerate release of the 52 already cleared by instructing the DoJ not to oppose the 10 active habeas petitions, and it warned that the House bill "would make it practically impossible to release new inmates to any destination."

The government was still exploring the Charleston Naval Brig and the Thomson Correctional facility as potential alternatives to Guantánamo. Sen. Scott (R-SC) found it "unbelievable" that the administration would consider the Brig, which was "right next to an elementary school and a residential neighborhood, as well as just a short drive from one of the biggest tourist destinations in the world." South Carolina's Sen. Graham also was opposed, and its governor, Nikki Haley, vowed to "do whatever it takes" to stop the plan. When the government revived the possibility of using Leavenworth, Gov. Brownback said: "the citizens of Kansas do not support moving terrorists to the heartland of America." Sen. Gardner and Rep. Tipton (both Colorado Republicans) were "absolutely" opposed to "any plan to bring terrorists to Colorado." When the administration sent officials to inspect Colorado prisons, Rep. Lamborn (R-Co) said "the people of Colorado do not want the world's worst terrorists in our own backyard" (ignoring those already in the Florence ADMAX). Rep. Peters (D-Ca) opposed transfer to Miramar. Sen. Kaine (D-Va) had not been briefed on the Naval Brig in Chesapeake.

The *New York Times* wrote in September that Guantánamo "has sat festering on the edge of the Caribbean and the Constitution … [has] had a powerful radicalizing effect, has severely tarnished America's standing as a nation of laws and has cost taxpayers more than $5.2 billion." It blamed Congress, but "in the end … the buck stops with the president." Yemenis could be sent to other countries. Criticizing the sluggish pace of certifications by Hagel and Carter, the *Times* said Obama "must insist that Mr. Carter move faster." "The government should prosecute or release the rest."

The conference committee draft NDAA prohibited the use of any funds to transfer or release detainees, construct or modify prisons in the USA, or close Guantánamo. It also banned transfers to Yemen, Somalia, Syria, and Libya, and required the administration to send Congress a plan to replace Guantánamo, including "specific facilities … that are intended to be used."[131] The White House again threated to veto the bill for using a supplemental war fund to avoid the Budget Control Act. In October the Senate passed it by a veto-proof 73–26 and the House by 227–156 (20 votes short of a veto override).

On October 22 Obama exercised his fifth veto because the bill "falls woefully short in three areas": respecting the sequester, preventing a wide range of reforms, and "specifically imped[ing] our ability to close Guantánamo in a way that I have repeatedly argued is counterproductive to our efforts to defeat terrorism around the world." Declaring it "well worth fighting" the battle "to put an end to an era of fiscal mismanagement," the *New York Times* also criticized "the unreasonable provisions that have stymied the administration's plan to shut down" Guantánamo. Sens. Ayotte, Capito (R-WV), and Scott declared Guantánamo the best place to hold detainees. Sen. Feinstein wrote in a *New York Times* op ed that it had "cost us billions of dollars and is a real threat to our security." Bush had released 532 of the 779 men he sent there. Whereas the few military commission convictions had resulted in light sentences, or were overturned, or were on appeal, 90 percent of the 580 civilian terrorism prosecutions led to convictions. The AI USA executive director wrote the *Times* that Feinstein's suggested transfer of the remaining detainees to the USA was "appalling." "The purpose of closing Guantánamo should be to end the human rights violation of indefinite detention without charge – not merely move it to a new location and change Guantánamo's zip code." Sen. Roberts put a hold on Obama's Secretary of the Army nomination to prevent any executive action to close Guantánamo. Sen. McCain complained again: "it's just unbelievable to me that all I'm asking for is a plan I can try and sell my colleagues. And they refuse to send one, and then they complain about the fact that we're not closing Guantánamo? It's hypocrisy."

The House passed a revised NDAA by a veto-proof 370–58 (bowing to Obama's budgetary objections but preserving the Guantánamo restrictions). CCR lawyer Shayana Kadidal wrote the *New York Times* that Obama "could instruct the DoJ to concede that release is appropriate in habeas corpus cases brought by the 53 detainees who are already cleared for transfer" and (as Hillary Clinton had suggested) "negotiat[e] guilty pleas with some of the remaining detainees in federal court[s]," which could "rule that the existing transfer restrictions were not intended by Congress to apply in such cases." White House Press Secretary Earnest warned: "we would like to work with Congress where we can, but if Congress continues to refuse, I wouldn't rule out the president using every element of his authority to make progress." Sen. Roberts expostulated: "why do we even have a Congress if the president can issue an executive order on anything?" McCain declared that Obama "lies when he says that he really wants to close Guantánamo with the cooperation of Congress, because he's never sent over a plan." Calling the White House threat "disgraceful," he retorted that if Obama "tr[ied] to do it by executive order ... you're going to see attempts by Congress to reverse that, including [through] funding mechanisms." House Homeland Security Committee chairman McCaul (R-Tex) said on *Fox News* that if Obama resorted to executive action, "I would hope the American people would rise up in numbers so strongly" he would back down.

Responding to rumors that DoD was considering the empty Centennial Correctional Facility, Sen. Gardner said "I will not sit idly by while the president uses political promises to imperil the people of Colorado by moving enemy combatants from Cuba, Guantánamo Bay, to my state of Colorado." "The pressure this would put on our judicial system in Colorado is real. The challenges that could be brought through the legal system we're not prepared for. I think that's another question on our federal judiciary in Denver ... Would they be transported to downtown Denver to the federal courthouse for a hearing?"

Concerned that the administration was still considering Leavenworth, Reps. Pompeo and Jenkins (both R-Kan) wrote Carter assailing Obama's "misguided policy." "We believe that state legislators, county commissioners, mayors and other local officials have the right to completely understand what their communities will face." The same day Sens. Gardner, Scott, and Roberts attacked the alleged plan. Gardner said Obama was "ignoring the plain letter of the law" and Hillary Clinton was "complicit." The Republican National Committee (RNC) was planning ads in Colorado, Kansas, the Carolinas, Iowa, Missouri, and Georgia linking Clinton to the alleged plan because a 2013 *Newsweek* story said she had "urged the president to shut down the prison unilaterally using 'national security waivers.'" Threatening to deploy "every weapon in our arsenal," Scott had identified "areas where we can place additional holds as well, including promotions."

After the Senate passed the revised NDAA 91–3, Josh Earnest said it had no "material impact on our ability to put together and send to Congress a thoughtful, carefully considered plan for closing the prison at Guantánamo Bay." Sen. Ayotte warned that any executive action "clearly would violate the law." Sen. McConnell said "the American people need to send a message by sending a new president a little over a year from now with a different view of what ought to be done ... it is very, very difficult to think of anything this administration hasn't screwed up whether at home or abroad." Rep. Ryan (R-Wisc) said the "language is very clear that he can't transfer the prisoners, and this is language that was put in the defense bill when [the Democrats] ran Congress ... The law is the law." But Sen. Durbin noted that Obama:

> time and again, has said that he wants to do everything in his power to close Guantánamo before he leaves. The Republicans in Congress

> continue to do everything in their power to stop it. I think there reaches a point where Congress is just being stubborn … and he has to make the decision in the best interests of the country, and I think closing Guantánamo is one of them …
>
> If the president [who is] a constitutional scholar … can find a constitutional path to that conclusion, I hope he can serve our country by closing Guantánamo once and for all.

Noting that the Bush administration "set it up by executive action," Sen. Feinstein said: "what you can build, you can take apart, too."

A variety of sources supported closure.[132] Gregory Craig and Clifford Sloan wrote in a *Washington Post* op ed that Article II gave Obama exclusive authority "to determine the facilities in which military detainees are held," rendering Congressional restrictions on closing Guantánamo "plainly unconstitutional." Retired Supreme Court Justice John Paul Stevens told Lawyers for Civil Justice that Congressional efforts to block transfers were "even more irrational" than the internment of Japanese Americans during World War II. Sens. Leahy, Feinstein, and Durbin urged Obama to transfer those already cleared and accelerate the PRBs, which at the current rate would not review all detainees until 2020. But Sens. Grassley (R-Ia), Graham, and Ayotte questioned DNI Clapper about recidivism, and the House Foreign Affairs Committee warned Secretary of State Kerry that the unrestrained ex-detainees in Uruguay posed a threat. After the November terrorist attack in Paris, Grassley said Obama's determination to close Guantánamo "was always based on the notion that softening America's image abroad would somehow soften our enemies' resolve. The headlines every day remind us that that's not the way it is." Sen. Inhofe agreed: "the propaganda war will simply shift to whatever facility these terrorists are brought to in the United States."

Th UK had first sought the release of Shaker Aamer in 2007; Obama's Task Force recommended it in 2009; and he had been a highly visible participant in the 2013 hunger strike.[133] After Prime Minister Cameron asked about him in January 2015, the White House promised to "prioritize" the transfer. In March, the British Parliament voted unanimously to demand his return. In May, four British Members of Parliament (two from each major party, including Jeremy Corbyn, who was elected leader of the Labour Party several months later) flew to Washington to meet Paul Lewis and Charles Trumbull (DoD and acting DoS envoys for Guantánamo) and Sens. McCain, Durbin, Feinstein, Leahy, and Manchin. The delegation wrote in a *New York Times* op ed that they "agree on almost nothing" except that Aamer "must be freed." They had been "astonished" by the "degree of incomprehension among the Senators we met from both parties." Lewis and Trumbull "were unable to adequately answer our questions." "If the president has any intention of closing Guantánamo, it will not be accomplished by complaining about Congress, whose members seem to have not been given even basic information about the detainees … or about the special case of Mr. Aamer." All this was "a slap in the face for America's staunchest friend." More than ninety prominent British figures wrote Obama requesting Aamer's return. Cameron again raised his release with Obama at the G7 summit in June. When DoD said at the end of September that he would be transferred, Rep. Thornberry expressed "grave concerns" because he did "not believe that the British government has the ability to hold or try him." Aamer returned to the UK on October 30. After the San Bernardino killings in December, he denounced extremists but also described in detail his abuse in Guantánamo. In February 2016 Sen. Cotton claimed that JCS chairman Dempsey had opposed the transfer because Aamer was "a dangerous man who seeks to harm the United States."

The ODNI report for the first six months of 2015 said 6 of the 121 detainees released by Obama had been confirmed as engaging in terrorism and 6 were suspected of doing so (5 percent each, compared with 21 and 14 percent of those released by Bush).[134]

Lawyers urged the DDC to order the release of Tariq ba Odah (approved in 2010), whom a hunger strike (since 2007) had reduced to 74 pounds, pushing him to the "precipice of death."[135] DoJ responded that the Guantánamo senior medical officer found Odah's condition was "dangerous" but "clinically stable." Although US District Judge Hogan had "no question that we have a seriously ill petitioner" and was "distressed at the failure of Congress and the executive to effectively provide the legislation" for judicial review of such cases (as the Supreme Court had directed in *Boumediene*), he told Odah's lawyers to seek DoD review first. When a country interested in accepting Odah sought his medical records, DoD balked for six weeks on grounds of patient privacy, forcing the delegation to cancel its visit. DoS officials seeking to negotiate transfers said DoD often obstructed their efforts, engaging in what the *New York Times* denounced as "insubordination." (Odah was finally sent to Saudi Arabia in April 2016, with eight other Yemenis.)

While welcoming the news of PRB clearances, the *New York Times* said: "there is no excuse for how slowly the DoD has moved to free dozens of men a panel of national security officials cleared for release years ago."[136] Although the White House promised in July to produce a closure plan, it "disappointingly" had not done so by October. That month a DoD team examined the three federal prisons in Florence, Colorado, and the 948-cell penitentiary in Canon City, which cost the state $20 million a year to keep empty. Florence officials and residents opposed Guantánamo detainees being transferred there. In November Josh Earnest again promised the Guantánamo plan "relatively soon," but DoD said there was "nothing imminent" because it was still costing different ideas. (It was later reported that Obama had rejected DoD's $600 million plan as too expensive.) McCain demanded a plan, warning that "this is all about" an excuse to use executive authority. But Attorney General Lynch assured the House Judiciary Committee (HJC) that "the current state of the law is that individuals are not transferred from Guantánamo to U.S. shores." The Attorneys General of Colorado, Kansas, and South Carolina wrote Obama, invoking the Paris attacks and declaring that using executive power to send detainees to those states would be "dangerous and illegal." Obama renewed his pledge to close Guantánamo, criticizing the "very strong tendency for us to get worked up around issues that don't actually make us safer, but make for good political soundbites." The *Washington Post* agreed with those who said Obama "should not and ... cannot close the prison unilaterally." In late November DoJ admitted in response to a question by US District Judge Lamberth that it would take "several more years" to review the remaining 107 detainees, and only 19 PRBs were scheduled. Since beginning in late 2013 they had completed just 18 cases and had 46 pending. Lamberth expressed exasperation: "obviously if the president cared, he could get this done in a year." Defense lawyers wrote Obama that their clients would consider pleading guilty in civilian court. In December a coalition of Kansas local, state, and federal officials wrote Obama opposing moving detainees to Leavenworth.

At the end of November Obama signed the NDAA 2016 – which preserved the ban on constructing prisons in the USA or transferring detainees there, and limited or barred other transfers – while noting that "under certain circumstances" the transfer restrictions might be unconstitutional.[137]

> Maintaining this site, year after year, is not consistent with our interests as a Nation and undermines our standing in the world. The continued operation of this facility weakens our national security by draining

> resources, damaging our relations with key allies and partners, and emboldening violent extremists. It is imperative that we take responsible steps to reduce the population at this facility to the greatest extent possible and close the facility.

On Guantánamo's fourteenth anniversary demonstrators at the US Embassy in London included the Labour shadow chancellor.[138] White House Chief of Staff McDonough said Obama would give Congress a closure plan. Sens. Ayotte and Graham called for a bar on further transfers and a Congressional investigation of all those under Obama. More than two years after the PRBs were established, they had heard only 24 cases, clearing 15 men for transfer (only six of whom had been resettled) and recommending 6 for continued detention; 3 decisions were pending, and 4 detainees were waiting for hearings. Senate Majority Leader McConnell said: "I'm a supporter of Gitmo. I think it ought to stay open. I think we ought to add more terrorists to it and we ought to interrogate them there." Donald Trump recently had said: "I would leave it just the way it is, and I would probably fill it up with more people that are looking to kill us." Marco Rubio agreed: "foreign terrorists caught overseas will receive a one-way ticket to Guantánamo." In his 2016 State of the Union message Obama said that Guantánamo "is expensive, it is unnecessary, and it only serves as a recruitment brochure for our enemies." Sen. Ayotte said: "any Obama administration decision to transfer a large number of Yemeni detainees from Guantánamo to Oman would represent a thinly veiled attempt to undercut the will of Congress and would further endanger the American people." But DoD transferred 10 Yemenis to Oman, reducing the population to 93.

Days later Defense Secretary Carter briefed Congress about the administration plan.[139] Rep. Jenkins (R-Kan) asked for details, and the Congressional Budget Office sought cost figures. After DoD transferred four detainees to Ghana, four members of the Senate Appropriations Committee threatened to cut the Pentagon's budget by $10 million for each one who escaped. HASC chairman Thornberry wrote Obama that the NDAA required the administration to send Congress by February 23 a "comprehensive strategy" for closing Guantánamo. Republicans retained lawyers to prepare a lawsuit to block transfers to the USA. The JCS wrote Rep. Pompeo that it would not violate the law by doing so.

Condemning Republicans' "reflexive and thoughtless" opposition, the *New York Times* said Obama could close the prison by the end of 2016.[140] Ten detainees might plead in federal court; others could be sent to other countries for prosecution, and PRBs might certify others for transfer. Reducing the population to "a very small number" would make it "increasingly hard to justify" the "cost of running the overseas prison": "an astounding $445 million" in FY2015.

Gordon England (Bush's Deputy Secretary of Defense 2006–09) wrote in a *Washington Post* op ed that recent releases were "endangering American lives as well as those of our friends and allies."[141] Acknowledging that he had "approved the transfer of too many higher-risk detainees who went on to kill again," he maintained that none of those remaining at the end of the Bush administration "would have been approved for release." Rubio elicited applause during a February RNC debate by declaring: "we should be putting people into Guantánamo, not emptying it out, and we shouldn't be releasing these killers who are rejoining the battlefield against the United States."

Obama finally sent Congress an eight-page plan on the February 23 deadline.[142] The 35 detainees already approved would be transferred; PRBs would be accelerated. Because civilian prosecutions were always "the preferred option," the administration was considering legislation to let detainees plead guilty in federal court. The 46 detainees not eligible for transfer or recommended for prosecution would be held in one of 13 US facilities, achieving a net saving of at least $335 million over 10 years and up to $1.7 billion over 20.

> [T]he detention facility at Guantánamo Bay does not advance our national security … It's counterproductive to our fight against terrorists, because they use it as propaganda … It drains military resources … harms our partnership with allies and other countries … is contrary to our values … undermines our standing in the world … [and] is viewed as a stain on our broader record of upholding the highest standards of rule of law.

Rubio predictably grandstanded: "Not only are we not going to close Guantánamo, when I am president, if we capture a terrorist alive, they are not getting a court hearing in Manhattan. They are not going to be sent to Nevada. They are going to Guantánamo, and we are going to find out everything they know."

House Speaker Ryan reiterated that "these detainees cannot come to American soil" because "the law is really clear." Attorney General Lynch and Defense Secretary Carter agreed. McCain dismissed the plan as "a Chinese menu. One from column a, one from column b, and 13 different sites." There was no proposal for detaining or interrogating future captures. Sen. Roberts released a video of himself crumpling up the plan and throwing it in the trash. Sen. Graham said he would hold a hearing on the "gibberish" plan. Sens. Graham, Ayotte, and McCain expected to join a House lawsuit to block transfers to the USA. Trump pledged to "keep Guantánamo open. We're going to fill it with bad dudes."

Although most Democrats supported the plan, some facing contested elections did not. And many human rights groups had reservations. However, 19 retired generals and admirals again backed closure. Rep. Thornberry said the 2017 NDAA should ban a handover of Guantánamo to Cuba (although Defense Secretary Carter had promised that would not happen). Rep. Walorski (R-In) accused Obama of underestimating recidivism. The latest poll found that 56 percent of Americans favored keeping Guantánamo open and only 40 percent wanted it closed, similar to the percentages in August 2015 (53/44) and March 2015 (60/39). The latest ODNI report found that 7 of Obama's 144 transfers were known to have engaged in militancy and 12 were suspected of doing so (5 and 8 percent), compared with 111 and 74 of Bush's 532 transfers (21 and 14 percent). Sen. Ayotte said this confirmed that "the Obama administration's misguided effort to empty and then close Guantánamo is putting terrorists back on the battlefield and making Americans less safe." Republican senators introduced a resolution rejecting the plan and another urging DoD to send captured ISIS (Islamic State of Iraq and Syria) fighters to Guantánamo. Paul Lewis (DoD envoy for detainees) told the House Foreign Affairs Committee that "unfortunately, there have been Americans that have died because of Gitmo detainees." But a week later an aide to Lee Wolosky (DoS envoy for detainees) said: "nobody transferred under this administration has been assessed to have killed any Americans. It's not by luck that we have a lower recidivism rate – it is due to the process we put in place." Nevertheless, Sen. Scott said this was a "clear admission" that closing Guantánamo would hurt national security. (It later emerged that 9 of the 12–15 detainees suspected of attacking Americans were dead or in custody.) DoD predicted that all detainees would receive a PRB hearing by December 20, but decisions could take months.

Sen. Ayotte introduced a bill (cosponsored by eight other Republicans) to prohibit the closure of Guantánamo, entrench the ban on transfers to the USA, and halt all transfers until October 2017.[143] Sen. Kirk (R-Ill) introduced another (with five cosponsors) to prohibit transfers to countries that were unstable or sponsored terrorism. Both expected difficult re-election campaigns. Sen. Johnson (R-Wisc), also facing a challenge, declared that Guantánamo detainees were the "worst of the worst" and should be "locked up forever." He introduced a bill to require the government to publicize transfers two weeks in advance. The websites of Sens. Toomey (R-Pa) and Portman (R-Oh) (also politically threatened) had petitions opposing closure. Sen. Gardner proposed an amendment closing US airspace to detainee flights. Criticizing the recent transfer of Libyans to Senegal, Sen. McConnell called this "precisely the wrong time to send experienced, hardened fighters back into the conflict." Rep. Jenkins introduced Ayotte's bill in the House because "reports indicate a terrifying number of released prisoners returning to the battlefield." Sen. Moran (R-Kan) sponsored a bill with five other Republicans requiring the Defense Secretary to certify before transfer that a detainee "no longer poses a continuing threat to the security of the United States" because "the current process is entirely subjective." Ayotte denounced the transfer of nine Yemenis to Saudi Arabia.

DoD accelerated PRBs from 2 to 3 a month to 2 a week, scheduling or conducting 21 in 2016 (and planning 2 more), almost twice the 12 completed in 2015. Sen. Roberts lifted his hold on Obama's Secretary of the Army nomination when the deputy defense secretary assured him that "the clock has run out" on transfers to Leavenworth. Although SASC drafted an NDAA amendment letting detainees plead in civilian court (and serve their sentences abroad), DoJ concluded that federal court rules barred defendants from pleading guilty to a felony without being physically present, and the administration feared that judges would not view detainees' pleas as voluntary. Sens. Kirk and Lankford (R-Ok) submitted an NDAA amendment to reduce aid to countries that "lose control" of transferred detainees. Sen. Moran (backed by five others) sought to remove any funding to plan and design alternatives to Guantánamo. Nine Republicans sponsored an amendment urging that ISIS detainees be sent to Guantánamo. After the Senate passed the NDAA 85–13, Obama threatened a veto. When the House passed a version banning all transfers, the White House repeated the threat. The *New York Times* called the failure to close Guantánamo "a shameful stain on Congress." Republicans continued to fan fears of recidivism. Airat Vakhitov, a Russian ex-detainee, was arrested in connection with the terrorist attack on the Istanbul airport. House Foreign Affairs Committee chair Royce called for a halt in transfers after Jihad Dhiab left Uruguay for Brazil; he later surfaced in Venezuela, declaring he wanted to travel to Turkey to see his family, and then took an abortive flight to South Africa, which refused to admit him. In mid-August the administration transferred 15 detainees to the UAE. In October PRBs approved the release of one detainee and the indefinite detention of five others; over the next two months they approved the release of two detainees and the indefinite detention of another.[144] The administration transferred one detainee to Cape Verde, four to Saudi Arabia, ten to Oman, and four to UAE.[145]

A week after his election, Trump declared that "I want to make sure, 100 percent sure, that if we're going to release people ... it's going to be safe to release them."[146] The next day Obama blamed his own failure to close the prison on "Congressional restrictions," but conceded that Trump "disagrees with me." Trump showed this by nominating as Homeland Security Secretary Marine Gen. John Kelly, who, as SOUTHCOM commander, had ordered the prison to stop disclosing the number of detainees on hunger strike and later declared it contained "no innocent men."

At the end of the Obama administration, the *Washington Post* said the failure to close Guantanamo "has something to do with Mr. Obama's reluctance to press his legal authority and something to do with the sluggishness of his appointees at the Pentagon; but it's mostly the result of obstructionism by Congress." After Trump tweeted that the remaining detainees were "extremely dangerous people and should not be allowed back onto the battlefield," the *New York Times* reiterated that "holding these prisoners at Guantanamo forever is untenable for a nation that claims to adhere to the rule of law." Ed Royce (R-Ca) said that the House Foreign Affairs Committee, which he chaired, had a "troubling new report" from intelligence that released detainees intended to rejoin the fight. *The Economist* called Guantánamo "one of Mr. Obama's most painful failures, putting an enduring stain on America's human-rights record." On his final day, Obama wrote the Speaker of the House and President Pro Tem of the Senate that Guantánamo "should never have been opened in the first place," and reiterated that Congressional restrictions on its closing "make no sense." At Guantánamo, 41 men remained: 3 were convicted and 7 were awaiting trial by military commission, five were cleared for transfer, and 26 were "forever prisoners."

Days after Trump's inauguration the White House drafted an executive order revoking Obama's orders to close Guantánamo, end secret prisons, and allow the ICRC access to all prisoners. Eleven Republican senators urged Trump to send more detainees there and eliminate the

PRBs (which had certified 37 detainees for transfer and 26 for continued detention). Trump's DNI nominee Dan Coats declared that "a significant number" of released detainees "have rejoined the fight." Trump tweeted his agreement: "122 vicious prisoners released by the Obama administration from Gitmo, have returned to the battlefield. Just another terrible decision." (ODNI said about half of the 121 "confirmed" to have engaged in terrorism were dead or back in custody. White House Press Secretary Sean Spicer acknowledged that Trump's numbers were wrong.) Attorney General Sessions said Guantánamo was the "perfect place" for detainees and had "plenty of space."

CONCLUSION

The Bush administration chose Guantánamo for its secrecy and inaccessibility, and because the OLC memos promised that noncitizen detainees in a prison outside US sovereignty would be unprotected by the Constitution and beyond the reach of federal courts. Consequently, those seeking to improve conditions of confinement, release prisoners, and close the base had to resort to other strategies. Exposure was an obvious first step, motivated by hope it would shame the administration into making changes. Freed detainees described abusive treatment; but the military retorted that they had been trained to lie by al-Qaeda (even though al-Qahtani's horrific interrogation was documented by the military itself). AI's condemnation of Guantánamo as "the gulag of our time" grabbed media attention, but was quickly dismissed as hyperbole; and Sen. Durbin was forced to apologize for analogizing the prison to those operated by the Nazis and the Khmer Rouge. The FBI, enlisted to assist interrogation (for which it had the most expertise), reported abuses up the chain of command (though much remained secret) and through the Schmidt–Furlow report; but only a few low-level interrogators were lightly disciplined, and the military repeatedly claimed to be exonerated by its numerous other investigations. The ICRC, as always, reported only to the USA, although it did take the unusual step of declaring "a discrepancy between the position of the United States and the ICRC." The one account with significant consequences was *Newsweek*'s *false* report of Koran desecration, which tragically led to mass demonstrations and numerous deaths and injuries throughout the Muslim world.

The Bush administration resolutely obstructed other modes of disclosure. It retaliated against whistle-blowers like Matthew Diaz, James

Yee, and the Afghan American interpreter and expelled investigative journalists. Forced by the Supreme Court to allow lawyers access, the administration created numerous obstacles: restricting the number and length of visits, undermining clients' confidence in their lawyers, seizing confidential lawyer–client communications and observing their interactions, harassing both clients and lawyers, and classifying much of what clients told lawyers.[147]

And the administration engaged in strenuous public relations campaigns, organizing Potemkin village tours, which convinced members of Congress (including some Democratic critics) that detainees (to whom they never spoke) enjoyed better conditions than they would in US prisons and received better medical care and food than they would at home (both low hurdles). But even the limited information available provoked criticism. Protesters demonstrated in major American and European cities, especially on the anniversaries of the prison's opening. UN organs, political leaders in allied countries, Nobel prizewinners, and of course human rights NGOs issued reports and sought closure. The only visible effect, however, was release of detainees to valued allies like the UK, France, Australia, and Saudi Arabia.

The detainees themselves, totally isolated except for their lawyers (who could achieve little), exploited their only resource – their bodies – by engaging in hunger strikes and attempting or committing suicide, seeking to transform vulnerability into strength. They resorted to these desperate measures to reclaim agency, express anger at abuses (especially rumors of Koran desecration) and despair at ever being released, mobilize external support, and shame the USA. There is a long history of such passive resistance, including Gandhi's hunger strikes for Indian independence, Martin Luther King Jr.'s nonviolent methods during the civil rights movement, hunger strikes by indefinite detainees during South Africa's Emergency, and IRA members' dirty protest in Belfast's Maze Prison. But some of those had significant advantages: widespread publicity and governments susceptible to moral suasion. Guantánamo detainees were dependent for publicity on the military (which systematically underestimated the number of hunger strikers and then stopped reporting them altogether) and their lawyers (whom the military accused of instigating the strikes and barred from visiting). Ironically, less moral outrage was provoked by the detainees' actions than by the military's harsh response. Perhaps fearing the anger and sympathy elicited by Bobby Sands's death in the Maze Prison, the

USA defied medical ethics and force-fed hunger strikers, keeping them alive (if barely). But the excessively harsh method – painfully inserting and removing metal-tipped feeding tubes twice a day into detainees shackled in restraint chairs, which made them soil themselves – aroused widespread condemnation from medical professionals, Democratic legislators, and federal judges. (In September 2017 detainees on hunger strike reported that they were no longer being force-fed unless in imminent danger of death.[148]) Repression also strengthened the resolve of strikers and solidarity among detainees. And though some suicides attracted little media attention, the administration's callous dismissal of the three June 2006 deaths produced a firestorm of criticism. (Several investigators argued that the detainees had died during harsh interrogation, but this story never secured widespread traction.) Although it is impossible to prove causation, it may be significant that transfers increased from 48 in the first six months of 2006 to 80 in the second (following the suicides); and though no one was transferred in the first half of 2013, 11 were transferred in the second half (when the hunger strike began) and 28 the next year.[149]

Two other institutions promised relief that proved to be illusory. The Bush administration responded to the Supreme Court's June 2004 *Rasul* decision by creating the fatally flawed CSRTs. These denied detainees legal representation and barred lay representatives from seeing the classified evidence on which decisions often were based. CSRTs heard *no* witnesses, outrageously claiming that not a single one was available. They relied on allegations by a few deeply untrustworthy, thoroughly discredited prisoners who curried favor by concocting patently false stories about dozens of detainees (most of whom they had never met). CSRTs based decisions on absurd evidence, like possessing a Casio watch worn by millions of others. The military directed CSRTs to find that detainees were ECs and ordered rehearings when the tribunals failed to do so. Judge Green offered a scathing critique of Murat Kurnaz's clearly erroneous CSRT. Even in the conservative DC Circuit, one panel declared it was unable to review a CSRT finding because the record was insufficient and another overruled a CSRT finding based on inadequate evidence. The Supreme Court held in *Boumediene* that CSRTs were an inadequate substitute for the habeas corpus hearings to which detainees were entitled. Perhaps most damning is the fact that, although 465 of the first 487 CSRTs found detainees to be ECs (95 percent), subsequent reviews by ARBs, the Obama Task Force, and PRBs determined that almost all of them should be released (approximately 95 percent of the nearly 800 ever detained). Indeed, even the Bush administration ignored the findings of the CSRTs it had created, releasing or transferring more than 500. It seems unlikely that the hardships of a decade or more in Guantánamo had rendered all these "terrorists" harmless.

If the CSRTs were discredited as a pliant tool of the military, the DDC exhibited the independence we expect of the judiciary; but judges found themselves largely powerless to offer redress. Judges Robertson and Urbina expressed deep sympathy for the Uighurs and profound frustration at being unable to transfer them to the USA (which might have helped convince other countries it was safe to accept detainees). The MCA stripped federal courts of jurisdiction over condition of confinement complaints. Judge Kessler could only order release of videotapes of forced feeding, but declined to enjoin the practice and was unable to free Dhiab, who had brought the action.

Although few of the strategies described above demonstrably improved detainees' conditions or extricated them from Guantánamo, they may have contributed to the growing consensus for closure. Bush had embraced this by 2006, and Rumsfeld reluctantly followed suit; Gates, who replaced him, agreed more enthusiastically, as did JCS chair Mullen. Bush's mother and wife concurred. Cheney gradually lost influence (though he continued to champion Guantánamo well into Obama's administration). In 2007 the new Democratic Congress called for closure. Both Democratic presidential aspirants (Obama and Clinton) and their Republican opponent (McCain) endorsed closure. And the pace of transfers dramatically increased from an annual average of 84 in 2003–05 to 128 in 2006 and 122 in 2007. But it fell to 30 in the 2008 election year, perhaps because Republicans feared a Willie Horton incident[150] if a former detainee committed a terrorist attack.

If the question until 2009 was how critics of Guantánamo fought the Bush administration, which created it, the question afterwards was why Obama failed to close the prison, especially during his first two years, when Democrats controlled both Houses of Congress. He reiterated his opposition to Guantánamo soon after being elected and, on his second day in office, dramatically issued an executive order that it be closed in a year. Although he and his officials repeated that promise over the next few months, he never fulfilled it. His Task Force missed its first deadline: screening all detainees in six months. Instead of closing the prison by the executive order's target date, the Task Force offered a plan very similar to what the administration finally presented to Congress six years later: prosecuting some, transferring others, and indefinitely detaining several dozen at an unspecified location. And though the 50 and 26 transfers in Obama's first two years were comparable to the 30 in Bush's last year, the pace then fell dramatically: just 1 in 2011, 4 in 2012, and 11 in 2013.[151]

There was considerable enthusiasm for closure. The *New York Times*, *Los Angeles Times*, and *Washington Post* strongly favored it (although the last wanted a national security court to identify those requiring indefinite detention). Former Bush administration officials like Waxman, Bellinger, and even Stimson endorsed closure. So did international organizations, the New York City Bar, and Afghan President Karzai. NGOs continued to campaign (although HRW and AI opposed institutionalizing indefinite detention in US prisons). Opinion polls were inconclusive and volatile, suggesting that a fully committed administration could have mobilized public support; but without such leadership, it declined.

Because there were so many actors, it is difficult to establish responsibility. But lack of political will seems to be part of the reason. (Obama said regretfully in March 2016 that if he could redo his presidency, "I would have closed Guantánamo on the first day," but the politics got tough and "the path of least resistance was just to leave it open."[152]) The Task Force review of detainees proceeded far more slowly than promised because the Bush administration's files were chaotic and incomplete; but investing more resources could have alleviated that problem. Obama, like Bush, abandoned the plan to free some Uighurs in the USA in the face of political opposition and did not transfer other detainees to US prisons when he could have done so, thereby weakening the argument that other countries should accept them. Having failed to secure local political backing for prosecuting the HVDs in New York, Holder abandoned the entire idea. After suspending the (inadequate) ARBs, the administration took years to replace them with PRBs, which then moved very slowly to approve detainees for transfer. DoD continued to defend Guantánamo.[153] Defense Secretaries Panetta, Hagel, and Carter dragged their feet in certifying transfers to Congress. But Obama was commander-in-chief: he could have ordered subordinates to act and fired those who refused. Instead, he seems to have husbanded his limited political capital for battles that he felt (rightly) were more important, such as the Affordable Care Act and the Iran nuclear deal. Obama could have directed DoJ to stop opposing habeas petitions (although this might have generated a confrontation between courts ordering releases and Congress obstructing transfers). And though Obama had promised as early as 2009 to give Congress a plan for closure, he did not produce it until 2016, and then was unwilling to run the political risk of selecting, or even prioritizing, US prisons.

Because the administration abandoned civilian prosecutions (later precluded by NDAA bans on transfers to the USA) and military commissions became mired in bitter adversarial clashes over the impossible task of constructing from scratch an entirely novel procedure to try death penalty defendants, the only way to close Guantánamo was to transfer detainees to other countries or US prisons. The first alternative required recipients. Many European allies initially seemed willing; some were even eager to repatriate citizens and residents.[154] But the US failure to transfer any detainees to its own soil angered potential recipients and aroused concern about the risks they were being asked to accept. The USA offered incentives: money to Palau, NATO membership to Albania, visa waivers to Bulgaria. But NDAA restrictions strongly (and effectively) discouraged Defense Secretaries from giving Congress the necessary assurances. And Abdulmutallab's attempted bombing induced Obama to suspend transfers of the large group of detainees from Yemen (where the bomber had trained).

Recidivism remained a central battleground in the struggle over Guantánamo. But Republican arguments often were factitious. They assumed (against the evidence) that all detainees *had been* terrorists (since otherwise they could not "*recidivate*"). "Known" recidivism sometimes included behavior no one would consider terrorism (such as making a film). The category of "suspected" terrorists was even more malleable, often depending on a single uncorroborated report about actions in inaccessible locales where it was impossible to obtain reliable information. Some of those released who did engage in terrorism were subsequently redetained or killed, thus posing no further threat. Republicans, who never objected to Bush's 525 transfers (an annual average of almost 90), assailed the 92 men Obama transferred in his first five years (an annual average of less than 20), overlooking the fact that the "recidivism" rate of Bush's transfers was three or four times higher than that of Obama's. And I remain baffled by the obsession with the threat posed by the handful of detainees being considered for transfer (which excludes the HVDs charged in military commissions), when the Taliban, al-Qaeda and its affiliates, ISIS, al-Shabab, and other organizations deploy tens or even hundreds of thousands of terrorists.

The prospect of transfers to the USA predictably provoked NIMBY resistance. Rep. Wolf blocked both presidents from freeing Uighurs in

Northern Virginia, even though the established Uighur community and philanthropic bodies wanted to host them. Proposals of civilian and military prisons in Montana, Illinois, Michigan, California, Virginia, Colorado, Kansas, and South Carolina provoked nearly hysterical reactions. Opponents refused to acknowledge that these prisons already contained far more dangerous inmates (including some convicted terrorists), none of whom had ever escaped. Instead, politicians stoked utterly unrealistic fears that visitors to maximum security prisons would pose threats or federal courts would simply release prisoners into the community.

The single greatest obstacle to closing Guantánamo, however, was opposition by Republicans (joined by some Democrats), who were impervious to arguments that closure was necessary to encourage allied cooperation and restore the country's international reputation. Although the cost per prisoner increased as the number declined, otherwise frugal Republicans were indifferent, declaring that no price was too great to detain terrorists. Closure proponents argued that the prison incited more terrorism than ex-detainees would commit; defenders replied that terrorists would find other reasons for their actions if Guantánamo were closed; neither offered any evidence. Civilian criminal procedure is grounded in the belief that it is better that ten guilty people go free than that one innocent person be convicted (even if practice falls woefully short of that ideal). But the "war on terror" embraced the opposite belief: it is better that ten innocent suspects be wrongly detained than that one be released to commit terrorism. And the deontological argument that indefinite detention without trial was not who we are attracted few converts.

Just four months after Obama's inauguration the Senate voted overwhelmingly against authorizing money for closure; by September Congress began considering legislation barring transfers to the USA. Early in Obama's second year the 2011 NDAA contained such restrictions, which grew increasingly stringent over the next few years. Although Obama voiced opposition and threatened vetoes, he ultimately confined himself to issuing bland signing statements (a practice for which he had criticized Bush). And even this mild opposition may have provoked Congress to tighten the restrictions and pass later NDAAs by veto-proof margins. Obama finally vetoed the 2016 NDAA, but did so for other reasons, and then signed a revised bill retaining transfer restrictions. The White House threat to close the prison by executive decree just backfired. That Republicans were determined to obstruct Obama over this issue (like all others) is shown by their criticism of trading Bergdahl for five Taliban – in which they were joined by McCain (who had been a POW for a similar length of time). They also used foreign terrorist attacks – *Charlie Hebdo*, the Stade de France, Brussels – as arguments against transfer (even though ex-detainees committed none of these atrocities).

Although Obama vowed not to leave Guantánamo for his successor to solve, he did just that.

CHAPTER FOUR

INTERROGATION

Torture – which the Bush administration, using typical Orwellian Newspeak, euphemized as "enhanced interrogation techniques" (EITs) – fueled one of the most emotional and enduring controversies in the "war on terror."[1] This chapter examines the struggle between proponents and critics of EITs, posing several questions. How did the OLC memos authorize torture? How did the presence or absence of legal authority influence governmental behavior? Why were the memos kept secret, how did that affect their legitimacy, how were they exposed, and with what consequences? What divisions emerged within the Bush administration, and which factions prevailed? What rhetorical arguments were mobilized for and against EITs, with what effect? How effective were Congress and its constituent committees in exercising oversight? In using confirmation hearings to expose and curtail EITs? In legislating limits or bans on EITs? What happened to criminal investigations? How did the electoral process affirm or repudiate EITs? How did the Obama administration differ from that of Bush?

THE BUSH ADMINISTRATION

The Bush administration secretly began building the legal structure for interrogation immediately after 9/11.[2] Some officials resisted (though this surfaced only years later). On January 26, 2002 Secretary of State Colin Powell objected to White House Counsel Alberto Gonzales's assertion that al-Qaeda and the Taliban were not POWs entitled to Geneva Conventions protections. A week later DoS Legal Adviser William H. Taft IV concurred. But Bush's February 7 memorandum declared that "common Article 3 of Geneva does not apply to either al Qaeda or Taliban detainees." On October 22, LtCol. Diane E. Beaver (SJA for Guantánamo's JTF 170) approved all the EITs, but urged that two harsher categories "undergo a legal, medical, behavioral science and intelligence review prior to their commencement." On November 27 DoD General Counsel Haynes also urged caution in authorizing some of the harsher techniques because the Armed Forces were trained in "a tradition of restraint." That month officials from all four branches raised objections. The Chief of the Army Intelligence Law Division warned that stress positions and sensory deprivation "cross the line of 'humane treatment'" and might "violate the torture statute." RAdm. Jane Dalton (legal counsel to JCS chair Gen. Richard Myers) began a new legal review. But after Donald Rumsfeld intervened, Myers told Dalton "that Mr. Haynes did not want this broad-based review to take place." On January 17, 2003 Haynes directed Air Force General Counsel Mary Walker to chair a working group to develop a legal policy for interrogation. MGen. Jack L. Rives (Air Force Judge Advocate General (JAG)) wrote that "several of the more extreme interrogation techniques, on their face, amount to violations of domestic law and the UCMJ" and are "violative of international law." That "simply is not how the U.S. armed forces have operated in recent history. We have taken the legal and moral 'high-road.'" RAdm. Michael F. Lohr (Navy JAG) asked how participation by the military in EITs would "affect their treatment when incarcerated abroad." The Army and Marine Corps JAGs also expressed opposition. But the working group's March 6 and April 4 Reports approved all the EITs. And on May 23 CIA General Counsel John Rizzo responded to a colleague who expressed concern that EITs violated the Geneva Conventions: "experience has demonstrated that this OLC has demonstrated an ingenious ability to interpret over, under and around Geneva, the torture convention, and other pesky little international obligations."

In December 2002 *Washington Post* reporters Dana Priest and Barton Gellman described beatings, stress positions, and sleep and sensory deprivation, mentioning a criminal investigation into the deaths of two detainees in Bagram, Afghanistan.[3] An official involved said: "if you don't violate someone's human rights some of the time, you probably aren't doing your job." Three months later the *New York Times* published an article (buried on page 14) about the dead detainees, now identified as Dilawar and Habibullah. Carlotta Gall said she had to wait a month for its publication, although her previous stories had appeared within a week. Roger Cohen said his "single greatest frustration as foreign editor was my [in]ability to get this story on page one" after pitching it four times.[4] On June 26, 2003, the UN's International Day in Support of Victims of Torture, President Bush declared that the USA was "committed to the worldwide elimination of torture and we are leading this fight by example." He vowed to prosecute and prevent "other cruel and unusual punishment." When a worried CIA General Counsel warned the White House that this could frighten interrogators, it secretly reaffirmed support for EITs. In March 2004 HRW published a report on abuses in Afghanistan.

The exposé of Abu Ghraib in April/May 2004 quickly prompted leaks of the OLC memos.[5] Gonzales declared in a *New York Times* op ed that "terrorists" were not protected by the Geneva Conventions but still would be treated "humanely." John Yoo confidently asserted that the "conflict with al Qaeda is not governed by the Geneva Conventions" and Congress's definition of "severe mental or physical pain – leaves room for interrogation methods that go beyond polite conversation." The *Times* summarized the January 9, 2002 Yoo–Delahunty memo advancing this view and Gonzales's January 25, 2002 memo to Bush declaring that "Geneva's strict limitations on questioning enemy prisoners" were "obsolete." The next day Secretary of State Powell objected that Gonzales wanted to "reverse over a century of U.S. policy and practice in supporting the Geneva Conventions and undermine the protections of the laws of war for our troops." After a summary of Jay Bybee's August 1, 2002 OLC "torture" memo appeared, Attorney General Ashcroft refused to provide or comment on the memos. At a press conference two days later Bush repeated his bland assurance "that anything we did would conform to U.S. law and would be consistent with international treaty obligations," but evaded questions about torture. Three days later the *Washington Post* published the full "torture" memo, which was promptly criticized by its columnist David Ignatius as well as legal academics and leading bar associations. Soon thereafter Gonzales said that memo and Haynes's March 6, 2003 memo were intended only to "explore the limits of the legal landscape" and had "never made it to the hands of soldiers in the field, nor to the president." But they had been discussed with Ashcroft and the DoJ Criminal Division as well as the White House Counsel's office and David Addington (Vice President Cheney's lawyer). In August the ABA House of Delegates condemned "any use of torture or other cruel, inhuman or degrading treatment" and urged the government to comply with the Constitution and laws and international treaties.

On November 30 the *New York Times* revealed that the previous July the ICRC had told the government that some military interrogations in Guantánamo Bay were "tantamount to torture."[6] Practices included "humiliating acts, solitary confinement, temperature extremes, use of forced positions," loud and persistent noise and music and "some beatings." The report called this "an intentional system of cruel, unusual and degrading treatment and a form of torture." MGen. Hood (GB commander) replied: "the detainees here have not been abused, they've not been mistreated, they've not been tortured in any way."

After Ashcroft resigned on Election Day 2004 Bush nominated Gonzales as Attorney General. Sen. Leahy (D-Vt) said the confirmation hearing "may be the only remaining forum in which to examine more fully the steps that were taken to weaken U.S. policy on torture in the period that led to the prison scandals at Abu Ghraib and Afghanistan."[7] Sen. Specter (R-Pa) (SJC chair) began the January 2005 hearing by quoting Gonzales's statement (above) that the limits set by the Geneva Conventions were "obsolete." Sen. Cornyn (R-Tex), who had published an op ed warning that "extending Geneva protections to al Qaeda would threaten the security of our soldiers, dramatically disable us from obtaining the intelligence needed to prevent further attacks … and badly undermine international law," called Gonzales "absolutely right." Gonzales now backtracked –"I consider the Geneva Conventions neither obsolete nor quaint" – but eagerly agreed with Cornyn that three federal courts had concluded that they did not apply to al-Qaeda. He told Sen. Kohl (D-Wisc) that following them "would be a dishonor." "We would have to provide … certain items of comfort, that could be used as weapons against our soldiers." Answering Specter's softball questions, he said he "absolutely" did not approve of torture. But pressed by Leahy, he conceded he did not "have a disagreement with the conclusions" of the OLC's August 2002 "torture memo." He repeatedly evaded the "hypothetical" question whether "the president has the authority to exercise a commander-in-chief override and immunize acts of torture." Asked by Sen. Durbin (D-Ill) whether the War Crimes Act always applied to US personnel, he sought an "opportunity to get back to you on that." Asked whether "U.S. personnel [can] legally engage in torture under any circumstances," he again "want[ed] to get back to you on that." In response to Sen. Kennedy (D-Mass), he denied any "specific recollection" of whether the CIA had requested approval for EITs, including waterboarding. When Sen. Graham (R-SC) noted that the UCMJ "makes it a crime to assault a detainee," Gonzales retorted that "we have good people at the Department of Justice who did the very best they could interpreting, in my judgment, a difficult statute." When Graham said the OLC had done "a lousy job," Gonzales replied that the August 2002 memo had been withdrawn but maintained that the memo's narrow definition of torture "was an arguable interpretation of the law." In later written responses, Gonzales said the CIA and other nonmilitary personnel were not covered by Bush's February 2002 promise to treat prisoners humanely, and the CAT did not apply to aliens overseas. He declined to define torture or prohibited interrogation techniques. If the administration "were to begin ruling out speculated interrogation practices we would fairly rapidly provide Al Qaeda with a road map concerning interrogation." Denouncing Gonzales's "very arrogant" responses, Kennedy said: "our committee should not acquiesce in such gross evasion and nonresponsiveness." Sen. Feinstein (D-Ca) said Gonzales's "legalistic" language made it hard to know "what he really thinks on the subject of torture."

John Yoo unsurprisingly backed Gonzales.[8] "The only way we can stop future attacks by Al Qaeda is by learning from [detainees] what their plans are. It doesn't make sense to take options off the table." When the USA ratified the CAT, Congress "consciously chose" not to adopt the "open-ended, vague phrase" "cruel, inhumane or degrading treatment." Whether waterboarding was torture "depends on the circumstances." "[I]llegal combatants," just like pirates and slave traders, did not "deserve the protection of the laws of war." Congress lacked the power to "tie the President's hands in regard to torture as an interrogation technique." Bush's re-election was "proof that the debate is over." "The public has had its referendum." The *New York Times* called Gonzales "The Wrong Attorney General." The "biggest strike" against him was the August 2002 memo, which gave "a disturbingly narrow definition of torture." His "attempts to distance himself from the memo have been unconvincing, especially since it turns out he was the one who requested that it be written." "Senate Democrats … should stand on principle and hold out for a more suitable attorney general." They did, but the SJC approved the nomination by a 10–8 party-line vote.[9] People for the American Way, Alliance for Justice, ACLU, HRW, HRF, AI, MoveOn, and True Majority continued to oppose the nomination; even the Congressional Hispanic Caucus did so after Gonzales refused to meet them. When Senate Democrats demanded at least ten hours of debate,

Sen. Hatch (R-Ut) accused them of making Gonzales a "scapegoat" for policies he did not control. Sen. McConnell (R-Ky) praised Gonzales for having "aggressively explored every possible legal means" to interrogate detainees; anything less would have been "dereliction." Kennedy said Gonzales had "advised the president that torture was an acceptable method of interrogation." Specter replied that Gonzales had been "very emphatic about his personal opposition to torture," but Leahy warned that Gonzales "views the president to have the power to override our law." Sen. Byrd (R-WV) could not support someone who "obviously contributed in large measure to … abominable legal decisions." Sen. Levin (D-Mich) accused Gonzales of "establishing the legal framework that set the stage for the torture and mistreatment of persons in the United States' custody." But Sen. Salazar (D–Co) was confident that as Attorney General, Gonzales would find torture "illegal and wrong." The Senate voted 60–36 to confirm (6 Democrats joining 54 Republicans), the smallest margin of Bush's second-term nominations and just two more than Ashcroft received. The *New York Times* found the outcome "depressing." Gonzales had "come to represent the administration's role in paving the way for the abuse and torture of prisoners." Confirmation sent "a terrible signal … to the rest of the world, and to American citizens concerned with human rights."

In order to ease Gonzales's confirmation, OLC acting head Daniel Levin (who replaced Jack Goldsmith) had formally repudiated the "torture" memo at the end of 2004 and declared that "torture is abhorrent both to American law and values and to international norms."[10] But immediately after being sworn in, Gonzales forced out Levin and chose Stephen Bradbury (who was being "auditioned" to head the OLC) to issue two secret opinions. James Comey (who was leaving the DoJ) approved one of these, authorizing 13 EITs, but told colleagues they would be "ashamed" of the other, which, for the first time, authorized multiple EITs.

In March CIA Director Porter Goss testified before the Senate Armed Services Committee: "I can assure you that I know of no instances where the intelligence community is outside the law on this. And I know for a fact that torture is not productive. That's not professional interrogation. We don't do torture."[11] When pressed, he reiterated: "At this time, there are no 'techniques' … that are being employed that are in any way against the law or … would be considered torture or anything like that." But he was "not able to tell" the committee whether torture had been used in the past. Asked by Sen. McCain (R-Az) about waterboarding,

Goss claimed it fell into "an area of what I will call professional interrogation techniques," which had had "documented successes." "I'd much rather explain why we did something than why we did nothing." In any case, the CIA now was "erring on the side of caution." A day later, fearing these equivocations might be misunderstood (or understood all too well), the Agency said: "all approved interrogation techniques, both past and present, are lawful and do not constitute torture." "C.I.A. policies on interrogation have always followed legal guidance from the Department of Justice" (which, of course, remained secret). "[L]awful interrogation of captured terrorists" is "a vital tool in saving American lives. It works and it is done with Congressional oversight, in keeping with American law." HRW's Reed Brody wrote the *New York Times* that Goss could not admit the CIA used waterboarding and also claim it did not torture.

In May Sen. Durbin attached a blanket prohibition on torture and cruel, inhuman, or degrading treatment to a supplemental military appropriations bill.[12] The Senate passed it unanimously, and the House overwhelmingly (420–2–3), and Bush signed it. In July the four JAGs testified at a SASC subcommittee hearing that they had expressed concerns about EITs to Walker's Working Group in March and April 2003. RAdm. McPherson (Navy JAG) said there were "differences of opinion" about the use of dogs, but leashing detainees, making them wear bras, and stripping them before women, though "juvenile," was not "inhumane." MGen. Romig (Army JAG) said those techniques violated the UCMJ and were "not in the spirit" of the Army Field Manual. The committee heard that the DoD had declared on March 17 that "the Report of the Working Group on Detainee Interrogations is to be considered a historical document with no standing in policy, practice or law."

In June Sens. Warner (D-Va), McCain, and Graham introduced amendments to the NDAA 2006 limiting interrogation to the Army Field Manual, prohibiting cruel, inhuman, or degrading treatment, and applying the Geneva Conventions to all detainees.[13] Bush promptly threatened a veto. On July 21 Cheney made a second attempt to dissuade the three senators. The amendments quickly received support from 14 former military officers, who wrote McCain: "the abuse of prisoners hurts America's cause in the war on terror, endangers U.S. service members who might be captured by the enemy and is anathema to the values Americans have held dear for generations." Majority Leader Frist temporarily withdrew the bill when he was unable to get 60 votes to cut off debate.

In July Bush nominated Timothy Flanigan to be Deputy Attorney General.[14] Questioned at the confirmation hearing about his role in drafting the OLC memos (as deputy White House Counsel through December 2002), he acknowledged participating in two briefings with Gonzales in summer 2002 about whether techniques "beyond the normal Q. and A. approach" were allowed, but denied seeing the August "torture" memo. Its rationale "sounded correct," but its conclusion that the president had the power to override the law was "sort of sophomoric." He now said that torture was "abhorrent," but whether mock executions and simulated drowning were appropriate "depends on all of the relevant facts and circumstances." "Inhumane treatment is not susceptible to a succinct definition." He could not say whether "degrading and abusive" treatment was humane. He withdrew his nomination when the SJC persisted in investigating his relationship with Jack Abramoff (who was later convicted of corruption as a lobbyist).

In September HRW issued a report on torture at Forward Operating Base (FOB) Mercury near Fallujah between September 2003 and April 2004.[15] Two sergeants described it as routine, one declaring they "were never briefed on the Geneva Conventions." A third sergeant and two physician's assistants substantiated the charges. But the key source was Capt. Ian Fishback, a deeply religious Christian, decorated West Point graduate, and son of a Vietnam War veteran, who had served two tours in Afghanistan and Iraq and whose wife was serving in Iraq. For 17 months he had tried to raise the issue with his chain of command, only to be told by superiors to "consider your career." After hearing Rumsfeld assert on television in May 2004 that DoD had "followed the spirit of the Geneva Conventions in Afghanistan, and the letter of the Geneva Conventions in Iraq … I knew something was wrong." He shared his concerns with West Point classmates and sought clarification of doctrine from his company and battalion commanders and several JAG lawyers. The company commander told him to "remember the honor of the unit is at stake. Don't expect me to go to bat for you on this issue." In response to his memo, the battalion commander said only: "I am aware of Fishback's concerns." When he described the abuses to the Army Secretary at a chance meeting he was told that "corrective action was already taken," which Fishback knew to be false. He asked the IG at Fort Bragg (where he was doing Special Forces training) for an analysis of the Geneva Conventions, but found the summary "very incomplete." The interpretation he obtained from the ICRC was "much closer to my West Point education." He also approached Democratic and Republican Congressmen and staff, a Guantánamo Bay interrogator, and the deputy head of the West Point department responsible for teaching the law of war. He was finally propelled to act after learning that one Iraq detainee had died during interrogation and another had a "saturating … sand bag" tied over his head. Inspired by the West Point Cadet Honor Code, he contacted HRW in summer 2005, met SASC staffers, and authorized them to publicize his story. On September 28 he wrote Sen. McCain that doctrinal "confusion contributed to a wide range of abuses" he had witnessed in Afghanistan and Iraq:

> including death threats, beatings, broken bones, murder, exposure to elements, extreme forced physical exertion, hostage-taking, stripping, sleep deprivation and degrading treatment …
>
> Some argue that since our actions are not as horrifying as Al Qaeda's we should not be concerned. When did Al Qaeda become any type of standard by which we measure the morality of the United States? We are America, and our actions should be held to a higher standard … the most important question that our generation will answer [is] do we sacrifice our ideals in order to preserve security?

The Army responded by opening a criminal investigation and denying him a pass to speak to Senate staff. When CIC pressed him to identify the two sergeants, he replied that he had come forward "because of the larger issue that prisoner abuse is systemic in the Army" and thus "a leadership problem." CIC said that without names they could do nothing more. The day after HRW notified his division it would release a report, CIC interrogated Fishback for six hours, demanding the sergeants' names and questioning his relationship with HRW. His command threatened to prosecute him for failing to disclose the names. Fishback went on ABC's *This Week* to reiterate that "we've got to make it clear to the world that America" does not torture, "and to the extent somebody's done something that they shouldn't have done, they'll be punished for it." After he provided additional information, McCain said: "I'm even more impressed by what a fine and honorable officer he is." But nothing came of the revelations.

In October the Senate voted 90–9 to approve the NDAA amendment prohibiting cruel, inhuman, or degrading treatment and requiring the armed forces to follow the Army Field Manual.[16] Reading Fishback's letter, McCain said: "our troops are not served by ambiguity. They are crying out for clarity." After quoting Colin Powell – "the world will note that America is making a clear statement with respect to the expected future behavior of our soldiers" – McCain said:

> [W]hat I do care very much about is ... what we lose when ... we allow ... our soldiers to forget that best sense of ourselves, our greatest strength – that we are different and better than our enemies, that we fight for an idea – not a tribe, not a land, not a king, not a twisted interpretation of an ancient religion – but for an ideal that all men are created equal and endowed by their Creator with inalienable rights.

This belief had sustained him and his comrades under torture in Vietnam. Sen. Alexander (R-Tn) agreed "it is time for Congress ... to clarify and set the rules for detention and interrogation." But Sen. Stevens (R-Ak) quibbled: "the techniques vary upon the circumstances and the physical location of people involved." "[S]ometimes ... intimidation is part of the system." And Sen. Sessions (R-Ala) denied any "systemic abuse of prisoners."

The *New York Times* praised the amendment for imposing "democratic values and the standards of behavior recognized by every other civilized nation" and helping "protect those in the nation's uniform."[17] "[T]orture yields worthless information and false confessions." The *Washington Post* praised the Senate for taking "a major step toward stopping the most damaging and shameful American conduct during the war on terrorism." Bush was seeking to "preserve the prerogative to subject detainees to cruel, inhuman and degrading treatment," which "threatens to declare to the world his administration's moral bankruptcy." The US Conference of Catholic Bishops urged the conference committee to adopt the Senate version. PBS aired a Frontline program on *The Torture Question* on October 18.

On October 20 Cheney and DCI Goss again unsuccessfully sought to dissuade McCain, or at least exclude the CIA from coverage, warning that the amendment could cost "thousands of lives."[18] If the USA captured another KSM who refused to disclose an imminent attack, "we have to be able to do what is necessary." The *Washington Post* accused Cheney of becoming "an open advocate of torture" and "proposing to legally authorize human rights abuses by Americans." Decrying the administration's "tireless ... efforts to legalize torture," the *New York Times* derided Cheney's proposal as "ludicrous," "absurd." Gen. Hoar (former CENTCOM commander) said on NPR that you could not "have one set of regulations that apply to uniformed Americans and another that applied to another agency in the government." But John Yoo warned that the amendment would limit interrogators to mere "questioning." Waterboarding could not be torture because it was administered to "basic training recruits." It was "clear legally, the Geneva Conventions do not apply to the war against al-Qaeda." DCI Goss wrote all staff that the *New York Times* and *Washington Post* editorials were "plain wrong." "We have not, we are not" torturing, and "we are not seeking such authorities." In a closed-door meeting, Cheney urged Republican Senators to exempt the CIA.

Fifteen House Republicans exhorted their conference committee member to pass the amendment.[19] The presidents of the American College of Physicians, American Psychiatric Association, and American Psychological Association endorsed the amendment. Declaring that "we aren't going to allow any weakening of language," McCain got a unanimous Senate vote to attach the ban to a related defense bill and threatened "to add it to every piece of important legislation voted on in the Senate until the will of a substantial bipartisan majority in both houses of Congress prevails." Sen. Graham refused to "entertain a retreat" or "an exception that washes away what we've been fighting for." DoD warned that "the kind of rigidity that comes with these kinds of amendments could restrict the president's flexibility in the global war on terror." Sen. Hagel (R-Neb) said the administration was "making a terrible mistake in opposing John McCain's amendment." But Sen. Hatch said the administration was "going to do everything in their power to make sure that our citizens in the United States of America are protected." McCain wrote a *Newsweek* op ed taking issue with the administration position "that the demands of this war require us to accord a lower station to the moral imperatives that should govern our conduct." Waterboarding was "very exquisite torture," which could make a person "say anything he thinks his captors want to hear." Tortured to provide the names of his flight squadron, he had given "the names of the Green Bay Packers' offensive line." In the midst of the controversy DoD approved (but did not announce) a new interrogations directive prohibiting "acts of physical or mental torture" and mandating "humane" treatment.

Partnership for a Secure America, a bipartisan group created by Sens. Rudman (R-NH) and former Rep. Lee Hamilton (D-In), strongly condemned CID treatment, which "makes us less safe, violates our nation's values, damages America's reputation in the world, and cannot be justified."[20] Gen. Pace (the new JCS chairman) agreed with McCain that "following our own rules certainly makes sense." But White House press secretary Scott McClellan refused to answer repeated questions about whether Cheney was seeking an exemption for the CIA. The *Los Angeles Times* published opposing op eds. David Gelernter (the Yale professor severely wounded by the Unabomber) argued that "if torturing terrorist X … is the only way to save lives, we have no right to refuse." Larry C. Johnson (a former CIA officer) said: "we should never use our fear of being attacked as a justification for dehumanizing ourselves or others." The *Wall Street Journal* deplored the debate as signifying a "flagging U.S. will to fight the war on terror." "[W]e know for a fact that information wrung from 9/11 mastermind Khalid Sheikh Mohammed and others has helped prevent further attacks on U.S. soil." EITs, including waterboarding, were just "psychological techniques designed to break a detainee."

In November the *New York Times* revealed that in spring 2004 CIA IG Helgerson issued a classified report finding that ten EITs authorized in 2002 and used against three dozen suspects in secret prisons around the world might be cruel, inhuman, or degrading treatment in violation of the CAT, which he believed applied even to noncitizens abroad.[21] Although eight of his ten recommendations for change had been accepted, only one CIA agent had been prosecuted. The CIA reiterated its statement eight months earlier that all interrogation techniques were lawful. Some former officers said that after Helgerson submitted his report, the Agency had limited interrogation practices in response to the Abu Ghraib revelations.

New evidence of abuses emerged days after the *Times* story was published. A former Army interrogator (later identified as Tony Lagouranis) said that in Iraq during the early months of 2004 prisoners were held in shipping containers, stripped, denied mattresses, placed in stress positions, subjected to dietary manipulation, deprived of sleep with music and lights, and frightened with barking dogs.[22] They "used hypothermia a lot." "[A]ccording to the interrogation rules of engagement, that was legal." "I was being told by my leaders that these people were not enemy POWs, and therefore, we could really sort of do whatever we wanted." But in more than 300 interrogations he only obtained "real intelligence" from about 20 "when I would sort of form a rapport with the person." At first he believed the intelligence reports that "these were bad guys … but later it became clear to me that … they were picking up just farmers." At FOB Calsu in August–October 2004, Marine Special Forces "would bring back prisoners who were bruised with broken bones, sometimes with burns" and "tell me that it was after their capture, while they were subdued." "One guy was forced to sit on an exhaust pipe of a Humvee … he had a giant blister, third degree burn on the back of his leg." The Army sent everyone to Abu Ghraib, even a man stopped at a checkpoint with a cell phone and shovel. The Marine major and a JAG lawyer ignored Lagouranis's objections. "When I would say they were innocent in my interrogation reports, they would send the prisoner up to Abu Ghraib without my interrogation report." He complained to CID five times in Iraq and again after returning to Fort Gordon, Georgia and gave a "Frontline" interview. But CID claimed never to have seen his reports.

ABC News reported that escapees from a CIA prison in Afghanistan confirmed the abuses.[23] CIA sources described six EITs instituted in March 2002: attention grab; attention slap; belly slap; long time standing (hands cuffed and feet shackled to the floor for more than 40 hours); cold cell (standing naked, periodically doused with cold water, in a 50-degree cell); and waterboarding (bound to an inclined board with feet raised and cellophane wrapped over the face as water is poured in the nose and mouth). At least three CIA officers refused training in the techniques. After being waterboarded and left naked in a cold cell overnight, Ibn al Shayk al Libi told interrogators that Saddam Hussein had weapons of mass destruction – a false claim he later retracted. ABC said at least three detainees had died during interrogation. A contemporaneous AI conference in London presented testimony about abuse by former Guantánamo detainees. Moazzam Begg described Korans pushed through airlocks and thrown on the ground. Ustad Badarzaman Badar, imprisoned for three months in Afghanistan, was stripped naked, shaved, and prevented from showering. Rustam Akhmiarov was held in a room cooled to the point that frost formed. Airat Vakhitov described "routine" beatings in Bagram and isolation for five months. "All of us have problems with our kidneys because we slept on the iron with air conditioning on."

In November the bipartisan 9/11 Commission faulted the administration for not following its recommendation that the USA develop "an approach toward the detention and humane treatment of capture terrorists" based on Geneva Convention Common Article 3.[24] It praised the revised Army Field Manual and the proposed NDAA ban on cruel, inhuman, or degrading treatment, which should "cover the treatment of detainees held by all elements of the U.S. government."

DCI Goss assailed the "huge amount of misinformation" about the Agency:

> We use lawful capabilities to collect vital information, and we do it in a variety of unique and innovative ways, all of which are legal and none of which are torture ...
>
> An enemy that's working in an amorphous network that doesn't have to worry about a bunch of regulations, chain of command, rule of law or anything else has got a huge advantage over a stultified, slow-moving, bureaucratic, by-the-book organization. So we have to, within the law and within all the requirements of our professional ethics in this profession, develop agility. And that means putting a lot of judgment in the hands of individuals overseas.

But the *Washington Post* said Goss's claim that the techniques were "not torture" would "open[] the way for the FBI to use cold cells and waterboarding on Americans." Noting that such practices "once were routinely condemned by the Department of State in its annual human rights report," the *Post* warned that "the Bush administration has so loosened and degraded the torture standard [that] the abuse of detainees will become far harder to prevent – not only in the CIA's clandestine cells but around the world." HRW renewed its call for an "independent bipartisan commission to examine interrogation practices" and "a special prosecutor to investigate criminal activity in the military and CIA."

Stanisfield Turner (a retired admiral and Carter's DCI) said on television he was "embarrassed that the United States has a vice president for torture" and followed this up with a letter signed by 32 members of the intelligence community.[25] Lawrence Wilkerson (a retired colonel who had been Colin Powell's chief of staff) said on television that "in the war of ideas, you cannot ... do things that that are in contradiction of your values." In a *Los Angeles Times* op ed HRF's Elisa Massimino urged passage of the McCain amendment, which had been supported by retired Gens. Powell and Shalikashvili (both former JCS chairmen) and more than two dozen retired senior officers. The *Washington Post* said it was "time for the GOP leadership, and President Bush, to stop resisting the overwhelming sentiment in Congress ... to put an end to the disgraceful abuse of foreign detainees." Sen. Graham wrote in a *Washington Post* op ed that "even during a time of war, we have chosen to be a nation of laws." An exception for the CIA might "set precedents that could jeopardize our troops in future conflicts." National Security Adviser Stephen Hadley tried to persuade McCain to protect CIA officers from prosecution. But Democratic Whip Rep. Steny Hoyer (D-Md) said McCain "ought to stick to his guns" because Cheney "wants to continue the option of torture."

The *New York Times* added the argument that torture "usually doesn't work" to the others that "it is morally wrong and illegal, damages the nation's image, and puts American soldiers … in mortal peril."[26] But David B. Rifkin Jr. and Lee A. Casey (former Reagan administration lawyers) wrote in the *Wall Street Journal* that coercive interrogation was "not inherently 'torture.'" "[A]ppropriate weight should be given to the rights and interests of the civilians who are the terrorists' preferred targets" in "assessing the moral and policy questions presented" by EITs. The *Washington Post* countered the next day that waterboarding "has been recognized as a torture technique since the time of Torquemada and the Spanish Inquisition."

The Senate balked at a House version offering blanket immunity to anyone who relied on the Attorney General's determination that an interrogation procedure was lawful.[27] Under pressure from Hadley, McCain was willing to grant only the immunity the UCMJ offered if "a person of ordinary sense and understanding would not know the practices are unlawful," for which "good faith reliance on advice of counsel shall be an important factor." The House approved this version 308–122, with the support of 122 Republicans. At a White House press conference with McCain, Bush said the law would "make clear to the world that this government does not torture and that we adhere to the international convention of torture [*sic*]." Hadley said the law would ban "cruel, inhuman or degrading treatment at home or abroad." To quell opposition DNI Negroponte assured Rep. Hunter (R-Ca) (HASC chair) that intelligence gathering would not suffer. The *Washington Post* praised the deal as an "important step toward curtailing the systematic human rights violations committed by the Bush administration in its handling of foreign prisoners." The *New York Times* wrote that "nothing should be more obvious for an American president than to support a ban on torture."

After the House passed the bill overwhelmingly Bush said in his signing statement that the executive branch would construe the provisions relating to detainees "in a manner consistent with the constitutional authority of the president to supervise the unitary executive branch and as commander in chief and consistent with the constitutional limitations on judicial power."[28] McCain expressed outrage at Bush "astonishing" claim that "whenever the president asserts that he's acting in the interests of national security, he's constitutionally permitted to violate any federal laws he finds inconvenient. Translated, Bush's statement says, 'I'll sign a law prohibiting cruel, inhumane and degrading treatment, but because I'm president, I can ignore it.'" Warner and he added:

> We believe the president understands Congress's intent in passing by very large majorities legislation governing the treatment of detainees … The Congress declined when asked by administration officials to include a presidential waiver of restrictions included in our legislation. Our committee intends through strict oversight to monitor the administration's implementation of the new law.

Graham went "a little bit further."

> I do not believe that any political figure in the country has the ability to set aside any … law of armed conflict that we have adopted or treaties that we have ratified. If we go down that road, it will cause great problems for our troops in future conflicts because [nothing] is to prevent other nations' leaders from doing the same.

The *Washington Post* warned that Bush was planning to ignore the law "whenever he chooses." "Even before the statement was issued, administration lawyers had taken the position that the McCain amendment would not necessarily end waterboarding."

Twenty-two retired Army, Navy, and Marine officers wrote Bush that the McCain amendment "will ensure that the United States has a single standard for interrogating enemy prisoners that is effective, lawful, and humane."[29] McCain said it was "critical" that the USA "observe basic human rights and obey the law that we just passed." "If the president wants to break the law he can do that. But we also have penalties for breaking the law."

In February 2006 Jane Mayer described the military's early opposition to EITs.[30] On December 17, 2002 NCIS director David Brant had told Alberto Mora (Navy General Counsel) that "we think people are being abused by the interrogators in Guantánamo in unlawful ways." Brant learned this from Brittain Mallow (head of the FBI CITF in Guantánamo) and Michael Gelles (an NCIS psychologist). Brant did not want his team to "observe, condone, or participate in any level of physical or in-depth psychological abuse … It was pretty basic, black and white to me." He ordered all CITF personnel to "stand clear and report" any abuse. Responding to Mora's request for more evidence,

Brant gave him the al-Qahtani interrogation transcript, saying that what it depicted was not "rogue activity" but was "rumored to have been authorized at a high level in Washington."

Mora was "appalled" by the "clearly abusive" behavior, which was "contrary to everything we were ever taught about American values." "If you make this exception, the whole Constitution crumbles." He called Steven Morello (Army General Counsel), who showed him other documents, including the October 11, 2002 memo by MGen. Michael Dunlavey (commander of Guantánamo's JTF-170) asserting that "the methods and techniques delineated in the accompanying memoranda will enhance our efforts to extract information." On December 2 Rumsfeld had approved the techniques on Haynes's advice after Morello "tried to stop it" without success. Finding Beaver's legal justification for EITs "wholly inadequate," Mora went to Navy Secretary Gordon England on December 20 and, with his authorization, to Haynes, warning that Rumsfeld's "jocular" comment that he often stood for 8–10 hours a day could encourage techniques exceeding even the memo's expansive boundaries. Believing he had convinced Haynes to revoke the memo, Mora left for a two-week Christmas holiday, only to learn from Brant on January 6, 2003 that the abuse of al-Qahtani had worsened. After complaining to Deputy Defense Secretary Paul Wolfowitz, Dalton, the DoD spokesperson, and Rumsfeld, he met with Haynes, who insisted "the techniques are necessary to obtain information" to prevent further attacks. Warning that DoD's legal justifications might not convince courts, Mora advised Haynes to "protect your client." But when Haynes relayed this to Rumsfeld, he just repeated his joke about standing for eight hours, insisting "that's not torture."

Because his warnings were ignored, Mora defied Haynes's instruction never to put anything in writing and drafted a memo he threatened to "sign out" on January 15 (making it an official document) unless EITs ended. At the end of that day Haynes told Mora that Rumsfeld was suspending the techniques and authorizing the Walker Working Group (including Mora) to develop guidelines. A week later, however, Haynes showed Mora an 81-page draft opinion by John Yoo, which Haynes had solicited, effectively superseding the Working Group. Convinced it contained "catastrophically poor legal reasoning," Mora wrote Walker that the "dangerous" opinion was "fundamentally in error." Walker replied that Haynes and she disagreed. Approached by Mora, Yoo reaffirmed on February 6 that "the President has the authority to order torture." Fearing that the Working Group's contributions were being "rejected if they did not conform to the OLC guidance," Mora told Haynes that Walker's report was "deeply flawed" and urged Rumsfeld to jettison it. But the Working Group approved the report at its last meeting on March 2. All four JAGs sent memos of dissent to Haynes, who immediately classified them secret. (In 2005 Sen. Graham – a former SJA – had released those memos, which he praised as written by "professional military lawyers," not "the ACLU" or "people who are soft on terrorism." MGen. Rives, the Air Force JAG, wrote: "we have taken the legal and moral 'high-road' in the conduct of our military operations." RAdm. Lohr, the Navy JAG, warned against "condoning practices that, while technically legal, are inconsistent with our most fundamental values." MGen. Romig, the Army JAG, declared that the OLC memo "will open us to international criticism that the 'U.S. is a law unto itself.'")

Mora waited to file his own dissent until Walker published her report, but it never appeared. When newspapers reported other abuses in June 2003, Sen. Leahy wrote Secretary of State Rice and received an assurance from Haynes that DoD had prohibited cruel, inhuman, or degrading treatment. Mora assumed this meant Rumsfeld had reversed his earlier policy, and was disabused only when the Abu Ghraib scandal broke in April 2004. During Senate hearings, Mora learned that Rumsfeld had signed Walker's report a year earlier without informing him. On July 7, 2004 he wrote Vice Adm. Church that "our government had adopted what only can be labeled as a policy of cruelty," which "disfigures our national character. It is incompatible with our constitutional order, with our laws, and with our most prized values … Where cruelty exists, law does not." Rumsfeld responded to Mayer's story by claiming he had not known of any objections to his policy until 4–6 weeks after he issued it. Once he learned of the objections, "we stopped it immediately." "Maybe" his comment about standing 8–10 hours a day "should have gone out" of the memo; but he added flippantly: "it did [not], and I wrote it and life goes on."

In March 2006 Condoleezza Rice said in a major foreign policy speech: "President Bush has stated unequivocally, as have I, that the United States is a nation of laws and we do not tolerate any American at home or abroad engaging in acts of torture."[31] But the same month AI published a 41-page report on abuses in Iraq, including harsh interrogation and torture. In April HRW sent the recently confirmed Attorney General a letter from more than a hundred legal academics urging him to issue "a clear public statement about specific legal standards applicable to detention and interrogation of detainees overseas" under NDAA 2006. They were "especially" concerned about his "failure to state that 'waterboarding' … constitutes torture" and urged him to clarify that "subjection to extreme temperatures, forced standing, binding in stress positions, and severe sleep deprivation" were unlawful cruel, inhuman, or degrading treatment. Soon thereafter, HRW, HRF, and the Center for Human Rights and Global Justice (CHRGJ) reported that at least 460 people had been abused, tortured, or killed in Afghanistan, Iraq, and Guantánamo; only 400 of the 600 suspects were investigated, and just a third had faced disciplinary action. In May the ACLU published an Army document dated several weeks before the Abu Ghraib scandal broke, listing 62 allegations of detainee abuse in Iraq and Afghanistan and a May 19, 2004 document in which a DIA officer said LGen. Sanchez had encouraged interrogators "to go to the outer limits to get information from the detainees."

When Michael Hayden deferred discussing waterboarding in a closed SSCI hearing on his nomination as CIA Director, the *Washington Post* reminded him that an "explicit" aim of the DTA ban on cruel, inhuman, or degrading treatment had been "to stop the CIA's use of waterboarding."[32] Such silence did "incalculable" damage "to America's global standing and long-term interests." But SSCI quickly voted for the nomination (12–3), and the Senate confirmed him (78–15).

Bush had nominated Haynes to the Fourth Circuit Court of Appeals in September 2003.[33] The SJC held hearings that November and voted him to the floor in March 2004 (before the Abu Ghraib scandal broke), but the 108th Congress adjourned without action (allegedly because of Graham's opposition). When Bush renominated Haynes in February 2005, McCain declared his opposition, and Graham voiced reservations based on the memos (quoted above) in which "military lawyers express grave concerns about confusing and legally flawed interrogation policies." RAdm. Guter (a retired Navy JAG) wrote Sen. Specter to oppose "the nomination of one who played such an integral role in creating this administration's 'unlawful combatant' policies." RAdm. Hutson (another retired Navy JAG) wrote Specter that Haynes "demonstrated himself to be deaf to the advice of senior military and civilian lawyers." Twenty-one retired military officers wrote the SJC to express "profound concern about the role Mr. Haynes played in establishing – over the objections of uniformed military lawyers – detention and interrogation policies … which led not only to the abuse of detainees in U.S. custody but to a dangerous abrogation of the military's long-standing commitment to the rule of law." But complaining that Haynes's record had been "distorted," Larry D. Thompson, James B. Comey, Jack Goldsmith, and Patrick F. Philbin (former high-ranking DoJ lawyers) maintained that he had sought to restrict EITs, brought the concerns of military lawyers to Rumsfeld's attention, and implemented OLC opinions simply because they "are binding on the executive branch." Leahy was unpersuaded, noting that Haynes had disingenuously written him on June 25, 2003 – soon after DoD approved EITs – that the CAT prohibited cruel, inhuman, or degrading treatment.

At the SJC hearing Haynes explained that enemies who "don't follow any rules" presented "difficult decisions." He was "glad" the August 2002 torture memo had been withdrawn. "I wasn't the decision maker. I was trying to be very clear about my role as the lawyer." Graham called Haynes's Working Group "a sham." Kennedy condemned Haynes's "shocking failure of legal and moral leadership." For Reid, the retired military officers' letter "says it all." Durbin asked "what message are we sending the world, in light of your role in promulgating abusive interrogation techniques, like the use of dogs, stress positions and forced nudity?" Haynes blamed Abu Ghraib on bad apples, "the work of the night shift, without any authority whatsoever." But the *New York Times* accused him of having been "closely involved in shaping some of the Bush administration's most legally and morally objectionable policies, notably on the use of torture. The last thing he is suited to be is a federal judge." The eight SJC Democrats asked for documents, including unredacted copies of the Church, Jacoby, and Formica reports.

All pending nominations expired with the August recess. But though the Democrats won the Senate in the November 2006 election, Bush renominated Haynes (among others), an action Sen. Schumer (D-NY) denounced as "a clear slap in the face of our request" for "the president to be bipartisan." Sen. Leahy (incoming SJC chair) accused Bush of "choosing partisanship over progress ... at the expense of a fair and independent judiciary." The *Washington Post* said Bush's action "strikes a discordant note." The *Los Angeles Times* went further: Bush had "kept the Hatfield–McCoy spirit alive." But when Congress convened in January 2007, the White House list of 33 proposed judges omitted Haynes. Schumer called it "the first whiff of conciliation." Leahy said Bush had made "the right decision."

Because the DTA subjected all military interrogations to the Army Field Manual, its revision engendered controversy over whether ECs in Guantánamo should be treated as POWs.[34] Asked during Senate hearings whether the new manual would impose a uniform standard and prohibit anything "that would be considered unlawful if it were employed against American service members," Rumsfeld said guardedly it would "comply with U.S. law." But in June 2006 the Army announced (over DoS opposition) that the manual would omit the Geneva Convention ban on "humiliating and degrading treatment." The *Los Angeles Times* warned that "this country harms its own image – and puts its troops in harm's way – when it humiliates and degrades prisoners." "Giving interrogators an inch of discretion" would encourage "some of them to take a mile." Letters to the *Times* called the proposed rules "unconscionable" and feared they would show "that the United States is definitely not a Christian country." The *New York Times* noted that "12 presidents and generations of military leaders" over more than seven decades had respected the Geneva Conventions. The administration's assurance of "humane treatment" did not offer "much comfort, since the Bush team has shown that it does not define humane treatment the way most people do." Cheney aides and some military officers wanted the rules to remain secret and permit different methods for "unlawful combatants," but they were opposed by human rights groups and Sens. McCain, Warner, and Graham. Gen. Abizaid (CENTCOM commander) and Gen. Schoonmaker (Army Chief of Staff) wanted clear regulations "so our corporals in the field can understand them." In August the DoD OIG issued a report on interrogations, which found that abuse allegations were not consistently reported, investigated, or managed; interrogation lacked unity and exceeded the Army Field Manual.

When the Army released the revised manual in September, the Army Deputy Chief of Staff for Intelligence acknowledged past "transgressions and mistakes" and asserted that "any piece of intelligence which is obtained under duress ... would be of questionable credibility, and additionally it would do more harm than good when it inevitably became known that abusive practices were used."[35] The Deputy Assistant Secretary of Defense for Detainee Affairs said the new policy "unambiguously articulates the values and traditions of our nation, values that John Adams called 'the policy of humanity,' which has been the cornerstone of the American ethics of warfare." As a former prosecutor, he had learned from Guantánamo interrogators that intelligence "is best derived through a period of ... long-term rapport-building." The manual prohibited "outrages upon personal dignity, in particular humiliating and degrading treatment," but added three methods to be used only on "unlawful combatants": good cop/bad cop; false flag (pretending the interrogation was in a foreign country); and separation. Appendix M explained that the last included solitary confinement, perceptual and sensory deprivation, sleep deprivation, fear and hopelessness, sensory overload, high and low temperatures, and emotional pride down.

Although the CIA had ensured that it was not governed by the manual, ODNI used Bush's contemporaneous transfer of the 14 HVDs from secret prisons to Guantánamo to declare that the Agency had "designed a new interrogation program that would be safe, effective, and legal" and "obtained legal guidance from the Department of Justice that none of the new procedures violated ... the U.S. Constitution, any U.S. statute, or U.S. treaty obligations."[36] All CIA interrogators were screened, experienced, trained and observed by nonparticipants, who could terminate any interrogation and had to report any deviation to the OIG and DoJ. The CIA claimed its interrogations had averted numerous terrorist attacks. At a press conference Bush also pronounced the interrogation procedures "tough ... safe, and lawful, and necessary," but refused to describe them because that "would help the terrorists learn how to resist questioning." He enumerated "some of the plots that have been stopped because of the information of this vital program."

Bush also promoted his Military Commissions Act, which not only responded to the Supreme Court's recent *Hamdan* decision on MCs but also authorized the CIA to use EITs generally prohibited to the military: sleep deprivation, stress positions, and extreme temperatures.[37] The Act adopted the Supreme Court's interpretation of the Fifth Amendment – prohibiting only practices that "shock the conscience" – rather than the Geneva Conventions ban on "outrages upon personal dignity," which the administration rejected as too vague. John Yoo praised the MCA for letting the CIA "operate with a freer hand." Yale Law School Dean Harold Koh denounced it for suggesting that "we are not prepared to make the same commitment that every other nation has made." The *Washington Post* criticized Bush's "full-throated defense of the CIA's 'alternative set of procedures' that the world properly regards as torture." The *Los Angeles Times* said the only "difference between torture and these 'alternative procedures' seems to be who's conducting the interrogation."

When HASC approved the MCA on September 13, 2006, Chairman Hunter exulted that there was "no better way to honor the fifth anniversary of Sept. 11."[38] Rep. Hoyer, the Minority Whip, replied that "the role of Congress is to bring to bear its own independent judgment." SASC resisted the administration proposals. Graham was "suspicious." McCain said "the overwhelming majority of retired military people" opposed them. Sen. Reed (D-RI) praised the "sincere effort" by Warner, McCain, and Graham to draft legislation "based on principle." DNI Negroponte warned that their bill "will not allow for the CIA high-value terrorist detention program to go forward" and insisted the MCA was not an attempt "to alter Geneva, nor to avoid the purposes of Geneva, but rather to give it the kind of clarity we felt [was] required." Gen. Vesey (who had retired as JCS chairman in 1985 after the longest active duty service on record) wrote McCain that the MCA "would undermine the moral basis which has generally guided o[u]r conduct in war" and "give opponents a legal argument for the mistreatment of Americans being held prisoner in time of war." But a senior administration official authorized to speak about legal issues (Gonzales) assured the CIA that the rules governing it were "context-specific," and "shocks the conscience" was a "flexible" standard. The *Wall Street Journal* applauded this assurance that the "threshold may be higher with the likes of KSM." The *Washington Post*, by contrast, warned against "legislation that would authorize the CIA to engage in interrogation tactics the world understands as torture" and "rewrite America's obligations under the Geneva Conventions." Speaking a week later about Maher Arar's ordeal, the *Post* reiterated that that EITs produced "unreliable" information and "can badly damage the honor and influence of the United States and its relations with allies."

The issue inevitably became a political football. In October, Sen. Clinton (D-NY) said about the "ticking bomb" hypothetical:[39]

> In the event we were ever confronted with having to interrogate a detainee with knowledge of an imminent threat to millions of Americans, then the decision to depart from standard international practices must be made by the president, and the president must be held accountable … that very, very narrow exception within very, very limited circumstances is better than blasting a big hole in our entire law.

A McCain spokesman was "shocked" that she "would try to have it both ways." At a campaign stop a few days later Bush warned that Democrats wanted to "shut down" the "CIA interrogation program." "We Republicans understand that we must give our professionals all the tools necessary to protect the American people." He warned that Nancy Pelosi, "the official third-in-line for the presidency" if Democrats won the House, was "against questioning terrorists in the CIA program." Bush repeated that refrain at an RNC reception the next day. At a campaign dinner a day later, Karl Rove said: "If leading Democrats have their way, our nation will be weaker and the enemies of our nation will be stronger."

But others continued to speak out against EITs, especially waterboarding.[40] A former Navy SEAL, who paid to have himself waterboarded on Current TV and lasted 24 minutes, was unambiguous: "It is torture." John Brennan (National Counterterrorism Center director) said it went "beyond the bounds of what a civilized society should employ." Joseph Margulies (a Northwestern University law professor) wrote a *Washington Post* op ed about the false confessions North Korean interrogators had extracted decades earlier from 36 downed US pilots. Sen. Kennedy had reminded the Senate that after World War II the USA had punished Japanese officers for waterboarding US civilians. Stephen Rickard (Open Society Institute) wrote in a *Washington Post* op ed that CIA interrogators had refused to continue using EITs after passage of the DTA. Sens. Graham, McCain, and Warner and Rep. Hunter maintained that the MCA banned waterboarding, hypothermia, stress positions, and sleep deprivation.

But on Bill O'Reilly's show President Bush was evasive.[41] "[W]e are not going to talk about the techniques we use in a public form [*sic*]." "[W]e won't torture. But we need to be in a position where we can interrogate." "The intelligence community believes strongly that the information we got from the detainee questioning program yielded information that made America safer, that we stopped attacks." "[T]he number of Democrats that opposed questioning people we picked up on the battlefield" was "an issue that they [would] have to explain to the American people" in the election three weeks later. When O'Reilly said Bush had been accused of violating human rights, the president chuckled, adding: "Look, after 9/11 I vowed to protect this country."

On October 24 MSNBC published two long articles detailing resistance to EITs in Guantánamo.[42] Col. Mallow (CITF commander 2002–05) said that in summer 2002 his agents had seen "silly and stupid" behavior, which he immediately related to superiors, including Haynes's office. FBI agents also reported their concerns up their chain of command, provoking their exclusion from the September 25, 2002 visit to Guantánamo by high administration lawyers and other officials, which planned the al-Qahtani interrogation. On October 11, 2002 MGen. Dunlavey (then GB commander) sought approval to interrogate al-Qahtani using 19 techniques banned by the Army Field Manual. Although CITF criticized these as "possibly illegal" and offered alternatives, the military began using them the next day, even without written approval. When MGen. Miller replaced Dunlavey on November 1, 2002 and soon thereafter authorized coercive techniques, Mark Fallon (Mallow's deputy and FBI Special Agent in Charge at Guantánamo 2002–04) balked and convinced Mallow to order CITF agents in writing to disengage from and report any inhumane interrogation. The Office of Military Commissions had warned that al-Qahtani's interrogation made him "unprosecutable." Mallow and Fallon had also blocked Haynes's plan to send al-Qahtani to Egypt or Jordan for "questioning." David L. Brant (NCIS director and Fallon's superior) told the Army "If there's anything that's beyond the boards, we'll just pull our people out." The Air Force Office of Special Investigations representative on CITF agreed. After Brant informed Mora (described above), the two flew to Guantánamo to persuade Miller to adopt rapport building, but were bluntly told: "if you want to be on the team, you've got to put on the same uniform." When Miller was sent to Abu Ghraib in September 2003 to advise on interrogation, Fallon dispatched FBI agent Blaine Thomas as a "chaperone" (whom Miller promptly sidelined). Mora now said he was "intensely proud of all these individuals" who declared "we will not be a party to this, even if we're ordered to do so." "We may have stopped some abuse on the DoD side, but it's clear we had no effect on national policy."

The day these articles appeared, Cheney pronounced on a conservative radio talk show that "dunking a terrorist in water" was a "no-brainer" if it "saves American lives."[43] "Our ability to interrogate high value detainees like KSM, that's been a very important tool that we've had to be able to secure the nation." "We wouldn't have that authority today if [Democrats] were in charge." Although he had been called "vice president for torture," he insisted "we don't torture." A spokesperson immediately clarified that Cheney was referring to "an interrogation program without torture." Several days later Cheney repeated that "this country does not torture," but "the interrogation program for a selected number of detainees" was "one of the most valuable intelligence programs we have." He maintained disingenuously: "I didn't say anything about water-boarding"; the interviewer "didn't even use that phrase." But a former CIA General Counsel said: "it's clear that the vice president didn't mean a friendly swim at the country club." White House Press Secretary Tony Snow also tried to extricate Cheney. "The

Vice President says he was talking in general terms about a questioning program that is legal to save American lives, and he was not referring to water boarding." Cheney was "not a guy who slips up, and he's also not a guy who does winks and nods about things that involve matters that you don't talk about for political reasons." Repeatedly asked whether Cheney disavowed waterboarding, Snow just reiterated that "he will disavow … torture, and he will not talk about specific techniques." Even after the controversy seemed to die down, former Republican House Majority Leader Tom DeLay said: "I don't think water boarding is torture," a concept he limited to "cutting their fingers, sticking things in their eyes." "Water boarding is a frightening experience, but the person does not have any physical damage."

Soon after assuming the SJC chairmanship Leahy announced an agenda of "restoration, repair and renewal," creating a subcommittee on human rights and the law.[44] He asked DoJ to release two OLC opinions on the CIA and "all directives, memoranda and/or orders … regarding C.I.A. interrogation methods." "I expect real answers, or we'll have testimony under oath until we get them." But DoJ refused to release the memos, claiming the information was classified and included confidential legal opinions that were privileged and whose disclosure would help the enemy. Leahy found it "disappointing that the DoJ and the White House have squandered another opportunity to work cooperatively with Congress." He planned to "pursue this matter further" as part of an oversight hearing. The *Los Angeles Times* said the administration was making a "mistake" by "stonewalling." "Congress … has a right to know."

In a February *Washington Post* op ed, Eric Fair, a civilian interrogator in Fallujah in summer 2004, described having seen detainees who had been beaten, held in solitary, and deprived of sleep, food, and light.[45]

As late as March, President Bush still had not issued an executive order authorizing CIA interrogation under the MCA (passed seven months earlier), partly because of DoS objections.[46] As a result, the CIA had been following the Army Field Manual ever since the DTA passed at the end of 2005. But DCI Tenet continued to maintain that "enhanced" interrogation:

> has saved lives. I know we've disrupted plots. I know this program alone is worth more than the FBI, the Central Intelligence Agency and the National Security Agency put together, have been able to tell us … Everybody forgets one central context of what we lived through: the palpable fear that we felt on the basis of the fact that

> there was so much we did not know ... Let me say that again to you. We don't torture people.

The CIA used EITs "because these are people who will never, ever, ever tell you a thing. These are people who know who's responsible for the next terrorist attack."

In the first Republican presidential primary debate, Sen. McCain warned that:

> the more physical pain you inflict on someone, the more they're going to tell you what they think you want to know ...
>
> When I was in Vietnam, one of the things that sustained us as we ... underwent torture ourselves – is the knowledge that if we had our positions reversed and we were the captors, we would not impose that kind of treatment on them. It's not about the terrorist; it's about us. It's about what kind of country we are. [47]

Sen. Rand Paul (R-Ky) was troubled by the "newspeak," which substituted EITs for torture. But Rudy Giuliani said he would tell interrogators "to use every method they could think of," though not "torture." Asked about waterboarding, he repeated himself, adding "even if it involves very high-pressure techniques." (A day later he said he would leave the decision to "the people who do it." Waterboarding was just "aggressive" interrogation.) Rep. Duncan Hunter (R-Ca) offered only "one sentence: 'get the information.'" Mitt Romney said EITs "have to be used." Rep. Tom Tancredo (R-Co) produced uproarious laughter and applause by joking that while "we're wondering about whether waterboarding would be ... a bad thing to do ... I'm looking for Jack Bauer." Brushing off "theoretical" objections to torture, Tancredo warned that if "we go under, western civilization goes under." The *Washington Post* said only McCain "got it right." Early in his presidential campaign, Sen. Obama (D-Ill) asked a Kansas City crowd: "why don't we say we don't torture ... that's not who we are as a people." America needed to express its "core decency" in order to remain a "beacon of hope."

In a *Washington Post* op ed Gens. Krulak (Marine Corps Commandant 1995–99) and Joseph P. Hoar (CENTCOM Commander 1991–94) reminded EIT apologists that it was "conduct we used to call war crimes."[48]

> Fear breeds panic, and it can lead people and nations to act in ways inconsistent with their character ... it is the duty of the Commander in Chief to lead the country away from the grip of fear, not into its grasp ...

> any degree of "flexibility" about torture at the top drops down the chain of command like a stone ... if we forfeit our values by signaling that they are negotiable in situations of grave or imminent danger, we drive those undecideds into the arms of the enemy ... [US rules for interrogation] will set the standard ... for what kind of treatment captured American soldiers can expect from their captors.

Gen. Kern (Ret.), who had authored one of the Abu Ghraib reports, wrote the *Post* to agree. "We undermine the values that built this country and the credibility of our armed forces when we stoop to the level of some of our enemies."

The Intelligence Science Board (which advised the DNI) issued a report (completed in August 2006 and leaked in January 2007) questioning the scientific basis for claims that EITs worked, and tracing EITs to practices attributed to the NKVD in the Soviet Union in a 1956 article.[49] Following the report's publication in May, the *Washington Post* said claims for the efficacy of EITs could not be evaluated "because the records of those interrogations have been kept secret." If Bush reauthorized them, he "will act in contravention of his administration's own expert advisers." The *Los Angeles Times* accused the administration of having "created ambiguity about a subject that cries out for clarity. Torture violates basic norms of American society." SSCI (all eight Democrats and four of the seven Republicans) demanded a legal review of the CIA's detention and interrogation program as part of the FY2008 Intelligence Authorization Bill. "More than five years after the decision to start the program the committee believes that consideration should be given to whether it is the best means to obtain a full and reliable intelligence debriefing of a detainee." Although the program "has led to the identification of terrorists and the disruption of terrorist plots," that should be "weighed against both complications it causes to any ultimate prosecution of these terrorists and the damage the program does to the image of the United States abroad." Although Feinstein and Whitehouse (D-RI) proposed to bar spending on interrogation techniques exceeding the Army Field Manual, Nelson (D-Fla) joined the Republicans in defeating it.

At SSCI's June confirmation hearing of John Rizzo as CIA General Counsel (he had been "acting" since March 2006), DCI Hayden acknowledged that President Bush still had not interpreted the Geneva Conventions, as required by the MCA.[50] Sen. Feingold (D-Wisc) said: "given this administration's willingness to violate the law and keep Congress in the dark … it is particularly important for Mr. Rizzo to provide assurances … that he will ensure that CIA respects the laws that Congress writes and will not rely on the administration's theory of inherent constitutional authority to violate the law." Feinstein expressed "serious concerns about this nomination." Noting that Rizzo had not objected to the 2002 "torture" memo, Sen. Wyden (D-Or) said: "I'm going to keep the hold until the detention and interrogation program is on firm footing, both in terms of effectiveness and legality." On July 20 Stephen Bradbury (acting OLC director) sent Rizzo a 79-page memo finding that six (redacted) EITs remained legal under the War Crimes Act, DTA, MCA, and Geneva Conventions. Bush withdrew the nomination on the day the committee had scheduled a vote. Rockefeller, SSCI chair, said the confirmation process "raised serious questions about whether [Rizzo] was the right person for the job." Bond, the Republican vice chair, agreed. (But Rizzo continued to be Acting General Counsel.)

Although SSCI postponed passage of the FY2008 Intelligence Authorization Act until Bush produced the documents it sought, the White House needed more "time to consider fully all legal and administrative aspects." Bush issued a classified order on July 20. Asked if it allowed waterboarding, a senior official said only that "it would be very wrong to assume that the program of the past would move into the future unchanged." The order guaranteed detainees "the basic necessities of life, including adequate food and water, shelter from the elements, necessary clothing, protection from extremes of heat and cold, and essential medical care." But another official acknowledged that "sleep is not among the basic necessities." The CIA still barred the ICRC from visiting detainees. McCain, Graham, and Warner wanted more information. Rockefeller repeated SSCI's demand that the White House produce the DoJ analysis of the new guidelines. DNI McConnell refused to discuss "specific measures," which "would aid those who want to resist those measures." "Because they believe these techniques might involve torture and they don't understand them, they tend to speak to us … [in] a very candid way." The program "has saved countless lives." But detainees "have adequate diet, [are] not exposed to heat or cold. They're not abused in any way." "[T]here would be no permanent damage." Bush's order prohibited torture, which it defined as "mutilation or murder or rape or physical pain." Attorney General Gonzales said techniques "would depend on circumstances."

The *Washington Post* warned that the order authorized techniques that "most people, including the world's democracies, regard as improper and illegal" and would expose "Americans captured by hostile governments" to "a new threat."[51] Gen. Kelley (Ret.) (Marine Corps Commandant 1983–87) and Robert F. Turner (former chair of the ABA Standing Committee on Law and National Security and former Reagan administration member) wrote in a *Washington Post* op ed that the order "has compromised our national honor" and might "promote the commission of war crimes by Americans." The *Los Angeles Times* urged Congress to "insist on a single standard for interrogation that will remove the 'but' from 'we do not torture.'" At its August meeting, the ABA House of Delegates (by a voice vote with a single nay) urged Congress to overrule Bush's order, which violated the Geneva Conventions and was inconsistent with the Army Field Manual. When all four JAGs warned that the order allowed CIA interrogators to engage in humiliating or degrading treatment unless they acted with specific intent, the DoJ repeated that the order was "consistent" with the Geneva Conventions. Turner called this "a con."

But DCI Hayden continued to resist, blaming the media for the unfortunate fact that "the broader political culture" was not "comfortable with the things we believe are both lawful and necessary to fight this war."[52] The CIA was not DoD and had not been "consulted about the Army Field Manual. No one ever claimed [the Manual] exhausted all the lawful tools America could have to protect itself." Days later, however, he revealed that in 2006 the Agency had banned waterboarding, to which only three men had been subjected in 2002–03. McCain exulted: "I have sought that result for years."

A few weeks later the *New York Times* disclosed Steven Bradbury's two secret opinions (described above), authorizing multiple painful tactics, including head slapping, simulated drowning, and cold, which the OLC had issued soon after Gonzales's confirmation.[53] Dan Froomkin wrote in his *Washington Post* column that this showed that "barbaric interrogation practices" had continued. The next day Rockefeller asked DoJ for the opinions, but Bond retorted that SSCI already had been briefed on the "legal justifications." The administration resisted Rockefeller on the ground that the opinions contained confidential advice. Leahy, whose SJC was about to hold a confirmation hearing for Michael Mukasey as Attorney General, also demanded the opinions, which he said had "reinstated a secret regime by, in essence, interpreting the law in secret." Specter (the ranking Republican) said the 2005 opinions "are more than surprising. I think they're shocking." Rep. Conyers (D-Mich) (HJC chair) also found "the alleged content of the opinions and the fact that they have been kept secret from Congress ... extremely troubling."

At a hastily organized press conference the next day, President Bush reiterated his mantra: "this government does not torture people." "The American people expect their government to take action to protect them from further attack. And that's exactly what this government is doing, and that's exactly what we'll continue to do." Rockefeller replied that the administration "can't say that Congress has been fully briefed while refusing to turn over key documents used to justify the legality of the program." Hayden denied "that the opinion opened the door to more harsh interrogation tactics" or "that information about the interrogation methods we actually have used has been withheld from our oversight committees." White House homeland security adviser Frances Fragos Townsend said "if Americans are killed because we failed to do the hard things, the American people would have the absolute right to ask why." Levin (SASC chair) asked Mukasey whether he would provide the memos if confirmed. Schumer commented sarcastically: "when the president says the Justice Department says it's o.k., he means Alberto Gonzales said it was o.k. Very few people are going to have much faith in that." McCain said he had been assured by the administration that waterboarding had ended.

The *Washington Post* observed that "presidential declarations can't change the facts" that the administration had "repeatedly authorized the CIA to use interrogation that the rest of the world – and every U.S. administration before this one – have regarded as torture." The OLC opinions were "highly questionable." "The administration has essentially been operating its own clandestine legal system, unaccountable to Congress or the courts." Congress should require that the Army Field Manual apply to all interrogations. The *New York Times* wrote that the USA used to "urge[] all nations to obey the letter and the spirit of international treaties." "The Bush administration has dishonored that history and squandered that respect." The public should ask whether we are "a nation that tortures human beings and then concocts legal sophistries to confuse the world and avoid accountability." Andrew Sullivan wrote in *The Times* of London that the phrase "enhanced interrogation" derived from the German *Versharfte Vernehmung*, "the exact term innovated by the Gestapo to describe what became known as the 'third degree.'" When the USA prosecuted this war crime in Norway in 1948, the Nazi defendants argued that "most of the injuries inflicted were slight and did not result in permanent disablement." Jimmy Carter told CNN that the USA "certainly" tortured detainees. "Our country for the first time in my lifetime has abandoned the basic principle of human rights." A reunion of US interrogators of German prisoners in the 1940s denounced the administration and refused its honors. Stuart Herrington, who had conducted interrogations in Vietnam, Panama, and the first Gulf War during his 30 years as an Army intelligence officer, said: "we never laid a hostile hand on a prisoner"; anyone who had done so "would have been disciplined and mostly likely relieved of his duties."

In response to a "ticking bomb" hypothetical proposed at the September 2007 Democratic presidential debate, Obama said:[54]

> America cannot sanction torture. It's a very straightforward principle, and one that we should abide by ... what we cannot do is have the President of the United States state, as a matter of policy, that there is a loophole or an exception where we would sanction torture. I think that diminishes us and it sends the wrong message to the world.

Sen. Biden (D-De) affirmed there was no "presidential exception." Hillary Clinton agreed: "we have to draw a bright line and say 'no torture – abide by the Geneva Conventions'." But though this seemed to repudiate the wriggle room she had given a president responding to a "ticking bomb" hypothetical, she soon reverted to that earlier position. All three had met with 17 flag officers, who had told Clinton: "in addition to the values that are so important for our country to exhibit ... there is very little evidence that it works." All the other Democratic candidates agreed.

But Republicans emulated Jack Bauer. Giuliani favored "aggressive questioning."[55] Whether waterboarding was torture "depends on how it's done ... on the circumstances ... on who does it." "The line between the two is very delicate and very difficult." "[W]hen you're dealing with terrorists ... you may have to use means that are a little tougher." He ridiculed Democrats for calling sleep deprivation torture: "on that theory, I'm getting tortured running for President of the United States. That's plain silly." His senior military intelligence adviser agreed: he had been waterboarded during training and felt "it falls into a gray area." McCain immediately retorted that waterboarding, which had been used by the Spanish Inquisition and Pol Pot in Cambodia, was "not a complicated procedure. It is torture." Although he would not waterboard "as a matter of course," Fred Thompson said officials sometimes had to "do what is necessary." (A man's got to do what a man's got to do.) "[A]ll I can say is that as president … the measures will always meet the circumstances." Romney said it was not "wise" to define "exactly what the line is on torture, because I don't think you want the enemy combatants to know what you're planning on doing."

After Gonzales announced his resignation as Attorney General, Democrats urged the White House to consult their Senate leadership on a replacement.[56] Specter wanted "somebody who understands the difference between being the president's lawyer and the chief law enforcement officer of the United States." Leahy sought a nominee with "a proven track record of independence to ensure that he or she will act as an independent check on this administration's expansive claims of virtually unlimited executive power." When Bush nominated Michael Mukasey, Biden said he would have to prove he was "not just the president's lawyer, but the country's lawyer." Four Harvard Law School Human Rights Program faculty urged Leahy to ask Mukasey: "will you commit to investigating and prosecuting those who have used, ordered, and authorized the use of waterboarding?" The *Los Angeles Times* said he should be asked whether he believed "that the humanitarian provisions of the Geneva Conventions apply less stringently to the CIA than to military interrogators?" Could the CIA subject suspected terrorists "to the simulated drowning known as water-boarding?" The *Washington Post* wanted him to be asked "do you approve of torture?" "Does he believe such methods as 'waterboarding' and sleep deprivation are unlawful?" The *New York Times* said he should be "made to explain which interrogation techniques he considers to be torture."

At the hearing Mukasey disavowed the (withdrawn) 2002 OLC "torture" memo, which "was worse than a sin, it was a mistake" because it was "unnecessary." He was not "aware of" a commander-in-chief power to immunize acts of torture that violated the law. If "the president has directed that the method of interrogation, notwithstanding a finding that it violates the law, should proceed anyway … I have no course but to follow the law." Leahy was "encouraged by the answers." The *Washington Post* complained that "few senators attempted to get beneath the surface of the judge's compelling but often incomplete answers." The *New York Times* said his "discussion of torture was good as far as it went, but it was too general."

The next day Mukasey evaded Whitehouse's question about whether waterboarding was torture prohibited by the Constitution:

> I think it would be irresponsible of me to discuss particular techniques with which I am not familiar when there are people using coercive techniques and who are being authorized to use coercive techniques. And for me to say something that is going to put their careers or freedom at risk simply because I want to be congenial, I don't think it would be responsible of me to do that. What I'm saying is that techniques can be authorized that are beyond the Army Field Manual and I should not get into a discussion of what they might be or in what combination they might be authorized ... I don't know what's involved in the technique. If waterboarding is torture, torture is not constitutional.

Denouncing that as "a massive hedge," Whitehead gave a brief description, but Mukasey refused to elaborate. Whitehouse was "disappointed" by this "purely semantic" answer. Noting that there was "nowhere near as bright a line today" as there had been the day before, Leahy asked "whether you received some criticism from anybody in the administration last night after your testimony." Mukasey denied this. But Feingold also observed that "overnight you've gone from being agnostic ... to holding what is a rather disturbing view" about the president's power to ignore the law. The White House said Mukasey was "not in a position to discuss interrogation techniques, which are necessarily classified."

Jonathan Turley (a George Washington University law professor) wrote in a *Los Angeles Times* op ed that "this confirmation vote should be about torture." Jed Rubenfeld (a Yale law professor) wrote in a *New York Times* op ed that Mukasey should be required to say whether the president could defy the law in the name of his authority "to defend the country," which would be "a dangerous confusion and distortion of the single most fundamental principle of the Constitution." Adam Cohen wrote in his *New York Times* column that Mukasey's claim that the president could defy laws when acting "to defend the country" created "a mighty large exception to the rule that Congress's laws are supreme." All ten SJC Democrats wrote Mukasey that it was "surprising that you are unfamiliar with waterboarding," which senior military leaders had described as torture. They asked for a "prompt response" to their question: "is the use of waterboarding, or inducing the misperception of drowning, as an interrogation technique illegal under U.S. law, including treaty obligations." Leahy said: "my vote would depend on him answering that question." Durbin called this a "seminal issue" on which his vote depended. Whitehouse (D-RI), Reid (D–Utah), and Sanders (D Independent–Vt) concurred. The next day Specter also sought

Mukasey's views "on the legality and propriety of waterboarding." The *Los Angeles Times* criticized Mukasey's "evasive testimony about torture." "[W]aterboarding, a feature of the Inquisition, isn't even a close call."

In his written response, Mukasey repeated that he had not been briefed, and an "*uninformed* statement of mine" [original emphasis] might be seen by interrogators as "a threat or a promise that could influence their performance" and might "provide our enemies with a window into the limits or contours of any interrogation program." "I was and remain loath to discuss and opine … at this stage." The White House praised this "very thorough" response. Leahy, however, remained "very concerned that Judge Mukasey finds himself unable to state unequivocally that waterboarding is illegal." Clinton was "deeply troubled by Judge Mukasey's continued unwillingness to clearly state his views on torture and unchecked executive power." Durbin said Mukasey "falls far short" on "precision … honesty and openness." Obama said: "we don't need another Attorney General who looks the other way on issues as profound as torture." Biden said: "anyone who thinks that waterboarding is not torture is not fit … to be Attorney General." By contrast, the nine SJC Republicans issued a news release urging the Senate to "stop playing politics with the Justice Department." Graham was heartened that Mukasey wrote that the DTA barred waterboarding by the military.

The *Washington Post* called it "a sad day in America when the nominee for Attorney General cannot flatly declare that waterboarding is unconstitutional." Mukasey should "renew his promise to review all Justice Department memos regarding detainee treatment and correct or eliminate those that don't comport with the law." Congress should require that all interrogations comply with the Army Field Manual. Dr. Allen S. Keller, director of the Bellevue/NYU Program for Survivors of Torture, said waterboarding and holding someone's head under water were torture. "Both mimic drowning … asphyxiation … waterboarding may be even more brutal than being submerged." Malcolm Nance, a master SERE (survival, evasion, resistance, escape) instructor, said: "waterboarding is unquestionably being used as a torture technique." "[A]nyone strapped down will say anything. Absolutely anything to get the torture to stop." Four retired flag officers wrote Leahy that waterboarding "is inhumane, it is torture, and it is illegal." As the four JAGs, they had told the SJC in 2006: "Waterboarding detainees amounts to illegal torture *in all circumstances*. To suggest otherwise … represents both an affront to the law and to the core values of our nation" [original emphasis].

Whitehouse asked on the Senate floor: "will we join that gloomy historical line leading from the Inquisition through the prisons of tyrant regimes, through gulags and dark cells, and through Saddam Hussein's torture chambers?" Durbin said: "if we are going to restore the image of the United States of America, the highest law enforcement officer should be clear, firm, unequivocal: that waterboarding and torture are unacceptable, un-American, illegal and unconstitutional." But Specter agreed with Mukasey that "an expression of an opinion … prior to becoming Attorney General would put a lot of people at risk." Graham and other Republicans expected Mukasey to declare waterboarding off limits once he had been briefed. (He never did.) McCain was "confident [Mukasey] would not condone such practice."

The *New York Times* was "stunned" that Mukasey "believes the president has the power to negate laws" and had suggested "he will not uphold standards of decency during wartime recognized by the civilized world for generations." His waterboarding comment was a "crass dodge." It published six letters decrying Mukasey's evasions. But the *Washington Post* now backtracked: for Mukasey to declare waterboarding illegal "would have been likely to bring him in conflict with existing Justice Department memorandums." He had promised to review them; "no nominee is likely to promise more in advance of confirmation."

Bush said Mukasey had been asked "unfair" questions because "he's not been read into the program." "If the Senate Judiciary Committee were to block Judge Mukasey on these grounds, they would set a new standard for confirmation that could not be met by any reasonable nominee … [and] would guarantee that America would have no Attorney General during this time of war." Specter asked the administration to brief the SJC on the CIA program; but Bush refused "to talk about techniques … the American people have got to understand the program is important and the techniques used are within the law." "On too many issues, Congress is behaving as if America is not at war." Speaking as a lawyer, Reid said: "if there were ever any indication of why people dislike lawyers, read the letter [Mukasey] wrote to us. It was so lawyerlike no one knew what he was saying." But Schumer was resigned that "no nominee from this administration will agree with us on torture … The best we can hope for is someone who will … remain independent." (Republicans noted that Schumer had recommended his fellow New Yorker.)

Leahy reiterated his opposition: "If an American was captured and waterboarded, would we consider it torture and want to raise bloody hell about it? Of course we would. There are fundamental issues that require moral and legal clarity and the willingness to act on our convictions, and this is one of them." But Schumer now said Mukasey was "far better than anyone could expect from this administration." He had made it clear in a closed meeting that he would enforce a law banning interrogation techniques, which Schumer hoped Congress would "soon pass." He wrote in a *New York Times* op ed that Mukasey "has demonstrated his fidelity to the rule of law." And declaring her support for Mukasey, Feinstein wrote in a *Los Angeles Times* op ed that Mukasey "is not Alberto R. Gonzales." His answers "were crisp and to the point, and reflected an independent mind." He did not "believe a president can be above the law." The *Washington Post* praised both senators for their "courage" and "moral fortitude to defy party politics and to take a stand on principle." The *Los Angeles Times* agreed that Mukasey "would represent a dramatic improvement" over Gonzales, and Feinstein "did the right thing." Specter also supported Mukasey for promising to enforce a law banning waterboarding. "[H]e is intelligent; he's really learned in the law. He's strong, ethical, honest beyond any question." The day after Schumer and Feinstein endorsed Mukasey (ensuring SJC approval), Bush repeated that Mukasey had declined to opine on waterboarding because he had not been briefed on it and did not want "an uninformed legal opinion to give terrorists a window into which techniques we may use, and we may not use, that could help them train their operatives to resist questioning."[57] The *Los Angeles Times* said Bush's "coyness about 'which techniques we may use' inevitably undercuts his repeated assertion that 'we do not torture.'" Congress should pass an "absolute and uniform" ban on torture "binding both the armed services and the CIA."

The SJC voted 11–8 for the nomination. Leahy dismissed as "empty argument" the assurances from fellow Democrats that Mukasey would enforce a law against waterboarding. Bush would veto such a law, and we "already have laws and treaty obligations against waterboarding." Kennedy called Mukasey's vow to enforce some future law "perhaps the most stunning and hollow promise reportedly made by a nominee for Attorney General in my 45 years in the Senate." "Enforcing the law is the job of the Attorney General. It's a prerequisite, not a virtue." Durbin accused Mukasey of a "legal dodge." "When the history of this time is written, the issue of torture will define America's values in the age of terrorism." Specter relied on the same assurance as

Schumer, while dismissing Mukasey's claim that he had not been briefed as "a flimsy excuse." Hatch objected that "it politicizes the Justice Department to demand that Judge Mukasey take a politically correct position on waterboarding." The *New York Times* published letters criticizing Democratic capitulation. But the *San Francisco Chronicle* called Mukasey "an intelligent, credible man" and blamed Congress for leaving the CIA a "legal loophole."

Late in the night of November 9 the Senate voted 53–40 to confirm Mukasey's appointment (the thinnest margin since 1952). Six Democrats and Lieberman (Independent D-Ct) joined the Republicans; the presidential candidates did not vote. In the preceding debate Feinstein said Mukasey was being treated unfairly. "This man has been a judge for 18 years. Maybe he likes to consider the facts before he makes a decision." Democrats should focus on shoring up the DoJ, not "pounding our chests" about torture. Assigning Democrats "a large measure of blame," the *New York Times* said cynically that "about all that is left of 'advice and consent' is the 'consent' part." The Senate had given the job of "chief law enforcement officer in the world's oldest democracy to a man who does not even have the integrity to take a stand against torture." Frank Rich wrote in his *New York Times* column that the vote "shows what pathetic crumbs the Democrats will settle for after all these years of being beaten down." The *Los Angeles Times* said that by withholding information about interrogation techniques, "Bush kept not only terrorists but [also] the American people guessing about whether waterboarding … is still an option." But swearing in Mukasey, Bush called him "the right man." Leahy said: "I want him to be as successful as possible." And Specter said "we're in for a clean slate."

While the nomination was pending, Democratic Reps. Nadler (NY) and Delahunt (Mass) introduced the law they hoped Mukasey would enforce: the "American Anti-Torture Act of 2007" banning torture by any US entity, including the CIA.[58] The House adopted it on November 13, but it died with the end of the Congress.

It was reported that Daniel Levin (then OLC acting head) became so worried about waterboarding as he prepared to issue the December 2004 opinion replacing the August 2002 "torture" memo, that he underwent the procedure at a military base, concluding it could be torture unless strictly limited and closely supervised.[59] Concerned that the administration had failed to offer clear guidelines, he had begun another memo imposing tighter controls when he was fired by Gonzales (whose confirmation was facilitated by Levin's 2004 memo) and replaced by the more pliant Bradbury. The *Washington Post* said Levin's "name can be added to the roster of accomplished conservative lawyers … who found themselves fighting to sustain the rule of law in an administration too often eager to suspend it." Mukasey should make "the eradication of this kind of disregard for principle and law … his first priority." But John Bellinger III (State Department Legal Adviser) temporized like Mukasey. Asked whether another nation would ever be justified in waterboarding an American, he said: "one would have to apply the facts to the law" (he meant the opposite) "to determine whether any technique … would cause severe pain and suffering." Pressed further, he was "not willing to include it or exclude it" because "our Justice Department has concluded that we just don't want to get involved in abstract discussions."

Henri Alleg, who had written a graphic account of being tortured by France during the Algerian war, now repeated: "no one can say, having passed through [waterboarding], that this was not torture."[60] Malcolm Nance told the HJC he had found waterboarding "an overwhelming experience that induces horror and triggers frantic survival instincts … I was being tortured."[61] But Rep. Franks (R-Az) said severe techniques were needed in emergencies, echoing the claim that KSM gave up important information about al-Qaeda after being waterboarded for just 90 seconds. Two days before Mukasey's confirmation vote the Army issued a "Strategic Communication Hot Topic" to "senior leaders" reiterating the ban on waterboarding.

John Kiriakou, a retired 14-year CIA veteran, boasted that waterboarding had broken abu Zubaydah in less than 35 seconds.[62] "It was like flipping a switch." Afterwards "he answered every question. The threat information he provided disrupted … maybe dozens of attacks." "[I]f we don't waterboard a person, and we don't get that nugget of information, and there's an attack … I would have trouble forgiving myself." But while acknowledging it was "inconsistent," Kiriakou also said waterboarding was "simply: torture." "We're Americans, and we're better than this." Kiriakou was interviewed by all the major media (but admitted the next day that he had not seen abu Zubaydah waterboarded). On the basis of this, Rush Limbaugh declared that waterboarding "works, is the bottom line." *National Review* editor Jonah Goldberg said that Kiriakou showed waterboarding was "right and certainly defensible." But retired FBI agent Daniel Coleman, who had helped to lead efforts against bin Laden until 2004 and supervised the examination of documents after abu Zubaydah's capture, said he had been only a "safehouse keeper" with mental problems, who claimed to know more than he did. Coleman had little confidence in anything abu Zubaydah said after being tortured, "because once you go down that road, everything you say is tainted." The CIA agreed with the FBI that abu Zubaydah had disclosed information about KSM and José Padilla *before* being subjected to EITs. But the Agency and the Bureau clashed bitterly over the use and efficacy of EITs.

On December 5, 2007 the *New York Times* informed DCI Hayden it would disclose the Agency's destruction of its EIT videotapes.[63] Hayden promptly told the Congressional oversight committees and Agency employees, repeating its justification for EITs: "Under normal questioning, Zubaydah became defiant and evasive. It was clear, in the President's words, that 'Zubaydah had more information that could save innocent lives, but he stopped talking.' That made imperative the use of other means to obtain the information – means that were lawful, safe, and effective." After the Agency "determined [the videotapes] were no longer of intelligence value" because the "documentary reporting was full and exacting," and that they were "not relevant to any internal, legislative, or judicial inquiries," it had destroyed them in 2005 because they "posed a serious security risk." Rockefeller said SSCI had been briefed on the existence and destruction of the tapes only in fall 2006 when it began to debate subjecting the CIA to the Army Field Manual. Hoekstra (who chaired the House Permanent Select Committee on Intelligence (HPSCI) in 2004–06) was never informed. After CIA General Counsel Scott W. Muller told some lawmakers about the planned destruction, Harman, the senior HPSCI Democrat in 2002–06, cautioned in writing "against destruction of any videotapes." Holt (D-NJ), a Committee member, said the CIA had repeatedly told him it did not tape interrogations. HJC chair Conyers wrote Mukasey that "withholding of evidence sought in fact-finding or criminal investigations could amount to obstruction of evidence." The 9/11 Commission protested it had never been told about the tapes despite its declared "interest in getting all the information we could on the detainees." The CIA had told Judge Brinkema (trying Zaccarias Moussaoui) that it had no videotapes of interrogations.

Jose A. Rodriguez Jr. (CIA Director of Clandestine Operations), who ordered the destruction, acted on the advice of two lawyers from his directorate (Steven Hermes and Robert Eitinger) but did not consult with DCI Goff or Acting General Counsel Rizzo. Comparing the destruction to "the 18½ minute gap in the tapes of President Richard Nixon," Sen.

Kennedy said the reason was "obvious – coverup." Calling Hayden's explanation "pathetic," Sen. Levin wanted a DoJ investigation. The *Washington Post* and Sens. Hagel and Biden said it could be obstruction of justice. House Minority Leader Boehner was "troubled"; Sen. McCain said: "it harms the credibility and moral standing of America in the world again." Even Mike Huckabee wondered if the destruction was "to cover somebody's rear end?" But instead of sending the matter to a prosecutor, Mukasey asked the DoJ and CIA IGs to conduct a joint investigation.

After Hayden briefed closed sessions of the two Intelligence Committees, members of both parties expressed outrage.[64] It emerged that four top administration lawyers had cautioned the CIA against the destruction: Gonzales, Addington, Miers, and Bellinger. The *New York Times*, Rep. Holt (D–NJ), and Sen. Reid called for an independent prosecutor. Reps. Reyes (D-Tex) and Hoekstra (R–Mich) (HPSCI chair and senior Republican) resisted the DoJ request to postpone their own inquiry until after its investigation because "the executive branch can't be trusted to oversee itself." DoJ also refused to tell SSCI if it had seen the tapes or provided legal advice because of "a long-standing policy of declining to provide nonpublic information about pending matters." When lawyers for Guantánamo detainees raised the destruction in a habeas hearing, DDC Judge Kennedy also deferred to the DoJ's investigation because "it is a law enforcement agency of this country." Two weeks after Kiriakou criticized the destruction, the CIA asked the DoJ to investigate whether he had disclosed classified information. At the end of 2007 the *New York Times* regretted that "men in some of the most trusted posts in the nation plotted to cover up the torture of prisoners by Central Intelligence Agency interrogators by destroying videotapes of their sickening behavior." The Agency retorted that the *Times* "does a great disservice to the men and women of the C.I.A." by describing "the lawful questioning of hardened terrorists as 'sickening behavior.'"

A month after the disclosure, Mukasey appointed John H. Durham (the senior Assistant US Attorney (AUSA) in Connecticut) to investigate.[65] The *New York Times* called this "a heartening, and unaccustomed, sign that the Attorney General is doing his duty to get to the bottom of a roiling scandal"; the *Washington Post* agreed it was "a welcome sign"; and the *Los Angeles Times* praised Mukasey's "commendable sensitivity to appearances." But following the referral, Rodriguez's lawyer said he would not testify before Congress without immunity.

Durham said he would review whether the government had violated any of the 17 orders in 21 lawsuits requiring preservation of evidence.

The *Washington Post* now reported that as early as September 2002 the CIA had briefed members of both Intelligence Committees (including Reps. Harman (D-Ca) and Goss (R-Fla) and Sens. Rockefeller (D-WV), Bob Graham (D–Fl), and Roberts (R-Kan)) about EITs.[66] One observer said no one had objected and at least two legislators had urged the CIA to push harder. Graham now claimed: "I was unaware of" waterboarding "so I couldn't object." In September 2006 the CIA briefed the entire committees for the first time, producing what DCI Hayden called a "rich dialogue." Goss (who had served on the House Committee until September 2004, when Bush made him DCI) agreed that those briefed had "a pretty full understanding of what the CIA was doing" and expressed "not just approval, but encouragement." Rep. Pelosi (D–Ca) (ranking minority member until January 2003) said the CIA represented the techniques as having been approved by lawyers but not yet operational. Rep. Harman (who replaced her) claimed to have sent the CIA a classified protest in February 2003. Because she had signed a second oath of secrecy as a committee member, "I was not free to disclose anything." Rockefeller said he had unsuccessfully urged an SSCI investigation. In May 2007 Sens. Feingold, Feinstein, Hagel, and Wyden had sent Hayden written objections about EITs after a classified hearing.

In December a conference committee of the two intelligence committees agreed that the 2008 authorization would limit all interrogation to the Army Field Manual, as Sens. Whitehouse (D-RI), Feingold, and Hagel had proposed.[67] Hagel, a decorated Vietnam veteran, said "inhumane, cruel variations of torture do not work." "That's not who we are as Americans." Rep. Harman said: "John McCain has persuaded me" that waterboarding is "something we should never do." But Sen. Bond (R-Mo) insisted waterboarding "is not torture" because "there are different ways of doing it." Setting any limits would let terrorists prepare for interrogations. The White House threatened a veto. The *New York Times* endorsed the proposal because Mukasey had "twisted himself into knots … refusing to say whether waterboarding was torture and therefore illegal." The *Los Angeles Times* concurred. Twenty-eight retired flag officers wrote both Intelligence Committees in favor. A week later the House passed the bill largely along party lines (222–199), mandating regular reports to Congress on CIA detention and interrogation methods and any DoJ legal justification. Rep. Reyes (HPSCI chair) declared that "the House is back in the business of conducting oversight of the intelligence community." But Rep. Hoekstra (his predecessor) complained that Congress was "giving al Qaeda ... our playbook." Bush repeated his veto threat, objecting to the limit on interrogation and the disclosure requirement. And Senate Republicans used a parliamentary maneuver to block the bill.

At the beginning of December 2007 Democratic presidential hopefuls Clinton, Obama, Dodd, Edwards, and Richardson, joined by Huckabee (the only Republican), met with a group of retired flag officers organized by HRF.[68] (Clinton, Biden, and Kucinich had met them in April.) BGen. Irvine told them there was "no conflict" between "protecting national security" and "the humane treatment of prisoners." In January 2008 the *New York Times* endorsed Clinton, who was "more prepared for the Herculean task of figuring out exactly where, how and how often the government's powers have been misused – and what must now be done to set things right," and McCain, who "stood up for the humane treatment of prisoners and for a ban on torture." The *Los Angeles Times* also endorsed McCain, who had "waged a principled and persistent effort to end the Bush administration's embrace of torture." But weeks later McCain voted against a bill to apply the Army Field Manual to CIA interrogations, strangely arguing that his own DTA banned CID treatment (though he knew it did not apply to the CIA).

Administration officials kept refusing to call waterboarding torture.[69] BGen. Thomas Hartmann (legal adviser to the military commissions) told Sen. Graham he was "not equipped to answer that question." DNI McConnell told *The New Yorker* it would be torture for him because he had a deviated septum and for others if you "get to the point that a person is actually drowning," but refused to say categorically it was torture. "Our policies are not torture." EITs had produced "tons" of meaningful information and saved "tons" of lives. "You can say that absolutely" KSM "would not have talked to us in a hundred years" without being waterboarded. "As soon as they start to talk we can tell in minutes if they are lying." The CIA called McConnell's statement "a very strong endorsement of the value of the CIA's detention and interrogation program" and echoed his statement that "the United States does not torture." A few days later Tom Ridge (DHS Secretary 2003–05) said there was "just no doubt in my mind – under any set of rules, waterboarding is torture." But at a press conference soon thereafter Mukasey continued to temporize about whether waterboarding was torture because he was still reviewing the "current program." "I won't say any more." He wrote Leahy before the SJC oversight hearing that the CIA was not presently authorized to waterboard.

> The principle that one should refrain from addressing difficult legal questions … has even more force as to this question … because any answer I could give could have the effect of articulating publicly – and to our adversaries – the limits and contours of generally worded laws that define the limits of a highly classified program … There are some circumstances where current law would appear clearly to prohibit the use of waterboarding. Other circumstances would present a far closer question.

Leahy criticized this "answer," which "did not address issues members of the Committee have asked him … such as whether he agrees that waterboarding is torture and illegal." Durbin said "there comes a time when he's running out of excuses for not answering."

Asked at the hearing whether Bush had violated laws against torture, Mukasey replied: "I don't know." The DTA had adopted the constitutional "shocks-the-conscience" standard, "a balancing test of the value of doing something as against the cost of doing it." He "clarified" this by saying he "meant the heinousness of doing it … balanced against … the value of the information you might get." Biden said "shocking the conscience had to do with what we consider to be basic societal values … civilized behavior," which should not be judged in "relationship to the end being sought." Schumer could not understand how Mukasey "would not be able to say that something that's repugnant should be outlawed." Durbin complained that Mukasey's words had "melted into the abstract." Mukasey replied that he had "carefully reviewed the limited set of methods that are currently authorized for use in the CIA program, and I've concluded that they are lawful." Leahy retorted that Mukasey "should be able to say" waterboarding "is illegal." Asked by Kennedy when "would waterboarding be legal," Mukasey declined to engage in "imagining facts and circumstances that are not present and thereby telling our enemies exactly what they can expect in those eventualities." Kennedy rebuked him for "refus[ing] to say anything whatever on the crucial question of what constitutes torture" and "ignor[ing] the fact that the CIA continues to use stress positions, sleep deprivation, other techniques that are every bit as abusive as waterboarding." Mukasey responded by conceding he "would feel" that waterboarding was torture if done to him.

The *New York Times* said Mukasey had "parroted the Bush administration's deplorable line" in this "disappointing debut."[70] He had "weaved and dodged questions from senators about whether [waterboarding] is torture when done to other people, and whether it is legal." The *Los Angeles Times* warned that Mukasey's "repugnant" "evasions … set a dangerous global precedent," making it "more likely that waterboarding and other forms of torture will be used against U.S. soldiers and civilians." His "refusal to declare the practice illegal suggests that the administration's top priority isn't setting clear rules for interrogations, it's making sure that U.S. officials who used the technique … are not prosecuted." It rejected his "legal and moral relativism" –"Torture is defined by what is done to the victim, not by the usefulness of the information obtained" – and urged the Senate to pass the Intelligence Authorization Act. Tim Rutten wrote in his *Los Angeles Times* column that Mukasey had exposed "the moral absurdity of the government's position" and replaced Gonzales as "Bush's hapless sycophant in chief." The *Wall Street Journal* responded to these attacks by accusing SJC of having "waterboarded" Mukasey, who had been "right to avoid hypothetical legal judgments."

A week later DCI Hayden publicly told SSCI for the first time that the Agency had waterboarded abu Zubaydah, al Nashiri, and KSM in 2002–03 in the "belief that additional catastrophic attacks against the homeland were inevitable."[71] Information from KSM and abu Zubaydah accounted for a quarter of all intelligence reports circulated by the CIA on al-Qaeda in the five years after 9/11. Applying the Army Field Manual to CIA interrogation made no more sense than applying it to CIA recruiting or rules about sexual orientation. Prohibiting EITs "would substantially increase the danger to America." Claiming *The New Yorker* quotations were taken out of context, he insisted waterboarding was "a legal technique used in a specific set of circumstances." But FBI Director Mueller told SSCI that the Bureau had obtained critical information from Saddam Hussein without coercion, and he believed the FBI's methods were effective. And Director LtGen. Maples said DIA had obtained valuable information without coercion.

The next day a White House spokesman confirmed that the CIA could still waterboard with the president's approval, which would "depend on the circumstances," including whether "an attack might be imminent."[72] Sen. Feinstein said "the White House is trying to give themselves as much of an open field here as possible" to "use the same kinds of tactics used by the most repressive regimes." Sen. Graham said the administration had assured him that the DTA prohibited waterboarding. McCain and he had recently written Mukasey that it was "beyond dispute that waterboarding 'shocks the conscience.'" Sen. Durbin asked Mukasey to investigate whether waterboarding had broken any laws; and he put a hold on Mark Filip as Associate Attorney General until Mukasey answered questions about interrogation methods and DoJ policies.

Testifying before the HPSCI a day later, Hayden distanced himself from DNI McConnell and the White House.[73] Although "all the techniques we've used have been deemed lawful," waterboarding was not part of the current program "and in my view, the view of my lawyers and the DoJ, it is not certain that the technique would be considered to be lawful under current statute." A CIA spokesman quickly backtracked, claiming Hayden had meant that waterboarding would have to be approved by the Attorney General and the president. A week later Hayden told CIA employees: "as befits a republic of laws, this vital counter-terror initiative [EITs] rests on a strong legal foundation."

Rejecting Durbin's request, Mukasey explained to HJC that CIA officers "cannot possibly be the subject of a Justice Department investigation because that would mean that the same Department that authorized the program would now consider prosecuting someone who followed that advice." The same day Cheney told the Conservative Political Action Committee (CPAC) it had been "a good thing we found out what [the detainees] knew." "Would I support those same decisions again today? You're damn right I would." The CIA had "a tougher program for tougher customers," which produced "information that has saved thousands of lives." The White House said waterboarding would occur in the future only if the Attorney General affirmed its legality and the president notified Congress. There were no "plans to use it." "We have made clear that the law has changed. That has given greater clarity to these questions." Durbin responded by lifting the hold on Filip, but said Mukasey's "refusal to repudiate waterboarding does tremendous damage to America's values and image and places Americans at risk of being subject to waterboarding by enemy forces."

Richard E. Mezzo, a six-year Navy veteran who had experienced waterboarding, wrote in a *Washington Post* op ed that it "is indeed torture."[74] "Pulling out my fingernails or even cutting off a finger would have been preferable." But a few days later Steven Bradbury (who had written the two secret OLC memos approving EITs) told a HJC subcommittee that waterboarding differed from the Spanish Inquisition's "water torture" because it was subject to "strict time limits, safeguards, restrictions." "Something can be quite distressing, uncomfortable, even frightening," but "if it doesn't involve severe physical pain, and it doesn't last very long, it may not constitute severe physical suffering" and therefore not be torture. And in one of his notorious *ex cathedra* pronouncements, Justice Scalia endorsed cost–benefit relativism:

> Is it obvious that what can't be done for punishment can't be done to exact [*sic* – read "extract"] information that is crucial to the syc [*sic* – read CinC]? I think it's not at all an easy question … is it really so easy to determine that smacking someone in the face to determine where he has hidden the bomb that is about to blow up Los Angeles is prohibited in the Constitution? … It would be absurd to say you couldn't do that. And once you acknowledge that, we're into a different game. How close does the threat have to be? And how severe can the infliction of pain be? … it would be absurd to say you couldn't … stick something under the fingernail.

In February 2008 the Senate voted 51–45 for the Intelligence Authorization Bill the House had approved in December 2007, applying the Army Field Manual to all federal agencies.[75] Although Republicans Hagel (Neb), Lugar (In), Collins (Me), Snowe (Me) and Smith (Or) joined all but one Democrat, all the other Republicans opposed it, even McCain, who claimed (falsely) "we always supported allowing the C.I.A. to use extra measures." And Bond warned the bill "would shut down the most prolific source of … useful actual information that the C.I.A. receives." Feinstein (one of the bill's sponsors) called it "a very big day. Torture is out." When the White House said presidential advisers recommended a veto, Schumer cautioned that Bush would "be voting in favor of waterboarding," and Reid urged the president to "show his own moral leadership." The *Washington Post* praised Congress for taking "an important step toward restoring the moral authority of the United Sates."

In a BBC interview Bush asked critics "which attack would they have hoped that we wouldn't have prevented?"[76] "We'll make sure professionals have the tools necessary to do their job." "I suspect the families" of the July 2007 London bombing victims "understand the nature of killers." "What people gotta understand is that we'll make decisions based upon law." "We believe in human rights and human dignity … We believe in freedom. And we're willing to take the lead … We're willing to accept responsibilities … And history will judge the decisions made during this period of time as necessary decisions."

McCain defended his vote a week later. "When we passed the Military Commission Act, we said that the C.I.A. should have the ability to use additional techniques. None of those techniques would entail violating the Detainee Treatment Act, which said that cruel, inhuman or degrading treatment are [*sic*] prohibited." That ban included waterboarding and "other extreme techniques." But the Field Manual "is not always directly translatable to use by intelligence officers." Declaring that McCain had been "untrue to his principles" and had "squandered some of his moral authority," the *Los Angeles Times* said his vote "belies his opposition to torture."

Bush vetoed the law "because it would take away one of the most valuable tools in the war on terror."[77] "We have no higher responsibility than stopping terrorist attacks." CIA interrogation "produced critical intelligence that has helped us prevent a number of attacks." The bill "would deprive the C.I.A. of the authority to use … safe and lawful techniques." The Army Field Manual was "not intended for intelligence professionals trained to question hardened terrorists."

In April 2008 ABC News revealed that the National Security Council's Principals Committee had approved the EITs, including waterboarding abu Zubaydah, and had described the August 2002 torture memo as the "golden shield."[78] DCIs Tenet and Goss briefed senior advisers, including Cheney, Rice, Rumsfeld, and Powell. Ashcroft agreed the policy was legal but wished senior White House advisers had been kept ignorant of the details, warning that "history will not judge this kindly." After the CIA captured a new suspect (al Nashiri), it asked the Principals Committee in summer 2003 to approve more EITs. Overriding Powell's growing concern, Rice (who chaired that meeting) told the CIA: "this is your baby. Go do it." Bush now acknowledged that he knew "our national security team met on this issue. And I approved" because people had been saying "the administration is not connecting the dots." The *New York Times* deplored that "with President Bush's clear knowledge and support … some of the very highest officials in the land not only approved the abuse of prisoners, but participated in the detailed planning of harsh interrogations and helped to create a legal structure to shield from justice those who followed the orders." It published a September 27, 2007 letter from Deputy Assistant Attorney General Brian Benczkowski to Sen. Wyden, opining that "to rise to the level of an outrage" prohibited by the Geneva Convention, conduct "must be so deplorable that the reasonable observer would recognize it as something that should be universally condemned." In March 2008

Benczkowski wrote: "the fact that an act is undertaken to prevent a threatened terrorist attack, rather than for the purpose of humiliation or abuse, would be relevant to a reasonable observer in measuring the outrageousness of the act." A Wyden spokesman called these claims "stunning" and "appalling." Defying Bush's earlier veto, the SSCI version of the 2009 Intelligence Authorization Act again applied the Army Field Manual to the CIA. Hayden responded: "We cannot have an approach to terrorism that only uses hated words 'renditions' and 'detentions' and 'interrogations'" and has "an on-off switch every other November."

The administration rebuffed Congressional efforts to investigate its involvement in interrogation. After learning from Phillippe Sands's book about Addington's role in approving interrogation in Guantánamo, Rep. Conyers asked him to testify before the House Judiciary Committee.[79] But his counsel said "Congress lacks any authority to examine" Cheney's or Addington's "behavior on the job." Yoo refused to talk about "deliberative communications." Ashcroft also declined, citing his workload (as a "consultant") and executive and attorney–client privilege. The HJC subcommittee on the Constitution, civil rights and civil liberties, chaired by Rep. Nadler, issued a subpoena for Addington, who spoke for just 72 seconds, warning: "no American should think we're free, the war is over, al Qaeda is not coming and they're not interested in getting us. Because that's wrong." He denied any legal or moral responsibility for interrogation tactics. Asked "could the president ever be justified in breaking the law," he said: "I'm not going to answer a legal opinion on every imaginable set of facts any human being could think of." Asked if an interrogator could torture a child to get information from a parent, he said: "I'm not here to render legal advice to your committee. You do have attorneys of your own." He claimed not to remember whether he had urged interrogators to use tougher techniques. Asked if waterboarding had been discussed, he said: "I can't talk to you. Al Qaeda may watch these meetings." Yoo could not say whether his torture memo had been implemented because the word implement "can mean a wide number of things." When the hearing resumed in July, Douglas Feith testified that the interrogation techniques approved by Rumsfeld in 2002 could be applied "in a humane fashion." "Removal of clothing doesn't mean naked," since interrogators could just remove top hats and monocles. American citizens were subject to "stress" in police stations every day. Asked how prisoners could be hooded and terrorized by dogs "humanely," Feith said multiple techniques "needed to be used in a carefully coordinated manner." Republican Reps. King (NY) and Issa (Ca) repeatedly obstructed Nadler's questioning, while Democrats fulsomely praised Ashcroft, who said the torture memos had been withdrawn "with both my knowledge and my approval." "I don't think I could, under oath, say that I've never had a second thought about it … if we've done something that we can improve, why would we not want to improve it?" In response to the softball question whether another attack would "not only be a probability but a certainty" without "our interrogation process," Ashcroft replied: "it could well have been."

In May 2008 DoJ offered the two Intelligence Committees the unredacted OLC opinions approving interrogation.[80] Sen. Feingold called this "certainly too late … and too little, as well." At a hearing of his SJC subcommittee, John P. Elwood (then OLC deputy head) said some opinions needed to be kept from the public because they were classified and officials had to be able to give confidential advice. But J. William Leonard, who had been in charge of document classification from 2002 to January 2008, said a March 2003 OLC opinion on interrogation should never have been classified. The *New York Times* said that "for more than a year, President Bush has refused to honor legitimate requests from the Democratic majority in Congress for legal documents that he used to justify ordering the abuse, humiliation and torture of prisoners." The *Washington Post* was pleased the administration was "gingerly mov[ing] toward comity and accountability" after having "jealously – and unjustifiably – guarded these documents for years." Feingold complained in a *Los Angeles Times* op ed that "the memos on torture policy that have been released or leaked hint at a much bigger body of law about which we know virtually nothing."

Also in May 2008 DoJ IG Glenn Fine published a report on the FBI's role in interrogation in Iraq, Afghanistan, and Guantánamo, whose release had been blocked for months by DoD.[81] Having reviewed more than 500,000 pages and conducted hundreds of interviews, the OIG praised the Bureau for refusing to engage in abusive interrogation, but criticized its slow response to agent reports of abuse. Nearly half the 450 FBI agents at Guantánamo reported observing interrogators outside the Bureau using harsh methods. After calling abu Zubaydah's interrogation "borderline torture," the FBI observed the CIA interrogation of Ramzi bin al-Shibh in Guantánamo, but continued debating whether to keep cooperating with the Agency, making a clean break only in 2003. FBI agents at Guantánamo began creating a "war crimes" file in 2002, but terminated it the next year because "investigating detainee allegations of abuse was not the F.B.I.'s mission." In July 2003 the head of the FBI's national security law unit wrote top officials that "were these enemy prisoners of war" the interrogations would "beyond doubt" be unlawful. Senior DoJ Criminal Division officials had raised concerns with the National Security Council.

The CIA retorted that the methods had been "found lawful by the DoJ itself." DoD said the report contained "nothing new," and in any case "the Department has been operating for a number of years now with new and improved guidance." A Rice spokesman called the report "pretty vague." But SASC chair Levin said it rebutted claims that abuse "was simply the result of a few bad apples acting on their own." HJC chair Conyers said he would ask Ashcroft, Yoo, Addington, Mueller, and Mukasey to testify. The *Washington Post* urged Congress to "vigorously" resist the administration's "long-running effort to circumvent the domestic anti-torture statute and the international Convention Against Torture." Declaring that "the report shows what happens when an American president, his Secretary of Defense, his Justice Department and other top officials corrupt American law to rationalize and authorize the abuse, humiliation and torture of prisoners," the *New York Times* called on Congress to "press for full disclosure." Rice now explained that "we were in an environment in which saving America from the next attack was paramount," but added: "I don't want anyone to believe that even when we were in that different place that we failed to ask the question: 'are we living up to our laws and to our treaty obligations?'" Fifty-six House Democrats wrote Mukasey citing "mounting evidence" that administration officials had authorized waterboarding and urging DoJ to appoint a special counsel. But in July Mukasey told the SJC he would not do so. A New York City Bar Task Force criticized Bush and the MCA for allowing the CIA to continue conducting EITs.

Several Congressional committees held hearings in June.[82] LtCdr. William C. Kuebler (who represented Omar Khadr before a military commission) told the SJC that a DoD manual directed employees to destroy evidence of harsh interrogation. Because the mission "has legal and political issues that may lead to interrogators being called to testify, keeping the number of documents with interrogation information to a minimum can minimize certain legal issues." FBI General Counsel Valerie Caproni testified she had never been allowed to see the OLC opinions. Glenn Fine told the House Foreign Affairs Committee that FBI agents had raised concerns about "the legality and effectiveness of

DoD techniques" and their impact on military commission prosecutions. But Rep. Rohrabacker (R-Ca) was dismissive: EITS "seem more like … hazing pranks from some fraternity than some well-thought-out policy of how do you torture someone and get information from them."

The same month SASC hearings revealed that in July 2002 DoD lawyers sought information on reverse engineering SERE.[83] Alberto Mora called the decision to use EITs "a mistake of massive proportions," a "policy of cruelty" that violated "our founding values, our constitutional system and the fabric of our laws, our overarching foreign policy interests, and our national security." Dr. Jerold F. Ogrisseg (a psychologist at the Air Force Survival School) remembered advising LtGen. Daniel J. Baumgartner Jr. (Joint Personnel Recovery Agency (JPRA) chief of staff) against waterboarding: "aside from being illegal, it was a completely different arena that we in the survival school didn't know anything about." Air Force Col. John R. Moulton II (Ret.) (JPRA commander March 2001–September 2004) testified that Air Force Col. Steven M. Kleinman (JPRA director of intelligence) had been withdrawn after he expressed "reservations" about EITs from Iraq and terminated a demonstration of "counter-resistance techniques with detainee." Kleinman (now retired) testified he told Moulton: "we are being asked to use a full range of SERE methods in the interrogation of detainees, and … these were violations of the Geneva Convention." Moulton said: "I believe now as I did during these events that JPRA should not be in the business of conducting interrogations or interrogator training." Kleinman described a recent meeting convened by HRF involving 14 of "America's most accomplished intelligence and law enforcement professionals," which concluded:

> [T]he most effective method for consistently eliciting accurate and comprehensive information from even the most defiant individuals … was through a patient, systematic, and culturally enlightened effort to build an operationally useful relationship … [whereas] coercive tactics … were, in the long run, not only ineffective but also counterproductive.

RAdm. Jane Dalton (JCS General Counsel at the time) testified that she had been prevented from conducting a legal review of the proposed techniques. LtCol. Diane E. Beaver (then SJA, JTF-GTMO) defended her memo as "the best work I could do under the constraints and circumstances." She testified that John Fredman, a senior CIA lawyer, told other administration lawyers visiting Guantánamo that whether harsh interrogation was torture "is a matter of perception." "If the detainee dies, you're doing it wrong." (Fredman later denied saying this.) Asked whether he had directed subordinates to get information about EITs, Haynes said: "my memory is not perfect." "I don't specifically remember when I saw this" memo on EITs' effects and "don't remember doing something with this information." "I cannot discuss it further without getting into classified information." He did "not recall" seeing the JAG memos objecting to EITs (but Dalton testified that Haynes "was aware that the services had concerns," and Mora said he had warned Haynes that his legal reasoning was inadequate). In two hours of testimony, Haynes said he did not recall 23 times, did not remember 22 times, did not know 16 times, and offered other evasions.

Levin warned: "if we use [SERE] techniques offensively against detainees, it says to the world that they have America's stamp of approval." Graham predicted that the OLC memos "will go down in history as some of the most irresponsible and shortsighted legal analysis ever provided to our nation's military and intelligence communities." Sen. Reed (a West Point graduate) told Haynes: "you did a disservice to the soldiers of this nation." Tim Rutten wrote in his *Los Angeles Times* column that SASC "has established definitively that the drive to make torture an instrument of U.S. policy originated at the highest levels of the Bush administration."

At a meeting convened by HRF and CSIS, experienced interrogators from the FBI, CIA, and military criticized EITs. Two weeks later it emerged that the SASC hearing had learned that a 1957 article on Communist Chinese brainwashing had been used in December 2002 to teach Guantánamo interrogators how the combination of sleep deprivation, stress positions, extreme temperatures, and diet manipulation "makes victim dependent on interrogator" and "weakens mental and physical ability to resist." Sen. Levin said Americans should be "shocked" at the use of such techniques "to get false confessions." DoD replied that "current D.O.D. policy" was to "treat all detainees humanely." The *Los Angeles Times* said the use of these techniques was "wrong and it doesn't work." It "also facilitates enemy recruitment … and deprives the United States of the standing to demand humane treatment of captured Americans."

In July 2008, a week after publication of intelligence reports showing the abuse of Omar Khadr in Guantánamo, his lawyers released a 10-minute video of the 16-year-old sobbing "help me" during interrogation.[84] A Canadian Department of Foreign Affairs report said an official who had visited Khadr (a Canadian citizen) heard he had been subjected to the "frequent-flier" program of sleep deprivation and kept in solitary for up to three weeks. Soon thereafter it was reported that the "frequent-flier" program persisted after being banned in March 2004. One detainee was moved 6 times a day for 12 days; another was subjected to repeated six-hour interrogations separated by four-hour breaks.

Rice informed SASC that the Principals Committee met in 2002–03 "to ensure that CIA's proposed interrogation program complied fully with U.S. legal obligations."[85] She remembered being told that the techniques to which military personnel were subjected in training did not "cause significant physical or psychological harm," but did not recall "specific discussions about withdrawing F.B.I. personnel from the abu Zubaydah interrogation." Bellinger remembered repeated reports from the DoJ criminal division about abuses in Guantánamo, but DoD assured him they were being investigated. Levin said these communications showed that officials "didn't care about … the validity of the confessions." Other administration officials refused to testify. Steven Kleinman recalled that a September 2003 interrogation in Iraq "had morphed into a form of punishment," but when he objected, interrogators "didn't seem to think it was a problem." And when Kleinman reported to his superior, he was told the techniques had been approved by Haynes or higher officials and these detainees were not protected by the Geneva Conventions.

In October 2008 James Clapper, Undersecretary of Defense for Intelligence, ordered that interrogations in military facilities be monitored to ensure they adhered to the Army Field Manual, even if they were being conducted by OGA (i.e., the CIA).[86] DoD reiterated that all its interrogations would conform to the Army Field Manual.[87]

Also in October the *Los Angeles Times* endorsed Obama.[88] McCain had "denounced torture as a senator but equivocated as a candidate, refusing to support legislation that would hold the CIA to the same interrogation guidelines used by the U.S. military," and had "redefined 'torture' in such a disingenuous way as to nearly embrace what he once abhorred."

THE OBAMA ADMINISTRATION

A week after Obama's election Rep. Holt urged him to issue an executive order "to put an immediate halt to our government's use of torture during interrogations."[89] Sen. Feingold proposed a ban on torture and cruel, inhuman, or degrading treatment. Obama declared: "I have said repeatedly that America doesn't torture, and I'm going to make sure that we don't torture." His Attorney General nominee, Eric Holder, said: "under the Geneva Conventions you are really limited in the amount of information that you can elicit from people." Even detainees who "are not prisoners of war" were "entitled to be treated in a very humane way and almost consistent with all of the dictates of the Geneva Conventions." Civil liberties groups called for a single standard for interrogation, and Feinstein agreed. John O. Brennan, who headed Obama's intelligence transition team and was a leading candidate for DCI, said EITs posed "a tough ethical question." Earlier he had "argue[d] for continuity." He withdrew his name after psychologists accused him of involvement in EITs (but was made Deputy National Security Adviser, which did not require confirmation).

Republicans were unrepentant.[90] Mukasey assailed the "relentless criticism of the very policies that have helped keep us safe." Michael Chertoff (Bush's DHS Secretary) declared that "the bottom line is that in the last seven-plus years we have not had a successful attack" in the USA. Cheney defended waterboarding. Rice claimed that "the United States has always kept to its international obligations," including "the convention on torture." But "information to prevent an attack is the long pole in the tent when you're dealing with terrorism." (The following April Rice answered a question about whether waterboarding was torture by declaring: "by definition, if it was authorized by the president, it did not violate our obligations under the CAT." A week later she reiterated that Bush was "very clear that we would do nothing, nothing, that was against the law or against our obligations internationally.") Bush pronounced that "there can be no debate about the results" of his policies "in keeping America safe." "America has gone more than seven years without another terrorist attack on our soil." Gonzales asked rhetorically: "what is it that I did that is so fundamentally wrong? I consider myself ... one of the many casualties of the war on terror." "People have this misperception that we as lawyers were responsible for the creation of policies that they don't like." He still could not say whether waterboarding was torture because it "requires an interpretation of the statute that is very vague."

Matthew Alexander (a pseudonym), who had conducted more than 300 interrogations and supervised a thousand, wrote in a *Washington Post* op ed (publicizing his book) that many "were based on fear and control" and "often resulted in torture and abuse."[91] Refusing to use

EITs, he had developed a methodology "based on building rapport with suspects, showing cultural understanding," which led to finding and killing al-Zarqawi. A long *Vanity Fair* article argued that the harsh interrogation of abu Zubaydah and KSM had produced no actionable intelligence. Asked in April 2008 if EITs had prevented any attacks, FBI Director Mueller said "I don't believe that has been the case."

In early December a group of retired military officers organized by HRF met with Obama administration officials, including Holder and White House Counsel Gregory Craig.[92] RAdm. Hutson (Ret.) denounced torture as "the technique of choice of the lazy, stupid and pseudo-tough." The USA should follow the "golden rule." Almost immediately afterwards Obama said: "I will abide by statutory prohibitions, and have the Army Field Manual govern interrogation techniques for all United States government personnel and contractors." Sen. Feinstein, incoming SSCI chair, planned to introduce a bill to mandate "a single, clear standard for interrogation across the federal government," one that would comply with "all laws and treaties."

SASC unanimously issued a report based on thousands of documents and more than seventy interviews (completed November 20 but not declassified for five months) accusing DoD of abusing detainees.[93] Rumsfeld's December 2002 authorization of EITs at Guantánamo was "a direct cause for detainee abuse" there and "influenced and contributed to the use of abusive techniques, including military working dogs, forced nudity and stress positions, in Afghanistan and Iraq." Bush's February 7, 2002 memo denied detainees in Afghanistan protection under the Geneva Conventions. "The use of techniques in interrogations derived from SERE resistance training created a serious risk of physical and psychological harm to detainees." JPRA "efforts in support of 'offensive' interrogation operations went beyond the agency's knowledge and expertise." OLC memos "distorted the meaning and intent of anti-torture laws" and "rationalized the abuse of detainees in U.S. custody." The report traced EITs from the SERE program and Guantánamo through Carolyn Wood at Bagram to Abu Ghraib in Iraq. Even after Lt.Gen. Sanchez revised his order, it still "contained ambiguities with respect to certain techniques, such as the use of dogs in interrogations, and led to confusion about what techniques were permitted." DoD had consulted with the CIA on interrogation, and the White House had reviewed CIA methods earlier and in more detail than had been acknowledged. The report did not urge further investigation or punishment.

SASC chair Levin said the abuses "cannot be chalked up to the actions of 'a few bad apples.'" McCain (the senior Republican) stressed "the inexcusable link between abusive interrogation techniques used by our enemies who ignored the Geneva Conventions" (alluding to his torture in Vietnam) "and interrogation policy for detainees in U.S. custody." Claiming that a dozen earlier investigations had exonerated DoD, a Rumsfeld aide called it "regrettable that Senator Levin has decided to use the Committee's time and taxpayer dollars to make unfounded allegations against those who have served our nation," condemning "irresponsible charges" in a "false narrative" that was "unencumbered by the preponderance of facts."

The *Wall Street Journal* agreed with Rumsfeld that "the real 'torture' disgrace" was the report on the "alleged 'torture' policies." Ever since 2002 "key Congressional leaders" had been "fully briefed by the CIA," yet "none of them saw fit to object." Levin's "real purpose is to lay the groundwork for war-crimes prosecutions." McCain's endorsement was a "mystery," which had "damaged his career." But the *Washington Post* said it "was obvious to many from almost the beginning of the scandal that the sickening photographs of naked, hooded prisoners being threatened by dogs and forced into humiliating poses were the direct result of policies adopted by ... Rumsfeld and other senior Bush administration officials." The report "delivers what ought to be a crushing blow to the continuing attempts of the Bush administration to deny, whitewash or obfuscate the truth behind the scandal." Because "the full story of the Bush administration's violations of international norms ... has yet to be told ... the next Congress and the Obama administration should agree to establish a full-fledged investigative commission."

Cheney patronized Obama with some unsolicited advice: "[B]efore you start to implement your campaign rhetoric, you need to sit down and find out precisely what it is we did and how we did it, because it is going to be vital to keeping the nation safe and secure in the years ahead."[94] The interrogation programs had been "absolutely essential to maintaining our capacity to interfere with and defeat all further attacks against the United States." DCI Hayden agreed: "do not allow others to say [harsh interrogation] didn't work. It worked." He "certainly would have considered [staying] if asked."

But at a January 9, 2009 press conference introducing Dennis Blair and Leon Panetta, his nominees for DNI and DCI, Obama said: "Under my administration, the United States does not torture. We will abide by the Geneva Conventions ... We will uphold our highest values and ideals. It is important for us to do that not only because that's who we are, but also, ultimately it will make us safer and will help in changing hearts and minds in our struggle against extremists."[95] A year earlier Panetta had written: "We cannot and must not use torture under any circumstances." A few months after that he had said "torture is illegal, immoral, dangerous and counterproductive." The *Los Angeles Times* and *New York Times* endorsed him for those views. But Hayden advised his successor: "Don't ever use the words CIA and torture in the same paragraph again … Torture is a felony."

Washington Post journalist Carol Leonnig reflected on how she reluctantly had been convinced that detainees had been tortured.[96] She initially was skeptical, and her editors reacted with "jaundiced disbelief." But by the end of 2004 "dozens of habeas petitions" described "horrible" abuse. Although the government repeatedly denied it, Judge Kessler declared in March 2006 that after reading numerous records, she had much less trust in the government. "I know it's a sad day when a federal judge has to ask a DoJ attorney this, but I'm asking you … why should I believe them?"

On his second full day as president Obama stood in the Oval Office with 16 retired generals and admirals (organized by HRF) and signed an executive order ending abusive interrogation.[97] Those flag officers had "made an extraordinary impression on me." "Our ideals give us the strength and moral high ground." "Our actions in defense of liberty will be as just as our cause, and we … will uphold our fundamental values as vigilantly as we protect our security." "We are willing to observe core standards of conduct not just when it's easy, but also when it's hard." He ordered government not to rely on any legal opinions on the subject produced after 9/11 and created a task force to determine whether the Army Field Manual offered adequate guidance.

At his confirmation hearing Blair said: "there will be no waterboarding … [or] torture on my watch."[98] Torture was "not moral, legal or effective." But he refused to call waterboarding torture, even when told that Holder had acknowledged at his confirmation hearing that it was; and Blair said the government would withhold the specifics of any future interrogation document so as not to provide "a training manual for our adversaries." (Gonzales had expressed "concern about [Holder] making a pronouncement like that.") Sen. Feinstein still sought to legislate a single standard.

At his confirmation hearing, Panetta said Obama's order had created "a single standard that would apply with [*sic*] interrogations with the

Army Field Manual."[99] Asked about the "ticking bomb" hypothetical, he replied that Mueller, McCain, and Petraeus all believed "that information can be obtained without having to resort to extraordinary measures." If "whatever was being used I felt was not sufficient, I would not hesitate to go to the president of the United States and request whatever additional authority I would need." But he reiterated that the president was bound by law, and "this president would do nothing that would violate the laws that were in place." The *Los Angeles Times* raised two concerns. First, "why concede the need for harsher measures" if, as Panetta said, "Obama would not violate any laws"? Second, Obama's appointment of a task force "raise[d] the possibility of a retreat from a single standard of interrogation." At his swearing-in Panetta said EITs "caused America to fall short of its founding principles" and "gave al Qaeda a powerful recruiting tool."

Obama's nomination of Dawn Johnsen to head OLC (where she had served under Clinton) elicited opposition from Republicans because of her criticism of the torture memos.[100] Rep. Smith (R-Tex) on the House Judiciary Committee said "her position on the intelligence community's ability to conduct interrogations and gather critical, time-sensitive intelligence to prevent terrorist attacks raises significant concerns." But after she told the SJC that torture was always illegal and waterboarding was torture, it voted along party lines to confirm her. The *Washington Post* supported her as "an outspoken critic of the Bush Justice Department's legal justification for harsh interrogation techniques." The *Los Angeles Times* pointed to the "overwhelming" irony that Republicans opposed her as "a partisan activist" because of "her caustic criticism of torture memos." But Republicans stalled the nomination until the end of the year. When Obama renominated her in 2010, she seemed to have the necessary 60 votes. The *Los Angeles Times* renewed its support. The *New York Times* called her "a highly qualified choice," dismissing "baseless" Republican objections. The *Washington Post* condemned Sen. Chambliss's (R-Ga) "obnoxious" hold. After Johnsen withdrew her name because "political opposition was prevent[ing] OLC from functioning at full strength," all three papers reiterated their support for her as "the ideal candidate" (*New York Times*), "eminently qualified" (*Los Angeles Times*) and "a nationally renowned legal scholar" (*Washington Post*), and criticized the administration and Congress.

Cheney persisted in maintaining that "if it hadn't been for what we did – with respect to the ... enhanced interrogation techniques for the

HVDs … then we would have been attacked again."[101] Replying in a *New York Times* op ed, Daniel P. Gregg (a 30-year CIA veteran who had been George H.W. Bush's National Security Adviser) said that during the Vietnam War he had obtained "a flood of actionable intelligence" from a prisoner who said nothing under South Vietnamese torture. An effective interrogator had "to recognize the prisoner's humanity, to understand his culture, background and language." In another *Times* op ed, Steven Kleinman and Matthew Alexander called Obama's torture ban "a major step toward reclaiming our heritage as a nation of laws and a people of character." The Army Field Manual methods had been "scientifically tested for effectiveness."

In March 2009 Cheney repeated his defense of EITs, invoking a classified report "that itemizes the specific attacks that were stopped by virtue of what we learned through these programs."[102] But *Washington Post* reporters concluded that abu Zubaydah had given up most of his limited information *before* being subjected to EITs. Although waterboarding produced a "torrent of names and alleged facts," almost all of it evaporated under further investigation. In response to repeated SSCI requests, the CIA never identified specific leads obtained by waterboarding him.

In February 2008 journalists reported that three months earlier the DoJ Office of Professional Responsibility (OPR) had submitted a draft report on its investigation of the OLC lawyers, begun in mid-2004.[103] It found that Yoo had blurred the lines between providing legal advice and policy advocacy, criticizing his use of a health benefits statute to narrow the definition of torture and his claim that the president could suspend the Fourth Amendment. But Mukasey and his deputy, Mark Filip, had strongly objected to the draft, insisting it include responses from Bybee, Yoo, and Bradbury. DoJ now said "the review process … likely will require substantial time and effort." Sens. Durbin and Whitehouse, who had learned about the investigation a year earlier, asked Holder to release the report, asserting that the decision to share the draft with the three lawyers "appears" to be a "departure from normal OPR practice."

At the end of February 2009 SSCI voted 14–1 to investigate the CIA's detention and interrogation policies and whether the Bush administration had withheld information from Congress.[104] An aide said Sen. Bond, the sole dissenter, "does not think that witch hunts and discussion of the legality of the memos are in any way helpful at this point." Panetta promised "to be transparent," but did "not support, obviously, an investigation or a prosecution of those individuals" who "did their job ... pursuant to the guidance that was provided."

In March the DoJ released more OLC memos approving use of the military inside the USA and rendition of detainees to countries where they might be tortured.[105] Echoing Obama's inaugural address, Holder said: "too often over the past decade, the fight against terrorism has been viewed as a zero-sum battle with our civil liberties. Not only is that thought misguided, I fear that in actuality it does more harm than good." The *New York Times* said: "a lot more transparency is needed. The documents do not include memos justifying harsh interrogations." Although the OLC "is supposed to ensure policies comply with the Constitution and the law," these memos "make it chillingly clear how quickly that office was rededicated to finding ways for Mr. Bush to evade, twist or ignore both." Tim Rutten wrote in his *Los Angeles Times* column that the memos show that "we came far closer" to "the brink of executive tyranny" than "even staunch critics of the White House believed." The *Washington Post* condemned "Mad Max's Justice Department." The memos show "how intellectually dishonest Bush-era lawyers were in coming to these preposterous conclusions."

On April 6 Mark Danner published the ICRC's 2007 confidential report to the USA on CIA abuse of the 14 HVDs in secret prisons, based on interviews after their transfer to Guantánamo.[106] Panetta reassured Congress that the CIA would obey Obama's executive order, conducting "debriefings using a dialogue style of questioning that is fully consistent with the interrogator approaches authorized and listed in the Army Field Manual."

On April 15 DoJ withdrew four OLC opinions (Bybee's August 2002 "torture" memo and Bradbury's three 2005 memos) and all others authorizing EITs issued between 9/11 and Obama's inauguration. The next day, over strong opposition from the intelligence community, Obama released those four opinions because this was "required by our commitment to the rule of law" and he had banned those methods, which had been "widely reported" and "publicly acknowledged" by the previous administration.[107] But he called this "a time for reflection, not retribution ... nothing will be gained by spending our time and energy laying blame for the past." "The men and women of the CIA have assurances ... that we will protect all who acted reasonably and relied upon legal advice from the DoJ." Holder agreed that release was "consistent with our commitment to the rule of law," but intelligence officials who relied in good faith on the memos would not be prosecuted.

Blair said that read now, "on a bright, sunny, safe day," EITs "appear graphic and disturbing." "But we will absolutely defend those who relied on these memos." Panetta concurred: "I will strongly oppose any effort to investigate or punish those who followed the guidance of the DoJ." But Sen. Leahy said the memos showed the need for an independent commission. And Rep. Conyers said those who ordered EITs "without proper legal authority" or "knowingly craft[ed] legal fictions to justify torture … should be criminally prosecuted." Sen. Feingold agreed. Rep. Nadler said: "we are legally required to investigate and, when appropriate, to prosecute those crimes." But Rahm Emanuel, Obama's chief of staff, said: "it's not a time to use our energy and our time in looking back." Dana Perino (Bush's press secretary) denounced the release as "reckless." EITs were the "reason" "we were not attacked again." House Minority Leader Boehner denounced the release as "clearly a political decision," which "ignored the advice of their DNI and their CIA director" and created "another sideshow." "I'm not going to allow our professionals and our allies around the world to get denigrated because they were working to keep our country safe."

Chertoff said it told terrorists what to expect during interrogation. Conceding it was "probably unrealistic" to pretend we could "keep it all a secret," Defense Secretary Gates's "first and foremost" concern was that protection be extended to CIA interrogators "who performed their duties in accordance with the legal guidance."

The *Washington Post* praised Obama for "courageously and wisely" striking "exactly the right balance."[108] The *New York Times* called the memos "a journey into depravity," written in "the precise bureaucratese favored by dungeon masters throughout history" in order "to provide legal immunity for acts that are clearly illegal, immoral and a violation of this country's most basic values." Lauding Obama's "commitment to transparency," the *Times* was "waiting to see an equal commitment to accountability" through an investigation of the memo authors, Yoo and Bybee. The *Los Angeles Times* called the "heartbreaking" memos a "bloodless legal exercise that can only be called surreal" and warned that Obama "continues to hedge about whether the CIA might once again be freed from the standards of conduct imposed on interrogators for the military."

Hayden and Mukasey assailed Obama in a *Wall Street Journal* op ed.[109] Releasing the opinions was "unnecessary as a legal matter," "unsound as a matter of policy," and would invite the "institutional timidity and fear of recrimination that weakened intelligence gathering in the past."

It violated Panetta's "sworn promise" to seek presidential authorization for EITs if necessary. Claims they did not work were "ignorant." "Any protestation of ignorance" by members of Congress was "pretense." The argument that EITs had "disgraced us before the world" was a "self-fulfilling prophecy." The Army Field Manual limits were inappropriate "for more experienced people in controlled circumstances with high value detainees." David Rivkin and Lee Casey (lawyers in the Reagan and Bush I administrations) wrote in another *Wall Street Journal* op ed that the memos revealed "a cautious and conservative Justice Department," which authorized EITS that "fall well short of 'torture'" and were "fully consistent with American values." Bybee was unrepentant: "The central question for lawyers was a narrow one; locate, under the statutory definition, the thin line between harsh treatment of a high-ranking al Qaeda terrorist that is not torture and harsh treatment that is. I believed at the time, and continue to believe today, that the conclusions were legally correct." But these defenses were weakened when the *New York Times* reported that the CIA had waterboarded abu Zubaydah 83 times in August 2002 and KSM 183 times in March 2003 (numbers that mistakenly had not been redacted in the memos and were reported by bloggers).[110] The *Washington Post* commented that "CIA interrogators were far from restrained in their use of this ancient and cruel technique." Several psychologists presented evidence of waterboarding's permanent effects.

Several days after releasing the memos Obama visited CIA headquarters to praise the "remarkable" courage of the Agency's "indispensable" employees and promise his "support and appreciation."[111] Rahm Emanuel said "those who devised policy" also "should not be prosecuted," but officials later claimed (implausibly) that he was referring to those who executed the policy, not the lawyers who wrote the memos. Sen. Feinstein asked Obama not to preclude prosecutions until SSCI had completed its investigation, in an estimated 6–8 months. Cheney asked the CIA to declassify "reports that show specifically what we gained as a result of this activity … that lay out the successes of those policies and point out in considerable detail all … that we were able to achieve." "Four former directors of the Central Intelligence Agency say" that after waterboarding, KSM "produced vast quantities of invaluable information about al Qaeda." Bush "knew a great deal about the program. He basically authorized it … this was a presidential-level decision." The *New York Times* ridiculed Cheney for suddenly getting "the full disclosure bug" when, as vice president, he "never acknowledged the public's right to know anything." Americans needed to know "who pushed the Justice Department lawyers to twist the law and the Constitution to excuse torture." The *Los Angeles Times* said the memos were "unlikely" to resolve whether "the information could have been gained more effectively through other means." Calling it "obvious" that OLC lawyers "deliberately contorted the law to justify decisions that had already been made," the *New York Times* urged Congress to impeach Judge Bybee and bar associations to disbar all three lawyers.

Conservatives pushed back.[112] Christopher Buckley warned against getting "too sanctimonious ... after watching nearly 3,000 innocent Americans endure god-awful deaths." Rush Limbaugh said: "I just slapped myself ... that's torture according to these people." "If somebody can go through waterboarding for 183 times ... it means it's not torture." Charles Krauthammer said that if "a face slap, or deprivation of sleep" was torture, "the word has no meaning." Bill Kristol called Obama "pathetic" to disavow "the good faith efforts of a previous administration to protect us in ways that I think were entirely appropriate." Bill O'Reilly said the *New York Times* viewed anything "beyond posing questions in an even voice" as torture. Karl Rove said torture claims revealed "the lunacy of the people on the left." Joe Scarborough called it "laughable" to characterize as torture "not letting terrorists sleep, and throwing cold water on them, and putting a caterpillar in a room." A *New York Post* editorial agreed. Three of the *Washington Post*'s conservative columnists offered justifications for EITs. Michael Gerson argued for relativism: "few Americans would object to the slapping of a terrorist during questioning." Marc Thiessen claimed that using EITs on KSM had prevented the attack on the Library Tower in Los Angeles (even though that plot was foiled before he was captured). Charles Krauthammer said EITs were justified if there was a "ticking time bomb" or "the extraction of information from a high-value enemy" was "likely to save lives."

Reps. Pelosi, Schakowsky (D-Ill), and Hoekstra urged further investigation.[113] HJC chair Conyers vowed to hold hearings. Sen. Feingold urged prosecution of the OLC lawyers and those who conducted EITs. But Sens. McCain, Lieberman, and Graham warned that prosecutions would have a "deeply chilling effect" on future administrations. And President Obama met Congressional leaders on April 22 and 23 to oppose a commission. Sen. Reid agreed that Congress should wait for the SSCI report, which he hoped "will come toward the end of this year." Sen. Feinstein said her committee was best equipped to investigate and expected the report's "completion within the next six to eight months." (It took *five years* longer to appear.)

Blair wrote his staff that "information gained from these techniques was valuable in some instances, but there is no way of knowing whether the same information could have been obtained through other means."[114] "The damage [EITs] have done to our interests far outweighed whatever benefit they gave us and they are not essential to our national security." He "like[d] to think I would not have approved those methods," but he "made clear that the CIA should not be punished for carrying out orders."

In a *New York Times* op ed, Philip Zelikow (9/11 Commission executive director) faulted the Bush administration for not having "thoughtfully considered those alternatives" that "rely on patience and skill."[115] He had earlier warned Obama not to preclude criminal investigations. "If a Republican president tried to do this, people would be apoplectic." Instead, the Attorney General should follow ordinary procedures to evaluate the evidence. In February 2006, as counselor to Secretary of State Rice, Zelikow had circulated a memo exposing the "absurdity" of Bradbury's May 30, 2005 memo, but the White House attempted to collect and destroy all copies. Ali Soufan (an FBI agent 1997–2005) wrote in a *New York Times* op ed that "for seven years I have remained silent about the false claims magnifying the effectiveness" of EITs. But he could not let Cheney's claims pass unchallenged. Soufan's interrogation of abu Zubaydah prior to waterboarding had elicited actionable intelligence about José Padilla and KSM. He saw EITs backfire "on more than a few occasions." When he told superiors that the CIA was using EITs on abu Zubaydah, the FBI withdrew him and its other agent. Andre Sauvageot, a retired Army colonel, wrote to the *New York Times* that in his seven years in Vietnam "there developed a de facto reciprocity in how we treated North Vietnamese prisoners and how the North Vietnamese treated ours."

The *Los Angeles Times* described the leaked 2003 CIA IG report.[116] Although IG Helgerson expressed concern about EITs and recommended an external review of their efficacy, Goss (who became DCI four months later) commissioned two former government officials with no interrogation experience. One (Newt Gingrich's national security adviser) produced a brief report calling the interrogation program "very structured and very disciplined," but it did not evaluate the methods. The other, by a former Deputy Defense Secretary, was similar. Former Bush administration officials denied seeing either. John Bellinger now characterized the failure to consider less coercive interrogation methods as "the greatest tragedy of the Bush administration's handling of detainee matters." *Times* columnist Doyle McManus called for public accountability, urging the Obama administration to release the IG report. Joseph Margulies wrote in a *Times* op ed that his client, abu Zubaydah, "suffers blinding headaches and has permanent brain damage."

The declassified SASC report provided additional information.[117] After abu Zubaydah's capture on March 29, 2002, the CIA proposed EITs (and waterboarding) to a meeting including Rizzo, Ashcroft, Rice, Hadley, Bellinger, and Gonzales. Rice insisted that Ashcroft provide not only OLC opinions on the legality of EITs but also his personal assurance. A July 13 meeting (including Chertoff and Wainstein) reviewed the interrogation plan, which Rice approved four days later. A year later the Principals Committee met with Bybee and Yoo to propose an interrogation plan for KSM, which Bush approved. The CIA started briefing the chairs and senior minority members of the two Intelligence Committees (the Gang of Four) in fall 2002, but briefed the full committees only in 2008. After the CIA IG's report in early 2004 expressed doubts about the legality of waterboarding, a new DoJ review led Ashcroft to assure the CIA on July 22, 2004 that all methods except waterboarding were legal. A month later Bradbury wrote that even waterboarding was legal if conducted with safeguards and reaffirmed this statement in his May 2005 memos. The *Washington Post* said the "well-documented report" showed that the EITs were "sought out and authorized by administration officials at the highest levels." Sens. Reid and Durbin withheld judgment because of the pending SSCI inquiry, but Rep. Pelosi urged a Congressional investigation. The *Washington Post* published a July 2002 memo from JPRA to Haynes (who forwarded it to the CIA), warning that EITs had "the potential to result in unreliable information" and "could be used by our adversaries as justification for the torture of captured U.S. personnel." A former official said the CIA never showed this to the Principals Committee, claiming instead that harsh interrogation "was safe and effective, and there was no alternative."

At a press conference marking his first hundred days, Obama said "waterboarding violates our ideals and our values. I do believe that it is torture."[118] During World War II "London was being bombed to smithereens [and] had 200 or so detainees. And Churchill said, 'We don't torture.' Churchill understood, you start taking shortcuts, and over time that corrodes … what's best in a people." Having read the classified CIA memos Cheney invoked, Obama expressed confidence that any information obtained through EITs "we could have gotten … in other ways." Ending EITs "takes away a critical recruitment tool that al Qaeda and other terrorist organizations have used" and "puts us in a much stronger position to work with our allies." Although the ACLU and AI said that Obama's acknowledgment that waterboarding was torture demanded a criminal investigation, a recent opinion poll found a clear majority of Americans opposed to this.

In a *Washington Post* op ed, former DCI Goss accused the Obama administration of having "crossed the red line between properly protecting our national security and trying to gain partisan political advantage."[119] Congress was "afflicted by amnesia." The CIA had briefed the Gang of Four on EITs when Goss chaired HPSCI in fall 2002. Now he was "slack-jawed to read that members claim not to have understood that the techniques on which they were briefed were to actually be employed." "We gave the CIA our bipartisan support." "[P]erhaps it is not amnesia but political expedience." "Circuses are not new in Washington, and I can see preparations being made for tents from the Capitol straight down Pennsylvania Avenue." "We can't have a secret intelligence service if we keep giving away all the secrets." "[F]or those" like Pelosi (then HPSCI's ranking minority member) "who now reveal having filed 'memorandums for the record' showing concern, real concern should have been expressed immediately … and not quietly filed away in case the day came when the political winds shifted."

DNI Blair and DCI Panetta sent HPSCI chair Hoekstra a chart showing a briefing including Pelosi on September 4, 2002 on abu Zubaydah's interrogation. She replied that "of the 40 C.I.A. briefings to Congress reported recently in the press, I was only briefed once … on the interrogation techniques the administration was considering using in the future." "[T]he only mention of waterboarding … was that it was not being employed." "The CIA was misleading the Congress … They mislead us all the time." Rep. Boehner (R-Oh) insisted: "it's pretty clear that they were well aware of what these enhanced interrogation techniques were; they were well aware that they'd been used." Sen. Bond (SSCI's senior minority member) declared it "outrageous that a member of Congress would call our terror-fighters liars." Pelosi replied: "my criticism of the manner in which the Bush administration did not appropriately inform Congress is separate from my respect for those in the intelligence community who work to keep our country safe." But the CIA now conceded it had said at that briefing that "waterboarding had not been used."

The chart also showed briefings of Sens. Bob Graham and Rockefeller in 2002, Rep. Harman (Pelosi's replacement) on February 4, 2003, and the two full committees in September 2006. A Rockefeller spokesman said he "was not presented with the full picture, nor was he told critical information that would have cast significant doubt on the program's legality and effectiveness." A week after being briefed, Harman asked the CIA General Counsel whether the methods "are consistent with the principles and policies of the United States." The answer "didn't address the issue I asked." Vicki Divoll (former deputy counsel to the CIA's Counterterrorism Center and SSCI general counsel) wrote in a *New York Times* op ed: "as a practical matter, there was very little, if anything, the Gang of Four could have done to affect the Bush administration's decision" on EITs.

Washington Post columnists piled on Pelosi. Charles Krauthammer insisted she "knew about the enhanced interrogation and said nothing." David Ignatius found it "pretty hard not to conclude that Pelosi is shading the truth to retrospectively cover her backside." The *Post* itself found Pelosi's "shifting accounts and faltering performance at her news conference ... far from reassuring." Sean Hannity accused her of "undermining our national security." Sen. Bond declared the CIA "would never lie to Congress." "[I]t's clear that they did tell" her. Rep. Hoekstra called her accusations "outrageous." DCI Panetta insisted that "C.I.A. officials briefed truthfully on the interrogation of abu Zubaydah." But former Sen. Bob Graham (who had chaired SSCI) said the CIA was wrong about three of the four dates on which it claimed to have briefed him, which was "just a small chapter of a long, long book of C.I.A. inaccuracies." The House voted 252–172 (mostly along party lines) to reject a Republican proposal to investigate Pelosi. Demanding that she apologize, Boehner declared: "I don't believe that the enhanced interrogation techniques were wrong. They helped us keep Americans safe." Rep. Rogers (R-Mich) concurred that Pelosi "owes the [intelligence] community an apology at the least." The chair of the House Democratic Caucus responded by accusing Republicans of playing "hypocritical political games."

House Republicans reported that a closed hearing of the HPSCI subcommittee on oversight and investigations heard evidence that EITs worked.[120] Rep. Kline (R-Mn) "came away with a very clear impression that we did gather information that did disrupt terrorist plots." Rep. Schakowsky (who had chaired the hearing) condemned those disclosures as "a violation of the rules." A month later, when House Democrats included a provision in the new Intelligence Authorization bill empowering Intelligence Committee chairs to decide when the entire membership should receive classified briefings, Obama threatened to veto it as an unconstitutional usurpation of executive power. The *New York Times* supported Obama.

On May 21, 2009 Obama gave a major speech at the National Archives.

> [T]he decisions that were made over the last eight years established an ad hoc legal approach for fighting terrorism that was neither effective nor sustainable – a framework that failed to rely on our legal traditions and time-tested institutions; that failed to use our values as a compass ... I banned the use of so-called enhanced interrogation techniques ... I reject the assertion that these are the most effective means of interrogation. What's more, they undermine the rule of law. They alienate us in the world. They serve as a recruitment tool for terrorists, and increase the will of our enemies to fight us, while decreasing the will of others to work with America. They risk the lives of our troops ... They are not who we are. [121]

Seeking to neutralize this, Cheney told the American Enterprise Institute the same day that the Bush administration had:

> understood that the safety of the country required collecting information known only to the worst of the terrorists. And in a few cases, that information could be gained only through tough interrogations ... [which] were legal, essential, justified, successful, and the right thing to do ... In my long experience in Washington, few matters have inspired so much contrived indignation and phony moralizing as the interrogation methods ... to completely rule out enhanced interrogation methods in the future ... is recklessness cloaked in righteousness.[122]

Liz Cheney said her father spoke out because Obama "suggested in the Oval Office itself that he would be open to the prosecution of former Bush administration officials." (She returned to the attack in September, asking Obama rhetorically: "in a ticking time-bomb scenario ... are you really unwilling to subject a terrorist to enhanced interrogation?" She called him "an American president who seems afraid to defend America" and insisted "waterboarding isn't torture.")

The *New York Times* revealed there had been divisions within the Bush administration.[123] After CIA IG Helgerson's report questioned the legality and effectiveness of EITs, DCI Tenet suspended the harshest methods. After the DTA became law, DCI Goss refused to conduct EITs without a new OLC assurance. When Bradbury began drafting such a memo in late 2006, Bellinger denounced it as a "work of advocacy," and Rice opposed reauthorization. Nevertheless, Bush reauthorized EITs in July 2007, while banning nudity and limiting sleep deprivation. Quoting Rice's defense of waterboarding – "by definition, if it was authorized by the president, it did not violate our obligations under the CAT" – the *Times* called that "just as ludicrous today as it was when Richard Nixon used it more than 30 years ago to excuse his own brand of lawbreaking."

At an SJC subcommittee chaired by Sen. Whitehouse, Ali Soufan testified anonymously that EITs were "ineffective, slow, and unreliable."[124] When Sen. Graham said "one of the reasons these techniques have survived for about 500 years is apparently they work," Soufan retorted that they persisted only because "it's easier to hit somebody than outsmart them." Questioning Pelosi's claim of ignorance, Graham asked: "Shouldn't we have Nancy Pelosi here?" Georgetown University law professor David Luban said OLC lawyers had "cherry pick[ed]" precedents and could not have had a "good faith belief" that their memos "accurately state the law." Calling the hearing "one of the most important of this year," Leahy renewed his plea for an independent commission. Whitehouse said that during the Bush administration, SSCI was not told "how badly the law was ignored, bastardized and manipulated by the DoJ OLC" or "how furiously government and military lawyers rejected the defective OLC opinions." Feingold declared: "nothing I have seen – including the two documents to which former Vice President Cheney has repeatedly referred – indicates that the torture techniques ... were necessary."

Calling itself the "Torture Truth Project," Accuracy in Media took a full-page advertisement in the *New York Times* urging the media to "stop misleading the world that our country condones torture," an accusation that was "losing the goodwill of people across the world" and "aiding al Qaeda in recruiting."[125] EITs did not produce enough "intense, lasting, brutal physical agony" to constitute torture. "Our own troops are subjected to waterboarding as part of their training." EIT critics, by contrast, denounced media euphemisms for torture. A reader objected that the *New York Times* "would not call bank robbery a 'brutal cash gathering technique.'" Ted Koppel said that "calling torture 'enhanced interrogation' is like calling rape 'enhanced seduction.'" A man who had undergone SERE training said that everyone "referred to what was done to us as 'torture.'" NPR's managing editor replied: "it is not for journalists to start labeling specific practices torture," which "suggests we've taken sides in the debate." But in August 2014 *New York Times* Executive Editor Dean Baquet said that henceforth the paper would use "torture" to describe the infliction of pain to elicit information because "the landscape has shifted." The CIA had waterboarded KSM 183 times; the DoJ was not prosecuting anyone. Hence "the disputed legal meaning of the word 'torture' is secondary to the common meaning."

Jesse Ventura (the former Minnesota governor and professional wrestler, who had been waterboarded as a SEAL) declared: "you give me a waterboard, Dick Cheney and one hour, and I'll have him confess to the Sharon Tate murders."[126] "If waterboarding's ok, why don't we let our police do it?" He urged prosecution of everyone involved "because torture is against the law." "[W]henever the government says it's time to move on, that means there's something they don't want you to know about." But the administration resisted further inquiry. DCI Panetta said he had cooperated with SSCI and would keep doing so because, as a former member of Congress, "I do believe it's important to learn the lessons from that period." But he was "most concerned" that this "doesn't become the kind of political issue that everything else becomes in Washington, D.C.," which would "interfere with the ability of these intelligence agencies to do our primary job."

When abu Zubaydah's lawyer, Brent Mickum, noted that his client had been captured on March 28, 2002, more than three months before the "torture" memo was issued, the CIA replied that it "was not the first piece of legal guidance for the interrogation program" (but did not disclose the earlier memo).[127] John Kiriakou said waterboarding began "at the very end of May or the very beginning of June." Psychologist James Mitchell sent daily reports to the CIA, which forwarded them to the White House, where Gonzales signed off on authorizations.

Opinion polls in 2009 found that the percentage favoring torture (which never reached half during the Bush years) rose after Obama's inauguration, while the proportion opposing it declined: 40/58 in January, 48/49 in April, and 50/46 in June; the percentage believing torture was sometimes justified rose to 54 by December but declined to 47 in December 2012.[128] (By contrast, three-quarters in China and India and two-thirds in Kenya and Nigeria thought it could be justified, compared to a quarter or less in Russia, Canada, Australia, Brazil,

Germany, Chile, Spain, Argentina, and Greece – mostly countries with experience of torture.)

When Bush first nominated LtGen. McChrystal as director of the Joint Chiefs of Staff in May 2008, SASC demanded more information about the treatment of detainees when he had been commander of Joint Special Operations Command (JSOC).[129] These concerns re-emerged when SASC took up the nomination again a year later. McChrystal claimed he had been "uncomfortable with interrogation techniques" and "immediately" began to moderate them when he became JSOC commander. The Senate quickly confirmed him when Majority Leader Reid took the floor to say that JCS chair Adm. Mullen had called to urge confirmation so McChrystal could go to Afghanistan that night, claiming he was "literally waiting by an airplane." (In his January 2013 memoir McChrystal admitted "mistakes." "As late as the spring of 2004, six months into my command [in Afghanistan], I believed our force needed the option of employing select, carefully controlled 'enhanced' techniques, including sleep management. I was wrong." By summer he had eliminated them.)

When rumors circulated in mid-July that Holder was considering a criminal investigation of EITs, Sens. Kyl (R-Az), Bond, and Sessions strenuously objected: "It is difficult to understand what rationale could drive DoJ now to reverse course, reopen a 5-year-old matter, and tarnish the reputations and lives of intelligence community professionals."[130] McCain warned it would give terrorists "more tools," and Rep. King (ranking member of the Homeland Security Committee) urged Republicans to adopt a "scorched earth policy" on all issues if there were any prosecutions. The *Washington Post* favored immunity for those who followed OLC guidelines. A DoJ official said Holder "has come reluctantly to consider" investigations. Panetta wrote a *Washington Post* op ed declaring it "time to move on." The intelligence chief of a major Western ally had asked him "a very good question": why was the USA "so consumed with what the CIA did in the past, when the most pressing national security concerns are in the present?" Panetta warned that "the focus on the past, especially in Congress, threatens to distract the CIA from its crucial core missions." White House Press Secretary Gibbs said the administration was eager to keep "going forward." "A hefty litigation looking backward is not what we believe is in the country's best interest." House Minority Leader Boehner warned against "a witch hunt designed to satisfy political allies," which will "have a chilling effect on the ability of our intelligence professionals to do their jobs." Sens. Kyl, Bond, and Sessions feared "that the true cost of this endeavor will ultimately be borne by the American people," who would be less safe. Sen. Leahy feared the investigation would constitute "scapegoating rather than true accountability" for "the lawyers and cabinet-level officials who approved the program in the first place."

But three important events occurred on August 24, 2009. First, OPR issued a report urging DoJ to reopen nearly half of the two dozen cases against the CIA the Department had declined to prosecute. In response, Holder directed John Durham (whom Mukasey had directed to investigate destruction of the CIA interrogation tapes) to conduct "a preliminary review into whether federal laws were violated in connection with the interrogation of specific detainees at overseas locations." CIA personnel "who acted in good faith and within the scope of the legal guidance" would not be prosecuted. Sen. Wyden thought the focus should be on OLC lawyers; Rep. Hoekstra said all the charges had been "exhaustively reviewed." Sen. McConnell called it a "poor and misguided decision." Sen. Lieberman said members of the intelligence community must "be free to do their dangerous and critical jobs without worrying that years from now a future Attorney General will authorize a criminal investigation of them for behavior that a previous Attorney General concluded was authorized and legal."

Sen. Bond issued a furious press release threatening to suspend Republican participation in the SSCI inquiry:

> First the White House usurps control over terrorist interrogations, signaling to the world they have lost confidence in Leon Panetta and our intelligence community, and now the Obama Justice Department launches a witch-hunt targeting the terror-fighters who have kept us safe since 9-11 … It looks like the administration is relying on the ACLU – and not our intelligence officials.

Seven former CIA directors urged Obama to abort Durham's investigation, which "creates an atmosphere of continuous jeopardy" and would "damage the willingness of many other intelligence officers to take risks to protect the country," disclose information that "can only help al Qaeda elude U.S. intelligence," and do "serious damage" to "the cooperation of foreign intelligence agencies." A month later SSCI Republicans carried out Bond's threat. Feinstein "candidly" wished "the Attorney General had waited." (Less than two months later the tables were reversed when Republicans demanded a Congressional investigation of the intelligence failure that had allowed the Fort Hood massacre, while Democrats objected that this might compromise the criminal prosecution of Hasan.)

The *Los Angeles Times* said the "wisdom" of Holder's decision was "vindicated" by the IG's report (discussed below), and it published letters castigating columnist Tim Rutten's criticism of the decision. The *Washington Post* believed the referral was "justified," but felt there was "something unsettling about telling operatives that they are off the hook, only to have that stance change with a new administration." The "real culprits" were Bush and Cheney, "who led America down the degrading path of state-sanctioned torture." Cheney repeated that CIA memos substantiated his claim that EITs had been essential; Holder's action "serves as a reminder, if any were needed, of why so many Americans have doubts about this administration's ability to be responsible for our nation's security." Days later he denounced the "outrageous political act," which "offends the hell out of me, frankly." He was "ok" even when interrogators exceeded the OLC guidelines. The *New York Times* replied that "the government owes Americans a full investigation," and "Mr. Cheney was at the center of each of these insults to this country's Constitution, its judicial system and its bedrock democratic values." The *Los Angeles Times* attacked "the bilious former vice president" and published critical letters.

The second event was the Obama Task Force's unanimous conclusion that the Army Field Manual should govern all interrogations, which would be conducted by FBI agents in the High-Value Detainee Interrogation Group under the National Security Council's direction.[131]

And third, the government finally released a heavily redacted version of IG Helgerson's 2004 report revealing that al Nashiri had been threatened with execution twice (with a gun and a power drill), subjected to threats to his family, and forced to hear what he thought was an execution in an adjoining cell.[132] The CIA now said that though it "in no way endorsed behavior … that went beyond formal guidance," DoJ had already reviewed those incidents and decided not to prosecute. (The agent was reprimanded but remained at the CIA until retirement and then continued training officers as a contractor.) The administration also released two secret 2004–05 reports Cheney had invoked concerning intelligence obtained through interrogation. Helgerson expressed disappointment that the government withheld his report's recommendations. He had found that repeated waterboarding was "inconsistent with the understanding between CIA and the DoJ" and OLC had never opined on whether EITs were CID treatment. "In fact, it appeared that certain of the techniques were designed solely because they were degrading." "Even at this late date, an independent panel of experts with backgrounds in interrogation should systematically evaluate the quality of the intelligence gained." Panetta said "the challenge is not the battles of yesterday, but those of today and tomorrow." But when he dismissed this "old story," the *Washington Post* replied it was "nonetheless revolting." The *New York Times* said the report "offers one more compelling reason for a far broader inquiry into Mr. Bush's lawless behavior." The *Los Angeles Times* called for "an encompassing inquest into what went wrong, and when."

At the end of August the administration declassified a Bradbury memo describing DCI Hayden's secret briefing of Sen. McCain and the full Intelligence Committees on September 6, 2006 (a month before the previously disclosed October 17 briefing) about six interrogation techniques, including sleep deprivation.[133] The memo claimed that "none of the members expressed the view that the CIA detention and interrogation program should be stopped, or that the techniques at issue were inappropriate." But a McCain aide said the senator had objected to Hayden and others at the time about sleep deprivation, which a friend had suffered in North Vietnam. SSCI said Feinstein and other members raised concerns. Nevertheless, the Bradbury memo used the CIA account of this briefing to argue that sleep deprivation did not "shock the conscience." The lack of objections was "a relevant measure of contemporary standards," even if it was "not conclusive on the constitutional question."

The Senate (with only one Republican vote) approved legislation requiring intelligence agencies to brief the Gang of Four. The bill easily passed the House (244–181). DNI Blair recommended a veto; the Office of Management and Budget (OMB) previously had recommended a veto of a similar House bill.[134]

In January 2010 Matthew Alexander wrote in a *New York Times* op ed that the Army Field Manual still let detainees be kept in indefinite "separation" (i.e., solitary confinement) and interrogated for 40 hours before being allowed to sleep for just 4, and did not explicitly prohibit stress positions or environmental manipulation.[135] Feinstein responded that the Manual allowed only 19 specific techniques. The following month HPSCI chair Reyes inserted provisions in the Intelligence Authorization Act to prohibit nudity, sexual acts, beatings, electrical shock, burns, waterboarding, military working dogs, hypothermia, sleep deprivation, dietary manipulation, threats, mock executions, religious desecration, denial of medical care, prolonged isolation, and exploiting phobias. Claiming credit for deleting that language, Rep. Hoekstra said Americans were "rightly outraged that Democrats would try to target those we ask to serve in harm's way." "The annual intelligence bill" should not be about "giving greater protection to terrorists."

Some 14 months after OPR completed its draft report on the OLC lawyers (whom it began investigating *six years* earlier), the DoJ released the revision, written by David Margolis, who had spent three decades in the Office.[136] Whereas the draft had found that Yoo and Bybee violated their professional obligations and recommended a referral to state disciplinary bodies, Margolis found they only showed "poor judgment." The *Washington Post* said this was the "right decision," but added that the lawyers "provided cover for reprehensible and abusive techniques that stained the country's reputation and diminished its moral standing in the world." The *Los Angeles Times* called the report "far from a vindication" of lawyers who "allowed themselves to serve as accessories to a policy that has caused incalculable damage to this country's moral authority." And the *New York Times* was incredulous that "government lawyers who abused their offices to give the president license to get away with torture did nothing that merits a review by the bar." All the Attorneys General and their Deputies for the previous 17 years wrote Sens. Leahy and Sessions praising "the wise counsel and good judgment of David Margolis." (When Margolis died six years later, the DoJ named its exceptional service award and a conference room after him.) But Sens. Leahy, Durbin, and Whitehouse and Rep. Conyers condemned Yoo and Bybee. Several weeks later OPR found that the CIA's "Effectiveness Memo," on which Bradbury had relied when approving EITs in 2005 and 2007, contained "plainly inaccurate information." Although the CIA had claimed that "[abu] Zubaydah's reporting led to the arrest of Padilla on his arrival in Chicago in May 2003," Padilla was arrested in May *2002*, abu Zubaydah was not waterboarded until August 2002, and the FBI elicited the information to arrest Padilla through traditional interrogation. Bradbury should have "demanded more specific information."

On the TV show *Meet the Press* on February 14, Biden rebutted Cheney's criticism of the administration's handling of Abdulmutallab (the Christmas Day "underwear bomber"). Cheney immediately retorted on ABC's *This Week* that all "capabilities," including waterboarding, should be "on the table." "I was a big supporter of waterboarding. I was a big supporter of the enhanced interrogation techniques." Biden replied on CBS's *Face the Nation*: "that's Dick Cheney. I mean thank God … the last administration didn't listen to him at the end." Biden could not envision "a time when waterboarding should be used on anyone." "It's not effective." A few months later Bush said about waterboarding KSM that he "would do it again to save lives."[137]

In February 2010 a CIA memo obtained through FOIA disclosed that at a briefing seven years earlier on EITs and planned destruction of the videotapes, SSCI chair Roberts raised no objections.[138] (SSCI's staff director at the time now said Roberts had been "in receive mode," i.e. inattentive, during the briefing.) When Sen. Bob Graham (then the senior Democrat) proposed that SSCI "undertake its own 'assessment' of enhanced interrogation," the Agency replied it would resist observation of interrogations or secret prisons. The CIA memo recorded: "Quickly, the Senator interjected that he saw no reason for the Committee to pursue such a request and could think of '10 reasons right off why it is a terrible idea.'" The same memo showed that Rep. Harman had asked pointed questions about interrogations at a July 2004 briefing, protested that HPSCI "had not been getting full and candid testimony on the detainee issue," and questioned whether EITs were necessary or effective.

On February 25 the House (with just one Republican vote) passed the Intelligence Authorization Act of 2010 (which the Senate already had passed), requiring the administration to inform all members of both Intelligence Committees of the "main features" of activities disclosed to the Gang of Eight (two from each party on each committee) and to notify the full Committees of every presidential directive to conduct covert action.[139] OMB recommended a veto, objecting that the "significant [intelligence] undertakings" that had to be disclosed were "vague and uncertain."

Conservatives continued defending EITs.[140] In his *Washington Post* column, Marc Thiessen claimed religious justification for "coercive interrogation" and declared that "no one" could maintain that slaps, diet manipulation, or "mild" sleep deprivation (for four days) were torture. (Because he had invoked religious authority, prominent Catholic theologians strongly refuted him.) Stuart Taylor said waterboarding was brutal but probably not torture. Karl Rove agreed and was "proud we used techniques that broke the will of these terrorists" and "kept the world safer." EITs were "appropriate, they're in conformity with our international requirements and U.S. law."

Judge Bybee testified in a closed-door HJC hearing that his OLC memo "was very very specific ... that there were ... certain factual assumptions that the CIA gave us, and that if they acted outside of those factual assumptions, that we had not issued an opinion to them." He had not been asked about or approved prolonged stress positions, dousing with cold water, "loud music to keep people from falling asleep," or "daily beatings."[141] But John Rizzo claimed that soon after the CIA got Bybee's "torture" memo, "Justice advised us that if ... the techniques are applied in the same way, the conclusions would be the same." Chairman Conyers sent the hearing transcript to DoJ, and the *Los Angeles Times* urged it to "prosecute the wrongdoers even if that creates political problems for President Obama." Commenting on Bybee's testimony, Bush said he had ordered waterboarding "because the lawyer said it was legal ... you gotta trust the judgment of people around you." "Using those techniques saved lives." He would make the same decision today. He wrote in his memoir that DoJ and CIA lawyers conducted "a careful legal review." "[C]riminalizing differences of legal opinion would set a terrible precedent for our democracy." Waterboarding was "tough," but "medical experts assured the CIA that it did no lasting harm." Bush reiterated that "information the detainees revealed constituted more than half of what the CIA knew about al-Qaeda," but he did not claim EITs had been necessary to elicit that information. The *Washington Post* found Bush's "cockiness ... a measure of how distorted his views ... remain on the subject of torture."

More information emerged about the CIA's destruction of the EIT videotapes (which Durham had been investigating for more than two years).[142] Through FOIA the ACLU had obtained emails from "John" (a CIA deputy) warning Executive Director Kyle "Dusty" Foggo that "we may have 'improperly' destroyed something." Jose Rodriguez (Director of the National Clandestine Service) had told "John" that "the heat from destroying is nothing compared to what it would be if the tapes ever got into the public domain ... out of context they would make us look terrible; it would be 'devastating' to us." Several days later Rodriguez said he and others "felt it was extremely important to destroy the tapes" and he would take "any heat." DCI Goss "laughed and said that actually, it would be he, PG, who would take the heat." "PG, however, agreed with the decision." "[Deputy General Counsel] Rizzo is clearly upset because he was on the hook to notify Harriet Miers [White House Counsel] of the status of the tapes ... Rizzo called Harriet this afternoon and she was livid." Rizzo now corroborated this account: White House officials "said don't do anything without telling them in advance." In July 2010 it was confirmed that Addington, Gonzales, and Bellinger had told CIA General Counsel Scott Muller in May 2004 not to destroy the tapes. Rodriguez had ordered the destruction just weeks after Dana Priest exposed the CIA's secret prisons on November 4, 2005.

In November 2010, just before the statute of limitations expired, Durham decided not to prosecute the destruction.[143] Rodriguez, Rizzo, and Panetta welcomed the decision. The *Washington Post* found it "difficult to discern" whether this was the right call and urged Congress "to address myriad unanswered questions." The *Philadelphia Inquirer* called the decision "disappointing." Regretting that this action "will make it more difficult to learn the facts about this inexcusable cover-up," the *Los Angeles Times* urged Congress to "determine to its own satisfaction how the decision to destroy the tapes evolved." The *New York Times* called the destruction "a serious affront ... to the rule of law" and complained that Durham had offered "no details" to explain his decision.

When Rep. Rogers (a former FBI agent and Army officer) became HPSCI chair after the Republicans won the House in 2010, he complained that "an FBI agent can use certain techniques against a gangster in New York City that the Army Field Manual would not allow a CIA case officer to use on a foreign terrorist sent here to blow up Americans."[144] He generally opposed Miranda warnings and the right to counsel. John Yoo and Robert Delahunty worried that "CIA agents will decline to interrogate prisoners, thanks to Mr. Holder's criminal investigations." In January 2011 Cheney repeated that Obama had endangered the nation by discarding "things like the enhanced interrogation techniques," which "had kept the nation safe for over seven years." Rumsfeld acknowledged in his memoir that the interrogation of al-Qahtani "may have gone beyond the techniques I had approved," but had no "regrets at all" because al-Qahtani "gave a lot of information" that "was very helpful ... to the United States government in saving lives." "Every single one" of the 12 reports after abu Ghraib "said there was not a shred of evidence that there was anything to do with senior military or senior civilian leadership that led to torture."

The CIA's internal mechanisms never significantly punished EITs.[145] After Gul Rahman died during interrogation in the Salt Pit in Afghanistan, the IG made a criminal referral of "Matt," the prison's top CIA officer, and "Paul," the Kabul station chief. But DoJ did not prosecute. And though the CIA review board recommended discipline for Matt (but not Paul), Executive Director Foggo decided against punishment. Paul became chief of the Near East Division, one of the Agency's most important jobs. "Albert," who conducted the mock execution of al Nashiri in Poland, received only a reprimand. "Mike," who operated that secret prison, retired during the investigation. "Ron," the station chief who had witnessed the abuse, became chief of the Central European Division, including all of Russia. After Manadel al-Jamadi died during a CIA interrogation in Abu Ghraib, "Steve," who ran the detainee unit, received a reprimand and retired but rejoined the CIA as a contractor. Station chief Gerry Meyer resigned. His deputy, "Gordon," temporarily banned from working overseas, ran the Pakistan–Afghanistan Department in the Agency's counterterrorism center.

In November 2011 Sen. Ayotte (R-NH) (with Chambliss and Graham) introduced an amendment to the NDAA 2012 to allow interrogation methods described in the Army Field Manual's classified Appendix M.[146] It failed after several dozen human rights organizations and two dozen retired flag officers voiced opposition.

When Abdulmutallab was arrested in the Detroit airport on Christmas Day 2009, the FBI questioned him before surgery for the burns he suffered in attempting to detonate a bomb.[147] After being read his Miranda rights following surgery, he asked for a lawyer and stopped talking (although he resumed after relatives intervened). DoJ responded by significantly expanding Miranda's "public safety" exception in an October 2010 memo, which the *New York Times* disclosed in March 2011. Interrogators could ask about future attacks, weapons, and accomplices, and continue questioning the suspect in "exceptional cases" with a supervisor's approval. The *Washington Post* approved the flexibility, which could let questioning proceed for days without a Miranda warning. The *Los Angeles Times* thought the guidelines were "so reasonable" they "should apply to any case." Outside the USA DoD could hold people nine weeks and then seek an extension. After Abdulmutallab pleaded guilty in October 2011, John Brennan said that his interrogation and that of Arbabsiar (see Chapter 2 on criminal prosecutions in the companion volume *Law's Trials*) "demonstrate that Miranda was not at all an impediment." The judge trying Abdulmutallab had refused to suppress statements he made before being Mirandized. But HJC chair Smith complained that "the Obama administration has sought to treat foreign terrorists the same way that they would treat U.S. citizens."

The May 2, 2011 bin Laden raid revived conservatives' claims that EITs worked.[148] Cheney "assume[d]" that they "led to bin Laden's ultimate capture." The Heritage Foundation headlined that interrogations had been "key." Karl Rove said the Bush administration's EITs "obviously served [Obama] well." John Yoo pronounced that "without the tough decisions taken by president Bush and his national security team, the United States could not have found and killed bin Laden." Jose Rodriguez asserted that information from KSM and al-Libi "about bin Laden's courier was the lead information that eventually led to the location of [bin Laden's] compound." "[T]he trail to bin Laden … stemmed from information obtained from hardened terrorists who agreed to tell us some … of what they knew after undergoing harsh but legal interrogation methods." Michael Mukasey made the same claim. Critics disagreed. KSM and al-Libi gave false information about bin Laden's courier. After EITs, Hassan Ghul revealed only the courier's *nom de guerre*. Information about his real name, where he operated, and where bin Laden was living did not come from detainees. An NSC spokesman said: "it took years of collection and analysis from many different sources." Even Panetta said it would always be an "open question" whether the CIA could have obtained the information in other ways. The *New York Times* denounced the "cynical and disturbing" "crowing by apologists and practitioners of torture," which was "immoral and illegal and counterproductive." The *Washington Post* said that even if information extracted through EITs had contributed to locating bin Laden, "the program wasn't justified – it still did America far more harm than good." Charles and Gregory Fried (father and son law professors at Harvard and Suffolk Universities) agreed in a *Washington Post* op ed. McCain repeated that waterboarding was torture and "prohibited by American laws and values." Both Panetta and SSCI staff had told him that the critical lead had come from a detainee who had not been tortured. "Ultimately, this is more than a utilitarian debate. This is a moral debate. It is about who we are."

(A year later Sens. Feinstein and Levin issued a statement calling claims that EITs had led to bin Laden "misguided and misinformed."[149] Jose Rodriguez repeated his assertions in a *Washington Post* op ed. Hayden equivocated: "information from C.I.A. detainees formed an important part of the narrative. Clearly other threads ultimately added to the final outcomes." Glenn L. Carle, CIA deputy national intelligence officer for transnational threats 2003–07, and Richard Killmer, executive director of the National Religious Campaign Against Torture

(NRCAT), wrote the *Post* that "torture is immoral and contrary to the teachings of all religions.")

At the end of June 2011, John Durham said that after reviewing "a tremendous amount of information" about 101 cases, he had decided to investigate only the deaths of Manadel al-Jamadi and Gul Rahman.[150] Holder accepted this recommendation. On his last day as CIA Director Panetta "welcome[d]" the news, noting that career prosecutors had already declined to proceed in those two cases. Rep. Rogers was pleased the decision "has finally substantially lifted an undeserved cloud of doubt and suspicion." A month earlier Mukasey had called the inquiry "absolutely outrageous" and "unconscionable." Sen. Grassley (R-Ia) hoped "the Attorney General will quit armchair quarterbacking." Civil liberties advocates were critical. At the release of HRW's 100-page report on torture by the Bush administration (partly in response to the debate about the efficacy of EITs, which had been revived by the bin Laden killing), director Kenneth Roth said: "there are solid grounds to investigate Bush, Cheney, Rumsfeld, and Tenet for authorizing torture and war crimes."

In his memoir published in August, Cheney again claimed that EITs had "worked" to save lives and were not torture.[151] Promoting the book, he endorsed waterboarding noncitizens. But in a September 16 speech at Harvard Law School on "Strengthening our Security by Adhering to our Values and Laws," John Brennan said:

> President Obama has directed that all our actions – even when conducted out of public view – remain consistent with our laws and values.
>
> For when we uphold the rule of law, governments around the globe are more likely to provide us with intelligence we need to disrupt ongoing plots … our counterterrorism tools are more likely to withstand the scrutiny of our courts, our allies, and the American people. And … it provides a powerful alternative to the twisted worldview offered by al-Qa'ida.

At the November 2011 foreign policy debate among Republican presidential hopefuls, Herman Cain said he would "return" to waterboarding.[152] "I don't see it as torture." "I will trust the judgment of our military leaders to determine what is and what is not torture." Michelle Bachmann called waterboarding "very effective" and accused Obama of having "essentially handed over our interrogation of terrorists to the ACLU." Rick Perry endorsed "using those techniques that we know will extract the information to save young American lives." Rick Santorum said EITs had "been proven to be successful in gathering information." With offensive presumption he added that McCain "doesn't understand how enhanced interrogation works. I mean, you break somebody, and after they're broken, they become cooperative." Newt Gingrich said "waterboarding is by every technical rule not torture." (A poll found that only 44 percent of Republicans thought waterboarding was torture, compared with 68 percent of all Americans.) After the debate a senior aid to Romney said waterboarding was not torture. (Two months earlier his national security advisers had urged him to rescind Obama's executive order banning EITs. A month after the debate Romney said: "we'll use enhanced interrogation techniques which go beyond those that are in the military handbook.") Only Jon Huntsman and Rand Paul opposed waterboarding. McCain was "very disappointed." After the debate Obama reiterated that waterboarding was "torture" and "contrary to America's traditions." The *New York Times* regretted that the candidates had "learned very little from the moral calamities" of the Bush administration and called Romney's refusal to renounce waterboarding "very disturbing." The *Washington Post* warned that Cain and Bachmann had "lost the moral authority" to argue against waterboarding Americans. "Torture leads to unreliable admissions," and "there is no evidence to suggest that such information could not have been gleaned using legal methods." Marc Thiessen replied in his *Washington Post* column that waterboarding American soldiers was illegal because they were "*lawful* combatants." Former DCI Hayden also pushed back in April 2012, declaring there was a need for "rough men," who "go where others cannot go and do what others cannot accomplish" and were willing to get "chalk on their cleats." Slapping and waterboarding were lawful. "Democracies cannot wage war over the long term on the basis of strict legalisms."

In August 2012 Holder decided not to file charges in the deaths of Gul Rahman and Manadel al-Jamadi because "the admissible evidence would not be sufficient to obtain and sustain a conviction beyond a reasonable doubt."[153] Rep. Rogers was pleased; civil libertarians were outraged. Finding "the implications for the rule of law … deeply troubling," the *New York Times* called for "a more detailed explanation." Holder gave Durham's team the 13th Distinguished Service Award.

Interviewed following publication of his memoir, Jose Rodriguez was "disgusted" to hear Obama describe him and other CIA employees as "torturers."[154] "We inflicted no severe and lasting pain, we broke no bones." "I totally rejected the President's statement that this was against our values." "[A]t the time it was legal, and you have to remember the times – we had been attacked." "Making a few of the worst terrorists on the planet uncomfortable for a few days during their first month of imprisonment is worth it in order to save thousands of lives." He dismissed the CIA's "meaningless letter of reprimand" for destroying the videotapes, which just told him "I had the courage to act to protect my officers when others around me did not." In an earlier interview Ali Soufan dismissed "every example given of claimed successes" for EITs as "factually incorrect." Sens. Feinstein and Levin also said Rodriguez's claims for the efficacy of EITs were "inconsistent with CIA records" and his destruction of the videotapes "was in violation of instructions from CIA and White House lawyers."

In December 2012 SSCI voted 9–6 to approve the 6,000-page report on CIA detention and interrogation (Snowe was the only Republican joining the eight Democrats).[155] Chambliss (the senior minority member) had wanted to give the CIA a chance to reply before the vote because the report contained "significant errors, omissions, assumptions and ambiguities – as well as a lot of cherry-picking." But McCain (a nonvoting member) said it "absolutely" should be made public because it demonstrated that "cruel, inhuman and degrading treatment of prisoners is not only wrong in principle and a stain on our country's conscience, but also an ineffective and unreliable means of gathering intelligence." Twenty-six retired flag officers agreed.

The contemporaneous release of *Zero Dark Thirty*, a feature film on the bin Laden killing, provoked a mixed reaction.[156] Sens. Feinstein, McCain, and Levin wrote Sony to express "deep disappointment" with the film's "inaccurate and misleading … suggestion that torture resulted in information that led to the location of Usama bin Laden." Acting DCI Michael Morell also told employees that the film's message that EITs "were the key to finding bin Laden" was "false." There had been "multiple streams of intelligence." "[I]mportantly, whether EITs were the only timely and effective way to obtain information … is a matter of debate that cannot and never will be definitely resolved." Ali Soufan wrote in a *New York Times* op ed that "torture led us away from bin Laden." Jose Rodriguez reiterated that he was "secure in the knowledge not only that our program worked – but that it was not torture." Kathryn Bigelow, one of the film's directors, said that "depiction [of torture] is not endorsement." Two months after its release the film had grossed $88 million.

When Obama nominated John Brennan as CIA Director (for the second time) in January 2013, Sen. McCain voiced "many questions and concerns … especially what role [Brennan] played in the so-called enhanced interrogation programs."[157] Declining the nomination four years earlier, Brennan claimed he had been "a strong opponent of many of the policies of the Bush administration," such as "coercive interrogation tactics, to include waterboarding." But several co-workers could not remember him voicing those concerns at the time. Still, prominent members of the first Obama administration (including Gregory Craig, David Kris, and Jeh Johnson) wrote that Brennan "has stood firmly with the president's efforts to ensure that interrogations are conducted in accord with the law and our values." The *New York Times* urged SSCI to "revisit" the issue. In written responses to the Committee Brennan said he had been "aware" of the EIT program "but did not play a role in its creation, execution, or oversight." He had expressed "significant concerns and personal objections" "privately with colleagues" and "publicly" after leaving the Agency, "but I did not try to stop it because it was something being done in a different part of the Agency under the authority of others." Even though DoJ had said EITs did not violate the law, they were "counterproductive to our overall efforts" and "would not be used again by the CIA if I were the Director." The night before the hearing Obama offered Feinstein, Chambliss, and Wyden two OLC opinions; SSCI had asked for another eight and permission for the staff to read all of them.

Code Pink protesters repeatedly interrupted the hearing until Feinstein cleared the room. Brennan said the (still secret) SSCI report raised "a number of very serious issues." "I had some visibility [*sic*] into some of the activities there. But I was not part of any type of management structure or aware of most of the details." Chambliss noted that John McLaughlin (who retired from the CIA as acting director in November 2004, after more than three decades) said he had never heard Brennan object. Buzzy Krongard, Brennan's boss at the Agency, said Brennan had a role in "helping to seek Justice Department approval for the techniques." "John would have been part and parcel of that process." Brennan "respectfully disagree[d]." Asked why he received at least fifty emails describing the abu Zubaydah interrogation, Brennan said he "was just cc'd … I wasn't an action officer on it." "[I]t was clearly my impression that there was valuable information coming" from EITs, which was "why I did say that they save lives." Sen. Rockefeller objected that the EIT program was "sold" with "grossly-inflated claims of professionalism and effectiveness." Sen. Mikulski (D-Md) complained that in more than ten years on SSCI "I've been jerked around by every CIA

Director" except Panetta, "misled, misrepresented, had to pull information out." In response to Levin, Brennan repeatedly refused to say whether waterboarding was torture and illegal, claiming he was not a lawyer; but he called it "reprehensible," "completely different" from SERE training, and declared it "should have been banned long ago." He also affirmed an earlier statement that waterboarding "is certainly subjecting an individual to severe pain and suffering, which is the classic definition of torture." He declined to support the claims for EITs advanced by Jose Rodriguez, Michael Hayden, and Michael Mukasey, and disagreed with Sen. Rubio's (R-Fla) criticism of prosecuting accused terrorists in criminal courts.

The *New York Times* found Brennan's responses "frequently unsatisfying." "It was incomprehensible that he did not acknowledge the obvious truth … that waterboarding is purely and simply torture" and "disheartening" that he "did nothing more to stop it because he did not have any oversight responsibility." John Rizzo said at a panel discussion on *Zero Dark Thirty* that Brennan "never expressed any concerns to me" about EITs, "and my office was 15 feet away from his." Sen. McCain did not want to put a hold on Brennan, "but the American people deserve answers" about his views on EITs. Nevertheless, SSCI voted 12–3 for the nomination. After the Senate voted 63–34 to confirm, the *Times* repeated its regret that Brennan "thinks there is some doubt still about whether the Bush administration tortured prisoners, hid its actions from Congress and misled everyone about whether coerced testimony provided valuable intelligence."

On April 16, 2013 the Constitution Project bipartisan Task Force published a 577-page report (tragically overshadowed by the previous day's Boston Marathon bombing).[158] It found that EITs "damaged the standing of our nation, reduced our capacity to convey moral censure when necessary and potentially increased the danger to U.S. military personnel taken captive." There was "no firm or persuasive evidence" that they produced valuable information that could not have been obtained by other means. It confirmed HRW reports that the CIA had waterboarded Libyans, something the Agency had never admitted. Under the headline "Indisputable Torture," the *New York Times* said the "sweeping report" provided a "necessary reckoning." Its "blunt language should help end a corrosive debate that has broken down on largely partisan lines." The *Times* urged publication of the SSCI report. Thomas Pickering (a Task Force member with four decades of government service in foreign affairs) wrote in a *Washington Post* op ed that the use of torture "undermined our values, principles and moral stature; eroded our global influence; and placed our soldiers, diplomats and intelligence officers in even greater jeopardy." The administration should declassify the six million pages examined by SSCI and publish its report; Congress should legislate against torture. Susan Brooks Thistlethwaite (former president of the Chicago Theological Seminary) wrote in a *Washington Post* op ed that to avoid a repetition of the mistakes after 9/11, we must "confront the truth of that time, its continuing corruptions of our moral and legal frameworks."

At the end of June 2013 the CIA sent SSCI a classified 122-page rebuttal.[159] A month later Feinstein said she planned to seek declassification of the executive summary after "making any factual changes to our report that are warranted." She was "appalled by the persistent media leaks by anonymous officials," which began three months before the CIA's response. Chambliss again called the report deeply flawed but said the executive summary could be published if accompanied by the CIA response and SSCI Republicans' dissent. Brennan opposed releasing any of it.

Obama's nomination of James Comey to direct the FBI prompted Sens. Durbin and Whitehouse to revive "an issue of great importance to our nation: torture."[160] In an April 27, 2005 email to his chief of staff, then Deputy Attorney General Comey had written that he agreed with one of Bradbury's OLC opinions, authorizing 13 EITs (including waterboarding and 180 hours of sleep deprivation), but said the "combined effects" approved by the other opinion were illegal. In another email he explained to Attorney General Gonzales "in stark terms ... what this would look like some day and what it would mean for the president and the government." A case could be made "that some of this stuff was simply awful." At his confirmation hearing a week after these emails were revealed, Comey said that "even though I as a person, as a father, as a leader thought, 'that's torture – we shouldn't be doing that kind of thing,' I discovered it's actually a much harder question to interpret this 1994 [anti-torture] statute, which I found vague." Gonzales presented Comey's objections to the Principals Committee, which rejected them. After the hearing, an aide said Comey had since changed his mind because both the DTA and Obama had banned waterboarding and the OLC opinions had been withdrawn. The *Los Angeles Times* said Comey "shouldn't have acquiesced in a reading of the law that purported to find [EITs] legal." The *New York Times* praised his "unequivocal rejection of waterboarding as a form of torture." The

Senate confirmed him, with only Rand Paul opposed. Nominated for DoD General Counsel, Stephen Preston told SASC: "I believe under current law waterboarding is torture." After Sen. Udall (D-NM) put a hold on the nomination until he got answers to seven questions, Preston said that under Bush, the CIA "fell well short" of keeping Congress informed. The Senate confirmed Preston.

In August 2013, in its periodic report to the UN Committee Against Torture, the DoS stated for the first time that "a time of war does not suspend the operation of the Convention [against Torture] as to matters within its scope," repudiating the position the USA had taken in 2006.[161]

A year after the SSCI report was completed, William H. Taft IV (DoS Legal Adviser under Bush) wrote a *Washington Post* op ed urging its publication.[162] EITs violated "U.S. values and law and compromised our moral leadership." "Until the report is publicly released, proponents of torture will continue to use the secrecy that surrounds the CIA's detention and interrogation program to distort the facts." In February 2014 the *Washington Post* observed that "more than a dozen years after the attacks of 9/11, it is time to treat government decisions made in the aftermath as history – to be debated and learned from."

During Caroline D. Krass's confirmation hearing as CIA General Counsel, Sen. Udall disclosed that two years earlier Panetta had ordered the CIA to produce an internal report, whose conclusions were "consistent with the Intelligence Committee's report." Udall threatened to put a hold on Krass's nomination until the Agency produced this "Panetta Review." Sen. Feinstein said SSCI would soon vote to adopt the committee report's executive summary, which would be subject to declassification before release. (SSCI wanted this conducted by the White House, not the CIA.) Much of the hearing concerned SSCI's request for two secret OLC memos. Krass (who was at OLC) resisted on the ground that they "represent pre-decision, confidential legal advice." The *New York Times* thought it "appalling" that all those memos were still secret. Obama's "expansive claims of secrecy" had denied "the country a reckoning necessary for the historical record, establishing accountability, and avoiding similar human rights violations in the future."

Accusing SSCI of having obtained the Panetta Review through unauthorized access to the Agency's databases, CIA asked the DoJ to investigate. SSCI parried with its own DoJ referral and a complaint to the CIA IG, alleging that the Agency had illegally monitored SSCI staff in violation of the 1986 Federal Computer Fraud and Abuse Act. Udall wrote Obama that the CIA's actions were "incredibly troubling for the committee's oversight responsibilities and for our democracy." "The CIA tried to intimidate the Intelligence Committee, plain and simple." A week later Feinstein also denounced the CIA's referral to the DoJ as "a potential effort to intimidate this staff," calling it a "defining moment" for oversight and warning: "I am not taking it lightly." In 2010 the CIA had removed 920 documents from the SSCI staff computer (located at a CIA facility), refusing to acknowledge impropriety or apologize. Because of the CIA's destruction of its interrogation videotapes in 2005, SSCI had placed its copy of the Panetta Review in a safe in the Hart Office Building. Denying Feinstein's charges, Brennan said "nothing could be further from the truth." "We wouldn't do that. I mean that's just beyond the scope of reason in terms of what we would do." Majority Leader Reid "unequivocally" supported Feinstein and was "disappointed" by the CIA's conduct. McCain called the allegations "very disturbing." Graham agreed that "if what they're saying is true about the CIA, this is Richard Nixon stuff. This is dangerous to a democracy. Heads should roll … The legislative branch should declare war on the CIA." Leahy said: "the members of the Senate must stand up in defense of this institution, the Constitution and the values upon which this nation was founded." But some Republicans urged an Ethics Committee review of their colleagues for disclosing internal Senate proceedings. Democrats called this a witch hunt. Udall said: "the only thing I've done is exercise vigorous oversight over senior intelligence officials who are all too often unwilling to cooperate with Congress."

The *New York Times* commented:

> It was outrageous enough when two successive presidents papered over the Central Intelligence Agency's history of illegal detention, rendition, torture and fruitless harsh interrogation of terrorism suspects. Now the head of the Senate Intelligence Committee … has provided stark and convincing evidence that the C.I.A. may have committed crimes to prevent the exposure of the interrogations.

USA Today said "attention should be paid" to Feinstein's "explosive charges." "If the CIA did what Feinstein alleges, its actions were an outrageous breach of law and the Constitution's separation of powers, and those involved must be held accountable." The *Washington Post* urged the CIA "to quickly work out an accommodation with the Senate that will permit use of the internal review." The *Denver Post* hailed its senator as "a leading supporter of declassifying as much as possible of the panel's report. If the Senate and White House fail to release the document ... it will only solidify growing public skepticism regarding proper oversight of America's clandestine activities."

Obama declared he was "absolutely committed to declassifying that report" as soon as it was completed (which had happened 15 months earlier), but declined to engage the present controversy, which Brennan had referred "to the appropriate authorities." Feinstein criticized Robert Eatinger, CIA Acting General Counsel, for making the DoJ referral, noting that he was one of the two lawyers, then in the clandestine service, who had approved the videotape destruction and was named more than 1,600 times in the SSCI report. Udall urged Eatinger to recuse himself from all matters concerning interrogations or SSCI. Graham did not "see a scenario ... that would justify what the C.I.A. is alleged to have done." Durbin deplored that "the C.I.A. is making it very difficult for Congress to fully carry out its oversight function." Heinrich now regretted having voted to confirm Brennan as DCI. Wyden effectively accused Brennan of lying. Rep. Schiff (D-Ca) (who chaired HPSCI) called Feinstein's charges "very serious" and expressed concern about how the CIA "pushed back without any kind of conciliation on this." Rep. Pelosi praised Feinstein's courage.

Deriding Brennan's allegation against SSCI staff as "patently absurd," Reid referred the controversy to the Senate Sergeant-at-Arms and asked the Director to ensure that the Agency contacted Senate staff only through the Sergeant-at-Arms.

> In my capacity as the leader of the U.S. Senate, the CIA's actions cause me great concern. The CIA has not only interfered with the lawful Congressional oversight of its activities, but has also seemingly attempted to intimidate its overseers by subjecting them to criminal investigation. The developments strike at the heart of the constitutional separation of powers between the legislative and executive branches. Left unchallenged, they call into question Congress's ability to carry out its core constitutional duties and risk the possibility of an unaccountable intelligence community run amok.

Reid wrote Holder that:

> the C.I.A. has produced no evidence to support its claims that Senate committee staff who have no technical training somehow hacked into the C.I.A.'s highly secure classified networks ... The CIA's decision to access the resources and work product of the legislative branch without

> permission is absolutely indefensible, regardless of the context … [and] stands as a categorically different and more serious breach.

Seeking to cool the controversy, Brennan wrote CIA employees in March 2014 that SSCI members "carry out their oversight responsibilities with great dedication and patriotism." Four months later DoJ declined to pursue either referral.[163] Feinstein was "pleased" this "will allow the committee to focus on the upcoming release of its report." But Udall criticized the decision for drawing "a false equivalency between congressional staff fulfilling their constitutional obligations and an executive branch agency potentially breaking the law." A few days later the CIA IG found that three Agency information technology officers and two lawyers "improperly accessed" the SSCI computer network, conducted a keyword search of all committee files, read staff emails, based the DoJ referral on "inaccurate information," and "displayed a lack of candor" in talking to the IG. Sen. Chambliss said these "serious violations" should be "dealt with very harshly." Graham called it "a very big deal," for which "an apology is not enough." Reid condemned the actions as "appalling and deeply threatening to our system of checks and balances." McCain called it "worse than criminal" and "clearly unconstitutional." Even Ayotte (a conservative Republican) said CIA hacking was "a huge, huge issue," potentially "of constitutional proportions." Udall and Heinrich (D-NM) demanded Brennan's resignation. Paul agreed, bragging: "I not only voted against Brennan, I filibustered his nomination." Asked by Wyden to reconsider its declination, the DoJ said it had known of the IG's findings when it made that decision. Several dozen public interest groups also demanded that Brennan resign. The *New York Times* said "the accountability and the apologies … will have to go much further." "[O]ne of those heads" that "should roll" "may need to Mr. Brennan's. If he knew about the break-in, then he blatantly lied. If he did not, then apparently he was unaware of the lawless culture that has festered within the C.I.A." SSCI's investigation had been "frustrated at many points by stonewalling from the agency, which provided misleading information, hid important facts inside a blizzard of excess documents, and forced endless delays in the declassification process." The Agency's "very core, and basic culture, needs a full overhaul."

But the White House praised Brennan for doing a "difficult job … extraordinarily well" and taking "responsible steps." At a press conference Obama acknowledged that "we tortured some folks." "I think any fair-minded person would believe" EITs "were torture, we crossed a line." "We did some things that were contrary to our values." But he had "full confidence" in Brennan. "It's important for us not to feel too sanctimonious in retrospect about the tough job that those folks had. A lot of those folks were working hard under enormous pressure and are real patriots." (Obama had earlier displayed anxiety about alienating the Agency. Panetta wrote in his memoir that when the CIA agreed in 2009 to give SSCI access to millions of documents, White House Chief of Staff Emanuel shouted: "the president wants to know who the fuck authorized this release to the committee. I have a president with his hair on fire.")

Two weeks later Brennan apologized in person to Feinstein and Chambliss and appointed an Accountability Review Board of three CIA employees and two outsiders (chaired by former Democrat Sen. Bayh (R-In)). Two weeks after Brennan met SSCI members behind closed-doors, some senators were so angry that they revealed he had refused to say who had authorized the intrusion into the committee's computers. Levin called such "disrespect towards the Congress" "arrogant" and "unacceptable." Heinrich said Brennan "continues to stonewall us on basic information." Udall renewed his call for Brennan's resignation. Brennan said: "if I've done something wrong, I'll stand up and admit it, but I'm not going to take … the allegations about hacking and monitoring and spying and whatever else." Wyden responded by accusing Brennan of encouraging a "culture of misinformation" at the CIA.

In October the Senate Sergeant-at-Arms ended his investigation without determining whether the CIA had done anything wrong. In January 2015 the Board found "clearly inappropriate" behavior but recommended no penalty because there had been no "malfeasance, bad faith, or the intention to gain improper access."[164] This effectively nullified the CIA IG report (released simultaneously), which found that right after an Agency employee told Brennan that SSCI had obtained the Panetta Review, the Director told a CIA lawyer he had "discussed the possible security breach" with White House chief of staff McDonough and ordered the lawyer "to use whatever means necessary to answer the question of how the documents arrived on the SSCI side of the [computer] system." Feinstein reasserted that "the decision was made to search the Committee computers, and someone should be found responsible for those actions." Wyden called it "incredible that no one at the CIA has been held accountable for this very clear violation of constitutional principles." Six months later he and Sens. Heinrich and Hirono (D-Hi) demanded that Brennan admit the CIA search had violated separation of powers and promise not to do so again.

John Rizzo (former CIA Acting General Counsel) urged publication of both the SSCI report and the Agency rebuttal, but continued to maintain that though "some of the techniques, particularly waterboarding … could be described as brutal … I don't think today that any of them rose to the legal threshold of torture." Cheney also insisted waterboarding was not torture and did not violate the Geneva Conventions, which anyhow did not apply to enemy combatants. "If I would have to do it all over again, I would. The results speak for themselves." Sen. King invited Cheney to "go through what those people went through, one of them a hundred plus-odd times." "[T]o say that it was carefully managed, and everybody knew what was going on, that's absolute nonsense."

In April 2014 SSCI voted to release its report, which still had to go to the White House for declassification.[165] Sen. King called the Agency's inaccurate statements to the president, NSC, and Congress "one of the most disturbing parts of this." SSCI declared that "the report exposes brutality that stands in stark contrast to our values as a nation." By documenting "deeply troubling" problems "with CIA's management of this program and its interactions with the White House, other parts of the executive branch and Congress," the report "shows why oversight of intelligence agencies in a democratic nation is so important." Chambliss (the ranking Republican) repeated that although the report had been "an expensive, partisan distraction" and contained significant errors, omissions and assumptions – as well as a lot of cherry-picking of the facts – I want the American people to be able to see it and judge for themselves." In a *Washington Post* op ed Jose Rodriguez defended the interrogation program for having "produced critical intelligence that helped decimate al-Qaeda and save American lives." "There was never any effort to mislead the administration or Congress." When former DCI Hayden accused Feinstein of being "emotional" about the report rather than "objective," Reid said the comment showed "Republicans' disregard for women." It emerged that after Vice President Biden had called for release of the report a year earlier, DoS sent Congress a classified letter warning that publication could endanger American lives abroad and harm foreign relations. But in February 2014 Biden declared: "I think the only way you excise [*sic* – read "exorcise"] the demons is you acknowledge … exactly that happened straightforward." Sens. Rubio and Risch (R-Id) now repeated the DoS warning about the dangers of the "one-sided, partisan report." Feinstein and Rockefeller wrote in a *Washington Post* op ed that the report's release "is the best way to ensure that this program … never happens again." Holder's August 2009 decision to expand DoJ's investigation of videotape destruction to the interrogations themselves had led DCI Panetta not to compel any employee to assist the SSCI study. This, not partisanship, provoked SSCI Republicans to withdraw their support. Forty House Democrats urged Obama to speed declassification. Feinstein asked Obama to limit the CIA's role in declassification because of its "clear conflict of interest on this issue and its demonstrated inability to face the truth about this program." Thirty retired generals wrote Obama seeking publication.

Some of those potentially implicated in EITs intensified their defense.[166] Rizzo reiterated they "were yielding detailed, valuable information into terrorist plots." He "absolutely reject[ed]" the claim that he "purposely misled the Department of Justice about what the techniques were and how they were being implemented." "This is strictly a political exercise by the Democratic side of the Intelligence Committee to castigate a Bush-era program." James Mitchell (the psychologist who had initiated the EITs) said it was "easy to forget in 2014 … that in 2002 we were hearing that the next attack was coming soon … the threat matrix was just on fire." EITs "were the 'bad cop' part of a more subtle, sophisticated and harsher version of the 'good cop/bad cop' approach to interrogation." Without having seen the report, he called it "a politicized rewriting of history" and was "highly skeptical" of its accuracy. At an NRA "Stand and Fight" rally, Sarah Palin ridiculed those who would coddle "enemies, who would utterly annihilate America, they who'd obviously have information on plots, to carry out jihad. Oh, but you can't offend them, can't make them feel uncomfortable, not even a smidgen. Well, if I were in charge, they would know that waterboarding is how we'd baptize terrorists."

Republicans leaped to defend the CIA.[167] On CBS's *Face the Nation* Sen. Chambliss said that "information gleaned from these interrogations was in fact used to interrupt and disrupt terrorist plots, including some information that took down bin Laden." Liz Cheney said on *Fox News* that Obama was "lying about what [the CIA] did, slandering them." On the same program former Acting DCI Morell said the CIA "had multiple legal opinions from the DoJ specifically saying [the EIT program] was not torture." But on CNN, Rep. King called it "nonsense" to "argue it wasn't torture." Rep. Rogers minimized searching CIA computers at a CIA facility as "a little bit different than spying on Congress." (The

CIA had *required* SSCI to use the Agency's computers at its facility.) In response to criticism that SSCI had not interviewed CIA employees, Michael Davidson (who had worked on the report for four years) said DoJ initially blocked SSCI interviews on the ground that Durham's criminal investigation was conducting them, then refused to give SSCI his interviews, and (after the report's release) resisted a *New York Times* FOIA request for the interviews on the ground that disclosure could affect the candor of law enforcement deliberations.

Retired military leaders again urged Obama to release the report. "The U.S. military's examination of torture in its ranks after the Abu Ghraib scandal was painful; it was also necessary to the health of the institution. The stakes are too high to allow the intelligence community to circle the wagons and launch a concerted campaign to undermine the report's credibility." MGen. Taguba (whose report exposed the Abu Ghraib abuses) wrote a *New York Times* op ed criticizing the "concerted effort to discredit" the report.[168] He knew "from experience that oversight will help the C.I.A."

Shortly before leaving the administration in 2013, DoS Legal Adviser Harold Koh wrote a 90-page memorandum declaring "it is not legally available to policy makers to claim" that the CAT does not apply to non-US citizens abroad – repudiating the position Gonzales had asserted in his 2005 confirmation hearing.[169] Perhaps because Gonzales's view still was shared by military and intelligence community lawyers, the administration rejected Koh's memo in March 2014. The *New York Times* warned Obama not to "consider any legal loophole that might permit an American official to engage in torture or cruelty, no matter where it takes place." A dozen Nobel Peace Prize laureates urged the president to "take the necessary steps to recover the standards on which the country was founded, and to once again adhere to the international conventions it helped to bring into being." Retired Archbishop Desmond Tutu (one of the signers) said their letter was inspired by "disturbing" news that the administration was thinking of embracing the "foul thinking" that "ghastly things," which were crimes at home, were permitted abroad. HRW and the ACLU exhorted the president to reaffirm the CAT's applicability to all official conduct, even outside the USA. Koh wrote Obama that doing so would "enshrine your legacy on one of the issues that most mattered to you when you first campaigned for president." Sens. Feinstein, Leahy, and Durbin told him: "it is crucial that the United States signals to the world that we have put the dark chapter of the Bush administration's torture program behind us."

Admitting at a meeting of the UN Committee on Torture that the USA "did not always live up to our own values," the acting DoS Legal Adviser now embraced the position that the CAT applied wherever the USA exercised governing authority (and even secret prisons – where it did not – were bound by domestic statutes and Obama's executive order). Tom Malinowski, Assistant Secretary of State for Human Rights (previously HRW advocacy director), reaffirmed that "torture, and cruel, inhuman and degrading treatment and punishment are forbidden in all places, at all times, with no exceptions." Committee members asked the USA whether the Army Field Manual's Appendix M allowed sleep or sensory deprivation. Five Libyan men whom Durham had not interviewed described their torture to the Committee, whose report, published at the end of November 2014, criticized EITs.

With Feinstein's agreement, former CIA Directors Tenet, Goss, and Hayden and Deputy Directors McLaughlin and Morell read the unredacted SSCI report.[170] Soon after SSCI voted to release the Executive Summary, Brennan convened a meeting of active and retired CIA employees who had participated in the program (presumably to plan a rebuttal). Increasingly unhappy with the delays and redactions, Wyden considered using the rarely employed device of reading the report on the Senate floor. Feinstein hoped it would be released in August 2014. But troubled that the White House redactions "eliminate or obscure key facts that support the report's findings and conclusions," she sent Obama a list of necessary changes. Levin agreed the redactions were "totally unacceptable." Udall warned that "strategically placed redactions can make a narrative incomprehensible." Heinrich analogized the redacted report to "reading a novel with 15 percent of the words blacked out." The White House defended the redactions as a "good-faith effort" to "protect national security." DNI Clapper maintained they were "minimal," half in the footnotes. But in October Wyden accused the intelligence leadership of "doing everything they can to bury the facts" by redacting pseudonyms, making the report much harder to understand; the CIA replied it was necessary to protect officers. In November Udall insisted he was "going to keep all options on the table to ensure the truth comes out." Michael Hayden said: "American embassies and other installations around the world have been warned to take defensive action in anticipation of this report being released." Feinstein reassured the public that there was only one remaining dispute about redactions. But agreement foundered on administration demands to eliminate pseudonyms. Heinrich complained: "if you take all the names out of a novel, it becomes very hard to understand that novel's narrative arc." Rockefeller declared the report was "being slow-walked to death. They're doing everything they can not to release it." McCain supported Feinstein's efforts.

Sen. Burr (R-NC) (who would chair SSCI in January, following Republicans' capture of the Senate) opposed releasing the report, which he condemned as full of unspecified inaccuracies. On December 5 Secretary of State Kerry asked Feinstein to delay release for three more days (although he had known of the controversy for months). ODNI also warned Congress about the risks of release. Jose Rodriguez anticipated the release with a *Washington Post* op ed, calling the report (which he had not seen) "a dishonest attempt to rewrite history." "We did what we were asked to do, we did what we were assured was legal, and we know that our actions were effective." Hayden said the SSCI claim that the CIA "lied to everyone about a program that wasn't doing any good ... beggars the imagination." Bush called CIA employees "patriots," "really good people." "[W]hatever the report says, if it diminishes their contributions to our country, it is way off base." Former Deputy and Acting CIA Director McLaughlin said the report "uses information selectively, often distorts to make its points." Rep. Rogers called the release "a terrible idea. Our foreign partners are telling us this will cause violence and death." Cheney said CIA employees "ought to be decorated, not criticized."

When the report finally was released on December 9, 2014, McCain made an eloquent speech on the Senate floor. EITs not only failed "to secure actionable intelligence to prevent further attacks" but also "actually damaged our security interests, as well as our reputation as a force for good in the world." In her hour-long speech, Feinstein said: "my words give me no pleasure." But history will judge the USA by its "commitment to a just society governed by law and the willingness to face an ugly truth and say, 'never again.'"[171] The same day HRF honored both with its Beacon Prize for "their leadership to end the use of torture and other cruel treatment of prisoners by the United States." Leahy said on the Senate floor that "this program did not make us safer." "As Americans, we cannot sweep our mistakes under the rug and pretend they did not happen." Whitehouse said the report "lays out in painstaking detail how the CIA under President Bush and Vice President Cheney turned down the dark path to torture, and then to cover its tracks misled Congress and executive officials about the efficacy of the torture program."

John Kerry said the report "affirms again that one of America's strengths is our democratic system's ability to recognize and wrestle with our own history, acknowledge mistakes, and correct course."[172] EITs "were at odds with our values." But the White House tried to play both sides. Press Secretary Earnest said: "the President believes that our men and women in the intelligence community are genuine patriots who put their lives on the line … to protect the American people." The administration was "not passing judgment" on the SSCI report "but expressing our full support for our men and women in the intelligence community." In a television interview later that day Obama repeated that EITs "constituted torture in my mind." "Some of these techniques … were not only wrong, but also counterproductive" because people will "say anything in order to alleviate the pain." In a formal statement he said the "troubling" program "did significant damage to America's standing in the world and made it harder to pursue our interests with allies and partners."

Brennan condemned the report as an "incomplete and selective picture."[173] While acknowledging "there were instances where representations about the program … were inaccurate, imprecise, or fell short of our tradecraft standards," he denied that "the Agency repeatedly, systematically, and intentionally misled others on the effectiveness of the program." EITs were "determined … to be lawful" by the DoJ and "duly authorized" by the administration. "Whatever your views are on EITs," the CIA "did a lot of things right." Brennan regretted the "unusual" fact that "no CIA personnel were interviewed" (ignoring that Panetta had told them they did not have to talk to SSCI). Despite this "flawed" process, however, many of the conclusions were "sound." "In a limited number of cases, Agency officers used interrogation techniques that had not been authorized, were abhorrent, and rightly should be repudiated by all. And we fell short when it came to holding some officers accountable for their mistakes." But the CIA had taken "steps to broaden the scope of our accountability reviews … systematically reexamine the legal opinions … and improve recordkeeping for interactions with the Congress." Although the program "produced useful intelligence that helped the United States thwart attack plans," Brennan conceded that "the cause and effect relationship between the use of EITs and useful information subsequently provided by the detainee is … unknowable." In any case, "effective non-coercive methods are available to elicit such information." He expressed a "fervent hope … that we can put aside this debate and move forward."

Feinstein said Brennan's remarks "showed that CIA leadership is prepared to prevent this from ever happening again." She repeated that "the report shows" that "information needed to stop terrorist attacks" was "obtained through other means." Furthermore, "the descriptions of interrogations that were finally provided to the committee did not accurately reflect reality." (Panetta equivocated similarly in his memoir: "we got important, even critical intelligence from individuals subjected to these EITs. What we cannot know – what we'll never know – is whether those were the only ways to elicit that information." "If a future president ever asked me whether we should go back to those techniques, I would say no.")

The 500-page Executive Summary (of a 6,700-page report based on more than six million pages of documents) found that EITs were "not an effective means of acquiring intelligence."[174] Twenty "of the most frequent and prominent examples of purported counterterrorism successes that the CIA has attributed to the use of" EITs were "wrong in fundamental respects." Interrogations were "far worse than the CIA represented to policymakers and others" and included "rectal rehydration" (disclosed for the first time). "The CIA repeatedly provided inaccurate information to the Department of Justice, impeding a proper legal analysis" of the program. The CIA "actively avoided or impeded" oversight by Congress, the White House and its own OIG. "CIA detainees were subjected to coercive interrogation techniques that had not been approved by the Department of Justice or ... authorized by CIA Headquarters." "The CIA rarely reprimanded or held personnel accountable" for abuses.

Several SSCI members added individual comments. Rockefeller, Wyden, Udall, and Heinrich berated the CIA for obstructing the Committee's investigation and oversight. Rockefeller found it "infuriating to realize that I was part of a box checking exercise." Wyden warned that "reliance on a secret body of law helped spawn a culture of misinformation." Udall said the CIA response "continues to be riddled with factual errors and misstatements." Heinrich accused the CIA of "taking years to dump millions of unsorted documents in a massive database, while resisting requests for additional information," and charged current and former officials with "anonymously misrepresenting the contents and the findings of the study in the press." King said: "the committee was continuously misled as to virtually all aspects of this program." Six Republicans wrote a 160-page rebuttal criticizing the report's "flawed analytical methodology," "decision not to interview key witnesses," and "strongly held biases." It insisted that EITs had been effective (devoting nearly 100 pages to that issue), "the CIA attempted to keep the Congress informed of its activities," and "most" of its representations were accurate. If presidential briefings were inadequate, "it was at the request of the White House – not the CIA, that only a broad description of the nature of the techniques would be provided." They concluded: "We have no doubt that the CIA's detention program saved lives and played a vital role in weakening al-Qa'ida."

Brennan and the CIA issued a lengthy response.[175] They agreed that because they had been "unprepared and lacked core competencies," there were "significant lapses in the Agency's ability to develop and monitor its initial detention and interrogation activities," but insisted these lasted no "more than a few months." The CIA "failed to perform a comprehensive and independent analysis on the effectiveness" of EITs. It let the psychologists who designed and directed the EITs assess "the fitness of detainees to be subjected to such techniques and the effectiveness of those same techniques." It "fell short when it came to holding individuals accountable for poor performance and management failures," but denied "there were many more instances of improper actions for which some form of accountability exercise should have been conducted." However, it disagreed with the SSCI claim "that the overall detention and interrogation program did not produce unique intelligence that led terrorist plots to be disrupted, terrorists to be captured, or lives to be saved," although it conceded that whether such intelligence "could have been obtained through other means … will forever remain unknowable." It rejected criticism that the Agency resisted oversight or intentionally misled anyone.

Immediately after the release, six former CIA directors and deputy directors wrote a long *Wall Street Journal* op end deploring the report's "lamentable … inaccuracies" and the "alarming" consequences these would have on the "public's understanding of the program."[176] The CIA's 30 "detailed and graphic" Congressional briefings had drawn "reactions that ranged from approval to no objection." "The CIA's aggressive counterterrorism policies and programs are responsible" for the fact that "the al Qaeda leadership has not managed another attack on the homeland in the 13 years since" 9/11. Those interrogations had led to "the capture of senior al Qaeda operatives … the disruption of terrorist plots and … added enormously to what we knew about al Qaeda."

In a full-page editorial calling the report "a portrait of depravity that is hard to comprehend and even harder to stomach," the *New York*

Times asked "why no one has ever been held accountable."[177] "The litany of brutality, lawlessness and lack of accountability serves as a reminder of what a horrible decision President Obama made at the outset of his administration to close the books on this chapter of our history." A week after publication the *Times* called for prosecution. Obama had "failed to bring to justice anyone responsible for the torture of terrorism suspects." Although he repeatedly said "we need to look forward as opposed to looking backwards," "the nation cannot move forward in any meaningful way without coming to terms, legally and morally, with the abhorrent acts ... These are, simply, crimes." There should be a full criminal investigation of Cheney, Addington, Tenet, Yoo, Bybee, Rodriguez, "the psychologists who devised the torture regimen; and the C.I.A. employees who carried out that regimen." The *Times* reiterated that demand in its summary of the "big issues" of 2014.

The *Washington Post* said the report "depicts the disgusting extremes." "That is not how Americans should behave. Ever." "[T]he argument over practical outcomes is mostly beside the point. Torture is wrong, whether or not it has ever 'worked.'" The *Los Angeles Times* said the report "documented ... outrageous conduct in stomach-turning detail" and "described new offenses to human dignity that border on the pornographic." It "amounts to an indictment of the CIA and its political enablers." The *Financial Times* said there was "no doubt" that the CIA "routinely practiced brutal forms of torture, misled Congress about what it was up to and made false claims about the benefits of 'EITs.'" Obama should reconsider his decision not to prosecute.

Thomas Friedman wrote in his *New York Times* column that "this act of self-examination is not only what keeps our society as a whole healthy, it's what keeps us a model that others want to emulate."[178] Andrew Rosenthal declared in his column that the CIA's actions were "disgusting and inexcusable." Most *Washington Post* columnists agreed. Ruth Marcus felt that "no one can review this account without feeling horror and shame, and without feeling anger at the degree to which public officials and the public itself were misled about what was being done in the name of national security." Paul Waldman said CIA employees "essentially had no idea what they were doing" and "generally made a mess of things." Walter Pincus found "plenty of blame to spread around inside and outside government for what went on in the name of America's security." But while acknowledging the need for "an honest public accounting," David Ignatius criticized the report as "overly prosecutorial," "a political document, not a dispassionate history."

Others also pushed back. Former CIA Deputy and Acting Director McLaughlin said "the most incredible and false claim … is that the program was neither necessary nor effective."[179] Former CIA spokesman Bill Harlow noted that the Agency had referred 20 cases of wrongdoing to the DoJ. The *Wall Street Journal* dismissed all the "outrage" as "politically convenient." "The report is more important for illustrating how fickle Americans are about their security, and so unfair to those who provide it." Jose Rodriguez admitted that "mistakes were made" (a huge understatement in the passive voice). Interrogation "was not our core skill." Because the CIA had put "a very young person" in charge of the Salt Pit, "the station dropped the ball and somebody froze to death there." "After August 2002, it was a well-managed program with specific instructions with what to do. Nevertheless, there were people who broke the rules." He "specifically" briefed Pelosi on abu Zubaydah's interrogation. The claim that EITs were inessential to finding Osama bin Laden was "total bullshit." John Yoo said the report "will assume a place in the annals of congressional recklessness." He was unmoved by critics "because I've been living in Berkeley so long I'm used to being surrounded by a sea of Marxists." EITs – even waterboarding – were legal. Former Bush adviser Karl Rove said the fully briefed Gang of Four had "encouraged the CIA to take every step." Sen. Chambliss said only three of 789 detainees were waterboarded: "There were 766 actionable intelligence reports written from abu Zubaydah. Common sense and logic would tell you that some of those reports were the result of statements abu Zubaydah made after he went through the EIT program." Rep. Rogers said it was "not a good decision" "to go back and ruin" the lives of CIA employees "over what we had already fixed." The USA should "push back" against any effort by other countries "to go after U.S. citizens who were working … to protect the United States." Rep. King insisted "the CIA did an excellent job" and was "responsible for stopping attacks against the United States." "[W]e have to stop this self-loathing." Even Rep. Schiff, a Democrat, said that as a former prosecutor he felt it would be "very difficult to make a case against someone who is following the advice of the Justice Department."

Hayden denounced the report as "a prosecutorial screed rather than a historical document." Rectal feeding was simply a "medical procedure" by which "you can get nourishment into a person." Protesting that "most of this stuff came before me," he complained that "I'm mentioned twice as much" in the report "as George Tenet – but George and Porter Goss had 97 detainees during their tenure, while I had two." Tenet declared twice on television: "we don't torture people." In a formal statement he said the "biased, inaccurate, and destructive" report "does damage to U.S. national security, to the men and women of the Central Intelligence Agency, and most of all to the truth." SSCI "consciously chose to denigrate the integrity and performance of men and women." The program was "directed by the President" and had "the legal authorization of the Attorney General." "[T]he Congressional leadership was regularly and accurately briefed." The program "was effective in saving American and allied lives."

Mukasey reiterated that "CIA interrogations followed the law."[180] Waterboarding could not be torture because it had been part of SERE training and KSM "came to know the precise limits of the procedure." "At last report, he is doing just fine." "More journalists have tried the experience of being waterboarded than terrorists were subjected to it. That wouldn't be the case if, for example, we were talking about needles under fingernails." Mukasey faulted the Supreme Court for extending the Geneva Conventions to those "who were never intended to be protected" and the Detainee Treatment Act for defining prohibited acts in "opaquely general terms" – i.e, "cruel, inhuman or degrading treatment or punishment." He favored a balancing test: what "shocks the conscience" for purposes of due process depended on "what is at stake – like, say, national security." He rebutted McCain by noting that other veterans with similar credentials "believe in the efficacy and morality of waterboarding." Mukasey's predecessor, Alberto Gonzales, blithely disclaimed responsibility. "Whether or not [the CIA] followed the [OLC] guidance, quite frankly, the oversight responsibility fell to the IG and General Counsel of the CIA. We just wouldn't know about it." "One of the lessons that one might get from all of this is the fact that war is a dirty business, and human beings sometimes they do things that they shouldn't do."

Cheney dismissed the report as "full of crap."[181] It was a "flat-out lie" that Bush did not know about EITs. But these did not violate human rights: "how nice do you want to be to the murderers of 3,000 Americans?" He would "do it again in a minute." "Torture is what the al Qaeda terrorists did to 3,000 Americans on 9/11 … there is no comparison between that and what we did with respect to enhanced interrogation." He had "no problem" with wrongfully detaining prisoners "as long as we achieve our objective." These comments provoked strong responses.

Andrew Rosenthal wrote in his *New York Times* column that "listening to Mr. Cheney sing the praises of waterboarding and other outrages is truly depressing." Noting that in 2005 Cheney had been able to persuade only six Republican senators to vote against the Detainee Treatment Act, Rosenthal commented: "Maybe the rest of us should take a cue from the others and stop paying attention to him ourselves." "Judging from my inbox," Ruth Marcus wrote in her *Washington Post* column, "Cheney's torture remarks are both too outrageous and ... too common to ignore." The *Washington Post* warned that "if Dick Cheney's views carry the day, releasing the Senate Intelligence Committee's horrifying account of CIA torture ... will hardly have been worth it." The ban on torture "must be a moral and political expectation, built into the country's mores."

The report provoked mixed reactions abroad.[182] Some of the worst human rights offenders seized the opportunity to indulge in hypocritical moralizing. China's Xinhua News Service denounced the "sheer hypocrisy" of America, which "is neither a suitable role model nor a qualified judge on human rights issues in other countries." Calling the report "confirmation of gross, systematic human rights violations," the Russian Commissioner for Human Rights, Democracy, and the Rule of Law urged the USA to disclose "the full spectrum of information about human rights abuses" and "bring those guilty to justice." Afghan President Ghani said the report "shows that our fellow countrymen have unfortunately been tortured and had their rights violated." Iran's Ayatollah Khamenei said "today, U.S. government is symbol of tyranny against humanity." Turkey's Foreign Minister denounced the "inhumane and really unacceptable torture." "Transparency is important" but "doesn't legitimize the torture that was inflicted."

A European Commission spokesperson said it "raises important questions about the violation of human rights by U.S. authorities." But though Members of the European Parliament (MEPs) called for an investigation of CIA torture in member countries, their former leaders predictably resisted. Aleksander Kwasniewski, president of Poland when the CIA tortured prisoners there, warned that "with this publication the Americans lose their potential as an ally." Thailand denied having had secret prisons (although abu Zubaydah had been tortured there). The former president of Lithuania maintained he had been "assured" that there was no prison in his country. The former head of Romanian intelligence admitted the CIA had black sites in his country, but insisted Romanians were ignorant of what happened there; several months later the former president said the same thing.

International bodies called for further action. Ben Emmerson, UN Special Rapporteur on counterterrorism and human rights, welcomed "the belated publication" of a report that "confirms" "there was a clear policy orchestrated at a high level within the Bush administration, which allowed it to commit systematic crimes and gross violations of international human rights law."[183] Those responsible "must face criminal penalties commensurate with the gravity of their crimes." Legal authorization "provides no excuse whatsoever." The USA "is legally obliged to bring those responsible to justice." The UN High Commissioner for Human Rights applauded the report, but added that the CAT "lets no one off the hook – neither the torturers themselves, nor the policy-makers, nor the public officials who define the policy or give the orders." The UN Special Rapporteur on torture said: "I was tortured. I know how important it is to hold the CIA accountable." Its actions had "been a big drawback in the fight against such practices in many other countries," which implicitly argued: "if the U.S. tortures, why can't we do it?" UN Secretary General Ban Ki-moon urged global action in response to the report. Even before it appeared the Chief Prosecutor of the International Criminal Court (ICC) said some EITs could "amount to cruel treatment, torture or outrages upon personal dignity as defined under international jurisprudence." Twenty-one NGOs asked the UN Human Rights Committee to seek "full accountability and transparency" for US torture. In 2014 AI demanded accountability, and the following year it published a 140-page report highlighting the SSCI report's findings, and calling for publication of the full report and prosecution of those implicated.

EIT critics also sought additional reforms.[184] Accusing the CIA of continuing to lie, Udall exhorted Obama to "purge" the Agency's leadership. Heinrich hoped for "a bit of housecleaning." Feinstein urged Obama to adopt measures to "make sure that the United States never again engages in actions that you have acknowledged were torture." UCI Law School Dean Erwin Chemerinsky said UC Berkeley Law Professor John Yoo should be prosecuted for writing the memo that "directly led to the torture policy." HRW executive director Kenneth Roth said the CAT "requires that torturers be prosecuted." Concerned that the EIT ban depended on an executive order that a future president could revoke, Rep. Nadler introduced the American Anti-Torture Act to limit interrogations to techniques authorized by the Army Field Manual.

Psychologist James Mitchell (called "Grayson Swigert" in the report, which identified him as the mastermind behind the EITs) protested:

"I was just a cog in the machine."[185] "The idea that I was managing things and running things is not true." But he could not resist boasting: "it would be a lie to say I didn't have influence." "[T]he whole point of the waterboard was to induce fear and panic." "[T]he moment [a detainee] was most susceptible to beginning to provide information was just before the next waterboarding session." He accused Senate Democrats of having "held a star chamber, decided I was guilty of something ... went into the CIA's six million pages of records, produced enough evidence to support their conclusion, and essentially issued a fatwa on me and Bruce" Jessen. The report "stirs up all the crazies and all the jihadists. So now we're getting death threats." "I do not mind giving my life for my country, but I do mind giving my life for a food fight for political reasons." "I'm very proud of the work we did. We saved lives. I don't care what the Senate says."

When the report appeared, 51 percent of Americans said EITs were justified and 56 percent believed they had elicited intelligence that prevented attacks.[186] Based on such polls, Marc Thiessen claimed in his *Washington Post* column that "the opponents of the CIA interrogation program were completely and utterly defeated" after "six sordid years of Democratic demagoguery and investigations." Of the 53 television talk show guests who offered opinions about EITs, 35 supported them and 18 were opposed.

As soon as he became SSCI chair (in January 2015), Burr asked Obama to "immediately" return all copies of the full SSCI report.[187] Feinstein "strongly disagree[d]." Burr appealed to the Senate referee: "it's a committee-sensitive report and it should have never found its way outside the halls of the committee without the minority and the majority not [*sic*] being informed." The administration rebuffed a FOIA request for the full report by claiming it was a congressional record. DoS and DoJ kept theirs unread in sealed envelopes; DoD let two officials read it. Two months after refusing even to accept the FBI's copy, Director Comey acceded to Feinstein's request that he read it, and said two other Bureau employees had done so.

The *New York Times* revealed that the Panetta Review (more than a thousand pages long) concluded that interrogating KSM had not produced intelligence that stopped attacks. An employee who worked on the Review complained in 2010 that the CIA had never withdrawn that claim (according to a CIA IG statement to SSCI). The CIA resisted a *New York Times* FOIA request for the Review, asserting it had ended abruptly in 2010, "had not been formally reviewed or relied upon by the C.I.A.'s senior leadership," and was consistently stamped "DELIBERATIVE PROCESS PRIVILEGED DOCUMENT" and "DRAFT." Burr intended to return the SSCI's copy of the Panetta Review to the CIA. US District Judge Boasberg denied FOIA requests for the Panetta Review in March and the full SSCI report in May.

McCain and Feinstein introduced an amendment to the 2016 NDAA requiring that *all* interrogations follow the Army Field Manual; the Senate passed it 78–21 (backed by all 46 Democrats voting and 32 Republicans), and Obama signed a later version containing that provision in November.[188] In September 2016 the High-Value Detainee Interrogation Group issued a report on noncoercive interrogation techniques.

A week before the 2016 presidential election, Donald Trump complained that "these savages are chopping off heads, drowning people … and then we can't do waterboarding?" Immediately after it, Sen. Cotton (R-Ark) endorsed waterboarding, which "isn't torture" because people in the military "volunteer" for it.[189] Trump was "a pretty tough guy, and I think he's ready to make those tough calls" to order waterboarding "if experienced intelligence professionals … say, 'we think this terrorist has critical information … and this is the only way we can obtain it.'" Jose Rodriguez said "of course [EITs] worked"; the SSCI "report is a farce. It's a like … Obamacare." Because EITs now "are well known to the enemy … we would have to come up with something else." James Mitchell, who had designed the EITs, advocated "somewhere between waterboarding and worse, and what's in the Army Field Manual." Trump's DCI nominee Mike Pompeo initially said waterboarding might resume, but before his confirmation hearing he assured Sen. Wyden that he would "absolutely not" comply with an order to use them. After Sen. McCain warned that any attempt to bring back waterboarding would be challenged in federal court, Vice President Pence responded that "we're going to have a president again who will never say what we'll never do." But after Trump was told by Marine Gen. James Mattis (soon to be nominated as Defense Secretary) that "I've never found [torture] to be useful. Give me a pack of cigarettes and a couple of beers [to give to the person being interrogated] and I'll do better," the president-elect rejected waterboarding, which was "not going to make the kind of difference that a lot of people are thinking." (As a Lieutenant General in Iraq in 2003, Mattis had ordered the investigation of the torture death of a suspect, which he called "the worst thing that happened" under him during the Iraq war.) Former

CIA General Counsel John Rizzo conceded that "restarting this would be extraordinarily difficult." Former DCI Michael Hayden said that if Trump wanted to waterboard someone he should "bring his own bucket." DCI Brennan warned that "the overwhelming majority of C.I.A. officers would not want to get back into that business." Trump received a letter from 176 retired flag officers stating that "the use of waterboarding or any so-called 'EITs' is unlawful under domestic and international law." Attorney General nominee Sessions acknowledged that waterboarding was "absolutely improper and illegal" and repeated this in his written replies to the SJC. The *Washington Post* took comfort in the comments by Pompeo and Sessions. But in his written replies to SSCI questions, Pompeo said that if the Agency told him that the limitation of using only methods approved in the Army Field Manual was "an impediment to gathering vital intelligence to protect the country," he would see if the law could be changed. An executive order drafted days after the inauguration would direct a review of the Army Field Manual to consider whether it should allow EITs. (White House Press Secretary Sean Spicer said the EO was "not a White House Document" and he had "no idea where it came from.") Sen. McCain retorted: "the law is the law. We are not bringing back torture in the United States of America." Trump reversed himself again. He had asked "people at the highest level of intelligence ... does torture work? and the answer was yes, absolutely." Waterboarding was "not pleasant" but "was just short of torture." "[A]ll of a sudden, they made it torture." The seven Democrats on SSCI urged Trump and other Executive Branch officials to read the full SSCI report. Sen. Warner promised to hold Pompeo and Mattis "to their sworn testimony to follow the law." Sen. Thune (R-SD), the third-ranking Republican, said the issue was "settled law." Both Senate Majority Leader Mitchell and House Speaker Ryan agreed. Trump named Gina Haspel CIA Deputy Director; she had run the secret prison in Thailand where the Agency first used EITs and the secret prison in Poland where abu Zubaydah and al Nashiri were waterboarded, and had executed Jose Rodriguez's order to destroy the EIT videotapes. (Trump nominated others with baggage from the Bush administration: Steven Bradbury, author of some of the OLC "torture" memos, as General Counsel of the Department of Transportation; Charles "Cully" Stimson, the Assistant Deputy Secretary of Defense who resigned after telling corporations to withdraw their business from law firms whose members represented Guantánamo detainees, as General Counsel of the Navy; and Christopher Wray, who may have covered up abuse at Abu Ghraib and

EITs in Afghanistan, Iraq, and Guantánamo while in the DoJ, as FBI Director.) A revised EO dropped the plan to revive Bush's 2007 order authorizing EITs and to rescind Obama's 2009 order requiring that all interrogations comply with the Army Field Manual. The High-Value Detainee Interrogation Group issued a report concluding "that the most effective practices for eliciting accurate information and actionable intelligence are non-coercive, rapport-based, information-gathering interviewing and interrogation methods."

The full SSCI report continued to generate controversy.[190] After the election Sens. Feinstein and Wyden asked Obama and Biden to declassify it (but there was not enough time). Sens. Levin and Rockefeller wrote a *New York Times* op ed urging Obama to protect the report. Obama's White House counsel assured Feinstein that the report would be preserved "under the Presidential Records Act" but remain classified for 12 years. The *New York Times* promptly published an editorial asking Obama to reconsider the lengthy classification. At the end of 2016 DDC Judge Lamberth issued an order (in al Nashiri's challenge to his Military Commission (MC)) that the report and the CIA response be deposited with the Court Security Officer, warning:

> [T]his Court has had a contempt trial and found an agency in contempt when it destroy an agency head's hard drive the day of a prior Inauguration [George W. Bush's]. This Court is confident that respondents will not want a contempt trial here when the Court's Order is crystal clear.

DoJ complied. Feinstein wrote both Defense Secretary Carter and MC Judge Pohl, urging that the Defense Department copy, which Pohl had ordered preserved, be given to the commission. But SSCI chair Burr directed his staff to retrieve all copies still held by Executive Branch agencies. And the DC Circuit, noting that "extremists have used Guantánamo Bay imagery in their propaganda and in carrying out attacks on Americans," reversed a 2014 order by DDC Judge Kessler that the DoD disclose videotapes of the forced cell extractions of Jihad Ahmed Mujstafa Diyab, who had been on hunger strike.[191]

CONCLUSION

This painful story illuminates the obstacles confronting resistance to abusive interrogation after 9/11. The OLC memos declaring that some detainees were not POWs protected by the Geneva Conventions and narrowly defining torture to exclude EITs clearly enabled those practices (and later were invoked by Bush and Mukasey, Obama and Holder to block criminal investigations). The cold, dispassionate legalese of Bybee, Yoo, and Bradbury evoked the notorious Wannsee conference at which the Nazis planned the Final Solution. The CIA required explicit legal protection and suspended use of EITs when this was delayed or ambiguous (for instance, after the 2004 CIA Office of the Inspector General (OIG) report and the 2005 DTA). That insistence implicated the Principals Committee and President Bush (even if he sought deniability by emulating Reagan's inattention to detail – an approach he took to naturally). The indispensability of legal forms suggests that OLC lawyers could have prevented use of EITs if they had not violated professional standards (as OPR found).[192] Yet there is also evidence that use of EITs preceded and exceeded the authorizing memos.

The effectiveness of OLC memos in legitimating EITs was compromised by the Bush administration's determination to keep them secret, based on its claim that this was essential to prevent terrorist groups from training members to resist interrogation. DNI McConnell wanted detainees to "believe these techniques might include torture" despite the administration's repeated protestations that "we do not torture" and the fact that those already detained – the vast majority of those ever interrogated – could no longer be trained. Therefore, the real reason for secrecy was fear of embarrassment, concern that the public would learn the abuses its government was committing and see the OLC legalese as callous and cruel. The memos thus confronted a fundamental contradiction: to authorize torture they had to describe it in detail; but public dissemination of such a description could delegitimate torture in the public eye.

Opposition to EITs, therefore, first had to expose the memos, a process that followed Chekhov's alleged observation about fiction's narrative trajectory: "if you say in the first chapter that there is a rifle hanging on the wall, in the second or third chapter it absolutely must go off."[193] As Sen. Wyden kept insisting, secret laws are anathema to democracy. Invocation of the OLC memos to justify EITs fueled demands for their publication. And as political advisers often warn, partial disclosures just intensify pressure for the full Monty. Indeed, secrecy can heighten the shock value of what is learned, as illustrated by leaks of the 2004 CIA OIG report and the 2006 ICRC report on the HVDs. And revelations about the harsh techniques authorized by the OLC memos prompted questions about what actually had been done to detainees.

Criticism of EITs emerged as soon as they were proposed. Understandably concerned about how they would be perceived outside the USA, DoS was one of the first governmental critics and remained the most consistent: Secretary of State Powell and his assistant, Col. Wilkerson (both ex-military) as well DoS Legal Adviser Taft (the former president's great-grandson).[194] The military was responsible for the largest number of abuses because it conducted the most interrogations, usually in war zones, often on or near the battlefield, using young, often raw, recruits who had been targeted by the enemy and had often been wounded or seen comrades injured or killed. But though DoD's civilian leaders, especially Rumsfeld and Haynes, aggressively promoted EITs, there was significant resistance from uniformed military lawyers: Beaver, Dalton, and maybe even Walker (whose review was aborted by Yoo's memo); the four Judge Advocates General; and especially Navy General Counsel Mora. A few military interrogators courageously exposed what they saw and did.[195] NCIS blew the whistle on EITs in Guantánamo. JPRA members played a more ambiguous role, some warning against reverse engineering SERE techniques, while others boasted of their unique interrogation expertise. The National Defense Intelligence College's own Intelligence Science Board concluded that EITs were ineffective. Among Republicans, Sen McCain – whose 5.5 years of detention and torture by North Vietnam conferred unique moral standing – fought against EITs in Congress, joined by fellow veterans Warner and Graham. One of HRF's most effective actions was to mobilize flag officers to oppose EITs and provide cover to Obama (who had no military credentials) when he issued his Executive Order banning them.

The FBI – for decades the CIA's rival and often antagonist – blew the whistle on the Agency's use of EITs in secret prisons and Guantánamo. Ali Soufan, who alerted the Bureau to the abuse of abu Zubaydah, wrote a book about his experience and clashed repeatedly with the CIA's Jose Rodriguez.[196] Even some CIA interrogators expressed reservations.[197] There are many possible explanations for the different responses of these various governmental entities. The CIA felt responsible for failing to anticipate and prevent 9/11; afterwards, it was charged with detaining and interrogating HVDs. But as the Agency later admitted, it was totally inexperienced in interrogation (as were the psychologists it chose as "expert" advisers). By contrast, the FBI had amassed a century of interrogating experience and, at least in recent years, had complied with legal restrictions.[198] And the military was the ultimate rule-bound bureaucracy, governed by its Field Manuals, the UCMJ, and the Geneva Conventions. Convinced of the rectitude of its own practices, the military argued that *all* government agencies should follow its example. (Some retrospective claims of opposition – by Bellinger, McChrystal, and Brennan, for instance – may have been convenient or wishful memories, just as after World War II so many French claimed to have fought in the Resistance and after 1994 so few white South Africans remembered supporting apartheid.)

EIT critics advanced a variety of arguments. Members of the military – preeminently McCain – embraced the deontological position that harsh interrogation was simply wrong, a betrayal of who Americans are, and therefore never acceptable. (His stance allowed Obama to echo that view.) DoD worried, with good reason, that EITs would expose captured colleagues to greater risks and help recruit and motivate jihadi fighters. DoS feared EITs would alienate allies. FBI interrogators believed their noncoercive tactics produced better, more reliable intelligence. EIT defenders typically resorted to utilitarian retorts: Muslim extremists would never respect the Geneva Conventions (making appeals to reciprocity pointless); allies (secretly) wanted the USA to employ every interrogation tactic. The clincher was the "ticking bomb" hypothetical. But like many law school hypotheticals, this one was fatally flawed.[199] First, cost–benefit calculus can justify inflicting unlimited torments if the threat is sufficiently great: forcing a detainee to watch his child being tortured or his wife or mother raped (behavior some interrogators threatened but no one publicly defended), even killing 1,000 innocents to save 1,001. Second, no advocate *ever* cited an occasion on which EITs had been necessary to avert an imminent danger. Indeed, they could not because the hypothetical is based on multiple unverifiable assumptions: the person interrogated possesses *unique* knowledge of a *certain* attack and will tell the *truth* but *only* under torture.

Nevertheless, defenders did succeed in forcing critics to adopt the discourse of utility rather than deontology.[200] Each dramatic event in the "war on terror" – Abdulmutallab's failed bombing attempt, the killing of bin Laden and its cinematic portrayal in *Zero Dark Thirty* – offered EIT defenders another opportunity to renew claims for their efficacy and indispensability. That may explain why SSCI devoted so much of its report to case studies purporting to show inefficacy, thereby inviting rebuttal by Republicans and the CIA. Cheney must have believed efficacy was a clincher when he demanded release of two CIA reports on that topic. Kiriakou even bragged that waterboarding had acted "like a switch" on abu Zubaydah. (But if it was so immediately effective, why was abu Zubaydah subjected to it 83 times and KSM a stunning 183?) Even Panetta, Brennan, and the CIA conceded that the utilitarian defense foundered on the unknowability of the counterfactual: what might interrogators have learned *without* using harsh techniques? Still, making efficacy the focus precluded a decisive resolution of the debate, allowing EIT supporters to propose a Pascalian wager: wouldn't you rather risk mistakenly torturing one person (who was probably guilty of something, even if he had no intelligence) than passively let terrorists kill thousands of innocents?[201]

Defenders used another tactic at least as often as the "ticking bomb" hypothetical: arguing by definition. While Bush endlessly mouthed the shibboleth "we do not torture," subordinates insisted that – since the president would never lie – what we did could not be torture and therefore was acceptable. The notorious "torture" memo facilitated such Orwellian Newspeak through its contorted definition of torture. (Other examples of Bush Newspeak included the comforting assurance that he was giving "professionals" in the intelligence "community" the "tools they need" – not recklessly allowing a conspiracy of rank amateurs to play with ineffective and superfluous instruments of torture. For a long time the media were complicit, avoiding the "T" word until critics shamed even the Gray Lady into jettisoning euphemisms.) Apologists adamantly avoided admitting that waterboarding was torture: Mukasey because, as a lawyer, he found the concept too vague; Brennan because, as a layperson, he could not presume to interpret such a technical term. EIT advocates pointed to the fact that SERE training included waterboarding – disregarding the fact that recruits knew they would not die, could stop at any time, and suffered it just once, not 183 times. Defenders contrasted it with the horrors of the Spanish Inquisition or Japanese torture in World War II, arguing that this made US actions acceptable. Cheney trivialized waterboarding as "dunking a terrorist in water" – as though it were a game children played, or water polo. Rumsfeld belittled stress positions by boasting that he stood at his desk eight hours a day (by choice – and I bet he leaned on the desk and took many breaks).

EIT opponents deployed a wide variety of strategies, the most common of which were exposés by the media (print journalism, PBS documentaries) and NGOs, Congressional investigations, interviews and books by former interrogators, and the testimony of former detainees. Many described discrete incidents or specific sites. The

Constitution Project offered the most comprehensive account, but unfortunately this appeared a day after the Boston Marathon bombing (which predictably prompted demands for better intelligence as well as cries for vengeance). The *New York Times*, *Los Angeles Times* and *Washington Post* repeatedly condemned EITs. All those examples of speaking truth to power strengthened the critical case, but their effects are hard to measure. Public opinion about EITs was almost evenly divided and changed little over time, paradoxically growing more favorable after Obama banned them. Outside the USA, exposure increased the defensiveness of allies complicit in the CIA's secret prisons, offered some of the worst human rights offenders a gratuitous chance to indulge in hypocritical anti-American diatribes, and prompted international organizations to reiterate unenforceable norms.

Because public shaming alone could not change the Bush administration's behavior, opponents deployed other tactics. Congress exercises oversight of the executive through its committees on intelligence, armed services, foreign relations, and the judiciary; but these fulfilled their responsibility only when the Democrats controlled the Senate (2007–15) and the House (2007–11). Committees and subcommittees held hearings, often reported in the media. But Bush administration officials obstructed their inquiries, refusing to produce documents (under the guise of various executive privileges) and either declining to testify or deflecting questions with vague responses or convenient amnesia. Such evasiveness sometimes resembled Bill Clinton's contortions concerning Monica Lewinsky – but unlike Clinton, Republicans generally got away with it (and it concerned torture, not consensual sex). By contrast, when the Bush "war on terror" was not under fire, oversight could be very effective, as in the Congressional response to medical neglect at Walter Reed Army Medical Center[202] and the mishandling of military remains at the Dover Air Force Base.[203]

It is instructive to contrast the SASC and SSCI investigations of interrogation. SASC's bipartisan effort completed a unanimous report in less than two years, to which DoD offered no rebuttal. Although SSCI voted 14–1 to study EITs, Republicans boycotted the process after Holder directed Durham to investigate abuses – and then shamelessly accused Democrats of engaging in a partisan witch-hunt, faulting the committee for not interviewing CIA employees whom DCI Panetta had excused from answering questions. The CIA's document dump of millions of pages and scorched earth fight over declassification (abetted by the White House) ensured that nothing would be published for nearly five years and then only a redacted Executive Summary, which still provoked fierce responses by the Republican minority and CIA (both of which had sought to undermine it in advance). The CIA minimized its own deficiencies, continuing to insist EITs had been effective and that it had never obstructed oversight by Congress or the executive.

There are a number of reasons for these differences. SASC's senior Republican, McCain, consistently voiced principled criticism of EITs. SASC reported during the Bush administration. DoD opposed EITs that exceeded its own rules or violated the Geneva Conventions. By contrast, SSCI's senior Republican was Burr, who shared his party's visceral hatred of Obama and its determination to obstruct and undermine him at every opportunity. As soon as he became chair, Burr tried to recall all copies of the SSCI report. Obama himself chose not to support his fellow Democrats in Congress. And both the CIA and the Obama administration were determined to preserve the government's authority to conduct EITs, even while repudiating past abuses and offering assurances that the Agency was not repeating them. The CIA and the Bush administration also sought to disarm criticism by accusing Congressional Democrats of having condoned EITs through their silence – and occasional enthusiasm – during briefings. Bradbury disingenuously invoked this in an OLC memo arguing that EITs did not "shock the conscience," although Congressional opinion was irrelevant to that constitutional standard. At the same time, both Republican and Democratic administrations resisted efforts to strengthen oversight through increased notification requirements, claiming these violated separation of powers.

Congressional efforts to exercise effective oversight were repeatedly diverted from the substantive question – the legality and appropriateness of EITs – by controversies over process. Such distractions are common: there is greater consensus on process, which seems less political than substance (as shown by the unresolved debate between EIT critics and defenders); and members of Congress (like all those who wield power) jealously guard their prerogatives. Cover-ups, paradoxically, often are harder to justify than the more egregious actions they seek to conceal. It was the Watergate break-in and 18-minute gap in the White House tapes that ultimately destroyed Nixon. Similarly, the CIA destruction of its videotapes elicited greater Congressional unanimity – and perhaps even outrage – than the horrendous EITs they depicted. Federal court orders for the preservation of evidence raised additional separation-of-powers questions. The Agency's justification – concern for the safety of the interrogators depicted – did not pass the laugh test. Was the nation's premier spy agency seriously arguing it could not keep secrets? In any case, the timing of the destruction (immediately after Dana Priest's exposé of the CIA's secret prisons), coupled with indiscreet comments in CIA emails, confirmed that this was a CYA (cover your ass) strategy. Like most cover-up attempts, however, this one ended by inflicting greater damage. Even Mukasey, a loyal Republican and "war on terror" hawk, felt obligated to order a DoJ investigation. The Agency break-in to the SSCI computers (at Brennan's behest) to determine how the Committee had obtained the Panetta Review generated even more acrimonious controversy, impelling members of both parties to denounce it as a violation of constitutional dimensions and prompting tit-for-tat referrals to DoJ, as well as investigations by the CIA OIG and Senate Sergeant-at-Arms. Yet both distractions ended inconclusively.

The constitutional requirement of "advice and consent" for presidential nominations gave the Senate another means of reviewing executive action – and one Democrats could employ even before they gained control in 2007. Yet Democrats were relatively ineffective in either blocking confirmations or extracting information about EITs. Bybee became a Ninth Circuit judge before his notorious OLC memos were leaked. Although the Senate never approved Bradbury as OLC head or Rizzo as CIA General Counsel, both served for years in an acting capacity.[204] Flanigan withdrew from consideration for Deputy Attorney General – but because of his ties to the convicted Jack Abramoff, not for writing the OLC memos. Haynes's nomination to the Fourth Circuit was blocked, first by Graham (whose state fell within the Circuit's jurisdiction and who objected to Haynes's central role in authorizing EITs for the military) and then by Democrats after they captured the Senate in 2006. Democrats failed to do more than expose Gonzales's incompetence during his 2005 confirmation hearing as Attorney General. Even after his eventual disgrace and the Democrats' capture of the Senate, they let Mukasey run circles around them, simply relieved he was not Gonzales. They praised him for promising to enforce a law banning EITs – not much of a concession by an Attorney General charged with enforcing *all* laws, especially when he knew Bush would veto this one. Schumer expressed confidence that his fellow New Yorker would observe the rule of law given its "plasticity" (hardly a comforting characterization). Democrats accepted Mukasey's refusal to answer "hypothetical" questions – something every student learns to do in the first week of law school. Senate Democrats were only slightly more effective under

Obama. Philip Mudd (who had been deputy director of the CIA's Office of Intelligence Analysis) withdrew from consideration as Obama's DHS undersecretary of intelligence and analysis rather than answer questions about involvement in EITs.[205] And Obama's nominees dutifully declared waterboarding was torture, thereby distinguishing themselves from their slippery predecessors.[206] But minority Republicans successfully blocked the superbly qualified Dawn Johnsen from heading OLC.

Although oversight and confirmation are vital powers, Congress's primary function is legislation, which also presents a mixed picture. The Senate's passage of the Detainee Treatment Act by a 90–9 vote represented an extraordinary rebuff to President Bush, whose vigorous opposition was reinforced by Cheney. This was a triumph for McCain (who may still have been smarting from his 2000 primary loss to Bush, especially the dirty South Carolina contest) and his fellow veterans in the Senate, Warner and Graham. The bill succeeded partly because these sponsors were Republicans with distinguished military records and partly because Abu Ghraib was still a vivid memory, whereas there had not been another attack in the four years since 9/11. Some lawmakers may have supported the bill because it also denied Guantánamo detainees the right to file habeas corpus petitions (apparently Graham's price for participating). Like so many "victories," this one was compromised, not only by the habeas ban (later invalidated by the Supreme Court), but also by exempting the CIA and allowing the military to engage in CID treatment of "unlawful combatants" (the Army Field Manual's secret Appendix M) and by Bush's signing statement reasserting his executive prerogatives. The following year Bush retorted with the Military Commissions Act, which not only entrenched that deeply flawed institution despite the Supreme Court's critical *Hamdan* decision, but also legislated the CIA's authority to use EITs (even though the Agency no longer held any prisoners). And though the CIA had not waterboarded anyone in three years, and McCain claimed Bush assured him the practice was banned, the president issued a secret executive order interpreting the Geneva Conventions, allegedly authorizing that technique. Bush also took the extraordinary step of vetoing the Intelligence Authorization Act 2008 because it extended the EIT ban to the CIA (a veto bizarrely supported by McCain).

Even without new legislation, EITs could be discouraged by prosecutions for violating existing laws, such as the Anti-Torture Act or the War Crimes Act.[207] But none was ever begun, much less completed. Mukasey, unsurprisingly, directed Durham to investigate only the videotape destruction (a potential obstruction of justice), not the far more serious crimes they evidenced. When Holder extended this investigation to the EITs themselves (seeking political cover from an OPR report criticizing an earlier declination), he excluded any actions approved by the OLC memos. Obama and Panetta concurred. The administration justified this limitation by arguing that – especially when policymakers remained immune – it would be unfair to prosecute those who implemented their directives (allegedly keeping us safe since 9/11), distract the CIA from its essential task, and discourage vigorous interrogation in the future. Critics exposed the flaws in these arguments (though to no avail). The OLC memos rested on patently faulty legal reasoning and fabricated "facts." More than half a century earlier the Nuremberg Trials categorically rejected the defense of following orders. Policymakers should be prosecuted as accessories or for conspiracy. The argument that defending lawsuits is an annoying distraction should be no more available to the CIA than it is to a private corporation. And the *purpose* of prosecution is to deter future crime (including EITs, if they are criminal). Yet Durham declined to prosecute any of the criminal referrals (giving no detailed reasons, as usual). And this second declination ensured that the cases would not be reopened when new evidence emerged (as it did in the SSCI report).

If the other two branches – legislature and judiciary – did little to restrain the executive, it did have internal checks. FBI agents complained about military EITs in Guantánamo, but the Army's CIC took no action. FBI agents in Thailand reported to their headquarters about the CIA's brutal interrogation of abu Zubaydah – and simply were withdrawn. The CIA refused to impose significant punishment on its interrogators, even when the Agency's review board recommended discipline after detainees died. The CIA kept the critical 2004 OIG report secret for years. OPR took *six years* to complete its investigation of the OLC lawyers. Furthermore, when internal monitors proposed significant remedial action, higher officials (who were political appointees) overturned those recommendations. DCI Goss handpicked two subordinates to produce reports, which predictably contradicted his IG. Mukasey appointed Margolis, who diluted OPR criticism of Bybee and Yoo, precluding their referral to state disciplinary bodies. (This closed the circle: foot soldiers could not be prosecuted because they followed orders; and those who gave the orders did nothing wrong.) After the CIA OIG found that the Agency had wrongfully penetrated the SSCI computer, DCI Brennan appointed an Accountability Board, which minimized the wrongdoing and recommended no action. And DoJ declined to pursue the dueling criminal referrals from the CIA and the Senate.

Democracy's ultimate check on government abuse is the electorate. Voters expressed no concern about the violation of core liberties in the 2002, 2004, or 2006 elections. In his 2004 campaign, John Kerry chose not to raise the Abu Ghraib scandal, which erupted just six months before the election. Anticipating the 2006 election, Bush emptied the secret prisons by transferring the 14 HVDs to Guantánamo and won passage of the MCA in an unsuccessful effort to play the national security card once again to preserve Republican control of the Senate (as he had done in 2004). EITs did become an issue in the 2008 primaries when Republicans Giuliani, Hunter, Romney, and Tancredo all endorsed waterboarding, often enthusiastically, and Clinton (characteristically) equivocated. But the issue disappeared once the two nominees, McCain and Obama, categorically opposed waterboarding. In 2012 Romney again endorsed EITs – as did most other Republican aspirants – but the issue never figured in the election.

Obama's 2008 victory was pivotal in the struggle to end EITs. John Yoo's dubious claim after Bush's 2004 re-election that "the public has had its referendum" on how to wage the "war on terror" was far more convincing four years later. Obama's executive order on his second full day in office banning EITs, together with his repudiation of secret prisons and vow to close Guantánamo, were one of the most dramatic official reaffirmations of the rule of law since 9/11. As in his first inaugural speech (and later speeches in Cairo, Oslo, and the National Archives), Obama displayed his considerable rhetorical powers, evoking Martin Luther King Jr. and Nelson Mandela among other heroes, and prompting apt comparisons to black preachers. Obama followed up by releasing more OLC memos authorizing torture (which his DoJ simultaneously rescinded), claiming to act under judicial compulsion. But he coupled these principled decisions with politically motivated assurances to the CIA that no one who had followed the discredited memos would be prosecuted and adamant opposition to an independent commission, justifying both actions by a call to look forward, not back (wrongly suggesting that those perspectives were mutually exclusive rather than complementary). This heightened an unresolved tension. Obama's repudiation of EITs, far from rendering judgment of the past superfluous, made it even more imperative. If EITs would be wrong in the future, they had been wrong in the past. Immunizing interrogators who followed orders just underlined the culpability of policymakers: Bush, his advisers (Cheney, Rumsfeld, Haynes, Gonzales, Rice, Addington), and the OLC lawyers. Publishing the memos further exposed the callous legal contortions of those who designed and rationalized torture. Even Obama's supporters could not ignore the growing gap between his soaring rhetoric and timid actions.

Whereas the challenge for EIT critics under Bush was preventing future abuses, the challenge under Obama was accounting for past abuses. Santayana famously wrote: "those who cannot remember the past are condemned to repeat it."[208] The impact of the SSCI report's devastating critique was weakened by Republican senators' boycott and dissent and the CIA rebuttal. By precluding an official, impartial, definitive determination that EITs had always been illegal – i.e., a successful prosecution – Obama preserved rhetorical space for future defenders. Even John Fredman was alleged to have commented cynically: "If the detainee dies, you're doing it wrong." But though at least five detainees did die during interrogation – Dilawar, Habibullah, Gul Rahman, Manadel al-Jamadi, and Abed Hamed Mowhoush – no one was prosecuted. Other debates over similarly fraught moral and legal issues have been decisively resolved. There are no reputable defenders of the crimes against Native Americans, slavery, internment of Japanese Americans, McCarthyism, discrimination on grounds of race or gender (and increasingly sexual orientation), anti-Semitism or Islamophobia (to offer only American examples). But even after the DTA prohibited EITs by the military, and especially after Obama banned them in all government agencies, apologists have continued to argue that they are moral, legal, and indispensable. Bush, Cheney, Rumsfeld, Addington, Bradbury, Rodriguez, Hayden, Tenet, McLaughlin, Rizzo, Yoo, Gonzales, Mukasey, and Mitchell, as well as a host of conservative commentators, remain unrepentant about past abuses and continue to advocate for EITs in the future.[209] Hayden confidently declared: "democracies cannot wage war over the long term on the basis of strict legalisms." Gonzales pronounced war "a dirty business" (as though that indisputable fact excused *all* dirt). After being confirmed, Mukasey reiterated that EITs should be evaluated by a utilitarian "balancing test." Even Obama's appointees hedged their bets. Blair and Panetta repudiated past EITs (in order to get confirmed), but asserted the possibility of using them in the future. Brennan resisted publication of the SSCI report, rightly fearing it would constrain his future actions. And in his successful 2016 campaign, Trump promised to bring back waterboarding and institute EITs that were "a hell of a lot worse." To invert Martin Luther King Jr., the arc of *this* moral universe, far from bending toward justice, resembles a sine curve, perpetually fluctuating between justice and injustice.

CHAPTER FIVE

ELECTRONIC SURVEILLANCE

Because the "war on terror" was fought against shadowy, often invisible, enemies who employed the full range of information technology to communicate, surveillance played an indispensable strategic role, including National Security Letters, roving wiretaps, business record searches, interception of international bank transactions, encryption, and even old-fashioned photographs of snail-mail envelopes.[1] This chapter, however, concentrates exclusively on NSA surveillance of electronic communications, especially phone and email. Because this was necessarily secret (indeed, wags said NSA stood for "No Such Agency"), it could be challenged only after being exposed – first by the *New York Times* and then by Edward Snowden. The struggle over surveillance raised many questions. How can law both legitimate and control secret government action? How was surveillance exposed; and how did the method of disclosure and the content of what emerged shape the responses of government and critics and change the nature of surveillance? How did public opinion about surveillance differ from attitudes concerning the other rule-of-law violations discussed in this volume? What roles did the following play: media, whistle-blowers, telecommunications and IT companies, other countries, and international organizations? How effective were Congressional oversight, the Senate's power to advise and consent to nominations, and legislative reforms? How did party affiliation shape the behavior of judges, legislators, and executive branch officials with respect to surveillance? How effective were FISC and Art. III courts in limiting surveillance, and how did they differ? How did surveillance actually change as a result of all these efforts to control it?

THE *NEW YORK TIMES*

On December 6, 2005, the *New York Times* published an exposé by James Risen and Eric Lichtblau of NSA's warrantless wiretapping of international communications involving hundreds, perhaps thousands, of people in the USA.[2] President Bush had secretly authorized this in 2002 based on John Yoo's November 1, 2001 OLC opinion asserting the president's Article II commander-in-chief powers.[3] (Yoo later wrote a 22-page letter to FISC presiding Judge Kollar-Kotelly justifying this surveillance program (codename STELLARWIND):[4] "We face a situation where the government's interest on one side – that of protecting the nation from direct attack – is the highest known to the Constitution. On the other side of the scale, the intrusion into individual privacy interests is greatly reduced due to the international nature of the communications." But these writings remained classified, and Yoo disingenuously declared in a December 2003 *Wall Street Journal* op ed that "nothing could be further from the truth" than the slander that the USA Patriot Act allowed NSA to target Americans.)

Others had challenged the program earlier. After NSA Director Hayden and DCI Tenet briefed the chairs and senior minority members of the Congressional Intelligence Committees (the "Gang of Four") on July 17, 2003, Sen. Rockefeller (D-WV) (SSCI's ranking Democrat) told Vice President Cheney: "Clearly, the activities we discussed raise profound oversight issues. As you know, I am neither a technician nor an attorney. Given the security restrictions associated with this information, and my inability to consult staff or counsel on my own, I feel unable to fully evaluate, much less endorse these activities." When FISC Chief Judge Kollar-Kotelly questioned whether information improperly obtained by NSA had been the basis for a Foreign Intelligence Surveillance Act (FISA) wiretap request, the agency suspended the program until the DoJ certified this was not the case. During an April 2005 hearing on renewing the Patriot Act, FBI Director Mueller said NSA "generally" was "not allowed to spy or to gather information on American citizens." The government defended wiretapping, claiming it had uncovered plots to destroy the Brooklyn Bridge (by Iyman Faris) and bomb British pubs and train stations.

New York Times Executive Editor Bill Keller said that when the newspaper uncovered the wiretaps more than a year earlier (before the 2004 election):

> the administration argued strongly that writing about this eavesdropping program would give terrorists clues about the vulnerability of their communications and would deprive the government of an effective tool for the protection of the country's security. Officials also assured senior editors of *The Times* that a variety of legal checks had been imposed that satisfied everyone involved that the program raised no legal questions. As we have done before in rare instances when faced with a convincing national security argument, we agreed not to publish at that time.

Over the following year the *Times* learned of misgivings within government and concluded it could publish without exposing "any intelligence-gathering methods or capabilities that are not already on the public record." Keller denied that the disclosure was "timed to the Iraqi election, the Patriot Act debate, Jim [Risen]'s forthcoming book or any other event." Byron Calame, the *Times*'s public editor, found the explanation for the delay "woefully inadequate," a view seconded by many readers.

Leaders of both parties demanded hearings.[5] Feinstein (D-Ca) (sitting on both SSCI and SJC) called the story "the most significant thing I have heard in my 12 years" in the Senate. Declaring that "it can't be condoned at all," SJC chair Specter (R-Pa) promised "oversight." Attorney General Gonzales replied that "winning the war on terror requires winning the war on information. And so we will be aggressive in obtaining that information." Sen. Lott (R-Mich) dismissed the concerns of "the libertarians. I want my security first. I'll deal with all the details after that." The *Washington Post* shared the *Times*'s concerns: "warrantless intelligence surveillance by an executive branch unaccountable to any judicial officer – and apparently on a large scale – is gravely dangerous." "[T]he administration appears to have taken the position that the president is entitled to ignore a clearly worded criminal law when it proves inconvenient in the war on terrorism."

Bush insisted the program was "critical to saving American lives" and "consistent with U.S. law and the Constitution."[6] Based on the recommendations of the Attorney General and White House counsel, Bush had renewed it every 45 days. He condemned the *Times*: "[O]ur enemies have learned information they should not have. And the unauthorized disclosure of this effort damages our national security and puts our citizens at risk. Revealing classified information is illegal." Secretary of State Rice supported him: "we simply can't be in a situation in which the president is not responding to this different kind of war on terrorism." Rep. Burton (R-In) complained that "the liberal media and its liberal allies are attacking the president" for legal acts. But Sens. Feingold (D-Wisc) and Leahy (D-Vt) accused Bush of acting as though he were "above the law," Sen. Levin (D-Mich) called the program "extremely dangerous," and Sen. Reid (D-Utah) said the "commander-in-chief does not trump the bill of rights."

Cheney, Tenet, and Hayden said they had informed the Gang of Four on October 25 and November 14, 2001.[7] Cheney reasserted that the program was "consistent with the president's constitutional authority as commander in chief" and the AUMF and had been "briefed to the Congress over a dozen times." But former Sen. Bob Graham (D-Fl) (then SSCI chair) remembered "no discussion about expanding" NSA wiretapping "to include conversations of U.S. citizens or conversations that originated or ended in the United States." "We cannot set aside the rule of law in a time of war." Rep. Pelosi (D-Ca) (also present) said the briefing described "unspecified activities" about which she had expressed "strong concerns." Sen. Feingold declared: "it doesn't matter if you tell everybody in the whole country if it's against the law." Sen. McCain (R-Az) said the briefings were "a legitimate part of the equation," but Bush had to explain why he ignored FISA.

The *New York Times* noted that on October 17, 2002 Hayden had properly urged "a sober national discussion about whether the line between liberty and security should be shifted"; instead, Bush had "secretly and recklessly expanded the government's powers in dangerous and unnecessary ways that eroded civil liberties and may also have violated the law."[8] The *Washington Post* warned that the program "defeats [FISA's] purpose by removing the independent court that is supposed to review the proposed surveillance and replacing it with unchecked executive discretion."

At a news conference Bush invoked his "obligation to protect" Americans in "a different era."[9] He opposed Congressional hearings, which "will say to the enemy, 'here's what they do, adjust.'" He claimed bin Laden had stopped using a satellite phone after news reports that it was being eavesdropped (but that was not a government leak). "This is not about wiretapping everybody. This is a very concentrated, very limited program focused on gaining information about our enemy." "This is really hurting national security ... we'll just have to wait and see" if there would be a leak investigation. (DoJ did launch one, claiming to act on behalf of NSA; the White House said this "is the way it should be.") Hayden explained that FISC approval was inefficient because it "involves marshaling arguments" and "lopping [*sic*] paperwork around." Gonzales said the administration had decided it "would be difficult, if not impossible" to obtain new legislation, and the AUMF was sufficient. But Sen. Feingold insisted nobody thought at the time "this was an authorization to allow wiretapping against the law of the United States." Sen. Reid claimed that "key details about the program apparently were not provided to me." Sen. Daschle (D-SD) was "surprised and disappointed that the White House would suggest that none of us informed of the program objected."

The *New York Times* retorted that none of the "phony choices" Bush advanced to defend his policies was as "absurd" as his latest: "save lives or follow the law."[10] "[M]ost bizarre" was his claim that the AUMF permitted wiretapping. "[A]ssurances that surveillance targets are carefully selected with reasonable cause don't comfort." Even conservative columnists were critical. George Will said the program "contravened a statute's clear language." "Now that the nation feels more secure," said David Ignatius, "we insist anew on the rule of law." Anne Applebaum called the rule of law "more fundamental in our national success than democracy or freedom." Richard Cohen warned that Bush was claiming "he is the state." "This is the Louis XIV school of government … such a president cannot be trusted." But Judge Richard Posner pronounced in a *Washington Post* op ed: "machine collection and processing of data cannot, as such, invade privacy." And *New York Times* columnist David Brooks feared that because "we will not be using our best techniques to monitor the communications of known terrorists … the odds of an attack on America just went up." The *Wall Street Journal* predictably praised Bush: "Thank You for Wiretapping." The founding fathers "recognized that a committee of 535 talking heads couldn't be trusted with such grave responsibility" for "national security."

Immediately after the *New York Times* revelation, DDC Judge Robertson resigned from FISC, fearing that information from illegal NSA wiretaps had been used to obtain FISA warrants.[11] Judge Kollar-Kotelly briefed the other FISC judges, some sharing Robertson's concerns. Contemporaneously, Republican Sens. Hagel (Neb), Snowe (Me), and Specter joined Democrats Feinstein, Levin, and Wyden (D-Or) in calling for hearings. But acting House Majority Leader Sen. Blunt (R-Mo) was "personally comfortable with everything I know about" the program.

Bush had said the previous April: "Any time you hear the United States government talking about wiretap … a wiretap requires a court order. Nothing has changed, by the way. When we're talking about chasing down terrorists, we're talking about getting a court order before we do so." The White House press secretary now claimed Bush had been talking only about the Patriot Act. DNI Negroponte wrote the intelligence community, denouncing "egregious" disclosure of the vital constitutional program.

Members of Congress disagreed about the adequacy of their briefing.[12] The National Security Act required written briefings but barred aides and note-taking. HPSCI chair Hoekstra (R-Mich) said he "couldn't help but conclude" from the briefing that the program "would have an impact on Americans." And Sen. Roberts (R-Kan) dismissed Rockefeller's claims of impotence: "a United States Senator has significant tools with which to wield power and influence over the executive branch." Cheney warned of a backlash "against those who are suggesting somehow we shouldn't have taken these steps in order to defend the country." Urging the appointment of a special counsel, the ACLU bought a full-page ad in the *New York Times*, pairing a photo of Nixon captioned "this man wasn't above the law" with one of Bush captioned "neither is this one."

On December 22, 2005 Assistant Attorney General Moschella warned the Gang of Four against "unauthorized disclosures in the media."[13] He claimed that the president's commander-in-chief power "includes the authority to order warrantless foreign international surveillance within the United States," and "the AUMF *clearly and unmistakably authorizes* such activities directed against communications of our enemy" [original emphasis]. "Foreign intelligence collection, especially in the midst of an armed conflict … fits squarely within the 'special needs' exception to the [Fourth Amendment's] warrant requirement." The *Washington Post* dismissed these unpersuasive arguments, and four law professors agreed. The Congressional Research Service said: "the Administration's legal justification … does not seem to be as well-grounded as the tenor of" Moschella's letter suggested.

Rep. Hoekstra maintained that "Congressional leaders at a minimum tacitly supported the program."[14] Sen. Roberts recalled that "Sen. Rockefeller expressed to the Vice President his vocal support of the program." But Sen. Daschle remembered voicing "grave concern" during the briefing, and Rep. Harman (D-Ca) now said the program "goes far beyond the measures to target al Qaeda about which I was briefed." Rep. Pelosi explained she could not make her earlier written objection public unless the government declassified it. Suzanne Spaulding, who had been General Counsel to both Intelligence Committees and CIA Assistant General Counsel, agreed "it is virtually impossible for any individual members of Congress, particularly members of the minority party, to take any effective action if they have concerns about what they have heard in one of these briefings," which reflected a "check the box" mentality. As Senate majority leader in 2001, Daschle had negotiated the AUMF with the White House counsel's office: "I can state categorically that the subject of warrantless wiretaps of American citizens never came up." The day after 9/11 the White House proposed an authorization "to deter and pre-empt any future acts of terrorism or aggression against the United States." But fearing this was too broad, Congress limited it to "all necessary and appropriate force against those nations, organizations, or persons [the President] determines planned, authorized, or committed or aided" the 9/11 attacks. Daschle remembered that "literally minutes before the Senate cast its vote, the administration sought to add the words 'in the United States and' after 'appropriate force' … I refused." He urged Congress to "fully investigate." (In March 2006 Moschella told Feinstein: "we do not recall such a discussion with former Senator Daschle." Daschle retorted: "it happened, and there is no question in my mind that the reason" for the administration's failed request was that Bush advisers "feared that they didn't have the authority" to act domestically without the language. Denis McDonough, then Daschle's foreign policy aide, said that David Crane, his counterpart in the office of then Senate Majority Leader Lott, told him "we'd like one last-minute change here" (which was rejected). It was clear to McDonough that the request "was coming from the White House." Crane had "no recollection," claiming he had been assigned to another task before the AUMF reached the Senate floor.)

A week after the initial story appeared, the press reported that NSA intercepted *all* overseas communications, checking for suspicious names, numbers, and words.[15] James Bamford, who had written two books about the Agency, said it intercepted "2 million pieces of communications in an hour." Hayden explained that dispensing with warrants gave NSA a "quicker" and "subtly softer trigger." After Bush's Executive Order, senior government officials persuaded the largest telecoms to provide access to their switches, through which many foreign-to-foreign communications were routed. A former technology manager at one telecom said they had been storing information on calling patterns and giving it to the government. John Dean (who should know) called Bush "the new Richard M. Nixon." "There can be no serious question that warrantless wiretapping, in violation of the law, is impeachable." But conservatives leaped to the president's defense.

Charles Krauthammer dismissed criticism as "yet another round of demagoguery." David Rivkin and Lee Casey declared: "the only outrageous thing about this policy is the outrage itself."

On New Year's Day 2006, Lichtblau and Risen reported that after Acting Attorney General Comey refused to issue a necessary certificate to continue electronic surveillance in 2004, White House counsel Gonzales and Chief of Staff Andrew Card sought it from Attorney General Ashcroft, who was in hospital recovering from gallbladder surgery.[16] When Ashcroft deferred to Comey, who had just arrived at his bedside, the program was temporarily suspended. Noting that Comey "can hardly be considered soft on terrorism," the *Los Angeles Times* denounced the program as "unnecessary" and "probably illegal." Bush's claim that "we're at war, and we don't have time to obey the law" was "an affront to the American system of checks and balances." Sen. Schumer (D-NY) said that when someone like Comey "had real doubts about the program, it calls into question the way the president and vice president went about changing it."

But Bush defended the program before an audience of wounded soldiers:[17]

> They attacked us before, they'll attack us again if they can. And we're going to do everything we can to stop them … If somebody from al Qaeda is calling you, we'd like to know why. We're at war with a bunch of cold blooded killers … and as commander in chief, I've got to use the resources at my disposal within the law to protect the American people.

The program had "been reviewed by Justice Department officials" and "members of the United States Congress." When he had said the previous April that wiretaps always needed warrants, "I was talking about roving wiretaps." The NSA program was "limited to calls from outside the United States to calls [*sic*] within the United States." The *New York Times* had caused "great harm to the United States." The "enemy out there … read the newspapers." Sen. McConnell (R-Ky) (second-ranking Republican) agreed that the focus of any Congressional investigation "should be on the leak." At the Heritage Foundation, Cheney defended the program as a "wartime measure … limited in scope to surveillance associated with terrorists." Had it been in place before 9/11, "we might have been able to pick up on two of the hijackers who flew a jet into the Pentagon." (But the 9/11 Commission found that the government failed to translate the intercepts it had made and did not know where the men were living.)

The *Times* replied to Republican attacks:[18] "A democratic society cannot long survive if whistle-blowers are criminally punished for revealing what those in power don't want the public to know – especially if it's unethical, illegal or unconstitutional behavior by top officials." The administration had used national security "as a catchall for any matter it wants to keep secret, even if the underlying reason for the secrecy is to prevent embarrassment to the White House." "Leak investigations are often designed to distract the public from the real issues by blaming the messenger."

Rep. Harman wrote Bush that briefing the "Gang of Eight" (majority and minority leaders of the two Houses and of their Intelligence Committees) did not satisfy the National Security Act of 1947, which authorized such limited briefings only for covert action, not wiretapping.[19] Rep. Hoekstra claimed that Congress had been "fully supportive of this program and the practice by which we have overseen it." Twenty-seven Democratic lawmakers asked Bush whether their communications or those of journalists had been intercepted. The Congressional Research Service (CRS) concluded that Bush lacked authority to order NSA to spy on US citizens or residents, prompting further criticism by Rep. Miller (D-Ca), head of the House Democratic Policy Committee, and Sen. Lautenberg (D-NJ). Even Thomas Kean (Republican co-chair of the 9/11 Commission) expressed doubts about the program's legality. Sen. Brownback (R-Kan), a staunch conservative, said "there was no discussion in anything that I was around" suggesting that the AUMF "gave the president a broad surveillance authority." Rep. Holt (D-NJ), a physicist on HPSCI, said NSA Director Alexander had falsely claimed at a December 6, 2005 briefing that the agency wiretapped Americans only after obtaining FISC warrants. Thirteen law professors and former government officials (including FBI Director Sessions and Deputy Attorney General Heymann) wrote that "the program appears on its face to violate existing law." The Acting DoD IG assured Democrats that the NSA IG was "actively reviewing aspects of that program"; but Rep. Lofgren (D-Ca) complained that the latter "has repeatedly reviewed this and okayed it."

Bush repeated that "I meant it when I said I'm going to uphold the Constitution," but added: "I have the right as commander in chief in a time of war to take action necessary to protect the American people."[20] He welcomed Congressional hearings "just so long as the hearing … doesn't tell the enemy what we're doing." Rep. Harman released a legal analysis by former CIA General Counsel Smith concluding that the case for the commander-in-chief's power was "weak" in light of FISA, and that the AUMF did not "justify warrantless electronic surveillance of United States persons in the United States." Acknowledging that the legal issues were "very knotty," Sen. Specter promised to "wear my skepticism on my sleeve" during the hearings. Sen. Feinstein maintained that FISC could authorize wiretaps with sufficient speed. A former FBI official and a former senior federal prosecutor dismissed the vast majority of NSA leads as worthless. The plots to destroy the Brooklyn Bridge and bomb British pubs and train stations were uncovered by other means. But DHS Secretary Chertoff asserted "without doubt" that wiretapping was "one of the critical tools we've used time and time again."

Observing that "in times of extreme fear, American leaders have sometimes scrapped civil liberties in the name of civil protection," the *New York Times* found it "hard to think of a more graphic example than President Bush's secret program of spying on Americans."[21] But Max Boot wrote in the *Los Angeles Times* that "all" Bush had done was "intercept communications between terrorists abroad and their contacts in the U.S. without a court order." A second CRS report produced at Rep. Harman's request found that the program violated the National Security Act.

Recalling on Martin Luther King Jr. Day at Constitution Hall that "for the last several years of his life, Dr. King was illegally wiretapped," Al Gore expressed the "shared concern that America's Constitution is in grave danger."[22] "Senator Ted Stevens [R-Ak] and Rep. Jim McGovern (D-Mass), among others, made statements during the [AUMF] debate clearly restating that the authorization did not operate domestically." But Attorney General Gonzales reiterated that DoJ had determined "the program is lawful." And half of Americans agreed that "wiretapping of telephone calls and e-mails without court approval" was acceptable. DoJ issued a 40-page White Paper defending the program. Steven G. Bradbury, acting OLC head, explained that "when it comes to responding to external threats to the country … the government would like to have a single executive who could act nimbly and agilely." But the *Washington Post* dismissed the White Paper as no "more convincing than its shorter predecessors." The same day the Democratic members of the Gang of Eight wrote Cheney demanding that the entire Intelligence Committees be briefed in the future. But he told the Manhattan Institute the program was "critical to the national security" and "within the president's authority." And White House press secretary

McClellan called wiretapping "a critical tool that helps us save lives and prevent attacks."

Sens. McCain, Durbin (D-Ill), and Kerry (D-Mass) and Rep. Harman said on television the administration should seek new legislation.[23] Mitt Romney (contemplating a 2008 run for president) dismissed criticism as limited to people "on the coasts … who are inclined to dislike the president," whose "primary responsibility" was "to protect the American people." Romney's "assumption" was that Bush did not break the law. Gen. Hayden (now Deputy DNI) said eavesdropping was no "driftnet" but rather "targeted and focused" on al-Qaeda. He echoed Cheney's claim that "we would have detected some of the 9/11 al Qaeda operatives in the United States" had the program been in place. Only "senior executives" who were "counter-terrorism and First Amendment question experts" made eavesdropping decisions. In another example of Orwellian Newspeak, Bush renamed warrantless wiretapping the "terrorist surveillance program" (TSP). The claim he had broken the law was "amazing." "If I wanted to break the law, why was I briefing Congress?" "Federal courts have consistently ruled that a president has authority under the Constitution to conduct foreign intelligence surveillance against our enemies." Although he was not a lawyer, "I can tell you what" the Supreme Court held in *Hamdi*: "Congress gave me the authority to use necessary force to protect the American people, but it didn't prescribe the tactics." In response to Democratic criticism, White House press secretary McClellan said FISA "was created in a different time period" and "didn't anticipate some of the technological issues that needed to be addressed."

At the National Press Club, Hayden characterized NSA employees as ordinary folk who "go shopping in Glen Burnie and their kids play soccer in Laurel. And they know the law. They know American privacy better than the average American, and they're dedicated to it."[24] Bush supported NSA employees "a hundred percent," warning that "operatives inside our country … blend in with the civilian population … get their orders from overseas, and then they emerge to strike from within. We must be able to quickly detect when someone linked to al Qaeda is communicating with someone inside of America." Attorney General Gonzales told Georgetown law students it was "imperative for national security reasons that we can detect reliably, immediately and without delay whenever communications associated with al Qaeda enter or leave the United States." The FISA process was too slow. Seven

Bush administration officials defended the program on television in the space of 24 hours.

The Gang of Eight Democrats called for hearings. Sens. Reid, Durbin, Kennedy (D-Mass), and Feingold separately wrote Bush that they were "gravely concerned" about the program. SSCI chair Roberts rebuked his Democratic colleagues for using "intelligence issues" as "fodder for political advantage" in "the middle of a war." But SJC chair Specter committed to holding public hearings. Sen. Clinton (D-NY) said the administration "argument that [the program was] rooted in the authority to go after al Qaeda is far-fetched" and the claim "that it's rooted in the Constitution inherently is kind of strange because we have FISA."

Rep. Harman wrote SSCI chair Roberts and ranking minority member Feinstein that in 2002 Sen. DeWine (R-Oh) had proposed a bill lowering the evidentiary standard for a search warrant from probable cause to "reasonable suspicion."[25] But an anonymous DoJ official said there had been "a conscious choice" not to have a public discussion about amending FISA to authorize NSA surveillance for fear of exposing the program. Hayden now conceded that NSA had replaced probable cause with a reasonableness standard. At a July 2002 hearing the DoJ counsel for intelligence policy had opposed the bill, telling Congress that the Patriot Act allowed the government "to use our expanded FISA tools more effectively to combat terrorist activity." Harman urged an investigation of "whether the failure to brief the Committee as required by law was compounded by testimony which was at best misleading, and at worst, false." Bush reiterated his claim to "a constitutional power," which he intended to use because FISA "was written in 1978," and now "it's a different world." If the effort to write a new law "is likely to expose the nature of the program, I'll resist it." The *Washington Post* condemned the Bush administration's "loathsome" "distortion, for political purposes, of the Democratic position on warrantless surveillance." The *Los Angeles Times* disparaged Bush's "weak case." In his world "only appeasers stand up for the Constitution." FISA had struck "the proper balance." But polls showed that more Americans supported wiretapping than civil liberties. In the last week of January 2006 Bush and senior aides asserted the program's legality at least 48 times, and DoJ issued a 27-page rebuttal of critics.

On January 29 the *New York Times* devoted its entire Sunday editorial page to a critique.[26] "Bush and his men" had promised a legal justification. "Instead, we got the familiar mix of political spin, clumsy historical misinformation, contemptuous dismissals of civil liberties concerns, cynical attempts to paint dissents as anti-American and pro-terrorist, and a couple of big, dangerous lies," including the unsupported claim that "Sept. 11 could have been prevented." Bush maintained that "only bad guys are spied on," but NSA "swept up vast quantities of email messages and telephone calls." Bush said "the spying is legal," but "the secret program violates the law as currently written." Bush said "just trust us," but "when Mr. Bush doesn't like the rules, he just changes them." Bush said "the rules needed to be changed," but he stopped Sen. DeWine from doing so. Bush said "other presidents did it," but his "time-line conveniently ended with F.D.R., rather than including Richard Nixon, whose surveillance of anti-war groups and other political opponents inspired FISA in the first place." "Congress has failed, tragically, on several occasions in the last five years to rein in Mr. Bush and restore the checks and balances that are the genius of American constitutional democracy. It is critical that it not betray the public once again on this score." University of Texas law professor Philip Bobbitt warned in a *Times* op ed that when the president "secretly decides a measure is unconstitutional and neglects to say so (much less why), he undermines the very system of public consent for which we are fighting."[27]

In his State of the Union address, Bush reiterated that the program was "based on authority given to me by the Constitution and by statute" (which he did not identify) and insisted that "appropriate members of Congress have been kept informed."[28] But DoJ refused to give SJC the two OLC opinions on the program's legality, and Sen. Feinstein released a letter from legal scholars rebutting the DoJ White Paper. Sen. Schumer said SJC should consider a subpoena. Calling Bush's legal justification "misleading," the *Los Angeles Times* warned that Republicans planned to argue in the forthcoming election: "if you think al Qaeda members have a right to privacy, vote Democratic." Indeed, six Republican senators defended NSA, and Sessions called wiretapping "absolutely necessary to prevent another 9/11 catastrophe."

DNI Negroponte refused to tell SSCI how many people were targeted, how phone calls and emails were intercepted, or whether there were any other "intelligence collection" programs.[29] Although Bush claimed only "a few" Americans' messages had been intercepted, DHS Secretary Chertoff admitted there had been "thousands." Warning that the leak had done "very severe" damage to national security, DCI Goss hoped "we will witness a grand jury investigation with reporters present, being asked to reveal who is leaking this information." At the end of the SSCI hearing chairman Roberts warned his Democratic colleagues: "you really don't have any civil liberties if you're dead." Afterwards, he expressed concern:

> that some of my Democratic colleagues used this unique public forum to make clear that they believe the gravest threat we face is not Usama bin Ladin [*sic*] and al Qaida but rather the President of the United States. There is no doubt in my mind that there are marching orders to the minority members of this committee to question and attack, at every opportunity, the President, the Vice President, the Secretary of State, the Attorney General, and now members of our intelligence services.

The SJC hearing began with a party-line vote rejecting a Democratic demand that Gonzales testify under oath.[30] When Feinstein quoted Bush's April 2004 Buffalo speech, Gonzales took "great issue with your suggestion that somehow the president of the United States was not being totally forthcoming with the American people." Gonzales insisted "that FISA does anticipate that another statute could permit electronic surveillance." Although some legislators did not intend to authorize surveillance by voting for the AUMF, "what matters is the plain meaning of the statute passed by Congress and signed by the president. And in this case, those plain words could not be clearer." Leahy disagreed: "this authorization is not a wiretap statute. We know what the wiretap statute looks like." Sen. Graham (R-SC) agreed: "when I voted for [the AUMF] I never envisioned that I was giving to this president or any other president the ability to go around FISA carte blanche." Invoking the internment of Japanese Americans during World War II, he said: "when the nation's at war … you need checks and balances more than ever, because within the law we put a whole group of people in jail who just looked like the enemy." When Gonzales asserted that FISA and the AUMF "complement each other," Specter retorted: "that just defies logic and plain English." Gonzales maintained that his interpretation was "fairly possible" and avoided constitutional problems. Feingold accused Gonzales of taking the device of "mincing words to a new high." Four Republicans expressed doubts about the president's authority. DeWine said: "it's in the country's best interest" for the White House to discuss the program with Congress and "see whatever changes in the law have to be made." Brownback said that since "we're going to be in this war on terrorism possibly for decades … to have another set of eyes looking at this surveillance technique is an important thing in maintaining the public's support for this."

Leahy pushed most aggressively.

LEAHY: If the president has that authority, does he also have the authority to wiretap Americans' domestic calls and e-mails? …

GONZALES: I am not comfortable, just off the cuff, talking about whether or not such activity would, in fact, be constitutional.

LEAHY: … Did it authorize the opening of first-class mail of U.S. citizens? That you can answer yes or no.

GONZALES: There is all kinds of wild speculation about what the—

LEAHY: Did it authorize it?

GONZALES: There is all kinds of wild speculation out there about what the president has authorized and what we're actually doing, and I'm not going to get into a discussion, Senator, about hypotheticals.

LEAHY: Mr. Attorney General, you're not answering my question. I'm not asking you what the president authorized. You're the chief law enforcement officer of the country. Does the law authorize the opening of first-class mail of U.S. citizens? …

GONZALES: Senator, I think that, again, that is not what is going on here …

LEAHY: … At least we have a press that tells us what you are doing, because you are not telling us … Of course, I'm sorry Mr. Attorney General, I forgot: you can't answer any questions that might be relevant to this … you mean you've been doing this wiretapping for three years and then suddenly you come up here and say, "Oh, by the way guys, could we have a little bit of authorization for this?" … Does this sound like a CYA on your part? It does to me.

Gonzales said Bush decided not to intercept domestic communications because "the reaction would have been twice as great."

> Our enemy is listening, and I cannot help but wonder if they aren't shaking their heads in amazement at the thought that anyone would imperil such a sensitive program by leaking its existence in the first place, and smiling at the prospect that we might now disclose even more or perhaps even unilaterally disarm ourselves of a key tool in the war on terror.

Asked why Bush did not seek Congressional authorization, Gonzales replied: "we didn't think we had to, quite frankly." (Three weeks later he wrote Specter and Leahy to qualify his statement that "all" Bush had authorized was wiretapping. Now he added: "I did not and could not address … any other classified intelligence activities." After Rep. Harman sought further clarification, Gonzales and his successor at the White House, Harriet Miers, assured her "there is not a broader program or an additional program out there involving surveillance of U.S. persons.")

After the hearing Specter said Gonzales's invocation of the president's commander-in-chief power was "not sound." "He's smoking Dutch Cleanser."[31] Rep. Harman called the claim that the AUMF authorized wiretapping "a bit of a stretch." "I don't think that's what most members of Congress felt they were doing." Sen. Biden (D-De) warned that the administration's rationalization could justify domestic wiretapping. Indeed, Sen. Kyl (R-Az) (ignoring the Constitution) advocated such an extension: "there is no less reason to do it than there is to intercept international communications with a potential terrorist warning of attack." Sen. Sessions (R-Ala) denied that the government was "going hog wild restraining American liberties. In fact, the trend has been to provide more and more protections." Sen. Hatch (R-Ut) claimed the administration had "more than made a persuasive case" that "this highly classified program is critical to the protection of the nation." Rep. Hoekstra wrote two letters to CRS, accusing it of having been "unwise at best and reckless at worst" to opine on classified matters about which it knew little. At a retreat, Bush exhorted House Republicans (believing journalists could not hear): "we must do everything in our power to protect the country." But Rep. Wilson (R-Az), chair of the HPSCI Subcommittee on Technical and Tactical Intelligence, expressed "serious concerns" about wiretapping. (An Air Force Academy graduate with a Ph.D. in international relations, she had been an NSC aide under George H.W. Bush.) Six Republicans joined her call for hearings, including Sens. Snowe and Hagel. Sen. Graham termed this "a Marbury v. Madison moment" (discussed in the companion volume *Law's Trials*). The *Los Angeles Times* felt "no great surprise that Alberto R. Gonzales sounded more like a White House spokesman than the country's chief law enforcement officer," building his case on "three wobbly pillars." "It's hard to say what's more disturbing, the Attorney General's unsound legal reasoning or his transparent efforts to avoid a legal conversation altogether in favor of emotional appeals aimed squarely at the court of public opinion." The *Washington Post* criticized Gonzales for refusing to "say how many Americans had been monitored, how widely the information collected had been shared within the government or whether permanent records had been kept," or to disclose whether the rules for wiretapping "had been reviewed either by Congress or a court." The *New York Times* said that though Roberts and Alito had "set new lows when it came to giving vague and meaningless answers to legitimate questions" during their Supreme Court confirmation hearings, "Gonzales made them look like models of openness." Having "forgotten" his promise to "stop acting like a hired gun helping a client figure out how to evade the law," he had given a "daylong display of cynical hair-splitting, obfuscation, disinformation and stonewalling." The

ACLU placed an ad in *USA Today* with photos of Bush and Gonzales, who took an oath "to preserve, protect and defend the Constitution of the United States." Polls by CNN/*USA Today* and CBS/*New York Times* showed that slightly more Americans disapproved than approved of Bush's program.

Under pressure from Republicans, Gonzales and Hayden gave a 3.5-hour closed-door briefing to HPSCI.[32] Harman said it was "a welcome thaw" but still did not comply with the National Security Act. Wilson called it "very forthcoming and very helpful," but regretted it left unanswered questions about "operational issues." The White House said NSA would brief SSCI but give "full details of the program" only to the Gang of Eight. Feinstein called it "sheer folly" for SSCI "not to be informed at this stage." Rockefeller dismissed the briefing as offering "nothing of substance." "Most of the questions that were asked were, in fact, not answered." Feinstein concurred. Feingold remained unpersuaded the program was legal. Wyden invoked Reagan's call to "trust but verify." The *Washington Post* acknowledged that the briefings were "a good first step," but added that "a framework for real oversight of the surveillance program remains necessary."

Cheney sought to fire up the CPAC convention: "with an important election coming up, people need to know just how we view the most critical questions of national security."[33] He warned against the "dangerous" "mind-set" of those "yielding to the temptation to downplay the threat and back away from the business at hand." The *Washington Post* accused the administration of having "patented the practice of taking a complicated policy issue and turning it into a club for the coming campaign."

Sens. Kennedy and Feingold asked the CEOs of AT&T, Sprint, Nextel, and Verizon to comment on a *USA Today* story that AT&T, Sprint, and MCI had cooperated with NSA spying.[34] AT&T (which had not denied an earlier allegation) now said equivocally it "abides by all applicable laws, regulations and statutes … and, in particular, with requests for assistance from governmental authorities."

On January 9, 2006 14 prominent constitutional law scholars across the political spectrum (including former government officials) had written Congressional leaders that DoJ's December 19, 2005 letter to Congress "failed to assert any plausible legal defense for the National Security Agency's domestic spying program."[35] They reiterated that conclusion on February 2, publishing their analysis in the *New York Review of Books* a week later. On February 13 the ABA, New York City

Bar, National Conference of Specialized Court Judges, and Beverly Hills Bar Association exhorted Bush "to abide by the limitations which the Constitution imposes" and urged Congress to conduct an open investigation of surveillance.

In mid-February *New York Times* Executive Editor Bill Keller said he was "not convinced" that "our reporting compromised national security."[36] Rather, it had provoked "an intense national debate about the proper balance between security and liberty," which members of both parties and all three branches of government "seem to regard as in the national interest." But *Commentary* accused the *Times* of having "compromise[d] the centerpiece of our defensive efforts in the war on terrorism," suggesting it could be prosecuted under the Espionage Act. The FBI had questioned many government employees in pursuit of the leaker. The *Times* said it could not "think of a president who has gone to the American people more often than George W. Bush has to ask them to forget about things like democracy, judicial process and the balance of powers – and just trust him." It also questioned Gonzales's "dedication to the truth." "In sworn testimony at his confirmation hearing last year, he dismissed as 'hypothetical' a question about whether he believed the president had the authority to conduct warrantless surveillance. In fact, Mr. Gonzales knew Mr. Bush was doing just that, and had signed off on it as White House counsel." Rep. Lofgren and 18 other House Democrats asked the White House to appoint a special prosecutor because their efforts to get answers to factual questions had been rebuffed "based on the feeblest of excuses."[37] The White House refused, telling Democrats instead to investigate the leak, which "has given the enemy some of our playbook."

The *New York Times* deplored the "familiar pattern" in which "President Bush ignores the Constitution and the laws of the land, and the cowardly, rigidly partisan majority in Congress helps him out by rewriting the laws he's broken."[38] After "Gonzales's refusal to answer questions," Specter "loyally produced a bill that actually grants legal cover, retroactively, to the one spying program Mr. Bush has acknowledged." "A far more noxious proposal" by Sen. DeWine "would entirely remove intelligence gathering related to terrorism" from FISA. Sen. Roberts "has refused to permit a vote on whether to investigate the spying scandal." Specter replied that his bill required FISC "to determine the program's constitutionality."

After a closed SSCI session, Roberts said he had invoked the committee's "nonpartisan tradition" to urge members to "fight the enemy, not each other."[39] As "an accommodation with the White House," SSCI created a subcommittee of four Republicans and three Democrats to oversee eavesdropping, thereby denying the other eight SSCI members any information. The usually mild Rockefeller exploded: "The Committee is, to put it bluntly, basically under the control of the White House through its chairman." Hagel dismissed Rockefeller's "laughable" criticism, boasting that DeWine, Snowe, and he (all on the subcommittee) were "three of the most independent Republicans" in the Senate. After Roberts denounced the insinuation that he was a "lap dog of the administration," complaining that Rockefeller "doesn't know how hard we worked" against "a lot of pushback," Rockefeller conceded the subcommittee was "a step in the right direction." Former Sen. Bob Graham deplored that "the extent of partisanship is of a different order than I ever saw" in his ten years on SSCI. Levin called the Republican Congress "simply too much of a rubber stamp for this administration"; Reid agreed that SSCI had "become an extension of the White House public relations operation." Thomas Kean also found the level of partisanship "new" and "distressful." Lashing back that Democrats' "stifling partisanship" was undermining SSCI, Majority Leader Frist (R-Tn) threatened to give Republicans another seat on the Committee and let each party hire its own staff. Snowe and Hagel supported DeWine's proposal to allow warrantless surveillance for 45 days, claiming that "we are reasserting Congressional responsibility and oversight." DeWine said the proposal would bring the program "into the normal oversight of the Senate Intelligence Committee." But Wyden compared it to a doctor diagnosing an unexamined patient. In the Senate Appropriations Committee, Specter threatened to reduce the administration's funding unless Gonzales answered more SJC questions. The *Washington Post* acknowledged "modest steps toward oversight," but thought DeWine's proposal "premature." "Congress cannot reasonably authorize or limit the NSA's program without knowing what sort of surveillance it encompasses and how it works." The *New York Times* accused Bush and Cheney of having "left FISA in tatters and the Senate Select Committee on its deathbed in just five years." The SSCI action was "breathtakingly cynical. Faced with a president who is almost certainly breaking the law, the Senate sets up a panel to watch him do it and calls that control." "[I]t was disappointing to see a principled Republican like Sen. Olympia Snowe go along." Though Specter was "righteously angry," he "has a sad habit of bowing to the right wing when the chips are down." The next day the *Times* contrasted the Republican "revolt against the president" over the UAE ports deal with the "collapse of congressional supervision of the executive branch" over "a major principle" like warrantless wiretapping. "With rebels like these who needs loyalists?" The *Los Angeles Times* warned that DeWine's proposal "would significantly expand the administration's power to intercept U.S. citizens' international phone calls and e-mails without obtaining a warrant."

Specter introduced the National Security Surveillance Act of 2006, which would let FISC authorize 45 days of unlimited interception of the identity, place of origin, and date of communications between a US person and someone abroad. Judge Robertson, who had resigned from FISC in protest, supported the proposal, as did four other former FISC judges. DeWine, Graham, Hagel, and Snowe introduced the Terrorist Surveillance Act of 2006, which would let the president authorize wiretapping for up to 45 days and impose harsh penalties on any government employee who disclosed "classified information" related to the program. Specter criticized their bill for letting the government "do whatever the hell it wants" for 45 days.[40] Roberts and Rockefeller expressed reservations.

Feingold submitted a resolution to censure Bush for violating the law, declaring on television that his actions were "reminiscent of what President Nixon … was basically removed from office for doing." Frist denounced this "crazy political move … at a time of war, when this president is out defending the American people with a very good, lawful, constitutional program."[41] Sen. Cornyn (R-Tex) wondered "how many of [Feingold's] Democratic colleagues will follow him off the cliff?" Warner called it "the worst type of political grandstanding." Specter said "the president may be wrong, but he has acted in good faith." Although Reid commended Feingold "for bringing this to the attention of the American people," Levin urged Congress to "wait until the investigation is completed." DNC Chairman Dean warned party members that "Republicans want you to think" that "Russ Feingold is a traitor." Sen. Allard (R-Co) had said that "time and time again [Feingold sided] with the terrorists." Feingold commented: "if such a crazy idea has such limited appeal, why do they have the attack dogs calling all over the country about this?" Pronouncing Feingold "a man of principle," Reid said: "people should cool their jets and let the process take its course." But Sen. Dodd (D-Ct) feared Feingold was "getting way down the road on this issue." Rush Limbaugh welcomed "such a gift" to conservatives. An RNC mailing to 15 million supporters declaring that "Dem Leaders 'Ecstatically' Embrace Sen. Feingold's Plan to Weaken the Tools to Fight the War on Terror" generated a greater response than any other issue in months. The *New York Times* shared Feingold's "frustration," but called censure a "bad idea." "Watching Mr. Feingold's fellow Democrats run for cover" showed "how effective" the Republican counter-attack had been. Because Roberts and Specter were "busy trying to give legal cover to the president's trampling on the law and the Constitution," Reid "should not be afraid to highlight that fact by shutting down the Senate's public business." Feingold wrote the *Times* that "there's nothing we could learn that would change the fact that by authorizing the program, the president broke the law." Specter reluctantly agreed to let the SJC hold hearings on the censure resolution, but proclaimed: "I am sure not going to sit back and have Feingold spout off." When Rep. Conyers (D-Mich) urged Congress to determine if there were grounds for impeachment (25 Democrats had backed his 2005 proposal), House Majority Leader Boehner (R-Oh) denounced such "political grandstanding of the very worst kind," which exposed "the soft underbelly of the Democrats' position on national security issues."

During the SJC's three-hour debate on Feingold's censure motion, only Leahy endorsed it, and Kohl (D-Wisc) (the only other Democrat present) left without speaking; Feinstein, Kennedy, and Biden skipped the meeting.[42] The five Republicans questioned so aggressively that witnesses could not complete their sentences. Hatch called the resolution "inflammatory" and "constitutionally suspect." Claiming "more expertise than anyone might wish" on the matter, John Dean said there was "lots of evidence" Bush violated FISA. Hatch retorted: "I don't think you have any." Cornyn dismissed Dean as "a convicted felon" trying to sell books. Graham called Nixon and Bush "apples and oranges." The three Republican witnesses said eavesdropping was authorized by the AUMF. Republicans urged supporters and talk show hosts to "tell Democrats to stop weakening our national security." The *New York Times* cautioned that censuring Bush "would probably not do much to make him follow the law."

Noting that President Wilson had authorized domestic wiretapping "based on the Constitution and his inherent role as commander in chief," Gonzales told the HJC he would not "rule [it] out," but refused to discuss other forms of surveillance.[43] Afterwards, DoJ insisted Gonzales had said nothing new. Rep. Sensenbrenner (R-Wisc) declared: "if we're properly to determine whether or not the program was legal and funded – because that's Congress's responsibility – we need to have answers, and we're not getting them." Rep. Schiff (D-Ca) said Gonzales had advanced "a wholly unprecedented assertion of executive power." Reading "between the lines" of the Attorney General's "maddeningly narrow talking points," the *New York Times* concluded that "the one warrantless N.S.A. spying program Mr. Bush has owned up to is not the only one going on." The *Washington Post* welcomed the "dramatic improvement," in which 11 Representatives and 6 Senators had received "comprehensive" briefings.

A day after House Republicans barred amendments expanding NSA oversight, Specter threatened to block funding "unless Congress is kept fully and currently informed" by briefings of all members of the Intelligence and Judiciary Committees.[44] "Where is the outrage? What's the use of passing another statute if the president won't pay attention to it?"

Bush's nomination of NSA Director Hayden to be DCI revived the debate.[45] Sen. Cornyn said "if the president's opponents hope to argue that we're doing too much to prevent terrorism … we look forward to taking that debate to the American people." But some Republicans expressed concern. House Speaker Hastert (R-Ill) complained he had not been consulted. The *New York Times* found it "hard … to quibble" with Rep. Hoekstra's view that Hayden, who had been "part of the White House's scripted defense of the program," was "the wrong person, the wrong place, at the wrong time." The *Times* hoped Specter, "who routinely promises to ask tough questions of nominees only to lie down and roll over once hearings are convened, will surprise the country this time and take a hard look at Gen. Hayden." Hayden promised to bring NSA surveillance "under federal law."

DoJ OPR, which had sought security clearance in order to investigate NSA surveillance, dropped the issue when this was denied in May.[46] Over three decades, OPR had never been denied clearance, which the administration had granted to many other DoJ officials (including those investigating the leak) and to the Privacy and Civil Liberties Oversight Board (PCLOB). In July OPR's chief lawyer wrote that "OPR has never been prevented from initiating or pursuing an investigation." Specter asked Gonzales "the obvious question of whether there was some interest on the part of the administration in not having that given." The Attorney General replied lamely that "every additional security clearance that is granted for the [program] increases the risk that national security might be compromised." When the White House said OPR "was not the proper venue," Rep. Hinchey (D–NY) (who had asked OPR to investigate) said he had been told by the DoJ IG that OPR *was* the appropriate unit. Reps.

Hinchey, Waxman (D-Ca), and Woolsey (D-Ca) asked Bush to "allow OPR to do its job." Rep. Lofgren said "the president's latest action shows that he is willing to be personally involved in the cover-up of suspected illegal activities." Bush's action underlined for Rep. Ruppersberger (D-Md) why courts and Congress needed to oversee the wiretapping program. The *New York Times* accused Bush of sending Gonzales to the SJC "to stonewall, obfuscate and spin fairy tales." The justification for refusing OPR security clearance "sounds nicely cloak-and-dagger, but does not explain why Mr. Bush granted immediate clearance to the lawyers charged with finding out who told *The Times* about the wiretapping in the first place." In March 2007 it emerged that before advising Bush to deny the OPR request, Gonzales had learned *he* would be the focus of investigators, who wanted to speak with Jack Goldsmith (the OLC head who opposed some warrantless wiretapping) and James A. Baker (the DoJ Office of Intelligence Policy and Review lawyer who had warned FISC Judge Kollar-Kotelly that officials had used information from warrantless wiretaps to obtain warrants).

In May 2006, *USA Today* elaborated its February story, reporting that NSA had records of "tens of millions" of phone calls from AT&T, Verizon, and BellSouth, which collectively served 224 million customers.[47] Verizon had informed customers that it disclosed confidential records "as required by law, legal process, or exigent circumstances." AT&T said it provided records to the government "strictly within the law." BellSouth denied providing any information "without proper legal authority." Only Qwest (with 14 million customers) had refused to cooperate. Warning that its obstinacy could compromise national security, NSA threatened to deny Qwest classified work, rebuffed Qwest's request that NSA seek FISC approval "because FISA might not agree" with the Agency, and declined to get a letter from the Attorney General. (On June 30 *USA Today* withdrew its claim that BellSouth and Verizon had given NSA phone records, but said 19 Members of Congress briefed on the program reaffirmed that NSA had domestic phone call data.)

More than fifty House Democrats demanded the appointment of a special counsel. Specter vowed to make the telecoms testify under oath. The *Washington Post* said: "it isn't clear how the companies could have turned over records of more than a trillion calls without violating consumer privacy laws." This "surveillance program of enormous magnitude" involved "presumptively private data of almost all Americans." "Is there any basis for confidence that telecommunication companies are not also turning over internet traffic data wholesale?" Congress should not legislate without "a comprehensive sense" of what the wiretapping program "is and how it fits into the Agency's larger domestic activities." The *New York Times* found "more reason than ever to be worried – and angry – about how wide the government's web has been reaching." The Senate should require Gonzales to testify under oath, "not roll over when [he] declines to provide answers," and use Hayden's confirmation hearing to conduct "a serious, thorough and pointed review." "Congress should pass legislation that removes any doubt that this kind of warrantless spying on ordinary Americans is illegal."

A few days after the article appeared, New Jersey's Attorney General subpoenaed five phone companies to investigate violations of state consumer protection laws.[48] Officials in Vermont, Maine, and Washington State had threatened similar investigations. DoJ immediately asked a federal court to block the subpoenas. New Jersey moved to dismiss the DoJ lawsuit, which would throw "an impenetrable cloak insulating the federal government's domestic surveillance activities from all judicial scrutiny." When Maine's Attorney General asked Verizon to provide a sworn statement that it had not disclosed phone records to NSA, the federal government obtained a TRO to stop this. In June 2009 ND Cal Judge Walker enjoined the investigations in Maine, New Jersey, Connecticut, Vermont, and Missouri, finding that the FISA Amendment Act 2008 (FAA) (discussed below) preempted state law.[49]

On May 11, 2006 Bush simply reiterated his earlier generalizations (and predictably stayed on message in his weekly radio address):[50] "[O]ur intelligence activities strictly target al Qaeda and their known affiliates … the government does not listen to domestic phone calls without court approval … We're not mining or trolling through the personal lives of millions of innocent Americans … every time sensitive intelligence is leaked, it hurts our ability to defeat this enemy." Rep. Hoekstra echoed him in a *Los Angeles Times* op ed. Eavesdropping "has been focused like a laser beam on al Qaeda and its known associates." Leakers committed "a breach of trust with the American public." The *Washington Post* condemned this "distressingly familiar" routine:

> A news organization reveals a secret operation by the Bush administration that employs a new means to fight the war on terrorism but also raises serious issues of civil liberties or human rights. The president starts off with a curt assertion that the actions are legal, even as his administration moves to head off any intervention by Congress. Resisting further

> requests for information, the White House countenances a public debate only to the extent it can be put to partisan use, as a means of casting Democratic critics as weak on national security.

Frank Rich wrote in his *New York Times* column that Bush was "aping the Nixon template." "It's the recklessness at the top of our government, not the press's exposure of it, that has truly aided the enemy, put American lives at risk and potentially sabotaged national security."

The *New York Times* reported that when Bush asked soon after 9/11 "is there anything more we could be doing, given the current laws," Hayden assured him "there is."[51] Cheney and Addington argued that NSA should intercept domestic communications, calling it "terrorist surveillance, not domestic surveillance," but NSA lawyers resisted. In January 2006 Hayden recalled telling NSA employees two days after 9/11 that standards for a "reasonable" intrusion into privacy changed "as smoke billowed from two American cities and a Pennsylvania farm field. We acted accordingly."

Specter said: "we're really flying blind on the subject, and that's not a good way to approach … the constitutional issues involving privacy."[52] Bush's denial of security clearance to the DoJ OPR was "incomprehensible." Feinstein feared "we are on our way to a major constitutional confrontation." Leahy felt it would be "a mistake to try to legislate knowing so little." Levin complained that "our briefings aren't complete." Graham urged "the administration to share the information necessary to construct a statute that would keep the program viable." Even House Majority Leader Boehner was "concerned." "I'm going to find out [the details], because I'm not sure why it would be necessary to keep and have that kind of information." But warning that the *USA Today* disclosure "threatens to undermine our nation's safety," Rep. Hoekstra regretted that "we are once again mired in a debate about what our intelligence community may or may not be doing." Sen. Lott (R-Miss) asked: "Do we want security … or do we want to get in a twit about our civil libertarian rights?" And Sen. Roberts dismissed "calls for further oversight [as] unnecessary."

Hayden insisted "everything that N.S.A. does is lawful and very carefully done." But the *Los Angeles Times* predicted his nomination "isn't likely to make much headway." "[N]o one in (or out of) Congress should have any faith in the administration's assurances about either its actions or its intentions under the program." Sen. Biden thought the disclosure was going to make confirmation "difficult." Hagel said Hayden "knows he's not going to be confirmed without answering those questions" about his role. Schumer declared that "a test of his independence" would be "whether he is able to answer some of these questions." But Reid tended to favor the nomination. A poll found that 63 percent of Americans supported the program and only 35 percent were opposed.

National Security Adviser Hadley said the program did not engage in "listening to domestic phone calls," but recorded only "who was called when, and how long did they talk."[53] Nevertheless, Rep. Harman accused the administration of "breaking the law," and Sen. Biden agreed. Specter was hopeful "we may get some answers" from the telecoms, which could not claim executive privilege. Rep. Markey (D-Mass) asked the Federal Communications Commission (FCC) to determine whether telecoms had broken the law. BellSouth said it had no contract with NSA "and we have not provided bulk customer calling records to the NSA"; but it later conceded NSA might have gotten them indirectly. Verizon said the same. AT&T reaffirmed its "obligation to assist law enforcement and other government agencies responsible for protecting the public welfare."

In anticipation of Hayden's confirmation hearing, NSA Director Alexander agreed to brief the full Intelligence Committees.[54] The *Los Angeles Times* said the "administration is doing the right thing for the wrong reason." But its columnist Max Boot dismissed FISA as "a luxury we can no longer afford." "This archaic law should be euthanized." In response to Specter, Gonzales said he had denied security clearance to OPR because "we don't want to be talking so much about the program that we compromise its effectiveness."

In his opening statement to SSCI, Hayden said "true accountability is not served by inaccurate, harmful, and illegal public disclosures."[55] Soon after 9/11 he had told NSA employees that Bush had approved wiretapping of international calls: "we're going to do exactly what he said, and not one photon or electron more." He assured the committee "that's what we've done." NSA lawyers "were very comfortable with the Article II arguments and the president's inherent authorities." There was no discussion of the AUMF. He denied Cheney had pushed NSA to eavesdrop on purely domestic calls but refused to tell Levin whether NSA had done more than had been disclosed. (In a commencement speech in May 2007, Hayden recalled telling SSCI: "I had a duty to play aggressively – 'right up to' the line. Playing back from the line protected me but didn't protect America. I made it clear I would always play in fair territory, but that there would be chalk dust on my cleats. Against a merciless enemy, we fight hard. I don't apologize for that.") The *New York Times* criticized Sen. Roberts for having "made it clear that this would be yet another rubber-stamp session." It was "clear that the one warrantless spying operation Mr. Bush has acknowledged … is not the only one." Hayden "could not explain coherently why he testified in 2002 that he had no authority to listen to Americans' phone calls without a warrant, when the president had already given him that authority." The *Los Angeles Times* repeated that the wiretapping was "all the more disturbing because the Bush administration refuses to submit any part of the program to judicial oversight." The Democratic Party asked supporters to tell their senators not to confirm Hayden.

A week later HPSCI attacked the *New York Times* and *Washington Post* for exposing the wiretapping, and some Republicans (though not Hoekstra) urged criminal prosecution.[56] When Rep. Renzi (R-Az) urged the Attorney General to "use all of the power of existing law to bring criminal charges," Rep. Harman retorted that anyone who wanted to imprison journalists should visit China, Cuba, or North Korea. *Commentary* senior editor Gabriel Schoenfeld called for prosecution of James Risen. "When it comes to programs that help to protect us from a second and more terrible 9/11, a little chilling effect on a media willing to recklessly disclose vital secrets would not be a bad thing." Gonzales acknowledged the "possibility" of prosecution under the Espionage Act 1917. "We have an obligation to enforce those laws. We have an obligation to ensure that our national security is protected" – statements the *Washington Post* warned "should chill the bones of every American who values a vigorous press." "The administration is seeking to convert a moribund WW I-era espionage law into an American version of Britain's Official Secrets Act." Gonzales responded by invoking the Supreme Court's 1979 decision in *Smith* v. *Maryland*,[57] which ruled that a police order requiring a phone company to install a "pen register" to record the numbers a suspect called did not violate privacy expectations protected by the Fourth Amendment. But he was focused more on leakers than journalists. (In July an ED Va grand jury investigating leaks of the NSA program subpoenaed Russell D. Tice, who claimed to have witnessed illegal activity, disclosed unclassified information to reporters, talked to Congressional staffers with security clearance, and tried to testify to Congress. NSA officials retaliated by questioning his mental health and withdrawing his security clearance.)

The *New York Times* found it "hard to say which was more bizarre about Attorney General Alberto Gonzales's threat to prosecute *The*

Times for revealing President Bush's domestic spying program: his claim that a century-old espionage law could be used to muzzle the press or his assertion that the administration cares about enforcing laws the way Congress intended." University of Chicago law professor Geoffrey Stone wrote in the *Los Angeles Times* that "the Bush administration is threatening a confrontation unprecedented in American history." Senior SJC members of both parties criticized US Attorney Matthew Friedrich for refusing to say whether the administration had ever considered prosecuting journalists for leaks. Leahy said: "you should be ashamed of yourself." The ACLU took out a full-page *New York Times* ad warning readers their phone companies might have sent their records to NSA and urging them to complain to the FCC and state Public Utilities Commissions. The ACLU itself complained to Public Utilities Commissions in 21 states. But the FCC declined to investigate because NSA activities were classified.

SSCI voted to confirm Hayden 12–3 (Feingold, Wyden, and Bayh (R-In) against).[58] Levin claimed Hayden "has shown some independence and some backbone and a willingness to say no to power." Feinstein called him "the leader and honest broker the CIA needs to regain its footing." The Senate confirmed 78–15. Specter (the only Republican) voted against to protest "the administration's policy of not informing the Congress." Clinton was opposed because the DCI should "show respect for the rule of law and recognition of the oversight role of Congress." Kennedy said his opposition reflected "very serious questions about the scope and legality of the N.S.A. domestic surveillance programs that [Hayden] helped design, implement and defend." The *Los Angeles Times* regretted the Senate's failure to translate "indignation on Capitol Hill … into action." But it endorsed the Feinstein–Specter bill, which would allow emergency wiretapping for seven days before the government had to seek FISC approval. The *Washington Post* opposed any legislation until Congress obtained a "firm sense of what the NSA surveillance program consists of."

Accusing Cheney of lobbying SJC members against having telecom executives testify, Specter threatened subpoenas.[59] Reid called the interference "deeply troubling." But Cheney was dismissive: "these communications are not unusual – they are the government at work." And Specter swallowed his pique after talking to Cheney and working out a compromise with Kyl to give blanket amnesty to anyone who authorized warrantless surveillance under the president's authority, and to consolidate the 29 federal court cases challenging spying in the Foreign Intelligence Surveillance Court of Review (FISCR) (whose decision could be appealed to the Supreme Court). Feinstein opposed "legislating in the dark" and insisted on a warrant requirement. The *New York Times* called it "time for the Senate to stop rolling over and start focusing on uncovering the extent of the spying and enforcing the law. A good place to start is by compelling the executives of the major telecommunications companies to testify." DeWine's "cynical" bill legalized the illegal. Feinstein's bill "leaves a gaping loophole for Mr. Bush to go on ignoring FISA." Specter's "convoluted" bill "still leaves too much room to evade court scrutiny and may actually widen the range of eavesdropping that can be done with a warrant." A few days later the *Times* said only one bill "remotely makes sense": Schumer's, which conferred standing on those seeking to challenge the law. Feinstein's proposal was "highly premature." DeWine's would give "the stamp of approval to Mr. Bush's claims of unlimited power." And Specter's was "fatally flawed" because it "would eliminate the vital principle that FISA's rules are the only legal way to eavesdrop on Americans." The *Los Angeles Times* criticized Specter for having "complicated matters by simultaneously pressing his own bill and signing on" to Feinstein's "superior" measure. Twenty-three Republican Representatives (including several conservatives) joined 183 Democrats in an unsuccessful attempt by Reps. Schiff and Flake (R-Az) to limit expenditures for domestic electronic surveillance to those complying with FISA. Rep. King called for investigations of the *New York Times*, *Los Angeles Times*, and *Wall Street Journal*.

The *New York Times* published a letter HPSCI chairman Hoekstra had written Bush the day before Hayden's confirmation hearing, mentioning "alleged Intelligence Community activities" not included in his committee's briefings and warning:[60]

> If these allegations are true, they may represent a breach of responsibility by the Administration, a violation of law, and, just as importantly, a direct affront to me and the Members of this committee who have so ardently supported efforts to collect information on our enemies … [Congress] should not have to play "Twenty Questions" to get information that it deserves under our Constitution. I want to reemphasize that the Administration has the legal responsibility to "fully and currently" inform the House and Senate intelligence committees of its intelligence and intelligence related activities.

Hoekstra now revealed "there was at least one major – what I consider significant – activity that we had not been briefed on." House Speaker Hastert shared his concerns. Hoekstra added: "This is actually a case where the whistle-blower process was working appropriately." A House committee had approved a bill to extend whistle-blower protections to intelligence agency employees, but these were excluded in the Senate version. (At the same time, Hoekstra and Sen. Santorum (R-Pa) had written a *Wall Street Journal* op ed on June 26 denouncing "people who leak the existence of sensitive intelligence programs ... to advance their political desires.")

In mid-July Specter announced that the administration endorsed his bill, which would let NSA wiretap without warrants for a week, authorize FISC to approve wiretapping *programs* (not just individual warrants), and consolidate all legal challenges in FISC.[61] DoJ could revise the program to meet FISC's requirements and appeal its decisions. Specter said "the bill recognizes the president's constitutional authority" and repeals statutory language making FISA the exclusive authorization. Rep. Harman denounced this "end run around the FISA," and Rep. Schiff called it "a further abdication" of Congress's role. Sen. Feingold opposed "any bill that would grant blanket approval for warrantless surveillance of Americans." Electronic Frontier Foundation (EFF) condemned it as a "rubber stamp" for eavesdropping. Declaring that the bill was no "compromise, except quite dramatically on the senator's part," the *Washington Post* said it gave "a green light for domestic spying" and "must not pass." Condemning this "license to wiretap," the *Los Angeles Times* said the government should be required "to secure the FISA court's approval for individual NSA surveillance operations." The *New York Times* warned that the bill would allow Bush "to go on ignoring the eavesdropping law." FISC "is not the right court to make the determination of constitutionality." The New York City Bar's president and the chair of its Committee on Civil Rights wrote the *Times* to agree. In February, the 550-member ABA House of Delegates had overwhelmingly adopted recommendations by its task force on domestic surveillance that the administration comply with or amend FISA, and that Congress conduct a comprehensive investigation of surveillance and affirm that the AUMF did not provide a statutory exception to FISA. Now complaining to HPSCI that "the administration continues to impede Congress," the ABA endorsed Harman's bill while opposing Specter's.

In a *Washington Post* op ed, Specter boasted he was one of the "civil libertarians" who "have insisted that the program must be subject to judicial review to ensure compliance with the Fourth Amendment."[62] Only FISC "has the expertise" to determine the program's legality. "Its closed proceedings and unblemished record for not leaking would make full consideration both possible and secure." Specter hailed "Bush's personal commitment to submit his program to FISC" as "a major breakthrough." The *Post* responded by attacking Specter's "very dangerous bill" as a "blank check to spy." It would address what Specter had called "a festering sore on our body politic" by "shooting the patient" and "legitimize not only whatever the NSA may now be doing but lots of other surveillance it might dream up." At the SJC hearing, DCI Hayden called Specter's proposal "a great opportunity to modernize intelligence gathering to 'protect our liberty and security.'" Director Alexander warned that if NSA had to get a warrant for every target, "you would be so far behind the target, if you were in hot pursuit, with the number of applications that you would have to make and the time to make those, you could never catch up." Feinstein (who had been briefed on the program as an SSCI member) retorted that it "is easily accommodatable to an individual warrant for U.S. persons." James X. Dempsey, policy director of the Center for Democracy and Technology, warned the proposal "would turn the clock back to an era of unchecked presidential power, warrantless domestic surveillance and constitutional uncertainty." A defensive Specter protested: "Have you ever gotten a concession from a president?"

Soon after briefing SSCI, NSA gave Roberts a set of "administration approved, unclassified talking points," which declared: "the program must continue," "there is strict oversight in place … now including the full Congressional intelligence committees," and "current law is not agile enough to handle the threat posed by sophisticated international terrorist organizations such as al-Qaeda."[63] The White House claimed that the failed plot to blow up planes flying from London to the USA showed "the importance of the approach that the administration has taken."[64] Sen. Cornyn asked "how much longer can we afford Democratic obstruction and opposition to important national security efforts?" Speaker Hastert said the plot "helps us push for stronger surveillance monitoring of terrorist movements."

SJC voted 10–8 (Graham and Specter joining the Democrats) to support bills by both Specter and Feinstein, although Kyl called them "totally contradictory."[65] Leahy complained that Specter's bill "makes compliance with FISA entirely optional." Rockefeller criticized "a cynical White House strategy [either] to prevent Congress from … acting or forcing it to legislate on vital national security and privacy issues in the dark." SJC also approved DeWine's proposal to require the administration to notify Congress of warrantless wiretaps. HJC canceled a vote on its own version (drafted by Wilson) because six conservative Republicans resisted efforts to weaken controls on eavesdropping.

The New York City Bar president wrote the majority and minority leaders of both Houses to oppose the Specter, DeWine, and Wilson bills and support Feinstein's. The *Los Angeles Times* agreed.[66] The *Washington Post* called the Specter and Wilson bills "disasters." But HPSCI and HJC approved Wilson's bill limiting surveillance to 60 days unless the president asked Congress for more time and described all the targets (Democrats supporting and most Republicans opposing). House Speaker Hastert expostulated: "for the second time in just two days, House Democrats have voted to protect the rights of terrorists." Rep. Boehner attacked "the Democrats' irrational opposition to strong national security policies." At a press conference Bush criticized "the vast majority of Democrats" for voting "against a program that would have institutionalized the capacity of this government to listen to al Qaeda phone calls." Sens. Feingold, Durbin, and Salazar (D-Co) opposed legislation that would "ratify an unlawful surveillance program." Former FBI and CIA Director William H. Webster, former FBI Director William Sessions, and 12 other former national security officials opposed "legislation that replaces the obligation to use the procedures of the FISA with broad language about relying upon the president's constitutional authority."

After Democrats won control of both Houses in November, Leahy said the SJC (which he would chair) would investigate how the program had operated and draft new legislation.[67] Specter predictably reversed himself, submitting a bill that would require warrants for eavesdropping on communications leaving but not entering the USA and fast-track challenges for Supreme Court review. Gonzales repeated that the program "does not invade anyone's privacy, unless you are talking to the enemy in this time of war." The DoJ IG, who had referred the issue to OPR a year earlier, now began his own investigation of DoJ "compliance with legal requirements governing the program," though not its constitutionality. The *New York Times* welcomed this "crack in the stone wall." The *Los Angeles Times* agreed that "NSA still needs more oversight."

As the Democratic-majority Congress convened, Gonzales told senior SJC members that DoJ had obtained a FISC order on January 10, 2007 allowing "the necessary speed and agility while providing substantial advantages. Accordingly ... the president has determined not to reauthorize the Terrorist Surveillance Program."[68] An official said the generic order had been signed by a judge just appointed to FISC, not presiding Judge Kollar-Kotelly. Gonzales refused to show members of Congress the order, but told Leahy it required probable cause to believe one communicant was a member or agent of al-Qaeda or an associated terrorist organization. Leahy and Specter asked Kollar-Kotelly to show them the order and make it public. The White House claimed it had been working on this proposal since spring 2005 (presumably worried the *New York Times* would publish the story it had suppressed under administration pressure the previous fall). Rockefeller (the new SSCI chair) still planned "to move forward with the committee's review of all aspects of this program's legality and effectiveness." The *New York Times* called warrantless wiretaps "one of the most egregious ... of the many ways that President Bush has trampled civil liberties and the balance of powers." The public still "needs to know why Mr. Bush broke the law for more than five years and what should be done to ensure there will be no more abuses of the wiretap statute." The *Los Angeles Times* expressed "relief that the rule of law has triumphed, suspicion that the administration's concession isn't all that it's cracked up to be and, most of all, anger at the president and his surrogates for suggesting that any criticism of their tactics was tantamount to treason."

A day later Bush insisted "nothing has changed in the program except the court has said we've analyzed it and it's a legitimate way to protect the country."[69] Gonzales also denied the program had been "terminated" and refused to give SJC more documents or explain why the administration reversed itself, claiming that only Bush could release the FISC opinion. Leahy called this "a little Alice in Wonderland." Schumer wanted to know whether FISC had authorized wiretapping of individuals or categories, "because if it is very broad-brush approval ... it doesn't do much good." Rep. Eschoo (D-Ca) said Gonzales had been "quite skittish," and Rep. Schiff called him "purposely evasive." The *Washington Post* compared the administration to "a traffic officer trying to hurry along bystanders at an accident scene: 'Move right along, folks, nothing to look at here.'" "Traveling down the rabbit hole with Mr. Gonzales is an endless frustrating journey, light on details, heavy on unsubstantiated assurances." Declaring that his views of the new program ranged "from skeptical to dubious," Rockefeller maintained that wiretapping still did not comply with FISA and wanted the government to obtain a separate warrant for every US resident targeted. SSCI designated eight staffers to examine the program and draft document requests. But Bond (the senior Republican) said the "new" program seemed "to meet all of our requirements."

A week after Rep. Reyes (the new HPSCI chair) threatened to subpoena the documents, the government agreed to give Congress the DoJ application to FISC and supporting briefs.[70] Congress was still seeking Bush's original order authorizing the program. Gonzales said: "it's never been the case where we've said we would never provide access." "All they have to do is ask." But the "highly classified" material could not be released to the public. The *Los Angeles Times* optimistically pronounced that the program "slowly but surely" was "being brought under the rule of law." But it still wanted to know whether FISC had approved only individual warrants or "just sign[ed] off on more general requests."

DNI McConnell circulated the administration bill to expand the powers under FISA by letting NSA monitor foreigners without FISC approval, extend FISA warrants for noncitizens to a year, allow surveillance without court order for a week, and give telecoms immunity from civil liability for cooperating with the government.[71] Specter called immunity "a pig in the poke" because the administration had never revealed "what these companies have done." At the SSCI hearing Rockefeller asked: "is the administration's proposal necessary?" Supported by Bond, Rockefeller requested all the legal opinions. "We cannot legislate in the blind." Whitehouse said: "the Attorney General has thoroughly and utterly lost my confidence." Feinstein complained that "there is nothing in this bill that confines the president to work within" FISA because McConnell had said that law "does not mean the president would not use" his commander-in-chief powers "in a crisis." The *New York Times* warned that the bill "would enact enormous, and enormously dangerous, changes" and "gut" FISA. It rejected the administration's "all-too-familiar dodge" that "the evidence of what is wrong with FISA was too secret to share with all Americans." The *Washington Post* urged Congress to proceed "with extreme caution." The "threshold issue" was whether the administration was "engaging in a farcical enterprise." The *Los Angeles Times* opposed immunity.

At the SJC on May 15 former Deputy Attorney General Comey offered a fuller account of the dramatic 2004 hospital incident.[72] Informed on March 4 that an OLC review of the program raised "concerns as to our ability to certify its legality," Ashcroft agreed changes had to be made. But that afternoon he was rushed to hospital with a severe case of gallstone pancreatitis and had his gallbladder removed on March 9. That day, after meeting with Gonzales, Card, and Addington, Cheney rejected the DoJ objections. The next day Comey refused to certify the program as its 45-day authorization was about to expire. That night he received an urgent notification from Janet Ashcroft, at her husband's bedside, that Gonzales and Card were on the way to persuade the Attorney General to reauthorize the program. Comey alerted FBI Director Mueller, and both raced to the hospital. Reaching the room minutes before Gonzales and Card, Comey found Ashcroft "pretty bad off." Mueller had ordered Ashcroft's security detail not to let Gonzales and Card eject Comey. Summoning his remaining strength, Ashcroft "lifted his head off the pillow and in very strong terms expressed his view of the matter, rich in both substance and fact," but added "that doesn't matter, because I'm not the Attorney General. There is the Attorney General." Gonzales and Card left without acknowledging the presence of Comey or Mueller. (Gonzales later claimed: "we went to the hospital to make sure that the attorney general had information about the approval of [the program by] the congressional leadership.") Card ordered an 11 p.m. meeting at the White House. When Comey explained he had brought Solicitor General Olsen as a witness because of "the conduct I had just witnessed," Gonzales shamelessly prevaricated: "What conduct? We were just there to wish him well." Early the next morning terrorist bombs killed more than 200 Spanish commuters. That day the White House approved the executive order for the program without a DoJ certification of its legality. Comey submitted his resignation effective March 12. "I couldn't stay if the administration was going to engage in conduct that the DoJ had said had no legal basis." (His letter, never sent but disclosed in September 2008, said he had encountered "an apocalyptic situation, where I and the DoJ have been asked to be part of something that is fundamentally wrong." He paraphrased Churchill –"this has been one of the institution's finest hours" – and Luther –"here I stand; I can do not [*sic*] other.") Comey's chief of staff, Ashcroft and his chief of staff, and Mueller had planned to join a mass resignation, which included US Attorney Rosenberg and OLC head Goldsmith. But after meeting separately that day with Comey and Mueller, Bush agreed to change the program.

Calling for Gonzales's resignation, Sen. Schumer said the story "crystallized Mr. Gonzales['s] view about the rule of law: that he holds it in minimum low regard." Schumer and three other Democratic senators reminded Gonzales that he had testified in 2006 that "there has not been any serious disagreement" about NSA wiretapping. Hagel said Gonzales "has failed this country" and "lost the moral authority to lead." But White House Press Secretary Snow insisted Bush had "full confidence in Alberto Gonzales." Comey's "splashy testimony" just rehashed "old conversations." "This is a program that saved lives, that is vital for national security, and furthermore has been reformed in a bipartisan way that is in keeping with everybody." The *Washington Post* found the account "so shocking it would have been unbelievable coming from a less reputable source" than "straight-as-an-arrow" Comey. The "bottom line" was "the administration's willingness ... to ignore its own lawyers." The next day the *Post* added that Gonzales "stonewalled Congressional inquiries and did [his] best to ensure that the shameful episode never came to light." Moschella had been similarly obstructive when he advised SJC in February that "in light of their inability to discuss ... confidential executive branch information ... we do not believe that Messrs. Ashcroft and Comey would be in a position to provide any new information." Even after Comey's testimony, Gonzales repeated: "I do not believe that these DoJ officials that you're identifying had concerns about this program." Publishing its third editorial in as many days, the *Post* said "it matters enormously ... whether the president was willing to have his White House aides try to strong-arm the gravely ill Attorney General into overruling the Justice Department's legal views." But Bush stonewalled: "I'm not going to talk about it." The *New York Times* said "the really big question" was what NSA had been doing *before* March 10, 2004. "The current Congress should resume a vigorous investigation of this egregious abuse of power."

DDC Judge Lamberth, who had been FISC chief judge, told the American Library Association:[73] "[Y]ou can fight the war and lose everything if you have no civil liberties left ... We still have to preserve our civil liberties. Judges are the kinds of people you want to entrust that kind of judgment to more than the executive." "What the president did with the NSA program" was "a worse way." Lamberth rebutted administration claims that the FISA process was too slow. Although FISC applications had been 40–50 written pages, after 9/11 he granted some "based on the oral briefing by the Director of the FBI." Within minutes after the attack on the Pentagon, "I had approved five FISA coverages on my cellphone."

Although Gonzales had assured HJC "all [you] have to do is ask," he disregarded its request for all the legal opinions about the program and his own account of the Ashcroft confrontation.[74] After OLC

Acting Director Bradbury also refused to produce the opinions, subcommittee chair Nadler threatened to subpoena them. "How can we begin to consider FISA legislation when we don't know what they are doing?" Three weeks later, after Kyl had blocked an SJC vote for a week, three Republicans joined the Democrats in approving subpoenas to Bush, Cheney, Hadley, and DoJ for the legal opinions and telecom agreements. Leahy said "the Committee has made no fewer than nine formal requests." The Deputy White House press secretary called it "unfortunate that Congressional Democrats continue to choose the route of confrontation."

In July 2007 Gonzales told SJC that the Gang of Eight had agreed on March 10, 2004 to continue the surveillance activity the DoJ had determined was illegal.[75] But two participants – Pelosi and Rockefeller – said there had been no consensus that the program should proceed; and three others maintained its legal foundation was not discussed. Gonzales also said the March 2004 confrontation did not involve the TSP but rather "other intelligence activities" he refused to describe. Claiming that Card and he "never had any intent to ask anything of [Ashcroft] if we did not feel that he was competent," Gonzales insisted the Attorney General had been "lucid" and did most of the talking. Rockefeller said Gonzales "once again is making something up to protect himself." Specter was going to review his testimony "to see if your credibility has been breached to the point of being actionable" (i.e., perjurious). Leahy announced: "I don't trust you … something I've never said to any cabinet member before." Whitehouse (D-RI) had "no choice but to believe that you intended to deceive us." Daschle said: "this appears to be another attempt to rewrite history." Feingold called Ashcroft's testimony "misleading at best." The *Washington Post* wrote that "something is terribly, terribly wrong when the Attorney General of the United States is called to testify under oath before Congress and much of the hearing revolves around his credibility – or lack thereof." He had lost "so much credibility that he should no longer serve in public office."

Two days later FBI Director Mueller told HJC that the 2004 confrontation concerned an NSA program about which he had "serious reservations."[76] After being briefed by Ashcroft, Mueller confirmed Comey's account of the incident. Schumer, Feingold, Feinstein, and Whitehouse asked DoJ to appoint a special prosecutor to investigate whether Gonzales had lied to Congress about the NSA program. Leahy raised the possibility of asking the DoJ IG to investigate Gonzales for perjury. White House press secretary Snow denounced this as "the latest in a long line of artful distortions by people who have spent the last six months hurling allegations at the Attorney General." A White House spokesman condemned "an out-of-control Congress which spends time … just trying to settle scores." The *New York Times* said "Americans have been waiting for months for Mr. Bush to fire Attorney General Alberto Gonzales, who long ago proved that he was incompetent and more recently has proved that he can't tell the truth." If the Solicitor General did not appoint a special prosecutor, Congress should impeach Gonzales. But Cheney declared himself "a big fan" of Gonzales, who "has done a good job under difficult circumstances," "testified truthfully," and "clearly" still had Bush's confidence. Paul McNulty, Gonzales's deputy, left to join Baker & McKenzie, observing cryptically: "it just couldn't be a better time to go into the private sector." When Mueller's notes confirming his recollection were released a month later, the *Washington Post* asked: "how many more times will Alberto R. Gonzales's credibility have to be shredded before his own sense of decency compels him to step down?"

In July 2007, the Sixth Circuit dismissed the first legal challenge to NSA wiretapping. Just weeks after the *New York Times* disclosure, the ACLU and the Michigan branch of the Council on American–Islamic Relations (CAIR) had sued in ED Mich on behalf of scholars, attorneys, journalists, and NGOs who communicated with the Middle East.[77] In May 2006 DoJ invoked state secrets and urged Judge Taylor not to consider the the plaintiffs' TRO motion, arguing that they lacked standing (because the plaintiffs could not know if they were targeted). But Taylor (appointed by Carter as the first black woman on the Detroit federal District Court) rebuffed DoJ, saying she would consider the TRO on June 11 and the DoJ motion to dismiss on July 10. When DoJ renewed its request, she replied: "you have conceded, have you not, that a program has been authorized?" DoJ objected that its White Paper was very general. Judge Taylor acknowledged not having read the classified parts of the government brief, which she could do only in Washington.

In August she found wiretapping illegal, describing it as "a secret program … which intercepts without benefit of warrant or other judicial approval … the international telephone and internet communications of numerous persons and organizations."[78] All the plaintiffs had a "well-founded belief" they were subjected to it. She rejected the invocation of the state secrets privilege to bar the lawsuit because of the government's "public admission" that the program existed; and she found that the privilege did not inhibit the government's ability to defend, since it claimed the program was authorized by the AUMF and the president's commander-in-chief powers. The plaintiffs alleged the program "had a significant impact on their ability to talk with sources, locate witnesses, conduct scholarship, engage in advocacy and communicate with persons who are outside the United States." It was "important to note" that if the court found no standing, the program "would be immunized from judicial scrutiny. It was never the intent of the Framers to give the President such unfettered control, particularly where his actions blatantly disregard the parameters clearly enumerated in the Bill of Rights." "Because of the very secrecy of the activity here challenged, Plaintiffs each must be and are given standing to challenge it." She found that the program violated the First and Fourth Amendments, FISA, and the separation of powers. The AUMF did not authorize it because that law "says nothing whatever of intelligence or surveillance" and, as a general statute, deferred to FISA. She rejected the argument that the president had inherent powers as commander-in-chief. "There are no hereditary Kings in America and no powers not created by the Constitution."

The ACLU agreed not to enforce the ruling before the government sought a stay (which Taylor denied but the Sixth Circuit granted). Sen. Reid welcomed the decision, which Kerry said showed that "no one is above the law," and Leahy and Schumer expressed support. The *New York Times* said the ruling "eviscerated the absurd notion" that the AUMF had authorized the program. Taylor's "careful, thoroughly grounded opinion" had achieved "what 535 members of Congress have so abysmally failed to do. She has reasserted the rule of law over a lawless administration." The *Washington Post* denounced the judgment as "a judicial misfire … full of sound and fury … neither careful nor scholarly, and … hard-hitting only in the sense that a bludgeon is hard-hitting." But it conceded Taylor "may well be correct in her bottom line." Law professors (even those sympathetic to the outcome) were generally critical of the reasoning. Rep. Hoekstra accused Taylor of "disarm[ing] America during a time of war." Bush "strongly disagree[d]" with the decision. Citing the plot to explode airplanes over the Atlantic, he said: "the American people expect us to protect them, and therefore, I put this program in place." The RNC issued a press release warning that "Liberal Judge Backs Dem Agenda to Weaken National Security" and circulated a petition against the judgment. Cheney told the Federalist Society that the decision was "an indefensible act of judicial overreaching."

After Bush ended the TSP, the government filed a brief in the Sixth Circuit (partly under seal) seeking dismissal on the ground that the case was moot "because no electronic surveillance is being conducted under the TSP."[79] It argued that any limit on eavesdropping "would be an unconstitutional encroachment on the executive's constitutional authority." The government also opposed release of the FISC order it claimed had superseded the TSP. The ACLU said the government "cannot argue that the case is moot because the government is currently in compliance with FISA, and at the same time expressly retain the authority to violate FISA tomorrow." James Bamford, a plaintiff (who had published two books critical of NSA), wrote in a *New York Times* op ed that the government's arguments were "a bit like a bank robber coming into court and arguing that, although he has been sticking up banks for the past half-decade, he has agreed to a temporary halt and therefore shouldn't be prosecuted." At oral argument Deputy Solicitor General Garre agreed with Judge Gilman that the government "could opt out at any time." Pressed by Judge Gibbons to explain how the plaintiffs had standing, the ACLU said lawyers representing Guantánamo detainees had to travel to the Middle East and Africa to do research they otherwise could have done by phone or email. When Garre called such standing "speculative," Gilman commented: "if the plaintiffs here don't have standing, who would possibly have standing?" The government refused to say if it had violated FISA, invoking state secrets.

In early July the Sixth Circuit reversed, finding that the plaintiffs lacked standing because they could not prove they had been wiretapped.[80] Although they might have a "reasonable" belief their communications were being intercepted, the "possibility remains that the NSA might *not* be intercepting." Therefore, "the anticipated harm is neither imminent nor concrete – it is hypothetical, conjectural, or speculative." Plaintiffs had failed to show "the exercise of governmental power … that directly regulates, proscribes, or compels" them. Their communicative ability would have been chilled even if the government had complied with FISA by obtaining a warrant. (Of course, it probably could not have gotten one.) Judge Batchelder quoted the Supreme Court: "The assumption that if respondents have no standing to sue, no one would have standing, is not a reason to find standing."[81] Judge Gilman dissented. The attorney plaintiffs had alleged that the program "forces them to decide between breaching their duty of confidentiality to their clients and breaching their duty to provide zealous representation." That was "sufficient to establish that they have suffered actual, imminent, concrete, or particularized harm." Whereas the majority asserted that "there is no evidence in the record from which to presume that the NSA is not complying with, or even exceeding, FISA's restrictions on the acquisition, retention, use, or disclosure" of communications, Gilman noted that Attorney General Gonzales and Principal Deputy DNI Hayden said the program had a "softer trigger" than FISA, using a "reasonable belief" standard rather than FISA's probable cause. Sen. Leahy regretted that the decision "closes the courthouse door." The *Washington Post* called it "sensible, carefully crafted and ultimately unsatisfying." "[T]hat the courts aren't likely to be the forum where we'll learn anything more … makes all the more compelling the need for Congress to closely monitor the program."

Bush submitted the Protect America Act (PAA) on July 28, 2007, warning that "every day that Congress puts off these reforms increases the danger to our nation … we are missing a significant amount of foreign intelligence." The Senate easily passed it on August 3 (60–28), the House the next day (227–183), and Bush signed it on August 5. The law (which expired in six months) dispensed with the requirement for a warrant if the DNI and Attorney General certified that a "significant purpose" of the interception was to obtain "foreign intelligence" and one communicant was "reasonably believed to be located outside of the United States." Telecoms were required to give NSA access, were compensated for this, and were granted immunity.

DNI McConnell told Congress in August that after the December 2005 exposé, the president acknowledged only NSA "targeting for interception without a court order of international communications of al Qaeda and affiliated terrorist organizations coming into or going out of the United States."[82] Democratic obstruction to revising FISA made McConnell's "blood pressure rise." Although the first FISC judge to hear an application in 2007 found the program "appropriate" and "legitimate," the second said: "if it's on a wire and it's foreign in a foreign country, you have to have a warrant." "It takes about 200 man hours to do one telephone number." In March "we needed thousands of warrants" from FISC, "but the most we could do was hundreds." The administration got a stay until the end of May, but then the National Intelligence Estimate reported a plan "to conduct terrorist operations to achieve mass casualties." At the end of May NSA was "losing capability." The White House insisted Congress strip FISC of jurisdiction over surveillance of foreigners. McConnell urged Congress to pass the administration's bill to extend PAA, warning that "we are actually missing a significant portion of what we should be getting." Democrats insisted on getting documents about the NSA program, "looking backwards," whereas he was a "forward-looking guy." McConnell also worried about telecom liability: "it would bankrupt these companies" if they lost "the suits at the value they're claimed" (discussed in Chapter 6 of the companion volume *Law's Trials*). The *New York Times* wished "McConnell had really wanted to enlighten the public." "Now we know the law was broken thousands of times." If each warrant application required 200 hours of paperwork, the "more than 218 top secret-cleared officials" would be "doing nothing all year but writing FISA applications."

On August 17 the White House asked SJC for more time to comply with its subpoena, but Leahy said "we've waited long enough" (nearly two months).[83] At the deadline three days later the White House counsel claimed that some documents might be covered by executive privilege and again sought more time. Returning to Washington after the August break, Leahy warned the White House not to "act like you're above the law." When the Senate reconvened, he planned to ask SJC to bring contempt charges. The White House accused him of "hyperbole." But the *Los Angeles Times* headlined its editorial "'Contempt' Is the Word," warning that the White House might be trying to "run out the clock until January 2009." Speaking to a group of lawyers, Kenneth Wainstein, Assistant Attorney General for National Security, said the president might claim constitutional authority to ignore any law Congress passed.

Gonzales resigned on August 27 (primarily because of the US Attorney scandal).[84] Bush praised him as "a man of integrity, decency and principle." Sen. Cornyn characterized Gonzales as "another casualty of the hyper-partisan atmosphere in Washington." But the *Washington Post* applauded the "unlamented exit," and the *New York Times* caustically said Gonzales "has finally done something important to advance the cause of justice" (evoking Malcolm's comment on the execution of the Thane of Cawdor in *Macbeth*, "nothing in his life became him like the leaving it," and Sydney Carter – another lawyer – accepting the guillotine in Dickens's *A Tale of Two Cities*: "it is a far, far better thing I do, than I have ever done"). The *Los Angeles Times* applauded the DoJ IG for continuing its investigation: although Gonzales's "excruciatingly belated resignation is welcome, it doesn't answer legitimate questions about whether and to what extent he misled Congress."

The September 5 HJC hearing again exhibited extreme political polarization.[85] Chairman Conyers urged his colleagues "to remember what truly makes this country different from those of our enemies is that we can begin by reading the Constitution and the Bill of Rights." Democrats eagerly accepted his challenge. Nadler (D-NY) deplored that the PAA – "rushed through Congress just before the August recess ... stampeded by administration fear-mongering and deception" – gave "unnecessary license for the administration to wiretap Americans without court supervision." "[N]o president, even this one, may become a law unto him or herself." He opposed telecom immunity because "suing the telecommunications companies might be the only way of getting into court" given that "the government is interposing a state secrets defense on any lawsuit" against it. Scott warned that the "vague notion of foreign intelligence ... includes information regarding trade deals, or international politics or any kind of diplomacy." In response to claims that warrants were too expensive, Delahunt (D-Mass) said: "to protect the Constitution and what we're concerned about in terms of our own values, no price is too high." "What we have found in the history of our country is that you can't trust the executive." Rep. Waters (D-Ca) was "frightened about the president of the United States and his ability to ignore the Constitution." Rep. Cohen (D-Tn) asked if any of the four witnesses knew "of any situations where the fact that some request for some surveillance went to the FISA court ... affected the security of this country?" Rep. Wasserman-Schultz (D-Fl) wondered if PAA would "allow the surveillance of an email between my child and an Iraqi child communicating ... about their views on the war." Criticizing DNI McConnell for claiming that "the debate in Congress means that some Americans are going to die," Rep. Johnson (D-La) asked: "how can there be a check and balance on the executive branch if there's no judicial oversight or legislative input into an executive function?" PAA authorized interception "if there was an American soldier in Iraq that sent an email to his girlfriend here in the United States." Rep. Sutton (D-Oh) accused the administration of "selectively releasing classified information when they think it will help their position." Rep. Susan Davis (D-Ca) said Republicans had "taken the position that if you don't agree [with the president] that somehow you're not sufficiently zealous in your concern for American security."

Republicans defended the administration. Rep. Smith (R-Tex) (the ranking member) complained that "the intelligence community has been hampered in gathering essential information." "Unfortunately, 90 percent of House Democrats voted to deny the director of national intelligence what he said he needed." Smith attacked "exaggerated claims of abuse or misleading claims of threats to civil liberties." Rep. Franks (R-Az) denounced "so-called civil liberties groups and liberal newspaper editors," who "have spent the last month spreading false allegations and misconceptions." It was important to "come back to earth a little bit" and remember "there were over 2,500 Americans that were almost instantaneously stripped of their right to live." The USA "face[d] a different kind of enemy than we've ever faced, an ideological one that lurks behind the shadows."

Telling the Senate Homeland Security and Governmental Affairs Committee that PAA had enabled NSA to learn about three men just arrested in a plot to attack US bases in Germany, DNI McConnell claimed that without it the USA would lose "50 percent of our ability to track, understand and know about these terrorists."[86] But other US and German officials said the terrorist cell had been discovered ten months earlier. McConnell also complained to HJC that it took too long to get FISC warrants: "we're falling further and further behind." The White House said Bush wanted the PAA made permanent.

Former OLC Director Goldsmith told SJC that Ashcroft, Comey, and the NSA General Counsel had never been fully briefed on the program.[87] When he led the internal DoJ review, Goldsmith "could not find a legal basis for some aspects of the program." "It was the biggest legal mess I had ever encountered." Comey and Ashcroft supported him. Addington had thundered that Goldsmith's obduracy might leave him with the blood of hundreds on his hands.

The HPSCI and HJC chairs drafted the RESTORE Act, authorizing FISC to issue one-year umbrella warrants, which the DoJ IG would audit, reporting quarterly to Congress.[88] A court order would be required to intercept communications with a domestic target. Telecoms received no immunity because the administration had not described their involvement. Rep. Hoyer (D-Md) explained: "at this point in time [it] would be blind immunity." Both committees approved the bill, voting along party lines. Calling it "a step backward," Bush insisted on immunity for "companies who are facing multibillion-dollar lawsuits." Rep. Harman accused him of playing "the fear card." The *Los Angeles Times* urged Bush to "make a full accounting of how – and on what supposed legal basis – the eavesdropping initiative was approved in the first place." The *Washington Post* praised the RESTORE Act as a "carefully crafted revision," but wanted immunity. Accusing the White House of "pumping out the same fog of fear and disinformation it used to push the bill through

Congress this summer," the *New York Times* supported immunity only if the administration disclosed "all surveillance conducted since 9/11." The White House threatened a veto. Democrats withdrew the bill after Republicans proposed an amendment authorizing unlimited surveillance of bin Laden and terrorist organizations, which Boehner said gave "Democrats a very simple choice: they can allow our intelligence officials to conduct surveillance on [the] likes of Osama bin Laden and al Qaeda or prohibit them from doing so and jeopardize our national security." Hoyer's spokesperson denounced this as a "cheap shot, totally political."

After nearly five hours of closed-door discussions, during which members got to see documents about the program, SSCI voted 13–2 for a bill granting immunity.[89] Feingold (who voted no with Wyden) said the documents "only further demonstrate that the program was illegal." Dodd (not on the committee) threatened to put a hold on the bill because of immunity. Leahy accused SSCI of "cav[ing]" in to the administration. He and Specter (SJC's ranking Republican) called the White House offer of documents in exchange for immunity "unacceptable." At the SJC hearing Leahy rejected immunity as "an after the fact free pass," and Specter agreed plaintiffs "ought to have their day in court." But former DoJ officials Ashcroft, Comey, Goldsmith, and Patrick Philbin urged Congress to grant "a just and fair protection for companies that allegedly responded to a call for assistance from the president in a time of national crisis." Ashcroft asserted in a *New York Times* op ed that immunity simply affirmed "longstanding principles of law," and denial would be "extraordinarily unfair." "A telephone company simply has no expertise in the relevant legal issues." (Ashcroft's consulting group was an AT&T lobbyist.) Feingold replied that "retroactive immunity sets a terrible precedent" if "we want companies and the government to follow the law in the future." The *Washington Post* equivocated: "the companies deserve some protection"; but lawmakers should "understand precisely what conduct they are immunizing." "[N]o lawmakers should accept this high-handed dismissal of Congress's legitimate needs." A few days later, however, the *Post* embraced the bill as a compromise. The administration offered to show the documents to Leahy, Specter, and SJC staffers with security clearance. Studs Terkel, a plaintiff in the Chicago wiretapping case, opposed immunity in a *New York Times* op ed. "By revealing the truth in a public forum, the American people will have the facts to play their historic, heroic role in putting our nation back on the path toward freedom." The *Los Angeles Times* favored the SSCI version but supported immunity only after the government made full disclosure.

Mark Klein, the former AT&T employee turned whistle-blower, spoke to the media for the first time when testifying against immunity.[90] He had seen documentation confirming that NSA was reading emails from 16 telecoms, many of which were unaware. "They're copying the whole internet." He decided to go public after Bush claimed the program just collected phone calls with suspected terrorists. Other evidence emerged that even before 9/11, NSA had been analyzing communications between the USA and Latin America for the Drug Enforcement Administration (DEA). NSA also had talked to AT&T about replicating its network center in New Jersey through a link to NSA headquarters, giving the agency access to *all* global phone and email traffic. A fiber optic line allegedly linked Verizon's New Jersey network center to the Quantico Marine Corps Base.

Just before Michael Mukasey was sworn in to replace Gonzales, OPR finally received security clearance.[91] Rep. Hinchey, who had sought the investigation, said "the new Attorney General understands that his responsibility is to the American people and the rule of law and not to any particular person, including the president." But hours later Mukasey joined DNI McConnell in opposing Leahy's bill. The same day the SJC voted 10–9 (Specter joining the Democrats) to eliminate immunity, and the House voted 227–189 along party lines to approve a bill without immunity. Bush again threatened a veto. James Woolsey, Bill Clinton's DCI, wrote in a *Los Angeles Times* op ed that if a "surveillance request made by the government is deemed improper, the government should be held accountable, not those who complied with its request." In the *New York Times*, DNI McConnell urged extension of the Protect America Act, which had "lived up to its name." "The intelligence community should spend its time protecting our nation, not providing privacy protections to foreign terrorists." "Those in the private sector who stand by us in times of national security emergencies deserve thanks, not lawsuits." Schumer objected that McConnell "does not explain why the administration continues to oppose … after-the-fact court oversight." Reps. Hoyer, Conyers, and Reyes (D-Tex) said the House bill "does precisely what Mike McConnell is asking for," but rejected immunity "because the administration refused to give us intelligence documents to explain what we'd be granting immunity for." Mukasey wrote a *Los Angeles Times* op ed supporting the SSCI bill. Criticizing FISC for refusing to release its decisions, the *New York*

Times declared: "the people have a right to know how [FISA], which is in the process of being revised, is being interpreted so they can tell their elected representatives what they think the law should be."

After a day-long Senate debate, Reid ruled there was insufficient time to consider the four bills: SSCI granting immunity, SJC denying it, Specter making the government liable, and Feinstein letting FISC decide immunity.[92] Dodd welcomed this "victory for American civil liberties." But DoJ declared it "absolutely urgent that legislation pass before the February 1 deadline," and the White House warned that "every day of delay brings us closer to reopening a dangerous intelligence gap." The *New York Times* accused Reid of trying to "shove a bad bill ... through the Senate." In August 2007 Bush, "as is his habit, falsely presented [PAA] as a matter of life and death." "The Constitution has been battered enough by rushing through major bills." The administration was pushing immunity "to make sure Americans never find out how much illegal spying the president ordered." The *Los Angeles Times* said making PAA permanent "would be a disaster for Americans' privacy." Mukasey again urged immunity: "we simply cannot afford to discourage the private sector from helping us to detect and prevent the next terrorist attack." But at a confirmation hearing for Mukasey's deputy, Leahy accused the Attorney General of having "no appreciation for the oversight role of Congress."

When Senate debate resumed in January 2008, Reid vowed to eliminate immunity, proposing a one-month extension of PAA "to allow lawmakers additional time to get this right."[93] Bush said: "we cannot afford to wait." But Reid dismissed the president's "irresponsible" veto threat as mere "posturing." Cheney warned the Heritage Foundation that Congress "must act now" or "our ability to monitor al Qaeda terrorists will begin to degrade." Asked how concerned he was on a scale of 1 to 10, Mukasey hyperbolically said "11." Sen. Bond (R-Mo) called delay "irresponsible" and "dangerous." When Reid began debate with the SSCI bill, the Senate voted 60–36 against eliminating immunity. Rockefeller said supportively: "the companies believed their cooperation was necessary, legal and would help stop future terrorist attacks." The administration finally gave the House the documents it had sought. The *New York Times* commented sarcastically: "the Senate (reportedly still under Democratic control) seems determined to help President Bush violate Americans' civil liberties and undermine the constitutional separation of powers." Reid, with the help of "other bullyable Democratic Senators like Mr. Rockefeller, Claire McCaskill,

Mary Landrieu and Ben Nelson," ensured the death of the superior SJC bill.

At the end of January two cloture motions failed.[94] Rockefeller now voted against, and Sens. Obama and Clinton left their presidential campaigns to do so. Both chambers unanimously extended PAA for 15 days. The same day Bush said in his State of the Union message that "the time to act is now"; but he signed the extension. Leahy accused Republicans of "obstructionism and delay." The *Los Angeles Times* supported the SSCI bill extending PAA for six years, which the Senate passed in mid-February (17 Democrats joining 49 Republicans and an Independent). Leahy accused "some people" of getting "cold feet when threatened by the administration." Praising the "good bill," Bush warned ominously: "at this moment, somewhere in the world, terrorists are planning new attacks on our country." Rep. Reyes said the legal documents recently provided by the administration "raise important questions, and it will take some time to gather enough information to make a determination on the issue of retroactive immunity." The House then rejected another 21-day extension of PAA (34 Democrats joining the Republicans). Rep. Hoyer called Bush's arguments a "basically dishonest" effort to "cover up … what might be disclosed" through lawsuits. When House Speaker Pelosi refused to schedule a vote, PAA expired. She contrasted FDR's rallying cry – "the only thing we have to fear is fear itself" – with Bush, who "tells the American people that he has nothing to offer but fear." Rep. Poe (R-Tex) said "there is probably joy throughout the terrorist cells throughout the world that the United States Congress did not do its duty today." Durbin accused Republicans of having "manufactured [a] political crisis" to "take [Americans'] minds off the state of the economy." Reid also charged Bush with a "reckless attempt to manufacture a crisis." Reyes wrote Bush: "if our nation is left vulnerable in the coming months, it will not be because we don't have enough domestic spying powers." Sen. Van Hollen (D-Md) said: "we have seen what happens when the president uses fearmongering to stampede Congress into making bad decisions. That's why we went to war in Iraq." Leading a walkout of scores of Republicans just before Democrats voted to cite John Bolton and Harriet Miers for contempt, Minority Leader Boehner protested that "we have space on the calendar today for a politically charged fishing expedition, but no space for a bill that would protect the American people from terrorists who want to kill us."

Bush left for Africa, warning that "our country is more in danger of an attack."[95] Boehner said: "the Democratic leaders ought to be held accountable for their inaction." But Reyes retorted that "there is no risk the program will go dark." Hoyer called the president's rhetoric "inaccurate" and "divisive – an attempt to stampede the House of Representatives to rubber-stamp legislation." Sen. McConnell accused Democrats of a payback for campaign contributions from trial lawyers suing the telecoms. "You're jeopardizing the entire existence of the [telecoms] by continuing to do this." Sen. Kennedy denounced this "dishonest and self-serving" allegation.

Mukasey and DNI McConnell warned the Intelligence Committees' Gang of Four that the country "is now more vulnerable to terrorist attack and other foreign threats ... these concerns are neither speculative nor theoretical."[96] Some telecoms had "delayed or refused compliance," and others threatened to do so. The Democratic chairs of the Intelligence and Judiciary Committees replied that the administration was "further politicizing the debate" by refusing the extension. Reid said "these latest scare tactics represent the president at his most unreasonable, irresponsible and misleading." Even after Mukasey and McConnell admitted that telecoms were still cooperating under orders authorized by the expired PAA, Bush reiterated that "the House's refusal to act is undermining our ability to get cooperation from private companies." The *Los Angeles Times* accused Bush of "characteristic exaggeration" but said House Democrats were "needlessly fixated" on the "sideshow" of immunity.

In May Sens. Whitehouse and Feinstein reported that John Yoo had said in his still-classified 2001 memo on wiretapping:[97] "[U]nless Congress made a clear statement in the FISA that it sought to restrict presidential authority to conduct warrantless searches in the national security area – which it has not – then the statute must be construed to avoid [such] a reading." Yoo ignored FISA's declaration that it provided the "exclusive means by which electronic surveillance ... and the interception of domestic wire, oral and electronic communications may be conducted." Whitehouse (a former US Attorney) said: "Once again, behind the veil of secrecy, OLC appears to have cooked up extravagant or misguided legal theories which would never survive the light of day." DoJ replied that "the 2001 statement addressing FISA does not reflect the current analysis of the Department" that the AUMF "confirmed and supplemented the President's Article II authority to conduct warrantless surveillance."

In June Sen. Bond warned that "we'll start losing intelligence capabilities" when the secret wiretapping orders issued under PAA expired in August.[98] His current proposal would let FISC grant immunity if "the Bush administration certifies that the companies were told the spying was legal." Mukasey said reverting to the old rules was "unthinkable" and passing a law was one of his highest priorities. The *New York Times* again accused Bush of "trying to scare Congress into expanding the president's powers to spy on Americans without a court order." His claim that FISA did not let NSA act quickly enough was "nonsense." Lawsuits against the telecoms "are the best hope of finding out the extent of Mr. Bush's lawless spying." Bush called Bond's "compromise" a "good bill" just before the House approved it, but Feingold denounced the "capitulation." The *Washington Post* "commended" both parties "for drafting legislation that brings the country's surveillance laws into the 21st century while protecting civil liberties and preserving important national security prerogatives." The *Los Angeles Times* said the House bill "takes a more realistic 'trust, but verify' approach," but hoped the Senate would improve it. The Senate voted 80–15 to debate it (thereby eliminating a filibuster threat by Feingold and Dodd). When Obama said he would vote for it, Paul Krugman accused him in a *New York Times* column of "showing disturbing signs of falling into the usual Democratic cringe on national security." The *Washington Post* said the attention given to immunity "far exceeds its underlying importance." The ACLU's Caroline Fredrickson accused the *Post* of ignoring the fact that the bill "would virtually do away with the role of the FISA court in overseeing new dragnet surveillance." Feingold warned that "Americans e-mailing relatives abroad or calling business associates could be monitored with absolutely no suspicion of wrongdoing by anyone." The *Post* acknowledged both of these points as "serious concerns, worth taking seriously," but still called the bill "a reasonable compromise." Morton Halperin wrote a *New York Times* op ed, repeating his warning two years earlier that the wiretapping program was "a far greater threat than the lawlessness of Richard Nixon" (who had targeted Halperin). The compromise bill "represents our best chance to protect both our national security and our civil liberties." The same day the *Times* urged the Senate to reject the bill, which "would needlessly expand the government's ability to spy on Americans and ensure that the country never learns the full extent of President Bush's unlawful wiretapping."

The FAA passed the House (293–129) on June 30 and the Senate (69–28, with 21 Democrats, including Obama – now the Democratic presidential candidate – joining the 47 Republicans and one Independent) on July 9; Bush signed it the next day.[99] Before the vote the RNC circulated Obama's December 17, 2007 statement that he "unequivocally opposes giving retroactive immunity to telecommunications companies" and would support a filibuster. Clinton, Reid, Durbin, and Biden voted no. Bond said the risk of US citizens being overheard was exaggerated "unless you have al-Qaeda on your speed dial." But Feingold (who sat on both SSCI and SJC) warned "that if more information is declassified about the program in the future … members of this body will regret that we passed this legislation." Section 702 allowed the Attorney General and DNI to authorize surveillance of non-US persons reasonably believed to be outside the USA. Without FISC approval, NSA could surveil US persons outside the United States for seven days if it had probable cause to believe they were agents of a foreign power. Telecoms received immunity.

In January 2009 FISCR published its August 2008 decision that under the (now expired) PAA, telecoms had to cooperate with government interception of the international phone calls and emails of US citizens.[100] The *Los Angeles Times* said the decision "vindicates Congress's decision to establish safeguards for such surveillance." Two ACLU lawyers wrote the *Times* that the FAA still "gives the executive branch virtually unchecked power to intercept Americans' international e-mails and telephone calls."

In April the DoJ and DNI semiannual certification of NSA programs to FISC (required by the FAA) disclosed "overcollection" of domestic communications between Americans, but claimed the problems had been corrected.[101] Members of both intelligence committees, however, expressed concern that NSA had ignored the law. The DoJ IG found "significant misconduct," including the wiretap of a Member of Congress who had visited the Middle East as part of an official delegation in 2005 or 2006. That was Rep. Harman, then ranking member of the House Intelligence Committee, who now expressed "outrage[]." A few days later it was reported that then DCI Goss had considered notifying Congress but had been blocked by Gonzales. In June Rep. Holt, chair of the House Select Intelligence Oversight subcommittee investigating the overcollection, said: "Some actions are so flagrant that they can't be accidental." A former NSA analyst described his 2005 training in "Pinwale," which archived foreign and domestic emails, letting NSA read a large number of messages to and from Americans as long as they fell within 30 percent of a permissible database search and Americans were not targeted. (This was thought to be the provocation for the Ashcroft hospital incident.) Two intelligence officials confirmed that the program was ongoing. The FAA authorized NSA to collect Americans' communications as an "incidental" by-product of investigating those "reasonably believed" to be made overseas. NSA was said to have exceeded FISC orders only 8–10 times; but each order involved hundreds of thousands of people. The *New York Times* wrote that "once again, the country is learning about how the federal government has been exceeding its legal authority and violating Americans' most basic rights." Congress should repeal the "deeply flawed" FAA.

In June the FAA aborted a lawsuit begun soon after the *New York Times* disclosures. At the end of January 2006 the EFF had sued AT&T in ND Cal on behalf of Tash Hepting and two other customers, alleging that the carrier had cooperated with NSA.[102] Kevin Bankston, EFF's lawyer, called the program "the biggest fishing expedition ever devised, scanning millions of ordinary Americans' calls and e-mails for suspicious patterns." One database was "Hawkeye," whose 312 trillion bytes contained nearly every telephone communication on the AT&T domestic network since 2001. In an affidavit for the plaintiffs, Mark Klein (the whistle-blower technician who retired from the company in 2004) said his employer had cooperated with NSA in 2003 to install equipment capable of "vacuum-cleaner surveillance" of internet traffic.[103] He described the room in which it was installed and interactions between AT&T colleagues and NSA; he had been told there were similar installations in San Jose, Los Angeles, San Diego, and Seattle. Four independent experts said Klein's documents identified equipment capable of monitoring large quantities of internet traffic, including email and phone calls, selecting messages by keywords, addresses, and countries of origin. The *New York Times* called on AT&T to "come clean, and stop immediately." The government filed a statement of interest and moved to dismiss for disclosure of state secrets.

On July 20, 2006 Judge Walker had denied a motion to dismiss this challenge to what he called "a massive warrantless surveillance program that illegally tracks the domestic and foreign communication records of millions of Americans."[104] Disregarding Klein's evidence and relying exclusively on statements by officials like President Bush and Attorney General Gonzales, Walker had concluded that the program's existence was not a secret. "The government has opened the door for judicial inquiry by publicly confirming and denying material information about its monitoring of communications content." "[T]he court takes seriously its constitutional duty to adjudicate the disputes that come before it … To defer to a blanket assertion of secrecy here would be to abdicate that duty … [and] sacrifice liberty for no apparent enhancement of security." Furthermore, the "plaintiffs could rely on many non-classified materials." By alleging that AT&T had given NSA access to its databases, the "plaintiffs have stated sufficient facts to allege injury-in-fact for all their claims." He also rejected AT&T's immunity claims.

But on August 21, 2008 the Ninth Circuit had reversed and remanded in light of the FAA grant of immunity to the telecoms.[105] And on June 3, 2009 Judge Walker dismissed this case (and the 32 others consolidated with it) because of this immunity, enacted "after months of election-year legislative exertion."[106] This "sui generis" law immunized "past, completed acts committed by private parties acting in concert with governmental entities that allegedly violated constitutional rights." Walker accepted the defendants' argument that plaintiffs retained the option of suing government officials, who were "the primary actors." He rejected the plaintiffs' separation of powers, nondelegation, due process and First Amendment challenges to FAA immunity. At the end of 2011 the Ninth Circuit affirmed, upholding the constitutionality of the immunity grant.[107]

Other judicial challenges failed for different reasons. On January 21, 2010, Judge Walker dismissed for lack of standing the lawsuit begun by Carolyn Jewel and others on September 18, 2008 against government employees (which would not be barred by FAA's grant of immunity to the telecoms).[108] The cases were "in essence, citizen suits seeking to employ judicial remedies to punish and bring to heel high-level government officials for allegedly illegal and unconstitutional warrantless electronic surveillance program[s]." But the plaintiffs merely alleged "interference with their telephone and/or broadband internet subscription," failing to "differentiate them[selves] from the mass of telephone and internet users." Both activities were "widespread on the scale of paying taxes." "The political process, rather than the judicial process may provide the more appropriate remedy for a widely shared grievance." The "requirement of concrete injury" to avoid unnecessary adjudication was "especially" important "when, as here, the constitutional issues at stake in the litigation seek judicial involvement in the affairs of the executive branch and national security concerns appear to undergird the challenged actions."

The Ninth Circuit reversed on December 29, 2011.[109] "Jewel alleged with particularity that *her* communications were part of the dragnet" at "AT&T's Folsom Street facility, through which all of

Jewel's communications allegedly passed" [original emphasis]. "[T]he harms Jewel alleges – invasion of privacy and violation of statutory protections – can be directly linked to this acknowledged surveillance program." "There is no real question about redressability." "[A]lthough the claims arise from political conduct and in a context that has been highly politicized, they present straightforward claims of statutory and constitutional rights, not political questions." On remand, Judge White (replacing Walker, who had retired) addressed a number of defenses on July 23, 2013.[110] "Given the multiple public disclosures of information regarding the surveillance program, the Court does not find that the very subject matter of the suit constitutes a state secret." "The Court finds that the state secrets privilege would apply to bar disclosure of significant materials relating to the alleged Program," but "may not set out precisely which matters." However, the court ruled that FISA preempted the privilege; and though sovereign immunity barred the plaintiffs' FISA damage claims, it did not bar those under the Wiretap Act and the Stored Communications Act.

But on February 10, 2015, Judge White granted the government summary judgment.[111] Having shown they were customers of AT&T, which helped NSA collect internet communications, the plaintiffs "have crossed the threshold requirement to establish that, should the program work as alleged, their communications would be captured in a dragnet Internet collection program." But they failed "to establish that the [§702] Upstream collection process operates in the manner in which the plaintiffs allege it does." Mark Klein "can only speculate about what data were actually processed and by whom in the secure room and how and for what purpose, as he was never involved in its operation." After reviewing the government's classified evidence, Judge White concluded that "adjudication of the standing issue could not proceed without risking exceptionally grave damage to national security." "The Court is frustrated by the prospect of deciding the current motions without full public disclosure of the Court's analysis and reasoning. However, it is a necessary by-product of the types of concerns raised by this case." Although Judge White certified his judgment for immediate appeal, the Ninth Circuit dismissed for lack of jurisdiction, remanding (for a second time) the undecided statutory and constitutional claims.[112]

In July 2009 the five Intelligence Community IGs (DoJ, DoD, CIA, DNI, and NSA) issued their Report on the President's Surveillance Program.[113] It suggested that the CIA crafted threat assessment memoranda to justify the surveillance activity and criticized the fact that

John Yoo was the only OLC official "read into" the program, with the result that his opinion was not peer-reviewed within OLC or approved by Director Bybee. Bush authorized the program *before* the first OLC memo, and Ashcroft approved it the day he was informed of the program. Yoo's memo mistakenly equated "interception of the international communications of U.S. persons in the United States" with permissible searches of people crossing borders. He asserted that the Fourth Amendment did not apply to surveillance in "direct support of military operations." Despite FISA, Yoo failed to discuss the Supreme Court's *Youngstown* opinion.[114] He did not accurately describe "Other Intelligence Activities" (beyond §215 surveillance). As early as 2002, DoJ was aware that prosecutors could have obligations to disclose to defense lawyers any information obtained through the program, but none was read into the program.

The report added details of the "hospital" incident. After replacing Yoo in May 2003, Philbin was read into the program, persuading Addington to read in Goldsmith as well. Concerned by Yoo's disregard of a critical FISA section undermining "the legality of certain aspects of the Other Intelligence Activities," the two communicated their doubts to Ashcroft and then to Addington. At Goldsmith's request, Comey was read into the program in January 2004 and soon agreed with those concerns. On March 5 (the day after Ashcroft's hospitalization) Goldsmith advised Comey that a "clear basis" existed for him to determine that he was Acting Attorney General and copied in Gonzales on the memo. Later that day Gonzales asked Goldsmith to confirm that Yoo's opinions "covered the program." Goldsmith, Philbin, and Comey "concluded that Yoo's memoranda did not accurately describe some of the Other Intelligence Activities." The next day (with Comey's approval) Goldsmith and Philbin told Addington and Gonzales these activities should stop. At a second meeting a day later, Addington and Gonzales expressed their disagreement to Goldsmith and Philbin. On March 9 Gonzales unsuccessfully tried to persuade Goldsmith to change his legal analysis or agree to a "30-day bridge." At noon that day Cheney told a meeting (which included Card, CIA Deputy Director McLaughlin, NSA Director Hayden, Gonzales, and FBI Director Mueller) that because Comey "has problems" with some activities, "the President may have to reauthorize without [the] blessing of DOJ." Mueller warned, "I could have a problem with that," and the FBI would "have to review legality of continued participation in the program." Comey, Goldsmith, and

Philbin were summoned to the White House and told by Cheney (in Gonzales's presence) that the program was "critically important" and "thousands" of lives would be at risk without it. Comey replied that as Acting Attorney General he could not authorize it, and White House officials refused to modify it. The next day the three DoJ officials reaffirmed their position. Later that day, at Bush's direction, Gonzales, Cheney, Card, Hayden, McLaughlin, and DCI Tenet briefed the Gang of Eight in the White House Situation Room. Gonzales claimed there was a consensus among the legislators that the program should continue; but three of the Democrats (Daschle, Rockefeller, and Pelosi) denied this. After the meeting Bush instructed Gonzales and Card to visit Ashcroft in the hospital. Card phoned, but Janet Ashcroft told an agent in her husband's security detail to tell Card that Ashcroft would not talk to him. Then, 25 minutes later, Card and Bush called to tell her Gonzales and Card were on their way. Comey (who had been informed) raced to the hospital, told his chief of staff to "get as many of my people as possible to the hospital immediately," and alerted Mueller and Philbin (who told Goldsmith). On arriving, Comey found Ashcroft "pretty bad off." Card and Gonzales appeared with the Presidential Authorization. After Ashcroft explained he was "not well," Gonzales said: "you know, there's a reauthorization that has to be renewed." Comey (now joined by Goldsmith and Philbin) advised Ashcroft "not to sign anything." Ashcroft expressed "very strong" reservations about the program's legal foundation, but added: "that doesn't matter, because I'm not the Attorney General. There is the Attorney General." Gonzales and Card left. Arriving soon thereafter, Mueller found Ashcroft "feeble, barely articulate, clearly stressed." Before leaving the hospital, Comey was called by a very upset Card and ordered to come to the White House immediately. Comey brought Solicitor General Olson, but the meeting was inconclusive.

The next morning, anticipating expiration of the Presidential Authorization, Bush signed with a certification by Gonzales, invoking the commander-in-chief's authority to disregard FISA and approve both the renewal and all previous authorizations. Later that day Gonzales told Goldsmith he could not challenge the president's authorization. At the same time Card met with Mueller, who warned that excluding DoJ from the meeting with the Gang of Eight and seeking Ashcroft's signature "gave the strong perception that the [White House] was trying to do an end run around the Acting" Attorney General. Card claimed (disingenuously) that Gonzales and he had been unaware Comey was Acting Attorney General. Comey drafted a resignation letter but was urged by Ashcroft's chief of staff to delay until the Attorney General, who was likely to resign with him, had recovered. Comey believed DoJ lawyers Charles Rosenberg, Daniel Levin, James Baker, David Ayres, and David Israelite also would resign. Goldsmith drafted a resignation letter citing the "shoddiness" of Yoo's opinions, "over-secrecy" of the program, and "shameful" hospital incident. Late that night Mueller also drafted a resignation. The next morning Comey and Mueller attended the regular White House daily threat briefing, after which Bush privately told Comey he had been unaware of the DoJ's legal concerns. Comey retorted that the president's staff had known them "for weeks." Bush said he only needed the program extended to May 6. After meeting with Mueller, Bush told the two to find a legal solution. Based on a memo from Goldsmith that the president could constitutionally rely on his commander-in-chief powers, Comey let the program continue. But four days later he wrote Gonzales that DoJ could not find legal authority for some Other Intelligence Activities, which had to stop immediately. Gonzales replied immediately that Comey had "a misunderstanding of the President's expectations regarding the Department of Justice." Gonzales was only "interested" in their "thoughts" about "alternative ways to achieve effectively" the goals the president had "addressed definitively." Nevertheless, Bush discontinued the disputed Other Intelligence Activities. On May 6, when the authorization expired, Goldsmith and Philbin submitted a 108-page memorandum finding that the AUMF authorized the president to order surveillance.

The *New York Times* said the "inescapable conclusion" of the IGs' "devastating" report was that "many of those programs could have been conducted just as easily within the law."[115] "A full accounting is the only way to ensure these abuses never happen again." Former DCI Hayden condemned the report's "hasty and deeply flawed judgments about the value and legality of what was a critical part of protecting America from further attack after 9.11." Yoo offered a lengthy justification of his discredited memo: "It is absurd to think that a law like FISA should restrict live military options against potential attacks on the United States." "The best way to find an al Qaeda operative is to look at all mail, text and phone traffic between Afghanistan and Pakistan and the U.S." The five IGs "were responding to the media-stoked politics of recrimination, not consulting the long history of American presidents who have lived up to their duty in times of crisis."

In September 2011 Sens. Wyden and Udall (D-NM) disclosed that DoJ had interpreted Patriot Act §215 – which allowed FISC to authorize the FBI to obtain "tangible things" – to empower NSA to obtain private information about people with no link to terrorism or espionage.[116] A recent DoJ statement that "section 215 is not a secret law, nor has it been implemented under secret legal opinions by the Justice Department" was "extremely misleading" because secret FISC opinions interpreted the law. Assistant Attorney General Weich replied: "we do not believe the executive branch is operating pursuant to 'secret law.'"

In May 2012 SSCI voted 13–2 (Wyden and Udall dissenting) to extend the FAA for five years.[117] A Wyden spokesman said: "before the Senate passes any long-term extension, we need to know how many law-abiding Americans are having their communications reviewed with these authorities." Feinstein also supported the SJC version of the extension, which required the ODNI IG to investigate its impact on US persons. Cautioning Congress "not so fast," the *Los Angeles Times* asked "whether Americans are being 'reverse-targeted' in operations purportedly aimed at foreigners abroad but actually designed to focus on someone in the U.S." The HJC approved the extension 23–11, but Rep. Conyers (ranking Democrat) warned that "the public does not yet have an adequate understanding of the extent of any adverse impact this Act has had on the privacy of American citizens." When the ODNI IG and NSA objected that such disclosure "would itself violate the privacy of U.S. persons," Wyden called this "one of the more remarkable statements I've heard in my time in public service." The NSA IG claimed that "such an estimate was beyond the capacity of his office." Robert Litt (ODNI General Counsel) said wiretaps could not target US persons. DNI Clapper had written to 11 Senate Democrats and two Republicans: "I strongly take exception to the suggestion that there is a 'loophole.'" The House voted 301–118 for the extension (74 Democrats joining almost all the Republicans in favor), which the *Washington Post* supported.

As expiration approached, Wyden threatened to block a vote unless the Senate debated additional safeguards for US persons.[118] Twelve senators joined him in asking how many US citizens had been surveilled. But both the administration and most Republicans backed the House bill, which the Senate passed 73–23 (30 Democrats joining all but three Republicans), after defeating both Wyden's proposal to require the DNI to tell Congress if NSA had collected any domestic communications (43–52) and an amendment by Merkley (D-Or) and

Lee (R-Ut) to require disclosure of significant FISC decisions (37–53). A few weeks later an ODNI review of FISC decisions concluded that *none* could be declassified.

In August the Ninth Circuit dismissed a lengthy legal challenge to eavesdropping. Eight years earlier the FBI had accidentally given a lawyer for Al-Haramain Islamic Foundation a copy of wiretapped conversations between its Saudi Arabian director (Suliman al-Buthe) and two of its American lawyers (Wendell Belew and Asim Ghafoor).[119] The recipient had circulated this to Belew and Ghafoor, another lawyer, and a director, discussed it with two more lawyers, and shared it with a *Washington Post* reporter. After discovering its mistake, the FBI had waited six weeks before demanding the document's return and had then seized Ghafoor's laptop to scrub the document. Prompted by the December 2005 *New York Times* exposé, Al-Haramain, Belew, and Ghafoor sued in federal court in Oregon in February 2006, seeking a declaratory judgment, injunction, and damages, and attaching the wiretap transcript (the "Sealed Document"). Three weeks later DoJ informed Jon Eisenberg, one of the plaintiffs' lawyers, that because the document "had not been properly secured," the FBI was on its way to the courthouse to take possession. Judge King refused to surrender it, asking "what if I say I will not deliver it to the F.B.I.?" AUSA Coppolino replied: "we obviously don't want to have any kind of a confrontation with you. But it has to be secured in a proper fashion." It was deposited in a "secure compartmented information facility" (SCIF) in Portland, but the FBI never retrieved the copies sent abroad. Observing at an August hearing that "it's probably gone many, many places," Judge King asked: "who is it a secret from?" The DoJ replied lamely: "it's a secret from anyone who has not seen it." "The document must be completely removed from the case, and plaintiffs are not allowed to rely on it to prove their claims." Judge King retorted: "There is nothing in the law that requires them to purge their memories." Channeling Orwell, Eisenberg objected: "they claim they own the portions of our brains that remember anything."

In September Judge King ruled that the plaintiffs could challenge the eavesdropping.[120] Because NSA's surveillance program had been disclosed by the president, Attorney General, and DoJ, it "is not a secret." King had "determined that there is no reasonable danger that the national security would be harmed if it is confirmed or denied that plaintiffs were subject to surveillance." Although he had returned the incriminating documents to the FBI, the plaintiffs could establish standing by sworn secret statements "attesting to the contents of the documents from their memories." "It is no longer a secret to plaintiffs whether their communications were intercepted as described in the sealed documents ... The existence of the surveillance program is not a secret, the subjects of the program are not a secret, and the general method of the program – including that it is warrantless – is not a secret." After the plaintiffs described the document in a sealed filing attached to their summary judgment motion, the DoJ complained to Judge King that the plaintiffs' lawyers had "mishandled information in the classified document" by preparing filings on their own computers and sought to inspect and delete the files.

In November 2007 the Ninth Circuit reversed and remanded.[121] Judge McKeown began by decrying that the administration had "spoon-fed" the public information about the TSP, moving "at lightning-speed to quell public concern" aroused by the *New York Times* disclosure. But "in light of extensive disclosures about the TSP, the government is hard-pressed to sustain its claim that the very subject matter of the litigation is a state secret." Nevertheless, "allowing Al-Haramain to reconstruct the essence of the document through memory ... countenances a back door around the privilege and would eviscerate the state secret itself." Without the Sealed Document, the plaintiffs could only "speculate" that they had been wiretapped and therefore lacked standing unless FISA preempted the privilege, a question the Circuit remanded to the District Court. In July 2008 Judge Walker (to whom the case had been transferred when several cases were consolidated in ND Cal) held that FISA did preempt the state secrets doctrine.[122] But in a Catch-22, he ruled that to claim under FISA §1810, the plaintiffs had to prove they were "aggrieved persons" without using the Sealed Document, which they had failed to do. Commenting wryly that "it is testament to the obstacles to seeking civil remedies for alleged violations of FISA that section 1810 has lain 'dormant for nearly thirty years,'" he allowed the plaintiffs to amend their complaint.

In March 2010 he granted the plaintiffs summary judgment, denying the defendants' motion to dismiss, which "largely ignored the court's prior rulings regarding FISA's displacement" of the state secrets privilege.[123] "[D]efendants contended that only the government's frank admission of the unlawful electronic surveillance ... would suffice" to prove standing. But in January 2009 he had found that the plaintiffs had made a prima facie case that they were aggrieved persons. In order that "the entire remaining course of this litigation [not be] ex parte," which "would deprive plaintiffs of due process to an extent inconsistent with Congress's purpose in enacting FISA's sections 1806(f) and 1810," he had directed the government to process security clearances for the plaintiffs' litigation team. Although he "directed defendants to review their classified submissions," they insisted *nothing* could be declassified. "What followed were several months of which the defining feature was defendants' refusal to cooperate with the court's orders punctuated by their unsuccessful attempts to obtain untimely appellate review." "In response to the court's directive to 'inform the court how [they intend] to comply with the January 5 order … defendants presented three similar-sounding alternatives, all of which appeared geared toward obtaining a stay of this court's proceedings pending review by the court of appeals." After the government found two of the plaintiffs' attorneys suitable for top secret/secure compartmented information clearances, the NSA Director and others "refused to cooperate with the court's orders, asserting that plaintiffs' attorneys did not 'need to know' the information that the court had determined plaintiffs attorneys would need." "[D]efendants refused to agree to any terms of the protective order proposed by plaintiffs and refused to propose one of their own."

In light of this, Walker ordered the defendants to show cause why they should not be prohibited from denying that the plaintiffs were "aggrieved persons" and why the court should not deem liability established. He directed the plaintiffs to rely only on nonclassified evidence; if the defendants relied on the Sealed Document or other classified evidence, he would produce it to those of plaintiffs' counsel with security clearance. "[T]o deem plaintiffs 'foreclosed' by … the court of appeals' 2007 opinion from building their case with later-disclosed, publicly-available evidence – especially in light of defendants' intransigence … and the limited progress made to date along the normal arc of civil litigation – would violate basic concepts of due process." He rejected the defendants' theory that "executive branch officials may treat FISA as optional and freely employ the SSP [state secrets privilege] to evade FISA, a statute enacted specifically to rein in and create a judicial check for executive-branch abuses of surveillance authority." In contending that "this is not a FISA case and defendants are therefore free to hide behind the SSP all facts that could help plaintiffs' case," especially the defendants' failure to obtain a warrant, "defendants take a flying leap and miss by a wide margin." "Defendants' possession of the exclusive knowledge whether or not a FISA warrant was obtained, moreover, creates such grave equitable concerns that defendants' must be estopped from arguing that a warrant might have existed." "Defendants' nit-picking of each item of plaintiffs' evidence, their remarkable insinuation (unsupported by any evidence of their own) that the al-Buthi/al-Timimi intercepts might have been pursuant to a FISA warrant and their insistence that they need proffer nothing in response to plaintiffs' prima facie case do not amount to an effective opposition to plaintiffs' motion for summary judgment." Having established liability, he gave the plaintiffs two weeks to decide whether to drop their other claims and submit a damages proposal. Even though the individual plaintiffs did not seek actual damages, he granted each one $20,400 liquidated damages and awarded the requested attorney's fees of $2,515,387.09 and $22,012.36 costs.

The *Los Angeles Times* applauded Walker for having "ratified a conclusion many Americans reached long ago – that the administration exceeded its legal authority in the war on terror" – and urged Holder not to appeal.[124] The *New York Times* said the ruling "provides a chilling account of the relentless efforts by the Bush administration and then the Obama administration to kill the civil lawsuit." Because presidential candidate Obama had pledged to reverse Bush's abuses, President Obama "should read this court ruling with chagrin and eliminate warrantless spying."

But in August 2012 the Ninth Circuit reversed, finding that FISA §1810 did not waive sovereign immunity.[125] Although this "effectively brings to an end the plaintiffs' ongoing attempts to hold the Executive Branch responsible for intercepting telephone conversations without judicial authorization," the court could not "let that occur without comment on the government's recent, unfortunate argument that the plaintiffs have somehow engaged in 'game-playing.'"

> In light of the complex, ever-evolving nature of this litigation, and considering the significant infringement on individual liberties that would occur if the Executive Branch were to disregard congressionally-mandated procedures for obtaining judicial authorization of international wiretaps, the charge of "game-playing" lobbed by the government is as careless as it is inaccurate. Throughout, the plaintiffs have proposed ways of advancing their lawsuit without jeopardizing national security … That their suit has ultimately failed does not in any way call into question the integrity with which they pursued it.

Another legal challenge failed months before Edward Snowden's disclosure. The day the FAA was enacted (July 10, 2008), AI sued to enjoin it. A year later SDNY Judge Koeltl dismissed for lack of standing.[126] The plaintiffs' alleged fear their communications would be monitored was "abstract," indeed "uniquely attenuated": "whether an order will be sought that affects the plaintiffs' rights, and whether such an order would be granted by the FISC, is completely speculative." For the same reason, plaintiffs could not base standing on the costs they incurred to avoid surveillance. Urging the Second Circuit to correct this "serious error," the *New York Times* said: "the chilling impact is neither trivial or [*sic*] merely speculative. Plaintiffs have had to take costly and inconvenient steps to safeguard their privacy, including travel to foreign countries to gather information." The New York City Bar, Reporters Committee for Freedom of the Press, and others filed amicus briefs.

In March 2011 the Second Circuit reversed.[127] Judge Lynch noted that the FAA did not require the government to identify "the particular target or facility to be monitored," and FISC merely verified that the government had made the proper certification. Plaintiffs could show standing by demonstrating "it was not unreasonable for them to incur costs" out of "an actual and well-founded fear" that "the government will intercept their communications." "They have asserted that the FAA permits broad monitoring through mass surveillance orders that authorize the government to collect thousands or millions of communications." It was "fanciful" to "question whether the government will ever undertake broad-based surveillance" since that was the FAA's declared purpose. The plaintiffs' fears "are by no means based on 'mere conjecture,' delusional fantasy, or unfounded speculation," but rather "on a reasonable interpretation of the challenged statute and a realistic understanding of the world." "It verges on the fanciful to suggest that the government will more than rarely fail to comply with the formal requirements of the FAA." In 2008 FISC approved all but one of the government's 2,082 applications. The plaintiffs' testimony that they had altered their conduct out of fear of surveillance was "uncontroverted." "The risk of being monitored by the government threatens the safety of their sources and clients, impedes their ability to do their jobs, and implicates the attorneys' ethical obligations." The *New York Times* hoped other challenges would follow, but feared the government would invoke state secrets.

In September the en banc Second Circuit denied rehearing (6–6).[128] Judge Raggi dissented (writing for Dennis, Jacobs, Cabranes, Wesley, and Livingston). Forbearance could confer standing only when a plaintiff would "*certainly*" be subject to surveillance [original emphasis]; mere "subjective fear" was insufficient. Otherwise "every mobster's girlfriend who pays for a cab to meet with him in person rather than converse by telephone would be acting on a not-irrational fear" and have standing. Plaintiffs seeking to nullify an act of Congress must satisfy an "especially rigorous" standing inquiry. Because they were not surveillance targets, they must make a "much more" convincing showing of standing. "In the absence of any evidence of actual surveillance practices," the court had to presume the government would conform to the statute and the Constitution. "[F]or the price of a plane ticket, plaintiffs can transform their standing burden from one requiring a showing of actual or imminent FAA interception to one requiring a showing that their subjective fear of such interception is not 'fanciful,' 'irrational' or 'clearly unreasonable.'" Whether the plaintiffs will ever be subject to surveillance "remains a matter of complete conjecture." "[H]ow reasonable can it be to interpret the FAA … to authorize, on its face, interceptions that invariably will violate that amendment?" There was "no reason to think that the Article III judges who serve on the FISA court will be timid in exercising" their authority. Judge Livingston wrote a dissenting opinion (joined by the other five) to emphasize that injury must be "actual or imminent," not merely "probabilistic." "[T]he Constitution sets limits not only on the power of Congress … but also on that of judges. It is thus not the 'glory of our system'" (as Judge Lynch claimed) "that elected leaders must answer to unelected judges whenever a challenge is asserted." The panel opinion "provokes a reasonable fear … not of an obstinate closure of courthouse doors" but "of judges arrogating to themselves a power inconsistent with both our constitutional design and the role of courts in a democratic society." Judge Jacobs dissented separately to offer a "glancing review of the merits." "These plaintiffs and their lawyers are claiming a policy-making role on matters that have no Fourth Amendment impact on them." "To support the otherwise-mysterious idea of injury to these plaintiffs (and causation), the panel opinion relies entirely (even credulously) on affidavits submitted by the plaintiffs, describing their supposed anxieties. But these affidavits employ all the lawyer's arts to convey a devious impression" and were "craftily worded to skirt actual falsehood" through "studied vagueness and anticipations of the conveniently unknown future."

> [T]he purpose of this lawsuit is litigation for its own sake – for these lawyers to claim a role in policy-making for which they were not appointed or elected, for which they are not fitted by experience, and for

> which they are not accountable. As far as I can see, the only purpose of this litigation is for counsel and plaintiffs to act out their fantasy of persecution … to make themselves consequential rather than marginal, and to raise funds for self-sustaining litigation … the frivolous nature of the claim … bears similarity to a *pro se* plaintiff's allegation that the CIA is controlling him through a radio embedded in his molar.

Defending his panel's decision, Judge Lynch replied that in deciding a summary judgment motion "the court's obligation to question assertions of fact does not extend permission for judges to substitute their own beliefs – derived from their own notions about what is and is not likely to be true" – for the plaintiffs' factual assertions, which "the government, which has ample resources to litigate those matters declines to challenge." Lynch found it "hard to take seriously" the dissenters' claim that the plaintiffs' fear "that their overseas contacts are likely to be government targets under the FAA" was merely "speculative." It was "the suggestion that the government is not certain to use" the authority conferred by the FAA that "is fanciful."

> To reject the plaintiffs' arguments not because they lack merit, but because we refuse to hear them, runs a much graver risk than whatever invasion of plaintiffs' privacy might be occasioned by the surveillance authorized by the challenged statute. The Constitution sets limits on the powers even of Congress. It is the glory of our system that even our elected leaders must defend the legality of their conduct when challenged. Short-circuiting that process risks not only that we will be governed by unconstitutional laws, but also that legitimate exercises of the lawmaking power will exist under a cloud, undispelled by the light of objective reasoning.

The *New York Times* applauded this "well-deserved setback to the Justice Department's accountability avoidance strategy." Chief Judge Jacobs's "gratuitous attack on the plaintiffs and their lawyers … embarrassed the Appeals Court he is supposed to lead and cast serious doubt on his judicial impartiality." In May 2012 the Supreme Court granted certiorari. In anticipation of oral argument, the *Times* argued that finding standing "would not require a legal stretch."[129] The lawyers and human rights, labor, legal, and media organizations had "taken expensive and burdensome steps to avoid the risk of government eavesdropping." Ethical rules required lawyers to do so. "Should the court acquiesce to the government's cramped reading of standing … it would foreclose any meaningful judicial review" and do "serious …

damage to the nation's system of checks and balances." When Justice Sotomayor asked during oral argument "is there anybody who has standing," Solicitor General Verrilli said there might be if the government prosecuted. But Justice Ginsburg did not "see a real person who would be subject to a federal charge who could raise an objection." Justice Scalia retorted that this "just proves that under our system of separated powers, it is none of our business." Verrilli evaded Justice Kagan's question about whether an ethical lawyer fearing surveillance should communicate with clients. Justice Kennedy said such a "lawyer would engage in malpractice if he talked on the telephone with some of these clients, given this statute." Kagan observed that "if you assume that information is the lifeblood of journalism … their sources and their information have dried up as a result of this statute."

In February 2013, the Supreme Court reversed 5–4, finding no standing.[130] Justice Alito (writing for Roberts, Scalia, Kennedy, and Thomas) held that the plaintiffs' future injury was based on a "highly speculative" fear, which was not traceable to the FAA. They "merely speculate and make assumptions" about FAA surveillance, but "cannot manufacture standing merely by inflicting harm on themselves based on their fears of hypothetical future harm that is not certainly impending." The FAA could be challenged by telecoms or criminal defendants. Justice Breyer dissented (joined by Ginsburg, Sotomayor, and Kagan). The harm the plaintiffs feared "is as likely to take place as are most future events that commonsense inference and ordinary knowledge of human nature tell us will happen." "Government has a strong *motive* to listen to conversations of the kind described." "Government's *past behavior* shows that it has sought, and hence will in all likelihood continue to seek, information about alleged terrorists and detainees through means that include surveillance." "Government has the *capacity* to conduct electronic surveillance" [original emphasis]. (Breyer was implicitly paraphrasing the police mantra that a suspect had motive, means, and opportunity.) FISC did not meaningfully limit this: in 2011 it approved all 1,674 applications. "The Court has often *found* standing where the occurrence of the relevant injury was far *less* certain than here." "[C]ourts have often found *probabilistic* injuries sufficient to support standing" [original emphasis]. "How could the law be otherwise?" The *New York Times* said the Court had "severely damaged the rule of law" by its "clear-cut abdication of its fundamental role in the American constitutional system of checks and balances."

EDWARD SNOWDEN[131]

On June 5, 2013 (after notifying the Obama administration) the *Guardian* reproduced an April order by FISC Judge Vinson under Patriot Act §215, directing Verizon to give NSA "on an ongoing daily basis" logs of all calls by tens of millions of customers "between the United States and abroad" or "wholly within the United States."[132] Although the source was not disclosed, this was the first publication of documents former NSA contractor Edward Snowden had shown to documentary filmmaker Laura Poitras, who had enlisted two journalists: the *Guardian*'s Glenn Greenwald and the *Washington Post*'s Barton Gellman. Minimizing its significance, Sen. Feinstein said the opinion involved a "lawful" program "briefed to Congress" and represented just "an exact three-month renewal of what has been the case for the past seven years." At the same time, newspapers revealed two other programs. PRISM (launched in 2007) extracted audio, video, photos, emails, documents, and collection logs from nine US internet companies (Microsoft, Yahoo, Google, Facebook, Paltalk, AOL, Skype, YouTube, and Apple), letting analysts track the movements of the communicator. The President's Daily Brief cited information from PRISM 1,477 times in 2012, constituting nearly one out of seven intelligence reports. A parallel program, BLARNEY, gathered metadata: "address packets and device signatures." DNI Clapper said PRISM "cannot be used to intentionally target any U.S. citizen or any other U.S. person." (It did not need to, since it was virtually universal.) FISC "only allows the data to be queried when there is a reasonable suspicion, based on specific facts, that the particular basis for the query is associated with a foreign terrorist organization." Snowden's leaks threatened "irreversible harm" to national security.

The ACLU promptly sued in SDNY to compel release of the FISC opinions.[133] Sixteen members of Congress (a majority of them Republicans) filed an amicus brief. Sen. Rand Paul (R-Ky) and five other Republican legislators sued to challenge the program's constitutionality.[134] Sens. Paul, Merkley, Wyden, and Udall called for more disclosure, which Wyden hoped would "force a real debate" on the Verizon program, something he could only hint about before.[135] But Graham said it would be "crazy" not to eavesdrop, and Chambliss claimed that "every member of the United States Senate has been advised of this." Feinstein concurred. Reid agreed "this isn't anything that is brand new." But Mikulski (D-Md) (Appropriations Committee chair) said: "'fully briefed' doesn't mean we know what's going on." Durbin echoed her: "to say that there's Congressional approval suggests a level of information and oversight that's just not there." Rep. King (R-NY) agreed: "people ought to have at least a general idea of what's going on." "It makes me nervous that all those phone records are in the possession of the National Security Agency." Paul called it "an astounding assault on the Constitution." But Reps. Rogers (R-Mich) and Ruppersberger (HPSCI chair and ranking Democrat) assured the public that the program "is consistent with the FISA … and approved by a federal court."

The *New York Times* said: "the Obama administration issued the same platitude it has offered every time President Obama has been caught overreaching in the use of his power: terrorists are a real menace and you should just trust us to deal with them." But "the administration has now lost all credibility."[136] A second editorial urged Congress to require that FISC publish its decisions and limit eavesdropping to "people suspected of terrorism." The *Washington Post* said: "for the public to be able to make a reasonable assessment of whether these programs are worth the security benefits, it needs more explanation," repeating this in a second editorial. Rep. Sensenbrenner concurred: "as the author of the Patriot Act, I am extremely troubled by the F.B.I.'s interpretation of this legislation." He wrote in a *Guardian* op ed that "the Patriot Act was never intended to allow the daily spying the Obama administration is conducting." "How can every call that every American makes or receives be relevant to a specific investigation?" "[M]ost" members of Congress, including himself, were not briefed. Reed Hundt (FCC chairman 1993–97) wrote the *New York Times* that "a founding principle of our jurisprudence is that you're innocent until proved guilty; data mining is based on the opposite principle." But the *Wall Street Journal* declared that "the data sweep is worth it if it prevents terror attacks." And former Attorney General Mukasey said "claims of pervasive spying … appear not merely exaggerated, but downright irrational."

Claiming to "welcome this debate," Obama reassured Americans that "nobody is listening to your telephone calls." "It's important to understand that your duly elected representatives have been consistently informed on exactly what we're doing." The *New York Times* felt the administration's "newfound interest in openness" was "a little hard to take seriously."[137] Before Congress had extended the FAA the previous December, Feinstein declared that eight recent terrorism cases "show the program has worked." The administration claimed it had uncovered Najibullah Zazi's plot by eavesdropping. But Sens. Wyden and Udall maintained that "all of the useful information that it has provided appears to have also been available through other collection methods that do not violate the privacy of law-abiding Americans." Nearly fifty legislators from both parties expressed concern. Three Democratic Representatives were critical: Merkley said the program was "not something that's briefed outside the Intelligence Committee," Ellison knew "almost nothing" about it, and Sinema protested that freshmen lawmakers had not been informed.

The exposé had global repercussions.[138] An Austrian MEP (president of the Socialists and Democrats group) asked the European Commission to determine whether EU laws had been broken, which would affect forthcoming trade talks. The EU Commissioner for Home Affairs sought more information. Viviane Reding, European Commission Vice President and EU Commissioner for Justice, wrote Attorney General Holder seeking "swift and concrete answers" to nine detailed questions about whether information on EU citizens had been gathered "on a large scale." German Chancellor Merkel's spokesman said that "this will be one of the things the Chancellor addresses when President Obama is in Germany." The German Interior Minister wanted to know whether Germans' right to privacy had been infringed, and the Justice Minister called the revelations "deeply disconcerting." After Snowden disclosed that NSA tapped Chinese mobile phone companies to read millions of text messages, and hacked computers at Tsinghua University and a major telecom headquartered in Hong Kong and Singapore, an editorial in the state-run *China Daily* said that "Snowden's crime, if any, pales in comparison with the actions of the U.S. officials who authorized and operated the cyberespionage program."

The second *Guardian* story showed that in March NSA had collected 97 billion pieces of data from the Internet, 3 percent (or nearly 3 billion) from the USA.[139] Responding to administration claims that the two Intelligence Committees has been briefed "multiple times," Wyden and Udall said the administration had misrepresented the use of its Patriot Act §215 "business records" authority. "Multiple senior officials have stated that the U.S. intelligence agencies do not collect information or dossiers on 'millions of Americans.'"

Public opinion was mixed, partly because the technical details were confusing. A WP/Pew Research Center poll after the story broke found that 56% felt the program was acceptable. CBS News found that nearly 60% disapproved of collecting ordinary Americans' phone records, but three-quarters approved tracking Americans suspected of terrorist activity. A later CBS poll found that 38% supported tracking phone records and 58% were opposed. A Gallup poll found that 53% disapproved of government surveillance and only 37% approved. A poll in early July found that 51% favored eavesdropping on all phone calls and 45% were opposed; 54% thought the program violated Americans' privacy, but 44% disagreed. Later that month three-fourths said the programs infringed privacy rights and half feared encroachments on their own privacy. A surprising 62% of Tea Party supporters disapproved of NSA eavesdropping. Another July poll found that 70% of Democrats and 77% of Republicans felt the programs invaded privacy and just over half of each believed this was unjustified. At the end of July a Pew Research Center poll found that 47% were more concerned that the government had gone too far in restricting civil liberties, while only 35% believed it had not gone far enough (the first time more were concerned about civil liberties than security since polling began in 2004). Almost twice as many conservatives as liberals were concerned about NSA spying.

Two days after the story broke Snowden announced: "I have no intention of hiding who I am because I know I have done nothing wrong."[140] "I am willing to sacrifice" career and personal life "because I can't in good conscience allow the U.S. government to destroy privacy, internet freedom and basic liberties for people around the world." Feinstein contemplated hearings, but added that "instances where this has produced good" intelligence were "all classified." She and Rep. Rogers felt Snowden should be prosecuted. Rep. Boehner called him a "traitor." Sen. McCain (R-Az) wanted him "prosecuted to the fullest extent of the law." On *Fox News*, Cheney called him a criminal and traitor. Rep King said Greenwald should be arrested (he lived in Brazil). Sen. Paul, by contrast, threatened a class action lawsuit against the internet and phone companies. The *Washington Post* called the eavesdropping debate "worthy" but criticized "grandstanding politicians" like Paul. Reid said senators had "had every opportunity" to be briefed. A poll found that 31% thought Snowden was a patriot and only 23% that he was a traitor; 35% thought he should not face charges, 25% that he should. Another poll found that 43% felt Snowden should be charged with a crime but 48% were opposed.

Many media voices were hostile. The *Wall Street Journal* said dismissively that NSA's "main offense so far seems to be the quality of those it trusts with security clearances." In his *New York Times* column Thomas Friedman expressed greater concern "about another 9/11" than about "potential government abuse of privacy," which "does not appear to have happened." Snowden was no "heroic whistle-blower." In his *Times* column, David Brooks accused Snowden of betraying "honesty and integrity," "his friends," and "employers," the cause of open government," "the privacy of us all," and the "Constitution." *Washington Post* columnists were equally vitriolic. Matt Miller deplored Snowden's "grandiosity." Those who called him a hero were "dead wrong." David Ignatius declared that "Snowden is challenging the rule of law." Marc Thiessen urged prosecution of Greenwald and the *Post* (his own employer) for publishing classified information on communications intelligence. But the *New York Times* decried the "false choice" between security and "democratic freedoms and basic rights." Government use of metadata "undermine[d] constitutional principles of personal privacy and freedom from constant government monitoring," was "totally at odds" with the Fourth Amendment, and "also attacks First Amendment values of free speech and association." The same day the *Times* criticized Boehner and Feinstein for "overcharging" Snowden with treason. Although he "clearly committed" some crimes, he "may well be going to jail for exposing practices that should never have been secret in the first place."

Two days later the USA charged Snowden in ED Va with violating the Espionage Act (which carried a possible death penalty) and stealing government property for the purpose of disclosing classified information, and it asked Hong Kong to extradite him. Days later Snowden flew to Moscow, probably hoping for asylum in Cuba, Venezuela, or Ecuador.[141] In response to a request to issue a provisional arrest warrant, Hong Kong claimed it never received the necessary information. The USA asked Russia to return Snowden, but the two countries had no extradition agreement.

An exchange at SSCI three months earlier now assumed greater significance.[142]

SEN. WYDEN: Last summer, the NSA director was at a conference and he was asked a question about the NSA surveillance of Americans. He replied … "The story that we have millions or hundreds of millions of dossiers on people is completely false" … I wanted to see if you could give me a yes or no answer … does the NSA collect any type of data at all on millions or hundreds of millions of Americans?

DNI CLAPPER: No, sir.

When Wyden expressed disbelief, Clapper added: "not wittingly. There are cases where they could inadvertently, perhaps, collect, but not wittingly." Wyden had sent his question to Clapper's office a day before the hearing and gave it a chance to correct any misstatements following the hearing. But only after Snowden's disclosure did Clapper write SSCI: "My response was clearly erroneous, for which I apologize." Clapper now explained that Wyden's question was "not answerable necessarily by a simple yes or no. I responded in what I thought was the most truthful or least untruthful manner, by saying, 'no.'" He later claimed the NSA program was like "looking at the Dewey Decimal numbers" of books in a library. "To me, collection of U.S. persons['] data would mean taking the books [*sic*] off the shelf, opening it up and reading it." Andrew Rosenthal responded in his *New York Times* column: "you have to wonder about giving a position of vast responsibility to someone who can beat Mr. Gonzales in dishonesty." But the White House backed the DNI: Obama "certainly believes that Director Clapper has been straight and direct in the answers that he's given and has actively engaged in an effort to provide more information about the programs." At the beginning of 2014, ODNI General Counsel Litt wrote the *New York Times* that Clapper had not lied. He had been "surprised" by the question and "focused his mind on the collection of the content of Americans' communications." Several days later Litt told a Wyden staffer that though Clapper "recognized his testimony was inaccurate, it could not be corrected publicly because the program involved was classified." In February 2016 Clapper reiterated: "I made a mistake. But I did not lie. There's a big difference." Collection "has a specific meaning, which may have a different meaning" to Wyden. "When Senator Wyden asked me the question, I simply didn't think of the [phone records] at the time stored by NSA and governed by section 215 of the Patriot Act … Instead, I thought of content – given his reference to 'dossiers' – which, in my mind, meant section 702 of the FISA which governs collection on non-U.S. persons overseas."

Claiming the program had stopped "dozens" of attacks, NSA Director Alexander accused Snowden of doing "grave harm."[143] "If the perspective is we're trying to hide something because we did something wrong, we're not." "I want the American people to know we're being transparent here." Rep. King called for prosecution of journalists who reported the story, especially Greenwald, whom he falsely accused of threatening to release the names of covert CIA agents. Feinstein promised legislation "which will limit or prevent contractors from handling highly classified and technical data" and said NSA would release information about attacks it had prevented, declaring "there are more than you think." After a briefing, Rep. Ruppersberger agreed the programs "thwarted 10 possible terrorist attacks." Rogers said the number "far exceeds 10." "If you can see just the number of cases where we've actually stopped a plot, I think Americans will come to a different conclusion than all the misleading rhetoric I've heard over the last few weeks." FBI Director Mueller told the Senate that one program had helped find a friend of the marathon bomber suspects. Had it been in place before 9/11, "we would have been able to identify that particular telephone number in San Diego" from which a hijacker had called an al-Qaeda safe house in Yemen. But Udall and Wyden had "not yet seen any evidence showing that NSA's dragnet collection of Americans' phone records has produced any uniquely valuable intelligence." "All of the plots [Alexander] mentioned appear to have been identified using other collection methods." Wyden was unpersuaded that the "collection of millions and millions of Americans' phone calls … is making us any safer." Obama said on PBS: "the one thing people should understand about all these programs … is they have disrupted plots, not just here in the United States but overseas as well." "What I can say unequivocally is that if you are a U.S. person, the NSA cannot listen to your telephone calls, and the NSA cannot target your emails." Of the hundreds of millions of records collected in 2012, only 300 were investigated after officials found a "reasonable suspicion" that the person was "associated with a specific foreign terrorist organization." The *New York Times* remained unconvinced. Obama's "promises lacked specificity, and some of his descriptions of domestic spy work verged on the misleading." FISC, which was "utterly opaque to the public," should publish its opinions.

Foreign observers were even more suspicious, especially after the *Guardian* revealed that the USA and UK had monitored email and phone communications of participants at two major international conferences in London, including then Russian President Medvedev.[144] China expressed concern. Peter Schaar, who enforced Germany's privacy rules, called the practices "monstrous." But at a joint conference with Merkel, Obama claimed: "we know of at last 50 threats that have been averted because of this information … lives have been saved." And Merkel acknowledged getting "very important information" from the USA. Nevertheless, a German Member of Parliament accused the USA of going "behind our backs to find out data about our citizens," a Spanish MEP assailed "a mass invasion of privacy with terrorism as the excuse," and a British MEP revealed that an "anti-FISA clause" had recently been removed from a proposed data protection reform at the insistence of the USA. European Commission Vice President Reding told Eric Holder the USA should acquire data through "mutual legal assistance" protocols, not PRISM, "which would be completely illegal in the EU."

Barton Gellman filled in the back story.[145] Under still-secret Executive Orders prepared by Addington, NSA had been getting email metadata and technical records of Skype calls from ATT, Sprint, and MCI (which later merged with Verizon). NSA lawyers had ruled that it did not "acquire" communications until analysts searched them, but Goldsmith and Comey disagreed. After Comey refused to sign off, the Bush administration replaced STELLARWIND with four other programs: PRISM collected phone calls; MAINWAY and MARINA processed metadata for phone calls and internet communications; and NUCELON looked at content. But after the *New York Times* exposed eavesdropping at the end of 2005, phone companies told NSA they "preferred to be compelled to do so by court order." In May 2006 FISC ruled that "business records" under Patriot Act §215 included a phone company's entire call database. Two months later FISC allowed NSA to resume bulk collection.

When SJC considered a proposal to make phone companies keep calling logs for five years, FBI Director Mueller objected that "it will take an awful long time" to subpoena them.[146] Asked by Leahy how often §215 had been critical in detecting terrorism, "because we're talking about billions of phone numbers," Mueller replied there were "anywhere from 10 to 12 [times] where 215 was important," though it had not been "instrumental" in all. "What you want is as many dots as you can. If you close down a program like this, you are removing dots from the playing field." Wyden and Udall acknowledged that "multiple terrorist plots have been disrupted at least in part because of information" from PRISM. But "saying 'these programs' have disrupted 'dozens of terrorist plots' is misleading if the bulk phone-records collection is actually providing little or no unique value."

Snowden disclosed that GCHQ (UK Government Communications Headquarters) tapped 200 of 1600 fiber optic communication lines (and hoped to tap 400), sharing all the internet traffic with the USA.[147] One document said GCHQ "produces larger amounts of metadata collection than the N.S.A." An NSA slide quoted Director Alexander joking during a 2008 visit to Menwith Hill Station (an NSA listening post in Yorkshire): "Why can't we collect all the signals all the time? Sounds like a good summer project for Menwith." NSA now said it "does not ask its foreign partners to undertake any intelligence activity that the U.S. government would be legally prohibited from undertaking itself."

Max Frankel wrote in the *New York Times* (where he had been a fixture for half a century) that privacy was an "inalienable right."[148] Snowden's leaks "stimulated a long-overdue public airing." FISC judges "function more as grand jury than court" and operate "entirely in secret." FISC "should inform the public about the nature of its cases and its record of approvals and denials" and "summon special attorneys to test the government's secret evidence in every case." Roger Cohen wrote in his *Times* column that had Snowden not leaked, "we would not know about PRISM, would not be debating it, would not have new legislation." Because "institutions at the core of the checks and balances that frame American democracy and civil liberties failed," Snowden had "performed a critical service. History ... will judge him kindly."

FISC critics noted that all 11 judges had been selected by Chief Justice Roberts; 10 had been appointed to District Courts by Republican presidents; 6 were former prosecutors.[149] FISC appointments by Chief Justices Burger and Rehnquist (both Republican appointees) had been ideologically more diverse. Chief Judge Walton replied that "the perception that the court is a rubber stamp is absolutely false." Deputy Attorney General James Cole told HPSCI that FISC judges "push back a lot." At the SSCI hearing Wyden said FISC had issued "pretty stunning rulings," which "are about as expansive as anything you can imagine." Blumenthal proposed that each of the 12 circuit chief judges select a FISC judge. Rep. Schiff introduced a bill that would let the president appoint them, and Rep. Cohen introduced another to let Congressional leaders pick 8 of the 12.

Urging Obama to declassify more information about the programs, the *Washington Post* said PRISM was "not a totally unexpected electronic dragnet."[150] If NSA "is using only a tiny fraction" of the data collected, as it claimed, "couldn't the public have known about the data collection before?" And "could the program work about as well with telecom firms keeping the data?"

Sen. Leahy introduced the FISA Accountability and Privacy Protection Act, cosponsored by four Democrats (Blumenthal (D-Ct), Tester (D-Mt), Udall, and Wyden) and one Republican (Lee).[151] It would accelerate FISA's sunset from December 2017 to June 2015, amend the Patriot Act to require the government to show that records it sought were relevant to an authorized investigation, and require an IG audit of §215 orders and other surveillance.

The *Guardian* published a secret 2009 NSA IG report, which found that the agency was vacuuming up the "metadata" logs of internet communications.[152] Telecoms voluntarily began providing data in November 2001 under STELLARWIND, which might have been the crux of the 2004 conflict between Comey and the administration. Judge Kollar-Kotelly's June 2004 order "essentially gave NSA the same authority to collect bulk internet metadata that it had under the PSP [President's Surveillance Program], except that it specified the datalinks from which NSA could collect and limited the number of people that could access the data." In November 2007 Assistant Attorney General Wainstein told Attorney General Mukasey that DoD wanted NSA to expand "contact chains," not stopping "when a chain hits a telephone number or [internet] address believed to be used by a United States person." Mukasey authorized that in January 2008. ODNI now said the internet program had been terminated in 2011 "for operational and resource reasons," but NSA kept collecting domestic "telephony metadata." Deputy Attorney General Cole told HPSCI: "phone records like this, that don't include any content, are not covered by the Fourth Amendment because people don't have a reasonable expectation of privacy in who [*sic*] they called and when they called." Wyden and Udall said the internet program was terminated in 2011 because intelligence officials repeatedly exaggerated its value in statements to Congress and FISC and then failed to demonstrate its utility in closed door hearings. FISC's redefinition of "relevant" under Patriot Act §215 was what they meant when referring to a secret interpretation of the law. Wyden said the administration's "statements gave the public a false impression of how these authorities were actually being interpreted," making it "impossible for the public or Congress to have a genuinely informed debate." Rep. Sensenbrenner called it a "stretch of the English language" to consider millions of records "relevant." Classified briefings had been a "rope-a-dope operation," giving lawmakers information they could not disclose. Rep. Mulvaney (R-SC) said: "if the administration has a policy to lie to Congress about classified materials in unclassified hearings, then you have to ask yourself what value the hearings have and whether or not anyone else is doing it."

Publication of the NSA IG report revived the debate about FISC's role.[153] Judge Kollar-Kotelly insisted she had "participated in a process of adjudication, not 'coordination' with the executive branch." NSA had briefed her on the technical aspects of metadata collection in May 2004, and she met Hayden twice that summer. He said that after the Agency modified its practices in response to her concerns, "the odds were greater that you'd pick up fewer protected communications of U.S. persons." In July (without informing the other FISC judges) she had approved the metadata program under a FISA provision for a "pen register/trap and trace." In May 2006 she had signed another order for bulk collection of phone metadata under Patriot Act §215. Other leaked FISC decisions expanded the "special needs" exception to the Fourth Amendment (in order to find that the collection and examination of Americans' communications were constitutional) and redefined "foreign intelligence" to include weapons of mass destruction (WMDs). The *New York Times* complained that FISC was "as opaque as it is powerful." Its blanket secrecy was "outrageous" and "the complete absence of any adversarial process" troubling. It had denied only one NSA petition in 2012. "It is possible that not a single one of these 1,788 requests violated established law, but the public will never know because no one was allowed to make a counterargument." Although the Chief Judge Walton warned that disclosing summaries would create "misunderstanding or confusion," the *Times* found it "difficult to imagine how releasing information would make the confusion worse."

A leaked document showed that the USA eavesdropped on the EU's UN mission and Brussels conference venue, as well as 38 embassies and missions in Washington.[154] UN Secretary General Ban Ki-moon observed that member states had an obligation to "protect the inviolability of diplomatic missions." The president of the European Parliament (EP) felt treated like an "enemy" and was "deeply worried and shocked." European Commission Vice President Reding said: "we cannot negotiate over a big trans-Atlantic market if there is the slightest doubt that our partners are carrying out spying activities on the offices of our negotiators." A German MEP wanted "to suspend upcoming negotiations with the U.S.A. and to review existing agreements." The EP Green Party leader called for investigation and cancelation of both SWIFT (for international bank transfers) and the exchange of international airline passenger data. The German chair of the EP Foreign Affairs Committee said the USA had "lost all balance – George Orwell is nothing by comparison." The president of Merkel's party warned that if the reports were true, "it would be sufficient to shatter mutual trust and to damage the close, trusting trans-Atlantic relationship." Baroness

Ashton (EU Foreign Affairs and Security Policy head) asked the USA for an explanation. The French Foreign Minister called spying "completely unacceptable." French President Hollande asked "that it stop immediately." France sought to suspend trade talks for two weeks. *Der Spiegel* reported that NSA monitored 500 million communications in Germany each month. Chancellor Merkel was "alienated" by eavesdropping.

But former DCI Hayden was contemptuous: "Any European who wants to go out and rend their garments with regard to international espionage should look first and find out what their own governments are doing." Obama agreed that "every intelligence service … [is] going to be trying to understand the world better and what's going on in world capitals." But he sought to mollify allies: "We work so closely together [with EU members] that almost no information is not shared between our various countries." And he promised that "if I want to know what Chancellor Merkel is thinking, I will call Chancellor Merkel." Secretary of State Kerry echoed his boss: "every country in the world … undertakes all kinds of activities to protect its national security." America's actions were "not unusual." Even the *New York Times* accused Europeans of "a touch of playacting." Their "outrage … seems overblown, as are their threats to suspend talks on a trans-Atlantic trade deal." But "antagonizing the citizens of some of our closest allies isn't a very promising strategy for increasing international security." The *Washington Post* agreed there was "much political theater in the European protests – and rather hypocritical theater at that." But it also felt there was a "kernel of genuine concern" because "much of what the NSA is accused of doing is unlawful in Germany."

After the French Foreign Minister declared at the US Embassy's July 4 reception that acts of spying "do not have their place between allies," *Le Monde* reported that the French DGSE (General Directorate for External Security) eavesdropped on French phones and internet traffic. The EP overwhelmingly passed a resolution that "strongly condemns the spying on E.U. representatives," demanded "full information on PRISM and other such programmes," and warned of their "potential impact on trans-Atlantic relations." After the *Guardian* revealed that "N.S.A. has for years systematically tapped into the Brazilian telecoms network and indiscriminately intercepted, collected and stored the mail and telephone records of millions of Brazilians," Brazil's Foreign Minister vowed to seek a UN measure "to impede abuses and protect the privacy" of international communications. *O Globo* said NSA was collecting data in Brazil, Colombia, and Mexico, some concerning the Venezuelan oil industry and the Mexican energy sector. Ambassador Shannon denied that the USA was conducting surveillance in Brazil.

Merkel rejected any comparison between NSA and the former East German Stasi. Intelligence work "has always been and will in future be essential for the security of citizens" in all democratic countries. But though she conceded that "our American partners need time for the examination," she also urged the EU to adopt legislation requiring that internet companies disclose what information they stored and with whom they shared it. Germany appeared resigned to (and possibly complicit in) NSA spying. Conceding that if "technical possibilities for spying exist, they will be used," its Interior Minister warned Germans to watch their data. PRISM conducted "very targeted" searches, and NSA had prevented five attacks in Germany. "All this talking and muscle-flexing" was "nonsense." But a Social Democrat Member of Parliament suggested Merkel had violated her oath of office to "keep damage from" the German people; and a Green Party Member of Parliament compared her to "the famous three monkeys: hear no evil, speak no evil and definitely see no evil."

Anger reignited when Snowden revealed that NSA had eavesdropped on Brazilian President Rousseff.[155] Vice President Biden phoned to apologize. (A year later Rousseff said she would meet Biden when he attended the World Cup: "I'm certain we can pick up our relations where we left off.") The Mercosur Foreign Ministers expressed their concern to UN Secretary General Ban Ki-moon. The Venezuelan who held Mercosur's rotating presidency said: "this practice absolutely violates international laws and the sovereignty and independence of nations, and … the fundamental human rights of the citizens of our countries." Biden also called Colombian President Santos to explain NSA's actions. Brazil's Foreign Minister told Kerry at a news conference that surveillance "cast a shadow of distrust" between the countries, and expressed "grave concern" after Britain detained David Miranda (a Brazilian citizen who was Greenwald's partner) for nine hours under its counterterrorism law during a London stopover on his way home from visiting Laura Poitras in Germany. Greenwald threatened: "I have many documents about the system of espionage of England, and now my focus will be there."

Snowden complained on the WikiLeaks website that Biden was pressuring "the leaders of [20] nations from which I have requested protection to deny my asylum petitions."[156] The *Washington Post* advised

Snowden that his "best solution" would be to "surrender to U.S. authorities" and negotiate a plea. Although he had not requested asylum from Bolivia, President Morales said in Moscow his country "is ready to take in people who denounce … espionage or monitoring." But when Morales flew home, France, Italy, and Portugal banned his plane from their airspace (presumably under US pressure). (France later apologized, saying it had reversed the ban on learning that Morales was on the plane.) When Spain conditioned permission to refuel in the Canary Islands on a search, the plane made an unscheduled stop in Vienna, where it was searched because the USA suspected it was carrying Snowden (an allegation confirmed by the Spanish Foreign Minister). After the incident Morales urged European leaders to "free themselves" from the USA. The Union of South American Nations called an emergency meeting. Argentine President Kirchner said the episode displayed "vestiges of a colonialism that we thought was completely over." President Correa of Ecuador (which had offered Snowden asylum) called it an "affront to all America." Colombian President Santos (a close US ally) declared "solidarity with Evo Morales because what they did to him is unheard-of" (even though the two leaders occupied opposite ends of the political spectrum and their countries engaged in border skirmishes). Venezuelan President Maduro and Nicaraguan President Ortega offered Snowden asylum. After the USA exhorted other Latin American nations not to grant asylum, the presidents of Brazil, Argentina, Uruguay, and Venezuela proposed a resolution expressing solidarity with the countries that had offered it.

Fearing he would be unable to accept asylum in Latin America, Snowden sought it in Russia, which allowed him to stay if he agreed "to fully stop activities causing damage to our American partners and Russian-American relations."[157] After a previously scheduled phone call between the two countries, which occurred within hours of Snowden's announcement, the USA accused Russia of having "facilitated a propaganda platform for Mr. Snowden." Putin retorted: "Russia has an independent foreign policy … I hope that our partners understand and react to this with calm, understanding." Sen. Graham urged the USA to boycott the Sochi Olympics if Russia granted Snowden asylum. McCain suggested expanding the number of people sanctioned for Russian human rights abusers. Instead, Holder sought to discourage Russia from granting asylum by assuring its Justice Minister that Snowden would not face the death penalty or torture. But at the end of July Russia granted Snowden asylum for a year. Schumer declared: "Russia has stabbed us in the back." McCain called the decision "a slap in the face of all Americans." The *New York Times* urged the president to boycott the St. Petersburg Group of 20 summit because Russia's "provocative" decision had "essentially [stuck] a thumb in Mr. Obama's eye." Snowden's fears of arrest and prosecution "do not qualify him for asylum." The *Washington Post* said Putin had "snubbed the United States." Obama canceled the meeting, pointing to Russia's "disappointing decision" as one factor. Greenwald said Snowden had "literally thousands of documents" containing "the instruction manual for how the NSA is built." They were encrypted, and Snowden would not make them public; but he was keeping them as "a way to protect himself against extremely rogue behavior on the part of the United States." Greenwald had increased his own security after a laptop was stolen from his Brazilian home.

FISC Chief Judge Walton granted Yahoo's request to declassify his 98-page 2008 decision approving broad collection of email and phone records and instructed DoJ to begin declassifying arguments on both sides.[158] Walton had concluded that "Congress obviously sought to strike the proper balance between the sometime conflicting interests of individual privacy and national security." When Yahoo refused to turn over the data while it appealed, DNI McConnell wrote Walton that "vital foreign intelligence information contained in communications to which only Yahoo has access will go uncollected." Walton promptly threatened Yahoo with a fine. FISCR said that "where the government has instituted several layers of serviceable safeguards to protect individuals against unwarranted harms and to minimize incidental intrusions, its efforts to protect national security should not be frustrated by the courts."

Rep. Amash (Mich) (a Tea Party Republican) sought to amend the NDAA to defund NSA.[159] At an HJC hearing Sensenbrenner interrupted Deputy Attorney General Cole to warn: "unless you realize you've got a problem that [§215 authority] is not going to be renewed." Conyers said the "unsustainable" "outrageous" programs "must be stopped immediately" because "this metadata collected in such a super-aggregated fashion can amount to a Fourth Amendment violation before you do anything else." Poe (another Republican) said: "I don't like 'Snowden' at all, but we would have never known what happened if he hadn't told us."

Sensenbrenner and Lofgren asked Holder and Clapper to let telecoms release more information about data requests. (A month earlier, hoping to forestall customer concerns, Google, Facebook, and

Microsoft had sought permission to reveal the FISA requests they had received.) A coalition of Silicon Valley companies (including Apple, Google, Facebook, and Twitter) and NGOs like the Center for Democracy and Technology, EFF, and the ACLU now asked Obama to provide more information and let the telecoms describe their involvement. But FISC renewed its order for bulk collection of phone call metadata. NSA Director Alexander lobbied against the Amash amendment, and the White House denounced the effort "to hastily dismantle" the program. Sens. Feinstein and Chambliss (R-Ga) opposed the amendment. But warning that Snowden's disclosures had exposed only "some" of what Wyden had been talking about, the senator accused the administration of "actively" misleading the public: NSA had invoked the same legal theory to authorize "secret surveillance programs that I and colleagues think go far beyond the intent" of the Patriot Act. The government believed its "essentially limitless" power could be used to gather medical, financial, credit card, and gun ownership records, even lists of "readers of books deemed subversive." Sen. Franken (D-Mn) introduced a bill to require the government to "disclose how many Americans' information is being collected and actually seen by federal officers or agents." After more than half a dozen top national security officials warned that "denying the N.S.A. such access to data will leave the nation at risk," the House narrowly defeated the Amash–Conyers amendment (205–217, with nearly equal numbers from both parties in favor) before passing the NDAA overwhelmingly (315–109). The *New York Times* observed that "a 51 percent majority in the House with strongly bipartisan opposition is hardly a vote of confidence in a program as intrusive as universal phone-record collection."

Jammed Carr (a senior ND Oh judge who had served on FISC in 2002–08) wrote a *New York Times* op ed urging that Congress authorize FISC "to appoint lawyers to serve the public interest when novel legal issues come before it" to argue in that court and appeal to FISCR and the Supreme Court.[160] Retired DDC Judge Robertson (who had resigned from FISC after the *New York Times* exposé) had proposed something similar, as had Sen. Blumenthal (a former Connecticut Attorney General). The *Washington Post* agreed. Rep. Schiff introduced a bill to authorize the PCLOB to decide whether to appoint opposing counsel and select them. Other bills would require the government to show "specific and articulable facts" demonstrating that the records it sought were relevant to a terrorism investigation and direct FISC to declassify all opinions that included a "significant construction or interpretation" of FISA. Sen. Paul went furthest, declaring that the Fourth Amendment "shall not be construed to allow any agency of the United States government to search the phone records of Americans without a warrant based on probable cause."

On July 27, 26 senators wrote Clapper, expressing concern about bulk collection and seeking information about its extent and efficacy in preventing terrorist attacks.[161] He acknowledged that NSA had "a number of compliance problems," which had been "previously identified and detailed in reports" to FISC "and briefings to Congress." But he insisted they "generally involved human error or highly sophisticated technology issues," not "intentional or bad-faith violations." The underlying legal opinions were "properly classified" – a claim Wyden said "just takes your breath away." In a *Washington Post* op ed Wyden and Udall urged the White House to terminate bulk collection of Americans' phone records. NSA's suspension of internet bulk collection in 2011 when it could not prove the program's usefulness "demonstrated to us that intelligence agencies' assessments of the effectiveness of particular collection programs are not always accurate." Their bill "would require the government to demonstrate that any private records obtained for intelligence purposes are in some way connected to terrorism or clandestine intelligence activities." "A few hundred court orders per year would not overwhelm the FISC, and emergency authorizations could be used in urgent circumstances." Reps. Sensenbrenner and Lofgren were drafting a bill limiting phone surveillance to named targets of terrorism investigations and authorizing internet companies to reveal their involvement in FISC cases. The *Washington Post* wanted telecoms to store phone data and NSA to give FISC good reasons before examining a phone number.

As administration officials prepared to testify before the SJC, Clapper declassified a highly redacted version of the secret order authorizing eavesdropping on Verizon customers.[162] At the hearing Deputy Attorney General Cole said: "nobody is listening to anybody's conversations through this program, and through this program nobody could." Feinstein warned: "we would place this nation in jeopardy if we eliminated those two programs." She wrote in a *Washington Post* op ed that "NSA recently disclosed that 54 terrorist 'events' have been interrupted in part because of information gleaned from this program" and PRISM. Although she knew "of no federal program for which audits, Congressional oversight and scrutiny by the Justice Department, the intelligence community and the courts are stronger or more sustained," she urged greater disclosure. Leahy responded that the administration overstated the success of the domestic phone call log program. NSA had not demonstrated that "dozens or even several terrorist plots" had been blocked. Many of the events Feinstein invoked had been detected by a program surveilling noncitizens abroad. NSA Deputy Director Inglis made the more modest claim that the domestic call tracking program had "contributed" to 13 investigations. Sen. Grassley (R-Ia) criticized Clapper for prior inaccurate statements: "nothing can excuse this kind of behavior from a senior administration official ... especially on matters of grave importance."

One case that NSA invoked involved Basaaly Moalin, a San Diego cab driver convicted of sending $8,500 to al-Shabaab.[163] Inglis told Congress: "you essentially have a range of tools at your disposal – one or more of these tools might tip you to a plot, other[s] might then give you an exposure as to what the nature of that plot is. Finally, the exercise of multiple instruments of power ... completes the picture and allows you to interdict that plot." But Udall retorted: "there's no reason why NSA needed to have its own database containing the phone records of innocent Americans in order to get the information related to Moalin. It could have just as easily gone directly to the phone companies, with an individualized court order." NSA also cited Najibullah Zazi's plot to bomb New York subways. But Wyden said: "in both cases, the government had all the information it needed to go to the phone company and get an individual court order." In September DNI Clapper, NSA Director Alexander, and Deputy Attorney General Cole told SSCI they would consider changing the search protocol, limiting contact chaining, shortening the length of data retention, and authorizing FISC to appoint an amicus.

The *Guardian* published a Snowden document showing that the XKeyscore program gave NSA analysts access to virtually all internet browsing activity in the world.[164] The *New York Times* said the "narrowly selected and heavily censored" documents the administration released "clarified nothing of importance." The *Washington Post* argued: "it should not have taken high-profile leaks to prod the government to reveal what it can." The next day it added: "not every leak is tantamount to treason." "Far too much information is classified." But the *New York Daily News* urged readers to "thank your lucky stars for aggressive signal intelligence programs." Connecting the dots "might yield a lead or two or three, and perhaps even disrupt attack plans in motion. This is precisely why we have a National Security Agency, and precisely what the Edward Snowdens of this world, and their champions, seem intent on unraveling."

Russell Tice, who had spent two decades collecting and analyzing data at NSA before being fired in 2005 for asking Congress to provide more whistle-blower protection, told *PBS Newshour* that former colleagues recently informed him the agency was collecting "contents word for word, everything of domestic communications in this country."[165] In 2002–03 NSA targets had included Judge Samuel Alito (then on the Third Circuit). William Binney, a whistle-blower who retired from NSA in 2001 after three decades, did not "believe … for a minute" the agency's claim that it collected only metadata. "That's why they had to build Bluffdale," where "you could store 100 years of the world's communications … content storage." NSA could store the world's metadata "in a 12-by-20-foot room … you don't need 100,000 square feet of space." Joel Brenner, a former NSA IG and senior legal counsel, insisted the program "only involves telephony metadata" and Binney and Tice "don't know what's going on inside the agency."

Snowden released documents confirming that NSA searched *all* email and text communications, and got FISC approval to read those of US people who cited information linked to foreign intelligence targets.[166] An NSA official maintained that the keywords used were "very precise." The *New York Times* condemned "the agency's inexhaustible appetite for delving into the communications of Americans. Time and again, the N.S.A. has pushed past the limits that lawmakers thought they had imposed to prevent it from invading basic privacy, as protected by the Constitution." The keyword search "could very well include innocent communications between family members expressing fears of a terror attack. Or messages between an editor and a reporter who is covering international security issues. Or the privileged conversation between a lawyer and a client who is being investigated." "Naturally, the FISC approved" NSA's "half-baked assertions with a secret opinion." "Despite President Obama's claim this week that 'there is no spying on Americans,' the evidence shows that such spying is greater than the public ever knew."

Claiming they had already lost business because of Snowden's revelations, US cloud computing companies feared they could forfeit $20–35 billion to foreign competitors over the next three years.[167] Even before the story broke, the EP required that data transfers from a European cloud to any other (but especially an American one) should notify customers of the privacy risk. The EU was considering rules banning the transfer of data unless it was protected under EU law or a new treaty with the USA complying with EU law. But the MEP who proposed them acknowledged that the EU had no power over national or EU security. The EP demanded termination of SWIFT because NSA eavesdropped on it.

Calling it "unfortunate" that "rather than an orderly and lawful process to debate these issues," leaks had "initiated the debate in a very passionate but not always fully informed way," Obama claimed: "we would have gotten to the same place" without them.[168] Snowden, who had been charged with three felonies, was no "patriot"; he should have gone to the Intelligence Committees rather than "putting at risk our national security." It was "not the case" that "we're out there willy-nilly just sucking in information on everybody and doing what we please with it." "America is not interested in spying on ordinary people … we show a restraint many governments around the world don't even think to do." Obama endorsed proposals to make FISC more adversarial "in appropriate cases" and increase oversight and audit of the phone database; and he appointed a task force on how to balance security and privacy. The administration also issued a White Paper declaring that the §215 program was constitutional and had been reauthorized by Congress. Rep. Boehner said: "transparency is important, but we expect the White House to insist that no reform will compromise the operational integrity of the program." Rep. Holt urged Obama to "acknowledge what a clear majority of Americans know: our government has violated the law by collecting the communications of millions of innocent U.S. citizens." The *New York Times* dismissed the administration's "weak agenda on spying reform." The problem was the programs' "existence," "not whether they are modestly transparent." At a minimum FISC should release unclassified summaries of its opinions.

House members complained that NSA obstructed oversight.[169] They could not take notes when reading classified documents and had to rely on Intelligence Committee staffers, many of them former NSA employees. Rep. Schakowsky (D-Ill) said bulk surveillance had not been "approved by a fully knowing Congress." Sensenbrenner repeated that classified briefings were a "rope-a-dope operation" intended to mislead "those who are on the trail of something that isn't right." Nadler asked: "how do you get political support to change a law when you can't say the reason?" Holt (a physicist) said NSA briefers "often delight in obfuscating behind a flurry of tech speak." But Rogers said that "very few members" took advantage of quarterly staff briefings. And Sen. Rockefeller said that the Obama administration had given SSCI the information it needed.

Snowden published a 2012 NSA audit finding that the agency violated the privacy rules for US persons 2,776 times in a year (but 1,904 of the incidents involved foreigners using their cell phones in the USA).[170] In one incident in February 2012, NSA retained 3,032 files (each containing an undisclosed number of phone call records) after FISC had ordered their destruction. Chief Judge Walton said FISC "does not have the capacity to investigate issues of noncompliance." In January 2008 NSA had collected metadata on numerous calls from the Washington DC area code (202), mistaking it for Egypt's country code (20). But its Director of Compliance said the number of willful errors was "miniscule" and even mistakes were in the "parts-per-million or parts-per-billion range." The White House claimed the documents "demonstrate that the NSA is monitoring, detecting, addressing and reporting compliance incidents." But Rep. Pelosi called the reports "extremely disturbing." David Firestone of the *New York Times* Editorial Board said the mistakes "amount to a serious abuse of government authority" and called the lack of oversight "staggering." The *Washington Post* wrote that "NSA must be more transparent in its error reporting." Sens. Wyden and Udall said the *Washington Post*'s "confirmation" of their earlier warnings was "just the tip of a larger iceberg." "The public should also be told more about why the FISC has said that the executive branch's implementation of §702 of the FISA has circumvented the spirit of the law." "This highlights the need for a robust and well-staffed public advocate" at FISC. In July the administration had declassified a February 2011 letter informing the HPSCI leaders of its bulk collection program. But though Assistant Attorney General Weich's cover letter said that making the material available to Congress would be an "effective way to inform the legislative debate about reauthorization" of the Patriot Act, the HPSCI leaders did not send it to the rest of the committee. A spokesman now said HPSCI had offered all members classified briefings. But Amash said he and dozens of others elected in 2010 lacked the information necessary to exercise oversight. Briefings were "like a game of 20 questions." "If you don't know about the program, you don't know what to ask." Rep. Grayson (D-Fl) denied Sen. Chambliss's claim that "all a member of Congress needs to do is ask for information, and he'll get it. Well I did ask, and the House Intelligence Committee said 'no,' repeatedly."

Bills proposed a variety of reforms: creating a special advocate before FISC (Sen. Blumenthal and Rep. Schiff); changing FISC's composition or selection process (Sen. Blumenthal and Reps. Cohen and Schiff); giving FISC judges technical advisers and making it easier for outsider groups to file amicus briefs (Rep. Schiff); requiring a warrant based on probable cause before any search of phone records (Sen. Paul); declassifying FISC decisions (Rep Sheila Lee (D-Tex)); repealing the Patriot Act authorization of surveillance (Rep. Holt); defunding collection of domestic call records (Reps. Amash and Conyers); and blocking bulk collection of domestic communications without a warrant (Rep. Lofgren).[171] Alan Raul (former PCLOB vice chair) urged the White House to create a privacy czar. Two former SSCI staffers called for an independent NSA IG. Reps. Van Hollen and Jordan (R-Oh) sought co-sponsors for the House version of Blumenthal's bill (supported by Paul, Udall, and Wyden).

In response to an EFF FOIA lawsuit, the administration released FISC Chief Judge Bates's 85-page 2011 opinion finding unconstitutional a program that had gathered domestic internet messages for three years.[172] Bates cited two other instances in which NSA had misled FISC, one by keeping logs of all domestic phone calls (and one redacted). As recently as April 2013, DoJ had said that releasing any part of the opinion would "cause exceptionally grave damage to the national security of the United States." Declassified FISC decisions released in response to EFF and ACLU lawsuits and Obama's directions showed that in 2011 the court reversed a 2008 ban on NSA searching communications between US persons and those allegedly involved in terrorist plots, and let NSA retain for six years rather than five communications with one end in the USA. Sen. Wyden accused FISC of abusing "an authority intended to target only foreigners." In March 2009 Judge Walton had strongly rebuked NSA. Every day it searched its entire phone call database for the 17,800 domestic and foreign numbers on an "alert list." Although it assured FISC that all those numbers met the legal standard of suspicion, only about ten percent did so. Walton had ruled that NSA "has compounded its noncompliance with the court's orders by repeatedly submitting inaccurate descriptions of the alert list process." Declaring that privacy safeguards "have been so frequently and systematically violated" that they "never functioned effectively," Walton imposed new limits. The *New York Times* cited this as further evidence "that the National Security Agency has frequently been unable to comprehend, let alone manage, its vast and continuing collection of Americans' telephone and internet records." In response to an ACLU motion, FISC Judge Saylor exhorted the government to review all FISC decisions for release. The *New York Times* applauded this. The *Washington Post* also urged greater transparency from NSA, "a huge organization of human beings with the same capacity to misunderstand, miscommunicate and misbehave as the rest of us." When the government declined to disclose a February 2013 FISC opinion two months later, Judge Saylor ordered it to give a detailed explanation.

At the end of August FISC Judge Eagen (named to the federal bench by George W. Bush and just appointed to FISC by Chief Justice Roberts) found NSA collection of bulk phone metadata constitutional and authorized by Patriot Act §215.[173] Although the Supreme Court's decision in *Smith* v. *Maryland* involved just one individual, "where one individual does not have a Fourth Amendment interest, grouping together a large number of similarly situated individuals cannot result in a Fourth Amendment interest springing into existence *ex nihilo*." FISC approved orders through a "structured adversarial process," although no recipient "has challenged the legality of such an Order." Under the Fourth Amendment "the required factual predicate for obtaining information in a case of special needs, such as national security, can be lower." "[T]he concept of relevance here is … broad … the government may meet the standard under Section 215 if it can demonstrate reasonable grounds to believe that the information sought to be produced has some bearing on its investigation of the identified international terrorist organizations." Eagen accepted the government's assertion that "'analysts know that the terrorists' communications are located somewhere' in the metadata produced under this authority, but cannot know where until the data is aggregated and then accessed by their analytic tools." Congress had "ratified" the program because the executive had provided "extensive and detailed information" to the Gang of Four. "It is unnecessary for the Court to inquire how many of the 535 individual Members of Congress took advantage of the opportunity to learn the facts" as long as "each Member was presented with an opportunity." In October FISC Judge McLaughlin approved an extension of the phone call log metadata program, endorsing Eagen's opinion.

Der Spiegel published a Snowden document showing that NSA decrypted the UN internal video conferencing system and spied on UN Missions from many countries as well as the EU.[174] The UN protested that "the inviolability of diplomatic missions … has been well-established international law." A few days later Greenwald released documents showing that NSA had spied on Enrique Peña Nieto during his successful campaign for Mexican president and on Brazilian President Rousseff. Another Snowden document confirmed that NSA had eavesdropped on the email of Mexican President Calderón and his Cabinet. Denouncing the practice as "unacceptable, illegitimate and against Mexican and international law," the Mexican Foreign Minister demanded an "exhaustive investigation." Obama assured Peña Nieto he had not authorized such spying. Brazil's Justice Minister condemned this "clear violation of Brazil's sovereignty." Calling such spying "plainly illegitimate," Rousseff indefinitely postponed her scheduled visit to Washington, even after Obama spent 20 minutes on the phone trying to persuade her to come. At the UN she called the spying "a breach of international law," a "grave violation of human rights and civil liberties," and especially "disrespect to national sovereignty." Brazil encrypted its email to block NSA spying and bought $4.5 billion worth of fighter jets from Belgium's Saab rather than Boeing, allegedly because of NSA spying.

At a news conference in Sweden, Obama denied the USA was spying on Europeans' emails or phone calls. But other documents revealed that NSA surveilled the Brazilian oil company Petrobras, Google, SWIFT, and the French Foreign Affairs Minister. Clapper maintained that NSA collected intelligence about financial matters but did not "use our foreign intelligence capabilities to steal the trade secrets of foreign companies on behalf of … U.S. companies." Allegations surfaced that NSA spied on the Austrian government in Vienna. India said NSA had bugged its Missions in Washington and the UN. After *Le Monde* reported that NSA taped more than 70 million French phone calls in a 30-day period at the end of 2012, targeting politicians, business people, and members of the administration, the Prime Minister and Interior Minister expressed shock. Clapper called the report "false." A September 2010 NSA memo referred to surveillance of France's Washington Embassy and UN Mission. The *New York Times* wrote that though "much of the public indignation by France and other governments is largely rhetorical … the very scale of America's clandestine electronic operations appears to be undercutting America's 'soft power.'" The *Washington Post* said the US responses – that the practice was necessary and everyone did it – were "reasonable answers, to a point." But targeting "top political leaders and diplomats … cannot be explained away as counterterrorism." And the "breezy" reply "overlooks the damage that revelations of spying are doing to important relationships."

When it was reported that NSA had listened to Merkel's cell phone, her spokesperson called it "a serious breach of confidence." Obama quickly telephoned her to deny it. His spokesman also denied eavesdropping on British Prime Minister Cameron. But when a (leaked) 2006 memo to the NSA Signals Intelligence Directorate urged senior officials in the White House, DoS, DoD, and other departments to share their "rolodexes," one official gave NSA 200 phone numbers (43 previously unknown) of 35 world leaders. After an Italian paper reported that NSA had spied on its government, Prime Minister Letta denounced the behavior as "inconceivable." Merkel and Hollande planned to negotiate a new agreement with the USA on intelligence. Spanish Prime Minister Rajoy told his Foreign Minister to summon the US Ambassador to respond to stories in *El País* and *El Mundo* that NSA had eavesdropped on 60 million Spaniards, including members of the government. US Ambassador Costos said NSA spied only for counterterrorism reasons, never economic advantage. The Swedish Prime Minister called it "completely unacceptable" to eavesdrop on an allied leader. The EP President said the EU should suspend negotiations on free trade. *Die Welt* maintained that targeting leaders was "not by accident but systematic and out of principle." The *New York Times* said Obama's efforts to reassure Hollande and Merkel "seem to have been as incomplete as the explanations the administration has given to the American public about the agency's excessive domestic surveillance." It urged the administration "to negotiate a formal pact that would set mutually acceptable surveillance guidelines."

Der Spiegel published NSA documents from Snowden indicating it had begun spying on Merkel from the US Embassy in 2002. *Bild am Sonntag* said NSA Director Alexander had informed Obama of this in 2010. An Italian magazine reported that NSA spied on the conclave of cardinals choosing the Pope. Rep. Rogers said the claim that 70 million French phone calls had been intercepted was "100 percent wrong" and reports that Merkel had been monitored did not "necessarily fit with what has actually happened." Rep. King said Obama should "stop apologizing, stop being defensive." The White House claimed it learned of the spying on allied leaders only after Snowden's revelations; but current and former intelligence officials said the White House and DoS had approved the spying. Claiming that SSCI had never been told, Sen. Feinstein said she was "totally opposed" to such spying. The *New York Times* dismissed the White House response as "a pathetic mix of unsatisfying assurances about reviews under way, platitudes about the need for security in an insecure age, and the odd defense that the president didn't know." But the *Wall Street Journal* found French outrage "especially hard to take seriously" since "the French intelligence agency … maintains its own robust data-collection program on domestic and foreign targets." Clapper insisted NSA did not "spy indiscriminately on citizens of any country." Alexander justified "information that we and our NATO allies have collected in defense of our countries and in support of military operations." But he also admitted to an EU delegation that NSA engaged in unilateral spying in Europe. At an HPSCI meeting, Rogers called it "disingenuous to imply that this committee did not have a full and complete understanding of activities of the intelligence community."

The furor extended to Asia. *Der Spiegel* reported that "STATEROOM" allowed the embassies and consulates of the "Five Eyes" (USA, UK, Canada, Australia, New Zealand) to spy on Asian governments. After a Snowden document revealed that Australia had tried to bug the phone of the President of Indonesia, it summoned the Australian and US ambassadors. The Chinese Foreign Ministry was "severely concerned." Clapper told HPSCI that in his 50 years in the intelligence business "leadership intentions in whatever form that's expressed is kind of a basic tenet of what we are to collect." Rep. Schiff replied: "if you're tapping the phone line of a foreign leader, an ally, that is a significant intelligence activity that should be reported to the committee."

Obama terminated spying on the IMF and World Bank headquarters in Washington. Wolfgang Ischinger, who had been German Ambassador to the USA in 2001–06, characterized transatlantic relations as worse than they had been since the start of the Iraq war, "a matter of broken trust and personal humiliation." While acknowledging it also spied on foreign diplomats, including those from the USA, Iran, and Russia, Brazil joined Germany in introducing a UN General Assembly resolution urging all countries to extend internationally guaranteed privacy rights to electronic communications and asking Human Rights Commissioner Pillay to report on privacy protections. After the Five Eyes lobbied against the resolution, the sponsors (now joined by 55 other nations) dropped the claim that surveillance violated human rights, but expressed deep concern about its "negative impact." Human rights groups supported the resolution, which the General Assembly adopted in December. In June 2014 Pillay issued a report on "The Right to Privacy in the Digital Age," deploring the "disturbing lack of transparency" in digital mass surveillance. Any limitation of privacy rights should be governed by "accessible, clear and precise" laws, not "secret rules and secret interpretations." Privacy rights did not end at a nation's boundaries. Bulk collection of metadata could be arbitrary unless it was necessary and proportionate to the threat, which did not justify mandatory third-party data retention. A year later, evaluating compliance with the ICCPR, the UN criticized the USA for not establishing adequate oversight for the protection of privacy rights, giving it the lowest grades for its failure to "ensure affected persons have access to effective remedies in case of abuse" or to "establish the responsibility of those who provided legal pretexts for manifestly illegal behavior."

After the Canadian Broadcasting Corporation published a Snowden document showing that NSA had cooperated with the Communications Security Establishment Canada in using the US Embassy in Ottawa to surveil a Group of 20 summit in Toronto, opposition politicians expressed outrage. Other documents revealed that the Australian spy agency shared citizens' data with NSA, and DGSE helped NSA spy in France. Despite a long-standing agreement among the Five Eyes to share intelligence, an NSA document revealed that it had considered unilaterally surveilling people in Australia, New Zealand, and Canada (presumably without their governments' knowledge). The EU Justice and Human Rights Commissioner warned that the Safe Harbor provision underlying commercial data exchanges, which were to expire in 2014, "seems not to be safe" and could be jettisoned. The EU Home Affairs Commissioner warned: "our co-operation with the US in the fight against terrorism has been put into question by the NSA revelations." Foreign countries also contemplated technological fixes. An alliance of German phone and internet companies sought to keep transmissions inside the country. Brazil considered requiring US companies to store Brazilian customers' data inside the country. EU leaders urged member countries to develop non-US cloud storage.

The controversy reignited in 2015.[175] After visiting the White House, Rousseff accepted the US promise "that friendly countries won't be spied on." Obama had assured her that "when he wants to know something, he'll call me." But two weeks later WikiLeaks reported that NSA had eavesdropped on Rousseff, her secretary and chief of staff, the central bank director and Foreign Minister, ambassadors, and military chiefs. It released other documents showing that NSA spied on at least three French presidents (Chirac, Sarkozy, and Hollande) between 2006 and 2012. After a Defense Council meeting, France called such behavior "unacceptable" and declared it would not "tolerate any actions that put French security and the protection of French interests in danger." The USA assured France it was not *at that time* surveilling its President, who was an "indispensable partner." Unmollified, the French Justice Minister condemned surveillance as an "unspeakable practice." Several days later WikiLeaks released documents showing that NSA had spied on Sarkozy's Economic and Budget Ministers as well as a hundred French companies, including the largest firms. Other documents revealed that NSA surveilled 35 targets in Japan, including the Cabinet Office, Finance and Trade Ministry, and Bank of Japan, as well as major companies like Mitsubishi and Mitsui, on topics including international trade and climate change. Prime Minister Abe told Vice President Biden that the allegations, if true, "could shake the relationship of trust in our alliance."

A bipartisan SJC group, including the two leaders (Leahy and Grassley), asked the Intelligence Community IG to investigate surveillance, but he pleaded insufficient resources.[176] In response to Leahy, Judge Walton said FISC rejected a quarter of initial applications but ultimately approved more than 99 percent (even Title III courts approved 99.96 percent of warrant requests in 2008–12). Sens. Feinstein and Chambliss (backed by their House counterparts Rogers and Ruppersberger) drafted the FISA Improvements Act to "change but preserve" surveillance. NSA would continue bulk collection of phone records, retaining them for five years; but FISC would require a "reasonable articulable suspicion" of a terrorist link before the government could run a number against that database. At the Cato Institute, Rep. Sensenbrenner denounced the bill as "a fig leaf." But SSCI approved it 11–4 while rejecting (7–8) a three-year cap on retaining phone records, a ban on bulk collection of cell-site information showing the caller's location, and publication of FISC decisions finding a constitutional violation. The *Washington Post* called for tougher controls. A rival bill by Wyden and Udall would ban bulk collection and systematic searches of Americans' international emails and texts "about" a target. Leahy and Sensenbrenner introduced the USA Freedom Act, ending bulk collection of phone records and requiring the government to delete information accidentally collected on Americans. It quickly garnered support from 16 senators and more than 70 representatives, as well as the 6 leading tech companies.

At an SJC Privacy Subcommittee hearing, NSA General Counsel Litt resisted a bill sponsored by Sens. Franken and Heller (R-Nv) to let internet companies disclose how many NSA demands they received and require NSA to reveal how many Americans it surveilled.[177] Franken found it "kind of troubling" that NSA did not know the latter figure. Litt warned that "the more detail we provide out there … the more easy it becomes for our adversaries to know where to talk and where not to talk."

A Snowden document showed that, since November 2010, NSA's MAINWAY program had mapped connections between foreign intelligence targets and US persons without obtaining a warrant, using bank codes, insurance information, Facebook postings, passenger manifests, voter registration rolls, GPS location, and property and tax records.[178] It also stored a year's worth of internet searches. In 2008 Gates and Mukasey had authorized the Defense Supplemental Procedures Governing Communications Metadata Analysis, invoking the Supreme Court's 1979 *Smith* v. *Maryland* decision. By 2011 that program was processing 700 million phone records and 1.1 billion cell phone records a day; its 2013 budget request sought to intercept 20 billion "record events" a day. NSA also collected hundreds of millions of address books from personal email and instant messaging accounts, many belonging to Americans. At an SSCI hearing, Alexander said that although NSA had the ability to collect GPS information based on cell phone tower data, it had not done so. In response to Leahy he conceded that only 13 out of the 54 instances of foiled plots he had cited had any nexus to the USA, and "these weren't all plots, and they weren't all foiled." In the end, he pointed to only four: Basaaly Moalin, Najibullah Zazi, David Coleman Headley, and Khalid Ouazzani.

Although American politicians called for prosecuting Snowden and his associates as traitors, many others honored them.[179] Snowden received the annual Sam Adams Award from retired US national security officers. The *Guardian* received Gannett Foundation awards for investigative journalism and watchdog journalism. The *Guardian* and Glenn Greenwald received the Leipzig Media Foundation Prize for Freedom and the Future of the Media. Snowden was voted *Guardian* Person of the Year. The Polk Awards went to Greenwald, Ewen MacAskill, and Laura Poitras of the *Guardian*, and Barton Gellman of the *Washington Post*. Snowden and Poitras received The Nation Institute's Ridenhour Prize for truth-telling. The *Guardian* was named newspaper of the year at the British Press Awards. Rostock University gave Snowden an honorary doctorate. Barton Gellman and the *Washington Post* won a Pulitzer Prize for public service. Sweden gave the Right Livelihood Award to Snowden and *Guardian* editor Alan Rusbridger. The *Guardian* won an Emmy for its coverage. The Motion Picture Academy gave Laura Poitras its best documentary award for *Citizenfour*. And the city of Dresden named a square after Snowden.

Snowden leaked a January 2013 memo describing how NSA (operating under EO 12333) engaged in backdoor overseas collection of millions of records a day from Yahoo and Google data centers, analyzing them using the Muscular program.[180] Both companies denied giving permission. Alexander maintained disingenuously: "I can tell you factually we do not have access to Google servers, Yahoo servers." But the journalists replied that NSA used *circuits*, not servers (because some data existed only in the cloud), thereby collecting even more. A later story speculated that NSA also had penetrated the internet cables of Verizon Communications, BT Group, Vodafone Group, and Level 3 Communications. Google and Yahoo sent unencrypted data through Level 3 (which was larger than Verizon and AT&T combined). Both Level 3 and Verizon said they complied with orders from the governments of countries where they operated. A Dutch newspaper published an NSA map showing that the Five Eyes intercepted internet cables across the Pacific in American territories, Singapore, and South Korea. A coalition of hundreds of groups (including ACLU, EFF, Occupy Wall Street NYC, and the Libertarian Party) collected 575,000 signatures urging Congress to "reveal the full extent of the NSA's spying programs" and sent thousands to protest at Capitol Hill.

An ACLU/EFF FOIA request secured release of a heavily redacted version of Judge Kollar-Kotelly's 2004 opinion approving bulk collection of email (citing *Smith* v. *Maryland*).[181] Authorizing NSA to search all email links from the suspect, she found that a relatively low standard of "relevance" was necessary to permit "the use of this very valuable investigative tool at the critical early stages of foreign intelligence and international terrorism investigations" since analysts "cannot know ahead of time ... exactly where" "terrorists' e-mails are located ... in the billions of data bits." The government also released Attorney General Gonzales's 2006 application to collect logs of all domestic phone calls – echoing John Yoo's OLC memo declaring that "the government's interest is the most compelling imaginable" and "the intrusion is minimal" – and a document acknowledging that the government had shut down the program for several months after it exceeded FISC authorization because of the "complexity" of collections. In 2009 NSA had admitted "that its compliance and oversight structure had not kept pace with its operational momentum."

DNI Clapper said nearly 2,000 pages of documents on surveillance had been declassified since Obama told him in June 2013 to "make public as much information as possible." The *New York Times* commented that FISC, which approved all but one of the previous year's 1,856 requests, was "not a court by any standard." The documents Clapper released "only highlighted the dubious grounds on which the programs have been approved, and how often and how systematically the N.S.A. violates the court's orders." Shareholders also pressed telecoms to reveal cooperation with NSA. The $161 billion NYS Common Retirement Fund demanded that AT&T publish reports on information it collected and shared; and the Fund joined with the $1.3 billion Trillium Asset Management to make a similar demand on Verizon. But in January 2014, Preet Bharara, US Attorney for SDNY, said the government would not turn over any more documents or reveal how many there were.

A February 2012 paper leaked by Snowden, "Sigint Strategy 2012–2016," declared that NSA would seek data from "anyone, anytime, anywhere" and try to decrypt or bypass encryption by influencing "the global commercial encryption market."[182] The Treasure Map program offered "a near real-time, interactive map of the global internet." It collected Wi-Fi network and geolocation data and 30–50 million unique internet provider addresses, many in the USA. Through the Packaged Goods program NSA gained access to "13 covered servers in unwitting data centers around the globe," including Germany, Poland, Denmark, South Africa, Taiwan, Russia, China, and Singapore.

In a *New York Times* op ed Sens. Wyden, Udall, and Heinrich (D-NM) called on the administration to "end the N.S.A. dragnet now."[183] "The bulk collection of Americans' telephone records" was "a clear case of a general warrant that violates the spirit of the framers' intentions." "We have yet to see any proof that [the program] provides real, unique value in protecting national security." The Feinstein–Rogers bill "would explicitly permit the government to engage in dragnet collection" and "give intelligence agencies wide latitude to conduct warrantless searches for Americans' phone calls and emails." Snowden documents revealed that, starting in 2007, NSA and GCHQ had collected data on age, sex, personal information, and location from hundreds of millions of cell phones outside the USA, some owned by US citizens. NSA General Counsel Litt said the agency was not collecting such data on calls made within the USA. But Wyden, Udall, and Mikulski offered an NDAA 2014 amendment to require the administration to say whether it planned to collect location data for "a large number of United States persons with no known connection to suspicious activity."

In a television interview at the beginning of December 2013, Obama said he would "be proposing some self-restraint on the NSA" and "some reforms that can give people more confidence."[184] Although he assured Americans that the agency "actually does a very good job about not engaging in domestic surveillance, not reading people's emails, not listening to the contents of their phone calls," he acknowledged that his assurances offered little comfort to foreigners because NSA was "not constrained by laws" outside the USA. More than 500 leading authors from 81 countries declared that "a person under surveillance is no longer free; a society under surveillance is no longer a democracy." "Surveillance is theft. This data is not public property, it belongs to us." They urged the UN to create an international bill of digital rights.

Also in December 2013 Google and Microsoft led other tech companies (including Apple, Yahoo, Facebook, Twitter, AOL, and LinkedIn) in publishing an open letter in leading newspapers calling on "the world's governments to address the practices and laws regulating government surveillance of individuals and access to their information."[185] "We are focused on keeping users' data secure, deploying the latest encryption technology to prevent unauthorized surveillance on our networks, and by pushing back on government requests to ensure that they are legal and reasonable in scope … Governments should limit surveillance to specific known users for lawful purposes, and should not undertake bulk data collection of internet communications."

Legislators invoked the letter to press for reform. Rep. Amash said: "businesses increasingly recognize that our government's out-of-control surveillance hurts their bottom line and costs American jobs." Rep. Sensenbrenner welcomed a letter from tech companies "directly impacted by NSA's overreach," which "helps add to the growing momentum for much-needed reform." Sen. Leahy warned that "the global competitiveness of the American technological industry has been undermined by revelations of massive dragnet surveillance programs." The Information Technology and Innovation Foundation estimated that US cloud computing could lose $35 billion by 2016. Forrester, a tech industry research firm, predicted losses by US ISPs of up to $180 billion by 2016. In March 2014 Microsoft reported losing customers, including the Brazilian government, which had joined with the EU to lay cables between Brazil and Portugal. IBM was spending more than $1 billion to build overseas data centers. Tech executives raised the issue with Obama at a March 2014 meeting. A survey of a thousand businesses worldwide found that almost 90 percent had changed how they used the cloud, nearly a third moving data to locations where they "know it will be safe." Edward J. Black, president and CEO of the Computer & Communications Industry Association, told the SJC in December 2013 that NSA surveillance and efforts to undermine encryption had damaged his members.

These pressures seemed efficacious. Deputy Attorney General Cole, NSA Director Alexander, and ODNI General Counsel Litt told SJC they had declassified several FISC orders and authorized telecoms to disclose some information about the orders they had received.[186] While reasserting that metadata collection raised no Fourth Amendment issues, the officials reaffirmed their willingness to limit contact chaining, reduce retention periods, and let FISC appoint amici. At a White House meeting convened by Obama to discuss the Affordable Care Act website, 15 technology executives shared the "principles on government surveillance that we released last week" and urged Obama "to move aggressively on reform" of NSA.

NSA Director Alexander told an SJC hearing that "there is no other way that we know of to connect the dots."[187] Fewer than 200 domestic numbers had been checked against NSA's database in 2013. Whitehouse agreed that ending the program would be "unilaterally disarming." But Leahy maintained that bulk collection had been "uniquely valuable" in just one terrorism case. And Grassley said some disclosures "call into serious question whether the law and other safeguards currently in place strike the right balance between protecting our civil liberties and our national security."

Obama's Review Group on Intelligence and Communications Technology (former CIA Deputy and Acting Director Michael Morell; law professors Geoffrey Stone, Peter Swire, and Cass Sunstein; and Richard A. Clarke, national security adviser to four presidents) reported in December 2013.[188] (Obama knew Stone and Sunstein from teaching at Chicago.) It endorsed bulk collection but recommended that phone companies retain the data, which NSA could obtain only by applying to FISC, where a "public interest advocate" would represent privacy and civil liberties. The entire Supreme Court would appoint FISC judges. NSA could not use "back doors" into hardware or software. Foreigners would enjoy the same protections as citizens under the Privacy Act 1974. The president should review the list of foreign leaders surveilled and the White House should regularly audit NSA collection activities. The Center for Democracy and Technology and the ACLU praised the report. The *New York Times* said the "remarkably thorough and well-reasoned" report's "most damning" conclusion was that bulk collection "was not essential to preventing attacks." The *Washington Post* found the recommendations "mostly valuable," but still favored NSA collection and storage of telephone metadata. Obama repeated that we "have lots of laws and checks and balances and safeguards and audits when it comes to making sure that the NSA and other intelligence communities are not spying on Americans." There was no evidence that NSA had "acted inappropriately." But he acknowledged the possibility "that some of the same information that the intelligence community feels is required to keep people safe can be obtained by having the private phone companies keep these records longer and to create some mechanism where they can be accessed in an effective fashion."

The *Times* found his response "disappointing." Declaring that the president should have suspended "the constitutionally questionable (and evidently pointless) collection of data on every phone call and email that Americans make," it urged Congress "to rewrite the relevant passage in the Patriot Act." Sen. Feinstein disagreed with the report's claim that "NSA's metadata program is 'not essential to preventing attacks.'" Rep. King deplored "a debate generated by the hysteria caused by Edward Snowden." "I don't think every one has to know what a spy agency is doing." Rep. Rogers feared "it opens up to more privacy violations when the companies hold" the metadata. The *Times* supported the Leahy–Sensenbrenner bill. "The way to restore" trust in government "is not through cosmetic touch-ups, but by Congress and the courts setting firm limits on all surveillance programs and ensuring that the administration complies." John McLaughlin (former Deputy and Acting CIA Director) expressed the fear in a *Washington Post* op ed that "we are going a little nuts in our dogged pursuit of the post-Snowden NSA." "Now is not the time to give up any tool in the counterterrorism arsenal." Former OLC lawyer Steven Bradbury warned in a *Washington Post* op ed that the recommendations of the "glib and unconvincing" report "would throttle the effectiveness of the program." But in January the New America Foundation published an analysis of 225 post-9/11 terrorism cases, concluding that §215 surveillance had "played an identifiable role in, at most, 1.8 percent"; most had relied on traditional law enforcement. NSA evidence was only instrumental in identifying Moalin; even then, the FBI then waited two months before tapping his phone.

Snowden documents revealed that NSA and GCHQ spied on more than a thousand targets (many unrelated to terrorism), including the Israeli Prime Minister and Defense Minister and two Israeli embassies, directors of UN and other relief programs, officials overseeing oil and finance ministries, French and German embassies, foreign energy companies, EU officials (one involved in antitrust battles with US tech companies), and African heads of state and family members.[189] The Knesset Speaker called this "a severe case."

At the end of 2013 Snowden declared he had "accomplished" his mission.[190] "I am not trying to bring down the NSA, I am working to improve the NSA." He had sought to do this internally, voicing concerns to two superiors in the technology directorate and two in the threat operations center's regional base in Hawaii in October 2012. (NSA denied this.) He showed them and 15 others that "we are collecting more in the United States on Americans than we are on Russians in Russia." British television carried Snowden's Christmas message that "privacy is what allows us to determine who we are and who we want to be."

Hayden accused Snowden of "treason" for offering the German and Brazilian governments documents in exchange for asylum. "This is the most serious hemorrhaging of America's secrets in the history of American espionage." Clemency would be "outrageous on its face." The *New York Times* countered that Snowden had "done his country a great service" and should be offered a plea bargain or clemency. "Mr. Snowden was clearly justified in believing that the only way to blow the whistle on this kind of intelligence-gathering was to expose it to the public and let the resulting furor do the work his superiors would not." No critic "has presented the slightest proof that his disclosures really hurt the nation's security." This editorial provoked more than 1,200 comments by midday, mostly hostile. The *Guardian* said Snowden "deserves" a pardon for an "act of some moral courage." But a bare majority of the public felt he did the "wrong thing" and should be charged with a crime. A majority of Obama's Review Group opposed exoneration. Sen. Paul said that if Snowden were punished, Alexander should be as well. Rep. King accused Paul of "creating this hysteria" by suing the NSA, "playing on some sort of scaremongering ... appealing to the lowest common denominator." He "doesn't deserve to be in the United States Senate."

At the end of January Holder rejected clemency but expressed willingness to negotiate a plea.

Five months later Snowden told Brian Williams on NBC News: "being a patriot doesn't mean prioritizing service to government above all. It means knowing when to protect your country, when to protect your Constitution, when to protect your countrymen from the violations and encroachments of adversaries … [which could be] bad policies."[191] He reiterated that he had expressed his concerns to superiors in Hawaii and NSA headquarters about the "real problems with the way the N.S.A. was interpreting its legal authorities" and had "more or less" been directed to "stop asking questions." NSA now responded by releasing what it said was his sole internal email, which sought clarification about the laws governing the agency. Snowden called this a "clearly tailored and incomplete leak," which omitted his correspondence with NSA compliance officials. On May 13, 2014 PBS's *Frontline* aired a program on the "United States of Secrets," interviewing the other whistle-blowers who exposed NSA surveillance: William Binney, Thomas Drake, Kirk Wiebe, Ed Loomis, and Diane Roark.

The EP Committee on Civil Liberties, Justice and Home Affairs produced a draft report, condemning "in the strongest possible terms the vast, systemic, blanket collection of the personal data of innocent people" and declaring that "trust has been profoundly shaken."[192] (Sixteen years earlier the EP had warned that "all e-mail, telephone and fax communications are routinely intercepted by" NSA.) "Data collection of such a magnitude" was probably guided by "motives such as political and economic espionage." It voted 36–2–1 to invite Snowden to testify by video link.

In January 2014 Obama spent 90 minutes discussing surveillance with members of Congress.[193] Declaring that the "critical question" was the value of the metadata program "weighed against the cost of collecting millions and millions of domestic call records of the American people," Rep. Schiff urged that telecoms hold their own data. Sen. Wyden read aloud the Review Group's conclusion that metadata "was not essential to preventing attacks and could readily have been obtained in a timely manner" using conventional means. HJC chair Goodlatte said Obama "needs to break his silence and clearly explain to the American people why" bulk collection of telephony metadata "is needed for our national security." At a White House meeting on January 10, tech companies said they did not want to hold internet metadata for the government.

In a public letter DDC Judge Bates, Director of the Administrative Office of the US Courts, warned that the proposed reforms would have a negative "operational impact" on FISC (where he had recently been chief judge). He recommended against changing the appointment of FISC judges and urged that a public advocate appear only at FISC's request. Providing unclassified summaries of FISC decisions would be "likely to promote confusion and misunderstanding." All of Obama's Review Group testified before SJC in favor of their recommendations. Sunstein said: "in our tradition … the judge doesn't decide whether one or another view gets a lawyer." At the hearing, Leahy agreed with the Group "that the section 215 program contributed to only a few of those cases and was not essential to preventing any terrorist attacks." But Grassley was concerned that having telecoms hold metadata "may create as many privacy problems as it solves," and that the panel proposals "appear to make it more difficult to investigate a terrorist than a common criminal." Sessions dismissed the panel as "mostly … civil libertarian." Rep. Schiff introduced the Telephone Metadata Reform Act, which would require telecoms to hold metadata and have the government request individual records.

On January 17, 2014 Obama proposed reforms closely tracking his Review Group's recommendations.[194] Metadata would be held by the companies that transmitted it; NSA would have to ask FISC for records except in an emergency and could see those two (not three) steps from a terrorism suspect. The USA would not eavesdrop on allied leaders. Data collected abroad would be deleted after a specified time. A panel of privacy and technology advocates would appear before FISC in novel cases. Wyden, Udall, and Heinrich called the proposal "a major milestone." The *New York Times* welcomed the "important new restrictions," but complained that Obama was "frustratingly short on specifics and vague on implementation." "Any public advocate must be free to decide what cases to argue." The *Washington Post* felt he "offered a usefully balanced view," but also found the proposals "less useful because they were vague." The *Los Angeles Times* urged Congress to consider "whether the metadata program is worth continuing even if the records are privately held." The *Wall Street Journal* warned that Obama's proposals "will do little to secure American privacy but they might make the country less safe."

A Task Force led by DIA Director LtGen. Flynn reported to Congress that Snowden had taken 1.7 million intelligence files.[195] Rep. Rogers declared that these "real acts of betrayal place America's military men and women at greater risk" and "are likely to have lethal consequences for our troops in the field." Rep. Ruppersberger said Snowden "handed terrorists a copy of our country's playbook." Rep. Rogers and Sen. Feinstein insinuated Snowden might have been working for Russian spy services while in Hawaii, but offered no evidence. Rep. McCaul (R-Tex) repeated that Snowden had been "cultivated by a foreign power." Snowden ridiculed these "absurd" "smears." In his annual report on threats facing the USA, DNI Clapper called on Snowden to return all the documents and accused him of hypocrisy for "choosing" to live in Russia. HASC chair McKeon (R-Ca) called Snowden "a traitor and a criminal"; vice chair Thornberry (R-Tex) said he was guilty of "espionage," which "compromise[d] the military capability and defense of the country" and would cost "billions to repair." In a *New Yorker* interview, Obama said Snowden's leaks had "put people at risk" while failing to show that NSA had acted illegally. "I actually feel confident that the way the N.S.A. operates does not threaten the privacy and constitutional rights of Americans and that the laws that are in place are sound."

NSA had implanted surveillance-facilitating software in nearly 100,000 computers worldwide, some through the Internet and some in hardware.[196] Four months after this was reported, Cisco CEO John Chambers wrote Obama: "We simply cannot operate this way; our customers trust us to be able to deliver to their doorsteps products that meet the highest standards of integrity and security."

On January 23 the PCLOB (former Federal Trade Commission Commissioner David Medine; retired DC Circuit Judge Patricia Wald; civil liberties advocate James Dempsey; and two Bush DoJ lawyers, Rachel Brand and Elizabeth Cook) issued a 238-page report recommending termination of the collection program:[197] "[It] lacks a viable legal foundation under section 215, implicates constitutional concerns under the First and Fourth Amendments, raises serious threats to privacy and civil liberties as a policy matter, and has shown only limited value." The Board found "no instance in which the program directly contributed to the discovery of a previously unknown terrorist plot or the disruption of a terrorist attack." FISC had not offered a detailed legal rationale for the program until 2013; and its argument that the Patriot Act authorized bulk collection "represents an unsustainable attempt to shoehorn a pre-existing surveillance program into the text of a statute with which it is not compatible." Bulk collection also violated the Electronic Communications Privacy Act. The *New York Times* observed that "once again, a thorough and independent analysis of the government's dragnet surveillance of

Americans' phone records has found the bulk data collection to be illegal and probably unconstitutional," as well as "virtually useless at stopping terrorism." The White House responded: "we simply disagree with the board's analysis of the legality of the program." So did Rep. Rogers. But Sens. Sanders (Independent-Vt) and Leahy called the program unconstitutional, and Reps. Schiff and Goodlatte (R-Va) demanded reform. The RNC urged a special committee to "reveal" the extent of NSA spying – "an intrusion on basic human rights that threatens the very foundations of a democratic society" – and "hold accountable those public officials who are found to be responsible for this unconstitutional surveillance." It also sought legislation prohibiting "blanket surveillance ... of any person residing in the U.S."

The government agreed to let tech companies disclose the number of FISC orders and National Security Letters (NSLs) (separately, in increments of 1,000) every six months, as well as the number of selectors.[198] In response, Google, Microsoft, Yahoo, and Facebook dropped their FISC lawsuits. Microsoft reported receiving 15–16,000 requests, Google 9–10,000, Facebook 5–6,000, and Yahoo 30–31,000. Objecting that the government was not letting telecoms reveal "nearly enough" information, the *New York Times* supported a bill sponsored by Sens. Franken and Heller requiring disclosure of all such orders.

Attorney General Holder told SJC that NSA was subject to a "great deal of oversight" and the issues this identified "have all been corrected."[199] But Sen. Wyden did not believe "this culture of misinformation can be easily fixed." (Two months later, in response to a question by Wyden, Clapper wrote that NSA had read US persons' communications with non-US persons reasonably believed to be outside the USA because Congress had declined to eliminate that authority when it reauthorized §702. Wyden and Udall called this "further evidence that the intelligence community will spy on Americans if it believes it has the legal authority to do so.") Steven Bradbury (former OLC acting head) warned HJC that Obama's proposed reforms "would severely constrain the effectiveness and utility of the NSA programs." But Rep. Sensenbrenner threatened Deputy Attorney General Cole that unless §215 "is fixed, you ... and the intelligence committee will get" no money; and Rep. Goodlatte said the programs needed "significant reform." When Rep. Rogers told an HPSCI hearing that journalists who published articles using leaked NSA documents were criminals "fencing stolen materials," FBI Director Comey responded that prosecuting them "could have First Amendment implications."

Warning HJC that "'Made in America' is no longer viewed as positive for customers of U.S. online services," Dean Garfield (president and CEO of the Information Technology Industry Council) called for greater transparency, a public advocate before FISC, and reform of §215 collection.[200] PCLOB and the Review Group repeated their criticisms.

A Danish newspaper published a Snowden document revealing that NSA intercepted information about other countries' positions before the 2009 Copenhagen climate summit to help US negotiators.[201] *Süddeutsche Zeitung* reported that NSA had monitored German Chancellor Schröder from 2002 and perhaps earlier. When Obama assured the French President a week later that the USA was "committed to making sure that we are protecting and concerned about the privacy rights ... of people around the world," Hollande said that "mutual trust has been restored." But Merkel planned to discuss with Hollande how to build communications networks within Europe "so that you don't have to go across the Atlantic with emails." Deutsche Telekom had introduced an encrypted internet service. Even after Obama promised to stop spying on Merkel, NSA increased surveillance of 320 German political leaders. The EP voted 621–10–22 to require search engines, social networks, and cloud storage companies to obtain permission from a citizen's national data protection authority before giving data to another country and to inform the citizen (but all 28 countries would have to agree for the rule to take effect). The EP passed (544–78–60) a nonbinding resolution condemning NSA spying and urging Europe to respect "democratic, judicial and parliamentary safeguards and oversight in a digital society." Snowden told the Council of Europe in April that NSA "specifically targeted" leaders and staff in NGOs, including AI and HRW, sometimes exclusively within the USA. That month the European Court of Justice (ECJ) held that bulk collection of phone records violated a fundamental right to privacy.

Perhaps responding to criticism of FISC's partisan political composition, Chief Justice Roberts named his first Democratic appointees – DDC Judge Boasberg and Ninth Circuit Judge Tallman – to FISC and FISCR, respectively.[202] (A later study found that Republican appointees had been a majority on FISC for 32 of the 34 periods since its creation in 1978.) FISC agreed to review each NSA phone record search, require a "reasonable, articulable suspicion" of a terrorist connection, and limit searches to two hops from the suspect. But ODNI General Counsel Litt told PCLOB that the "operational burden" of requiring court approval to intercept Americans' communications would be so great that FISC "would be extremely unhappy." And NSA General Counsel Rajesh De acknowledged that because the government identified foreign targets from email content, not just addresses, "there is a greater likelihood" of intercepting communications involving Americans or those that were wholly domestic.

Snowden documents revealed that the Australian Signals Directorate monitored the Mayer Brown law firm while it was representing Indonesia in trade disputes with the USA and shared the information with NSA, warning that it might contain privileged attorney–client communications.[203] ABA President James Silkenat told NSA Director Alexander that "the interception and sharing of attorney–client privileged communications by government agencies" risks "chilling the full and frank discussion between lawyer and client that is essential for effective legal representation." Alexander assured him that "NSA has afforded, and will continue to afford, appropriate protection to privileged attorney–client communications."

NSA helped GCHQ conduct the "Optic Nerve Program," which intercepted and stored images (some sexually explicit) from more than 1.8 million Yahoo customers' webcam chats.[204] Sens. Wyden, Udall, and Heinrich were "extremely troubled." The Computer and Communications Industry Association said this "indicates government privacy violations have reached an alarming new level of intrusiveness."

A bipartisan group of 181 representatives introduced the Email Privacy Act to amend the Electronic Communications Privacy Act 1986 by requiring a warrant to search email.[205] A similar bill introduced by Leahy and Lee passed SJC, but the Securities and Exchange Commission (SEC) and other agencies warned it would obstruct their investigations.

Snowden documents revealed that NSA had spied on former Chinese President Hu Jintao and China's Trade Ministry, banks, and telecoms, especially Huawei (which the USA had blocked from American business deals, accusing it of wanting to create backdoors to let the Chinese government or businesses steal secrets).[206] An NSA spokesperson insisted "we do not give intelligence we collect to U.S. companies." NSA also spied on Pacnet (the Hong Kong-based operator of undersea fiber optic cables), state oil companies in Saudi Arabia, Africa, Iran, and Mexico, and the European Commission Antitrust Commissioner. China lodged a complaint. When President Xi Jinping raised the issue, Obama said: "the United States does not engage in espionage to gain a commercial advantage." Less than two months later the

USA charged members of the Chinese People's Liberation Army in ED Pa with stealing trade secrets from US companies and others with using Blackshades to remotely control computers. Holder said: "the alleged hacking appears to have been conducted for no reason other than to advantage state-owned companies and other interests in China, at the expense of businesses here in the United States." China responded by ending talks with the USA on norms of internet behavior. Its State Internet Information Office planned to require "internet security assessments for important internet information technology products and their suppliers entering the Chinese marketplace." The Chinese State Council Information Office's Internet Media Research Center said it had confirmed Snowden's claims that "U.S. monitoring operations have involved the Chinese government and leaders, Chinese companies and scientific research institutions, ordinary internet users and many mobile phone users." Accusing Cisco of complicity with NSA, China banned it and other leading American firms, including Apple, from its government purchasing list.

Obama directed DoJ and the intelligence community to design a plan to end NSA's bulk collection, leaving call logs with the phone companies and requiring that NSA obtain a FISC order to search each suspect (and others two hops away).[207] The administration would seek one renewal of the 90-day FISC order about to expire. In January 2014 Obama had started requiring prior FISC approval except in emergencies, a rule NSA found workable. The *New York Times* observed that Obama "doesn't need to ask the permission of Congress … He can just end [bulk collection] immediately." The proposed standard of "reasonable, articulable suspicion" was "unacceptably weak." FISC should disclose when it granted NSA requests. The *Miami Herald* said it was "a good, if belated, start," but "doesn't go far enough." FISC should follow an adversarial process. The *Washington Post* also called it "a good start." HPSCI proposed something very similar, and Sen. Feinstein endorsed the administration proposal.

A Snowden document showed that NSA eavesdropped on leaders of 122 countries, naming Germany, Malaysia, Peru, Somalia, Guatemala, Colombia, Belarus, Ukraine, Malawi, and Syria.[208] FISC apparently had approved collecting everyone's calls in Germany, China, Mexico, Japan, Venezuela, Yemen, Brazil, Sudan, Guatemala, Bosnia, and Russia. (Another document revealed that MYSTIC recorded metadata on all calls, even those by Americans, in Mexico, Philippines, Kenya, and at least one other country. A later Snowden leak revealed that SOMALGET allowed NSA to record the *content* of every cell phone call in the Bahamas – to interdict drugs – and another unnamed country, later revealed to be Afghanistan.) A Bundestag committee was investigating NSA spying in Germany and planned to have Snowden testify. The USA denied an official German request for NSA records of Merkel's phone calls and refused to conclude a "no-spying" agreement with Germany because it had none with any country (even the Five Eyes), and it would therefore have to offer the same to other allies. Germany abandoned an effort to increase intelligence sharing with the USA. At a joint press conference during Merkel's visit to the White House, Obama called her "one of my closest friends on the world stage ... we have gone a long way in closing some of the gaps." But Merkel said it was too soon to return to "business as usual," partly because of the "[dis]proportionality" of surveillance. Germany terminated Verizon's contract for internet service, fearing it facilitated NSA surveillance.

In January 2014 an unnamed phone company (later revealed as Verizon) asked FISC Judge Collyer to stop making it give records to NSA.[209] On March 20 she denied the request, rejecting Judge Leon's analysis in *Klayman* (see below) on the ground that *Smith* v. *Maryland* governed and disregarding the PCLOB conclusion that the Patriot Act did not authorize bulk collection. Collyer called this the first telecom challenge to §215, quoting FISC Judge Eagen's August 2013 opinion: "To date, no holder of records who has received an order to produce bulk telephony metadata has challenged the legality of such an order." In fact, Sprint had resisted a similar §215 order before FISC Judge Bates in January 2010, noting it had raised questions about the program as early as July 2009. Sprint complied with Bates's order after reading secret FISC opinions, including one by Chief Judge Kollar-Kotelly holding that the relevance standard "does not require a statistical 'tight fit' between" bulk collection and the "much smaller proportion" of relevant data.

The House of Representatives considered rival bills. In HJC, Sensenbrenner's USA Freedom Act would compel NSA to get FISC approval for every search; in HPSCI, the FISA Transparency and Modernization Act by Rogers and Ruppersberger would require that FISC approve only new surveillance programs but let it deny NSA searches retroactively.[210] The HJC bill required a reasonable articulable suspicion that the data related to counterterrorism; the SSCI bill permitted searches to detect espionage, WMD proliferation, and other national security threats. The HJC bill allowed FISC to appoint a "special advocate" but dropped language letting telecoms issue detailed reports about government data requests. Both committees unanimously approved a compromise requiring phone companies to keep call logs for 18 months and letting NSA seek FISC approval to search records two links from the suspect. After weakening the USA Freedom Act to let NSA search using a "discrete term" that would "limit the scope of the information or tangible things sought" rather than a "specific selection term … used to uniquely describe a person, entity or account," the House passed it 303–121. The *New York Times* regretted that the bill "does not live up to its title." The administration's last-minute amendment could let NSA "demand records for an entire ZIP code, state or region."

In a *New Yorker* interview as he was about to retire as NSA Director, Alexander repeated his assertion (which the magazine had disproved) that the metadata program would have let the agency prevent 9/11 by identifying Khalid al-Mihdhar, the San Diego-based hijacker.[211] He also reiterated the discredited claim that the program had disrupted 54 "plots, funding, and giving money." Metadata was "the least intrusive, most efficient way" to do that. He insisted the USA was now "at greater risk." His successor, Adm. Michael Rogers, said: "if we do anything against U.S. persons, we have specific legal constraints that we must apply." Although he had seen terrorist groups change their communications strategy because of Snowden's disclosures, "you have not heard me as the director say, 'oh, my God, the sky is falling.'" The number of targets for whom NSA could no longer collect data was more than half a dozen, "but not in the hundreds."

On June 18 a group of nearly forty civil liberties and privacy NGOs withdrew their support for the Act because the House Rules Committee had broadened selectors (including "about" targets), reduced transparency and disclosure of FISC opinions, and weakened provision for an amicus. On the anniversary of Snowden's revelations, the Reform Government Surveillance coalition of nine leading tech companies published an open letter in the *New York Times* and *Washington Post* warning that the Act "could permit bulk collection of internet 'metadata'" and urging the Senate to reject the bill.[212] The same day the head of a major technology trade association warned SSCI that NSA's activities could have "seriously damaging long-term implications" for the global economy. Later that month more than thirty civil liberties and human rights organizations wrote Sens. Reid, McConnell, Leahy, Grassley, Feinstein, and Chambliss opposing the bill. Microsoft's general counsel said FISC was unaccountable, not "inclined to promote justice" because "only one side gets to tell its story," and made law "the American public is not permitted to read."

In a late night session the House voted 293–123 for an NDAA amendment sponsored by Lofgren, Sensenbrenner, and Massie (R-Ky) eliminating funds for the NSA to use FISA §702 to conduct searches targeting Americans or to ask hardware makers and software developers to build backdoor access.[213] But the House then passed the NDAA 340–73 without the amendment. At the end of June ODNI issued its first transparency report, indicating that NSA had targeted nearly 90,000 people and organizations under FISA §702; but it did not reveal how many were US persons or report on activity under EO 12333.

A document released by Snowden, signed by Attorney General Holder and approved annually by FISC, authorized NSA to intercept information "concerning" 193 countries (all but the other four Eyes) as well as the World Bank, IMF, EU, and International Atomic Energy Agency.[214] After the leak of a 2011 FISC opinion estimating that NSA annually collected up to 46,000 wholly domestic emails containing a target's address or phone number, Wyden complained that NSA "is scooping up huge amounts of Americans' wholly domestic communications." On July 2, 2014 PCLOB opined that the FISA §702 program met the Fourth Amendment's reasonableness standard, but added that the "unknown and potentially large scope of the incidental collection of U.S. persons' communications, the use of 'about' collection ... and the use of queries to search for the communications of specific U.S. persons ... push close to the line." It urged that targeting procedures specify criteria for determining the expected foreign intelligence value and that NSA report annually the number of phone calls and emails that began or terminated in the USA and the number of queries on US persons' data.

The *Washington Post* substantiated these concerns. Using Snowden's material, it analyzed 160,000 emails and instant message conversations and 7,900 documents from more than 11,000 online accounts, all intercepted by NSA under FAA §702.[215] If a target entered an online chat room, NSA collected every posting; 90 percent of those surveilled were not intended targets, and many were US persons. NSA supervisors told analysts that PRISM and upstream collection had a "lower threshold for foreignness 'standard of proof,'" requiring only "reasonable belief," not probable cause. One analyst found the standard met because the communication was not in English; another presumed that someone on the chat "buddy list" of a known foreign national also was foreign. A supervisor had instructed analysts that "the best foreignness" selector was a foreign IP address, although millions of Americans lived or traveled abroad or routed their traffic through foreign IPs. The intercepted content included accounts of romance, sexual liaisons, mental health crises, political and religious conversions, and financial anxieties, as well as photos. Whereas the recent ODNI transparency report said nearly 90,000 people were targeted under §702 in 2013, the *Post* estimated that ten times as many were surveilled. DNI General Counsel Litt dismissed such "incidental interception." "The most you could conclude from these news reports is that each valid foreign intelligence target talks to an average of nine people." But the PCLOB said NSA procedures under §702 "may allow a substantial amount of private information about U.S. persons to be acquired by the government, examined by its personnel, and used in ways that may have a negative impact on those persons." Four senators led by Tester urged Clapper to erase all American communications collected "incidentally" and explain "incidental" collection.

Markus R, 31, a mid-level employee of the German federal intelligence agency (BND) arrested for spying for Russia on July 2, 2014, confessed to accepting €25,000 from the USA for 218 German intelligence documents concerning the Bundestag investigation of NSA spying in Germany.[216] The CIA knew of the arrest before Obama phoned Merkel (about NSA eavesdropping on her cell phone), but did not inform the White House. German President Gauck said if the reports were true, "that is really a gamble with friendship … one really has to say, enough is enough." Traveling in China, Merkel said it would be "a serious case," "a clear contradiction as to what I consider to be trusting cooperation between agencies and partners." Emphasizing that "we are not talking about something minor," Foreign Minister Steinmeier summoned the US Ambassador and demanded "swift clarification." Germany expelled the CIA station chief, an action no ally had ever taken before but one that Steinmeier said was "a necessary and an appropriate reaction to the breach of trust." Hans-Christian Ströbele, a member of the Bundestag inquiry, called it "a necessary symbolic act to show our friends on the other side of the Atlantic how serious this matter is." The Interior Minister said: "the political damage is already disproportionate and serious." Merkel also justified the expulsion: "the important thing is to show how we view things … it is not a co-operative partnership when such things take place." The *Washington Post* said: "one clear lesson from the dust-up over Ms. Merkel's cellphone

… was that such operations against allies are almost certainly not worth the damage caused when they are revealed." But former CIA Acting General Counsel Rizzo dismissed the outage as hypocritical. The BND "has long assumed that other countries, including the U.S., were seeking to obtain secret inside information on Germany's plans."

Both sides tried to repair the damage. Kerry and Steinmeier issued a joint statement vowing continued cooperation. Obama discussed intelligence cooperation with Merkel, who affirmed that Germany and the USA were close partners "and nothing about this will change." Obama sent his chief of staff and counterterrorism adviser to meet their counterparts and the BND head in Berlin. But Patrick Sensburg, who chaired the Bundestag inquiry, complained that, a year after Snowden's revelations, the USA still had not explained why it spied on allies. Vice Chancellor Gabriel said the USA had threatened to end intelligence sharing if Germany offered Snowden asylum or even let him address the Bundestag in person. *Der Spiegel* revealed that an October 2013 BND investigation found that at least 2,000 items in the NSA selector list targeted Western European and German interests, including the European Aeronautic Defence and Space Company (EADS), Eurocopter, and French agencies, in violation of a 2002 agreement between the USA and Germany not to surveil each other.

Reviving its investigation at the request of the Left and Green Parties, BND found 40,000 suspicious search parameters, some targeting European governments and companies. *Süddeutsche Zeitung* reported that BND cooperated with NSA in watching "top officials at the French Foreign Ministry, the Elysée Palace and the European Community," prompting two Bundestag committees to investigate. Airbus (one alleged target) filed an espionage complaint. In a decision confirmed but not publicly announced, Germany limited cooperation with the USA on data gathering after learning that BND had not questioned the NSA search terms. A German spokeswoman offered assurances that the Bundestag inquiry was "not something that will jolt German–American relations in any way." But the Bundestag committee leaked emails between Germany and the USA showing that efforts to stop US surveillance in Germany after Snowden's revelations had been a sham. The German federal prosecutor terminated his investigation into eavesdropping on Merkel's phone because NSA refused to cooperate. But three weeks later WikiLeaks published documents confirming eavesdropping, beginning in the 1990s, of 56 phone numbers, including Merkel's top aides and senior figures in the administrations of Gerhard

Schröder and Helmut Kohl; 48 numbers were still in use, including those of Merkel's intelligence coordinator and chief of staff. The latter told the US Ambassador that "established violations are pursued" and "such repeated incidents harm the cooperation between German and American intelligence agencies." The Finance Minister condemned the actions. But the federal prosecutor refused a Green Party request to reopen the investigation.

Analyzing a Snowden document containing 7,485 email addresses monitored by NSA in 2002–08, *The Intercept* found a Rutgers University professor who was president of the American Iranian Council, CAIR executive director Nihad Awad, a Muslim lawyer who defended those accused of terrorism, another Muslim lawyer who represented Sudan in a lawsuit brought by terrorist victims, and the national chair of the American Muslim Alliance.[217] Rep. Keith Ellison (D-Mn), the only Muslim member of Congress, expressed concern. But DoJ and ODNI called it "entirely false that U.S. intelligence agencies conduct electronic surveillance of political, religious or activist figures … for exercising constitutional rights."

Sen. Leahy introduced an alternative to the USA Freedom Act requiring NSA to "narrowly limit the scope of the tangible things to be sought to the greatest extent practical" and directing FISC to publish opinion summaries containing enough information to reveal their impact on civil liberties.[218] The White House was "strongly" supportive. The *New York Times* called it "a significant improvement over the halfhearted measure passed by the House." NSA should have to obtain FISC permission before examining Americans' communications collected "incidentally." The *Washington Post* said it "represents a careful, politically achievable balance." After Judge Bates wrote in support of the House bill as Director of the Administrative Office of U.S. Courts, Nancy Gertner (D Mass Judge 1994–2011) objected that he was unauthorized to speak for the judiciary. Holder and Clapper supported the House bill. A coalition of tech industry groups and dozens of civil liberties organizations urged Congress to pass it "and then immediately turn your attention to more meaningful and comprehensive reform of the [NSA's] overreaching and unconstitutional surveillance practices." But Sen. Coats (R-In) advocated for SSCI's FISA Improvements Act in a *USA Today* op ed. Hayden and Mukasey wrote in the *Wall Street Journal* that "only ISIS" could love Leahy's bill. The Senate's 58–42 vote for the USA Freedom Act was insufficient to overcome a filibuster. Rubio voted against it, declaring that proponents of NSA reform "cannot cite a single example of this program ever being abused." Chambliss exhorted fellow Republicans: "you guys are going to be in charge next year. You're the ones who ought to write this bill." The White House planned to reintroduce it in the next Congress. Leahy wrote Obama the day before a key NSA program expired, urging him not to seek renewal. But NSA obtained FISC's approval.

John Napier Tye (who had just quit DoS after three years to be a whistle-blower) warned in a *Washington Post* op ed that "Americans should be even more concerned about the collection and storage of their communications under EO 12333 than under section 215."[219] There was no limit on collecting information on Americans outside the USA, and many internet servers were located abroad. PCLOB promised to investigate.

Ben Emmerson, UN Special Rapporteur for the promotion and protection of human rights and fundamental freedoms while countering terrorism, said in a report to the General Assembly that "bulk access technology is indiscriminately corrosive of online privacy and impinges on the very essence of the right" guaranteed by ICCPR Art. 17 that "no one shall be subjected to arbitrary or unlawful interference with his or her privacy, family, home and correspondence."[220] Any internet user should have standing to "challenge the legality, necessity and proportionality" of surveillance. Germany and Brazil offered a new resolution condemning unlawful or arbitrary surveillance as "highly intrusive" and asking the UN Human Rights Commission to consider appointing a special rapporteur on privacy rights. The Commission adopted the proposal (which had 65 sponsors) by consensus. The European Commissioner for Human Rights issued a 120-page report, "The Rule of Law on the Internet in the Wider Digital World," declaring that "suspicionless mass retention of communications data is fundamentally contrary to the rule of law … and ineffective." The director of the European Commission's Department of Justice complained that "the law … which empowers the NSA to basically grab everything which comes from outside the United States is a real trade barrier to a European digital company to provide services to Americans inside America."

EFF and *New York Times* FOIA requests uncovered two conflicting FISC decisions.[221] After the *Times* exposed the NSA program and a federal judge in Boston found it illegal, in January 2007 the administration persuaded FISC Judge Howard to approve an expansive definition of probable cause to believe that "facilities" – which could include the high-capacity switches through which telecoms routed international communications – were being used by a foreign target. But when the program came up for renewal three months later, FISC Judge Vinson rejected a government request to target foreigners communicating through US facilities, finding it did not meet the probable cause standard. The following month, however, Vinson allowed the existing surveillance to continue by approving a long list of specific addresses. After Bush signed the PAA on August 5, 2007, Vinson approved the NSA application.

In December 2014 Congress eliminated a provision inserted by Reps. Massie and Lofgren in the Intelligence Authorization Act, banning NSA searches of Americans' communications.[222] But the Act as passed prohibited the government from holding for more than five years any communications "reasonably anticipated" to involve a US person and obtained without a court order or subpoena (even those collected overseas under EO 12333). In a case involving a man accused of illegally exporting goods to Iran without a license, DoJ disclosed that DEA retained metadata on calls between the USA and other countries even without evidence of criminal activity. Leahy asked Holder not to revive the program, which had been suspended in September 2013 and later terminated. In April 2015 HRW sued because its staff regularly called countries linked to the drug trade.

At the end of January 2015 PCLOB complained that "many of the recommendations directed at the administration [a year earlier] have yet to be fully satisfied, with the administration having taken only partial steps, at most, toward implementing them."[223] Although it had made "substantial progress" toward implementing the recommendations on internet surveillance, it "has not implemented the Board's recommendation to halt the NSA's telephone records program." (The following year PCLOB said all 22 of its 2014 recommendations "have been implemented in full or in part, or the relevant government agency has taken significant steps toward adoption and implementation.") Days later Obama ordered deletion of any incidentally collected communication by a US person unless it was determined to be "relevant to foreign intelligence"; and he institutionalized regular White House review of NSA monitoring of foreign leaders. At her SJC confirmation hearing for Attorney General, Loretta Lynch told Graham that NSA surveillance was "constitutional and effective"; but she temporized on releasing the OLC memos, including those on EO 12333. In February FISC reauthorized bulk telephony metadata collection under §215 only after it found "a reasonable, articulable suspicion that the requested selection term is associated with an international terrorist organization approved by the Court," and it limited queries to two hops.

As §215 was about to expire, a coalition of major tech firms and privacy groups wrote Obama and senior lawmakers opposing any legislation authorizing bulk collection.[224] Presidential aspirant Rand Paul promised to end warrantless surveillance. Reps. Massie and Pocan (D-Wisc) introduced the Surveillance State Repeal Act to repeal both the Patriot Act and the FAA. Senate Majority Leader McConnell and SSCI chair Burr (R-NC) introduced a bill to extend §215 through 2020. And Leahy and Lee reintroduced the USA Freedom Act in the Senate, while Goodlatte and Conyers did so in the House. With support from House Speaker Boehner, HJC passed the last of these 25–2. The *New York Times* regretted that many provisions were "weaker than in earlier versions of the bill, and weaker than they need to be." Although HRW, EFF, and the Information Technology Industry Council supported it, the ACLU wanted a tighter definition of selector terms, limits on retaining information, and an advocate before FISC. Reps. Goodlatte, Conyers, Sensenbrenner, and Nadler wrote the *New York Times* that the bill "represents the most sweeping set of reforms to government surveillance practices in nearly 40 years."

On May 7 the Second Circuit held in *ACLU* v. *Clapper* (discussed below) that §215 did not authorize bulk surveillance. The *New York Times* said the decision's "most important message" was that "Congress could not have intended to approve a program whose scope almost no one outside the National Security Agency fully comprehended."[225] Republicans seeking to renew §215 ignored this "most important rebuke yet of the government's abuses under that law." Sponsors of the USA Freedom Act said the ruling confirmed that "bulk collection of data is not authorized under the law and is not accepted by the American people." But Sen. Corker (R-Tn) declared it was "beyond belief how little data is part of the program." McConnell repeated the CIA's claim that NSA surveillance "would have likely prevented 9/11." Reid asked him rhetorically: "how can you reauthorize something that is illegal?" Burr called the decision "a joke." Graham said that "it would be pretty hard to diminish this program right now based on a court ruling that's not binding" (a bizarre statement for a lawyer). Presidential candidates Paul, Clinton, and Cruz (R-Tex) supported the USA Freedom Act. Paul promised to filibuster any renewal of §215 and end bulk collection "on day 1" as president. But other contenders defended the program. Rubio

(R-Fla) accused critics of "lying" when they claimed that "the United States government is listening to your phone calls or going through your bills as a matter of course." Christie insisted that "no one has a single example of our intelligence services misusing this program for political or other nefarious purposes" (as though misconduct like Nixon's was the only issue). Bush supported §215. The *Washington Post* endorsed the USA Freedom Act, urging McConnell to revise his claim that §215 authorized bulk collection, a view that had been "barely" tenable even before the decision.

Instead, McConnell introduced a bill to extend the deadline a month. After the House passed the USA Freedom Act 338–88 and adjourned until after §215 expired on June 1, the *Washington Post* again urged McConnell to permit a vote on this "carefully crafted compromise." The latest poll found that 60 percent of Americans (even 59 percent of very conservative voters) wanted §215 modified. McConnell agreed to let the Senate vote. DoJ told Congress it would start closing the surveillance program on May 22, 2015. Rand Paul filibustered for 10.5 hours on the night of May 20–21, supported by Lee, Cruz, Daines (R-Mt), and Manchin (D-WV). The *New York Times* applauded Paul's "singular service … particularly since so many of his rivals prefer to slide off the issue by endorsing a compromised and faulty renewal." The next day the Senate voted 57–42 for the bill, failing to reach the necessary 60 votes but also failing to pass McConnell's extension. Obama warned that "a whole range" of "noncontroversial" authorities in the Patriot Act "are at risk of lapsing." Sen. Cotton (R-Ark) predicted that loss of "this critical tool would lead to attacks on the United States." But noting that "the government has not offered persuasive evidence that bulk collection of phone records has been crucial to foiling plots," the *New York Times* declared that a hiatus "would be perfectly fine." The Patriot Act provisions expired after Paul blocked an extension during a rare Sunday session. But the Senate voted 77–17 to take up the House bill, passing it the next day 67–32, and Obama signed it.

The Act ended bulk collection after a 180-day transition period. NSA promised to expunge all its data when the program expired on November 29. Two weeks later Hayden belittled its effect: "what you're going to be required to do is … go to court and get access to [telephony metadata] from the companies … And this is it after two years? Cool!" A month after the Act passed, FISC Judge Mosman let NSA resume bulk collection during the transition period, rejecting the Second

Circuit's *ACLU* v. *Clapper* opinion.[226] That court denied an ACLU motion to enjoin NSA from surveilling the organization during the transition period, finding that Congress knew it was authorizing this. "We need not, and should not, decide such momentous constitutional issues based on a request for such narrow and temporary relief."

Declaring that Snowden's "dangerous decision to steal and disclose classified information had severe consequences for the security of our country and the people who work day in and day out to protect it," the White House rejected a petition by 167,000 urging a pardon.[227] Snowden said he got no response to his offer to serve time in prison; without a deal he would be tried by a judge under the Espionage Act and receive a sentence of at least 30 years.

Chris Christie was applauded at a Republican presidential debate in August 2015 when he declared: "we have to give more tools to our folks to be able to" eavesdrop, "not fewer, and then trust those people and oversee them to do it in the right way."[228] A few days later Jeb Bush said the balance between privacy and security "has actually gone the wrong way." Encryption "makes it harder for the American government to do its job." In October Hillary Clinton said Snowden should be prosecuted because he "stole very important information that has unfortunately fallen into a lot of the wrong hands." Bernie Sanders agreed Snowden should suffer a "penalty," but said "what he did in educating us should be taken into consideration"; and Sanders vowed to end NSA surveillance.

Snowden documents revealed that in September 2003 AT&T gave NSA a " 'live' presence on the global net," letting it collect 400 billion metadata records a month and send more than a million emails a day to its keyword selection system.[229] By 2011 AT&T was giving NSA 1.1 billion domestic cell phone call records a day. DNI Clapper acknowledged that Snowden's leaks had "forced some needed transparency, particularly on those programs that affected the civil liberties and privacy in this country"; but Clapper regretted that they had forced the shutdown of surveillance in Afghanistan, where "it was the single most important source of force protection and warning." NSA Director Rogers told SSCI that bulk collection was essential, citing a National Academy of Sciences study. Wyden replied that the White House Review Group had come to the opposite conclusion.

The ACLU and EFF praised FISC for appointing five amici curiae to argue in cases presenting "a novel or significant interpretation of the law": a criminal defense lawyer, a former OLC acting director, a Georgetown law professor, a former Holder aide, and an information security lawyer.[230] In the first case where an amicus appeared (the former Holder aide), Judge Hogan granted the surveillance applications but also criticized NSA for failing to comply with minimization procedures and the FBI for not establishing review teams for targeted persons facing criminal charges.

In October 2015 (in a case brought by an Austrian graduate student) the European Court of Justice invalidated the Safe Harbor agreement governing data transfers between the USA and EU because Snowden's leaks revealed that NSA had almost unfettered access to internet data; and it ruled that data protection regulators in each of the 28 EU countries had to approve privacy protections.[231] The USA and EU had been negotiating a new agreement for two years; and a bill was pending in Congress to let Europeans challenge privacy infringements in US courts. Attorney General Lynch said the "particularly disappointing" ECJ decision was "based on inaccurate and outdated media reports." In February 2016 (just before the deadline) negotiators announced an agreement – the EU–US Privacy Shield – prohibiting "indiscriminate" or "arbitrary" use of data and creating a complaints ombudsperson. Congress and all 28 countries had to approve it.

After the November 2015 Paris attacks, DCI Brennan denounced "hand-wringing" over surveillance, declaring that Snowden's leaks had made it harder to identify ISIS's "murderous sociopaths."[232] Hayden said bulk collection of metadata had done no harm and was designed to identify "unknown people inside the homeland who are communicating with terrorists abroad." "In the wake of Paris, a big stack of metadata doesn't seem to be the scariest thing in the room." Former Acting DCI Morell said: "ISIS went to school on how we were collecting intelligence on terrorist operations by using telecoms technologies. And when they learned that from the Snowden disclosures, they were able to adapt to it and essentially go silent." He was "fairly confident" they were using encryption. "Much more damaging: the Snowden disclosures created this perception that people's privacy was being put at significant risk." The media "made the public more concerned about the privacy issue than the legitimate facts should have done." "I believe [Snowden] contributed to the rise of ISIS." Former DCI Woolsey said: "the blood of a lot of these French young people is on [Snowden's] hands." Espionage was "still a capital crime, and I would give him the death sentence, and I would prefer to see him hanged by the neck until he's dead, rather than merely electrocuted." Condemning Cruz for supporting the USA Freedom Act, Rubio said it "left our intelligence community with fewer tools to protect the American people and needlessly created more vulnerabilities and gaps in information gathering used to prevent terrorist attacks at home and abroad." Cruz retorted that Rubio "is not willing to protect the Fourth Amendment privacy rights of law-abiding citizens." Christie said: "it's not a coincidence that [the Paris attack] happened in the aftermath of restricting these programs and … demoralizing the intelligence community." He attacked Cruz and Paul for supporting FISA reform. The *New York Times* condemned Brennan's remarks as "a new and disgraceful low." "What he calls 'hand-wringing' was the sustained national outrage following the 2013 revelations by Edward Snowden." "Indiscriminate bulk data sweeps have not been useful." The *Times* opposed "unquestioning acceptance of ineffective and very likely unconstitutional tactics that reduce civil liberties without making the public safer." Paul said that when politicians and officials "stand up on television and say the tragedy in Paris means you have to give up your liberty, we need more phone surveillance – bullshit." After the San Bernardino attack, Sen. Cotton introduced legislation to undo the USA Freedom Act.

But NSA Director Rogers told a group of industry and intelligence officials that having phone companies keep the metadata "is working well so far."[233] An NSA IG report obtained by the *New York Times* said the agency was getting much less data from Americans' international communications than privacy advocates feared. The NSA official who investigated Snowden's leak claimed that about a thousand intelligence targets had since "taken steps to remove themselves from our visibility." But he liked the new program, even though it was more expensive and slower. Rubio, however, said at a Republican presidential debate that the USA Freedom Act "did … take away a valuable tool … to see who terrorists have been calling." Paul disagreed: "we are not any safer through the bulk collection of all Americans' records. In fact, I think we're less safe." The Conservative Solutions Project, which backed Rubio, published photos of Cruz, Paul, and Sanders with the caption: "these senators have defended Snowden's actions."

The USA Freedom Act did not eliminate privacy concerns. In March 2016 the Brennan Center reported that "the majority" of NSA electronic surveillance occurred through EO 12333, using broad selectors like "Yemen."[234] FISC had no supervisory authority over such collection, and data could be retained for more than five years and shared with foreign governments. HPSCI investigated whether NSA had intercepted communications between members of Congress and Israeli officials. Hoekstra tweeted: "very disturbing. Actually outrageous. Maybe unprecedented abuse of power." "NSA and Obama officials need to be investigated and prosecuted if any truth to WSJ reports. NSA loses all credibility." Cruz said: "this administration views Congressional Republicans and sometimes even Democratic members of Congress as their enemy … At times, it seems like they view the American people as their enemy." NSA also allegedly had recordings of Israeli Prime Minister Netanyahu and his aides leaking negotiations for the Iranian nuclear ban in the hope of torpedoing it.

Several legal challenges to surveillance paralleled these legislative reforms, which ultimately disposed of them. The day after the *Guardian* published Snowden's revelations, Larry Klayman, a conservative lawyer and gadfly, sued the government and 12 internet companies in DDC for invasion of privacy on behalf of himself and other individuals, seeking $23 billion damages.[235] In mid-December 2013 Judge Leon issued a preliminary injunction, ordering the government to stop collecting Klayman's phone call data and destroy its records (but stayed the order to let the government appeal).[236] Although 15 FISC judges had issued 35 orders authorizing the program, "the Government has nonetheless acknowledged, as it must, that failures to comply with the minimization procedures set forth in the orders have occurred." Leon noted that since the Supreme Court's decision in *Clapper* v. *Amnesty International*,[237] "news reports revealed the existence and scope of certain NSA surveillance activities." Plaintiffs could "point to strong evidence that, as Verizon customers, their telephony metadata has been collected for at least seven years … and will continue to be collected." A declassified FISC opinion "confirms that the NSA has indeed collected telephony metadata from Verizon." Although the government claimed that FISC's order mentioned only Verizon Business Network Services (VBNS), not Verizon Wireless (Klayman's carrier), it "makes this argument at the same time it is describing in its pleadings a bulk metadata collection program that can function *only* because it 'creates an historical repository that permits retrospective analysis of terrorist-related communications across *multiple telecommunications networks*.'" If the government claims to have created "a *comprehensive* metadata database … NSA *must* have collected metadata from Verizon Wireless, the single largest wireless carrier in the United States" [original emphasis]. "[T]he Government asks me to find that plaintiffs lack standing based on the theoretical possibility that the NSA has collected a universe of metadata so incomplete that the program could not possibly service its putative function. Candor of this type defies common sense and does not exactly inspire confidence." The plaintiffs also had standing to challenge NSA's querying procedures: "The Government … describes the advantages of bulk collection in such a way as to convince me that plaintiffs' metadata – indeed *everyone's* metadata – is analyzed, manually or automatically, whenever the Government runs a query using as the 'seed' a phone number or identifier" [original emphasis].

Leon concluded that the plaintiffs were likely to prevail on their Fourth Amendment claim because "the evolutions in the Government's surveillance capabilities, citizens' phone habits, and the relationship between the NSA and telecom companies" had "become so thoroughly unlike those considered by the Supreme Court thirty-four years ago that a precedent like *Smith* [*v. Maryland*] simply does not apply." The pen register in *Smith* functioned for only 13 days, and there was no indication the data were retained. "[T]here is the very real prospect that the [NSA] program will go on for as long as America is combating terrorism, which realistically could be forever." "It is one thing to say that people expect phone companies to occasionally provide information to law enforcement; it is quite another to suggest that our citizens expect all phone companies to operate what is effectively a joint intelligence-gathering operation with the Government." "[T]he almost Orwellian technology that enables the Government to store and analyze the phone metadata of every telephone user in the United States is unlike anything that could have been conceived in 1979" (when *Smith* was decided). Because "people in 2013 have an entirely different relationship with phones than they did thirty-four years ago … the metadata from each person's phone 'reflects a wealth of detail about her familial, political, professional, religious, and sexual associations.'" When he ruled on the merits, Leon expected to find that "people have a reasonable expectation of privacy that is violated when the Government, without any basis whatsoever to suspect them of any wrongdoing, collects and stores for five years their telephony metadata for purposes of subjecting it to high-tech querying and analysis without any case-by-case judicial approval."

Considering whether "special needs" rendered a warrantless search "reasonable," Leon noted that "no court has ever recognized a special need sufficient to justify continuous, daily searches of virtually every American citizen without any particularized suspicion." Although the government claimed the NSA program was faster than other investigative tools, it "does not cite a single instance in which analysis of the NSA's bulk metadata collection actually stopped an imminent attack, or otherwise aided the Government in achieving any objective that was time-sensitive in nature," and none of the three instances it cited "involved any apparent urgency." Leon therefore had "serious doubts about the efficacy of the metadata collection program."

The plaintiffs were likely to prevail on the merits: "Surely, such a program infringes on 'that degree of privacy' that the Founders enshrined in the Fourth Amendment. Indeed, I have little doubt that the author of our Constitution, James Madison, who cautioned us to beware 'the abridgement of freedom of the people by gradual and silent encroachments by those in power,' would be aghast." Leon declared that the plaintiffs would suffer irreparable harm without injunctive relief, quoting the DC Circuit: "It has long been established that the loss of constitutional freedoms 'for even minimal periods of time, unquestionably constitutes irreparable injury.'" Because he was unpersuaded "that the NSA's database has ever truly served the purpose of rapidly identifying terrorists in time-sensitive investigations," he was "*certainly* not convinced that the removal of two individuals from the database will 'degrade' the program in any meaningful sense" [original emphasis].

The *New York Times* hailed the decision as "an enormous symbolic victory for opponents of the bulk-collection program, and a reminder of the importance of the adversarial process." The *Washington Post* said bulk collection was "a potentially powerful tool," but "could, if abused, reveal sensitive facts about nearly every American's life." The *Los Angeles Times* praised the "powerful opinion," which "effectively refutes … the government's principal argument for the constitutionality of the program."

Eight months later the DC Circuit vacated Leon's preliminary injunction and remanded for further investigation of standing.[238] Judge Brown said that "although one could reasonably infer from the evidence presented [that] the government collected plaintiffs' own metadata, one could also conclude the opposite." Judge Williams wrote that the "plaintiffs' contention that the government is collecting data from Verizon Wireless … depends entirely on an inference from the existence of the bulk collection program." Given "the government's representation that it has never collected 'all, or even virtually all' call records, I find plaintiffs' claimed inference inadequate to demonstrate a 'substantial likelihood' of injury." The "plaintiffs' inference … rests on an assumption that NSA prioritizes effectiveness over all other values" and "fails to account for the possibility that legal constraints, technical challenges, budget limitations, or other interests prevented NSA from collecting metadata from Verizon Wireless." Judge Sentelle would not only vacate the preliminary injunction but also dismiss for lack of standing. "*Clapper* cuts their claims out entirely."

A few days later Judge Leon said the plaintiffs could amend their complaint to include customers of VBNS, which was known to have participated in NSA spying. "This court believes that tens of millions of Americans' constitutional rights have been – and are being – violated. If the court finds jurisdiction, I don't have to write another opinion on the merits ... It is written." He directed DoJ lawyers to cancel their vacation plans and be ready for oral argument on short notice. Aware that the NSA program was about to expire, Leon was "not going to stand by and let you run the clock out if I can avoid it." He told Klayman to ask the Circuit Court to issue its mandate, but said he could grant a motion to amend the complaint before then. A DoJ lawyer said terminating bulk collection – even less than two months before it was scheduled to end in December – would create an imminent national security risk; but the lawyer could not name a single attack the program had prevented. Leon complained that the government had offered only "wonderful high lofty expressions, general vague terms."

After Klayman amended his complaint to add as plaintiffs a California lawyer and law firm using VBNS, Leon enjoined further collection, denying the government's motion to delay a status conference.[239] He had stayed his December 13, 2013 order, having "assumed that the appeal would proceed expeditiously," but the Circuit did not act until nearly three months after the USA Patriot Act lapsed. Although the government had warned of an "intelligence gap" if the USA Patriot Act procedure was enjoined before the USA Freedom Act procedure took effect, "the Government has failed to identify any concrete consequences that would likely result." For "obvious political reasons" Congress did not authorize a continuation of the old procedure during the transition period, but "the Government conveniently went immediately" to FISC for an extension. Although the Second Circuit in *Clapper* (discussed below) had declined to reach the "momentous constitutional issues" because the program was about to expire, Judge Leon did "not suffer the same time constraints," since his analysis of these issues "began nearly two years ago." "[T]his Court cannot, and will not, sit idle in the face of likely constitutional violations for fear that it might be viewed as meddling with the decision of a legislative branch that lacked the political will, or votes, to *expressly* and unambiguously authorize the Program for another six months" [original emphasis]. "Barring some unimaginable circumstances, it is overwhelmingly likely that [plaintiffs'] telephone metadata was indeed warehoused by the NSA." Leon "wholeheartedly" disagreed with the government's claim that there was no evidence that NSA had accessed these records. "[E]very single time the NSA runs a query … it must 'analyze metadata for *every* phone number in the database'" [original emphasis].

> [N]othing in our Circuit Court's opinion precludes me from inferring, based on the NSA's past collection of VBNS subscriber data, that it continues to collect bulk telephony metadata from that *same* provider, pursuant to the *same* statutory authorization, to combat the *same* potential threats to our national security … common sense leads to that precise conclusion here … By the Government's own admission, it is marshaling all available investigative tools to combat a threat it believes to be [at] least as menacing as it was in 2013 [original emphasis].

"Typically, searches not conducted pursuant to a warrant based on the requisite showing of probable cause are '*per se* unreasonable.'" The "special needs" doctrine required Leon to balance privacy and security. "Plaintiffs have a very significant expectation of privacy in an aggregated collection of their telephony metadata," which could reveal "embedded patterns and relationships, including personal details, habits, and behaviors." The 92 percent of American adults owned cellphones did not have the "diminished expectation of privacy that typically characterizes 'special needs' incursions." Leon found the plaintiffs' privacy interests "robust" and rejected the government's claim that the intrusion was "minimal and finite." Rather, the "sweeping, and truly astounding program … targets millions of Americans arbitrarily and indiscriminately." It was "absurd to suggest that the Constitution favors, or even tolerates, such extreme measures!" The "Government has made *no* attempt to tailor its program at all." "[T]here continues [*sic*] to be *no minimization procedures* applicable at the collection stage." "[D]espite changes to the Program, the Government is still, in effect, asking this Court to sanction a dragnet of unparalleled proportions." "To date, the Government has still not cited a single instance in which telephone metadata analysis actually stopped an imminent attack." Its claims that the program "*can* be an important component" and "*can* provide information" were "not exactly confidence inspiring!"

To the government's "bootstrap argument that the enactment of the USA FREEDOM Act confirms the importance of this Program," Leon sarcastically retorted: "Please!" He again quoted a DC Circuit opinion: "enforcement of an unconstitutional law is always contrary to the public interest." Congress was "of course … *not* permitted to prioritize any policy goal over the Constitution" [all original emphasis]. "This Court simply cannot, and will not, allow the Government to trump the Constitution merely because it suits the exigencies of the moment." Leon concluded with a warning: "[T]his case is perhaps the last chapter in the judiciary's evaluation of this particular program's compatibility with the Constitution. It will not, however, be the last chapter in the ongoing struggle to balance privacy rights and national security interests under our Constitution in an age of evolving technological wizardry."

Although he had stayed his original order, "I will not do so today" because "it has been almost two years since I first found that the NSA's Bulk Telephony Metadata Program likely violates the Constitution and because the loss of constitutional freedoms for even one day is a significant harm." DoJ filed an emergency request for a stay, which the DC Circuit granted.[240] The en banc Circuit denied a motion for emergency review.[241] The government successfully moved to vacate the preliminary injunction and dismiss the appeal as moot because the USA Freedom Act ended bulk collection.

The divergent trajectory of a second lawsuit exposed dramatic differences in judicial perspective. Less than a week after Snowden's revelations, the ACLU sued in SDNY to enjoin NSA surveillance.[242] During oral argument Judge Pauley expressed skepticism about the government's claim that the program raised no constitutional issues. When the government maintained that Congress had been fully informed, Pauley noted that several legislators denied knowing about it. Rep. Sensenbrenner filed an amicus brief to that effect. But two weeks after Judge Leon enjoined bulk collection, Judge Pauley dismissed the ACLU lawsuit (as he had AI's). He began:

> The September 11th terrorist attacks revealed, in the starkest terms, just how dangerous and interconnected the world is. While Americans depended on technology for the conveniences of modernity, al-Qaeda plotted in a seventh-century milieu to use that technology against us … And it succeeded because conventional intelligence gathering could not detect diffuse filaments connecting al-Qaeda.

Pauley claimed that the challenged program would have let NSA connect the 9/11 hijacker Khalid al-Mihdhar to a known al-Qaeda safe house in Yemen and pass this information to the FBI. (In fact, the CIA knew of the connection but did not tell the FBI.) Pauley declared: "the effectiveness of bulk telephony metadata collection cannot be seriously disputed," citing three cases: Adis Medunjanin, Khalid Ouazzani, and David Headley. (Others argued that NSA surveillance had not been essential in any of them.) Pauley acknowledged that the "blunt tool" of bulk collection could "reveal a rich profile of every individual as well as a comprehensive record of people's associations with one another." And the plaintiffs clearly had standing. But the USA Patriot Act barred their statutory claim, and their constitutional challenge failed under *Smith* v. *Maryland*, where the plaintiff's privacy concerns had been "far more individualized." Because metadata belonged to Verizon, not the plaintiffs, querying it "does not implicate the Fourth Amendment – anymore [*sic*] than a law enforcement officer's query of the FBI's fingerprint or DNA databases." The Supreme Court's decision in *AI* v. *Clapper* "compels the conclusion that the bulk metadata collection does not burden First Amendment rights substantially." Pauley noted that "fifteen different FISC judges have found the metadata collection program lawful a total of thirty-five times." He quoted Justice Jackson's statement that "the Bill of Rights is not a suicide pact." "Every day, people voluntarily surrender personal and seemingly-private information to transnational corporations." The *New York Times* said this "deeply troubling decision" was "perplexing in its near-total acceptance of the claim by the government that it almost always acts in accordance with the law." Pauley showed "an alarming lack of skepticism," particularly in light of Clapper's misrepresentation to SSCI in March "that the N.S.A. was not collecting any type of data at all on hundreds of millions of Americans."

In May 2015 the Second Circuit reversed, finding that §215 did not authorize bulk collection of metadata.[243] Judge Lynch noted that because metadata could reveal a "startling amount of detailed information," which "could traditionally only be obtained by examining the contents of communications," metadata was "often a proxy for content" about "civil, political or religious affiliations" and "intimate relationships," and could reveal that an individual was a victim of rape or domestic violence, suffering from addiction, or contemplating suicide. It was "virtually impossible for an ordinary citizen to avoid creating metadata about himself on a regular basis." The FISC order published by the *Guardian* "requires Verizon to produce call detail records, every day, on all telephone calls." The government "does not seriously dispute ... that all significant service providers in the United States are subject to similar orders." Unlike *Amnesty International* v. *Clapper*, "here, appellants' alleged injury requires no speculation whatsoever." "[T]he government admits that, when it queries its database, its computers search all of the material stored" and thus "necessarily searches [*sic*] appellants' records." The ACLU's "associational rights are being violated," and it suffered "a 'chilling effect' on clients and donors." "[T]he government relies on bits and shards of inapplicable statutes, inconclusive legislative history, and inferences from silence in an effort to find an implied revocation of the Administrative Procedure Act's authorization of challenges to government actions."

> [T]he government takes the position that the metadata collected – a vast amount of which does not contain directly "relevant" information ... – are nevertheless "relevant" because they may allow the NSA, at some unknown time in the future, utilizing its ability to sift through the trove of irrelevant data it has collected up to that point, to identify information that is relevant ... such an expansive concept of "relevance" is unprecedented and unwarranted.

"The sheer volume of information sought is staggering." "The government can point to no grand jury subpoena that is remotely comparable." "[A]ll examples [of subpoenas] of which we are aware, are bounded either by the facts of the investigation or by a finite time limitation." Furthermore, §215 required that information be "relevant to an authorized investigation," but "the government has not attempted to identify to what particular 'authorized investigation' the bulk metadata of virtually all Americans' phone calls are relevant." "[T]he government effectively argues that there is only one enormous 'anti-terrorism' investigation, and that any records that might ever be of use in developing any aspect of that investigation are relevant to the overall counterterrorism effort." "If the government is correct, it could use §215 to collect and store in bulk any other existing metadata data available anywhere in the private sector, including metadata associated with financial records, medical records, and electronic communications (including email and social media information) relating to all Americans."

Lynch rejected the government's ratification argument. "Congress cannot reasonably be said to have ratified a program of which many members of Congress – and all members of the public – were not aware." "[I]t is a far stretch to say that Congress was aware of the FISC's legal interpretation." Indeed, "the widespread controversy that developed, in and out of Congress, upon the public disclosure of the program makes clear that this is not a situation in which Congress quietly but knowingly adopted the FISC's interpretation." Having concluded that §215 did not authorize the program, the court did not address the "weighty constitutional issues." Although the ACLU had demonstrated "a certainty" of success on the merits, the court remanded to Pauley to decide whether to issue a preliminary injunction, since §215 was "scheduled to expire in just several weeks" and it was "prudent to pause to allow an opportunity for debate in Congress."

Judge Sack agreed with "the primary role that should be played by [Congress] in deciding … whether such programs … are appropriate and necessary," but wrote separately "to ensure that that statement is not read to devalue or minimize the role of the courts in determining the meaning of any such legislation … or its propriety under the Constitution." He also wanted to distinguish "quotidian" federal courts from FISC, which displayed "neither transparency nor a true adversary system." Noting the crucial role counsel for the *New York Times* had played in convincing Judge Gurfein in 1971 not to enjoin publication of the Pentagon Papers, Sack thought it "worth considering that the participation of an adversary to the government at some point in the FISC's proceedings could similarly provide a significant benefit to that court." He ended by quoting Alexander Hamilton's warning in the *Federalist Papers*: "to be more safe" during wartime, nations "become more willing to run the risk of being less free."

On June 9, 2015, a week after Congress passed the USA Freedom Act, the Circuit Court stayed its ruling pending briefs.[244] In October it denied a preliminary injunction during the transition period (ending in December), deferring to Congress's "reasonable decision" to authorize bulk metadata collection during the transition and declining to reach the constitutional issues.

Two other cases reached similar dead ends. In June 2014 a challenge by Anna Smith (represented by her lawyer husband) was dismissed by D Idaho Judge Winmill (a Quixotic example of tilting at windmills), who found that under *Smith* v. *Maryland* she had "no expectation of privacy in the telephone numbers that she dials."[245] He was more troubled by NSA's collection of the time and duration of calls, musing: "Would most citizens want to keep private the fact that they called someone at one in the morning and talked for an hour or two?" They also might want to conceal their location and movements (but he accepted NSA's representation it was not collecting that information). He praised Judge Leon's different conclusion "as a template for a Supreme Court opinion" and noted that Justice Sotomayor had questioned *Smith* v. *Maryland* (but observed that it had not been overruled). In March 2016 the Ninth Circuit found the case moot because NSA had stopped collecting metadata the previous November.

WikiMedia, criminal defense lawyers, journalists, and NGOs sued NSA in March 2015, challenging FISA §702 "upstream" surveillance and the use of "about" selectors.[246] D Md Judge Ellis dismissed in October, following the Supreme Court's *Clapper* decision. The plaintiffs "depend on suppositions and speculation, with no basis in fact, about how the NSA implements Upstream surveillance." They "merely speculate" that NSA was "intercepting all communications passing through ... chokepoints." Analogizing NSA's technological capabilities to a car able to do 200 mph but driving at only 70 mph, Ellis declared that NSA might not be "using the surveillance equipment to its full potential." FISC review ensured that NSA surveillance "must comport with the Fourth Amendment." Furthermore, " 'about surveillance' is targeted insofar as it makes use of only those communications that contain information matching the tasked selector." Interceptions were more likely to occur under PRISM (which this lawsuit did not challenge). WikiMedia claimed that upstream surveillance was "virtually certain" because NSA captured over a trillion communications annually. Unimpressed, Ellis sought to display his superior mathematical sophistication. "One trillion is plainly a large number, but size is always relative. For example, one trillion dollars are of enormous value, whereas one trillion grains of sand are but a small patch of beach." "Plaintiffs conclude that there is a greater than 99.9999999999% chance that NSA has intercepted at least one of their over one trillion communications on the basis of an arbitrary assumption, namely that there is a 0.00000001% chance that the NSA will intercept any particular Internet communication." "Plaintiffs seem to presume a string of zeros buys legitimacy. It does not." What if the chance were lower? "Mathematical gymnastics of this sort do not constitute 'sufficient factual matter' to support a 'plausible' allegation." Where "a court is confronted with substantial uncertainty about the predicates of standing, the risk of a false positive is of greater concern" than any violation of civil liberties "because it implicates an existential question about ... the limits of the judiciary's power in relation to the other branches of government." "[E]stablishing standing to challenge Section 702 in a civil case is plainly difficult. But such difficulty comes with the territory. It is not a flaw of a classified program that standing to challenge that program is not easily established."

But in May 2017 the Third Circuit reversed.[247] The plaintiffs' allegations made "plausible the conclusion that the NSA is intercepting, copying, and reviewing at least some of Wikimedia's communications." "And because Wikimedia has self-censored its speech and sometimes forgone electronic communications in response to Upstream surveillance, it also has standing to sue for a violation of the First Amendment."

Defendants accused of or convicted of terrorism also sought to expose electronic surveillance. During Supreme Court argument of AI's challenge to the FAA in February 2013, Solicitor General Verrilli resisted Justice Sotomayor's suggestion that *no one* would have standing to challenge the law if these plaintiffs did not, by assuring her that prosecutors would notify defendants if evidence had been obtained through warrantless wiretapping.[248] In his opinion dismissing the case for lack of standing, Justice Alito relied on Verrilli's representation to declare that "if the government intends to use or disclose information obtained or derived from" FISA surveillance, "it must provide advance notice of its intent, and the affected person may challenge the lawfulness of the acquisition." Sens. Wyden, Udall, and Heinrich wrote Verrilli questioning his representation. During the December 2012 debate over renewing the FAA, Feinstein had cited cases in Fort Lauderdale and Chicago as evidence that the law had "worked." In spring 2013 prosecutors rebuffed a defense request to confirm that the FAA had been used. When the *New York Times* reported this in June 2013, the embarrassed Solicitor General asked DoJ National Security division lawyers why they had not flagged the issue when reviewing his briefs and preparing him for argument. They claimed disclosure was required only if the evidence was introduced. But after Verrilli overruled them, backed by the FBI, NSA, and ODNI, prosecutors filed statements in the Chicago and Fort Lauderdale cases that they did not intend to use evidence obtained under the FAA. The *Washington Post* welcomed this "long-overdue policy at Justice" and expressed confidence that "at least one open case is likely to result in an actionable constitutional claim against the government's warrantless wiretapping authority." Attorney General Holder said in November 2013 that the DoJ was reviewing cases to decide when to disclose information. That month it notified Mohamed Mohamud (convicted of planning to bomb a Portland, Oregon Christmas celebration) that his trial had included such evidence. Judge King postponed sentencing while defense lawyers sought discovery. But the Ninth Circuit upheld his conviction on the ground that Mohamud had a "diminished" expectation of the privacy of communications sent abroad and the government had acted reasonably to prevent a terrorist attack.[249]

Lawyers for other defendants (including Reaz Qadir Khan, Basaaly Moalin, Abdella Ahmad Tounisi, and Adel Daoud) asked prosecutors to reveal whether their own or their clients' communications had been wiretapped.[250] ND Ill Judge Coleman accepted the government's assurance it did not plan to use surveillance evidence at Daoud's trial, but withdrew that ruling days later. When prosecutors offered to show her their wiretap evidence in camera, she ordered them to disclose it to Thomas A. Durkin (a defense lawyer with security clearance) because "an accurate determination of the legality of the surveillance is best made in this case as part of an adversarial proceeding." She found "unpersuasive" "the government's only response at oral argument … that it has never been done." The Seventh Circuit reversed Coleman's order. Judge Posner said: "Terrorism is not a chimera. With luck, Daoud might have achieved his goal of indiscriminately killing hundreds of Americans." (Actually, an undercover informant had given him inert explosives.) Coleman's claim that "adversary procedure is always essential to resolve contested issues of fact" was "an incomplete description of the American judicial system." Durkin's security clearance did not resolve concerns about disclosure. Defense lawyers "might in their zeal to defend their client … or misremembering what is classified … inadvertently say things that would provide clues to classified materials." (So might judges.) "There are too many leaks of classified information." The president's review panel "study of the classified material has convinced us that there are indeed compelling reasons of national security for their being classified" and "that the investigation did not violate FISA."

In October 2013 prosecutors told lawyers for Jamshid Muhtorov, an Uzbek charged in 2012 in D Colorado with material support to the Islamic Jihad Union, that they would use evidence obtained from NSA surveillance.[251] In January 2014 defense lawyers moved to bar the evidence, but in November 2015 the judge upheld the 2008 FAA. In October 2014 EDNY Judge Gleeson allowed Agron Hasbajrami to withdraw his 2012 guilty plea to material support (sending money to a Pakistani militant group), for which he had been sentenced to 15 years. The government disclosed it had monitored his communications without a warrant, and Gleeson found that Hasbajrami "was not sufficiently informed of the facts."[252] In February 2015 Gleeson denied a motion to suppress the evidence. In June 2015 Hasbajrami entered a second plea, which allowed him to appeal on the ground of surveillance. A month later he sought to withdraw the plea.

> [M]y pleas was unvoluntarily due to the pressure of my attorney Steve Zissou. His statements to me speaks better: "You will plea guilty. If you don't plea I am not coming to trial with you you will go pro-se. Even if I come I'll say you are guilty." He even disparaged me by saying: "do you have a mental problem that you don't want to plea." So I was forced to accept it.

Gleeson denied the motion.[253] Although he acknowledged that "few things are more unsettling than the idea that a government is spying on its own citizens" and listed prior abuses, there was "no denying" after 9/11 that "there are individuals and groups dedicated to inflicting grave harm on our nation." He found "the intelligence gathering here is reasonable under the Fourth Amendment." Hasbajrami "had a diminished – if not nonexistent – expectation of privacy" in emails with non-US persons outside the USA. In August, Gleeson re-sentenced Hasbajrami, this time to 16 years. He appealed to the Second Circuit.

In anticipation of the expiration of §702 at the end of 2017, SJC held a hearing in May 2016.[254] Chairman Grassley acknowledged concerns about the interception of communications between a targeted foreigner and someone inside the USA. Ranking member Leahy complained that "we *still* do not know how much of our data is collected under this authority" [original emphasis]. Ten months later, John Conyers, HJC's ranking Democrat, said "the intelligence community has not so much as responded to our letter" requesting the number of Americans incidentally surveilled. He and Chairman Goodlatte told DNI Coats the estimate was "crucial." After declassification of a long FISC opinion by Judge Collyer exposing abuses raising a "very serious Fourth Amendment issue," NSA stopped collecting messages "about the target." Coats told Congress he had given up trying to estimate how many US communications were incidentally collected because the effort would divert resources and invade Americans' privacy (*sic*). At the SJC hearing, Graham angrily asked: "am I entitled to know if my communications were collected?" Durbin wondered "how are we supposed to believe we have great transparency if you can't even identify for us how many Americans have been swept up?" Chairman Grassley told Graham: "I want you to proceed until you get an answer."

In September 2016 HPSCI issued a three-page executive summary of a report, finding that Snowden, "a serial exaggerator and fabricator," "caused tremendous damage to national security," handing over "secrets that protect American troops overseas and … provide vital defenses against terrorists and nation-states."[255] A group of 31 prominent authors took a *New York Times* ad urging Obama to pardon Snowden. Snowden defended himself: "By partnering with journalists, I sought to exercise our democratic system of checks and balances." By contrast, Gen. Petraeus "shared information that was far more highly classified … with his biographer and lover for personal benefit," receiving a "very light" punishment. Snowden did not "think things are fixed." FISA was "a rubber stamp." But Obama said: "I can't pardon somebody who hasn't gone before a court and presented themselves." After Obama commuted Chelsea Manning's sentence, the *New York Times* wrote that Snowden also "acted in the spirit of a whistle-blower" and "should be offered at least a plea agreement that would allow him to return home." But Mike Pompeo (whom Trump named DCI) had said the previous February that Snowden "should be brought back from Russia and given due process, and I think the proper outcome would be that he would be given a death sentence for having put friends of mine, friends of yours, who served in the military today, at enormous risk." And in April 2014 Trump had called Snowden "a spy who has caused great damage to the U.S. A spy in the old days, when our country was respected and strong, would be executed."

CONCLUSION

Bush responded to the 9/11 attacks (which not only inflicted devastating human and economic losses but also deeply embarrassed him) by asking if NSA could do more to anticipate further attacks (even though he had ignored his August 6 President's Daily Briefing entitled "Bin Laden Determined to Strike in US"). When the agency proudly hyped its technological capability (seeing an unparalleled opportunity to boost its budget and status), the president deliberately chose not to seek new legislation. Although the administration later claimed doing so would have alerted al-Qaeda, terrorists already had ample incentive to safeguard their communications, aware the USA wanted to intercept them. Bush knew he would not be denied expanded surveillance powers by a Congress that had just passed the AUMF with a single dissent. Rather, he must have feared that revealing the enormous scope of US surveillance would provoke criticism at home and abroad (the same reason that the administration concealed OLC torture memos). To forestall this, everything about the new program had to be hidden, even (indeed, especially) its legal authority. White House counsel Gonzales conveniently elicited OLC opinions obviating the need for legislation. John Yoo's memos (which are still mostly secret) advanced several bizarre arguments: the president's commander-in-chief powers trumped both the Fourth Amendment and FISA; surveillance was authorized by the AUMF (whose legislative history clearly showed it did not apply within the USA); and that very general law amended the far more specific FISA.

The fundamental flaws in Yoo's legal analysis were obvious to the few insiders who saw the memos, even those supporting the administration's "war on terror." The secret report of the five intelligence community IGs demolished his reasoning. Within DoJ, both Comey and Ashcroft supported the refusal by Jack Goldsmith (all three of them conservatives) to contravene FISA; and they and other DoJ officials threatened to resign in protest. Had the memos been published when written, they clearly would have sparked the debate democracy demands, which the Bush administration was determined to evade.

Secrecy successfully insulated electronic surveillance from criticism for four years. Even the *New York Times* suppressed its explosive story for over a year. (Was it actually persuaded publication would endanger national security? Did it fear being accused of seeking to influence the 2004 election – at a moment when Bush was shamelessly playing the national security card?) The *Times* may ultimately have published only because Risen's book was about to scoop his employer. Secrecy obstructed Congressional oversight: most legislators did not know what questions to ask; the few Democrats informed about surveillance (Wyden, Udall, Rockefeller, Pelosi) could not publicize their information. Yet secrecy can never be hermetic, and each leak inspired others: by NSA, AT&T, and DoS insiders, or media competitors like *USA Today* (not known for political courage or investigative journalism), the *Washington Post*, the *Guardian*, and other European newspapers. The *Times* story also provided the necessary foundation for successful FOIA requests by human rights advocates and journalists. Although public relations advisers regularly warn clients that full disclosure is the best way to contain a scandal, government's instinct is to stonewall. Therefore, the strategy adopted by Snowden and his journalist collaborators of responding to each denial with a new leak – often revealing an even more egregious privacy violation – was particularly effective.

Whereas photographs of naked prisoners abused at Abu Ghraib or shackled detainees in orange smocks kneeling behind barbed wire at Guantánamo sparked widespread outrage, the response to privacy violations was more complex. Surveillance was widely condemned by editorials and op eds in leading newspapers, legal scholars and bar associations, and former government officials. But public opinion remained almost evenly divided, perhaps because many mistakenly believed – as the administration kept declaring – that only "terrorists" were surveilled. Furthermore, NSA's activities were technical, often opaque; and the multiplicity of programs (under FISA, the Patriot Act, PAA, FAA, and EO 12333) let the government claim it was terminating one without acknowledging it was secretly continuing others.

Unlike the *Times* exposé, Snowden's disclosures provoked opposition from other countries and IT companies. Foreign critics were uninhibited by the belief that NSA spying enhanced *their* security. Public insults to national honor forced leaders to respond to domestic outrage they may not have shared. The heavy-handed attempt to block Morales's plane (thought to be spiriting Snowden out of Russia) infuriated not just Bolivia but also other Latin American countries (even some that detested Morales's politics), as well as European allies in the flight path. NSA's overwhelming technological superiority fostered both dependence and resentment. National leaders Obama had befriended felt betrayed (notably Merkel). Germany (as well as other countries) had painful memories of surveillance under Nazism and Communism. When the USA protested it was motivated solely by national security concerns, Snowden showed that it also sought economic advantage in negotiations over trade and the environment (and even spied on the Vatican conclave of cardinals).

But if Snowden's steady stream of embarrassing revelations succeeded in stoking foreign anger, there were few consequences. As NSA defenders kept emphasizing, many of the countries protesting the loudest also spied on foreigners. This was unsurprising: the object of intelligence is to uncover other nations' goals, strategies, and capabilities. More importantly, foreign countries had little power to change the hegemon's behavior. Many depended on NSA for information crucial to their own national security. Technological retaliation risked Balkanizing the web. Criminal prosecutors were unable to penetrate NSA's proverbial *omertà*. Still, European nations could and did raise objections to spying in negotiations over other common concerns – international bank transfers (SWIFT), air travel security, or safe harbor provisions for commercial data exchange – securing marginally better privacy protections.[256] Supranational organizations were less effective. The UN passed resolutions and produced reports but lacked teeth. The EP postured but wielded little power. The ECJ could not enforce its decrees.

Whereas almost all telecoms actively cooperated with NSA (while perhaps oblivious to its backdoor surveillance), IT companies responded to Snowden's exposé with public anger and collective action. They were America's economic superstars – innovative, fabulously wealthy, global – and generally sympathetic to the Obama administration. But the very ease of operating across national boundaries, which they eagerly exploited in order to grow, exposed them to retaliation by countries fearing their data were unsafe in American hands. Having promised customers privacy, IT companies worried about losing market share to foreign competitors less vulnerable to NSA scrutiny and domestic rivals promising better encryption. They sought permission to reveal what they had been compelled to do (perhaps to stimulate public agitation, since the information itself did little to allay privacy concerns). NSA tampering with computer hardware and software turned manufacturers and programmers into IT companies' allies. The ongoing controversy over encryption further exacerbated resistance. Given the growing prominence of technology in the American economy, the industry wielded real clout.

The administration deployed various strategies to defend surveillance. It sought to undercut Democrats' criticism by claiming that the Intelligence Committees' senior minority members had known about the programs and not only failed to object but even expressed enthusiasm. Democrats retorted that secrecy disabled them from using the limited information they received. The Bush administration also emphasized what it did *not* do – read the content of all communications – hoping to distract attention from what it *did* do – search that content using multiple terms. Bush falsely claimed that every wiretap required a warrant and surveillance was limited to communications with al-Qaeda; administration officials maintained the program was narrowly targeted when it actually intercepted *every* phone call and email; NSA denied having backdoors in telecom "servers" – because its backdoors were located in telecom circuits (which transmitted far more information than any server); Clapper lied to Wyden that NSA did not "wittingly" collect data "on millions or hundreds of millions of Americans." Although some of these misrepresentations were themselves initially secret, subsequent leaks exposed all of them, further damaging the administration's credibility.

Both administrations undermined assurances that they scrupulously protected the privacy of US persons by boasting – to intelligence and other executive officials, Congress, and the public – about the efficacy and comprehensiveness of surveillance. If the challenge was finding needles in haystacks (a constant post-9/11 mantra), NSA needed to collect and examine *all* communications, using a wide array of search terms. The flaw in this argument was that most searches turned up hay, not needles: the FBI complained that only 1 percent of STELLARWIND data significantly advanced investigations, which meant that the other 99 percent wasted its time. Bureaucratic impatience with FISA was predicated partly on the burden of repeated applications to search records. And since surveillance raised constitutional questions, defenders had to exaggerate both future national security threats and the essential contribution of surveillance to foiling past plots. No matter how often their claims were discredited, administration officials continued to maintain that NSA could have prevented the 9/11 attack and did frustrate 54 other terrorist "events" (one of which was the risible plan to demolish the Brooklyn Bridge by cutting its cables with a welding torch). But such counterfactuals (like those used to justify EITs) are logically unverifiable. Even NSA Director Alexander could name only 4 of the 54 alleged "events" and was unable to show that surveillance was indispensable to aborting any of them. But such debunking did nothing to discourage similar claims in response to each new attack. Without bothering to offer any evidence, defenders blithely blamed Snowden for the rise of ISIS and its Paris attacks, and the USA Freedom Act for the San Bernardino lone wolf attacks (even though NSA surveillance persisted through those attacks and the Agency expressed satisfaction with the Act's new procedures).

Both administrations also resorted to the classic strategy of shooting the messenger. Bush officials denounced the *New York Times* (whose story they successfully suppressed for a year) and threatened to prosecute both it and the leaker(s). Snowden's actions, which were clearly illegal, prompted demands for his prosecution (even execution), leading to criminal charges, including those under the arguably inappropriate 100-year-old Espionage Act, and futile requests that Russia extradite him. But though critics sought to impugn Snowden's motives, he and his media collaborators were inundated with speaking invitations and showered with honors, especially in Europe.

Because the details of surveillance were highly technical and its legal authority murky, the 2004 Ashcroft hospital incident acquired an outsized importance by personalizing the issues. Administration lawyers like Goldsmith and Comey, whom Gonzales assumed were "loyal Bushies," demonstrated admirable backbone and fidelity to law; even Ashcroft, who had signed off on the surveillance program, backed subordinates in defying the president. And DoJ's refusal to affirm the program's legal foundation led Bush to suspend it temporarily. At the same time, Comey ultimately did find authority for the §215 program in the president's commander-in-chief powers. The threat of mass resignations at DoJ revived painful memories of the Saturday Night Massacre three decades earlier and Nixon's ignominious resignation. And the incident contributed to Bush replacing Gonzales, who could no longer take refuge in convenient memory lapses and verbal evasions. Still, Gonzales remained unrepentant to the end, defiantly declaring that Bush was uninterested in DoJ legal opinions (a bizarre statement for an Attorney General). And Hayden and Yoo stubbornly maintained the program's legality, dismissing criticism by the five intelligence community IGs. The controversy further shredded the veil of secrecy protecting surveillance when participants hinted that the contested program was *not* PRISM (the only one the *New York Times* had outed); but they never identified the real suspect. Like other leaks, this one continued its corrosive drip, putting the Bush administration on the defensive every time new details emerged. But as often happens, attention was diverted from substantive issues (how surveillance violated privacy and whether it was lawful) to procedural missteps (Gonzales's outrageous behavior in pressuring the stricken Ashcroft and falsely claiming not to not know that Comey was Acting Attorney General).

Partisan politics inevitably played a central role in the controversy, if the divisions did not perfectly reflect party lines. Although members of both parties initially expressed outrage at what the *New York Times* disclosed, most Republicans quickly rallied behind their president, who hoped (unsuccessfully) to repeat his 2004 victory by shamelessly accusing both the *Times* and Democratic critics of endangering national security. Bush felt so confident of his political footing that he nominated Hayden, who had led surveillance as NSA Director, to be DCI. But some Republicans – centrists like Snowe, those with a military background (Graham, McCain, Hagel, Heather Wilson), and Sensenbrenner (who claimed authorship of the USA Patriot Act) – sought to obtain more information and modify the program. Specter characteristically blustered and then caved. Feingold's censure motion and Conyers's reiteration of his earlier impeachment proposal just stoked Republican grassroots anger; Cornyn provocatively invited a fight on this terrain. In the end, many Democrats supported the very limited reforms embodied in the PAA and FAA (discussed below).

Politics played out differently in response to Snowden's revelations. Republicans who had defended surveillance programs under Bush attacked the same programs under Obama. Having led the challenge to surveillance under Bush, Democrats displayed much less loyalty to their president than Republicans had shown to theirs; and some Tea Party members (Amash, Paul) expressed their libertarian principles by championing privacy, culminating in the House falling just seven votes short of defunding NSA. But the biggest difference was Obama himself. Although he had had criticized surveillance as a candidate, he defended it as president, claiming (unconvincingly) that he would have reformed it without Snowden's exposé. But then he took a characteristic step (one Bush never would have contemplated), appointing a Review Group of two prominent national security experts who had served Republicans and three law professors (including two of his former University of Chicago colleagues). Its recommendations, seconded by the PCLOB – an institution Bush had not even bothered to staff for years, which now included two ex-Bush lawyers as well as other highly respected former officials – provided the political cover that allowed Obama to endorse the bipartisan USA Freedom Act.

The other two branches encountered significant obstacles in seeking to restrain the executive. Efforts by Congressional Democrats to uncover information were largely unsuccessful.[257] While Republicans controlled the Senate, Roberts stopped Democrats from raising the issue in SSCI (repudiating that committee's long tradition of nonpartisanship); even the hearing to confirm Hayden as DCI produced no new insights into NSA's behavior under his directorship. Closed-door briefings did nothing for transparency. When Specter called Gonzales before the SJC, the Attorney General persisted in ducking and weaving. Members of Congress showed real spine only when they felt the executive had violated their own prerogatives by providing insufficient or misleading information.

Because (as I discuss below) most Art. III courts refused to address constitutional challenges, and FISC almost always bought the administration line on FISA, Congress represented the only effective check on surveillance. Unlike legislators' profound differences about EITs, extraordinary rendition, Guantánamo, and targeted killing, virtually every member of Congress agreed NSA should engage in *some* surveillance. But some legislators grandstanded: Feingold by pursuing a futile motion to censure Bush, Paul by filibustering the USA Freedom Act. And some Tea Party Republicans, moved by libertarian sentiments, joined Democratic reformers: the surprising Amash–Conyers alliance – between two Michigan Representatives divided by half a century in age and the entire political spectrum – nearly ended surveillance. Legislative debates, however, quickly became mired in highly technical questions: whether there is a privacy interest in metadata, the permissible number of "hops" from a target or the number of years that data could be retained, search by a "discrete" rather than "specific" selection term, the scope of searches "about" a target, how "reasonable articulable suspicion" differed from probable cause, and whether FISC would control the rare participation of an amicus. The result was a multiplicity of competing bills, making it difficult to mobilize popular sentiment around the issues. Even civil liberties organizations vacillated about whether to endorse some limited reforms. Administrations found the Intelligence Committees more pliant than the Judiciary Committees. Congress kept protesting it could not legislate in ignorance – and then did just that (although looming sunset clauses threatening NSA with going dark sometimes extracted grudging administration disclosures). Seeking to forestall action by the new Democratic Congress, Bush declared at the beginning of 2007 that he had suspended the TSP (knowing he had obtained a secret FISC order making it *easier* to engage in bulk collection and that other secret programs were unaffected). His declaration came dangerously close to the negative pregnant of admitting that NSA *had* engaged in arguably illegal surveillance. Only when a second FISC judge required NSA to seek individual warrants did Bush propose the PAA. The administration played a game of chicken with Congress, securing temporary extensions by warning that the alternative was *no* surveillance (raising the specter of an "intelligence gap" echoing the Cold War's fictitious "missile gap"). But criticism of FISA as too slow and cumbersome exposed the administration to accusations that it had simply disregarded the statute. And temporary measures forced it to keep returning to Congress. Nevertheless, most of the reforms changed *how* NSA obtained authority to surveil while placing few limits on *what* it saw or heard (as in the compromise to have telecoms rather than

NSA store intercepted communications). For instance, PAA let NSA eavesdrop if a communication concerned "foreign intelligence" (a category far broader than al-Qaeda and associated forces) and the agency "reasonably believed" that one participant was outside the USA. The Bush administration successfully conferred immunity on telecoms that had cooperated with NSA (making arguments like those Obama later advanced for not investigating EITs that had acquired a false patina of legality from OLC memos). And the Obama administration made some easy concessions, such as publishing FISC opinions. Just as the administration subjected EITs to the Army Field Manual while retaining authority for harsher interrogations in Appendix M, so EO 12333 surveillance remained secret and unregulated after the USA Freedom Act. Indeed, the new NSA Director experienced little difficulty in operating under the USA Freedom Act. Still, limited reforms did prompt renewed calls for more stringent regulation, as did discovery of NSA "errors."

A quarter century earlier, Congress had responded to the Church Committee's exposure of surveillance by enacting FISA, making FISC responsible for protecting privacy. But though in rare instances judges rejected or modified NSA requests, FISC – like other specialized courts and administrative agencies captured by the industries they regulate – overwhelmingly deferred to the administration. Soon after 9/11, in a decision with enormous ramifications, Judge Kollar-Kotelly accepted John Yoo's arguments that NSA could use a very low standard of "relevance" and that *Smith* v. *Maryland* exempted metadata from Fourth Amendment protection. Just as legislators tended to resist only when the executive violated *their* prerogatives, so FISC judges were more likely to take umbrage when the executive sought warrants without revealing the use of surveillance. Robertson resigned from the court over this; and Lamberth, otherwise supportive of NSA, castigated it for deceiving him. But even when FISC operated as Congress had intended, it was fatally flawed. Its secret opinions could not legitimate surveillance by showing Congress and the public that NSA was following the rules. Its decisions could not be validated or corrected through review by regular Art. III courts. And FISC did not have a way of discovering whether NSA was complying with its orders. Secrecy blinkered even FISC judges, who could not retain copies of the OLC opinions purportedly authorizing NSA surveillance. Former judges criticized the lack of an adversary process (since the telecoms, which could contest FISC orders, had little interest in alienating a government with which they had lucrative contracts just to champion the rights of customers unaware their privacy had been breached). The presiding judge had the power to retain cases, rather than assigning them randomly. FISC was never representative of the Art. III judiciary and became even more politically partisan under Chief Justice Roberts. Because many of these deficiencies were indefensible, critics were able to force changes. Roberts selected two judges appointed by Democratic presidents (still grossly outnumbered by the nine Republican appointees). Congress introduced a limited adversary process. And redacted FISC opinions were published (without endangering national security).

Federal courts were the last resort for those challenging NSA surveillance. But rather than producing authoritative answers to litigants' questions, judges split sharply along ideological lines, which closely tracked the party of the appointing president (see Table 5.1).[258]

Table 5.1 Judges' Rulings in NSA Surveillance Cases, by Appointing President's Party

Appointing President	# Decisions for Plaintiff	% Decisions for Plaintiff	# Decisions for Defendant	% Decisions for Defendant	Total Decisions
Democrat	25	68	12	32	37
Republican	6	17	29	83	35
Total	31	43	41	57	72

Chi-Square = 18.65, p<.00002

Civil libertarian judges found that plaintiffs had standing because NSA and the administration had boasted that the program was comprehensive – indeed, insisted it must be in order to be effective – thereby admitting that it surveilled *everyone*. Calling this mere common sense, these judges expressed concern that if these plaintiffs lacked standing, no one would have it. Executive-minded judges, by contrast, were ready, even eager, to find that no one might have standing, explicitly relegating plaintiffs to a political process that had already failed them. These judges indulged in ungrounded speculation that NSA *might* not have surveilled *this* plaintiff, knowing full well that the plaintiff could not offer a rebuttal because the program was secret (a perfect Catch-22). Judge Ellis advanced a bizarre analogy between someone driving a car more slowly than it could go and NSA choosing to overlook some communications. (Ellis also exposed his embarrassing innumeracy.) In another Catch-22, these judges reasoned that the government could collect metadata because that was not a search, and then could search the metadata because the government, not the customer, now owned it. These judges prohibited plaintiffs from relying on memories of secret government documents they had legally read. Judges disagreed about whether FISA preempted state secrets. Some judges found that lawyer plaintiffs had been harmed by being forced to travel abroad in order to protect client confidentiality. Other judges mocked such "mysterious" injuries, arguing that they would have occurred even if surveillance had been legal. (So what?) One judge declared that "probabilistic" injuries could not confer standing, even though courts routinely compensate them (e.g., the cost of medical surveillance following exposure to risk). Judges disagreed about whether *Smith v. Maryland* applied to NSA surveillance and was still good law. Some judges parroted the discredited claim that NSA surveillance could have exposed the 9/11 hijackers and prevented that attack and others. But their brethren voiced skepticism about the efficacy and necessity of surveillance. Judges disagreed about whether the more specific FISA trumped the more general AUMF. Some judges extolled judicial review as "the glory of our system." Others reviled it as "judges arrogating to themselves a power inconsistent with both our constitutional design and the role of courts in a democratic society." Some judges privileged constitutional rights; others insisted that judicial action in the absence of a narrowly cabined standing was a greater danger than surveillance itself. Some judges derided their colleagues' opinions as "fanciful" and "hard to take seriously." Some lauded plaintiffs' lawyers as champions of the Constitution; others accused them of "act[ing] out their fantasy of persecution," "mak[ing] themselves consequential," and "rais[ing] funds for self-sustaining litigation." Some invoked the Founding Fathers by name, proudly proclaiming that America had "no hereditary kings." Others eagerly deferred to the president's commander-in-chief powers. When all else failed, judges dismissed cases on grounds of immunity: sovereign in the case of the government, granted to the telecoms by the FAA. Courts failed to transcend these essentially political differences. But the bottom line was clear: the judiciary never struck down a surveillance program.

CHAPTER SIX

IUS IN BELLO

War not only permits but demands actions that would be criminal in peacetime: seizing, detaining, killing, even assassinating enemies. But while authorizing such actions, the Law of Armed Conflict (LOAC) also imposes limits.[1] Warfare must "distinguish between the civilian population and combatants"; "loss of life and damage to property incidental to attacks must not be excessive in relation to the concrete and direct military advantage to be gained"; injuries must be "absolutely necessary"; and warfare may not "cause superfluous injury or unnecessary suffering."[2] This chapter examines efforts to restrain actions the USA took abroad in its "war on terror": in arenas where it openly waged war (Afghanistan, Iraq, Pakistan, and Yemen) and in nations that were complicit with US extraordinary renditions (Sweden, Italy, Germany, Macedonia) or hosted its secret prisons (Poland, Romania, Lithuania).

THE US DEBATE OVER TARGETED KILLING[3]

Less than a month after 9/11, CENTCOM launched a drone attack on the Taliban leader Mullah Omar, accused of sheltering the al-Qaeda planners; but it killed only some bodyguards.[4] Although President Bush authorized many more drone strikes, the US debate caught fire only after Obama took office. It raised many questions: How were drones and their legal authorization, initially secret, brought to public attention? What were the differences between drones and other weapons of war and between targeting US citizens and others? Who criticized drones, what troubled them, what arguments did they make (both legal and strategic), and how did the government respond? What divisions emerged within government? How did Congress and the courts respond? How, if at all, did this debate influence drone warfare?

On his third full day in office, President Obama was briefed in the Situation Room about a strike in Pakistan the previous day, which had missed its target – a Taliban hideout – but hit the compound of a tribal elder belonging to a pro-government peace committee, killing him and four family members, including two children.[5] Steven Kappes, CIA Deputy Director, justified such "signature strikes" (where the targets' identities were unknown): "we can see that there are a lot of military-age males down there, men associated with terrorist activity, but we don't always know who they are." Obama replied "that's not good enough for me," but allowed signature strikes to continue. In March, JCS chairman Mullen briefed him on a "kinetic opportunity" in Somalia – a high-level Shabab operative would attend a ceremony for recruits completing training – and suggested killing them all. Obama demurred, agreeing with a four-star general who said "carpet bombing a country is a really bad precedent."

In a March 2009 speech at the University of Minnesota, Seymour Hersh referred to a JSOC "executive assassination ring," but would not expand.[6] A few months later the *Wall Street Journal*, *New York Times*, *Washington Post* and *Los Angeles Times* all reported that after 9/11 the CIA had planned and possibly trained for targeted killings in Afghanistan.[7] Bush made a finding authorizing them if capture was too dangerous; Vice President Cheney insisted that Congress not be told. Although no operation was conducted, the plan was never shelved. Learning about it in June, CIA Director Panetta immediately canceled the program and notified Congress. Sen. Bond (R-Mo) said: "if the CIA weren't trying to do something like this, we'd be asking 'why not?'" Rep. Hoekstra (R-Mich) was equally unconcerned. But Sen. Feingold (D-Wisc) expressed "deep concerns" to Obama, adding that "individuals who ordered that Congress be kept in the dark should be held accountable." Sen. Durbin (D-Ill) objected that "to have a massive program that is concealed from leaders in Congress is not only inappropriate, it could be illegal." The *New York Times* encouraged Congress "to assess Cheney's actions and, if appropriate, turn over its evidence to the Justice Department." A month later the *Times* reported that the CIA had paid Blackwater USA several million dollars to find and kill al-Qaeda members. But warning Congress that its focus on the past "threatens to distract the CIA from its crucial core missions," Panetta called it "time to move on." HPSCI investigated why it had not been told about the program. Two months later it was reported that in 2008 the USA had added some fifty Afghan drug traffickers with "proven" insurgent "links" to the list of those to be captured or killed, provoking protests from the Afghan Interior Ministry and Director General for Prosecution.

A December 17, 2009 air strike in Yemen killed Yemenis, Saudis, Pakistanis, and Egyptians associated with AQAP. By late 2009 the USA had added Anwar al-Awlaki – a US citizen and leading al-Qaeda propagandist – to JSOC's list of "high value individuals" it sought to capture or kill.[8] A December 24 strike on his house missed him but killed the AQAP leader and deputy leader and about thirty other militants gathered to discuss retaliation for the earlier drone strike.[9] In an interview posted on the Al Jazeera website on December 23, al-Awlaki had praised Maj. Nidal Hasan for the Fort Hood killings on November 5. Al-Awlaki's father Nasser said his son "should face trial if he's done something wrong." But "if Obama wants to kill my son, this is wrong." The Yemeni government said the USA had provided insufficient evidence for an arrest, but it was watching Anwar al-Awlaki closely. Foreign Minister al-Qirbi claimed that all the air strikes had been conducted by his country, provoking AQAP's incredulity. After his abortive attempt to bomb an airline landing in Detroit on Christmas Day, Umar Farouk Abdulmutallab told the FBI that Anwar al-Awlaki had helped plan the attack and offered religious justifications. Obama promised that AQAP "will be held to account" for the attempt. The Yemeni government asked Nasser al-Awlaki to persuade his son to turn himself in for prosecution in connection with the Fort Hood bombing. At the end of January 2010 Anwar al-Awlaki claimed Abdulmutallab as "one of my students," adding: "I did not tell him to do this operation, but I support it."

In February 2010 DNI Blair declared that the USA could kill American citizens outside the country if they were "taking action that threatens Americans."[10] DoD followed "a set of defined policy and legal procedures that are very carefully observed." NSC had to approve the inclusion of an American on the kill list. In March DoS Legal Adviser Harold Koh told the American Society of International Law that "U.S. targeting practices … comply with all applicable law, including the laws of war," observing the principles of distinction (limited to military objectives) and proportionality (collateral damage not excessive in relation to the anticipated military advantage). "[I]ndividuals who are part of … an armed group are belligerents and, therefore, lawful targets." Such targeted killings were not assassinations.

In April the administration approved killing al-Awlaki. The *Washington Post* praised Koh for having "rightly rejected the absurd notion that enemy targets must be provided 'adequate process' before the strike occurs." But Vicki Divoll (former SSCI General Counsel and CIA Assistant General Counsel) wrote in a *Los Angeles Times* op ed that it was perverse to require judicial approval to eavesdrop on al-Awlaki but not to kill him. At the end of April Divoll repeated this statement in the first Congressional hearing on targeted killing, held by the subcommittee on national security of the House Committee on Oversight and Government Reform.

Philip Alston, UN Special Rapporteur on extrajudicial, summary, or arbitrary executions, said killing should be entrusted to the armed forces, which provided "quite abundant accountability as demonstrated by what happens when a bombing goes wrong in Afghanistan," rather than the CIA, which would "not provide any information and not do any follow-up."[11] The USA should disclose the legal justifications for such killings, the criteria and safeguards in selecting targets, and the process for investigating civilian deaths. He criticized the USA for putting drug lords on its kill list and rejected "pre-emptive self-defense."

On July 7, 2010 Nasser al-Awlaki retained the ACLU and CCR to challenge the decision to target his son.[12] But three days later the Treasury Department's Office of Foreign Assets Control (OFAC) labeled Anwar al-Awlaki a "specially designated terrorist," making it a crime for Americans to engage in transactions for his benefit without a license. Nasser al-Awlaki's lawyers applied for a license and, when the government did not respond, sued to be allowed to represent Anwar al-Awlaki. The *Los Angeles Times* said the proposed assassination "raises profound legal and moral issues that at the very least ought to be debated in a court of law." The *Washington Post* disagreed: such killings might be necessary "when a target is hiding in a lawless state"; the President should approve them, notify Congress, and consider making the "general criteria" public. The *New York Times* said, "particularly in the case of American citizens ... the government needs to employ some due process before depriving someone of life," perhaps by getting "the equivalent of a judicial warrant" from a court like FISC. Jameel Jaffer of the ACLU and Pardiss Kebriaei of CCR (Nasser al-Awlaki's lawyers) wrote in the *Times* that a court should "require the government to disclose the standards under which it adds terrorism suspects ... to government kill lists, and ensure that those standards are consistent with domestic and international law."

When OFAC lifted its ban on representation, Nasser al-Awlaki sued in DDC to enjoin the killing.[13] The *Los Angeles Times* said courts should "rule on when killing an American located far from a battlefield passes constitutional muster." "In the absence of an imminent threat, the aim should be to capture Awlaki and return him to the United States." It rejected claims that "litigation would reveal state secrets or that the targeting of Americans is a decision to be made by the executive branch." The *New York Times* praised the drone program as "very effective," but felt "the government needs to do a better job of showing the world that it is acting in strict compliance with international law." The administration "must explain how targets are chosen, demonstrate that attacks are limited and are a last resort, and allow independent authorities to oversee the process." The *Washington Post* disagreed: "courts have traditionally and correctly left decisions on combat operations to the military and executive branch experts constitutionally tasked with defending the country." The government moved to dismiss on grounds of state secrets, lack of standing, and political question, and because courts should not bind the actions of future presidents. At oral argument in November, Judge Bates called the case "extraordinary and unique," wondering why the government needed a warrant to eavesdrop but not to kill. But he also questioned whether Anwar al-Awlaki had authorized Nasser al-Awlaki to sue. About the same time Anwar al-Awlaki posted a video pronouncing: "don't consult with anyone in fighting the Americans; fighting the devil doesn't require consultation or prayers or seeking divine guidance." The *New York Times* saw "a strange symmetry between Awlaki's taped argument that killing is acceptable even in the absence of a religious fatwa, and the U.S. government's argument that killing is acceptable without oversight or due process." Because "we live under the rule of law … we must hold ourselves to the standards we have set even when it is inconvenient, difficult or dangerous to do so." In his *Washington Post* column, David Ignatius agreed that "a clear international legal regime has never been more needed." Even the conservative *Washington Times* said Obama had "exceeded his power in ordering Awlaki's assassination." In December Judge Bates dismissed Nasser al-Awlaki's lawsuit for lack of standing (since he had failed to prove he represented Anwar al-Awlaki's best interests or that Anwar could not sue himself) and because the case raised a nonjusticiable political question. The *Los Angeles Times* criticized this as "the latest case in which procedural roadblocks have prevented judicial scrutiny of questionable tactics in the fight against terrorism." Although the *New York Times* had always thought the lawsuit "a little shaky," it said "the administration should remain very worried about the moral implications of its policy."

At the end of October 2010 the USA intercepted bombs sent from Yemen to destroy planes landing in Philadelphia and Newark, for which AQAP claimed responsibility.[14] Yemen charged Anwar al-Awlaki, his cousin Otham al-Awlaki, and Hesham Mohammed Asem with "forming an armed group to carry out criminal acts targeting foreigners" in connection with the October 6 killing of a French engineer in Sanaa.[15] A Yemeni judge ordered Anwar al-Awlaki "arrested by force, dead or alive" after he failed to appear at the November 2 trial. Asem denied all the charges, claiming he had been tortured to confess.

In February 2011 John Rizzo (former CIA Acting General Counsel) explained that some ten lawyers in the Agency's Counterterrorism Center would prepare a five-page finding on whether an individual posed a danger to the USA.[16] He had seen about one new proposal a month; about thirty people were targeted at any given time. "The agency was very punctilious about … tr[ying] to minimize collateral damage, especially women and children."

The debate over drones intensified after a March 17 strike: the USA claimed it had killed 20 militants, but Pakistan said the more than 40 dead included innocent civilians.[17] Cameron Munter, the new US Ambassador, urged more judicious use of "signature" strikes. JCS chairman Mullen also questioned them, and National Security Adviser Donilon expressed concern. The next month DCI Panetta told Director Pasha of Pakistan Inter-Services Intelligence (ISI) the USA would give Pakistan advance notice of any strike expected to kill more than twenty people. The killing of bin Laden a month later provoked Pakistan to demand an end to signature strikes. Defense Secretary Gates feared Pakistan would block military shipments to Afghanistan. DoS Legal Adviser Koh defended the bin Laden operation by invoking his 2010 speech to the American Society of International Law (ASIL).[18] Munter asked Secretary of State Clinton to give him greater control over the strikes and explain them to Pakistan, but the CIA blocked Clinton's efforts to do so. The next month Obama instituted an appeals process giving the DoS a greater say. If the ambassador to Pakistan objected, there would be a discussion with the DCI or a deputy. If they could not agree, the Secretary of State would talk to the DCI, who had the final say. The USA gave Pakistan more advance notice and suspended strikes when Pakistani officials were visiting the USA. Pakistan responded by increasing intelligence cooperation with the USA and reducing opposition to drone strikes.

In May 2011 the USA again fired at al-Awlaki, but missed.[19] The next month it killed a mid-level al-Qaeda operative and several other suspected militants in southern Yemen, together with four civilians. On September 30 it finally succeeded in killing al-Awlaki as well as Samir Khan (another US citizen, who had not been targeted) and two other alleged al-Qaeda operatives. Obama accused al-Awlaki of having taken "the lead role in planning and directing the efforts to murder innocent Americans." The administration released a 50-page June 2010 OLC opinion principally drafted by David Barron and Martin Lederman authorizing the killing of a target who could not be captured and posed an imminent risk (including someone committed to attacking the USA whenever possible, even if not engaged in doing so at that time). NSC made the initial choice of targets, which were approved by the Principals Committee and ultimately the president. (In September 2011 DDC Judge Collyer had denied an ACLU FOIA request for the "legal basis" of targeted killing and information about target selection, numbers killed and injured, and geographic limits, finding that Panetta had "never acknowledged the CIA's involvement in such program.")

Rep. McCaul (R-Tex) gloated that Khan was "a bonus," a "twofer." Hailing the "good strike," Cheney urged the Obama administration to "reconsider some of the criticism they offered about our policies." Rep. Ron Paul (R-Tex) said it would be "sad" if "the American people accept this blindly and casually." Rep. Harman (D-Ca) and Sens. Feinstein (D-Ca) and Levin (D-Mich) asked the White House to release the pertinent legal memos, although the latter two supported the killing.

Media opinion was divided. The *New York Times* said the "detailed and cautious memorandum" was still "an insufficient foundation for a momentous decision by the government to kill one of its citizens." It wanted a FISC-like hearing. Its public editor said: "cracking the government's silence, specifically on its legal rationale, should be a high priority for the paper." In a *New York Times* op ed Jack Goldsmith (OLC director under Bush) called it "a just act of war" not "an assassination." The prior reviews by lawyers and policy makers were "wholly unprecedented in war" and "exceed anything the law requires." The *Washington Post* said the strike "was clearly justified, both legally and morally," but urged the administration to give appropriate members of Congress the OLC memo and publish a redacted version because the incorrect claim that the killing was illegal was "not easily or intuitively dismissed." *Washington Post* columnist David Ignatius was only "partly reassure[ed]" by the process, preferring a FISC-like review. John Bellinger III (former legal adviser to the NSC and DoS) wrote in a *Washington Post* op ed that al-Awlaki had received "sufficient due process," but "the administration should provide more information about the strict limits it applies to targeting and about who has been targeted." Even a conservative *Washington Post* columnist who had yelled "a little 'yippee'" at the news wanted "to hear the Attorney General or the President explain why" it was okay. The *Los Angeles Times* said: "the secret, unilateral, targeted assassination of a U.S. citizen far from the battlefields of Iraq and Afghanistan is hardly something to celebrate." "There was no transparent, legal, reviewable process." Killing someone "who poses no immediate danger is morally obnoxious. It is also impossible to harmonize with the U.S. Constitution." "[A]ll nations ought to think long and hard before gunning down their enemies in other countries." But its columnists disagreed. Max Boot dismissed the objections of "a few civil libertarians"; Jonah Goldberg called al-Awlaki's US citizenship irrelevant. George Washington University law professor Jonathan Turley wrote in a *USA Today* op ed that "no republic can long stand if a president retains the unilateral authority to kill citizens whom he deems a danger to the country." Notre Dame law professor Mary Ellen O'Connell wrote in a CNN op ed that "extrajudicial killing of terrorist suspects ... is no more efficacious, lawful or moral than torture." Yale law professor Bruce Ackerman said the White House had "conducted nothing resembling a fair-minded process." But Berkeley law professor John Yoo declared that "every member of the enemy armed forces and leadership is a legitimate target in wartime, regardless of whether they can be caught or whether they pose an imminent threat." Five leading newspapers published 96 articles on the killing within a month after al-Awlaki's death, and many more discussed legal and ethical issues.

In mid-October 2011 five drone strikes in Yemen killed seven people, including two al-Qaeda leaders, but also Anwar al-Awlaki's 16-year-old son Abdulrahman, an American citizen, who had been searching for his father, and four other members of the al-Awlaki clan.[20] The NSC coldly observed: "over the past year, the Department of State has publicly urged U.S. citizens not to travel to Yemen and has encouraged those already in Yemen to leave." Nearly two weeks later DoS claimed it still had not confirmed Abdulrahman's identity. Nasser al-Awlaki called the killings "murder by a state gone mad." The *Washington Post* regretted that:

> no one in the administration has spoken publicly about what additional factors – if any – must be weighed when an American is the target. And no mention has been made about whether any special consideration must be given to an American who may become "collateral damage." The administration also has not publicly addressed how age may factor into a decision to strike.

Attacks "must be subject to rigorous checks," but "U.S. citizens who take up arms with the enemy forfeit their rights to due process." It again urged the administration to release the OLC memo. But on October 27 the CIA responded to a *New York Times* FOIA request for the OLC opinion by refusing to acknowledge its existence.

In a November 2011 *New York Times* op ed, Clive Stafford Smith (a lawyer for Reprieve) described an Islamabad Jirga (assembly of leaders), which displayed the damage from drone strikes.[21] Soon thereafter another strike killed Tariq Ali, 16, whom Stafford Smith had met at the event, together with his 12-year-old cousin Waheed Khan and Jahi Zardullah's four nephews. "None of these were harmful people. Two were still in school and one was in college." Saadullah, who lost both legs and an eye, had wanted to be a doctor. Paul D. Miller (NSC director for Afghanistan 2007–09) wrote in a *Washington Post* op ed that "it is a mistake to invest the president – any president – with the unreviewable power to kill any American whom he deems to represent a threat to national security." Former DNI Blair urged that drone strikes be transferred from the CIA, where they were secret, to the military, which had "a set of procedures that are open, known for how you make decisions about when to use deadly force or not, levels of approval, degrees of proof." (This view was one reason for his ouster.) When Koh had proposed in 2010 that the administration disclose the legal justification for targeted killing, an official recalled that "the immediate reaction was you can't talk about covert programs." National Security Adviser Brennan had said in September that "we have the authority to take action against al-Qaeda and its associated forces without doing a separate self-defense analysis each time." But Bellinger said: "if we don't explain our legal rationale and the limitations we apply now, then we're opening the door to other countries to do the same thing." DCI Petraeus and DNI Clapper wanted the legal reasoning revealed. In a December debate among Republican presidential hopefuls, Romney,

Gingrich, Huntsman, and Perry supported targeted killing; only Paul dissented. Gingrich insisted that such killings were consistent with the rule of law because those targeted had been "found guilty by a panel."

The administration continued to offer justifications in 2012. Defense Secretary Panetta said:[22]

> [W]e're required under a process of law, to be able to justify that despite the fact that person may be a citizen, he is first and foremost a terrorist who threatens our people, and for that reason, we can establish a legal basis on which we oughta go after that individual … because their goal is to kill our people, and for that reason we have to defend ourselves … when an enemy combatant holds a gun at your head, you fire back.

Obama claimed the drone program was "kept on a very tight leash" and used for "very precise, precision strikes against al Qaeda and their affiliates." "Drones have not caused a huge number of civilian casualties." The *Los Angeles Times* felt this public acknowledgment "puts new pressure on the administration to defend the policy openly." Holder needed to be "specific" about "the killing of American citizens without due process" and release the OLC memo. Former DCI Hayden warned that "there isn't a government on the planet that agrees with our legal rationale for these operations, except for Afghanistan and maybe Israel." "We need a court order to eavesdrop" on al-Awlaki, "but we didn't need a court order to kill him." Doyle McManus wrote in his *Los Angeles Times* column that it was "past time" that the administration "explained how [targeted killing of citizens] squares with the Constitution's guarantee of due process."

The London-based Bureau of Investigative Journalism (BIJ) said that at least fifty civilians had been killed in follow-up strikes when they rushed to help the injured, and another twenty or more at funerals.[23] In the 260 strikes since Obama took office, there were "credible" reports of 282–535 civilian deaths, including more than sixty children. The USA rejected these figures as much too high, but conceded several dozen civilian deaths. The *Los Angeles Times* regretted that "the American media scarcely noticed" the report and that the program's legality "has never been considered by a U.S. court and is seldom discussed by Congress." If the report was correct, US strategy "seems to have been borrowed from the playbook of Islamist terrorists." "It is past time for U.S. courts and the United Nations to explore the legal issues involved in targeted assassination." The numbers were hotly contested. In April 2009 a US official had claimed that only 5% of the 400 deaths were civilians; a year later a US counterterrorism official said just 6% of the more than 500 deaths were civilians; and in August 2011 a senior official said only 2.5% of the 2,000 killed were civilians. In June 2011 Brennan went further: "there hasn't been a single collateral death because of the exceptional proficiency, precision of the capabilities we've been able to develop." He later said that "for more than a year … the U.S. government has not found credible evidence of collateral deaths … outside of Afghanistan or Iraq." And ten months after that he repeated "that over a period of time before my public remarks … we had no information about a single civilian … being killed." During similar time periods, however, the New America Foundation identified 66, the Long War Journal 44, the University of Massachusetts, Dartmouth 24 and BIJ about 200. A study of ten major drone strikes since 2010 found that 56 of the 194 killed were civilians or tribal police. NPR reporter Kelly McEvers said "more often than not, it's civilians who were killed in these strikes, [rather] than militants." Still, DoD continued to insist that "the number of civilian casualties is very, very low," though it would not offer a number. But defenders of drones argued that in conventional warfare civilian casualties were higher, on the order of 40%. And BIJ reported that civilians were a declining percentage of drone deaths in Pakistan: 28% in 2008, 16% in 2011, and just 2% in the first six months of 2012. Clive Stafford Smith wrote the *New York Times* that the issue was not what proportion of deaths were civilians but rather that "targeting militants in Pakistan without declaring war is illegal," and "drones drastically lower the threshold at which politicians are willing to kill." But Americans were unconvinced: 83% supported the program (77% of liberal Democrats). A later poll found that 62% of Americans approved of drone strikes, compared with just 21% of the public in Japan and 6% in Egypt.

Sen. Wyden (D-Or) wrote Holder:

> For the executive branch to claim that intelligence agencies have the authority to knowingly kill American citizens (subject to publicly unspecified limitations) while at the same time refusing to provide Congress with any and all legal opinions that delineate the executive branch's understanding of this authority represents an indefensible assertion of executive prerogative.

On February 22, 2012 DoD General Counsel Jeh Johnson repeated Koh's justifications in a speech at Yale Law School.[24] He analogized targeted killing to the US Navy shooting down the plane of Admiral

Yamamoto, commander of the Japanese navy, in 1943. Neither was an "assassination." US citizens enjoyed no immunity. Targeting decisions were "core functions of the Executive Branch" and "not appropriate for submission to a court."

Two weeks later Holder insisted it was "entirely lawful ... to target specific senior operational leaders of al Qaeda and associated forces."[25] Also citing the Yamamoto killing, he denounced use of the "loaded term" assassinations as "misplaced." Targeting an American citizen "who is actively engaged in planning to kill Americans would be lawful" if the threat was imminent, capture infeasible, and the killing complied with the principles of necessity, distinction and proportionality and would not inflict unnecessary suffering. "National security operations are core functions of the Executive Branch."

Calling Holder's speech "long on generalities and short on specifics," the *Washington Post* urged the administration to release the legal memos.[26] In his *New York Times* column, Andrew Rosenthal criticized both speeches for "reject[ing] any role for the courts in deciding when to kill American citizens." A week later he also called for release of the legal memos, dismissing Holder's "laughable" claim that Congress had engaged in a "robust" review. Media company Bloomberg said Holder's speech "left exposed a gaping hole in the administration's counterterrorism policy: the justification for targeted killings." "Life-and-death issues demand consistency and openness." The *Los Angeles Times* was "more concerned [than ever] that this nation is heading down a dangerous path." It was "uncomfortable with the [president's] broad powers ... to act as judge, jury and executioner ... on the basis of secret evidence." The "definition of 'imminent threat' is extremely vague." "We have to wonder how supporters of this position would feel if another country such as China or Russia were to take this approach in killing its enemies around the world." The *New York Times* wrote:

> President Obama, who came to office promising transparency and adherence to the rule of law, has become the first president to claim the legal authority to order an American citizen killed without judicial involvement, real oversight or public accountability ... Perhaps most disturbing, Mr. Holder utterly rejected any judicial supervision of a targeted killing ... The executive acting in secret as the police, prosecutor, jury, judge and executioner is the antithesis of due process.

The *Times* called for release of the legal memo, "unable to imagine why Mr. Obama would want to follow the horrible example set by Mr. Bush in withholding such vital information from the public." Leonard Pitts Jr. wrote in his *Miami Herald* column that the USA had killed al-Awlaki "without trial. Without due process. Without hesitation." Obama had set himself up as "judge, jury and executioner of every accused terrorist." Vicki Divoll wrote in a *Los Angeles Times* op ed that Congress should determine whether the president should "be able to order the killing of an American citizen with no review outside his own executive branch advisers." But in a *Wall Street Journal* op ed, John Yoo praised Holder for having "embraced the legal theories of the Bush administration ... that the Constitution designed the president to act alone" while faulting the Attorney General for making "a fundamental mistake by conceding that terrorists on the battlefield have due process rights at all." And three weeks after its cautious criticism, the *Washington Post* said "Obama was on solid ground in relying on" domestic and international law in the strike on al-Awlaki, although "the legitimacy of such targeted strikes against U.S. citizens would be bolstered by additional review."

At the end of April 2012 Deputy National Security Adviser Brennan explained that "in full accordance with the law – and in order to prevent terrorist attacks on the United States and to save American lives – the United States conducts targeted strikes against specific al-Qaeda terrorists."[27] "We only authorize a strike if we have a high degree of confidence that innocent civilians will not be injured or killed, except in the rarest of circumstances."

In a *New York Times* op ed New America Foundation director Peter Bergen deplored that Obama "became the first president to authorize the assassination of a United States citizen."[28] Drone strikes in Pakistan had increased from one every 43 days under Bush to one every four under Obama. *Washington Post* columnist Michael Gerson defended them as "some of the most precise applications of force in the history of warfare." But *Los Angeles Times* columnist Doyle McManus objected that the administration still had not said "who makes the decision ... or how many levels of review such a decision gets." The *New York Times* found Obama's claimed authority to choose targets "very troubling." "How can the world know whether the targets chosen by this president or his successors are truly dangerous terrorists and not just people with the wrong associations," or be confident that the president "truly pursued all methods short of assassination?" ACLU president Anthony Romero warned in a letter to the *Times* that "if President Obama is allowed to execute American citizens without judicial review and outside the theater of war, that astonishing power will forever reside in the hands of future presidents." But *Washington Post* columnist Charles Krauthammer declared drone strikes "fully justified ... in principle."

HRF urged Obama to declare "that the United States will not target individuals solely on the basis of their membership in or association with particular groups."[29] Brennan's "claim that all members of 'al Qaeda, the Taliban and associated forces' are targetable with lethal force is a misstatement of the relevant international law." The chairs and senior minority members of both Intelligence Committees exhorted the administration "to fully, fairly and impartially investigate" drone strikes. AI criticized the administration for treating "the entire world as a battlefield," "radical[ly]" reinterpreting the concept of "imminence," viewing "military-age males" as "guilty until proven innocent," and refusing to disclose "key factual and legal details of the killing programme."

In June UN Human Rights Commissioner Navi Pillay said in Islamabad that drone strikes raised "serious questions about compliance with international law" and suggested Pakistan invite an investigation by Christof Heyns, UN Special Rapporteur on extrajudicial, summary or arbitrary executions.[30] Heyns urged the USA to "clarify the procedures in place to ensure that any targeted killing complies with international humanitarian law and human rights" and ensure "prompt, thorough, effective and independent public investigation of alleged violations." He cited reports by the Pakistan Human Rights Commission that 30 percent of the thousand deaths since 2010 were civilian and told a conference organized by the ACLU that "current targeting practices weaken the rule of law." Ben Emmerson, UN Special Rapporteur for counterterrorism, said the USA was obligated to investigate and report every death, and announced he would study civilian casualties. Susan Rice, US Ambassador to the UN, questioned the "appropriateness" of Heyns's and Emmerson's proposed inquiries. At the UN Human Rights Council, Russia and China led other countries in issuing a statement condemning drone attacks. Pakistan Foreign Minister Khar told the UNHRC that strikes violated international law and sovereignty. In his March 2013 report, Emmerson said Pakistan had "emphasized its consistently-stated position that drone strikes on its territory are counter-productive, contrary to international law, a violation of Pakistan's sovereignty and territorial integrity, and that they should cease immediately."[31]

> Officials stated that reports of continuing tacit consent by Pakistan to the use of drones on its territory by any other state are false and confirmed that a thorough search of government records had revealed no indication of such consent having been given … Since mid-2012 (and to date) the government has regularly sent *Notes Verbales* to the US embassy in Islamabad protesting the use of drones.

During a SJC hearing in July, Sen. Grassley (R-Ia) complained that "we don't know the legal basis for the license to kill Americans" because the administration refused to provide the legal memos.[32] Declaring that "all of us are troubled … about the use of targeted killings that involve American citizens," Cornyn introduced an amendment to require the administration to give several committees the OLC memos. "[W]e're not mere supplicants of the Executive Branch. We are a coequal branch of government with the Constitutional responsibility to conduct oversight." (This failed on a 10–8 party-line vote.) *New York Times* columnist Andrew Rosenthal said Cornyn's request "makes sense."

In September Obama reiterated that criteria for strikes were "very tight and very strict."[33] The target had to be "authorized by our laws" and "a threat that is serious and not speculative." "It has to be a situation in which we can't capture the individual before they move forward on some sort of operational plot against the United States." "[W]e are very careful about avoiding civilian casualties." American citizens were "subject to the protections of the Constitution and due process."

In November the *Washington Post* said that though "scores – maybe hundreds – of civilians" had been among the 3,000 killed by more than 400 drone strikes, these were "a more effective and – yes – humane way" to combat "an irregular enemy."[34] "That drones do not put the lives of U.S. soldiers at risk and cause fewer collateral deaths are virtues, not evils." But though strikes in Pakistan, Yemen, and Somalia "meet tests for domestic and international legality," they "stoke popular hostility." "Drone strikes should be carried out by military forces rather than by the CIA … they should be publicly disclosed and subject to Congressional review. The process and criteria for adding names to kill lists in non-battlefield zones should be disclosed and authorized by Congress."

Fearing a loss in the November election, the administration sought to institutionalize its targeted killing policy.[35] Obama said in mid-October: "we've got to … put a legal architecture in place, and we need Congress's help … to make sure that not only am I reined in but any other president's reined in." After his re-election, the *New York Times* feared "the world may never see" the new rules. "Any rules should specify that no one can be killed unless actively planning or participating in terror, or helping lead al Qaeda or the Taliban." "Killing should be a last resort." Standards for preventing collateral damage "should be detailed and thorough." "[I]f an American citizen operating abroad is targeted, due process is required." A FISC-like court should "review the evidence … before [a] person is placed on a kill list." The AI USA executive director wrote the *Times* that "international human rights law and humanitarian law" should govern targeted killing. CCR's Pardiss Kebriaei and ACLU's Hina Shamsi wrote that the Constitution and international law were sufficient legal architecture.

In December 2011 the *New York Times* had sued the DoJ in SDNY seeking documents authorizing the killing of three US citizens in Yemen.[36] In April 2012 Judge McMahon granted Holder's personal request for more time to respond (the government's second) and agreed to keep secret DNI Clapper's declaration. DoJ said that "even to describe the numbers and details of most of these documents would reveal information that could damage the government's counterterrorism effort." CIA National Clandestine Service director John Bennett said the Agency "can now publicly acknowledge that it possesses records responsive to the ACLU's FOIA request," but refused to produce them. Judge McMahon dismissed the action on January 3, 2013. "Most of what is sought in the facially overbroad request … was properly withheld" under exemptions for "confidential and operational information." But requests for "the precise legal justification" for the targeted killings "implicate serious issues about the limits on the power of the Executive Branch … and about whether we are indeed a nation of laws, not of men." The administration had discussed the issue "in cryptic and imprecise ways."

> More fulsome [*sic*] disclosure of the legal reasoning on which the Administration relies to justify the targeted killing of individuals, including United States citizens, far from any recognizable "hot" field of battle, would allow for intelligent discussion and assessment of a tactic that (like torture before it) remains hotly debated. It might also help the public understand the scope of the ill-defined yet vast and seemingly ever-growing exercise in which we have been engaged for well over a decade, at great cost in lives, treasure, and (at least in the minds of some) personal liberty.
>
> However, this Court is constrained by law, and under the law, I can only conclude that the Government has not violated FOIA … The Alice-in-Wonderland nature of this pronouncement is not lost on me,

> but … I can find no way around the thicket of law and precedents that allow the Executive Branch of our Government to proclaim as perfectly lawful certain actions that seem on their face incompatible with our Constitution and laws, while keeping the reasons for its conclusion a secret.

The *New York Times* objected that "various government officials have spoken publicly about the American role in killing Mr. Awlaki," which "should have been deemed a waiver of the government's right to withhold its legal rationale from public scrutiny." A month later *NBC News* published a redacted version of the 16-page DoJ White Paper on targeted killing, which largely repeated the justifications offered above.

On appeal, the Second Circuit affirmed in part, reversed in part, and remanded.[37] Judge Newman found that Koh's ASIL speech, Johnson's Yale Law School speech, Holder's Northwestern University speech, Brennan's Wilson Center speech and testimony at his confirmation hearing for DCI, and the DoJ White Paper had waived the lawyer–client privilege with respect to the OLC memorandum. "We need not fear that OLC will lack for clients." But Newman's opinion graphically illustrated the contradictions McMahon had deplored: "One of those reasons concerns [redacted] the Government persuasively argues warrants continued secrecy. [redacted] We will redact all references to that [redacted]." The *New York Times* urged the administration not to seek further review. "For years now, the Obama administration has been playing a self-serving and duplicitous game over its power to kill people away from any battlefield and without judicial oversight or accountability." The Second Circuit had found the government's "overwrought claims of national security … seriously wanting." The administration should not be able "to have it both ways … cherry-picking information to share while keeping its underlying legal reasoning secret."

On remand on July 16, 2015, Judge McMahon expressed "deep[] regret that the Court of Appeals was not more definitive in its discussion of how closely an official acknowledgment had to track information contained in a document that would otherwise be exempt from disclosure."[38] But redactions rendered her reasoning just as opaque as Newman's:

> [W]hile the extensive and explicit publicity about whether the CIA should continue to play any "operational role" in targeted killings using drones give me great pause on the subject, I am unable to conclude that the Government has waived FOIA exemptions … If I were

> writing on a clean slate, I would rule that the [redacted] have been "officially acknowledged," and that FOIA protection is accordingly waived. [redacted] I believe it is for the Circuit to decide in the first instance [redacted] waive FOIA protection for documents discussing those [redacted]. The Court of Appeals now has the benefit of my view on the matter.

(But readers did not.) The Second Circuit affirmed on October 22. "[I]t would be difficult to explain in detail why the context of the legal reasoning ... differs from the context of the public explanation ... without revealing matters that are entitled to protection." In January 2016 the Second Circuit dismissed a FOIA action by City University of New York (CUNY) Law School seeking the NSC list of drone targets.

The ACLU also sued the CIA for the memos in DDC. In September 2011 Judge Collyer denied the FOIA request, finding that Panetta "never acknowledged the CIA's involvement in such a program."[39] The National Security Act exempted "intelligence sources and methods." "The Court has no reason to second-guess the CIA as to which programs that may or may not be of interest implicate the gathering of intelligence." "[L]eaving hostile groups guessing as to the CIA's possible interest or involvement in, or control over, drone strikes could itself be of eminent benefit." "Courts 'have consistently deferred to executive affidavits predicting harm to the national security, and have found it unwise to undertake searching judicial review.'" During oral argument on appeal, DC Circuit Chief Judge Garland asked whether Brennan's statement that the government targeted terrorists was not "an official acknowledgement that the CIA is involved in the drone program?" Stuart F. Delery, Acting Assistant Attorney General, said Obama's statements were insufficient. Judge Tatel asked about Panetta's 2010 claim that "the more we continue to disrupt al-Qaeda's operations, and we are engaged in the most aggressive operations in the history of the CIA in that part of the world, and the result is that we are disrupting their leadership." But Delery said Panetta did not mention drones.

In March 2013, the Circuit Court reversed.[40] Judge Garland wrote: "The CIA has proffered no reason to believe that disclosing whether it has any documents at all about drone strikes will reveal whether the Agency itself ... operates drones." "The President of the United States has himself publicly acknowledged that the United States uses drone strikes." So had Brennan: "Given these official acknowledgments ... it is neither logical nor plausible for the CIA to maintain that it would reveal anything not already in the public domain to say that the Agency 'at least has an intelligence interest' in such strikes. The defendant is, after all, the Central Intelligence Agency." "But there is more." Brennan "stated that, in deciding whether to carry out a strike, '[w]e … draw[] on the full range of our intelligence capabilities.'" "And there is still more." Then DCI Panetta boasted that the strikes had been "very effective because they have been very precise." Garland observed: "It is hard to see how the CIA Director could have made his Agency's knowledge of … drone strikes any clearer." "[A] s it is now clear that the Agency does have an interest in drone strikes, it beggars belief that it does not also have documents relating to the subject." "[T]he CIA asked the courts … to give their imprimatur to a fiction of deniability that no reasonable person would regard as plausible. 'There comes a point where … Court[s] should not be ignorant as judges of what [they] know as men' and women." "[T]he official statements of the President and Messrs. Brennan and Panetta render it impossible to believe that those two speeches are the only documents related to drone strikes in the agency's files." But on remand, Judge Collyer again dismissed on June 18, 2015, finding that the records sought "could reveal the scope of the drone program, its successes and limitations, the 'methodology behind the assessments and the priorities of the agency' and more," and were protected by FOIA exemptions for classified information and the deliberative process, and attorney–client and presidential communication privileges.

After Obama nominated Brennan as DCI, the ACLU said the Senate should investigate his role in targeted killing, and HRF urged it to "get commitments from him that the drone program is conducted lawfully."[41] The *New York Times* agreed he should be "deeply questioned" about drone strikes. Sen. Wyden asked him to provide government files on the killing of Americans. In a *New York Times* op ed Vicki Divoll accused Democrats of not having "fought this president" to get the documents, "even though Congress has the absolute power under the Constitution" to see them. The *Washington Post* reported that the Principals Committee had merely approved regulations Brennan had drafted, specifying the process for placing names on the kill list, principles governing the targeting of US citizens, and approvals necessary for operations outside war zones; but these did not govern CIA strikes in Pakistan. The Council on Foreign Relations published a report urging Obama to end signature strikes or explain their legal justification and disclose the targeting criteria.

In February 2013 *NBC News* published the DoJ White Paper on targeted killing, provided to the Senate Intelligence and Judiciary Committees in summer 2012, which found it lawful to kill a US citizen pursuant to "public authority" if "an informed high-level official" reasonably decided the target was a high-ranking al-Qaeda member who posed a "continued" and "imminent threat of violent attack against the United States" and capture was infeasible.[42] In response, AI urged the administration "to disclose further legal and factual details" about targeted killings, "end claims that the USA is authorized by international law to use lethal force anywhere in the world," and "recognize the application of international human rights law," "respecting the rule that if there is doubt as to whether a person is a civilian, the person is to be considered a civilian" and "ensuring independent and impartial investigations." But though the proportion of Americans surveyed in February 2013 who viewed targeted killing of US citizens as illegal was twice that of those believing it was legal (48 versus 24 percent), the proportion who generally approved drone attacks "on people and other targets deemed a threat to the U.S." was six times that of those disapproving (75 versus 13 percent).

White House Press Secretary Carney said Congress should be satisfied with the White Paper, but the chairs of the both Intelligence Committees still wanted to see the OLC opinions. The *New York Times* found the DoJ lawyers' "twisted logic" "disturbing." The White Paper "redefined the word 'imminent' in a way that diverges sharply from its customary meaning" and felt "no need to explain" the targeting decision "to Congress, the courts or the public – or, indeed, to even acknowledge that the killing took place." *Washington Post* columnist James Downie called the White Paper "a chilling document, full of twisted definitions, gaping loopholes and hints that the White House still isn't sharing its full justification for killing citizens without due process." In anticipation of Brennan's confirmation hearing, the administration agreed to give the OLC memo to the Intelligence Committees. Wyden had threatened to "pull out all the stops to get the actual legal analysis … laws in our country and their interpretation are not supposed to be confidential." Denying the committees the memo would make "a mockery … of the oversight process." Feinstein agreed that "it is critical for the committee's oversight function." The *New York Times* welcomed the "overdue push for greater accountability and transparency." "For years, Mr. Obama has stretched executive power." Notre Dame law professor Mary Ellen O'Connell wrote in a *New York Times* op ed that the Senate should hold Brennan "to account for one of the administration's gravest failings: its refusal to openly discuss the legal basis for America's campaign of targeted killing of terrorism suspects." "The Justice Department has concocted an elastic definition of necessity – attempting to justify force in the absence of an immediate threat – without citing any treatise or decision by an international court." The *Washington Post* said Brennan's confirmation hearing gave "senators an opportunity to air a host of pent-up questions about the Obama administration's secret warfare, including drone strikes in Pakistan, Yemen, and Somalia."

Brennan's written statement to SSCI promised "transparency" about "the legal basis as well as the thresholds, criteria, processes, procedures, approvals, and reviews" of "the use of lethal force outside the 'hot battlefield' of Afghanistan."[43] In response to a pre-hearing question, he said any strike had to satisfy the law of war principles of necessity, distinction, proportionality, and humanity, and claimed that drones "dramatically reduce the danger to U.S. personnel and to innocent civilians." After clearing the room of demonstrators, Feinstein objected that staffers could not see the two memos disclosed and sought the other seven. Brennan replied that it was "rather exceptional" to disclose *any* OLC opinion. But Wyden "made it clear that we've got to see any and all of those legal opinions … before the vote." Feinstein complained that forbidding disclosure of the number of civilian casualties meant that "for the public" the drone campaign "doesn't exist." (She later said the number of civilian deaths was "very low," "in the single digits" each year.) Brennan agreed that "we need to acknowledge" civilian deaths. "[W]e only take such actions as a last resort, to save lives when there is no other alternative." Al-Awlaki was "not just a propagandist" but "part of the operational effort that is known as al-Qa'ida in the Arabian Peninsula" and "intimately involved in activities that were designed to kill innocent men, women and children." Rep. King (R–NY) said: "having the executive being the prosecutor, the judge, the jury and the executioner all in one is very contrary to the traditions and the laws of this country" and suggested a special court to oversee targeted killings. Brennan replied that the administration had "wrestled" with the idea, which was "certainly worth[y] of discussion," but targeting decisions were "an inherent Executive Branch function." He conceded that American citizens "are due much greater due process than anybody else." Wyden complained that the CIA had never identified the countries where it conducted targeted killings. Brennan responded that "we need to … optimize transparency … but at the same time optimize secrecy and the protection of our national security." He agreed that "we need to [ac]knowledge" mistakes "to our foreign partners" and do so "publicly." In response to Sen. Collins (R-Me), he declared "unequivocally … there's never been occasion … where we had the opportunity to capture a terrorist and … we decided to take a lethal strike." When she warned that backlash from the strikes caused more harm than any good they achieved, Brennan said "in many areas … the people are being held hostage to al-Qa'ida … and have welcomed the work that the U.S. Government has done with their governments to rid them of the al-Qa'ida cancer that exists." At the end of the hearing Rockefeller (D-WV) said: "I quite honestly do not recall anybody who was more forthright, more direct, more accommodating … more open to the possibility of working with this Committee." Responding to written questions after the hearing, Brennan said "there should be an interagency review process when making policy decisions associated with such strikes." The government should reveal "overall numbers of civilian deaths" as far as consistent with "national security."

Brennan won over most media commentators.[44] The *New York Times* endorsed him, but hoped "he does not forget that the heightened danger does not free the executive branch from oversight or the normal system of checks and balances." The *Times* did not "buy the administration's claim to have the authority to kill Americans, and other suspects, far beyond any battlefield with no oversight and no review." And the assertion that the government used lethal force only when "there is no other alternative" was "at odds with reports of vastly increased drone strikes." *Times* columnist David Brooks accepted that "acting brutally abroad saves lives at home," but wanted an "independent judicial panel to review the kill lists" and "an independent panel of former military and intelligence officers issuing reports on the program's efficacy." *Washington Post* columnist Michael Gerson said drones were "a technology that allows the most discriminate application of force in the history of warfare." *Post* columnist Charles Krauthammer urged even fewer constraints. It was "nonsense" to require an "imminent attack." Krauthammer spouted his own nonsense: "A sleeping Anwar al-Awlaki could lawfully be snuffed not because of imminence but because he was self-declared al Qaeda and thus an enemy combatant." In a *Post* op ed, civil liberties lawyer David Cole conceded that targeted killing "beats the tragically untargeted killing used in the World War II bombings" and might be permissible against citizens on "extraordinary occasions," but it always had to be acknowledged. *USA Today* agreed that "drones beat the alternatives," but claimed it would be "easy to create" a FISC-like court to "review kill lists of Americans in non-imminent situations." The *New York Times* also endorsed a specialized court and "clear and public standards for how a suspect can be named an enemy combatant." But some remained skeptical. The ACLU's Hina Shamsi and Christopher Anders wrote that the *Times*'s proposal would "legitimize" the "executive branch's claimed killing authority." *Post* columnist Dana Milbank warned that Brennan would "play[] God … even more frequently once he moves to Langley." The drone program was "an extraordinary assertion of the executive's powers … crying out for Congressional oversight." While conceding that al-Awlaki was "a legitimate target," *Post* columnist Eugene Robinson denied "that the president or a 'high-level official' gets to make the call without judicial oversight."

Former Defense Secretary Gates declared himself a "big advocate" of drones because "the numbers" of civilians killed "are extremely small" and you "have the ability to limit that collateral damage more than with any other weapon system that you have."[45] But it was "worth giving serious consideration" to having "a panel of three judges or one judge" determine there was "a compelling case … to launch an attack against an American citizen." Sen. Rand Paul (R-Ky) said "there needs to be a trial for treason" before targeting an American citizen. Former South African Archbishop Desmond Tutu wrote the *New York Times* that he was "deeply, deeply disturbed" that judicial review of targeted killings might be limited to US citizens. "Do the United States and its people really want to tell those of us who live in the rest of the world that our lives are not of the same value as yours?" John Yoo wrote in a *Wall Street Journal* op ed that the White Paper should "have simply … stated that under the laws of war U.S. military units can kill any enemy soldiers at any time." Giving "enemy combatants on the battlefield" any "due-process rights" reduces the "U.S. military's speed and decisiveness" and "dissipates the rights of the law-abiding at home." Sen. Graham (R-SC) said: "sometimes you hit innocent people, and I hate that, but we're at war, and we've taken out some very senior members of al-Qaeda."

James Robertson (who had resigned from FISC after the *New York Times* disclosed warrantless wiretapping in 2005 and retired from the DDC in 2010) wrote in a *Washington Post* op ed that judicial review of targeted killing was "a very bad idea" because it would require an "advisory opinion" and "severely compromise[]" judicial independence.[46] In a *New York Times* op ed, Georgetown University law professor Neal Katyal agreed that a drone court was "a mistake." "It is hard to think of something less suitable for a federal judge to rule on than the fast-moving and protean nature of targeting decisions." In a *Wall Street Journal* op ed, Michael Mukasey denounced the proposal as a "feel-good prescription ... devoid of substance." "Judges have no basis or background that suits them to review targeting decisions and no way to gather facts independently." But Jane Harman (D-Ca) (former HPSCI ranking minority member) wrote in a CNN op ed that "a FISA-like process ... would protect individual civil liberties ... while confronting a supercharged threat environment."

Feinstein said SSCI "receives notifications with key details of each strike shortly after it occurs" and "holds regular briefings and hearings on these operations."[47] After she said she had "reached an agreement with the White House to provide the committee access to all OLC opinions related to the targeted killing of Americans in a way that allows members to fulfill their oversight responsibilities," SSCI voted 12–3 to confirm Brennan. Joining the majority, Wyden, Udall (D-NM), and Collins declared that "this sets an important precedent for applying our American system of checks and balances to the challenges of 21st-century warfare." Paul threatened to filibuster after Holder explained that though the administration had "no intention" of conducting such strikes in the USA, in a 9/11-style "emergency" he "would examine the particular facts and circumstances before advising the president on the scope of his authority." Paul worried aloud: "say you're an Arab-American in Dearborn, Michigan, e-mailing your brother in the Mideast, and they think your brother is a terrorist. Does that mean they can use a drone to kill you?"

Paul (assisted by Sens. Cruz (R-Tex) and Lee (R-Ut)) staged a 13-hour filibuster, focusing on whether the government could target a US citizen, on US soil, who did not pose an imminent threat.[48] He was praised by Tea Party conservatives, Senate Majority Leader McConnell (R-Ky), and Code Pink. RNC chairman Priebus called the filibuster "completely awesome." *New York Times* columnist Gail Collins agreed that the "fact that the president was ordering the death of American citizens anywhere without oversight was worrying." *Washington Post* columnist Eugene Robinson lauded Paul "for grabbing us by the lapels." *Post* columnist David Ignatius said Paul's "argument for clearer limits on drones is absolutely right." The *Post* itself hedged: Paul "was rightly taken to task for gross and irresponsible mischaracterizations of the Obama administration's policy," but the administration "has never revealed even [the] outlines" of its "process for adding names to a target list." NYU law professor Ryan Goodman said in a *New York Times* op ed that the administration's "overly broad definition" of "engaged in combat," including drug traffickers and al-Qaeda financiers, "stretches the laws of war beyond recognition." Sen. McCain (R-Az) defended drones and attacked Paul, complaining that "it's always the wacko birds on right and left that get the media megaphone." Rep. Amash (R-Mich) taunted McCain: "Did you come up with that at #dinnerwithbarack?" The Senate confirmed Brennan 63–34. Afterwards, Paul wrote in a *Washington Post* op ed that his filibuster "was the beginning of a fight to restore a healthy balance of powers." "[N]o American should be killed by a drone without first being charged with a crime." Cruz and he introduced a bill "to prohibit the use of drones to kill citizens of the United States within the United States" unless the individual "poses an imminent threat of death or serious bodily injury to another individual."

At an SJC oversight hearing, chairman Leahy (D-Vt) considered subpoenaing the OLC opinions, and Grassley (the ranking Republican) expressed frustration that they had been given only to SSCI.[49] Holder first told Cruz that killing someone not posing an immediate threat would be "inappropriate," but then conceded under pressure it would be unconstitutional. When Cruz proposed to draft a bill barring the use of drones to kill Americans in the USA, Holder warned that might violate separation of powers. Feinstein observed that shooting down a plane hijacked by terrorists in the USA would be lawful. Holder agreed with Graham that the AUMF did not exclude action against terrorists in the USA (even though former Sen. Daschle (D-SD) said Congress had rebuffed the administration's request to add "in the United States" to the authorization). Lee said the requirements of "imminence" and "unfeasibility" of capture were so loose as to be meaningless. After the hearing Holder emailed Paul that the president did not "have the authority to use a weaponized drone to kill an American not engaged in combat on American soil."

The *New York Times* reported more details about the antecedents of the al-Awlaki killing.[50] After Abdulmutallab revealed that al-Awlaki had assisted the Christmas Day plot, OLC lawyers Barron and Lederman wrote a memo finding him a lawful target because he participated in war on behalf of al-Qaeda and threatened the USA. They justified military action under the AUMF and CIA action as "national self-defense," drawing an analogy to a high speed police chase. But after discovering a 1994 statute barring the killing of Americans overseas, with no national security exception, they prepared a more comprehensive 63-page memo. Based on intelligence reports linking al-Awlaki to the May 2010 Times Square bomb attempt and the October 2010 attempt to bomb cargo planes flying to the USA, they concluded that he was planning further attacks. They interpreted a 1997 District Court decision to hold that "Congress did not intend to criminalize justifiable or excusable homicides." The White Paper was based on this memo. This prompted the *Times* to call for repeal of the AUMF, in part because Obama had relied on it "to use drones to kill terrorists far from the Afghan battlefield, and to claim an unconstitutional power to kill American citizens in other countries based only on suspicion that they are or might become terrorist threats, without judicial review." Obama again rebuffed requests for the drone memos by Sens. Leahy and Rockefeller.[51] John Podesta (Clinton's chief of staff, now chair of the Center for American Progress) wrote in a *Washington Post* op ed that Obama should release the memos.[52] Rep. McCarthy (R-Ca), the third ranking Republican, said the House should subpoena the OLC memos that had been given to the Senate.[53] "How is somebody being able to make those decisions without a check and balance?"

Jane Harman (former HSPCI ranking member, now director of the Woodrow Wilson Center) warned in a *New York Times* op ed that "the tactic of taking out bad guys may ultimately create more of them."[54] The FISA framework should be extended to targeted killings. But at Fordham Law School, Jeh Johnson expressed skepticism about a FISC-type court, questioning whether judges should provide "top cover" for "death warrants" based on secret evidence in *ex parte* hearings. He had seen the "feasibility of capture of a particular objective change several times in one night." In April 2013 ten human rights groups urged Obama to publicly disclose the standards for targeted killing, ensure compliance with international law, facilitate judicial review and Congressional oversight, and investigate and report civilian casualties.

After the administration acknowledged for the first time in May 2013 that the USA had killed four citizens outside battlefields, Obama issued a new classified policy guidance authorizing strikes in such zones only if there was "a continuing, imminent threat to Americans" and the target could not feasibly be captured.[55] Sens. Rubio (R-Fla) and King (R-NY) introduced the Targeted Strike Oversight Reform Act, requiring an independent analysis before the government targeted a citizen. In July Nasser al-Awlaki wrote a *New York Times* op ed about the drone strike that killed his grandson Abdulrahman and a cousin (both teenagers) and at least five other civilians eating in an open air restaurant. "The Obama administration must answer for its actions and be held accountable." "No court ever reviewed the government's claims" against his son Anwar, "nor was any evidence of criminal wrongdoing ever presented to a court. He did not deserve to be deprived of his constitutional rights as an American citizen and killed."

Following AI and HRW reports of civilian casualties from drone strikes in Pakistan and Yemen (discussed below), the White House Press Secretary "strongly disagree[d]" with the "claim that the U.S. has acted contrary to international law."[56] It took "extraordinary care" and was "mindful of the absolute need to limit civilian casualties and to ... reach a standard of near certainty that no civilians will be killed or injured." Operations were "precise," "lawful," and "effective. But the *New York Times* called for "greater transparency and accountability." Former Defense Secretary Gates warned the Association of the US Army's annual conference that drones had led many in the White House and Congress to view war as "bloodless, painless and odorless," whereas it "is inevitably tragic, inefficient and uncertain." UN Special Rapporteurs Emmerson and Heyns presented reports on drones, reminding the USA of the rules of international law and international humanitarian law. Pakistan had told Emmerson that of the 2,200 people killed by drones, 600 definitely were civilians and another 200 probably were. In Yemen, 21–58 of the 268–393 killed were civilians. *Lawfare* published four estimates finding civilian deaths a significant fraction of all drone deaths in Pakistan in 2011: 57–65/392–604 (New America Foundation), 30/435 (Long War Journal), 52–146/447–600 (BIJ), and 72–155/456–661 (Columbia Human Rights Clinic). For the period 2004–13 the figures were 258–307/2,039–3,370 (New America Foundation) and 411–890/2,566–3,570 (BIJ).

SSCI voted on November 5 to require the administration to disclose how many civilians and militants were killed by drones each year and impose additional requirements before the president could authorize strikes against US citizens or resident aliens.[57] The number of strikes nearly halved from 2012 to 2013 (from 42 to 22 in Yemen and from 46 to 25 in Pakistan), and Feinstein said civilian deaths were "significantly lower" than critics claimed. At a February 2014 HSPCI hearing, Schiff said the USA should publish an annual report on the number of combatants and noncombatants killed by drone strikes. His amendment to do so had failed the previous year; Feinstein offered the Targeted Lethal Force Transparency Act again in 2014.

Although the administration sought to transfer all drone strikes from the CIA to the military, the House and Senate Appropriations Committees expressed their misgivings by including a secret provision in the budget bill requiring the administration to certify that the military met standards in drone operations.[58] Feinstein said she had seen the CIA "exercise patience and discretion specifically to prevent collateral damage" and "would really have to be convinced that the military would carry it out that well." An aide said SSCI "recently reviewed this issue, and Senator Feinstein believes her views are widely shared on the committee." SASC chair McCain responded angrily on the Senate floor that "the Appropriations Committee has no business making these decisions. The job of the Armed Services Committee and the job of the Intelligence Committee is to authorize these things." After the December 12, 2013 strike on a Yemeni wedding party (discussed below), that government prohibited JSOC strikes but allowed those by the CIA. Nevertheless, Rep. Schiff (D-Ca) urged in a *New York Times* op ed that drone strikes be transferred to the military. "We must hold ourselves accountable by being more open about the effect of our drone strikes," and the "administration must go further to explain what protections are in place to ensure due process for any American who may be targeted."

Sen. Grassley said "targeted killing of American citizens by their own government should be one of the most fundamental reasons to ensure checks and balances are in place."[59] The government had "been hiding behind a Cliff's [*sic*] Notes version of the justification that gave no legal analysis for the killings." SJC should see "unredacted copies of any and all legal opinions." The committee had voted 10–8 for Barron's nomination to the First Circuit Court of Appeals before the *New York Times* described the memo he wrote with Lederman. Now the administration postponed a Senate vote until it decided what to disclose and whether to appeal the DC Circuit decision ordering release of the OLC memos (discussed above). Sens. Paul, Udall, and Wyden opposed the nomination without such disclosure. The White House offered to show the memos to the full Senate but not the public. The *New York Times* objected that "the administration has never explained in detail the legal justification for the killing" of al-Awlaki. "Senators have a right to see the quality of a nominee's legal analysis, particularly when he is trying to make a case for a morally questionable activity." The public "also has the right to evaluate one of the Obama administration's most important national security decisions, and the quality of the people it is nominating to the bench." It joined more than twenty organizations urging the administration not to appeal.

Rand Paul wrote in a *New York Times* op ed that "killing an American citizen without a trial is an extraordinary concept and deserves serious debate."[60] "The Bill of Rights is clear." Al-Awlaki "should have been tried – in absentia, if necessary." "[L]egal arguments that affect the rights of every American should not have the privilege of secrecy." Declaring himself "not satisfied" with Barron's memos, which pointed to "no valid legal precedent to justify the killing of an American citizen not engaged in combat," Paul threatened to filibuster the nomination. Even after Solicitor General Verrilli decided not to appeal the Second Circuit opinion and release much of the memo, Paul still vowed to filibuster unless the Senate got all the memos and the public saw redacted versions. The Senate voted 52–43 to proceed with the nomination. Praising Paul's "impassioned and articulate defense of the centrality of due process even for the most reviled," the *New York Times* objected that a vote on the nomination before disclosure of the memos "would shut the public out of the debate." But on May 22, 2014 the Senate narrowly confirmed Barron (53–45).

In June the DC Circuit released a redacted version of the OLC's July 2010 memo approving the killing of al-Awlaki (omitting the first 11 pages containing evidence that he was an operational terrorist).[61] It found that the statute outlawing "Foreign murder of United States nationals" barred only "unlawful killings," which excluded those conducted under a public authority justification. This killing would be done in the "lawful conduct of war" under the AUMF because al-Awlaki was a "leader of AQAP forces," which were "part of al-Qaida forces" or "associated with" al-Qaeda. AQAP's activities "pose a 'continued and imminent threat' of violence to United States persons and interests." "[T]he targeted nature of the operation would help to ensure that it would comply with the principle of distinction, and DoD has represented to us that it would make every effort to minimize civilian casualties." The authors understood "that an operation by [DoD or CIA] to capture al-Aulaqi in Yemen would be infeasible at this time." Even though he was a US citizen, the Fifth Amendment "would not require the government to provide further process," and "the Fourth Amendment 'reasonableness' test is situation-dependent."

Sen. Udall called the release "a victory for government transparency," but planned to press for additional disclosure. The *New York Times* said the legal rationale "provides little confidence that the lethal action was taken with real care." The memo was a "slapdash pastiche of legal theories – some based on obscure interpretations of British and Israeli law – that was clearly tailored to the desired result." The public authorities doctrine was "a dangerous concept if expanded because it could be used to justify all kinds of government misdeeds." Awlaki's "due-process rights are dealt with summarily." Dawn Johnsen (a former OLC head) defended the memo, which exhibited "careful, high-quality analysis" and conducted "a thorough review of all relevant legal authorities." Writing in a *USA Today* op ed, HPSCI chair Rogers (R-Mich) dismissed criticism: "the legal reasoning behind a drone strike … is simple: Nations have the right to use force against legitimate enemy targets." "American men and women would have to be put at unreasonable risk to capture a terrorist in largely ungoverned areas of the Yemen desert." "Constitutional due process protections do not and should not extend to al-Qaeda terrorists who plot to kill us." But in a second editorial the *Times* repeated that "there are grave moral and legal questions going unanswered in the government's use of armed drones to kill people considered terrorist threats." "Drone operations need to be subject to credible oversight" and be conducted by the DoD.

The memo's release did little to end debate. SSCI dropped a provision requiring the president to disclose the number killed or injured by drones after opposition by DNI Clapper.[62] But the House version of the NDAA threatened to withhold 25 percent of the Special Operations budget unless Secretary Hagel complied with the provision in the previous year's budget that he provide detailed information about the process for selecting and approving drone targets. The *New York Times* criticized Obama for having "shifted military actions to the shadows by authorizing drone campaigns in Pakistan, Yemen and Somalia," policies that were "too similar to his predecessor's for our comfort." But Americans remained split, 52 percent approving drone strikes and 41 percent disapproving; approval was greater only in Israel and Kenya, and no other country had a majority in favor.

"Signature strikes" in Pakistan in January 2015 killed two hostages – Warren Weinstein (a US citizen) and Giovanni Lo Porto (an Italian) – as well as alleged terrorists Ahmed Farouq and Adam Gadahn (both US citizens).[63] Because the CIA had not known the latter were present at the target, they had not undergone the requisite DoJ vetting; but a classified addendum to Obama's 2013 directive exempted the CIA's drone program in Pakistan from the "imminent threat" requirement (though not the requirement of "near certainty" to avoid civilian casualties). Obama offered his "deepest apologies" for the first two deaths and ordered a "full review." "One of the things that sets America apart from many other nations, one of the things that makes us exceptional is our willingness to confront squarely our imperfections and to learn from our mistakes." The *New York Times* praised Obama's "candor and remorse," but emphasized the "questionable legality" of targeted killing. These strikes raised "serious questions about just how much intelligence officers have before dropping bombs into remote areas by hitting a switch half a world away." The response to the hostages' deaths "stands in contrast to the silence [the administration] usually maintains about the civilian victims of drone strikes." Sen. Feinstein claimed that "the number of civilian casualties that have resulted from such strikes each year has typically been in the single digits." Pakistanis objected that the USA did not apologize when their compatriots were killed or wounded. Complaining a year later that nothing had happened, Lo Porto's family filed briefs with the Italian state prosecutor, arguing that the strike had been illegal and asking the prosecutor to seek information from the USA. Accusing the administration of refusing to negotiate compensation, the Weinstein family sought the $10,000-a-day the USA was giving the Iran embassy hostages for the 1,251 days Weinstein had been held before being killed. Ten human rights organizations urged Obama to conduct the same "thorough independent review" promised the Weinstein and Lo Porto families for *all* strikes, and offer those victims' families the same compensation. Prompted by Obama's apology, Faisal bin Ali Jaber, whose brother-in-law and nephew had been killed in a drone strike in Yemen, joined others seeking a declaratory judgment in DDC that the strike was unlawful. The Yemeni government gave the families of those victims $155,000, which probably came from the USA.

In the aftermath of these strikes Sen. McCain renewed his effort to transfer the drone program to the military.[64] The CIA was "called the intelligence agency" for a reason; the armed forces were "obviously the people that are supposed to be carrying out military operations." Gov. John Kasich (a potential Republican presidential candidate) agreed. The *Washington Post* favored the transfer, but said the program itself "shouldn't be up for review." "There is little question that drones are the least costly means of eliminating militants whose first aim is to kill Americans." A recent poll found that 60 percent of Americans generally favored drone strikes and only 13 percent were opposed; but only 47 percent approved strikes threatening innocent Americans. In

January 2016 Congress had added a classified measure to a spending bill, restricting the administration from using money to transfer control to the military.

On February 19, 2016 former DCI Hayden wrote a *New York Times* op ed entitled: "To Keep America Safe, Embrace Drone Warfare."[65] He said that claims "that a high percentage of the people killed in drone strikes are civilians" were "totally at odds with the intelligence I have received." "[T]he targeted killing program has been the most precise and effective application of firepower in the history of armed conflict." He "deeply regret[ted] a strike that killed a child," but his grandfather had a garage full of dangerous chemicals, and he intended to use them, perhaps on Americans." "Civilians have died, but in my firm opinion, the death toll from terrorist attacks would have been much higher if we had not taken action." Hayden claimed in his memoir that "the intelligence on which these strikes were conducted was exquisite" and "intelligence for signature strikes was quite robust." UN Special Rapporteur Heyns replied in the *Times* that Hayden "fails to reckon with the very real concerns raised by a global targeted killing program carried out according to secret rules and with no real accountability" and "does not address the repeated, well-documented reports of numerous civilian casualties." "The message the drone program sends could not be clearer: western lives are precious. Foreign Muslims' lives are cheap." Farea al-Muslimi, co-founder of the Sana'a Center for Strategic Studies, wrote the *Times* that "Hayden's views [were] completely at odds with the reality in my country," which was that "many of those killed by the United States were civilians."

A day later the USA acknowledged that an air strike against ISIS in Libya killed 32, including two Serbian hostages, even though weeks of observing the site disclosed "no indications of any civilians present."[66] The USA offered condolences, but alleged that the Serbs had been killed by a criminal group who had kidnapped them and sought to cover this up by presenting them as victims of the air strike. Protests were filed by Serbia and Libya's internationally recognized parliament in Tobruk, which called the strikes "a clear and flagrant violation of the sovereignty of the Libyan state."

Publishing a 17-month "Report Card" on implementation of the recommendations of its 2014 report, the Stimson Center gave the administration grades of D or F for improved transparency in strikes, releasing information on strikes or their legal basis, transferring responsibility to the military, and greater accountability for strikes outside traditional battlefields.[67] Reprieve issued a report claiming that "multiple attempts to kill just 41 individuals have resulted in total fatalities of 1,147 people overall, including 150 children." The ACLU's Jameel Jaffer and Bret Max Kaufman wrote in a *New York Times* op ed that the Obama administration had "killed as many as 5,000 people" by drone strikes, "possibly 1,000 of them civilians." Obama should publish his Presidential Policy Guidance and the OLC memos, acknowledge all strikes, investigate those that killed civilians and pay compensation, and shift responsibility to the military. When Lisa Monaco, Obama's counterterrorism and homeland security adviser, said the administration planned to produce an annual assessment of drone strike casualties "outside areas of active hostilities" (Iraq, Afghanistan, and Syria), the *New York Times* called the promised transparency "too little, too late." DCI Brennan defended the strikes:

> This administration has made the criteria very rigorous … there are lots of reports about hundreds upon thousands of innocents who have been killed as a result of these strikes. I can tell you with great confidence that those are exceptionally exaggerated reports … the number of civilians killed relative to the number of terrorists killed is a very small portion.

At a press conference at the end of the Nuclear Security Summit, Obama acknowledged:[68]

> legitimate criticism that … the legal architecture around the use of drone strikes or other kinetic strikes wasn't as precise as it should have been, and there's no doubt that civilians were killed that shouldn't have been … What I can say with great confidence is that our operating procedures are as rigorous as they have ever been and that there is a constant evaluation of precisely what we do.

Several days later he said at University of Chicago Law School:

> My hope is that by the time I leave office, there is not only an internal structure in place that governs these standards that we've set, but there is also an institutionalized process whereby the actions that the U.S. government takes through drone technology are consistently reported on an annualized basis … in the first couple of years of my presidency, the architecture – legal architecture, administrative architecture, command structures – around how these were utilized was under-developed relative to how fast the technology was moving … it is not true that this has been this sort of willy-nilly, "let's bomb a village." That's not how folks have operated. What I can say with great certainty is that the rate of

> civilian casualties in any drone operation are [sic] far lower than the rate of civilian casualties that occur in traditional war.

There were only seven CIA strikes in the first six months of 2016, just two in Pakistan, and more responsibility was transferred from the CIA to DoD (after the fall of the Yemeni government that had banned DoD strikes).

In July, after months of promises, the administration revealed data on air strikes outside the war zones of Afghanistan, Iraq, and Syria: 473 strikes in 2009–15 killed an estimated 2,372–2,581 "combatants" and 64–116 civilians.[69] The Long War Journal and BIJ estimated far more civilian deaths: 200–800. The following month the administration released the rules governing targeted killing.[70] DoD and CIA could propose a target after review by their top lawyers. The Deputies Committee (number two officials at national security departments and agencies) then considered whether the threat to the USA could be prevented in other ways and evaluated the strike's impact on "the broader regional and international political interests of the United States." The killing could occur if they recommended it, the Principals Committee unanimously agreed, and the target was not a US citizen; otherwise, the president decided. He could waive these rules in "extraordinary cases" when there was a "fleeting opportunity," no time for a full review, or the target "poses a continuing, imminent threat to another country's persons."

In an October interview Obama displayed typical ambivalence.[71] He was "sincerely … glad the left pushes me on this," but "much of the time" their critiques were not "fair or fully informed," failing to "recognize the degree to which the civilian-casualty rate … is significantly lower than what happens in a conventional war." But "having these nonprofits continue to question and protest ensured that, having made that initial decision" to disclose casualty figures, "it got pushed all the way through."

A month before he left office, Obama directed national security departments and agencies to prepare a formal report on the legal and policy frameworks guiding the use of military force and to update it annually.[72] At a press conference at MacDill Air Force Base in Tampa the next day, he reiterated that "under rules that I put in place and that I made public, before any strike is taken outside of a war zone, there must be near certainty that no civilians will be killed or injured." The Trump administration promptly reconsidered these restraints, provoking objections by three dozen members of the national security establishment, as well as the *New York Times*.[73] But Trump's national security advisers proposed to allow drone strikes on foot soldiers as well as leaders and to drop the requirement that all strikes be approved at the highest level.[74]

Analysis

For most of the first decade of the "war on terror" drone attacks attracted little attention or criticism. That was unsurprising – and of course deliberate. To paraphrase Neville Chamberlain, they occurred in faraway countries about which Americans knew little (Pakistan and Yemen), directly endangered no Americans, and were secret; indeed, until recently the CIA would neither admit nor deny they had occurred. Although the United States routinely killed thousands, it took exceptional circumstances to arouse public interest: the deaths of American citizens, large numbers of civilians, or identifiable innocent victims.

One reason for widespread indifference is the difficulty of distinguishing targeted killings from conventional warfare, whose goal, after all, is to kill enemies. Throughout much of history killing was intimate. Aerial bombing campaigns in World War II – especially the firebombing of Dresden and nuclear attacks on Hiroshima and Nagasaki – led critics to warn that modern warfare's impersonality and distance made killing too easy. These concerns intensified during carpet bombing in the Vietnam War. To justify its "war on terror" the Bush administration consistently invoked "self-defense," which it stretched to include "pre-emptive self-defense." Drones are far more precise and selective than bombs (though both depend on accurate intelligence); and snipers also engage in "targeted killing." Yet many observers remain troubled by drone warfare's premeditation and asymmetry of risk and the fact that civilians (ultimately the president) make the final targeting decisions.

Only after more than ten years of targeted killing did the Obama administration belatedly allow glimpses into its legal foundation and restrictions. Before then, however, there were many efforts to limit such operations. One method was exposure. Seymour Hersh, who (with CBS) had broken the Abu Ghraib story, casually mentioned a CIA assassination program after a 2008 talk at the University of Minnesota. But he acknowledged being unable to document it, and his comment attracted no attention. The program became public only when Panetta learned of it soon after taking over the CIA in 2009, promptly informed Congress, and canceled it. By then it had been tainted by its origin in the Bush administration, its use of contractors (including the notorious Blackwater), and especially its concealment from Congress (allegedly on Cheney's orders).

Any human activity is prone to mistake.[75] Military mistakes are distinctive in that they kill or maim, often many people. Although the USA suspended drone strikes after killing Pakistani soldiers at the Afghan border and large numbers of civilians within Pakistan, they soon resumed. A drone that killed 15 civilians after operators disregarded warnings about children elicited little response. Obama responded indirectly to criticisms by insisting that drone strikes were "very precise," kept on a "very tight leash," targeted "active terrorists who are trying to go in and harm Americans," and "have not caused a huge number of civilian casualties." By contrast, the Navy produced a 381-page report recommending corrective action after a drone strike killed a US marine and a navy hospitalman.

Policy concerning targeted killing was contested among the DoD, CIA, and DoS. JSOC and the CIA had different command structures and legal constraints. Donald Rumsfeld had been determined to displace the CIA (which had taken the lead in Afghanistan after 9/11) and to dominate intelligence gathering and analysis. Some in the Agency were uncomfortable with its growing paramilitary role. Critics felt lethal force should be governed by the military chain of command (whose members were subject to the UCMJ), and were particularly concerned by the CIA's use of contractors. But the authority of JSOC to conduct assassinations without notifying the Ambassador or CIA station chief troubled both DoS and Agency headquarters. Obama gave DoS a greater role, even though the CIA could still overrule the Ambassador.

Targeting US citizens created further complications. Commentators and letter writers to the *New York Times* cited the Fifth Amendment prohibition on depriving someone of life without due process of law. Some legislators responded with a bill to strip "terrorists" of citizenship. The *Washington Post* seemed to feel this was unnecessary because Americans who "take up arms with the enemy" forfeit due process rights. But some conservatives passionately opposed the use of lethal force against citizens within the USA (a red herring no one contemplated). Sen. Cruz planned to table a bill to outlaw this. Some outside observers had the opposite reaction. Former Archbishop Desmond Tutu felt that condoning drone strikes only against noncitizens echoed the infamous *Dred Scott* decision treating slaves as nonpersons.

The plan to kill Anwar al-Awlaki and its ultimate execution brought these objections to a climax. The administration sought to anticipate criticism by asserting its authority to kill an American citizen outside the USA while declining to name the target and remaining vague about how the decision would be made. Then the Treasury Department labeled al-Awlaki a "specially designated global terrorist," an inescapably public determination that diverted attention to whether CCR and the ACLU could represent him in a legal action challenging his assassination. An embarrassed administration quickly backed down; how could it require an American citizen to obtain a license in order to seek judicial review of his own execution? Yemeni President Saleh also sought to assist his indispensable American ally by staging a prosecution of al-Awlaki in absentia for complicity in the killing of a French employee of an Austrian oil company. Although the court quickly convicted him, the actual killer complained that his confession had been extracted by torture and insisted he had acted for purely personal reasons.

After the assassination the USA offered various justifications. Obama accused al-Awlaki of complicity in Abdulmutallab's 2009 Christmas Day bomb attempt and the 2010 attempt to blow up cargo planes landing in the USA. (Al-Awlaki defiantly claimed credit for the first, as well as for inspiring the Fort Hood massacre.) Critics objected that if the administration had evidence of such past crimes, it should have sought Yemen's assistance in capturing and extraditing al-Awlaki to stand trial in the USA. The administration declined to publish or even summarize evidence that he was planning future crimes against Americans. It asserted disingenuously that he could have avoided assassination by surrendering to the USA, but there was no outstanding indictment or warrant for his arrest, and police cannot constitutionally execute suspects. The *Washington Post* bought the administration argument, declaring al-Awlaki an "enemy belligerent" who had "forfeited constitutional protections by directing hostile forces against his homeland." But that obscured the distinction between past and future crimes. The *New York Times* and *Los Angeles Times* found the administration arguments unconvincing. Law professors Bruce Ackerman at Yale and Noah Feldman at Harvard independently suggested that al-Awlaki might have been exercising his First Amendment right of free speech – exactly the kind of question a court should decide before an assassination. The administration did not argue that either of the other two American citizens it killed – Samir Khan and al-Awlaki's son Abdulrahman – could lawfully be targeted. It treated the former's death as legitimate "collateral damage" and (hypocritically) offered condolences. It advanced tenuous arguments about the latter: the USA had urged its citizens to leave Yemen (but all of the 16-year-old's family lived there); it had not received confirmation of his death (his grief-stricken grandfather, Nasser al-Awlaki, asked incredulously how he could identify a body that had been blown to bits). The two killings transformed Nasser al-Awlaki from a lifelong American supporter into another implacable enemy.

The assassination of Anwar al-Awlaki provoked pundits to join a chorus of cheerleading that was appalling in its misinformation and vacuity. New York University (NYU) law professor Richard Epstein said al-Awlaki was "fair game … and ought to know it." Harvard law professor Jack Goldsmith said an "attack on enemy soldiers is not an assassination." (What was Goldsmith's definition of "enemy soldier," and which forum found al-Awlaki one, using what process and evidence?) Berkeley law professor John Yoo said anyone who "takes up arms with the enemy" forfeits any right to due process. (Who decided that al-Awlaki had "take[n] up arms" and based on what evidence?) John Bellinger III (who had been legal adviser to the National Security Council and DoS) said the Constitution empowered the administration to put down an "insurrection," and al-Awlaki was an "insurrectionist." (Who found that those legal categories applied?)

The media were worse. Max Boot (*Los Angeles Times*) analogized the assassination to killing Confederate soldiers during the Civil War. Al-Awlaki and Khan "gave up the benefits of American citizenship by taking up arms against their country." (Decided by whom, according to what law, and based on what evidence? Even the administration did not claim legal authority to target Khan for killing.) Jonah Goldberg (*Los Angeles Times*) declared al-Awlaki's citizenship irrelevant: "if you're a terrorist, you're a terrorist." (Is that a legal category? And who decides? Even the administration acknowledged that citizens were different.) Charles Krauthammer (*Washington Post*) cavalierly dismissed any interest in the "imminence" of the threat allegedly posed by al-Awlaki (a requirement of international law). He saw no difference between bombing North Vietnam and assassinating an American citizen.

Politicians and government officials (past and present), who should have been restrained by the power they exercised, were the most irresponsible. As Republican presidential candidate, Mitt Romney said anyone who joins "a group that declares war on America … is fair game." (The USA can assassinate *every* member of al-Qaeda and its affiliates? Then why bother trying them in military commissions or federal courts?) Newt Gingrich exhibited his usual verbal diarrhea. The government could kill anyone "who was found guilty under review of actively seeking the death of American citizens ... It is the rule of law. If you engage in a war against the United States, you are an enemy combatant. You have none of the civil liberties of the United States. You cannot go to court ... waging war on the United States is outside criminal law." Leon Panetta (who served as both DCI and Defense Secretary, as well as President Clinton's Chief of Staff) was equally incoherent. Someone: "who wants to attack our people and kill Americans ... is a terrorist ... we have to defend ourselves ... out there on a battlefield ... that person is an enemy combatant, and when an enemy combatant holds a gun at your head, you fire back."

Sen. Graham (a lawyer) wrongly claimed the AUMF authorized drone strikes in the USA. Attorney General Holder agreed. Former Sen. Daschle had to remind them that Congress had explicitly rejected the Bush administration's attempt to add "in the United States" to the AUMF. As an administration critic (and likely presidential candidate), Sen. Paul let demagoguery trump precision, caricaturing the decision process. Obama had been "flipping through flash cards" and saying "do you want to kill him? ... Yea, let's go ahead and kill him." He accused Holder of asserting the administration could use a drone to kill an American citizen in Dearborn for emailing his brother in the Mideast who was suspected of terrorism.

Both before and after the killing the Obama administration (unlike its predecessor) repeatedly offered justifications. DoS Legal Adviser Koh, DoD General Counsel Johnson, and Attorney General Holder all gave speeches sketching the drone policy's contours and legal foundation. But UN Special Rapporteur Philip Alston found these inadequate. President Obama explained that drone strikes were directed against "active terrorists who are trying to go in and harm Americans" and claimed they "have not caused a huge number of civilian casualties." Chief counterterrorism adviser John O. Brennan maintained that the government engaged in targeted killing only "as a last resort, to save lives when there is no alternative." But because the administration withheld the OLC memos, these arguments remained unpersuasive.

Conservatives supported the policy, accusing the Obama administration of timidity. Michael Gerson claimed in the *Washington Post* that the strikes "protect the U.S. people from violence." John Yoo felt vindicated by the new administration's embrace of his own theories of executive power, but attacked Holder for adopting a criminal justice approach to the "war on terror." Sens. Graham and McCain, who had sought to restrain some Bush policies (EITs), strongly endorsed drone strikes.

But many others questioned them, especially signature strikes, including HRW, the National Association of Criminal Defense Counsel, *Nation* editor Katrina vanden Heuvel, Micah Zenko (Council on Foreign Relations), and liberal Democrat Sen. Wyden. The UN's Secretary General Ban Ki-moon, Human Rights Commissioner Navi Pillay, its Human Rights Council, and Special Rapporteurs Cristof Heyns, Philip Alston, and Ben Emmerson all challenged the legality of targeted killing. Critics included a surprising number of establishment figures: DNI Blair, Cameron Munter (Ambassador to Pakistan), National Security Adviser Donilon, JCS chairman Mullen, Defense Secretary Gates, and John Podesta (President Clinton's chief of staff). Gen. Petraeus preferred smaller strikes, and Gen. McChrystal worried that drones were "hated on a visceral level" and contributed to a "perception of American arrogance." After retiring as DCI, Michael Hayden observed that only Afghanistan had agreed to targeted killings; and he was troubled by the anomaly that the government needed judicial authority to eavesdrop on al-Awlaki but not to kill him. The *Washington Post* converged with the *New York Times* and *Los Angeles Times* in questioning targeted killing. Even some conservatives spoke out against drones. Many called for greater disclosure of the policy and a more independent targeting process: David Rivkin (who served in the Reagan and Bush I administrations), *Washington Post* columnists David Ignatius and Richard Cohen, and the *Washington Times*. Sen. Paul's filibuster generated extensive press coverage and plaudits from unlikely sources, such as Code Pink.

The debate was not limited to the legality of drone strikes. Defenders argued they killed terrorist leaders; critics claimed that most victims were easily-replaced foot soldiers. The circumstances of the killings made it difficult, even impossible, to resolve this dispute. Critics complained that the Obama administration preferred to kill rather than capture. This eliminated the risk to Americans and avoided the problem of where to hold prisoners (created by Obama's disavowal of secret prisons and pledge to close Guantánamo). But it sacrificed the intelligence value of interrogations – an even greater loss if, as the administration claimed, the dead were al-Qaeda leaders. Gregory Johnsen (a Yemen scholar), David Rhode (*New York Times*), Peter Osborne (*Telegraph*), David Kulcullen (an architect of the Iraq surge), Sir Sherard Cowper-Coles (British special representative to Afghanistan and Pakistan), Abdul Ghan al-Iranyi (a Yemeni political analyst), Robert Wright (*The Atlantic*), Robert Grenier (former head of the CIA Counterterrorism Center and Pakistan station chief), Ibrahim Mothana (a Yemeni opposition leader), Lette Taylor (HRW researcher), James Traub (*Foreign Policy*), Andrew Cockburn (*Los Angeles Times*), and many others claimed that targeted killings – and the extreme vulnerability felt by those forced to listen to drones hovering overhead for days or weeks – drove people into the arms of al-Qaeda and the Taliban. Supporters praised drones for not exposing Americans to risk; critics warned that such asymmetry could make the administration, targeters, and drone operators trigger-happy.

Efforts to question targeted killing outside the political process – in the courts – were no more successful. The DDC found that Nasser al-Awlaki lacked standing to challenge the government's plan to assassinate his son Anwar. (Only Anwar would have had standing? How would he have sued, or even authorized his father, since any communication would have exposed him to immediate death?) Civil damage actions for the deaths of Anwar al-Awlaki, his son Abdulrahman, and Samir Khan were blocked by sovereign immunity. Although polls revealed widespread opposition to drone strikes in other countries, the US public was generally supportive, even if it had reservations about killing citizens, especially in the USA. That may help to explain why Congressional oversight was so ineffective. The two Intelligence Committees seem to have been satisfied with being notified after killings. HPSCI's one hearing had no visible effect.

If opposition to the strikes themselves seemed ineffective, critics gained traction by raising process issues, especially secrecy. While admitting the need to conceal operational details, they asserted that Congress and the public were entitled to know and debate the criteria and procedure for choosing targets and the identity of those killed. As always, leaks about these issues increased pressure for further disclosure, if only to correct misinformation. The media naturally supported calls for transparency. There were fissures within the administration, with DoS favoring greater disclosure and the CIA and DHS Secretary Napolitano advocating secrecy. Obama championed transparency in his first inaugural address and again in his 2013 State of the Union address. The administration confronted a frequent dilemma: how could it boast about the success of drone attacks – especially the death of al-Awlaki – without revealing information about them; but such revelations inevitably led to demands for more information and weakened invocations of state secrets.

The fight came to a head over the OLC memos justifying, and limiting, targeted killing. Although the administration adamantly resisted disclosure, it was embarrassed by its own release of Bush-era OLC memos justifying EITs. The ACLU brought two actions: in SDNY (seeking memos related to the al-Awlaki assassination) and in DDC (seeking all relevant memos). Both District Judges found that the government had not acknowledged the program, although Judge McMahon conceded the "irony" of concealing DNI Clapper's declaration in support of government secrecy. (Indeed, even Clapper favored disclosure of the general rules governing drone strikes, if not the details of the al-Awlaki assassination, and was seconded by Koh and Johnson, legal advisers to DoS and DoD.) But though the Second and DC Circuits reversed, ruling that government boasts about and legal justifications for drone strikes constituted official acknowledgment, the District Judges again dismissed on remand because of FOIA exceptions. At first the administration refused to release even the White Paper, calling it a draft covered by the executive branch's "deliberative process." Once that had been leaked to NBC, the administration said Congress should be satisfied and not get the OLC memos. Even media supporters like the *Washington Post* could not swallow such intransigence. It was the need to secure Brennan's confirmation as DCI that ultimately forced the administration to give SSCI two OLC memos. (The hearing itself produced little new information, and the Senate confirmed Brennan nearly 2:1.) Then, of course, the administration also had to release them to HPSCI. But those disclosures were begrudging: staffers (on whom busy senators depended) still could not see the memos, and senators could not retain them. Still, those partial releases provoked SSCI to seek the other seven OLC memos and both Judiciary Committees to insist on equal access.

Controversy over access to the memos coincided with debate over the process for selecting targets. A wide variety of commentators, including Jane Harman and Robert Gates, and media ranging from *USA Today* to the *New York Times* and the *Washington Post* quickly embraced the idea of adapting FISC to review assassinations. Even Brennan conceded during his confirmation hearing that the idea was "worthy of discussion." But it provoked immediate criticism. The ACLU opposed FISC's secrecy. James Robertson (the former federal judge who had resigned from FISC in protest) said it would be inappropriate for a court to sign a death warrant in a non-adversarial process or offer advisory opinions. Judicial independence would be "severely compromised." Death warrants were not like search warrants. Declaring that courts could not act quickly enough and generalist judges lacked expertise, Georgetown law professor Neal Katyal proposed a new "national security court" within the executive branch. Bush Attorney General Mukasey agreed. But Yale law lecturer Eugene Fidell said that would not be a court at all. (Indeed, FISC operated *ex parte* and approved more than 99 percent of government applications.)

In the end, none of the efforts succeeded in constraining executive power to order assassinations.

LAW ON THE BATTLEFIELD

Since 9/11 the USA has waged war in four countries: Afghanistan, Iraq, Pakistan, and Yemen. (Air strikes in Somalia and Libya are outside the scope of this book.) In doing so, the USA has killed and wounded civilians (and sometimes soldiers) of those countries, violated their sovereignty, and dishonored Islam. The responses to these actions raise the following questions: How did private individuals and governments react? What explains differences among the four countries and between civilian casualties and affronts to honor or sovereignty? How did the USA justify its actions and deal with local grievances? How different were its responses to "friendly-fire" injuries to its own military or citizens of close allies, imprisonment of its own citizens, or injuries inflicted by contractors? What effect, if any, did actions within these countries have on the USA's conduct of its war?

Afghanistan

Because the United States began fighting in Afghanistan less than a month after 9/11 and did not invade Iraq for another 18 months, the Afghan war shaped responses to war crimes and civilian casualties.

Abdul Rashid Dostum

In late November 2001 thousands of Taliban surrendered to Gen. Dostum in Kunduz and were imprisoned.[76] Survivors and witnesses told American journalists in 2002 that prisoners died after being stuffed into metal shipping containers without food or water for three days or were shot by guards; all were buried in a mass grave. A 2002 DoS intelligence report put the number at 1,500. Afghan witnesses were later tortured or killed. When Pierre-Richard Prosper (US Ambassador-at-Large for War Crimes) investigated, Dostum claimed that just 200 died from combat wounds or disease and any suffocations were accidental. The Karzai government also rebuffed Prosper: "We have had decades of war crimes. Where do you start?" After Zalmay Khalilzad, White House coordinator for Afghanistan, "raised the political implications" of the investigation, Prosper suspended it. PHR, which discovered the mass grave in 2002, said "repeated efforts to protect witnesses, secure evidence and get a full investigation have been met by the U.S. and its allies with buck-passing, delays and obstruction." In late 2002 a NATO military commander rejected the ICRC's request to investigate. A few months later Dell Spry, a senior FBI official at Guantánamo, said about ten Afghans detained there independently told agents Dostum supervised suffocations and shootings. Although a January 2003 FBI report confirmed this, a senior FBI official at headquarters told Spry to drop the matter, which was the military's responsibility. CENTCOM conducted an "informal inquiry"; but when special forces working with Dostum denied knowledge of the mass killing, DoD ended the investigation. A former defense official remembered Deputy Defense Secretary Wolfowitz saying in early 2003: "we are not going to be going after" Dostum. PHR obtained documents through FOIA showing that Wolfowitz had resisted others' efforts to do so. As early as 2006 satellite photos showed that the burial site had been disturbed. In 2008 a UN medical forensics team found excavations suggesting that bodies had been removed from the mass grave.

When the media revived the story in mid-2009, Prosper (now retired) urged the Obama administration to investigate. On July 10 it said there were no grounds to do so because "only foreigners were involved and the alleged killings occurred in a foreign country." PHR replied that the USA "has a legal obligation to find out what U.S. officials knew, where U.S. personnel were, what involvement they had, and the actions of U.S. allies during and after the massacre." The *New York Times* added the refusal to investigate "to the Bush administration's sordid legacy." Dostum reiterated his denial on a Radio Free Europe/Radio Liberty website. The station's newsroom director said a rebuttal it had solicited "indicate[d] very strongly that many detainees – possibly hundreds – died while in the custody of Dostum's forces." Claiming he had just seen "the indications that this had not been properly investigated," Obama directed his national security team to "collect the facts." Salon now reported that Spry had heard but did not believe allegations that US forces had been present. In April 2016 Dostum (now Afghan vice president) was barred from the USA days before a planned visit to New York and Washington, during which he was to address the UN General Assembly on narcotics trafficking.[77] He claimed that the tenuous security situation in Afghanistan required him to cancel. Three years earlier Secretary of State Kerry had rebuffed Rep. Rohrabacher's request that Dostum be given a visa.

Pat Tillman

Tillman, a former NFL player who patriotically turned down a multi-million-dollar contract with the Arizona Cardinals to enlist after 9/11, died in Afghanistan on April 22, 2004.[78] Troops knew immediately that he had been killed by friendly fire, and by April 31 an investigation confirmed that the death was caused by "gross negligence." But his body armor and uniform were burned, allegedly because they were a bloody "biohazard." The truth was concealed from his brother, Kevin, another Army Ranger fighting near the attack, and not publicly disclosed until May 29, nearly four weeks after the nationally televised May 3 memorial service at which Tillman was posthumously awarded a Silver Star. DoD began an investigation in response to complaints by his family and Sen. McCain. More than a year after the death Army Special Operations Command confirmed the facts stated above. Seven soldiers received administrative reprimands resulting in pay cuts and loss of rank. The *New York Times* criticized the army for having "kept the sorry secret and [having] pursued a misbegotten public relations strategy." In March 2007 two DoD reports criticized nine officers, including four generals. Acting Army Secretary Pete Geren issued an apology. Declaring that the reports contained "more questions than answers," Rep. Honda (D-Ca) (who represented Tillman's district) asked HASC to hold hearings. Tillman's family said the reports "attempt to impose closure by slapping the wrists of a few officers."

A month later Tillman's father, Pat, told the House Oversight and Government Reform Committee that "a terrible tragedy" had been "transformed into an inspirational message." Kevin testified at the hearing that evidence had been destroyed, witness testimony "disappeared into thin air," and the autopsy did not conform to regulations. The *New York Times* said: "Congress must press forward." But the White House rejected a document request from Rep. Waxman (D-Ca) and the committee's senior Republican. The *Times* urged

Waxman to continue "his dogged efforts to get to the bottom of this convoluted and troubling case." The army censured LtGen. Kensinger for failing to follow SOPs to notify the family and top officials about the investigation and for lying to investigators; and it issued a memorandum of concern to three brigadier generals and two lower officers. Gen. McChrystal had told DoD investigators that when he approved a Silver Star, he suspected Tillman had been killed by friendly fire and a day later warned top generals and the president to avoid using the citation's language of "devastating enemy fire." DoD Acting IG Gimble said McChrystal should be held "accountable for the inaccurate and misleading assertions" in the Silver Star recommendation and for failing to notify officials. But Gen. Wallace, commander of training, concluded that McChrystal had behaved reasonably in assuming that the supporting material he received was accurate. Tillman's mother Mary dismissed the punishments even before they were issued and again accused the military of a cover-up. At the committee's second hearing Defense Secretary Rumsfeld said "the Tillmans were owed the truth," but he denied "any evidence of a coverup." Kensinger refused to testify. Gen. Abizaid said: "there was never any intention to keep the idea of fratricide from the family or the public." The *New York Times* complained that "we still don't know who concocted a phony story about how Corporal Tillman died and whether the White House knew it was happening." The *Washington Post* urged Congress to insist that interviews of administration officials be transcribed. Twenty members of the military who had fought in Iraq and Afghanistan asked NFL Commissioner Goodell to help get the Tillman case documents. Mary Tillman wrote a book about her son to pressure the NFL to act.[79]

A year later, the House committee's draft report said it was "frustrated" by senior officials' "near universal lack of recall." With respect to both Tillman and Jessica Lynch: "affirmative acts created new facts that were significantly different than what the soldiers in the field knew to be true. And in both cases, the fictional accounts proved to be compelling public narratives at difficult times in the war." The *New York Times* deplored the "widespread – and, we suspect, self-induced – amnesia among high officials." Rep. Waxman said: "a terrible tragedy that might have further undermined support for the war in Iraq was transformed into an inspirational message that served instead to support the nation's foreign policy wars in Iraq and Afghanistan." Gen. Wallace, who investigated the case, ordered punitive action against seven officers but cleared three, including McChrystal. When McChrystal resigned two years later after speaking disrespectfully about Obama administration officials, Mary Tillman said in a *Los Angeles Times* op ed that his actions following her son's death "should have been grounds for firing him back then." (Other friendly-fire deaths provoked similar scrutiny.)[80]

Desecration of Corpses

In October 2005 Australian television screened a videotape of American soldiers from the 1st Battalion, 508th Infantry Regiment, 173rd Airborne Brigade burning the bodies of Taliban members they had killed the previous night in a village north of Kandahar.[81] Islam forbids cremation. The soldiers cited hygiene for refusing to let villagers give the bodies a Muslim burial. But psychological operations soldiers said the cremation was intended to provoke a Taliban attack. The video showed a PsyOps (psychological operations) specialist saying in the local language over a loudspeaker directed toward the village: "Attention Taliban: You are all cowardly dogs. You allowed your fighters to be laid down facing west [toward Mecca] and burned. You are too scared to retrieve the bodies. This just proves you are the lady boys we always believed you to be." Another shouted: "Your time in Afghanistan is short. You attack and run away like women. You call yourself Talibs but you are a disgrace to the Muslim religion, and you bring shame on your family. Come and fight like men instead of the cowardly dogs you are."

CENTCOM promised to investigate. The State Department called the allegations "very serious." President Karzai ordered an independent inquiry. The Afghan Independent Human Rights Commission said such desecration was "against the Islamic beliefs and traditions of Afghanistan and a violation of the Geneva Conventions and of international humanitarian law." The four soldiers involved received reprimands, and their unit commander was reassigned.

Civilian Casualties[82]

Civilian casualties are inevitable in warfare; but the number, identity, and circumstances can affect whether they violate the laws of warfare, requiring the military to respond. After a suicide bomber attacked the Marine Fox Company in Nangarhar Province on March 4, 2007, slightly wounding one soldier, Marines killed and wounded many civilians.[83] The USA initially said the convoy "reported receiving enemy fire from a number of locations" and "believed they saw folks with weapons." But when hundreds of Afghans protested and President Karzai condemned the casualties, Army MGen. Kearney, Special Operations commander for the Middle East and Central Asia, opened an investigation, which concluded that the Marines had sprayed the countryside with machine guns while racing ten miles back to base, a response that was "out of proportion to the threat." Kearney said: "We found … no brass [shells] that we can confirm that small-arms fire came at them. We have testimony from Marines that is in conflict with unanimous testimony from civilians at the sites … My investigating officer believes those folks were innocent … we were unable to find evidence that those were fighters."

Broken glass indicated that Marines had kept on firing three miles from the ambush site. The Afghan Independent Human Rights Commission (AIHRC), which interviewed 50 witnesses and the local police force but could not question Marines, said the 12 dead civilians included an infant, a 16-year-old girl, and a 75-year-old man. A car stopped by the side of the road was riddled by 250 bullets, killing three passengers, 80, 75, and 16 years old. Four were killed in a minibus stopped at a gas station. The use of "indiscriminate force" constituted "a serious violation of international humanitarian standards." CENTCOM forwarded its report to Adm. Fallon, the senior American officer in the region. Victims' families wanted those responsible tried under Islamic law and executed.

Two months later Army Col. Nicholson, brigade commander, told families of the 19 killed and 50 wounded: "I stand before you today, deeply, deeply ashamed and terribly sorry that Americans have killed and wounded innocent Afghan people." "This is a terrible, terrible mistake, and my nation grieves with you for your loss and suffering. We humbly and respectfully ask for your forgiveness." The USA paid $2,000 for each of the dead. A week later Gen. Conway, Marine Corps commander, said Nicholson should not have apologized because he might have to review charges against the soldiers involved.

In January 2008 Nathaniel Travers, who had been in the convoy, testified at an Art. 32 hearing under a grant of immunity that "there were a lot of people who died who didn't need to. They were just driving their cars." Gunners fired until the platoon leader radioed a command to stop. Three Marine sergeants and an Afghan interpreter in the first two cars said gunners had fired methodically, only in response to incoming fire, and approaching cars that seemed threatening. Three witnesses said Sgt. Peter Brooks fired careful warning shots into the pavement to stop two Afghan cars. Sgt. Joshua Henderson, who released more than 200 rounds, said he had identified at least three gunmen firing on the convoy and returned fire at two "mams" (military age males). "Everyone I fired at … [was] positively identified firing at the … convoy with a gun." "I was threatened constantly with oncoming traffic, failure to slow down and pull off the road." Sgt. Heriberto Beccera-Bravo said Henderson fired at least ten times but not wildly or indiscriminately. Four other gunners who had fired their weapons refused to testify without immunity. NCIS Investigator David Kurre said: "we're not sure of anything." One panel member called that "the most accurate statement I've heard in the court so far." The prosecutor conceded: "we're dealing with the fog of war."

Haji Liwani Qumandan, a tribal elder, said his car had been sprayed by "thousands of bullets," killing his father and wounding his 12-year-old nephew. An American soldier said he saw a "Kalashnikov type" weapon on the ground next to that car. Qumandan denied they were armed but gave inconsistent testimony about observing the IED and once claimed a fourth person had been in the car. Defense lawyers accused him of faking his wounds. Nanglyi, driving another car, said he had obeyed hand signals to pull over but Marines still shot, wounding him and his 15-year-old nephew.

Col. Nicholson testified that the Marine company often entered his assigned area without coordinating with him, as Maj. Galvin, the Marine commander had done that day. Nicholson later learned that Galvin had informed him of only five to six of the more than thirty operations Marines had conducted in that area. This incident had damaged the relations he had carefully nurtured with local tribes; and Marines had undermined the investigation by fleeing the scene of a gunfight, "something we never do." Right after the incident Galvin told Nicholson the unit had left "five or six bodies." Nicholson admitted under cross-examination that US troops found no dead or wounded at the scene 30 minutes later, but explained that Afghans collect and bury their dead quickly and might have taken the wounded to the nearby hospital. Lt. Wicks, leader of the Army MP platoon investigating immediately after the incident, also saw no dead or wounded, but was told they had been removed. Investigators found bullet damage to trees along the highway but could not identify the source. Afghan police inspected the hillside but discovered no evidence of small-arms fire. One car was struck by at least 200 bullets. MPs collected 125 bullet casings, but the week before NCIS arrived (two months later) these were discarded and burned. Two other witnesses described tensions between Army Special Operations and Marines. SFC Jason Mero was "100% certain" that small-arms fire struck the second Humvee and several days later saw bullet marks on the vehicle. Air Force Col. Patrick Pihana, in charge of the investigation, initially agreed, but changed his mind after talking to Afghan civilians and wanted Mero "to buck up his opinion."

Although Col. Nicholson made cash payments to the families of 17 victims, only five corpses of adult men were described by witnesses, and there was no evidence they had been shot by Marines. Nicholson also paid 25 people who had been wounded; Afghan hospital officials said they had treated at least two dozen that day, but could not say how many had been wounded by Marines. Defense lawyers denounced a "culture of fraud."

LtGen. Helland, CENTCOM Marine commander, concluded that everyone had "acted appropriately and in accordance with the rules of engagement and tactics, techniques and procedures in place at the time in response to a complex attack." Following the first Marine Corps court of inquiry in more than fifty years, Maj. Galvin, Capt. Noble, and Capt. Robert Olsen were to face administrative action for "administrative, manning, and training issues."

In late April 2007 a three-day battle between coalition forces and the Taliban in Shindand District, Herat Province, killed up to thirty civilians.[84] Local residents rioted, storming government buildings; some were wounded by police. President Karzai said the government "can no longer accept" civilian casualties. Local officials visiting the site on May 2 reported that 45–51 civilians had been killed; bodies were still being dug out of a mud house destroyed by US-led bombing raids. The US military claimed it had killed 136 suspected Taliban and no civilians. The upper house of the Afghan parliament passed a bill directing the coalition to cease military operations unless it had had been attacked or had consulted the Afghan National Army, government, or police; and it set a timetable for the departure of foreign forces.

In May a US Special Forces air strike in Helmand Province killed at least 21.[85] The USA said a "significant" number were militants, and it did not "have any report of civilian casualties." A day later Afghans said the toll was 50–80 and brought 21 bodies – mostly women and children – to the Sangin District governor.

On June 17 an unsuccessful attempt to capture or kill Abu Laith al-Libi, a top al-Qaeda commander, included a rocket attack that destroyed a madrassa, killing seven children.[86] Special Operations then shot six men dead from helicopters and detained others. The governor told angry villagers the tragedy "could have been prevented had the people exposed the presence of insurgents in the area," but he promised compensation. A week later Karzai declared: "Afghan life is not cheap and should not be treated as such." More than a hundred civilian deaths had been reported in the previous week. "You don't fight a terrorist by firing a field gun from 37 km away into a target." "Either this cooperation and coordination [with the Afghan government] will be created and applied, or Afghanistan will take its decision in this regard." But five days after that four more civilians were killed.[87] Lal Gul, chair of the Afghanistan Human Rights Organization, said soldiers "blew out the door of the house that belongs to Haji Muhammad Jan, who was about 80 years old, killing him and two of his sons and a grandson." The USA claimed to have found rocket-propelled grenade (RPG) launchers and grenades, had killed three militants, and taken 16 prisoners; but Gul said they were "mostly farmers," not Taliban.

Following a 12-day visit to Afghanistan in 2008, Philip Alston, UN Special Rapporteur on extrajudicial, summary or arbitrary executions, criticized units operating out of Camp Ghecko outside Kandahar and in Nangarhar, finding that coalition forces had killed about 200 civilians in the first four months of 2008.[88]

On July 4, 2008 a US air strike in Nuristan province killed at least sixteen civilians.[89] Two days later an air strike killed 47 people, mostly women and children in a wedding party accompanying a bride to a neighboring village in Eastern Nangarhar Province. Gen. McKiernan and President Karzai flew there to apologize. About a week later an attack by Special Forces and Afghan National Army (ANA) commandos killed civilians in Zerkoh Valley near Shindand in Herat Province. On July 20 an air strike in Farah Province killed at least eight Afghan police. A government spokesman said: "we would like the incidences of civilian casualties brought to an absolute minimum." The ROEs had been revised after Marines killed 19 civilians in March 2007 and an air strike the next month killed another 57 (including women and children); and they were revised again in April 2008. The top military lawyer at the air operations center said "we explicitly guarantee extra benefits to civilians" and claimed that many casualty reports were Taliban propaganda.

On August 26 the USA said an air strike requested by ANA commandos near Azizabad in Shindand District, Herat Province killed 30 Taliban, including its target, Mullah Sadiq.[90] "We're confident we struck the right compound." But Karzai said 70 civilians had been killed, and ANA said the 90 dead included 60 children and 19 women. The local police chief who visited the village the next morning saw 76 bodies, including 50 children, 19 women, and 7 men (others were still buried by rubble). His spokesman insisted "there were no Taliban." Several Afghan observers said the group had been commemorating an anti-Taliban militia commander killed the previous year. The commander of the ANA division involved in the raid agreed that 60 children, 19 women, and more than a dozen men had been killed. The local member of parliament (chair of the parliamentary defense committee and member of the government investigation) said the 60 children were killed in their sleep. Villagers blamed tribal enemies for false intelligence. Kai Eide, UN Special Envoy to Afghanistan, said eyewitnesses reported 90 civilians killed. But the USA insisted it had killed 25 militants and just five civilians (who might have been related to the Taliban commander), dismissing "outrageous" reports by local residents who either supported or feared the Taliban. Afghan and US forces seized several assault rifles, 4,000 rounds of ammunition, mines, bomb-making materials, grenades, $4,000, and photos of the exteriors of several nearby US bases. Gen. Conway, the Marine commandant, said "this is a dirty game being played, but … we are as precise as we can [be]." Gen. McKiernan, commander of NATO forces, said "this was a legitimate insurgent target." The civilian dead were "nowhere near the number reported in the media, and … there was a very deliberate information operation orchestrated by the insurgency." The USA agreed to a joint investigation with Afghanistan.

The Afghan government drafted a document requiring better coordination with Afghan security forces. Russia circulated a draft UN "Security Council press statement" declaring that US air strikes had caused "numerous civilian casualties, including women and children" and "killing and maiming civilians is a flagrant violation of international humanitarian law and human rights law." The *Washington Post* regretted the "woeful familiarity" of "the dueling accounts." The Afghan investigation confirmed that the air strikes had killed 60 children, 15 women and 15 men, none of them "foreign or internal Taliban." After Gen. McKiernan saw UN and ANA videos showing dozens of dead children, he sent a CENTCOM general to review the initial investigation. *New York Times* reporter Carlotta Gall saw a cell phone video of at least 11 dead children among 30–40 bodies in a village mosque and counted 42 freshly dug graves, 13 for children and another 13 for women. Villagers identified relatives in graves whose names matched those given by elders. An Afghan doctor who ran a nearby clinic counted 50–60 dead civilians, mostly women and children. The Shindand district chief, who was on good terms with US and NATO forces, had counted 76 bodies on the day of the strike and believed more had been found later. Villagers denied the US claim that Special Forces visited the village the next day. A Special Forces major saw 6 burial sites within a 6-mile radius but only one with 18–20 freshly dug graves. But a villager said the main graveyard had 24 fresh graves and no member of the US military had returned since the raid. A day after Bush expressed regrets to Karzai, the Afghan president visited Azizabad to pay his respects, condemn the air strikes, and vow to arrest the Afghan who misled US forces.

In October the US inquiry found that the raid had killed 22 militants and 33 civilians: 8 men, 3 women, 12 children, and 10 unidentified. The Special Operations inquiry conducted four days after the raid had not accurately counted the dead. But the USA concluded that "there is no culpability" because the raid was "a valid military action" with "a legitimate target" based on "credible intelligence" that militants were gathering for a commemoration. Charges that US or ANA forces violated the ROE were "unsubstantiated." "The use of force was in self-defense, necessary and proportional." "Unfortunately and unknown to the U.S. and Afghan forces," militants "chose fighting positions in close proximity to civilians." LtGen. Martin Dempsey (acting CENTCOM commander) said: "as we have seen all too often, this ruthless enemy routinely surround themselves with innocents." DoD claimed that "no military in history has gone to greater lengths to avoid civilian casualties." Two years later a SASC report found that the house where the Taliban leader Mullah Sadiq was suspected of holding a meeting actually belonged to the brother of a local warlord who had been hired by the US contractor ArmorGroup in 2007. The bombing raid was a by-product of complex relationships between Afghan contractors and the Taliban.

In September HRW reported in detail on 6 air strikes inflicting civilian casualties, adding that 13 in 2006 killed 116 civilians, 22 in 2007 killed 321, and 12 in the first 7 months of 2008 killed 119.[91] Civilian casualties were much more common in rapid response air strikes than in those that were planned. At the beginning of the month NATO acknowledged that forces taking fire in Paktika Province had called in artillery support, killing two children and injuring seven others.[92] NATO said it "deeply regrets this accident." In a second incident near Kabul, an Afghan police officer said US troops backed by

Afghan intelligence killed a man and two children; the USA denied any American troops had participated. A few days later a drone missile killed 6–12, including Arab men, 2 women and 3 children. Speaking to US military officers on September 9, President Bush said: "regrettably ... our pursuit of the enemy will result in accidental civilian deaths. This has been the case throughout the history of warfare."

A few days later Gen. McKiernan released a "revised tactical order" requiring Afghan forces to lead house searches, mandating information from multiple sources before attacks, and regulating the use of lethal force.[93] He repeated that "never in history has a military coalition taken greater measures to try and avoid civilian casualties," but acknowledged that 156 civilians had been killed so far that year, compared with 161 in all of 2007 (the latter was half the HRW figure). A subordinate said it would be "an absolute rule that we acknowledge our mistakes when they happen." Battlefield commanders would report civilian casualties within 24 hours; and a civilian-led unit would monitor "credible allegations" of civilian deaths by Afghans, aid agencies, and journalists. Families would receive condolence payments of $2,500, more in the discretion of commanders. But none of this applied to US Special Forces or the ANA's 145,000 soldiers. Contemporaneously, the UN Commissioner for Human Rights reported 1,445 civilian deaths in the first eight month, blaming 800 on the Taliban and insurgents, leaving the coalition responsible for 645 – four times McKiernan's figure. (The UN Assistance Mission in Afghanistan (UNAMA) later reported that air strikes were responsible for 64 percent of the 828 civilian deaths attributed to pro-government forces in 2008.) Meeting President Karzai in Kabul, Defense Secretary Gates expressed "personal regrets" for civilian casualties and ordered immediate condolence payments. "While no military has ever done more to prevent civilian casualties, it is clear we have to work even harder." He accepted a proposal by the Afghan Defense Minister to create a permanent Afghan–American investigating board. But a day later Australian Special Forces, claiming they had come under fire (although no Australian was wounded), killed the former Urozgan Province police chief and a tribal leader and military commander who had been a Karzai ally.

An October 16 air strike in a village near Lashkar Gah (capital of Helmand Province) killed 25–30 civilians.[94] Villagers took the bodies of at least eighteen women and children to the governor's compound. A few days later coalition forces mistakenly attacked an ANA checkpoint that had been in place for ten days on the main highway in Khost Province, killing nine and injuring others. A November 3 air strike in Shah Wali Kot village in Kandahar killed 40 civilians and wounded 28, mostly women and children attending a wedding party. The USA claimed it had killed nine militants and accused insurgents of forcing civilians to remain in the area during the firefight. After Obama was elected the next day, Karzai declared: "we cannot win the fight against terrorism with air strikes." His "first demand" of the new US president was "to put an end to civilian casualties." A day later estimates of the dead rose to 90. The USA acknowledged 37 dead civilians and 35 injured and paid compensation. Fighting and air strikes in Badghis Province on November 6 killed seven civilians and 15 Taliban. A few days later coalition forces killed 14 civilians guarding a road construction project in Khost Province. Soon after that an attack on a US military convoy resulted in the deaths of at least eight bystanders. In a news conference with NATO Secretary General Jaap de Hoop Scheffer at the end of November, Karzai said: "We have no power to stop the planes. I wish I could intercept the planes."

A few days later Special Forces killed 7 Afghan police and wounded 13 in Qalat, the capital of Zabul Province.[95] Coalition forces called it "a tragic case of mistaken identity on both parts," but the deputy police chief said his men had been inside their station when Americans had come under fire from another building. The provincial deputy governor said "special forces didn't inform the police that they were going to that village," apparently for fear the police would alert the Taliban. A few days later, when a bus heading toward US soldiers in central Wardak Province failed to stop after warning shots, soldiers killed four passengers and wounded at least ten. Just before Christmas a raid in Khost Province killed a father, mother, and male relative, while a woman and a four-year-old boy were bitten by an attack dog. The USA said the raid detained an al-Qaeda operative and found grenades, an AK-47, pistols, and a shotgun, and the dead had shown "hostile intent." Karzai condemned the operation in front of government leaders and foreign diplomats: "entering by force to our people's houses is against the government of Afghanistan." After a second raid in Kandahar Province, the USA said it had killed 11 armed Taliban and found dozens of land mines, grenades, and bomb-making materials; but local leaders said four of the dead were civilians.

This sequence of events provoked an extraordinary outburst from Karzai:[96]

> [T]he coalition forces began to employ thugs, and went with those thugs into the homes of hundreds of elders and community people, frightened into running away from Afghanistan …
>
> For years I've been saying that the war on terrorism is not in Afghanistan, it's in the training camps, it's in sanctuaries [in Pakistan]. Rather than going there, the coalition went around the Afghan villages, burst into people's homes and … [has been] committing extrajudicial killings in our country. The latest example was the day before yesterday in Khost, where a man, a woman and a 12-year-old boy were killed. Were they al Qaeda? And even if they were, was there a court order to shoot them down in their homes? And if they were, was the 12-year-old boy al Qaeda too? Or the woman? And if this continues, we will be in a deeper trench than we are in today. And the war against terrorism will end in a disgraceful defeat … [The coalition] hired [Afghan] thugs … or warlords or whatever. They created militias of those people who had no limits to misbehavior and who were sent to people's homes to search their homes, to arrest them and to intimidate them. And we've been trying to tell them for seven years now that this is wrong … this has to stop if you want to succeed … if they go to the Afghan homes and burst in and arrest or kill, does that leave the Afghan people with the feeling that they have a government? No. That is actually the destruction of the Afghan government. If Afghanistan is a sovereign country, if Afghanistan has an elected government, if Afghanistan has a constitution, if Afghanistan has laws, and if there is a slogan of strengthening Afghan democracy and institutions, then the Afghan sovereignty and the Afghan laws must be respected, and not violated in such an extreme manner as it is being done today. Therefore my plea to the international community and to the American government is … that we want to sit down and redraw the map of relations in which we take responsibility for what's gone wrong in my government … and I would like the international community also to commit strongly to respecting the Afghan sovereignty and Afghan laws in conducting the war on terrorism with the right tools and the right attitude … I was talking for a long time about regaining the trust of the communities, meaning, in the first stage, to stop harassing them, to stop bursting into their homes. To stop arresting them at will and to stop bombing villages.

In early January 2009 an artillery shell killed 11 civilians and wounded 9 near Tirin Kot, the capital of Urozgan Province.[97] A raid on a village north of Kabul on January 19 killed a militant commander and 14 civilians. Without admitting their innocence, the USA paid $2,500 for each death, $500 for each of the two wounded, and $1,500 for village repairs. After discussing with CENTCOM commander Gen. Petraeus the problem of civilian deaths, deployments, ROEs, and a ban on NATO searches of Afghan homes, Karzai told the opening of parliament he had sent NATO a draft agreement two weeks earlier, but coalition forces had disregarded his call to stop air strikes near civilians. The speaker of the Senate complained that Special Forces gave Afghans no advance warning of raids. After a firefight in Laghman Province a few days later, village elders said 22 civilians were killed, but the USA claimed the 15 dead were Taliban. Troops found automatic rifles, RPGs, hand grenades, and ammunition. Soon thereafter the USA said it actually had killed 32 Taliban, insisting the alleged "civilians" were Taliban "sentries." "[T]he enemy placed the whole village in harm's way by operating the way they do." But two of the wounded told a different story: during a house search on January 7, coalition troops had killed 13 civilians and wounded 9. A January 23 raid in the same place killed at least 16, including 2 women and 3 children. The provincial governor said villagers were armed because there were no police. Two days later hundreds of angry villagers marched to the provincial capital, and Karzai called for an end to house raids.

An attack in Laghman Province on January 24, targeting a Taliban commander who had left months earlier, killed 16 civilians, including 2 women and 3 children, and wounded dozens.[98] Although the USA claimed most of the dead were militants and one woman had been firing an RPG, it paid $2,000 to the victims' families, acknowledging "there was some potential that some of those killed were civilians." A raid in Ghazni Province in early February killed two men whom villagers said were civilians; but the USA claimed they were militants who had barricaded themselves in the targeted house. Hundreds demonstrated. A survey several days later found that a quarter of Afghans believed attacks on Americans were justifiable, twice the proportion in 2006. Eighty percent called coalition air strikes unacceptable, whereas only 28 percent blamed the Taliban for hiding among civilians. The USA said an air strike in Herat Province a few days later killed 15 militants; but villagers claimed the dead were 3 militants and 13 civilians, including 3 children and 6 women. BGen. Ryan, who led the inquiry, said weapons and ammunition had been found. Four days later a night raid in Logar Province killed one man and arrested four others (three of whom were released days later). The next morning hundreds of protesters blocked a nearby highway, appearing on television that evening. A February 22 night raid on the Imam Sahib village mayor's house in Kunduz Province killed five alleged militants. But the mayor – a member of an anti-Taliban faction, who was hiding in his house at the time – said those killed were his driver, cook, and bodyguard, and two guests. The provincial governor bitterly criticized US forces. Vice Adm. McRaven, JSOC head, disclosed (after it ended) that he had ordered a two-week halt in most commando missions because of civilian deaths.

An early March Special Operations raid in Logar Province killed five people, who the USA said were armed militants but a delegation from the provincial governor claimed were civilians.[99] Police shot and wounded two villagers protesting at a government office. A raid in Khost Province killed at least four civilians, including a woman and a 14-year-old boy. But NATO said "multiple intelligence sources" identified the dead as "four to eight enemy fighters." Soon thereafter a NATO air strike in Kumar Province killed 6 civilians, including 2 children, and wounded 14. According to a member of the provincial council, May 4 air strikes in two villages in Farah Province killed an estimated 70, including women and children. Villagers brought the bodies to Farah, the provincial capital. The USA said: "the Taliban are using civilians' houses for their own protection and as a shield." Meeting with Obama and Pakistani President Zardari in Washington, Karzai called the deaths "unacceptable." The ICRC said dozens of noncombatants had been killed in two locations. The provincial governor told the Afghan Parliament on May 6 that up to 130 civilians had been killed. The local member of parliament said the governor had told him that "villagers have brought two tractor trailers full of pieces of human bodies to his office." Someone he knew counted 113 bodies being buried, and more were being pulled from the rubble. One provincial council member said there were 147 dead; another compiled a list of over 150. But the USA acknowledged only 12 civilians killed. The chair of parliament urged the government to present a new status of forces agreement within a week. But the commander of the International Security Assistance Force (ISAF), Gen. McKiernan, said he had "information that leads us to distinctly different conclusions about the cause of the civilian casualties," citing reports that they had been killed by Taliban grenades. The USA acknowledged these reports were "thinly sourced," but did not withdraw them. Police fired on hundreds of Afghans protesting outside police stations and at the governor's office, wounding three. Shopkeepers in the provincial capital vowed to remain closed until the air strikes were fully investigated. When the local member of parliament visited one village, residents threatened to beat him and other officials. Residents of both villages said the Taliban had left before the air strikes occurred. Afghan government officials accepted villagers' handwritten lists of 147 dead civilians. After interviewing 21 villagers, AIHRC identified 117 dead, including 26 women and 61 children. It criticized both the Taliban for fighting among civilians and the USA for using excessive force, but villagers blamed the USA.

After meeting with Obama, Karzai said most of the casualties had been caused by US bombs, telling NBC's *Meet the Press*: "Civilian casualties are undermining support in the Afghan people for the war on terrorism and for relations with Americans." JCS chairman Adm. Mullen said: "we cannot succeed in Afghanistan … by killing Afghan civilians," but "we can't tie our troops' hands behind their backs." Retired LtGen. Karl W. Eikenberry, the new US Ambassador to Afghanistan, flew with Karzai to the mosque in Farah to tell several hundred elders and village representatives that the bombing was a tragedy and to promise new tactics. He questioned the wisdom of dropping 2,000 lbs. bombs on houses without knowing who was inside. Karzai said the USA had pledged to stop bombing villages and raiding houses. Nearly three weeks later the USA still maintained it had killed 60–65 Taliban and only 20–30 civilians. Video "clearly depicts insurgents entering the buildings which were then targeted." But villagers said that Taliban had left at least 90 minutes before the air strikes; any subsequent movements were civilians fleeing the first attack. The military report concluded that every target was a legitimate threat, but in "several instances … the choice of how to deal with that threat did not comply with the standing rules of engagement." After the principal combat had ended, an Air Force B-1 circled back along an "elongated approach" and bombed a building where it believed Taliban were massing without reconfirming the target. But though this violated rules requiring a more imminent threat before endangering nearby dwellings, DoD found "no indication" that this targeting gap "resulted in civilian casualties." The USA insisted that civilian deaths were "greatly outnumbered by the Taliban killed."

During a SASC hearing, Sen. McCain said a mission's success should be measured by "the number of Afghans shielded from violence," not the number of enemy fighters killed. A military victory would be "hollow and unsustainable" if it provoked popular resentment. (Indeed, the military stopped releasing the number of militants killed.) A new report a month later acknowledged that the May attack killed at least 26 and possibly many more, but said it was impossible "conclusively to determine the number of civilian casualties." CENTCOM maintained that air strikes did not violate the laws of war, but conceded they were inconsistent with the goal of "providing security and safety for the Afghan people." JCS chairman Mullen found no grounds for disciplinary action. Gen. McChrystal (McKiernan's successor as ISAF commander) ordered a review of the mission and planned to meet with provincial leaders and villagers. Air strikes would be used only to protect US and Afghan forces from being overrun and would not be conducted in populated areas, and special care would be taken before attacking houses and compounds where insurgents were believed to have taken cover. "Any entry into an Afghan house should always be accomplished by Afghan National Security Forces, with the support of local authorities." After meeting with McChrystal and NATO defense ministers, Defense Secretary Gates called killing civilians "one of our greatest strategic vulnerabilities." The *New York Times* agreed that "protecting Afghan civilians and expanding the secure space in which they can safely go about their lives and livelihoods must now become the central purpose of American military operations in Afghanistan."

But a July air strike in Kandahar Province killed at least 5 civilians and wounded 13, including 2 women and 4 children. They had been sleeping at the time, and there had been no fighting and no Taliban were present.[100] And in August a helicopter killed four men in Kandahar Province. The USA said they had been riding motorcycles and were armed and carrying plastic jugs (which could be used for IEDs); but an uncle said the four brothers, aged 12 to 21, had been sleeping. Angry villagers carried the bodies to the provincial governor's guest house. In a separate incident in Kandahar, a US helicopter killed five civilians. The USA said they were loading weapons, but villagers claimed the "weapons" were cucumbers.

ISAF reported that following McChrystal's new orders, civilian deaths in July and August fell to 13 and 6 from 92 and 59 a year earlier. But in September up to ninety were killed in a US air strike that German soldiers had requested on two fuel tankers stuck in a riverbed near Kunduz after being hijacked by the Taliban.[101] The Afghan government said 72 were dead, about 30 of them insurgents; the German military claimed a video from an American fighter plane showed 100 Taliban, some armed, and all 57 dead were fighters. The provincial public health officer reported that a medical team saw 80 dead, "most of them ... civilians and villagers." Local villagers explained that some had been conscripted by the Taliban to unload the fuel, while others had been collecting it for themselves. McChrystal immediately sent a video message, translated into Dari and Pashto, declaring that he took "this possible loss of life or injury to innocent Afghans very seriously" and had ordered an investigation. The next day he flew to Kunduz, walked to the bombing site, and visited the injured in hospital. The German Defense Minister said the Taliban had threatened an attack before the September 27 German election.

On the eve of a Stockholm meeting on expanding the war in Afghanistan, European leaders called the bombing a "tragedy" and a "big mistake." Germans, however, were cautious. Chancellor Merkel told the Bundestag that she "deeply regrets" any innocent victims but opposed "premature judgments." Foreign Minister Steinmeier (a Social Democrat challenging Merkel in the forthcoming election) also rejected "premature judgments." The German Defense Ministry said: "we continue to consider the military strike correct." But Defense Minister Jung now claimed only that "the predominant share [of the dead] were Taliban." The NATO investigation found that about 125 had been killed, at least a dozen of whom were not insurgents. Based on interviews with survivors, AIHRC said 60–80 had been killed. The provincial governor's office said just five were civilians. Karzai's investigator found 69 Taliban and 30 civilians killed and 11 Taliban and 9 civilians wounded. At the end of November the new German Defense Minister revealed that a German general and a senior Ministry officer resigned after *Bild* reported that information on civilian casualties had been withheld. A day later Jung (now Labor Minister) also resigned. In April 2013 the Bonn Regional Court allowed the victims' lawsuit to proceed, finding that the German colonel who ordered the air strike might have violated the Geneva Conventions.

In September 2009 McChrystal criticized the military for being "preoccupied with protection of our own forces."[102] But others warned that civilian deaths had been reduced at the expense of military deaths (which had grown from 42 in July–August 2008 to 96 in the same months of 2009). Sen. Collins said: "I am troubled if we are putting our troops at great risk in order to go to such extremes to avoid Afghan casualties" and urged DoD to determine whether the new ROE were unnecessarily endangering US troops. Coalition troops came under fire 30 percent more often in summer 2009 than 2008, and air munitions dropped fell by half. Defense Secretary Gates conceded that as a result of McChrystal's orders, "our troops take some additional risk to themselves to avoid innocent Afghan casualties." JCS chairman Mullen agreed that the risk to US forces was "up higher now." He was replying to a letter (forwarded by Collins) from John Bernard (a retired Marine whose Marine son was in Helmand) complaining that "the marines and soldiers that are 'holding' territories … without reinforcement, denial of fire-support and refusal to allow [US troops] to hunt and kill the very enemy we are there to confront are nothing more than sitting ducks." After his son was killed a month later, Bernard wrote: "We've hamstrung ourselves in fear of angering a population that hates us anyway." Collins said US military policy had passed "a tipping point" where "you are asking them to be so cautious in their approach that you almost guarantee they will incur wounds or even be killed." SASC chair Levin complained that four Marines had been killed in an ambush after their unit was denied air and artillery support. Some US commanders said insurgents were taking advantage of the new ROE by fighting from Afghan homes.

A month later the *New York Times* described McChrystal's response when a European general reported at an ISAF morning briefing that a Hellfire missile had obliterated an Afghan compound.[103]

> *McChrystal*: I would like for you to explain to me the process you used to shoot a Hellfire missile into a compound that might have had civilians in it … Were there civilians in that compound?
> *General*: I'm sorry, but the system is not responsive enough for us to get that kind of information quickly.
> *McChrystal*: We bomb a compound, and I don't know about it until the next morning? … I'm being a hard-ass about it.
> *General*: It seems it was not a Hellfire missile but a 500-pound bomb.
> *McChrystal* [taking off his reading glasses and looking around the room]: Gentlemen, we need to understand the implications of what we are doing. Air power contains the seeds of our own destruction. A guy with a long-barrel rifle runs into a compound, and we drop a 500-pound bomb on it? Civilian casualties are not just some reality with the Washington press. They are a reality for the Afghan people. If we use air power irresponsibly, we can lose this fight.

He had previously directed the military to "think how you would expect a foreign army to operate in your neighborhood, among your families and your children, and act accordingly."

Two months later an Army Special Forces officer complained about excessive bureaucratic restraint in a *New York Times* op ed.[104] "Decisions move through the process of risk mitigation like molasses. When the

Taliban arrive in a village … it takes 96 hours for an army commander to obtain necessary approvals to act." His company was "stopped on 70 percent of our attempts because we could not achieve the requisite 11 approvals in time."

Civilian casualties persisted.[105] A September 2009 air strike killed at least five in Helmand Province. In October a military convoy shot and killed two women, a child, and a young man, and wounded two other women and a man when a car failed to stop on command. During a search for two missing American soldiers, an air strike killed seven Afghan soldiers and a civilian in November. A NATO raid in December killed a dozen people in Laghman Province. Although NATO claimed it had killed seven militants and had no "reports to substantiate those claims of harming civilians," it conceded several days later that "there could possibly have been some civilians killed in a confusing situation." Afghan security forces stopped hundreds of protesting villagers from entering the provincial capital, killing one and wounding two. Several weeks later a joint Afghan–US force killed at least nine in Kunar Province. A senior NATO official claimed they were known Taliban, who smuggled IEDs. But after Karzai insisted eight were schoolboys and was confirmed by the provincial governor and a member of parliament, coalition forces stopped maintaining that all the dead were insurgents. NATO initially denied participating in the raid and then said it had been a joint operation with the ANA; but the Afghan Defense Minister said only US Special Forces had been involved. Karzai's office said his investigation confirmed the deaths of eight schoolboys, 12–17 years old, from one extended family. ISAF took them from three homes "and shot them dead." The school principal, whose grandchildren were among the dead, said "all of them are students in my school and they were here until late afternoon." Two other dead were an elderly man and a local farmer. Karzai called on ISAF to turn over "those responsible for the deaths." NATO replied that several of the dead had beards and the joint ISAF–Afghan operation had come under fire. Kai Eide retorted that "eight of those killed were students enrolled in local schools," but conceded there was "evidence to strongly indicate that there were insurgents in the area at the time." The killing prompted protesters in Kabul to chant "Stop Afghanicide" "Obama! Take your soldiers out of Afghanistan."

At the beginning of 2010 a NATO missile killed 5–7 civilians, including 3 children, in Helmand Province.[106] When American forces inspecting an engineering project in Nangarhar Province stopped to toss candies to Afghan children, a large explosion killed two schoolboys, two adults, and a policeman. Although US forces blamed unexploded ordnance and themselves suffered nine wounded, local residents demonstrated for several hours, convinced Americans had deliberately caused the explosion, and 5,000 marched in Jalalabad. After spreading a rumor in Helmand Province that US servicemen had desecrated the Koran and defiled a local woman, the Taliban organized a demonstration of several thousand, who overturned cars, burned down a school, and stormed the National Directorate of Security (NDS) office. The dead included an NDS officer, two police, and eight demonstrators; a dozen others were wounded. A raid in Ghazni Province killed four men (who the USA said were insurgents) and a 13–15-year-old boy (who the USA said reached for a gun and showed "hostile intent"). But declaring all were civilians, village residents took the bodies to Ghazni city to protest, shouting slogans against Americans and the government. Two days after a suicide bombing near Kabul, a US convoy "fired on what appeared to be a threatening vehicle," killing Mohammad Yunis, a cleric waiting to drive his sons to an Islamic school. ISAF apologized and offered compensation. A few days later, during a nighttime firefight involving the ANA and US Special Forces, the USA called in an air strike, killing four ANA soldiers and wounding seven. In Ghazni Province, US soldiers shot at a car approaching a checkpoint, killing two civilians and wounding another. A February 21 drone strike in Daikundi province killed between one and two dozen people; McChrystal apologized to Karzai; several weeks later US military apologized to villagers, paying survivors $2,900 and victims' families $4,800.

The UN reported that civilian deaths caused by coalition forces declined 28 percent in 2009 (to 596), crediting tighter rules for air strikes (which accounted for 359).[107] US commanders also limited night raids, observing:

> In Afghan culture, a man's home is more than just his residence. It represents his family, and protecting it is closely intertwined with his honor. He has been conditioned to respond aggressively whenever he perceives his home or honor is threatened. We should not be surprised that night operations elicit such a response, which we then often interpret as the act of an insurgent.

As Pat Tillman's death demonstrated, the US military treated its own friendly fire casualties much more seriously than those it inflicted on Afghan civilians, recommending letters of reprimand or other disciplinary actions following three ambushes in 2008 and 2009.[108] At least five battlefield commanders were reprimanded or investigated in January 2010. A retired colonel whose son was killed pressed DoD for a new probe for more than a year, prompting Gen. Petraeus to direct an investigation by a three-star marine general, whose 4,000-page report recommended discipline against company, battalion, and brigade commanders. The USA also disciplined commanders for errors that let the Taliban inflict casualties on US troops.

Before the February 2010 coalition assault in Marja, Helmand Province, BGen. Nicholson observed that "in counterinsurgency, the people are the prize."[109] He asked a dozen of Marja's most important elders to tell people to stay indoors when the fighting began and promised to repair or compensate for any property damage. Gen. McChrystal said: "until we can operate so the Afghan people believe that we are here to protect them in every way, we still have improvements to make." The day prior to the assault Karzai demanded "absolute caution" to avoid killing civilians. But even before it began, a stray artillery shell killed 12, including 5 women and 5 children. The marine battalion commander stood with victims' relatives and a local elder, declaring: "I bring my deepest condolences and will provide all my support." McChrystal told Karzai: "we deeply regret the tragic loss of life." He suspended use of the targeting device "until a thorough review of this incident has been conducted." But after it was determined that the problem was faulty intelligence, the ban was lifted. It turned out that three of the dead were Taliban insurgents who had seized the house as a fighting position. The AIHRC later reported that 28 civilians had been killed in the Marja offensive.

The *New York Times* published an op ed by a self-described "intelligence analyst" (actually a Georgetown graduate student moonlighting as a defense contractor), who claimed that "air support to American and Afghan forces" in the Marja operation "has been all but grounded by concerns about civilian casualties."[110] Troops "under heavy attack have had to wait an hour or more for air support." A similar delay in Kunar Province in September 2009 had led to the deaths of four Marines, eight ANA soldiers, and an Afghan interpreter, and 22 had been wounded. "Clearly … the pendulum has swung too far in favor of avoiding the deaths of innocents at all cost." "[N]o past war has ever supplied compelling proof" that "dead civilians are harmful to the conduct of war." The "lofty ideal" at the heart of McChrystal's directive was an "immoral" "lie" that "pretends that war can be fair and humane."

Two days later a NATO air strike in Kunduz Province killed seven Afghan police officers and wounded two more.[111] A few days after that, NATO accidentally killed 16 civilians. Addressing the opening of parliament, a furious Karzai displayed the photo of an 8-year-old girl whose 12 family members had been killed. Soon thereafter a NATO missile in Urozgan Province struck two overloaded minibuses and a truck, killing at least twenty-seven, including women and children, and wounding more than a dozen. ISAF said the target was "a group of suspected insurgents, believed to be en route to attack a joint Afghan–ISAF unit." But an official conceded there had been "no danger to coalition forces." "Apoplectic" at this flagrant violation of his directive, McChrystal again expressed "sorrow and regret" to Karzai. "I have made it clear to our forces that we are here to protect the Afghan people." Karzai "reminded the NATO commander that the issue of civilian casualties was a major hurdle against an effective war on terror and it must stop." His Cabinet "strongly condemn[ed]" NATO's "unjustifiable" and "repeated" killing of civilians. A week later JCS chairman Mullen said the military must use force "in a precise and principled manner." The battlefield was "in the minds of the people." McChrystal published part of his classified January order, making Afghans the leaders of night raids, but Karzai still sought an absolute ban. McChrystal also brought Special Operations (which he had previously commanded) under his control for the first time and gave it a new directive.

More than three months later a military report criticized the drone operators involved in the Urozgan air strike for claiming that the convoy contained only military-age men when intelligence analysts monitoring the video feed twice warned the operators and ground command posts that children were visible.[112] Although a Special Operations team turned the bodies of civilians over to local Afghans after the attack, officers on the ground failed to report civilian casualties. Four officers, including the brigade and battalion commanders, received reprimands, and two junior officers were disciplined. McChrystal said "inadvertently killing or injuring civilians is heartbreaking and undermines their trust and confidence in our mission. When we make a mistake, we must be forthright." He announced new training measures and asked Air Force commanders to investigate the Predator operators. Karzai expressed satisfaction with the investigation and remedial steps. The Air Force subsequently disciplined Predator (remotely piloted aircraft) crew members for failing to relay warnings from intelligence analysts to battle commanders. Wanting to support ground forces, the Predator pilot "had a strong desire to find weapons," which "colored – both consciously and unconsciously – his reporting of weapons and children." US military officers later went to the village to apologize and pay $2,900 to each wounded survivor and $4,800 to the families of each deceased.

On February 12, US Special Operations and Afghan Special Forces raided a house late at night in Paktia Province.[113] The local police chief and district prosecutor were killed when they emerged from the house to investigate, armed with Kalashnikov rifles; three women (two pregnant) were killed when they came to the men's aid. ISAF initially said the women had been bound and gagged after being killed execution-style; but it subsequently admitted the wrappings were the traditional burial garment. The lead investigator decided not to visit the scene in order to avoid "re-awakening emotional and political turmoil." The USA continued to maintain it was "not sure anyone will ever know how [the women] died," claiming they had knife punctures and slashes, suggesting they had been murdered before the assault. But an eyewitness saw an American using a knife to extract bullets from the bodies (as part of a cover-up). The military report explained that "the ground force was confused by the unfamiliar sight of women prepared so quickly for burial" (which Islam requires). It concluded that the "assumption" that the women had been killed by Afghans was an "honest assessment" resulting from "lack of cultural understanding." Noting that the family had been entertaining more than 25 guests to celebrate naming a new child, a senior Afghan official asked angrily: "in what culture in the world do you invite … people for a party and meanwhile kill three women?" Witnesses, including the Gardez University vice chancellor, insisted that uniformed Americans had conducted the raid, entering the compound before Afghan forces. He and his relatives threatened to burn themselves to death in protest. A spokesman for the Afghan Defense Minister complained that US "special forces were not accountable to anyone in the country." UNAMA's 2009 report declared: "these forces often operate with little or no accountability and exacerbate the anger and resentment felt by communities." It found that survivors of the raid "suffered from cruel, inhuman and degrading treatment." The chair of the Afghan Parliament's Defense Committee, who had participated in joint US–Afghan investigations of civilian deaths, said "in most of the cases … special forces are involved." But when he asked McChrystal "if there are individuals who do not obey [you] then what are they doing in this country," the general replied, "there are no operators in this country that I am not absolutely comfortable do exactly what I want them to do." Following the investigation he ordered, however, military personnel were disciplined and Adm. McRaven visited the victims' compound, offering to sacrifice a sheep to ask for forgiveness and paying $175,000 compensation.

NATO promised a joint forensic investigation, but then said this was impossible because the bodies had been buried the same day. Alleging evidence-tampering, Afghan investigators claimed that NATO soldiers had "dug bullets out of their victims' bodies" and "washed the wounds with alcohol before lying to their superiors about what happened." The head of the victims' family said the hallways where four of the five were killed had been repainted and at least two bullet holes replastered. NATO conceded "there was evidence of tampering at the scene, walls being washed, bullets dug out of holes in the walls," and investigators "couldn't find bullets from the wounds in the body." But "nothing pointed conclusively to the fact that our guys were the ones who tampered with the scene," and NATO "strongly den[ied] having dug any bullets out of bodies."

> We deeply regret the outcome of this operation, accept responsibility for our actions that night, and know that this loss will be felt forever by the families. The force went to the compound based on reliable information in search of a Taliban insurgent, and believed that the two men posed a threat to their personal safety. We now understand that the men killed were only trying to protect their families.

Senior US military officials apologized to family members and opened a new investigation to resolve differences with the Afghan Interior Ministry findings.

A *Los Angeles Times* account of the debriefing of a bombing raid stressed the precautions taken to avert civilian casualties.[114] After a pilot code-named Thurman dropped a 500 lb bomb on a Taliban target during his 12-hour mission, he immediately underwent two cross-examinations, the second attended by RAdm. Davidson (commander of the USS *Dwight D. Eisenhower* strike group), who said "often, in this war, it's the bombs that you don't drop that are the most important." The *Eisenhower* expected to drop just a fraction of the 66,000 lbs of bombs it had dropped during its previous deployment. Thurman said: "Afghans believe the planes are omnipotent and that when we have civilian casualties that we did it on purpose." "I've never been told that I caused civilian casualties. I don't want that on my conscience." Before this deployment pilots were briefed extensively on McChrystal's new rules.

The commander of carrier Air Wing Seven said: "we're here to protect people, and that means limiting civilian deaths."

But McChrystal's new rules did not reduce casualties at checkpoints, where 30 Afghans were killed and 80 wounded between summer 2009 and March 2010.[115] In a video he cautioned troops that during his more than nine months in "not a single case where we have engaged in an escalation of force incident and hurt someone has it turned out that the vehicle had a suicide bomb or weapons in it, and in many cases [it] had families in it." He added, however, that "nothing has changed to limit your right or responsibility to defend yourself." Two weeks later US troops fired on an Afghan bus, killing up to five civilians and wounding 18, many seriously. The USA claimed troops had first shot flares and then fired in early morning light, unaware it was a passenger bus. The driver denied there had been any signal, insisting troops had fired from 60–70 yards. Hundreds protested at the bus station where the damaged vehicle had been taken, shouting "Death to America" and condemning Karzai, who called the shooting "unjustifiable." The governor of Kandahar Province said the military commander should be prosecuted. A few days later a NATO convoy shot to death two shopkeepers, a police officer, and a 12-year-old student returning from a sports event in Khost Province. NATO claimed the dead were two insurgents and their "associates" and that the convoy "attempted to flag the vehicle down and flashed its lights," but the driver "responded by turning off the vehicle's headlights and accelerating toward the convoy," even after warning shots were fired. A day later, however, NATO apologized for "this tragic loss of life," admitting it had wrongly described two of the dead as "known insurgents" and the biometric data it had invoked "has not yet determined to be relevant."

Two raids by a joint US–Afghan force in Logar Province provoked anger.[116] On April 23, NATO said it killed five Afghan insurgents who displayed "hostile intent," retrieving AK-47s, pistols, and Pakistani passports. But Abdul Ghani said NATO killed two of his brothers and arrested two others. A raid the next day killed a cleric, a high school headmaster, and two others. The following day an angry crowd burned 12 trucks. A few days later in Nangarhar Province, NATO killed a man related to member of parliament Safia Sidiqi. NATO said the victim emerged from his house with a shotgun and "clearly presented hostile intent." Sidiqi joined demonstrators blocking the main road to Kabul and shouting "Death to Americans, Long Live the Taliban." When they tried to storm a government building, police killed one protester and wounded two others.

Ninety Afghan civilians were killed by coalition forces in the first four months of 2010, nearly 2.5 times as many as a year earlier.[117] Although deaths from air strikes had decreased, at least 28 Afghans had been killed and 43 wounded in convoy and checkpoint shootings during those months, compared with 8 and 28 a year earlier (and 36 for all of 2009). Since summer 2009, none of those killed or wounded posed a danger to coalition troops. Commanders responded with new guidelines instructing troops to practice drills "that include decisions to disengage," construct checkpoints that allow more space to maneuver, consult local Afghan leaders, not "automatically take the easy safe route when doing so requires the use of standoff weapons or indirect fire," and remain at the scene of shootings, if possible, and take responsibility. But LtGen. Rodriguez, operational commander of coalition forces, said "the last thing you want to do is put people, because of the pressure or the guidance, into positions where they are losing their lives because they don't think they have the right of self-defense." A UN report a month later confirmed that civilian deaths from coalition forces had declined; contemporaneously, NATO said that civilian casualties in March–May were down 44 percent compared with the previous year.

On May 14 a joint US Special Operations–Afghan nighttime raid to arrest a Taliban subcommander in Nangarhar Province claimed to have killed him and at least nine other insurgents.[118] Afghan interpreters with bullhorns repeatedly urged people to come out of the house. But Rafuddin Kushkaki, who owned it, said "my brother ran out to see what was happening; he was killed right away. My son ran out too and was shot as well." The alleged Taliban was just a young farm laborer. "We thought they were thieves, raiders," because voices were drowned out by a storm. A mortar sight "found" in the house had been planted by Afghan raiders; an ammunition vest belonged to household guards who patrolled the property; and a military uniform was used by a man who drove for local police. All were Tajiks not affiliated with the predominately Pashtun insurgency. Kushkaki worked as a driver for Zahir Qadir, a former Afghan general whose father had fought the Taliban alongside Karzai. Qadir convened a gathering of tribal elders, who condemned the raid, insisting all the dead were civilians. The district police chief, who had not been warned in advance, arrived in response to a phone call while the gunfight was in full swing, but was kept away. Although the Afghan Defense Ministry agreed all those killed were terrorists, the Afghan Interior Ministry investigation failed to confirm the identity of the alleged Taliban or the involvement of any other insurgents. Member of parliament Sidiqi visited the survivors and said all the victims were farmers. The only weapons found were rifles, which everyone had.

If McChrystal's orders saved Afghan lives, they angered US troops.[119] A marine infantry lieutenant said he had stopped seeking air support during the Marja offensive because it took too much time. Infantrymen said pilots could not attack a building or tree line from which troops were taking fire unless they could see insurgents shooting. Troops were ordered into the open to draw such fire. When Gen. Petraeus was nominated at the end of June to replace McChrystal (who was removed for disrespecting civilian superiors), he echoed these criticisms: "I want to assure the mothers and father of those fighting in Afghanistan that I see it as a moral imperative to bring all assets to bear to protect our men and women in uniform. Those on the ground must have all the support they need when they are in a tough situation." Karzai and other Afghan leaders "are in full agreement with me on this."

> I am keenly aware of concerns by some of our troops on the ground about the application of our rules of engagement and the tactical directive … If confirmed, I would continue the emphasis on reducing loss of civilian life in the course of operations to an absolute minimum while also ensuring that we provide whatever assets are necessary to ensure the safety [of coalition forces].

In early July an air strike killed at least five civilians in Ghazni Province as a result of a miscommunication.[120] The next day an errant artillery shell killed six civilians in Paktia Province. A NATO air strike in Helmand Province in late July allegedly killed 52 civilians, including 7 women and 17 children. Karzai and his Cabinet condemned the strike "in the strongest possible terms." NATO responded that "any speculation at this point of an alleged civilian casualty … is completely unfounded." After initially denying any civilian deaths, ISAF claimed six civilians and eight Taliban had been killed when the latter had seized the roof of a house, trapping the civilians inside. Following an investigation by provincial and local officials, Karzai said 39 civilians had been killed in the house, where Taliban had been fighting. He "once again insisted that under any conditions civilian casualties are not acceptable to him." In Kabul at the end of the month an SUV carrying four US Embassy contractors struck a car of Afghans, killing one and seriously injuring two more. Hundreds rioted, chanting "Death to America" and "Death to Foreigners," burning that SUV and another that rushed to rescue it. Three Afghans were injured. The next day several hundred Afghans marched through central Kabul to protest all the civilian deaths.

In August Gen. Petraeus issued a new tactical directive restricting artillery strikes and aerial bombardment of buildings, tree lines, and hillsides, and the use of small-arms fire when civilians might be present, while emphasizing that "nothing in this paragraph is intended to hinder an individual's right of self-defense."[121] He sought to correct junior field commanders' misperceptions that air strikes were effectively prohibited and forbade them to impose further restrictions on the use of force "without my approval." Military operations should normally be partnered with Afghan forces and commanders notified in advance of any exceptions. "Avoid spinning, and don't try to 'dress up' an ugly situation. Acknowledge setbacks and failures, including civilian casualties, and then state how we'll respond and what we've learned." A separate Counterinsurgency Guidance said: "We can't win without fighting, but we also cannot kill or capture our way to victory. Moreover, if we kill civilians or damage their property in the course of our operations, we will create more enemies than our operations eliminate. That's exactly what the Taliban want. Don't fall into their trap."

A National Bureau of Economic Research study found that killing two Afghan civilians provoked six revenge attacks. Karzai's Deputy National Security Adviser said Petraeus's approach was "basically … not very different" from McChrystal's, which the IACHR found had resulted in fewer civilians killed by US forces in 2010. UNAMA's semi-annual report agreed that civilian casualties inflicted by Afghan or coalition forces declined 40 percent in the first half of 2010 and deaths from NATO aerial bombings declined 64 percent. Petraeus said: "every Afghan death diminishes our cause."

Afghans said an August air strike in Nangarhar Province killed 32 civilians, though NATO claimed it had killed 2 senior Taliban leaders, 15–20 insurgents, and just 4–12 civilians.[122] A week later an air strike in Helmand Province killed five civilians. After discussing the issue during an hour-long video conference with Obama, Karzai said he had asked for a "strategic review" of the NATO campaign based on "rightful demands of the people of Afghanistan that terrorism cannot be fought in Afghan villages." Later that month a house raid in Nangarhar

Province killed a man and his son after NATO forces searching for a Taliban commander drew gunfire. Hundreds of residents in Jalalabad blocked the main highway in protest. In Jowzjan Province, NATO helicopters killed 4 Afghan police and wounded 13 more. An air strike in Farah Province killed a woman and two children. A nighttime raid in Baghlan Province killed 8 civilians, including 2 women and a child, and injured 12.

In September in Takhar Province, NATO jets fired twice on a convoy of election campaign workers in vehicles covered with political posters, killing 12 and wounding the candidate and others.[123] The USA said the target was a senior Islamic Movement of Uzbekistan leader and claimed NATO had expended "a great deal of time and patience" to ensure the strike occurred in a remote area without civilians. An air strike in Laghman Province, which the USA claimed killed more than 70 Taliban, allegedly also killed civilians, prompting more than a hundred local residents to protest angrily in the provincial capital. In October a US air strike killed the Taliban shadow governor of Helmand Province and several other Taliban commanders, but also killed three civilians and wounded three boys. The USA acknowledged killing two civilians, one an eight-year-old girl, and wounding two boys in an exchange of fire with insurgents in Logar Province. A few days later NATO helicopters killed five armed men in Helmand Province. NATO claimed they were insurgents, but the local Afghan government said they were private security guards.

US defensiveness in response to Afghan claims of civilian casualties contrasted sharply with its contrition after inadvertently killing Linda Norgrove, a British aid worker, during a raid to free her from the Taliban.[124] Immediately afterwards, NATO said she had been killed by a captor detonating an explosive. Although Special Operation troops had reported using a grenade, this was not passed "up the military chain of command." But after watching the video, the Special Operations commander told Petraeus he had seen "someone throwing a hand grenade into the area where Miss Norgrove was being held." Petraeus explained that "the error came to light only after viewing the sharper image on the hard drive." Members of the team had been disciplined "for failing to provide a complete and full account of their actions." After Petraeus promised "a full U.S./U.K. investigation," Prime Minister Cameron said it was "clear that the best chance of saving Linda's life was to go ahead." "From the moment Linda was taken hostage, Gen. Petraeus has treated her as if she was a U.S. citizen." The raid had been approved by Foreign

Secretary Hague, who later called it "an incredibly difficult operation that was carried out with the utmost courage by elite U.S. forces."

Charles J. Dunlap Jr., a retired Air Force general, wrote in a *Washington Post* op ed that "the controversial policy restricting airpower in the Afghan war may be ripe for review," blaming it for "a staggering 31 percent increase" in Afghan civilian deaths in 2010 (most inflicted by the Taliban) and the fact that US and ISAF casualties "have reached all-time highs."[125] "Airpower reduces the need to put our precious soldiers in the path of the improvised explosive devices that are killing and maiming more ISAF troops than anything else." He quoted an "Afghan expert," claiming that though the Afghan government used civilian casualties as leverage with ISAF, many local officials "tend actually not to be too concerned with this to a degree." Sarah Holewinski, executive director of the Campaign for Innocent Victims in Conflict, replied in the *Post* that her group, HRW, and OSI had found that "Afghans are intensely critical of U.S. and NATO forces because of air strikes harming civilians." UNAMA reported that civilian deaths from fixed-wing aircraft fell from 54 during the first ten months of 2009 to 19 during the same period in 2010, even though there were more air strikes, but deaths from helicopter fire rose from 3 to 37 (leaving the totals unchanged).

On November 14 Karzai told the *Washington Post* that "the time has come to reduce military operations … the presence of, you know, boots in Afghanistan … the intrusiveness into daily Afghan life."[126] "[B[ursting into homes at night, arresting Afghans" was "terrible," not "the business of any foreign troops." Special Operations raids had increased to 200 a month, six times the level of 18 months earlier. Was capturing "Talib A … so important to have 10 more people killed, civilians … children and women?" "I can never talk in favorable terms about planes that are shooting people or bombing people … it is not desirable for the Afghan people either to have 100,000 or more foreign troops going around the country endlessly." He was not a "partner" of the USA if that meant "someone who will keep quiet when a village is bombed … I will speak for Afghanistan … if you're looking for a stooge and calling a stooge a partner, no." Petraeus expressed "astonishment and disappointment." Secretary of State Clinton said: "the use of intelligence-driven, precision, targeted operations against high-value insurgents and their networks is a key component of our comprehensive civilian–military operations." NATO Ambassador Sedwill complained that Karzai's criticism just before a summit meeting on Afghanistan was "not helpful." Obama expressed his displeasure: "if we're ponying up billions of dollars to ensure that President Karzai can continue to build and develop his country, then he's got to also pay attention to our concerns as well." Civilian deaths were "an entirely legitimate issue," but Karzai had "to understand that I've got a bunch of young men and women in a foreign country being shot at," who "need to protect themselves." It was not "acceptable" for them to be "just sitting ducks for the Taliban."

But *Washington Post* columnist David Ignatius documented the war's unpopularity among Afghans.[127] Polls in Kandahar and Lashkar Gah in October found that 50 percent thought recent military operations were bad for the Afghan people; 65 percent said foreign forces killed more civilians than the Taliban did (which was grossly erroneous); and 72 percent felt foreigners disrespected their religion. The *Washington Post* published supporting quotations from Helmand: "Americans are just making life worse and worse"; "the more infidels who come to our country, the more Afghans die, and the less safe we become"; "I believe the British and American troops are more cruel than the Taliban"; the Taliban "are our brothers, our cousins, our relatives … If somebody attacks from one house, the Americans bomb the whole place." NATO had actually razed hundreds, perhaps thousands, of homes around Kandahar booby-trapped by Taliban (paying compensation, though both sides disputed the amount).

After Karzai's interview, NATO artillery landed short of their target in Kunar Province, killing three civilians and wounding four.[128] In an operation capturing a Haqqani militant in Paktia Province in December, NATO troops killed seven men, who the local police chief believed were civilians. Fearing they were threatened, NATO soldiers called in an air strike in Helmand Province, killing four who turned out to be ANA soldiers. NATO killed another five civilians in Helmand during a firefight in a compound. A NATO helicopter fired on a convoy of cars driving to an event hosted by the head of the local council in Faryab Province, killing a police officer and a lawmaker's brother. Acting on faulty intelligence, a NATO night raid in Kabul killed two Afghan private security guards and wounded three others. Karzai's spokesman said "this was an irresponsible way of dealing with an issue in Kabul city." The Kabul Police director of criminal investigations called it "murder."

Karzai banned private security contractors effective December 17, 2010, though the Afghan National Security Council (under pressure from Petraeus) exempted military bases, embassies, diplomatic residences, and convoys (but not development organizations).[129] When asked to extend the deadline, Karzai stormed out of a meeting with top US officials, declaring that contractors "violate the law, they kill people." His chief of staff said Karzai had been objecting to contractors for five years "but nobody listened to him." Karzai had issued his order after security guards collided with civilian cars the previous August, killing an Afghan and provoking protests. A few days later he relented, creating a committee to prepare a timeline for the transition. But he told the *Washington Post* that "one of the important elements of the transition that we're working on is to end ... the violence and the violation of our laws that these private security firms cause." The government allowed private security contractors to work for development organizations until their contracts expired. In February 2011 Karzai said foreign governments should stop using private security contractors, declaring that "Afghanistan belongs to Afghans." In March the government said ISAF and the US Agency for International Development (USAID) would have to stop using private security guards. In September the Interior Ministry started auditing security firms. In January 2012 Afghan police arrested two British contractors for possession of 30 unlicensed AK-47s (whose serial numbers had been removed).

A January 2011 air strike in Daykundi Province killed three Afghan police officers traveling to meet US Special Forces for a joint patrol.[130] NATO claimed they were "setting up what appeared to be an ambush position." A February 17 air strike in Kunar Province killed what Governor Wahidi said was "13 armed opposition, 22 women, 26 boys and 3 old men." The local hospital reported three women, four children and two men wounded. Karzai declared he would "take any steps necessary to prevent and stop civilian casualties in this country." RAdm. Smith, the strategic communications chief, maintained there were no signs of civilian casualties. His unit had overheard Taliban talking about reporting civilian casualties to local authorities: "that's where the civilian casualty thing came from." Three days later Petraeus dismissed allegations by Karzai's office and Wahidi, claiming that Afghans might have invented stories or even burned their own children. Even after Wahidi's investigation team had brought victims with burns and shrapnel wounds to the provincial capital, including a man, a woman, and five youths under 17, Smith stuck to the US line: "We have observed increased reporting of children being disciplined by having their hands and feet dipped into boiling water. No one is claiming that this is the case in this instance, but it may well be." At the National

Security Council meeting, a participant said Petraeus again "claimed that in the midst of the [operation] some pro-Taliban parents in contact with a government official decided to create a civilian casualty claim to pressure international forces to cease the [operation]. They burned hands and legs of some of their children and sent them to the hospital." An incensed Afghan official declared that "killing 60 people and then blaming the killing on those same people, rather than apologizing for any deaths? This is inhuman." But Smith maintained that "reports from elders in the region appear unrealistically high and unsupported by anything we know to date." Shuja ul-Mulik, a member of the investigating team and former member of parliament, counted 27 graves in the village and saw the trench where most had died. "I saw women and children's garments. I saw blood-stained walls of the trench. I saw pieces of blankets and cotton from the quilts the villagers wrapped themselves in because of the cold weather." But human rights organizations conceded it was difficult to determine the age of the blood stains and graves.

A NATO air strike in Kunar Province at the beginning of March killed nine children collecting firewood.[131] Petraeus said "we are deeply sorry for this tragedy and apologize." NATO would investigate and discipline if necessary. He had ordered all air crews "to be rebriefed on tactical directives, reinforcing the need to be sure we protect the lives of innocent Afghans as we pursue a ruthless enemy." He apologized to the Afghan people at an Afghan National Security meeting. But some members of parliament demanded that Petraeus appear before parliament. Although the Afghan President's office said Obama expressed "deep regret" in a video conference, Karzai himself said: "the people of Afghanistan are tired of these incidents and excuses, and condemnations cannot relieve their pain. I am asking you on behalf of the people of Afghanistan that there be no repetition of this incident." Defense Secretary Gates used a news conference with Karzai to say "this breaks our heart. Not only is their loss a tragedy for their families, it is a setback for our relationship with the Afghan people." Karzai said: "I trust [Gates] fully when he says he's sorry." There were protests in the district capital and Kabul after this third civilian killing in two weeks. Contemporaneously, ISAF shot dead Mohammad Khan, a cousin of Karzai's father, during a night raid in Kandahar; it quickly apologized. At a memorial service for relatives and neighbors of the Kunar Province victims Karzai wept openly and said: "With great honor and with great respect, and humbly rather than with arrogance, I request that NATO and America should stop these operations on our soil. This war is not on our soil. If this war is against terror, then this war is not here, terror is not here … our demand is that this war should be stopped." But his spokesman said the president was referring to civilian casualties, not the war.

At the end of March a NATO air strike targeting a vehicle carrying insurgents in Helmand Province killed two men, two women, and three children, and wounded five others.[132] A NATO raid on the wrong house in Nangarhar Province in May killed a 12-year-old girl and her uncle, who was a police officer. NATO apologized but explained it had "suspected" the girl had a gun and the uncle had "threatened the security force with a pistol." At the end of the month a night raid in Takhar Province killed four civilians, including two women. Thousands of protesters attacked a police headquarters and a NATO base, leaving 12 dead. Karzai had recently said that "to avoid arbitrary and uncoordinated operations by foreign forces in Afghanistan," he had ordered the Ministry of Defense to bring them under Afghan control. But NATO said that though it "fully supports President Karzai's intent to have Afghan forces increasingly in the lead for operations," "we would not have seen the gains and progress made to date without the conduct of targeted intelligence-driven night operations."

Days later a NATO air strike in Helmand Province killed civilians in a compound from which insurgents were firing.[133] A US spokesman said: "while I know there is no price on human life, we will ensure that we make amends with the families in accordance with Afghan culture." Karzai said the dead included two men, two women, and ten children, and others were wounded. A contemporaneous air strike in Nuristan Province allegedly killed more than twenty police wearing civilian clothes. Night raids were averaging 300 a month (Reuters estimated 19 a night between December 2010 and February 2011); the USA claimed it hit its targets 80 percent of the time, inflicting civilian casualties less than one percent of the time. Karzai said: "NATO and American forces have been warned repeatedly that their arbitrary and improper operations are the causes of killing innocent people." Doing so "for the last time," he threatened "unilateral action," declaring: "Such attacks will no longer be allowed." Afghanistan "has a lot of ways of stopping" them. "If they continue their attacks on our houses, then their presence will change from a force that is fighting against terrorism to a force that is fighting against the people of Afghanistan. And in that case, history shows what Afghans do with trespassers and occupiers."

NATO offered a bland response: "Gen. Petraeus has repeatedly noted that every liberation force has to be very conscious that it can, over time, become seen as an occupation force. We are in agreement with President Karzai on the importance of constantly examining our actions in light of that reality – and we are doing just that." Karzai subsequently told Gates: "the people of Afghanistan do not wish or want to see their houses being bombarded, civilians being killed and lives lost." This was their "demand." Gates replied that "the vast majority of civilian casualties are caused by the Taliban."

A month later NATO forces pursuing a leader of the Haqqani network in Khost Province called in an air strike killing "several" insurgents as well as "a number of associated family members," whose presence had been "unknown to the security forces."[134] The provincial police chief said the dead included three women and six children. In August, after drawing fire from a compound in Helmand Province, ISAF called in an air strike, killing the owner, his wife, and seven children. Days later US soldiers in Kandahar shot at Afghan police, killing seven and wounding the commander and another.

In September 2011 the Open Society Foundation reported that raids had increased fivefold, from about four a night (2/09–12/10) to 19 a night (12/10–2/11).[135] The UN reported that civilian deaths in such raids dropped slightly from 98 in 2009 to 90 in 2010.[136] ISAF claimed that less than one percent of raids inflicted civilian casualties, and no shots were fired in 80 percent.

In November Karzai told the loya jirga that in exchange for letting the USA remain on military bases after the 2014 withdrawal, he would demand an end to house searches and night raids by foreign troops and full respect for national sovereignty.[137] The head of the coalition's joint command responded that night raids were "very important" and "safe for the populace as well … because they're done at night when there is very little civilian activity." But the loya jirga (90 percent of whose delegates had been chosen by Karzai) affirmed his demand.

Days later a NATO air strike in Kandahar Province killed two insurgents and six children and injured two others.[138] Karzai's office held NATO responsible, but also disseminated a letter by Gen. Allen declaring he had "issued direct orders for all units to conduct retraining on our methods of employing force against insurgents while protecting Afghan civilians." But in Nangarhar Province about the same time ISAF killed two men whom relatives called "ordinary laborers" with "no link with al-Qaeda." Disregarding Karzai's complaints, ISAF conducted about a dozen raids each night.

Although negotiations for a long-term strategic agreement had begun in March 2011, they were stalemated in December by Afghan insistence on abolishing or greatly limiting night raids, whose frequency had doubled since 2010.[139] NATO said "95% of all night operations at this stage are already partnered. So basically the recommendation of the traditional loya jirga is already put in action." But a Karzai spokesman complained that the USA did not tell Afghan security forces in advance "where they are going, which house they are searching and who is the target." Adm. McRaven, JSOC commander, said: "night raids are very valuable when you are trying to get someone who is trying to hide." In January 2012 Karzai told more than 250 members of parliament: "too many of our civilians, soldiers and security forces lost their lives in order to defend this country."

On January 22 a video surfaced on the Internet showing four members of the 3rd Battalion, 2nd Marines urinating on three dead Taliban, one covered in blood, in Helmand Province between March and September 2011.[140] One Marine sneered: "have a great day, buddy." The Taliban (who had been contemplating peace talks) "strongly condemn[ed] the inhuman act of wild American soldiers." Defense Secretary Panetta promptly telephoned Karzai, regretting the "utterly deplorable" conduct and assuring him it would be investigated and punished. Calling the act "condemnable in the strongest possible terms," Karzai said he had asked the USA to punish the perpetrators severely. Secretary of State Clinton expressed "total dismay," saying those involved "must be held fully accountable."

The next month an air strike in Kapisa Province killed eight 11–15-year-olds who had been grazing goats and sheep and collecting firewood.[141] Holding up photos of the victims with bloodied faces, an adviser appointed by Karzai to lead an investigation said to the press: "I call on the human rights community and the world community: who will speak up for the rights of these children?" NATO insisted it had "precisely" followed "all tactical directives" in bombing "a group of armed men that we observed engaging in unusual behavior" by "moving in open terrain in a tactical fashion, clearly keeping distance from each other," thereby posing "an imminent threat to the Afghan National Police and Coalition forces in the valley." A NATO official later claimed they were "adult-sized," and he had "no doubt they were carrying weapons." But he conceded: "we may never know what they were doing lined up under that rock that day."

An even more inflammatory event occurred later that month.[142] Two US soldiers took a truckload of debris from Parwan Prison to a burn pit at Bagram Airfield, where an Afghan soldier observed them throwing new Korans into the fire and tried to intervene. A crowd of more than 2,000 assembled – some shouting "Death to America" and singing Taliban songs – closing government buildings and preventing people from entering the city center. Gen. Allen apologized, insisting the action was "not intentional in any way." "The material recovered will be properly handled by appropriate religious authorities." He ordered every coalition solider to complete training within ten days "in the proper handling of religious materials." The US Embassy suspended all staff travel, and NATO took military vehicles off the streets. US Deputy Defense Secretary Ashton Carter met Karzai, whom Obama also wrote "to express my deep regret" and to "extend to you and the Afghan people my sincere apologies." Parliament issued "a resolution strongly condemning this act and demanded punishment of the culprits." Several members of parliament urged Afghans and police to wage jihad against the USA.

A second day of demonstrations left four dead in Parwan, and one dead at each of Bagram, Jalalabad, and Logar Province, and dozens injured. On the third day of demonstrations (now including Laghman and Baghlan Provinces) six more Afghans were killed and at least fifty-five wounded; a man wearing an ANA uniform killed two NATO soldiers. Karzai convened both Houses of Parliament. At a meeting attended by 300, a member of parliament for Parwan Province, where at least four demonstrators had died, called Americans "invaders" and (joined by about twenty others) asked mullahs and religious leaders "to urge the people from the pulpit to wage jihad against Americans." The Kabul police chief did "not blame people for throwing rocks at us because this is their right to protest their anger about dishonoring our holy Koran." A fourth day of demonstrations continued in Kabul and six other provinces following Friday prayers. Six protesters and a police officer died in Herat, and dozens were wounded. Hundreds burned cars and shops in Khost. Although Karzai had told parliament the act was a mistake "and we will accept [the American] apology," he also said: "whoever did this should be punished." Some members of parliament said the Taliban were exploiting the incident to stoke anger at the USA, Pakistan, and Iran. Gen. Allen opened an AR 15–6 inquiry and was cooperating with an Afghan investigation; the Ulema Council and some members of parliament were also investigating. After two US officers were shot dead inside the Interior Ministry, Gen. Allen ordered NATO to withdraw all advisers from Kabul ministries. Defense Secretary Panetta said the Afghan Defense Minister had offered condolences; and the Interior Minister apologized and offered to cooperate in an investigation.

When Newt Gingrich called Obama's apology "astonishing" and an "outrage," and Rick Santorum complained that it showed weakness, the *Los Angeles Times* criticized their "shameless[]" behavior. Apologizing was not only "the decent thing to do but … may have prevented an even worse backlash than the one that has cost four American lives so far." The *New York Times* found it "unfathomable" that after a decade in Afghanistan some US troops did not know that "Muslims consider destruction of the holy book blasphemous." But it urged Karzai to remind Afghans who engaged in "violent rampages" about "the horrors of Taliban repression and the high price Americans have paid defending them."

Continuing massive protests in Kunduz, Herat, and Laghman Provinces led to more deaths and injuries. At least six US military were wounded in northern Afghanistan. Calling it retaliation for the burning, the Taliban claimed responsibility for a suicide bomb killing at least nine at the Jalalabad airport and another at Parwan killing two children. A civilian teaching Afghan army literacy courses and an ANA soldier killed two Americans and wounded a third in Kandahar before being shot dead. The UN Secretary General's special representative in Afghanistan said the UN "rejected and condemned" the burnings. "It doesn't matter that it was a mistake." "[T]here must be a second step … of disciplinary action."

The AR 15–6 inquiry found that two Afghan interpreters, who had been asked to identify prison library books that might be a security risk, selected 1,652, including Korans and other religious texts containing handwritten notes. A US military official explained: "we overly rely around here on linguists." But the Ulema Council and a member of parliament said the notes were just detainees' "memories of their imprisonment" and translations from Arabic into Pashto or Dari. Because the prison lacked storage capacity, it decided to burn the books. After meeting with Karzai, the Ulema Council called the act "unforgivable" and "antihuman," declaring that "this evil action cannot be forgiven by apologizing. The personnel of the mentioned crime should be put on a public trial as soon as possible." The clerics also blamed "the illegal management of the prison," urging the USA to hand over all prisons to the Afghan government. A spokesman said Karzai "has requested from U.S. officials ... a trial and punishment." Ambassador Crocker and Gen. Allen. proposed to transfer all detention centers in six months, but Karzai demanded immediate transfer and an end to night raids. At this explosive moment, SSgt. Robert Bales massacred 16 Afghans near Kandahar (discussed in Chapter 3 on courts-martial in the companion volume *Law's Trials*). Afterwards, Karzai again denounced the Koran burnings as "satanic acts that will never be forgiven by apologies." The Ulema Council also called them a "satanic act," "unforgivable, wild and inhuman." The protests causing 29 Afghan and 6 American deaths expressed "justifiable emotions."

After emotions subsided, Afghanistan resumed negotiations for a strategic partnership agreement with the USA[143] When signed in April 2012, it required that all "special operations" (except those by the CIA) be reviewed and approved by a panel including NDS and the Defense and Interior Ministries. An Afghan court had to issue a warrant within 72 hours of the raid, but could do so after the raid when intelligence required immediate action. Afghans would lead house searches but could invite US forces to join them. Raids still relied heavily on US intelligence, and the two countries disagreed about whether the USA could temporarily detain and interrogate those captured.

Days later the *Los Angeles Times* exposed a two-year-old incident.[144] In February 2010 grinning US soldiers posed for photos while holding the severed legs of a suicide bomber. A few months later the platoon did this again, holding a dead man's hand with a raised middle finger and putting the platoon's patch next to other remains. A soldier from the platoon had given 18 photos to the *Times*, which published the two least inflammatory ones over objections by the military. Denouncing the "disgusting act" and warning that "similar incidents of an odious nature" had provoked violent responses, Karzai sought "accelerated and full transition of security responsibilities to Afghan forces." DoD opened an investigation. Defense Secretary Panetta "strongly condemned" the incident, telling troops at Fort Benning, Georgia, that the actions of a few soldiers who "lack judgment, lack professionalism, lack leadership" could have huge consequences. The same day JCS chairman Dempsey said "we have to reconnect leader to led, and hold leaders accountable at every level." Gen. Amos, Marine Corps commandant, wrote all officers that it was imperative to stop such episodes. Gen. Odierno, Army chief of staff, also spoke to officers and noncommissioned officers about discipline. Andrew Bacevich wrote a *Washington Post* op ed, listing other acts of "barbarism" and deploring the lack of "command accountability."

More than a dozen times in April and May Afghan commanders refused to conduct night raids for fear of civilian casualties, delaying attacks until civilians (and presumably Taliban) had left.[145] Karzai had told Interior Ministry officials: "if you have any doubt about an American intelligence report, do not conduct any operation based on it." But air strikes in May and June continued to kill civilians: 14 in Baghdis Province, a family of 6 in Helmand Province, a family of 8 in Paktia Province, 18 in Logar Province (half of them children). In the last incident Taliban stayed overnight in a house celebrating a marriage. When a joint NATO–Afghan contingent surrounded it, the Afghans called on civilians to leave, but the Taliban prevented them. After taking fire, the NATO–Afghan force called in an air strike. The US military spokesman (who had seen a video of the operation) said: "as an infantryman myself, I will tell you that [NATO forces] backed off, they tried every measure, they tried call-out, they did the proper steps in trying to clear the building and were repelled back by insurgent fire." However, a member of the delegation Karzai sent to investigate said the air strike "was not acceptable at all" because, though he could see a man firing from the roof of the house in the video, "you could also see women and children clearly."

Gen. Allen told the Logar provincial governor: "I wanted to come immediately to see you after this tragedy and to offer you, personally, my apologies, my condolences and my regrets." He said to victims' relatives and local officials: "I know no apology can bring back the lives of the children or the people who perished in this tragedy, and this accident, but I want you to know that you have my apology and we will do the right thing by the families." The governor replied: "we are accepting his apology, but the people who did this … should be punished." Local residents agreed. After an Afghan investigation, Karzai concluded that US troops had called in the air strike without waiting for Afghan units surrounding the house to flush out the Taliban. This was the fifth instance of civilian casualties inflicted by unilateral US action since the memorandum of understanding (MOU) that had been signed earlier that spring. Karzai said "the expectation of the Afghan government and the Afghan people was that a new page would open between Afghanistan and the United States." He would view further violations as breaking the agreement and treat US troops as part of an "occupation."

NATO agreed that "given our commitment to protect Afghan civilians, restricting the use of air-delivered munitions against insurgents within civilian dwellings is a prudent and logical step in the progression in the campaign." But Gen. Allen insisted: "that doesn't obviate our inherent right to self-defense. We will always … do whatever we have to do to protect the force." Only 32 of the more than 1,300 air strikes in 2012 damaged civilian dwellings, and just five caused civilian deaths. NATO had inflicted 124 civilian casualties in the first five months of 2012, compared with 256 during that period the previous year. Within days, however, Karzai declared: "an agreement has been reached clearly with NATO that no bombardment of civilian homes is allowed for any reason … even when [coalition forces] are under attack." Such strikes were "an absolutely disproportionate use of force and an illegitimate use of force."

> There are police operations every day in the United States in various localities. They don't call in airplanes to bomb those places. There was a police action in Toulouse, when they were going to neutralize the terrorist … they didn't call the French air force to bomb the house … airstrikes are not used in civilian areas. If they don't want to do it in their own country, why do they do it in Afghanistan?

DoD promised "a more serious effort to use other means." Gen. Allen "agreed that we would not apply air fire to civilian dwellings," but again insisted on the right of self-defense. Karzai, however, said air strikes were "just completely banned. Absolutely banned. Absolutely."

At the end of August the US military issued letters of reprimand to the three soldiers involved in the Koran-burning incident, finding they had acted without "malicious intent" but failed to follow proper procedures, did not receive clear guidance from leaders, and were ignorant of the Koran's importance.[146] It also imposed nonjudicial punishments on the three noncommissioned officers who pleaded guilty to urinating on corpses, recording the video, and making a false statement. A month later it court-martialed two staff sergeants involved, who pleaded guilty and were reduced in rank. In February 2013 a sergeant and a captain were court-martialed. SSgt. Chamblin, who had pleaded guilty to dereliction of duty and wrongfully urinating on a body, was reduced in rank and given a $500 fine. He had sought "revenge" for a buddy killed by an IED and expressed no regrets. "Now these insurgents see what happens when you mess with us." "Do you want the Marine Corps to be a group of boy scout pretty boys or do you want guys that will go out there and kill the people that are trying to take advantage of your country and kill Americans?" In October a panel recommended that Capt. Clement be discharged for substandard performance in the urination incident. But the military dismissed the charges shortly before Clement's lawyer, Maj. Weirick, was to testify about alleged misconduct in the case, including improper classification of material potentially helpful to the defense. John Fitzpatrick, director of the US Information Security Oversight Office, was investigating Weirick's complaint about classification after Rep. Walter Jones (R-NC) complained to Fitzpatrick that "this corruption, at the highest level of the USMC [US Marine Corps], is unlike anything I have witnessed in my 20 years in Congress." Fitzpatrick rejected the complaint because disseminating the photos could encourage attacks on troops.

Coalition forces continued to kill civilians.[147] In Urozgan Province in September, Australian soldiers killed a 70-year-old man and his 30-year-old son (whom the USA called "military-aged" insurgents); ISAF said the provincial government had approved the raid, which involved Afghan forces. NATO forces killed eight women collecting firewood in Laghman Province during a 2 a.m. firefight with insurgents. ISAF killed three children collecting dung for fuel and claimed they might have been planting IEDs. In a firefight with the Taliban, ISAF killed four children grazing sheep and goats in Logar Province.

UNAMA reported that air strikes in 2012 had killed 126 civilians and wounded 78, 42 percent less than the previous year.[148] Civilian casualties from search operations also continued to decline to 54 deaths and 21 injuries, 33 percent less than the previous year, partly because Afghan forces had begun leading such operations in July. There also was a 26 percent decrease in civilian casualties from escalation of force incidents, leading to 14 deaths and 35 injuries. Many were attributed to Afghan National Security Forces; those involving ISAF fell from 15 to 5, partly because it adopted a new SOP.

Negotiations for a Bilateral Security Agreement (BSA) governing US forces after 2014 stalled over the question of immunity.[149] Karzai said he was "willing to go to the Afghan people … and argue for" immunity if the USA handed over all detainees, shut its prisons, surrendered control over Afghan airspace, and ended raids on villages.

A February 2013 NATO air strike in Kunar Province hit two houses, killing four women, five children, and a man, and wounding four teenagers, three of them girls.[150] The provincial governor said he had not been informed of the mission, which was not coordinated with Afghan security forces. But Karzai said Gen. Dunford had expressed condolences and said the strike had been requested by NDS. Asking an audience at the Afghan National Military Academy "how do you call for an air strike from foreigners on your own people," Karzai forbade such actions. A month later a NATO helicopter shot and killed two 11- and 12-year-old brothers gathering firewood with donkeys in Urozgan Province. Gen. Dunford again apologized to Karzai. The UN Committee on the Rights of the Child said the USA had killed hundreds of children over the previous four years through the "lack of precautionary measures and indiscriminate use of force."

After villagers in Wardak Province complained of being tortured by US Special Forces, Karzai ordered them to leave the province within two weeks.[151] A February 13 raid detained a veterinary student, whose "dead body was found three days later in the area under a bridge." Nine men had disappeared after an earlier raid. Sixty tribal leaders were detained by US Special Forces and "Afghan Special Forces," taken to a base, and beaten. Afghan officials had given ISAF photos and videos of the principal suspects – Afghan American translators wearing ANA commando uniforms – but ISAF maintained those men had disappeared or never worked for them. Karzai initially said "our Afghan people are not safe in their houses" because of Afghan troops. "Why should I blame foreigners?" But a few days later he canceled a joint news conference with US officials, denouncing both Special Forces and US control over detainees. Claiming that an engineering student in Kandahar had been badly abused at a US prison after being detained by Afghan forces backed by the CIA, Karzai asked the Agency to hand over the Afghans who had conducted the arrest and interrogation.

After Karzai's deadline for withdrawing Special Forces from Wardak passed, Gen. Dunford said plans for the transition were evolving "in a responsible, deliberate way." The next day, however, an Afghan police officer opened fire on US Special Forces and their Afghan counterparts, killing two Americans. Several days later Dunford noted that Karzai "has not issued a directive to the [US] force, and he realizes that we're working this as quickly as we can." But the Ulema Council said the USA had to withdraw Special Forces from Wardak and transfer Bagram Prison to Afghanistan or it "will be considered as an occupation." "As the Koran says: almighty Allah has never paved the road for infidels to rule and govern Muslims." A demonstration in Wardak involved 300 people, including relatives holding photos of the disappeared. Dunford said Karzai and he had come to an agreement, and Special Forces began to withdraw from Wardak at the end of March.

Air strikes in March and April continued to kill civilians: five in Nangarhar, two children, and then four police and two civilians in Ghazni Province.[152] An air strike in Kunar Province killed a commander and 6 other alleged Taliban, but also 12 children, 4 women, and a man. The CIA admitted that one agent had been killed and three others seriously wounded. But after the US military said the operation had been directed by the NDS, Karzai fired its head in Kunar. Another air strike in Kunar Province in June killed two women and a child, although NATO denied this. A third air strike in Kunar Province in September killed eight women and children; ISAF initially said ten "enemy forces" had died, but agreed to investigate. Karzai denounced the attack as "against all internationally agreed principles."

The USA and Afghanistan still had not concluded the BSA in October, partly because of Afghan anger at unilateral US military operations.[153] Karzai's spokesman said "killing people in homes and killing people in villages is bringing the war on terror to Afghans." "After 2014 will any foreign military be free to go where it pleases and operate the way it pleases in Afghanistan? The answer is no." A few days later Karzai said: "they want us to keep silent when civilians are killed. We will not, we cannot." "The worsening of relations began in 2005 where we saw the first incidents of civilian casualties … the U.S. and NATO forces were conducting operations in Afghan villages, causing harm to Afghan people." As the two sides approached agreement, Karzai said immunity for US troops would be decided by the loya jirga. Secretary of State Kerry assured him that US forces would not conduct any unilateral operations after 2013. Although the US military wanted to be able to enter homes "on extraordinary occasions," Karzai refused: "if that is needed, show us your intelligence and we will go in alone." But the USA was reluctant to share intelligence with Afghans.

Aimal Faizi, Karzai's spokesman, said Kerry had phoned on November 19, offering to write a letter acknowledging military errors. Karzai offered to drop his opposition to US raids on homes if Obama signed it. National Security Adviser Susan Rice said: "there is not a need for the United States to apologize to Afghanistan. Quite the contrary." But the White House Press Secretary said Obama would express "regret" for civilian deaths. The draft agreement gave US military personnel immunity from prosecution. But where Afghanistan had proposed that "no detention or arrest shall be carried out by United States forces. The United States forces shall not search any homes," the agreement now said Afghans would take the lead, but US operations would "complement and support them" and show "full respect for Afghan sovereignty and full regard for the safety and security of the Afghan people, including in their homes." "U.S. forces shall not enter Afghan homes for the purposes of military operations except under extraordinary circumstances involving urgent risk to life and limb of U.S. nationals."

Karzai postponed signing the BSA. In the middle of the loya jirga he said the governor of Nangarhar Province had reported that "U.S. Special Forces raided a house of twin brothers … martyring both," a mason and a plumber. An ISAF spokesman replied they had killed "two armed insurgents after being fired upon." Furthermore, the operation "was Afghan-led with 100 Afghan national security force personnel and 17 coalition advisers." But Afghan officials maintained the raid was conducted by US Special Forces, and the only Afghans present were US employees or mercenaries. Faizi said Karzai was seeking additional "guarantees" that US forces would not enter Afghan homes and would nullify the BSA if there was one more raid. Karzai told the loya jirga: "from this moment on, America's searching of houses, blocking of roads and streets, military operations are over, and our people are free in their country." The White House called the latest draft its "final offer." If it were not adopted by the end of the year, it "would be impossible for the United States and our allies to plan for a presence post-2014." The chair of the loya jirga, which had approved the BSA, urged Karzai to sign it. But the president replied: "on your behalf we will try to bargain more with the Americans … give me a chance to do politics and don't give this agreement for free to the Americans." After Rice threatened a complete and final withdrawal by the end of 2014, Karzai said he would sign the BSA only if the USA released all Guantánamo Bay detainees. During a dinner with Rice, he expressed "very strong and intense" anger at Ambassador Cunningham, who had insisted Guantánamo detainees were unrelated to the BSA. Rice declared the USA had ended negotiations and would terminate all Western aid, including $4 billion for the military and another $4 billion for economic development.

A few days later Gen. Dunford called Karzai, conceded that a drone strike had killed and wounded civilians, "expressed deep regrets for the incident and any civilian casualties, and promised to convene an immediate joint investigation."[154] One of two strikes in Helmand Province missed the target, killing a child and severely wounding two women.

Karzai now demanded the BSA also ban drone strikes. "This attack shows that American forces do not respect the lives and security of the people of Afghanistan and the loya jirga." "There will be no security agreement between Kabul and Washington, if these unilateral military operations by arrogant and oppressive foreign troops on our people continue." His Defense Minister warned that the "entire cabinet is against him on this." But Faizi retorted:

> President Obama assured President Karzai that the U.S. will "make every effort to respect the sanctity and dignity of Afghans in their homes and in their daily lives, JUST AS WE DO FOR OUR OWN CITIZENS." That is how the U.S. respects the sanctity and dignity of homes in the U.S., bombing a residence for an individual? [original emphasis]

Kerry warned a NATO conference "this is not fooling around. This is serious business." Budget cycles required ISAF's 50 members to plan now for equipment and deployment. NATO Secretary General Rasmussen agreed. In a *New York Times* op ed Gen. Allen (a former commander of coalition forces in Afghanistan) and Michael O'Hanlon (Brookings Institution director of research) urged the USA to "ignore Karzai's arrogant insults." In a *Washington Post* op ed John Podesta (Clinton's chief of staff) and two members of the Center for American Progress (which Podesta directed) condemned Karzai's "manufactured crisis." SASC chair Levin said the USA should wait and sign the BSA with Karzai's successor, who was "likely to be more reliable." Defense Secretary Hagel visited Afghanistan but met only the Defense Minister, who said the agreement "would be signed … in a very timely manner." Karzai denounced the USA for "absolutely" acting like a colonial power by threatening that "we won't pay salaries, we'll drive you into a civil war." Abdullah Abdullah, who had run for president in 2009 and planned to do so in 2014, accused Karzai of "wasting the time of the nation." The Acting Director of the Afghan Chamber of Commerce and Industries said: "if the B.S.A. is not signed, things will turn back to the dark days of the past." JCS chairman Dempsey said: "it's not our intention to reopen the text and to renegotiate that which had been already discussed." Karzai retorted: "we are not a nation known for giving into intimidation." "Afghanistan, as poor as it is, is not a country that takes threats." Ending drone strikes and raids on homes was "an absolute prerequisite." Members of the Meshrano Jirga (parliament's upper house) exhorted Karzai to sign. The longtime Iraq Foreign Minister urged Karzai to accept the deal: "don't be under the illusion that no matter what you do the Americans are here to stay." The White House press secretary said: "the negotiation is over. There are no changes that are going to be made."

Claiming that eight civilians had been killed in a drone strike in Parwan Province in January 2014, Faizi said: "this is exactly about one of our conditions about the signing" of the BSA, "but it seems like it is not understood. How many more innocent Afghans have to die so it gets the attention of U.S. officials?"[155] An Afghan investigation found that 13 civilians had been killed, including 3 women and 4 children. Insisting "the operation was requested by the Afghans and approved by the Afghans," the USA said only two civilians were killed. Karzai demanded an end to all air strikes and ground operations by foreign forces. Although the lead Afghan investigator said at least 14 civilians had been killed, the Parwan governor retorted that fewer than ten had been and denounced those claiming higher numbers as "supporters of the Taliban." Some of the photos of bodies offered by the official investigation were years old and had been posted on the Taliban website. At a briefing the next day to rebut this, one of the villagers, Alif Shah Ahmadzai, claimed to identify neighbors attending the funeral from a photo, but it had been taken four years earlier at a village hundreds of miles away. Searched by security guards before the event, Ahmadzai had about 100,000 Afghans in cash ($2,000), which he said Karzai's advisers had given him as compensation for relatives of the dead. "Do you think we lie for 100,000 Afghanis?" Karzai also blamed the USA for insurgent attacks, including one on a Lebanese restaurant in Kabul, even though the Taliban claimed credit for many of them. After Ambassador Cunningham called this "a deeply conspiratorial view that's divorced from reality," Faizi denied Karzai had said it. The *New York Times* denounced Karzai's "perfidies" and refusal to sign the BSA. In March he said he still cried about meeting a four-year-old girl who had lost half her face in the January strike. "Afghans died in a war that's not ours" but was waged "for the U.S. security and for the western interest." He "was forced to yell" to "get attention." During a 2010 visit to the White House he had showed Obama a photo of a family "just gazing with fright and fear" during a US-led night operation. "I said, 'President, this is what I'm trying to end, the intimidation of Afghan families at night.'" Because Obama's response was unsatisfactory, "we really are an angry people."

UNAMA found that drone strikes in 2013 killed 45 civilians, which was at least a third of all civilian air strike deaths and three times as many as in the previous year.[156] AI reported an investigation of civilian deaths in 2009–13 based on interviews with 125 witnesses.[157] In nine of ten incidents in which a total of at least 140 civilians died, including at least 50 children, no survivor had been interviewed by the USA, as required by international law.

On February 27, 2014 US soldiers raided Radio Paigham-e-Milli (a pro-government station supported by US military commercials) in Logar Province, ransacking the premises, damaging much of the broadcasting equipment, seizing computers and phones, and confiscating two AK-47s and an RPG (which station employees said were for defensive purposes).[158] They detained three employees, one of whom said he was beaten and threatened with death. ISAF claimed the raid was largely Afghan-led. But the Afghan Interior and Defense Ministries denied this, and local police were unaware until it was underway. The local journalists association threatened to strike. Air strikes continued to inflict casualties, killing five Afghan soldiers and wounding eight in Logar Province in March, killing a woman and two children in Khost Province in April, killing at least four civilians, including two women, in Shindand District in August, and killing 14 and wounding 13 in Kunar Province in September.

In his final address to Parliament Karzai claimed the Afghan military protected 93 percent of the country and was ready to take over, warning "foreign countries who maybe out of habit … want to interfere, that they should not interfere."[159] Obama told Karzai the 32,000 US troops in Afghanistan would be cut to 9,800 by the end of the year, half that by the end of 2015, and limited to protecting the embassy by the end of 2016. The day after being sworn in as president in September, Ashraf Ghani signed the BSA and Status of Forces Agreement (SOFA), allowing US and NATO troops to remain and immunizing US military personnel (but not contractors) from Afghan prosecution. Parliament approved the agreements 152–5. The government lifted the ban on nighttime raids by Afghan Army Special Forces (who could be accompanied by US forces). In February 2015 the police chief of Eastern Nangarhar Province said that more than 17 drone attacks in the previous two months had killed 29 militants and wounded 11 without inflicting any civilian casualties. "It is only the drones that can target the Taliban militants without posing a harm to civilians." The Kunar police chief also said drones had been effective. A spokesman for the Ministry of Defense agreed they played a "crucial role" and could "eliminate targets accurately." By contrast, fire from US helicopters in

Logar Province in July killed at least seven Afghan troops and wounded five. A similar incident in March 2014 had killed at least five Afghan troops. In September the Afghanistan Deputy Interior Minister for Counternarcotics said an air strike on an official convoy in Helmand Province had killed 11 from the agency and wounded 4.

On October 3, 2015 a US air strike on the Médecins sans frontières (MSF) hospital in Kunduz killed 12 staff and 10 patients (including 3 children) and wounded at least 37.[160] The bombing persisted for 30 minutes after MSF contacted the military, to which it had earlier given the hospital's coordinates. Obama offered condolences for "the tragic incident." Ghani expressed only "sorrow" because Gen. Campbell had apologized. Campbell opened an AR 15–6 investigation and "directed the entire force to undergo in-depth training in order to review all of our operational authorities and ROEs." After initially claiming that the strike "was conducted against insurgents who were directly firing upon U.S. service members," he conceded it was Afghans who had been threatened and called for help. Immediately after the attack the Afghan National Security Adviser told a European diplomat that Ghani had authorized him to declare that Afghanistan would take responsibility because "we are without doubt, 100 percent convinced the place was occupied by Taliban." A local member of parliament said: "I know that there were civilian casualties in the hospital, but a lot of senior Taliban were also killed." The acting provincial governor said: "the hospital campus was 100 percent used by the Taliban … We tolerated their firing for some time" before responding. The Afghan Defense Minister said the hospital "was a place [the Taliban] wanted to use as a safe place because everybody knows that our security forces and international security forces were very careful not to do anything with a hospital." "The compound was being used by people who were fighting there," and a Taliban flag was on a hospital wall. But MSF insisted "the compound was not entered by Taliban soldiers with weapons."

The UN High Commissioner for Human Rights called the strike "utterly tragic, inexcusable, and possibly even criminal." The ICRC condemned it. MSF left Kunduz "disgusted" by Afghanistan's attempt to justify the attack by the "claim that members of the Taliban were present. This amounts to an admission of a war crime." The *New York Times* called the military's initial characterization of the incident as collateral damage "outrageous and dehumanizing." Obama telephoned MSF president Dr. Joanne Liu with a rare apology, but expressed confidence in the three military investigations by the USA, NATO, and a joint

US–Afghan group. Liu repeated an earlier demand for an independent investigation, which Afghanistan rejected. MSF general director Christopher Stokes denounced the "grave violation of international humanitarian law." In a *New York Times* op ed, the executive director of MSF in the USA again sought an international investigation, because the other three "will understandably be rooted in the context of military doctrine and practice, not international humanitarian law."

A day before the air strike a senior officer in the Army Green Berets had written that the hospital was under control of insurgents and a US objective was to "clear the trauma center" of enemy forces. But MSF said that two days before the attack it had denied to the USA that "our hospital had a large group of Taliban fighters in it." A US official said it was actually an Afghan Health Ministry hospital a short distance away that had been overrun by the Taliban. A month after the attack the provincial governor was still claiming that 300 insurgents had been in the hospital, from which "they were opening fire on our soldiers." A senior Afghan official was "glad" it had been bombed because "they treated hundreds of Taliban there." The head of Afghan Police Special Forces in Kunduz insisted there were "huge numbers of Taliban inside the MSF hospital." "We gave all this information to our foreign allies. We were begging them to launch the airstrikes." The US military "indicated a willingness to do condolence payments as soon as we can when the investigations are done," but maintained these were "symbolic gestures," not an admission of guilt or "paid to compensate anyone for a loss."

CENTCOM's 3,000-page report concluded that "the personnel involved did not know they were striking a medical facility." The "tragic incident was caused by a combination of human errors, compounded by process and equipment failures." "[C]ertain personnel failed to comply with the rules of engagement and the law of armed conflict," but this was not a war crime. There had been inadequate briefing for an emergency air strike that took off 69 minutes early, lacking video and electronic messages because the satellite radio failed, and diverging from its flight path to avoid a missile. The targeting system became misaligned and had the wrong coordinates; the hospital roughly matched a visual description of the intended target; and even after the targeting system was fixed and correctly aligned with the intended target, the crew still focused on the hospital. Minutes before firing, the crew told Bagram airfield headquarters the target's coordinates; but though officials there had a no-strike list showing those coordinates, they did not connect that with the information from the crew. Although MSF contacted US officials 11 minutes into the strike, it continued for another 19 minutes because information had to pass through several layers to get to military officials on the ground, and even then they did not immediately stop the strike. Of the 16 service members involved, 12 (including the general officer) received suspensions, removals from command, letters of reprimand, formal counseling, and retraining. The five directed out of theater got letters of reprimand and admonishment. Condolence payments were made to more than 170 people, and $5.7 million was approved to rebuild the MSF facility. Complaining that "the U.S. version of events presented today leaves M.S.F. with more questions than answers," the group delivered a petition with 545,000 signatures to the White House calling for an independent investigation and raised the death toll to 14 staff, 24 patients and 4 patients' relatives. The MSF President called the report "an admission of an uncontrolled military operation in a densely populated urban area, during which U.S. forces failed to follow the basic rules of law."

Gen. Nicholson, the new commander of US and NATO forces in Afghanistan, went to Kunduz to "stand before the families and people of Kunduz, to deeply apologize for the events" that led to the bombing and "humbly and respectfully ask for your forgiveness." But the *New York Times* complained that "after more than six months, the Pentagon has yet to fully explain what went wrong." The $6,000 for each of the dead and $3,000 to each of the wounded were "insulting," an "utterly inadequate recompense for the lives and livelihoods lost in one of the most monumental mistakes of the recent wars." "Taking stock of the needs of the survivors and coming up with a reasonable plan to help them rebuild their lives could have been done in a matter of days." Nicholson's apology "should have come months earlier." "A callous response to a blunder of the magnitude of the Kunduz attack is unjustifiable and entirely avoidable." The latest briefing disclosed that a "torrent of mistakes" had "resulted from gross negligence." The military made the "ridiculous" claim it could not disclose the identities of those found culpable and their punishments out of concern for their privacy and because some were still deployed. The decision not to prosecute was "deeply troubling." "Under the American military code and international laws of war, fatal mistakes that result from recklessness and gross negligence can constitute crimes." Eugene Fidell wrote in a *New York Times* op ed that the military could have convened a court of inquiry, which "would have fostered greater confidence in the results." It could have charged reckless destruction of property, reckless or wanton operation of aircraft, murder, manslaughter, or dereliction of duty.

Matthieu Aikins, an investigative reporter, offered evidence in the *New York Times* that Afghan forces had deliberately encouraged the air strike (strengthening suspicions raised by comments made immediately afterwards, quoted above).[161] Col. Abdullah Gard, head of the Kunduz police quick-reaction force, had complained to Aikins in November that MSF staff "give [Taliban] medicine, they transport and treat their injured. Their existence is a big problem for us." "All their most important leaders were inside the hospital, especially Tajiks, Uzbeks and high-ranking Pakistanis. They had raised their flag and established their headquarters there." Yaftali, commander of the Afghan Army's Special Operations Force (KKA), said his unit had picked up Taliban transmissions from inside the hospital. "We located about 10 to 15 radios from there. The Taliban were inside and outside the hospital." "They were firing R.P.G.s at us from the direction of the hospital." A provincial council member said: "the general perception was that M.S.F. supported the Taliban." A Green Beret who participated in the fighting wrote afterwards: "There were enemy in there." Taliban "were using it as a [command and control] node. They had already removed and ransomed the foreign doctors, and they had fired on partnered personnel from there." The previous July Afghan police commandos, believing abu Huzaifa (a Taliban commander) had been wounded and taken to the MSF hospital, forced their way inside, assaulted staff, and fired weapons in the air. MSF closed admissions for five days until the Afghan government provided assurances hospitals would be respected. Gard, whose commandos had participated in the hospital invasion, said MSF "hid [abu Huzaifa]. The people who work there are traitors, all of them." The US military treated the Afghan commandos as Persons With Designated Special Status, bringing them inside the alleged claim of "self-defense." Maj. Hutchinson, commander of the 1st Battalion, 3rd Special Forces Group, used this designation to launch offensive "pre-assault fire." The special status designation obviated the need for anyone other than him or the aircraft commander to approve firing. Hutchinson was relieved of his command and reprimanded, but then appointed as his battalion's executive officer.

Disputes about casualties continued under Ghani. In April a drone hit a truck in Paktika Province, killing an anti-Taliban local elder on his way to mediate a land dispute, together with four bodyguards and seven others.[162] A second strike killed two who went to pick up the bodies; and a third killed three who had climbed a hill to see what had happened. The District Governor said the dead were civilians; the provincial police chief said they were Taliban; and the Afghan Defense Minister said they were al-Qaeda. The USA said: "there was no evidence to indicate that there were any civilian casualties at all." In September 2016 an air strike hit a home in Achin District, Nangarhar Province, where a group had assembled to welcome home a tribal leader from the haj, killing 13 and wounding another 12; there was disagreement about whether any ISIS supporters were among them.[163] In an October battle to recapture Kunduz, a NATO air strike killed civilians, estimated at 26 by the media but at over a hundred by local government officials, prompting a denunciation by former president Karzai.[164] An operation the following month killed 33 civilians and wounded 27.[165] But because the Taliban "were using civilian houses as firing positions," the USA paid no compensation. In April 2017 a US air strike killed at least nine civilians: an elderly couple, their daughter-in-law, and six grandchildren.[166] A week later it dropped its largest conventional bomb on ISIS caves. Calling Ghani an "accomplice" and "traitor," Karzai condemned the "brutal misuse of our country as testing ground for new and dangerous weapons." In August air strikes killed more than a dozen civilians in Shindand District and a dozen in Logar Province.[167] US forces dropped nearly 70 percent more bombs and other ordnance in the first six months of 2017 compared with the previous year.

Analysis

The killing or wounding of Afghans and insults to Islam, committed by the US military, provoked fierce anger. Despite the many differences among these myriad incidents, responses tended to follow a common trajectory: public outcry, uncertainty about who killed or injured whom and under what circumstances, a promise to investigate, an apology, derisively low compensation, and no clear resolution.

The first US response typically was denial: there had been no civilian casualties or far fewer than alleged; the victims were not civilians but Taliban, or at least MAMs (military age males – an age group that encompassed everyone from pre-teens to the elderly). The fallback was justification: US forces had responded proportionately to a threat: drivers failed to stop at roadblocks; victims had been armed (most Afghan men carried guns for protection, given endemic violence and inadequate policing); intelligence had been flawed, often concocted by Afghans pursuing a grudge. The US constantly boasted it did more to avoid civilian casualties than any country had done in any war.

The USA also blamed the Taliban for hiding among and thereby endangering civilians in order to hinder the coalition response and fabricating or inflating civilian casualties to inflame Afghan anger at Americans. There was evidence for some of those charges. The USA noted – accurately – that the Taliban inflicted four or five times as many civilian casualties as did coalition forces, often intentionally, and never apologized. But it was clear that injuries caused by forces viewed as infidel foreign invaders provoked far greater resentment. True, this civil war (like all others) bred bitter animosities. But unlike Americans, the Taliban could communicate with their Afghan adversaries, who were fellow Muslims and would remain (and quite possibly rule) after the inevitable American departure. This may also explain why more serious abuses committed by Afghan police seemed to spark less anger than lesser accidental harms inflicted by Americans.

Despite their impotence, or perhaps because of it, Afghans regularly resorted to direct action. They carried victims' bodies to the nearest Afghan government headquarters to prove that innocent civilians had died and let their wounds cry out for vengeance. But these expressive acts produced no result. Although the USA invariably promised to investigate, the process rarely satisfied victims or the Afghan government. It dragged on for weeks, months, even years. Evidence was ambiguous and contradictory, and Americans lacked the linguistic skills and cultural knowledge to acquire or interpret it. Site visits often seemed too dangerous. Forensic evidence either was never collected or was lost. Islam mandated that bodies be buried quickly and neither exhumed nor autopsied. Afghans (sometimes accurately) accused Americans of destroying incriminating evidence by removing bullets from bodies. The USA disregarded or rejected the more exhaustive investigations conducted by entities like the AIHRC.

As the British often intone, justice must not only be done but must also be seen to be done. Afghans wanted to confront the alleged perpetrators, but the USA failed to identify them or hastily spirited them out of the country. Afghans wanted suspects tried by Islamic law in Afghan criminal courts and subject to the death penalty; but SOFA immunized the US military from prosecution by the Afghan legal system. In the rare instances when US military justice took its halting invisible course, the accused were exonerated or received derisory punishment after secret administrative proceedings. The inadequacy of these investigations and prosecutions contrasted sharply with the much faster, more thorough, transparent response to friendly fire incidents or alleged errors leading to the deaths of US troops.

Although American officials often apologized personally, promptly, and profusely, superiors sometimes reprimanded subordinates for doing so prematurely and repudiated their actions: e.g., Marines criticizing the Army following the Nangarhar killings; Chancellor Merkel rebuking Gen. McChrystal following the German bombing of the hijacked oil tankers. Apologies may have salved the honor of victims and their families, but many dismissed apologies without punishment as meaningless.

The USA readily offered compensation. From the American perspective, the few thousand dollars paid to the injured or victims' kin were a trivial expense, especially given the hundreds of billions lavished on the war. For most Afghans, by contrast, such payments were an extraordinary windfall, many times their annual incomes. But accepting solatia also threatened to trivialize the harm suffered, vividly demonstrating that Afghan lives were cheap, while strengthening US accusations that greedy Afghans exaggerated the number killed or injured.

As these tragedies recurred with numbing frequency, it took something distinctive to generate outrage: an unusual number killed or injured; victims who were women, children, elderly, or relations of Afghan officials; seeming indifference to civilian safety; and especially willful or gratuitous violence or offense (echoing the Abu Ghraib travesty). Americans could not understand why burning Korans provoked more intense anger than killing dozens of innocent civilians. (In 2017 a US propaganda leaflet showing a lion, representing the Coalition, chasing a dog – seen as dirty in Islam – wrapped in a Taliban flag provoked a revenge suicide attack.)[168] Afghans persisted in attributing malice to the perpetrators (perhaps influenced by the antics of the publicity-seeking Florida pastor who threatened to burn the Koran), whereas they were prepared to accept some civilian casualties as unintentional. Knowing this, the Taliban ruthlessly exploited the burning. Similarly, urinating on or desecrating Taliban bodies or body parts could only be intended to offend – and succeeded brilliantly, even with Afghans nominally loyal to the regime. The repeated outcry by Afghans (and other Muslims) that religion meant more to them than life itself may help to explain the muted reaction to SSgt. Bales's massacre of 16 civilians.

Karzai and other Afghan politicians angrily denounced civilian casualties, making bold but empty threats against the USA and

NATO. Karzai's fiery rhetoric echoed Lear's piteous outcry after being humiliated by his two older daughters: "I will do such things – what they are yet I know not, but they shall be the terrors of the earth."[169] But Karzai shared that foolish king's impotence. The upper house of parliament ordered ISAF to cease military operations unless they were attacked or had previously consulted with Afghan authorities; and it set a unilateral timetable for foreign troops to withdraw. Karzai prohibited Afghan forces from calling in US air strikes. The real audience for these pronouncements, however, was not the USA – which angrily denounced Afghan ingratitude for its allies' economic and human sacrifices and simply disregarded the demands – but domestic opponents who reviled Karzai as an American lackey. As a nuclear power and essential conduit for materiel shipments to Afghanistan, Pakistan wielded considerable leverage in opposing drone attacks. Afghanistan, by contrast, was totally dependent on the USA; even negotiations over the strategic partnership agreement were little more than a charade. Other organizations denounced civilian casualties: the UN, HRW, AIHRC, and EU. Even Russia cynically sought a propaganda advantage, despite its own brutal conquest and occupation of Afghanistan. But these criticisms had no visible effect.

Strategic considerations may have been more influential than international law (especially since the USA insisted it was compliant). Afghans, human rights advocates, and eventually US military officials like Gen. McChrystal argued that night raids on homes and air strikes recruited more insurgents than they captured or killed. Major tragedies sometimes influenced the USA to modify policies. But the net impact of such policy shifts was unclear. The USA reduced air strikes – limiting them to force protection – when the surge increased boots on the ground. But this augmented the number of civilian casualties inflicted by gun battles. When pressured to curtail the latter by requiring that the Afghans lead attacks and restricting the use of lethal force, the USA once again asserted its unchallenged control of the sky, deploying both piloted and unmanned aircraft. Efforts to reduce civilian casualties were condemned for endangering US troops. Green-on-blue killings (attacks on coalition forces by Afghan forces) increased suspicion of Afghan "allies," provoking more blue-on-green killing. It was easier to modify ROEs for air strikes (which did not endanger US pilots) than for ground battles (where restraint increased the risk to American troops). The Afghans demanded control over night raids and air strikes in order to assert sovereignty, as well as reduce civilian casualties. But the USA resisted sharing intelligence with the Afghans or giving them advance notice of operations for fear of leaks to the Taliban. Even the strategic partnership agreement had little effect. It required that a court order be sought within 72 hours of a raid (not the 48 Afghans wanted), but this could be obtained retroactively (and, like a FISC eavesdropping warrant, was unlikely to be denied). Afghans conducted home searches – but based on American intelligence. Afghans interrogated suspects – but posed questions drafted by the USA. Gen. Dunford withdrew Special Forces from one district but not the entire province, as Karzai had demanded. As US military ended night raids in response to Karzai's demands, these operations were conducted by even-less-constrained Afghan militias directed by Special Operations forces and the CIA.

The quantity and quality of scrutiny devoted to Pat Tillman's death contrasted sharply with the casual, callous response to Afghan deaths. As always, the cover-up (for which there could be no justification) attracted greater attention and provoked more anger than the friendly fire itself (which could be blamed on the fog of war). The military conducted its own investigation. The media (especially the *New York Times*) refused to let the matter drop; the NFL agitated. There was a documentary film. Tillman's parents were indefatigable and effective advocates; his mother wrote a book. They mobilized members of Congress to insist on hearings, leading to two more military investigations, by the DoD IG and CIC. But amnesia conveniently obstructed a full accounting; and the White House withheld suspicious emails and restricted official testimony. Although officers were found to have committed misconduct in both causing and investigating the death, punishment was mild, and the highest ranks were not held responsible. Although McChrystal made inaccurate and misleading assertions in his Silver Star recommendation, he was found to have behaved reasonably in relying on the supporting material provided. But embarrassment about the response to Tillman's death may have accelerated the investigation of Linda Norgrove's.

Iraq

Military Detention

In September 2006 the USA held an estimated 13,000 prisoners in Iraq, whose detention was approved by the Combined Review and Release Board (CRRB) in secret hearings without granting them legal representation.[170] Prominent Iraqis could secure their freedom.[171] The USA released and apologized to Amar Abdul Aziz al-Hakim, who had been arrested on his return from Iran with seven AK-47s, 14 pistols, and more than $6,000 in currency. His father was one of the most powerful Shiite leaders, and thousands protested throughout Iraq. He complained afterwards on television that a soldier had "kicked me violently against the wall ... handcuffed me ... [and] bound my eyes." President Talabani sharply criticized the detention.

Americans were mistreated far less often by their own military than were Iraqis and were more likely to obtain relief from legal remedies. Cyrus Kar – a dual US–Iranian citizen visiting Iraq to make a documentary film about his namesake King Cyrus the Great – was detained in May 2005 when a search of his taxi found "a large number of washing machine timers, a device frequently used to make improvised explosive devices."[172] An MI interrogator told him: "You're in big trouble. You're an American terrorist enemy combatant. You're the next John Walker Lindh" (a US citizen captured as an enemy combatant during the war in Afghanistan). Guards in Abu Ghraib cursed him, and a soldier smashed his face into a cinder block wall. The FBI said he was entitled to a lawyer, but "the last guy who requested one is still waiting two years later, in Afghanistan." A month later FBI agents returned items they seized from his Los Angeles apartment and told relatives: "he's cleared." After being held in solitary for 54 days, he was released two days before a hearing on the habeas petition filed for him by the ACLU. The US military in Iraq claimed: "this case highlights the effectiveness of our detainee review process." The DoD spokesman said defensively: "these are serious matters of life and death, and there's a process – which takes some time – to gather all the information." Numan Adnan al-Kaby, an Iraqi-born US resident, was arrested in Baghdad in April 2005 after a mortar attack on US forces.[173] In July the CRRB found him uninvolved and recommended his release; but claiming it had received additional information, the military detained him until September, two days after a habeas petition was filed.

Iraqi Journalists

Iraqi journalists suffered far worse: 23 had been killed by US forces and insurgents in 2004 and another 15 in the first nine months of 2005.[174] The CPJ called Iraq "the most dangerous place in the world to work." US soldiers killed Reuters television soundman Waleed Khaled, claiming he was driving suspiciously, and wounded and detained another cameraman. They shot Abdul Ameer Younis Hussein, an Iraqi cameraman for CBS News filming the aftermath of a suicide bombing in Mosul, and arrested him in hospital, claiming he had tested positive for explosive residue and had "knowledge of future terrorist attacks." Just before he was scheduled to go before the CRRB, he was transferred to the Iraqi Central Criminal Court; but when Iraq declined to prosecute, his case was returned to the Board, which still had not heard it five months after his arrest. CBS had spent tens of thousands of dollars on his behalf, but was denied access to him, his medical records, and the film he shot. The Iraqi Minister of Justice criticized US detentions of Iraqi journalists and urged an end to the immunity of US troops from prosecution under Iraqi law. Hussein was still in prison a year later, having spent most of the time in solitary. The USA held AP photographer Bilal Hussein for five months, accusing him of "close relationships with persons known to be responsible for kidnappings, smuggling, improvised explosive device attacks."[175] AP President Tom Curley wrote the *New York Times* that the military "has shown us no evidence … and given us no chance to refute the evidence it claims to have." Although the military conducted what it called three "independent, objective reviews," Hussein was not allowed a lawyer at any of them. The USA detained Reuters cameraman Ibrahim Jassam in September 2008. Although an Iraqi court ordered his release in November for lack of evidence, the USA continued to hold him a year after his capture.[176] The 2009 SOFA required the USA to release "low threat" detainees in a "safe and orderly" manner and refer "high threat" cases to the Iraqi Justice Ministry by the end of the year. Foreign journalists fared no better. After an eight-day inquest into the shooting death of British journalist Terry Lloyd, Oxfordshire Deputy Coroner Andrew Walker found there was "no doubt" that the US military had committed "an unlawful act."[177] The USA refused to let troops testify, and Walker excluded anonymous "self-serving statements." Lloyd's Lebanese interpreter also had been killed, and his French cameraman was missing and presumed dead.

Military Contractors

When contractors killed or injured Iraqis there was no internal discipline, no criminal prosecution by Iraq (because of immunity), and no judicially ordered compensation. Perpetrators were spirited out of Iraq, and some employers made an ex gratia payment.

Contractors played an unprecedented role in the Iraq war.[178] In December 2004 US government agencies and reconstruction firms had spent more than $766 million on contracts for security. In fall

2005 there were at least 52 licensed firms (36 foreign and 16 Iraqi) and another 50 illegal firms, with an estimated 25,000 employees. In summer 2007 the 21 private security companies in the CENTCOM database employed 10,800, but the private security industry estimated the total at three times that figure.[179] BGen. Horst, Deputy Commander of the 3rd Infantry Division responsible for security in Baghdad, complained that contractors "run loose in this country and do stupid stuff. There's no authority over them." At least a dozen shootings of civilians between May and July 2005 had killed six Iraqis and wounded three. Contractors protecting the US Embassy engaged in 122 shootings between July 2004 and September 2005, only three of which led to disciplinary measures. In May 2005 the Iraqi Deputy Interior Minister in charge of private security directed the registered companies to obey local law. After shootings that month, Horst reminded representatives of registered firms of the military philosophy: "make no new enemies." But "they don't have to think about the consequences of what they do." The next day 16 American and 3 Iraqi employees of Zapata Engineering, a North Carolina contractor, shot indiscriminately on both sides of the road as they passed Abu Ghraib (guarded by Horst's soldiers), "doing what we call 'clearing by fire.'" On July 14 Ali Ismael was shot to death in his car while driving behind a convoy of four Chevrolet Suburbans believed to belong to a US security contractor. The USA said: "the evidence clearly indicates the vehicle was fired on from the rear." But the Iraqi director of security police called this "three pages of lies to try to cover up that their company was involved." He was "1 million percent sure" that Ismael had been shot from in front.

In October 2007 in Baghdad, Unity Resources Group (URG) security guards killed two Armenian Christian women in their car, which had at least 35 bullet holes.[180] The brother of one wanted the perpetrators "punished accordingly with the Torah … 'an eye for an eye.'" Those guards had seriously wounded a man driving on the same road four months earlier. URG ended that investigation because it could not identify the victim. Its employees also had been investigated for the March 2006 killing of a 72-year-old agriculture professor whose vehicle allegedly failed to stop at a checkpoint. USAID disclaimed responsibility because it had hired RTI International, which had subcontracted with URG. In November a DynCorp guard killed an Iraqi taxi driver. But though DoS confirmed the shooting and the Interior Ministry opened an investigation, DynCorp claimed to be ignorant of any injuries.

In October 2010 the *New York Times* reported other incidents involving contractors, extracted from cables released by WikiLeaks.[181] In December 2004 Custer Battles employees fired five shots into a crowded minibus, handing out cash compensation payments though no one was hurt. In March 2005 Global employees killed a Filipino driving a cement truck for KBR. Blackwater employees killed a man driving his car and wounded his wife and daughter in May 2005, killed an Iraqi ambulance driver in May 2006, and killed an Iraqi in the backseat of a vehicle in Kirkuk in August 2006. In 2006 employees of Danubia Global killed three Iraqis in Falluja.

Just before Christmas 2006 a drunk Blackwater employee in the Green Zone killed a guard for Vice President Adel Abdul Mahdi. The Vice President angrily demanded that Ambassador Khalilzad come to his house, confronted him with the victim's family, insisted on the name of the killer and his employer, and asked that the killer be handed over. Khalilzad identified the killer as Andrew J. Moonen, but quickly spirited him out of the country and paid $20,000 compensation (the usual amount was $3,000 for accidental deaths, $5,000 for aggravated circumstances). The Assistant Secretary of State for the Bureau of Diplomatic Security (BDS) explained "there was no reason for [Moonen] to stay in Baghdad." Blackwater withheld his $13,000 bonus and made him pay his airfare home. Within weeks, however, he had been sent to Kuwait by Combat Support Associates, which said the killing had not appeared on Moonen's record. In October 2010 DoJ declined to charge him because of the problems that aborted the Nisour Square prosecution (discussed below): he had given a statement to the Regional Security Office after being promised immunity and threatened with being fired if he did not talk.

In Chapters 2 and 6 of the companion volume *Law's Trials* I deal with the criminal prosecutions and civil damage actions arising out of the September 16, 2007 Nisour Square massacre, in which Blackwater killed 17 Iraqi civilians and wounded more than 20; here I analyze other responses.[182] A DoS report (written by a *Blackwater contractor* that day and leaked ten days later) claimed the company had "returned defensive fire" and mentioned no civilian casualties. The US military investigation the same day reached the opposite conclusion: there was "no enemy activity involved" and "every indication of an excessive shooting." Dozens of US soldiers went door-to-door, offering victims condolence payments and stressing they had not been involved. (Iraq later demanded $8 million for each death; DoS offered $10–12,500, denying this was "an admission of culpability." Many families angrily rejected it.) Two days later Iraq banned the company, but it was soon back at work, and a senior adviser to Prime Minister al-Maliki admitted the government could not expel it (because DoS, unlike DoD, did not require contractors to be licensed). Secretary of State Rice phoned al-Maliki to apologize and promise an investigation. The Interior Minister called it "a big crime." The National Security Adviser sought to end immunity. Al-Maliki said "this company's activities [should] be frozen" and it "should be held accountable" for its "crime." A week later he called Blackwater "a serious challenge to the sovereignty of Iraq," which "cannot be accepted." The USA and Iraq created a joint investigating commission, but DoS warned: "you would have to have a precise set of facts in order to be able to determine the various applicable legal authorities and whether or not there were any laws that were broken." The *Los Angeles Times* said the ROE were "in need of an overhaul" and the USA should let the guards be tried in Iraq if the joint investigation found they had broken Iraqi law.

This massacre revived interest in other Blackwater shootings that year. On February 4 its guards had shot an Iraqi journalist near the Foreign Ministry. On February 7 a Blackwater sniper had shot three security guards at the government-run Iraq Media Network (IMN). An investigation by the Justice and Interior Ministries, Iraqi Police, and IMN found Blackwater responsible, but DoS concluded that the actions "fell within approved rules governing the use of force." On February 14 Blackwater guards had smashed automobile windshields. In May they had killed a person near the Interior Ministry. On September 9 they had killed five and wounded ten near the Baghdad municipal building. Three days later they severely wounded five in east Baghdad. (Even a DoS report found that Blackwater convoys fired their weapons twice as often as those of DynCorp International or Triple Canopy.) The Deputy Interior Minister deplored that there had been "no concrete results" in response to his complaints about these incidents.

The report by the Interior, National Security, and Defense Ministries (which also examined six other incidents in which Blackwater killed 10 and wounded 15) concluded that the Nisour Square massacre was "a terrorist action against civilians," and recommended that all foreign security companies be replaced by Iraqi companies (without immunity), Blackwater employees be prosecuted, and the company pay compensation.[183] The Interior Minister called Blackwater "100 percent guilty," and al-Maliki "demanded" DoS fire it. Instead, DoS resumed travel outside the Green Zone, protected by Blackwater. A spokesman for the Iraqi security forces warned that expelling the company would leave a "security gap." An investigation by the House Committee on Government Oversight and Reform identified 195 "escalation of force" incidents involving Blackwater since early 2005, but DoS prohibited the company from cooperating, and the committee did not discuss the Nisour Square killings after DoJ warned this could compromise the FBI investigation. The *New York Times* said the incident had made "the dangers of this privatized approach to the war … frighteningly clear." The *Washington Post* said CPA Order 17 "needs to be corrected" to "ensure that those who kill innocent Iraqis or engage in other criminal excesses can be held legally accountable."

Rep. Price (D–NC) and Sens. Edwards (D-NC) and Obama (D-Ill) sponsored legislation to extend the scope of the Military Extraterritorial Jurisdiction Act (MEJA) from DoD contractors (who had been included by a September 2006 law, though it was not implemented for two years) to all contractors and require FBI investigation.[184] Obama said: "This is about our claims to moral leadership in the world. We cannot win a fight for hearts and minds when we outsource critical missions to unaccountable contractors." Despite strong White House opposition, the House overwhelmingly passed the bill (389–30), which had been endorsed by the International Peace Operations Association (which included Blackwater). Applauding the legislation, the *New York Times* found it "clear" that Blackwater guards "have been allowed to run amok with no concern about being held accountable under the law." Sen. Brownback (R-Kan) asked DoS to conduct a broad investigation of contractor behavior because an action like Blackwater's "undermines the efforts of our diplomats to affirm the importance of human rights and advance our national interests."

Even though Blackwater refused access to employees or its disabled vehicles, the US military investigation found that guards had opened fire without provocation and used excessive force.[185] The Prime Minister's commission concluded that the Blackwater convoy had not been fired on "directly or indirectly." "This is a deliberate crime against civilians. It should be tried in court and the victims should be compensated." Iraq asked the USA to surrender the guards and drafted a law to make all contractors liable in Iraqi courts. "It is not a matter of compensation but rather the penalties that this company must pay for violating the law and human rights." The father of a dead 10-year-old boy rejected the compensation offered: "My father is a tribal sheik, and we're not used to taking any amount unless the concerned will come and confess and apologize." Other families concurred. Grand Ayatollah Ali al-Sistani called for sanctions against Blackwater. But DoS refused to waive immunity for contractors or share information with DoD or Iraqi investigators, and resisted DoD's request for exclusive authority over all contractors.

At the end of October Rice testified for three hours before the House Committee on Oversight and Government Reform, expressing "regret that we did not have the kind of oversight I would have insisted upon" and promising "we now will have that oversight."[186] She conceded that management of contractors had been "inadequate," but declined to "second-guess people on the ground" and did not "think that people have been either reckless nor have they been trying somehow to shield people in this circumstance." Ambassador Crocker, who had strongly defended security contractors in Congressional testimony before Nisour Square, continued to praise them: "these guys guard my back. I have to say they do it extremely well." Rep. Schakowsky (D-Ill) introduced a bill to replace armed contractors with military or BDS personnel. The Interior Minister threatened to authorize raids on security firms to check compliance with weapons licensing and declared (wrongly) that victims could sue in Iraq despite CPA Order 17. The *Los Angeles Times* criticized Rice for not acknowledging "that the State Department had been aware of that 'hole'" in MEJA "for at least two years and has rejected Pentagon suggestions to plug it by making security contractors subject to military law."

In May 2008 DoS renewed Blackwater's contract for another year without even seeking other bids.[187] The *New York Times* had "hoped the Bush administration would rethink the folly of relying on mercenaries, who have no accountability to Iraqi or American law." In response to Nisour Square, BDS created the Force Investigation Unit (FIU) to investigate security contractors' misuse of force. Although federal regulations prohibited contractors from performing "inherently governmental functions," including "the direct conduct of criminal investigations," BDS hired a private contractor to staff the FIU. Three weeks after Sen. Feingold challenged Rice about this, DoS canceled the contract. Partly because of Nisour Square, the new SOFA granted contractors no immunity after 2008. On January 23, 2009 the Interior Ministry said Blackwater had to leave the country as soon as the joint Iraqi–US committee completed guidelines for contractors. DoS awarded Triple Canopy a five-year contract starting in May;

but lacking adequate personnel, it hired some former Blackwater employees. As Blackwater's contract was about to expire in September, DoS extended it. In November the *New York Times* disclosed that in December 2007 Blackwater executives had authorized about $1 million in secret payments to Interior Ministry officials for their support after Nisour Square. The Interior Minister implausibly promised to investigate. An Iraqi lawyer hired by Blackwater at the time said that after getting approval from al-Maliki, Blackwater gave 40 Nisour Square victims' families about $800,000, which it hoped would "moisten the situation with the Iraqi government to get the license." Victims' families confirmed the payments.

Anticipating the US military withdrawal at the end of 2011, Iraqi police detained several hundred contractors, examining visas, weapons permits, and authorizations to drive routes.[188] After the withdrawal Iraq stopped issuing and renewing weapons licenses and other permits and limited visas. An adviser to President Talabani said: "we have to apply our own rules now." An adviser to Prime Minister al-Maliki said foreigners have to enter the country "legally and in a way that respects that Iraq now has sovereignty and control over its land." In May 2013 a 200-page report by a subcommittee of the DoD's Defense Legal Policy Board recommended placing all contractors in war zones under military jurisdiction.

Documents filed in a lawsuit against Blackwater in June 2014 revealed that DoS had begun investigating the company on August 1, 2007 (six weeks before Nisour Square).[189] On August 20, Jean Richter (the BDS special agent leading the inquiry) was told the Embassy had been asked to document her "inappropriate behavior." The next day Daniel Carroll, Blackwater's senior project manager in Iraq (and a former SEAL), threatened "he could kill" her and "no one could or would do anything about it." She "took Mr. Carroll's threat seriously. We were in a combat zone where things can happen quite unexpectedly." Others had told her to be "very careful" because the review could jeopardize the jobs of Blackwater employees. The Embassy's acting regional security officer told DoS that Richter had become "unsustainably disruptive to day-to-day operations and created an unnecessarily hostile environment for a number of contract personnel." She was recalled to Washington the next day. Her August 31 report documented Blackwater misconduct, warning that inadequate oversight had created "an environment full of liability and negligence." Because "Blackwater contractors saw themselves as above the law," they, "instead of

Department officials, are in command and in control." On October 5 DoS recorded her statement but took no further action. The panel Rice appointed to examine Nisour Square never interviewed her. Patrick Kennedy, who chaired it, told reporters on October 23 that the panel had found no communications from the Embassy raising concerns about Blackwater. "We did not find any ... significant pattern of incidents ... that the embassy had suppressed in any way."

Interrogation

Although Abu Ghraib attracted most media attention (partly because of the photographs), abuses occurred throughout Iraq.[190] Capt. Ian Fishback and two sergeants exposed those at Forward Operating Base Mercury near Fallujah. A detainee's leg was broken with a baseball bat, and others were beaten and kicked ("fucking a PUC" [person under control]). Detainees were made to hold stress positions until they passed out ("smoking a PUC"), had chemicals applied to skin and eyes, were subjected to heat and cold, denied food and water, and deprived of sleep. MI ordered MPs to soften up detainees for interrogation, telling soldiers "those guys were IED trigger men last week"; but some beat prisoners just to vent frustrations. Medical staff lied that the injuries had been incurred during capture. Fishback said, "we knew where the Geneva Conventions drew the line, but then you get that confusion when the Secretary of Defense and the President made that statement" that the Geneva Conventions did not apply to detainees. A sergeant claimed they "were never briefed on the Geneva Conventions." For more than 17 months Fishback tried to raise his concerns with superiors and obtain clear orders, but was repeatedly told to "consider your career" and warned that "the honor of the unit is at stake." He asked the Army IG at Fort Bragg for an analysis of the Geneva Conventions, but what he got was "very incomplete and provides no information that I need." A deeply religious Christian and West Point graduate, with a Vietnam veteran father and wife serving in Iraq, Fishback tried to follow the Cadet Honor Code: "A cadet shall not lie, cheat, steal or tolerate those who do." He reported the abuses to Army Secretary Harvey, who brushed him off, saying "corrective action was already taken." After learning that one detainee had died during interrogation in Iraq and another had been waterboarded, Fishback contacted HRW, which put him in touch with staffers for Sens. McCain and Warner (D-Va) (both veterans and SASC members); but the military denied a pass to meet them. A few days later Army CID and the Army IG interviewed him, but said they could do nothing unless he named the subordinates involved (to whom he had promised anonymity). McCain said: "we've got to have it stopped. It is hurting America's image abroad." "It's not about prisoners. It's about us." Rumsfeld claimed: "the Army is taking it seriously." If "somebody's done something that they shouldn't have done, they'll be punished for it." But no one was. Eric Fair, who had worked with the 82nd Airborne as a contract interrogator in summer 2004, described similar abuses.

The ACLU released documents obtained through FOIA showing that the US military detained women to force their husbands to surrender for interrogation.[191] One email asked: "have you tacked a note on the door and challenged [the husband] to come get his wife?" A secret DIA memo said Task Force 6–26 had detained the mother of three young children (one still nursing): "it was recommended that if the wife were present, she be detained and held in order to leverage the primary target's surrender." The US military responded that "when you see an individual email note, it's oftentimes very confusing to figure out how that particular case fits into an overall larger puzzle." But a woman detained for four months told a US journalist that she and eight others had been held for that purpose. Interrogated in prison, Charles Graner admitted such practices were "the other big Geneva Convention violation" at Abu Ghraib. "They were picking up, you know, Joe Snuffy's wife to get Joe Snuffy … [it] happened a lot."

Civilian Casualties

In June 2007 a helicopter attack in Khalis, about ten miles from Baqubah (where the USA was fighting al-Qaeda), killed 17 men, who residents said were members of the village guard force.[192] After the USA claimed to have killed 26 militants in Sadr City, Baghdad a few days later, Prime Minister al-Maliki said his government "refuse[d]" to let the USA "carry out any military operation in any Iraqi province or city without first acquiring permission from the leadership of the Iraqi forces," which it had not done. In October US troops searching for a leader associated with the Iranian Quds Force said they had killed at least fifteen criminals transporting weapons in another Shiite town in Khalis. Iraqis replied that the dead, though armed, were defending their town from al-Qaeda in Mesopotamia. The local hospital reported treating eight children, four of whom died. Two weeks later the USA said it had killed up to 49 militants during a lengthy battle in Sadr City and was "unaware of any innocent civilians being killed"; but the Iraqi Interior Minister said 13 civilians were dead and 69 wounded.

A freelance correspondent saw the corpses of a woman and two small children and interviewed two wounded boys; another man reported two dead 18-month-old children. In a separate incident US helicopters fired on men they claimed were planting IEDs north of Baghdad, but the 16 dead included 6 women and 3 children, and another 14 were wounded. An air strike 80 miles north of Baghdad killed 15 farmers working in their field before dawn, including 5 women, 4 teenagers, and 2 toddlers. Members of parliament discussed restricting US military operations as part of the reauthorization for US forces required by the end of the year. (The previous June parliament had passed a resolution over al-Maliki's objections requiring the government to seek its permission before authorizing an extension of the US troop presence.) The Parliamentary Speaker's Office, which included Shiites, Sunnis, and Kurds, said "the Iraqi Parliament condemns these violations that are against the basics of military work and human rights" and "touch[] the life and dignity of Iraqis." A November air strike killed 40 armed Sunni men wearing reflective bands provided by the USA to identify them as friendly forces at night. The US military commented: "we had some people on the ground who identified these individuals as bad guys ... there is really no change in our posture since then." LtGen. Odierno, second in command in Iraq, was confident "we hit the right place" because there were "al Qaeda operatives ... heavy weapons ... some suicide vests." The USA said it had arrested 21 suspects, but a brother of one of the dead said they were council members and 13 had since been released. Hundreds of residents protested. In Muthanna Province, US soldiers shot at motorists trying to avoid the military caravan, killing two and seriously wounding others, including local police guarding a councilman, and destroying a truckload of sheep. Later that month US soldiers killed civilians in at least three highway incidents. The more than one thousand civilians killed in 2007 were over four times the 229 killed in 2006. In two separate incidents in February 2008, US forces killed Sons of Iraq – Sunnis who manned checkpoints for the USA.

After US troops withdrew from Radwaniya in May 2008, Iraqi police found a Koran perforated with bullet holes. MGen. Hammond, the commander in Baghdad, addressed tribal leaders: "In the most humble manner, I look in your eyes today and I say, please forgive me and my soldiers."[193] He also read an apology from the unidentified soldier (who was disciplined and removed from Iraq). Another officer kissed a Koran and gave it to the tribal leaders, who accepted the apology. The Iraqi Cabinet condemned the shooting but acknowledged the apology. When unmollified Iraqis tried to storm a military base, police killed three and wounded seven. A week later the USA apologized for a Marine who handed out coins with a biblical verse at a checkpoint in violation of military regulations prohibiting religious proselytizing, removing him from duty and promising discipline.

In June US forces killed civilians in two separate incidents in a single day.[194] After Iraqis shot in the air to repel men they believed were thieves, the USA responded with an air strike, killing a man and his wife and three children, and wounding others. US soldiers also "returned" fire at "criminals," forcing their car to run off the road and crash, killing three bank employees on their way to work. The USA claimed that "a weapon was recovered from the wreckage," but the Iraqi armed forces general command called it cold-blooded murder. A week later the military offered $10,000 to each family, all of whom refused, demanding a written apology. (The next month the USA apologized, admitting soldiers had not been fired on and no weapon had been found, but still maintaining they had followed proper "escalation of force" measures even though some had injured civilians in other checkpoint encounters.) The day after this incident a team of 60 US soldiers raided a house in al-Maliki's home town, killing the president's cousin. During a raid the following month US Special Operations shot to death the son and nephew of Hamad al-Qaisi, governor of Salahuddin Province, while they slept in their home. Al-Qaisi suspended all cooperation with the USA and threatened to resign. The Deputy Governor said there had been at least two similar US attacks in the area. At the end of July, US soldiers killed a man and his two sons and wounded his daughter, claiming to have been fired on; but none of the dead had a weapon.

In August Navy guards beat two detainees and confined eight others in a cell overnight, closing the vents and subjecting them to pepper spray. The guards were administratively punished.[195] In September an Iraqi security force guarding a Tigris River bridge shot at a US military boat by mistake. In the ensuing gun battle, US soldiers killed three Iraqi soldiers, two police, and two paramilitary Sons of Iraq. The Iraqi Army called it "unbelievable" that the USA did not know there was an Iraqi checkpoint at the bridge. "The American forces could have identified themselves … through turning the boat lights on or making a certain noise." Later that month US forces chased a suspect to his home, killed him, and then called in an air strike, killing five innocent men (a policeman, gym owner, lawyer, and two college students) and three women, and wounding a child. After 400 demonstrated, the

USA said: "sadly, this incident again shows that the … terrorists repeatedly risk the lives of innocent women and children to further their evil work." Following a raid in which the USA killed a senior member of the Iraqi Islamic Party (the largest Sunni Arab grouping) and arrested five others, the party complained it had been targeted (in anticipation of the January 2009 provincial election) because of its success in forging alliances with others, and suspended all contact with the USA until the perpetrators were punished and it received an apology.

At the beginning of 2009, a day after the USA and Iraq signed a new security agreement extending immunity from prosecution under Iraqi law for American soldiers (unless the USA certified they had committed premeditated grave felonies off base and off duty), a US soldier shot a 24-year-old woman editor of a Baghdad television channel for "acting erratically."[196] Her employer condemned an act done "in cold blood." At the end of the month US forces raided a house, killing a retired colonel and his wife and wounding their daughter. The USA claimed the woman had reached under the mattress, where they found a gun, and the man had attacked them. The provincial police chief denied the US claim that it had conducted the raid with Iraqi forces (as required since the beginning of the year). Hundreds attended the funeral, shouting "Death to America." Two weeks later the USA apologized and offered compensation after killing an eight-year-old girl and wounding several other civilians in a crowd of Shiite pilgrims. After two Iraqis were killed and six arrested (including a police captain) in an April raid, the USA apologized but insisted the operation targeting suspected Shiite militants in the Mahdi Army and Promise Day Brigade was "fully coordinated and approved by the Iraqi government." Declaring that the USA had violated SOFA, Prime Minister al-Maliki called on it to "hand over those responsible for this crime to the courts" (in contravention of SOFA). Hundreds of demonstrators, including police, chanted "no, no" to America, occupation, and Israel. In July a US military convoy repairing a disabled vehicle shot to death an Iraqi truck driver who failed to halt after a signal. Several weeks later US soldiers chasing insurgents raided houses, killing two adults and a 14-year-old, and wounding four, including two children. The senior Iraqi army commander at the scene ordered his men to apprehend the US soldiers, but then capitulated to US pressure while maintaining that "what happened is a crime." The USA said its soldiers' response "was within the rules of engagement, appropriate and proportionate to the attack on them." In September, claiming they had come under fire, US soldiers killed two men (whose bodies exhibited dog bites) and detained an Iraqi intelligence officer, after using explosives to break down gates and doors to a home.

In April 2010 WikiLeaks released a video of an American helicopter killing a Reuters photographer and driver in July 2007.[197] Within days it was viewed more than three million times on YouTube and replayed hundreds of times on television. (Reuters had tried to get it for two years.) In the audio one pilot said "look at those dead bastards," while the other replied "nice." Watching a wounded man crawl away, a pilot exhorted: "all you got do is pick up a weapon" – so the pilot could shoot him. Soon after a van arrived to collect the wounded, the pilots opened fire. One said callously: "well, it's their fault for bringing their kids into a battle." When a US armored vehicle seemed to roll over a corpse, a pilot chuckled: "I think they just drove over a body." At the time the USA had said: "there is no question that coalition forces were clearly engaged in combat operations against a hostile force." A US military investigation found its forces had no reason to know the dead were journalists because they "made no effort to visibly display their status as press or media representatives and their familiar behavior with and close proximity to the armed insurgents and their furtive attempts to photograph the coalition ground forces made them appear as hostile combatants to the Apaches that engaged them." The USA accused WikiLeaks of editing the video to obscure the fact that the helicopters were supporting soldiers who had drawn small-arms fire and RPGs. But the CPJ said the video "confirms our long-held view that a thorough and transparent investigation into this incident is urgently needed." The *Los Angeles Times* agreed that the video "certainly raises enough [questions] to warrant further investigation."

In September 2014 Haider al-Abadi, the new prime minister, said that after he "raised the issue of the sovereignty of Iraq," his government had to approve any air strike.[198] "We don't want to happen in Iraq what happened in Yemen and Pakistan." After investigating 18 allegations of civilian casualties from air strikes in Iraq and Syria between August 8 and December 30, 2014, CENTCOM concluded that 13 were not credible and maintained there had been *no* civilian casualties. When the Syrian Observatory for Human Rights (SOHR) said a May 1 strike in Syria killed at least 64 civilians, including 31 children, CENTCOM replied that it had "no information to corroborate allegations that coalition air strikes resulted in civilian casualties." Days later, however, it admitted for the first time that a strike against ISIS in November 2014 had killed two children. An August strike in Idlib Province killed five fighters of the Free Syrian Army (which the USA supported) and eight women and children. In September CENTCOM admitted that a March 13 strike in Hatra, Iraq had killed two women and three children. SOHR said air strikes had killed 181 civilians: 26 in one Syrian village, including at least 7 children and 4 women; more than a dozen were missing. In August AirWars reported that 57 air strikes against ISIS in Iraq and Syria during the previous 12 months had killed more than 15,000 militants, but also at least 459 civilians. A December 18 strike against IS allegedly killed 25 Iraqi soldiers and wounded 37. Defense Secretary Carter immediately called Prime Minister al-Abadi, saying: "it seemed to be a mistake that involved both sides." He acknowledged the deaths of nine soldiers and an officer, expressed condolences, and offered to conduct a joint investigation. Although al-Abadi accepted this account and hoped other politicians would not exploit the incident, they promptly did. Obama said on NPR on December 21: "if the suggestion is that we kill tens or hundreds or thousands of innocent Syrians and Iraqis, that is not who we are, and that would be a strategy that would have an enormous backlash against the United States." AirWars listed 405–553 civilians killed by the US coalition in 76 separate incidents based on two or more generally credible sources. In January 2016 the USA admitted that 5 air strikes against IS in Iraq and Syria between March 12 and July 4, 2015 had killed 8 civilians and wounded 3, claiming that just 14 civilians had died since bombing began in summer 2014. But AirWars said 135 incidents killed 815–1149 civilians between August 8, 2014 and January 12, 2016. SOHR reported that US air strikes had killed 38 civilians in Syria in February. An April air strike in Syria killed several members of the Korasan Group, but also one civilian bystander, and injured ten others. In April the USA admitted killing 20 civilians and wounding 11 in 9 air strikes between September 10, 2015 and February 2, 2016 (more than twice as many as previously acknowledged for that period); earlier it admitted killing 21 and wounding 17 between August 2014 and September 2015 and was investigating 23 other allegations.

In April 2016 CENTCOM delegated to its commander in Iraq authority to order strikes in several areas when there was a probability of ten civilian casualties. In June the USA claimed that during nearly two years of fighting ISIS in Iraq and Syria it had killed 20,000 fighters but only 41 civilians; but it reopened an investigation of a 2015 strike in Mosul that killed nine women and children. In July SOHR said air strikes on the ISIS-controlled villages of Tokhar and Hoshaniyeh in Syria killed at least 56 civilians, including 11 children, and wounded dozens, a day after coalition strikes on Manbij killed at least 15 civilians. Estimates of the deaths during the fight for Manbij (mostly from coalition bombing) ranged from 500–700 (Free Manbij Media Centre), to 368 (Manbij Coordination Committee) and 190 (Airwars). A later strike allegedly killed 28 civilians, including women and children, in al-Ghandour, 23 km from Manbij. Airwars head Chris Woods wrote in a *New York Times* op ed that the coalition had killed at least 1,500 civilians; SOHR and Iraq Body Count offered similar or higher numbers. "Official White House data on counterterrorism actions in Pakistan, Yemen and elsewhere show civilians dying on average once every seven airstrikes ... Yet we are simultaneously asked to accept that civilians are about 35 times less likely to die in the campaign against the Islamic State." In September the USA acknowledged that it might have killed civilians in three strikes over six days. Days later it admitted that an air strike in Deir al-Zour Province targeting ISIS actually killed Syrian troops; the attack was quickly stopped after a warning from Russia, which claimed at least 62 dead and 100 injured; the USA expressed its regrets to the Syrian government and appointed a brigadier general to investigate. In November the coalition acknowledged 119 civilian deaths in Syria and Iraq between August 2014 and July 2016, but the Syrian Observatory for Human Rights said coalition air strikes had killed at least 680 civilians, including 169 children.[199] In December the USA increased its estimate to 173 and promised monthly reports.

On March 16, 2017 the USA bombed the Omar Ibn al-Khatab mosque near al-Jinah village in Aleppo province, killing at least 38.[200] (Three months later, the DoD investigation claimed the only civilian casualty was a child who had accompanied an adult to an al-Qaeda meeting.) Another strike hit a school in Raqqa province, where civilians were taking shelter; claiming it had killed 30 fighters, the USA called it "a clean strike." A third strike in Mosul was said to have killed up to 200 civilians; the USA accused ISIS of "smuggling civilians into buildings so we won't see them and trying to bait the coalition to attack." HASC chair Thornberry (R-Tex) said: "obviously ISIS is trying to use human beings as shields to protect themselves." He defended the Trump administration's loosened ROEs, compared to those of Obama: "it did not work to have NSC staffers approving each strike." Noting that Trump had declared during the campaign that the USA should "take out" militants' families and "bomb the shit" out of IS, Rep. Ted Lieu

(D-Ca) – a former JAG – questioned "whether the Trump administration is violating the Law of War." After first denying it had dropped a bomb, the USA then claimed that the damage had been aggravated by explosives stored there by ISIS, which had "gathered" the victims there; local residents denied this. Airwars reported 1,058 civilian deaths in March, compared with 465 in the last full month of the Obama administration. In April a US-led air strike killed 18 Syrian fighters allied with it. Prompted to reinvestigate, in May the USA discovered another 80 deaths it had not previously reported; in June it acknowledged another hundred civilian deaths. A group of former Obama administration lawyers sued the Trump administration seeking all documents asserting the authority for the mosque strike. Two strikes in Deir al-Zour province late May allegedly killed 42 ISIS prisoners; another strike days later killed at least 30. The UN Independent International Commission of Inquiry on the Syrian Arab Republic reported in mid-June that 300 civilians had been killed in air strikes since March 21. Airwars reported that the US coalition dropped 5,775 bombs, shells and missiles on Raqqa in August, killing 433 civilians, and had killed more than a thousand since the assault began on June 6.[201]

Analysis

As in Afghanistan, US citizens were more successful in securing some (if imperfect) redress through the law: release from detention following a habeas petition in US courts, compensation for accidental or intentional injuries inflicted by contractors. Iraqi journalists, by contrast, languished in American prisons or, worse, went uncompensated for injuries or death. Contractors unconstrained by the military chain of command and exempt from even the military's flawed disciplinary system wreaked havoc on Iraqi civilians. It took an atrocity of the magnitude of Nisour Square to prompt the first significant investigation of civilian injuries and deaths. But this was hopelessly compromised from the start. Even before Nisour Square, DoS bowed to Blackwater pressure and aborted its inquiry. After that massacre, DoS hired contractors to investigate contractors, granted immunity to witnesses (greatly complicating criminal prosecutions), and successfully frustrated Congressional scrutiny. Because the USA squandered so much money on the Iraq war, both it and Blackwater were profligate in paying compensation in the hope of appeasing victims. And though both the US military and the contractors' trade association were desperate to dissociate themselves from Blackwater, DoS retained the company as long as possible and then replaced it with another that blithely hired ex-Blackwater guards. In the aftermath, though contractors lost their immunity from Iraqi law, none was ever prosecuted in Iraq. Abuses by contractors declined, but only because their numbers decreased.

The US military inflicted civilian casualties with even greater impunity, readily offering apologies and compensation (responses that cost little but sometimes were rebuffed for reasons of honor) while resisting Iraqi oversight. As in Afghanistan, the USA invoked the fog of war, treated "escalation of force" killings as justifiable, and blamed insurgents for endangering civilians. Even after WikiLeaks released the videotape of helicopter pilots gloating about killing Iraqi journalists, the US investigation found no wrongdoing. And when the USA eventually agreed to joint operations with the Iraqis, it sought to blame *them* for civilian casualties. Insults to Islam lacking any military justification – such as shooting at Korans or Christian proselytizing – elicited greater scrutiny, but still produced no visible punishment. And though the USA acceded to Iraqi jurisdiction over the US military in the vanishingly rare case of a premeditated grave felony off base and off duty, none was ever prosecuted.

Pakistan

Whereas the USA openly waged wars endorsed (if ambivalently) by the governments of Afghanistan and Iraq, it had no public permission to engage in military actions in Pakistan.[202] And whereas SOFAs immunized US military from prosecution under Afghan and Iraqi law, Americans enjoyed no immunity in Pakistan. Therefore, the CIA engaged in a secret drone campaign under an arrangement requiring Pakistani approval of each target. Although Pakistan unconvincingly claimed credit for the first drone strike in South Waziristan in June 2004, which killed a Taliban ally (whose grave became a pilgrimage site) and two children, it quickly denounced the next strike 18 months later on what the CIA believed was a meeting of high-level al-Qaeda and Taliban members, killing 13–22 people, many of them apolitical.[203] The Foreign Office summoned Ambassador Crocker for a rebuke, and the Federally Administered Tribal Areas (FATA) Secretariat began documenting civilian casualties, later claiming that five women and five children had been killed.

In July 2008 President Bush secretly authorized Special Operations to conduct ground assaults in Pakistan after informing the government but not seeking its approval.[204] The USA said the Pakistani army privately consented (having previously agreed to let US forces in Afghanistan penetrate six miles into the country in "hot pursuit"). A day after Asif Ali Zardari was sworn in as president in September, a ground operation and air strike by three Special Operations helicopters killed about two dozen men. The USA suspected they were al-Qaeda, but the Foreign Minister said no "high value target or known terrorist was among the dead, only innocent civilians, including women and children." The provincial governor denounced the "outrage." Gen. Kayani, Army Chief of Staff, declared that "no external force is allowed to conduct operations inside Pakistan." "There is no question of any agreement or understanding with coalition forces whereby they are allowed to conduct operations on our side of the border." NATO agreed that the UN mandate for the Afghan war did not include "ground or air incursions" into Pakistan. Prime Minister Gilani condemned the raid. Calling it a "grave provocation" and a violation of sovereignty, Pakistan summoned the US Ambassador, filed a "strong protest," and reserved the right of "self-defense." In North Waziristan a few days later a drone killed 4 alleged militants and at least 16 others, including 4 women and 2 children, and injured another 15, mostly women and children. Soon thereafter another drone in North Waziristan killed 12, including women and children. The Pakistani military said retaliation against US forces was "possible" because Pakistan had "a right of self-defense." In an editorial headlined "Enough, Uncle Sam," *The News* (Pakistan) called such attacks "the best recruiting sergeant the extremists ever had." But the *Washington Post* said it was "clear that Pakistani army and security forces lack the capacity to defeat the extremists" and "Kayani was briefed by senior U.S. commanders." Such attacks "must continue," even though they might "destabilize Mr. Zardari's democratically elected administration," because "no risk to Pakistan's political system or its U.S. relations is greater than that of a second 9/11 attack staged from the tribal territories."

JCS chairman Mullen met with Kayani and Gilani separately in Pakistan several days later and "reiterated the U.S. commitment to respect Pakistan's sovereignty." A Pakistani military spokesman threatened that were there another ground raid or air strike, "which is definite, no ambiguity," the "orders are clear … open fire." But Pakistani authorities said the source had been misquoted. A few days later Zardari said in his first speech to a joint session of parliament: "We will not tolerate the violation of our sovereignty and territorial integrity by any power." Members of parliaments loudly thumped their desks in support.

The *New York Times* warned it "would be catastrophic for both countries" if Pakistani troops shot American troops; but it also called Bush's authorization of such raids "a desperation move." "[A] rising number of civilian deaths, on both sides of the border, is driving more people into the hands of the repressive Taliban." "Any revised plan must do a lot more to avoid civilian casualties and support, rather than undermine, Pakistan's civilian leaders." Within days these fears seem to be realized. On September 23 Pakistan said two US helicopters had entered North Waziristan from Afghanistan but retreated under fire; the USA denied this. The next day Pakistan said soldiers and tribesmen had shot down a US drone in South Waziristan; the USA denied this, too. A few days after that Pakistani troops fired on two US helicopters, prompting them and ground troops to return fire. The USA denied the helicopters had crossed the border. Zardari told the UN General Assembly: "we cannot allow our territory and our sovereignty to be violated by our friends."

At the end of September a drone in North Waziristan killed 21 insurgents, 2 women and a child.[205] Several weeks later a drone in Dande Darpakhel village, North Waziristan, missed its target – the madrassa of Jalaluddin Haqqani – but hit another madrassa, killing at least ten local students and teachers. The Pakistan Lawyers Foundation demonstrated, and parliament unanimously demanded an end to such strikes. A few days later the Foreign Minister summoned Ambassador Patterson and insisted on an immediate halt to the "counterproductive" missile strikes, giving her a copy of the parliamentary resolution. When Gen. Petraeus visited Pakistan as CENTCOM commander in November, the Defense Minister said the strikes created "bad blood," and Zardari called them "difficult to explain by a democratically elected government." (But there was evidence of hypocrisy. An August 23 cable disclosed by WikiLeaks two years later said Interior Minister Malik had told Ambassador Patterson: "I don't care if they do it [drone strikes] as long as they get the right people. We'll protest in the National Assembly and then ignore it." *Washington Post* columnist David Ignatius said that, during a September visit to Washington, Zardari secretly agreed to a list of targets *he* wanted killed and said in November: "kill the seniors [i.e., al-Qaeda leaders]. Collateral damage worries you Americans. It does not worry me.") Days after these protests a North Waziristan strike killed 13, allegedly including 8 local people, prompting condemnation by Zardari and Gilani. A week later a strike killed 11, including 3 relatives of a local resident who allegedly sheltered foreign fighters. After a strike in Northwest Frontier Province (the first outside Waziristan) killed six (who locals said were not militants), a presidential spokesman complained: "it looks like the Americans are not listening." The head of Jamaat-e-Islami vowed to block NATO supply lines to Afghanistan if the strikes continued. But in November *The Times* (London) reported the CIA had lowered the threshold for drone strikes from a 90 percent chance of success to 50 percent.

An air strike in North Waziristan in January 2009 killed a house owner and his two brothers and three nephews.[206] Another in South Waziristan killed seven, including three children. Senior Pakistan officials said a hundred civilians had been killed since the summer. After a third attack, in North Waziristan, killed 18, only 5 of whom were said to be militants, hundreds demonstrated against the USA in Islamabad. Zardari declared that the "day was not far away when these attacks will be stopped." He, Foreign Minister Qureshi, and Gen. Kayani criticized the strikes to Richard Holbrooke (US Special Representative for Afghanistan and Pakistan). But in an SSCI hearing Sen. Feinstein expressed surprise at this, claiming the strikes "are flown out of a Pakistan base," a fact the CIA confirmed. Pakistani air defense controllers coordinated with the US Embassy to ensure that Pakistani F-16 fighter bombers did not mistakenly hit drones or CIA officers on the ground. When Pakistan complained that the strikes targeted only al-Qaeda and the Haqqani network, the USA launched two at Baitullah Mehsud, after ISI provided intelligence on his location. But the Northwest Frontier Province governor reiterated that "these strikes are unproductive" and "attract more jihadis." After meeting Gen. Kayani and ISI head Gen. Pasha, DCI Panetta said: "nothing has changed our efforts to go after terrorists, and nothing will change those efforts." Soon after succeeding Hayden, Panetta had said that the targeted killing program in Pakistan was "very precise and it is limited in terms of collateral damage and, very frankly, it's the only game in town in terms of confronting or trying to disrupt the Al Qaeda leadership."

David Kilcullen, a former Australian army officer who advised Gen. Petraeus in Iraq, told HASC that "we need to call off the drones" for strategic reasons.[207] "Since 2006, we've killed 14 senior al Qaeda leaders using drone strikes; in the same time period, we've killed 700 Pakistani civilians in the same area ... deeply aggravating ... the population," which was "coalesc[ing] ... around the extremists." With Andrew Exum (a former US army officer in Iraq and Afghanistan), he wrote a *New York Times* op ed urging a "moratorium on drone strikes into Pakistan."

Instead, the USA gave Pakistan a say in choosing targets and supplemented CIA strikes with those by the military, which would focus on the Taliban threat to Pakistan.[208] But in December the USA authorized the CIA to launch more drones from a base in Baluchistan and asked Pakistan for permission to strike in Quetta (which was never granted). Pakistan dropped the restrictions on the drone program it had sought in fall 2009 in exchange for conducting a ground offensive against militants in South Waziristan, which the USA had requested. An anonymous US official said 80 drone strikes in the previous two years had killed "more than 400" enemy fighters with "just over 20" civilian casualties – "people who were either at the side of major terrorists or were at facilities used by terrorists." The CIA said "press reports suggesting that hundreds of Pakistan civilians have somehow been killed" were "flat-out false." But the New America Foundation said that since 2006 drone strikes had killed at least 500 militants and 250 civilians; the Long War Journal estimated 885 military and 94 civilian deaths; and the Pakistan Institute for Peace Studies said the "vast majority" of the 667 killed by drones in 2009 were civilians. Panetta boasted that 22 CIA drone strikes in the two-and-a-half months after a December 30, 2009 suicide bombing killed seven CIA agents and contractors near Khost, Afghanistan were "one of the most aggressive operations that CIA has been involved in in our history."[209] (There had been just 53 strikes in all of 2009.) One strike killed Hussein al-Yemeni (an organizer of the suicide bombing) in Miram Shah, the first in a populated locale, sending a "very important signal that they are not going to be able to hide in urban areas." Panetta also claimed "we've had much better relations" with Pakistan, which had been "much more tolerant of the operations we have there."

At the end of September 2010 NATO helicopters based in Afghanistan attacked 600 feet into Pakistan, killing about fifty members of the Haqqani network, but also killing three Pakistani paramilitary soldiers and wounding three others.[210] Pakistan said NATO knew of its checkpoint. The Foreign Ministry called it "a clear violation and breach of the U.N. mandate," which had "no agreed 'hot pursuit' rules." NATO insisted "the ROE were followed. They were acting in self-defense." Gilani was "profoundly concerned." Pakistan expected "its partners to respect its territorial sovereignty." Zardari's office told Panetta (who was visiting Islamabad) that "the government of Pakistan strongly disapproves any incident of violation of its sovereignty." Parliament unanimously denounced the attack. Pakistan closed the most important border crossing at Torkham, though Holbrooke called it "inconceivable" the closure "would continue for more than a short period." NATO oil tankers were burned in Shikarpur, Baluchistan, and Islamabad. NATO's Secretary General apologized to Foreign Minister Qureshi and hoped the border would be reopened soon. But the attacks continued. Gunmen destroyed half the 40 tankers stalled near Quetta and shot at trucks on their way to the one open border crossing at Chaman. Pakistan demanded an apology for the attack. NATO offered only regrets, but Ambassador Patterson offered "our deepest apology," and JCS chairman Mullen phoned Gen. Kayani with an official but private apology. A joint Pakistani–NATO inquiry viewed 2.5 hours of video, which showed two helicopters approaching the frontier post (200 yards from the border) from *inside* Pakistan and attacking after Pakistani soldiers fired a warning shot, but not toward the helicopters. The helicopters returned four hours later and fired seven more missiles. Pakistan reopened the border after ten days. Two weeks later Obama joined a meeting of his top advisers with Kayani and Qureshi in an effort to repair relations.

On January 27, 2011 Raymond Davis was arrested after shooting dead two men on a motorcycle, Faizan Haider and Faheem Shamshad, at a traffic signal in Lahore.[211] The US Embassy said: "we regret that this incident resulted in loss of life. However, eyewitness reports on the day of the incident showed the American diplomat acted in self-defense. There is no doubt he has diplomatic immunity, and we are working with the government of Pakistan to resolve the issue." The Lahore police chief said only one man had pointed a gun, which had no bullets, and the other was shot in the back while trying to flee. "We have proved this was a cold-blooded murder." The police said Davis first fired from inside his car and then got out and shot Haider twice more as he ran away; they collected ten bullet casings. Autopsies found that each had been shot two or three times from behind. The men, known members of a robbery gang, had currency from Pakistan, Japan, Oman, and the Philippines. Davis photographed them, called the US Consulate, and fled in his car. When apprehended, he lied to police about the encounter. His cell phone and camera contained photos of bridges, markets that had been bombed, and government installations near the Indian border. A consular vehicle sent to extricate him from the police sped the wrong way down a one-way street, killing a motorcyclist and then fleeing, leaving behind 100 bullets, gloves, a compass and a black face mask. (When Pakistan demanded the surrender of those in the car, the USA said they had left the country.)

Sen. Kerry (D-Mass), who enjoyed good relations with Pakistan, flew there to express remorse and promise an investigation, but added: "that doesn't mean the law of immunity is not to be respected." Zardari cautioned Kerry the case was "not as simple as it was sometimes being portrayed." After meeting Kerry, Qureshi (who had been removed as Foreign Minister for refusing to give Davis "blanket immunity") and the main Punjab opposition party leader said domestic courts should decide the case. Obama expressed concern "about the loss of life," but insisted "there's a broader principle at stake that I think we have to uphold," namely immunity for Davis, whom Obama repeatedly called a "diplomat." There were demonstrations in Karachi against Obama and Kerry. A Lahore student leader vowed to "create a movement that would turn into a revolution." HASC chair McKeon (R-Ca) warned Pakistani leaders that some members of Congress might try to withhold nearly $3 billion in economic and military aid unless Davis was released. Senior House Republicans made a similar threat to Ambassador Haqqani.

After the Punjab Advocate General filed a "double murder case" against Davis, a Pakistan court gave the government three weeks to decide whether he had immunity. Ambassador Munter apologized, but said the USA was "disappointed" that immunity had not been granted immediately. On the day of the killings the US Embassy had told the Foreign Ministry that Davis was a consular employee, who would not enjoy immunity; but a week later it claimed that its application to the Ministry in late 2009 had called him a "technical and administrative" official at the Embassy, who would have immunity. Ten days after the shooting a Pakistani official called Davis a CIA agent. US officials countered that he was a longtime CIA contractor who collected intelligence and conducted surveillance for agents, and was engaged in "area familiarization" at the time of the shooting. His visa described him as a "regional affairs officer," a common CIA cover. (It later emerged that Davis had been involved in a covert effort to penetrate Lashkar-e-Taiba.) Obama reiterated that diplomats "are not subject to … local prosecutors." But a 1963 treaty allowed prosecution of consular staff for a "grave crime."

Invoking diplomatic immunity, Davis refused to participate in his court hearing. The Pakistan government told the court that the Foreign Minister had not clearly acknowledged Davis's immunity. The Ministry admitted that it attempted to register him as a diplomat only the day after the shootings, but confirmed that he held a diplomatic passport. Pakistani investigators told reporters that Davis's car had a GPS device that could direct drone strikes in North Waziristan. Using information found on him, Pakistan intelligence was "rolling up" CIA cells and operatives throughout the country and had apprehended 45 Pakistanis in contact with him. ISI (which questioned Davis for 14 days) demanded information about CIA contractors (but the Agency had withdrawn all of them). Pakistan security officials increased surveillance of US vehicles and officials, detaining three Americans with illegal license plates.

Less than two months after the shootings Davis was whisked out of the country after the USA paid $2.3 million to his victims' families, as authorized by Sharia law. Ambassador Munter said DoJ had opened an investigation (but it was never mentioned again). Hundreds protested at the US Consulate in Lahore. Opposition parties walked out when Zardari addressed parliament. Gen. Kayani told the USA to withdraw 335 persons, including CIA officers and contractors and Special Operations forces. The family of the dead motorcyclist was denied any remedy.

In February 2011 it was reported that after an August 2010 strike killed 13 Afghan Taliban but also four women and three children, the USA changed its targeting policy.[212] A US official claimed no civilian had been killed in the more than 75 subsequent strikes. The New America Foundation said fewer than 20 civilians had been killed, and just 6 percent of drone strike deaths in 2010 were civilian, compared to 25 percent in previous years. The USA aborted an attack on Sirajuddin Haqqani because of the presence of women and children, and Pakistan said two missiles had been diverted from their targets to avoid civilians. But on March 17, the day after Davis's release, the USA resumed drone strikes, which it had paused on January 23. The four missiles missed their target, striking a jirga in Data Khel, North Waziristan, convened to settle a dispute over a chromite mine. Pakistan said 45 were killed. Gen. Kayani said the jirga "was carelessly and callously targeted with complete disregard to human life." Gilani denounced "such irrational behavior." Pakistan withdrew from talks with the USA and Afghanistan in Brussels. Islamist parties organized protests. Foreign Minister Basher told Ambassador Munter that the strikes "constituted a flagrant violation of humanitarian norms and law." At a meeting with DCI Panetta and JCS chairman Mullen in Washington on April 11, ISI director Gen. Pasha said he and Gen. Kayani considered drone strikes out of control. A month later – a day after Mullen asked Kayani to intensify his fight against the Taliban in western Pakistan, accusing ISI of protecting the

Haqqani network – a strike in North Waziristan killed 24, including 4 women and 5 children. There were demonstrations in Peshawar, where opposition leader Imran Khan (the former cricket star and most popular politician in Pakistan) succeeded in blocking trucks carrying supplies to NATO in Afghanistan. But though Mullen told Kayani the USA would not reduce drone strikes until Pakistan launched an operation against the Haqqani network, it did impose restrictions.

Several lawsuits sought redress for drone attacks. Mirza Shahzad Akbar, representing victims of the March 17 strike, outed the CIA station chief in legal documents seeking police help in keeping him in the country until a lawsuit could be filed.[213] He promptly left Pakistan. Akbar sued in Peshawar High Court, asking the government to categorize such strikes as war crimes and appeal to the UN Security Council and Human Rights Council and the International Commission of Jurists. In response to a lawsuit in the UK by Reprieve alleging British complicity with the USA in choosing targets, the British Foreign Office said any disclosure would endanger intelligence sharing with the USA. The trial court dismissed. In May Akbar wrote about the deaths in a *New York Times* op ed.

On May 2, 2011 US Special Operations raided the Abbottabad compound, killing Osama bin Laden.[214] Pakistan responded by leaking the name of the CIA station chief in Islamabad (who had clashed with ISI head Gen. Pasha over Davis), forcing him to leave, and restricted the movement of embassy personnel. The leader of the main opposition party called for an independent judicial commission to determine why Pakistan was not given advance notice. Although ISI had stopped conducting surveillance for the CIA or granting visas to its agents after the Davis killings, it resumed granting visas in July. But days later Pakistan arrested five CIA informants and detained Dr. Shakil Afridi, who had used a vaccination program to seek access to bin Laden's compound. Save the Children withdrew eight workers for fear they might be accused of links to Afridi. A government commission investigating the raid recommended that he be prosecuted for treason. Rep. Rohrabacher (R-Ca) responded by nominating him for a Congressional gold medal. Despite pleas by Panetta and Sens. Levin and McCain, Afridi was tried under the colonial Frontier Crimes Regulations on charges of cooperating in war against the state and interfering with state affairs. In the Khyber Agency tribal court he could not have a lawyer, present evidence, or cross-examine witnesses. A government official advised by tribal elders found him guilty and sentenced him to 33 years. Secretary of State Clinton regretted both the conviction and sentence. The Senate Appropriations Committee cut aid to Pakistan by $33 million ($1 million for each year of his sentence). Sen. Paul planned to introduce a bill to eliminate all aid to Pakistan. When Afridi began a hunger strike, the USA reiterated its calls for his release. In August 2013 Pakistan said Afridi would be retried because the original judge had been unauthorized to hear the matter. Under pressure from Congress, Prime Minister Sharif agreed to review the case. But a few weeks later the mother of a boy who died when Afridi took out his appendix filed a complaint leading to a murder charge. When Obama signed the bill withholding $33 million in aid, the Foreign Ministry defiantly declared Afridi would not be released under pressure. The Commissioner of Frontier Crimes Regulation reduced his sentence to 23 years, but he sought a new trial. His lawyer quit in May 2014, after a "final" warning from militants, saying that undue US pressure had hurt Afridi. (In March 2015 the lawyer was killed by a faction of the Pakistani Taliban.) In May 2014 the USA bowed to pressure from public health officials and declared it would not use vaccinations as an espionage device. After Afridi was exposed, dozens of public health workers had been killed in Pakistan; the previous year 83 new polio cases were reported. The *New York Times* said "the fakery … should never have been used." Although Trump had boasted during his election campaign that it would take him "two minutes" to free Afridi, Pakistan's Foreign Minister retorted: "Pakistan is not a colony of the United States of America."

Drone strikes resumed soon after the bin Laden raid.[215] To rebuild trust, the USA twice gave the Pakistani military information on insurgent bomb-making factories, based on drone surveillance. (The USA could not use drones for bombing because of the danger of civilian casualties.) But the buildings were abandoned before the military arrived, suggesting the intelligence had been leaked. A month after the bin Laden raid Gen. Kayani again called for an end to drone strikes, which "were not acceptable under any circumstances." At the end of June, Deputy National Security Adviser Brennan claimed that in the previous six months "there hasn't been a single collateral death because of the exceptional proficiency, precision of the capabilities that we've been able to develop." But British and Pakistani journalists said a May 6 strike, which the USA claimed killed nine militants in a pickup truck, actually killed 12 militants and 6 civilians in a religious school. BIJ said at least forty-five civilians had been killed during that period; and the Long War Journal said the "claim of zero civilian casualties in a year is absurd." The *New York Times* was equally skeptical: "perfection is rare in life; in war, rarer still." At an Aspen Security Forum, former DNI Blair urged the USA to end the drone campaign, or at least give Pakistan a greater role in targeting, and repeated this in a *New York Times* op ed, declaring that "no issue is more controversial than American drone attacks in Pakistan territory." But Panetta lauded the campaign, and former Rep. Harman called the attacks "a crucial tool in our counter-terrorism arsenal." In August the BIJ reported that more than 160 of the more than 2,292 people killed in drone strikes since 2004 were children, but noted that just 45 civilians had died in 10 strikes during the previous year.

In September JCS chairman Mullen accused ISI of complicity in the Haqqani network's June 28 attack on the US Embassy in Kabul, which killed 16, and the truck bombing of a NATO outpost outside Kabul, which killed 5 coalition soldiers and wounded 77.[216] The *New York Times* urged the administration "to ratchet up the pressure" on Pakistan. Interior Minister Malik "categorically" denied the accusation, refusing to let the USA conduct a ground operation against the Haqqani network (as it had threatened to do when ISI Director Pasha visited Washington). The USA "must respect our sovereignty." Foreign Minister Khar said it was "not acceptable" for the USA "publicly to recriminate [Pakistan], to humiliate it." Defense Minister Mukhtar declared Pakistan was a sovereign nation "which cannot be threatened." Gen. Kayani called the claim "disturbing" and "not based on facts." Gilani accused the USA of ignoring the "feelings" of Pakistanis who wanted "to defend their motherland and its sovereignty." But Defense Secretary Panetta said: "the first order of business right now is to, frankly, put as much pressure on Pakistan as we can to deal with this issue from their side."

After meeting the Chinese Vice Premier, Gilani said "China categorically supports Pakistan's efforts to uphold its sovereignty, independence and territorial integrity." Kayani canceled a visit to Britain to meet with top commanders, after which leaks warned of "stern responses" to an American attack. Pasha flew to Saudi Arabia, a close ally. Several retired army officers urged Pakistan to sever diplomatic relations with the USA. A senior aide to Mullen said: "the chairman stands by every word of his testimony." But the next day the White House Press Secretary said Mullen's claim that the Haqqani network was a "veritable arm" of ISI was "not the language I would use." Nevertheless, Secretary of State Clinton told Khar at the UN that the USA remained committed to attacking any threats, "in particular [from] those who have taken up safe havens inside Pakistan."

After Gilani, Kayani, and Pakistani JCS chairman Wynne met with more than 50 politicians from 32 parties for 9 hours, the government rejected the US's "baseless" allegations and promised full support to the armed forces "in defeating any threat to national security." Pasha told the meeting that though Pakistan "did not want to take relations with the United States to the point of no return, it also was capable to [*sic*] defending itself in case of an attack." Imran Khan said Pasha "told the participants that Haqqani network has three wings and ISI does not maintain contacts with Haqqani's militant wing." On television Gilani stressed his determination "to defend the sovereignty, independence and territorial integrity of our sacred motherland." In his weekly radio address Obama assured Pakistan the USA would have "no boots on the ground." But whether Pakistan's support for the Haqqani network was active or passive, "they've got to take care of this problem." Zardari wrote in a *Washington Post* op ed that "the recent accusations against us have been a serious setback to the war effort and our joint strategic interests." He also assailed drone strikes: "The Pakistani street … ask[s], is our blood so cheap? Are the lives of our children worthless?"

After former Afghan President Rabbani was assassinated in his home on September 20, Afghanistan declared the assassin was Pakistani and accused ISI of complicity.[217] The Pakistan Foreign Ministry rejected this, maintaining that Gilani had personally "offered cooperation in the investigation." The *Washington Post* said "the message to Pakistan should be one-dimensional and clear: eliminate the sanctuaries or expect stepped-up U.S. efforts to do so." The Afghan NDS claimed it had foiled a plot to kill President Karzai involving al-Qaeda and the Haqqani network. At a news conference Obama accused Pakistanis of "hedging their bets" by "having interactions with some of the unsavory characters who they think might end up regaining power in Afghanistan." A week later four separate drone strikes killed the number three leader of the Haqqani network and 17 others. National Security Adviser Donilon had warned Kayani in Saudi Arabia that Pakistan had to either kill the Haqqani leadership, help the USA to do so, or persuade them to join a peaceful Afghan government. But Kayani told two parliamentary defense committees that "the real problem lies in Afghanistan, not Pakistan." Although ISI had contacts with the Haqqani network, so did the CIA and MI6. The USA should think "10 times" before launching another operation like the bin Laden killing because Pakistan was not Iraq or Afghanistan.

Secretary of State Clinton said that, in relation to Afghanistan, "we must send a clear, unequivocal message to the government and people of Pakistan that they must be part of the solution, and that means ridding their country of terrorists who kill their own people and who cross the border to kill people in Afghanistan." She had offered condolences to Rabbani's son. In a press conference with Khar in Islamabad, Clinton declared: "for too long extremists have been able to operate here in Pakistan and from Pakistani soil." "It is a fact" that the Haqqani network was "operating out of safe havens in Pakistan." Kayani told the parliamentary defense committees that the USA "keep [*sic*] throwing this damn aid [threat] at us time and again. We don't want their military aid." Karzai defied the USA: "if fighting starts between Pakistan and the U.S., we are beside Pakistan." Sen. Levin said at the Council on Foreign Relations that Pakistan's failure to renounce the Haqqani network would be a "show-stopper." "We have the right to target not only forces and artillery attacking our forces in Afghanistan across the border in Pakistan but to target the people controlling those forces as well." (US forces in Afghanistan had taken fire from Pakistan at least fifty-five times since the bin Laden raid, compared with just twice in 2010.)

Imran Khan declared Pakistan "will not accept any slavery. We will help you in a respectable withdrawal of your troops from Afghanistan, but we will not launch a military operation in Pakistan for you."[218] Gilani told Pakistani expatriates in Perth, Australia that "there is no such permission" for drone strikes. "Unlike the policies of the past when things started rolling with a single telephone call from the United States, now we seek the mandate of the Parliament and take decisions with consensus." Four days later a drone strike killed two Haqqani network members. In a *New York Times* op ed, Clive Stafford Smith described a strike that had killed a 16-year-old boy he had met and wounded the victim's 12-year-old cousin, who lost both legs and an eye. In November the Long War Journal reported that after the USA imposed restrictions on drone strikes the previous summer, 5.5 percent of those it killed (13/235) were significant al-Qaeda figures or militant commanders, compared with 2.2 percent in 2010 (18/801) and a similar proportion in the first half of 2011.

On November 26 NATO helicopters crossed the Afghan border into Northwest Pakistan and attacked two checkpoints (one twice), killing 25 soldiers (including 2 officers) and wounding 14.[219] Gilani said the government was taking it up "in the strongest terms with NATO and the U.S." "Business as usual will not be there." Zardari condemned the strikes. Kayani attended the victims' funerals. Pakistan announced the closure of the Torkham border crossing, which Interior Minister Malik said would be permanent, and ordered the CIA to remove its drone operations from Shamsi air base within 15 days. Gen. Allen offered "my most sincere and personal heartfelt condolences," promising that "this incident has my highest personal attention." Clinton, Panetta, and NATO Secretary-General Rasmussen offered their "deepest condolences." But when Clinton phoned, Foreign Minister Khar expressed the "deep sense of rage across Pakistan," saying that the episode "negates the progress made by the two countries on improving relations and forces Pakistan to revisit the terms of engagement." There were demonstrations in major cities, some by religious parties and banned militant groups. A headline in Pakistan's *The News* called the incident a "slaughter." Imran Khan urged the government to withdraw from "America's war." Ambassador Munter "pledged that the United States will work closely with Pakistan to investigate this incident." NATO said a preliminary investigation found that allied and Afghan troops had come under fire from unknown enemies before calling in air strikes. "The Durand Line [international border between Pakistan and Afghanistan] is not always 100 percent clear." But a spokesman said Pakistan had given grid locations of all border posts to the USA, whose forces had penetrated 1.5 miles into its territory.

Gen. Nadeem, director general of military operations, called it "an unprovoked attack of blatant aggression," denying Pakistan had fired first. "It is not possible that the ISAF/NATO forces did not know the location of Pakistani posts." Gen. Mattis, CENTCOM commander, appointed a senior Special Operations officer to lead the inquiry. When the USA did not respond to Pakistan's demands for an apology, it boycotted the international conference on Afghanistan in Bonn. The *New York Times* said "Pakistan's leaders seem most interested in fanning popular anger" and "Pakistan's army is far too cozy with the Taliban"; but it added that "the Obama administration and NATO have wasted precious time allowing the crisis to escalate." Ambassador Munter told the White House Obama had to make a formal statement to prevent relations from worsening. DoS agreed, but DoD was opposed. Obama called Zardari but did not formally apologize. Gen. Kayani gave Pakistani forces authority to return fire against NATO "aggression" without orders from superiors. The *New York Times* said Pakistan's refusal to cooperate with the US/NATO investigation or attend the Bonn meeting was "self-defeating," but reiterated that Obama's eight-day delay in speaking "further fueled the crisis."

The USA vacated the Shamsi air base. Rockets were fired at more than twenty NATO fuel trucks near Quetta, though it was unclear whether this was retaliation. Gilani said Pakistan might continue to block NATO convoys and was writing "new rules of engagement with the United States … with the aim of providing more respect to our sovereignty." After Gen. Allen spoke to Gen. Kayani for the first time (more than two weeks after the attack), Pakistan reinstated the liaison officers it had withdrawn, but imposed a $2,500 tax on each container crossing the border and other charges on fuel tankers.

The US military investigation attributed the attack to "inadequate coordination by U.S. and Pakistani military officers" and "incorrect mapping information."[220] But Gen. Clark said that "given what information they had at the time," US troops "acted in self-defense and with appropriate force after being fired upon." DoD expressed "deepest regret" and "sincere condolences," but did not apologize because "there was no intentional effort to target persons or places known to be part of the Pakistan military." In a 25-page rejoinder, Pakistan rejected any responsibility, calling the US report "factually not correct." The chair of the Pakistan Senate Defense Committee (a former ISI chief) called it "a coverup that will only make it worse." DoD was prepared to make bereavement payments, but a senior Pakistani security official rejected "blood money." Petraeus offered advance notice of future drone strikes and limits on targets, but Pasha demanded they be ended. A few days later Clinton told Khar the USA reserved the right to attack anyone who posed a direct threat to US national security. Calling this a violation of sovereignty, Khar warned that any unauthorized aircraft risked being shot down. Gilani said a parliamentary committee was conducting a "full review of the terms of cooperation" with the USA. "Pakistan's sovereignty and territorial integrity are not negotiable." But Pakistan's leverage was reduced by NATO's ability to ship supplies by other routes.

In early January 2013 the CIA canceled a strike in North Waziristan when Pakistan denied permission, but resumed strikes on January 10, after the longest lull in three years, killing three. By mid-March there had been 10 confirmed strikes; but local media reported that only 1 of the 59 dead was a civilian. The leader of the opposition said: "they must be stopped forthwith." The chair of Pakistan's cross-party national security committee read a report declaring "no overt or covert operations inside Pakistan shall be tolerated." Government and opposition united to demand that drone strikes end. Gilani told Parliament: "I assure you we will get these enforced in letter and spirit." When the CIA conducted its first strike in a month at the end of April, the Foreign Minister condemned it as "violative of [Pakistan's] territorial integrity and sovereignty." After two separate strikes in late May killed 11–14 suspected militants, the Foreign Affairs Ministry reiterated that they were "illegal, counterproductive and totally unacceptable." Parliament had made ending them a condition of reopening supply lines to Afghanistan. But days later two drone strikes killed another nine people. Peter Osborne, chief political correspondent of *The Telegraph* (UK), said it was "almost impossible to overestimate the anger and distress" caused by drone strikes, which were one reason why Ambassador Munter resigned after less than two years.

During a special session of parliament in March, convened by Zardari to discuss ties with the USA, the leader of the opposition said: "the drones are killing innocent bystanders, including children and women. They must be stopped forthwith."[221] The chair of the cross-party national security committee declared: "no overt or covert operations inside Pakistan shall be tolerated." Those responsible for the November 26 attack "should be brought to justice," and the USA should make an unconditional apology. There should be no private security contractors or intelligence operatives, no verbal agreements about national security, repudiation of all earlier agreements, and no transportation of arms or ammunition through Pakistan. But the USA shelved plans to apologize after its soldiers burned Korans in Afghanistan (discussed above) and refused to discipline anyone. At a meeting with Gilani in Seoul, Obama acknowledged "strains" in the relationship, but insisted Pakistan respect US concerns for "national security and our needs to battle terrorists." Furious the government had promised to reopen supply lines, opposition parties prevented parliament from resuming debate. The CIA conducted less than half as many strikes in the first quarter of 2012 as it had during that quarter the two previous years. But when the USA offered a $10 million reward for Hafiz Saeed, the alleged mastermind of the 2008 Mumbai attack living openly in Lahore, Gilani said: "such negative messages will increase the trust deficit." The leader of the opposition warned: "today, Hafiz Saeed has been targeted. Tomorrow, any ordinary Pakistan citizen can get the same treatment." The head of the Lahore District Bar Association told a lawyers' convention that "it is President Obama who is a terrorist."

On April 12 Gilani told parliament: "today's resolution" banning strikes "will enrich your respect and dignity; I assure you that we will get these enforced in letter and spirit." The opposition leader said Pakistan's relationship with the USA "cannot be ... imbalanced." But after the US blamed attacks in Kabul on April 15 on the Haqqani network (which the USA accused Pakistan of sheltering), the administration ruled out an apology and conducted another drone strike less than two weeks later. The Foreign Minister said: "the policy of the government is very, very clear." A member of parliament who had sat on the committee that drafted the resolution averred: "in no case would we allow the NATO supplies now." The Foreign Ministry condemned a second strike soon thereafter as a violation of sovereignty and international law.

But a week later Foreign Minister Khar called it time to reopen the border: "Pakistan has made a point and now can move on."[222] It wanted to attend the May 20 NATO summit, for which an agreement with the USA was a prerequisite. The Information Minister insisted that "no decision on NATO supplies will be made under any pressure." Pakistan now demanded $5,000 for each container, claiming this represented damage to infrastructure and security costs (and confident the USA was paying twice as much for the alternative northern route). Invoking the billions of dollars it had given Pakistan over the previous decade, the USA said it would provide no more aid. Pakistan claimed it was owed more than $3 billion; the USA contended the amount was just $1.3 billion. At the NATO meeting in Chicago, Obama refused to meet Zardari, who had come for that sole reason. Pakistani Ambassador Rehman published a *Chicago Tribune* op ed listing five demands, which annoyed Obama.

Four strikes at the beginning of June killed 27, including Abu Yahya al-Libi, deputy leader of al-Qaeda.[223] The Foreign Ministry summoned the US Chargé d'Affaires to say that "drone strikes were unlawful, against international law and a violation of Pakistan's sovereignty." The *Wall Street Journal* retorted that "protestations of sovereignty would be more credible if Pakistan controlled its territory – and if its military hadn't allowed and abetted the creation of the world's leading terrorist sanctuary." It bestowed rare praise on Obama, whose "decision to expand the drone program into Pakistan and Yemen ... is one of his finest accomplishments. These precision strikes are also the most humane weapon invented to date in aerial warfare, producing relatively few civilian casualties." The *New York Daily News* and John Yoo also cheered al-Libi's death.

The numbers game continued.[224] A Pakistani researcher said 14 percent of the 700 drone deaths were civilians. The USA reported much lower proportions: 5 percent (20/420, April 2009), 6 percent (30/530, May 2010), 2.5 percent (50/2,000, August 2011). After National Security Adviser Brennan denied in June 2011 that there had been "a single collateral death," he "adjusted the wording" to claim no deaths in more than a year. He hedged further in April 2012: "we had no information about a single civilian … being killed," but "unfortunately, in war, there are casualties, including among the civilian population." The BIJ advanced the wildly different estimate of 830 civilian deaths in Pakistan.

The border closure cost the USA $100 million a month. After Obama thanked Central Asian nations and Russia for facilitating shipment of materiel through countries north and west of Afghanistan, Panetta insisted in New Delhi that drone strikes would continue, dismissing claims about sovereignty and declaring the USA was "reaching the limits of our patience" with Pakistan.[225] The *Washington Post* warned that Panetta was "oversimplifying some of the very complex issues," calling his statements "misplaced and unhelpful." But Gen. Dempsey also said the USA was "extremely dissatisfied" with Pakistan's efforts to contain the Haqqani network. In early June the USA withdrew its negotiating team after a fruitless 45 days. Munter resigned as ambassador after failing to persuade the administration to end "signature" strikes against unidentified targets. In the seventh week of negotiations, Pakistan reduced its demand from $5,000 to $3,000 a container and the USA raised its offer from $250 to $1,000, while agreeing to repave highways. But Pakistan continued to insist on repairs to the port of Karachi, an indemnity waiver if US cargo were damaged, and a formal apology for the November 26 strike. The USA agreed to the port repairs but refused indemnity waivers. When negotiations resumed on July 1, Kayani proposed a new draft apology, provoking the US Deputy Secretary of State to explode in anger. Two days later, after a seven-month border closure costing the USA $1 billion, it reached an agreement with Pakistan. Clinton telephoned Khar with a message, negotiated with the White House and DoD, which carefully avoided the word "apology," but "acknowledged the mistakes" and declared that "America respects Pakistan's sovereignty." The USA would pay $250 per truck (compared with the $17,000 it was paying for trucks using the northern route) and refurbish 130 miles of road. The administration would ask Congress to reimburse Pakistan for the $1.2 billion cost of 150,000 Pakistani troops fighting in the counterinsurgency and was likely to resume military aid to Pakistan. The *New York Times* welcomed an agreement ending a "needless dispute." The Information Minister dismissed "this useless issue of which word has been used. The reality is that the nation has been able to bring the world superpower to offer an apology." But the Defense of Pakistan Council (a coalition of Islamic parties) brought 8,000 demonstrators to Lahore, where a speaker declared: "we are here to rid Pakistan of American slavery." At the end of July the USA and Pakistan signed an MOU on supply routes through 2015.

Drone strikes had continued throughout this period. In August, on his first visit to Washington as ISI director, Gen. ul-Islam said Pakistani planes could conduct the strikes instead of US drones.[226] After three strikes in as many days killed 18 people, Foreign Minister Khar summoned US diplomats and denounced the strikes as "illegal, unproductive ... a violation of our sovereignty and territorial integrity and in violation ... of international laws." She told the Asia Society they were "illegal and unlawful." "This has to be our war ... As the drones fly over the territory of Pakistan, it becomes an American war and the whole logic of this being our fight, in our own interest, is immediately put aside and again it is a war which is imposed on us." Pakistan's Ambassador to the UN said drones violated sovereignty and were illegal: "thousands of innocent people ... have been murdered in these indiscriminate attacks." But in September the *Wall Street Journal* reported that about once a month the CIA described to ISI the broad areas it intended to target; Pakistan did not respond but cleared the airspace. US officials said that from 2009 until early 2012 it had Pakistan's consent to its "foreign internal defense mission." Imran Khan threatened to lead 100,000 demonstrators to South Waziristan, a closed area. He was joined by 32 international peace activists, including Americans from Code Pink. Although the group was blocked at the South Waziristan border, Khan declared "we have achieved the goal ... our message of peace has reached the world."

At the end of October Foreign Minister Khar opened the UN Human Rights Council's universal periodic review by condemning drone strikes.[227] In January 2013 she told the US Senate they violated her country's sovereignty, repeating this to the Pakistani Senate. The

Chair of the latter's Defense Committee complained about a "perpetual war by drones." The USA suspended strikes during the first two months of the year, resuming them only after Brennan was confirmed as DCI. Ben Emmerson, UN Special Rapporteur on the protection and promotion of human rights while countering terrorism, reported that Pakistan told him that a "thorough search of government records" uncovered no evidence of consent to the attacks, which therefore violated its sovereignty. (But Musharraf, who had been president in 2006–08, confirmed newspaper reports that ISI had approved CIA strikes and helped choose targets.) Pakistan confirmed at least 400 civilian deaths and suspected another 200. Other sources reported comparable numbers. Using data from the BIJ and the New America Foundation, Pitch Interactive found 535 civilian deaths (including 175 children) and 2,348 other deaths (only 47 of them high-profile targets).

In April the Peshawar High Court Chief Justice ruled that the March 2011 strike on the jirga had been illegal since there was no armed conflict in FATA.[228] International humanitarian law (which applied in the absence of armed conflict) made every victim a civilian and the strikes war crimes. The court declared that "the government of Pakistan must ensure that no drone strike takes place in the future" by tabling a UN resolution and, if the USA vetoed it, "think about breaking diplomatic ties." Mirza Shahzad Akbar, who brought the lawsuit, denounced the strikes in a *New York Times* op ed. AI published a report on their impact, documenting civilian casualties and the US failure to fulfill its obligation to investigate.

Drone strikes decreased in 2013, perhaps to avoid influencing Pakistan's May 11 general election.[229] A month after commencing his third term as Prime Minister, Sharif declared that strikes "shall stop now. If we respect the sovereignty of other nations, these nations shall also respect the sovereignty of our country." But three days later a strike killed at least seven people. After the second strike in little more than a week, Sharif directed the US Chargé d'Affaires to meet with the Foreign Minister, who reasserted the demand that strikes end. Pakistan Tehreek-e-Insaf (PTI: Imran Khan's Justice for Pakistan party, which controlled Khyber Pakhtunkhwa Province) submitted an anti-drone resolution in both the Punjab and the National Assembly, urging the government to use military force. Karzai said: "I fully will stand with Pakistan against any activity by any foreign power that causes civilian casualties in Pakistan." In July Pakistan's UN ambassador said drones "violate Pakistan's sovereignty" and "the principles of distinction and proportionality." Secretary of State Kerry said on Pakistani television in August: "I think the [drone] program will end as we have eliminated most of the threat and continue to eliminate it." But DoS quickly hedged: these were "changes that we expect to take place in that program over the course of time, but there is no exact timeline." Strikes had fallen from 122 in 2010 to just 16 in the first 7 months of 2013. After a strike killed six people a few days later, however, the Foreign Ministry said it set "dangerous precedents," and 2,000 attended the senior Haqqani network commander's funeral. At the end of September Sharif told the UN General Assembly the USA should end drone attacks. Several days later at least five more people were killed in North Waziristan. Days after that another strike killed four and wounded others, provoking the Foreign Minister's condemnation. Nobel laureate Malala Yousafzai said that when she met Obama in the Oval Office in October, "I also expressed my concerns that drone strikes are fueling terrorism. Innocent victims are killed in these acts, and they lead to resentment among the Pakistani people." In October the USA gave Pakistan more than $1.5 billion in outstanding aid.

The *Washington Post* published secret CIA documents and Pakistani diplomatic memoranda confirming that the two countries had an agreement on drone strikes and had shared information about at least sixty-five.[230] A Foreign Ministry spokesman said: "whatever understandings there may or may not have been in the past, the present government has been very clear regarding its policy on the issue. We regard such strikes as a violation of our sovereignty as well as international law." Sharif had stressed to Obama "the need for an end to such strikes," after which they issued a joint statement that "our enduring partnership is based on the principles of respect for sovereignty and territorial integrity." A day later Gilani (prime minister 2008–12) called it "totally absurd" to suggest that his government had acquiesced in such attacks. "During my government, there was no such support given to drone strikes whatsoever." But he could not rule out secret communications between the CIA and ISI under conditions set by President Musharraf. "After 9/11, the U.S. rang up Musharraf and said, 'you are either with us or your [*sic*] not with us,' and he said 'we are with you.'" In a 2012 CNN interview, Musharraf had admitted authorizing "a few" strikes. Hussain Haqqani, Pakistan's former ambassador to the USA, wrote in his memoir *Magnificent Delusions* that in 2008 the USA had killed Baitullah Mehsud, the Pakistan Taliban commander, at the Pakistan military's request.

Less than a week after Sharif met Obama a strike killed three people. For the second time in days Imran Khan threatened to block NATO supply routes if these attacks persisted. After a drone killed Hakimullah Mehsud, his uncle, and a bodyguard, the Pakistan Taliban aborted planned peace talks with Sharif, calling his government "fully complicit." The Interior Minister denounced the strike as a calculated blow to the peace process. Imran Khan declared he would block withdrawal of US and NATO materiel from Afghanistan. His PTI said: "the government, as a last resort, should target drones." Jamat-e-Ismali (another party) agreed. The USA assured Pakistan there would be no more strikes during peace talks with the Taliban. But a day later a drone hit an Islamic seminary in Northeast Hangu District (the first strike outside the tribal region), killing two teachers and four students and wounding others. Imran Khan led about 10,000 protesters in blocking NATO convoys over the weekend (when there were few trucks). When traffic resumed on Monday, police dispersed the blockade but let it resume a day later. The PTI Information Secretary Mazari identified the CIA station chief, demanding the government stop him from leaving the country so he could be prosecuted. After another drone strike in North Waziristan, Mazari accused the USA of showing "nothing but contempt for Pakistan's leadership." The USA stopped sending trucks through Torkham Gate and also through Baluchistan after that route was bombed. Visiting Pakistan, Defense Secretary Hagel warned that blocking supply lines could jeopardize $100 million in US military aid. Sharif promised the routes would be reopened, but Khan insisted the blockade would remain until strikes ended. The National Assembly unanimously resolved that strikes stop immediately. The blockade was still in place a week after Pakistan promised Hagel it would take "immediate action" to lift it. In January 2014 PTI continued its blockade at Torkham and threatened to extend it to the port of Karachi. Sharif's Information Minister denounced Khan as a demagogue "trying to divert the attention of people from his failures" in his own province. At the end of February PTI ended its three-month blockade a day after the Peshawar High Court declared it unconstitutional. Noting there had been no strikes since December 2013, PTI claimed that "the pressure of the blockade has already resulted in a shift in the Obama administration's drone policy."

The battle of numbers continued. NBC News published classified documents describing 114 drone strikes.[231] Although they described the dead as "other militants" in 26 and "foreign fighters" in 4, those categories really meant the CIA did not know their identities; it acknowledged only 1 of the approximately 600 killed as a civilian. The BIJ released a leaked Pakistan government report on 75 drone strikes and 5 NATO attacks in FATA in 2006–09, finding that of the 746 killed, at least 147 were civilians (94 of them children). The Defense Ministry said that 317 strikes in the previous five years had killed 2,000 suspected terrorists and 67 civilians (but none since January 2012). *Dawn* wrote that "regardless of whose figures are correct, the death of civilians is deplorable." "America's unilateral drone strikes violate Pakistan's sovereignty and are not legitimate." Less than a week later the Ministry admitted its figures were "wrong and fabricated." In March the Foreign Ministry had told the UN that the 330 strikes since 2004 had killed about 600 civilians. In early 2013 FATA had said 1,450 civilians had been killed in the previous five years. The BIJ said strikes in 2013 killed 112–193 militants but fewer than 5 civilians, down from 13–63 in 2012. Since 2004, 381 strikes had killed 416–951 civilians. After a June 2012 strike, the CIA showed US politicians overseeing the program a video depicting a drone killing only Abu Yahya al-Libi. But contemporaneous news reports and investigations by AI and BIJ uncovered three strikes, which AI said killed 10–16, including 6 civilians who sought to rescue victims of the initial blast. A new Pakistan government document also claimed ten deaths. Even after the *New York Times* published the BIJ investigation naming the ten dead, the USA continued to insist all were armed terrorists. In May 2014 BIJ reported that 61 percent of drone strikes targeted domestic buildings, killing an estimated 1,500 people in the previous 18 months, including at least 222 civilians. The overall and civilian casualty rates were highest for religious buildings (accounting for nearly half of all civilian deaths). Nevertheless, there were just 27 drone strikes in 2013, down from 128 in 2010, and no civilian casualties.

After pausing strikes in December 2013, the USA resumed in mid-May 2014, with the first in North Waziristan in mid-June (following Bowe Berdahl's release), killing about 100 people.[232] Pakistan voiced the usual objections. But Reuters reported that two high officials said the government had given "express approval" following the collapse of peace talks with the Taliban and its attack on the Karachi airport. By mid-July the USA had conducted four strikes. After it launched nine in ten days in October, *Dawn* said Pakistan's "relative silence can be interpreted as, at the very least, tacit acceptance and, possibly, active cooperation between the countries." But following the sixteenth strike of 2014, the Foreign Ministry said "the government of Pakistan is itself taking decisive action against terrorist elements and therefore believes that such strikes are unnecessary and need to be stopped." After the fourth strike in FATA in January 2015, Pakistan again denounced all strikes. In April the Islamabad High Court ordered the filing of criminal charges against Jonathan Bank, the former CIA station chief, and John Rizzo for a drone attack killing the brother and son of Kareem Khan, whose 2013 civil action had been dismissed for lack of jurisdiction. The prosecution was dismissed because the attack did not occur in the jurisdiction of the Islamabad police, but police planned to refile it in FATA.

On May 21, 2016 a JSOC drone strike in Baluchistan killed Mullah Akhtar Muhammad Mansoor, leader of the Afghan Taliban.[233] The USA said he posed a "continuing, imminent threat" to its personnel. Sharif condemned the violation of Pakistan's sovereignty because he had not been notified in advance. The Foreign Ministry summoned Ambassador Hale to protest. The Interior Minister said: "the justification provided by America to the world for this drone attack is illegal, unjustified, unacceptable, against Pakistan's independence and sovereignty, and completely against the U.N. Charter and international law." But the USA said it had disclosed weeks earlier that Mansoor was a target, and Pakistan had provided information on his general location though not his movements. The *New York Times* said: "the attack might not have been necessary had Pakistan cooperated in the first place and worked with the Americans to defeat the Taliban."

Analysis

Unlike the Karzai and al-Maliki administrations in Afghanistan and Iraq, the Pakistani government was not fighting for survival, had not invited the USA to join its fight against domestic enemies, and denied having consented to drone strikes in its territory. This denial – constantly reiterated by the highest officials – was aimed at a reflexively anti-American public further inflamed by the US wars in Afghanistan and Iraq. Determined that it (not India) would dominate Afghanistan after the inevitable US departure, Pakistan infuriated its American ally by refusing to attack the Taliban or Haqqani faction, which used their FATA refuge to strike Afghan and US targets across the border (allowing the USA to justify its own strikes as self-defense). The USA even suspected ISI of sharing intelligence with militants, helping them evade drone strikes. Although the Afghan government often accused Pakistan of sheltering cross-border attackers, it also joined its much larger neighbor – which it expected would ultimately dominate the region and with which it shared religion, ethnicity, and language – in resisting the American hegemon. Opposition politicians (preeminently the hugely popular Imran Khan) fanned that hostility, embarrassing the government into spouting nationalistic slogans (and even boasting, unconvincingly, that *it* had conducted the air attacks). Russia and China jumped at the chance to back Pakistan in this dispute, supporting its call for a UN investigation of drone strikes.

But practice belied the fiery rhetoric. Journalists repeatedly disclosed that Musharraf, Zardari, and Gilani had secretly granted permission for the strikes, some of which were launched from Pakistan's Shamsi air base. Partly because Pakistan was a nuclear power and had been a Cold War ally against the Soviet-backed India, the USA offered it a semblance of sovereignty by entrusting strikes to the secretive CIA rather than the highly visible US military. (But DCI Panetta could not resist bragging about the number and intensity of the Agency's drone strikes in retaliation for the December 2009 suicide bombing killing seven agents in Afghanistan.) The CIA notified Pakistan of some strikes in advance, canceled others in response to objections, and occasionally received an acknowledgment or even information about potential targets (some of whom, like the Mehsuds, Pakistan wanted dead).

These tacit understandings were periodically disrupted (and strikes temporarily suspended) following particularly egregious insults to Pakistan's sovereignty (Raymond Davis's killing of two robbers – for which the USA paid a staggering $2.3 million in compensation; the Osama bin Laden raid; and the killing of the Afghan Taliban leader Mansour) and other incidents triggering Pakistani resentment, such as accidental killings of its soldiers in cross-border raids and civilian drone casualties (after an August 2010 strike killed four women and three children, drone policy changed and civilian deaths decreased). Pakistan's honor demanded a public apology, which Obama was reluctant to give for fear of offering ammunition to Republican critics. Pakistan blocked the movement of materiel to and from Afghanistan through the Torkham border crossing (costing the USA an additional $100 million a month), outed CIA station chiefs and agents, and even responded with military force when its own troops suffered casualties. But however vehemently Pakistani leaders asserted their sovereignty, they depended on US civilian and especially military aid and support against domestic terrorists and in the interminable conflict with India.

Although all wars inflict "collateral damage," drone strikes provoked a distinctive response. In conventional warfare, civilians who suffer casualties could be accused of harboring or secretly being fighters. Drone strikes rarely prompted such justifications. Instead, contention focused on the ratio of civilian casualties to those of known or suspected militants. But this number could not be established conclusively. The USA rarely acknowledged the secret strikes, which occurred in remote areas like Waziristan, whose inaccessibility was the reason militants hid there and the USA deployed drones rather than ground forces. And some victims exhibited ambiguous loyalties, assisting al-Qaeda or the Taliban at times while opposing them at others. Estimates of the proportions varied widely. After one attack, the USA claimed 2 militants and 8 civilians dead, whereas an NPR reporter found no militants and 17–26 civilians dead. BIJ published figures at the high end, adding that some civilians had been killed by a second strike while rescuing victims or attending funerals – a practice that elicited widespread condemnation. The Pakistan Human Rights Commission claimed that "thousands of innocent people" had been murdered. Pakistan sought to personalize these tragedies with names, biographies, photos, and accounts by bereaved relatives. US estimates, unsurprisingly, occupied the opposite extreme. Brennan claimed civilian casualties were "extremely rare"; in June 2011 he denied there had been a single civilian death in Pakistan or Yemen for more than a year. Feinstein maintained that the number of civilians killed annually was in the "single digits." The USA highlighted the militant leaders it killed. Defenders argued (accurately) that the proportion of civilian casualties in drone strikes was far lower than in bombing raids or ground warfare. But this advantage was repeatedly eclipsed by a few tragic incidents inflicting many civilian casualties. Strikes ultimately diminished, less because of Pakistani opposition than because of the absence of suitable targets and hope the Taliban would enter peace negotiations.

Yemen[234]

On November 3, 2002, a US drone killed Qaed Sinan Harethi and five others (including Ahmed Hijazi, an American citizen). The UN called it "an alarming precedent" and "a clear case of extrajudicial killing" in violation of international law and treaties.[235] Two days later (and a day before the Congressional election) Deputy Defense Secretary Wolfowitz boasted that a "successful tactical operation [had] gotten rid of somebody dangerous." President Saleh banned armed drones, saying "this is why we are reluctant to work closely" with a government that does not "consider the internal circumstances in Yemen."

In December 2009 Obama ordered missile strikes against a suspected al-Qaeda training camp north of Sana'a and another in Abyan Province, where "an imminent attack against a U.S. asset was being planned."[236] The Yemeni Embassy in Washington said its government had "planned and executed" the attacks, killing up to 120 people. Yemen said at least 34 were militants, but opposition leaders insisted many were civilians. A tribal leader saw "parts of bodies, mostly women and children." A parliamentary inquiry found that the strike had killed at least forty-one members of two families, and three more civilians were killed and nine wounded when they stepped on cluster bombs. Later that month a missile strike in Shabwa Province missed Anwar al-Awlaki but killed at least thirty suspected militants gathered to discuss attacking Yemeni and foreign sites in retaliation for the earlier drone strikes. Foreign Minister al-Qirbi again claimed the strike had been conducted exclusively by his government (provoking derision from AQAP, the target). He said the USA "should learn from its experiences in Pakistan and Afghanistan and not repeat the mistakes in Yemen, both in dealing with the government of Yemen and confronting al-Qaeda." A drone strike in Marib Province on May 25, 2010 killed al-Qaeda members and also the deputy governor, who had been trying to persuade them to surrender. President Saleh took responsibility and paid blood money for this fourth secret US strike since December 2009. Yemen again banned further strikes. In November al-Qirbi claimed US drones engaged only in "surveillance," providing "intelligence information" for Yemeni Air Force strikes.

The following month Saleh assured John Brennan (whom he had known as the CIA's Riyadh station chief) that "Yemen's national territory is available for unilateral counterterrorism operations by the U.S."[237] "I have given you an open door on terrorism, so I am not responsible." WikiLeaks had published a cable in which Yemen promised the USA after the December 2009 strikes: "we'll continue saying the bombs are ours, not yours." And Deputy Prime Minister al-Alimi had assured the USA that any "munitions found at the sites … could be explained away as equipment purchased from the U.S." Denouncing the publication by WikiLeaks as a "despicable criminal act," Brennan called Saleh to apologize. After Saleh was severely injured by a June 11 rebel rocket attack, the USA felt freer to conduct strikes.

Yemeni tribal leaders, victims' relatives, and human rights activists warned that civilian deaths fueled anti-American sentiment while increasing sympathy for al-Qaeda.[238] A businessman mourned his dead brothers: a teacher and cell phone repairman. A strike claiming to have killed Fahd al-Quso, a militant, actually killed Nasser Salim, who had been tending his farm when al-Quso arrived. A strike in Bayda in March 2012 killed at least thirty; the USA claimed all were militants, but Yemenis said many were civilians. An adviser to former President Saleh said an offer to bury the dead "made people even more grateful and appreciative of al Qaeda," which vowed to "take revenge on your behalf." Ansar al-Sharia (AQAP in southern Yemen) claimed a bomb killing a hundred in Sana'a as its retaliation. An August strike killed three al-Qaeda members but also a man who had opposed AQAP and a police officer. NPR declared that civilians were killed "more often" than militants. Although a strike claimed to have killed two militants and eight civilians, "we found zero militants killed, between 17 and 26 civilians killed." Gregory Johnsen, a Yemen expert, said AQAP had grown from 200–300 at the end of 2009 to about a thousand in mid-2012, partly because of drone strikes. Robert Grenier, former head of the CIA Counterterrorism Center, warned that if the USA killed "young men, who are typically armed … indiscriminately you are running the risk of creating a terrific amount of popular anger." A Yemeni writer and politician wrote in a *New York Times* op ed that "when a U.S. drone missile kills a child in Yemen, the father will go to war with you." An HRW researcher reported "a much stronger sense of anger about the drone program" than four years earlier.

A September strike missed its target but killed 14, including 3 women and 2 children. The victims' families and tribesmen affiliated with al-Qaeda closed the main roads, stormed government buildings, and tried to take the bodies to the president's palace. AQAP displayed photos of the dead on its websites and offered compensation. At the funeral mourners cried: "America is a killer." The Yemeni government claimed it had conducted the strike, which killed only militants; but tribal leaders (and later Yemeni officials) said all were civilians and blamed the USA, which eventually accepted responsibility. The government publicly apologized and sent 101 guns to tribal leaders, but its promised investigation went nowhere. After visiting Washington, President Hadi praised drones as "technologically … more advanced than the human brain," maintaining that the USA and Yemen had taken "multiple measures to avoid mistakes of the past." Drones "pinpoint the target and have zero margin of error, if you know what target you're aiming at." "Every operation, before taking place, they take permission from the president." Brennan claimed that "Yemeni partners are more eager to work with us" because drone strikes freed them "from the hellish grip of A.Q.A.P." But Gregory Johnsen replied in a *New York Times* op ed that Brennan's claim that there was "little evidence that [strikes] are generating widespread anti-American sentiment or recruits for A.Q.A.P" was "either shockingly naïve or deliberately misleading." A Yemeni had told Johnsen he "would not be surprised if a hundred tribesmen join al-Qaeda as a result of the latest drone mistake."

Although drone strikes increased from 18 in 2010 to 53 in 2012, the rate fell by half in the first months of 2013.[239] A January 2013 strike killed a university student and a teacher who had accepted money to transport strangers (who turned out to be al-Qaeda). Although Obama had declared in his National Defense University speech that the USA would strike only if there was a "near-certainty that no civilians will be killed or injured," and Secretary of State Kerry added a week later, "we do not fire when we know there are children or collateral[s]," a June 9 drone strike killed suspected militants in a car but also one of their brothers. Nabeel Khoury (US deputy chief of mission in Yemen 2004–07) wrote that "drone strikes take out a few bad guys to be sure, but they also kill a large number of innocent civilians. Given Yemen's tribal structure, the U.S. generates roughly forty to sixty new enemies for every AQAP operative killed by drones." In October HRW published a report documenting civilian casualties in six drone strikes. Reprieve and Code Pink arranged for Faisal bin Ali Jaber, a Yemeni government engineer, to visit the USA to describe the August 29, 2012 strike that killed his brother-in-law (an imam who had denounced al-Qaeda) and nephew, as well as a local police officer and three others. Those deaths provoked two local teenage boys to join AQAP. Jaber sought an investigation and compensation for the village. HPSCI rejected two amendments by Adam Schiff to require the administration to report the number of combatants and noncombatants killed by drones. In July 2014 the Yemeni National Security Bureau gave the family $100,000 (which came from the USA, according to Reprieve).

A December 12 drone strike hit a wedding motorcade, killing 15 and wounding 5.[240] The Supreme Security Committee, led by Hadi, claimed the deceased were "top leaders who plotted several terrorist attacks." But after interviewing locals two days later, a Yemeni human rights activist said the dead were shepherds and khat farmers carrying weapons that were traditional at Yemeni weddings. Parliament banned drone attacks. The Yemeni government gave relatives 101 Kalashnikov rifles and 24–32 million Yemeni riyals ($110–159,000; a later account put the figure at more than $1 million, or about $60,000 per death). The CIA said it had questioned the intelligence prior to the JSOC strike. Based on two investigations, DoD concluded that only al-Qaeda members were killed, but refused to release the reports. An HRW investigation found that the attack killed at least twelve men and wounded at least 15 others, some of whom may have been AQAP. Yemen banned JSOC from conducting further strikes. The Yemeni Minister for Human Rights wrote in a *Washington Post* op ed that the drone killed at least 14 civilians and injured 22 others, more than a third seriously. Because "the U.S. government has issued no admission of responsibility, nor any apology ... it has left the Yemeni government to clean up another bloody mess." "Drones tear at the fabric of Yemeni society." Ansar al-Shariah in Yemen distributed propaganda videos showing informants admitting planting tracking microchips in militants' cars and civilians killed in drone strikes. In August 90 percent of the members of Yemen's National Dialogue Conference felt drones should be criminalized. BIJ said that 11–29 civilians were among the 61–99 killed by 16 strikes in Yemen in 2013; the Open Society Institute identified 55 civilians killed in 11 strikes between May 2012 and April 2014.

Days after President Trump's inauguration, drone strikes killed what Yemeni officials said were at least seven women and seven children, including Anwar al-Awlaki's 8-year-old daughter, as well as tribal leaders working with the displaced Yemeni government, which the USA supported.[241] Trump had given DoD authority to declare three Yemeni provinces areas of "active hostilities," in which battlefield rules were more relaxed. The USA initially replied that "there were a lot of female combatants who were part of this," but later conceded the civilian casualties. White House Press Secretary Sean Spicer said the raid, which Trump had approved over dinner with Jared Kushner and led to the death of a Navy SEAL, was "very, very well thought-out and executed." "When you think of the loss of life throughout America and institutions and in terms of the world, in terms of what some of the individuals could have done, I think it is a successful operation by all standards." But Gen. Votel, CENTCOM commander, said: "we lost a lot on this operation. We lost a valued operator; we had people wounded; we caused civilian casualties; lost an expensive aircraft." Yemen responded by withdrawing permission for US ground operations (but then reconsidered).

Analysis

Like Pakistan, Yemen faced death from the sky, but in very different circumstances. Although the USA claimed that targets like al-Awlaki threatened the American homeland, it seems to have put him on the kill list before it had evidence of this. Hence it had to rely on the AUMF rather than self-defense to justify most of the strikes (even though Yemen was far from any US battlefield). Unlike Pakistani Presidents Musharraf and Zardari, Yemeni President Saleh was totally dependent on the USA and very insecure (indeed, he was forced out of office after being severely wounded). In a futile attempt to hide this dependence, he initially took responsibility for the missile strikes, implausibly claiming the USA had sold him munitions. (But Wolfowitz, like Panetta, could not refrain from boasting about the November 2002 strike.) Unlike Pakistan, where fear of embarrassment by opposition parties restrained open cooperation with the USA, Yemen explicitly authorized and even welcomed the strikes, since militants threatened not only Western targets but also the regime itself. President Hadi even praised the technological perfection of drone targeting "if you know what you're aiming at" (a big "if"). He, too, was dependent on the USA, which greatly increased strikes in 2012 to help him regain territory from AQAP. Yemen responded to civilian casualties by paying compensation (with US funds), promising investigations (which never occurred), and declaring meaningless bans on strikes. Perhaps because it was so accommodating, Yemen successfully resisted the US request to conduct "signature strikes," which would have risked far more civilian casualties. But al-Qaeda effectively exploited the strikes for propaganda, burying the dead, compensating relatives, and encouraging demonstrations. And commentators warned that Yemen's tribal structure ensured that each strike would drive relatives of the dead to seek revenge by supporting or joining AQAP. Therefore Yemen, like Pakistan, felt compelled to criticize the strikes at the same time it was providing intelligence for them.

EXTRAORDINARY RENDITIONS AND SECRET PRISONS[242]

Countries where the USA declared war – Afghanistan and Iraq – or waged war without declaring it – Pakistan and Yemen – were sites of resistance to civilian casualties and other abuses. Other countries were implicated in US extraordinary renditions (Sweden, Canada, Italy, and Germany) and secret prisons (Poland, Romania, and Lithuania). Those operations raised several questions. What were the differences among and within the first four countries to complaints about extraordinary renditions? How were secret prisons exposed? What were the differences among and within the latter three countries to those exposés? How effective were European regional institutions in changing those practices and redressing the injuries they inflicted?

Sweden

On December 18, 2001 Sweden denied asylum to Ahmad Agiza and Muhammad al-Zery, accepted Egyptian assurances they would not be tortured, and handed the men to the CIA, which flew them to Egypt, where they were detained and tortured.[243] Both alerted the Swedish ambassador a month later. In June 2003 Agiza complained to the UN Committee against Torture, which found in May 2005 that Sweden had violated the CAT. The ECHR rejected his case as untimely. After the UN Human Rights Committee found that Sweden knew of al-Zery's mistreatment, that country paid him 3 million kronor ($502,000) in July 2008 and Agiza the same in October.

Canada

On September 26, 2002, the USA detained Maher Arar, a Canadian citizen in transit at JFK Airport from Zurich to his home in Montreal.[244] After interrogating him for 13 days, the USA rendered him to Jordan, which delivered him to Syria (his birthplace), where he was detained and tortured for a year. Canada established a Commission of Inquiry, which reported in July 2006 that the Royal Canadian Mounted Police had given the USA incorrect information. The Prime Minister apologized, and Canada gave Arar Can$10.5 million compensation plus his legal costs. The USA kept Arar on its "no-fly" list, preventing him from testifying in person at a joint hearing of the House Foreign Affairs Committee's Subcommittee on International Organizations, Human Rights and Oversight and the Judiciary Committee's Subcommittee on the Constitutional, Civil Rights and Civil Liberties. After he testified by phone, many members apologized. But US courts denied his civil damages claim (see Chapter 6 in the companion volume *Law's Trials*).

Italy

On February 17, 2003 CIA agents seized Hassan Mustafa Osama Nasr (aka abu Omar) as he walked to a Milan mosque, took him to the US Air Force base at Aviano, flew him to Ramstein, Germany, and rendered him a week later to Egypt (his birthplace).[245] His wife reported him missing, and an Egyptian woman witnessed the abduction. But the Italian General Investigation and Special Operations Division (DIGOS) dropped the case in March when the CIA lied to it that abu Omar was in the Balkans. After the Egyptian government released him from prison on April 20, 2004 he phoned his wife in Italy on May 8. Italian secret police, who had been developing a criminal terrorism case against him and sharing intelligence with the CIA, were furious at the agency's betrayal. Armando Spataro, Milan's deputy chief prosecutor, called the CIA actions "a serious breach of Italian law." But former CIA agents said the Rome station chief, who directed the operation, had briefed his counterpart in Italian military intelligence (SISMI), who cleared it with Prime Minister Berlusconi. Promptly denying this, the Prime Minister summoned the US ambassador and demanded the USA show "full respect for Italian sovereignty." The Minister for Parliamentary Affairs said it was "not even imaginable" that Italy had authorized the seizure. The Milan prosecutor obtained arrest warrants for 22 Americans (all of whom had left the country). A police raid on the home of Robert Seldon Lady, the CIA's Milan substation chief, found a computer with surveillance photos of abu Omar on the block where he was abducted, research on routes from Milan to Aviano, and evidence that Lady had gone to Cairo four days after the abduction and remained there through the start of the interrogation. Prosecutors and judges had signed extradition requests for the 22 in November; but Justice Minister Roberto Castelli (from the Northern League) did not immediately give his approval (usually a formality); and after meeting Attorney General Gonzales, Castelli denounced Spataro as a leftist "militant," whose work had to be reviewed carefully. But the judge who had approved the arrest warrants said the evidence "removes any doubt about [Lady's] participation." A Milan court issued European arrest warrants for the 22 Americans. A member of the Democratic Left Party asked the Parliamentary Intelligence Oversight Committee to question the Interior and Defense Ministers. Implicitly acknowledging complicity, Berlusconi declared that governments should not be expected to fight terrorism "with a law book in hand."

In December 2005 John Brennan (then director of the CIA Counterterrorism Center) defended extraordinary renditions:

> [I]t's rather arrogant to think we're the only country that respects human rights. I think that we have a lot of assurances from these countries that we hand over terrorists to that they will, in fact, respect human rights. [Consider an Egyptian citizen. The Egyptians] have a longer history in terms of dealing with them and they have family members and others that they can bring in, in fact, to be part of the whole interrogation process … a lot of times it makes more sense to have that person in a country where the local … intelligence and security service can in fact have a long process that's going to be able to elicit that information.

Michael Scheuer, a 22-year CIA veteran who had been closely involved with the bin Laden unit until he resigned in 2004, was more candid.[246] "It is easier to let the Egyptians or Jordanians do the dirty work … People are treated differently in Cairo and Milwaukee."

In April 2006, just after Berlusconi lost his re-election bid, Castelli refused to seek extradition.[247] Spataro had documents showing participation by Lt. Luciano Pironi (code-named Ludwig) of the Carabinieri (national military police), but they claimed he acted alone. Gen. Pollari, chief of SISMI, denied his agency's participation, but was removed from his position in November 2006 in what the government called a "natural rotation." In December prosecutors sought indictments of 26 Americans. *Corriere della Sera* published the 11-page affidavit abu Omar gave Italian prosecutors describing his abduction by the CIA and torture in Egypt, observed by an American. His wife said Egyptian officials had offered him $2 million from a "foreign intelligence service" (presumably the CIA) "to say that he had not been kidnapped and to say that he had come of his own free will."

In 2007, when Judge Interlandi began hearing the charges against the 26 Americans (in absentia) and 9 Italians, some defendants made an unsuccessful effort to terminate the proceedings on constitutional grounds.[248] Pironi admitted stopping abu Omar and asking for his ID so the CIA could seize him; Lady had assured Pironi the operation had "cover" and rewarded him with a six-day trip to the USA, including a visit to CIA headquarters, where top officials for European operations thanked him. Gen. Pignero, a former senior SISMI official (who knew he was dying), said that in late 2002 Pollari was visited by the CIA Rome station chief Jeffrey Castelli, who identified ten men he wanted captured. Pollari gave the list to Pignero, indicating the CIA wanted abu Omar given priority. "It was clear that the project envisioned the capture of terrorists, and of abu Omar in particular, with procedures that were outside the law." Although Pollari and he were opposed, they cooperated. Pignero documented abu Omar's movements. Marco Mancini (formerly number two at SISMI, now in jail for corruption and a defendant in this case) was heard discussing the abduction in two taped conversations (one of which he made to document his innocence). Pollari denied any involvement. Judge Interlandi issued the indictments declaring: "it's a question of principle. Today, it's Abu Omar. Tomorrow, it could be my daughter. These are fundamental human rights, and we have to respect them."

Abu Omar, who had been jailed again after telephoning his wife, was freed on February 11, 2007.[249] A few days later Italy decided to try 26 Americans and 5 Italians. The government had asked the Constitutional Court whether the prosecution had illegally ordered wiretaps of Italians' phone calls. The Deputy Prime Minister accused the prosecution of endangering national security; but the Minister for State Prosecutions disagreed and criticized the government for not requesting extradition. Two Italians had admitted guilt: Pironi got a suspended sentence; a former journalist got six months, commuted to a fine. CIA agents had carelessly left abundant evidence: copies of their passports and frequent flier cards, records of cell phone conversations, and hotel and restaurant credit card bills. DoS claimed Italy did not know their identities; but others called the aliases transparent. Warning that "these continuing investigations can harm intelligence cooperation," the USA refused to extradite anyone.

Judge Magi granted a motion on behalf of Pollari and Mancini ordering Berlusconi, Prodi, and other senior officials to testify about whether they had approved the abduction.[250] Abu Omar's wife described his torture. Bruno Megale, head of anti-terrorism police in Milan, who had been investigating abu Omar, first learned of his disappearance when his wife and friends reported him missing. He interviewed two witnesses to the abduction but made no progress until abu Omar phoned from Egypt after his first release from prison. Megale found cell phone calls near the site from Lady, a US Air Force colonel, five American diplomats, and SISMI officers, some to Virginia "where the Central Intelligence Agency has its headquarters." In March 2009 the Constitutional Court finally ruled that files seized from a SISMI apartment in Rome and an Italian military policeman's admission that he had participated in the kidnapping at Lady's request were inadmissible state secrets; but it admitted wiretaps of intelligence agents.

When the trial resumed in May, Col. d'Ambrosio, SISMI head in Milan, testified that Lady had said in October 2002 that the CIA (over his objections) was going to render abu Omar to Egypt to make him an informant.[251] Lady had terrible relations with Rome station chief Jeffrey Castelli, who had sent his deputy to Milan to ensure that Lady followed orders. After urging his boss Mancini to abort the operation, d'Ambrosio was transferred to Rome; Lady claimed this was Castelli's doing. Lady (who had retired from the CIA) told *Il Giornale*: "I'm only responsible for carrying out orders that I received from my superiors." "I worked in intelligence for 25 years and almost no activity I did in those 25 years was legal in the country where it happened." "I wasn't at the scene and I didn't organize the thing." "It happened in my jurisdiction but it was absolutely not under my control." The CIA had been "so unprofessional" because "there were too many people involved."

At the end of the trial prosecutors sought 10–13-year sentences for most of the Americans.[252] Abu Omar and his wife asked for €10 and €5 million damages respectively. The judge denied a request by Joseph Romano, head of security at Aviano, to transfer his case to a court-martial; some CIA defendants sought diplomatic immunity. In early November Magi convicted 23 Americans, sentencing Lady to eight years and the others to five, and convicted three Italians (including two former SISMI members Pompa and Seno), sentencing them to three years. The Americans would not be considered fugitives, and their European arrest warrants were valid only in Europe. Magi granted diplomatic immunity to three of the highest ranking CIA agents (Castelli, Medero, and Russsomando) and acquitted the five Italians who worked for SISMI (Pollari, Mancini, di Troia, di Gregori, and Ciorra) under the state secrets doctrine. Magi ordered those convicted to pay €1 million to abu Omar and €500,000 to his wife (though this never happened). The *Los Angeles Times* praised Magi for calling extraordinary rendition "by its real name – 'illegal,'" even though the decision was "largely symbolic." The editors did not "like renditions and generally [thought] even the most dangerous criminals are entitled to due process." The *New York Times* said "the Italian court got it right" and "the American court got it miserably wrong" in dismissing Arar's damage action "on flimsy grounds."

In his 200-page judgment published three months later, Judge Magi found that the CIA's ability to act with impunity "leads to the presumption that such activity was carried out at least with the knowledge (or maybe with the complicity)" of SISMI; but it was "not possible" to prove that because of the Constitutional Court's ruling that the evidence was a state secret – which Magi called "a logical and juridical paradox."[253] The Milan Court of Appeal convicted the five Italians who were originally acquitted, sentencing Pollari to 10 years, Mancini to 9, and the others to 6, but the Constitutional Court annulled the first two sentences, and the Court of Cassation overturned the remaining convictions because the case involved classified information. An appellate court convicted the three CIA agents who had been granted diplomatic immunity in the original trial.

In July 2013 Lady was detained by Panama border guards acting on an international arrest warrant issued by Italy the previous December, but was soon released because Panama had no extradition treaty with Italy.[254] Lady asked President Napolitano for a pardon, declaring: "I never intended to disrespect Italy's sovereignty." At the end of 2015 President Mattarella pardoned him and Bernie Medero; President Napolitano had already pardoned Joseph Romano.

Sabrina de Sousa (one of the convicted Americans) was detained in October 2015 as she tried to leave Portugal to visit her mother in Goa.[255] After a Portuguese court approved her extradition to Italy, she lost her appeal to the Supreme Court, and the Constitutional Court declined to hear her case. De Sousa protested that "this rendition was funded by Congress with approval of senior government officials in the U.S., Italy and Egypt." Her only role was to interpret at a meeting a year before the kidnapping when a CIA officer met Italian intelligence to discuss the logistics of renditions generally; Omar was never mentioned. She had sued the USA in November 2014, seeking documents showing that the rendition had been approved by higher officials and asking why she had not been included in the pardon request. As Portugal was about to extradite her to Italy, a partial presidential pardon reduced her sentence to three years, allowing her to petition successfully to serve it by teaching English twice a week to minors in state care.

Italy reactivated the charges against Abu Omar of criminal association and aiding illegal emigration with a goal of terrorism.[256] After one day of evidence in a closed door fast track trial, he was convicted in absentia and sentenced to six years. In February 2016 the ECHR ruled that "Italian authorities had a duty to take the appropriate measures to ensure that the persons within their jurisdiction were not subjected to torture or to inhuman or degrading treatment or punishment," and ordered Italy to pay €70,000 to abu Omar, €15,000 to his wife and €30,000 costs.

Germany

Khaled el-Masri, a Turkish-born German citizen, was seized on vacation at the Macedonian border and taken to Skopje on January 23, 2004.[257] Because the head of the CIA's Counterterrorism Center mistook him for someone with the same name who had been associated with the 9/11 hijackers, the USA rendered him to Kabul, holding him in the Salt Pit for six weeks and subjecting him to EITs. Although by March the Center realized that suspicions that he had a forged passport were wrong, it continued to hold him. In May Secretary of State Rice twice ordered his release, but only at the end of the month was he dumped in Albania. A week earlier a German had told el-Masri he would be unable to prove what had happened and the USA would never admit it. The US ambassador to Germany briefed Interior Minister Schily, but asked him to keep it secret. Chancellor Merkel said Rice admitted the mistake in December 2005, declaring "we work very hard and as quickly as possible to rectify" errors. But aides claimed Rice conceded only that *if* mistakes were made would they be corrected.

In February 2006 police and prosecutors in Neu-Ulm (el-Masri's home) began an investigation into German complicity.[258] A senior Macedonian official involved in the detention said that soon after el-Masri's capture Macedonian officials notified the German Embassy, but the Foreign Office denied this. El-Masri told German police he was 90 percent certain that the man who interrogated him three times in Afghanistan was a German senior police official calling himself "Sam" (later identified as Gerhard Lehmann of the German Federal Police). After el-Masri picked him out from a ten-man line-up, "Sam" claimed he had been "on holiday" in Germany at the time of the alleged interrogation but could not remember the location. The Interior Minister denied that any member of the secret services had seen el-Masri and insisted "Sam" "has never been to Afghanistan."

Although Germany initially claimed it had learned of the abduction only when el-Masri returned home, its spy agency (Bundesnachrichtendienst or BND) told a parliamentary inquiry in June 2006 that a mid-level employee at the Skopje embassy had been informed at the time of el-Masri's seizure.[259] In September Hans-Christian Ströbele (a Green Party member of parliament and member of the inquiry), supported by a Free Democratic Party colleague, criticized the police for not issuing arrest warrants. The German television station NDR published the names and aliases of the 13 CIA operatives. The Munich state prosecutor August Stern sought arrest warrants, which were issued on January 31, 2007. *Süddeutsche Zeitung* declared that "the great ally is not allowed to simply send its thugs out into Europe's streets." The *Los Angeles Times* argued that in addition to the "legal and moral" arguments against "snatching terrorism suspects off the streets of Europe and shipping them to unsavory countries to be tortured," this "disastrous" policy would make European allies "less inclined to cooperate." "Due process remains a fundamental western value, and outrage about violations is a sign of democratic health." (In February 2007 the *Times* disclosed details of the plane crew that had flown el-Masri from Macedonia to Afghanistan.)

In 2010 the media reported a secret February 2007 cable in which John M. Koenig (deputy chief of mission) told DoS he had "reiterated" to German Deputy National Security Adviser Rolf Nikel "our strong concerns about the possible issuance of international arrest warrants in the al-Masri [*sic*] case."[260] Nikel "underscored the independence of the German judiciary" and said "from a judicial standpoint, the facts are clear, and the Munich prosecutor has acted correctly," but added that "politically speaking … Germany would have to examine the implications for relations with the U.S." Because of "intense pressure from the Bundestag and the German media … this case 'will not be easy.' The chancellery would nonetheless try to be as constructive as possible." The day after the arrest warrants were issued, US diplomats went on the offensive. Stern, the Bavarian state government, and the Federal Justice Ministry (Bundesministerium für Justiz, or BMJ) opposed an investigation. Stern told an American diplomat he "felt compelled to act due to media pressure." The Bavarian Chancellery and the offices of the state governor and his cabinet made unsolicited calls to the Embassy emphasizing that the Chancellery had been "surprised and displeased" by the warrants and played "no role in the actions of the prosecutor, who is independent." The Bavarian Justice Minister also expressed surprise. BMJ assured the Embassy that international arrest warrants could be issued only after it had evaluated both their legal validity and "foreign policy implications." But it also warned that US interference "might be perceived as an admission of involvement by CIA agents." The Foreign Ministry state secretary expressed doubt about the warrants' legality and promised the USA that his Ministry would take foreign policy considerations into account. Later that year the BMJ decided to drop the case after the USA made clear it would not arrest or hand over the agents. In June 2008 Wolfgang Kaleck and other human rights lawyers sued to compel the German government to pursue the extradition, but in December 2010 the Cologne Administrative Court upheld the decision not to proceed.

The ACLU filed el-Masri's petition against the USA in the Inter-American Commission on Human Rights, which agreed to hear it in August 2009. In May the Spanish Audiencia Nacional prosecutor's office asked Judge Moreno to issue arrest warrants for the 13 CIA agents who stopped in Majorca on their way to get el-Masri in Skopje. In June 2010 the ECHR agreed to hear OSI's case on behalf of el-Masri against Macedonia. On October 8 the court ordered Macedonia to answer and invited Germany to comment. In December 2012 the 17-judge Grand Chamber unanimously found that el-Masri's account was "established beyond reasonable doubt" and ordered Macedonia, which "had been responsible for his torture and ill-treatment," to pay him €60,000.[261]

The CIA IG's 2004 report on EITs (portions of which were published in June 2016) found that though the Agency "quickly concluded [el-Masri] was not a terrorist" and the "prolonged detention of el-Masri was unjustified," two officers defended it "despite the diminishing rationale, by insisting that they knew he was 'bad.'"[262] DCI Tenet "was informed about the ... rendition shortly after it happened and then again in late April 2004." Three CIA lawyers received an "oral admonition." The IG referred the case to the DoJ, but the ED Va US Attorney declined to prosecute in May 2007. I discuss el-Masri's failed US damages action in Chapter 6 of the companion volume *Law's Trials*.

Secret Prisons

On November 2, 2005 the *Washington Post* revealed that the CIA had detained more than a hundred terrorism suspects, including "high-value detainees," rendered some to third countries, and subjected others to EITs in secret "black site" prisons in eight countries, including Thailand and Afghanistan (the *Post* did not name the others at the request of the USA).[263] Parliaments in Canada, Italy, France, Sweden, and the Netherlands had opened investigations into renditions involving their territories. At his November 7 press conference President Bush was unapologetic: "We are finding terrorists and bringing them to justice ... We are trying to disrupt their plots and plans ... any activity we conduct, is within the law." After the CIA asked DoJ to investigate the source of the leaks, Sen. Frist (R-Tn) and Rep. Hastert (R-Ill) urged the two Intelligence Committees to do so as well. Sen. Roberts (R-Kan), SSCI chair, thought the culprit was a Republican senator who had attended a briefing by Vice President Cheney a day before the article appeared. Two Republicans, Rep. Shays (Ct) and Sen. Graham, said any investigation should focus on the prisons themselves. The *New York Times* criticized "Republican leaders of Congress" for "piously demanding a full investigation into the sources." Any damage had been "caused by the administration's underlying acts and policies, not by the news media's disclosures." On November 17 a spokesman said DoS had briefed Spain and Norway on the issue but refused to discuss other countries: "I cannot provide for you every day answers to this country and that country and whatever the country of the day is." Austria, Denmark, Iceland, and Norway now launched investigations. At the end of November the USA told the EU it needed more time to confirm whether renditions had crossed member states' territory.

EU Justice and Home Affairs Commissioner Franco Frattini warned that any member state found to have operated a secret prison could lose its voting rights. Terry Davis, Council of Europe Secretary General, gave member states three months to disclose what they knew about renditions and secret prisons. On January 18, 2006 the EP voted 359–127 to create a temporary committee on the alleged use of European countries by the CIA for the transport and illegal detention of prisoners (TDIP), consisting of 46 members from all political groups. In the UK Sir Menzies Campbell (Liberal Democrat deputy leader and foreign affairs spokesman) said: "we need full disclosure by our government." He and members of parliament Andrew Tyrie (Conservative) and Chris Mullen (a former Labour Minister for Foreign Affairs) created an All-Party Group on Extraordinary Renditions to investigate. But the British Foreign Office said "we are not aware of the use of U.K. territory or airspace for the purpose of extraordinary renditions." The Council of Europe appointed Dick Marty, a Swiss prosecutor, to conduct an investigation. He asked the EU satellite center for photos of the past three years of Sczytno-Szymany airport in Poland and Mihail Kogalniceanu air base in Romania, and Eurocontrol (the European Aviation Authority) for itineraries of 31 aircraft used by the CIA. At the end of January 2006 he had found no prisons but had enough evidence to continue his investigation. He believed the prisoners had been moved to Morocco a month earlier (because of the *Post* exposé), but the Moroccan government said: "we have no knowledge about this subject." Marty issued three reports in 2006, 2007, and 2011.[264] Journalists and NGOs documented numerous flights through Europe by aircraft associated with the CIA, but there was little evidence that a particular flight had carried detainees to secret prisons or rendered them to torture.[265]

Former Romanian Defense Minister Ioan Mircea Pascu said parts of the Mihail Kogalniceanu air base, used by the USA in 2003, had been closed to Romanians.[266] Planes carrying US prisoners might have made stopovers, but there was no secret prison. The base commander denied there had ever been prisoners. The USA left the base in June 2003. Spanish officials acknowledged that an April 2004 flight from Guantánamo stopped in Tenerife on its way to Romania. When Secretary of State Rice visited Romania on December 6, 2006 President Traian Basescu denounced "speculation about the landing of certain airplanes." "If there is the wish by anyone to visit any place suspected to be destined for detention and torture, Romania puts at their disposition its entire territory." Reporters visiting the base found no prisons. The Romanian parliament established a Senate Committee of Inquiry in 2005 co-chaired by a member of parliament and the head of the Romanian Intelligence Service, which produced a classified report; a Romanian government secret inquiry found there had been no prison.

On the eve of her departure for Europe on December 5, Rice declared:[267]

> For decades, the United States and other countries have used "renditions" to transport terrorist suspects from the country where they were captured to their home country or to other countries where they can be questioned, held or brought to justice … where … the local government cannot detain or prosecute a suspect, and traditional extradition is not a good option … the local government can make the sovereign choice to cooperate in a rendition … [which] are permissible under international law and are consistent with the responsibilities of those governments to protect their citizens.

The *New York Times* commented that "what most Americans think when they hear talk about 'bringing the terrorists to justice'" was that they would be "charged in courts, put on trial, convicted and sentenced." They did not visualize "predawn abductions, blindfolded prisoners on plane rides and years of torture in distant lands without any public reckoning." ABC News reported that when HRW revealed the existence of secret prisons in Poland and Romania, these were immediately closed and the 11 HVDs flown to Morocco. Polish Defense Minister Sikorski said: "my president has said there is no truth in these reports." After Rice answered questions at a dinner for 32 Foreign Ministers and NATO representatives on December 7, the French Foreign Minister lauded Americans as "our friends and our allies." The Dutch Foreign Minister said "we have gotten guarantees and all the satisfactory answers we can hope for"; the prisons were "pure speculation." The NATO Secretary General said Rice's comments "cleared the air." A week later her predecessor, Colin Powell, said "our European friends cannot be shocked that this kind of thing takes place … we have, over the years, had procedures in place that would deal with people who are responsible for terrorist activities."

Before the latest revelations, outgoing Polish President Kwasniewski maintained "there never have been" and "are no such prisons or such prisoners on Polish territory."[268] But on December 10 *Gazeta Wyborcza* reported that planes belonging to the CIA or FBI had landed at Szczytno-Szymany airport at least five times since December 2002, standing on the runway without refueling as they were approached by border control officials and minivans from Kiejkuty, the site of a Polish intelligence service training school. Prime Minister Marcinkiewicz said he had ordered a "detailed" inquiry to "check if there is any proof that such an event took place in our country." A Parliamentary Committee for Special Services concluded there had been no prison.

In January 2006 a Swiss newspaper disclosed that the previous November Swiss intelligence had intercepted a fax from Egypt's Foreign Minister to its London embassy discussing 23 detainees from Iraq and Afghanistan interrogated at Mihail Kogalniceanu air base, and mentioning "similar interrogation centres in Ukraine, Kosovo, Macedonia and in Bulgaria."[269] The Romanian Defense Ministry and the Bulgarian Foreign Affairs Minister categorically denied this. A few days later the *Sunday Times* (London) reported that the USA was helping build a prison for the Moroccan secret police near Rabat.[270] Dick Marty had found documentation of flights between Washington, Guantánamo Bay, and the Rabat military airport. French intelligence and diplomatic sources confirmed that in the first week of December 2005 (when the secret European prisons were hastily emptied in the wake of the *Post*'s disclosures) four suspects were led blindfolded and handcuffed from a Boeing 737 at that airport to a fleet of American vehicles.

In April the EU anti-terrorism chief told TDIP that the existence of secret prisons "does not appear to be proven beyond reasonable doubt."[271] But a few days later rapporteur Claudio Fava issued the first interim report, concluding that "the CIA has, on several occasions, clearly been responsible for kidnapping and illegally detaining alleged terrorists on the territory of member states, as well as for extraordinary renditions." "The committee deplores the fact that … the CIA has used aircraft registered under fictitious company names or with private companies to secretly transfer terror suspects to other countries including Egypt, Jordan, Syria and Afghanistan." A week later DoS legal adviser John Bellinger complained that "the suggestion that intelligence flights are somehow engaged in illegal activity really undermines the cooperation between the United States and Europe." The report was "hysterical in its hyperbole" for concluding that all CIA flights had "nefarious intent." It was "absurd" to allege that they carried detainees. The report contained so many errors that the USA had decided not to respond. Fava replied that his report said "some" flights had detainees, not all. Asked why the USA did not give the ICRC access to all prisoners, DoS asserted that some individuals "forfeit their rights under Geneva Convention protections." Two weeks later SSCI proposed legislation requiring the administration to report the location of secret prisons (Snowe (R-Me) and Hagel (R-Neb) joining the Democrats). In June DoS again dismissed the report as just a "sort of rehash" without "solid facts." The Polish Prime Minister called the accusations "slanderous" and "not based on any facts." The head of the Romanian Parliamentary Committee on Foreign Intelligence said: "there is no evidence there were such detention bases in Romania." British Prime Minister Tony Blair said it contained "absolutely nothing new."

The final report in November found that 11 countries had been involved in renditions or secret prisons. Poland first said it had not retained logs of the 11 CIA-operated flights, then that they had been destroyed, and finally that they had been "saved in an unspecified place." The former Szymany airport director said strangers visited at least six times in 2002–03, offering large amounts of cash to land planes from Afghanistan and elsewhere. Each parked at the end of the runway, waiting in the dark for an unmarked minivan. But the Polish Ministry for Special Services dismissed the report as based on "commonly repeated assumptions, suspicions and probabilities." TDIP also found evidence of a prison in Romania (where CIA planes had landed 21 times), considered it "highly likely" that the Italian secret services knew about the rendition of abu Omar, and accused Sweden of wrongly relying on "diplomatic assurances" that Egypt would not torture Agiza and al-Zari. The EP approved the report 382–256, but narrowly concluded (356–323) it was "not possible to acknowledge or deny that secret detention centres were based in Poland." "No definitive evidence has been provided to contradict any of the allegations concerning the running of a secret detention facility on Romanian soil."

Although the USA repeatedly denied the existence of secret prisons, Bush had to acknowledge them in September 2006 when he declared them empty after transferring 14 HVDs to Guantánamo.[272] Poland and Romania again denied they ever had such prisons. René van der Linden, President of the Council of Europe Parliamentary Assembly, declared that "kidnapping people and torturing them in secret ... is what criminals do, not democratic governments." Sen. Rockefeller (ranking Democrat) said SSCI had not been told the locations of the secret prisons. Claudio Fava criticized Romania's "superficial" investigation. Ioan Talpes, former head of its foreign intelligence service, said Romanians were excluded from the military portions of Kogalniceanu air base under a 2002–03 agreement with the USA. An airport officer said "there was no transfer of prisoners by American armed forces in the base" (but of course the CIA conducted the operation). A former Jeppesen International Trip Planning employee remembered managing director Bob Overby boasting at a meeting, "we do all of the extraordinary rendition flights – you know, the torture flights" for the CIA.

In February 2007 the *Chicago Tribune* reported that in late 2002 and early 2003 many planes registered to American companies (mostly Gulfstreams favored by the CIA) flew from Afghanistan to Szymany airport, parked at the end of the runway, were met by government vehicles, and left after an hour or two for Morocco, Uzbekistan, or Guantánamo Bay.[273] The airport manager said: "everything was unusual, from beginning to end. I was told to accept these flights even when the airport was closed" and "not to organize full ground service. They said to send everyone home and keep only one technical service worker." Planes paid landing fees in cash at 2–4 times the going rate. Regional border guards checked passengers based on a list provided by the aircraft and ordered airport authorities not to approach. Customs formalities were secretly conducted on the plane. Cars with tinted windows took passengers to Stare Kiejkuty, 12 miles away. The then head of Polish military intelligence said CIA flights landed at the airport and the Agency controlled a "special zone" inside Stare Kiejkuty. A British intelligence memo said Prime Minister Blair told Polish Prime Minister Miller to withhold the information from his own government.

In March 2007 Rep. Markey (D-Mass) introduced the "Torture Outsourcing Prevention Act" to end renditions. At an April joint hearing of two House Foreign Affairs Committee subcommittees, Rep. Delahunt (D-Mass) (who organized it) said renditions "are utterly inconsistent with our broader foreign policy goals" and "violate our obligations under the UN Convention Against Torture and other international treaties" and "fundamental American values."[274] Claudio Fava called the rendition program "an illegal instrument." But Michael Scheuer said renditions were "the single most effective counterterrorism operation ever conducted by the United States government," and denied that "a single target of rendition has ever been kidnapped by CIA officers." He would not "be surprised if [detainees'] treatment [in "Middle Eastern prisons"] was not up to U.S. standards," but "this is a matter of no concern." "If you accepted an assurance from any of the Arab tyrannies who are our allies that they weren't going to torture someone, I have got a bridge for you to buy." "If mistakes were made, I can only say that that is tough, but war is a tough and confusing business." The USA did not owe an apology to Arar or anyone else seized by mistake. "They're not Americans. I really don't care." "I never got paid ... to be a citizen of the world." "If I had the same sheet of information about Maher Arar today, I would go after him again." Rep. Rohrabacher said the CIA had made "maybe three" mistaken arrests. "I do not put that on a list of atrocities." European obsession with due process could have "the unfortunate consequence" of helping al-Qaeda kill tens of thousands in London. "If somebody were to set off a dirty bomb in New York or in Boston Harbor or in Los Angeles ... there would be millions of Americans whose lives would be lost." He declared bizarrely: "There are no Afghans in ... Guantánamo," which "has been inspected by Amnesty International and a plethora of human rights organizations and not found to be inhumane." Neither Scheuer nor Rohrabacher cared if "these terrorists rot in prison." At a private luncheon at the German Embassy in Washington a month earlier DCI Hayden had denounced European criticism as "hypocrisy."

In June AI, Cageprisoners, CCR, HRW, the NYU Center for Human Rights and Global Justice, and Reprieve published a list of 39 people believed to be secretly imprisoned by the USA.[275] The next day TDIP published its final report confirming that Poland and Romania had hosted secret CIA prisons. The CIA said: "Europe has been the source of grossly inaccurate allegations." "When you see words like 'apartheid' and 'torture' in the document, that tells you it's biased and distorted."

Polish President Kaczynski said that since he took office in December 2005, "there has been no secret prison." "I am assured there never were any in the past either." In September DCI Hayden called the report "wild speculation." "The suggestion that even a substantial number of those 1,245 flights were carrying detainees is frankly absurd on its face."

In October (at the request of Reprieve) the All Party Group on Extraordinary Renditions investigated whether the British base on Diego Garcia in the Indian Ocean had hosted rendition flights.[276] Andrew Tyrie complained that whenever members of parliament asked, the government responded that US authorities "have repeatedly given us assurances" that no suspect had ever been held there. But a Gulfstream jet regularly used by the CIA flew there from Washington on September 11, 2002, soon after the capture of Ramzi bin al-Shibh. In January 2008 the government refused to give the Group the minutes of September 2007 UK/US political-military talks in Washington, claiming release "would prejudice the defence" of the territory and damage diplomatic relations. But less than a month later Foreign Secretary David Miliband admitted that two US planes carrying detainees had refueled on Diego Garcia en route to Guantánamo Bay and Morocco in 2002. John Bellinger explained that the flights came to light after the USA re-examined past operations, interviewed former employees, and conducted a "more exhaustive search" of records, blaming "an administrative error in the way the searches were conducted previously." Miliband did "not believe the U.S. government set out to mislead the British government. I believe they told us in good faith they had no evidence of the use of Diego Garcia." In 2005, 2006, and 2007 Jack Straw (Miliband's predecessor) and Tony Blair had denied any layovers. Now Prime Minister Brown said: "it is unfortunate that this was not known and it is unfortunate it happened without us knowing." Liberal Democrats, Conservatives, and Labour backbenchers were highly critical. DCI Hayden called these "rendition operations, nothing more." The Agency had been "in the wrong" about the information and it was important to "take responsibility for errors and to learn from them." The *Los Angeles Times* said: "the Bush administration should be ashamed for misleading Britain." In June 2008 Miliband said the USA had studied a list of 391 flights and assured him there had been no other renditions through British territory.

In November 2007 Ana Gomes, a Portuguese MEP, obtained flight logs suggesting that CIA planes flew nearly 700 detainees across Greece,

Italy, Spain, and Portugal to Guantánamo from a Turkish military airbase or the US air base at Incirlik.[277] Thomas Hammarberg, Council of Europe (CE) Commissioner for Human Rights, said: "what happened at Guantánamo was torture and it is illegal to provide facilities or anything to make this torture possible." Turkish agencies "reached no findings regarding any unacknowledged deprivation of liberty conducted by foreign agencies within the territory of the Republic of Turkey or any transport by aircraft or otherwise of the persons deprived of their liberty." In January 2008 Terry Davis, CE Secretary General, complained that no member country had implemented his 2006 recommendations that it supervise foreign intelligence agents, stop the abuse of diplomatic immunity, and monitor airports and airspace. In February the EU Commissioner for Justice and Home Affairs accused Poland and Romania of evading requests to clarify their involvement with the CIA. Three times in 2004 and twice in 2005 a plane landed at Kogalniceanu air base in the middle of the night, exchanged large parcels resembling bundled-up detainees with a black bus, and then flew to North Africa. The planes filed either no flight plan or a bogus one. Other planes arrived from Iraq and parked in a restricted area off the runway, pretending to have technical problems but making no repairs. President Basescu's office said dismissively: "what business do we have with this?" Former Defense Minister Ioan Mircea Pascu called it a "closed subject."

In November *El País* published a government document showing the USA had asked the Spanish Foreign Minister in January 2002 to let a CIA flight land at Móron air base on its way to Guantánamo.[278] Foreign Minister Moratinos had told parliament in November 2005 he had no knowledge of US planes stopping in Spain and told TDIP in September 2006 that the USA had assured the Zapatero government it knew of no CIA planes stopping in Spain between Kabul and Guantánamo. Spain now promised to investigate, but in January 2015 an appellate court sustained the Audiencia Nacional decision to suspend the investigation because the CIA's refusal to identify the personnel made it impossible to pursue the case.

After the EP again condemned renditions as "an illegal instrument" in February 2009, the new Obama administration created a task force to study rendition policy.[279] DCI Panetta said in April that the "CIA no longer operates detention facilities or black sites" but "retains the authority to detain individuals on a short-term transitory basis." "We anticipate that we would quickly turn over any person in our custody to U.S. military authorities or to their country of jurisdiction." In August the president's Interrogation and Transfer Policy Task Force approved renditions with better oversight. The *Los Angeles Times* regretted the failure to make a "clear break with the past." The administration continued to resist disclosure of Bush's September 2001 order authorizing the CIA to create secret prisons.

In April 2009 it was revealed that for more than a year Warsaw public prosecutor Robert Majewski had been investigating the Miller administration's complicity in operating the secret prison.[280] Prosecutors also were investigating whether Polish intelligence made 20 agents available to the CIA, as reported in *Rzeczpospolita.* Two members of the parliamentary investigative committee saw a 2005 document confirming this, which had since disappeared. Journalist Mariusz Kawalewski had found the flight record books from Szymany airport, which had been declared lost, and had reconstructed flight routes based on refueling receipts. In August the *New York Times* reported information from two CIA officials about Kyle "Dusty" Foggo, who had headed the Agency's main European supply base and overseen construction of three secret prisons in Bucharest, Morocco, and Poland.[281]

That month ABC News reported that a secret CIA prison outside Vilnius, Lithuania had housed up to eight suspects for more than a year until the *Washington Post*'s disclosure led the CIA to remove them.[282] Although the Agency had filed false flight plans, flight logs showed its planes moving detainees among Lithuania, Thailand, Afghanistan, Poland, Romania, Morocco, and Guantánamo. A former CIA official said that because Lithuania sought better relations with the USA, we "didn't have to" offer any incentives. The Lithuanian government promptly denied everything. Faldas Adamkus (president 2004–09) was "absolutely sure that there was no CIA prison in Lithuania." But two months later the newly elected President Grybauskaite (who also held the foreign and defense policy portfolios) said the earlier parliamentary finding that there had been no prison was a mere formality because of the lack of "political will." A month after that ABC News reported it had discovered the prison at a horseback riding academy, which Elite, LLC (a CIA front) bought in March 2004. Lithuania had agreed to host the prison after Bush visited in 2002 and pledged to support Lithuania's NATO application, which succeeded in April 2004. Locals seeking work at the site were rebuffed by English-speaking guards. When the site was sold to the Lithuanian government in 2007, a former Lithuanian counterintelligence officer said: "everybody knew this was handed to us by the Americans." The Parliamentary Committee on National

Security and Defense (CNSD) visited the site and declared it had "all rights and tools to ultimately clarify the situation." But after a joint meeting with the Committee on Foreign Affairs, it found insufficient information for a full investigation.

When he met Grybauskaite soon thereafter, Hammarberg said flight logs had been doctored and warned Lithuania: "it is quite likely that further information might leak from the United States, so they should hurry up and do their own investigation now." When the president acknowledged "indirect suspicions" that the prison existed, parliament directed CNSD to conduct a full investigation. After questioning more than fifty people, including two former presidents, CNSD found evidence that the site contained a prison, but not that it had held any prisoners. Although it published no report, CNSD asked prosecutors to investigate. Prime Minister Kublius said "the strategic partnership with the United States cannot be an excuse to essentially operate under Soviet methods." Grybauskaite removed a former State Security Department director from his post as ambassador to Georgia; and the current director and Foreign Secretary resigned. In May 2010 Kublius said at a press conference with Secretary of State Clinton in Washington: "all the investigations which we were able to do were done in Lithuania by Lithuanian Parliament, and we have nothing to add." In June the European Committee for the Prevention of Torture visited the prison; its May 2011 report concluded ambiguously that "the premises did not contain anything that was highly suggestive of a context of detention," but "could be adapted for detention purposes." In September 2010 Reprieve sent the Prosecutor General evidence that abu Zubaydah had been held there, but Grybauskaite said the information had to be reviewed in the USA. In November 2010 AI published its own detailed analysis of the prison. But in January 2011 the Prosecutor General closed the investigation because of the absence of data on airplane passengers, the statute of limitations, and the fact that the three named State Security Department officials were no longer with the Department. In January 2014 the Vilnius Regional Court overruled prosecutors, directing them to investigate the complaint on behalf of al-Hawsawi by the Human Rights Monitoring Institute and Redress.

Two days after the initial ABC News report on Lithuania, Romania's deputy chief of mission in Washington wrote the *New York Times*:[283]

> The Romanian authorities have cooperated in good faith and with utmost transparency with all the investigative international mechanisms

> and bodies created with the aim to clarifying the alleged existence in Romania of C.I.A. secret detention centers. In addition to the undertakings of the Romanian government in this regard, the Senate of Romania established in 2005 a special committee tasked to investigate these allegations. The report issued by the committee – adopted by the Senate on April 22, 2008 – has concluded that the allegations are unfounded.

In December 2011 Romania's Foreign Affairs Minister told the CE that "no public official ... has been involved in the unacknowledged deprivation of any individual, or transport of any individual while so deprived of their liberty," and "no such activities took place on Romanian territory."

In February 2010 the Helsinki Foundation for Human Rights and OSI found flight logs showing that six CIA flights landed at Szymany airport in 2003, five from Kabul and one from Morocco.[284] Four years earlier Poland had told TDIP there were no logs. In July 2007 documents had been found showing flights between December 5, 2002 and September 22, 2003 (when the prisoners were transferred to Romania). Then Prime Minister Miller now reiterated there were "no secret CIA prisons in Poland." In October 2010 Polish prosecutors granted the status of victim to Abd al-Rahim al Nashiri, who had been tortured in the secret prison, and later did the same for abu Zubaydah. DoJ refused to cooperate with the Polish prosecutors.

In January 2012 Poland secretly charged Zbigniew Siemiatkowski, chief of intelligence 2002–04, with exceeding his powers, breaching international law, unlawful deprivation of liberty, and corporal punishment of POWs; it also planned to charge his deputy, who dealt with the CIA.[285] The Polish intelligence agency had given prosecutors an agreement Siemiatkowski had signed, with a "cc to Prime Minister" Miller. President Komorowski said he wanted "to finally get to the bottom of the question of the existence of CIA prisons in Poland." Prime Minister Tusk said: "Poland is a democracy where national and international law must be observed. This issue must be explained." But former Prime Minister Miller said: "I won't shed tears for murderers." Prosecutors had been preparing a request to the head of parliament to bring Miller (now leading an opposition party) before the state tribunal. But the general prosecutor transferred the investigation from Warsaw to Krakow. (A year earlier the general prosecutor had demoted one Warsaw prosecutor and taken the other off the case.) In March Komorowski reiterated that "the reputation of Poland is at stake ... it is the task of the legal apparatus to clarify this." But the Polish lawyer representing al Nashiri said prosecutors refused to give him documents. And in February 2013 prosecutors dropped the charges. In October 2013 the Polish prosecutor general granted Walid Mohammad bin Attash the status of an "injured person" in the investigation of the secret prison.[286]

In April 2012 six members of the EP Committee on Civil Liberties, Justice and Home Affairs toured the alleged Lithuanian prison and criticized the two investigations for concluding that the prison had never held anyone, even though CIA flights had landed in the country 29 times.[287] The Committee voted 50–2 to approve a report that Lithuania, Poland, and Romania should investigate secret prisons and renditions; the EP agreed overwhelmingly (568–34).

In August 2012 the Open Society Justice Initiative applied to the ECHR on behalf of al Nashiri against Romania.[288] In March 2013 Interrights and American and Polish lawyers applied to the ECHR on behalf of abu Zubaydah against Poland. On July 23, in a 164-page ruling, the ECHR ordered Poland to pay €130,000 to abu Zubaydah and €100,000 to al Nashiri. Miller, who had been prime minister at the time, called it "unjust and immoral" to "put the rights of murderers above the rights of victims." The judgment was "based on rumors, speculation and slander." He had "said many times that such a prison did not exist." A Foreign Ministry spokesman said Poland should have been given a chance to conduct its own investigation. (For a decade it had prevented its own prosecutors from doing so.) The White House said "the overriding point … is that this program no longer exists." In October Poland said it would appeal the ruling that it had not cooperated with the investigation; it had been unable to do so because the requested documents were classified. But in February a panel of five judges rejected Poland's appeal in the joint cases of al-Nashiri and abu Zubaydah, and it agreed to pay.

After the release of the SSCI Report's Executive Summary on December 9, 2014 and AI's deciphering of the transparent "color code" identifying the countries hosting CIA prisons, former President Kwasniewski admitted that "the U.S. side asked the Polish side to find a quiet site where it could conduct activity that would allow [it] to effectively obtain information from persons who had declared readiness to cooperate with the U.S. side. We gave our consent to that," but not to torture.[289] He insisted that the money the USA had given Poland was unrelated funding for intelligence services, not payment for hosting the prison. Ioan Talpes, former head of intelligence, acknowledged the

CIA had "centers" in Romania, and "it is probable that people were imprisoned and treated in an inhumane manner." Romania had "explicitly taken no interest in knowing what the CIA did there." "In such situations it is better not to interfere." Although former President Illiescu denied knowledge of the prisons, Talpes said he had told the president in 2003–04 that the USA was carrying out "certain activities" in Romania. Several weeks later Iliescu again confirmed Romania had hosted CIA "black sites," but denied this was in exchange for US support for Romania's application to join NATO (which succeeded in 2004), or that he had known what the CIA was doing in the prison. Former Lithuanian President Adamkus said: "I was assured by top-ranking officials of our security agencies that there is no prison in Lithuania and that nobody ever delivered the prisoners. Until I see documents before my eyes about someone secretly bringing prisoners into Lithuania, I will stick to my position."

Analysis

The response of countries to allegations of complicity with US extraordinary renditions and secret prisons spanned the gamut from flat denial and cover-up to frank admission and remedy. Canada and Sweden conducted serious investigations, acknowledged responsibility for extraordinary rendition and torture – Arar to Syria, Agiza and al-Zery to Egypt – and paid substantial compensation (a stunning Can$10.5 million to Arar). By contrast, Italy and Germany initially (if unconvincingly) denied any involvement with the well-documented American abuses of abu Omar and el-Masri. (The CIA was so confident of impunity that agents in Italy and Majorca blithely used their real names, IDs, credit cards, and cell phones.) But though low-level officials in Italy admitted involvement, and career prosecutors and judges there and in Germany courageously exposed their government's culpability, politicians and higher courts obstructed any authoritative legal accounting and pardoned those convicted. The USA significantly contributed to this outcome, exerting pressure behind the scenes and, of course, refusing to extradite suspects. Italy never paid abu Omar and his wife the €500,000 its court provisionally awarded them and, indeed, sentenced him (in absentia) to six years. Sabrina de Sousa, the only American facing a prison term (for a conviction in absentia), was also the least culpable. Arar and el-Masri found their damage actions blocked in US courts and even were denied visas to observe their cases or testify before Congress.

Equally stark contrasts characterized responses to disclosure of the CIA's secret prisons in Poland, Romania, and Lithuania, each of which had succumbed to US inducements of monetary aid or NATO membership. Bush's August 2006 decision to close the prisons by transferring 14 HVDs to Guantánamo (to ease passage of the MCA following the Supreme Court's *Hamdan* decision) contained the negative pregnant that they had been open. Years later the SSCI report confirmed the media accounts of detention and abuse. Low-level officials in the three countries implicated disclosed suspicious evidence; CIA planes left a paper trail that was hard to erase; and political parties were motivated to embarrass rivals who had been in power when the prisons operated. But the governments repeatedly issued blanket denials, conducting superficial inquiries clearly intended to whitewash, and blocking investigations by career prosecutors. Partly out of anger that it had been deceived by its closest ally, the UK eventually acknowledged that detainees had been aboard US ships briefly docked in Diego Garcia. By contrast with national denials and evasions, European regional institutions and NGOs vigorously investigated, unambiguously finding governmental responsibility (though they lacked enforcement power). And the ECHR awarded damages to abu Zubaydah and al-Nashiri against Poland (as well as abu Omar and el-Masri against Italy and Macedonia).

CONCLUSION

The USA waged its "war on terror" in foreign countries as well as at home. It deployed troops in Afghanistan and Iraq, conducted air attacks there and in Pakistan and Yemen (as well as Somalia and Libya) using drones and manned aircraft, seized alleged terrorists in the USA, Sweden, Italy, and Macedonia, rendering them to prisons for torture, and detained and tortured alleged terrorists in secret prisons in Poland, Romania, and Lithuania (as well as Thailand and Morocco). All these activities threatened and sometimes violated the rule of law. This chapter has examined the variety of ways in which it was defended.

Drone strikes raised new and distinctive questions. Critics analogized them to assassinations because of their deliberation and expressed concern that targets were chosen by civilians (including the president); those condemned to live in dread for days or weeks under their audible threat deeply resented the asymmetric risk. Although (as apologists noted correctly) drone strikes were more selective and precise than aerial bombing, they depended on intelligence, which was never perfect and sometimes deliberately distorted. Resistance within the USA took many forms. Fearing allies and their populace were being alienated, DoS clashed with DoD and the CIA; even some high-ranking military and intelligence officials worried that the strategic costs of killings exceeded their benefits. Libertarians like Rand Paul joined opposition by Democratic lawmakers and human rights NGOs. Perhaps because Obama was a lawyer, his administration bowed to pressure to release some (but not all) of the memos asserting authority for drone strikes and delineating the legal parameters. But courts' refusal to hear challenges to targeted killings, before or after the fact, left the fundamental legal questions unresolved, letting defenders continue to advance unfounded, often deeply flawed, justifications. As elsewhere, it was easier to challenge process – how targets were chosen, which branches of government would be informed and when – than to question targeted killing itself. But though critics stressed the apparent anomaly that wiretapping but not killing required judicial scrutiny, proposals for a FISC-type court were still-born. Leading media – the *New York Times* and *Los Angeles Times*, and sometimes the *Washington Post* – raised objections to both all targeted killing and particular operations. But perhaps because the public accepted targeted killing (according to opinion polls), Congress remained passive. Hence domestic resistance was ineffective.

Outside the USA, efforts to defend the rule of law fared no better. A particularly blatant failure was repudiation of a fundamental tenet – equal justice under law – emblazoned on the pediment of the US Supreme Court, embodied in iconic statues of blindfolded Justice, and epitomized in the English boast that the law is "no respecter of persons." The USA consistently favored its citizens (and those of its allies) over those on whose behalf it claimed to be waging the "war on terror." The families of Tillman (American) and Norgrove (British) were granted a much more meaningful legal process than any bereaved Afghan family. Americans who suffered accidental injuries (e.g., friendly-fire casualties, electrocutions in showers) were treated better than Afghans or Iraqis deliberately killed or raped by Americans; and the culprits were sanctioned more harshly. Although drone strikes on US citizens (notably al-Awlaki) aroused loud domestic criticism, the process by which he was targeted was much more public and deliberative than that used for others – a glaring disparity provoking South Africa's Archbishop Tutu to draw parallels with apartheid. Unlike the tens of thousands of foreigners who languished in US detention, US citizens detained abroad by their own government secured release after seeking habeas. The USA successfully insisted on immunity for members of the military coalition. Contractors unconstrained by military training, command structures, or criminal justice either enjoyed immunity or were spirited to safety in the USA. These profound inequalities evoked discomforting memories of the humiliating extraterritoriality Western nations imposed on nineteenth-century China.

Differences among the four principal battlegrounds of the US "war on terror" – Afghanistan, Iraq, Pakistan, and Yemen – shaped those nations' responses to the grievous casualties and abuses their citizens suffered.[290] Karzai – a Pashtun fighting a predominately Pashtun Taliban while deflecting challenges from other ethnic groups (Tajik, Hazara, Uzbek) – was totally dependent on the USA to wage that war and support his government (and he greatly enriched himself and his family in the process). Al-Maliki – a Shiite trying to suppress a Sunni insurgency with support from uncertain Shiite allies (clerics, militia, and Iran, all jockeying for influence) while resisting Kurdish demands for greater autonomy – was equally dependent on the US military. Saleh and his successor Hadi survived only by perpetually "dancing on the heads of snakes" – Yemen's ancient clan rivalries, further complicated by threats from AQAP and Houthi rebels (allegedly supported by Iran).[291] Pakistan enjoyed much more leverage: it was a long-standing Cold War ally and nuclear power; it never (publicly) consented to US military operations (and therefore did not grant the immunity extracted from Afghanistan and Iraq as the price of US intervention); and it could block essential materiel shipments to and from Afghanistan. But Pakistan had its own problems: threats from religious extremists and Baluchi separatists, bitter enmity with India (periodically erupting in fighting over Kashmir and terrorist attacks elsewhere in India), and its determination that Pakistan (not its Indian rival) would dominate Afghanistan after the inevitable US departure (leading it to tolerate and even assist the Taliban and Haqqani faction).

Despite these differences, the four countries exhibited similar responses. Relatives and supporters of the dead flouted the religious mandate of a quick burial by taking the bodies to local authorities to strengthen demands that perpetrators be tried under Islamic law. Of course, this never happened. Such protests may have increased pressure on the USA to investigate, but that process was opaque and protracted, almost always exonerating the military (when it reached *any* public conclusion). Although investigations by national or local governments and NGOs often were more critical of the USA, they had no visible effect. In the fog of war, facts were hard to establish: sites were geographically inaccessible and dangerous to visit; Western investigators faced linguistic and cultural differences for which they were ill-trained; the laws of war did not clearly differentiate between legitimate and illegitimate casualties; most adult men carried guns (making them suspect as "MAMs"); civilians in all four countries often sympathized with insurgents, sometimes actively helping them; and (as the USA complained) the Taliban deliberately endangered civilians and exploited or exaggerated casualties for propaganda purposes. Because criticism of air strikes (necessarily) was framed in terms of the relative proportions of legitimate military and illegitimate civilian casualties, it devolved into inconclusive arguments about indeterminate numbers. As deaths and injuries mounted, it took particularly grievous incidents involving large numbers of civilians – especially women, children, and the elderly – to provoke significant protest. Although insurgents inflicted many more civilian casualties, often deliberately, these generated less visible outrage than the much smaller number blamed on the foreign infidel invader, whose apparent omnipotence made local populations skeptical about claims that the deaths were "accidental." The long-standing animus against the USA sparked violent protests when Islam was insulted (desecration of the Koran or the dead) or national honor and sovereignty were violated (border incursions, friendly-fire casualties, Davis's killings, the bin Laden raid). In all four countries, political leaders repeatedly denounced air and ground attacks, demanding they cease. But this rhetoric was directed primarily to domestic audiences (often in response to criticism by political rivals), sometimes prompting implausible claims that the national military, not the USA, had conducted the strike. Although leaders' denunciations and mass protests occasionally produced pauses, these always were temporary; and restraint in deploying one strategy often just meant shifting to another (e.g., between ground and air attacks). The USA was profligate with apologies and compensation, both of which cost it little. Bereaved kin (understandably) rejected apologies without justice (by which they meant prosecution under Islamic law); but almost all accepted the money offered, which often greatly exceeded their annual incomes (feeding US accusations that claims were fabricated). Only Pakistan had sufficient leverage to elicit an extended suspension of drone strikes. Otherwise, declines in civilian casualties were attributable primarily to the diminishing number of significant targets coupled with concern that killings were recruiting more insurgents than they eliminated. The Trump administration has, if anything, showed even less concern about civilian casualties and protests by victims' governments in its "wars" in Afghanistan, Iraq, Syria, and Somalia.[292]

Complicity by Western allies with extraordinary renditions and secret prisons played out differently. Some countries were motivated by loyalty: Canada with respect to Arar, the UK (which may have been deceived) concerning US ships with prisoners stopping at Diego Garcia. Others responded to bribes: NATO membership for Lithuania and Romania (Albania accepted five Uighurs from Guantánamo for the same reason), foreign aid for Poland. Macedonia may simply have submitted to bullying. Investigative reporters played an indispensable role in exposing renditions and prisons. Nations responded very differently to the revelations. Canada and Sweden conducted scrupulous investigations and generously compensated the victims. Poland, Romania, and Lithuania indulged in transparent whitewashes, obstructed investigations by career prosecutors, and persisted in denying incontrovertible facts. Political leaders in Italy and Germany aborted prosecutorial efforts; instead of paying abu Omar the compensation ordered by its court, Italy convicted him in absentia. European regional institutions, by contrast, ferreted out complicity by member states and ordered three of them to pay compensation. But the USA simply stonewalled: its courts dismissed lawsuits by Arar and el-Masri; even after they were conclusively exculpated immigration continued to bar them; and the USA successfully obstructed prosecutions in Germany and Italy, and of course refused to extradite CIA agents to stand trial there.

CHAPTER SEVEN

THE RESILIENCE OF THE RULE OF LAW

The introductory chapter reviewed the extensive literature on the defense of the rule of law in a wide variety of times and places to frame questions about the US response to the 9/11 attacks. This concluding chapter begins by briefly reprising those questions.

The rule of law is defined and protected by official norms: constitutions, statutes, treaties, regulations, and judicial decisions. Whereas much of the literature addresses when and why states first adopt such norms and progressively conform to them, the USA waged its "war on terror" within a well-established and highly elaborated normative environment it had helped promulgate, pledged to respect, and boasted about following. How did those norms differ in pedigree, acceptance, consistency, comprehensiveness, clarity, specificity, and visibility? Who invoked, applied, and contested them? Were they interpreted narrowly or broadly, following precedent or innovatively?

Most of the literature focuses on the susceptibility of relatively weak nations to political, economic, or moral pressure to obey norms exerted by more powerful nations (often the USA) and supranational bodies. Was the American hegemon influenced by those forces?[1] In a global economy, even the USA is vulnerable to fluctuations in international trade (imports of essential raw materials, exports of goods and services). It also has a stake in the viability of international organizations it played a crucial role in creating (though administrations vary in their commitment). Did the USA grant international observers access to investigate alleged rule-of-law abuses? It is bound to other nations by treaties, friendships, common interests and culture, the loyalties of immigrant populations, and strategic considerations. And it takes pride in disseminating, strengthening, and modeling international norms of behavior, many of which have deep roots in US history. Which domestic actors, nations, and international bodies invoked which treaties, provoking what responses by which US officials? Were those other nations moved by normative commitments, strategic interests, or concern for their nationals? Did the USA resile from existing treaty commitments? How did it justify this? Was it moved by moral suasion or shaming?

The literature rightly emphasizes the role of NGOs (many US-based), which may be the only civil society institutions capable of challenging authoritarian regimes. How did the identity of human rights victims in the US "war on terror" influence NGOs' willingness to champion them? What were the consequences for NGOs of doing so? Did NGOs with an active membership (like AI) behave differently from those (like the ACLU) that relied on mass donations but centralized decision-making and action? Which tactics did NGOs employ, e.g., conducting investigations, issuing reports, writing letters, engaging in direct action, petitioning officials, litigating, lobbying legislators? How did NGOs frame their claims: choosing victims (because they were innocent or especially appealing, unique or numerous, anonymous or famous), depicting them (through photos, videos, films, biographies, personal testimony), characterizing rule of law violations (in terms of intent, causation, repetition), and choosing whom to blame? How did they inspire empathy in Americans for victims separated by physical and cultural distance? How did they address compassion fatigue? How did NGOs ensure the accuracy of their factual claims? Did they offer governments a veil of secrecy? Did this increase access? Did they claim neutrality or avow partisanship? Did they focus on process or substance? Did these choices affect their influence? How did they use the media? What kinds of publicity were most effective? What explains differences in NGOs' overall impact? Did this vary with the particular US administration in power? How did the success or failure of particular campaigns affect NGOs' resources and influence? How were these influenced by external events (terrorist attacks, human rights abuses, affirmations of rule of law norms, regime changes)?

Other civil society institutions also may defend the rule of law: the clergy on behalf of religious values, doctors for patients, and especially lawyers for clients (avoiding moral taint by invoking their essential role in an adversarial system) and for legality itself. Celebrities may exploit their visibility. The media play an indispensable role in informing the public and shaping opinion.[2] Their ability to do so depends on capable, courageous investigative journalists and risk-taking publishers, both motivated by competition for scoops. How does the government respond to media disclosures? Do the media seek to protect the anonymity of whistle-blowers? Are they successful?

Because the executive branch claims preeminence in responding to national security threats, its actions crucially affect the vicissitudes of the rule of law. Men as different as Lincoln, Wilson, FDR, and Obama, who had urged caution as lawyers, all sought to expand executive power once they became wartime presidents. The executive can resist judicial limits on its actions (for instance, by suspending habeas corpus or transferring cases from civilian to military courts); alternatively, it can ameliorate harsh punishments of dissidents (through pardons or clemency, although courts can overturn amnesties). (As I wrote this, an Israeli court convicted a soldier of manslaughter for killing a wounded Palestinian assailant lying unarmed on the ground; but a member of Netanyahu's cabinet immediately called for a presidential pardon and was quickly seconded by the Prime Minister; while the nationalist Foreign Minister Avigdor Lieberman urged the public to respect the court's decision.[3]) Even wartime presidents may display commitment to the rule of law. Nations learn from experience: Germany greatly values privacy because it suffered from Nazi and Communist totalitarianism. How has the American experience of wartime injustice (e.g., internment of Japanese Americans in the Second World War) influenced American leaders confronting national security threats? As even advocates of the theory of a unitary executive recognize, that branch is not monolithic. Civilian and military leaders differ in how they are socialized and the contingencies and incentives they encounter. The two principal intelligence agencies were rivals from the start and operate by different modalities in different realms: the CIA covertly abroad, systematically defying the laws of host countries; the FBI at home, often openly, proclaiming (if not always exhibiting) fidelity to US law. The executive branch necessarily functions through a vast bureaucracy. When do subordinates resist rule-of-law violations ordered by superiors? Engage in whistle-blowing? Which ones do so? Do prosecutors voluntarily disclose exculpatory evidence or potentially fatal procedural errors? What happens to objectors, violations, and violators? How successful is the executive in concealing its misconduct? What happens when cover-ups are exposed? How do personnel changes affect compliance with the rule of law? Do administrative agencies created to protect national security observe the due process guarantees other agencies routinely provide?

Legislators may passively acquiesce in, actively abet, or resist rule-of-law violations by passing, modifying, or obstructing legislation initiated by them or the executive. Members of the executive's own party may revolt; more often, the opposition (which may be divided) seeks political advantage by doing so. (Opponents may even precipitate the government's fall in parliamentary systems.) Legislatures can ask the executive for information and even demand it (threatening to refuse necessary funds). Legislatures can deploy their own investigative powers either to invade civil liberties (by harassing constitutionally protected behavior) or expose executive misconduct. They can pass legislation like FOIA, empowering civil society to compel disclosure of rule-of-law violations (but the efficacy of such mechanisms depends on both executive compliance and judicial interpretation).

Finally, the literature reveals the unpredictable fate of the rule of law when a nation fears for its security. Rule-of-law defenders may forge alliances among long-standing adversaries, such as religious and secular activists or libertarians and leftists. Adventitious events like wars or terrorist attacks may prompt sudden changes of direction. New leaders may have different policy priorities from those they replace and feel uncommitted to previous courses of action, or even repudiate them for political reasons. Perhaps most importantly, campaigns to redress abuses and restore the rule of law can take decades, even generations.

The five chapters analyzing US rule-of-law violations in the aftermath of the 9/11 attacks address many (if not all) of these questions while generating some of their own. This concluding chapter looks across those five domains – Abu Ghraib, Guantánamo Bay, interrogation, surveillance, and warfare – to tease out insights into the successes and failures of efforts to defend the rule of law.

LAW MATTERS

Readers may be surprised by and resist this judgment, given the appalling rule-of-law violations the USA has committed since 9/11. My point, however, is that most governments, including the American government, can act only through law, which entails giving reasons for the exercise of power. What cannot be justified cannot be authorized. And the power to authorize is inseparable from the power to prohibit: asserting the legality of *some* behavior implies (or at least increases the risk) that *other* behavior is illegal. The United States' need to cloak its actions in legal garb therefore empowered law to shape those actions.

The issue was not whether to embrace new legal constraints but how to construe those the USA already acknowledged. For that interpretation to provide effective legal cover, it had to include detailed descriptions of the actions authorized. Had this legal advice been exposed to public scrutiny, the ensuing criticism (of both the reasoning and the behavior authorized) might have made the government more cautious, prompting it to seek other opinions or simply reject the earlier advice. The Bush administration responded to this danger by jealously guarding the secrecy of all its legal opinions. Even FISC decisions remained secret (unlike those of Art. III courts). That, however, rendered them incapable of publicly legitimating the actions they authorized. Perhaps in recognition of this Obama – a constitutional lawyer – vacillated between transparency and secrecy, disclosing some of the OLC memos but not all.

There is ample evidence that law influenced government action in myriad ways. Both administrations sought legal opinions before they began abusing Abu Ghraib prisoners, sending detainees to Guantánamo, experimenting with EITs in the Thai secret prison, greatly expanding electronic surveillance, and conducting targeted killings. DoD acknowledged law-of-war constraints on its use of lethal force; and changes in ROEs seem to have reduced civilian casualties. (But the extraterritoriality the USA demanded from Afghanistan and Iraq immunized its military from those countries' laws; and the military's own justice system usually exculpated those accused or treated leniently those found guilty.) As these novel and legally dubious programs generated other questions, the administration sought additional advice, which further shaped behavior. The Bush administration secured the legal opinions it sought by packing the government with "loyal Bushies."[4] White House counsel Alberto Gonzales (whom Bush, as Texas Governor, had appointed to the state Supreme Court) and Vice President Cheney's counsel David Addington told the ideologues whom Attorney General Ashcroft had appointed to the OLC – Yoo, Bybee, and Delahunty – what they wanted the CIA, NSA, and military to do, and those apparatchiki designed the desired legal garb. Critics within the government were blindsided, sidelined, or ignored: Secretary of State Colin Powell, DoS legal adviser William Taft IV, and the general counsels and JAGs of the four DoD branches. Donald Rumsfeld abruptly aborted a review of EITs by military lawyers that seemed about to find legal limitations. Jack Goldsmith resigned as OLC head days after leaks of memos written under his predecessor (although he had planned his return to academia months earlier). Acting Attorney General Comey followed Goldsmith's advice that FISA did not permit some of NSA's electronic surveillance practices. (Congress had passed FISA in response to the Church Committee's exposure of Nixon's abuses.) The hospitalized Ashcroft deferred to Comey; and even Bush was unprepared to risk mass resignations at the DoJ (which might, embarrassingly, remind observers of Nixon's Saturday Night Massacre). Seeking to distinguish himself from his predecessor, Obama – visibly backed by retired flag officers, many of them military lawyers – issued Executive Orders on his second day in office, ending legal authority for EITs and closing secret prisons.

The exposure of Abu Ghraib encouraged leaks of the OLC memos, which now were read against the background of both their prior concealment and the lurid abuses at that prison. The flimsiness of the legal reasoning provoked immediate condemnation across the political spectrum. After Gonzales wrote a *New York Times* op ed defending the memos, Harvard law professor Detlev Vagts dismissed them as "an effort to find loopholes that could be used to avoid responsibility."[5] A representative of the UN High Commissioner for Human Rights castigated the description of detainees as "terrorists" as a "plain disregard of the presumption of innocence." The New York City Bar's Committees on International Human Rights and on Military Affairs and Justice declared "there is no blanket exception [from the Geneva Conventions] for so-called 'unlawful combatants.'" HRW's Tom Malinowski said the opinion authors "were contemplating … the commission of war crimes and looking for ways to avoid legal accountability." The *New York Times* published letters denouncing "the arrogance and shortsightedness" of the opinions, which were "at best absurd."[6] Bush "has thrown the Geneva Conventions, the only civilized aspect of war, into the trash bin." "We cannot be a country based on the rule of law if our nation does not obey the law." A writer whose parents had survived the Holocaust was "shocked and ashamed by the Bush administration's parsing of what is and what is not torture."

Repeatedly challenged at a June 10 press conference, Bush declared:[7] "The instructions went out to our people to adhere to law. That ought to comfort you. We're a nation of law. We adhere to laws. We have laws on the books. You might look at those laws, and that might provide comfort for you." But rejecting Bush's "small comfort," the *Washington Post*'s David Ignatius wrote that Bybee's August 1, 2002 "torture memo" "in its dry, lawerly way, is as shocking as the Abu Ghraib photographs."[8] Two law professors wrote a *Washington Post* op ed exposing Bybee's "stunning legal contortions."[9] Indeed, the OLC withdrew Bybee's memo just ten days after it was leaked.[10] Promptly getting cold feet, the CIA suspended EITs three days later (and did not resume them until Bradbury's 2005 memos offered it new legal cover).[11] The June 28 Supreme Court decisions demolished the OLC claim that federal courts lacked jurisdiction to investigate detention in Guantánamo Bay. Ruth Wedgwood (professor of international law and diplomacy at Johns Hopkins University) and R. James Woolsey (DCI 1993–95), both conservatives, wrote in a *Wall Street Journal* op ed that the memos did "not give an adequate account of the law."[12] *The Nation* denounced them as Abu Ghraib's "smoking guns."[13] At the ABA annual conference on August 9, its House of Delegates condemned "any use of torture or other cruel, inhuman or degrading treatment."[14] The DoJ formally replaced the "torture memo" in December in order to ease Gonzales's confirmation as Attorney General.

Legal norms both enabled and restricted abuses. Memos prospectively permitted EITs and electronic surveillance; Bush, Obama, their Attorneys General and Congress retrospectively immunized interrogators and telecommunication companies acting under those authorizations. OLC memos laid the foundation for sending detainees to Guantánamo. Anticipating and responding to the Supreme Court's decision in *Rasul*, DoD established CSRTs to review the legal grounds for holding detainees; but these rubberstamped almost every detention and were found by the Supreme Court in *Boumediene* to be constitutionally flawed. DoD appears to have welcomed the DTA ban on EITs; by contrast, the CIA vigorously resisted being limited to the Army Field Manual. Congress "reformed" FISA after the *New York Times* and Snowden exposés of electronic surveillance; but NSA devised ways to keep doing what it wanted to do. The Obama administration's OLC memos and White Paper on targeted killing do not seem to have prevented any drone attacks. At the end of the day, it was the MPs, who could only point to hints and winks to justify abusing detainees at Abu Ghraib – but no written orders, who were hung out to dry.

When DoJ lawyer David Margolis (tasked by Bush's Attorney General Mukasey) rejected the OPR recommendation to transmit charges against the OLC lawyers to state disciplinary authorities, the circle of impunity snapped shut: lawyers could not be punished for grossly distorting the law in their opinions; and both administrations immunized anyone who conducted EITs or electronic surveillance while following those fundamentally flawed opinions. This circular reasoning eviscerated the core meaning of the rule of law. It encouraged the executive to handpick lawyers who would treat laws the way Humpty Dumpty did words:

> "When I use a word," Humpty Dumpty said in a rather scornful tone, "it means just what I choose it to mean – neither more nor less." "The question is," said Alice, "whether you can make words mean so many different things." "The question is," said Humpty Dumpty, "which is to be master – that's all." [15]

By such reasoning law becomes infinitely malleable, indistinguishable from politics, inviting precisely the nihilism with which conservatives charged critical legal studies.

SUNSHINE IS THE BEST DISINFECTANT

As the discussion of legal opinions makes clear, the necessary first step in challenging rule-of-law violations is exposure. Like all executives, both administrations sought to conceal their actions behind a veil of secrecy, justifying this in the name of national security. At Abu Ghraib, the CIA hid "ghost prisoners" from the ICRC; the military made BGen. Karpinski sign its response to the ICRC to disguise the fact that MI, not her MPs, controlled the prison; ICRC reports of abuse were not transmitted up the chain of command and were not supposed to circulate outside the US government. The military's Art. 32 preliminary hearings were secret, as was Taguba's investigation. Other military investigation reports were heavily redacted. Those who participated in or observed the Tier 1A abuses did not blow the whistle for fear of seeming uncool or ratting on friends; their passivity and that of their superiors convinced others the behavior was acceptable, even approved. Only because the culprits shamelessly courted notoriety by sharing photographs did evidence of their escapades ultimately surface. But another thousand photographs and videos remain secret despite a decade-long campaign to obtain them.

The Bush administration chose to house detainees in Guantánamo precisely because it totally controlled that remote prison: initially denying access to lawyers and then severely limiting what they could say; refusing to let UN investigators speak to detainees (with the predictable, and presumably intended, result that the UN declined to visit); and staging Potemkin Village junkets for credulous American lawmakers. The military drastically restricted journalists' movements within Guantánamo, forbade communication with detainees, fought every FOIA request, and even expelled some of the most persistent reporters. Too little happened most of the time to justify a permanent reporter, and seats on flights to the base were rationed when there was a crisis (like detainee protests or suicides). The military stopped revealing the number of hunger strikers and prohibited photos in response to the global outrage at those of hooded, shackled, orange-suited detainees kneeling in front of barbed wire. Foreign countries visited only their own detainees and depended on the USA to release them. The USA sought to discredit ex-detainees' reports and naturally refused to publicize ICRC reports. EITs were restricted to the CIA's secret prisons and military prisons in Afghanistan, Iraq, and Guantánamo – all closed sites. The CIA destroyed videotapes of its interrogations. FBI personnel observed CIA abuses in Guantánamo but reported only to headquarters. A few interrogators confessed their use of EITs after leaving the military. Only after years of controversy was the Democrat-controlled SSCI able to publish a redacted version of the 500-page executive summary of its nearly 7,000-page report; their Republican successors tried to recall and destroy all copies of the latter.

The secrecy of surveillance makes it difficult for individuals to prove they have been surveilled. The Bush administration refrained from seeking the FISA amendments it knew Congress would approve for fear of exposing what NSA was doing. It briefed only the intelligence committees' Gang of Four, who were forbidden to disclose what they learned. It successfully pressured the *New York Times* to delay exposing NSA wiretapping for a year. Most telecoms covertly collaborated with NSA because they depended on government contracts. Foreign governments that engaged in similar behavior were understandably reluctant to denounce their American ally.

It is hardest to conceal the damage inflicted by warfare – since its purpose is to kill, maim, destroy, and terrorize. Indeed, the military broadcasts its achievements, both out of pride and to justify its budget. Tensions within the military (Army, Marines, and Special Forces) and between it and the CIA could also prompt exposure. But "war on terror" victims were isolated in remote areas of Afghanistan, Iraq, Pakistan, Yemen, Somalia, and Libya and lacked the linguistic skills, cultural knowledge, and technology to publicize their injuries. Western journalists and NGOs encountered similar difficulties in reporting on air strikes, house raids, traffic stops, and drone attacks. Only the most dramatic collateral damage – multiple casualties, patently innocent victims, or protected targets like MSF hospitals – garnered significant coverage in the US media.

Potential whistle-blowers had reason to fear retaliation. Governments seek to divert attention from disclosures of their own misdeeds by shooting the messengers. In the 1970s Daniel Ellsberg was prosecuted for leaking the Pentagon Papers, escaping punishment only because the Nixon administration "Plumbers" burgled his psychiatrist's office. A military imam who befriended Guantánamo detainees and a military lawyer who gave their names to CCR were disciplined. Chelsea Manning was sentenced to 35 years for disclosing evidence of possible US war crimes (though one of Obama's last actions was to commute this to seven years). Edward Snowden seems permanently exiled to Russia for exposing massive NSA surveillance. Other NSA employees have been investigated or prosecuted. Yet the military (hypocritically) claimed Joseph Darby as a hero for revealing the photos of Abu Ghraib abuses (which it hoped to keep secret). And no one was ever blamed for leaking the OLC memos. Principled resistance may be less dangerous than people fear: even in Nazi Germany, judges who opposed the regime suffered no serious punishment.[16]

If the government may temporarily escape scrutiny by concealing abuses, secrecy can also create vulnerability. It can never be hermetic because many want to know and some wish to disclose (for personal, political, or principled reasons). Furthermore, the media – to whom we owe our knowledge of all five rule-of-law violations (as the footnotes in those chapters thoroughly document) – thrive on exposure. Government efforts to conceal information perversely magnify its importance when it surfaces, as illustrated by exposés of Abu Ghraib, EITs, secret prisons, extraordinary renditions, and surveillance. Congress is deeply resentful when the executive fails to keep it informed, especially when it is deceived (for instance, by the CIA or NSA). Cover-ups often are harder to justify than the behavior they seek to conceal (partly because process appears to be a shared neutral value, whereas policy expresses personal preferences susceptible to challenge as subjective). Exposure upends prophylactic efforts to preserve deniability and alters the balance of power between government and whistle-blowers. Each leak weakens arguments for further secrecy and motivates others to blow the whistle. Graner's extreme narcissism and his generation's exhibitionism led him to record and publicize his misdeeds. Competition for a scoop between CBS and *The New Yorker* produced near simultaneous publication of the photographs and Taguba's report. The Abu Ghraib scandal prompted the OLC memos to leak. ICRC reports circulate too widely within government for all of them to remain secret. If governments are necessarily bureaucratic (as Weber showed), the military is the ultimate bureaucracy. Bureaucracies cannot function without records, which can leak, e.g., the Abu Ghraib log books documenting who knew what and when, or al-Qahtani's Guantánamo interrogation transcript detailing the EITs. Courts-martial are public proceedings. Motivated by pride, rivalry, or budgetary need, government agencies boast about their capabilities and achievements: detaining the "worst of the worst" in Guantánamo, extracting intelligence by EITs and surveillance, vanquishing enemies on the battlefield, killing bin Laden and al-Awlaki.

Sunshine may let the body cure itself, but exposure alone does not heal self-inflicted social wounds. Its effects varied among the five domains. Abu Ghraib provoked intense outrage across a broad political spectrum – more anger than had been expressed since the USA launched its wars in Afghanistan in 2001 and Iraq in 2003, and started sending detainees to Guantánamo in 2002. There are many possible explanations. Two-and-a-half years had elapsed since 9/11 without another attack on the homeland. Bush's claim of WMDs had been exposed as a false pretext for overthrowing Saddam Hussein. The Sunni uprising made the Iraq war increasingly unwinnable and unpopular. The administration did not – indeed, could not – claim that detainee abuse in Abu Ghraib had produced useful intelligence because that would raise (plausible) suspicions that it had been ordered. The flagrantly sexual behavior both aroused the public and strengthened the administration's disavowal of complicity. Graner's and England's lack of contrition made them attractive scapegoats. Perhaps most importantly, the abuses were embodied in immediately comprehensible photographs: the pyramid of naked bodies, the detainee led on a leash, the hooded man with "electrodes" on hands outstretched in a simulacrum of crucifixion. These quickly joined earlier iconic photographs: the Spanish Republican soldier falling to his death after being shot, soldiers raising the US flag in Iwo Jima, black schoolchildren spat upon while integrating a school, other civil rights demonstrators attacked by dogs or firehoses, a naked Vietnamese girl on fire from napalm, the South Vietnamese Chief of National Police executing a handcuffed Viet Cong prisoner, a girl at Kent State University keening over the body of an anti-war protester killed by National Guard troops. For all these reasons, Bush, Rumsfeld, and other high civilian and military leaders quickly condemned the behavior as aberrational, blaming a few bad apples while (falsely) promising it would be thoroughly investigated and all those responsible punished. The (flawed) efforts to do so conveniently distracted attention from other systemic rule-of-law violations.

Photos of Guantánamo Bay detainees, though published as widely as those of Abu Ghraib, could not sustain public interest in the prison, beginning its fifteenth year as I write. Although the Bush administration's release of more than 500 prisoners gave the lie to its tired mantra that these were the "worst of the worst," the transfer of 16 HVDs to Guantánamo in 2006 helped sustain anger at the detainees, as did the often misleading figures disseminated by both administrations about alleged "recidivism" by ex-detainees (many of whom could not "fall back" into a terrorism they had never committed). But drastic restrictions on information, especially visuals, have helped keep the prison out of public consciousness. No one claims detainees still possess "actionable intelligence" after a decade and a half. Yet it is difficult to arouse the public on behalf of the 10 convicted or on trial before military commissions, the 26 "forever" prisoners, and the few others cleared but not transferred at the end of the Obama administration.

Descriptions of EITs, especially waterboarding, provoked widespread revulsion. The CIA anticipated the potentially explosive impact of visuals of these procedures by destroying its videotapes. Jose Rodriguez, who ordered the destruction, wrote subsequently:[17]

> We knew that if the photos of CIA officers conducting authorized EIT ever got out, the difference between a legal, authorized, necessary, and safe program and the mindless actions of some MPs [at Abu Ghraib] would be buried by the impact of the images. The propaganda damage to the image of America would be immense … I was not depriving anyone of information about what was done or what was said. I was just getting rid of some ugly visuals that could put the lives of my people at risk.

The SSCI report's detailed documentation, including the euphemistic "rectal hydration," reignited criticism, but this had limited impact because Obama had banned EITs. The Bush administration (and those who continued to defend EITs after Obama's ban) responded that tens of thousands of US air force personnel underwent waterboarding during SERE training (hardly the same thing), and it was used on only a few detainees, elicited essential intelligence, and was justified by the "ticking bomb" hypothetical.

The (necessary) invisibility of surveillance inhibited public anger at its exposure. Those subject to it could perceive no consequences beyond an abstract loss of privacy – which Americans already had blithely surrendered to commercial enterprises simply by using cell phones and the Internet. (But Wikipedia searches for the terms al-Qaeda, Hezbollah, dirty bomb, chemical weapon, and jihad fell dramatically after Snowden's revelations.[18]) American IT companies, competing with each other and especially with European rivals in protecting customer privacy, took a stronger stance against surveillance. Both administrations advanced unverifiable claims that surveillance had obtained intelligence that could not have been gathered in other ways and had been critical to preventing terrorist attacks. A few allied leaders felt compelled to denounce *lèse-majesté*; but their grievances were compromised by their own intelligence services' surveillance of other countries (though this seemed to embarrass European regional institutions less).

Since the purpose of war is to defeat enemies by destroying their forces, and American anger at Islamic terrorism was constantly refueled by successful and attempted attacks in the USA and abroad, civilian casualties rarely elicited sympathy unless the victims were unambiguously innocent or numerous. Targeted killing was an anomalous exception to this general indifference, presumably because it was premeditated; and discomfort increased when the target was a US citizen, even one as generally detested as al-Awlaki.

These responses reveal some surprising patterns. The degree of outrage seems to vary *inversely* with the number of people victimized by rule-of-law violations. To be effective, surveillance had to cast the largest net, one that caught all Americans; but it inflicted the least perceptible damage. Drones terrified all those forced to listen to the insistent whine for days or weeks; air strikes, ground combat, and traffic stops killed, injured, and frightened tens of thousands. About 700 were detained in Guantánamo; about 100 were subjected to EITs (less than a dozen to waterboarding), held in secret prisons or rendered to foreign countries; and only a handful were abused in Abu Ghraib. It also is paradoxical that most of those surveilled were Americans, whereas all other victims were Muslims (none a US citizen except the four killed by drones, three of whom were declared terrorists), almost all living in countries where the USA was waging its "war on terror." Outrage, perversely, also seems to vary directly with the precision with which each practice distinguished between its intended (arguably legitimate) target and others. Drones are more discriminating than manned air strikes, ground combat, or traffic stops (assuming good intelligence). Most of those subjected to the harshest EITs probably once possessed some useful intelligence. The fact that almost all Guantánamo detainees were released, many of them years after interrogation had ended, strongly suggests they could have been freed earlier, and some never should have been detained. And NSA's frequent invocation of the challenge of finding a needle in a haystack rightly acknowledged that almost all those surveilled never should have been targeted. But it may be the wholly gratuitous nature of the abuse inflicted in Abu Ghraib that explains its virtually universal vehement condemnation.

THE BUCK STOPS HERE[19]

Because the executive is charged with primary responsibility for national security, it has the greatest power to violate or defend the rule of law. Bush blamed the Abu Ghraib abuses on a few MPs, thereby diverting responsibility from everyone else (including Rumsfeld). Bush established the Guantánamo Bay prison to deny the 700 detainees any constitutional rights, preclude judicial scrutiny, and minimize publicity. When the Supreme Court rejected the OLC's arguments, the administration devised the flawed CSRTs, which sought to give indefinite detention a veneer of legality. But these tribunals denied detainees legal representation, access to the government's classified evidence, and a meaningful opportunity to call witnesses (*none* of whom ever appeared); they relied on testimony from a few venal prisoners eager to curry favor with their keepers by fabricating transparent fictions; and the few panels obstinately concluding that detainees were not enemy combatants were simply replaced by more pliable substitutes, which promptly found they were. But despite Rumsfeld's rants about the "worst of the worst," the Bush administration released or transferred more than 500 detainees; and Bush's wife and mother, Gates, Mullen, and even Rumsfeld and the president himself ultimately favored closure.

On his second day in office Obama vowed to close Guantánamo within a year. But unsurprisingly, given his background as a constitutional law professor, he created a highly deliberative review process, which failed to meet that deadline, partly because of the chaotic records inherited from his predecessor. Believing in reason and the possibility of reaching consensus, Obama seems to have been unprepared for the virulent Republican hostility. Rep. James Clyburn (the third most powerful Democrat in Congress) said in 2012 that Congressional Republicans "met on the night that he was sworn-in, and took a blood oath to each other that they would be obstacles to [Obama's] administration."[20] Vice President Biden later reported that informants told him that Senate Minority Leader McConnell (R-Ky) had said: "for the next two years, we can't let you succeed in anything. That's our ticket to coming back." House Appropriations Committee Chair Obey said the senior minority member of his committee, Jerry Lewis, told him: "It doesn't matter what the hell you do, we ain't going to help you. We're going to stand on the sidelines and bitch."[21] Focused on the Affordable Care Act, Obama delayed action on Guantánamo until Republicans won control of the House and began erecting ever-greater obstacles to closure. His Defense Secretaries then dragged their feet in signing the certifications Congress mandated before transfers. William Blackstone wrote 250 years ago that the criminal justice system "holds it better that ten guilty persons escape, than that one innocent party suffer."[22] Guantánamo inverted that venerable maxim by detaining hundreds of innocent men because false positives cost the administration nothing, whereas a single false negative risked a Willie Horton moment. Obama failed for seven years to give Congress the closure plan it requested, ultimately producing one that lacked crucial details (perhaps to avoid provoking NIMBY objections from states with federal prisons). The administration ineptly failed to lay the political groundwork for trying the HVDs in federal court, ensuring that the novel, inexperienced military commissions would drag on for years without even starting trials. Still, at the end of Obama's second term Guantánamo contained just 45 detainees: 10 convicted or on trial, 29 declared "forever" prisoners, and 6 certified for release but not transferred.

Bush bears full responsibility for the EITs, despite his transparent efforts to preserve deniability. The FBI resisted them in the CIA's secret prison in Thailand and again in Guantánamo (partly motivated by rivalry with and suspicion of the CIA); ODNI's Intelligence Science Board found EITs unnecessary and the intelligence they extracted unreliable. Obama decisively ended them on his second day in office. Both administrations defended NSA surveillance (which Obama had criticized as a senator and presidential candidate). But subordinates like Goldsmith and Comey (backed by Ashcroft) insisted on fidelity to law (although Comey ultimately found a way to authorize what NSA wanted to do). Although Obama was criticized for greatly increasing the use of drones, these arguably improved the ability to strike legitimate targets while minimizing collateral damage.

This brief review confirms beyond doubt that the identity of the chief executive can make a difference to the fate of the rule of law. In addition to ending EITs and almost closing Guantánamo, Obama published many of the Bush-era OLC opinions (to expose their tendentious arguments, disavow those policies, and claim the moral high ground) and even some of his own (in the interest of transparency – if also under pressure). He claimed (unconvincingly) he would have curtailed NSA surveillance even without Snowden's revelations and appointed critics to review those activities, accepting many of their recommendations. Obama's actions can be attributed, in part, to his many differences from Bush: biography, race, class, education, personality, policies, and principles. But he also took office in 2009, after more than seven years without a domestic terrorist attack. (Indeed, Bush had declared his desire to close Guantánamo and had stopped waterboarding detainees.) But if Obama was far more principled than Bush, he was less successful in implementing those principles. Some of this can be blamed on Congress: under Bush, Republicans controlled both Houses for four years and the Senate for another two; under Obama, Democrats controlled both Houses for only the first two years and the Senate for another four. Some of Obama's inefficacy, however, reflects his relative reticence in exercising executive power: Bush repeatedly issued signing statements and threatened and used vetoes; Obama repudiated signing statements and, while sometimes threatening to veto the NDAA, did so only once and then not to protect the rule of law.

Given the president's central importance to the fate of the rule of law, one would expect that issue to figure prominently in elections. Indeed, John Yoo claimed that Bush's 2004 re-election was a referendum on EITs, which the American people had embraced. That argument is as flimsy as the OLC opinions Yoo concocted to authorize the rule-of-law violations. Even though John Kerry had a distinguished military record (while Bush had evaded the draft), and Abu Ghraib broke just six months before the election, Kerry did not accuse Bush of responsibility, perhaps because of the scurrilous "Swift boat" attack,[23] perhaps because the public sees Republicans as more reliable on national security issues – despite Bush's catastrophic decision to invade Iraq. Bush moved the HVDs to Guantánamo in September 2006 partly because the secret prisons had been outed, but also to play the fear card again, holding a press conference on 9/11 with victims' families, promising to bring the terrorists to justice. News coverage typically featured a dated photo of a glowering, disheveled KSM. But if elections are referenda, that one rejected the Republicans (though Bush continued to insist that the MCA allowed the CIA to use EITs). In the 2008 election McCain and Obama both opposed EITs, although Romney (and other Republican hopefuls) embraced them in 2012. That year only Rand Paul unsuccessfully sought to make an issue of surveillance and targeted killing. Donald Trump spouted typically contradictory messages about EITs in 2016. Electoral politics seem an inhospitable arena in which to defend the rule of law.

IS MILITARY JUSTICE AN OXYMORON LIKE MILITARY MUSIC?

Although subordinate to the president as commander-in-chief, the military has an independent responsibility to respect the rule of law.[24] Despite earlier reports of abuses, even deaths, at military prisons in Afghanistan, Abu Ghraib constituted a profound shock. DoD responded by circling the wagons. Aside from Taguba's report (which was supposed to remain secret), the dozen others were whitewashes. Rumsfeld handpicked those who investigated him: two previous Defense Secretaries, a general, and a former Republican Congresswoman who vindicated him before seeing any evidence. All the investigations blamed bad apples at the bottom of the barrel and deficiencies in training and communication, not superiors' orders or suggestions. Courts-martial of MPs were procedurally fair and sentenced two ringleaders to lengthy prison terms. But most pleaded guilty, securing lenient sentences (even without testifying against others). A perfect storm of bureaucratic finger-pointing – between MPs and MI, officers and enlisted personnel, the military and the CIA – ended without a single officer convicted, partly because military judges were punctilious about procedural niceties. None of this is surprising. Nearly two thousand years earlier, Juvenal asked rhetorically "quis custodiet ipsos custodes?" – "who will watch the watchmen?" An English saying warns against setting a fox to guard the henhouse. And the experience of self-regulation by lawyers, doctors, clergy, politicians, and police hardly inspires confidence.

The military had a mixed record on other rule-of-law violations. It carefully controlled information about resistance by Guantánamo detainees – disturbances, hunger strikes (which it simply stopped reporting), and especially deaths – and drastically restricted journalists' access. It defended force-feeding, which the World Medical Association had denounced. It conducted the flawed CSRTs and military commissions. But it also strongly supported the Geneva Conventions, believing that adherence protected its own members. Senior military lawyers resisted the EITs, as did NCIS in Guantánamo; the Army Field Manual always prohibited EITs. And the military accepted law-of-war restrictions on combat, investigated alleged violations, apologized to and compensated victims, and modified ROEs to reduce collateral damage.

AN IRON CAGE

That governments, especially the military, must act through bureaucracies has important consequences for the rule of law. Officials follow rules; subordinates obey superiors; every action is recorded (e.g., Abu Ghraib abuses by the Detainee Assessment Branch). Everyone seeks to avoid responsibility for violations, sometimes by blaming others, sometimes by covering up. MPs at Abu Ghraib claimed to be doing what superiors wanted, but could not cite written orders; they also saw the brutal actions of CIA personnel and contractors as freeing them to treat detainees harshly. Although some critics called Guantánamo lawless, detainee treatment actually was minutely regulated (if not subject to judicial review). Unlike the military or FBI, the CIA experimented with EITs (including waterboarding) because it had no experience with interrogation and relied on equally ignorant contractors. FISA and other laws regulated surveillance. The technological innovation of weaponized drones introduced the novel tactic of targeted killing, which required new regulations and prompted debate over whether it should be conducted by the CIA (which operated secretly and followed no visible rules but may have been more cautious) or the military (which operated in public according to rules).

Some subordinates resisted rule-of-law violations in each of the five domains. Darby gave superiors the Abu Ghraib abuse photos; Taguba wrote a scathing report blaming officers (but all later reports were whitewashes). Some FBI agents and military guards and psychologists opposed abuses at Guantánamo and in the CIA's secret prisons. Some interrogators and military lawyers objected to EITs. A few NSA employees (including Snowden) blew the whistle on surveillance. Career prosecutors in Italy and Germany sought to hold the CIA and their own governments accountable for extraordinary rendition but were overruled by superiors. Lower level officials in Poland, Romania, and Lithuania probed for evidence of secret CIA prisons, which superiors tried to cover up. These examples, though hardly conclusive, suggest that those at the bottom of the bureaucratic hierarchy were more likely to follow rules – for good as well as bad – whereas those at higher levels either subordinated rules to personal ambition or truly believed in *raison d'état*. At the same time, lower level officials were much more likely than superiors to be blamed for rule-of-law violations. Sabrina de Sousa, arguably the least culpable CIA officer, was the only one threatened with punishment for the rendition of abu Omar. Only MPs were held responsible for the Abu Ghraib scandal. And as the Tillman case showed, the higher the official, the less likely he was to be held responsible.

THE PEOPLE'S HOUSES

Although Congress tends to be highly deferential to the executive, it responded differently to each of the five categories of rule-of-law violations. Congressional Republicans were swept up by the initial wave of outrage at Abu Ghraib. Veterans like Sens. Warner, McCain, and Graham were particularly vehement about the stain on the military's honor. But though SSCI chair Warner held hearings, these ended inconclusively. And Congress failed to assign responsibility to any superior officer, much less demand Rumsfeld's resignation. The Republican-backed DTA and MCA both stripped federal courts of jurisdiction to hear habeas petitions by Guantánamo detainees. Congressional delegations eagerly joined DoD junkets to the island, and even Democrats waxed enthusiastic about conditions of confinement. Democrats did not push to close Guantánamo, even after winning control of Congress. Either because they were committed to the prison or obsessed with opposing Obama at every turn, Republicans blocked his efforts to transfer detainees to the USA – Uighurs to Virginia, HVDs for trial in federal court, and ultimately any detainee to any federal prison, civilian or military – greatly complicating efforts to persuade other countries to accept detainees. Republicans also repeatedly erected roadblocks to Obama administration transfers abroad, even though they never objected to Bush's release of more than 500 detainees (who displayed higher recidivism rates).

Congressional Democrats offered no effective resistance to EITs under Bush. Because only the Gang of Four were briefed and could not share concerns with others, the oversight charade became a ruse to coopt Congress and neutralize opposition. The most dramatic rebuff to Bush was the Senate's stunning 90–9 vote for the DTA, reflecting leadership by the three Republicans with military experience. McCain, who enjoyed unique moral stature as a torture survivor, may have felt lingering resentment at Bush's treatment of him during the 2000 primary. Graham was determined to immunize military decisions from judicial review. The taint of Abu Ghraib, less than two years earlier, also may have encouraged Congressional action. Two years later Republicans joined Democrats in passing the MCA, extending the EIT ban to the CIA. But in both instances Bush issued signing statements asserting his power to disregard the will of Congress. Obama's Executive Order banning EITs may have led Democrats to procrastinate, with the result that McCain and Feinstein were only able to enact the ban in 2015. Although the SSCI investigation began as a bipartisan effort (reflecting the intelligence committees' historical nonpartisanship), Republicans revolted when Holder expanded the DoJ investigation of the CIA's destruction of its EIT videotapes (ordered by his predecessor Mukasey) to include the EITs themselves. Republicans issued a stinging minority dissent and, once they regained control of the Senate, sought to recall and destroy all copies of the still secret full report. Even under Obama the executive blocked SSCI efforts to have the entire report declassified. The CIA predictably resisted SSCI: its Director excused employees from testifying (blaming the DoJ investigation); CIA employees broke into the SSCI computer; and the Agency wrote a strong dissent.

By arguing aggressively that Democrats in the Gang of Four had acquiesced in NSA eavesdropping – indeed, demanded more – Republicans diverted attention from the surveillance itself to the question of who knew what and when. The exclusion of Congressional staffers was even more disabling on these technical issues. Alberto Gonzales's outrageous attempt to extract a signature from the hospitalized Attorney General Ashcroft generated more Congressional interest than the program he declined to authorize. Republicans, surprisingly, may have resisted surveillance more vigorously under Obama than Democrats did under Bush, partly because Snowden's revelations were more dramatic, partly just to undermine the president, and partly out of libertarian sentiment (certainly true of Paul). Congress played almost no role in restraining the executive's conduct of the war beyond demanding the legal memos governing targeted killing.

Congress was most vociferous (if still ineffective) in response to Abu Ghraib because the Bush administration itself condemned the behavior. Congress also pushed back against EITs because of the leadership of Republicans with military backgrounds. All members of Congress agreed surveillance had to be regulated (after all, their predecessors had enacted FISA). But though Congress passed legislation limiting surveillance under both administrations, it placed few significant restrictions on NSA actions. Congressional Republicans obstructed Obama's efforts to close Guantánamo (and even he wanted to detain some indefinitely in federal prisons). Congressional oversight was seriously compromised by executive insistence on secrecy. Even in the minority, Democrats did take advantage of mandatory confirmation hearings, but only succeeded in extracting limited information (such as OLC memos) from a reluctant executive. This sorry record of timidity and complaisance is highlighted by comparison with Congress's thorough investigation of problems at Walter Reed Army Medical Center (leading to its closure in 2011) and Dover Air Force Base Port Mortuary (exposing "gross mismanagement" and forcing out those responsible). And Congress vividly exhibited its bitter political polarization in Republicans' unfounded charges against Secretary of State Clinton for the attack on the Benghazi embassy and her handling of emails.

The inadequate Congressional response to rule-of-law violations exhibited a pattern found elsewhere: process-based challenges have more leverage than those addressing substantive issues. Gonzales's inexcusable behavior in Ashcroft's hospital room overshadowed discussion of NSA surveillance. Unfavorable comparison with Art. III courts led to reforms of FISC but no reduction in surveillance. The CIA's destruction of its interrogation videotapes and breach of the SSCI computer were easier targets than the EITs themselves. Congress readily voiced resentment of CIA deceit and concealment, e.g., of the assassination program; and SSCI expanded briefings from the Gang of Four to the Gang of Eight, and ultimately the full committee. FISC judges castigated the FBI for filing misleading warrant applications, but did not stop approving them. Critics demonstrated flaws in the CSRTs and military commissions, but could not free Guantánamo detainees or ensure that trials were held in Art. III courts. Critics could expose problems in how drone targets were chosen but not end the killings.

UNBALANCING THE SCALES OF JUSTICE

The companion volume *Law's Trials* describes how the judiciary responded to rule-of-law violations. Here I discuss how the "war on terror" affected, and arguably distorted, a range of judicial and quasi-judicial institutions. The Bush administration instituted CSRTs after the Supreme Court held in *Rasul* that Guantánamo detainees had a right to habeas corpus. But these tribunals were conducted by nonlawyers and did not let detainees have legal counsel, see classified evidence, or present witnesses. They uncritically relied on a few detainees whose testimony was clearly not credible and on "facts" like wearing a commonly available Casio watch. As *Law's Trials* shows, US District and Circuit Court judges criticized and rejected CSRT findings, and the Supreme Court in *Boumediene* reaffirmed that detainees could seek habeas. Perhaps most damning is the fact that Obama's Task Force and his PRBs reversed most CSRT judgments, and all but 45 of the nearly 700 detainees whom CSRTs had approved for indefinite detention ultimately were released or transferred. The Bush administration created the military commissions (discussed in *Law's Trials*) because it feared that the EITs to which it had subjected defendants would make convictions difficult, and that courts-martial conferred too many rights on the accused (who in every other case were military). The chaos that inevitably ensued when a brand-new institution heard death penalty cases ensured that all detainees were still years away from trial at the end of the Obama administration. Because FISC was staffed by judges handpicked by (Republican-appointed) Chief Justices, it was even more partisan than the Republican-packed federal judiciary. Only the government appeared; proceedings and opinions were secret; and FISC approved virtually all applications. The Obama administration made very limited reforms: a public advocate in selected cases, publication of some opinions but not all, and a slightly less unrepresentative bench. Given these flaws, it is fortunate that proposals to use FISC as a model for a national security court that would review Guantánamo detention or choose drone attacks targets were unsuccessful. Art. III judges hearing challenges to surveillance divided sharply along ideological lines. But courts ultimately approved every program, sometimes by making implausible factual assumptions (e.g., that *this* plaintiff was not wiretapped even though NSA boasted of wiretapping *everyone*), sometimes simply by deferring to the government in national security matters. And most of the issues discussed in this volume were nonjusticiable in

Art. III courts: the Abu Ghraib abuses (whose victims had no access to US lawyers), detention and conditions of confinement in Guantánamo and military prisons in Afghanistan and Iraq, extraordinary rendition, secret CIA prisons, targeted killing, and other military operations.

CIVIL SOCIETY

As the introductory chapter revealed, NGOs devote significant effort to shaping public opinion by investigating and documenting rule-of-law violations.[25] The difficulty is that most Americans are indifferent to these issues most of the time. The opinions they do have tend to track basic divisions in American society and strenuously resist falsification (as shown by denials of Obama's citizenship or climate change). Abu Ghraib strongly engaged public attention because of the appalling images of sexualized abuse; but its effect was ephemeral and significantly neutralized by Bush administration condemnations of the behavior and the flurry of military investigations. Photographs of humiliated Guantánamo detainees also disturbed many; but it was hard to sustain interest in their plight over 14 years. Partly because no one was prosecuted for EITs, prominent Republicans (including Trump) persisted in endorsing waterboarding and other abuse, giving the public permission to do the same. Americans seem complacent about being surveilled, either because they feel no injury or because they are confident only terrorists are targeted. Furthermore, the line between acceptable and unacceptable surveillance turns on technical questions most people feel incapable of addressing. Although targeting Americans for killing made many of their fellow citizens queasy, military operations rarely generated widespread outrage. It is illuminating to contrast public passivity on these momentous issues with the vehement, and ultimately successful, opposition to transferring Uighurs to Virginia, trying HVDs in New York City or Alexandria, and imprisoning Guantánamo detainees in Michigan, Illinois, Kansas, South Carolina, or Colorado. Demonstrating once again that all politics are local, savvy (and unscrupulous) politicians in those locales leveraged fear and Islamophobia to their advantage.

Criticism of US rule-of-law violations tended to be stronger and more unified abroad, partly because of widespread resentment of American hegemony (which local politicians could stoke). Foreign countries sought to extract nationals from Guantánamo and refused to extradite terrorism suspects to the USA without a guarantee that they would not be sent to the island. Signatories of the Convention Against Torture condemned EITs. Residents of countries surveilled by NSA expressed outrage that they, and even their leaders, had been wiretapped. Targeted killing excited widespread condemnation, especially since the USA enjoyed a monopoly of the drone technology. But foreign criticism was necessarily tempered by the fact that many countries cooperated with the USA on counterterrorism, were complicit in extraordinary rendition and secret prisons, engaged in warfare (sometimes killing civilians), and conducted surveillance (if on a smaller scale). Although NGOs also appealed to regional and international bodies, the USA was not subject to the ICC or ECHR and disregarded the powerless IACHR. But though Bush and Bolton (his UN ambassador) showed contempt for the world institution, the Obama administration engaged seriously with the UN Council on Human Rights.

NGOs' experience in pressing the USA to respect the rule of law by appealing to public opinion does not offer much comfort. There is little evidence that the public, or even government officials, read or are swayed by the numerous NGO reports carefully documenting US violations. Only those capable of shame can be embarrassed. But there may be other justifications for "speaking truth to power": as an expressive act declaring the speaker's fidelity to ideals, bearing witness to good and evil, answering future generations' inevitable questions, documenting who knew what when, and laying the foundation for remedial actions that may take a generation to achieve.[26]

INTERPOSING BODIES

Scholars have characterized direct action as the power or weapon of the weak.[27] Gandhi pioneered "satyagraha" as leader of the Indian movement for independence from Britain. Martin Luther King Jr. embraced nonviolence in the US civil rights movement, repeatedly going to jail for civil disobedience; African Americans sat in at segregated lunch counters and rode buses in the South, suffering beatings and imprisonment. IRA members in Northern Ireland's Maze Prison resorted to a "dirty protest," smearing their cells and bodies with their feces; Bobby Sands starved himself to death. South Africans experienced cycles of peaceful demonstrations, police killings, and mass funerals in their struggle against apartheid. Buddhists immolated themselves to protest the South Vietnamese government. President Kennedy said of Malcolm Browne's iconic photo of Thích Quảng Đức burning to death: "No news picture in history has generated so much emotion around the world as that one."[28] Nearly 150 Tibetans sought to immolate themselves between February 2009 and July 2015 to protest Chinese rule.[29] The USA has recently experienced several years in which police killings of African Americans have led to massive demonstrations, spawning the Black Lives Matter movement.

The victims of rule-of-law violations in the US "war on terror" took the limited actions available and inspired action by others. Those abused at Abu Ghraib were completely helpless (as were others subjected to extraordinary rendition or held in military and secret CIA prisons). Guantánamo detainees refused to leave their cells, threw bombs of vomit, feces, and urine at guards, mutilated themselves, engaged in hunger strikes, and attempted and committed suicide. They were punished with loss of privileges, denial of comfort items and clothes, and solitary confinement, subjected to forcible cell extraction, and painfully force-fed while strapped to chairs so they soiled themselves. (The last practice compounded the outrage among medical professionals, Democratic legislators, and even some federal judges.) Even though the military sought to silence these protests by denying them the fuel of publicity (a major reason the Bush administration chose Guantánamo), they sometimes secured improved conditions of confinement if not their real goal: transfer or release. Tragically, false reports of Koran desecration in Guantánamo provoked massive demonstrations across the Muslim world, leading to hundreds of deaths and injuries at the hands of local police – but no changes in Guantánamo. Demonstrations in the USA and abroad on the 15 anniversaries of the prison's January 11 opening had no visible effect. Many subjected to EITs refused to talk, though few could hold out against repeated waterboarding (if they still could lie). Individuals and companies (even without knowing they had been targeted) and especially the IT industry tried to prevent surveillance by encrypting communications or routing or transmitting them in other ways. (Osama bin Laden relied exclusively on couriers during his last years.) Civilian casualties and nighttime house raids provoked Afghans to demonstrate before local leaders, often displaying the bodies of those killed. In a clientelist, clan-based society, the authority of these leaders rested on their ability to care for followers; failure to do so dishonored leaders, exposing them as mere puppets. But because the leaders had little power, and Afghan villagers could not appeal directly to the central government, much less the USA or its NATO allies, these protests were limited to expressions of grief and rage. It is instructive to compare direct action in its two most common settings: Guantánamo and Afghanistan. Both confronted an alien Western culture. Guantánamo detainees often had to act individually; Afghans always acted collectively. Detainees could hurt only themselves; Afghans could threaten others. Detainees had no visible audience; Afghans appealed to countrymen in district and provincial capitals, local leaders, and national and international media, sometimes eliciting a visit or comment by President Karzai. For these reasons, Afghans do seem to have influenced the US military to modify its tactics and ROEs, sometimes reducing civilian casualties and offenses to Afghan honor.

EQUAL JUSTICE UNDER LAW

This is arguably the most fundamental tenet of the rule of law: engraved on the pediment of the Supreme Court, personified by the iconic figure of a blindfolded woman holding the scales of justice, and embodied in the English assurance that "the law is no respecter of persons." Yet the US "war on terror" repeatedly transgressed it. Immediately after 9/11 the USA seized, held, and abused hundreds of undocumented immigrants believed to be Muslim or Arab (some just because of their darker skins) and deported almost all. (Needless to say, it did not treat the other 11 million undocumented immigrants in the same way.) It required tens of thousands of legally documented Muslims to register. Only noncitizens were detained in Guantánamo (Hamdi was quickly moved to the USA when it emerged he was born there), subjected to EITs (although Padilla was treated brutally in the brig), tried by military commissions, or subjected to extraordinary rendition. Conservative critics argued that terrorists apprehended in the USA, such as Abdulmutallab, Shahzad, Ghailani, Tsarnaev, abu Ghaith, and Rahimi, should have been tried by military commissions; and Republicans aborted the SDNY trial of five HVDs. NSA claimed that it only read the communications of noncitizens abroad (where the Fourth Amendment did not apply). US military personnel in Afghanistan and Iraq enjoyed immunity from local prosecution. Military contractors shared that for a period, and those without it were spirited out of the country before they could be prosecuted: Blackwater contractors after the Nisour Square massacre, CIA contractor Raymond Davis after he killed two Pakistanis. The CIA built secret prisons abroad, where US law could not reach: Thailand, Poland, Romania, Lithuania, and

Morocco. The USA refused to cooperate when Italy and Germany investigated extraordinary renditions or sought to extradite CIA agents to stand trial. The USA applied different rules to the targeted killing of citizens and others. The USA paid little or no compensation for killing or wounding Afghans, Iraqis, Pakistanis, Yemenis, and Somalis (though it paid $1.3 million for each of two deaths to extricate Davis from Pakistan and substantial amounts after a drone strike in Yemen to prop up President Saleh). The USA devoted far more energy to investigating the deaths of its military (Tillman) or allied civilians (Norgrove) from friendly fire or contractor negligence (electrocutions) than the much more numerous instances of "collateral damage." It provided more due process to US citizens detained in military prisons than to foreigners. It refused to compensate those detained in Guantánamo by error (or for too long), or mistakenly rendered to foreign prisons (el-Masri), but paid $2 million to Brandon Mayfield, an American wrongly jailed in Portland for just three weeks. In none of these instances did the paramount norm of equality offer any leverage.

CLASH OF CIVILIZATIONS

Unable to compete with the West economically, technologically, or militarily, Islam demanded respect. Many Muslims saw the "war on terror" as a struggle for dignity, a demand that the West acknowledge the crimes of the Crusades and accept Islam, with its 1.6 billion believers, as the equal of Christianity and Judaism (just as Islam recognized those two other "peoples of the book"). Both al-Qaeda's 9/11 attacks and later ISIS atrocities sought to spark a war between Islam and the West. US conduct of this "war" exacerbated those feelings. Bush callously called it a crusade, offensively linking Iraq and Iran (traditional enemies) with North Korea in an "axis of evil." Neoconservatives foretold an inevitable "clash of civilizations."[30] Both the 9/11 attacks and the US response intensified American Islamophobia, expressed in dramatically increased numbers of hate crimes and bizarre campaigns against a nonexistent threat to impose sharia. Many antiterrorism tactics (not just the Abu Ghraib abuses) deliberately insulted or mocked Islam: stripping detainees naked, accusing them of homosexuality, and making them simulate homosexual acts. Interrogators forced detainees to embrace Christianity or wrapped them in the Israeli flag. The military insulted Islamic beliefs by violating the modesty of women during nighttime house raids. Soldiers routinely denigrated Muslims as rag heads or hajis. Some posed for photos with Taliban body parts or urinated on corpses. Others proselytized for Christianity. An American minister burned the Koran; another American (of Egyptian Coptic origin) made a film mocking Islam. The false rumor of Koran desecration in Guantánamo and the accidental burning of Korans in Afghanistan provoked mass demonstrations across the Muslim world, many of which turned violent; credulous belief in the former and conviction that the latter event was intentional revealed the depth of Muslim distrust and resentment. Americans found it hard to grasp that Muslims were more offended by insults to Islam than physical injuries, as illustrated by the passionate responses to the cartoons of Mohammed in the Danish newspaper *Jyllands-Posten*, caricatures of the Prophet in *Charlie Hebdo*, and (decades earlier) the fatwa against Salman Rushdie for *The Satanic Verses*. Part of the explanation could be found in the terrorist taunt "we love death more than you love life," enacted in the 9/11 attacks and numerous suicide bombings, and related to the belief that a jihadi who died in an attack was guaranteed entry to paradise. All this meant that none of the remedies the USA offered for rule-of-law violations salved victims' sense of dishonor. Even apologies and compensation (when given) could not satisfy the demand for Islamic justice conducted by Islamic governments before the entire population.

WHICH MORAL DISCOURSE?

A central issue for defenders of the rule of law was the choice of a moral discourse. Few deployed deontological rhetoric, even though it was potentially the most powerful. Sen. McCain, having survived torture, condemned it by declaring: "it's about us. It's about who we were, who we are and who we aspire to be."[31] Some human rights advocates categorically rejected indefinite detention without trial. Sen. Paul invoked libertarian principles in criticizing NSA surveillance and targeted killing (at least of US citizens). Pacifists opposed the wars in Afghanistan, Iraq, Pakistan, Yemen, Somalia, Libya, and Syria. But the reticence of most to use nonconsequentialist language was unsurprising. A defining feature of modernity is the displacement of deontological arguments by a hegemonic utilitarianism, which substitutes questions of "more or less" for "either/or." (We can see the dominance of utilitarianism by noting the exceptions. Abortion and marriage equality opponents invoke religious values. Libertarians oppose sumptuary taxes on cigarettes or soft drinks or mandatory motorcycle helmet laws. The National Rifle Association champions the "right to bear arms," disregarding the carnage of gun violence. Most people recoil from utilitarian arguments that slavery was good for African Americans or polygyny was good for women.) Weber analyzed how rational authority superseded tradition and charisma. Utilitarian rhetoric presents itself as scientific: if we do x, then y will follow. Lawyers argue for rules and judges justify them by appealing to what Cardozo termed sociological arguments.[32] The debate over the death penalty often is framed in terms of whether it deters more powerfully than a life sentence. Tort law is full of such facile arguments: holding tortfeasors liable for damages encourages them to spend the optimally efficient amount of money on safety; granting immunity to government employees protects their essential exercise of discretion.

The problem with utilitarian reasoning is that its empirical claims almost never are tested and often cannot be. But because it was the dominant discourse, rule of law defenders felt compelled to engage its arguments. This choice was fraught. Consequentialist justifications for rule-of-law violations in the "war on terror" were particularly powerful because of their inherent asymmetry: the benefits of counterterrorist strategies typically accrued to the USA, while the costs were inflicted on others (those detained in Guantánamo or secret prisons, subjected to EITs or rendered to torture abroad, surveilled, or killed, injured, or damaged by air strikes or ground warfare). The Bush administration and Republicans under Obama made several utilitarian arguments for Guantánamo. Detainees disclosed intelligence. But some knew nothing (having been seized by mistake or handed over for a bounty); all could have been interrogated in Afghanistan or Iraq; and few were interrogated for more than a few months – certainly none for the 15 years some languished in the prison. Defenders therefore fell back on the justification of incapacitation: it was necessary to hold detainees in Guantánamo to prevent them from returning to terrorism. They inverted Blackstone's deontological position (above) to assert it was better that hundreds of innocent men be detained than that one be released to engage in terrorism. But the empirical predicates of this proposition were missing. Some detainees had never engaged in terrorism. "Recidivism statistics" were highly manipulable and unreliable. (They also showed higher levels for those released by Bush – to which no Republican ever objected.) Guantánamo defenders failed to explain why they were obsessed with a few hundred detainees when tens or hundreds of thousands were waging jihad in Afghanistan, Iraq, Pakistan, Yemen, Libya, and Syria. US forces never attempted to capture all of them and released most they did, without provoking the furor accompanying transfers from Guantánamo. Military leaders understood that the USA could not defeat terrorism by killing or capturing all the terrorists. Guantánamo defenders cited the law of war to justify detention until the "war on terror" ended. But they never said who would decide when termination occurred and by what criteria. Conservatives and radical Islamists tragically seemed to agree that the "war" could end only with the (inconceivable) triumph of one side or the other.

Guantánamo critics responded with their own utilitarian arguments. Echoing opponents' warnings about recidivism, they asserted that detention was more likely to radicalize than rehabilitate. They declared that Guantánamo's mere existence recruited many more jihadists than the prison held. And they claimed Guantánamo alienated allies. But critics offered no empirical support for these propositions, which would have been very difficult to test and even more to quantify. Critics also cited Guantánamo's cost, which had reached an astronomical $8 million/prisoner/year in October 2016 and an estimated $10 million/prisoner/year for the few remaining at the end of the Obama administration – more than *300 times* the $30,000 it would cost to house detainees in a federal prison.[33] But defenders (many claiming to be fiscal conservatives) simply jettisoned their utilitarian pretensions, proclaiming that cost was no consideration when Americans' safety was at stake. Although critics could never win this debate, release of all but 45 of the nearly 700 held in Guantánamo seemed to acknowledge that a utilitarian calculus did not justify indefinite detention.

EIT defenders responded to critics' deontological argument that torture was *never* permissible – a position enshrined in international treaties and domestic law – with their trump card: the ticking bomb hypothetical. If torture was the only way to make a suspected terrorist disclose unique information that alone would let the government interdict a WMD that would kill X innocent people (pick your own scary number), it must be justified. Opponents have decisively dismembered that argument. There is no way of knowing that only under torture will the terrorist disclose unique truthful information that is necessary and sufficient to stop an attack otherwise certain to occur. (This essential premise contains at least seven unknowns.) No one has ever identified an actual situation. Furthermore, if utilitarianism justifies some torture, it justifies all torture, e.g. forcing the suspect to watch his wife being raped or his child burned alive. After all, utilitarianism can justify killing 1,000,000 of "them" to save 1,000,001 of "us" (advocated by the nuclear deterrence strategy of mutual assured destruction, or MAD). But those logical demolitions did little to diminish the argument's rhetorical power, as shown by the fact that SSCI felt compelled to devote much of its 500-page report to trying to show the inefficacy or superfluity of torture, thereby exposing itself to rebuttals by the Republican minority and the CIA. Torture critics advanced their own utilitarian arguments: EITs were likely to elicit lies rather than truth (interrogatees will say anything to stop the torture); rapport-building was more effective; and EITs motivated jihadis to join the fight, increased the risk US troops would be tortured if captured, and alienated allies. But critics offered no evidence for any of these propositions, and certainly could not prove them. Each new terrorist attack and counterterrorism operation revived calls for more EITs, accompanied by claims they could have prevented terrorism or did so. But no evidence was offered for either assertion; and the arguments were strangely hermetic, pairing claims that both the success *and* the failure of counterterrorism operations demonstrated the indispensability of EITs. Defenders also invoked attacks to remind the US of their potential cost and exaggerate their probability, while citing successful counterterrorism operations to demonstrate they were cheap, feasible, and effective.

Defenders of surveillance made similar arguments that it had prevented terrorist attacks and only it could have done so. Once more, however, they did not and could not offer any evidence. NSA claimed it could have prevented 9/11 had it surveilled the two future hijackers in San Diego. Critics retorted that the CIA had known about them but failed to inform the FBI. Since NSA asserted it had to comb the entire haystack to find a single needle, utilitarian defenders necessarily contended that the loss of privacy suffered by every American was trivial. Utilitarian critics again advanced unsubstantiated empirical assertions, e.g., that surveillance alienated allies, making essential cooperation less likely.

The law of warfare employs a utilitarian calculus to prescribe how the military may inflict the greatest damage on enemy forces while doing the least harm to civilians. But because the ratios do not and cannot have precise numerical values, critics of military operations could advance only vague objections that civilian casualties had been excessive or unnecessary. Consequently, the debate devolved into an inconclusive numbers game: comparisons of how many and which insurgents and civilians had been killed and under what circumstances. Furthermore, the inherently ambiguous distinction between insurgents and civilians was rendered more opaque by the US military's capacious category of "MAMs" (military age males, ranging from pre-teen to elderly) and the CIA's conduct of signature strikes (against people whose identities were unknown). Given the remoteness of most operations and the greatly elevated danger (to journalists and NGOs) of visiting the scene of recent attacks, the US military possessed the best and often the only information (through mandatory reports by those involved and videotapes from drones and manned aircraft); but it also was strongly motivated to exculpate itself. The debate over targeted killing took a somewhat different form. Defenders advanced the utilitarian argument that drones were more precise (true only if intelligence was correct). Critics offered a deontological argument against deliberation (which typically increases the seriousness of crimes), comparing targeted killing to assassination. Defenders replied that military snipers also pick their targets and wait for the best shot.

Defenders of all five categories of rule-of-law violations resorted to a peculiar utilitarian trope: look at what we refrain from doing, not what we do; applaud us for not acting worse than we did and not as badly as others. (This resembled the child's protest against a parental admonition: look at what a sibling or friend did.) MP misconduct at Abu Ghraib was a unique aberration; other countries and fighters behave that way all the time. Conditions at Guantánamo Bay were better than those at many, perhaps most, US prisons (an embarrassingly low bar). Detention there was not as harsh as the internment of Japanese Americans (although it lasted much longer) and was much less evil than Nazi concentration camps. EITs were not as painful as other interrogation techniques and certainly not torture (using the Spanish Inquisition as the baseline); and only a few detainees were subjected to them. Because NSA had the ability to read virtually every communication in the world, it should be commended for doing less. American military might so greatly exceeded that of any adversary in the "war on terror" that the US should be praised for exercising restraint. Look at all the civilians that could have been killed but haven't been, all the drone targets that are not obliterated. And to highlight American benignity, the US emphasized the horror of its adversaries' malignity: the 9/11 attack and especially ISIS atrocities.

Despite their flaws, utilitarian arguments against rule-of-law violations seem to have gained some traction. The Bush administration was profoundly embarrassed by Abu Ghraib, fearing its impact on the wars in Iraq and Afghanistan, the US reputation in the Muslim world, and allied cooperation. Toward its end, the administration seems to have been persuaded that Guantánamo did more harm than good, ultimately releasing or transferring more than 500 detainees. In a few instances, the USA had to promise not to send terrorism suspects to Guantánamo in order to persuade other countries to extradite them. Congressional Republicans' continued opposition to the prison's closure may have been motivated more by their determination to block *every* Obama initiative than national security concerns. The CIA closed several secret prisons for fear they were about to be exposed. Utilitarian arguments against EITs confronted two obstacles: skepticism that adversaries in the "war on terror" would reciprocate our restraint, and the fact that they held few if any US prisoners. And though professional interrogators consistently maintained that rapport secured better intelligence, EIT advocates insisted on trusting their instinct that brute force could always extract the truth. The anger voiced by allied leaders (especially Angela Merkel) at being surveilled seems to have convinced Obama to order NSA to be more cautious. And the power of both IT companies and European nations (individually and collectively) to evade or obstruct surveillance by moving operations abroad or encrypting communications forced the USA to modify its eavesdropping policies. Utilitarian arguments may have had the greatest effect on the military, whose actions must be pragmatic, given their life or death consequences. Drone strikes, civilian casualties, night raids, and traffic stops could anger local populations, denying the USA accurate intelligence and transforming civilians and even military allies into adversaries, endangering American lives and prolonging the war. Drone strikes diminished partly because of the lack of targets and hopes that the Taliban would negotiate.

THE BOTTOM LINE

At the end of the day, defenders of the rule of law achieved only partial victories – all that is ever possible. A few foot soldiers were punished for the abuses at Abu Ghraib but not their superiors, and certainly not those whose orders encouraged the abuses. Detention in Guantánamo was significantly reduced to 10 convicted or on trial in military commissions, 29 "forever" prisoners, and a few approved for transfer; but the failure to close it was an invitation to Trump to fulfill his campaign pledge to "load it up with some bad dudes."[34] Its existence also means that the seriously flawed military commissions rather than Art. III courts will continue to conduct trials. Obama's PRBs offered a far better screening mechanism than Bush's CSRTs and certified for transfer almost all they reviewed. Shutting the CIA's secret prisons will make it more difficult to open new ones. Criticism of extraordinary rendition to countries that torture makes such operations riskier. Obama and Congress prohibited EITs (although the Army Field Manual Appendix M may preserve a loophole). And though Trump indulged in characteristic demagoguery by threatening to "bring back waterboarding, and ... a hell of a lot worse than waterboarding," his Cabinet appointees may resist (and so may the CIA).[35] Surveillance remains a contested arena: the FAA authorizes a great deal (and the scope of EO 12333 remains unclear), while privacy advocates, the IT industry, and European nations and institutions continue to resist. As the wars in Afghanistan, Iraq, Yemen, Syria, Somalia, and Libya drag on indefinitely, the US military will continue to draw imperfect lines between acceptable and unacceptable civilian casualties. Trump might view Obama's expansion of drone strikes as a license to choose new targets.

LOOKING BACKWARD TO MOVE FORWARD

Perhaps the greatest defeat of rule-of-law defenders was their inability to persuade either administration to prosecute the most egregious violators. Although Bush condemned the Abu Ghraib abuses, his administration suppressed the Taguba report, which alone held officers responsible; and courts-martial convicted none of them. Bush's FAA was infected with a crucial compromise immunizing telecommunications companies complicit in NSA surveillance. Shortly before his first inauguration, Obama told a television interviewer he believed "we need to look forward as opposed to looking backwards."[36] "[P]art of my job is to make sure that, for example, at the C.I.A., you've got extraordinarily talented people who are working very hard to keep Americans safe. I don't want them to suddenly feel like they've got [to] spend their [*sic*] all their time looking over their shoulders." He maintained that position throughout both his terms of office. Directing John Durham to investigate the CIA's EITs, Attorney General Holder promised not to prosecute anyone "who acted in good faith and within the scope of the legal guidance given by" Bush administration lawyers (already found to be flawed and repudiated).[37] Consequently, none of them was prosecuted. *New York*

Times columnist Thomas Friedman praised these decisions because any prosecution "taken to its logical end here would likely require bringing George W. Bush, Donald Rumsfeld and other senior officials to trial, which would rip our country apart."[38]

This was a tragic error.[39] William Faulkner wrote that "the past is never dead. It's not even past."[40] George Santayana warned that "those who cannot remember the past are condemned to repeat it."[41] Courts alone are empowered to give authoritative answers to legal questions. Exercising this authority was essential in the "war on terror" because the OLC – whose opinions bind the executive – had approved many rule-of-law violations. Even though Republicans had succeeded in packing the federal judiciary, its members' lifetime tenure gave them greater independence than that displayed by Bush's OLC apparatchiki. Durkheim maintained that deviance performs the essential social function of enabling the state to reaffirm the violated norm; but this can happen only if the state actually punishes the violator.[42] Hegel argued that society owes punishment to the offender.[43] Jurists warn that leaving transgressions unpunished weakens the legitimacy of both the law violated and the entire legal system, and can lead to nullification: Prohibition, drug use, income tax evasion, even speeding are examples. The Nuremberg Trials made an indispensable contribution to affirming and strengthening international law; the ICC is trying to do something similar today. There are numerous domestic examples of criminal trials that conclusively established the illegality of hotly contested, politically freighted actions: Lt. William Calley for the My Lai massacre, the Watergate "Plumbers," Oliver North for Iran–Contra.

In the absence of such an authoritative decision, rule-of-law violators can keep claiming their actions were legal. After the SSCI report documented the CIA's horrific abuses, John Yoo reiterated his discredited opinions on torture.[44] Just weeks before Donald Trump was inaugurated, Alberto Gonzales (Bush's disgraced Attorney General and White House counsel) repeated that "the Bush administration insisted that interrogation techniques, such as waterboarding, were not torture." He advised Trump:[45] "[T]he president is head of the executive branch, and he could have the final say if he chooses to exercise his authority on the law. And he may decide that the law passed by Congress is unconstitutional given certain circumstances that may unduly restrict his authority as commander-in-chief to protect this country."

Dissenting in *U.S.* v. *Korematsu* – one of the Supreme Court's greatest self-inflicted wounds – Justice Jackson excoriated his colleagues.

> [O]nce a judicial opinion rationalizes [a military order] to show that it conforms to the Constitution, or rather rationalizes the Constitution to show that the Constitution sanctions such an order, the Court for all time has validated the principle of racial discrimination in criminal procedure and of transplanting American citizens. The principle then lies about like a loaded weapon, ready for the hand of any authority that can bring forward a plausible claim of an urgent need. Every repetition imbeds that principle more deeply in our law and thinking and expands it to new purposes.[46]

Prosecutorial and judicial abstention can be as toxic as action. It is the failure of courts to rule that torture is illegal under domestic and international laws, and declare that the president has no constitutional power to ignore those laws, that is the greatest threat to the rule of law.

APPENDIX: TABLES

Chapter 5

Table A1 Electronic Surveillance

Case	Court	Judge	Appointing President's Party	For Plaintiff
New Jersey Challenge	ND Cal	Walker	R	N
CAIR Challenge	ED Mich	Taylor	D	Y
	6th Cir.	Gibbons	R	N
		Batchelder	R	N
		Gilman	D	Y
Hepting	ND Cal	Walker	R	Y
	9th Cir.	Pregerson	D	N
		Hawkins	D	N
		McKeown	R	N
	ND Cal	Walker	R	N
Jewel	ND Cal	Walker	R	N
	9th Cir.	Pregerson	D	Y
		Hawkins	D	Y
		McKeown	R	Y
	ND Cal	White	R	N
Al-Haramain	D Ore	King	D	Y
	9th Cir.	McKeown	R	N
		Pregerson	D	N
		Hawkins	R	N
	ND Cal	Walker	R	Y
	9th Cir.	Pregerson	D	N
		Hawkins	R	N
		McKeown	R	N

(continued)

Table A1 (*continued*)

Case	Court	Judge	Appointing President's Party	For Plaintiff
Amnesty International	SDNY	Koeltl	D	N
	2nd Cir.	Lynch	D	Y
		Calabresi	D	Y
		Sack	D	Y
	2nd Cir. en banc	Raggi	R	N
		Hall	R	N
		Jacobs	R	N
		Cabranes	D	N
		Wesley	R	N
		Livingston	R	N
		Lynch	D	Y
		Calabresi	D	Y
		Sack	D	Y
		Katzman	D	Y
		Pooler	D	Y
		Chin	D	Y
	USSC	Alito	R	N
		Roberts	R	N
		Scalia	R	N
		Thomas	R	N
		Kennedy	R	N
		Ginsburg	D	Y
		Breyer	D	Y
		Sotomayor	D	Y
		Kagan	D	Y
Klayman	DDC	Leon	R	Y
	DC Cir.	Brown	R	N
		Williams	R	N
		Sentelle	R	N
	DDC	Leon	R	Y

Table A1 *(continued)*

Case	Court	Judge	Appointing President's Party	For Plaintiff
ACLU	SDNY	Pauley	D	N
	2nd Cir.	Lynch	D	Y
		Sack	D	Y
		Broderick (DJ)	D	Y
Smith	D Id	Winmill	D	N
WikiMedia	D Md	Ellis	R	N
	3rd Cir.	Diaz	D	Y
		Motz	D	Y
		Davis (DJ)	R	Y
Adel Daoud	ND Ill	Coleman	D	Y
	7th Cir.	Posner	R	N
		Kanne	R	N
		Rovner	R	N
Jamshid Muhtorov	D Colo	Kane	D	N
Agron Hasbajrami	EDNY	Gleeson	D	N
Mohamed Mohamud	D Ore	King	D	Y
	9th Cir.	Pregerson	D	N
		Bea	R	N
		Owens	R	N

NOTES

In order to avoid distracting readers with the numerous citations, they are grouped together in notes that contain all the sources for one or more related paragraphs.

ACRONYMS

ABA	American Bar Association
ACLU	American Civil Liberties Union
AFP	Agence France-Presse
AG	Attorney General
AI	Amnesty International
AIHRC	Afghan Independent Human Rights Commission
AP	Associated Press
BG	*Boston Globe*
BS	*Baltimore Sun*
BSA	Bilateral Security Agreement
CCR	Center for Constitutional Rights
CE	Council of Europe
CFR	Council on Foreign Relations
CID	Criminal Investigation Command (Army); Cruel, inhuman and degrading (treatment)
CJTF	Combined Joint Task Force
CSM	Christian Science Monitor
CSRT	Combatant Status Review Tribunal
CT	*Chicago Tribune*
DoD	Department of Defense
DoJ	Department of Justice
DoS	Department of State
DT	*Daily Telegraph* (UK)
EIT	Enhanced interrogation technique
FAIR	Fairness & Accuracy in Reporting
FISC	Foreign Intelligence Surveillance Court

FOIA	Freedom of Information Act
FP	*Foreign Policy*
FR	*Federal Register*
FT	*Financial Times* (UK)
G	*Guardian* (UK)
GAO	General Accountability Office
GCHQ	Government Communications Headquarters (UK)
HRF	Human Rights First
HRW	Human Rights Watch
I	*Independent* (UK)
ICC	International Criminal Court
ICRC	International Committee of the Red Cross
IG	Inspector General
IMF	International Monetary Fund
INGO	international nongovernmental organization
ISAF	International Security Assistance Force
ISI	Inter-Services Intelligence (Pakistan)
JAG	Judge Advocate General
JCS	Joint Chiefs of Staff
LAT	*Los Angeles Times*
LOAC	Law of Armed Conflict
LtCol.	Lieutenant Colonel
LtGen.	Lieutenant General
MGen.	Major General
MI	Military Intelligence
MH	*Miami Herald*
MSF	Médecins sans frontières (Doctors Without Borders)
NATO	North Atlantic Treaty Organization
NCIS	Naval Criminal Investigation Service
NDAA	National Defense Authorization Act
NPR	National Public Radio
NSA	National Security Agency
NYRB	New York Review of Books
NYT	*New York Times*
O	*Observer* (UK)
ODNI	Office of the Director of National Intelligence
OIG	Office of the Inspector General
OLC	Office of Legal Counsel, Department of Justice
Pfc.	Private first class

PHR	Physicians for Human Rights
PTI	Pakistan Tehreek-e-Insaf
SA	Senate Amendment
SASC	Senate Armed Services Committee
Sgt.	Sergeant
SJC	Senate Judiciary Committee
SSCI	Senate Select Committee on Intelligence
ST	*Sunday Times* (UK)
T	*Times* (UK)
TDIP	Temporary Committee on the Alleged Use of European Countries by the CIA for the Transport and Illegal Detention of Prisoners
UNAMA	United Nations Assistance Mission in Afghanistan
VOA	Voice of America
WP	*Washington Post*
WSJ	*Wall Street Journal*

PREFACE

1 "Deciderization 2007 – a Special Report," Introduction to *The Best American Essays 2007* (New York: Houghton Mifflin, 2007).

CHAPTER 1 DEFENDING THE RULE OF LAW

1 For histories, critiques and apologetics of this period, see Leone & Anrig (2003); Sidel (2004); Ricks (2006); Risen (2006, 2014); Paust (2007); Savage (2007, 2015); Ball (2007); Cohn (2007); Gore (2007); Lichtblau (2008); Honigsberg (2009); Blum & Heymann (2010); Baker (2013); Brooks (2016); Cheney & Cheney (2011); Priest & Arkin (2011); Chertoff (2009); Draper (2007); Schmitt & Shanker (2011); Feingold (2012); Gellman (2008); Margulies (2010); Greenberg (2016); Herman (2011); Shipler (2012); Margulies (2013); Scahill (2013); Morrell & Harlow (2015); Ohlin (2015); Danner (2016).
2 Hunt (2007).
3 Bingham (2011: 19).
4 Fisher (2008: 5, 8).
5 Bingham (2011: 24, 27).
6 Bingham (2011: 15); Hunt (2007).
7 Martinez (2012); Keck & Sikkink (1998: 44–51).
8 Keck & Sikkink (1998: 80–89).
9 Krygier (2014).

10 European Commission for Democracy through Law (2011).
11 Dicey (1959); cf. Wade (1967); Raz (1979: 214–18).
12 Agamben (2005: 24); see the debates in Ramraj (2008); Dyzenhaus (2008); Gross (2008), Hussain & Sarat (2010b). For an attempt to delineate a middle ground, see Lazar (2009).
13 Schmitt (2005); Douglas et al. (2014: 6).
14 Fatovic (2009: 3).
15 *Terminiello* v. *City of Chicago*, 337 U.S. 1, 36 (1949). When the Court invalidated a Chicago ordinance criminalizing speech that might move hearers to attack the speaker – the "heckler's veto" – Jackson declared in dissent that the Bill of Rights is not a "suicide pact."
16 Rossiter (1948: 5).
17 Rajagopal (2003).
18 Goldstein (2001: 56, 61–68).
19 Hope (2004); Steyn (2004).
20 Moeckli (2010); Johns (2005); Aradau (2007); Husssain (2007); Fitzpatrick & Joyce (2007).
21 Quoted in Bingham (2011: 8).
22 See Gearty (2007: 10–15).
23 Neumann (1942: 362–63).
24 Kirchheimer (1967).
25 Berlin (1991).
26 Krygier (2011: 79–80; 2012a: 238, 242; 2013).
27 Palombella (2010).
28 Cahn (1949); Shklar (1998); Gutmann (2001: ix, xvii–xix); Waldron (2010: 228, 232); see also Friedman (2011: 19).
29 Raz (1979); Böckenförde (1991).
30 Ignatieff (2001a: 16; 2001b: 55–57, 88–89).
31 Krygier (2011: 79–80; 2012a: 238, 242; 2013).
32 Waldron (2011: 15).
33 *Grundgesetz*, Art. 1 (1949).
34 *McNabb* v. *U.S.*, 318 U.S. 322, 347 (1943).
35 Quoted in Levy (1968: ix).
36 Fuller (1969).
37 Cass (2001: 4).
38 MacCormick (2005).
39 Waldron (2011: 6); cf. Fiss & Resnick (1988). One of the Warren Court's defining contributions was conforming criminal procedure to the rule of law; see West (2011).
40 Thompson (1975: 259–68).
41 See also Fine (1984).
42 Oakeshott (1991: 389).
43 Quoted in Abel (1995: 7).
44 Gordimer (1999: vii).
45 Forewords to Abel (1995: viii, x).
46 Wiesel (1999: 3).
47 Ignatieff (2001a: 53).

48 Annan (1999).
49 Johnson (1999).
50 Tamanaha (2004: 1–2); Cheesman (2015).
51 Abel (1995: 12–13, 16).
52 Gewirtz, "What China Means by Rule of Law," NYT (10.20.14); Forsythe, "China's Chief Justice Rejects an Independent Judiciary, and Reformers Wince," NYT (1.18.17).
53 Sang-hun, "North Korea Says Reports of Abuse Are Produced by Political 'Racket,'" NYT (9.14.14); Bruce, "North Korea Agrees to Weigh Steps on Human Rights," NYT (9.20.14).
54 "North Korea Praises Rights Record in Draft Resolution," AP (10.15.14).
55 Sanger, "North Korea Challenges U.N. Report on Violations," NYT (10.20.14).
56 Hubbard & Yeginsu, "Turkish Leader Declares a State of Emergency," NYT (7.21.16).
57 Lyon & Olson (2012).
58 E.g., Waltz (1979).
59 E.g., Donnelly (2003).
60 Quataert (2009: 5).
61 Farrall (2007: 22).
62 Barkun (1968); Kratochwil (1989).
63 Ignatieff (2001a: 55).
64 Williams (2007: 14).
65 Hayek (1944: 54).
66 Call (2007); Weingast (2010), cited in Krygier (2012b).
67 Shue (1979); Rejali (2007).
68 Waldron (2010: 243).
69 Cited in Hunt (2007: 80). An article in Diderot's *Encyclopedia* made a similar argument. Ibid. 104.
70 Tyler (1990: 170–78).
71 Seron et al. (2004).
72 E.g., Kristof, "Liberal Reality Check," *Pittsburgh Post-Gazette* (6.3.02) ("as risks change, we who care about civil liberties need to realign balances between security and freedom"); Dershowitz (2002a; 2002b); Yoo (2005; 2006).
73 Shue (1979: 11–15); Waldron (2010: 12).
74 Waldron (2010: 12), following Nozick (1974) and Dworkin (1977).
75 Mutua (2002); Peerenboom (2004); Hopgood (2013); see also Sarat & Kearns (2011).
76 Dicey (1959).
77 Thibaut & Walker (1975: 118–19).
78 Jacobs & Buckley, "China Moves to Reinforce Rule of Law, With Caveats," NYT (10.24.14).
79 347 U.S. 483 (1954); Wechsler (1959).
80 *Kelo* v. *City of New London*, 545 U.S. 469 (2005).
81 *Citizens United* v. *Federal Election Commission*, 558 U.S. 310 (2010).

82 *Burwell* v. *Hobby Lobby Stores, Inc.*, 134 S.Ct. 2751 (2014).
83 For lawyers' critiques of the Bush administration response, see Silkenat & Shulman (2007).
84 Marx (1947): "Until now, philosophers have sought only to interpret the world in various ways; the point, however, is to change it" (from "Theses on Feuerbach").
85 Selznick (1959; 1968).
86 I am following the path of grounded theory. Glaser & Strauss (1967). In his introduction to the collection of essays entitled *Rights in Context*, Banakar (2010: 3) describes its focus as "how rights are employed by various actors and interest groups as a strategic tool to create and recreate social relations and structures over time."
87 On efforts to enforce human rights in the USA, see Armaline et al. (2011); Hertel & Libal (2012).
88 Keys (2014: 22–26).
89 Anderson (2003); Simmons (2009: 44).
90 Hunt (2007: 179).
91 Simmons (2009: 72–75, 82–87, 100–107, 276–77); Goodman & Jinks (2003).
92 Hathaway (2002); Hafner-Burton & Tsutsui (2005); Hafner-Burton et al. (2008); Keith (1999); Gilligan & Nesbitt (2009).
93 Finnemore (1996: 2).
94 Simmons (2009: 14–16, 137, 144, 161, 165–74, 181–83, 192–94, 257, 273–76, 278, 281, 326–35); Keith (1999; 2002); Landman (2005); Hathaway (2002).
95 Downs & Jones (2002).
96 Dudziak (2000).
97 Keys (2014: 35).
98 Anderson (2003); Simmons (2009: 44).
99 Keys (2014: 45).
100 Risse & Sikkink (1999, 2013); Risse & Ropp (1999; 2013); Jetschke & Liese (2013); Simmons (2013); Risse et al. (2013).
101 Sikkink (2011: 88–96, 245–54).
102 Keck & Sikkink (1998: 7); Risse-Kappen (1995: 22). On Argentina, see Robben (2004).
103 Neier (2012: 109–12). On appeals to these bodies, see Huang (2008). On the effect of publicity, see Clark (2013).
104 Becker (2013: 77–92); Piccone (2010: ix–x, 2, 5–7, 13–18, 22, 27–37); Quataert (2009: 74–92, 118–36).
105 But an AI report suggests that police abuses continued, although at lower levels. "Rights Group: Police Torture in Philippines Rife," WP (12.5.14). And two years later President Duterte boasted that as mayor of Davao "I used to do it personally," i.e. kill suspected drug dealers and users, "just to show the guys that if I can do it, why can't you?" Goldman, "Rodrigo Duterte on Killing Criminal Suspects: 'I Used to Do It Personally,'" NYT (12.14.16).
106 Keys (2014: 53, 80–146, 161–75, 206, 210–75).

107 O'Donnell & Schmitter (1986); Whitehead (1996); Lutz & Reiger (2009); Goldsmith & Krasner (2003); Snyder & Vinjamuri (2004).
108 Sikkink (2011: 134–86); Kim & Sikkink (2010); but see Olsen et al. (2010).
109 Tolley (1990–91); Soohoo (2008); AI (2014c); Cole (2016).
110 Keck & Sikkink (1998: 89–101 and Table 1 p. 11). The total number of INGOs increased from 973 in 1956 to 5471 in 1996: Welch (2001a: 1).
111 Walker (1990: 11, 67, 168, 268); Finan (2007: 135).
112 Stone (2004: 238).
113 Prouvez & Bovay (2001).
114 Power (2001: chap. 4); Neier (2012: 187–89); Clark (2001b: 6, 13–17).
115 Neier (2012: 3, 8–12).
116 Ibid. 235–39.
117 Quataert (2009: 94–100); Neier (2012: 205–27).
118 Walker (1990: 206–207, 326, 329, 342, 363).
119 Chokshi, "Nonprofits Opposed to Trump's Ideology See a Surge in Donations," NYT (11.17.16).
120 Mauro, "Former ACLU Leaders Quarrel with Current Leadership over Campaign Finance," *Legal Times* (9.8.14).
121 Power (2001: chap. 5).
122 Welch (2001b); Power (2001: 135, 141–42, 234).
123 Clark (2001b: 101–19).
124 Ibid. 43–67; Power (2001: 138).
125 Walker (1990: 312).
126 Keck & Sikkink (1998: 15); Neier (2012: 187–89); Clark (2001b: 6, 13–17).
127 Chafee (1919, 1920).
128 Walker (1990: 47, 62, 64, 116).
129 Hopgood (2006: 73–77, 81–83, 93–98, 103, 114–19).
130 Forsythe (1977: 43, 45–47, 59, 63, 66–67, 76ff.). But the country must release the entire report if it publicizes any part.
131 Tolley (1994: 80–83, 86, 125).
132 Korey (1998).
133 Tolley (1994).
134 Scoble & Eisenberg (1976); Scoble (1984).
135 Quataert (2009: 112–16, 121, 130).
136 Walker (1990: 264–65).
137 Keck & Sikkink (1998: 16–17, 20–23, 28–29); Neier (2012: 187–89); Clark (2001b: 6, 13–17).
138 Keck & Sikkink (1998: 27); Stone (1989).
139 Neier (2012: 94).
140 Keck & Sikkink (1998: 52–58).
141 Quataert (2009: 14).
142 www.operationsmile.org.
143 Cohen (2001: 173–74).
144 Hopgood (2006: 73–77).
145 Moeller (1999); see also Wilson & Brown (2009).

146 Hopgood (2013: 105–108).
147 Cieply, "Divining Why One Film Spurs Activism, While Others Falter," NYT (7.7.14).
148 Cohen (2001: 180–83, 203–19, 249–50, 265).
149 Oliner & Oliner (1988); Fogelman (1994).
150 Power (2001: chap. 4).
151 Keck & Sikkink (1998: 60–72).
152 Roth, "The End of Human Rights?" NYRB 72 (10.23.14).
153 Welch (2001a: 10).
154 Power (2001: 134–35, 141–42, 150–54 and chap. 7); Keys (2014: 203–04).
155 Hopgood (2013: 105–08).
156 Power (2001: chap. 2).
157 Becker (2013: chap. 6).
158 Brysk (1994: 10–12, 37, 40–86); Keck & Sikkink (1998: 103–10); Sikkink (2011: 60–79).
159 Clark (2001a).
160 Sikkink (2011: 37–59); Clark (2001b: 38–41).
161 Becker (2013: chap. 7).
162 Becker (2013: chap. 8).
163 Walker (1990: 359–60).
164 Silkenat & Shulman (2007).
165 Walker (1990: 15); Stone (2004: 202ff.).
166 Walker (1990: 21).
167 *Schenck* v. *U.S.*, 249 U.S. 47 (1919).
168 *Abrams* v. *U.S.*, 250 U.S. 616 (1919).
169 Healey (2013).
170 Walker (1990: 111–13.
171 Ibid. 189–90, 194; Stone (2004: 422–23).
172 Halliday et al. (2007: 9).
173 Stone (2004: 158–59).
174 Lawrence (1974).
175 Stone (2004: 225).
176 Auerbach (1976).
177 Walker (1990: 186–88, 201–02, 208–09); Stone (2004: 420–21).
178 Luckham (1981); bin Abas et al. (1989); Wong, "Lawyers Defend Hong Kong Rule of Law in Show of Unity against Beijing," NYT (6.27.14).
179 Cooke (2007); Press (2012).
180 Stone (2004: 502–14); Weiner (2012: 294–95); Walker (1990: 289–90); Lewis (2007: 147); Fisher (2008: 53–54); *New York Times Co.* v. *United States*, 403 U.S. 713 (1971).
181 Stone (2004: 471, 488–96); Weiner (2012: 293); Medsger (2014).
182 Stone (2004: 384); Walker (1990: 212).
183 Scott (2013: 28–30, 69–90, 95–133).
184 *U.S. v. Progressive, Inc.*, 467 F. Supp. 990 (W.D. Wis. 1979); Walker (1990: 197–98); Harding (2014).
185 Stone (2004: 462, 468).

186 Schwarz & Hug (2008); Posner & Vermeule (2011); Walker (2012), Edelson (2016).
187 Stone (2004: 88, 111, 122; Neff (2010: chaps. 2, 6).
188 Stone (2004: 145–46).
189 Ibid. 137, 223ff.
190 Lewis (2007: 83–88); Stone (2004: 248–50).
191 The supply of food, oil and materiel to the Allies during World War II in return for leases on army and naval bases in Allied territory, thus effectively ending the USA's pretense of neutrality.
192 Stone (2004: 296–96).
193 Stone (2004: 443).
194 Lewis (2007: 451).
195 Weiner (2008: 386–87).
196 Weiner (2008: 72–73, 111, 165, 181, 186, 198–99, 208, 214, 223, 250ff., 269, 314, 329, 365–66, 587).
197 Lewis (2007: 20).
198 Stone (2004: 124); Murphy (1979); Work (2005).
199 Lewis (2007: 128–29); Weiner (2012: 37–42, 58–66); Honig (2009: chap. 3).
200 Stone (2004: 231); Walker (1990: 56).
201 Stone (2004: 239, 248–50); Lewis (2007: 83–88); Finan (2007: 135, 138, 142).
202 Lewis (2007: 122–23, 160–62); Stone (2004: 293–95).
203 Stone (2004: 247–65); Fisher (2008: 132–33).
204 Finan (2007: 154–55).
205 Lewis (2007: 335–43, 348).
206 Weiner (2012: 195–97, 265, 291).
207 Weiner (2012: 309–39); Walker (2012: chap. 9).
208 Weiner (2008: 371ff., 379, 388–89, 413, 466); Shane (2009: 85).
209 Weiner (2012: 363–65); Walsh (1997); Lewis, "Lawrence E. Walsh, Prosecutor in Iran–Contra Scandal, Dies at 102," NYT (3.20.14).
210 On relations between Congress and the executive with respect to warmaking, see Barron (2016).
211 Thompson (1975: 21).
212 Lewis (2007: 17–18).
213 Stone (2004: 124).
214 Weiner (2012: 171).
215 Abel (1995: 17).
216 Walker (1990: 120); Fisher (2008: 138–44).
217 Stone (2004: 244–46).
218 Ibid. 224.
219 Finan (2007: 34–35).
220 Lewis (2007: 126).
221 Stone (2004: 54).
222 Ibid. 147–48.
223 *Olmstead* v. *U.S.*, 277 U.S. 438 (1928); Weiner (2012: 76).
224 Stone (2004: 244–46).

225 Scott (2013: 142–43).
226 Weiner (2012: 185–96, 377–91); Stone (2004: 384); Walker (2012: chaps. 5–6); Schrecker (1998).
227 Rowland, "Arthur Miller Casts His Spell," NYRB 58 (9.25.14), citing Norton (2002).

CHAPTER 2 ABU GHRAIB

1 Gall, "U.S. Military Investigating Death of Afghan in Custody," NYT (3.4.04).
2 Amman (2005); Benvenisti (2004); Strauss et al. (2004); Wypijewski (2006); Winkler (2009).
3 Serrano & Miller, "Documents Provide New Details of Abuse," LAT (5.23.04); Serrano, "Soldier 'Bewildered' Over Abuse," LAT (8.7.04); Zernike, "At Abuse Hearing, No Testimony That G.I.'s Acted on Orders," NYT (8.7.04); "Whistleblower Threatened," NYT (8.18.04); Darby, "Prisoner of Conscience," GQ (9.06); Benjamin, "Sympathy for Charles Graner," Salon.com (12.1.08); Gourevitch & Morris (2008: 232, 234, 243–45).
4 Hersh, "Chain of Command," *The New Yorker* 38 (5.17.04); Gourevitch & Morris (2008: 247–48).
5 Karpinski & Strasser (2005: 19–20, 23).
6 Quoted in Remnick, "Introduction," in Hersh (2004: xviii); see Risen, "Command Errors Aided Iraq Abuse, Army Has Found," NYT A1 (5.2.04); Karpinski & Strasser (2005: 220).
7 Hersh, "Torture at Abu Ghraib," *The New Yorker* 42 (5.10.04); Hersh, "Chain of Command," *The New Yorker* 38 (5.17.04); Hersh, "The Gray Zone," *The New Yorker* 38 (5.24.04).
8 Maj. Gen. Antonio Taguba, Article 15–6 Investigation of the 800th Military Police Brigade, in Greenberg & Dratel (2005: 405–50).
9 Risen, "Command Errors Aided Iraq Abuse, Army Has Found," NYT (5.2.04); Jehl & Schmitt, "The Struggle for Iraq," NYT (5.5.04).
10 On the involvement of Rumsfeld, see Cockburn (2007); Graham (2009).
11 Chan, "U.S. to Cut Iraq Prison Population," WP (5.5.04); McDonnell, "New Chief of Prisons Defends His Role in Iraq," LAT (5.9.04).
12 Chen, Hendren & Hook, "Bush Scolds Rumsfeld on Abuse Inquiry," LAT (5.6.04); Fassihi & Hitt, "On Arab TV, Bush Tries to Appease Anger Over Abuse," WSJ (5.6.04); Reynolds, "Bush Issues an Apology on Prisoners," LAT (5.7.04).
13 Report of the International Committee of the Red Cross (ICRC) on the Treatment by the Coalition Forces of Prisoners of War and Other Protected Persons by the Geneva Conventions in Iraq During Arrest, Internment and Interrogation (February 2004), in Greenberg & Dratel

(2005: 383); Cloud, Robbins & Jaffe, "Red Cross Found Widespread Abuse of Iraqi Prisoners," WSJ (5.7.04); Lewis & Lichtblau, "Red Cross Says That for Months It Complained of Iraq Prison Abuses to the U.S.," NYT (5.7.04); Drogin, "Red Cross Blew Whistle on Abuses," LAT (5.8.10); Cloud, "Red Cross Cited Detainee Abuse Over a Year Ago," WSJ (5.10.04); Cloud & Fassihi, "Red Cross Told Powell of Abuse of Iraqi Prisoners in January," WSJ (5.11.04).

14 Lewis, "Red Cross Found Abuses at Abu Ghraib Last Year," NYT (5.11.04); Jaffe & Cloud, "Officials in Iraq Knew Last Fall of Prison Abuse," WSJ (5.19.04); Jehl & Schmitt, "Officer Says Army Tried to Curb Red Cross Visits to Prison in Iraq," NYT (5.19.04); Schmitt, "Two U.S. Generals Outline a Lag in Notification on Reports of Abuse in Iraqi Prison," NYT (5.20.04); Jehl & Lewis, "U.S. Military Disputed Protected Status of Prisoners Held in Iraq," NYT (5.23.04); Warren, Sworn Statement to CID (6.18.04); Gourevitch & Morris (2008: 33–34).

15 "Iraq Prison Scandal: Excerpts from Rumsfeld's Remarks," LAT (5.8.04); "Testimony of Secretary of Defense Donald Rumsfeld before the Senate and House Armed Services Committees (5.7.04).

16 Graham (2009: 464).

17 Slater, "Iraq Prison Scandal: Press Release Made No Waves," LAT (5.8.04).

18 Miller, "Assessment of DoD Counterterrorism Interrogation and Detention Operations in Iraq"; Schmitt, "Pentagon Official Says Asking Army to Help Iraq Interrogators Did Not Lead to Prison Abuse," NYT (5.11.04); Schmitt, "Rumsfeld Aide and a General Clash on Abuse," NYT (5.12.10); Cockburn (2007: 193–94).

19 Graham (2009: 467).

20 Copeland, "Prison Revolt," WP (5.10.04); Higham, Stephens & White, "Prison Visits General Reported in Hearing," WP (5.23.04); Jehl & Schmitt, "General Says Sanchez Rejected Her Offer to Give Address to Iraqis About Abuses," NYT (5.24.04).

21 "The Abu Ghraib Spin," NYT (5.12.04).

22 Robbins, Jaffe & Cloud, "Interrogation Rules Were Issued Before Iraq Abuses," WSJ (5.13.04).

23 Shanker, "At Iraqi Prison, Rumsfeld Vows to Punish Abuse," NYT (5.14.04).

24 Spinner, "Hundreds Freed at Abu Ghraib," WP (5.22.04); Spinner, "Abu Ghraib Prisoners Freed During Sit-In," WP (5.25.04); Hauser, "To Frenzied Scenes, Abu Ghraib Frees 624 Prisoners," NYT (5.29.04); Spinner & Sebti, "U.S. Frees Hundreds from Abu Ghraib," WP (5.29.04); Glanz, "U.S. Releases More Prisoners: Bombings Kill at Least 21 Iraqis," NYT (6.7.04); Spinner, "For Freed Iraqis, Mixed Emotions," WP (6.15.04).

25 Johnson & Golden, "Rumsfeld and Aide Backed Harsh Tactics," NYT (5.16.04); Hamburger, "Wider Abuse Inquiry Sought," LAT (5.17.04); Richter, "U.S. Issues Report on Human Rights," LAT (5.18.14); "Transcript: Senate Hearing on Iraq Prison Abuse," WP (5.19.04); Tierney, "Hot Seat Grows Lukewarm Under Capital's Fog of War," NYT (5.20.04); Schmitt, "Two U.S. Generals Outline a Lag in Notification on Reports of

Abuse in Iraqi Prison," NYT (5.20.04); Schrader, "General Blames Poor Guidance for Prison Abuse," LAT (5.20.04); Higham, Stephens & White, "Prison Visits General Reported in Hearing," WP (5.23.04); Miller, Sworn Statement to CID (June 2004); Remnick in Hersh (2004: xix); Mahler, "After the Imperial Presidency," NYT (11.9.08).

26 LtCol. Phifer to Commander, Joint Task Force 170, "Request for Approval of Counter-Resistance Strategies" (10.11.02) in Greenberg & Dratel (2005: 227–28); Haynes to Rumsfeld, "Counter-Resistance Techniques" (11.27.02), Memo 21 in Greenberg & Dratel (2005: 237); Rumsfeld to Commander USSOUTHCOM, "Counter-Resistance Techniques" (1.15.03), Memo 23 in Greenberg & Dratel (2005: 239); Working Group Report on Detainee Interrogations in the Global War on Terrorism (4.4.03), Memo 26 in Greenberg & Dratel (2005: 286, 341–43); Rumsfeld to Commander USSOUTHCOM, "Counter-Resistance Techniques in the War on Terrorism" (4.16.03), Memo 27 in Greenberg & Dratel (2005: 360).

27 Gourevitch & Morris (2008: 51–53); Sanchez, "CJTF-7 Interrogation and Counter-Resistance Policy" (10.12.03), in Greenberg & Dratel (2005: 460).

28 Graham & Babington, "2 GOP Chairmen at Odds over Hill Abuse Hearings," WP (5.19.04); "An Abu Ghraib Investigation," NYT (5.22.04).

29 Lewis, "Justice Memos Explained How to Skip Prisoner Rights," NYT (5.21.04); Jehl & Schmitt, "Dogs and Other Harsh Tactics Linked to Military Intelligence," NYT (5.22.04); Cloud & Jaffe, "General Advised on Use of Dogs in Iraq Prison, Army Report Says," WSJ (5.26.04); Pappas to Sanchez, "Request for Exception to CJTF-7 Interrogation and Counter Resistance Policy" (11.30.03), in Greenberg & Dratel (2005: 466).

30 Milbank, "Bush Seeks to Reassure Nation on Iraq," WP (5.25.04); Hendren & Serrano, "Pentagon Intends to Replace Ground Commander in Iraq," LAT (5.25.04); McDonnell, "Sanchez Takes His Leave as Commander of Coalition Troops," LAT (7.2.04).

31 Fassihi & Stecklow, "Behind Bars: Finding U.S. Abuse in Iraq Left Red Cross Team in a Quandary," WSJ (5.21.04); Serrano, "Nov. 6 Red Cross Report to Military Detailed Abuse," LAT (5.29.04); Zernike & Rohde, "Forced Nudity of Iraqi Prisoners Is Seen as a Pervasive Pattern, Not Isolated Incidents," NYT (6.8.04).

32 Jehl & Schmitt, "C.I.A. Bid to Keep Some Detainees Off Abu Ghraib Roll Worries Officials," NYT (5.25.04); Jehl & Elliott, "Cuba Base Sent Its Interrogators to Iraqi Prison," NYT (5.29.04).

33 Jehl & Zernike, "Scant Evidence Cited in Long Detention of Iraqis," NYT (5.30.04); Serrano, "General Detailed Conditions at Prison," LAT (6.3.04).

34 Serrano & McDonnell, "Witness Faults Actions of Prison Interrogators," LAT (5.13.04); Higham & Stephens, "New Details of Prison Abuse Emerge," WP (5.21.10); Testimony of Capt. Carolyn Wood (5.21.04); Serrano & Miller, "Documents Provide New Details of Abuse," LAT (5.23.04); Higham, Stephens & White, "Prison Visits General Reported

in Hearing," WP (5.23.04); Zernike & Rhode, "Forced Nudity of Iraqi Prisoners Is Seen as a Pervasive Pattern, Not Isolated Incidents," NYT (6.8.04); Sanders, "Judge Orders Army Leaders Questioned," LAT (6.22.04); Wong, "Top Commanders Face Questioning on Prison Abuse," NYT (6.22.04); Serrano & Schmitt, "Files Show Bush Team Torn Over POW Rules," LAT (6.23.04); "US Military Judge Threatens to Suspend Iraq Prison Abuse Hearing," AFP (8.23.04); "Prison Abuse Figure Blames 'Secret Services,'" LAT (8.30.04); Wong, "Trial Date Set for Another Reservist in Prison Abuse Case," NYT (10.22.04); Oppell, "Judge Rejects Bid for Testimony from Top Officers in Abuse Trial," NYT (10.23.04); "Ex-Chief of Iraq Prisons Must Testify," LAT (12.5.04); Gourevitch & Morris (2008: 38–39).

35 Myers, "Why Military Justice Can Seem Unjust," NYT (6.6.04); Serrano, "Soldier Tells of Prison Abuse," LAT (8.31.04); "Ex-Soldier Testifies in Abuse Hearing," NYT (8.31.04).

36 Fleishman, "Abu Ghraib Informer Feared a Cover-Up," LAT (6.15.04).

37 Schmitt & Elliott, "Abu Ghraib Inquiry Is Said to Focus on Head of Its Interrogation Center," NYT (6.4.04); Schmitt, "Officer in Charge of Questioning Iraqi Inmates Had No Interrogation Training," NYT (6.9.04); Serrano, "Interrogation Center Chief Created 'Chaotic Situation,'" LAT (8.27.04); Jehl, "Inmates Were Reportedly Kept Off Books to Speed Transfer," NYT (10.9.04).

38 Simon, "House Democrats Begin Iraq Abuse Inquiry," LAT (6.4.04); Myers & Schmitt, "Wide Gaps Seen in U.S. Inquiries on Prison Abuse," NYT (6.6.04).

39 Miller, "Abu Ghraib Intelligence Soldier Describes Iraq Abuse in Detail," LAT (6.4.04).

40 Working Group on Detainee Interrogations in the Global War on Terrorism, Assessment of Legal, Historical, Policy, and Operational Considerations (3.6.03); Lewis & Schmitt, "Lawyers Decided Bans on Torture Didn't Bind Bush," NYT (6.8.04); Lewis, "Ashcroft Says the White House Never Authorized Tactics Breaking Laws on Torture," NYT (6.9.04).

41 "Twisting American Values," LAT (6.9.04); "The Roots of Abu Ghraib," NYT (6.9.04); Tepperman, "An American in The Hague?" NYT (6.10.04); Gregg, "Fight Fire with Compassion," NYT (6.10.04); "All's Fair," NYT (6.20.04); Ignatieff, "Mirage in the Desert," NYT (6.27.04).

42 Hendren & Mazzetti, "Pentagon to Broaden Its Abuse Inquiry," LAT (6.11.04); Smith & White, "General Granted Latitude at Prison," WP (6.12.04); SASC, Inquiry into the Treatment of Detainees in U.S. Custody 2003–04 (Report No. 06-INTEL-10) (11.20.08); Constitution Project (2013: 105).

43 Elliott, "Unit Says It Gave Earlier Warning of Abuse in Iraq," NYT (6.14.04); Elliott, "Documents Are Said to Show Earlier Abuse at Iraq Prison," NYT (6.19.04).

44 Finnegan, "Kerry Raises Iraq Abuse Questions," LAT (6.16.04); Elliott, "Documents Are Said to Show Earlier Abuse at Iraq Prison," NYT (6.19.04); H.R. 700; H. Con. Res. 472.

45 Stevenson, "White House Says Prisoner Policy Set Humane Tone," NYT (6.23.04); Serrano & Schmitt, "Files Show Bush Team Torn over POW Rules," LAT (6.23.04); Chen, "Harsher Methods Fruitful, U.S. Says," LAT (6.23.04); Johnston & Risen," Aides Say Memo Backed Coercion Already in Use," NYT (6.27.04); Zernike, "Defining Torture: Russian Roulette, Yes. Mind Altering Drugs, Maybe," NYT (6.27.04); "The White House Papers," NYT (6.24.04).
46 Serrano, "Prison Commander Testifies in Scandal," LAT (6.25.04); Filkins, "Testimony Ties Key Officer to Concealing of Iraqi Death," NYT (6.25.04); Spinner, "More GIs at Prison May Face Charges," WP (6.26.04).
47 Simon, "S.C. Republican Digging for Iraq Abuse Answers," LAT (6.29.04).
48 "Abu Ghraib, Stonewalled," NYT (6.30.04).
49 Elliott, "Capture of Hussein Aides Spurred U.S. Interrogators," NYT (7.3.04); Gourevitch & Morris (2008: 211).
50 Waxman, "Free Pass from Congress," WP (7.6.04); "Unanswered Questions," WP (7.11.04).
51 White & Smith, "House Panel Reviews Iraq Prison Reports," WP (7.15.04).
52 Serrano, "Officials Accuse Each Other in Prison Scandal," LAT (7.15.04).
53 Gourevitch & Morris (2008: 165–69).
54 Mikolashek, "Department of the Army Inspector General Inspection Report on Detainee Operations" (7.21.03), in Greenberg & Dratel (2005: 629–907); Schmitt, "Army Report Says Flaws in Detention Did Not Cause Abuses at Abu Ghraib," NYT (7.23.04); White & Higham, "Army Calls Abuses 'Aberrations,'" WP (7.23.04); Ackerman, "Prisoner Interrogations Too Harsh, A Report Says," MH (7.23.04); "Abu Ghraib, Whitewashed," NYT (7.24.04); Sevastopoulo, "Military Finds 94 Abuse Cases in Iraq and Afghanistan," FT (7.26.04).
55 White, "Ex-Guard to Face More Charges," WP (7.9.04); Martz, "Army to Present Evidence on Iraq Abuse," *Atlanta Journal-Constitution* (8.3.04); White, "U.S. Soldiers Abused Prisoners 'Just for Fun,' Prosecutors Say," MH (8.4.04); Breed, "Prosecutors Say Abuse Was 'For Fun,'" *Charlotte Observer* (8.4.04); Gibson, "Army Portrays England as Rogue Soldier," BS (8.4.04); Zernike, "The Woman With Leash Appears in Court on Abu Ghraib Abuse Charges," NYT (8.4.04); Serrano, "Abused Iraqi Detainees Said to Hold No Intelligence Value," LAT (8.4.04); Fuoco, "Pfc. England a Bad Soldier, Iraq Abuse Hearing Told," *Pittsburgh Post-Gazette* (8.5.04); Ackerman, "Prosecutor Strengthens Case Against Soldier in Iraq Abuse," *Charlotte Observer* (8.5.04); Breed, "Iraq Abuse Went Unreported," *Chicago Sun-Times* (8.6.04); Ackerman, "Elusive Captain Describes Jail Tactics," MH (8.6.04); "Soldier's Account Disputed," Newsday (8.7.04); Ackerman, "New Evidence Shown in Iraq Abuse Hearing," *Bradenton Herald* (8.7.04); Serrano, "Efforts to Halt Prison Abuse Told," LAT (8.5.04); Zucchino & Miller, "Officer Was at Crossroads of Abu Ghraib Command," LAT (8.1.04); "Iraq Prisoner Abuse Case May End Generals' Careers," *Akron Beacon Journal* (8.31.04); White, "Colonel Urges Court-Martial for England," WP (9.16.04).

56 Hedges, "Army Reserve General Says Iraq Prison Abuse Probe Will Let Top Brass Off Hook," CT (8.20.04).

57 Williams, "Soldier to Plead Guilty to Prison Abuse Charges," *Milwaukee Journal Sentinel* (8.24.04); Richissin & Gibson, "Memo Purportedly Foresaw Iraq Abuses," BS (8.24.04); "US Soldier to Plead Guilty on Some Iraq Prison Abuse Charges," AFP (8.24.04).

58 Richissin & Gibson, "Memo Purportedly Foresaw Iraq Abuses," BS (8.24.04); "Third US Soldier Faces Judge over Iraq Prison Abuses," AFP (8.24.04).

59 Independent Panel to Review Department of Defense Detention Operations, "Final Report," in Greenberg & Dratel (2005: 908–75); Schmitt, "Defense Leaders Faulted by Panel in Prison Abuse," NYT (8.24.04); Serrano & Mazzetti, "Prison Abuse Panel Faults Leaders," LAT (8.25.04); Schmitt, "Abuse Panel Says Rules on Inmates Need Overhaul," NYT (8.25.04); "Findings on Abu Ghraib Prison: Sadism, 'Deviant Behavior' and a Failure of Leadership," NYT (8.25.04); Jehl, "A Trail of 'Major Failures' Leads to Defense Secretary's Office," NYT (8.25.04); "Talk of the Nation," NPR (8.26.04).

60 Ackerman & Strobel, "Pentagon Officials Share Blame over Abuses," MH (8.25.04); Burns, "Iraq Abuse Report Faults Pentagon Leadership," *The Columbian* (8.25.04).

61 LtGen. Anthony R. Jones & MGen. George R. Fay, "Investigation of Intelligence Activities at Abu Ghraib," in Greenberg & Dratel (2005: 987–1131); Gertz, "27 Tied to Iraq Prisoner Abuses," *Washington Times* (8.26.04); Graham, "The Scope of a Scandal Gets Wider," WSJ (8.27.04); Jaffe, "Army Blames Confusion for Iraq Abuse," WSJ (8.27.04); Schmitt, "Abuses at Prison Tied to Officers in Intelligence," NYT (8.26.04); "Latest Report on Abu Ghraib: Abuses of Iraqi Prisoners 'Are, Without Question, Criminal,'" NYT (8.26.04); Elliott, "Perilous Conditions Led Up to Abuses at Baghdad Prison," NYT (8.26.04); Jehl, "Some Abu Ghraib Abuses Are Traced to Afghanistan," NYT (8.26.04); Serrano, "Pentagon Cites Widespread Involvement in Prison Abuses," LAT (8.26.04); Miller, "CIA Spurned Prison Rules, Report Says," LAT (8.26.04); Mazzetti, "Prison Abuse Reports May Insulate Bush from Blame," LAT (8.26.04); "Holding the Pentagon Accountable: For Abu Ghraib," NYT (8.26.04); "Abu Ghraib, the Next Step," NYT (8.27.04); "Path of Arrogance in Iraq," LAT (8.27.04).

62 Obtained by the ACLU and posted: www.truthout.org/docs_2005/printer_040405F.shtml (last accessed June 1, 2005); Smith, "Army Memos Reveal Beginnings of Prison Abuse," MH (8.30.04) (from WP).

63 Liptak, "Report Is Likely to Prompt Criminal Charges," NYT (8.27.04); Schmitt, "Rumsfeld Denies Abuses Occurred at Interrogations," NYT (8.28.07).

64 Mazzetti, "Reforms in Place at Abu Ghraib," LAT (9.4.04); Filkins, "General Says Less Coercion of Captives Yields Better Data," NYT (9.7.04); Onishi, "Transforming a Prison with U.S. Image in Mind," NYT

(9.16.04); Krane, "Army General Says Iraq Abuse Report Set Her Up," *Lexington Herald-Leader* (9.5.04).

65 Schwartz, "Independent Panel on Abu Ghraib Is Urged," LAT (9.9.04); Schmitt & Jehl, "Army Says C.I.A. Hid More Iraqis Than It Claimed," NYT (9.10.04); Hendren, "CIA May Have Held 100 'Ghost' Prisoners," LAT (9.10.04); Jehl, "C.I.A. Cites Order on Supervised Interrogations," NYT (9.11.04); "No Accountability on Abu Ghraib," NYT (9.10.04).

66 McDonnell, "Military Intelligence Soldier Sentenced in Abu Ghraib Case," LAT (9.12.04); Onishi, "Military Specialist Pleads Guilty to Abuse and Is Jailed," NYT (9.12.04).

67 "Remember Abu Ghraib?" WP (10.15.04); Garamone, "Detainee Panel Tells Senate Not to Overlook Forest," DoD News (9.9.04).

68 Bernstein, "Reservist to Plead Guilty to Some Charges in Mistreatment of Iraqi Prisoners," NYT (8.24.04); Morin, "GI Pleads Guilty to Iraq Jail Charges," LAT (10.21.04); Oppel, "Sergeant in Abu Ghraib Case Pleads Guilty to 8 Counts," NYT (10.21.04); Spinner, "MP Pleads Guilty to Abuse at Iraq Prison," WP (10.21.04); Allam, "U.S. GI Pleads Guilty to Jail Abuse," MH (10.21.04); Wong, "Trial Date Set for Another Reservist in Prison Abuse Case," NYT (10.22.04); Morin, "GI Gets 8-Year Sentence after Guilty Plea in Abuse Scandal," LAT (10.22.04).

69 White, "Abu Ghraib Guards Kept a Log of Prison Conditions, Practices," WP (10.25.04).

70 "Abu Ghraib Soldier Arraigned," LAT (8.14.04); "3 Charges Dismissed in Case of Iraq Prison Abuse Suspect," LAT (8.26.04); Jehl, "G.I. in Abu Ghraib Abuse Is Spared Time in Jail," NYT (11.3.04); Serrano, "4th Soldier Guilty in Prison Scandal," LAT (11.3.04); "GI Pleads Guilty to Dereliction of Duty," CT (11.3.04); White, "Prison Abuse Witness Demoted," WP (11.3.04); Gourevitch & Morris (2008: 142).

71 "G.I. Accused of Prison Abuse in Iraq Faces Military Trial," NYT (1.10.05); Zernike, "Central Figure in Iraq Abuse Goes on Trial," NYT (1.11.05); Serrano, "Guard Enjoyed Beating Iraqis, Three Testify," LAT (1.11.05); Reid, "Case Against Soldier Is Presented," WP (1.12.05); Serrano, "Guard Was 'Primary Torturer,' Prisoner Says," LAT (1.12.05); Zernike, "Detainees Describe Abuses by Guard in Iraq Prison," NYT (1.12.05); Rich, "On Television, Torture Takes a Holiday," NYT (1.12.05); Karpinski & Strasser (2005: 233); Benjamin, "Sympathy for Charles Graner," Salon.com (12.1.08); Gourevitch & Morris (2008: 157).

72 Zernike, "Reservist to Offer Guilty Plea in Jail Assault," NYT (1.28.05); "Former Guard Pleads Guilty in Abuse Case," NYT (2.2.05); "Abu Ghraib Called Filthy and Volatile at Army Hearing," LAT (2.3.05); "Abu Ghraib Prison Guard Seeks Leniency in Sentencing," LAT (2.4.05); "6 Months in Prison for Abu Ghraib Guard," LAT (2.5.05).

73 Mazzetti, "Lack of Oversight Led to Abuse of Detainees, Investigator Says," LAT (3.9.05); Schmitt, "New Interrogation Rules Set for Detainees in Iraq," NYT (3.10.05); "Abu Ghraib, Whitewashed Again," NYT (3.11.05); Schmitt, "Official Declines to Pin Blame for Blunders in

Interrogations," NYT (3.11.08); Miller & Hendron, "No Need for CIA Abuse Probe, Republican Says," LAT (3.11.08).

74 Schmitt, "Former Intelligence Officer Clear in Iraq Abuse," NYT A7 (3.12.05); "Harsh Tactics Were Allowed, General Told Jailers in Iraq," NYT A8 (3.30.05); ACLU, "Army Memo Released by ACLU Suggests Perjury in Lt. Gen. Sanchez Sworn Testimony on Torture" (3.31.05) at www.aclu.org/SafeandFree/SafeandFree.cfm?ID=17688&c=206 (last accessed February 16, 2018); Schmitt, "Four Top Officers Cleared by Army in Prison Abuses," NYT (4.23.05); White, "Top Army Officers Are Cleared in Abuse Cases," WP (4.23.05).

75 Zernike, "Plea Deal Is Set for G.I. Pictured in Abuses in Iraq," NYT (4.30.05); "Reservist Pleads Guilty in Prison Abuse, Cites Peer Pressure," LAT (5.3.05); Cornwell, "Lynndie England's Abu Ghraib Plea Bargain Thrown Out," I (5.5.05); Blumenthal, "Judge Tosses Out Abuse Plea after the Ringleader Testifies," NYT (5.5.50); Hart & Serrano, "Abu Ghraib Guilty Plea Is Dismissed," LAT (5.5.05); Blumenthal, "Private Will Face New Charges over Abuse of Prisoners in Iraq," NYT (5.6.05); Zernike, "Behind Failed Abu Ghraib Plea, a Tale of Breakups and Betrayal," NYT (5.10.05); "Soldier Gets Closer to Abuse Retrial," NYT (5.25.05); "England Gives up Right to Hearing," LAT (5.25.05); "Soldier's Statements Excluded from Retrial," NYT (7.9.05).

76 Serrano & Mazzetti, "General Demoted over Prison Scandal," LAT (5.6.05); "General Who Ran Prison Is Demoted," NYT (5.6.05); Schmitt, "Army Moves to Advance 2 Linked to Abu Ghraib," NYT (6.29.05); Dillon, "War on Terror Dominates Talks Given at Graduations," NYT (6.12.05); Schmitt, "No Criminal Charges for Officer at Abu Ghraib Interrogations," NYT (5.12.05); Serrano, "Abu Ghraib Intelligence Chief Is Reprimanded," LAT (5.12.05); Karpinski & Strasser (2005: 143–44); Sanchez & Phillips (2008).

77 "Rebuilding in the Gulf: Did Rumsfeld Order Abu Ghraib Rough Stuff?" WorldNetDaily.com (8.3.05); Cohn, "Janis Karpinski: Exclusive Interview," Truthout.org (8.24.05); *Democracy Now!* (10.26.05); Karpinski & Strasser (2005: 197–98, 203).

78 Bajaj, "Court-Martial Opens in an Iraqi Abuse Case," NYT (5.13.05); "Abu Ghraib Defendant Says Photo Was a Shared Joke," LAT (5.13.05); "Witness Clears Abu Ghraib Guard of Some Abuse," NYT (5.14.05); "Another Abu Ghraib Guard Is Found Guilty," LAT (5.17.05); "Reservist Gets Six-Month Sentence for Abusing Iraqis at Abu Ghraib," NYT (5.18.05); "Soldier in Abu Ghraib Photos Is Sentenced," LAT (5.18.05); Gourevitch & Morris (2008: 74–75, 110).

79 Serrano, "Two Army Dog Handlers Charged in Abuse Scandal," LAT (6.3.05); "2 Sergeants Charged in Iraq Prison Abuse," NYT (6.3.05); White, "Abu Ghraib Dog Tactics Came from Guantanamo," WP (7.27.05); White, "Army General Advised Using Dogs at Abu Ghraib, Officer Testifies," WP (7.28.05); Cho, "Allegations against Dog Handlers Are Described," LAT (7.27.05); Cho, "Dogs Called General's Proposal,"

LAT (7.28.05); "Ex-Warden Tells of Use of Dogs," NYT (7.28.05); "The Truth about Abu Ghraib," WP (7.29.05).

80 "Soldier 'Instructed' to Abuse Abu Ghraib Prisoners," ABCOnLine (8.21.05).

81 Cloud, "G.I.'s Role in Detainee Abuse Is Starkly Contrasted at Retrial," NYT (9.22.05); "Testimony on Abu Ghraib," NYT (9.24.05); Gerstenzang & Serrano, "Female Reservist Guilty of Abu Ghraib Abuse," LAT (9.27.05); Cloud, "Private Found Guilty in Abu Ghraib Abuse," NYT (9.27.05); White, "Reservist Sentenced to 3 Years for Abu Ghraib Abuse," WP (9.28.05); "Convicted US Soldier Says 'Worse Things' Have Happened at Abu Ghraib," AFP (10.3.05); Beavers, "England Back in Mineral County," *Cumberland Times-News* (3.2.07); Nestle, "Abu Ghraib's Grasp," *The Daily* (3.19.12).

82 Goodman, "Col. Janis Karpinski, the Former Head of Abu Ghraib, Admits She Broke the Geneva Conventions but Says the Blame 'Goes All the Way to The Top,'" *Democracy Now!* (10.26.05).

83 The US Military produced a deck of cards showing details of the most wanted members of Saddam Hussein's regime to aid their identification by troops.

84 White, "General Asserts Right Not to Incriminate Himself in Abuse Case," WP (1.12.06); "A General's Dishonor," WP (1.15.06); Serrano & Mazzetti, "Charges Sought against Officer at Abu Ghraib," LAT (1.13.06).

85 White, "Former Abu Ghraib Guard Calls Top Brass Culpable for Abuse," WP (1.23.06).

86 "U.S. Senators to Probe General's Abu Ghraib Testimony," NYT (2.7.06); Benjamin, "Not So Fast, General," Salon.com (3.7.06).

87 "SBS Broadcasts Graphic Abu Ghraib Images," *Sydney Morning Herald* (2.15.06); White, "Australia Airs Images of Prison Abuse in Iraq," WP (2.16.06); Stout, "More Abu Ghraib Pictures Broadcast on Australian TV," NYT (2.16.06); Benjamin, "The Abu Ghraib Files," Salon.com (2.16.06); Walsh, "The Abu Ghraib Files," Salon.com (3.14.06).

88 Walker, "ACLU Challenges Latest U.S. Move to Block Release of Detainee Abuse Photos," *Newsweek* (1.10.15).

89 White, "Detainee in Photo with Dog Was 'High-Value' Suspect," WP (3.13.06); "Abu Ghraib Guard Says He Followed Orders," LAT (3.14.06); Timiraos, "Army Officer OKd Dogs in Interrogations," LAT (3.16.06); White, "Officer Says He Wrongly Approved Use of Dogs," WP (3.16.06); White, "Dog Handler Found Guilty of Abu Ghraib Abuse," WP (3.22.06); Timiraos, "Army Dog Handler Guilty of Prisoner Abuse in Iraq," LAT (3.22.06); Schmitt, "Iraq Abuse Trial Is Again Limited to Lower Ranks," NYT (3.23.06); "Abu Ghraib Dog Handler Sentenced," LAT (3.23.06); Benjamin & Sherer, "'Big Steve' and Abu Ghraib," Salon.com (3.31.06); "The Joy of Being Blameless," NYT (3.23.06).

90 Benjamin, "No Justice for All," Salon.com (4.14.06).

91 Schmitt, "Judge Orders a Top Officer to Attend Abuse Trial," NYT (4.19.06); White, "Top Officer Ordered to Testify on Abuse," WP (4.19.06); Smith & White," Abuse Trial Revives Old Questions," WP

(5.22.06); Shamsi, HRF blog (5.23.06; 5.25.06; 5.26.06; 6.2.06); Lewis, "Court in Prisoner Abuse Case Hears Testimony," NYT (5.25.06); "Military Jury Weighs Dog Handler's Fate," NYT (5.31.06); "Dog Handler Convicted in Abu Ghraib Abuse," NYT (6.2.06); "Abu Ghraib Dog Handler Sentenced," LAT (6.3.06).

92 Sworn statement, probably by Capt. Carolyn Wood (5.21.04); Arnesen, "Lieutenant Colonel Faces Hearing in Abu Ghraib Case," CNN.com (10.16.06); Wood, "Colonel's Role at Abu Ghraib Is Scrutinized," BS (10.17.06); Dishneau, "Command Roles at Abu Ghraib Questioned," BS (10.17.06); Pelton, "Abu Ghraib Commander Told Superiors He Lacked Training," BS (10.18.06); Dishneau, "Ex-Commander Talks at Abu Ghraib Hearing," BS (10.18.06); Dishneau, "Abu Ghraib Interrogator Testifies at Hearing," BS (10.18.06); Pelton, "Strife at Prison Is Shown," BS (10.19.06); Marbella, "Abu Ghraib Grew from Wretched Conditions," BS (10.20.06); Anderson, "Abu Ghraib Command Structure Detailed," BS (10.20.06); Dishneau, "Officer Awaits Fate in Abu Ghraib Case," BS (10.20.06); Kiehl, "No Tie to Abuse, Defense Argues," BS (10.21.06); "Officer to Face Court-Martial on 8 Charges in Abu Ghraib Abuse," NYT (1.27.07); White, "Conflicting Portraits of Officer Charged over Abu Ghraib," WP (7.31.07).

93 "2 Abu Ghraib Charges Dropped," NYT (8.21.07); White, "Abu Ghraib Officer Cleared of Detainee Abuse," WP (8.28.07); White, "Reprimand Is Sentence for Officer at Abu Ghraib," WP (8.30.07); White, "Army Officer Is Cleared in Abu Ghraib Scandal," WP (1.10.08).

94 "Penalty for Prison Abuse Is Upheld," NYT (7.17.08); "Military High Court Upholds Abu Ghraib Convictions," LAT (2.5.10).

95 Sentilles (2008); see generally Mitchell (2011).

96 Philip Zimbardo strongly contested this when testifying for Frederick in the penalty phase. Zimbardo (2008: chaps. 14–15).

97 Rumsfeld (2011).

98 Danner (2004: 5, 20), quoting from Serrano, "Three Witnesses in Abuse Case Aren't Talking: Higher-Ups and a Contractor Out to Avoid Self-Incrimination," *San Francisco Chronicle* (5.19.04) and Report of the ICRC on the Treatment by the Coalition Forces of Prisoners of War and Other Protected Persons by the Geneva Conventions in Iraq during Arrest, Internment and Interrogation (February 2004).

CHAPTER 3 GUANTÁNAMO BAY

1 For accounts by and about detainees, translators, MI, and imams, see Rose (2004); Saar & Novak (2005); Yee (2005); Meeropol (2005); Worthington (2007); Begg & Brittain (2006); Kurnaz & Kuhn (2008); Khan (2008); Fletcher & Stover (2009); Margulies (2009); Hicks (2010); Slahi (2015); Boumediene & Idir (2017). For accounts by lawyers, see Denbeaux & Hafetz (2009); Hafetz (2016). See generally

Murphy et al., "Guantánamo: An Oral History," *Vanity Fair* (1.11.12). For legal critiques, see Amann (2004); Denbeaux & Denbeaux (2006c); Johns (2013); Greenberg (2010); Goldsmith (2012); ABCNY, Committee on Federal Courts (2004). For historical comparisons, see Springer (2010); Burrows (2010).

2 Granger (2010).

3 Philbin to Haynes, "Possible Habeas Jurisdiction over Aliens Held in Guantánamo Bay, Cuba" (12.28.01), Memo 3 in Greenberg & Dratel (2005: 29).

4 542 U.S. 466 (2004).

5 Hendren, "Detainees May be Moved Off Cuba Base," LAT (6.30.04); Marquis, "Pentagon Will Permit Captives at Cuba Base to Appeal Status," NYT (7.8.04); Hendren & Mazzetti, "Pentagon Reportedly Aimed to Hold Detainees in Secret," LAT (7.9.04); Gearan, "Prisoner Gets First Chance to Tell Story," *The State* (Columbia, SC) (7.31.04).

6 "4 Detainees Refuse U.S. Review Hearings," *Belleville News-Democrat* (8.5.04); Jehl, "Pentagon Seeks to Transfer More Detainees from Base in Cuba," NYT (3.11.05); "U.S. Judge Bars Transfer of 13 Guantánamo Detainees," NYT (3.15.05); Johnston, "Judge Limits the Transfer of 13 from Guantánamo," NYT (3.30.05); "Guantánamo Detainee Wins Order against Transfer," LAT (4.15.05); Serrano, "Military Report on Guantánamo Highlights Danger of Al Qaeda," LAT (4.18.05); Gall, "17 Afghans Freed from Guantánamo Prison," NYT (4.20.05); "18 Released from Guantánamo," LAT (4.20.05). For critiques of the government's assessment, see Denbeaux & Denbeaux (2006b; 2006d); for defenses, see Felter & Brachman (2007a; 2007b).

7 Kaufman & Witt, "Returning Afghans Talk of Guantanamo," WP (3.26.03).

8 Frankel, "Three Allege Guantánamo Abuse," WP (8.5.04); Torriero, "Gitmo Prisoner Abuse Reported," *Orlando Sentinel* (8.5.04); Butler, "Britons Allege Abuse at Guantánamo," *Lexington Herald-Leader* (8.5.04); Dodd & Branigan, "US Abuse Could Be War Crime," G (8.4.04); "3 Ex-Guantánamo Detainees Allege Abuses in Documents," *Belleville News-Democrat* (8.5.04); Whittle, "Guantánamo Facility Is Humane," *Dallas Morning News* (8.8.04); Serrano, "Gitmo 'Lifetime,' Interrupted," LAT (4.14.05); Northam, "Leaving Guantánamo: Enduring a Harsh Stay," NPR (5.22.06); Warrick, "Detainees Allege Being Drugged, Questioned," WP (4.22.08); Al-Dossari, "I'm Home but Still Haunted by Guantánamo," WP (8.17.08); Denbeaux et al. (2010); Kaye & Leopold, "DoD Declassifies Report on Alleged Drugging of Detainees," Truthout (7.11.12).

9 Benjamin, "Did Chertoff Lie to Congress about Guantánamo," Salon.com (8.28.07); Lewis & Schmitt, "Inquiry Finds Abuses at Guantánamo Bay," NYT (5.1.05); Serrano, "Report Details Discipline for Guantánamo Abuses," LAT (5.7.05); Schmidt & Furlow (2005).

10 Barry, "Gitmo: Southcom Showdown," *Newsweek* (5.8.05); "Muslims See a Coverup for U.S.: White House Demands Full Retraction," MSNBC (5.16.05) www.msnbc.msn.com/id/7870840 (last accessed February 16,

2018); Seelye, "Newsweek Apologizes for Report of Koran Insult," NYT (5.16.05); "Muslims Skeptical over Newsweek Back-Track on Koran," NYT (5.16.5); Schmitt, "Newsweek Backtracks on Koran Report," LAT (5.16.05); Seelye & Lewis, "Newsweek Retracts Account of Koran Abuse by U.S. Military," NYT (5.17.05); McGrath, "Reporter on Retracted Newsweek Article Put Monica on the Map," NYT (5.17.05); Rainey & Mazzetti, "Newsweek Retracts Its Article on Koran," LAT (5.17.05); Bumiller, "White House Presses Newsweek in Wake of Koran Report," NYT (5.18.05); "Newsweek Apology 'Not Enough,'" LAT (5.18.05).

11 "A Sudden Taste for Openness," NYT (5.18.05); Serrano & Daniszewski, "Dozens Have Alleged Koran's Mishandling," LAT (5.22.05); Eggen & White, "Inmates Alleged Koran Abuse," WP (5.26.05); Lewis, "Documents Say Detainees Cited Abuse of Koran by Guards," NYT (5.26.05); White & Eggen, "Pentagon Confirms Koran Incidents," WP (5.27.05); Hendren, "Military Probe Finds Some Mishandling of Koran," LAT (5.27.05); Shanker, "Inquiry by U.S. Finds 5 Cases of Koran Harm," NYT (5.27.05); Friedman, "Just Shut It Down," NYT (5.27.05); Masood, "Reports of Mishandling Koran Bring Protest Worldwide," NYT (5.28.05); "Muslims Across World Protest Koran Reports," LAT (5.28.05); Serrano, "Pentagon: Koran Defiled," LAT (6.4.05); "Possible Detainee Abuse Documented," LAT (1.3.07); Eggen, "FBI Reports Duct-Taping, 'Baptizing' at Guantánamo," WP (1.3.07); Apuzzo, "FBI Details Detainee Abuse," G (1.3.07).

12 Norton-Taylor, "Guantánamo Is Gulag of Our Time, Amnesty Says," G (5.25.05); Cowell, "U.S. 'Thumbs Its Nose' at Rights, Amnesty Says," NYT (5.25.05); "President's Press Conference," May 31, 2005, at www.whitehouse.gov/news/releases/2005/05/20050531.html (last accessed June 1, 2005); Gerstenzang, "Bush Calls Criticism of Guantánamo Detainee Treatment Absurd," LAT (5.31.05); "USA: Response to President Bush," Press Release, 05/31/2005, at news.amnesty.org/mavp/news.nsf/print/ENGAMR510872005 (last accessed June 1, 2005); "Rumsfeld: Criticism of Gitmo Inaccurate," *USA Today* (6.2.05); Alvarez, "Rights Group Defends Chastising of U.S.," NYT (6.4.05); "Un-American by Any Name," NYT (6.5.05); "Biden Urges U.S. to Take Steps to Close Prison at Guantánamo," NYT (6.6.05); Neubauer, "Biden Says U.S. Should Shut Guantánamo Prison," LAT (6.6.05); "Carter Says U.S. Should Close Detention Center at Guantánamo," NYT (6.8.05); "Apology Demanded for Remark on U.S.," NYT (6.17.05); Stolberg, "Leading Democrat Apologizes for Prisoner Abuse Remark," NYT (6.22.05).

13 "Bush Opens Door to Possible Closing of Guantánamo," NYT (6.8.05); Shanker, "Rumsfeld Says Guantánamo Isn't Being Considered for Closing," NYT (6.9.05); "Rumsfeld Favors Repatriating Detainees," NYT (6.10.05); "Beyond Guantánamo," WP (6.12.05); "Cheney Argues for Keeping Guantánamo Open," NYT (6.13.05); McDonough, "Cheney Responds to Gitmo Critics," AP (6.13.05); "Senate GOP: Closing Gitmo Not the Answer," NYT (6.14.05).

14 Bumiller, "Cheney Calls Guantánamo Prison Essential," NYT (6.14.05); "Rumsfeld Says No Alternatives Exist for Gitmo Prison," NYT (6.15.05); "Guantánamo Inmates Can Be Held 'In Perpetuity,' – US," NYT (6.15.05); Press Briefing by Scott McLellan (6.15.05), at www.whitehouse.gov/news/releases/2005/06/20050615-3.html#c (last accessed July 1, 2005); "Who We Are," NYT (6.18.05); Bush Press Conference (6.19.05) at www.whitehouse.gov/news/releases/2005/06/20050620-19.html (last accessed July 1, 2005).
15 Zagorin & Duffy, "Inside the Interrogation of Detainee 063," *Time* (6.20.05); Lewis, "Guantánamo's Long Shadow," NYT (6.21.05).
16 Cloud, "Guantánamo Reprimand Was Sought, an Aide Says," NYT (7.13.05); Mazzetti, "General Rejects Call to Penalize Ex-Guantánamo Prison Chief," LAT (7.13.05); "Report Discredits F.B.I. Claims of Abuse at Guantánamo Bay," NYT (7.14.05); "Senators Hear of 'Degrading' Interrogations," LAT (7.14.05); "The Women of Gitmo," NYT (7.15.05); Allen, "Lawmaker Tours Become Part of Guantánamo Life," WP (8.6.05).
17 Jehl, "Some Republicans Seek Prison Abuse Panel," NYT (6.22.05); "Cheney: Iraq Will Be 'Enormous Success Story,'" CNN (6.24.05); Kirkpatrick, "Senators Laud Treatment of Detainees in Guantánamo," NYT (6.28.05); Daly, "Senators Seek Rules for Guantánamo Detainees," Napanews.com (6.28.05); Lewis, "Guantánamo a Thorny Issue for Democrats on Committee," NYT (6.30.05); Hendren, "Witnesses Support Guantánamo," LAT (6.30.05); Rauch, "Guantánamo's Problem Isn't In Cuba. It's In Washington," *National Journal* (7.8.05); Zerrougui et al., Situation of Detainees at Guantánamo Bay (UN Economic and Social Council E/CN.4/2006/120) (2.15.06); "Bush Speaks of Closing Guantánamo Prison," NYT (5.9.06); Rosenberg, "President's Guantánamo Comments Raise Policy Question," MH (5.8.06); Cody, "China Demands that Albania Return Ex-U.S. Detainees," WP (5.1006); "The Gitmo 'Decider,'" LAT (5.10.06); McWalters, "British Official Urges Guantánamo Closure," LAT (5.11.06); Cowell, "Briton Wants Guantánamo Closed," NYT (5.11.06); Rosenberg, "'I Received No Direction to Change Things,'" MH (5.28.06); Higgins, "U.N. Human Rights Experts Chastise U.S.," WP (7.17.06).
18 Allen, "House Democrats to Target Guantánamo Prison, Abu Ghraib in Iraq," Politico.com (1.23.07); Shanker & Sanger, "New to Pentagon, Gates Argued for Closing Guantánamo Prison," NYT (3.23.07); "The President's Prison," NYT (3.25.07); "Gates Signals Willingness to Close Prison," NYT (3.30.07); "The Cloud of Gitmo," LAT (4.2.07).
19 Barnes, "Feinstein Seeks to Close Guantánamo," LAT (5.1.07); Cornwell, "House Demands Plan for Guantánamo Detainees," WP (5.17.07); Pincus, "Powell Calls for Closure of Military Prison at Guantánamo," WP (6.11.07); Richter, "Powell Says It's Time to Close Guantánamo," LAT (6.11.07); "Restore America's Values," LAT (6.13.07).
20 Sherwell, "Straight-Talking McCain Vows to Fix World's View of the 'Ugly American,'" *Sunday Telegraph* (3.19.07); Schor, "Most Presidential

Hopefuls Give only Lip Service to Closing Guantánamo," *The Hill* (6.12.07); Levey, "Closing Guantánamo Lockup Looks Increasingly Unlikely," LAT (9.24.07); Freidman, "9/11 Is Over," NYT (9.30.07).

21 "Closing Guantánamo," WP (6.26.07); Davis, "The Guantánamo I Know," NYT (6.26.07); Letters to the Editor, NYT (6.27.07).

22 Lee, "White House Decision Near to Close Gitmo," AP (6.21.07); White & Wright, "Guantánamo Splits Administration," WP (6.22.07); Shanker & Johnson, "Legislation Could Be Path to Closing Guantánamo," NYT (7.4.07); Sevastopoulo, "Gates Admits Rift over Guantánamo," FT (10.2.07); Glaberson, "New Detainee Rights Weighed in Plans to Close Guantánamo," NYT (11.4.07); Bowker & Kaye, "Guantánamo by the Numbers," NYT (11.10.07).

23 Walck, "Guantánamo Chief Blasts Critics in Comments to Savannah Audience," *Savannah Morning News* (1.23.08); Buzby, "Guantánamo Is a Model Prison (Really)," WSJ (6.4.08); Williams, "New Incentive Dangled at Guantánamo," LAT (8.3.08).

24 Barnes, "Guantánamo Closure Not an Easy Prospect," LAT (4.14.08); Letter to the Editor, NYT (10.28.08); Letter to the Editor, NYT (11.9.08).

25 See Fletcher & Stover (2008).

26 Ambah, "Episode at Guantánamo Leaves Family at a Loss," WP (3.11.07).

27 Center for Constitutional Rights, The Guantánamo Prisoner Hunger Strikes & Protests: February 2002 – August 2005 (2005); Kazem, "Freed Afghans Decry Guantánamo Conditions," LAT (7.21.05); "Some Guantánamo Prisoners Have Gone on Hunger Strike," NYT (7.22.05); Savage, "Lawyers Cite Guantánamo Concessions," BG (8.13.05); Savage, "89 Prisoners Resume Hunger Strike at Guantánamo," BG (8.26.05); Leonnig, "More Join Guantánamo Hunger Strike," WP (9.13.05); Jacobs, "Hunger Strike Spreads at Guantánamo Bay," WP (9.15.05); "National Briefing," NYT (9.22.05); "Judge Is Urged to Deny More Access to Detainees on Hunger Strike," NYT (10.15.05); Lewis, "Striking Guantánamo Detainees Gain in Ruling," NYT (10.27.05); White, "Guantánamo Desperation Seen in Suicide Attempts," WP (11.1.05); Isikoff & Hosenball, "More Problems at Gitmo," *Newsweek* (11.16.05); White, "Detainee's Condition Upheld," WP (11.17.05); White, "Suicidal Guantánamo Inmate Moved Out of Isolation," WP (12.17.05); Bonner, "Terror Suspect's Ordeal in U.S. Custody," NYT (12.18.05).

28 "A Package of News Briefs from the Caribbean," MH (7.17.07).

29 "National Briefing," NYT (12.30.05); Golden, "Tough U.S. Steps in Hunger Strike at Camp in Cuba," NYT (2.9.06); Schmitt & Golden, "Force-Feeding at Guantánamo Is Now Acknowledged," NYT (2.22.06); Wilner, "American Gulag," LAT (2.26.06); White, "Guantánamo Force-Feeding Tactics Are Called Torture," WP (3.1.06); White & Leonnig, "U.S. Cites Exception in Torture Ban," WP (3.3.06); Lewis, "Guantánamo Detainee Seeks Court Action," NYT (3.3.06); "Forcefeeding and Restraint of Guantánamo Bay Hunger Strikers," 367 *The Lancet* 811 (3.11.06); *Al-Adahi* v. *Obama*, CA No. 05-280 (DDC 2.10.09).

30 Williams, "4 Guantánamo Prisoners Attempt Suicide in One Day," LAT (5.19.06); Golden, "U.S. Should Close Prison in Cuba, U.N. Panel Says," NYT (5.20.06); Williams, "U.N. Panel Wants Cuba Jail Closed," LAT (5.20.06); Carrell, "Breaking Point: Inside Story of the Guantánamo Uprising," I (5.21.06).
31 Sutton, "75 Prisoners Join in Hunger Strike at U.S. Base in Guantánamo Bay," WP (5.30.06); "75 Detainees Go on Hunger Strike," LAT (5.30.06); "Hunger Strike at Guantánamo Prison Grows to 89 Inmates," LAT (6.2.06); "New U.S. Rules Allow Gitmo Force-Feeding," NYT (6.6.06).
32 Risen & Golden, "Three Prisoners Commit Suicide at Guantánamo," NYT (6.11.06); Barnes & Williams, "Guantánamo's First Suicides Pressure U.S.," LAT (6.11.06); White, "Three Detainees Commit Suicide at Guantánamo," WP (6.11.06); "Guantánamo Suicides a 'PR Move,'" BBC News (6.11.06); Roche, "Suicides Fuel More Calls for Closure of Guantánamo," WP (6.12.06); Sutton, "Suicides Prompt New Calls to Shut Guantánamo," WP (6.12.06); "The Deaths at Gitmo," NYT (6.12.06); "U.S. Distances Itself from Gitmo Remarks," NYT (6.12.06); Cloud & Lewis, "Prisoners' Ruse Is Suspected at Guantánamo," NYT (6.12.06); Ignatius, "A Prison We Need to Escape," WP (6.14.06); Ambah, "Family of Guantánamo Detainee Doubts He Took His Own Life," WP (6.14.06); Cage, "Suicides Bring New Calls to Closes Gitmo," WP (6.13.06); Benchellali, "Detainees in Despair," NYT (6.14.06); Gordon, "Guards Tighten Security to Prevent More Deaths," *Charlotte Observer* (6.13.06); "Close Guantánamo," *Le Monde* (6.13.06) (in French); Dodd, "Military Launches Guantánamo Inquiry," *Charlotte Observer* (6.14.06); Dodd, "Observer Journalists Ordered to Leave Guantánamo Bay," *Charlotte Observer* (6.14.06); "Gitmo, Get Real!" *Charlotte Observer* (6.16.06); Rosenberg, "Guantánamo Detainees Unaware of Defense Lawyers," MH (6.16.06); Gordon, "Career Crisis Hovers over Guantánamo Commander," *Charlotte Observer* (6.18.06); Rainey, "Journalists Forced Off Guantánamo," LAT (6.15.06); Williams, "Kicked Out of Gitmo," LAT (6.18.06); Bosman, "Evictions Raise the Tension Level at Guantánamo," NYT (6.19.06); Denbeaux & Denbeaux (2006a; 2006e); White, "Guards' Lapses Cited in Detainee Suicides," WP (8.23.08); Denbeaux (2009); Hickman (2015).
33 Norah O'Donnell Interview, "Hardball with Chris Matthews," MSNBC (6.23.06).
34 Shane, "Seeking an Exit Strategy for Guantánamo," NYT (6.18.06); "Imprisoned in Chaos," WP (6.18.06); "The Detention Dilemma," WP (6.19.06); Stolberg, "Bush's Visit to Vienna Is Marked by Tension," NYT (6.21.06); "Close Guantánamo?" WP (6.22.06); Williams, "Guantánamo Officials Say They Can't Stop All Suicides," LAT (6.28.06); White, "Signs of Detainees' Planning Alleged," WP (7.8.06); Cave, "U.S. Says Inmate Legal Notes May Have Aided Suicide Plot," NYT (7.9.06); Schwartz, "Pentagon Suspects Lawyer Involvement in Deaths," *Legal Times* (7.17.06); CCR Press Release (8.29.06); Golden, "The Battle for Guantánamo," NYT (9.17.06); Williams, "At Guantánamo: Hard Time

and a View of What Could Have Been," LAT (10.7.06); "Gitmo Detainees Going to New Prison," MSNBC.com (12.8.06); Golden, "Military Taking a Tougher Line with Detainees," NYT (12.16.06); "Saudi Detainee at Guantánamo Commits Suicide," LAT (5.31.07); "Detainee Who Killed Himself Is Identified," LAT (6.1.07); Glaberson & Williams, "Pentagon Files Offer Details on Detainee in Suicide," NYT (6.1.07); Vitello, "Terrorism: Where's the Gruel?" NYT (12.22.07).

35 AI (2007); "Guantánamo Conditions 'Worsening,'" BBC News (4.5.07); Golden, "Guantánamo Detainees Stage Hunger Strike Despite Force-Feeding Policy," NYT (4.9.07); Williams, "Hunger Strike at Guantánamo," LAT (4.9.07); Williams, "Guantánamo Suicide Attempt Confirmed," LAT (12.5.07).

36 Wilber, "Judge Orders Exam for Detainee," WP (12.20.08).

37 Rosenberg, "Hunger Strikers Surge to 10 Percent at Guantánamo," MH (1.8.09).

38 Kaye, "Recently Released Autopsy Reports Heighten Guantánamo 'Suicides' Mystery," Truthout (3.1.12).

39 Savage, "Guantánamo Detainee, a Former Hunger Striker, Dies," NYT (9.11.12); Rosenberg, "Dead Guantánamo Detainee Won, Then Lost Court-Ordered Release," MH (9.11.12); Falkoff, "A Death at Gitmo," LAT (9.20.12); Rosenberg, "NCIS Still Investigating Yemeni Prisoner's Guantánamo Death," MH (12.18.12); Poitras, "Death of a Prisoner," NYT (1.10.13); Savage, "Suicide by Pills Is Cited in Death of Guantánamo Detainee," NYT (6.29.13); Finn & Tate, "Guantánamo Detainee Died from Drug Overdose, Report Finds," WP (6.29.13).

40 UN Commission on Human Rights, Draft Report: Situation of Detainees at Guantánamo Bay (2.15.06) (Future/E/CN.4/2006.120); Coughlin, "U.N. Inquiry Demands Immediate Closure of Guantánamo," DT (2.13.06); Farley, "Report: U.S. Is Abusing Captives," LAT (2.13.06); "The Guantánamo Disgrace," LAT (2.14.06); Hoge, "U.N. Report Calls for End to Guantánamo Detentions," NYT (2.16.06); Farley, "U.S. Rejects Guantánamo Report," LAT (2.17.06); Hoge, "Investigators for U.N. Urge U.S. to Close Guantánamo," NYT (2.17.06); Tavernise, "Gunmen in Iraqi Army Uniforms Kidnap a Wealthy Banker and His Son," NYT (2.18.06); "The Shame of the Prisons," NYT (2.18.06); Cowell, "Blair Calls Camp in Cuba an 'Anomaly,'" NYT (2.18.06); Ward & Perry, "Bush Poised to Shut Down Guantánamo," *Daily Mirror* (2.22.06); Morris, "Horrors of Camp Delta Are Exposed by British Victims," I (2.22.06); Charter, Gledhill & Hurst, "Blair Condones Amin-Style Tactics against Terrorism, Says Archbishop," T (2.24.06); Letter to the Editor, NYT (4.30.06); "Top Australian Lawyers Condemn Guantánamo Bay Detention," AFP (6.3.06); Council of Australian Law Deans, Incarceration without Trial at Guantanamo Bay of David Hicks (June 2006); Sciolino, "Spanish Judge Calls for Closing U.S. Prison at Guantánamo," NYT (6.4.06); Sales (2007).

41 Campagna, "The Enemy: Sami al-Haj's Story," Romanesko (10.3.06); Kristof, "Sami's Shame, and Ours," NYT (10.17.06); Heller, "The Sad Case of Sami al-Haj," Opinio Juris (9.15.07).

42 DoD Press Release (5.2.08); "Al Jazeera Journalist Is Freed after 6 Years at Guantánamo," LAT (5.2.08); Glaberson, "Cameraman Is Released from Guantánamo," NYT (5.2.08); Kristof, "A Prison of Shame, and It's Ours," NYT (5.4.08); Martinez, "U.S. Challenges Condition of Gitmo Detainee," ABC Website (5.2.08); Stelter, "From Guantánamo Cell to a Desk at al Jazeera," NYT (12.23.09).

43 Savage, "Military Tribunal Ordered Release of Chinese Muslims," BG (12.13.05); White, "Court May Hear Chinese Detainees," WP (12.13.05); White & Wright, "Detainee Cleared for Release Is in Limbo at Guantánamo," WP (12.15.05); *Qassim* v. *Bush*, 407 F.Supp.2d 198 (DDC 2005); "China: U.S. Sends Chinese Guantánamo Detainees to Albania," NYT (5.6.06); Higgins, "Tale of 5 Muslims: Out of Guantánamo and into Limbo," WSJ (6.2.06); Konviser, "A Strange Kind of Freedom," *Toronto Star* (6.13.06); Lewis, "5 Men Leave Guantánamo for a Bleak, Uncertain Future," NYT (8.15.06); Golden, "Chinese Leave Guantánamo for Albania Limbo," NYT (6.10.07); "New Zealand Refuses Guantánamo Detainees," NYT (8.20.07); Gillies, "Canada Balked at Guantánamo Refugees," WP (8.15.07); Willett (2016).

44 Denniston, Scotusblog (10.1.08); Wilber, "Uighur Detainees May Be Released to U.S.," WP (10.5.08); Glaberson, "Despite Ruling, Detainee Cases Facing Delays," NYT (10.5.08); Savage, "Judge Orders 17 Chinese Muslims Released from Guantánamo Bay," LAT (10.8.08); Wilber, "Chinese Muslims Ordered Released from Guantánamo," WP (10.8.08); Glaberson, "In Blow to President, Judge Orders 17 Detainees at Guantánamo Freed," NYT (10.8.08); Glaberson, "Appeals Panel Issues Stay of Order Freeing Detainees," NYT (8.9.08); "Appeals Court Postpones Release of Guantánamo Detainees," LAT (10.9.08).

45 "17 Detainees," WP (10.9.08); "The Shadow of Guantánamo," LAT (10.12.08); "The Rule of Law in Guantánamo," NYT (10.11.08); Glaberson, "Release of 17 Guantánamo Detainees Sputters as Officials Debate Risk," NYT (10.16.08); Wilber, "Appeals Court Halts Release of 17 Guantánamo Detainees," WP (10.20.08); Glaberson, "Appeals Court Stops Release of 17 Detainees in U.S.," NYT (2.19.09); Wilber, "Court Reverses Ruling Bringing 17 Detainees to US," WP (2.18.09); Spiegel, "Court Reverses Guantánamo Ruling," LAT (2.19.09); Wilber, "Appeals Court Halts Release of 17 Guantánamo Detainees," WP (10.20.08); "Free the Uighurs," WP (2.19.09); "Free the Uighurs," LAT (2.23.09); *Kiyemba* v. *Bush*, 2008 WL 4898963 (DC Cir. 2008); *Kiyemba* v. *Obama*, 555 F.3d 1022 (DC Cir. 2009).

46 Finn & Kornblut, "Guantánamo Bay: Why Obama Hasn't Fulfilled His Promise to Close the Facility," WP (4.24.11).

47 Gall, "Delegation Seeks Release of Afghans Being Held at Guantánamo," NYT (6.15.06); Whitlock, "82 Inmates Cleared but Still Held at Guantánamo," WP (4.29.07); Glaberson, "Hurdles Frustrate Effort to Shrink Guantánamo," NYT (8.9.07).

48 Morris, "Guantánamo Inmates Not Entitled to UK Help, Court Rules," I (5.5.06); "Premier Asks U.S. to Free 5 Prisoners," LAT (8.8.07);

Bonner, "Britain Asks to Take Back 5 Guantánamo Detainees," NYT (8.8.07); Stringer, "UK Asks US to Release 5 from Guantánamo," WP (8.7.07); Dodd, "Guantánamo Man's Family Release 'Torture' Dossier," G (8.11.07); Williams, "U.S. to Free 4 British Men from Guantánamo," LAT (12.8.07); Attweill, "Former Guantánamo Detainees Fight Extradition to Spain," G (1.9.08); Verkaik, "Photos 'Show UK Guantánamo Detainee was Tortured,'" I (12.10.07).

49 Chivers, "Russian Freed from Guantánamo Is Killed by Police near Chechnya," NYT (6.28.07); White, "Libyan Detainee, Fearing Torture, Fights Transfer Home," WP (6.15.07); Rosenberg, "Rights Groups Criticize Guantánamo Releases," MH (6.20.07); White "Detainee Transfers Concern Senators," WP (7.14.07); Glaberson, "Judge Halts Transfer of Guantánamo Detainee," NYT (10.10.07); "Tunisian Court Jails Former Inmate of Guantánamo Bay," LAT (10.25.07).

50 "White, "Red Cross Meets with 14 Moved to Guantánamo Bay," WP (10.13.06); Dedman, "In Limbo: Cases Are Few against Gitmo Detainees," MSNBC (10.24.06); Williams, Connell & Lopez, "Saudi Prisoner Release Gives U.S. Pause," LAT (10.25.06); Witte, "Taliban Leader Once Held by U.S. Dies in Pakistan Raid," WP (7.25.07); White, "Lawyers Assert that Pentagon Overstates Ex-Detainee Threat," WP (12.11.07); Denbeaux (2007); Denbeaux et al. (2007; 2008a; 2008b); Rubin, "Former Guantánamo Detainee Tied to Mosul Suicide Attack," NYT (5.8.08); Rubin, "Bomber's Final Messages Exhort Fighters against U.S.," NYT (5.9.08). For critiques of the government's numbers, see Denbeaux et al. (2008a; 2008b; 2009).

51 Stockman & Walsh, "Detainees Not Given Access to Witnesses," BG (6.18.06); Walsh, "Guardian Finds Afghan Witnesses U.S. Couldn't," G (6.20.06).

52 Whitlock, "At Guantánamo, Caught in a Legal Trap," WP (8.21.06); Northam, "Tapes Provide First Glimpses of Secret Gitmo Panels," NPR (11.21.06).

53 Hegland, "Empty Evidence," *National Journal* (2.3.06); Hegland, "Who Is at Guantánamo Bay," *National Journal* (2.3.06); Hegland, "Guantánamo's Grip," *National Journal* (2.3.06).

54 "National Briefing," NYT (8.30.05); Preston, "Judge Orders U.S. to Supply Prisoner Names," NYT (1.24.06); Neumeister, "Judge Orders Release of Gitmo Detainee IDs," WP (1.23.06); White, "Pentagon to Identify Detainees," WP (2.25.06); Shanker, "Pentagon Plans to Tell Names of Detainees," NYT (2.26.06); White & Tate, "Pentagon Releases Detainees' Names," WP (3.4.06); White & Tate, "In Guantánamo Bay Documents, Prisoners Plead for Release," WP (3.5.06); Golden, "Voices Baffled, Brash and Irate in Guantánamo," NYT (3.6.06); "They Came for the Chicken Farmer," NYT (3.8.06); Umansky, "A Fate Worse than Guantánamo?" WP (3.5.06); "Pentagon Releases More Names," WP (4.4.06); "Nearly 30 Percent at Guantánamo Jail Cleared to Go," Reuters (4.21.06); Williams, "U.S. to Free 141 Terror Suspects," LAT (4.25.06); Golden, "U.S. Says It Fears Detainee Abuse in Repatriation," NYT (4.30.06); Weisman, "U.S. to

Turn over 16 Saudis from Guantánamo to Riyadh," NYT (5.18.06); Williams, "U.S. to Free 16 Saudi Terrorism Suspects," LAT (5.18.06).

55 Golden, "For Guantánamo Review Boards, Limits Abound," NYT (12.31.06); Taylor, "America's Silent Hearings," *St. Louis Dispatch* (4.1.07); Selsky, "Files Raise Questions on Gitmo Decisions," WP (10.3.07).

56 Denbeaux & Denbeaux (2006a); Glaberson, "Guantánamo Detainees' Suit Challenges Fairness of Military's Repeat Hearings," NYT (5.15.07); "Gitmo: A National Disgrace," NYT (6.6.07); Glaberson, "Pentagon Study Sees Threat in Guantánamo Detainees," NYT (7.26.07).

57 Glaberson, "Reserve Officer Criticizes Process of Identifying 'Enemy Combatants' at Guantánamo," NYT (6.23.07); Leonnig & White, "An Ex-Member Calls Detainee Panels Unfair," WP (6.23.07); Glaberson, "Military Insider Becomes Critic of Hearings at Guantánamo," NYT (7.23.07); Glaberson, "Critic and Ex-Boss Testify on Guantánamo Hearings," NYT (7.27.07).

58 "U.S. Military Reviews Guantánamo Enemy Combatant Hearings That Kept Hundreds Behind Bars," AP (10.11.07).

59 "No Reporters at Detainees Hearings," LAT (3.7.07); Barnes, "Guantánamo Decision Is under Fire," LAT (3.8.07); White, "Alleged Architect of 9/11 Confesses to Many Attacks," WP (3.15.07); Spiegel, "9/11 Planner Confesses to Many Plots," LAT (3.15.07); Letters to the Editor, NYT (3.16.07); Liptak, "Confession at Guantánamo by 9/11 Mastermind May Aid other Qaeda Defendants," NYT (3.16.07); Linzer & White, "Probe of al-Qaeda Leader's Handling Sought," WP (3.17.07); White, "Al-Qaeda Suspect Says He Planned Cole Attack," WP (3.20.07); Rich, "Terrorism Suspect Alleges 'Mental Torture,'" WP (5.16.07); Glaberson, "Terror Suspect Testifies of Torture in Custody," NYT (5.16.07); White, "Detainees Ruled Enemy Combatants," WP (8.10.07).

60 *Bismullah* v. *Gates*, 501 F.3d 178 (DC Cir. 2007), rehearing denied, 503 F.3d 137 (DC Cir. 2007), en banc rehearing denied, 514 F.3d 1291 (DC Cir. 2008); Glaberson, "Court Tells U.S. to Reveal Data on Guantánamo," NYT (7.21.07); White, "Government Must Share All Evidence on Detainees," WP (7.21.07); Glaberson, "Security Chiefs Cite Danger in Revealing Detainee Data," NYT (9.12.07); Leonnig, "Intelligence Chiefs Back a Guantánamo Reversal," WP (9.12.07); Glaberson, "U.S. Mulls New Status Hearings for Guantánamo Inmates," NYT (10.15.07).

61 *Parhat* v. *Gates*, 532 F.3d 834 (DC Cir. 2008); White & Wilber, "Appeals Court Invalidates Detainee's 'Enemy' Status," WP (6.24.08); Glaberson, "U.S. Court in a First, Voids Finding by Tribunal," NYT (6.24.08); Meyer, "Court Rules in Favor of Detainee," LAT (6.24.08); "Another Rebuke on Guantánamo," NYT (6.25.08); Glaberson, "Evidence Faulted in Detainee Case," NYT (7.1.08); Wilber & White, "Judges Cite Need for Reliable Evidence to Hold Detainees," WP (7.1.08); "A Home for a Detainee," WP (8.16.08).

62 Leonnig, "Evidence of Innocence Rejected at Guantánamo," WP (12.5.07).

63 "Mr. Mukasey's Justice," NYT (7.27.08).

64 Serrano, "WikiLeaks Releasing Documents on Guantánamo," LAT (4.25.11); Rosenberg & Lasseter, "Wikileaks: Secret Guantánamo Files Show U.S. Disarray," McClatchy (4.24.11); Lasseter & Rosenberg, "Just 8 at Gitmo Gave Evidence against 235 Others," McClatchy (4.25.11); Calderone, "Wikileaks' Guantánamo Bay Documents," HuffPost (4.25.11); "The Guantánamo Papers," NYT (4.26.11); Letter to the Editor, NYT (4.28.11).

65 See Stafford Smith (2007); Denbeaux & Hafetz (2009); Khan, "My Guantánamo Diary," WP (4.30.06); Khan (2008); Rosenberg, "For Reporters, the Rules at Guantanamo Change Daily," McClatchy (7.26.10).

66 Wiltrout, "Navy Lawyer Once Posted at Cuba Base Is Charged," *Virginian-Pilot* (8.29.06); "Prosecutor: A Valentine Held Names of Detainees," LAT (5.15.07); Egerton, "'Moral Decision' Jeopardizes Navy Lawyer's Career," *Dallas Morning News* (5.17.07); Rosenberg, "Lawyer: U.S. Policy Shielded List of Captives," MH (5.17.07); "Virginia: Navy Lawyer Is Guilty of Communicating Secret Information," NYT (5.18.07); Horton, "A Tale of Two Lawyers," *Harper's* (5.20.07); Brooks, "The Good, the Bad and the Prosecuted," LAT (5.25.07); Golden, "Naming Names at Gitmo," NYT Magazine (10.21.07); Milburn, "Former Navy Lawyer Goes before Kansas Supreme Court," *Wichita Eagle* (10.26.12); "Kansas: Supreme Court Disbars Former Navy Attorney," WSJ (11.21.12).

67 Leonnig, "U.S. Wants to Limit Guantánamo Detainees' Access to Lawyers," WP (4.27.07); "Bar Criticizes Proposed Detainee Rules," NYT (4.30.07); "After the Lawyers," NYT (4.27.07); "Ban All the Lawyers," WP (4.29.07); "Gitmo: Still a 'Legal Black Hole,'" LAT (5.1.07); Glaberson, "U.S. Won't Limit Detainees' Visits with Attorneys," NYT (5.12.07); "U.S. Won't Limit Lawyers' Visits to Guantánamo," MH (5.11.07); "Lawyers Access to Gitmo Restricted," AP (9.22.07).

68 Wilber, "Legal Logjam May Be Ahead," WP (8.20.08); Stafford Smith (2007); Bonner, "A New Threat at Guantánamo: Smuggled Speedos and Briefs," NYT (9.28.07); Stafford-Smith, "An Incursion of Briefs at Guantánamo," WP (10.2.07); Stafford Smith, "Gitmo: America's Black Hole," LAT (10.5.07); *In re Guantanamo Bay Detainee Litigation*, 953 F.Supp.2d 40 (DDC 2013), rev'd, *Hatim* v. *Obama*, 760 F.3d 54 (DC Cir. 2014).

69 Glaberson, "Many Detainees at Guantánamo Rebuff Lawyers," NYT (5.5.07); Kinney, "Pursuing Their Duty in a Legal Netherworld," *Philadelphia Inquirer* (1.20.08).

70 NYT (11.10.08); Apuzzo & Jordan, "Obama Planning US Trials for Guantánamo Detainees," AP (11.10.08); Finn, "Guantánamo Closure Called Obama Priority," WP (11.12.08).

71 CCR Press Release (11.10.08); CCR, Abandoned at Guantánamo (11.08); Finn, "Guantánamo's Yemeni Detainees Epitomize a U.S. Security Concern," WP (11.19.08); Jordan, "UN Expert: 100 Guantánamo Inmates Need New Homes," AP (11.20.08); "Few Americans Would Close Guantánamo," Angus Reid Global Monitor (11.28.08); Cloonan & Mendelson, "How to Close Guantánamo," WP (11.30.08); Sisk, "Defense

Secretary Robert Gates: Closing Guantánamo Bay Prison a 'Priority,'" *Daily News* (12.2.08); Abramowitz, "Portugal Urges E.U. to Accept Former Guantánamo Detainees," WP (12.12.08); Finn, "Plans Being Drawn to Close Guantánamo Prison," WP (12.19.08); "Germany Says It May Offer to Take Some Guantánamo Bay Inmates," NYT (12.23.08); Wilner, "We Don't Need Guantánamo Bay," WSJ (12.22.08); Foley & McDonald, "Australia and Britain Are Reluctant on Detainees," NYT (1.3.09); Shanker & Cooper, "A New Chapter: Europe Is Ready to Work with Obama," NYT (1.4.09).

72 Jakes, "Advisers Say Obama Preparing to Close Gitmo," AP (1.12.09); Glaberson & Cooper, "Obama to Order Cuba Prison Shut on 1st Day," NYT (1.13.09); "Guantánamo Prison Closure Tops Obama's List," LAT (1.13.09).

73 Moore, "Pentagon Studies Bases as Possible Guantánamo Replacement; Lawmakers Object," NYT (1.17.09).

74 "Closing Guantánamo," NYT (1.18.09); Glaberson, "Rulings of Wrongful Detentions in Cuba as the Bush Era Closes," NYT (1.19.09).

75 Executive Order 13492, Closure of Guantánamo Detention Facilities, White House (1.22.09).

76 Williams, "Obama Moves to Close Guantánamo Prison," LAT (1.22.09); "Justice and Security," WP (1.22.09); Cohen & Agiesta, "Public Supports Closing Guantánamo," WP (1.22.09); Shane, Mazzetti & Cooper, "Obama Reverses Key Bush Policy, but Questions on Detainees Remain," NYT (1.23.09); Mazzetti & Shane, "Where Will Guantánamo Detainees Go?" NYT (1.24.09); Talev & Rosenberg, "9/11 Families Applaud Obama at Meeting on Guantánamo," McClatchy (2.6.09); Rosenberg, "Top Navy Official Reviews Conditions at Guantánamo," MH (2.5.09).

77 Abu-Nasr, "Gitmo Closure A Welcome Decision but Late," AP (1.20.09); Whitlock, "E.U. Willing to Help U.S. on Guantánamo," WP (1.27.09); Rotella, "Detainees Pose a Challenge for Europe," LAT (1.8.09).

78 Worth, "Freed by U.S., Saudi Becomes a Qaeda Chief," NYT (1.23.09); Worth, "2 Ex-detainees in Qaeda Video," NYT (1.25.09); Wallsten, "McCain Leads GOP Charge against Obama," LAT (1.26.09); Selsky, "U.S. Defends Transfer as Ex-Detainees Vow Terror," WP (1.27.09); Worth, "Saudis Issue List of 85 Terrorism Suspects," NYT (2.4.09); "Saudi Arabia: Guantánamo Ex-Inmate Is in Custody," NYT (2.18.09).

79 DeYoung & Finn, "Guantánamo Case Files in Disarray," WP (1.25.09); Finn, "4 Cases Illustrate Guantánamo Quandaries," WP (2.16.09).

80 Rosenberg, "Top Navy Official Reviews Conditions at Guantánamo," MH (2.5.09); Letter from ACLU to Joseph A. Benkert, Assistant Secretary of Defense (2.6.09); Letter from CCR to Sandra Hodgkinson (Deputy Assistant Secretary of Defense for Detainee Affairs) and Alan Liotta (Principal Director of Office of Detainee Affairs) (2.14.09); DoD, Review of Department Compliance with President's Executive Order on Detainee Conditions of Confinement (2009); Finn & Wilber, "Review Finds Detainees' Treatment Legal," WP (2.21.09); Meyer, "Pentagon Calls Guantánamo Humane," LAT (2.21.09); Glaberson, "Pentagon

Finds Guantánamo Follows Geneva Conventions," NYT (2.21.09); DoJ Press Release (2.20.09); Chu, "Guantánamo Inmate Returns to Britain," LAT (2.24.09); CCR, Current Conditions of Confinement at Guantánamo: Still in Violation of the Law (2.23.09).

81 Baker, "Guantánamo Abuse Has Worsened Since Obama – Lawyer," Reuters (2.25.09); Richey, "Yasin Ismail's Case Highlights the Difficulty of Verifying Conditions of Confinement," CSM (2.23.09); "Guantánamo Detainee Claims Abuse," Al Jazeera (4.15.09).

82 Finn, "British Officials to Visit Detainee in Cuba," WP (2.12.09); Bonner, "Detainee to Return to Britain, as Efforts to Prove Torture Claims Continue," NYT (2.23.09); Sullivan, "Former Guantánamo Detainee Returns to London," WP (2.23.09); "Freed Detainee Arrives Back in UK," BBC (2.23.09).

83 McConnell, "Don't Close It," WP (3.15.09).

84 "High-Level Officials Hold Meeting on Guantánamo," WP (3.20.09); Glaberson & Landler, "Top Diplomat to Be Named Special Envoy on Guantánamo," NYT (3.12.09).

85 Glaberson & Erlanger, "Europe's Hedging on Inmates Clouds Plans for Guantánamo," NYT (3.16.09); Glaberson, "U.S. and European Officials Discuss Detainees," NYT (3.16.09).

86 AG Holder, Remarks in Berlin (4.29.09); Whitlock, "Europe Seen Willing to Take Detainees," WP (4.30.09); Goldstein, "Swedish Court Secures Ex-Guantánamo Uighur's Asylum Quest," CSM (4.30.09); "France to Accept Guantánamo Detainee," NYT (5.7.09).

87 Schlesinger, "Obama's Increasingly Unpopular Guantánamo Bay Decision," US News (4.3.09).

88 Bumiller & Glaberson, "Gates Says Up to 100 Detainees May Be Held in U.S.," NYT (5.1.09); Hook, "Doing Hard Time over Guantánamo," LAT (5.7.09).

89 "Holder Says Getting OLC Nominee Confirmed Is His Top Priority," *Legal Times* (5.7.09); Frieden, "Holder: Suspected Gitmo Terrorists Won't Be Freed in U.S.," CNN (5.7.09); Bacon, "Lawmakers Balk at Holding Guantánamo Detainees in U.S.," WP (5.8.09); "Bill Would Bar Move of Inmates to the U.S.," LAT (5.14.09); Herszenhorn, "Unease Grows for Democrats over Security," NYT (5.14.09); Herszenhorn, "House Orders Obama to Provide Plan for Closing the Guantánamo Center," NYT (5.15.09); Johnson, "At Hearing, Assurance on Fate of Detainees," WP (5.15.09); Herszenhorn, "In Shift, Leaders of Senate Reject Guantánamo Aid," NYT (5.20.09); Hook, "Guantánamo Plan on Hold," LAT (5.20.09); Barnes & Meyer, "Obama Still on Course to Close Guantánamo," LAT (5.21.09); Stolberg, "Obama Is Said to Consider Preventive Detention Plan," NYT (5.21.09); "Lawmakers Demand a Plan on Guantánamo," LAT (5.25.09).

90 Remarks by the President on National Security, White House (5.21.09). For an insider's critique of Obama's policies, see Brooks (2016).

91 Bumiller, "1 in 7 Detainees Rejoin Jihadists, Pentagon Finds," NYT (5.21.09); Elliott, "NYT Reporter: Maybe 1 in 7 Detainees Didn't 'Return' to Terrorism," TPM Muckraker (5.21.09); "US: At Least One 'Recidivist'

Tortured to Confess to Terrorism," HRW (5.21.09); "Some Former Detainees Return to Terrorism," LAT (5.27.09); Bergen & Tiedemann, "Inflating the Guantánamo Threat," NYT (5.29.09); Hoyt, "What Happened to Skepticism?" NYT (7.7.09); Fletcher & Stover, "There's No Escaping Guantánamo," LAT (6.11.09); Fletcher & Stover (2008, 2009).

92 Whitlock & DeYoung, "Europe Objects Anew to Detainees," WP (5.29.09); Brand, "EU Expects to Take 'Several Dozen' from Guantánamo," WP (6.4.09); "A Home for Detainees," LAT (6.18.09); Finn & Tate, "CIA Mistaken on 'High-value' Detainee, Document Shows," WP (6.19.09); "Bloc Gains on Guantánamo Policy," NYT (6.16.09).

93 "Military Gitmo Detainee Dies of Apparent Suicide," AP (6.2.09); CCR Statement (6.2.09); Rosenberg, "Military Still Quiet on Suicide of Yemeni Guantánamo Detainee," MH (6.3.09); Mohamed, "Was Detainee's Death a Suicide?" MH (6.11.09); Valtin, "Murder at Guantánamo?" Daily Kos (11.22.09).

94 Sidoti, "Poll: US Divided over Torture, Closing Guantánamo," AP (6.3.09).

95 Landler, "U.S. Hopes to Move 17 Detainees from Guantánamo to Palau, Officials Say," NYT (6.10.09); Barnes, "Palau Agrees to Take Some Guantánamo Detainees," LAT (6.10.09); Jacobs & Otterman, "China Protests Moving of Detainees," NYT (6.12.09); Barnes, "Palau Deal May Not End Uighur Issue," LAT (6.11.09); Rosenberg, "Surprise: Four Chinese Detainees Sent from Guantánamo to Bermuda," MH (6.11.09); Barnes & Hook, "U.S. Retreats on Accepting Detainees," LAT (6.12.09); Glaberson, "6 Guantánamo Detainees Are Released to Other Countries as Questions Linger," NYT (6.12.09); Finn & Somashekhar, "Obama Bows on Settling Detainees," WP (6.12.09); Chu, "Europeans Balk at Taking Guantánamo Detainees," LAT (6.13.09); "Three Saudis Moved from Guantánamo," WP (6.13.09); Glionna, "Palau President Is Calm as Storm Brews on Island," LAT (6.15.09); "A Home for the Uighurs," WP (6.16.09); Beck, "The Myth of the $12 Million Uighur," NYT (6.20.09); Hosaka, "Gitmo Uighurs Reluctant to Move to Palau," AP (6.17.09); "The Meaning of Freedom," WP (9.29.09); DoD, Press Release (9.26.09); Raghavan & Finn, "U.S. Sees Saudi Program as an Option for Detainees," WP (10.14.09); Pelofsky & Ficini, "Rejecting Chinese Requests, U.S. Sends 6 Uighur Detainees to Palau," WP (11.1.09).

96 "Bush Hopes Closing Won't Harm Security," NYT (6.19.09); Becker, "Senate Widely Approves Emergency Funds for Wars," NYT (6.19.09); Johnston & Baker, "Shift Possible on Holding Terror Suspects," NYT (6.27.09); Linzer & Finn, "White House Weighs Order on Detention," WP (6.27.09); "Hypocrisy on the Hill," WP (7.5.09); Johnston & Bumiller, "Obama's Plan for Closing Guantánamo Faces Legal and Logistical Hurdles," NYT (7.14.09); Miller & Savage, "Obama to Miss Detainee Deadlines," LAT (7.21.09); Johnston, "Panels Miss a Deadline in Reviewing Guantánamo," NYT (7.21.09); Finn, "Reports on U.S. Detention Policy Will Be Delayed," WP (7.21.09); Perez & Weisman, "U.S. Expected to Miss Deadline on Detainee Policy," WSJ (7.20.09); "Get Moving on Gitmo," LAT (7.27.09); Richburg & Johnson, "Victims' Families United

in Tragedy, Divided in Views," WP (8.4.09); Ackerman, "Pat Roberts Will Shut the Senate Down over Closing Guantánamo," *Washington Independent* (8.4.09); Baker, "Obama to Use Current Law to Support Detentions," NYT (9.23.09); "Two-Tiered Justice for Terror Suspects?" LAT (9.26.09); "Mr. Obama Punts," WP (9.27.09); Baker & Johnston, "Guantánamo Deadline May Be Missed," NYT (9.28.09); Wittes, "Obama's Dick Cheney Moment," WP (9.29.09); Meyer, "U.S. May Not Make January Deadline for Closing Guantánamo," LAT (10.7.09); "Guantánamo Fever," WP (10.9.09); Stout, "House Allows Guantánamo to Transfer Some to U.S.," NYT (10.16.09); "Close Gitmo and Give Detainees Their Day in Court," LAT (10.29.09); Crabtree, "Holder Vows Gitmo Defendants Wouldn't Be Released in the U.S.," *The Hill* (11.13.09); Savage, "Illinois Site May Be Path to Closing Cuba Prison," NYT (11.16.09); Bacon, "In Senate Vote, Signs of Shift on Detainees," WP (11.18.09); Davey, "Village Split on Detainees as Neighbors," NYT (11.18.09); Calabresi & Weisskopf, "The Fall of Greg Craig," *Time* (11.19.09); Slevin & Lydersen, "Prison Holds Promise for Job-Strapped Town," WP (11.21.09); Slevin & Finn, "Illinois Prison Likely to House Detainees," WP (12.6.09); Parsons, "U.S. to House Guantánamo Detainees in Illinois, Officials Say," LAT (12.15.09); Savage, "U.S. Said to Pick Illinois Prison to House Detainees," NYT (12.15.09); Cooper & Johnston, "Obama Tells Prison to Take Detainees," NYT (12.16.09); Slevin, "Obama Administration to Buy Illinois Prison for Guantánamo Detainees," WP (12.16.09); "Guantánamo Must Be Closed," NYT (12.18.09); "The Plan to Move Gitmo Detainees to the U.S. Has a Gaping Hole," WP (12.19.09); Avila & Schorsch, "Officials Seek to Reassure Illinois Residents on Guantánamo Prison Transfer," LAT (12.23.09); Savage, "Plan to Move Guantánamo Detainees Faces New Delay," NYT (12.23.09); "Guantánamo at Crossroads," LAT (12.27.09).

97 Gerstein, "Bomb Plot Complicates Gitmo Plan," Politico (12.26.09); Savage, "Yemen's Ties to al Qaeda Complicate Guantánamo Plans," LAT (12.30.09); Raghavan, "Former Guantánamo Detainees Fuel Growing al-Qaeda Cell," WP (12.30.09); "How to Fight al-Qaeda's Offshoot in Yemen," WP (12.30.09); "Brennan: Some Guantánamo Detainees Will Go to Yemen," CNN (1.3.10); DeYoung & Fletcher, "Attempt to Bomb Airliner Could Have Been Prevented, Obama Says," WP (1.6.10); Barnes & Parsons, "More Former Guantánamo Detainees Returning to Militant Activity, Pentagon Says," LAT (1.7.10); Kadidal, "New York Times Re-Runs Retracted Story on Guantánamo Detainees' 'Return to Terror,'" HuffPost (1.7.10); "Call to Keep Certain Countries from Getting Terrorism Suspects Is Too Broad," WP (1.19.10); DeYoung, "Brennan Says No Recidivism among Guantánamo Detainees Released by Obama," WP (2.3.10); Laessing, "25 Saudi Guantánamo Prisoners Return to Militancy," Reuters (6.20.10).

98 Finn & Wilson, "New Detainee Site in U.S. Is Considered," WP (8.3.09); Meyer & Barnes, "Hybrid U.S. Prison Considered," LAT (8.3.09); Ackerman, "Pat Roberts Will Shut the Senate Down over Closing Guantánamo," *Washington Independent* (8.4.09); "Michigan: Officials Tour

Prisons," NYT (8.14.09); "War Games," NYT (8.16.09); "Getting Out of Gitmo," LAT (9.30.09); "More Than Half Guantánamo Inmates Can Be Transferred," AFP (12.3.09).

99 Guantánamo Bay Task Force Final Report, www.justice.gov/ag/Guantánamo-review-final-report.pdf (last accessed February 16, 2018); Finn, "Justice Task Force Recommends about 50 Guantánamo Detainees Be Held Indefinitely," WP (1.22.10); Savage, "Detainees Will Still Be Held, But Not Tried, Official Says," NYT (1.22.10); "Panel Recommends Transfer to U.S. for 82 Guantánamo Detainees," LAT (1.24.10); "The Case for Clear Standards on Holding the Worst of the Detainees," WP (2.6.10); ACLU Press Release (1.22.10); Greenwald, "ACLU's Anthony Romero," Salon (1.24.10); Gerstein, "Senator: White House Mulls Indefinite Detention," Politico (2.15.10); Kornblut, "Graham Proposes Framework for Handling Terrorism Suspects," WP (3.23.10); "The K.S.M. Files," NYT (4.15.10); Milbank, "Eric Holder's Guantánamo Morass," WP (4.15.10); Savage, "Closing Guantánamo Fades as a Priority," NYT (6.27.10).

100 Filkins & Shah, "After Arrests, Taliban Promotes a Fighter," NYT (3.25.10).

101 Macedo, "More Guantánamo Detainees Are Returning to Terror upon Release," Fox News (3.29.10).

102 Rosenberg, "Poll: Americans Don't Want U.S. to Empty Guantánamo," MH (3.30.10).

103 HR 5136; S. 1033. Savage, "House Panel Rejects a Plan to Shift Detainees to Illinois," NYT (5.21.10); "Politics and Fear-Mongering Keep Guantánamo Open," WP (5.27.10); Finn, "Most Guantánamo Detainees Low-Level Fighters, Task Force Report Says," WP (5.29.10); "Washington: Another Blow to Guantánamo Plan," NYT (5.29.10); "The Gitmo Detention Dodge," WP (6.20.10); "Plans to Buy Prison Proceed," NYT (6.22.10); Higham & Finn, "At Least $500 Million Has Been Spent since 9/11 on Renovating Guantánamo Bay," WP (7.7.10); Goldsmith, "A Way Past the Terrorist Detention Gridlock," WP (9.10.10).

104 "House Republican Calls for Keeping Guantánamo Prison Open," *Legal Times* (11.3.10); Finn, "2 Released from Guantánamo Bay by Obama Administration Return to Terrorism, Report Says," WP (12.7.10).

105 Savage, "Holder Denounces a Bill to Ban Detainee Transfers," NYT (12.10.10); Yoo & Delahunty, "The Collapse of the Guantánamo Myth," WSJ (12.11.10); "Look in the Mirror," WP (12.13.10); Markon, "Transfer Ban for Guantánamo Detainees Tucked into Spending Bill," WP (12.13.10); Slajda, "Democrats Added Ban on Gitmo Detainee Transfer to Omnibus Spending Bill," TPM Muckraker (12.13.10); "Guantánamo Must Go," LAT (12.14.10); Savage, "Detainee Review Proposal Is Prepared for President," NYT (12.22.10); Savage, "Vote Hurts Obama Push to Empty Prison," NYT (12.23.10); "Where Mr. Obama's Order on Terrorism Detentions Falls Short," WP (12.25.10); "A Step toward Fairness," NYT (12.28.10); "Mr. Obama's Detainee

Mess," WSJ (12.26.10); "The Guantánamo 48," LAT (12.29.10); "Our List of Wishes for 2011," LAT (1.1.11); Guiora & Blank, "Don't Deny Detainees Their Day in Court," LAT (1.4.11); Malinowski, "A Legacy Obama Should Avoid," WP (1.7.11); "The Rule of Law," NYT (1.7.11); Finn & Kornblut, "Obama Decries Curbs on Trying Detainees in U.S.," WP (1.7.11); "President Obama Should Fight Barriers to Guantánamo Civilian Trials," WP (1.7.11); "Going Nowhere on Gitmo," LAT (1.12.11).

106 Shane & Landler, "Obama Clears Way for Guantánamo Trials," NYT (3.8.11); Finn & Kornblut, "Obama Creates Indefinite Detention System for Prisoners at Guantánamo Bay," WP (3.8.11); Milbank, "Obama's New Gitmo Policy Is a Lot like Bush's Old Policy," WP (3.8.11); Stern, "Obama's Decision on Guantánamo Detainees Roundly Criticized on Right, Left," *CQ Today* (3.7.11); Serrano, "Obama to Resume Military Trials for Guantánamo Detainees," LAT (3.8.11); "The Prison that Won't Go Away," NYT (3.9.11); "Mr. Obama's Gitmo Order Is a Half Step in the Right Direction," WP (3.9.11); "Mired in Guantánamo," LAT (3.9.11); Linzer, "Obama Counterterrorism Adviser Slams Congressional Efforts to Block Guantánamo's Closure," ProPublica (3.18.11).

107 Mikva et al., "Beyond Guantánamo," CT (10.7.11); Stimson, "Common-Sense Principles for Detainee Policy," Heritage Foundation (10.17.11); "Peddling Fear," NYT (10.23.11); "Congress's Chance to Rewrite Rules for Fighting Terrorism," WP (10.31.11); Cohen, "Detainee Legislation Compromise," *The Atlantic* (10.28.11); "Politicizing Terrorism, Again," BG (11.7.11); Finn, "Guantánamo Detainees Cleared for Release but Left in Limbo," WP (11.9.11); Executive Office of the President, Statement of Administration Policy (on NDAA 2012) (11.17.11); Finn, "Veto Threatened over Detention Provisions," WP (11.18.11); "Congress Overreaches on Terrorism," WP (11.21.11); Levin & McCain, "Defense Bill Offers Balance in Dealing with Detainees," WP (11.27.11); Ukman, "Stage Set for Fight over Detainee Legislation," WP (11.29.11); Udall, "Defense Bill Gives Military Too Much Responsibility for Detainees," WP (11.29.11); Cassata, "FBI Director Raises Concerns with Detainee Policy," AP (11.29.11); Savage, "Senate Approves Requiring Military Custody in Terror Cases," NYT (11.30.11); Mascara, "Senate Vote Sets up Fight over Terrorism Detainees," LAT (11.30.11); Savage, "Senate Declines to Clarify Rights of American Qaeda Suspects Arrested in U.S.," NYT (12.2.11); Cassata, "Congress, White House at Odds over Defense Bill," AP (12.2.11); Reilly, "White House Still Threatening Veto over Terrorists in Military Custody Mandate," TPM Muckraker (12.1.11); Herb, "White House Stands by Veto Threat Despite Senate Compromise Bill," *The Hill* (12.3.11); "Don't Retreat from Freedoms," *Philadelphia Inquirer* (12.6.11); Waxman & Bellinger, "A Problematic Terrorist Detention Bill," Council on Foreign Relations (12.5.11); "Hobbling the Fight against Terrorism," NYT (12.8.11); "Military Detention of All Terror Suspects Deserves a Veto: View," Bloomberg News (12.9.11); Sonmez, "Lawmakers Try to

Ease White House Concerns about Detainee Rules," NYT (12.13.11); Gerstein, "Defense Bill Revised in Bid to Avoid Veto," Politico (12.13.11); "House and Senate Agree on Sweeping Defense Bill," AP (12.13.11); "Congressional Meddling on Terror Cases, to Little Effect," WP (12.14.11); Jackson, "Obama to Sign Defense Bill, after Detainee Changes," *USA Today* (12.14.11); Savage, "Obama Drops Veto Threat over Military Authorization Bill after Revisions," NYT (12.15.11); Sonmez, "White House Drops Defense Bill Veto Threat after Lawmakers Rework Detainee Provisions," WP (12.15.11); "Military Bill on Spending Is Approved by Congress," NYT (12.16.11); Rosenthal, "More Rubble from the Military Detention Cave-In," NYT (12.16.11); "A Wrong Turn in Terror Fight," LAT (12.16.11); "Politics over Principle," NYT (12.16.11); Savage, "Obama Challenges Provisions in Budget Bill," NYT (12.24.11); Landler, "After Struggle on Detainees, Obama Signs Defense Bill," NYT (1.1.12); Nakamura, "Obama Signs Defense Bill, Pledges to Maintain Legal Rights of U.S. Citizens," WP (1.1.12); Nicholas, "Obama Signs Defense Bill but Balks at Terrorism Provisions," LAT (1.1.12), "President Obama Signs Indefinite Detention Bill into Law," ACLU (12.31.11); "Detention Hour," CT (1.3.12).

108 Boumediene, "My Guantánamo Nightmare," NYT (1.8.12); Kurnaz, "Notes from a Guantánamo Survivor," NYT (1.8.12).

109 Borger & Boone, "Taliban Leaders Held at Guantánamo Bay to Be Released in Peace Talks Deal," G (1.3.12); Rosenberg, "Taliban Opening Qatar Office, and Maybe Door to Talks," NYT (1.4.12); "The Risks of Talking to the Taliban," WP (1.5.12); "Talking with the Taliban," NYT (1.5.12); Borger, "U.S. Denies Deal on Freeing Taliban Prisoners from Guantánamo," G (1.4.12); Thiessen, "Don't Let These Taliban Leaders Loose," WP (1.9.12); Finn & Tate, "On 10th Anniversary, Guantánamo Bay's Future Is Unclear," WP (1.11.12); Hosenball & Cornwell, "U.S. Assessing Risks of Taliban Transfer: Petraeus," CT (2.1.12); Bennett & Mascaro, "GOP Criticizes Plan to Transfer 'High-level' Guantánamo Detainees," LAT (2.2.12).

110 Finn, "Guantánamo Detainees Protest on Anniversary," WP (1.9.12); Wittes, "How the Next 10 Years at Guantánamo Should Look," WP (1.12.12); Kennedy, "100s Protest on 10th Anniversary of Guantánamo Prison," LAT (1.12.12); Turley, "10 Reasons the U.S. Is No Longer the Land of the Free," WP (1.14.12); Fouhy, "Candidates Disagree over Indefinite Detention," BG (1.17.12); "U.N. Rights Chief: U.S. Must Close Guantánamo," AP (1.24.12).

111 Savage & Rosenberg, "Republican Report Criticizes Transfers from Guantánamo," NYT (2.9.12); "Intelligence Report Finds only 16 Percent of Released Gitmo Detainees Rejoin Terror War," WP (3.5.12).

112 Herb & Munoz, "Fight Looms over Detainee Provisions," *The Hill* (5.13.12); "House Backs Indefinite Detention of Suspected Terrorists, Even U.S. Citizens," WP (5.17.12); Weisman, "House Vote Upholds Indefinite Detention of Terror Suspects," NYT (5.18.12); "A New Attack on the Constitution," NYT (5.18.12).

113 *Hedges* v. *Obama*, 2012 WL 1721124 (SDNY 2012), 2012 WL 2044565 (SDNY 2012), 890 F.Supp.2d 494 (SDNY 2012), 2012 WL 4075626 (2nd Cir. 2012); 724 F.2d 170 (2nd Cir. 2013), cert den. 134 S.Ct 1936 (2014); Savage, "Judge Blocks Controversial Indefinite Detention Law," NYT (9.13.12); "Detention Wars, Continued," WP (9.16.12); "Obama Appointee vs. Obama," WSJ (9.17.12); Savage, "U.S. Appeals Judge Grants Stay of Ruling on Detention Law," NYT (9.19.12); "Federal Judge Wrongly Blocks President from Holding Terrorism Supporters," *New York Daily News* (9.20.12).

114 Adams, "Democrats 2012 Platform Policy Comes Complete with Rolled-Back Rhetoric," G (9.5.12); GAO, "Guantánamo Bay Detainees: Facilities and Factors for Consideration If Detainees Were Brought to the United States" (GAO 13–31) (November 2012); "Close Guantánamo Prison," NYT (11.26.12).

115 McAuliff, "Senators Make Bid to End Indefinite Detention in NDAA," HuffPost (11.28.12); "Government Report Supports Closing Guantánamo," NYT (11.29.12); Savage, "Senate Votes to Curb Indefinite Detention," NYT (11.30.12); Herb, "Senate Passes $631b Defense Policy Bill 90-0," *The Hill* (12.4.12); Herb, "President Obama's Pledge to Close Gitmo in Second Term Faces Difficult Test," *The Hill* (12.13.12).

116 "Mr. Obama's Inertia on Guantánamo," WP (12.22.12); Savage, "Signing Defense Bill, Obama Challenges Detainee Provisions," NYT (1.4.13); "Rights and the 'War on Terror,'" LAT (1.6.13); Daskal, "Don't Close Guantánamo," NYT (1.10.13); Letters to the Editor, NYT (1.21.13); Savage, "Office Working to Close Guantánamo Is Shuttered," NYT (1.30.13); Gerstein, "State Dept. Shutters Guantánamo Closure Office," Politico (1.28.13).

117 Rosenberg, "Lawyers: Conditions Deteriorating at Guantánamo Prison," MH (3.4.13); Finn & Tate, "Guantánamo Bay Detainees' Frustrations Simmering, Lawyers and Others Say," WP (3.17.13); "U.S. Military Says Hunger Strike at Guantánamo Has Grown to 21 Detainees, but No Lives in Danger," AP (3.18.13); Savage, "Number of Hunger Strikers Surges at Guantánamo," NYT (3.21.13); Savage, "More Join Hunger Strike at Guantánamo Prison," NYT (3.26.13); Rosenberg, "Red Cross in Guantánamo a Week Early to Check on Hunger Strikers," MH (3.26.13); Valery, "Guantánamo Hunger Strikers Ready for Death: Lawyer," AFP (3.30.13); Finn & Tate, "Hunger Strike at Guantánamo Bay Spreads," WP (4.1.13); "Hunger Strike at Guantánamo," NYT (4.6.13); "U.S. Names New Commander at Guantánamo Bay Prison as Hunger Strike Amind Hunger Strike [*sic*]," WP (4.12.13); Rosenberg, "Washington: Troops Forcibly Move Hunger Strikers at Guantánamo into Cells," MH (4.13.13); Savage, "Mounting Tensions Escalate into Violence during Raid at Guantánamo Prison," NYT (4.14.13); Moqbel, "Gitmo Is Killing Me," NYT (4.15.13); Rosenberg, "Guantánamo Hunger Strikers: The Dilemma of Forced Feeding," MH (4.13.13); Savage, "Officials Describe Chaos at Guantánamo in Weeks that Preceded Raid on Prison," NYT (4.17.13); Rosenberg, "Almost a Third of Guantánamo Captives Now

Considered Hunger Strikers," MH (4.18.13); "Guantánamo Bay Prison Enters a Tense New Phase with Most Prisoner [*sic*] Locked Down after Clash," WP (4.20.13); Savage, "Military Says Hunger Strike by Detainees Is Growing," NYT (4.20.13); Rosenberg, "Nearly Half of Guantánamo Prisoners on Hunger Strike," MH (4.22.13); Savage, "Despair Drives Guantánamo Detainees to Revolt," NYT (4.25.13); "The Guantánamo Stain," NYT (4.26.13); "Number of Prisoners on Hunger Strike in Guantánamo Rises to 97," WP (4.26.13); Rosenberg, "Feinstein Urges U.S. to Resume Guantánamo Transfers," MH (4.25.13); "Military Says 100 of 166 Prisoners Now on Hunger Strike at Guantánamo Bay," WP (4.27.13); Goodman, "A Desperate Situation at Guantánamo," *Democracy Now!* (4.29.13); Nocera, "The Detainees' Dilemma," NYT (4.30.13); Sutton, "American Medical Association Questions Guantánamo Force-Feeding," Reuters (4.30.13); Savage, "As Hunger Strike Grows, Guantánamo Adds Medical Staff," NYT (4.30.13); Savage, "Amid Hunger Strike, Obama Renews Push to Close Cuba Prison," NYT (5.1.13); "The President and the Hunger Strike," NYT (5.1.13); "President Obama Must Make Closing Guantánamo a Priority," WP (5.1.03); "Erasing the Stain of Guantánamo," LAT (5.1.13); Olsen, "Afghanistan's Karzai Urges Closure of Guantánamo," ABC News (5.2.13); Serrano, "Guantánamo Detainee Says Prison 'Shakedown' Sparked Hunger Strike," LAT (5.4.13); "The Guantánamo Dilemma," CT (5.6.13); Shimkus, "Guantánamo Medical Providers Face Dilemma," MH (5.8.13); Gerstein, "Levin Calls for White House Guantánamo Envoy," Politico (5.10.13); "In Guantánamo Have We Created Something We Can't Close?" NPR's *All Things Considered* (5.11.13); "Physician Dismisses Force-Feeding Concerns," Al Jazeera (5.21.13); Rosenberg, "Guantánamo's Military Defense Lawyers Cite My Lai Massacre in Plea to Hagel," MH (5.22.13); Rosenberg, "Guantánamo Filmed Guards Searching Qurans for Contraband, but You Can't See It," MH (7.28.14).

118 "The Future of Our Fight against Terrorism," Lawfare (5.23.13); "Obama Drone Speech Delivered at National Defense University," HuffPost (5.23.13); Herb, "GOP's Chambliss: Obama Speech Will Be 'Viewed by Terrorists as Victory,'" *The Hill* (5.23.13); Ackerman, "Guantánamo Bay Strikers Demand New Doctors in Letter of Protest," G (5.31.13); Nocera, "Is Force-Feeding Torture?" NYT (6.1.13); "Yemen Says Obama Must Back Up Guantánamo Promise with Action," HuffPost (6.3.13); Lardner, "GOP House Bill Would Block Guantánamo Closing," BG (6.4.13); Herb, "Dem. Blasts Gitmo Spending in House Bill," *The Hill* (6.3.13); Rosenberg, "Southcom General Has Nothing to Offer Guantánamo Hunger Strikers," MH (6.5.13); Barnes, "Retired Military Brass Press Obama on Guantánamo Closure," WSJ (6.4.13); Baker, "Amid Hunger Strike, Senators Lead Delegation to Prison at Guantánamo," NYT (6.8.13); Herb, "White House Threatens Veto of Defense Bill," *The Hill* (6.11.13); Cassata & Lardner, "House $638b Defense Bill Keeps Guantánamo Prison," MH (6.15.13); Savage, "Kerry Associate Chosen

for Post on Closing Guantánamo Prison," NYT (6.17.13); Rosenberg, "FOIA Suit Reveals Guantánamo's Indefinite Detainees," MH (6.18.13); Carter & Liptak, "Doctors to Obama: Let Us Treat Hunger-Striking Detainees at Guantánamo," CNN (6.19.13); Townsend, "U.S. Steps Up Effort to Break Guantánamo Hunger Strike," O (6.23.13); Savage, "Bill to Ease Transfers of Guantánamo Detainees Moves through Senate," NYT (6.25.13); Reprieve, Down the Tubes: The 2013 Hunger Strike at Guantánamo Bay (July 2013); Rosenberg, "Lawyers Ask Judges to Halt Guantánamo Forced-Feeding," MH (7.1.13); Faraz, "A Letter from Guantánamo," HuffPost (7.2.13); Rosenberg, "Guantánamo Prison to Synchronize Force-Feedings to Ramadan Fast," MH (7.2.13); Rosenberg, "Feinstein, Durbin ask Obama to Halt Guantánamo Forced-Feedings," WP (7.11.13); Rosenberg, "Guantánamo: 2 Detainees Quit Hunger Strike," MH (7.11.13); Kember, "Guantánamo Bay Hunger Strike Might Be Ending," WP (7.13.13); Savage, "15 Held at Guantánamo Are Said to Quit Hunger Strike," NYT (7.15.13); "A Force-Feeding Disgrace at Guantánamo," LAT (7.14.13); McFadden, "U.S.: More Prisoners End Hunger Strike at Guantánamo," BG (7.18.13); Nocera, "Guantánamo Rulings Change Little," NYT (7.23.13); Kasperowicz, "House Protects Guantánamo Bay, Missile Programs in DoD Spending Bill," *The Hill* (7.23.13); Lardner, "Senate Panel Shows Deep Division on Guantánamo," MH (7.24.13); Savage, "U.S. to Send 2 at Guantánamo Back to Algeria, Saying Security Concerns Are Met," NYT (7.27.13); "Hunger Strike at Guantánamo Bay Shows Signs of Weakening," Reuters (7.31.13); Rose, "Why We Should Shut Down Guantánamo," *Mail on Sunday* (7.4.13); Wilson, "Security Threat from Yemen Complicates Obama's Guantánamo Plan," WP (8.8.13); Grisham, "After Guantánamo, Another Injustice," NYT (8.10.13); Feinstein & Durbin, "How to Close Gitmo," LAT (8.14.13); Rosenberg, "Alleged 9/11 Conspirator Complains about Food Service at Guantánamo," MH (8.20.13); Rosenberg, "U.S. Sends Two Algerians [*sic*] Prisoners Home from Guantánamo," MH (8.29.13); Savage, "Guantánamo Hunger Strike Largely Over, U.S. Says," NYT (9.24.13); Savage, "Pentagon Denies Money for Guantánamo Overhaul," NYT (9.25.13); Savage, "Pentagon Names Envoy for Guantánamo's Closing," NYT (10.9.13); "Obama Recommits to Closing Guantánamo Bay," CBS News (11.4.13); Hudson, "Amid Lingering Hunger Strike Guantánamo Abuses Press On," Truthout (11.9.13); Perez, "Obama Faces Crucial Guantánamo Votes," CNN's Security Clearance (11.18.13); "A Glimmer of Sense on Guantánamo," NYT (11.26.13); "Politics Keeps Getting in the Way of Closing Guantánamo," WP (11.30.13); Rosenberg, "Guantánamo Ends Daily Hunger-Strike Reports," MH (12.3.13); "U.S. Sends 2 Guantánamo Prisoners Back to Algeria," WP (12.5.13); Savage, "Two Guantánamo Detainees Are Involuntarily Repatriated to Algeria," NYT (12.6.13); "A Bad Decision at Guantánamo," NYT (12.7.13); Townsend, "William Hague Letter Brings Hope to Shaker Aamer in Guantánamo," G (12.7.13); Leopold, "Gitmo Media Blackout Hopes to Undermine

Hunger Strikers," Al Jazeera America (12.11.13); "U.S. Sends 2 Guantánamo Prisoners to Saudi Arabia," WP (12.16.13); Savage, "Two Saudi Prisoners Sent Home from Guantánamo," NYT (12.17.13); Osman, "Sudanese Guantánamo Detainee Says He Was Tortured," AP (12.19.13); "Obama Signs Defense Law, Calls It a 'Welcome Step' Toward Closing Guantánamo Bay Prison," WP (12.26.13); "U.S. Sends 3 Uighur Guantánamo Prisoners to Slovakia," WP (12.31.13); Rosenberg, "Last 3 Uighurs Leave Guantánamo," MH (12.31.13); Rosenberg, "House Committee Earmarks $69 million for New Secret Prison," MH (5.9.14).

119 Rosenberg, "71 Guantánamo Prisoners Will Get Parole-Style Hearings, Pentagon Says," WP (7.21.13); Rosenberg, "Guantánamo's Forever Captives to Make Pitch for Freedom in Secret," MH (11.15.13).

120 "Judge Denies Gitmo Detainee's Humanitarian Bid for Relief, Citing Lack of Jurisdiction," WP (4.15.13); *Aamer* v. *Obama*, 953 F.Supp.2d 213 (DDC 2013).

121 *Aamer* v. *Obama*, 742 F.3d 1023 (DC Cir. 2014); Savage, "Appeals Court Allows Challenges by Detainees at Guantánamo Prison," NYT (2.12.14); Ackerman, "Members of Congress Demand to see Guantánamo Detainee Force-Feeding Videos," G (10.30.14).

122 Savage, "Videos Said to Show Force-Feeding of Detainees at Guantánamo Bay," NYT (5.14.14); "Force-Feedings at Guantánamo," NYT (5.16.14); Doyle, "Judge: Produce Guantánamo Videos, Medical Records," MH (5.21.14); "Guantánamo Force-Feeding Causing 'Agony,' Says US Judge," Reprieve Press Release (5.23.14); Ahmed, "Lawyers File for Emergency Restraining Order against Gitmo Staff," Al Jazeera America (6.16.14); Doyle, "Judge in Guantánamo Force-Feeding Case Wants More Evidence," MH (6.18.14); "Journalists Seek Public Access to Guantánamo Force-Feeding Videotapes," MH (6.20.14); Rosenberg, "Navy Nurse Refuses to Force-Feed Guantánamo Captive," MH (7.15.14); "Judge Orders Independent Health Exam for Guantánamo Hunger-Striker," *Stars and Stripes* (8.12.14); Doyle, "Judge Demands Answers on Guantánamo Force-Feeding," MH (8.14.14); Rosenberg, "Nurse Who Refused to Force-Feed Sent Home from Guantánamo," MH (8.22.14); Rosenberg, "No Court Martial for Nurse Who Refused to Give Force-Feeding at Guantánamo," MH (9.15.14); Gerstein, "Judge Won't Close Guantánamo Force-Feeding Hearing," Politico (10.2.14); Savage, "Judge Orders Disclosure of Guantánamo Videos," NYT (10.4.14); Rosenberg, "Federal Court Hearing Examines Guantánamo Hunger-Strike Policy," MH (10.5.14); Savage, "A Practice Goes On Trial," NYT (10.7.14); Zapotsky, "Guantánamo Bay Detainee Seeks Changes in Force-Feeding," WP (10.7.14); Zapotsky, "Guantánamo Bay Detainee Force-Feeding Case Continues," WP (10.8.14); Rosenberg, "Guantánamo 'Experiment' Didn't Break Hunger Strike but Gets Judge's Attention," MH (10.9.14); Ackerman, "Judge Grants 30-Day Delay in Release of Guantánamo Force-Feeding Videos," G (10.16.14); Rosenberg, "Judge Upholds Guantánamo's Treatment of Hunger-Striker Waiting to Go," MH (11.9.14); Rosenberg, "Top Nursing Group

Backs Navy Nurse Who Wouldn't Force-Feed at Guantánamo," MH (11.19.14); Ackerman, "U.S. to Appeal Judge's Ruling on Guantánamo Bay Force-Feeding Videos," G (12.2.14); Rosenberg, "Pentagon Fears Blowback from 'Humane' Guantánamo Video Release," MH (12.3.14); "Release the Guantánamo Force-Feeding Videos," NYT (12.8.14); Leopold, "Pentagon Panel Proposes Sweeping Changes That Could Impact Guantánamo Force-Feeding," Vice News (3.23.15); Doyle, "Court Hears Debate over Release of Guantánamo Detainee Force-Feeding Videos," MH (5.8.15); Rosenberg, "Navy Nurse Who Refused to Force-Feed at Guantánamo Keeps His Job," MH (5.13.15); Jacobs & Ackerman, "Judge Pushes to Speed Release of Force Feeding Videos at Guantánamo Bay," G (7.9.15); Walker, "Judge Orders U.S. to Prepare Guantánamo Force-Feeding Tapes for Release," *Newsweek* (7.10.15); Ackerman, "Guantánamo Force-Feeding Videos Released to U.S. Court in Redacted Form," G (9.14.15); Defense Health Board, Ethical Guidelines and Practices for U.S. Military Medical Professionals (2015); Doyle, "Judge Sticks by Decision to Release Guantánamo Force-Feeding Videos," MH (10.27.15); *Dhiab* v. *Obama* (DDC Judge Kessler 10.27.15); Pradhan (2016).

123 Savage & Cooper, "Under Pressure, Hagel Promises to Act on Guantánamo Transfers," NYT (5.30.14); Savage, "Decaying Guantánamo Defies Closing Plans," NYT (9.1.14); "Limbo and Cruelty at Guantánamo," NYT (9.7.14); Rosenberg, "Estonia Agrees to Resettle a Guantánamo Detainee," MH (10.10.14); Marcos, "House Republican Urges Administration to Stop Gitmo Transfers," *The Hill* (11.3.14); Savage, "Kuwait Released from Guantánamo under New Review System," NYT (11.6.14).

124 Gearan & Londono, "U.S. Seeks Prisoner Swap with Taliban to Free Army Sgt Bowe Bergdahl," WP (2.18.14); Schmitt & Savage, "Bowe Bergdahl, American Soldier, Freed by Taliban in Prisoner Trade," NYT (6.1.14); Hamburger & Sieff, "Joy about Bergdahl Release Gives Way to Questions," NYT (6.1.14); "Trading with the Taliban," WSJ (6.1.14); "Was Price to Win Release of an American Soldier from Taliban Captivity Too High?" WP (6.2.14); Savage & Sanger, "Deal to Free Bowe Bergdahl Puts Obama on Defensive," NYT (6.3.14); Bolton, "Graham Warns of Republican Impeachment Push over Gitmo," *The Hill* (6.4.14); Mazzetti et al., "Behind P.O.W.'s Release: Urgency and Opportunity," NYT (6.5.14); Sanger & Baker, "Fears for Sgt's Life Led to Secrecy about Swap, Obama Official Says," NYT (6.5.14); "The Rush to Demonize Sgt. Bergdahl," NYT (6.6.14); Gearan, "Sources Outline Conditions on Taliban Leaders Release in Exchange for Bergdahl," WP (6.6.14); Farenthold & Fuller, "The Bergdahl Boomerang," WP (6.6.14); Knowlton, "With Tough Tone, Kerry Defends Swap for Bergdahl," NYT (6.8.14); Weisman, "Bergdahl Briefing Fails to Allay Senators' Doubts," NYT (6.11.14); Connelly, "Bergdahl Prisoner Swap Stirs Concern," NYT (6.11.14); Berman, "GOP Takes Steps to Rein in Obama," *The Hill* (6.10.14); "The Milk Carton Guy," NYT (6.15.14); Rosenberg,

"Pentagon Prosecutor: Guantánamo Detainees in Bergdahl Swap Couldn't Be Successfully Prosecuted," MH (6.15.14); Cassata, "House Panel Weighs Limits on Guantánamo Transfers," MH (6.16.14); Marcos, "House Votes to Ban Gitmo Transfers," *The Hill* (6.19.14); Tiron, "House Passes $570b Defense Bill Rejecting Cost Cuts," Bloomberg (6.20.14); Rosen, "Military Leaders Back Bergdahl Prisoner Exchange," McClatchy (7.10.14); Cassata, "House Panel Condemns Obama for Guantánamo Prisoner Swap," MH (7.29.14); "Prisoner Swap with Taliban Was Illegal, Investigators Say," NYT (8.20.14); Marcos, "22 Dems Vote for Bergdahl Resolution," *The Hill* (9.19.14); Starr, "Officials: Detainees Swapped for Bergdahl Suspected of Militant Activities," CNN (1.30.15); Ryan, "Republicans Say Detainees Released in Bergdahl Swap Are Still Security Risks," WP (5.16.15); Nordland, "For Swapped Taliban Prisoners from Guantánamo Bay, Few Doors to Exit Qatar," NYT (6.1.15); Harris & Youssef, "Congress: Bowe Bergdahl Swap Was FUBAR," Daily Beast (12.7.15); Ryan, "Lawmakers Accused White House of Concealment in Bowe Bergdahl Prisoner Swap," WP (12.10.15); Goldsmith (2016).

125 Al-Tamimi, "Moroccan Ex-Guantánamo Detainee Mohammed Mizouz Identified in Syria," Syria Comment (12.22.13); "Former Guantánamo Detainee Implicated in Benghazi Attack," WP (1.8.14); Roggio, "Former Guantánamo Detainee Killed While Leading Jihadist Group in Syria," *Long War Journal* (4.4.14).

126 Savage, "Panel Recommends Transferring Yemeni from Guantánamo," NYT (1.10.14); "U.S.: Detained Yemeni May Rejoin al Qaeda If Freed," WP (1.28.14); Savage, "Military Is Asked to Return Guantánamo Inmate to Yemen," NYT (1.29.14); Savage, "Military Board, in a First, Says Yemeni Should Stay Detained," NYT (3.12.14); Savage, "Military Repatriates Algerian Detainee from Guantánamo Bay," NYT (3.13.14); Josceyn, "Review Board Recommends Indefinite Detainee at Guantánamo Be Transferred," *Long War Journal* (4.26.14); "Prisoner Boycotts Guantánamo Hearing over Search," AP (5.3.14); Rosenberg, "Board Oks Release of Sickly 'Forever Prisoner' Who Learned Yoga at Guantánamo," MH (5.29.14); Rosenberg, "Panel Clears Kuwait 'Forever Prisoner' for Repatriation from Guantánamo," MH (7.25.14); Savage, "Board Says Saudi Detainee Should Be Repatriated," NYT (10.20.14); Savage, "Kuwait Released from Guantánamo under New Review System," NYT (11.6.14); Savage, "5 Guantánamo Inmates Are Sent to Eastern Europe," NYT (11.21.14); "Saudi Detainee Is Released from Guantánamo Bay after 12 Years," NYT (12.23.14); Rosenberg, "Saudi Arabia Fetches Former 'Forever Prisoner' from Guantánamo," MH (11.23.14); "Another Yemeni 'Forever Prisoner' at Guantánamo Is Cleared for Release," MH (12.10.14); Rosenberg, "4 Afghans Returned Home from Guantánamo," MH (12.20.14); Wong, "Inhofe: Gitmo Release Will 'Embolden Terrorists,'" *The Hill* (12.22.14); Cooper, "Five Guantánamo Prisoners Are Released to Kazakhstan," NYT (12.31.14); Rosenberg, "Guantánamo Parole Board OK's Release of Obese Egyptian Captive," MH (2.25.15); Rosenberg, "Parole Board Clears another

Guantánamo 'Forever Prisoner,'" MH (4.17.15); Savage, "6 Guantánamo Detainees from Yemen Are Transferred to Oman," NYT (6.13.15); Rosenberg, "Amputee Libyan 'Forever Prisoner' Cleared for Release," MH (9.15.15); Savage, "U.S. Repatriates Moroccan from Guantánamo and Approves a Kuwaiti's Transfer," NYT (9.18.15); Savage, "Saudi Held at Guantánamo Is Repatriated, Reducing Number of Detainees to 114," NYT (9.23.15); Rosenberg, "Guantánamo Frees 9-Year Hunger Striker to Saudi Arabia," MH (9.22.15); Rosenberg, "Guantánamo Parole Board Clears another 'Forever Prisoner,'" MH (9.24.15).

127 "Uruguay's President Offers to Resettle Guantánamo Detainees," MH (3.20.14); "Mujica Confirms Uruguay Will Accept Guantánamo Prisoners as 'Refugees,'" Mercopress (3.21.14); Parks, "Uruguay's Leader Agrees to Take up to Six Guantánamo Prisoners," WSJ (5.7.14); "Uruguay Agrees to Take 8 to 12 Guantánamo Prisoners," Mercopress (5.13.14); Sheridan, "Uruguayan President Agrees to Take Six Detainees from Guantánamo," WP (5.16.14); Savage, "U.S. Is Said to Plan to Send 6 Detainees to Uruguay," NYT (7.17.14); Savage, "Decaying Guantánamo Defies Closing Plans," NYT (9.1.14); Savage, "U.S. Transfers 6 Guantánamo Detainees to Uruguay," NYT (12.7.14); Goldman, "Six Guantánamo Detainees Transferred to Uruguay as Obama Works to Close Prison," WP (12.7.14); Savage, "Uruguay Accepts 6 Detainees Held at Guantánamo," NYT (12.8.14); "Uruguay's Guantánamo Letter," NYT (12.13.14); Partlow, "After 12 Years in Guantánamo, Ex-Detainees Find Little Solace in Uruguay," WP (3.22.15); "Uruguay's New President Wants U.S. to Assist Ex-Guantánamo Detainees," MH (4.8.15); "Ex-Guantánamo Detainees Keep up Protest in Uruguay," WP (4.26.15); "Former Guantánamo Detainees in Day 4 of Protest at U.S. Embassy in Uruguay," MH (4.28.15); Haberkorn & Prengaman, "Uruguay Urges Former Guantánamo Detainees to Sign for Housing," MH (4.28.15); Haberkorn & Prengaman, "Uruguayans Frustrated by Protest of Ex-Guantánamo Detainees," WP (5.8.15); Leopold, "U.S. Manipulates Number of Gitmo Hunger Strikers, Says Detainee," Al Jazeera America (5.15.14); Haberkorn & Prengaman, "Former Guantánamo Detainees Quit Protest at U.S. Embassy in Uruguay," MH (5.20.15); Rosenberg, "Guantánamo Medics: Forced-Feedings Aren't Torture," MH (9.26.14).

128 Savage, "U.S. Report Addresses Concern over Obama's Plan to Close Guantánamo," NYT (5.16.14); Gerstein, "White House Again Threatens Veto over Guantánamo Limits," Politico (5.21.14); Cassata, "Obama Win on Guantánamo Prison May Be Short-Lived," MH (5.23.14); Cipriano, "Poll: Most Oppose Closing Guantánamo Prison," Real Clear Politics (5.27.14); Savage & Cooper, "Under Pressure, Hagel Promises to Act on Guantánamo Transfers," NYT (5.30.14); Marcos, "House Rejects Bid to Allow Gitmo Transfer," *The Hill* (5.30.14); Savage, "Decaying Guantánamo Defies Closing Plans," NYT (9.1.14); "Limbo and Cruelty at Guantánamo," NYT (9.7.14); Rosenberg, "Estonia Agrees to Resettle a Guantánamo Detainee," MH (10.10.14); Firestone, "Pat Roberts's Latest Campaign Tactic: Guantánamo Fear-Mongering," NYT

(10.28.14); Marcos, "House Republican Urges Administration to Stop Gitmo Transfers," *The Hill* (11.3.14); Savage, "Kuwaiti Released from Guantánamo under New Review System," NYT (11.6.14); Cooper, "Hagel Resigns under Pressure as Global Crises Test Pentagon," NYT (11.25.14); Gerstein, "Guantánamo Added to White-House-Hagel Friction," Politico (11.25.14); Barnes & Crittenden, "Pentagon Legislation Won't Include Language Allowing Guantánamo Closure," WSJ (12.1.14); "Congress Deals Blow to Plan to Shut Guantánamo Prison," Reuters (12.1.14); Collinson, "McCain Prepared to Help Obama Close Guantánamo," CNN (12.14.14); Sink, "Obama on Gitmo: 'I'm Going to Be Doing Everything I Can to Close It,'" *The Hill* (12.22.14); Cooper, "Cliff Sloan, Guantánamo Envoy, Quits amid Delays in Prisoner Releases," NYT (12.22.14); Ryan & Goldman, "U.S. Prepares to Accelerate Detainee Transfers from Guantánamo Bay Prison," WP (12.24.14); Sloan, "The Path to Closing Guantánamo," NYT (1.6.15); Gerstein, "Even in Legacy Mode, Obama's Unlikely to Close Gitmo," Politico (1.12.15); "Dempsey Thinks U.S. Can Do More to Fight Terror, Backs Closing Guantánamo," Fox News (1.11.15); Lenhert, "I Helped Create Gitmo. Now I Want to Shut it Down," Politico (1.11.15).

129 Cassata, "Top GOP Senators Look to Restrict Obama on Guantánamo," AP (1.13.15); Cooper, "U.S. Moves Five Yemenis from Guantánamo," NYT (1.15.15); Speier, "Guantánamo Prison Is Wasteful and Un-American. Shut It Down," WP (1.16.15); Wong, "GOP Senators Want Greater Transparency on Gitmo Transfers," *The Hill* (1.1.5.15); "Perpetuating Guantánamo's Travesty," NYT (1.18.15); Rosenberg, "Obama to Congress: Guantánamo Prison Makes No Sense," MH (1.21.15); "Sen. Cotton Unloads on Guantánamo," Real Clear Politics (2.5.15); Reichmann, "Fiery Debate Continues in Senate over Guantánamo Prison," MH (2.5.15); Levine, "Tom Cotton: U.S. Should Be 'Proud' of How It Treats Guantánamo Detainees," HuffPost (2.9.15); Reichmann, "Gitmo Prison Closure Hampered by Freed Detainee's Turn to IS," AP (2.11.15); Ryan & Tate, "Senate Measure Would Sink Obama's Plan for Closing Guantánamo," WP (2.12.15); Foster & Parker, "Should All Gitmo Detainees 'Rot in Hell'?" *The Hill* (2.16.15); Good, "Marco Rubio Would Reopen Gitmo, Reverse Obama Foreign Policy," ABC News (4.13.15).

130 Ryan & Goldman, "Facing Threat in Congress, Pentagon Races to Resettle Guantánamo Inmates," WP (4.22.15); Rosenberg, "Stage Not Yet Set for Resumption of Guantánamo Detainee Releases," MH (4.23.15); Rosenberg, "GOP's First Draft of Defense Policy Could Stifle Guantánamo," MH (4.28.15); Wong, "House Panel Passes $612b Defense Bill," *The Hill* (4.30.15); Rosenberg, "Defense Bill Adds Restrictions on Transfers from Guantánamo," MH (5.1.15); O'Toole, "McCain Brokers Compromise that Would Let Obama Close Gitmo," Defense One (5.15.15); Marcos, "House Rejects Bid to Close Gitmo," *The Hill* (5.14.15); Marcos, "House Rejects Allowing Gitmo Transfers," *The Hill* (6.3.15); Carey, "Senate Showdown on Guantánamo," *The Hill*

(6.5.15); Ryan & deBonis, "Senate Passage of Defense Bill Sets Stage for Showdown with White House," WP (6.19.15); Carney, "McCain Expects Pentagon Plan on Closing Gitmo," *The Hill* (6.18.15); Savage, "Obama's Plan for Guantánamo Is Seen Faltering," NYT (7.22.15); "Brennan, Ash Carter: Not Confident Gitmo Can Be Closed by End of Obama's Presidency," CBS News (6.23.15); O'Toole, "White House in 'Final Stages' of Plan to Close Guantánamo," Defense One (7.22.15); Wong, "Obama Aide Outlines Plan to Close Gitmo," *The Hill* (7.27.15); "While Guantánamo Logjam Endures, Some Prisoners Could Be Freed," NYT (7.30.15); Spetalnick & Rohde, "U.S. Steps Up Efforts to Meet Obama's Goal to Close Guantánamo Prison," Reuters (8.7.15); Mak & Youssef, "The Pentagon Is Keeping Half of Gitmo Locked up – Against the White House's Wishes," Daily Beast (8.9.15); Goldman & Ryan, "Issue of Where to Move Guantánamo Detainees Threatens Closure Plan," WP (8.10.15); Rosenberg, "Pentagon Surveying Potential U.S. 'Guantánamo North' Lockups," MH (8.15.15); Savage, "U.S. Is Poised to Oppose Freeing Guantánamo Hunger Striker," NYT (8.15.15); Resnikoff, "South Carolina Governor Vows to Block Gitmo Prisoner Transfer," Al Jazeera America (8.20.15); O'Toole, "As Search for 'Gitmo North' Heats Up, Lawmakers Go Full NIMBY," Defense One (9.11.15); Baldor, "Bid to Shut Guantánamo Roils Pentagon, White House, Congress," MH (9.12.15); "How to Close Guantánamo," NYT (9.20.15); Wright, "White House Reiterates NDAA Veto Threat," Politico (9.30.15); Rosenberg, "Defense Legislation Forbids Moving Guantánamo Captives to U.S. and Returning Base to Cuba," MH (10.1.15); Wong, "Pentagon Chief Recommends Veto of Defense Policy Bill," *The Hill* (9.30.15); Savage, "U.S. Studies Moving Guantánamo Detainees to Colorado Prison," NYT (10.3.15).

131 Demirjian, "Defense Policy Bill Advances in the Senate," WP (10.6.15); "Mr. Obama Is Right to Veto Defense Bill," NYT (10.23.15); Zengerle, "U.S. Budget Deal Could Complicate Plans to Close Guantánamo," Reuters (10.27.15); Demirjian, "New Defense Authorization Deal Struck," WP (11.3.15); O'Toole, "White House Won't Rule Out Vetoing Defense Authorization Bill (Again) over Guantánamo," Defense One (11.4.15); Reichmann, "Kansas Senator Puts Hold on Obama Nominee over Guantánamo," MH (11.4.15); Feinstein, "Let's Finally Close Guantánamo," NYT (11.5.15); O'Brien, "Obama Unlikely to Veto NDAA a Second Time over Gitmo," CQ *Roll Call* (11.5.15); Kadidal, Letter to the Editor, NYT (11.5.15); Zengerle, "Revised U.S. Defense Bill Sails through House, despite Guantánamo," Reuters (11.5.15); Hattem, "McCain: 'Disgraceful' That Obama Would Close Gitmo Unilaterally," *The Hill* (11.5.15); Baldor & Hennessey, "Pentagon Plan to Close Guantánamo Expected in Coming Week," MH (11.7.15); Sullivan, "Homeland Chairman Predicts Obama Will Unilaterally Close Gitmo," *The Hill* (11.8.15); Hawkins, Letter to the Editor, NYT (11.10.15); Kheel, "Kansas Lawmakers Push for Guantánamo Visit," *The Hill* (11.10.15); Carney, "Senate Republicans Tie Hillary Clinton to Gitmo

Fight," *The Hill* (11.10.15); Herszenhorn, "Senate Passes Military Bill that Bans Transfers of Guantánamo Detainees," NYT (11.11.15); Wong, "Ryan: Obama Can't Unilaterally Close Gitmo," *The Hill* (11.11.15); Demirjian, "Democrats Hint They Are Ready for Obama to Shut Down Gitmo Alone," WP (11.12.15).

132 Craig & Sloan, "The President Doesn't Need Congress's Permission to Close Guantánamo," WP (11.6.15); Berman, "John Paul Stevens Says Some Guantánamo Bay Detainees Should Be Given Reparations," WP (5.6.15); Hoskinson, "House Committee Says Gitmo Detainees Released to Uruguay Still a Threat," Townhall.com (5.6.15); Reichmann, "Critics: Changing Guantánamo Prison's Zip Code Isn't a Fix," MH (11.13.15).

133 Verkaik, "The Last Briton in Guantánamo," *Daily Mail* (10.6.12); Pecquet, "Britain Hopeful for Guantánamo Detainee's Release after U.S. Election," *The Hill* (10.30.12); Aamer, "I'm a Bit of a Professional Hunger Striker, I've Done It So Often," *New Statesman* (April 2013); Bravin, "U.K. Delegation Presses for Release of U.K. Resident Held at Guantánamo Bay," WSJ (5.21.15); Drury, "Special Relationship between UK and US 'at Risk' over Case of Guantánamo Briton Shaker Aamer," *Daily Mail* (5.23.15); Corbyn, Davis, Mitchell & Slaughter, "Obama's Slap in Britain's Face," NYT (6.7.15); Savage & Erlanger, "Shaker Aamer Is Released from Guantánamo Prison after 13 Years," NYT (10.30.15); Goldman, "Former British Resident Released from Prison at Guantánamo Bay," WP (10.30.15); "Open Letter to Barack Obama Requesting Return of Shaker Aamer to the UK," G (7.3.15); Savage, "Pentagon Says High-Profile Guantánamo Detainee Will Be Sent to Britain," NYT (9.26.15); Goldman & Ryan, "Shaker Aamer, Longtime Guantánamo Bay Detainee, to Be Freed to Britain," WP (9.26.15); Cobain, "Shaker Aamer 'Suffered Profound Disruption of His Life' at Guantánamo," G (11.2.15); "Ex-UK Guantánamo Detainee Denounces Extremism," NYT (12.18.15); "Guantánamo Briton Shaker Aamer Relives his 14-Year Nightmare of Savage Abuses," *Daily Mail* (12.14.15); Wong, "GOP: Carter Overruled Joint Chiefs Chairman on Gitmo Transfer," *The Hill* (2.24.16).

134 "U.S. Suspects More Freed Guantánamo Inmates Returned to Battlefield," Reuters (9.3.15); ODNI, Summary of the Reengagement of Detainees Formerly Held at Guantánamo Bay, Cuba.

135 CCR News Release (9.11.15); Rosenberg, "Federal Judge: Guantánamo Hunger Striker May Be Entitled to Medical Review," MH (10.15.15); Levinson & Rohde, "Pentagon Thwarts Obama's Effort to Close Guantánamo," Reuters (12.29.15); "The Pentagon's Insubordination on Guantánamo," NYT (1.3.16); Savage, "9 Guantánamo Prisoners from Yemen Are Sent to Saudi Arabia," NYT (4.16.16); Farah (2016).

136 Rosenberg, "Guantánamo Parole Board Clears Afghan," MH (10.7.15); Goldman, "Mauritanian Detainee Held at Guantánamo Bay Is Transferred Home," WP (10.29.15); "Guantánamo Releases Ramp Up," NYT (11.2.15); Rosenberg, "Guantánamo Parole Board Clears Yemeni 'Forever Prisoner,'" MH (11.3.15); Rosenberg, "Pentagon Team in

Colorado in Quest for 'Guantánamo North,'" MH (10.13.15); Healy, "Prison Town in Colorado Doesn't Want Guantánamo Detainees," NYT (11.17.15); O'Toole, "White House Delays Plan to Close Guantánamo, Again," Defense One (11.16.15); Gerstein, "Lynch Douses Talk of Obama Going Rogue on Guantánamo Closure," Politico (11.18.15); Bender & Toosi, "Obama Administration Delays Gitmo Closure Plan," Politico (11.19.15); Hattem, "States Hint at Lawsuits over Gitmo Detainees," *The Hill* (11.19.15); Nakamura, "In Wake of Paris Attacks, Obama Vows to Close Guantánamo," WP (11.19.15); Rosenberg, "Obama: Paris Doesn't Change Determination to Close Guantánamo Prison," MH (11.19.15); "Obama Cannot Go It Alone on Guantánamo," WP (11.21.15); Roberts, "Obama Administration Admits Review of Guantánamo Cases Will Take Years," G (11.24.15); Lubold & Lee, "White House Rejects Pentagon Plan to Close Guantánamo As Too Costly," WSJ (12.1.15); Savage, "Frustrated in Efforts to Close Guantánamo Prison, Officials Look to Reduce Population," NYT (12.3.15); Wheeler, "Kansas Officials to Obama: Don't Close Guantánamo," *The Hill* (12.14.15).

137 Savage, "Obama Signs Defense Bill, Despite Guantánamo Objections," NYT (11.26.15).

138 Ryan, "Saudi Inmate Repatriated as Protesters Mark Guantánamo Milestone," WP (1.12.16); Ackerman, "Inbuilt Delays in Case Reviews Make Prospect of Guantánamo Closure Recede," G (1.11.16); Smith, "Mitch McConnell Pledges to Fight to Keep Guantánamo Bay Open," G (1.13.16); Ryan & Goldman, "In Milestone, Guantánamo Population to Fall Below 100 for First Time in 14 Years," WP (1.14.16); Savage, "Guantánamo Population Drops to 90 after 10 Prisoners Go to Oman," NYT (1.15.16).

139 O'Toole, "Pentagon Sends Obama Plan to Close Guantánamo, Move Detainees to US," Defense One (1.14.16); Kheel, "Kansas Congressman Demands to See Obama's Guantánamo Plans," *The Hill* (1.22.16); Kheel, "Republican Wants Price Tag for Closing Gitmo," *The Hill* (1.27.16); Wong, "Senators Threaten to Cut Aid for Ghana if Gitmo Detainees Escape," *The Hill* (2.1.16); Kheel, "GOP Chairman Warns Obama of Deadline for Gitmo Plan," *The Hill* (2.4.16); French, "House Republicans Eye Potential Lawsuit on Gitmo Transfers," Politico (2.10.16); Wong, "Joint Staff: We Won't Break Law to Close Gitmo," *The Hill* (2.16.16).

140 "The Plan to Shut Down Guantánamo," NYT (2.23.16).

141 England, "The Defense Secretary Should Refuse to Release Guantánamo Detainees. Here's Why," WP (2.6.16).

142 Remarks by the President on Plan to Close the Prison at Guantánamo Bay, White House (2.23.16); DoD, Plan for Closing the Guantánamo Bay Detention Facility (2.23.16); Savage & Davis, "Obama Sends Plan to Close Guantánamo to Congress," NYT (2.23.16); Kheel, "Democrats Call for Congress to Consider Obama's Gitmo Plan," *The Hill* (2.23.16); Kheel, "Human Rights Groups Pan Obama's Gitmo Proposal," *The Hill* (2.23.16); Marcos, "GOP Lawmaker Introduces Resolution to Authorize Gitmo Lawsuit," *The Hill* (2.23.16); Tailor, "Speaker Paul Ryan: Legal

Steps to Stop Obama from Closing Guantánamo Prison," MH (2.24.16); Hattem, "Attorney General: Transferring Detainees to US Still Illegal," *The Hill* (2.24.16); Wong, "GOP: Carter Overruled Joint Chiefs Chairman on Gitmo Transfer," *The Hill* (2.24.16); Kheel, "Armed Services Republicans: Obama's 'Gibberish' Gitmo Plan Will Get Hearings," *The Hill* (2.24.16); Wong, "Overnight Defense: Officials Grilled on Gitmo, Budget," *The Hill* (2.25.16); Wong, "How the White House Lost McCain on Gitmo," *The Hill* (2.25.16); O'Toole, "Hillary Clinton's Preemptive Strike on the GOP over Guantánamo," FP (2.25.16); Carney, "Democratic Candidates Buck Obama on Guantánamo," *The Hill* (2.27.16); Wong, "Pentagon Chief: Gitmo Detainees Can't Come to US 'Unless Congress Acts,'" *The Hill* (3.1.16); Kheel, "GOP Rep Seeks to Prevent Turning over Guantánamo to Cuba," *The Hill* (3.2.16); Kheel, "House Republican: Obama 'Underestimates' Gitmo Recidivism," *The Hill* (3.2.16); Hensch, "Poll: Over Half of Americans Oppose Closing Gitmo," *The Hill* (3.4.16); CNN/ORC International Poll (3.4.16); Savage, "Several More Ex-Guantánamo Detainees Suspected of Militancy, Report Says," NYT (3.8.16); Wong, "Overnight Defense: GOP Digs In against Gitmo Plan," *The Hill* (3.8.16); Wong, "GOP Introduces Resolution Rejecting Obama's Gitmo Plan," *The Hill* (3.8.16); Hattem, "Lynch: No Gitmo Transfers to US without Change in Law," *The Hill* (3.9.16); Wong, "GOP Resolution Calls for Sending Captured ISIS Fighters to Gitmo," *The Hill* (3.10.16); Lamothe, "Pentagon Official: Release of Guantánamo Detainees Has Led to American Deaths," WP (3.24.16); Rosenberg, "Guantánamo Limbo: Dozens Still Waiting for First Review Obama Ordered in 2011," MH (3.28.16); Savage, "2 Libyan Guantánamo Inmates Are Transferred to Senegal," NYT (4.4.16); Goldman & Ryan, "At Least 12 Released Guantánamo Detainees Implicated in Attacks on Americans," WP (6.8.16).

143 Carney, "Senate GOP Would Halt Gitmo Transfers," *The Hill* (4.5.16); Savage, "Republicans Seize on Guantánamo Fears in Re-election Races," NYT (4.8.16); Carney, "GOP Senator Wants to Tie Gitmo Fight to Aviation Bill," *The Hill* (4.8.16); Kheel, "House GOP Bill Would Freeze Gitmo Transfers," *The Hill* (4.11.16); Carney, "GOP Looks to Tighten Rules for Gitmo Transfers," *The Hill* (4.12.16); Savage, "9 Guantánamo Prisoners from Yemen Are Sent to Saudi Arabia," NYT (4.16.16); Wong, "GOP Angry about Weekend Gitmo Transfer," *The Hill* (4.18.16); Wong, "Administration Speeds Up Review Boards for Guantánamo Detainees," *The Hill* (5.3.16); Schmidt, "Army Secretary Nomination Is Blocked by a G.O.P. Senator," NYT (5.11.16); Savage, "Measure Would Let Guantánamo Detainees Enter Pleas in Civilian Court," NYT (5.13.16); Schmidt & Savage, "Eric Fanning Confirmed as Secretary of the Army," NYT (5.18.16); Kheel, "Senate Defense Bill Includes Funding to Design Guantánamo Alternative," *The Hill* (5.20.16); Carney, "Senate GOP Gears Up for Fight over Gitmo Transfers," *The Hill* (5.24.16); Wong, "GOP Senators Propose Sending ISIS Fighters to Gitmo," *The Hill* (5.25.16); Demirjian, "Senate Passes Defense Bill, Setting Up Tough

Negotiations with the House over Budget and Social Policy Issues," WP (6.14.16); Kheel, "House Votes to Ban All Gitmo Transfers," *The Hill* (6.15.16); Ryan & DeYoung, "White House, Citing Long List of Objections, Threatens Veto of Defense Bill," WP (6.7.16); "The Broken Promise of Closing Guantánamo," NYT (6.20.16); Levinson, "Justice Department Opposes New Obama Proposal on Guantánamo," Reuters (6.21.16); Tlisova, "Russian Ex-Guantánamo Detainee Linked to Turkey Airport Attack," VOA (7.5.16); Savage & Romero, "Disappearance of Ex-Guantánamo Bay Prisoner Raises Alarms," NYT (7.7.16); Savage, "Transfer Policy Questioned after Former Guantánamo Detainee Goes Missing," NYT (7.8.16); Ryan, "Former Guantánamo Detainee in Venezuela, Hopes to Travel to Turkey," WP (7.29.16); "US Transfers 15 Prisoners from Guantanamo Bay to UAE," Al Bawaba (8.16.16); "Who's Still Held at Guantánamo," MH (8.24.16); Currier & Williams, "Who's Left at Guantánamo? Fates of Dozens of Prisoners Are Undecided," The Intercept (9.9.16); "Ex-Guantanamo Detainee Leaves Uruguay for South Africa," NYT (12.16.16); "South Africa Turns Away Former Hunger-Striking Guantanamo Detainee," MH (12.16.16).

144 Rosenberg, "Guantanamo Parole Board Oks Release of Afghan, Approves 25th 'Forever Prisoner,'" MH (10.17.16); Rosenberg, "Parole Board Says 2 Former CIA Prisoners Are Too Dangerous to Leave Guantanamo," MH (10.25.16); Rosenberg, "Parole Board Declares Never-Charged Abu Zubaydah a Forever Prisoner," MH (10.27.16); Rosenberg, "Guantanamo Parole Board Approves 21st Captive for Release, 29th 'Forever Prisoner,'" MH (11.29.16); Rosenberg, "Guantanamo Board Approves Release of Another Yemeni 'Forever Prisoner,'" MH (12.10.16).

145 Savage, "Guantanamo Detainee Is Sent to Cape Verde in First Transfer since Trump Victory," NYT (12.5.16); Savage, "4 Yemeni Detainees at Guantanamo Are Transferred to Saudi Arabia," NYT (1.5.17); Savage, "10 More Detainees Are Transferred from Guantanamo Prison," NYT (1.16.17).

146 Trump (11.14.16); "Obama Blames Congress for Not Closing Guantanamo," MH (11.15.16); "Trump Taps Kelley for Homeland Security, Third General for Top Post," Reuters (12.7.16); Ordonez, "Trump Pick to Head Homeland Security Oversaw Guantanamo Prison," MH (12.7.16); "The Failure to Close Guantanamo," WP (1.3.17); Lamothe, "Trump Says No More Detainees Should Be Released from Guantanamo Bay Prison," WP (1.3.17); "The Clock Is Ticking on Guantanamo," NYT (1.4.17); Lederman, "Lawmaker: Intelligence Shows Gitmo Transfers Aiming to Rejoin Fight," MH (1.10.17); "Guantánamo Remains a Stain on America's Reputation," *Economist* (1.14.17); Obama to House Speaker and Senate President Pro Tem (1.19.17); Savage, "Trump Poised to Lift Ban on C.I.A. 'Black Site' Prisons," NYT (1.25.17); Savage, "White House Pulls Back from Bid to Reopen C.I.A. 'Black Site' Prisons," NYT (2.4.17); Savage, "ISIS Detainees May Be Held at Guantanamo, Document Shows," NYT (2.8.17); Rosenberg, "GOP Senators Write to Trump on Guantanamo Prison: Keep It, Grow It," MH (2.14.17); Savage, "The Fight over Guantanamo's Parole Board,

Explained," NYT (2.18.17); Savage, "President Has It All Wrong on Guantanamo," NYT (2.28.17); Savage, "Sessions Say Guantanamo Is a 'Very Fine Place' for New Suspects," NYT (3.10.17).

147 For more on the lawyers, see Prabhat (2016: chap. 4).

148 Savage, "Military Is Waiting Longer before Force-Feeding Hunger Strikers, Detainees Say," NYT (10.11.17); Qassim, "I Am in Guantanamo Bay. The US government Is Starving Me to Death," G (10.13.17); Rabbani, "Dear President Trump, Close Guantanamo Bay and Give Us a Fair Trial," *Newsweek* (10.12.17); Khan, "A Pakistan Man Is Starving to Death in Guantanamo. We Have a Duty to Stop It," WP (10.19.17).

149 Transfer data from "The Guantánamo Docket," NYT www.projects.nytimes/com/Guantánamo/timeline (last accessed January 1, 2015).

150 When George H.W. Bush opposed Michael Dukakis in the 1988 presidential election, Bush successfully used the fact that Horton had been released on parole during Dukakis's governorship of Massachusetts and then committed more crimes to smear Dukakis as soft on crime – and defeated him in the election. Dukakis had nothing to do with the release.

151 For a careful analysis of the length of detention, see Dorison (2011).

152 Bruck (2016).

153 Ibid.

154 On efforts by US allies to protect their citizens from abuse, see Banham (2017).

CHAPTER 4 INTERROGATION

1 The definitive work on torture is Rejali (2007). See also Otterman (2007); Stritzke et al. (2009); Pallitto (2011). For earlier US involvement in torture, see Harbury (2005). For legal and ethical analyses, see Greenberg (2006); Jaffer & Singh (2007); Gross (2009); Cohn (2010); Fried & Fried (2010); Kelly (2011); Lokaneeta (2011); Shipler (2012); Johns (2013); Luban (2014); Gordon (2014). For analyses of media representations, see Flynn & Salek (2012).

2 Bush, "Memorandum: Humane Treatment of al Qaeda and Taliban Detainees" (2.7.02); Greenberg & Dratel (2005: Memos 8, 10, 18, 21, 24–26); Lewis, "Military's Opposition to Harsh Interrogation is Outlined," NYT (7.28.05); Benjamin, "Bush's Top General Quashed Torture Dissent," Salon (6.30.08); See Cole (2009); Denbeaux et al. (2015).

3 Priest & Gellman, "U.S. Decries Abuse but Defends Interrogations," WP (12.26.02); Gall, "Threats and Responses: Prisoners," NYT (3.4.03); HRW (2004). See also Mackey & Miller (2004); Matthews (2008); Cole (2009); Parry (2010); Umansky (2014); Mazzetti & Shane, "Debate over Interrogation Methods Sharply Divided the Bush White House," NYT (5.4.09); Ladin, "In Secret Email, CIA's Chief Lawyer Mocked 'Pesky Little International Obligations,'" ACLU (7.21.16); Arsenault (2017). For accounts by soldiers who conducted EITs, see Sharrock (2010); McKelvey (2007).

4 Early reports of abusive interrogation included Smith, "U.S. Account of a Battle with Taliban Is Disputed," NYT (1.27.02); Schmitt & Shanker, "U.S. Releasing 27 Captured in Raid," NYT (2.7.02); Gall, "Released Afghans Tell of Beatings," NYT (2.11.02); Knickmeyer, "Survivors of Raid by U.S. Forces Say Victims Were Among America's Best Friends," AP (2.6.02); Moore, "Villagers Released by American Troops Say They Were Beaten, Kept in 'Cage,'" WP (2.11.02); Slater, "U.S. Forces Beat Afghans after Deadly Assault, Ex-Prisoners Say," LAT (2.11.02); Hanley, "Finally Freed, Afghans Say They Were Kicked and Abused in U.S. Hands," AP (3.23.02). I am grateful to John Sifton for these citations. See Umansky (2006).

5 Gonzales, "The Rule of Law and the Rules of War," NYT (5.15.04); Lewis, "Justice Memos Explained How to Skip Prisoner Rights," NYT (5.21.04); Yoo, "Terrorists Have No Geneva Rights," WSJ (5.26.04); New York City Bar's Committees on International Human Rights and on Military Affairs and Justice, Supplement to Human Rights Standards Applicable to the United States' Interrogation of Detainees (6.4.04); Priest & Smith, "Memo Offered Justification for Use of Torture," WP (6.8.04); Senate Judiciary Committee, Hearing (6.8.04); Allen & Priest, "Memo on Torture Draws Focus to Bush," WP (6.9.04); White House Press Conference (6.10.04); Priest, "Justice Dept. Memo Says Torture 'May Be Justified,'" WP (6.13.04); Ignatius, "Small Comfort," WP (6.15.04); Clark & Mertus, "Torturing the Law," WP (6.20.04); Locy & Biskupic, "Interrogation Memo to Be Replaced," *USA Today* (6.23.04); Allen & Schmidt, "Memo on Interrogation Tactics Is Disavowed," WP (6.23.04); Priest, "CIA Puts Harsh Tactics on Hold," WP (6.27.04); Wedgwood & Woolsey, "Law and Torture," WSJ (6.28.04); Report to the ABA House of Delgates (8.9.04) www.abanow.org/2004/08/aba-house-of-delegates-torture-resolution-2004/ (last accessed March 5, 2018).

6 "Red Cross Finds Detainee Abuse in Guantánamo," NYT (11.30.04).

7 "Gonzales Will Face Questions on Iraq and the Death Penalty," *Belleville News-Democrat* (11.12.04); "Senate Judiciary Confirmation Hearing," NYT 1.6.05); Lichtblau, "Gonzales Says '02 Policy on Detainees Doesn't Bind C.I.A.," NYT (1.19.05); Richter & Schmitt, "Cabinet Votes Stall in Senate," LAT (1.20.05); Lichtblau, "Senate Panel Delays Vote on Gonzales," NYT (1.20.05).

8 Efron, "Torture Becomes a Matter of Definition," LAT (1.23.05); "The Wrong Attorney General," NYT (1.20.05); Mayer, "Outsourcing Torture," *The New Yorker* (2.14 & 21.05).

9 Lichtblau, "Senate Panel Approves Gonzales on a Party-Line Vote," NYT (1.27.05); Emails from PFAW Activist Network (1.31.05), ACLU of Southern California Take Action (2.1.05); Alliance for Justice (2.1.05); MoveOn.org (2.1.05); Lichtblau, "Democrats Oppose a Gonzales Filibuster," NYT (2.2.05); Reynolds, "Democrats Extend Debate on Gonzales," LAT (2.2.05); "Senate Plans to Confirm Gonzales," NYT (2.3.05); "GOP Sees Breakthrough in Gonzales Confirmation," LAT (2.3.05); Reynolds, "Senate Ratifies Attorney General," LAT (2.4.05); Lichtblau, "Gonzales Is Confirmed in a Closer Vote Than Expected," NYT (2.4.05); "The Senate and Mr. Gonzales," NYT (2.4.05).

10 Shane, Johnston & Risen, "Secret U.S. Endorsement of Severe Interrogations," NYT (10.4.07); Greenberg & de Vogue, "Former Attorney General Accused of Playing Politics with Justice," ABC News (6.19.08); Shane & Johnston, "U.S. Lawyers Agreed on Legality of Brutal Tactic," NYT (6.7.09); Froomkin, "How Cheney Bent DoJ to His Will," WP (6.8.09).

11 "CIA Directors Stands Behind U.S. Interrogation Practices," LAT (3.18.05); Jehl, "Questions Left By C.I.A. Chief On Torture Use," NYT (3.18.05); Jehl, "C.I.A. Says Approved Methods of Questioning Are All Legal," NYT (3.19.05); Letter to the Editor, NYT (3.21.05).

12 Lichtblau, "Congress Adopts Restriction on Treatment of Detainees," NYT (5.11.05); White, "Military Lawyers Fought Policy on Interrogations," WP (7.15.05).

13 Earle, "Senate Republicans Push Military Prison Oversight," *The Hill* (6.29.05); "Detainee Rules May Lead to Veto," LAT (7.22.05); White & Smith, "White House Aims to Block Legislation on Detainees," WP (7.23.05); Schmitt, "Cheney Working to Block Legislation on Detainees," NYT (7.24.05); HRF letter (7.25.05); Kuhnhenn, "Frist Pulls Defense Bill to Avoid Votes on Treatment of Detainees," KnightRidder Newspapers (7.26.05); "GOP Pushes Detainee Treatment Rules over Veto Threat," LAT (7.26.05); Gerstenzang, "GOP Pressure over Detainee Policy Leads to Defense Bill Delay," LAT (7.27.05).

14 Lichtblau, "Justice Nominee Is Questioned on Department Torture Policy," NYT (7.25.05); Lichtblau, "Bush's Nominee for No. 2 Justice Post Withdraws," NYT (10.8.05).

15 HRW (2005); Zagorin, "Pattern of Abuse," *Time* (9.23.05); Serrano, "Officer's Road Led Him Outside Army," LAT (9.25.05); Schmitt, "3 in 82nd Airborne Say Beating Iraqi Prisoners Was Routine," NYT (9.24.05); "World Briefing," NYT (9.26.05); Serrano, "New Iraq Abuse Allegations Get McCain Moving," LAT (9.26.05); White, "Reservist Sentenced to 3 Years for Abu Ghraib Abuse," WP (9.28.05); Schmitt, "Officer Criticizes Detainee Abuse Inquiry," NYT (9.28.05); Fishback Letter to McCain, WP (9.28.05); Schmitt, "Soldier Reports More Abuses to Senator," NYT (10.5.05).

16 Sidoti, "Senate Approves Detainee Treatment Rules," WP (10.5.05); Babington & Murray, "Senate Supports Interrogation Limits," WP (10.6.05); Schmitt, "Senate Moves to Protect Military Prisoners Despite Veto Threat," NYT (10.6.05); Lederman, "Beware the 'Augmented' McCain Amendment" (10.15.05) https://balkin.blogspot.co.uk/2005/10/beware-augmented-mccain-amendment.html (last accessed February 18, 2018).

17 "Binding the Hands of Torturers," NYT (10.8.05); "End the Abuse," WP (10.7.05), US Conference of Catholic Bishops, Letter (10.14.05).

18 Smith & White, "Cheney Plan Exempts CIA from Bill Barring Abuse of Detainees," WP (10.25.05); Schmitt, "Exception Sought in Detainee Abuse Ban," NYT (10.25.05); Klaidman & Isikoff, "Cheney in the Bunker," *Newsweek* (11.14.05); "John Negroponte Ducks Questions

on Vice President Cheney's Lobbying on Capitol Hill to Have CIA Exempted from McCain Legislation Banning Mistreatment of Detainees," *Time* (11.6.05); "Vice President for Torture," WP (10.26.05); "Legalized Torture, Reloaded," NYT (10.26.05); Conan, "Analysis: Administration Wants CIA Exemption on Torture Bill," NPR (10.26.05); "Cheney Urges Exception to Torture Ban for CIA," MSNBC (11.4.05).

19 Schmitt, "House Delays Vote on U.S. Treatment of Terrorism Suspects," NYT (11.4.05); Letter to the Editor, NYT (11.4.05); Hirsch, "Truth about Torture," *Newsweek* (11.7.05); Hendren, "McCain Vows to Add Torture Ban to All Major Senate Legislation," LAT (11.5.05); Schmitt, "Senate Votes Again for Ban on Abusing Prisoners," NYT (11.5.05); "Hagel: Torture Exemption Would Be Mistake," AP (11.6.05); Schmitt & Golden, "Pentagon Plans Tighter Control of Interrogation," NYT (11.8.05); DoD Directive #5115.09 (11.3.05); McCain, "Torture's Terrible Toll," *Newsweek* (11.21.05).

20 Partnership for a Secure America, "Bipartisan Group Condemns Cruel Treatment of Prisoners" (11.5.05); www.pbs.org/newshour/bb/middle-east/july-dec05/pace_11.07.html (last accessed January 1, 2006); www.whitehouse.gov/news/releases/2005/11/20051108.html (last accessed January 1, 2006); Gerlernter, "When Torture Is the Only Option," LAT (11.11.05); Johnson, "… And Why It Should Never Be One," LAT (11.11.05); "A Tortured Debate," WSJ (11.12.05).

21 Jehl, "Report Warned C.I.A. on Tactics in Interrogation," NYT (11.9.05).

22 "Former U.S. Army Interrogator Describes the Harsh Techniques He Used in Iraq," *Democracy Now!* (11.15.05); Lagouranis & Mikaelian (2007).

23 Ross & Esposito, "CIA's Harsh Interrogation Techniques Described," ABC News (11.18.05); Diamond, "CIA Chief: Interrogation Methods 'Unique' but Legal," *USA Today* (11.20.05); HRW, "CIA Whitewashing Torture" (11.21.05); "Director for Torture," WP A18 (11.23.05); Oliver, "'They Couldn't Take Away my Dignity,'" G (11.19.05); see also Begg & Brittain (2006).

24 "9/11 Commissioners Fault Administration," NYT (11.14.05); Kean, "Report on the Status of 9/11 Commission Recommendations. Part III: Foreign Policy, Public Diplomacy, and Nonproliferation" (11.14.05); Eggan, "U.S. Is Given Falling Grades by 9/11 Panel," WP (12.6.05).

25 "Ex-CIA Boss: Cheney Is 'Vice President for Torture,'" CNN (11.18.05); "Powell Aide: Torture 'Guidance' from VP," CNN (11.20.05); Massimino, "Heading toward the 'Dark Side,'" LAT (11.21.05); "What Congress Should Do," WP (12.5.05); Graham, "Rules for Our War," WP (12.6.05); Schmitt & Sanger, "White House and McCain Near Deal on Torture," NYT (12.7.05).

26 "Illegal, Immoral and Pointless," NYT (12.10.05); Rifkin & Casey, "The McCain Amendment Is Flawed," WSJ (12.10.05); "Torture and the Constitution," WP (12.11.05).

27 Hulse & Schmitt, "Negotiators Say Differences over Ban on Abuse Remain," NYT (12.12.05); Sanger & Schmitt, "Bush Says He's Confident that He and McCain Will Reach Agreement on Interrogation Policy," NYT (12.13.05); Knowlton, "Bush and McCain Reach Deal on Treatment of Terror Suspects," NYT (12.15.05); White & Babington, "House Supports Ban on Torture," WP (12.15.05); "White House Near Deal on Anti-Torture Measure," Reuters (12.15.05); Rogers, "Bush Accepts McCain's Torture-Ban Amendment," WSJ (12.16.05); White, "President Relents, Backs Torture Ban," WP (12.16.05); Schmitt, "President Backs McCain Measure on Inmate Abuse," NYT (12.16.05); "A Blow against Torture," WP (12.16.05); "Ban Torture, Period," NYT (12.16.05).

28 Sidoti, "House Approves Sweeping Defense Bill," WP (12.19.05); www.whitehouse.gov/news/releases/2005/12/20051230-8.html (last accessed January 15, 2006); Savage, "3 GOP Senators Blast Bush Plan to Bypass Torture Ban," BG (1.5.06); Brooks, "McCain to Bush: 'Don't Try It, Pal,'" LAT (1.6.06); "Unchecked Abuse," WP (1.11.06).

29 "Bush Urged to Specify U.S. Policy on Torture," LAT (1.20.06); "McCain Unsure if U.S. Interrogations Lawful," AP (1.27.06).

30 Mayer, "The Memo," *The New Yorker* (2.27.06); Mayer (2008: 213–37); Cloud, "Concerns Led to Revisions, Rumsfeld Said," NYT (2.22.06); see also Mora, Memorandum for IG, Dept. of Navy: Statement for the Record: Office of General Counsel Involvement in Interrogation Issues (7.7.04); "Memo: Pentagon Concerned About Legality of Interrogation Techniques," ABC News (6.15.05).

31 "Rice Denies U.S. Is World's Jailer," BBC News (3.31.06); AI (2006); Schmitt, "Few Punished in Abuse Cases," NYT (4.27.06); Brown, "Report Claims Torture Is Widespread at U.S. Jails Abroad," MH (4.27.06); Neumeister, "Army Knew of Iraq Abuse Claims," G (5.2.06).

32 "New Face, Old Evasion," WP (5.20.06).

33 Bolton, "Nominee Is Held Up by Graham," *The Hill* (5.24.06); Hernandez, "Bush Nominee Tries to Calm Torture Furor," NYT (7.12.12); Totenberg, "Detainee Questions Trip Federal Court Nominee," NPR's Morning Edition (7.12.06); Dowd, "He Let the Dogs Out!" NYT (7.12.06); "Abu Ghraib, Rewarded," NYT (7.17.06); Lewis, "New Democratic Majority Throws Bush's Judicial Nominations into Uncertainty," NYT (11.12.06); Savage, "Bush Revives Stalled Judicial Nominations," LAT (11.16.06); Lewis, "Bush to Put Nominations Back on Table," NYT (11.16.06); Lewis, "A Somber Annual Meeting for Conservative Lawyers," NYT (11.19.06); "A Symbolic Step on Judges," WP (11.17.06); "Hope for Bipartisan Nominations," LAT (11.24.06); Lewis, "Bush Drops Plans to Resubmit 3 Judicial Nominees," NYT (1.10.07); Savage & Weinstein, "4 White Flags Fly in Courts Fight," LAT (1.10.07); Smith, "4 Nominees to Appeals Courts Are Dropped," WP (1.10.07).

34 Schmitt, "Profile of Cambone," NYT (5.10.06); Barnes, "Army Rules Put on Hold," LAT (5.11.06); "Rumsfeld Reveals Split of Interrogations," NYT (5.18.06); Barnes, "Army Manual to Skip Geneva Detainee Rule,"

LAT (6.5.06); "No Defense for Degrading Prisoners," LAT (6.6.06); "Letters to Editor, "Detainee Interrogation Policy Is Bad for U.S.," LAT (6.7.06); Wright, "Soldiers Already Know What Is Right," Army 24 (June 2006); Schmitt, "Pentagon Rethinking Manual with Interrogation Methods," NYT (6.14.06); "Pentagon to Disclose Interrogation Tactics," NYT (6.14.06); DoD Deputy IG for Intelligence, Review of DoD-Directed Investigations of Detainee Abuse (8.25.06) (06-INTEL-10).

35 Army Field Manual for Human Intelligence Collector Operations (FM-2-222-3), Directive 2310.01E; Stolberg, "Looking to Elections, Bush and Democrats Spar on National Security," NYT (9.6.06); White, "New Rules of Interrogation Forbid Use of Harsh Tactics," WP (9.7.06); DoD Press Conference (9.7.06); Kaye, "How the U.S. Army's Field Manual Codified Torture – and Still Does," www.alternet.org/rights/117807 (last accessed February 18, 2018).

36 ODNI, Summary of the High Value Terrorist Detainee Program (probably 9.7.06); "President Discusses Creation of Military Commissions to Try Suspected Terrorists," White House Press Release (9.6.06).

37 Liptak, "Interrogation Methods Rejected by Military Win Bush's Support," NYT (9.8.06); Barnes, "CIA Can Still Get Tough on Detainees," LAT (9.8.06); "Ending the Lawlessness," WP (9.7.06); "Tortured Logic," LAT (9.13.06).

38 Schmitt, "Senate Panel Sends a Mixed Message on Wiretapping," LAT (9.14.06); Weisman, "GOP Leaders Back Bush on Wiretapping, Tribunals," WP (9.14.06); Lichtblau & Zernike, "Panel in Senate Backs Bush Plan for Monitoring," NYT (9.14.06); "A Crucial Choice," WP (9.14.06); Smith, "Behind the Debate, Controversial CIA Techniques," WP (9.16.06); "Torture by Mistake," WP (9.20.06).

39 "McCain Team Mocks Hillary Torture Loophole," *New York Daily News* (10.16.06); Abramowitz & Goldfarb, "Rove Road-Tests Tougher Attack on Democrats," WP (10.22.06).

40 Meek, "He Is Water-Tortured to Make Waves," *New York Daily News* (10.1.06); Margulies, "The More Subtle Kind of Torment," WP (10.2.06); Pincus, "Waterboarding Historically Controversial," WP (10.5.06); Rickard, "Interrogators Beware," WP (10.17.06).

41 Froomkin, "A Question Bush Can't Answer," WP (10.18.06).

42 Dedman, "Gitmo Interrogations Spark Battle over Tactics," MSNBC.com (10.24.06); Dedman, "Can the '20th Hijacker' of Sept. 11 Stand Trial?" MSNBC.com (10.24.06); for a fuller account, see Fallon (2017).

43 "Interview of the Vice President by Scott Hennen, WDAY at Radio Day at the White House (10.24.06) http://georgewbush-whitehouse.archives.gov/news/releases/2006/10/20061024-7.html (last accessed February 18, 2018); Eggen, "Cheney's Remarks Fuel Torture Debate," WP A9 (10.27.06); Landay, "Cheney Confirms that Detainees Were Subjected to Water-Boarding," McClatchy Newspapers (10.25.06); Lewis, "Furor over Cheney Remark on Tactics for Terror," NYT (10.28.06); Gerstenzang, "Cheney Calls Dunking of Terror Suspects a 'No-Brainer,'" LAT (10.28.06); Eggen, "Cheney Defends 'Dunk in the Water' Remark,"

WP A2 (10.28.06); Winslow, "DeLay Promotes His Vision," *Newsday* (12.12.06).

44 "Leahy Seeks Documents on Detention," WP (11.18.06); Johnston, "Senate Democrats Revive Demand for Classified Data," NYT (11.24.06); Johnston, "New Judiciary Subcommittee Is to Focus on Civil Liberties," NYT (12.14.06); Schmitt, "Congress, Bush Poised for 1st Friction," LAT (1.3.07); "Make Them Talk," LAT (1.4.07); Johnston, "Stormy Outlook as Gonzales Faces Senate Democrats," NYT (1.13.07).

45 Fair, "An Iraq Interrogator's Nightmare," WP (2.9.07). He expanded on his experience in Fair (2016).

46 Mazzetti, "C.I.A. Awaits Rules on Interrogation of Terror Suspects," NYT (3.25.07); "Tenet: 'Slam Dunk' Comment Misused," CBS News (4.26.07).

47 Wallsten, "GOP Candidates Divided on Detainees," LAT (5.17.07); "First-in-the-South Republican Primary Debate Begins with Shared Views on Iraq," Fox News (5.15.07); Brooks, "Don't Tell These Guys Torture's Wrong," LAT (5.18.07); "A Question of Torture," WP (5.17.07); Hunter, "Obama Does It Truman Style – Giving 'Em Hell over Iraq," *Chicago Sun Times* (5.13.07).

48 Krulak & Hoar, "Fear Can Be a Strong Motivator," WP (5.17.07); Kern, "Letters to the Editor: What Torture Could Cost Us," WP (5.23.07).

49 Intelligence Science Board (2006); Brumfield, "Interrogation Comes Under Fire," Nature (1.24.07); Shane, "Soviet-Style 'Torture' Becomes 'Interrogation' in the War on Terror," NYT (6.3.07); Hinkle & Wolff, "Communist Interrogation and Indoctrination of 'Enemies of the State': Analysis of Methods Used by the Communist State Police," 76 *Annals of Neurology and Psychology* 115 (1956); Shane & Mazzetti, "Interrogation Methods Are Criticized," NYT (5.30.07); "Bad Methods," WP (6.1.07); Miller, "Panel Is Critical of Secret CIA Jails," LAT (6.1.07); Pincus, "Senators Seek Legal Review of CIA Methods," WP (6.1.07); Shane, "Senate Committee Attacks C.I.A. Detentions," NYT (6.1.07); Shane, "Senate Committee Attacks C.I.A. Detentions," NYT (6.11.07); "Do We Use Torture?" LAT (6.18.07).

50 DeYoung, "Administration Struggles with Interrogation Specifics," WP (6.19.07); Mazzetti & Shane, "Question Time for Nominee Linked to Interrogations," NYT (6.19.07); Mazzetti, "Nominee for C.I.A. Counsel Offers Few Details in his Senate Confirmation Hearing," NYT (6.20.07); Bradbury to Rizzo, "Application of the War Crimes Act …" (7.20.07); Mazzetti, "Rules Lay out C.I.A.'s Tactics in Questioning," NYT (7.21.07); DeYoung, "Bush Approves New CIA Methods," WP (7.21.07); "Meet the Press," NBC (7.22.07); "Senator Says He Will Block C.I.A. Nomination," NYT (8.16.07); Senate Select Committee on Intelligence, Press Release (9.25.07); Mazzetti, "Nominee for C.I.A. Counsel Withdraws," NYT (9.26.07).

51 "A Return to Abuse," WP (7.25.07); Kelley & Turner, "War Crimes and the White House: The Dishonor in a Tortured New 'Interpretation' of the Geneva Conventions," WP (7.26.07); "The Torture Mystery," LAT (7.26.07); Weinstein, "ABA Urges Override of CIA Interrogation Techniques," LAT (8.13.07); Savage, "Military Cites Risk of Abuse by CIA," BG (8.25.07).

52 Miller, "It Feels 'Like Sept. 10,' CIA Director Says," LAT (9.8.07); Ross, Esposito and Raddatz, "CIA Bans Water-Boarding in Terror Interrogations," ABC News (9.14.07); Ross & Esposito, "Only Three Have Been Waterboarded by CIA," ABC News (11.2.07).

53 Shane, Johnston & Risen, "Secret U.S. Endorsement of Severe Interrogations," NYT (10.4.07); Froomkin, "Torture, Continued," WP (10.4.07); Johnston & Shane, "Debate Erupts on Techniques Used by C.I.A.," NYT (10.5.07); Eggen & Abramowitz, "Congress Seeks Secret Memos on Interrogation," WP (10.5.07); Stolberg, "Bush Defends Interrogations, Saying Methods Aren't Torture," NYT (10.6.07); Miller & Schmitt, "Bush Denies CIA Torture of Suspects," LAT (10.6.07); Abramowitz & Warrick, "Bush Defends Interrogations," WP (10.6.07); "More Torture Memos," WP (10.7.07); "On Torture and American Values," NYT (10.7.07); Sullivan, "Bush's Torturers Follow Where the Nazis Led," T (10.7.07); "Carter: America Tortures," CNN (10.10.07); Dvorak, "Fort Hunt's Quiet Men Break Silence on WWII," WP (10.6.07); Herrington, "Two Problems with Torture," *Pittsburgh Post-Gazette* (10.21.07).

54 www.ontheissues.org/2007_Dem_primary_Dartmouth.htm (last accessed February 18, 2018); Kornblut & Balz, "Clinton Cites Lessons of Partisanship," WP (10.10.07); "What Did Hillary Really Say to the Washington Post about Torture?" (10.10.07), www.talkingpointsmemo.com/horsesmouth (last accessed November 1, 2007).

55 Cooper, "Giuliani Questioned on Torture," NYT (10.25.07); "McCain Rebukes Giuliani on Waterboarding Remark," NYT (10.26.07); Santora, "3 Top Republican Candidates Take a Hard Line on the Interrogation of Detainees," NYT (11.3.07).

56 Shenon & Myers, "2 Sides Push Smooth Process on Naming Attorney General," NYT (8.30.07); Shenon & Johnston, "Bush Is Nearing a Choice to Lead the Justice Department," NYT (9.12.07); Eggen, "Reid Says Senators Would Block Olson," WP (9.13.07); Stolberg & Shenon, "Bush to Appoint Ex-Judge as Head of Justice Dept.," NYT (9.17.07); Schmitt, "Restoring Morale a Crucial Test for Mukasey," LAT (10.17.07); Shenon and Johnston, "Democrats to Press Justice Dept. Pick on Independence," NYT (10.17.07); "Two Questions for Mukasey," LAT (10.17.07); "The Mukasey Hearing," WP (10.17.07); "Pressing Mr. Mukasey, "NYT (10.17.07); Schmitt, "Mukasey Pledges Justice Dept. Reform," LAT (10.18.07); Eggen & Kane, "Mukasey Vows Not to Bow to Political Power," WP (10.18.07); Shenon, "Attorney General Choice Treads Careful Line at Senate Hearing," NYT (10.18.07); Herszenhorn, "Warmth for a Nominee Viewed as Unlike His Predecessor," NYT (10.18.07); "Mr. Mukasey's Answers," WP (10.18.07); "The Attorney General Nominee," NYT (10.18.07); Schmitt, "Mukasey Hearing Turns Prickly," LAT (10.19.07); Eggen & Kane, "On Day 2, Democrats See Change in Mukasey," WP (10.19.07); Shenon, "Senators Clash with Nominee over Torture and Limits of Law," NYT (10.19.07); Turley, "Mukasey's Confirmation: A Vote about Torture," LAT (10.24.07);

Rubenfeld, "Lawbreaker in Chief," NYT (10.24.07); Shenon, "A Top Republican Joins in Question for Nominee," NYT (10.25.07); "Mukasey's Take on Torture," LAT (10.25.07); "Senators Balk at Mukasey's Torture Reply," LAT (10.26.07); "Written Questions of Senator Patrick Leahy, Chairman, Senate Judiciary Committee, for Michael B. Mukasey, Nominee for Attorney General of the United States" (10.30.07); Cohen, "Honey, They Shrank the Congress," NYT (10.30.07); "AG Nominee Unsure about Waterboarding," AP (10.30.07); Schmitt, "Mukasey's Reply Draws More Fire," LAT (10.31.07); Eggen, "Mukasey Losing Democrats' Backing," WP A1 (10.31.07); Shane, "Nominee Describes Harsh Interrogation as Repugnant," NYT (10.31.07); "The Waterboarding Dodge," WP (10.30.07); Haberman, "Bearing Witness to Torture," NYT (10.30.07); Nance, "Waterboarding Is Torture … Period," *Small Wars Journal and Mother Jones* (10.31.07); Quoted by Michael Posner in "Letter to the Editor: End Cruel Tactics," *USA Today* (11.20.07); Schmitt, "Democrats' Resistance to Mukasey Grows," LAT (11.1.07); Eggen & Kane, "Two More Democrats to Oppose Mukasey," WP (11.1.07); Shane, "Nominee's Stand May Avoid Tangle of Torture Cases," NYT (11.1.07); Smith, "McCain Defends Mukasey on Waterboarding," WP (11.1.07); "Torture and the Attorneys General," NYT (11.1.07); "Mr. Mukasey and Torture," WP (11.2.07); Schmitt, "Bush Raises Stakes on Mukasey," LAT (11.2.07); Eggen & Kane, "Undecided Schumer May Be Key to Mukasey's Chances," WP (11.2.07); Stolberg, "Bush, Defending Justice Nominee, Sees Unfairness," NYT (11.2.07); Herszenhorn, "Taking All the Credit, and then Counting the Cost," NYT (11.2.07); Letters to the Editor, NYT (11.2.07); Schmitt, "Mukasey All but a Shoo-In for Approval," LAT (11.3.07); Eggen & Kane, "Democratic Defections Clear Path for Mukasey," WP (11.3.07); Shenon & Herszenhorn, "Justice Nominee Gets 2 Key Votes from Democrats," NYT (11.3.07); Feinstein, "Judge Mukasey Has My Vote," LAT (11.3.07); "Two for Mr. Mukasey," WP (11.4.07); "Confirm Mukasey – and Stop Torture," LAT (11.5.07); "Committee Republican Backs Mukasey Despite Concerns," NYT (11.5.07); Schumer, "A Vote for Justice," NYT (11.6.07); Schmitt, "Committee Sends Mukasey Nominee to Senate Floor," LAT (11.7.07); Eggen & Kane, "Mukasey Bid Survives Division on Senate Panel," WP (11.7.07); Shenon, "Senate Committee Approves Mukasey Nomination," NYT (11.7.07); Letters to the Editor, NYT (11.7.07); "Mukasey Moves Forward," *San Francisco Chronicle* (11.8.07); Schmitt, "Senate Confirms Mukasey as Attorney General," LAT (11.9.07); Eggen, "Senate Confirms Mukasey by 53–40," WP (11.9.07); Hulse, "Mukasey Wins Vote in Senate, Despite Doubts," NYT (11.9.07); "Abdicate and Capitulate," NYT (11.11.07); Rich, "The Coup at Home," NYT (11.11.07); "Time Bomb Fizzles," LAT (11.13.07); Schmitt & Neuman, "New Attorney General Sworn In," LAT (11.14.07); Shenon, "Challenges Awaiting, Mukasey Takes Ceremonial Oath," NYT (11.15.07); Kellman, "New Attorney General Mukasey Shows Savvy," AP (11.17.07).

57 "Time Bomb Defense Fizzles," LAT (11.13.07).

58 "Nadler, Delahunt to Introduce 'American Anti-Torture Bill,'" CBS News (10.24.07); "House Adopts Nadler-Delahunt Anti-Torture Provision," nadler.house/gov/press release (11.14.07).
59 Greenburg & de Vogue, "Bush Administration's Internal Waterboarding Debate," ABC News (11.2.07); Shane, "A Firsthand Experience before Decision on Torture," NYT (11.7.07); "The View from the Waterboard," WP (11.6.07); Pilkington, "Top US Legal Adviser Refuses to Rule Out 'Torture' Technique," G (11.5.07).
60 "French Journalist Henri Alleg Describes His Torture Being Waterboarded by French Forces during Algerian War," *Democracy Now!* (11.5.07).
61 White, "Waterboard Is Torture, Says Ex-Navy Instructor," WP (11.9.07); Khanna, "Army Reiterates That Waterboarding Is Torture, Since Mukasey Won't," Alternet and Think Progress (11.13.07).
62 Ross, "'CIA-Abu Zubaydah': Interview with John Kiriakou," ABC News (12.10.07); Esposito & Ross, "Coming In from the Cold: CIA Spy Calls Waterboarding Necessary but Torture," ABC News (12.10.07); Warrick & Eggen, "Waterboarding Recounted," WP (12.11.07); Froomkin, "Did Torture Work?" WP (12.11.07); Eggen & Pincus, "FBI, CIA Debate Significance of Terror Suspect," WP (12.18.07); Stelter, "How '07 ABC Interview Tilted a Torture Debate," NYT (4.28.09); Suskind (2006); Kiriakou (2012); compare Soufan & Freedman (2011) with Rodriguez & Harlow (2012).
63 Hayden, Message to CIA Employees (12.6.07); SSCI, Chairman Rockefeller's Statement on the CIA Decision to Destroy Tapes of Early Interrogations (12.6.07); Miller, "CIA Says Interrogation Tapes Were Destroyed," LAT (12.7.07); Eggen & Warrick, "CIA Destroyed Videos Showing Interrogations," WP (12.7.07); Mazzetti, "C.I.A. Destroyed 2 Tapes Showing Interrogations," NYT (12.7.07); Karl, "Harriet Miers Knew of Destruction of Interrogation Tapes," ABC News (12.7.07); SSCI (12.7.07); Senator Carl Levin Press Conference (12.7.07); Miller, "Democrats Demand Probe into Destruction of Tapes," LAT (12.8.07); Eggen & Warrick, "Inquiry Sought on CIA Tapes," WP (12.8.07); Lichtblau, "Congress Looks into Obstruction as Calls for Justice Inquiry Rise," NYT (12.8.07); Richey, "Destroyed CIA Tapes Spur Probes," Christian Science Monitor (12.10.07); "The Torture Tapes," WP (12.8.07); Fiore & Neubauer, "Destruction of CIA Tapes Raises Bipartisan Concerns," LAT (12.10.07); "A Weekly Roundup of the Buzz from the Sunday Talk Shows," WP (12.10.07); "White House Mum on Destroyed CIA Tapes," CBS News (12.10.07); "Senators Slam CIA Tape Destruction," CBS News (12.9.07); Meyer, "CIA Watchdog Launch Inquiry," LAT (12.9.07); Mazzetti & Johnston, "Justice Dept. and C.I.A. Watchdog Start Inquiry of Interrogation Videos' Destruction," NYT (12.9.07); Benjamin, "For the CIA's Eyes Only," Salon.com (12.8.07); Mazzetti, "Uneasy Spotlight for Ex-Official of C.I.A.," NYT (12.10.07); Mazzetti, "9/11 Panel Study Finds that C.I.A. Withheld Tapes," NYT (12.22.07); Warrick & Eggen, "CIA Tapes Were Kept from 9/11 Panel, Report Says," WP (12.23.07); Kean & Hamilton, "Stonewalled by the CIA," NYT (1.2.08).

64 "Lawmakers Investigate CIA Interrogation Tape Disposal," *Jim Lehrer's NewsHour* (12.11.07); Miller, "Senate Widens Probe of Destroyed Tapes," LAT (12.12.07); Eggen & Pincus, "Hayden Tells Panel He Can't Answer Every Question about Tapes," WP (12.12.07); Mazzetti & Johnston, "C.I.A. Director Says Others Made Decisions about Tapes," NYT (12.12.07); Letter from Rush Holt to Michael Mukasey (12.11.07); Abramowitz & Warrick, "White House Lawyers Told of Videotapes," WP (12.20.07); Mazzetti, "C.I.A. Chief Cites Agency Lapse on Tapes," NYT (12.13.07); Pincus, "CIA Chief: Hill Should Have Been Told More," WP (12.13.07); Jordan, "Attorney General Denies Details in CIA Tapes Inquiry," AP (12.14.07); Schmitt & Miller, "Justice Moves to Control Tapes Probe," LAT (12.15.07); Eggen & Warrick, "Congress's Probe of CIA Tapes Resisted," WP (12.15.07); Shane, "Court Inquiry on Tape Case Is Opposed," NYT (12.15.07); Johnston & Mazzetti, "Delay Is Sought by Justice Dept. on C.I.A. Inquiry," NYT (12.15.07); "Legal Fight Breaks Out over Destroyed CIA Tapes," LAT (12.16.07); Eggen, "Destruction of CIA Tapes Defended," WP (12.16.07); Schmitt, "Judge Rebuffs Justice Dept., Will Look into CIA Tapes," LAT (12.18.07); Eggen, "Judge Schedules Hearing on CIA Tape Destruction," WP (12.19.07); Meyer, "Judge Reluctant to Probe Tapes Case," LAT (12.22.07); Stout & Johnston, "No Immediate Ruling on Judicial Inquiry," NYT (12.22.07); Leonnig, "Detainee Evidence Probe Weighed," WP (12.22.07); Mazzetti & Shane, "Bush Lawyers Discussed Fate of C.I.A. Tapes," NYT (12.19.07); "Ex-CIA Agent: Waterboarding 'Saved Lives,'" CNN Politics (12.11.07); Baker & Warrick, "CIA Seeks Investigation of Ex-Officer's Claims," WP (12.21.07); "Looking at America," NYT (12.31.07); Mansfield, Letter to the Editor, NYT (1.7.08).

65 Mukasey Statement (1.2.08); "U.S. Announces Criminal Inquiry into C.I.A. Tapes," NYT (1.3.08); Schmitt, "Justice Dept. to Probe the CIA," LAT (1.3.08); Johnston, "An Inquiry Seen as Payback in a Rivalry," NYT (1.4.08); Eggen & Warrick, "Criminal Probe on CIA Tapes Opened," WP (1.3.08); Jordan, "Attorney General Nixes Special Prosecutor in CIA Case," AP (1.25.08); "The Right Move on the C.I.A. Tapes," NYT (1.3.08); "Mr. Mukasey's Move," WP (1.3.08); "Careful, Congress," LAT (1.4.08); Eggen & Warrick, "Ex-CIA Official May Refuse to Testify about Videotapes," WP (1.10.08); Shane, "Prosecutor to Review Official Handling of C.I.A. Tapes," NYT (2.10.08).

66 Warrick & Eggen, "Hill Briefed on Waterboarding in 2002," WP (12.9.07).

67 Hess & Flaherty, "Lawmakers Agree to Limit CIA Interrogators to Military-Approved Technique, Bar Waterboarding," AP (12.6.07); Shane, "Lawmakers Back Limits on Interrogation Tactics," NYT (12.7.07); "In Arrogant Defense of Torture," NYT (12.9.07); "Senators Slam CIA Tape Destruction," CBS News (12.9.07); "Lawmakers Investigate CIA Interrogation Tape Disposal," *Jim Lehrer's NewsHour* (12.11.07); "The CIA Tapes," LAT (12.13.07); Pincus, "CIA Chief: Hill Should Have Been Told More," WP (12.13.07); Jordan, "Attorney

General Denies Details in CIA Tapes Inquiry," AP (12.14.07); "House Passes Bill to Outlaw CIA's Use of Waterboarding," LAT (12.14.07); Warrick & Pincus, "House Passes Bill to Ban CIA's Use of Harsh Interrogation Tactics," WP (12.14.07); Shane, "House Passes Restrictions on Interrogation Methods," NYT (12.14.07).

68 Tiron, "Huckabee, Democrats to Meet Retired Officers on Torture," *The Hill* (11.30.07); "Primary Choices: Hillary Clinton," NYT (1.25.08); "Primary Choices: John McCain," NYT (1.25.08); "Barack Obama," LAT (2.3.08); Cooper, "McCain Draws Criticism on Torture Bill," NYT (2.17.08).

69 Hearing of the Subcommittee on Terrorism, Technology and Homeland Security of the Senate Judiciary Committee, C-Span (11.11.07); "Intelligence Chief Couches Reference to Waterboarding as 'Torture,'" WP (1.13.08); Wright, "The Spymaster," *The New Yorker* (1.21.08); "Washington: Former Secretary on Waterboarding," NYT (1.19.08); Shenon, "So Is Waterboarding Torture? Mukasey May Never Say," NYT (1.26.08); Shenon, "Tough Senate Hearing Awaits Mukasey," NYT (1.30.08); Mikkelsen, "U.S. Attorney General Says CIA Interrogations Legal," Reuters (1.30.08); Frieden, "Attorney General to Skip 'Waterboarding' in Testimony," CNNPolitics.com (1.30.08); Eggen, "Mukasey Holds Back on Torture Issue," WP (1.30.08); Schmitt, "Is Waterboarding Torture? Mukasey's Still Not Ready to Say," LAT (1.30.08); Cohen, "Michael Mukasey's Magic Words," CBS News (1.30.08); Lithwick, "Thank You. Now Go to Hell," *Slate* (1.30.08); Shenon, "Mukasey Will Not Rule Out Waterboarding," NYT (1.31.08); Schmitt, "Democrats Decry Mukasey's Waterboarding Silence," LAT (1.31.08); Schor, "Take That, Mukasey," G (1.31.08); TPM Muckraker (1.30.08); Shenon, "Mukasey Will Not Rule Out Waterboarding," NYT (1.31.08); Schmitt, "Democrats Decry Mukasey's Waterboarding Silence," LAT (1.31.08); Rutten, "Mukasey's Confession," LAT (2.2.08); Miller, "CIA Chief Confirms Use of Waterboarding," LAT (2.6.08).

70 "A Disappointing Debut," NYT (1.31.08); "It's Torture; It's Illegal," LAT (2.2.08); Rutten, "Mukasey's Confession," LAT (2.2.08); "'Waterboarding' Mukasey," WSJ (1.31.08).

71 Miller, "CIA Chief Confirms Use of Waterboarding," LAT (2.6.08); Mazzetti, "Intelligence Chief says al Qaeda Improves Ability to Strike in U.S.," NYT (2.6.08).

72 Eggen, "White House Defends CIA's Use of Waterboarding in Interrogations," WP (2.7.08); Miller, "Waterboarding Is Still an Option," LAT (2.7.08).

73 Shane, "C.I.A. Chief Doubts Tactic to Interrogate Is Still Legal," NYT (2.8.08); Gorman, "CIA Let Contractors Perform Waterboarding," WSJ (2.8.08); Eggen, "Justice Dept. 'Cannot' Probe Waterboarding, Mukasey Says," WP (2.8.08).

74 Mezzo, "Why It Was Called 'Water Torture,'" WP (2.10.08); "Scalia Says He Sees a Role for Physical Interrogations," NYT (2.13.08); "Scalia Accepts Infliction of Pain to Get Key Information," LAT (2.13.08); Eggen, "Justice Official Defends Rough CIA Interrogations," WP (2.17.08).

75 Herszenhorn, "Senate Votes to Ban Harsh Interrogations," NYT (2.13.08); Miller, "Senate OKs Limits on Interrogations," LAT (2.14.08); Herszenhorn, "Bill Curbing Terror Interrogators Is Sent to Bush, Who Has Vowed to Veto It," NYT (2.14.08); "Moral Barrier, the President Stands in the Way of a Ban on Torture," WP (2.15.08).

76 MacAskill, "London Bombs Justify 'Torture,' Says Bush," G (2.15.08); "Shame, Sen. McCain," LAT (2.19.08).

77 "Bush on Veto of Intelligence Bill," NYT (3.8.08).

78 Greenburg, Rosenberg & Vogue, "Sources: Top Bush Advisors Approved 'Enhanced Interrogation,'" ABC News (4.9.08); Eggen, "Bush Approved Meetings on Interrogation Techniques," WP (4.12.08); Thomas, "Bush Admits He Approved Torture," *Seattle Post-Intelligencer* (5.2.08); "The Torture Sessions," NYT (4.20.08); Warrick, "Secretive Agency under the Spotlight," WP (7.5.08); Mazzetti, "Letters Outline Legal Rationale for C.I.A. Tactics," NYT (4.27.08); Warrick, "Administration Says Particulars May Trump Geneva Protections," WP (4.27.08); "Panel Wants Limits on Interrogations," LAT (4.30.08).

79 "Cheney Lawyer Claims 'Congress Lacks Constitutional Power' to Investigate Vice President's Role in Torture Approval," ThinkProgress (4.29.08); Johnson, "Lawmaker Threatens Subpoenas for Aides," WP A4 (4.29.08); Shane, "House Panel Backs a Subpoena for Cheney's Chief of Staff," NYT (5.7.08); Johnson, "Panel Will Subpoena Assistant to Cheney," WP (5.7.08); Barnes, "Cheney Aide Digs in at Hearing," LAT (6.27.08); Milbank, "When Anonymity Fails, Be Nasty, Brutish and Short," WP (6.27.08); Lithwick, "Faith in the System," Slate.com (7.15.08); Milbank, "Let the Games Begin!" WP (7.16.08); Benjamin, "Ashcroft Suggests CIA Sought Legal Approval after Torture Began," Salon (7.17.08); "Ashcroft Disclaims Legal Reasoning for Waterboarding," LAT (7.18.08); Milbank, "John Ashcroft, Riding Back on a White Horse," WP (7.18.08); Sands (2005, 2008).

80 Shane & Johnstone, "Justice Dept. Will Share Interrogation Options," NYT (5.1.08); Johnson, "Lawmakers to See Secret Documents," WP (5.1.08); "Notes from the War on Terror," NYT (5.2.08); "Coming Clean on Torture," WP (5.5.08); Feingold, "Government in Secret," LAT (5.8.08).

81 "Coming Clean on Torture," WP (5.5.08); Lichtblau, "F.B.I. Gets Mixed Review in Report on Interrogation," NYT (5.17.08); "Unanswered Questions," ABC News Blog (5.20.08); Lichtblau & Shane, "Report Details Dissent on Guantánamo Tactics," NYT (5.21.08); Schmitt, "Military Tactics Worried FBI Interrogators," LAT (5.21.08); Johnson & White, "Audit Finds FBI Reports of Detainee Abuse Ignored," WP (5.21.08); "What the F.B.I. Agents Saw," NYT (5.22.06); Lee, "Rice Defends Post-9/11 Interrogation Techniques," AP (5.23.08); Warrick, "Lawmakers Urge Special Counsel Probe of Harsh Interrogation Tactics," WP (6.8.08); ABCNY Task Force on National Security and the Rule of Law (2008); Johnson, "Right the Ship or Hold the Course?" WP (7.20.08).

82 Ryan, "DoJ Official Describes 'Abusive' Interrogation," ABC News (6.4.08); Warrick, "Lawmakers Urge Special Counsel Probe of Harsh Interrogation Tactics," WP (6.8.08); Williams, "Guantánamo Criticism Intensifies," LAT (6.11.08); Shane, "Congress Seeks Answers on Harsh Interrogations," NYT (6.11.08).

83 SASC, Statements of Daniel J. Baumgartner Jr. (6.17.08), Alberto J. Mora (6.17.08); Jane G. Dalton (6.17.08); Diane E. Beaver (6.17.08); Jerald Ogrisseg (6.17.08), Steven M. Kleinman (9.25.08), John R. Moulton II (9.25.08); SASC Holds Hearing on Detainee Interrogation Techniques, CQ Congressional Transcripts (9.25.08); Warrick, "Report Questions Pentagon Accounts," WP (6.17.08); Milbank, "Abu Ghraib? Doesn't Ring a Bell," WP (6.18.08); Flaherty, "Probe: Pentagon Lawyers Sought Harsh Interrogations," AP (6.18.08); Warrick, "CIA Played Larger Role in Advising Pentagon," WP (6.18.08); Mazzetti, "Ex-Pentagon Lawyers Face Inquiry on Interrogation Role," NYT (6.17.08); Kravitz, "Psychology of Suffering Detainees Examined," WP (6.18.08); Rutten, "Torture Began at the Top," LAT (6.18.08); Mazzetti & Shane, "Notes Show Confusion on Interrogation Methods," NYT (6.18.08); "Harsh Interrogation Methods Stain U.S. Image, Endanger Soldiers: Experts," AFP (6.18.08); Benjamin, "Bush's Top General Quashed Torture Dissent," Salon.com. (6.30.08); Shane, "China Inspired Interrogations at Guantánamo," NYT (7.2.08); "Torture, Made in China," LAT (7.7.08); Taylor, "Opening Argument; Inconvenient Facts and Detainee Abuse," *National Journal* (1.10.09).

84 Noronha, "Video of Interrogation of Gitmo Prisoner Released," WP (7.15.08); White, "Tactic Used after It Was Banned," WP (8.8.08).

85 Miller, "Rice Admits Bush Officials Held White House Talks on CIA Interrogations," LAT (9.24.08); Mazzetti, "Bush Aides Linked to Talks on Interrogations," NYT (9.25.08); Warrick, "Top Officials Knew in 2002 of Harsh Interrogations," WP (9.25.08).

86 Barnes, "Pentagon Tightens Rules on Detainee Interrogation," LAT (10.15.08).

87 DoD Directive 3115.09, "DoD Intelligence Interrogations, Detainee Debriefings, and Tactical Questioning" (10.9.08).

88 "Bringing Us Together," LAT (10.14.08); "Barack Obama for President," LAT (10.19.08).

89 223 *HRF Law and Security Digest* (11.14.08); Cohen, "Democratic Pressure on Obama to Restore the Rule of Law," NYT (11.14.08); Robinson, "After the Torture Era," WP (11.18.08); Greenwald, "Eric Holder Talking to Paul Zahn," Salon (11.19.08); Oliphant, "Civil Liberties Groups Have a Wish List for Obama," LAT (11.20.08); Ambinder & Sullivan, "No Way, No How, No Brennan," Atlantic Monthly Online (11.21.08); Miller, "John Brennan Withdraws Name from Consideration as CIA Director," LAT (11.26.08); Mazzetti & Shane, "After Sharp Words on C.I.A., Obama Faces a Delicate Task," NYT (12.3.08); Baker, "Obama Is Reported Set to Revise Counterterrorism Efforts," NYT (1.8.09); Mazzetti, "Building Bridges over Troubled Waters at C.I.A.," NYT (1.9.09). For a profile of

Brennan, see Johnsen, "The Untouchable John Brennan," BuzzFeed (4.23.15).

90 Meyer, "Mukasey Collapses during Speech," LAT (11.21.08); La Corte, "Washington Judge Yelled 'Tyrant' at Attorney General Michael Mukasey before He Collapsed," LAT (11.26.08); Hsu, "Chertoff Urges Tighter Security," WP (12.4.08); Miller, "Cheney Was Key in Clearing CIA Interrogation Tactics," LAT (12.16.08); NPR Interview (12.10.08); Eggen, "Bush Says His Post-9/11 Actions Prevented Further Terrorism," WP (12.18.08); Slater, "Former Attorney General Alberto Gonzales to Wall Street Journal: 'I Consider Myself a Casualty,'" WSJ (12.31.08); Perez, "Gonzales Defends Role in Antiterror Politics," WSJ (12.31.08); Stolberg, "A Somber Bush Says Farewell to the Nation," NYT (1.16.09); Eviatar, "Actually, Condi, When the President Breaks the Law, It's Still Illegal," *Washington Times* (5.1.09); Dowd, "How Character Corrodes," NYT (5.3.09); MacGillis, "4th-Grader Questions Rice on Waterboarding," WP (5.4.06).

91 Alexander, "I'm Still Tortured by What I Saw in Iraq," WP (11.30.08); Rose, "Tortured Reasoning," *Vanity Fair* (12.16.08); Alexander, "Talk, Not Torture, Gets the Information," LAT (12.30.08); Alexander & Brunning (2008).

92 Finn, "Retired Officers Meet with Obama Aides on Interrogation Policy," WP (12.4.08); "Obama Legal Team Meets with Anti-Torture Generals," AP (12.3.08); Sherer, "Rollback on Torture? Not So Easy for Obama," *Time* (12.5.08).

93 SASC (2008); Miller & Barnes, "Rumsfeld Blamed in Detainee Abuse Scandals," LAT (12.12.08); Warrick, "Rumsfeld Responsible for Torture, Report Says," WP (12.11.08); Warrick & DeYoung, "Report on Detainee Abuse Blames Top Bush Officials," WP (12.12.18); Shane & Mazzetti, "Senate Panel Report Links Top Bush Administration Officials to Abuse of Detainees," NYT (12.12.08); "Policy of Abuse," WP (12.14.08); "The Real 'Torture' Disgrace," WSJ (12.19.08).

94 Abramowitz, Warrick & Pincus, "Obama under Pressure on Interrogation Policy," WP (1.10.09); Miller, "Departing CIA Chief Defends Interrogations," LAT (1.16.09).

95 Panetta, "Americans Reject Fear Tactics," *Monterey County Herald* (3.9.08); "Quantum of Politics," LAT (1.7.09); "Not a Company Man," NYT (1.10.09); Abramowitz, Warrick & Pincus, "Obama under Pressure on Interrogation Policy," WP (1.10.09); Hess, "Obama Intelligence Nominee Says No Torture on His Watch," AP (1.22.09); Ryan, "Intel Pick Holds Back on Waterboarding," ABC News (1.22.09); Woodward (2010); quoted in Rutten, "Unraveling the Torture Knot," LAT (10.9.10).

96 Leonnig, "The Stories of Torture Sounded Made Up. They Weren't," WP (1.18.09).

97 Shane, "Obama Orders Secret Prisons and Detention Camps Closed," NYT (1.22.09); Shane, Mazzetti & Cooper, "Obama Reverses Key Bush Policy, But Questions on Detainees Remain," NYT (1.23.09); Miller & Barnes, "Obama Sets New Rules in War on Terror," LAT (1.23.09);

Warrick & DeYoung, "Obama Reverses Bush Policies on Detention and Interrogation," WP (1.23.09); Pincus, "Intelligence Pick Calls Torture Immoral, Ineffective," WP (1.23.09); HRF, "Statement from 16 Retired Admirals and Generals" (1.22.09); "Obama at Signing of Executive Orders," 230 *HRF Law and Security Digest* (1.23.09).

98 "Statement of Dennis C. Blair before SSCI (1.22.09); Pincus, "Intelligence Pick Calls Torture Immoral, Ineffective," WP (1.23.09); "Ex-Attorney General Gonzales: 'I Should Have Been More Engaged,'" NPR's Tell Me More (1.26.09).

99 SSCI, "Additional Prehearing Questions for The Honorable Leon E. Panetta upon His Selection to Be the Director of the Central Intelligence Agency"; SSCI Confirmation Hearing, CQ Transcriptions (2.5.09); 232 *HRF Law and Security Digest* (2.6.09); "Not Even a Little Torture," LAT (2.14.09); Shane, "Biden Says Bush Gave al Qaeda Recruiting Tool," NYT (2.20.09).

100 Hunt, "Obama Doesn't Need Cheney's Advice on Terrorism," Bloomberg (2.23.09); Lewis, "Justice Dept. Nominee Avoids Confrontation at Hearing," NYT (2.26.09); Horton, "The Woman Who Could Nail Bush," Daily Beast (3.26.09); Horton, "Are Republicans Blackmailing Obama?" Daily Beast (4.5.09); "Confirm Dawn Johnsen," WP (4.30.09); "Defending Dawn Johnsen," LAT (5.11.09); O'Keefe & Butterworth, "Senate Conforms More than 30 U.S. Posts, Sends Six Back," WP (12.25.09); "GOP Blocks Controversial Obama Nominee Dawn Johnsen before Recessing," Fox News (12.25.09); "Dawn Johnsen to Be Re-nominated, Confirms White House," HuffPost (1.7.10); Savage, "President Is Said to Decide to Renominate Six Choices," NYT A14 (1.8.10); Johnson, "Specter Now Says He'll Support Dawn Johnsen for OLC," WP (1.13.10); Raju, "DoJ Nominee Appears to Have 60 Votes," Politico (1.12.10); "The Senate Should Confirm Dawn Johnsen," LAT (1.28.10); "An Unreasonable Delay," NYT (2.4.10); Savage, "Nominee to Legal Office Withdraws," NYT (4.10.10); Stein, "Dawn Johnsen, Key Obama Justice Nominee, Withdraws Her Nomination," HuffPost (4.9.10); "Politics 1, Rule of Law 0," NYT (4.13.10); "Legal Counsel Limbo," LAT (4.12.10); "The Office of Legal Counsel Still in Limbo," WP (4.15.10).

101 Harris, Allen & VandeHei, "Cheney Warns of New Attacks," Politico (2.4.09); Falcone, "Cheney Predicts 'Probability' of Attack," NYT (2.5.09); Gregg, "Speaking with the Enemy," NYT (2.8.09); Kleinman & Alexander, "Try a Little Tenderness," NYT (3.11.09).

102 Finn & Warrick, "Detainee's Harsh Treatment Foiled No Plots," WP (3.29.09).

103 "Waterboarding Advice Is Probed," LAT (2.23.08); Leopold, "DoJ Probe on Yoo Memos 'Damning,' Senators Demand Answers," *The Public Record* (2.15.09); Shane, "Justice Dept. Is Reviewing Interrogation under Bush," NYT (2.17.09); Johnston, "Senators Seek Ethics Findings," WP (2.17.09); Leopold, "DoJ Report Blasts Yoo for Not Citing High Court Opinion in Torture Memos," *The Public Record*

(2.22.09); Isikoff, "A Torture Report Could Spell Big Trouble for Bush Lawyers," *Newsweek* (2.23.09); Leopold, "DoJ Watchdog 'Revising' Critical Report on Jon Yoo's Legal Work on Torture," *The Public Record* (3.31.09).

104 Mazzetti, "Senate Panel to Pursue Investigation of C.I.A.," NYT (2.27.09); Miller, "Senate Panel to Probe CIA Methods," LAT (2.27.09); Warrick, "Senate Panel to Examine CIA Detainee Handling," WP (2.27.09); Warrick, "Senate Panel Reaches Terms for Probe of CIA Detentions," WP (3.6.09).

105 Lewis, "Memos Released by Justice Dept. Show Wide View of Bush's Power," NYT (3.3.09); Meyer & Barnes, "Memos Gave Bush Overriding Powers," LAT (3.3.09); Smith & Eggen, "Post-9/11 Memos Show More Bush-Era Legal Errors," WP (3.3.09); "The Tortured Memos," NYT (3.4.09); Savage, "Bush-Era Memos Stun Legal Experts," LAT (3.4.09); Rutten, "Bush's Executive Tyranny," LAT (3.4.09); "Mad Max's Justice Department," WP (3.4.09).

106 ICRC Report on the Treatment of Fourteen "High Value Detainees" in CIA Custody (February 2007); Danner, "The Red Cross Torture Report; What It Means," NYRB (4.6.09); Warrick & Tate, "Report Calls CIA Detainee Treatment 'Inhuman,'" WP (4.7.09); Panetta, "Message from Director: Interrogation Policy and Contracts," CIA (4.9.09); Miller, "Panetta Sets New CIA Standards," LAT (4.10.09).

107 Barron, "Memorandum for the Attorney General," ACLU (4.15.09); Shane, "Debating Release of Interrogation Memos," NYT (4.1.09); Isikoff, "'Holy Hell' over Torture Memos," *Newsweek* (4.4.09); President Obama, Press Release (4.16.09); DoJ, Press Release (4.16.09); Mazzetti, "Obama Releases Interrogation Memos, Says C.I.A. Operatives Won't Be Prosecuted," NYT (4.16.09); Mazzetti & Shane, "Interrogation Memos Detail Harsh Tactics by the C.I.A.," NYT (4.17.09); "Attorney: Justice Memos Prove U.S. Did Not Torture," Fox News (4.17.09); Mazzetti, "C.I.A. Memos Could Bring More Disclosures," NYT (4.18.09); Shanker, "Gates Voices Concerns about Release of Interrogation Memos," NYT (4.24.09); Smith, "Emanuel Rejects Trial for Memos' Authors," WP (4.20.09); "President Obama Delivers Remarks to CIA Employees," WP (4.20.09); Warrick, "Obama Cites CIA's Possible 'Mistakes' but Vows Support," WP (4.21.09); "Boehner: Memos Outline 'Torture Techniques,'" HuffPost (4.23.09).

108 "Dealing with a Disgrace," WP (4.17.09); "The Torturer's Manifesto," NYT (4.18.09); "Close the Torture Loophole," LAT (4.18.09).

109 Hayden & Mukasey, "The President Ties His Own Hands on Terror," WSJ (4.17.09); Rivkin & Casey, "The Memos Prove We Didn't Torture," WSJ (4.19.09); Lewis, "Official Defends Signing Interrogation Memos," NYT (4.29.09).

110 Shane, "Waterboarding Used 266 Times on 2 Suspects," NYT (4.19.09); "Shocking the Conscience," WP (4.21.09); Gantz & Meyerson, "Damage from CIA Tactics Is Disputed," LAT (4.20.09); Walsh, "Waterboarding: A Mental and Physical Trauma," *Time* (4.20.09).

111 Baker & Shane, "Pressure Grows to Investigate Interrogations," NYT (4.20.09); "Cheney Calls for Legal Memos to be Declassified," Fox News (4.20–21.09); "In the Spirit of Openness," NYT A24 (4.23.09); Eggen, "Cheney Requests Release of 2 CIA Reports on Interrogations," WP (4.25.09); "Is Cheney Right about the Memos?" LAT (5.1.09); "The Lawyers," NYT (5.7.09); CBS, *Face the Nation* (5.10.09) www.cbsnews.com/htdocs/pdf/FTN_051009.pdf (last accessed February 18, 2018); Kane & Warrick, "Cheney Oversaw Briefings on Interrogation Methods," WP (6.3.09).

112 Amira, "Who Defends 'Torture'?" *New York Magazine* (4.21.09); Gerson, "Lines on a Slippery Slope," WP (4.27.09); Noah, "More Library Tower Nonsense," *Slate* (4.27.09); Krauthammer, "Torture? No, except…" WP (5.1.09).

113 Balz & Bacon, "Congress Debates Fresh Investigation of Interrogations," WP (4.23.09); Herszenhorn, "Lawmakers Push Interrogation Inquiries," NYT (4.25.09); "As Report Shows Bybee's Torture Culpability, Conyers Says, 'We're Coming After These Guys,'" HuffPost (4.21.09); Herszenhorn & Hulse, "Obama Resisting Push for Interrogation Panel," NYT (4.24.09).

114 "Seeing the Upside of Interrogations," LAT (4.22.09); Warrick, "Intelligence Chief Says Methods Hurt U.S.," WP (4.22.09).

115 Baker & Shane, "Pressure Grows to Investigate Interrogations," NYT (4.20.09); Zelikow, "A Dubious C.I.A. Shortcut," NYT (4.24.09); Soufan, "My Tortured Decision," NYT (4.23.09); Ghosh, "A Top Interrogator Who's Against Torture," *Time* (4.24.09); Sauvageot, Letter to the Editor, "How to Treat a Prisoner," NYT (4.24.09); Isikoff, "We Could Have Done This the Right Way," *Newsweek* (5.4.09); Benjamin, "CIA Torture May Have Hindered Intelligence Gathering," Salon (5.14.09); Zelikow, "The OLC 'Torture Memos': Thoughts from a Dissenter," Foreign Policy Blog (4.21.09); Baumann & Corn, "A Cheney Cover-Up?" *Mother Jones* (5.6.09); Warrick & Finn, "Internal Rifts on the Road to Torment," WP (7.19.09); "Memo Shows US Official Disagreed with Bush Administration's View on Torture," G (4.3.12). Zelikow's February 15, 2006 memo was entitled "The McCain Amendment and U.S. Obligations under Article 16 of the Convention Against Torture."

116 Miller, "CIA Reportedly Declined to Closely Evaluate Harsh Interrogations," LAT (4.26.09); McManus, "Examining Torture in the Bush Era," LAT (4.26.09); Margulies, "Abu Zubaydah's Suffering," LAT (4.30.09).

117 Shane & Mazzetti, "In Adopting Harsh Tactics, No Inquiry into Past Use," NYT (4.22.09); Warrick & Finn, "Harsh Tactics Readied before their Approval," WP (4.22.09); Knowlton, "Report Gives New Detail on Interrogation Approval," NYT (4.22.09); Barnes, "Military's Role in CIA Tactics Cited," LAT (4.22.09); Sifton, "New Torture Report Details Bushies' Role," Daily Beast (4.22.09); Smith & Finn, "Harsh Methods Approved as Early as Summer 2002," WP (4.23.09); Balz & Bacon, "Congress Debates Fresh Investigation of Interrogations," WP (4.23.09);

"Eyes Wide Shut," WP (4.25.09); Finn & Warrick, "In 2002, Military Agency Warned against 'Torture,'" WP (4.25.09); Rizzo, "I Could Have Stopped Waterboarding Before It Happened," Politico (1.5.14).

118 Wallsten & Miller, "Obama Gives Nuanced Defense of his Stance on Torture," LAT (4.30.09); Transcript of Press Conference (4.29.09).

119 Goss, "Security before Politics," WP (4.25.09); Emptywheel, "CIA Lying to ABC about Torture. Again. ABC Reporting It Uncritically. Again," Firedoglake (5.7.09); "Intelligence Report: Pelosi Briefed on Use of Interrogation Tactics in Sept. '02," ABC News (5.7.09); Miller, "Leaders Were Told of CIA's Methods," LAT (5.8.09); Shane & Hulse, "Chart Shows Top Democrats Briefed on Interrogations," NYT (5.9.09); Kane, "Memo Says Pelosi Knew about Harsh Tactics," WP (5.8.09); Divoll, "Congress's Torture Bubble," NYT (5.13.09); Krauthammer, "The Torture Debate, Continued," WP (5.14.09); Ignatius, "Pelosi up a Tree," WP (5.15.09); Hulse, "Pelosi Says She Knew of Waterboarding by Early 2003," NYT (5.15.09); Miller, "CIA Misled Congress, Pelosi Says," LAT (5.15.09); "Pelosi Says She Was Misled on Waterboarding," WSJ (5.14.09); Milbank, "Nancy Pelosi's Fancy Footwork," WP (5.15.09); Kane, "Accusations Flying in Interrogation Battle," WP (5.15.09); Hulse, "On Interrogations, A Rare Dent in Pelosi Armor," NYT (5.16.09); Miller, "Panetta Disputes Pelosi's Charge," LAT (5.16.09); Beacon & Warrick, "CIA Chief Rebuts Pelosi' Charges," WP (5.16.09); "What Ms. Pelosi Knew," WP (5.16.09); Graham, "Eyes Forward on Intelligence," WP (5.21.09); Hulse, "Republican Call for Inquiry on Pelosi Claim Is Rejected," NYT (5.22.09); Kane & Warrick, "Definitive Account of Briefings Still Elusive," WP (5.22.09); "Topic A: Is Pelosi in Trouble?" WP (5.21.09); FAIR (5.20.09).

120 Allen, "Intel Firestorm: GOP Reveals Briefing Info," *The Hill* (6.4.09); Kane, "House Intelligence Chairman Reyes Says CIA Lied to Committee," WP (7.9.09); "Sharing Secrets in the Capitol," NYT (7.10.09).

121 "Obama National Archives Speech," HuffPost (5.21.09).

122 Rutenberg, "A 'Freer' Cheney Makes Case (With Dual Focus)," NYT (5.21.09); Edwards & Byrne, "Fear of Prosecution Caused Cheney to Speak Out, Daughter Says," Raw Story (5.22.09); Leibovich, "New Cheney Taking Stage for the G.O.P.," NYT (9.28.09).

123 Mazzetti & Shane, "Debate over Interrogation Methods Sharply Divided the Bush White House," NYT (5.4.09); "The Torture Debate. The Missing Voices," NYT (5.7.09).

124 Meyer, "Senator Backs Inquiry on Interrogations," LAT (5.14.09); Johnston, "Bitter Start to a Hearing on Interrogation Tactics," NYT (5.14.09); Johnson, "Former Official: Treatment of Terror Suspects a 'Collective Failure,'" WP (5.13.09); Horton, "Torture Smoking Gun?" Daily Beast (5.14.09).

125 NYT (5.14.09); Petersen, Letters to the Public Editor, NYT (5.3.09); BBC (5.12.09); NPR Ombudsman (6.22.09); Letters to the Public Editor, NYT (6.5.11); Baquet, "The Executive Editor on the Word 'Torture,'" NYT (8.8.14).

126 Larry King (5.12.09); Sarlin, Interview with Ventura, Daily Beast (5.22.09); Zavis, "Panetta Urges Focus on Threats to U.S.," LAT (5.19.09).

127 Shapiro, "Did White House OK Earliest Detainee Abuse?" NPR's *All Things Considered* (5.20.09); "U.S. 'Waterboarding' Row Rekindled," BBC News (7.13.09).

128 Cohen & Agiesta, "Public Supports Closing Guantánamo," WP (1.22.09); Sidoti, "Poll: US Divided over Torture, Closing Guantánamo," AP (6.3.09); WP/ABC News Poll (6.25.09); Greenwald, "America's Regression," Salon (12.3.09); Gronke & Rejali (2010); Lobe, "U.S. Poll Tracks Shifts in Public Attitudes since 9/11," IPS News (9.2.11); Swanson, "Torture Poll: Most Americans Say Torture Is Justifiable at Times," HuffPost (12.14.12); Amnesty International, Attitudes to Torture (2014).

129 Dreazen, "Lawmakers Hold Up a Top General's Nomination," WSJ A6 (5.1.08); "Questions for General McChrystal," NYT A18 (6.1.09); Schmitt & Shanker, "U.S. Report Finds Errors in Afghan Airstrikes," NYT (6.3.09); Shanker & Schmitt, "General Given Pick of Military in Afghan War," NYT (6.11.09); McChrystal (2013).

130 Cushman, "Attorney General May Call for Interrogation Inquiry," NYT (7.12.09); Johnson, "Probe of Alleged Torture Weighed," WP (7.12.09); "Interrogations and Prosecution," WP (7.27.09); Miller & Meyer, "Criminal Investigation into CIA Treatment of Detainees Expected," LAT (8.9.09); Miller, "GOP Senators Warn Holder against CIA Abuse Inquiry," LAT A16 (8.20.09); "Top Prosecutor Orders Probe into Interrogations," CNN (8.24.09); Panetta, "Congress and the CIA: Time to Move On," WP (8.24.09); Etheridge, "Did Cheney Blink?" NYT (8.25.09); Kane & Johnson, "GOP Leader Calls CIA Probe 'Witch Hunt,' Democrats Say It's Too Narrow," WP (8.26.09); "Enhanced Interrogation," LAT (8.26.09); Rutten, "We Don't Need the Pain of Torture Indictments," LAT (8.26.09); Letters to the Editor, "We're Still a Nation of Laws," LAT (8.30.09); Miller, "Interrogation Documents Provide Fodder to Both Sides," LAT (8.26.09); Etheridge, "Did Cheney Blink?" NYT (8.25.09); Meyer, "Cheney Calls CIA Probe 'Outrageous,'" LAT A12 (8.31.09); Swarns, "Cheney Defends C.I.A. Methods on Detainees," NYT A1 (8.31.09); Monstrous, "Cheney: Interrogations Probe Is a 'Political Act,'" WP (8.31.09); Roth, "Democrats Urge Holder to Allow Torture Probe to Go Further," TPM Muckraker (8.24.09); Kane & Johnson, "GOP Leader Calls CIA Probe 'Witch Hunt'; Democrats Say It's Too Narrow," WP (8.26.09); "Dick Cheney's Version," NYT (9.3.09); "Torture's Fallout," LAT (9.3.09); Letters to the Editor: "Tortured by Cheney," LAT (9.4.09); Johnson, Markon & Tate, "Inquiry into CIA Practices Narrows," WP (9.19.09); Baker, "C.I.A. Chiefs Ask Obama to Abandon Abuse Inquiry," NYT (9.19.09); Finn, "GOP Senators Pull Out of Inquiry into CIA Program," WP (9.26.09); Kane, "Republicans Criticize Obama's Call to Delay Inquiries on Fort Hood," WP (11.18.09); Shane & Johnston, "Republicans Seek Inquiry on Fort Hood," NYT (11.18.09).

131 Kornblut, "Obama OKs Team to Interrogate Terrorists," LAT (8.24.09); Report of the Special Task Force on Interrogation and Transfer Policies (8.24.09).

132 CIA IG, Special Review: Counterterrorism Detention and Interrogation Activities, September 2001–October 2003 (2003-7123-IG 7 May 2004); Warrick & Smith, "CIA Used Gun, Drill in Interrogation," WP (8.22.09); Hosenball & Isikoff, "Report Reveals CIA Conducted Mock Executions," *Newsweek* (8.21.09); Warrick & Smith, "CIA Officer Disciplined for Alleged Gun Use in Interrogation," WP (8.23.09); Finn, Warrick & Tate, "CIA Report Calls Oversight of Early Interrogations Poor," WP (8.25.09); Smith, "Two Administrations Drew Different Lessons from 2004 CIA Report," WP (8.25.09); "Following the Torture Trail," WP (8.25.09); "The Torture Papers," NYT (8.26.09); "Enhanced Interrogation," LAT (8.26.09); Goldman, "Ex-CIA Officer Accused of Electric-Drill Torture Now Training CIA Operatives as a Contractor," Huffpost (9.7.10); Goldman & Apuzzo, "At CIA, Mistakes by Officers Are Often Overlooked," WP (2.9.11); "At CIA, Grave Mistakes, Then Promotions," AP (2.9.11).

133 Scherer & Ghosh, "McCain Denies Giving O.K. to a CIA Torture Tactic," *Time* (8.31.09).

134 Nakashima, "Intelligence Oversight Bill Faces Obstacles," WP (9.18.09); Miller, "With Bill at Obama's Desk, Congress Aims to Renew Oversight of CIA Operations," WP (9.30.10).

135 Alexander, "Torture's Loopholes," NYT (1.21.10); Feinstein, "Letter to the Editor," NYT (1.31.10); Crabtree, "Intelligence Bill Pulled over Controversial Added Interrogation Provision," *The Hill* (2.25.10).

136 Isikoff & Klaidman, "Holder under Fire," *Newsweek* (1.29.10); Johnson, "No Sanctions for Bush Lawyers Who Approved Waterboarding, Report Will Say," WP (1.31.10); "Durbin and Whitehouse React to Report on Torture Authorizations" (2.19.10); Comment of Sen. Patrick Leahy (2.19.10); "Conyers Releases Report on Torture Lawyers" (2.19.10); Lichtblau & Shane, "Report Faults 2 Who Wrote Terror Memos," NYT (2.20.10); Serrano, "Waterboarding Memo Authors Committed No Misconduct, Report Says," LAT (2.20.10); Johnson & Tate, "Authors of Waterboarding Memos Won't Be Disciplined," WP (2.20.10); "No Punishment for Torture Memos' Authors, But No Exoneration Either," WP (2.23.10); "John Yoo and Jay Bybee's Disgrace," LAT (2.23.10); "The Torture Lawyers," NYT (2.25.10); Palazzolo, "Former Justice Officials Rally Around Margolis," Main Justice (3.5.10); Isikoff, "Justice Report: CIA Memo Used by Cheney to Justify Waterboarding Was Inaccurate," *Newsweek* (2.21.10); Nakashima & Horwitz, "FBI Director James B. Comey and Senior Justice Officials Eulogize Beloved Colleague David Margolis," WP (11.2.16).

137 "Bush Defends Waterboarding al Qaeda's Professed 9/11 Mastermind," AP (6.2.10).

138 Shane, "Destroying C.I.A. Tapes Wasn't Opposed, Memo Says," NYT A16 (2.23.10).
139 Pincus, "White House Threatens Veto on Intelligence Activities Bill," WP A4 (3.16.10); Stein, "White House Agrees to Share Covert Operations Information with More Members of Congress," WP (9.27.10); Miller, "With Bill at Obama's Desk, Congress Aims to Renew Oversight of CIA Operations," WP (9.30.10).
140 Thiessen, "A Middle Ground for Interrogations," WP (2.22.10); Taylor, "Brutal, Yes, 'Torture,' Probably Not," *National Journal* (2.27.10); Oppenheimer, "Catholic Defender of Waterboarding Gets an Earful from Critics," NYT (2.27.10); "Rove 'Proud' of U.S. Waterboarding," BBC News (3.12.10).
141 Savage & Shane, "Bush Aide Calls Some Methods Used by C.I.A. Unauthorized," NYT (7.16.10); Dilanian, "Author of 'Torture Memos' Says CIA Exceeded Limits in Interrogations," LAT (7.15.10); Markon & Finn, "Ex-Justice Official Says Limits on Detainee Questionings May Have Been Exceeded," WP (7.16.10); "Investigating the Interrogators," LAT (7.21.10); Kornblut, "Bush Defends Iraq War, Use of Waterboarding," WP (11.9.10); Bush (2010); "Why George W. Bush Can Confess to Approving Torture," WP (11.15.10).
142 Finn & Tate, "2005 Destruction of Interrogation Tapes Caused Concern at CIA, E-Mails Show," WP (4.16.10); Mazzetti, "C.I.A. Leader Backed Destroying Tapes in '05," NYT (4.16.10); "E-Mail: Ex-CIA Director Porter Goss Agreed with Destroying Waterboarding Tapes, Miers 'Livid,'" AP (4.16.10); Apuzzo & Goldman, "Key Omission in Memo to Destroy CIA Terror Tapes," AP (7.26.10).
143 Johnson, "No Charges in CIA Interrogation Tape Case," NYT (11.9.10); DoJ Press Release (11.9.10); Mazzetti & Savage, "No Criminal Charges Sought over C.I.A. Tapes," NYT (11.10.10); Markon, "No Charges in Destruction of CIA Videotapes, Justice Department Says," WP (11.10.10); Dilanian, "U.S. Won't Charge CIA Officers in Destruction of Tapes," LAT (11.10.10); "The CIA Tapes: Case Not Closed," WP (11.12.10); "But Was It a Crime?" *Philadelphia Inquirer* (11.15.10); "Waffling on Waterboarding," LAT (11.16.10); "A Case for Accountability," NYT (1.26.11).
144 Yoo & Delahunty, "The Collapse of the Guantánamo Myth," WSJ (12.11.10); "Movers and Shakers: Rep. Rogers to Interrogate White House over Interrogations," Fox News (12.31.10); Gangel, "Interview with Dick Cheney on NBC," HuffPost (1.17.11); Shanker & Savage, "In Book, Rumsfeld Recalls Bush's Early Iraq Focus," NYT (2.3.11); Klein, "Rumsfeld to Diane Sawyer: 'Would've Been Better Off If I Had Resigned after Abu Ghraib'," ABC News (2.8.11); Rumsfeld (2011).
145 Goldman & Apuzzo, "At CIA, Grave Mistakes, Then Promotions," AP (2.9.11).
146 SA 1068 (11.18.11); Letters (11.22.11, 11.28.11).
147 Hsu & Agiesta, "Intelligence Chief Says FBI Was Too Hasty in Handling of Attempted Bombing," WP (1.21.10); Savage, "Delayed Miranda

Warning Ordered for Terror Suspects," NYT (3.25.11); "In Terror Probes, More Flexibility on Miranda Rights Is Needed," WP (4.7.11); "Miranda Rights and Terror Suspects," LAT (4.4.11); Dozier, "Terror Suspects Held Weeks in Secret," AP (4.8.11); Savage, "Developments Rekindle Debate over Best Approach for Terrorism Suspects," NYT (10.14.11).

148 McCarter, "Republicans Say Torture Led U.S. to bin Laden. Facts Say Otherwise," Daily Kos (5.2.11); Rubin, "Time to Reopen the Interrogation Debate," WP (5.9.11); Mukasey, "The Waterboarding Trail to bin Laden," WSJ (5.6.11); Shane & Savage, "Bin Laden Raid Revives Debate on Value of Torture," NYT (5.3.11); Dilanian, "Trail to bin Laden Began with CIA Detainee, Officials Say," LAT (5.5.11); "The Torture Apologists," NYT (5.5.11); "The Tracking of bin Laden Is No Vindication for Torture," WP (5.10.11); Yoo, "Tough Interrogations Worked," *USA Today* (5.10.11); Fried & Fried, "Torture Apologists Stain Triumph over bin Laden," WP (5.5.11); McCain, "Bin Laden's Death and the Debate over Torture," WP (5.11.11); Rodriguez, "The Path to Bin Laden's Death Didn't Start with Obama," WP (4.30.12).

149 Shane, "Role of Torture Revisited in bin Laden Narrative," NYT (5.1.12); Rodriguez, "The Path to bin Laden's Death Didn't Start with Obama," WP (4.30.12); Letter to the Editor, WP (5.8.12); see Carle (2011).

150 Zagorin, "Haunted by Homicide: Federal Grand Jury Investigates War Crimes and Torture in Death of 'The Iceman' at Abu Ghraib," *Time* (6.13.11); Statement of Attorney General Regarding Investigation into the Interrogation of Certain Detainees, DoJ (6.30.11); Finn & Tate, "Justice Department to Investigate Deaths of Two Detainees in CIA Custody," WP (6.30.11); Dilanian, "Most CIA Interrogation Cases Won't Be Pursued," LAT (6.30.11); Panetta, "Message from the Director; DoJ Investigations Moving toward Closure" (6.30.11); Lichtblau & Schmitt, "U.S. Widens Inquiries into 2 Jail Deaths," NYT (6.30.11); Roth, "The Books Aren't Closed on Bush's Torture Policy," WP (7.11.11); HRW (2011); CCR (2011); "A Debate on HRW's Call for Bush Administration Officials to be Tried for Torture," *Democracy Now!* (7.12.11).

151 Savage, "Cheney Says He Urged Bush to Bomb Syria in '07," NYT (8.25.11); Wilson & DeYoung, "In Memoir, Cheney Defends Decisions, Bush as President," WP (8.26.11); "Former VP Cheney Says Waterboarding Justified in Interest of Protecting National Security," WP (8.30.11); Cheney & Cheney (2011; 2015).

152 "Fact Check: A Tortured Look at Torture and Other Missteps in GOP Foreign Policy Debate," WP (11.13.11); Swerwer, "Bachmann: The ACLU Is Running the CIA under Obama," *Mother Jones* (11.13.11); "Two 'Rule of Law' Republicans Dissent on Torture and Assassinations," *The Atlantic* (11.13.11); Cohen, "Crazy Talk on Torture? Blame Obama," (11.13.11); "Obama Disagrees with GOP Presidential Candidates on

Waterboarding," WP (11.15.11); Woodward, "Fact Check: Hyperbole on Terror Investigations," WP (11.23.11); "The Torture Candidates," NYT (11.15.11); "The Problem with Republican Support for Waterboarding," WP (11.15.11); Thiessen, "On Waterboarding, Let's Stick to the Facts," WP (11.16.11); "Where the Republican Candidates Stand on Issues," NYT (12.31.11); Sullivan, "The Moral Scandal of Rick Santorum and 'EITs,'" Daily Beast (2.22.12); Savage, "Election May Decide When Interrogation Amounts to Torture," NYT (9.28.12); Pearlstein, "Former CIA Director Hayden on Interrogation, Common Article 3," *Opinio Juris* (4.19.12).

153 Statement of Attorney General Eric Holder on Closure of Investigation into the Interrogation of Certain Detainees, DOJ (8.30.12); Shane, "No Charges Filed on Harsh Tactics Used by the C.I.A.," NYT (8.31.12); Miller, "Justice Closes CIA Probe without Charges," WP (8.31.12); "No Penalty for Torture," NYT (9.5.12); Emptywheel (10.18.12).

154 Rodriguez & Harlow (2012); Davidson, "Q. & A.: Ali Soufan," *The New Yorker* (5.17.12); Davidson, "'I Really Resent You Using the Word 'Torture,'" *The New Yorker* (7.19.12); Joint Statement from Sens. Feinstein and Levin (4.27.12).

155 Hosenball, "Senators to Vote on Probe of CIA Interrogation Program," Reuters (12.6.12); Shane, "Portrayal of C.I.A. Torture in bin Laden Film Reopens a Debate," NYT (12.13.12); Shane, "Senate Panel Approves Findings Critical of Detainee Interrogations," NYT (12.14.12); Miller, "Report Finds Harsh CIA Interrogations Ineffective," WP (12.14.12).

156 Bruni, "Bin Laden, Torture and Hollywood," NYT (12.9.12); "McCain Rejects Torture Scene in 'Zero Dark Thirty,'" AP (12.19.12); Letters to the Editor, NYT (12.21.12); "Senators Say C.I.A. Misled Filmmakers," NYT (1.4.13); Rodriguez, "A CIA Veteran on What 'Zero Dark Thirty' Gets Wrong about the bin Laden Manhunt," WP (1.5.13); Wolf, "A Letter to Kathryn Bigelow on Zero Dark Thirty's Apology for Torture," G (1.5.13); Ignatius, "The Moral Choices on Interrogations," WP (12.13.12); Cieply, "Hollywood Makes Case for 'Zero Dark Thirty,'" NYT (1.20.13); Soufan, "Torture, Lies and Hollywood," NYT (2.24.13); Freedman, "'Zero Dark Thirty,' Through a Theological Lens," NYT (2.23.13).

157 SSCI, Questions for the Record, Mr. John Brennan (2013); Shane & Mazzetti, "Choice to Lead C.I.A. Faces a Changed Agency," NYT (1.8.13); "Nominations for Defense and the C.I.A.," NYT (1.8.13); SSCI, Open Hearing on the Nomination of John O. Brennan to Be Director of the Central Intelligence Agency (2.7.13); Mazzetti & Shane, "Drones Are Focus as C.I.A. Nominee Goes before Senators," NYT (2.8.13); "A Long Overdue Discussion," NYT (2.8.13); "John Rizzo. Former Top CIA Lawyer, Says John Brennan Never Objected to Waterboarding," HuffPost (2.12.13); DeYoung, "McCain Renews Threat to Hold Up Brennan Conformation to CIA Post," WP (2.24.13); Shane, "C.I.A.'s History Poses Hurdles for an Obama Nominee," NYT (3.7.13); "Mr. Brennan's Excuse," NYT (3.8.13).

158 Shane, "U.S. Practice Torture after 9/11, Nonpartisan Review Concludes," NYT (4.16.13); Constitution Project (2013); "Indisputable Torture," NYT (4.17.13); Pickering, "America Must Atone for the Torture it Inflicted," WP (4.17.13); Thistlethwaite, "Terror, Torture, and Truth," WP (4.18.13).

159 Miller & Tate, "CIA Report Refutes Senate Panel's Criticism of Agency's Harsh Interrogation Methods," WP (6.27.13); Mazzetti & Shane, "Senate and C.I.A. Spar over Secret Report on Interrogation Program," NYT (7.20.13).

160 Shane, "2 Senate Democrats Seek Comey's Views on Waterboarding," NYT (7.4.13); "Senate Judiciary Committee Holds Confirmation Hearing on the Nomination of James B. Comey, Jr. to Be FBI Director," CQ Congressional Transcripts (7.9.13); Schmidt, "F.B.I. Nominee Explains How View Has Changed on Interrogation Tactic," NYT (7.10.13); "A New Leader for the F.B.I.," NYT (7.10.13); "OK to Head the FBI, Except…" LAT (7.16.13); Peters, "Senate Backs F.B.I. Chief and Considers Other Picks," NYT (7.30.13); Munoz, "DoD Nominee Admits Waterboarding Was Torture," *The Hill* (7.25.13); Mayer, "Top C.I.A. Lawyer Sides with Senate Torture Report," *The New Yorker* (10.17.13).

161 Compare U.S. Department of State, Periodic Report of the United States of America to the United Nations Committee Against Torture ¶14 (8.12.13) with U.N. Committee Against Torture, Consideration of Reports Submitted by States Parties under Article 19 of the Convention ¶14 (7.25.06).

162 Taft, "Reveal What U.S. Torture Cost Us," WP (12.13.13); Harris & Hudson, "CIA Torture Report Posed for Release – At Least Some of It," FP (12.13.13); Mazzetti, "Senate Asks C.I.A. to Share its Report on Interrogations," NYT (12.18.13); Zengerle, "Mark Udall Demands CIA Report amid Dispute over Torture Study," Reuters (12.18.13); "Release the Torture Reports," NYT (12.20.13); "Declassify the Senate Report on CIA Interrogation Methods," WP (2.7.14); Mazzetti, "C.I.A. Employees Face New Inquiry amid Clashes on Detention Program," NYT (3.5.14); Landay, "Probe Sought of CIA Conduct in Senate Study of Secret Detention Program," McClatchy (3.4.14); Mazzetti, "Computer Searches at Center of Dispute on C.I.A. Detentions," NYT (3.6.14); Landay et al., "Senate Staffers Slipped Secret CIA Documents from Agency's Headquarters," McClatchey (3.6.14); Nakashima, "CIA Draws Scrutiny over Searching Senate Panel's Computers for Interrogation Report," WP (3.6.14); Mazzetti, "Behind Clash between C.I.A. and Congress, A Secret Report on Interrogations," NYT (3.8.14); Mazzetti, "Feinstein Publicly Accuses C.I.A. of Spying on Congress," NYT (3.11.14); Mazzetti & Weisman, "Conflict Erupts in Public Rebuke on C.I.A. Inquiry," NYT (3.11.14); "The C.I.A. Torture Cover-Up," NYT (3.11.14); Lewis, "Obama: White House Won't Wade into CIA Torture Report Dispute at This Time," G (3.12.14); Everett, "Saxby Chambliss Breaks with Dianne Feinstein on CIA Allegations," Politico (3.12.14);

James, "Feinstein's CIA Outrage Splits Senate," NPR (3.11.14); Raju & Bresnahan, "Mark Udall at Center of Senate–CIA Spat," Politico (3.12.14); "CIA Has a Lot of Explaining to Do: Our View," *USA Today* (3.12.14); Mazzetti, "Amid Bitter Rift, Senate Approves Pick for Top C.I.A. Lawyer," NYT (3.13.14); "The CIA Should Cooperate with the Senate on Torture Report," WP (3.16.14); Lillis, "Lawmaker 'Taken Aback' by CIA's Tough Response to Spying Allegations," *The Hill* (3.15.14); "Ex-CIA Top Lawyer: Release the 'Black Site' Report," Daily Beast (3.14.14); Denson, "Sen. Ron Wyden Scorches Senior CIA and NSA Officials and Their 'Pattern of Deception,'" *The Oregonian* (3.19.14); Lesniewski, "Reid Orders Probe of CIA Spying," RollCall.com (3.20.14); Hudson & Harris, "Agent Provocateur," FP (3.17.14); Joachim, "Reid Orders Computer Review to Defend Senate Committee in Rift with C.I.A.," NYT (3.21.14); O'Keefe, "Reid Asks CIA to Allow Senate Investigators to Examine Computers," WP (3.21.14); Miller, "Amid CIA's Battle with Senate Intelligence Committee, Brennan Strikes Conciliatory Note," WP (3.22.14); Goodman, "A Debate on Torture," *Democracy Now!* (3.28.14).

163 Watkins, "Justice Declines to Pursue Allegations That CIA Monitored Senate Intelligence Staff," McClatchy (7.10.14); Wong, "DoJ Won't Probe CIA-Senate Spy Charges," *The Hill* (7.10.14); Sen. Udall Statement (7.10.14); "Senate-CIA Dispute Unsettled As Final Investigation into Torture Report Ends," HuffPost (10.24.14); Leopold, "The Google Search That Made the CIA Spy on the US Senate," Vice.com (8.14.15); CIA IG, Report of Investigation: Agency Access to the SSCI Shared Drive on RDINet (7.18.14); Mazzetti & Hulse, "Inquiry by C.I.A. Affirms It Spied on Senate Panel," NYT (7.31.14); Everett, "2 Democrats: CIA Director John Brennan Should Resign," Politico (8.1.14); Miller, "CIA Director John Brennan Apologizes for Search of Senate Committee's Computers," WP (8.1.14); "The C.I.A.'s Reckless Breach of Trust," NYT (8.1.14); Rampton & Hollland, "Obama Says That after 9/11, 'We Tortured Some Folks,'" Reuters (8.1.14); Hulse & Mazzetti, "Obama Expresses Confidence in C.I.A. Director," NYT (8.2.14); McAuliff, "Senators Slam CIA Spying as 'Worse Than Criminal,'" HuffPost (8.1.14); Miller, "CIA Director under Fire from Lawmakers after Agency's Search of Senate Computers," WP (8.2.14); Everett, "Rand Paul: Fire Brennan," Politico (8.1.14); Watkins, "New Sparks Fly between CIA, Senate Intelligence Committee," McClatchy (9.12.14); Ackerman, "CIA Chief: 'If I've Done Something Wrong, I'll Stand Up and admit It,'" G (9.18.14); Sledge, "Ron Wyden Hits CIA Director John Brennan Over 'Culture of Misinformation,'" HuffPost (9.19.14); Stein, "What Former CIA Head Leon Panetta Says Now about Torture," *Newsweek* (10.9.14); Landay, Watkins & Taylor, "Senate's Inquiry into CIA Torture Sidesteps Blaming Bush, Aides," McClatchy (10.16.14); Pincus, "Coexistence of Aggressive Interrogation and Civil Liberties," WP (10.20.14); Panetta (2014); Bruck, "The Inside War," *The New Yorker* (6.22.15).

164 Final Report of the Rendition, Detention, and Interrogation Network Agency Accountability Board (1.14.15) www.cia.gov.library/reports/Redacted-December-2014-Agency-Accountability-Board-Report.pdf (last accessed January 1, 2015); Apuzzo & Mazzetti, "Panel to Advise against Penalty for C.I.A.'s Computer Search," NYT (12.20.14); Mazzetti & Apuzzo, "C.I.A. Officers Are Cleared in Senate Computer Search," NYT (1.15.15); Miller, "CIA Finds No Wrongdoing in Agency's Search of Computers Used by Senate Investigators," WP (1.15.15); Watkins, "White House Knew CIA Snooped on Senate, Report Says," HuffPost (1.15.15); Gerstein, "Reports Detail White House Role in CIA-Senate 'Spying Flap,'" Politico (1.15.15); "Feinstein Corrects Record on CIA Accountability Board Report," News from Dianne Feinstein (1.27.15); Hattem, "Federal Judge Denies FOIA Request for Secret CIA Document," *The Hill* (3.31.15); Ntahobari, "Dick Cheney Denies War Criminal Allegations at KPU Event," *The Eagle* (American University) (3.28.14); Cole, "Waterboard Cheney!" The Raw Story (4.7.14).

165 Mazzetti, "Senators Clear Path for Release of Detention Report on C.I.A.," NYT (4.3.14); Joachim, "Senate Panel Votes to Reveal Report on C.I.A. Interrogations," NYT (4.4.14); Miller & Goldman, "Senate Panel Votes to Release CIA Interrogation Report," WP (4.4.14); Watkins, Taylor & Lightman, "Senate Panel Finds CIA Illegally Interrogated Terror Suspects after Sept. 11," MH (4.3.14); Coleman, "Heinrich Votes to Declassify CIA Report," *Albuquerque Journal* (4.3.14); Rodriguez, "I Ran the CIA Interrogation Program," WP (4.5.14); Rogin, "Secret State Department Letter Warned: Don't Release CIA Torture Report," Daily Beast (4.7.14); Everett, "Michael Hayden under Fire for Dianne Feinstein Comment," Politico (4.7.14); Feinstein & Rockefeller, "Why the Senate Report on the CIA's Interrogation Program Should Be Made Public," WP (4.11.14); Shabad, "House Democrats Urge Obama to Quickly Declassify CIA Report," *The Hill* (4.10.14); "Senate Intelligence Committee Investigating Leak to McClatchy, Feinstein Says," McClatchy (4.12.14); Jordan, "Generals Want CIA Torture Report Declassified," Military.com (5.1.14).

166 Rosen, "CIA's Former Top Lawyer Fires Back at Senate Report, Criticizes Feinstein," McClatchy (4.16.14); Leopold, "James Mitchell: 'I'm Just a Guy Who Got Asked to Do Something for His Country,'" G (4.18.14); Altman, "Pasco Man, Behind CIA Interrogation Program, Defends Actions," *Tampa Tribune* (4.22.14); "Sarah Palin: 'Waterboarding Is How We'd Baptize Terrorists' If I Were in Charge," HuffPost (4.27.14).

167 Lynch & Chiacu, "Saxby Chambliss: CIA Interrogation Tactics Helped Get Osama bin Laden," Reuters (8.3.14); Zezima, "CIA Director Chastised by Some, Defended by Others on Sunday Shows," WP (8.4.14); "CIA Torture Debate Continues Smoldering Ahead of Senate Report," CBS News (8.3.14); Bolton, "Chambliss Slams Senate CIA Report as Partisan," *The Hill* (8.3.14); Savage, "U.S. Tells Court that Documents from Torture Investigation Should Remain Secret," NYT (12.11.14).

168 Taguba, "Stop the C.I.A. Spin on the Senate Torture Report," NYT (8.6.14).

169 Savage, "Obama Could Reaffirm a Bush-Era Reading of a Treaty on Torture," NYT (10.19.14); "Close the Overseas Torture Loophole," NYT (10.21.14); Savage, "Peace Prize Laureates Urge Disclosure on U.S. Torture," NYT (10.27.14); Koh, "Memo to the President: Say Yes to the Torture Ban," Politico (11.5.14); Savage, "U.S. to Revise Bush Policy on Treatment of Prisoners," NYT (11.12.14); DeYoung, "United Nations Asks United States to Clarify its Position on Torture," WP (11.12.14); Ackerman, "Former CIA Detainees Claim US Torture Investigators Never Interviewed Them," G (11.12.14); Savage, "U.S. Tells U.N. Panel of Steps to Revise Interrogation Policy," NYT (11.13.14); Savage, "U.N. Commission Presses U.S. on Torture," NYT (11.14.14); "UN Panel Raps US Record on Torture," WP (11.28.14); Cumming-Bruce," U.N. Panel Cites Concerns with U.S. Security Practices," NYT (11.29.14).

170 Mazzetti, "Ex-Chief of C.I.A. Shapes Response to Detention Report," NYT (7.26.14); Dilanian, "Some in 'Torture' Report Denied Chance to Read It," WP (7.28.14); Lesniewski, "Wyden Ponders Release of CIA Torture Report without White House Consent," *Roll Call* (7.25.14); Everett, "Senate's CIA Report Could Come Out in August," Politico (7.29.14); Feinstein Statement (8.5.14); Mazzetti, "Senator Denounces Redactions of Report on C.I.A. Detention Program," NYT (8.6.14); Miller, "Senate, CIA Clash over Redactions in Interrogation Report," WP (8.6.14); Rosenthal, "C.I.A. Hires Yossarian to Censor Torture Report," NYT (8.7.14); Doyle & Taylor, "Since Its Founding the CIA Rarely Has Met a Secret It Doesn't Like," *Stars and Stripes* (8.7.14); Dilanian, "Senator Says CIA Is Trying to 'Bury the Facts' from Torture Report," AP (10.23.14); Trujillo, "Udall: 'All Options' on Table with CIA Report," *The Hill* (11.13.14); "Former CIA Director Warns Torture Report Release May Endanger Overseas Personnel," HuffPost (11.17.14); "Dianne Feinstein Says Torture Report almost Ready for Release after Months of Delay," HuffPost (11.18.14); "Senate Torture Report Talks Break Down as Administration Pushes for Redactions," HuffPost (11.20.14); Mazzetti & Hulse, "Democratic Squabbling on C.I.A. Torture Report," NYT (11.21.14); "Torture Report Fight Erupts in Chaos," HuffPost (11.21.14); Firestone, "Time's Running Out for Torture Report," NYT (11.22.14); Rogin, "Kerry Puts Brakes on CIA Torture Report", Bloomberg (12.5.14); Mazzetti & Hulse, "Senate Panel Faces New Obstacle to Release of Torture Report," NYT (12.6.14); Rodriguez, "Today's CIA Critics Once Urged the Agency to Do Anything to Fight al-Qaeda," WP (12.5.14); Baker, "Bush and C.I.A. Ex-Officials Rebut Torture Report," NYT (12.8.14); "House Intelligence Committee Chair Mike Rogers on Candy Crowley," CNN (12.7.14); Landler & Baker, "White House and Republicans Clash over C.I.A. Torture Report," NYT (12.9.14); "Floor Statement by Sen. John McCain on Senate Intelligence Report on CIA Interrogation Methods" (12.9.14); White House Press Briefing (12.9.14); Mazzetti, "Panel Faults C.I.A. over Brutality and

Deceit in Terrorism Interrogations," NYT (12.10.14); Miller, Goldman & Tate, "Senate Report on CIA Program Details Brutality, Dishonesty," WP (12.10.14).

171 Hulse, "For Dianne Feinstein, Torture Report's Release Is a Signal Moment," NYT (12.10.14); Statement by Sheldon Whitehouse on SSCI Report (12.9.14).

172 Statement by John Kerry on SSCI Report (12.9.14).

173 Stein, "What Former CIA Head Leon Panetta Says Now about Torture," *Newsweek* (10.9.14); Landay, Watkins & Taylor, "Senate's Inquiry into CIA Torture Sidesteps Blaming Bush, Aides," McClatchy (10.16.14); Pincus, "Coexistence of Aggressive Interrogation and Civil Liberties," WP (10.20.14); Panetta (2014).

174 SSCI (2014).

175 Brennan to Feinstein & Chambliss (6.27.13); CIA, Comments on the Senate Select Committee on Intelligence's Study of the Central Intelligence Agency's Former Detention and Interrogation Program (June 2013).

176 Tenet et al., "Ex-CIA Directors: Interrogations Save Lives," WSJ (12.10.14); Shane, "After Senate Report's Release, Political Divide about C.I.A. Torture Remains," NYT (12.10.14).

177 "The Senate Report on the C.I.A.'s Torture and Lies," NYT (12.10.14); "The Horrors in America's 'Dungeon' Should Never Have Happened," WP (12.10.14); "Torture Report: Our Post-9/11 Shame, in Stomach-Turning Detail," LAT (12.10.14); "A Tortured Legacy of the 9/11 Terrorist Attacks," FT (12.10.14); "Prosecute Torturers and their Bosses," NYT (12.22.14); "Torture, Race, Marijuana and 12 other Big Issues of 2014," NYT (12.28.14).

178 Friedman, "We're Always Still Americans," NYT (12.10.14); Rosenthal, "Here Come the Torture Apologists," NYT (12.10.14); Ignatius, "The Senate's CIA Report Is a Necessary Public Accounting," WP (12.10.14); Marcus, "Exposing the CIA's Stain on America," WP (12.10.14); Waldman, "The Gigantic Disaster of the CIA's Torture Program," WP (12.10.14); Pincus, "Tortured Roots of Enhanced Interrogations," WP (12.17.14).

179 Yoo, "The Feinstein Report Cannot Deny a Clear Record of Success," *Time* (12.9.14); McLaughlin, "Senate Interrogation Report Distorts the CIA's Success at Foiling Terrorist Plots," WP (12.10.14); Roston, "CIA Says It Policed Its Interrogators," Buzzfeed (12.8.14); "Spooks of the Senate," WSJ (12.10.14); Baker, "Obama Catches Blame on Tactics of Torture That He Ended," NYT (12.11.14); Murphy, "CIA Chief: 'Unknowable' Whether Ordinary Interrogation Would Bring Same Intelligence Gains," WP (12.11.14); Dozier, "CIA Interrogation Chief: 'Rectal Feeding,' Broken Limbs Are News to Me," Daily Beast (12.11.14); Reilly, "Defenders of the CIA's Torture Program Dig In," HuffPost (12.10.14); Yoo, "Ignoring Risks to National Security," *National Review* (12.10.14); Stolberg & Lichtblau, "Ex-Chief Leads Vocal Defense of C.I.A.," NYT (12.12.14); Lamothe, "Former Bush Lawyer: U.S. Did Not Consider Cumulative Effects of 'Enhanced Interrogation,'" WP

(12.13.14); Shane, "Backing C.I.A., Cheney Revisits Torture Debate from Bush Era," NYT (12.15.14); "Sunday Show Wrap-Up: CIA in Spotlight," *The Hill* (12.14.14); Hattem, "Congress Won't Push Prosecutions," *The Hill* (12.14.14).

180 Mukasey, "The CIA Interrogations Followed the Law," WSJ (12.16.14); Dilanian, "Bush Officials Did Little Oversight of CIA Program," AP (12.20.14).

181 Rosenthal, "John McCain: The Anti-Cheney on Torture," NYT (12.17.14); Marcus, "Dick Cheney's Tortured Logic," WP (12.17.14); "America Should Set Torture Out of Bounds," WP (12.17.14).

182 Witte, "CIA Interrogation Report Marks Another Hit for U.S. Global Standing," WP (12.10.14); "Ex-Leader: Poland Agreed to CIA Site, Not Torture," WP (12.10.14); Herszenhorn, "Russia Denounces U.S. over Torture Report," NYT (12.11.14); Goldstein & Gladstone, "Afghan Leader Expresses Shock at Torture Revelations," NYT (12.11.14); "U.S. Allies Condemn Torture," WP (12.11.14); Feng, "Chinese Coverage of C.I.A. Torture Report Says It Highlights U.S. Hypocrisy," NYT (12.12.14); "Report Unleashes Global Criticism of CIA Interrogation Methods," Radio Free Europe (12.12.14); Hodal, "Thailand Denies It Ran Secret Prison for CIA or Allowed Torture on Its Territory," G (12.12.14); Connolly, "Romanian Ex-Spy Chief Acknowledges CIA Had 'Black Prisons' in Country," G (12.14.14); Ahmed, "From Blame Game to Half Confessions," HuffPost (12.15.14); Marinas & Lowe, "U.S. Torture Report Puts Romania's Role under Scrutiny," Reuters (12.16.14); "Torture: MEPs Call for Investigation into EU Countries' Role in CIA Practices" (12.17.14), www.europa1.europa.eu/news (last accessed January 1, 2015); "It's Been a Year since Senators Voted to Reveal CIA Torture. What Do We Have to Show for It?" G (4.3.15); Sytas & Lowe, "Lithuanian Prosecutors Restart Investigation into CIA Jail," Reuters (4.2.15); "Former Romania President Admits Allowing CIA Site," Al Jazeera (4.27.15); "U.S. Snubs Poland Request for CIA Secret Prison Documents," AP (6.13.15).

183 Sengupta, "Americans Involved in Torture Can Be Prosecuted Abroad, Analysts Say," NYT (12.11.14); Cumming-Bruce, "Torture Fight Set Back by U.S. Failure to Prosecute, U.N. Official Says," NYT (12.12.14); "UN Chief: US Torture Report Must Spur Global Action," WP (12.18.14); Pizza, "If Obama Won't Prosecute CIA Torture, Can the ICC?" Al Jazeera America (12.17.14); "It's Been a Year since Senators Voted to Reveal CIA Torture. What do we have to Show for It?" G (4.3.15); Mendez, "I Was Tortured," Politico (6.23.15); AI (2014c, 2015).

184 Baker, "Obama Catches Blame on Tactics of Torture That He Ended," NYT (12.11.14); Wiener, "Prosecute John Yoo, Says Law School Dean Erwin Chemerinsky," *The Nation* (12.12.14); Miller, "Feinstein, after Release of CIA Report, Urges Measures to Ban 'Abusive' Interrogations," WP (1.6.15); Hudson & Ratnan, "CIA Chief Won't Rule Out a Return of Torture Techniques," FP (12.11.14).

185 Risen & Apuzzo, "C.I.A. on Path to Torture, Chose Haste over Analysis," NYT (12.16.14); Leopold, "Psychologist James Mitchell Admits He Waterboarded al Qaeda Suspects," Vice (12.15.14); Campbell, "The 'Architect' of the CIA Torture Program Says Senate Report Put His Life in Danger," Business Insider (12.16.14).

186 "About Half See CIA Interrogation Methods As Justified," Pew Research Center for the People and the Press (12.15.14); Thiessen, "Democrats Lose the 'Torture' Debate,'" WP (1.15.15); "Torture Advocates Outnumbered Critics 2–1," FAIR (1.7.15).

187 Mazzetti, "C.I.A. Report Found Value of Brutal Interrogation Was Inflated," NYT (1.21.15); Everett, "Richard Burr Takes CIA Report Fight to Senate Referee," Politico (1.21.15); Hawkins, "SSCI Chairman to CIA: We'll Hide Your Documents If You Hide Ours," OpentheGovernment.org (1.23.15); Hattem, "FBI Chief Not Sure Where 'Torture Report' Is," *The Hill* (3.12.15); Gerstein, "No Obligation to Release Senate Interrogation Report, Judge Rules," Politico (5.20.15).

188 "John McCain Leading Quiet Effort to Include Torture Laws in Defense Authorization," HuffPost (5.12.15); Hattem, "McCain, Feinstein Seek to Add Anti-Torture Measure to Defense Bill," *The Hill* (6.9.15); "Senate Passes Bipartisan Amendment to Prevent Torture," HRF (6.16.15); Huetteman, "Senate Votes to Turn Presidential Ban on Torture into Law," NYT (6.17.15); High-Value Detainee Interrogation Group, Interrogation: A Review of the Science (September 2016).

189 Kheel, "Cotton: Trump Can Make 'Tough Calls' on Waterboarding," *The Hill* (11.9.16); Dozier, "Trump Backer Pushes for New CIA 'Enhanced Interrogation,'" Daily Beast (11.14.16); Wang, "Mike Pence Doesn't Rule Out Waterboarding under Trump Administration," WP (11.21.16); Shear, Hirschfield & Haberman, "Trump in Interview, Moderates Views but Defies Conventions," NYT (11.22.16); Apuzzo & Risen, "Donald Trump Faces Obstacles to Resuming Waterboarding," NYT (11.29.16); Bilefsky, "C.I.A. Chief Warns Donald Trump against Tearing Up Iran Nuclear Deal," NYT (12.1.16); Watkins, "The CIA's Torture Architect Says Harsh Interrogations Needed More Than Ever," BuzzFeed (12.6.16); Fink & Cooper, "Inside Trump Defense Secretary Pick's Efforts to Halt Torture," NYT (1.3.17); Letter to Trump from 176 Retired Flag Officers (1.6.17); Zapotsky, Horwitz & Nakashima, "Sessions Emphasizes the Primacy of the Law over His Political Views," WP (1.10.17); Demirjian & Warrick, "Trump's Pick for CIA Leader Says He Would Refuse to Restart EITs," WP (1.12.17); "Trump's Nominees Are Right: The United States Can't Go Backward on Torture," WP (1.14.17); Sen. Sessions Written Replies to SJC (1.17.17); Dozier, "Trump CIA Pick Leaves Door Open to Waterboarding, More Spying on Americans," Daily Beast (1.20.17); Davis, Sanger & Haberman, "Trump to Order Mexican Border Wall and Curtail Immigration," NYT (1.25.17); Miller, "White House Draft Order Calls for Review on Use of CIA 'Black Site' Prisons Overseas," WP (1.25.17); Mayer, "Trump's Tough-Guy Talk on Torture Risks Real Lives," New Yorker Blog (1.25.17); Mazzetti &

Savage, "Leaked Draft of Executive Order Could Revive C.I.A. Prisons," NYT (1.26.17); Wright, "Mattis, Pompeo Stunned by CIA 'Black Sites' Report," Politico (1.25.17); Bolton, "In Break with Trump, GOP Leaders Say Torture Should Remain Illegal," *The Hill* (1.26.17); Greenwood, "Trump: Waterboarding Isn't Torture," *The Hill* (1.26.17); Carney, "Intelligence Committee Democrats to Trump: Read Torture Report," *The Hill* (1.26.17); Nakamura, "Trump Says 'Torture' Works, but He'll Defer on Decision over Tactics to His Defense Secretary," WP (1.27.17); CIA Press Release (2.2.17); Miller, "CIA Officer with Ties to 'Black Sites' Named Deputy Director," WP (2.3.17); Savage, "White House Pulls Back from Bid to Reopen C.I.A. 'Black Site' Prisons," NYT (2.4.17); High-Value Detainee Interrogation Group, "Interrogation: A Review of the Science" (2016); Lawfare (6.8.17); Savage, "Trump Nominee Who Wrote Bush-Era Torture Memos Is Scrutinized," NYT (6.28.17); Grazee, "Who Is Christopher Wray, Trump's Pick for FBI Director," PBS NewsHour (7.12.17).

190 Gerstein, "Feinstein Still Pressing Obama to Declassify 'Torture Report,'" Politico (11.29.16); Levin & Rockefeller, "The Torture Report Must Be Saved," NYT (12.10.16); Letter from W. Neil Eggleston to Dianne Feinstein (12.9.16); "Declassify the Senate Torture Report," NYT (12.13.16); *al-Nashiri* v. *Obama* (D.D.C. 12.28.16); Rosenberg, "Senator Asked Pentagon Chief to Give the War Court His Copy of CIA 'Torture Report,'" MH (2.1.17); Mazzetti, Rosenberg & Savage, "Torture Report Could Remain Under Wraps," NYT (6.3.17); DeYoung, "Republican Senator Moves to Retrieve Copies of Secret Report on CIA's Brutal Detention Program," WP (6.3.17).

191 Savage, "Judge Orders Disclosure of Guantanamo Videos," NYT (10.3.14); Savage, "Videos of Force-Feeding at Guantanamo Will Stay Secret, Court Rules," NYT (4.1.17); *Dhiab* v. *Obama*, 70 F.Supp.3d 486 (D.D.C. 2014), rev'd 852 F.3d 1087 (D.C. Cir. 2017).

192 See also Luban (2014: chaps. 8–9).

193 Chekov wrote this in an 1889 letter to Aleksandr Semenovich Lazarev. In his "Memoirs," S. Shchukin reproduces the full quote: www.writingclasses.com/toolbox/ask-writer/whats-this-business-about-chekhovs-gun (last accessed March 12, 2018).

194 For a recent example of this view, see Johnson et al. (2016).

195 Fishback, Letter to McCain, WP (9.28.05); Lagouranis & Mikaelian (2007); Alexander & Brunning (2008); Edmonds (2015); Fair (2016).

196 Soufan & Freedman (2011).

197 Kiriakou & Ruby (2012); Carle (2011).

198 Compare Weiner (2007) with Weiner (2012).

199 Brecher (2007); Ginbar (2008); Allhoff (2012); Luban (2014: chaps. 3–4); APT (2007).

200 See, e.g., O'Mara (2015).

201 Elshtain (2004).

202 President's Commission on Care for America's Returning Wounded Warriors (2007).

203 Sonez, "Dover Mismanagement Requires Congressional Action, Some Lawmakers Say," WP (11.10.11); Whitlock, "Abizaid to Head Inquiry into Dover Mortuary Scandal," WP (11.22.11); Shanker, "Air Force Apologizes for Disposal of Remains," NYT (12.9.11); Whitlock, "Dumping of Partial Remains of War Dead in Va. Landfill Spurs Wider Probe," WP (12.9.11); Davenport, "Congressman Calls for Review of All 131 Military Cemeteries," WP (1.27.12); Bumiller, "9/11 Victims' Remains Disposed of in Landfill," NYT (2.29.12); Whitlock, "Portions of 9/11 Victims' Remains Taken to Landfill, Report Says," WP (2.29.12); Whitlock, "Dover Mortuary Officials Punished for Retaliating against Whistleblowers," WP (5.22.12).

204 Shenon & Lichtblau, "White House Renews Battle over Lawyer Who Signed Interrogation Memos," NYT (1.24.08); Shenon, "Tough Senate Hearing Awaits Mukasey," NYT (1.30.08).

205 Hess & Sullivan, "Obama Nominee Tied to CIA Interrogation," AP (6.4.09); Sullivan, "DHS Nominee Philip Mudd Drops Out over Ties to CIA Interrogation Tactics," HuffPost (6.5.09); Finn & Pincus, "Nominee Pulls Out as Role at CIA Is Studied," WP (6.6.09); Thompson, "Nominee Declines Position over Interrogation Program," NYT (6.6.09).

206 Munoz, "DoD Nominee Admits Waterboarding Was Torture," *The Hill* (7.25.13).

207 18 U.S.C. §§ 2340–41, 2441.

208 Santayana (1905).

209 Cockburn (2007); Rodriguez & Harlow (2012); Rizzo (2014); Harlow (2015); Mitchell & Harlow (2016).

CHAPTER 5 ELECTRONIC SURVEILLANCE

1 See Finan (2007: chap. 9); Harris (2010); Solove (2011); Horton (2015); Schneier (2015).

2 Risen & Lichtblau, "Bush Lets U.S. Spy on Callers without Courts," NYT (12.16.05); Eggen, "Bush Authorized Domestic Spying," WP (12.16.05); Farhi, "At the Times, A Scoop Deferred," WP (12.17.05); Kurtz "Bush Presses Editors on Security," WP (12.26.05); Calame, "Behind the Eavesdropping Story, a Loud Silence," NYT (1.1.06); Letters to the Public Editor, NYT (1.8.06); Leonnig, "Secret Court's Judges Were Warned about NSA Spy Data," WP (2.9.06); Lizza, "State of Deception," *The New Yorker* (12.16.13); "The War on Leaks," CBS News (10.12.14). For histories of the NSA before 9/11 see Bamford (1983, 2002); Aid (2009).

3 All but 13 lines of the 7-page memo are redacted. On the dangers of secret law, see Gotein (2016).

4 Yoo to Kollar-Kotelly (5.17.02); Savage & Lichtblau, "Classified 2002 Letter on N.S.A. Eavesdropping Is Made Public," *The Hill* (3.1.16).

5 Eggen & Lane, "On Hill, Anger and Calls for Hearings Greet News of Stateside Surveillance," WP (12.17.05); "Spying on Americans," WP

(12.18.05); Milbank, "Bush's Fumbles Spur New Talk of Oversight on Hill," WP (12.18.05).

6 Baker, "President Acknowledges Approving Secretive Eavesdropping," WP (12.18.05); Knowlton, "In Oval Office Speech, Bush Presses Defense of Iraq War," NYT (12.18.05); Sanger, "In Address, Bush Says He Ordered Domestic Spying," NYT (12.18.05); Lichtblau & Risen, "Eavesdropping Effort Began Soon after Sept. 11 Attacks," NYT (12.18.05); Risen & Lichtblau, "Rice Defends Domestic Eavesdropping," NYT (12.19.05); Canellos, "Bush's Counsel on Spying Now under Close Scrutiny," BG (12.27.05).

7 Gellman & Linzer, "Pushing the Limits of Wartime Powers," WP (12.18.05); Yen, "Lawmakers Call for Domestic Spying Probe," AP (12.18.05); Yen, "Probe Sought on NSA Surveillance," WP (12.19.05).

8 "This Call May Be Monitored…" NYT (12.18.05); "Unauthorized Snooping," WP (12.20.05).

9 Baker & Babington, "Bush Addresses Uproar over Spying," WP (12.20.05); Lichtblau & Sanger, "Administration Cites War Vote in Spying Case," NYT (12.20.05); Johnston & Greenhouse, "'01 Resolution Is Central to '05 Controversy," NYT (12.20.05); "U.S. to Probe Disclosure of NSA's Domestic Surveillance," LAT (12.30.05); "Justice Dept. Opens Inquiry into Leak of Domestic Spying," NYT (12.30.05); "U.S. Probes Eavesdropping Leak," Reuters (12.30.05); Meyer, "Leak in Domestic Spy Program Investigated," LAT (12.31.05); Eggen; "Justice Dept. Investigating Leak of NSA Wiretapping," WP (12.31.05).

10 "The Fog of False Choices," NYT (12.20.05); Will, "Why Didn't He Ask Congress?" WP (12.20.05); Posner, "Our Domestic Intelligence Crisis," WP (12.21.05); Ignatius, "The Revolt of the Professionals," WP (12.21.05); Applebaum, "Hollow Rhetoric on 'Rule of Law,'" WP (12.21.05); Brooks, "When Big Brother Is You," NYT (12.22.05); Cohen, "Trust Him with our Rights? No," WP (12.22.05); "Thank You for Wiretapping," WSJ (12.20.05).

11 Leonnig & Linzer, "Spy Court Judge Quits in Protest," WP (12.21.05); "Secret Court to Be Briefed on Spying," NYT (12.22.05); Leonnig & Linzer, "Judges on Surveillance Court to Be Briefed on Spy Program," WP (12.22.05); Hutcheson & Kuhnhenn, "Senators Demand Spying Probe," MH (12.21.05).

12 Jehl, "Spy Briefings Failed to Meet Legal Test, Lawmakers Say," NYT (12.21.05); NYT (12.22.05).

13 Moschella to Sens. Roberts and Rockefeller and Reps. Hoekstra and Harman (12.22.06); Johnston & Lewis, "Defending Spy Program, Administration Cites Law," NYT (12.23.05); "The Power to Spy," WP (12.25.05); Liptak, "Little Help from Justices on Spy Program," NYT (12.23.05); Bazan & Elsea (2006).

14 Jehl, "Among Those Told of Program, Few Objected," NYT (12.23.05); Daschle, "Power We Didn't Grant," WP (12.23.05); Gellman, "Daschle: Congress Denied Bush War Powers in U.S.," WP (12.23.05);

Spaulding, "Power Play," WP (12.25.05); Gellman, "Administration Revives Dispute over Eavesdropping Authority," WP (3.4.06).

15 Savage, "Wiretaps Said to Sift All Overseas Contacts," BG (12.23.05); Krauthammer, "Impeachment Nonsense," WP (12.23.05); Lichtblau & Risen, "Spy Agency Mined Vast Data Trove, Officials Report," NYT (12.24.05); Rivkin & Casey, "Unwarranted Complaints," NYT (12.27.05); Dean, "George W. Bush as the New Richard M. Nixon," FindLaw (12.30.05).

16 Lichtblau & Risen, "Justice Deputy Resisted Parts of Spy Program," NYT (1.1.06); "The Spy Plan's Spoiler," LAT (1.4.06).

17 Lichtblau, "Bush Defends Spy Program and Denies Misleading Public," NYT (1.2.06); Roche & Chen, "Bush Says Terrorism Warrants Spying in U.S.," LAT (1.2.06); VandeHei & Eggen, "Cheney Cites Justifications for Domestic Eavesdropping," WP (1.5.06).

18 "On the Subject of Leaks," NYT (1.4.06).

19 Shane, "Key Democrat Says Spying Violated Law," NYT (1.5.06); Shane, "Republican Senator Defends Briefings on Domestic Spying," NYT (1.6.06); Gorman, "Legal Support for Bush's Spy Actions Is Thin, Report Says," LAT (1.7.06); Lichtblau & Shane, "Basis for Spying in U.S. Is Doubted," NYT (1.7.06); Leonnig, "Report Rebuts Bush on Spying," WP (1.7.06); "Attorney General Is Asked to Testify on Spy Program," LAT (1.9.06); Lichtblau, "Judges and Justice Dept. Meet over Eavesdropping Program," NYT (1.10.06); Eggen, "Probe Set in NSA Bugging," WP (1.11.06).

20 Sanger, "In Shift, Bush Says He Welcomes Inquiry on Secret Wiretaps," NYT (1.12.06); Gerstenzang, "Bush Calls Spying Inquiry Inevitable," LAT (1.12.06); Jehl, "Specter Vows a Close Look at Spy Program," NYT (1.16.06); Reynolds, "Specter Remains Doubtful of Spy Program's Legality," LAT (1.16.06); Bergman, Lichtblau, Shane & Van Natta Jr., "Spy Agency Data after Sept. 11 Led F.B.I. to Dead Ends," NYT (1.17.06).

21 "Spying on Ordinary Americans," NYT (1.18.06); Boot, "The Wiretaps Shouldn't Bug Us," LAT (1.18.06); Eggen, "Congressional Agency Questions Legality of Wiretaps," WP (1.19.06); Shane, "Report Questions Legality of Briefings on Surveillance," NYT (1.19.06).

22 Cillizza, "Gore Says Bush Broke the Law with Spying," WP (1.17.06); Baker, "White House Disputes Gore on NSA Spying," WP (1.18.06); OLC, Legal Authorities Supporting the Activities of the National Security Agency Described by the President (1.19.06); Leonnig, "Administration Paper Defends Spy Program," WP (1.20.06); Schmitt, "Domestic Spying Gets a Boost," LAT (1.20.06); Lichtblau & Risen, "U.S. Officials Cite Legal Rationale on Spying Effort," NYT (1.20.06); Gerstenzang, "GOP Praises Eavesdropping Program," LAT (1.21.06); Lichtblau & Risen, "More Attacks and Meetings on a Program under Fire," NYT (1.21.06); "The President's End Run," WP (1.23.06).

23 Richter, "Lawmakers Debate New Limits on Spying," LAT (1.23.06); Nagourney, "Delicate Dance for Bush in Depicting Spy Program as Asset," NYT (1.23.06); Eggen & Pincus, "Campaign to Justify Spying Intensifies,"

WP (1.24.06); Sanger & Lichtblau, "Administration Starts Weeklong Blitz in Defense of Eavesdropping Program," NYT (1.24.06); Gerstenzang, "In Long Address, Bush Defends Spying Program," LAT (1.24.06).

24 Shane, "Leader Who Worked to Reshape Agency's Image Is on the Defensive," NYT (1.24.06); Eggen, "Gonzales Echoes Defense of Wiretaps," WP (1.25.06); Lichtblau, "Gonzales Invokes Actions of Other Presidents in Defense of U.S. Spying," NYT (1.25.06); Bumiller & Lichtblau, "Bush Visits Security Agency and Defends Surveillance," NYT (1.26.06); VandeHei, "Rift between Parties over NSA Wiretapping Grows," WP (1.26.06); Reynolds, "Alito Debate Focuses on Executive Power," LAT (1.26.06); Gerstenzang, "In the Eye of the Spying Storm," LAT (1.26.06).

25 Savage, "Words, Deeds on Spying Differed," LAT (1.26.06); Eggen & Pincus, "Varied Rationales Muddle Issue of NSA Eavesdropping," WP (1.27.06); Bumiller, "Bush Sees No Need for Law to Approve Eavesdropping," NYT (1.27.06); "A Discredit to the GOP," WP (1.27.06); "Spying by Another Name," LAT (1.26.06); Brownstein, "Bush's Rating Sink, but Trust Remains," LAT (1.27.06); Lichtblau & Liptak, "Bush Presses on in Legal Defense for Wiretapping," NYT (1.28.06).

26 "Spies, Lies and Wiretaps," NYT (1.29.06).

27 Bobbitt, "Why We Listen," NYT (1.30.06).

28 Bush, "We Strive to Be a Compassionate, Decent, Hopeful Society," NYT (2.1.06); "A Comfort Speech," LAT (2.1.06); Lichtblau, "Senate Panel Rebuffed on Documents on U.S. Spying," NYT (2.1.06); Babington, "Lawmakers Urge More Executive Branch Oversight," WP (2.3.06).

29 Miller, "Officials Closemouthed on Eavesdropping," LAT (2.3.06); Shane, "Senate Session on Security Erupts in Spying Debate," NYT (2.3.06); Senator Roberts Issues Statement Following the Intelligence Committee's Open World-Wide Threat Hearing (2.2.06).

30 SJC Hearing, "Wartime Executive Power and the NSA's Surveillance Authority" (2.6.06); Schmitt, "Gonzales Also Ends Up Defending his Credibility," LAT (2.7.06); Reynolds, "Gonzales Defends Spying as 'Limited and Lawful,'" LAT (2.7.06); Eggen, "Gonzales Defends Surveillance," WP (2.7.06); "Excerpts from Senate Hearing on Eavesdropping Program," NYT (2.7.06); Liptak, "In Limelight at Wiretap Hearing: 2 Laws, but Which Should Rule?" NYT (2.7.06); Lichtblau & Risen, "Top Aide Defends Domestic Spying," NYT (2.7.06); Babington, "Gonzales Denies More Extensive Domestic Spying," WP (3.3.06).

31 Babington, "Activists on Right, GOP Lawmakers Divided on Spying," WP (2.7.06); Eggen, "Limiting NSA Spying Is Inconsistent with Rationale, Critics Say," WP (2.8.06); "The President's Mouthpiece," LAT (2.7.06); "Compromise on Spying," WP (2.7.06); MoveOn Email (2.7.06); Lichtblau, "Republican Who Oversees N.S.A. Calls for Wiretap Inquiry," NYT (2.8.06); "The Art of Saying Nothing," NYT (2.8.06).

32 Shane & Lichtblau, "Full House Committee Gets Briefing on Eavesdropping," NYT (2.9.06); Reynolds, "Lawmakers Hear Details of Spy Program," LAT (2.9.06); Reynolds, "Consensus Grows for Curbs

on Surveillance," LAT (2.10.06); Babington, "Patriot Act Compromise Clears Way for Senate Vote," WP (2.10.06); "Another Set of Eyes," WP (2.10.06).

33 VandeHei, "Cheney Says NSA Spying Should Be an Election Issue," WP (2.10.06); Gerstenzang, "Conservatives' Reunion Is Less than United this Year," LAT (2.10.06); "Irresponsible Rhetoric, Again," WP (2.12.06).

34 Shane, "Attention in N.S.A. Debate Turns to Telecom Industry," NYT (2.11.06).

35 Nolan et al., Letter to Congressional Leaders (2.2.06); Nolan et al., "On NSA Spying: A Letter to Congress," NYRB (2.9.06); ABA et al. (2006).

36 Johnston, "Inquiry into Wiretapping Article Widens," NYT (2.12.06); "The Trust Gap," NYT (2.12.06); "Times Files Suit Seeking Documents," NYT (2.28.06); "Times Lawsuit Dismissed," NYT (7.3.07).

37 "Eighteen Members of Congress Call for NSA Special Counsel, as White House Rebuffs Calls," Raw Story (2.27.06).

38 "Kabuki Congress," NYT (3.6.06); Specter, Letter to the Editor, NYT (3.8.12).

39 Pincus, "Senate Panel Blocks Eavesdropping Probe," WP (3.8.06) Kirkpatrick & Shane, "G.O.P. Senators Say Accord Is Set on Wiretapping," NYT (3.8.06); Miller & Reynolds, "Republicans Kill Request for Spy Program Inquiry," LAT (3.8.06); Shane & Kirkpatrick, "G.O.P. Plan Would Allow Spying without Warrants," NYT (3.9.06); "Authorizing Surveillance," WP (3.9.06); "The Death of the Intelligence Panel," NYT (3.9.06); Miller, "On a Senate Committee, Partisanship Boils Over," LAT (3.10.06); "About That Rebellion…" NYT (3.11.06); "A Blank Check for Snoops," LAT (3.12.06); Babington, "Senate Intelligence Panel Frayed Bipartisan Infighting," WP (3.12.06).

40 Babington, "Bill Would Allow Warrantless Spying," WP (3.17.06); Lichtblau, "Judges on Secretive Panel Speak Out on Spy Program," NYT (3.29.06); Lederman, "Kris Testimony on NSA Surveillance and Possible Amendments to FISA," Balkinization (3.28.06).

41 Remarks of Senator Russ Feingold Introducing a Resolution to Censure President George W. Bush (3.13.06); Files, "Senator to Propose Censure of Bush over Spy Program," NYT (3.13.06); Simon, "Democrat Plans to Ask Senate to Censure Bush," LAT (3.13.06); "Feingold Seeks Censure of Bush," WP (3.13.06); Babington, "Feingold Pushes to Censure President," WP (3.14.06); Hulse, "Democrats Beat Quick Retreat on Call to Censure President," NYT (3.14.06); "Censure of Bush Is Debated," LAT (3.14.06); Murray, "A Senate Maverick Acts to Force an Issue," WP (3.15.06); "'Cowering' Democrats Scolded," LAT (3.15.06); Kirkpatrick, "Call for Censure Is Rallying Cry to Bush's Base," NYT (3.16.06); "Time for Facts, Not Resolutions," NYT (3.17.06); Feingold, Letter to the Editor, NYT (3.18.06); Reynolds, "Introducing Mr. McDean?" LAT (3.19.06); Hulse, "Call for Censure of Bush to Get Senate Hearing," NYT (3.25.06).

42 Babington, "Senators Debate Move to Censure Bush," WP (4.1.06); Kirkpatrick, "Call to Censure Bush Is Answered by a Mostly Empty Echo," NYT (4.1.06); Brownstein, "Seats Notably Empty at Censure Hearing," LAT (4.1.06); "Resolving the Wiretap Debate," NYT (4.6.06).

43 Eggen, "Warrantless Wiretaps Possible in U.S.," WP (4.7.06); Lichtblau, "Gonzales Suggests Legal Basis for Domestic Eavesdropping," NYT (4.7.06); "Adventures in Testifying," NYT (4.11.06); "A Start on NSA Oversight," WP (4.10.06).

44 Pincus & Babington, "Specter Wants More Debate on Spying," WP (4.28.06); Miller, "Wiretap Funding Cutoff Is Warned," LAT (4.28.06).

45 Wallsten & Hook, "Selection Ensures Welcome Revival of Wiretap Debate," LAT (5.9.06); "Shuffling Spies Around," NYT (5.9.06); Babington, "CIA Pick Open to Wiretap Oversight," WP (5.11.06).

46 Shane, "With Access Denied, Justice Department Drops Spying Investigation," NYT (5.11.06); "Security Issue Kills Domestic Spying Inquiry," *USA Today* (5.11.06); Eggen, "Bush Thwarted Probe into NSA Wiretapping," WP (7.19.06); Lewis, "Bush Blocked Ethics Inquiry, Gonzales Says," NYT (7.19.06); Schmitt, "Bush Blocked Internal Probe of Wiretaps," LAT (7.19.06); "Tap-Dancing as Fast as He Can," NYT (7.20.06); Shane, "Experts Differ about Surveillance and Privacy," NYT (7.20.06); Waas, "Aborted DoJ Probe Probably Would Have Targeted Gonzales," *National Journal* (3.15.07).

47 Cauley, "NSA Has Massive Database of Americans' Phone Calls," *USA Today* (5.11.06); Gellman & Mohammed, "Data on Phone Calls Monitored," WP (5.12.06); "More Domestic Spying," WP (5.12.06); "Ever-Expanding Secret," NYT (5.12.06); Markoff, "Questions Raised for Phone Giants in Spy Data Furor," NYT (5.13.06); Belson, "Qwest's Ex-Chief Is Suddenly Cast as Defender of Privacy," NYT (5.13.06); Savage, "Phone Firms Questioned," LAT (5.13.06); Richtel, "Newspaper Hedges on Report of Phone Companies and Data," NYT (7.1.06).

48 Chen & Richtel, "New Jersey Demands Data on Phone Call Surveillance," NYT (6.16.06); "Trenton: State Defends its Subpoena Effort," NYT (9.12.06); "Maine: Lawsuit over Phone Records," NYT A17 (9.22.06); *U.S. v. Adams*, 473 F.Supp.2d 108 (D.Me 2.8.07).

49 *In re: National Security Agency Telecommunications Records Litigation*, 630 F.Supp.2d 1092 (ND Ca 2009).

50 "Transcript of Bush's Comments on NSA Phone Monitoring," CNN (5.11.06); Hoekstra, "Keeping Secrets, Keeping Safe," LAT (5.13.06); Menn & Meyer, "Justice Department Asks U.S. Judge to Dismiss AT&T Suit," LAT (5.14.06); "A Pattern of Excess," WP (5.14.06); Rich, "Will the Real Traitors Please Stand Up?" NYT (5.14.06).

51 Shane & Lichtblau, "Cheney Pushed U.S. to Widen Eavesdropping," NYT (5.14.06).

52 Lichtblau & Shane, "Bush Is Pressed over New Report on Surveillance," NYT (5.12.06); Brownstein & Reynolds, "Congress 'Flying Blind' on NSA Issue, Some Say," LAT (5.12.06); Menn & Granelli, "As Technology

Advances, Privacy Laws Lag," LAT (5.12.06); Miller, "New Furor over NSA Phone Logs," LAT (5.12.06); "A Call to Account," LAT (5.12.06); Davis, "Hayden Nomination Seems Safe from NSA Furor," BS (5.13.06); Hulse, "Democrats See an Opening to Debate Security Issues," NYT (5.13.06).

53 Meyer, "Questions on NSA Abound," LAT (5.15.06); "FCC Member Voices Concern on Wiretaps," LAT (5.16.06); Belson, "BellSouth Denies It Gave Records to N.S.A.," NYT (5.16.06); Belson & Richtel, "Verizon Denies Turning Over Local Phone Data," NYT (5.17.06); Tumulty, "Inside Bush's Secret Spy Net," *Time* (5.22.06).

54 "Full Panels to Get Surveillance Briefing," NYT (5.17.06); Miller & Menn, "President Backs Off Wiretap Secrecy," LAT (5.17.06); Spiegel, "NSA Briefs Spy Panels on Surveillance," LAT (5.18.06); Mazzetti & Stolberg, "Wider Briefing for Lawmakers on Spy Efforts," NYT (5.18.06); Linzer & Babington, "Lawmakers Reexamine Hayden," WP (5.18.06); Tumulty, "Inside Bush's Secret Spy Net," *Time* (5.22.06); "Calling on Congress," LAT (5.18.06); Boot, "Forget Privacy, We Need to Spy More," LAT (5.17.06).

55 "Opening Statement by Michael V. Hayden before the Senate Select Committee on Intelligence" (5.18.06); "CIA Nominee Complains Embattled Agency Has Become a 'Political Football,'" MSNBC.com (5.18.06); "The Senate and the General," NYT (5.19.06); "White House Hopes to Get Senate Vote of Approval Next Week," MSNBC (5.19.06); Miller, "Hayden Defends Spying by NSA," LAT (5.19.06); Stolberg, "Senators Left Out of the Loop Make their Pique Known," NYT (5.19.06); Linzer & Babington, "Hayden Urges CIA Critics to Refrain," WP (5.19.06); Priest & Pincus, "Nominee Has Ability to Bear Bad News," WP (5.19.06); Lichtblau, "Nominee Says N.S.A. Stayed within Law on Wiretaps," NYT (5.19.06); Mazzetti, "C.I.A. Choice Says He's Independent of the Pentagon," NYT (5.19.06); "Terrorist Phone Tag," LAT (5.20.06); Hayden, "CIA Director's Address at Duquesne University Commencement" (5.4.07).

56 Liptak, "Panel Is Told Disclosures Pose Danger to Security," NYT (5.27.06); Schoenfeld, "Weak on Leaks," LAT (5.21.06); Pincus, "Prosecution of Journalists Is Possible in NSA Leaks," WP (5.22.06); Liptak, "Gonzales Says Prosecutions of Journalists Are Possible," NYT (5.22.06); "Official Secrets: Be Careful What You Read," WP (5.23.06); Pincus, "Gonzales Defends Phone-Data Collection," WP (5.24.06); "A Sudden Taste for the Law," NYT (5.24.06); Stone, "The U.S. Can Keep a Secret," LAT (6.6.06); Pincus, "Silence Angers Judiciary Panel," WP (6.7.06); NYT A5 (5.24.06); Belson, "A.C.L.U. Seeks States' Help on Phone Records Inquiry," NYT (5.25.06); Shane, "Leak of Classified Information Prompts Inquiry," NYT (7.29.06); Eggen, "Grand Jury Probes News Leaks at NSA," WP (7.29.06).

57 442 U.S. 735 (1979).

58 Mazzetti, "Senate Panel Endorses C.I.A. Nominee," NYT (5.24.06); Babington, Intelligence Panel Backs Hayden as CIA Director," WP

(5.24.06); Shane, "Senate Overwhelmingly Confirms General to Be Director of CIA," NYT (5.27.06); Babington, "Hayden Confirmed as CIA Chief," WP (5.27.06); "Make No Law," WP (5.25.06); "Regulate the Spooks," LAT (6.8.06).

59 Miller, "Specter Says Cheney Tried to Derail Hearings," LAT (6.8.06); Hulse & Rutenberg, "Specter's Uneasy Relationship with White House Is Revealed in a Letter to Cheney," NYT (6.8.06); Stolberg, "Cheney Defends Passing Senator in Defense of Eavesdropping," NYT (6.9.06); Pincus, "Specter Offers Compromise on NSA Surveillance," WP (6.9.06); "Blind Man's Bluff," NYT (6.11.06); "A Leap of Faith, Off a Cliff," NYT (6.15.06); "A Glimmer from the Hill," LAT (6.24.06); Kornblut, "Court Review of Wiretaps May Be Near, Senator Says," NYT (6.26.06).

60 Babington, "Bush Is Pressed on Reporting Domestic Surveillance," WP (7.9.06); Lichtblau, "Ally Warned Bush on Keeping Spying from Congress," NYT (7.9.06); Puzzanghera & Miller, "Republican Complains of Secrecy," LAT (7.10.06); Lichtblau & Shane, "Congressman Says Program Was Disclosed by Informant," NYT (7.10.06); Babington, "Hoekstra Urges Bush to Impart Intelligence Details," WP (7.10.06); Ackerman, "Pete Hoekstra, Intelligence Officials, and al Qaeda," TNR Online (7.13.06).

61 Babington & Baker, "Bush Compromises on Spying Program," WP (7.14.06); Mondics, "Bush Agrees to Deal on Spying Program," *Philadelphia Inquirer* (7.14.06); Schmitt & Gerstenzang, "Bush Agrees to Review of Domestic Spying Program," LAT (7.14.06); Lichtblau, "Bush Would Let Secret Court Sift Wiretap Process," NYT (7.14.06); "Wiretap Surrender," WP (7.15.06); "A License to Wiretap," LAT (7.16.06); "The Real Agenda," NYT (7.16.06); Kamins & Risdeitcher, Letter to the Editor, NYT (7.21.06); Reynolds, "Specter Sees Pluses in His Spying Bill," LAT (7.23.06); Statement of Michael S. Greco, ABA President, before Permanent Select Committee on Intelligence, House of Representatives, on FISA (7.19.06).

62 Specter, "Surveillance We Can Live With," WP (7.24.06); "Blank Check to Spy," WP (7.26.06); Lichtblau, "Administration and Critics, in Senate Testimony, Clash over Eavesdropping Compromise," NYT (7.27.06); Pincus, "Officials Urge Law to Allow Eavesdropping," WP (7.27.06).

63 Pincus, "Democrats Call NSA's Input to Senate Panel Inappropriate," WP (9.13.06).

64 Rutenberg, "Bush Aides Foresee Gains on Eavesdropping and Guantánamo," NYT (8.12.06).

65 Schmitt, "Senate Panel Sends a Mixed Message on Wiretapping," LAT (9.14.06); Weisman, "GOP Leaders Back Bush on Wiretapping, Tribunals," WP (9.14.06); Lichtblau & Zernike, "Panel in Senate Backs Bush Plan for Monitoring," NYT (9.14.06); Federation of American Scientists, Secrecy News (9.06).

66 Weisman, "Republican Rift over Wiretapping," WP (9.6.06); "No Rubber Stamp for Bush," LAT (9.17.06); "Wrong Turn on Eavesdropping," WP

(9.20.06); "House Panel Approves Wiretapping Bill," NYT (9.21.06); Weisman, "Wiretap Bill Moves Closer to Passage," WP (9.26.06); Simon & Schmitt, "Wiretap, Tribunal Bills Get Senatorial Shuffle," LAT (9.26.06); Lichtblau, "G.O.P. Reaches Tentative Deal on Domestic Spying Legislation," NYT (9.26.06); Weisman & Leonnig, "No Compromise on Wiretap Bill," WP (9.27.06); Hulse & Zernike, "Deal Is Likely on Detainees but Not on Eavesdropping," NYT (9.27.06); Schmitt, "House OKs Expanded Wiretap Program," LAT (9.29.06); Lichtblau, "House Approves Power for Wiretaps without Warrants," NYT (9.29.06); Babington & Weisman, "Senate Approves Detainee Bill Backed by Bush," WP (9.29.06); Rutenberg, "President Sees Signs Favoring G.O.P. Victory," NYT (10.12.06).

67 Lichtblau, "With Power Set to Be Split, Wiretaps Re-Emerge As Issue," NYT (11.10.06); Lichtblau, "Despite Year of Ire and Angst, Little Has Changed on Wiretaps," NYT (11.25.06); Lichtblau, "Justice Official Opens Spying Inquiry," NYT (11.28.06); "Crack in the Stone Wall," NYT (11.30.06); "NSA Still Needs More Oversight," LAT (12.12.16).

68 Transcript of DoJ Background Briefing (1.17.07); Schmitt, "U.S. Ceases Warrantless Spy Operation," LAT (1.18.07); Lichtblau & Johnson, "Court to Oversee U.S. Wiretapping in Terror Cases," NYT (1.18.07); Shane, "White House Retreats under Pressure," NYT (1.18.07); Eggen, Court Will Oversee Wiretap Program," WP (1.18.07); "A Spy Program in from the Cold," NYT (1.18.07); "'Never Mind' on Spying," LAT (1.19.07).

69 Johnston & Shane, "Senators Demand Details on New Eavesdropping Rules," NYT (1.19.07); Schmitt, Miller & Savage, "Court to Oversee U.S. Wiretapping in Terror Cases," LAT (1.19.07); Savage, "Administration Stays Course in Legal War," LAT (1.20.07); "A Retreat on Wiretapping?" WP (1.21.07); Miller, "Panel Chairman Wants Strict New Wiretap Rules," LAT (1.24.07).

70 Mazzetti, "Key Lawmakers Getting Files about Surveillance Program," NYT (2.1.07); Serrano, "U.S. to Give Congressional Records on Spying," LAT (2.1.07); Eggen, "Records on Spy Programs Turned Over to Lawmakers," WP (2.1.07); "It Hears Us," LAT (2.6.07).

71 Shrader, "McConnell Seeks to Boost U.S. Spy Powers," WP (4.10.07); Risen, "Legislation Seeks to Ease Rules on Domestic Spying," NYT (4.14.07); Pincus, "Administration Seeks to Expand Surveillance Law," WP (4.14.07); Sniffen, "Senators Cautious about Wiretap Proposal," WP (5.2.07); "Spying on Americans," NYT (5.2.07); "Fixing FISA," WP (5.7.07); "Wiser Intelligence," LAT (5.9.07).

72 Eggen & Kane, "Gonzales Hospital Episode Detailed," WP (5.16.07); Schmitt, "Panel Told of a Sickbed Face-Off," LAT (5.16.07); "Mr. Comey's Tale," WP (5.16.07); "The Gonzales Coverup," WP (5.17.07); "Caller ID," WP (5.18.07); "Mr. Gonzales's Incredible Adventure," NYT (5.17.07); Schmitt, "Now We Know Why Jim Comey Left," LAT (5.17.07); Shane & Johnston, "Loyal to Bush but Big Thorn in G.O.P. Side," NYT (5.17.07); Eggen, "Official: Cheney Urged Wiretaps," WP (6.7.07); Lederman, "'An Apocalyptic Situation': Jim Comey's (Signed but Unsent) Resignation

Letter," Balkinization (9.14.08); Gellman, "Conflict over Spying Led White House to Brink," WP (9.14.08); Gellman, "Cheney Shielded Bush from Crisis," WP (9.15.08); "Ex-Attorney General Gonzales: 'I Should Have Been More Engaged,'" NPR's Tell Me More (1.26.09); "The Director," CBS News (10.12.14).

73 "Judge Criticizes Wiretap Program," NYT (6.25.07); "U.S. Judge Takes Bush to Task over Warrantless Surveillance," LAT (6.24.07); Sniffen, "Ex-Surveillance Judge Criticizes Warrantless Taps," WP (6.24.07).

74 Risen, "Democrats May Subpoena Eavesdropping Documents," NYT (6.8.07); "Subpoena Vote Is Set in Wiretap Inquiry," NYT A14 (6.13.07); "Senator Blocks Vote on Subpoenas over Eavesdropping," NYT (6.15.07); Fletcher, "Senators Subpoena the White House," WP (6.28.07); Risen, "Subpoenas Sent to White House on Wiretapping," NYT (6.28.07); Meyer, "Wiretap Subpoenas Prod Administration," LAT (6.28.07).

75 Eggen & Kane, "Gonzales, Senators Spar on Credibility," WP (7.25.07); Schmitt, "Gonzales Loses Ground on the Hill," LAT (7.25.07); Johnston & Shane, "Gonzales Denies Improper Pressure on Ashcroft," NYT (7.25.07); "Credibility Collapse," WP (7.25.07); Waas, "What Did Bush Tell Gonzales?" *The Atlantic* (9.26.08); Waas, "The Case of the Gonzales Notes," *The Atlantic* (9.26.08).

76 Eggen & Kane, "FBI Chief Disputes Gonzales on Spying," WP (7.27.08); Schmitt, "FBI Chief Undercuts Gonzales' Testimony on Bush Wiretapping," LAT (7.27.07); Johnston & Shane, "Gonzales Dealt Blow in Account by F.B.I. Director," NYT (7.27.07); Rutenberg, "Chatty Senator on Air Force One Pushes Rules – and Buttons," NYT (7.27.07); Shane & Johnston, "Mining of Data Prompted Fight over U.S. Spying," NYT (7.29.07); Eggen, "Data Mining Figured in Dispute over NSA," WP (7.29.07); Schmitt, "Why Controversy over Gonzales' Testimony Continues to Boil," LAT (7.30.07); "Mr. Gonzales's Never-Ending Story," NYT (7.29.07); Eggen, "Cheney Disputes Libby Verdict, Voices Support for Gonzales," WP (7.31.07); Eggen, "FBI Director's Notes Contradict Gonzales's Version of Ashcroft Visit," WP (8.17.07); Johnston & Shane, "Notes Confirm Pressure on Ashcroft over Spying," NYT (8.17.07); "The Hospital Visit, Revisited," WP A14 (8.20.07).

77 "Domestic Spying Challenged in Court," NYT (1.17.06); Baker, "White House Disputes Gore on NSA Spying," WP (1.18.06); Weinstein, "Domestic Spying Program Comes under Legal Scrutiny," LAT (6.12.06); Karush, "ACLU Tries to Stop Warrantless Wiretapping," WP (6.12.06); Liptak, "Arguments on Spy Program Are Heard by Federal Judge," NYT (6.13.06).

78 *ACLU* v. *NSA*, 438 F.Supp.2d 754 (E.D. Mich. 2006); Liptak & Lichtblau, "U.S. Judge Finds Wiretap Actions Violate the Law," NYT (8.18.06); Eggen & Linzer, "Judge Rules Against Wiretaps," WP (8.18.06); "Ruling for the Law," NYT (8.18.06); "A Judicial Misfire," WP (8.18.06); Liptak, "Many Experts Fault Reasoning of Judge in Surveillance Ruling," NYT (8.19.06); Lichtblau, "Bush Predicts Appeals Court Will Lift Ban on

Wiretaps," NYT (8.19.06); "Surveillance Can Continue amid Court Appeal," LAT (10.5.06); "Bush Team States Spy Case," LAT (10.14.06); Abramowitz & Hsu, "Cheney Rejects Idea of Iraq Withdrawal," WP (11.18.06).

79 Liptak, "Secrecy at Issue in Suits Opposing Domestic Spying," NYT (1.26.07); Eggen, "Dismissal of Lawsuit against Warrantless Wiretaps Sought," WP (1.26.07); Weinstein, "ACLU Wants Access to Sealed Wiretap Filings," LAT (1.27.07); Weinstein, "Surveillance Case to Pit Strong Views," LAT (1.31.07); Bamford, "Bush Is Not Above the Law," NYT (1.31.07); Liptak, "Judges Weigh Arguments in U.S. Eavesdropping Case," NYT (2.1.07); Weinstein, "Court Hears Arguments on Wiretap Programs," LAT (2.1.07).

80 *ACLU* v. *NSA*, 467 F.3d 590 (6th Cir. 2007), cert. denied, 552 U.S. 1179 (2008); Liptak, "Panel Dismisses Suit Challenging Secret Wiretaps," NYT (7.7.07); Goldstein, "Lawsuit against Wiretaps Rejected," WP (7.7.07); Weinstein, "Court Supports Bush in Wiretap Suit," LAT (7.7.07); "Not in this Court," WP (7.7.07).

81 *Schlesinger* v. *Reservists Comm. To Stop the War*, 418 U.S. 208, 227 (1974).

82 Warrick & Pincus, "How the Fight for Vast New Spying Powers Was Won," WP (8.12.07); Roberts, "Transcript: Debate on the Foreign Intelligence Surveillance Act," *El Paso Times* (8.22.07); Miller, "Spy Chief Reveals Details of Operations," LAT (8.23.07); "The Spy Chief Speaks Out," NYT (8.26.07).

83 "More Time Sought on Spy Subpoena," LAT (8.18.07); Risen & Lichtblau, "Concerns Raised on Wider Spying under New Law," NYT (8.19.07); "Lichtblau, "Senator Threatens to Charge White House with Contempt," NYT (8.21.07); Eggen, "Cheney's Office Says it Has Wiretap Documents," WP (8.21.07); "'Contempt' Is the Word," LAT (8.22.07).

84 Eggen & Fletcher, "Embattled Gonzales Resigns," WP (8.28.07); Palz & Abramowitz, "In the End, Realities Trumped Loyalty," WP (8.28.07); Meyer & Hamburger, "Gonzales' Legacy of Controversy," LAT (8.28.07); Schmitt, "Alberto Gonzales Resigns as Attorney General," LAT (8.28.07); Lichtblau, "Attorney General Held Firm on War Policies," NYT (8.28.07); Shenon & Johnston, "A Defender of Bush's Power, Gonzales Resigns," NYT (8.28.07); "An Unlamented Exit," WP (8.28.07); "The House Lawyer Departs," NYT (8.28.07); Eggen & Kane, "Justice Dept. Probing Whether Gonzales Lied," WP (8.31.07); Shenon, "Inspector General at the Justice Dept. Is Investigating Gonzales' Testimony," NYT (8.31.07); "Gauging Gonzales," LAT (9.6.07).

85 HJC Hearing, "Warrantless Surveillance and the Foreign Intelligence Surveillance Act" (9.5.07).

86 Warrick & Pincus, "U.S. More Prepared but Faces Ongoing Threat," WP (9.11.07); Schmitt, "New U.S. Law Credited in Arrests Abroad," NYT (9.11.07); Spiegel, "Spy Chief Says Wiretap Powers Needed," LAT (9.19.07); Risen, "Warrantless Wiretaps Not Used, Official Says," NYT (9.19.07).

87 Eggen, "White House Secrecy on Wiretaps Described," WP (10.3.07); Lewis, "Panel Is Told of 'Mess' over Eavesdropping," NYT (10.3.07).

88 Nakashima, "Democrats to Offer New Surveillance Rules," WP (10.7.07); Lichtblau, "Immunity Crucial in Talks on Eavesdropping Rules," NYT (10.10.07); Nakashima, "GOP Opposes Attempt to Revise Wiretap Law," WP (10.10.07); Miller, "House Panels Pass Spy Restrictions," LAT (10.11.07); Eggen, "White House Fights Democratic Changes to Surveillance Act," WP (10.11.07); Labaton, "House Panels Vote for More Scrutiny over Foreign Eavesdropping," NYT (10.11.07); "It's Bush's Call," LAT (10.13.07); "Surveillance Update," WP (10.14.07); "Spies, Lies and FISA," NYT (10.14.07); "Veto Threat on Wiretapping Bill," NYT (10.17.07); "House GOP Derails Spy Measure," LAT (10.18.07); Weisman & Nakashima, "Senate and Bush Agree on Terms of Spying Bill," WP (10.18.07); Lichtblau, "Tentative Deal in Senate on Eavesdropping Bill," NYT (10.18.07).

89 Miller, "Senate Panel OKs Spying Legislation," LAT (10.19.07); Nakashima & Murray, "Senate Panel Approves News Surveillance Bill," WP (10.19.07); Shane & Lichtblau, "Panel Approves Eavesdropping Compromise," NYT (10.19.07); Nakashima, "Senators Say White House Cut Deal with Panel on FISA," WP (10.23.07); Lichtblau & Shane, "Phone Companies Seeking Immunity Gave to Senator," NYT (10.23.07); "The Price of Admission," WP (10.23.07); "Senate Panel to See Papers on Agency's Eavesdropping," NYT (10.26.07); "Progress on Surveillance," WP (10.27.07); Terkel, "The Wiretap This Time," NYT (10.29.07); Lichtblau, "Key Senators Raise Doubts on Eavesdropping Immunity," NYT (11.1.07); "A Promising Senate Surveillance Plan," LAT (11.2.07); Ashcroft, "Uncle Sam on the Line," NYT (11.5.07); Feingold, Letters to the Editor, NYT (11.7.07).

90 Nakashima, "A Story of Surveillance," WP (11.7.07); Risen & Lichtblau, "Ex-Worker at AT&T Fights Immunity Bill," NYT (11.7.07); Lichtblau, Risen & Shane, "Wider Spying Fuels Aid Plan for Telecoms," NYT (12.15.07).

91 Schmitt, "Justice Wiretap Probe Restarted," LAT (11.14.07); Eggen, "Justice Dept. Reopens Surveillance Probe," WP (11.14.07); Shane, "Bush Approves Clearances for N.S.A. Inquiry," NYT (11.14.07); Shenon, "Challenges Awaiting, Mukasey Takes Ceremonial Oath," NYT (11.15.07); Risen, "Senate Drops Immunity from Eavesdropping Bill," NYT (11.15.07); Woolsey, "When the CIA Comes Calling," LAT (11.15.07); McConnell, "Help Me Spy on al Qaeda," NYT (12.10.07); Letters to the Editor, NYT (12.12.07); Mukasey, "A FISA Fix," LAT (12.12.07); "The Court That May Not Be Heard," NYT (12.15.07).

92 Lichtblau, "Democrats Delay a Vote on Immunity for Wiretaps," NYT (12.18.07); Weisman & Kane, "Telecom Immunity Issue Derails Spy Law Overhaul," WP (12.18.07); "Senate Delays Eavesdropping Vote," LAT (12.18.07); "Bad Bill Now, Bad Bill Later," NYT (12.19.07); Shenon, "Mukasey Signals He'll Be a Strong Bush Advocate," NYT (12.20.07); "Reid Retreats on Eavesdropping Bill," LAT (12.22.07).

93 Lichtblau, "Democrats Try to Delay Eavesdropping Vote," NYT (1.23.08); Eggen, "Senate Opens Debate on Wiretap Measure," WP (1.24.08); Hess, "Senate Delays Eavesdropping Vote," AP (1.24.08); Alarkon, "Battle over Wiretapping Is Heating Up on the Hill," *The*

Hill (1.24.08); Jones, "White House Wants Immunity for Electronic Surveillance," *Information Week* (1.24.08); Miller, "Senate Spy Bill Still Shields Telecoms," LAT (1.25.08); Lichtblau, "In Senate, a White House Victory on Eavesdropping," NYT (1.25.08); Schwartz, "Mukasey Pushes for Electronic Surveillance," US News (1.25.08); "The FISA Follies, Redux," NYT (1.26.08); Eggen, "Veto of Wiretap Measure Is Threatened," WP (1.27.08).

94 "Senate Fails to Pass New Spying Law," LAT (1.29.08); Leahy Statement (1.28.08); Alarkon, "Senate Votes to Keep Debate Open over Foreign Surveillance Bill," *The Hill* (1.29.08); Ferraro, "Lawmakers Extend Spy Bill Amid Immunity Fight," Reuters (1.29.08); Koffler, "Surveillance and Subservience," G (1.29.08); Eggen, "Surveillance Law Extended for 15 Days," WP (2.1.08); "Trust, but Verify," LAT (2.4.08); Lichtblau, "Senate Votes for Expansion of Spy Powers," NYT (2.13.08); Kane, "Senate Authorizes Broad Expansion of Surveillance Act," WP (2.13.08); Miller, "Senate OKs Bill to Extend Wiretaps," LAT (2.13.08); Reichmann, "Bush Warns of Attacks While Backing Bill," WP (2.13.08); Lichtblau, "Eavesdropping Law Likely to Lapse," NYT A25 (2.14.08); Eggen, "Senate Passes Ban on Waterboarding, Other Techniques," WP (2.14.08); Hulse, "House Leaves Surveillance Law to Expire," NYT (2.15.08).

95 Herszenhorn, "Sharp Exchanges over Surveillance Law," NYT (2.16.08); Weisman and Eggen, "Surveillance Law Set to Expire Today," WP (2.16.08).

96 Miller, "Standoff Intensifies over Spying Legislation," LAT (2.23.08); Lichtblau, "More Sharp Words Traded over Lapsed Wiretap Law," NYT (2.23.08); Eggen & Nakashima, "Spy Law Lapse Blamed for Lost Information," WP (2.23.08); "Focus on FISA," LAT (2.23.08).

97 Barnes, "Sentence in Memo Discounted FISA," WP (5.23.08).

98 Lichtblau, "Return to Old Spy Rules Is Seen as Deadline Nears," NYT (6.10.08); Johnson, "Lawmakers Near Deal on Surveillance Bill," WP (6.14.08); "Mr. Bush v. The Bill of Rights," NYT (6.18.08); "Bush Urges Passage of Bill to Overhaul Spy Powers," NYT (6.20.08); Eggen & Kane, "Surveillance Bill Offers Protection to Telecommunication Firms," WP (6.20.08); Miller, "Accord Reached on U.S. Wiretaps," LAT (6.20.08); Lichtblau, "Deal Is Struck to Overhaul Wiretap Law," NYT (6.20.08); "A Better Surveillance Law," WP (6.20.08); "Better Tapping," LAT (6.23.08); Kane, "Senate Debates Rewrite of' 78 Law that Created Secret Intelligence Court," WP (6.26.08); Krugman, "Rove's Third Term," NYT (7.4.08); Soderberg, "A Good-Enough Spy Law," LAT (7.5.08); "FISA Follies," WP A16 (7.3.08); Fredrickson, "Letter to the Editor," WP (7.8.09); "FISA's Fetters," WP (7.9.08); Halperin, "Listening to Compromise," NYT (7.8.08); "Compromising the Constitution," NYT (7.8.08).

99 Murray, "Obama Joins Fellow Senators in Passing New Wiretapping Measure," WP (7.10.08); Lichtblau, "Senate Approves Bill to Broaden Wiretap Powers," NYT (7.10.08); Finnegan & Barabak, "Party Takes Obama Shift in Stride," LAT (7.10.08); "Bush Signs Eavesdropping Law," NYT (7.11.08).

100 Risen & Lichtblau, "Court Affirms Wiretapping without Warrants," NYT (1.15.09); Savage, "Court Calls Warrantless Wiretaps Legal," LAT (1.16.09).
101 Lichtblau & Risen, "Scale of U.S. Wiretapping Exceeded Law, Officials Say," NYT (4.16.09); Mazzetti & Lewis, "Wiretap Said to be Viewed as Serious in Late 2005," NYT (4.24.09); Risen & Lichtblau, "Extent of E-mail Surveillance Renews Concerns in Congress," NYT (6.17.09); "The Eavesdropping Continues," NYT (6.18.09).
102 *Hepting* v. *AT&T Corp.*, 439 F.Supp.2d 974 (ND Ca 2006); Menn, "Lawsuit Targets AT&T over Domestic Spying Program," LAT (2.1.06); Singel, "AT&T Sued over NSA Eavesdropping," *Wired News* (1.31.06).
103 "Court Filings Tell of Internet Spying," NYT (4.7.06); Markoff & Shane, "Documents Show Link between AT&T and Agency in Eavesdropping Case," NYT (4.13.06); Singel, "Whistle-Blower Outs NSA Spy Room," *Wired News* (4.7.06); "AT&T and Domestic Spying," NYT (4.17.06); Markoff, "U.S. Steps into Wiretap Suit against AT&T," NYT (4.29.06); Menn & Meyer, "Justice Department Asks U.S. Judge to Dismiss AT&T Suit," LAT (5.14.06); "Bush Administration Wants Spy Lawsuits Dismissed," LAT A30 (5.28.06); Caruso, "White House Invokes Privilege in Spy Cases," *Baltimore Sun* (5.27.06); Markoff, "U.S. Pushes for Dismissal of Lawsuit against AT&T," NYT (6.24.06).
104 Markoff, "Judge Declines to Dismiss Privacy Suit against AT&T," NYT (7.21.06); Liptak, "Judge Rejects Customer Suit over Records from AT&T," NYT (7.26.06); "California: Spying Lawsuits Are Consolidated," NYT (8.11.06); "California: Judge Denies Request to Unseal Records," NYT (2.21.07).
105 *Hepting* v. *AT&T Corp.*, 539 F.3d 1157 (9th Cir. 2008), cert. denied, 133 S. Ct 421 (2012).
106 *In re National Security Agency Telecommunications Records Litigation*, 633 F.Supp.2d 949 (N.D. Calif. 2009).
107 *In re National Security Agency Telecommunications Records Litigation*, 671 F.3d 881 (9th Cir. 2011); Walker, "Telecom Companies Granted Immunity in Wiretap Case," NationofChange (12.30.11); "Court Upholds Law that Protects Companies Aiding U.S. Surveillance," NYT (12.30.11); Savage, "U.S. Supreme Court Ends Suit against Telecom Firms for Aiding NSA," LAT (10.10.12).
108 Shane, "Agency and Bush Are Sued over Domestic Surveillance," NYT (9.19.08); Greenwald, "What in the Hell Is Going On in This Administration?" Salon (4.6.09); *Jewel* v. *National Security Agency*, 2010 WL 235075 (ND Ca 2010).
109 *Jewel* v. *National Security Agency*, 673 F.3d 902 (9th Cir. 2013).
110 *Jewel* v. *National Security Agency*, 965 F.Supp.2d 1090 (ND Ca 2013).
111 *Jewel* v. *NSA*, 2015 WL 545925 (ND Ca 2015); "Court Upholds NSA Snooping," *The Hill* (2.11.15).
112 *Jewel* v. *NSA*, 810 F.3d 622 (9th Cir. 2015).
113 OIGs of DoD, DoJ, CIA, NSA and ODNI, Unclassified Report on the President's Surveillance Program (7.10.09).

114 *Youngstown Steel & Tube Co.* v. *Sawyer*, 343 U.S. 579 (1952).
115 Meyer, "Bush-Era Surveillance Went Beyond Wiretaps," LAT (7.11.09); Lichtblau & Risen, "U.S. Wiretapping of Limited Value, Officials Report," NYT (7.11.09); Johnson & Nakashima, "'Inappropriate' Secrecy Hurt Surveillance Effort, Report Says," WP (7.11.09); Hess, "Bush Surveillance Program Was Massive," AP (7.11.09); "Illegal, and Pointless," NYT (7.17.09); Yoo, "Why We Endorsed Warrantless Wiretaps," WSJ (7.16.09).
116 Savage, "Public Said to be Misled on Use of the Patriot Act," NYT (9.22.11).
117 Nakashima, "Senate Panel Votes to Extend Government's Broader Surveillance Authority," WP (5.23.12); "Not So Fast on FISA," LAT (5.25.12); Yager, "House Judiciary Panel Votes to Extend Overseas Surveillance Powers," *The Hill* (6.19.12); Johnson, "Lawmakers Tangle over Renewing Surveillance Law," NPR (7.30.12); Kasperowicz, "House Votes to Allow Surveillance of Overseas Terrorists without Court Permission," *The Hill* (9.12.12); "FISA Needs to Balance Security and Liberty," WP (10.29.12).
118 Nakashima, "Sharp Debate Expected on Electronic-Intercept Law," WP (12.8.12); Cox, "Senate GOP Objects to Considering FISA Bill, Calls for Vote on House Version," *The Hill* (12.19.12); Pear, "Federal Power to Intercept Messages Is Extended," NYT (12.29.12); Nakashima, "No Classified FISA Court Rulings Made Public as a Result of Review," WP (1.20.13).
119 Leonnig & Sheridan, "Saudi Group Alleges Wiretapping by U.S.," WP (2.2.06); *Al-Haramain Islamic Foundation* v. *Bush*, 451 F.Supp.2d 1215 (D. Or. 2006); Liptak, "Secrecy at Issue in Suits Opposing Domestic Spying," NYT A1 (1.26.07); Eggen, "Dismissal of Lawsuit against Warrantless Wiretaps Sought," WP (1.26.07); Weinstein, "ACLU Wants Access to Sealed Wiretap Filings," LAT (1.27.07).
120 Liptak, "Judge Allows Islamic Group to Challenge Wiretapping," NYT (9.8.06).
121 *Al-Haramain Islamic Foundation* v. *Bush*, 507 F.3d 1190 (9th Cir. 2007). Al-Haramain had been consolidated with Hepting on April 26, 2007, but the 9th Circuit severed them. *Hepting* v. *AT&T Corp.* 508 F.3d 898 (9th Cir. 2007).
122 *In re National Security Agency Telecommunications Records Litigation*, 564 F.Supp.2d 1109 (N.D. Ca 2008).
123 *In re National Security Agency Telecommunications Records Litigation*, 700 F.Supp.2d 1182 (N.D. Ca 2010); Savage & Risen, "N.S.A. Wiretaps Were Unlawful, Judge Rules," NYT (4.1.10); Risen & Savage, "Court Ruling on Wiretap Is a Challenge for Obama," NYT (4.2.10).
124 "The Limits of 'State Secrets,'" LAT (4.3.10); "We Can't Tell You," NYT (4.4.10).
125 *Al-Haramain Islamic Foundation* v. *Obama*, 690 F.3d 1089 (9th Cir. 2012), superseded by 705 F.3d. 845 (9th Cir. 2012); Gerstein, "Appeals Court Tosses Warrantless Wiretapping Suit," Politico (8.7.12).

126 *Amnesty International* v. *McConnell*, 646 F.Supp.2d 633 (SDNY 2009); "Spying, Civil Liberties and the Courts," NYT (4.16.10).
127 *Amnesty International* v. *Clapper*, 638 F.3d 118 (2nd Cir. 2011); Lichtblau, "Court Revives Lawsuit over Government Surveillance," NYT (3.22.11); "The Right to Sue over Wiretapping," NYT (3.23.11); Lichtblau, "Split Decision and Barbed Comments Show a Court Deeply Divided on Wiretapping," NYT (9.22.11).
128 *Amnesty International* v. *Clapper*, 667 F.3d 163 (2nd Cir. 2011); "Accountability Avoidance," NYT (10.6.11).
129 "Surveillance and Accountability," NYT (10.29.12); Liptak, "Challenge to Wiretaps Heard by Justices," NYT (10.30.12).
130 *Clapper* v *Amnesty International*, 133 S. Ct. 1138 (2013); Liptak, "Justices Turn Back Challenge to Broader U.S. Eavesdropping," NYT (2.27.13); "Unbridled Secrecy," NYT (2.27.13); Savage, "Supreme Court Rules Out Secret Surveillance Lawsuits," LAT (2.26.13).
131 Epstein (2016); Hertsgaard (2016).
132 Savage & Wyatt, "U.S. Is Secretly Collecting Records of Verizon Calls," NYT (6.6.13); Nakashima, "Verizon Providing All Call Records to U.S. under Court Order," WP (6.6.13); Gellman & Poitras, "U.S. Intelligence Mining Data from Nine U.S. Internet Companies in Broad Secret Program," WP (6.6.13); Savage, Wyatt, Baker & Shear, "Spy Chief Calls Leaks on U.S. Surveillance 'Reprehensible,'" NYT (6.7.13); Baker, "Despite Ambivalence, a Strong Embrace of Divisive Security Tools," NYT (6.7.13); Weisman, "Sounding the Alarm, but with a Muted Bell," NYT (6.7.13); Gerstein & Mak, "White House: Obama 'Welcomes' Surveillance Debate," Politico (6.7.13). On the background of the disclosures, see Rusbridger, "The Snowden Leaks and the Public," NYRB (11.21.13); Reitman, "Snowden and Greenwald: The Men Who Leaked the Secrets," *Rolling Stone* (12.4.13); Greenwald (2014); Harding (2014); Bamford (2014).
133 Savage, "A.C.L.U. Files Lawsuit Seeking to Stop Collection of Domestic Phone Logs," NYT (6.12.13); Nakashima & Wilson, "ACLU Sues over NSA Surveillance Program," WP (6.12.13); Rosenthal, "How Can We Debate a Secret Law?" NYT (3.13.16).
134 Milbank, "The Left Turns Compliant on Violating Civil Liberties," WP (6.14.13).
135 Nakashima & Finn, "Lawmakers Who Warned Vaguely of Phone Record Surveillance Call for More Disclosure," WP (6.14.13).
136 "President Obama's Dragnet," NYT (6.7.13); "The Government Needs to Explain about the NSA's Phone Data Program," WP (6.7.13); "Thank You for Data-Mining," WSJ (6.7.13); "Congress Can Stop Privacy Abuse," NYT (6.8.13); Hundt, Letter to the Editor, NYT (6.8.13); "U.S. Public Should Know about Government Collection of Phone, Internet Records," WP (6.9.13); Sensenbrenner, "This Abuse of the Patriot Act Must End," G (6.9.13); Mukasey, "Leaking Secrets Empowers Terrorists," WSJ (6.10.13).
137 "A Real Debate on Surveillance," NYT (6.11.13); Schmitt, Sanger & Savage, "Administration Says Mining of Data Is Crucial to Fight

Terror," NYT (6.8.13); Pfanner & Kanter, "U.S. Internet Spying Draws Anger, and Envy," NYT (6.8.13); Baker & Sanger, "Obama Calls Surveillance Programs Legal and Limited," NYT (6.8.13); Finn & Nakashima, "Obama Defends Sweeping Surveillance Efforts," WP (6.8.13); Kane, "Debate about Surveillance Programs Scrambles Usual Lineups in Congress," WP (6.8.13); Kessler, "Obama's Claim that 'Every Member of Congress' Was Briefed on Telephone Surveillance," WP (6.11.13).

138 Kanter, "E.U. Official Pushes U.S. to Explain its Surveillance," NYT (6.12.13); Mullany & Shane, "U.S. Petitions for Extradition in N.S.A. Case," NYT (6.23.13).

139 Weisman & Sanger, "White House Plays Down Data Program," NYT (6.9.13); Shane & Weisman, "Debate on Secret Data Looks Unlikely, Partly Due to Secrecy," NYT (6.11.13); Kopicki, "Poll Finds Disapproval of Record Collection but Little Personal Concern," NYT (6.12.13); Newport, "Americans Disapproved of Government Surveillance Programs," Gallup Politics (6.12.13); Vasilogambros, "Americans Shift Their View against U.S. Surveillance Programs," *National Journal* (7.10.13); Cohen & Balz, "Poll: Privacy Concerns Rise after NSA Leaks," WP (7.24.13); Clement, "Tea Party Privacy Concerns Skyrocket, Poll Finds," WP (7.27.13); Blake, "A Turning Point in the Political Debate over Surveillance," WP (8.17.13).

140 Shapiro, "Edward Snowden NSA: Guardian Reveals Identity of Whistleblower behind NSA Revelations," HuffPost (6.9.13); Mazzetti & Schmidt, "Ex-Worker at C.I.A. Says He Leaked Data on Surveillance," NYT (6.10.13); Knowlton, "Feinstein 'Open' to Hearings on Surveillance Programs," NYT (6.10.13); Gellman, Blake & Miller, "Edward Snowden Comes Forward as Source of NSA Leaks," WP (6.10.13); "In NSA Programs, Democracy Works in Secret," WP (6.11.13); "Snowden's 'Conscience,'" WSJ (6.11.13); Shane & Weisman, "Earlier Denials Put Intelligence Chief in Awkward Position," NYT (6.12.13); Friedman, "Blowing a Whistle," NYT (6.12.13); Brooks, "The Solitary Leaker," NYT (6.11.13); Miller, "Edward Snowden's Grandiosity," WP (6.11.13); "Surveillance: A Threat to Democracy," NYT (6.12.13); "Surveillance: Snowden Doesn't Rise to Traitor," NYT (6.12.13); Nakashima & Wilson, "ACLU Sues over NSA Surveillance Program," WP (6.12.13); Ignatius, "Edward Snowden's Misplaced Idealism," WP (6.13.13); Sullivan, "More Americans See Man Who Leaked NSA Secrets as 'Patriot' Than Traitor: Poll," Reuters (6.13.13); Shane & Somaiya, "New Leak Indicates Britain and U.S. Tracked Diplomats," NYT (6.17.13); Broder, "Cheney Defends Surveillance and Says Leaks Were Traitorous," NYT (6.17.13); Thiessen, "Glenn Greenwald Committed a Crime," WP (6.17.13); Clement & Sullivan, "Poll: Public Wants Congressional Hearings on NSA Surveillance," WP (6.19.13); Shane, "Ex-Contractor Is Charged in Leaks on N.S.A. Surveillance," NYT (6.22.13); Mullany & Shane, "U.S. Petitions for Extradition in N.S.A. Case," NYT (6.23.13); Zetter, "Pro-privacy Senator Wyden on

Fighting the NSA from Inside the System," *Wired* (10.23.14); Greenwald (2014: 197–99).

141 Bradsher & Barry, "N.S.A. Leaker Leaves Hong Kong on Flight to Moscow," NYT (6.23.13); Baker & Gladstone, "U.S. Rebukes China, Russia and Ecuador over Snowden," NYT (6.24.13).

142 Milbank, "Edward Snowden's NSA Leaks Are Backlash of Too Much Secrecy," WP (6.11.13); "Sen. Wyden Notes Previous Administration Denial of Widespread Collection of Data on Americans," WP (6.11.13); Rosenthal, "Making Alberto Gonzales Look Good," NYT (6.12.13); Miller, "Misinformation on Classified NSA Programs Includes Statements by Senior U.S. Officials," WP (7.1.13); Reitman, "Q&A: Senator Ron Wyden on NSA Surveillance and Government Transparency," *Rolling Stone* (8.15.13); Lizza, "State of Deception," *The New Yorker* (12.16.13); Litt, Letter to the Editor, NYT (1.4.14); Hattem, "Spy Head: I Didn't Lie to Congress," *The Hill* (2.17.16).

143 Sanger, Savage & Schmidt, "N.S.A. Chief Says Phone Logs Halted Terror Threats," NYT (6.13.13); Nakashima & Markon, "NSA Director Says Dozens of Attacks Were Stopped by Surveillance Program," WP (6.13.13); Sanger & Peters, "A Promise of Changes for Access to Secrets," NYT (6.14.13); Miller & Horwitz, "U.S. Officials Fear NSA Leaker Has More Classified Documents," WP (6.13.13); O'Keefe, "How Far Is Too Far for NSA? (and What Is Congress Doing This Week?)," WP (6.17.13); Baker, "Obama Defends Authorization of Surveillance Programs," NYT (6.18.13); Isikoff, "U.S. Intelligence Officials: 'Dozens' of Terror Plots Disrupted by NSA Surveillance," NBC News (6.15.13); Savage, "N.S.A. Chief Says Surveillance Has Stopped Dozens of Plots," NYT (6.19.13); "Details on Spying Not More Assurances," NYT (6.19.13).

144 Bradsher, "Ex-N.S.A. Contractor's Disclosures May Draw China's Attention," NYT (6.14.13); Nocera, "This Isn't How to Stop Hacking," NYT (6.15.13); Shane & Somaiya, "New Leak Indicates Britain and U.S. Tracked Diplomats," NYT (6.17.13); Fiaola, "The Guardian: Britain, United States Spied at Summits," WP (6.17.13); Cohen, "Obama's German Storm," NYT (6.18.13); Calmes, "Merkel Challenges Obama on Surveillance," NYT (6.19.13); Calmes, "Obama Says Surveillance Helped in Case of Germany," NYT (6.20.13); Gallagher, "European Commission Squares Up to Eric Holder over 'Completely Illegal' Surveillance," *Slate* (6.19.13).

145 Gellman, "U.S. Surveillance Architecture Includes Collection of Revealing Internet, Phone Metadata," WP (6.16.13).

146 Savage, "F.B.I. Director Warns against Dismantling Surveillance Program," NYT (6.20.13); Nakashima, "Senators Say NSA Phone Records Played Little Role in Stopping Terror Plots," WP (6.20.13).

147 Shane, "Ex-Contractor Is Charged in Leaks on N.S.A. Surveillance," NYT (6.22.13); "Guardian: Leaked Documents Expose Massive UK Spying Operation Involving 200 Fiber Optic Cables," WP (6.22.13).

148 Frankel, "Where Did Our 'Inalienable Rights' Go?" NYT (6.23.13); Cohen, "The Service of Snowden," NYT (6.28.13).

149 Wallsten, Leonnig & Crites, "For Secretive Surveillance Court, Rare Scrutiny in Wake of NSA Leaks," WP (6.23.13); Savage, "Roberts's Picks Reshaping Secret Surveillance Court," NYT (7.26.13).
150 "Debate over Government's Use of Electronic Data Has Been Helpful," WP (6.23.13).
151 Kasperowicz, "Leahy Offers Bill to Sunset FISA Provisions," *The Hill* (6.24.13).
152 NSA OIG, Working Draft (3.24.09); Savage & Risen, "New Leak Suggests Ashcroft Confrontation Was over N.S.A. Program," NYT (6.28.13); Greenwald & Ackerman, "NSA Collected US Email Records in Bulk for More Than Two Years under Obama," G (6.27.13); O'Harrow & Nakashima, "President's Surveillance Program Worked with Private Sector to Collect Data after Sept. 11, 2001," WP (6.28.13); Risen, "Lawmakers Question White House Account of an Internet Surveillance Program," NYT (7.4.13); Valentino-Devries & Gorman, "Secret Court's Redefinition of 'Relevant' Empowered Vast NSA Data-Gathering," WSJ (7.8.13); Walsten, "Lawmakers Say Administration's Lack of Candor on Surveillance Weakens Oversight," WP (7.11.13).
153 Leonnig, Nakashima, & Gellman, "Secret-Court Judges Upset at Portrayal of 'Collaboration' with Government," WP (6.30.16); Lichtblau, "In Secret, Court Vastly Broadens Powers of N.S.A.," NYT (7.7.13); "The Laws You Can't See," NYT (7.9.13).
154 MacAskill & Borger, "New NSA Leaks Show How US Is Bugging Its European Allies," G (6.30.13); Shane & Sanger, "Job Title Key to Inner Access Held by Snowden," NYT (7.1.13); Castle & Schmitt, "Europeans Voice Anger over Reports of Spying by U.S. on Its Allies," NYT (7.1.13); Gordon, "Kerry Says Snowden Affair Will Not Upset China Relations," NYT (7.1.13); Nakamura, "Obama Defends U.S. Intelligence Gathering in Wake of E.U. Outrage," WP (7.1.13); DeYoung, "Kerry in Brunei, Faces European Anger over Snowden's NSA Disclosures," WP (7.1.13); Birnbaum, "E.U. Fury on Allegations of U.S. Spying," WP (7.1.13); "Obama Says All Nations Seek Intelligence, but U.S. Will Respond to European Concerns about Spying," WP (7.1.13); Erlanger, "Outrage in Europe Grows over Spying Disclosures," NYT (7.2.13); Lynch & Nakashima, "U.S. Seeks to Calm Europe over Spying Reports," WP (7.2.13); "Listening In on Europe," NYT (7.3.13); Birnbaum, "Spying Allegations Could Delay U.S.–E.U. Trade Talks," WP (7.3.13); Erlanger, "France, Too, Is Sweeping Up Data, Newspaper Reveals," NYT (7.5.13); "U.S. Needs to Deal with E.U. Concerns about NSA Spying," WP (7.5.13); Lee, "Why 'We Only Spy on Foreigners' Doesn't Work Any More for the NSA," WP (7.7.13); Richter, "Brazil Voices 'Deep Concern' over Gathering of Data by U.S.," NYT (7.8.13); Eddy, "For Western Allies a Long History of Swapping Intelligence," NYT (7.10.13); Forero, "Paper Reveals NSA Operations in Latin America," WP (7.10.13); "Germany's Merkel Rejects Parallel between NSA Activities and Stasi," WP (7.10.13); Eddy & Kanter, "Merkel Urges Europe to Tighten Internet

Safeguards," NYT (7.16.13); Birnbaum, "European Anger over NSA Spying Turns Inward," WP (7.17.13); "Germany's Merkel Faces Pre-election Turbulence as Opposition Pounces on U.S. Surveillance," WP (7.17.13); "Germany's Merkel Calls for Patience on Answers from Washington on U.S. Surveillance Programs," WP (7.19.13).

155 "Brazil Says U.S. Vice President Biden Telephoned President Rousseff about Surveillance Disclosures," WP (7.20.13); "South American Ministers Tell UN Chief of Alarm at Alleged U.S. Spying in Region and World," WP (8.6.13); "Colombia's President Seeks U.S. Clarification on Electronic Spying," WP (8.9.13); Romero, "In Brazil, Kerry Is Told Spying Sows 'Distrust,'" NYT (8.13.13); Savage & Schwirtz, "Britain Detains the Partner of a Reporter Tied to Leaks," NYT (8.19.13); "Journalist Pledges Not to Be Silenced by Partner's Detention at Heathrow Airport in London," WP (8.19.13); Erlanger, "Britons Question Whether Detention of Reporter's Partner Was Terror-Related," NYT (8.20.13); Kember & Adam, "U.S. Had Advance Notice of Britain's Plan to Detain Reporter Glenn Greenwald's Partner," WP (8.20.13); "U.K. Defends Detention of Journalist's Partner as Part of Duty to Protect National Security," WP (8.20.13); Romero, "Brazilian President Rejects Criticism over World Cup," NYT (6.3.14).

156 Gladstone & Neuman, "Snowden Is Said to Claim U.S. Is Blocking Asylum Bids," NYT (7.2.13); "Plugging the Leaks in the Edward Snowden Case," WP (7.2.13); Gladstone, Neuman & Eddy, "Bolivian President's Plane Leaves Austria after Diplomatic Scramble," NYT (7.3.13); Lally & Forero, "Plane Ferrying Bolivian President from Europe Is Caught Up in Snowden Saga," WP (7.3.13); Neuman & Smale, "Barring of Bolivian Plane Infuriates Latin America as Snowden Case Widens," NYT (7.4.13); Miller, "Suspicion of Manhunt Follows Snowden Case," WP (7.4.13); "Bolivia's Morales Says Plane Dispute Was Used by the U.S. to Intimidate Other Leaders," WP (7.5.13); Neuman & Herszenhorn, "Venezuela Offers Asylum to Snowden," NYT (7.6.13); Diaz, Forero & Englund, "Venezuela Says It Will Shelter Snowden," WP (7.6.13); "Snowden's Fate Up in Air after Nicaragua, Venezuela Say They're Willing to Grant Asylum," WP (7.6.13); Herszenhorn & Archibold, "Russian Official Says Venezuela Is the 'Best Solution' for Snowden," NYT (7.7.13); Neuman & Archibold, "U.S. Is Pressing Latin Americans to Reject Snowden," NYT (7.12.13); Barry & Roth, "Snowden Renews Plea for Moscow to Grant Asylum," NYT (7.13.13).

157 Mackey, "First Image of Snowden in Moscow Emerges from Meeting with Rights Group," NYT (7.12.13); Barry & Roth, "Snowden Renews Plea for Moscow to Grant Asylum," NYT (7.13.13); Herszenhorn, "Russia Has Received No Asylum Request from Snowden, Officials Say," NYT (7.13.13); Englund, "Snowden Says He Will Seek Asylum in Russia," WP (7.13.13); Fisher, "The White House Is Turning Up the Pressure on Moscow over Snowden," WP (7.14.13); "Snowden Has 'Blueprints' to NSA, Journalist Says," NYT (7.15.13); Herszenhorn, "Putin Does Not

Expect Ties with U.S. to Be Harmed by Snowden Case," NYT (7.17.13); Herb, Pecquet & Sink, "Sen. Graham Suggests U.S. Boycott Winter Olympics in Russia over Snowden," *The Hill* (7.16.13); Schmidt & Myers, "U.S. Letter Says Leaker Won't Face Death Penalty," NYT (7.27.13); Kramer, "Russia Grants Snowden 1-Year Asylum," NYT (8.1.13); Gorst, "Edward Snowden Receives Temporary Asylum in Russia, Leaves Moscow Airport," WP (8.1.13); Gorst & Warrick, "Snowden Granted Asylum in Russia, Leaves Moscow Airport," WP (8.2.13); "What's the Point of a Summit?" NYT (8.7.13); Rucker, "Obama Cancels Upcoming Meeting with Putin," WP (8.7.13); Baker & Myers, "Ties Fraying, Obama Drops Putin Meeting," NYT (8.8.13); "President Obama Must Find His Voice on Russia," WP (8.8.13).

158 Leonnig, "FISA Court Seeks Release of Declassified Filing in Secret Yahoo Case," WP (7.16.13); "Court Orders Declassification of Decision on Surveillance," NYT (7.17.13); Goel, "Government Push for Yahoo's User Data Set Stage for Broad Surveillance," NYT (9.13.14).

159 Miller, "3 Tech Giants Want to Reveal Data Requests," NYT (6.12.13); Herb, "GOP Leaders Pushed to Allow House Vote on Defunding the NSA," *The Hill* (7.15.13); Risen, "Bipartisan Backlash Grows against Domestic Surveillance," NYT (7.18.13); Horwitz & Branigin, "Lawmakers of Both Parties Voice Doubts about NSA Surveillance Programs," WP (7.18.13); Shane, "Surveillance Court Renews Order for Phone Call Data," NYT (7.20.13); Risen & Savage, "N.S.A. Director Lobbies House on Eve of Critical Vote," NYT (7.24.13); Franken, "We Need Transparency on Domestic Surveillance," CNN (7.23.13); Weisman, "House Defeats Effort to Rein In N.S.A. Data Gathering," NYT (7.25.13); "A Bipartisan Warning on Surveillance," NYT (7.26.13).

160 Carr, "A Better Secret Court," NYT (7.23.13); "Reforming the FISA Court," WP (7.24.13); Jakes, "Court Would Hear Opposing Views in Spy Cases," BG (7.25.13).

161 Wallsten, "NSA Surveillance Program Has Had Compliance Problems, Intelligence Official Says," WP (7.27.13); Udall & Wyden, "The White House Should End the Bulk Collection of Americans' Phone Records," WP (7.27.13); Weisman, "Momentum Builds against N.S.A. Surveillance," NYT (7.29.13); "How to Reform the NSA's Metadata Program," WP (7.29.13).

162 Horwitz & Nakashima, "Government Unveils Secret Order to Verizon," WP (7.31.13); Feinstein, "Make NSA Programs More Transparent," WP (7.30.13); Shane & Sanger, "Senate Panel Presses N.S.A. on Phone Logs," NYT (8.1.13); Nakashima, "Newly Declassified Documents on Phone Records Program Released," WP (8.1.13); "More Fog from the Spy Agencies," NYT (8.1.13); "Americans Deserve Greater Transparency on Intelligence Gathering," WP (8.1.13); "Not Every Leak Is Tantamount to Treason," WP (8.2.13); "A Lesson on Listening," *New York Daily News* (8.6.13).

163 Nakashima, "NSA Cites Case as Success of Phone Data-Collection Program," WP (8.9.13); Clapper et al., Joint Statement for the Record, SSCI (9.26.13); Schwartz, "The Whole Haystack," *The New Yorker* (1.26.15).
164 Greenwald, "XKeyscore: NSA tool collects 'nearly everything a user does on the internet,'" G (7.31.13).
165 "NSA Collects 'Word for Word' Every Domestic Communication, Says Former Analyst," *PBS Newshour* (8.5.13).
166 Savage, "N.S.A. Sifting Broader Set of Data Crossing U.S. Border," NYT (8.8.13); "Breaking Through Limits on Spying," NYT (8.9.13).
167 Arthur, "Fears over NSA Surveillance Revelations Endanger U.S. Cloud Computing Industry," G (8.8.13); Hakim, "Europe Aims to Regulate the Cloud," NYT (10.7.13); Traynor, "New EU Rules to Curb Transfer of Data to US after Edward Snowden Revelations," G (10.17.13); Traynor, "Freeze US–EU Pact Aimed at Tracking Terrorism Funds, Advises Strasbourg," G (10.23.13).
168 "Bulk Collection of Telephony Metadata under Section 215 of the USA Patriot Act (8.9.13); President Obama's News Conference (8.9.13); Savage & Shear, "President Moves to Ease Worries on Surveillance," NYT (8.9.13); "A Weak Agenda on Spying Reform," NYT (8.9.13); Nakashima & Barnes, "Administration Asserts Broad Surveillance Powers," WP (8.9.13).
169 Wallsten, "Lawmakers Say Obstacles Limited Oversight of NSA's Telephone Surveillance Program," WP (8.10.13).
170 Savage, "N.S.A. Often Broke Rules on Privacy, Audit Shows," NYT (8.16.13); Gellman, "NSA Broke Privacy Rules Thousands of Times per Year, Audit Finds," WP (8.16.13); Leonnig, "Court: Ability to Police U.S. Spying Program Limited," WP (8.16.13); Savage, "N.S.A. Calls Violations of Privacy 'Miniscule,'" NYT (8.17.13); Firestone, "What Happens When the N.S.A. Gets Sloppy," NYT (8.17.13); Wyden & Udall Statement (8.16.13); Wallsten, "House Panel Withheld Document on NSA Surveillance Program from Members," WP (8.17.13); Nakashima, "Lawmakers, Advocates Call for Reforms at NSA," WP (8.17.13); "Understanding the NSA's Errors," WP (8.18.13); Grayson, "Congressional Oversight of the NSA Is a Joke. I Should Know, I'm in Congress," G (10.25.13).
171 Wallbank, "Push to Limit Spy Programs Gains Momentum in Congress," CT (8.19.13); Peterson, "The House Is Divided over Almost Everything. But FISA Court Reform Might Be Able to Unite It," WP (10.2.13); Sasso, "Rep. Schiff Pushes Bill to Create FISA Privacy Advocate," *The Hill* (9.20.13); Raul, "After NSA Revelations, a Privacy Czar Is Needed," WP (9.23.13); Snider & Battaglia, "The National Security Agency Needs an Independent IG," WP (9.27.13).
172 Savage & Shane, "Secret Court Rebuked N.S.A. on Surveillance," NYT (8.21.13); Nakashima, "NSA Gathered Thousands of Americans' E-mails before Court Ordered It to Revise Its Tactics," WP (8.22.13);

Nakashima, "Government to Release Annual Totals of Surveillance Orders," WP (8.31.13); Nakashima, "Obama Administration Had Restrictions on NSA Reversed in 2011," WP (9.8.13); Shane, "Court Upbraided N.S.A. on Its Use of Call-log Data," NYT (9.11.13); "More Mistakes at the N.S.A.," NYT (9.12.13); Shane, "Judge Urges U.S. to Consider Releasing N.S.A. Data on Calls," NYT (9.13.13); "NSA, Other Government Agencies Should Be More Transparent," WP (9.16.13); "Steps Toward a Less Secret Court," NYT (9.18.13); Gerstein, "Surveillance Court Chafes at Obama Administration Secrecy," Politico (11.20.13).

173 *In re Application of the Federal Bureau of Investigation for an Order Requiring the Production of Tangible Things*, FISC BR 13–109 (8.29.13); Savage, "Extended Ruling by Secret Court Backs Collection of Phone Data," NYT (9.18.13); Savage, "N.S.A. Plan to Log Calls Is Renewed by Court," NYT (10.18.13); *In re Application of the Federal Bureau of Investigation for an Order Requiring the Production of Tangible Things*, FISC BR 13–158 (10.11.13).

174 "German Magazine: NSA Decrypted, Spied on, United Nations' Internal Video Conferencing System," WP (8.25.13); Smale, "Surveillance Revelations Shake U.S. German Ties," NYT (8.26.13); "UN Says Nations Are Barred from Spying on It, Will Address US about Snowden Leak on Hacking," WP (8.27.13); "N.S.A. Said to Have Spied on Leaders of Brazil and Mexico," NYT (9.2.13); Romero & Archibold, "Brazil Angered over Report N.S.A. Spied on President," NYT (9.3.13); "Obama: US Not Spying on Europeans' Emails or Phone Calls, Surveillance Programs under Review," WP (9.4.13); Chappell, "Mexico Summons U.S. Ambassador, Seeking Answers to Spying Claims," NPR (9.3.13); Romero, "Obama Tries to Sooth Brazil and Mexico over Spying Reports," NYT (9.7.13); Romero, "N.S.A. Spied on Brazilian Oil Company, Report Says," NYT (9.9.13); Romero, "Brazil: Answers Are Sought on N.S.A. Spying," NYT (9.10.13); "Allegations That NSA Has a Listening Post in Vienna Turn into Austrian Affair of State," WP (9.13.13); Romero, "Brazil's Leader Postpone State Visit to Washington over Spying," NYT (9.18.13); Saxena, "NSA Planted Bugs at Indian Missions in D.C., U.N.," *The Hindu* (9.25.13); Barbara, "Have a Nice Day, N.S.A.," NYT (9.27.13); "Brazil Announces Secure Email to Counter U.S. Spying," AFP (10.1.13); Gluesing, Poitras, Rosenbach & Star, "Fresh Leak on US Spying: NSA Accessed Mexican President's Email," Spiegel Online (10.20.13); Ford, "Mexico Lashes Out against Report of U.S. Spying," CNN (10.21.13); "France Seeks Explanation after 'Shocking' US Spying Claims," AFP (10.21.13); Chrisafis & Jones, "Snowden Leaks: France Summons US Envoy over NSA Surveillance Claims," G (10.21.13); Rubin, "French Condemn Surveillance by N.S.A.," NYT (10.21.13); Traynor & Chrisafis, "MEPs Tighten Up Draft Data Privacy Rules after Snowden Revelations," G (10.22.13); Rubin, "France: U.S. Wiretapped Envoys, Newspaper Reports, Citing Leaks," NYT (10.22.13); "New Leaks, New Repercussions," NYT (10.22.13);

"Diplomat: Obama Promises US Probe into Reported Spying on Mexico Presidential Email System," WP (10.22.13); "James Clapper: Reports US Tapped French Phones 'False,'" BBC News (10.23.13); Shoichet, "Mexico to Summon U.S. Ambassador over Spying Allegations," CNN (10.23.13); "The U.S. Needs to Adjust Its Policy toward Spying on Allies," WP (10.22.13); "Readout of the President's Phone Call with Chancellor Merkel of Germany," White House (10.23.13); Traynor, Ottermann & Lewis, "Angela Merkel's Call to Obama: Are You Bugging My Mobile Phone?" G (10.23.13); Sanchez, "US Denies Spying on David Cameron," DT (10.24.13); Smale, "Anger Growing among Allies on U.S. Spying," NYT (10.23.13); Ball, "NSA Monitored Calls of 35 World Leaders after US Official Handed Over Contacts," G (10.24.13); "Report: US and UK Spied on Italian Government," Al Jazeera America (10.24.13); Spiegel & Peel, "Merkel Floats EU–US Privacy Pact as Anger Mounts over Spying," FT (10.24.13); Smale, "Amid New Storm in U.S.–Europe Relationship, a Call for Talks on Spying," NYT (10.25.13); Spiegel & Fontanella-Khan, "Merkel and Hollande to Change Intelligence Ties with US," FT (10.25.13); "Alleged Electronic Targeting of Allies Must End, French President Says," WP (10.25.13); "European Leaders Denounce Alleged US Spying on EU Allies," WP (10.24.13); Bilefsky, "Indignation in Europe over Claims that U.S. Spied on Merkel's Phone," NYT (10.24.13); "N.S.A. Snooping and the Damage Done," NYT (10.25.13); "Brazil Seeks UN Resolution to Guarantee Internet Privacy amid Anger over US Surveillance," WP (10.25.13); Smale, Eddy & Sanger, "Data Suggests Push to Spy on Merkel Dates to '02," NYT (10.27.13); Knowlton, "Lawmaker Offers Strong Defense of U.S. Surveillance Efforts in Europe," NYT (10.27.13); Birnbaum, "Merkel May Have Been Monitored by U.S. since 2002, Magazine Reports," WP (10.27.13); Gorman & Entous, "Obama Unaware as U.S. Spied on World Leaders: Officials," WSJ (10.28.13); "NSA 'Monitored 60 Million Spanish Calls in a Month,'" BBC News (10.28.13); Gold, "Peter King: Obama Should Stop Apologizing for NSA," Politico (10.27.13); Dilanian & Stobart, "White House OKd Spying on Allies, U.S. Intelligence Officials Say," LAT (10.28.13); Wilson & Gearan, "Obama Didn't Know about Surveillance of U.S.–Allied World Leaders until Summer, Officials Say," WP (10.28.13); Minder, "Spain Summons American Ambassador on New Reports of N.S.A. Spying," NYT (10.28.13); "The White House on Spying," NYT (10.28.13); "Birds, Bees and NSA Spies," WSJ (10.28.13); Sasso, "Security Chiefs Seek to Soothe Outrage over NSA Surveillance," *The Hill* (10.29.13); Harris, Shachtman & Groll, "Intelligence Vets: Of Course Obama Knew about NSA Spying," FP (10.29.13); Higgins & Kanter, "As It Denounces U.S. Spying, Europe Delays Privacy Protection at Home," NYT (10.29.13); "US 'Spied on Vatican in Run-Up to Conclave,'" Al Jazeera (10.30.13); "China, Other Asian [countries] Angry over Embassy Spy Reports," G (10.31.13); "James Clapper: Spying on Leaders Not Significant Enough to Tell Congress," HuffPost (10.29.13); Perlez, "Australia Said to Play

Part in N.S.A. Effort," NYT (11.1.13); Cochrane, "Indonesia Summons Australian Envoy on Spying Reports," NYT (11.1.3); Wan, "Outrage at Alleged U.S. Spying Efforts Gathers Steam in Asian Capitals," WP (11.1.13); Gerstein, "EU: NSA Chief Alexander Acknowledged Spying in Europe," Politico (10.30.13); Hosenball, "Obama Halted NSA Spying on IMF and World Bank Headquarters," Reuters (10.31.13); Ischinger, "Restoring Trans-Atlantic Trust," NYT (11.2.13); Romero, "Brazil Acknowledges Spying on Diplomatic Targets," NYT (11.4.13); "Brazil and Germany Introduce UN Resolution to Protect Internet Privacy from Eavesdroppers," WP (11.7.13); "Spain: U.S. Ambassador Says NSA Acts Legally in Spain, Respects Citizens' Privacy, Spanish Law," WP (11.8.13); Cochrane, "N.S.A. Spying Scandal Hurts Close Ties between Australia and Indonesia," NYT (11.20.13); "Rights Groups Urge UN to Back Privacy Protection," WP (11.22.13); Lynch, "Inside America's Plan to Kill Online Privacy Rights Everywhere," FP (11.20.13); MacAskill & Ball, "UN Surveillance Resolution Goes Ahead despite Attempts to Dilute Language," G (11.21.13); "UN Advances Internet Privacy Resolution," WP (11.27.13); Austen, "Ire in Canada over Report N.S.A. Spied from Ottawa," NYT (11.29.13); MacAskill, Ball & Murphy, "Revealed: Australian Spy Agency Offered to Share Data about Ordinary Citizens," G (12.1.13); Root, "French Intelligence Involved in NSA Spying in France, Monde Says," Bloomberg (11.29.13); Ball & Farrell, "NSA Considered Spying on Australians 'Unilaterally,' Leaked Paper Reveals," G (12.4.13); Soto & Winter, "Saab Wins Brazil Jet Deal after NSA Spying Sours Boeing Bid," Reuters (12.18.13); Traynor, "NSA Surveillance: Europe Threatens to Freeze US Data-Sharing Arrangements," G (11.26.13); Scott, "Europe Urges U.S. to Handle Data Privacy with Care," NYT (11.28.13); Birnbaum, "Germany Looks at Keeping its Internet, E-mail Traffic Inside its Borders," WP (11.1.13); UN High Commissioner for Human Rights, "The Right to Privacy in the Digital Age" (6.30.14); McLaughlin, "U.N. Gives U.S. Flunking Grades on Privacy and Surveillance Rights," The Intercept (7.28.15).

175 Bevins, "Why Did Brazil's President Change Her Tune on Spying," FP (6.16.15); Alcindor, "WikiLeaks: U.S. Wiretapped Brazilian Presidents," *USA Today* (7.4.15); "Wikileaks Files Said to Show N.S.A. Spied on French Leaders," NYT (6.24.15); Rubin, "France Denounces Revelations of Spying by N.S.A.," NYT (6.24.15); McLaughlin, "French Justice Minister Says Snowden and Assange Could Be Offered Asylum," The Intercept (6.25.15); "Wikileaks Says NSA Spied on Top French Companies," France24 (6.30.15); Moritsugi, "WikiLeaks Says U.S. Spied on Japanese Government, Companies," WP (7.31.15); Fifield, "WikiLeaks Says U.S. Spied on Another Ally – This Time, Japan," WP (8.1.15); "Japan's Abe Asks Biden for Investigation of Possible U.S. Spying," Reuters (8.5.15); Hongo, "Abe Asks U.S. to Investigate Alleged NSA Spying on Japanese Government," WSJ (8.26.15).

176 Savage, "Senators Call for Surveillance Inquiry," NYT (9.24.13); Sasso, "Judiciary Chairman Takes Aim at NSA," *The Hill* (9.24.13);

Savage, "Senators Push to Preserve N.S.A. Phone Surveillance," NYT (9.27.13); Sasso & Tummarello, "House Intelligence Panel Working on Bill to Save NSA Spying," *The Hill* (10.8.13); Sasso & Tummarello, "Patriot Act Author Preps Freedom Act to Rein in NSA," *The Hill* (10.9.13); Nakashima, "NSA Bills Set up a Choice in Congress: End Bulk Collection of Phone Records or Endorse It," WP (10.28.13); Sasso, "Lawmakers Propose USA Freedom Act to Curb NSA's Powers," *The Hill* (10.29.13); Serwer, "Former NSA Supporters Join Critics in Calling for Reform," MSNBC (10.28.13); Timberg & Nakashima, "Amid NSA Spying Revelations, Tech Leaders Call for New Restraints on Agency," WP (11.1.13); Nakashima, "Senate Bill Would Approve NSA Program but Try to Curb It," WP (10.31.13); "NSA Oversight Should be Tough, Clear and Fair," WP (11.2.13); Romm, "Intelligence IG Rebuffs Hill on Surveillance Probe," *The Hill* (11.6.13); Gerstein, "Intelligence Panel Sharply Split on Surveillance Reforms," Politico (11.15.13).

177 Gerstein, "Obama Aides: Transparency Plans Could Harm Security," Politico (11.13.13).

178 Risen & Poitras, "N.S.A. Gathers Data on Social Connections of U.S. Citizens," NYT (9.29.13); Ball, "NSA Stores Metadata of Millions of Web Users for up to a Year, Secret Files Show," G (9.30.13); Savage, "In Test Project, N.S.A. Tracked Cellphone Locations," NYT (10.3.13); Nakashima, "NSA Had Test Project to Collect Data on Americans' Cellphone Locations, Director Says," WP (10.3.13); Lennard, "NSA Director Admits to Misleading Public on Terror Plots," Salon (10.2.13); Gellman & Soltani, "NSA Collects Millions of E-mail Address Books Globally," WP (10.15.13); Elliott & Meyer, "The NSA's Big Terrorism Claim Doesn't Hold Up," ProPublica (10.23.13); Maas, "The Intercept's Laura Poitras Wins Academy Award for 'Citizenfour,'" The Intercept (2.23.15).

179 "Edward Snowden Says Mass Surveillance Programs Are Making People Less Safe," WP (10.13.13); "Awards for Guardian," G (10.21.13); Rice-Oxley, "Edward Snowden Voted Guardian Person of the Year 2013," G (12.9.13); "Snowden Awarded Swedish 'Alternative Nobel,'" Al Jazeera (9.24.14); Barron, "Polk Awards Honor Articles on N.S.A. Surveillance," NYT (2.17.14); Cohen, "Snowden to Receive Truth-Telling Prize," NYT (4.6.14); Lewis & Ottermann, "Angela Merkel Denied Access to Her NSA File," G (4.10.14); Davidson, "The Guardian Wins an Emmy for Coverage of NSA Revelations," G (9.30.14); MacAskill, "Edward Snowden Wins Swedish Human Rights Award for NSA Revelations," G (12.1.14); Noack, "The Global Cult of Edward Snowden Keeps Growing," WP (6.24.15).

180 Gellman & Soltani, "NSA Infiltrates Links to Yahoo, Google Data Centers Worldwide, Snowden Documents Say," WP (10.30.13); Gellman, Soltani & Peterson, "How We Know the NSA Had Access to Internal Google and Yahoo Cloud Data," WP (11.5.13); Perlroth & Markoff, "N.S.A. May Have Penetrated Internet Cable Links," NYT (11.26.13); Dorling, "Singapore, South Korea Revealed as Five Eyes

Spying Partners," *Sydney Morning Herald* (11.25.13); "U.S. Protesters Call for End to Spying," Al Jazeera America (10.26.13).

181 Savage & Risen, "Latest Release of Documents on N.S.A. Includes 2004 Ruling on Email Surveillance," NYT (11.18.13); Nakashima & Miller, "Official Releasing What Appears to Be Original Court File Authorizing NSA to Conduct Sweeps," WP (11.19.13); Chen "AT&T and Verizon Pressed to Detail Roles in U.S. Surveillance Efforts," NYT (11.21.13); "Surveillance Goes on Trial," NYT (11.23.13); Ackerman, "U.S. Withholding FISA Court Orders on NSA Bulk Collection of Americans' Data," G (1.21.14).

182 Risen & Poitras, "N.S.A. Report Outlined Goals for More Power," NYT (11.23.13).

183 Wyden, Udall & Heinrich, "End the N.S.A. Dragnet, Now," NYT (11.25.13); Glanz, "Documents Say Phones Outside U.S. Are Tracked," NYT (12.5.13); Gellman & Soltani, "NSA Tracking Cellphone Locations Worldwide, Snowden Documents Show," WP (12.5.13); Glanz, Larson & Lehren, "Spy Agencies Tap Data Streaming from Phone Apps," NYT (1.28.14); Esposito, Cole, Shone & Greenwald, "Snowden Documents Reveal British Spies Snooped on YouTube and Facebook," NBC News (1.28.14).

184 Gerstein, "Obama Plans New Limits on NSA Surveillance," Politico (12.5.13); Taylor & Hopkins, "World's Leading Authors: State Surveillance of Personal Data is Theft," G (12.9.13).

185 Wyatt & Miller, "Tech Giants Issue Call for Limits on Government Surveillance of Users," NYT (12.9.13); Timberg, "Major Tech Companies United to Call for New Limits on Surveillance," WP (12.9.13); "An Open Letter to Washington," NYT (12.9.13); Lewis, "Demands for 'NSA reform' intensifying," G (12.9.13); Gustin, "NSA Spying Scandal Could Cost U.S. Tech Giants Billions," *Time* (12.10.13); Tummarello, "Silicon Valley Warns NSA Surveillance Poses Threat to Overseas Growth," *The Hill* (12.10.13); Statement of Edward J. Black to Senate Judiciary Committee (12.11.13); Miller, "Revelations of N.S.A. Spying Cost U.S. Tech Companies," NYT (3.22.14); Joachim, "Obama and Tech Executives to Meet Again on Privacy Issues," NYT (3.22.14); Taylor, "NSA Revelations 'Changing How Businesses Store Sensitive Data,'" G (3.30.14).

186 Cole et al., Joint Statement to SJC (12.11.13); Calmes & Wingfield, "Tech Leaders and Obama Find Shared Problem: Fading Public Trust," NYT (12.18.13); Kang & Nakashima, "Tech Executives to Obama: NSA Spying Revelations Are Hurting Business," WP (12.18.13).

187 Nakashima, "At Senate Hearing, NSA Director Defends Spying Program," WP (12.12.13).

188 President's Review Group on Intelligence and Communications Technologies (2013); Sanger, "Obama Panel Said to Urge N.S.A. Curbs," NYT (12.12.13); Rosenthal, "Restraining the N.S.A.," NYT (12.14.13); Clarke et al., "Protecting Citizens, and Their Privacy," NYT (12.19.13); Sanger & Savage, "Obama Is Urged to Sharply Curb

N.S.A. Data Mining," NYT (12.19.13); "Turn Off the Data Vacuum," NYT (12.19.13); Nakashima & Soltani, "Panel Urges New Curbs on Surveillance by U.S.," WP (12.19.13); "Mr. Obama's Disappointing Response," NYT (12.21.13); Rucker & Miller, "Obama Promises Review of NSA Spying Program, Possible Reforms," WP (12.21.13); Statement by Sen. Feinstein on President's Review Group Findings (12.20.13); "NSA Could Improve Transparency without Harming Security," WP (12.21.13); Huetteman, "Debating the N.S.A.'s Data Collection and a Panel's Findings," NYT (12.22.13); Gibson, "Leahy, Peter King Debate NSA," Politico (12.22.13); "Bad Times for Big Brother," NYT (12.21.13); McLaughlin, "NSA Intel-Gathering Programs Keep Us Safe," WP (1.2.14); Bradbury, "Don't Limit the NSA's Effectiveness," WP (1.4.14); Bergen et al., "Do NSA's Bulk Surveillance Programs Stop Terrorists?" New America (1.13.14); Nakashima, "NSA Phone Record Collection Does Little to Prevent Terrorist Attacks, Group Says," WP (1.13.14).

189 Glantz & Lehren, "N.S.A. Spied on Allies, Aid Groups and Businesses," NYT (12.21.13); Nakashima, "NSA, British Spy Agency Targeted Many Foreign Interests, Including Allies, Aid Agencies," WP (12.21.13); Eglash, "In Israel, Officials Use U.S. Spying Revelation to Bring New Focus to Pollard Case," WP (12.22.13); "Israeli Ministers Demand End to U.S. Spying," WP (12.22.13).

190 Gellman, "Edward Snowden, after Months of NSA Revelations, Says His Mission's Accomplished," WP (12.23.13); Castle, "TV Message by Snowden Says Privacy Still Matters," NYT (12.25.13); CBS's *Face the Nation* (12.29.13); "Edward Snowden: Whistle-Blower," NYT (1.2.14); "Snowden Affair: the Case for a Pardon," G (1.1.14); Sullivan & Clement, "Clemency for Edward Snowden? The Public Is Skeptical," WP (1.3.14); Baker, "Moves to Curb Spying Help Drive the Clemency Argument for Snowden," NYT (1.5.14); Knowlton, "Senators Differ Sharply on Penalty for Snowden," NYT (1.6.14); *This Week* Transcript, ABC News (1.4.14); Cohen, "Make a Deal with Snowden," WP (1.7.14); Richinick, "Rep. Peter King: Rand Paul Creating 'Hysteria,'" MSNBC (1.6.14); Kenny, "U.S. Willing to Hold Talks If Snowden Pleads Guilty," NYT (1.24.14).

191 Schneider & Kenney, "Defending His Actions, Snowden Says He's a Patriot," NYT (5.29.14); Sanger, "N.S.A. Releases Email That It Says Undercuts Snowden's Whistle-Blower Claim," NYT (5.30.14); Nakashima & Gellman, "U.S. Officials, Snowden Clash over E-mail Records," WP (5.30.14).

192 European Parliament, Committee on Civil Liberties, Justice and Home Affairs, Draft Report (1.8.14); Bilefsky, "E.U. Panel Invites Snowden to Testify on Privacy Breaches," NYT (1.10.14); European Parliament, Scientific and Technological Options Assessment, "An Appraisal of Technologies of Political Control" (1.6.98), cited in Bamford (2008: 16 and notes).

193 Baker & Savage, "Obama Seeks Balance in Plan for Spy Programs," NYT (1.10.14); Harris & Hudson, "Inside the White House Meetings

to Reform the NSA," FP (1.9.14); Rep. Goodlatte, Statement (1.9.14); Bates to Feinsten (1.13.14); Nakashima, "Tech Firms: We Don't Want to Keep Internet Metadata for the Government," WP (1.13.14); Baker & Savage, "Obama to Place Some Restraints on Surveillance," NYT (1.15.14); Gerstein, "Surveillance Critics, Defenders Square Off on Hill," Politico (1.14.14); Shabad, "Schiff Unveils NSA Metadata Reform Bill," *The Hill* (1.14.14).

194 Remarks by the President on Review of Signals Intelligence (1.17.14); Presidential Policy Directive/PPD-28 (1.17.14); Landler & Savage, "Obama Outlines Calibrated Curbs on Phone Spying," NYT (1.18.14); "The President on Mass Surveillance," NYT (1.18.14); "Obama's Political Surveillance," WSJ (1.19.14); "Grading President Obama's NSA Speech," WP (1.18.14); "Obama's NSA Reforms: A Significant Step," LAT (1.19.14).

195 Munsil, "'Lethal Consequences' Seen in NSA Leak," Politico (1.9.14); Schmitt & Sanger, "Congressional Leaders Suggest Earlier Snowden Link to Russia," NYT (1.20.14); Tsukayama, "NSA Program Defenders Question Snowden's Motives," WP (1.20.14); Savage, "Snowden Denies Suggestions That He Was a Spy for Russia," NYT (1.22.14); Kessler, "Is Snowden Working for the Russians?" WP (1.22.14); Goldman, "Snowden Denies Receiving Assistance from Russian Intelligence with NSA Leaks," WP (1.22.14); Mazzetti & Sanger, "Top Intelligence Official Assails Snowden and Seeks Return of N.S.A. Documents," NYT (1.30.14); Peralta, "Lawmaker Says Snowden Leaks Will Cost Country 'Billions to Repair,'" NPR (2.5.14); Remnick, "Going the Distance," *The New Yorker* (1.27.14).

196 Sanger & Shanker, "N.S.A. Devises Radio Pathway into Computers," NYT (1.15.14); "Cisco Chief Urges Obama to Curb NSA Surveillance Activity," Reuters (5.18.14).

197 PCLOB (2014a); Savage, "Watchdog Report Says N.S.A. Program Is Illegal and Should End," NYT (1.23.14); Nakashima, "Independent Review Board Says NSA Phone Data Program Is Illegal and Should End," WP (1.23.14); "End the Phone Data Sweeps," NYT (1.24.14); Nakashima, "Obama Disagrees with Watchdog Group's Conclusion That NSA Phone Program Is Illegal," WP (1.23.14); Tummarello, "Privacy Board Report Last Straw on NSA Surveillance Program, Lawmakers Say," *The Hill* (1.23.14); Republican National Committee, Resolution to Renounce the National Security Agency's Surveillance Program; "Republican National Committee Denounces NSA Spying, Calls for Investigation," G (1.24.14).

198 Tillman, "DoJ, Tech Companies Reach Deal on Disclosure of Surveillance Data," *National Law Journal* (1.27.114); Apuzzo & Perlroth, "U.S. Relaxes Some Data Disclosure Rules," NYT (1.28.14); "Making Surveillance a Little Less Opaque," NYT (2.2.14); "Web Companies Give First Look at Secret Government Data Requests," Reuters (2.3.14).

199 Hattem & Tummarello, "Officials Defend NSA, Decry Snowden," *The Hill* (1.29.14); Ruger, "Congress Pushed NSA Reforms, Dechert Lawyer Objects," *National Law Journal* (2.4.14); Savage, "Republicans Spar

on Leaks and Surveillance, Underscoring Partisan Shake-Up," NYT (2.5.14); Savage, "Letter Tells of U.S. Searches for Emails and Calls," NYT (4.2.14); Ackerman, "NSA performed Warrantless Searches on Americans' Calls and Emails – Clapper," G (4.1.14); Hattem, "Lawmakers Incensed over NSA 'Loophole,'" *The Hill* (4.1.14); Nakashima, "NSA Searched Americans' Communications without a Warrant, Intelligence Director Says," WP (4.1.14).

200 Garfield, Testimony to HJC hearing "Examining Recommendations to Reform FISA Authorities" (2.4.14).

201 "For the NSA, Espionage Was a Means to Strengthen the U.S. Position in Climate Negotiations," *Information* (Denmark) (1.30.14); Smale, "German Paper Says U.S. Kept Tabs on Leader," NYT (2.5.14); Goldfarb & Nakamura, "Obama and French President Hollande Discuss NSA Spying at Joint News Conference," WP (2.12.14); Scott, "E.U. Leaders Seek Way to Protect Individuals' Data," NYT (2.19.14); "U.S. Now Bugging German Ministers in Place of Merkel – Report," Reuters (2.23.14); Jolly, "European Union Takes Steps toward Protecting Data," NYT (3.12.14); Harding, "Edward Snowden: US Government Spied on Human Rights Workers," G (4.8.14).

202 Ruger, "Chief Justice Roberts Names Two Judges to Surveillance Court," *Legal Times* (2.7.14); "NSA Gets under 30 Percent of Phone Data," WP (2.8.14); Nakashima, "Official: Court's Sign-Off for Queries on Americans' Data Would Be Impractical," WP (3.20.14); Wheeler, "The Changing Composition of the FISC and What if Anything to Do About It," Lawfare Research Paper Series (2016); Ruger, "Study Finds Surveillance Court Skews Republican," *Legal Times* (6.6.14).

203 Risen & Poitras, "Spying by N.S.A. Ally Entangled U.S. Law Firm," NYT (2.16.14); Gordon, "Indonesia Takes Aim at Australia over Spying, but Not the U.S.," NYT (2.17.14); Ruger, "ABA Presses the NSA over Attorney–Client Privilege," *Legal Times* (2.21.14); Alexander, letter to Silkenat (3.10.14).

204 Ackerman & Ball, "Yahoo Webcam Images from Millions of Users Intercepted by GCHQ," G (2.27.14); Tummarello, "Tech Industry Slams NSA Webcam Spying," *The Hill* (2.27.14); Ackerman, "Senators to Investigate NSA Role in GCHQ 'Optic Nerve' Webcam Spying," G (2.28.14).

205 Tummarello, "An End to Warrantless Email Searches?" *The Hill* (2.2.14).

206 "Targeting Huawei: NSA Spied on Chinese Government and Networking Firm," Spiegel Online (3.22.14); Sanger & Perlroth, "N.S.A. Breached Chinese Servers Seen As Security Threat," NYT (3.23.14); Nakashima, "NSA Targeted Network of Chinese Tech Firm Huawei, Leaked Document Shows," WP (3.23.14); Wan, "China Demands U.S. Explanation about Reports of NSA Hacking into Huawei," WP (3.24.14); Jacobs, "After Reports on N.S.A., China Urges End to Spying," NYT (3.25.14); Hennessey, "Obama Defends NSA Spying in Meeting with Chinese President," LAT (3.24.14); Schmidt, "U.S. to Charge Chinese Army Personnel with Cyberspying," NYT (5.19.14); Sanger, "With Spy

Charges, U.S. Draws a Line that Few Others Recognize," NYT (5.20.14); Sanger, "Fine Line Seen in U.S. Spying on Companies," NYT (5.21.14); Buckley, "China Threatens Security Checks for Tech Firms after U.S. Indictments," NYT (5.2.14); Buckley, "Beijing Levels New Attack at U.S. Cyber-Spying," NYT (5.27.14); Ramzy, "China Pulls Cisco into Dispute on Cyberspying," NYT (5.27.14); Denyer, "China Removes Top U.S. Tech Firms from Government Purchasing List," WP (2.28.15).

207 Savage, "Obama to Call for End to N.S.A.'s Bulk Data Collection," NYT (3.25.14); Nakashima, "White House Plan Would End NSA's Bulk Collection of Americans' Phone Data," WP (3.25.14); Savage, "Obama Says N.S.A. Curbs Would Address Worries," NYT (3.26.14); "Mr. Obama's Limits on Phone Records," NYT (3.26.14); Throp, "House Intel Panel Unveils NSA Metadata Overhaul Bill," NBC News (3.25.14); Nakashima, "White House Pushes Congress to Quickly Pass Changes to NSA Data Collection Program," WP (3.28.14); "Limiting NSA's Reach," MH (3.27.14); Knowlton, "Feinstein Gives Tentative Nod to Data Curbs," NYT (3.31.14); "Congress Needs to Reach a Deal on the NSA Phone Program," WP (3.31.14).

208 Poitras, Rosenbach & Stark, "'A' for Angela: GCHQ and NSA Targeted Private German Companies and Merkel," Spiegel Online (3.29.14); Faiola, "Germany Opens Hearings on U.S. Spying," WP (4.4.14); Lewis & Ottermann, "Angela Merkel Denied Access to her NSA File," G (4.10.14); Sanger, "U.S. and Germany Fail to Reach a Deal on Spying," NYT (5.2.14); Landler, "Merkel Signals That Tension Persists over U.S. Spying," NYT (5.3.14); "German Lawmakers Want to Interview Snowden," WP (5.8.14); "Fearing NSA Surveillance, German Government Ends Verizon Contract for Internet Service," US News (6.26.14); Glanz, "Leaked File Details U.S. Phone Monitoring Abroad," NYT (3.19.14); Gellman & Soltani, "NSA Surveillance Program Reaches 'Into the Past' to Retrieve, Replay Phone Calls," WP (3.19.14); Ackerman, "U.S. Tech Giants Knew of NSA Data Collection, Agency's Top Lawyer Insists," G (3.19.14); Devereaux, Greenwald & Poitras, "Data Pirates of the Caribbean," The Intercept (5.19.14); Cartwright-Carroll, "Government Wants Answers on U.S. Spy Claims," *Nassau Guardian* (5.20.14).

209 Savage, "Phone Company Bid to Keep Data from N.S.A. Is Rejected," NYT (4.26.14); Savage, "Phone Company Pushed Back against N.S.A.'s Data Collection, Court Papers Show," NYT (5.15.14); Nakashima, "U.S. Revealed Secret Legal Basis for NSA Program to Sprint, Documents Show," WP (5.15.14).

210 Tummarello, "Rival NSA Bills Put Boehner on the Spot," *The Hill* (5.5.14); Savage, "Rival House Bills Aim to Rein In N.S.A. Phone Data Program," NYT (5.7.14); Nakashima, "Surveillance-Bill Compromise Close in House, Would End Mass NSA Collection of Phone Data," WP (5.7.14); Savage, "House Panel Advances Bill on N.S.A. Collection of Phone Data," NYT (5.9.14); Savage, "Changes to Surveillance Bill Stoke Anger," NYT (5.21.14); Weisman & Savage, "House Passes Restraints

on Bulk Data Collection," NYT (5.23.14); "A Surveillance Bill that Falls Short," NYT (5.23.14); Nakashima & Peterson, "House Approves Bill that Would End NSA's Collection of Americans' Phone Records," WP (5.23.14).

211 "The Al-Qaeda Switchboard," *The New Yorker* (1.13.14); Schwartz, "'We're at Great Risk': Q&A with General Keith Alexander," *The New Yorker* (5.15.14); Nakashima, "New NSA Chief Seeks to Reassure Public on Surveillance," WP (6.3.14); Sanger, "New N.S.A. Chief Calls Damage from Snowden Leaks Manageable," NYT (6.30.14).

212 Hattem, "Tech Titans Tell Senate to Go Big on NSA Overhaul," *The Hill* (6.4.14); Ovide, "Microsoft's Top Lawyer Assails Secret Court," WSJ (6.24.14).

213 Greenberg, "House Votes to Cut Key Pursestrings for NSA Surveillance," *Wired* (6.20.14); Marcos, "In Surprise Vote, House Backs NSA Limits," *The Hill* (6.19.14); Tiron, "House Passes $570 billion Defense Bill Rejecting Cost Cuts," Bloomberg (6.20.14); Nakashima, "U.S. Releases Data on Sensitive Surveillance Programs for First Time," WP (6.28.14).

214 Nakashima & Gellman, "Court Gave NSA Broad Leeway in Surveillance, Documents Show," WP (7.1.14); "The N.S.A. Can Spy on These 193 Foreign Governments," NYT (7.2.14); Nakashima, "Independent Panel: NSA Surveillance Program Targeting Foreigners Is Lawful," WP (7.2.14); PCLOB (2014b).

215 Gellman, Tate & Soltani, "In NSA-Intercepted Data, Those Not Targeted Far Outnumber the Foreigners Who Are," WP (7.6.14); Gellman, "How 160,000 Intercepted Communications Led to Our Latest NSA Story," WP (7.12.14); Pincus, "Oversight Board Says NSA Data Mining Puts Citizens' Privacy at Risk, but Sees No Abuse," WP (7.15.14); Nakashima, "4 Senators Raise Alarm about NSA Collection of Americans' E-mails, Phone Calls," WP (7.26.14).

216 Smale, "German Arrested on Suspicion of Passing Secrets," NYT (7.4.14); Faiola, "Fresh U.S. Spying Allegations Could Damage Relations with Germany," WP (7.6.14); Smale, "Ties Strained, Germans Press U.S. to Answer Spy Allegations," NYT (7.7.14); Perlez, "Spy Scandal Tails Merkel All the Way to Beijing," NYT (7.8.14); Mazzetti & Landler, "Spying Case Left Obama in the Dark, U.S. Officials Say," NYT (7.9.14); Smale & Eddy, "Germany Expels Top U.S. Intelligence Officer," NYT (7.10.14); "Germany Dumps 70-year No-Spying Pact," Daily Beast (7.7.14); Smale, Mazzetti & Sanger, "Germany Demands Top U.S. Intelligence Official Be Expelled," NYT (7.11.14); Miller & Kirchner, "Germany Orders CIA Station Chief to Leave over Spying Allegations," WP (7.11.14); "German Foreign Minister to Meet Kerry to Discuss Spying Claims," WP (7.11.14); "Merkel Blasts U.S. Spying, Hopes Washington Will Change Tack," NYT (7.12.14); "U.S. Does Pointless Damage to its Relationship with Germany," WP (7.12.14); Smale, "Behind German Spy Cases, Twists Worthy of Films," NYT (7.13.14); "U.S., Germany Vow Cooperation Despite Espionage Spat," WP (7.13.14); Shear, "In Call, Obama and Merkel Discuss 'Cooperation' on Intelligence," NYT

(7.16.14); Rizzo, "Don't Be Fooled, Germany's Outrage at U.S. Spying Is Just for Show," *Time* (7.15.14); "Germany's Merkel Seeks 'Sensible' US Spy Talks," WP (7.18.14); Baker & Eddy, "Obama Sends Aide to Soothe German Allies," NYT (7.23.14); DeYoung & Faiola, "A Year after U.S. Spying Revelations, German Officials Say Questions Remain Unanswered," WP (7.23.14); Greenwald, "U.S. Threatened Germany over Snowden, Vice Chancellor Says," The Intercept (3.19.15); "Spying Close to Home: German Intelligence under Fire for NSA Cooperation," Spiegel online (4.24.15); "Berlin Spied on France for the NSA, German Media Say," (4.30.15) www.france24.com/en/20150430-berlin-spied-france-usa-nsa-german-media-elysee (last accessed February 19, 2018); Eddy, "Germany Is Accused of Helping N.S.A. Spy on European Allies," NYT (5.1.15); Faiola, "NSA Scandal Rekindles in Germany, with an Ironic Twist," WP (5.1.15); Smale & Eddy, "Pressure Mounts on Merkel to Explain German Role in N.S.A. Espionage," NYT (5.7.15); Smale, "Germany Limits Cooperation with U.S. over Data Gathering," NYT (5.8.15); "Germany: No Damage to US Relations from Spy Affair," WP (5.8.15); Smale & Sanger, "Another Spying Scandal Adds to Political Crisis for Merkel," NYT (5.21.15); "Snowden NSA: Germany Drops Merkel Phone-Tapping Probe," BBC News (6.12.15); Eddy, "File Is Said to Confirm N.S.A. Spied on Merkel," NYT (7.2.15); Smale & Eddy, "Germany, Again, Calls on U.S. to Answer Spying Accusations," NYT (7.3.15); Smale, "German Aides' Phone Numbers Appear on U.S. Intelligence Documents," NYT (7.9.15).

217 Savage & Apuzzo, "U.S. Spied on 5 American Muslims, a Report Says," NYT (7.10.14); Nakashima, "U.S. Is Said to Have Monitored Muslims' E-mails," WP (7.10.14).

218 Bates, Comments of the Judiciary on Proposals Regarding the Foreign Intelligence Surveillance Act (1.10.14); Savage, "Senator's Bill Is Stricter on N.S.A. Than House's," NYT (7.25.14); "A Stronger Bill to Limit Surveillance," NYT (7.28.14); "Senate Bill Strikes a Balance between Core Intelligence Needs and Civil Liberties," WP (8.2.14); Vladeck, "Judge Bates (Unintentionally) Makes the Case for FISC Reform," Just Security (8.7.14); Hattem, "Holder, Spy Chief Support Senate NSA Reform Bill," *The Hill* (9.3.14); Hattem, "Pressure Mounts on Senate for NSA Vote," *The Hill* (9.9.14); Gertner, "Who Speaks for the Bench about Surveillance?" *National Law Journal* (9.15.14); Hattem, "Civil Liberties Groups: Don't Stop on NSA Reform," *The Hill* (10.7.14); Coats, "Don't Take Away Anti-Terror Tools," *USA Today* (10.21.14); "A Crucial Vote on the Surveillance Bill," NYT (11.18.14); "The Senate Should Approve a Bipartisan Proposal to Reform the NSA," WP (11.18.14); Hayden & Mukasey, "NSA Reform that Only ISIS Could Love," WSJ (11.18.14); Wilhelm, "White House Says It 'Strongly Supports' the Senate's NSA Reform Bill," TechCrunch (11.17.14); Savage & Peters, "Bill to Restrict N.S.A. Data Collection Blocked in Vote by Senate Republicans," NYT (11.19.14); Ackerman, "White House to Revive NSA Surveillance Legislation during Next Congress," G (11.20.14); Nakashima & O'Keefe,

"NSA Reform Legislation Blocked in Senate amid Renewed Fears of Terrorist Attacks," WP (11.20.14); Firestone, "There's No Proof of Surveillance Abuse?" NYT (11.21.14); Hattem, "Leahy to Obama: End NSA Program Now," *The Hill* (12.4.14).

219 Tye, "Meet Executive Order 12333: The Reagan Rule that Lets the NSA Spy on Americans," WP (7.18.14); Nakashima & Soltani, "Privacy Watchdog's Next Target: The Least-Known but Biggest Aspect of NSA Surveillance," WP (7.23.14); Savage, "Reagan-Era Order on Surveillance Violates Rights, Says Departing Aide," NYT (8.13.14).

220 Bowcott & Ackerman, "Mass Internet Surveillance Threatens International Law, UN Report Claims," G (10.14.14); Nichols, "Germany, Brazil Push the U.N. to Be Tougher on Digital Spying," Reuters (11.7.14); Sengupta, "U.N. Urges Protection of Privacy in Digital Era," NYT (11.26.14); Cumming-Bruce, "U.N. Panel Cites Concerns with U.S. Security Practices," NYT (11.29.14); Bowcott, "Mass Surveillance Exposed by Snowden 'Not Justified by Fight Against Terrorism,'" G (12.8.14); Fioretti, "NSA's Surveillance a 'Trade Barrier' for EU Companies: EU Official," Reuters (12.8.14).

221 Nakashima, "Records Reveal Why Court Shut Down Bush-Era Spy Program," WP (12.13.14); Savage, "F.B.I. Is Broadening Surveillance Role, Report Shows," NYT (1.12.15); Savage, "Documents Show N.S.A.'s Moves on Surveillance before Congress's Approval," NYT (1.27.15).

222 "Backroom Move Strips 'Backdoor' NSA Spying Ban from Spending Bill," HuffPost (12.10.14); Nakashima, "Congress Sets Limits on Overseas Data Collection," WP (12.18.14); Schmidt & Apuzzo, "U.S. Discloses New Trove of Phone Call Records," NYT (1.17.15); Reynolds, "HRW Sues Feds over Mass Surveillance," Courthouse News Service (4.8.15).

223 PCLOB, Recommendations Assessment Report (1.29.15); Bennett, "Watchdog: White House Has Done Little on Surveillance Reform," *The Hill* (1.29.15); Sanger, "President Tweaks the Rules on Data Collection," NYT (2.2.15); Nakashima, "As Obama Tightens Surveillance Guidelines, Uncertainty Lingers on NSA Program," WP (2.4.15); Nelson, "Privacy Board Will Do 'Deep Dive' on NSA, CIA Practices," *US News* (4.8.15); SJC Hearing (1.28.15); White House Office of the Press Secretary, Statement on Reauthorization of the Collection of Bulk Telephony Metadata under Section 215 of the USA Patriot Act (2.27.15); Volz, "NSA Spying Wins another Rubber Stamp," *National Journal* (2.27.15); PCLOB, Recommendations Assessment Report (2.5.16).

224 Nakashima, "Tech Firms and Privacy Groups Press for Curbs on NSA Surveillance Powers," WP (3.24.15); Trujillo, "Paul Vows to End NSA Program If Elected," *The Hill* (4.7.15); Ackerman, "NSA and FBI Fight to Retain Spy Powers as Surveillance Law Nears Expiration," G (4.15.15); Nakashima, "McConnell Bill Would Extend NSA Surveillance," WP (4.22.15); Nakashima, "With Deadline Near, Lawmakers Introduce Bill to End NSA Program," WP (4.29.15); "More Excuses on the Patriot Act," NYT (5.2.15); Goodlatte et al., Letter to the Editor, NYT (5.7.15).

225 *ACLU* v. *Clapper*, 785 F.3d 787 (2nd Cir. 2015); Savage, "N.S.A. Phone Data Collection Illegal, Appeals Court Rules," NYT (5.7.15); "The Illegal Phone-Data Sweeps," NYT (5.7.15); Byers & Tummarello, "NSA Ruling Puts Lawmakers on Edge," Politico (5.7.15); Clark, "NSA Ruling Splits Republican Presidential Hopefuls," McClatchy (5.7.15); Hattem, "Clinton Breaks Silence, Supports NSA Reform Bill," *The Hill* (5.7.15); Weisman & Steinhauer, "Court Ruling on N.S.A.'s Data Collection Jolts Both Defenders and Reformers," NYT (5.9.15); "New Rules for the National Security Agency," WP (5.11.15); Peters, "Rand Paul Tries to Stake Territory as Lone Candidate Who'd Guard Civil Liberties," NYT (5.12.15); Nakashima & Debonis, "White House Backs Bill that Would End NSA Bulk Collection of Phone Records," WP (5.12.15); Steinhauer, "House Votes to End N.S.A.'s Bulk Phone Data Collection," NYT (5.14.15); Fox, "Sen. Corker, NSA Should Do Far More with Your Phone Data," Defense One (5.13.15); Hattem, "McConnell Files Short-Term NSA Bill," *The Hill* (5.14.15); "Congress vs. Terrorism," WP (5.18.15); Peoples & Dilanian, "Republicans Clash over NSA Surveillance Powers," ABC News (5.18.15); Ackerman & Siddiqui, "NSA Surveillance Opposed by American Voters from All Parties, Poll Finds," G (5.18.15); deBonis & Nakashima, "GOP Division Puts Congress on Brink of Ending NSA Surveillance Program," WP (5.20.15); deBonis & Nakashima, "NSA May Need to Begin Winding Down Surveillance Program This Week," WP (5.20.15); Kim & Byers, "Rand Paul Calls It a Night after 10½ Hours," Politico (5.21.15); "Rand Paul's Timely Takedown of the Patriot Act," NYT (5.22.15); Steinhauer, "Senate Blocks Bill on N.S.A. Collection of Phone Records," NYT (5.23.15); Baker, "Obama Warns Senators on Lapse in Surveillance," NYT (5.27.15); Savage, "Reality Checks in Debate over Surveillance Laws," NYT (5.28.15); "Let Patriot Act Provisions Expire," NYT (5.28.15); Steinhauer & Weisman, "Senate to Take Up Spy Bill as Parts of Patriot Act Expire," NYT (6.1.15); Steinhauer & Weisman, "Senate Approves Bill to Rein In N.S.A. Surveillance," NYT (6.2.15); Steinhauer & Weisman, "U.S. Surveillance in Place since 9/11 Is Sharply Limited," NYT (6.3.15); Savage, "General Hayden's Offensive," NYRB (5.26.16).

226 Nakashima, "With Court Approval, NSA Resumes Bulk Collection of Phone Data," WP (7.1.15); Savage, "A.C.L.U. Asks Court to Stop Part of NSA's Bulk Phone Data Collection," NYT (7.15.15); McLaughlin, "NSA Will Destroy Archived Metadata When Program Stops," The Intercept (7.27.15); Savage, "NSA Won't Be Ordered to Stop Bulk Collection Early," NYT (10.30.15); Nakashima, "Federal Appeals Court Allows NSA Phone Data Collection to Run through November," WP (10.30.15).

227 Harris, "U.S. Rejects Petition Seeking Pardon for Edward J. Snowden," NYT (7.29.15); MacAskill, "Edward Snowden: US Has Not Offered Me Plea Deal," G (10.6.15).

228 Fung, "Chris Christie Actually Wants to Expand NSA's Spying Powers," WP (8.7.15); Williams, "Bush Calls for Broader Government Surveillance," *The Hill* (8.19.15); Adam, "Clinton and Sanders: Snowden Should Face Prosecution," WP (10.14.15).

229 Angwin, Savage, Larson, Moltke, Poitras & Risen, "AT&T Helped U.S. Spy on Internet on a Vast Scale," NYT (8.15.15); "U.N. Says Expects States to Respect Privacy after AT&T Spying Report," Reuters (8.17.15); Nakashima, "Top Spy Bemoans Loss of Key Info-gathering Program," WP (9.10.15); Hattem, "NSA Head: We Need Bulk Collection," *The Hill* (9.24.15); Sanger, "Report Finds No Substitute for Mass Data Collection," NYT (1.16.15).

230 McLaughlin, "Secret Surveillance Court Picks First Outsider to Get a Look In," The Intercept (9.25.15); Hattem, "Spy Court Appoints New Advisers," *The Hill* (11.25.15); Savage, "Judge Rejects Challenge to Searches of Emails Gathered Without Warrant," NYT (4.19.16).

231 Scott, "Data Transfer Pact between U.S. and Europe Is Ruled Invalid," NYT (10.6.15); Williams, "US, EU Get Three Months to Cut New Privacy Deal," *The Hill* (10.16.15); Holden, "Attorney General Lynch Chides European Decisions to Restrict Data Sharing," Reuters (12.10.15); Fioretti, "EU Wants Stricter Controls over U.S. Snooping Powers in Data Pact Talks," Reuters (1.18.16); Scott, "U.S. and Europe in 'Safe Harbor' Data Deal, but Legal Fight May Await," NYT (2.2.16); Fioretti, "United States Sets out Limits on Its Spying as Part of New Data Pact with EU," Reuters (2.27.16).

232 Shane, "After Paris Attacks, C.I.A. Director Rekindles Debate over Surveillance," NYT (11.17.15); "Mass Surveillance Isn't the Answer to Fighting Terrorism," NYT (11.18.15); Hirsh, "It's All Back in Snowden's Lap," Politico (11.17.15); Carney, "Rubio Backs Push to Delay NSA Reforms after Paris Attacks," *The Hill* (11.18.15); Richardson, "Ex-CIA Director: Snowden Should Be 'Hanged' for Paris," *The Hill* (11.20.15); Brynes, "Rand Paul: 'Bull – –' to Ramp up NSA Surveillance Post-Paris," *The Hill* (11.20.15); Hattem, "Christie: 'Paris' Intelligence Failure' Rooted in Limits to Surveillance," *The Hill* (11.24.15); Flegenheimer, "Ted Cruz Attacks Marco Rubio on Privacy and Immigration," NYT (11.29.15); Rubin, "The NSA Vote Comes Home to Haunt Cruz," WP (12.7.15).

233 Nakashima, "The Head of the NSA Just Undercut Rubio's Claims Last Night at the Debate," WP (12.17.15); "Backers of Marco Rubio Target Ted Cruz for Stance on Edward Snowden," NYT (12.19.15); Savage, "N.S.A. Gets Less Web Data Than Believed, Report Suggests," NYT (2.17.16); Kelly, "NSA: Fallout from Snowden Leaks Isn't Over, but Information Is Getting Old," NPR (3.17.16).

234 Toh et al. (2016); Entous & Yadron, "U.S. Spy Net on Israel Snares Congress," WSJ (12.29.15); Wong, "House Looking at Whether NSA Collected Lawmakers' Communications," *The Hill* (12.30.15); Entous & Yadron, "The Cold War-Era Rules Designed to Protect U.S. Lawmakers Communications," WSJ (12.29.15).

235 "Sen. Wyden Notes Previous Administration Denial of Widespread Collection of Data on Americans," WP (6.11.13); Hicks, "Former Justice Attorney Seeks $23 billion in Damages for NSA Surveillance," WP (6.13.13).
236 *Klayman* v. *Obama*, 957 F.Supp.2d 1 (DDC 2013); Savage, "Judge Questions Legality of N.S.A. Phone Records," NYT (12.17.13); "A Powerful Rebuke of Mass Surveillance," NYT (12.17.13); Nakashima & Marimow, "Judge: NSA's Collecting of Phone Records Is Probably Unconstitutional," WP (12.17.13); "The NSA Must Disclose More to Make its Case," WP (12.17.13); Shear, "Score One for the Legal Thorn in Government's Side," NYT (12.17.13); "The NSA vs. the Constitution," LAT (12.18.13).
237 568 U.S. 398 (2013).
238 *Obama* v. *Klayman*, 800 F.3d 559 (D.C. Cir. 2015); Risen, "Setback for Suit against N.S.A. on Phone Data," NYT (8.29.15); Hsu, "Judge Lays Out Path to Revive Challenge to NSA Phone Surveillance Program," WP (9.2.15); McLaughlin, "Government Likens Ending Bulk Surveillance to Opening Prison Gates," The Intercept (10.8.15); Savage, "Judge Deals a Blow to N.S.A. Data Collection Program," NYT (11.9.15); Hattem, "Appeals Court Clears Hurdle for NSA," *The Hill* (11.11.15); Gerstein, "Appeals Court Lets NSA Phone Program Continue," Politico (11.17.15).
239 *Klayman* v. *Obama*, 2015 WL 6873127 (D.D.C. 2015).
240 *Klayman* v. *Obama*, 2015 WL 9010330 (D.C. Cir. 2015).
241 *Klayman* v. *Obama*, 805 F.3d 1148 (D.C. Cir. 2015).
242 *ACLU* v. *Clapper*, 959 F.Supp.2d 724 (SDNY 2013); Liptak & Peters, "Congress and Courts Weigh Restraints on N.S.A. Spying," NYT (11.19.13); Liptak & Schmidt, "Judge Upholds N.S.A.'s Bulk Collection of Data on Calls," NYT (12.28.13); "This Week, Mass Surveillance Wins," NYT (12.28.13); Horwitz, "NSA Collection of Phone Data Is Lawful, Federal Judge Rules," WP (12.28.13); Peterson, "The Most Kafkaesque Paragraph from Today's NSA Ruling," WP (12.28.13). For a detailed analysis of what the government did and did not know about Mihdhar, see Bamford (2008).
243 *ACLU* v. *Clapper*, 785 F.3d 787 (2nd Cir. 2015); Savage, "N.S.A. Phone Data Collection Illegal, Appeals Court Rules," NYT (5.7.15); "The Illegal Phone-Data Sweeps," NYT (5.7.15); Byers & Tummarello, "NSA Ruling Puts Lawmakers on Edge," Politico (5.7.15); Clark, "NSA Ruling Splits Republican Presidential Hopefuls," McClatchy (5.7.15); Hattem, "Clinton Breaks Silence, Supports NSA Reform Bill," *The Hill* (5.7.15); Weisman & Steinhauer, "Court Ruling on N.S.A.'s Data Collection Jolts Both Defenders and Reformers," NYT (5.9.15); "New Rules for the National Security Agency," WP (5.11.15); Peters, "Rand Paul Tries to Stake Territory as Lone Candidate Who'd Guard Civil Liberties," NYT (5.12.15); Nakashima & Debonis, "White House Backs Bill that Would End NSA Bulk Collection of Phone Records," WP (5.12.15); Steinhauer, "House Votes to End N.S.A.'s Bulk Phone Data Collection," NYT

(5.14.15); Fox, "Sen. Corker, NSA Should Do Far More with Your Phone Data," Defense One (5.13.15); Hattem, "McConnell Files Short-Term NSA Bill," *The Hill* (5.14.15); "Congress vs. Terrorism," WP (5.18.15); Peoples & Dilanian, "Republicans Clash over NSA Surveillance Powers," ABC News (5.18.15); Ackerman & Siddiqui, "NSA Surveillance Opposed by American Voters from All Parties, Poll Finds," G (5.18.15); deBonis & Nakashima, "GOP Division Puts Congress on Brink of Ending NSA Surveillance Program," WP (5.20.15); deBonis & Nakashima, "NSA May Need to Begin Winding Down Surveillance Program This Week," WP (5.20.15); Kim & Byers, "Rand Paul Calls It a Night after 10½ Hours," Politico (5.21.15); "Rand Paul's Timely Takedown of the Patriot Act," NYT (5.22.15); Steinhauer, "Senate Blocks Bill on N.S.A. Collection of Phone Records," NYT (5.23.15); Baker, "Obama Warns Senators on Lapse in Surveillance," NYT (5.27.15); Savage, "Reality Checks in Debate over Surveillance Laws," NYT (5.28.15); "Let Patriot Act Provisions Expire," NYT (5.28.15); Steinhauer & Weisman, "Senate to Take Up Spy Bill as Parts of Patriot Act Expire," NYT (6.1.15); Steinhauer & Weisman, "Senate Approves Bill to Rein In N.S.A. Surveillance," NYT (6.2.15); Steinhauer & Weisman, "U.S. Surveillance in Place since 9/11 Is Sharply Limited," NYT (6.3.15).

244 *ACLU* v. *Clapper*, 2015 WL 4196833 (2nd Cir. 2015); 804 F.3d 617 (2nd Cir. 2015).

245 Markon, "Snowden's Surveillance Leaks Open Way for Challenge to Programs' Constitutionality," WP (7.16.13); *Smith* v. *Obama*, 24 F.Supp.3d 1005 (D. Id. 2014), vacated as moot, 2016 WL 1127087 (9th Cir. 2016); Kerr, "Another Federal Judge Rules on Legality of NSA Surveillance," WP (6.3.14); Lessmiller, "Ninth Circuit Tosses Challenge to NSA Spying," Courthouse News Service (3.22.16).

246 Wales & Treitkov, "Stop Spying on Wikpedia Users," NYT (3.10.15); *WikiMedia Foundation* v. *NSA*, 143 F.Supp.3d 344 (D. Md. 2015); Duncan, "Judge Dismisses Wikipedia Lawsuit over NSA Surveillance Program," BS (10.23.15).

247 *Wikimedia Foundation* v. *National Security Agency*, 857 F.3d 193 (3rd Cir. 2017).

248 Savage, "Door May Open for Challenge to Secret Wiretaps," NYT (10.16.13); "High Court to Rule on Warrantless Wiretapping," WP (10.20.13); Horwitz, "Justice Is Reviewing Criminal Cases That Used Surveillance Evidence Gathered under FISA," WP (11.15.13); Savage, "Warrantless Surveillance Continues to Cause Fallout," NYT (11.21.13); Johnson, "Judge Suspends Sentencing of Would-Be Bomber after NSA Revelations," NPR (11.26.13); Savage, "Judge Upholds 2008 Surveillance Law," NYT (11.20.15).

249 Savage, "Terrorism Conviction of a Wiretapped American Is Upheld on Appeal," NYT (12.6.16); *U.S.* v. *Mohamud*, 843 F.3d 420 (9th Cir. 2016).

250 "Terrorism Suspect's Lawyer Seeks Clarity on Possible U.S. Surveillance Overreach," CBS (7.30.13); Goudie, "Government Wins Major Spy Ruling in Chicago Terror Case," ABC News (8.28.13); "Judge Undoes

Key Ruling on NSA Evidence in Bomb Plot Case," CBS Chicago (9.3.13); Janssen, "Attorney for Teen Terror Suspect Wants to See Secret Evidence," *Chicago Sun-Times* (11.29.13); Vitka, "The Dragnet's Day in Court," *Slate* (9.30.13); Sharma, "San Diego Somalis Want New Trial after NSA Revelations," KPBS (12.13.13); *United States* v. *Daoud*, 2014 WL 321384 (N.D. Ill. 2014), rev'd, 755 F.3d 479 (7th Cir. 2014); Meisner, "Judge Rejects Looking into If Surveillance Program Led to Terrorism Charge," CT (1.20.14); Savage, "Warrantless Surveillance Challenged by Defendant," NYT (1.30.14); "Feds Appeal Secret Documents Order in Illinois Terror Case," NYT (2.11.14); Barrett, "DoJ Notifies Terror Suspect Evidence Gathered through NSA Program," WSJ (4.3.14); Nakashima, "Appeals Court Overturns Lower Court Order Permitting Disclosure of Secret FISA Material," WP (6.16.14).

251 *U.S.* v. *Muhtorov*, 187 F.Supp.3d 1240 (D. Colo. 2015); Barnes & Nakashima, "U.S. Tells Terror Suspect It Will Use Surveillance Evidence, Setting up Possible Legal Challenge," WP (10.25.13); Savage, "Federal Prosecutors in a Policy Shift, Cite Warrantless Wiretaps as Evidence," NYT (10.26.13); Savage, "Warrantless Surveillance Challenged by Defendant," NYT (1.30.14).

252 *Hasbajrami* v. *United States*, 2014 WL 4954596 (EDNY 2014); Raymond, "Albanian Who Challenged Warrantless Surveillance to Face U.S. Terror Trial," Reuters (3.2.115); Ax, "Challenge to U.S. Warrantless Surveillance on Tap after Guilty Plea," Reuters (6.26.15); Farivar, "In 2016, Terror Suspects and 9-Eleven Thieves May Bring Surveillance to Supreme Court," Ars Technica (1.1.16).

253 *United States* v. *Hasbajrami*, 2016 WL 1029500 (EDNY 2016).

254 Statements of Sens. Grassley and Leahy (5.10.16); Uchill, "House Judiciary Signals Reauthorization of NSA Surveillance Powers with Privacy Tweeks," *The Hill* (3.1.17); Volz, "U.S. Lawmakers Ask for Disclosure of Number of Americans under Surveillance," Reuters (4.7.17); Nakashima, "NSA Halts a Controversial Email Collection Practice to Preserve Larger Surveillance Program," WP (4.29.17); Savage, "How Trump's N.S.A. Came to End a Disputed Type of Surveillance," NYT (5.12.17); Johnson, "Secret Court Rebukes NSA for 5-Year Illegal Surveillance of U.S. Citizens," MH (5.26.17); Huetteman & Savage, "Top Officials Evade Senate on Trump and Russia," NYT (6.8.17); Nakashima & Demirjian, "Intelligence Officials Rogers and Coats Say They Won't Discuss Specifics of Private Conversations with Trump," WP (6.7.17); Nakashima, "Spy Agencies Seek Permanent Authority for Contested Surveillance Program," WP (6.27.17); Savage, "N.S.A. Warrantless Surveillance Aided Turks after Attack, Officials Say," NYT (6.27.17).

255 House of Representatives, Review of the Unauthorized Disclosures of Former National Security Agency Contractor Edward Snowden (9.15.16); Pardonsnowdennow.org, NYT (11.22.16); "Edward Snowden: 'Do I think Things Are Fixed? No,'" NYT (12.7.16); Fabian, "Obama Suggests Snowden Pardon Unlikely," *The Hill* (11.18.16); Pompeo, C-Span's Washington Journal (February 2016); Shelbourne,

"Snowden: Petraeus Disclosed More 'Highly Classified' Information Than I Did," *The Hill* (12.4.16); Isikoff, "Snowden Says Petraeus Disclosed 'Far More Highly Classified' Secrets 'Than I Ever Did,'" Yahoo News (12.4.16); "President Obama's Last Chance to Show Mercy," NYT (1.19.17); Roth, "As One Whistleblower's Sentence Is Commuted, Snowden Gets More Time in Russia," WP (1.19.17).

256 See Baker (2010); Miller (2016).

257 See Zegart (2011).

258 See Table A1 in the Appendix.

CHAPTER 6 *IUS IN BELLO*

1 For soldiers' accounts of LOAC violations, see Wright (2004); Fick (2005); Williams & Staub (2005); Bellavia & Bruning (2006); Rieckhoff (2006); Gordon & Trainor (2006); Massing, "Iraq: The Hidden Human Costs," NYRB (12.20.07); Gopal (2014); Edmonds (2015). On the pervasiveness of LOAC violations, see Smith & Brecher (2005); Ferguson (2006). On the relative roles of the CIA and DoD Special Forces, see Hastings (2012); Mazzetti (2013).

2 Additional Protocol I to 1949 Geneva Conventions, Articles 35.2, 48 (1977); Army FM27-10 (July 1956); Solis (2010: 258).

3 For analyses of their legality and strategic consequences, see Bergen & Tiedemann (2009); Gross (2009); Alston (2010, 2011); Finkelstein et al. (2012); Gurule (2013); Ahmed (2013); Williams (2013); Bashir & Crews (2012); Strawser (2013); Evangelista & Shue (2014); Bergen & Rothenberg (2014); Cockburn (2015); Shane (2015); Horton (2015); Kaag & Kreps (2014); Cortwright et al. (2015); Woods (2015); Wittes & Blum (2015); Chayes (2015); Scahill & Staff of The Intercept (2016); Fisk & Ramos (2016); Gusterson (2016); Powell (2016); Kreps (2016); Columbia Law School Human Rights Clinic and Sana'a Center for Strategic Studies (2017). Film treatments include Robert Greenwald, *Unmanned* (2013); Rick Rosenthal, *Drones* (2013); Madhia Tahir, *Wounds of Waziristan* (2013); Andrew Nicol, *Good Kill* (2014); Tonje Shei, *Drone* (2014); Gavin Hood, *Eye in the Sky* (2015); and Sonia Kennebeck, *National Bird* (2016).

4 Woods (2015: 23–26, 55–61).

5 Klaidman (2012: 39–43, 49–51).

6 Black, "Investigative Reporter Seymour Hersh Describes 'Executive Assassination Ring,'" Reuters (3.11.09).

7 Gorman, "CIA Had Secret al Qaeda Plan," WSJ (7.13.09); Barnes, "Clamor Grows over CIA Secrets," LAT (7.13.09); Gorman, "CIA Had Secret al Qaeda Plan," WSJ (7.13.09); Mazzetti, "After 9/11 C.I.A. Had Plan to Kill Qaeda's Leaders," NYT (7.14.09); Miller, "CIA Planned Assault Teams," LAT (7.14.09); Warrick & Pershing, "CIA Had Program to Kill al-Qaeda Leaders," WP (7.14.09); "Checking Cheney's Story," NYT (7.15.09); Miller, "CIA's Assassination Puzzle," LAT A1 (7.16.09); Warrick, "CIA Assassin Program Was Nearing New Phase,"

WP (7.16.09); Panetta, "Congress and the CIA: Time to Move On," WP (8.2.09); Senate Committee on Foreign Relations, "Afghanistan's Narco War: Breaking the Link between Drug Traffickers and Insurgents" (8.10.09); Mazzetti, "Outsiders Hired as C.I.A. Planned to Kill Jihadists," NYT A1 (8.20.09); Smith & Warrick, "Blackwater Disclosure Adds to CIA Worries," WP (8.21.09); Whitlock, "Afghans Oppose U.S. Hit List of Drug Traffickers," WP (10.24.09).

8 Shane (2015).

9 Raghavan, "Yemeni Air Strike May Have Killed Cleric Linked to Ft Hood Attack," WP (12.24.09); Miller, "Yemen Airstrikes Hit Suspected al Qaeda Members," LAT (12.25.09); Healy & Shane, "Yemen Says It Attacked a Meeting of al Qaeda," NYT (12.25.09); Schmitt & Worth, "U.S. Widens Terror War to Yemen, al Qaeda Bastion," NYT (12.28.09); Raghavan, "Al-Qaeda Group in Yemen Gaining Prominence," WP (12.28.09); Meyer, "U.S.-Born Cleric Linked to Airline Bombing Plot," LAT (12.31.09); Baker, "Obama Says al Qaeda in Yemen Planned Bombing Plot, and He Vows Retribution," NYT (1.3.10); DeYoung, "Yemen to Revamp Visa Procedures in Wake of Failed Christmas Day Airliner Bombing," WP (1.21.10); Priest, "U.S. Military Teams, Intelligence Deeply Involved in Aiding Yemen on Strikes," WP (1.27.10); Worth, "Cleric in Yemen Admits Meeting Airliner Plot Suspect, Journalist Says," NYT (2.1.10).

10 Nakashima, "Intelligence Chief Acknowledges U.S. May Target Americans Involved in Terrorism," WP A3 (2.4.10); Koh, "The Obama Administration and International Law" (3.24.10); Shane, "U.S. Approves Targeted Killing of Radical Muslim Cleric Tied to Domestic Terror Suspects," NYT (4.7.10); Miller, "Muslim Cleric Aulaqi Is the 1st U.S. Citizen on List of those CIA Is Allowed to Kill," WP (4.7.10); "Defending Drones: The Laws of War and the Right to Self-defense," WP (4.13.10); Divoll, "U.S. Targets an American Abroad," LAT (4.23.10); Shane, "A Legal Debate as C.I.A. Stalks a U.S. Jihadist," NYT (5.14.10). For an account by a Dane who claimed to have helped the CIA locate al-Awlaki, see Storm (2014).

11 Savage, "U.N. Official Expected to Call on U.S. to End C.I.A. Drone Strikes in Pakistan," NYT (5.28.10); Savage, "U.N. Official Expected to Call on U.S. to End Warning of Use by Others," NYT (6.3.10).

12 Charlie Savage, "Lawyers Seeking to Take Up Terror Suspect's Legal Case Sue U.S. for Access," NYT (8.4.10); Gerstein, "Treasury to Allow al-Awlaki Lawsuit," WP (8.3.10); David Savage, "ACLU Sues to Represent Suspected Terrorist in Yemen," LAT (8.4.10); "Lawyers Win Right to Aid U.S. Target," NYT (8.5.10); "An Illegal Bulls-Eye?" LAT (8.7.10); "Whether to Use Drones on Americans Linked to al-Qaeda," WP (9.16.10); "Lethal Force under Law," NYT (10.8.10); Jaffer & Kebriaei, Letter to the Editor, NYT (10.18.10). See www.aclu.org/targetkillings (last accessed January 1, 2011).

13 "Rights Groups File Challenge to Targeted Killing by U.S.," ACLU Press Release (8.30.10); Savage, "U.S. Weighs How to Block Suit on Targeted

Killing," NYT (9.16.10); "A Better Way to Get Awlaki," LAT (9.20.10); Hsu, "Obama Invokes 'State Secrets' Claim to Dismiss Suit against Targeting of U.S. Citizen al-Aulaqi," WP (9.25.10); Savage, "State Secrets Cited in Effort by White House to Block Suit," NYT (9.25.10); Hsu, "U.S. Officials Defend 'State Secrets' Claim in al-Aulaqi Suit," WP (9.26.10); "Lethal Force under Law," NYT (10.10.10); "The U.S. Courts Should Not Have a Say in Drone Strikes," WP (10.23.10); Shane & Worth, "Challenge Heard on Move to Kill Qaeda-Linked Cleric," NYT (11.9.10); "Targeting an American," LAT (11.10.10); Ignatius, "Dazzling New Weapons Require New Rules for War," WP (11.11.10); "Obama's Assassination List," *Washington Times* (11.20.10); Hsu, "Judge in D.C. Tosses Suit Challenging Placement of Yemeni Cleric on Terrorist List," WP (12.7.10); Savage, "Suit over Targeted Killings Is Thrown Out," NYT (12.8.10); "Punting on Awlaki?" LAT (12.8.10); "Judicial Scrutiny before Death," NYT (12.13.10); *Al-Aulaqi* v. *Obama*, 727 F.2d 1 (DDC 2010).

14 Bennett, "'Credible Terrorist Threat' Seen in U.S.-Bound Packages," LAT (10.29.10); Robbins & Shear, "Obama Says Explosives Were U.S.-Bound," NYT (10.29.10); Shane, "U.S. Hunts for More Suspicious Packages," NYT (10.30.10); Hauser, "Explosives in Cargo Renew Debate on Screening," NYT (10.30.10); Mazzetti & Worth, "U.S. Sees Complexity of Bombs as Link to al Qaeda," NYT (10.31.10); Berger, "Nations Halt Air Cargo from Yemen," NYT (11.1.10); Shane & Worth, "Earlier Flight May Have Been Dry Run for Plotters," NYT (11.2.10).

15 Finn & Miller, "Cargo Plane Bombs More Lethal Than Xmas Day Attempt; Yemen Charges Aulaqi in Absentia," WP (11.2.10); Mazzetti & Shane, "In Parcel Bomb Plot, 2 Dark Inside Jokes," NYT (11.3.10); Schmitt & Shane, "Saudis Warned U.S. of Attack before Parcel Bomb Plot," NYT (11.6.10); Al-Haj, "Yemen Orders U.S.-Born Cleric Found 'Dead or Alive,'" WP (11.6.10).

16 McKelvey, "Inside the Killing Machine," Daily Beast (2.13.11).

17 Entous, Gorman & Barnes, "U.S. Tightens Drone Rules," WSJ (11.4.11); Dilanian, "U.S. Put New Restrictions on CIA Drone Strikes in Pakistan," LAT (11.8.11); Traub, "Silent but Deadly," FP (11.16.12). Seymour Hersh (2016) claimed that Pakistan had protected bin Laden and assisted the SEAL operation.

18 Koh, "The Lawfulness of the U.S. Operation against Osama bin Laden," Opinio Juris (5.19.11).

19 Mazzetti, "U.S. Is Intensifying a Secret Campaign of Yemen Airstrikes," NYT (6.9.11); Mazzetti, Schmitt & Worth, "Two-Year Manhunt Led to Awlaki Death," NYT (10.1.11); Shane, "Judging a Long, Deadly Reach," NYT (10.1.11); Finn, "Secret U.S. Memo Sanctioned Killing of Aulaqi," WP (10.1.11); Wilson, "Obama Pushes Boundaries in Targeting of al-Aulaqi," WP (10.1.11); "Yemen: Fingerprints Confirmed Identities of Awlaki and Khan," LAT (10.1.11); President Obama, "Remarks on the Death of Awlaki at the Retirement of Adm. Mike Mullen as Chair of the JCS" (9.30.11); Goldsmith, "A Just Act of War," NYT (10.1.11);

"Killing of Anwar al-Aulaqi Was Clearly Justified," WP (10.1.11); "Anwar Awlaki: Targeted for Death," LAT (10.2.11); Boot, "Yemen after Awlaki," LAT (10.2.11); Goldberg, "Obama's Terrorist Dilemma," LAT (10.4.11); Ignatius, "A Hint of Deterrence in U.S. Drone-War Strategy," WP (10.4.11); Bellinger, "Will Drone Strikes Become Obama's Guantanamo?" WP (10.3.11); "Administration Should Do More to Defend Awlaki Strike," WP (10.6.11); Warrick, "Cheney: After Yemen Strike, Obama Owes Apology to Bush," WP (10.3.11); Fox, "Anwar al-Aulaqi Killing Praised in Washington," WP (10.1.11); Turley, "Why We Should Wince over al-Awlaki's Death," *USA Today* (10.5.11); O'Connell, "Killing Awlaki Was Illegal, Immoral and Dangerous," CNN (10.5.11); Finn, "Political, Legal Experts Want Release of Justice Dept. Memo Supporting Killing of Anwar al-Awlaki," WP (10.8.11); Brisbane, "The Public Editor: The Secrets of Government Killing," NYT (10.9.11); Cohen, "Who Signed al-Awlaki's Death Warrant?" WP (10.11.11); Ackerman, "Obama's Death Panel," FP (10.7.11); "Iran's Plot – and a U.S. Double-Standard?" LAT (10.12.11); Hosenball, "Secret Panel Can Put Americans on 'Kill List,'" Reuters (10.6.11); Funk, "Family of al Qaeda Blogger Samir Khan 'Appalled' by U.S. Actions," *Charlotte Observer* (10.6.11); Savage, "Secret U.S. Memo Made Legal Case to Kill a Citizen," NYT (10.9.11); "Justifying the Killing of an American," NYT (10.12.11); DeYoung, "Secrecy Defines Obama's Drone War," WP (12.20.11); McKelvey, "Media Coverage of the Drone Program," Joan Shorenstein Center on the Press Politics and Public Policy (Discussion paper 77) (February 2013).

20 "Yemen Says US Airstrike Kills Media Chief for al-Qaeda's Yemeni Branch, 6 other Militants," WP (10.15.11); Finn & Miller, "Anwar al-Awlaki's Family Speaks Out against His Son's Death in Airstrike," WP (10.18.11); Finn, "Awlaki Family Releases Teen's Birth Certificate," WP (10.19.11); "When Is It OK to Kill Americans Abroad?" WP (10.21.11); Finn, "Awlaki Family Angered by U.S. Silence," WP (10.27.11); Kennedy, "Dad of U.S. Terrorist Anwar al-Awlaki: 'My Son's Blood Will Not Go in Vain,'" *New York Daily News* (12.5.11).

21 Stafford Smith, "For Our Allies, Death from Above," NYT (11.4.11); Greenwald, "The Human Toll of the U.S. Drone Campaign," Salon (11.2.11); Miller, "When Will the U.S. Drone War End?" WP (11.18.11); Gerstein, "Ex-DNI Dennis Blair: Get CIA Out of Long-Term Drone Campaigns," Politico (11.30.11); Miller, "Under Obama, an Emerging Global Apparatus for Drone Killing," WP (12.28.11); DeYoung, "Secrecy Defines Obama's Drone War," WP (12.20.11); Klaidman, "Obama Team to Break Silence on al-Awlaki Killing," Daily Beast (1.23.12); Savage, "In G.O.P. Field, Broad View of Presidential Power Prevails," NYT (12.30.11); "Two 'Rule of Law' Republicans Dissent on Torture and Assassinations," *The Atlantic* (11.13.11).

22 Serwer, "Panetta: Decision to Kill Americans Suspected of Terrorism Is Obama's," *Mother Jones* (1.30.12); Landler, "Civilian Deaths Due to Drones Are Not Many, Obama Says," NYT (1.31.12); Parsons & Memoli, "Obama Opens Up about Drone Strikes in Pakistan," LAT (1.31.12);

"America's Drone Wars," LAT (2.1.12); McManus, "Who Reviews the U.S. 'Kill List'?" LAT (2.5.12).

23 Shane, "U.S. Said to Target Rescuers at Drone Strike Sites," NYT (2.6.12); "Regarding U.S. Drones," LAT (2.7.12); Nakashima, "Democrat Balks over Secrecy on Awlaki Killing," WP (2.9.12); Wilson & Cohen, "Poll Finds Broad Support for Obama's Counterterrorism Policies," WP (2.9.12); Woods, "Fresh Evidence of CIA Civilian Deaths in Pakistan Revealed," Bureau of Investigative Journalism (2.27.12); Zenko, "How Many Civilians Are Killed by U.S. Drones," CFR (6.4.12); Harris, "Drone Attacks Create Terrorist Safe Havens, Warns Former CIA Official," G (6.5.12); Taintor, "Americans Are the 'Clear Outliers' in Support for Drone Strikes," TPMDC (6.13.12); McEvers, "Reporting from Yemen amid Ongoing Drone Attacks," NPR (7.9.12); Shane, "The Moral Case for Drones," NYT (7.15.12), "Letters to the Editor," NYT (7.20.12).

24 Jeh Charles Johnson, "National Security Law, Lawyers and Lawyering in the Obama Administration," Yale Law School (2.22.12).

25 Eric Holder, Remarks at Northwestern University Law School (3.5.12).

26 "It's Time to Release the Drone Memos," WP (3.6.12); Rosenthal, "Reviving the Constitution," NYT (3.6.12); Rosenthal, "Targeted Killing," NYT (3.13.12); "Holder's Terrorism Talk Leaves Us in the Dark on Drones," Bloomberg (3.7.12); "Holder's Troubling Death-by-Drone Rules," LAT (3.7.12); "The Power to Kill," NYT (3.11.12); Yoo, "The Good and Bad in Eric Holder's Drone Defense," WSJ (3.12.12); Pitts, "Where Is the Outrage against Obama's Tactics in the War on Terror?" MH (3.13.12); "Additional Review for Drone Killings," WP (3.24.12); Divoll, "Targeted Killings: Who's Checking the Executive Branch?" LAT (3.25.12).

27 Miller, "Brennan Speech Is First Obama Acknowledgement of Use of Armed Drones," WP (4.30.12); Savage, "Top U.S. Security Official Says 'Rigorous' Standards Are Used for Drone Strikes," NYT (5.1.12).

28 Bergen, "Warrior in Chief," NYT (4.29.12); Gerson, "America's Remote-Controlled War on Terror," WP (5.4.12): McManus, "Coming Clean on Drones," LAT (5.6.12); "Too Much Power for a President," NYT (5.31.12); Letters to the Editor, NYT (6.1.12); Krauthammer, "Barack Obama: Drone Warrior," WP (6.1.12).

29 Klaidman, "Drones: How Obama Learned to Kill," *Harper's Magazine* (5.28.12); Becker & Shane, "Secret 'Kill List' Proves a Test of Obama's Principles and Will," NYT (5.29.12); Klaidman (2012); Shane, "U.S. Attacks, Online and from the Air, Fuel Secrecy Debate," NYT (6.6.12); AI (2012).

30 Morley, "UN Rights Chief Calls for Drone Probe," Salon.com (6.7.12); Nebehay, "U.N. Investigator Decries Use of Killer Drones," Reuters (6.19.12); Bowcott, "Drone Strikes Threaten 50 Years of International Law, Says UN Rapporteur," G (6.21.12); Shane, "Drone Strikes to Be Investigated," NYT (10.26.12); "Drones Violate Sovereignty, Pakistan Tells UN," *Pakistan Tribune* (10.31.12); Pecquet, "US Open to

Cooperating with UN Probe into Drone Strikes," *The Hill* (11.12.12); Bowcott, "UN to Examine UK and US Drone Strikes," G (1.24.13); Burns, "U.N. Panel to Investigate Rise in Drone Strikes," NYT (1.25.13).

31 Emmerson statement (3.14.13).

32 Serwer, "Congress Wants to See Obama's 'License to Kill,'" *Mother Jones* (7.31.12); Rosenthal, "John Cornyn Makes Sense," NYT (8.2.12); "Cornyn Called Targeted Killing a 'Program,' Too," EmptyWheel (8.10.12).

33 Shachtman, "Obama Finally Talks Drone War, But It's Almost Impossible to Believe Him," Wired's Danger Room (9.7.12).

34 "Pulling the U.S. Drone War Out of the Shadows," WP (11.1.12).

35 Shane, "Election Spurred a Move to Codify U.S. Drone Policy," NYT (11.25.12); "Rules for Targeted Killing," NYT (11.30.12); Letters to the Editor, NYT (11.30.12, 12.7.12).

36 Katz, "U.S. Officials Debating Response to 'Targeted Killing' Suit," Reuters (4.24.12); "Obama Administration Rejects Requests for 'Targeted Killing' Papers, Citing National Security," WP (6.20.12); "Appeals Court Judges Seem Skeptical of CIA Secrecy on Drone Program," WP (9.20.12); "Misplaced Secrecy on Targeted Killing," NYT (1.4.13); *N.Y. Times Co.* v. *Dep't of Justice*, 915 F.Supp.2d 508 (S.D.N.Y. 2013); DoJ White Paper: Lawfulness of a Lethal Operation Directed against a U.S. Citizen Who Is a Senior Operational Leader of Al-Qa'ida or an Associated Force; Isikoff, "Justice Department Memo Reveals Legal Case for Drone Strikes on Americans," NBC News (2.4.13).

37 *N.Y. Times Co.* v. *U.S. Dep't of Justice*, 756 F.3d 100 (2nd Cir. 2014); "Transparency on Targeted Killings," NYT (4.22.14).

38 *ACLU* v. *Dep't of Justice*, 2015 WL 4470192 (S.D.N.Y. 2015), aff'd, 806 F.3d 682 (2nd Cir. 2015); Savage, "Appeals Court Rules Memos on Targeted Killings Can Stay Classified," NYT (11.24.15); Trujillo, "Court Slaps Down Effort to FOIA Obama's List of Drone Targets," *The Hill* (1.26.16).

39 *ACLU* v. *CIA*, 808 F.Supp.2d 280 (D.D.C. 2011).

40 *ACLU* v. *CIA*, 710 F.3d 422 (D.C. Cir. 2013); Finn & Tate, "Appeals Court Rejects CIA's Argument over Acknowledging Drone Opinions," WP (3.15.13); Bailey, "ACLU Loses Bid for CIA's Charts on Drone Strikes," Courthouse News Service (6.22.15); *ACLU* v. *CIA*, 109 F.Supp.3d 220 (D.D.C. 2015). The D.C. Circuit affirmed on April 21, 2016.

41 Shane & Mazzetti, "Choice to Lead C.I.A. Faces a Changed Agency," NYT (1.8.13); Landler, "Obama Nominates Hagel as Defense Secretary and Brennan as C.I.A. Chief," NYT (1.7.13); Shane, "Senator Asks to View Files on Killings of Americans," NYT (1.15.13); Divoll, "Who Says You Can Kill Americans, Mr. President?" NYT (1.17.13); Miller, Nakashima & DeYoung, "CIA Drone Strikes Will Get Pass in Counterterrorism 'Playbook,' Officials Say," WP (1.20.13); Zenko (2013).

42 Department of Justice, White Paper: Legality of a Lethal Operation by the Central Intelligence Agency against a U.S. Citizen (5.25.11);

Savage & Shane, "Memo Cites Legal Basis for Killing U.S. Citizens in al Qaeda," NYT (2.5.13); DeYoung, "Justice Dept. Document Justifies Killing Americans Overseas If They Pose 'Imminent Threat,'" WP (2.5.13); Shane & Savage, "Report on Targeted Killing Whets Appetite for Less Secrecy," NYT (2.6.13); "To Kill an American," NYT (2.6.13); Downie, "The Justice Department's Chilling 'Targeted Killings' Memo," WP (2.6.13); Shear & Shane, "Congress to See Memo Backing Drone Attacks on Americans," NYT (2.7.13); DeYoung & Miller, "Obama Will Allow Lawmakers to See Secret Memo on Targeted Killings," WP (2.7.13); "Drone Strikes under Scrutiny," NYT (2.7.13); O'Connell, "The Questions Brennan Can't Dodge," NYT (2.7.13); AI (2013a); Fairleigh Dickinson University's Public Mind, "Public Says It's Illegal to Target Americans Abroad as Some Question CIA Drone Attacks" (2.7.13).

43 "Feinstein: Senate Staffers 'Banned from Seeing' Vital Information," HuffPost (2.7.13); Mazzetti & Shane, "Drones Are Focus as C.I.A. Nominee Goes before Senators," NYT (2.8.13); Miller, "Brennan Defends Drone Strike Policies," WP (2.8.13); Shane, "Debating a Court to Vet Drone Strikes," NYT (2.9.13); "Lawmakers Propose Giving Federal Judges Role in Drone Strikes, but Hurdles Await," WP (2.8.13).

44 "A Long Overdue Discussion," NYT (2.8.13); Brooks, "Florence and the Drones," NYT (2.8.13); Milbank, "'Trust Me' Is Not Enough on Drone Warfare," WP (2.8.13); Robinson, "Assassinations by Remote Control," WP (2.8.13); Gerson, "Obama's Drone Policy, Rooted in Self-Defense," WP (2.8.13); Cole, "President Obama, Did or Did You Not Kill Anwar al-Awlaki?" WP (2.9.13); "Drones Beat the Alternatives," *USA Today* (2.10.13); "A Court for Targeted Killings," NYT (2.14.13); Krauthammer, "In Defense of Obama's Drone War," WP (2.14.13); Letter to the Editor, NYT (2.21.13).

45 "Ex-Pentagon Chief Gates Finds 'Merit' in Idea of Creating Special Court to OK Drone Strikes," WP (2.10.13); Strauss, "Gates Backs More Oversight of Drones," *The Hill* (2.10.13); Tanfani, "Ex-Defense Chief Calls for Review before Drone Strikes on Americans," LAT (2.11.13); "Letters to the Editor," NYT (2.13.13); Yoo, "The Real Problem with Obama's Drone Memo," WSJ (2.7.13); "US Senator Says Drones Death Toll Is 4700," DT (2.21.13).

46 Robertson, "Judges Shouldn't Decide about Drone Strikes," WP (2.16.13); Katyal, "Who Will Mind the Drones?" NYT (2.21.13); Mukasey," How to Untangle an Incoherent Drone Policy," WSJ (2.18.13); Harman, "Drone Courts Can Work," CNN (2.19.13).

47 Feinstein Press Release on Intelligence Committee Oversight of Targeted Killings (2.13.13); Shane & Mazzetti, "Strategy Seeks to Ensure Bid of C.I.A. Pick," NYT (2.21.13); Shane, "Nominee to Lead C.I.A. Clears Hurdle after Release of Drone Data," NYT (3.6.13).

48 Stevenson & Parker, "A Senator's Stand on Drones Scrambles Partisan Lines," NYT (3.8.13); Weiner, "McCain Calls Paul, Cruz, Amash 'Wacko Birds,'" WP (3.8.13); Shane & Shear, "Visions of Drones Swarming U.S. Skies Hit Bipartisan Nerve," NYT 3.8.13); Ewing, "Rand Paul Pulls Plug

on Nearly 13-hour Filibuster," Politico (3.6.13); Collins, "Talk of the Town," NYT (3.7.13); Robinson, "Rand Paul Makes the Right Call with Filibuster," WP (3.8.13); "More Oversight and Disclosure on Drones," WP (3.8.13); Paul, "My Filibuster Was Just the Beginning," WP (3.9.13); Ignatius, "Drones: A Weapon that Needs a Holster," WP (3.9.13); Goodman, "The Drone Question Obama Hasn't Answered," NYT (3.9.13).

49 Savage, "Senators Press Holder on Use of Military Force," NYT (3.7.13); Statement by Sen. Leahy, Senate Judiciary Committee Hearing on Oversight of the DoJ (3.6.13); Robinson, "Rand Paul Makes the Right Call with Filibuster," WP (3.8.13).

50 Mazzetti, Savage & Shane, "How a U.S. Citizen Came to Be in America's Cross Hairs," NYT (3.10.13); "Repeal the Military Force Law," NYT (3.10.13).

51 McAuliff, "Obama Rebuffs Dems on Drone Kill Memos, Asserts Executive Secrecy Prerogative," HuffPost (3.13.13).

52 Podesta, "Obama Should Lift Secrecy on Drones," WP (3.14.13).

53 Tiron, "McCarthy Says House Should Subpoena Documents on Drones," Bloomberg (3.15.13).

54 Harman, "Remote-Control Warfare Requires Rules," NYT (3.18.13); Johnson, "A 'Drone Court': Some Pros and Cons" (3.18.13); Savage, "Former Pentagon Lawyer Offers Pros and Cons of Drone Court," NYT (3.18.13); ACLU et al., Letter to President Obama (4.11.13).

55 Savage & Baker, "Obama, in a Shift, to Limit Targets of Drone Strikes," NYT (5.23.13); DeYoung & Finn, "U.S. Acknowledges Killing of Four U.S. Citizens in Counterterrorism Operations," WP (5.23.13); Klapper, "Rand Paul Threatens to Hold Up James Comey FBI Nomination over Drones," Huffpost (7.10.13); Al-Awlaki, "The Drone That Killed My Grandson," NYT (7.18.13).

56 Walsh & Mehsud, "Civilian Deaths in Drone Strikes Cited in Report," NYT (10.22.13); Whitlock, "Drone Strikes Killing More Civilians than U.S. Admits, Human Rights Groups Say," WP (10.22.13); Herb, "Carney: U.S. Drone Strikes 'Precise,' 'Lawful,'" *The Hill* (10.23.13); "The Death of Innocents," NYT (10.23.13); Jaffe, "Former Defense Secretary Gates Warns against Lure of Drone Warfare," WP (10.23.13); Heyns, Report of the Special Rapporteur on Extrajudicial, Summary or Arbitrary Executions (9.13.13); Emmerson, Report of the Special Rapporteur on the Promotion and Protection of Human Rights and Fundamental Freedoms While Countering Terrorism (9.18.13); "A Meta-Study of Drone Strike Casualties," Lawfare (7.22.13).

57 Dilanian, "U.S. Drone Strikes Down since Curbs Were Imposed," LAT (11.17.13); Firestone, "How Many Non-combatants Are Killed by Drones?" NYT (2.5.14).

58 Miller, "Lawmakers Seek to Stymie Plan to Shift Control of Drone Campaign from CIA to Pentagon," WP (1.16.14); O'Keefe, "McCain Responds Angrily to Report on Drones," WP (1.16.14); Schmitt,

"Congress Restricts Drone Program Shift," NYT (1.17.14); Schiff, "Let the Military Run Drone Warfare," NYT (3.12.14); "The Lawyer behind the Drone Policy," NYT (5.8.14).

59 Cox, "Grassley Wants 'Unredacted' Memo Justifying Killing of U.S. Citizen," *The Hill* (4.22.14); Peters, "Judicial Nominee's Memos on Drones Stirring Bipartisan Concern in the Senate," NYT (5.6.14); Gerstein, "White House Offers Drone Memo to Whole Senate," Politico (5.6.14); Openthegovernment.org (5.12.14); Savage, "U.S. Seeks to Censor More of Memo that Approved Drone Strike on American," NYT (5.29.14).

60 Paul, "Show Us the Drone Memos," NYT (5.12.14); Rubin, "Rand Paul Links Arms with ACLU vs. Drone Use," WP (5.16.14); Parker, "Memo Approving Targeted Killing of U.S. Citizen to Be Released," NYT (5.21.14); O'Keefe, "David Barron's Judicial Nomination Clears Procedural Hurdle," WP (5.21.14); "The Senate Foolishly Rushes In," NYT (5.22.14).

61 Barron, Memorandum for the Attorney General Re: Applicability of Federal Criminal Laws and the Constitution to Contemplated Lethal Operations Against Shaykh Anwar al-Aulaqi (7.16.10); Savage, "Court Releases Large Parts of Memo Approving Killing of American in Yemen," NYT (6.23.14); "A Thin Rationale for Drone Killings," NYT (6.23.14); Rogers, "In Defense of Killing a U.S. Citizen," *USA Today* (6.30.14).

62 Mazzetti, "Senate Drops Bid to Report on Drone Use," NYT (4.29.14); DeYoung, "Obama's Revamp of Anti-Terror Policies Stalls," WP (5.22.14); "President Obama and the World," NYT (5.4.14); Fuller, "Americans Are Fine with Drone Strikes," WP (7.15.14).

63 Miller, "Hostages' Deaths Raise Wider Questions about Drone Strikes' Civilian Toll," WP (4.23.15); Whitlock, Ryan & Miller, "Obama Apologizes for Attack that Killed Two Hostages," WP (4.23.15); Baker & Davis, "Amid Errors, Obama Publicly Wrestles with Drones' Limits," NYT (4.25.15); "Regret over a Drone's Deadly Damage," NYT (4.25.15); Miller & Tate, "U.S. Government's Refusal to Discuss Drone Attacks Comes Under Fire," WP (4.25.15); Mazzetti & Apuzzo, "Deep Support in Washington for C.I.A.'s Drone Missions," NYT (4.26.15); Entous, "Obama Kept Looser Rules for Drones in Pakistan," WSJ (4.26.15); Shahzad & Hurst, "Pakistanis See Double Standard in Drone Strikes," WP (5.1.15); Shane, "Families of Drone Strike Victims in Yemen File Suit in Washington," NYT (6.7.15); Currier, "One Year On, No Justice for Italian Hostage Killed in U.S. Drone Strike," The Intercept (3.15.16); O'Toole, "Family of U.S. Hostage Killed in Botched Strike Blasts the White House," FP (4.22.16).

64 Acosta, "Obama to Make New Push to Shift Control of Drones from CIA to Pentagon," CNN (4.27.15); "Drone Strikes Are Bad; No Drone Strikes Would Be Worse," WP (5.2.15); Dilanian & Swanson, "AP Poll: Americans Approve of Drone Strikes on Terrorists," *Sacramento Bee* (5.1.15); Hattem & Matishak, "Drone Fight Simmers in Congress," *The Hill* (5.2.15).

65 Hayden, "To Keep America Safe, Embrace Drone Warfare," NYT (2.19.16); Hayden (2016: 337); Heyns, Letter to the Editor, NYT (2.26.16); al-Muslimi, Letter to the Editor, NYT (3.2.16).
66 Walker & Alizway, "Serbian Hostages Killed in U.S. Airstrikes against ISIS in Libya," NYT (2.21.16); Ryan, "Serbia Says a U.S. Strike in Libya Killed Two of Its Diplomats: Here's Why the Pentagon Thinks It Didn't," WP (2.24.16).
67 Stimson Center (2014, 2016); Mazzetti, "Use of Drones for Killings Risks a War without End, Panel Concludes in Report," NYT (6.26.14); "Reining in the Drones," NYT (7.7.14); Johnsen, Letter to the Editor, NYT (7.7.14); Jaffer & Kaufman, "Limit the Next President's Power to Wage Drone Warfare," NYT (3.8.16); Ackerman, "White House to Reveal Death Toll of U.S. Drone Strikes for First Time," G (3.7.16); "Transparency in the Drone Wars," NYT (3.20.16); Johnson, "Protests Shut Down CIA Director's Talk at Penn," *Daily Pennsylvanian* (4.1.16); Reprieve, "The Truth About Drone Strikes: Opaque Transparency" (2016).
68 Michaels, "Obama: Drone Strikes Have Become More Precise," *USA Today* (4.2.16); Hattem, "Obama Outlines Hopes for Legacy on Drone Strikes," *The Hill* (4.7.16) Miller, "Why Drone Strikes Have Plummeted," WP (6.16.16).
69 Savage & Shane, "U.S. Reveals Death Toll from Airstrikes outside War Zones," NYT (7.2.16); Miller, "Why the White House Claims on Drone Casualties Remain in Doubt," WP (7.2.16); Shane, "Drone Strike Statistics Answer Few Questions, and Raise Many," NYT (7.4.16); Zenko, "Do Not Believe the U.S. Government's Official Numbers on Drone Strike Civilian Casualties," FP (7.5.16).
70 Savage, "U.S. Releases Rules for Airstrike Killings of Terror Suspects," NYT (8.7.16).
71 Chait, "Five Days that Shaped a Presidency," *The New Yorker* (10.2.16).
72 Presidential Memorandum – Steps for Increased Legal and Policy Transparency Concerning the United States Use of Military Force and Related National Security Operations, White House Press Release (12.5.16); Remarks by the President on the Administration's Approach to Counterterrorism, White House Press Release (12.6.16); Report on the Legal and Policy Frameworks Guiding the United States' Use of Military Force and Related National Security Operations, White House (December 2016).
73 Savage & Schmitt, "Trump Administration Is Said to Be Working to Loosen Counterterrorism Rules," NYT (3.13.17); Jaffe & Young, "Trump Administration Reviewing Ways to Make It Easier to Launch Drone Strikes," WP (3.14.17); Lubold & Harris, "Trump Broadens CIA Powers, Allows Deadly Drone Strikes," WSJ (3.13.17); "Preventing a Free-For-All with Drone Strikes," NYT (3.16.17).
74 Savage & Schmitt, "Trump Poised to Drop Some Limits on Drone Strikes and Commando Raids," NYT (9.21.17).
75 Perrow (1999).

76 Lasseter, "As Possible Afghan War-Crimes Evidence Removed, U.S. Silent," McClatchy (12.11.08); Risen, "U.S. Inaction Seen after Taliban P.O.W.'s Died," NYT A1 (7.11.09); PHR, "President Obama Orders National Security Team to Investigate Dasht-e-Leili Massacre and Alleged Cover-Up," (7.12.09); "The Truth about Dasht-i-Leili," NYT A20 (7.14.09); Oppel, "Afghan Warlord Denies Links to '01 Killings," NYT A6 (7.18.09); Benjamin, "Did U.S. Forces Watch Afghan Massacre?" Salon (7.22.09).

77 Rosenberg, "Afghanistan's Vice President Is Barred From Entering U.S.," NYT (4.29.16).

78 White, "Army Withheld Details About Tillman's Death," WP (5.4.05); "Report: Army Knew How Tillman Died," LAT (5.4.05); "National Briefing," NYT (8.25.05); "Facing Up to the Tragedy of War," NYT (5.24.05); White, "Criminal Probe in Tillman Case Set to Open," WP (3.5.06); Davey & Schmitt, "2 Years after Soldier's Death, Family's Battle Is with Army," NYT (3.21.06); Cloud, "Pentagon Faults 9 Officers for Aftermath of Tillman Death," NYT (3.27.07); Tyson, "9 Officers Blamed in Tillman Death, But No Coverup Found," WP (3.27.07); Barnes & Spiegel, "Army Lied about Tillman's Death, Report Says," LAT (3.27.07); Zucchino, "Tillmans Level Unfriendly Fire at Pentagon," LAT (3.28.07); McKinley, "Family Strongly Criticizes Query into Tillman's Death," NYT (3.28.07); Tyson, "General's Memo Urged Caution after Tillman Death," WP (3.31.07); "Army's Documents Detail Secrecy in Tillman Case," NYT (4.21.07); Juo, "Panel Hears about Falsehoods in 2 Wartime Incidents," NYT (4.25.07); Schreck, "Tillman's Brother Lashes Out," LAT (4.25.07); "Corporal Tillman Haunts the Pentagon," NYT (4.27.07); White, "White House Denies Request for Documents in Ex-NFL Player's Death," WP (7.14.07); "Seeking the Truth about Pat Tillman," NYT (7.27.07); Lewis, "Retired General Is Censured for Role in Tillman Case," NYT (8.1.07); Havemann, "Censure in Death of NFL's Tillman," LAT (8.1.07); Lauer & Neuman, "Rumsfeld Denies Tillman Coverup," LAT (8.2.07); Von Zielbauer, "Panel Queries Rumsfeld on Tillman Battle Death," NYT (8.2.07); "White House Will Allow Interviews in Tillman Investigation," LAT (8.3.07); Lindlaw & Mendoza, "General Suspected Cause of Tillman's Death," WP (8.4.07); "Waiting for the Truth on Cpl Tillman," NYT (8.4.07); "A 'Path Forward?'" WP (8.8.07); "Request for Release of Tillman Documents," NYT (8.14.07); Zirin, "The Tillman Offenses," LAT (6.8.08); White, "Unanswered Questions in Tillman Report," WP (7.15.08); "Investigation of Pat Tillman Misinformation Goes Nowhere," LAT (7.15.08); "Who Spread False Tales of Heroism?" NYT (7.16.08); Waxman Statement (7.17.08); Shanker, "Choice of Commander for Afghan War Revives Questions in Tillman Case," NYT (5.26.09); Tillman, "Pat Tillman's Mother on Army Gen. Stanley McChrystal: I Told You So," LAT (8.8.10); Karpel, "Whitewash in Wartime," NYT (8.15.10); House Committee on Oversight and Government Reform, Misleadinig Information from the Battlefield: The Tillman and Lynch Episodes (7.17.08); Krakauer (2009); Ordona, "Getting to the Truth of Pat Tillman's Death," LAT (8.18.10).

79 Tillman & Nacchino (2008).
80 Lamothe & Gibbons-Neff, "U.S. Military Launches Investigation into Deaths of Army Rangers, Citing Potential Friendly Fire," WP (4.28.17); Cooper, "'Friendly Fire' May Have Killed 2 U.S. Soldiers in Afghanistan Raid," NYT (4.29.17).
81 Serrano, "U.S. Looks into Videotaped Desecration of Taliban Corpses by Army Unit," NYT (10.20.05); Schmitt, "Army Examining an Account of Abuse of 2 Dead Taliban," NYT (10.20.05); Gall & Schmitt, "Taliban Step Up Afghan Bombings and Suicide Attacks," NYT (10.21.05); Munadi, "Karzai Condemns Burnings of Afghan Bodies by U.S. Troops," NYT (10.22.05); "U.S. Soldiers Reprimanded for Burning Bodies," CNN.com (11.26.05).
82 Tirman (2012).
83 Cloud, "U.S. Military Opens Inquiry into Whether Marines Killed 10 Afghans after Attack on Convoy," NYT (3.24.07); "Probe Finds Excess Force in Afghanistan Incident," LAT (4.12.07); Gall, "Marines' Actions Called Excessive in Afghanistan," NYT (4.15.07); Saidi & King, "Panel Calls Marines' Action Illegal," LAT (4.15.07); Tyson & White, "Excessive Force by Marines Alleged," WP (4.14.07); Tyson & White, "Marines Killed Civilians, U.S. Says," WP (4.15.07); Von Zielbauer, "Killings of Afghan Civilians Recall Haditha," NYT (4.20.07); Cloud, "U.S. Pays and Apologizes to Kin of Afghans Killed by Marines," NYT (5.9.07); Spiegel, "Apology Wrong, General Says," LAT (5.18.07); Von Zielbauer, "Afghan Civilians Were Killed Needlessly, Ex-Marine Testifies," NYT (1.9.08); Von Zielbauer, "4 Say Marines Took Fire in Attack on Afghans," NYT (1.10.08); Zucchino, "Marine Shooter Seeks Immunity in Afghan Case," LAT (1.11.08); Zucchino, "Frustration in Marines Shooting Inquiry," LAT (1.18.08); Zucchino, "2 Afghans Testify in Marine Inquiry," LAT (1.22.08); Zucchino, "Army Colonel again Criticizes Marine Unity," LAT (1.24.08); Zucchino, "Marine Humvee Was Shot At, Army Expert Testifies," LAT (1.26.08); Zucchino, "No Answers in Marine Inquiry," LAT (1.29.08); Zucchino, "Did Marines Kill Wildly, or Not?" LAT (2.5.08); "No Charges for Two Marines in Deaths of Afghans," WP (5.24.08).
84 Constable, "Karzai Says Civilian Toll Is No Longer Acceptable," WP (5.3.07); "Afghan Bill Restricting Foreign Forces Advances," LAT (5.9.07).
85 "Afghans Report Civilian Toll in Airstrikes," LAT (5.10.07); Gall, "Afghans Say Civilian Toll in Strikes Is Much Higher than Reported," NYT (5.11.07).
86 "The Afghan Struggle: A Secret Archive," NYT (7.26.10) (WikiLeaks); Chatterjee, "The Secret Killers, Assassination in Afghanistan and Task Force 373," TomDispatch (8.19.10); Bearak, "Karzai Calls Coalition 'Careless,'" NYT (6.25.07).
87 Bearak & Wafa, "U.S. Account of Afghan Deaths at Odds with Head of Rights Group," NYT (6.30.07).

88 Gall, "U.N. Official Raises Alarms over Killing in Afghanistan," NYT (5.16.08).
89 Gall, "Joint Operation Kills 2 Afghan Tribal Leaders, U.S. Says," NYT (7.18.08); Shanker, "Civilian Risks Curbing Strikes in Afghan War," NYT (7.23.08); Gall, "U.S. and NATO Forces Kill 13 Afghans in Strikes Said to Be Mistakes," NYT (7.21.08); Rondeaux, "Civilian Airstrike Deaths Probed," WP (7.25.08).
90 Rondeaux & Hamdard, "U.S. Probes Afghan Assertions that Raid Killed 70 Civilians," WP (8.24.08); Gall, "Afghan President Assails U.S.-led Airstrike That He Says Killed 95," NYT (8.24.08); "U.N. Says Has Evidence Air Strikes Killed 90 Afghans," WP (8.26.08); "U.N. Cites Evidence That U.S. Attack in Afghanistan Killed 90 Civilians," LAT (8.27.08); Rondeaux & DeYoung, "U.N. Finds Airstrike Killed 90 Afghans," WP (8.27.08); Gall, "U.S. Killed 90 in Afghan Village, Including 60 Children, U.N. Finds," NYT (8.27.08); Schmitt, "U.S. Officials Describe Afghan Airstrike," NYT (8.28.08); Tyson, "Pentagon Reports U.S. Airstrike Killed 5 Afghan Civilians, not 90," WP (9.29.08); Gall, "Joint Inquiry on Deaths of Afghans Is Proposed," NYT (8.30.08); Faiez & King, "Joint Investigation Planned in Disputed Afghanistan Death Toll," LAT (8.31.08); Hamdard & Rondeaux, "Joint Inquiry Sought into US-led Strike in Afghan Town," WP (8.31.08); "Collateral Killing: Too Many Innocent Afghans Are Dying in U.S. Airstrikes," WP (8.31.08); "Afghan Officers Say Troops in Raid Were Fired on First," LAT (9.1.08); "U.S. Will Review Afghan Death Toll Investigation," LAT (9.8.08); Gall, "Trail of Evidence Points to High Civilian Toll in Afghan Raid," NYT (9.8.08); Rondeaux & DeYoung, "U.S. Team to Reinvestigate Deadly Strike in Afghanistan," WP (9.9.08); Schmitt, "U.S. Inquiry Is Said to Conclude 30 Civilians Died in Afghan Raid," NYT (10.8.08); Barnes, "U.S. Military Acknowledges Higher Civilian Toll in Afghanistan Attack," LAT (10.9.08); DeYoung, "Military Justifies Attack That Killed At Least 33 Afghan Civilians," WP (10.9.08); Risen, "Afghans Linked to Taliban Guard U.S. Bases," NYT (10.8.10).
91 HRW (2008).
92 Faiez & King, "2 Afghan Children Killed in Western Artillery Strike," LAT (9.2.08); "NATO Forces and Afghans Kill Children in Two Attacks," NYT (9.2.08); "World Briefing," LAT (9.3.08); Rondeaux & Hamdard, "U.S. Rejects Claims of Afghan Deaths," WP (9.3.08); Gall, "U.S. Airstrike Inquiry at Odds with Reports of More Afghan Deaths," NYT (9.3.08); Shah & Perlez, "U.S. Missiles Killed at least Six People on Afghan–Pakistan Border, Residents Say," NYT (9.6.08); Gerstenzang, "Bush to Focus on Afghan Civilian Deaths, U.S. Troop Transfers," LAT (9.9.08); Gall, "More Afghans Being Killed, Report Says," NYT (9.9.08).
93 Barnes, "NATO Commander in Afghanistan Seeks to Curb Civilian Deaths," LAT (9.17.08); Shanker, "NATO Tries to Reduce Afghan Casualties," NYT (9.17.08); Barnes, "Afghans' Toll Shakes Generals," NYT (10.19.08); Barnes, "Defense Secretary Robert Gates Apologizes for

Afghan Civilian Casualties," LAT (9.18.08); Shankar, "Gates Tries to Ease Tension in Afghan Civilian Deaths," NYT (9.18.08); "Afghanistan: World Briefing," LAT (9.19.08); UNAMA, Afghanistan: Annual Report on Protection of Civilians in Armed Conflict, 2008 (January 2009).

94 Burns, "Afghan Officials Say Airstrike Killed Civilians," NYT (10.17.08); "Afghanistan: Civilian Deaths Probed," WP A16 (10.18.08); King, "Afghanistan Officials Say 17 Civilians Killed in Fighting," LAT (10.18.08); King, "Coalition Friendly-Fire Incident Kills 9 Afghan Soldiers," LAT (10.23.08); Faiez & King, "U.S. to Investigate Report of Airstrike Hitting Afghan Wedding Party," LAT (11.6.08); Rondeaux, "End Civilian Deaths, Karzai Tells Obama," WP (11.6.08); Wafa & Burns, "Afghan Officials Say U.S. Strike Killed 40 at Wedding Party," NYT (11.6.08); Wafa & Rahimi, "Amid New Accounts of Civilian Deaths, U.S. Says Taliban Put Afghans in Line of Fire," NYT (11.7.08); Faiez & King, "U.S. Acknowledges 37 Afghan Civilians Killed in Fighting Last Week," LAT (11.9.08); Wafa & Rahimi, "Amid New Accounts of Civilian Deaths, U.S. Says Taliban Put Afghans in Line of Fire," NYT (11.7.08); Faiez & King, "Afghan President Karzai Accuses Western Forces of Killing 14 Civilians," LAT (11.11.08); Faiez & King, "Afghanistan Struggle Takes a Heavy Toll on Civilians," LAT (11.14.08); Semple, "Afghan Leader, Showing Impatience with War, Demands Timetable from NATO," NYT (11.11.08); Semple, "U.N. Official in Afghanistan Tells Allies to Ease Attacks," NYT (12.8.08).

95 "Mistaken U.S. Strike Kills 6 Afghan Police," LAT (12.10.08); Rondeaux, "U.S. Troops Mistakenly Kill Six Afghan Policemen," WP (12.11.08); Semple, "U.S. Forces Cite Errors in Killings of 7 Afghans," NYT (12.11.08); "4 Killed in Shooting at a Bus Carrying Afghans," NYT (12.13.08); Ellick, "Tensions Rise as Afghans Say U.S. Raid Kills Civilians," NYT (12.19.08); "Afghanistan: Protests over Raid," NYT (12.27.08).

96 Barker, "Afghanistan's President Karzai Laments Use of 'Thugs,'" LAT (12.22.08).

97 "Afghanistan: 11 Civilians Killed," NYT A14 (1.8.09); "Afghanistan Seeks More Control of Nato Troops," LAT (1.21.09); Faiez, "Afghans Dispute Toll in U.S. Raid," LAT (1.25.09); Wallstein, "Afghanistan Warning Sounded," LAT (1.26.09); Gall, "Afghans, from Hospital Beds, Dispute U.S. Account of Raid," NYT (1.26.09); "Afghanistan: Payments Made for Victims of U.S. Raid," NYT (1.28.09).

98 "Afghanistan: Villagers Protest Deadly U.S. Raid," LAT (2.2.09); "Afghans Rally Against U.S. after Strike Kills Two," WP (2.2.08); Barker, "Civilian Deaths Roil Afghans," LAT (2.18.09); Cohen & Agiesta, "Poll of Afghans Shows Drop in Support for U.S. Mission," WP (2.10.09); "Airstrike Killed 13 Afghan Civilians, U.S. Says," LAT (2.22.06); Oppel, "Revising Initial Claim, U.S. Concedes Afghan Attack Mainly Killed Civilians," NYT (2.22.09); Constable, "Tactical Success, Strategic Defeat," WP (3.2.09); Mazzetti & Schmitt, "U.S. Halted Some Afghan Raids over Concern on Civilian Deaths," NYT (3.10.09); Wafa & Gall, "U.S. Kills 5 Afghans in Raid on House," NYT (3.23.09).

99 "U.S.-Afghan Mission Kills 5," LAT (3.15.09); Oppel & Wafa, "Civilians Died in Airstrike by Nato, Afghan Says," NYT (4.15.09); King, "U.S. Investigating Afghan Claims of 70 Civilian Deaths," LAT (5.6.09); Shah & Gall, "Afghans Say U.S. Raids Killed 30 Civilians," NYT (5.6.09); King, "Red Cross Backs Reports of Afghan Civilian Deaths," LAT (5.6.09); King, "Dozens of Afghan Civilians Killed, Red Cross Confirms," LAT (5.7.09); Gall & Shah, "Civilian Deaths Imperil Support for Afghan War," NYT (5.7.09); Jaffe, "Joint Probe Planned of Deadly U.S. Strike in West Afghanistan," WP (5.7.09); Jaffe, "Civilian Deaths Create Difficulties for U.S. Strategy in Afghanistan," WP (5.7.09); Bumiller & Gall, "U.S. Officials Admit Civilians Died in Afghan Air Raids," NYT (5.8.09); King, "Afghans Protest Civilian Deaths; U.S. Raises Doubts," LAT (5.8.09); Cooper, "Afghan President Insists He's Fighting Corruption," NYT (5.9.09); Barnes, "Afghan Toll Is Much Lower, U.S. Officials Say," LAT (5.9.09); Hsu, "More Airstrikes Against Taliban Possible, Says U.S. Official," WP (5.11.09); Gall & Shah, "Afghans Recall Airstrike Horror, and Fault U.S.," NYT (5.15.09); King, "What Happened Here?" LAT (5.17.09); Barnes & King, "Mullen Cites Danger of Civilian Losses," LAT (5.19.09); Wafa & Bumiller, "Afghan Leader's Brother Survives Ambush; U.S. Offers Details on Lethal Airstrikes," NYT (5.19.09); Gall, "U.S. Envoy Vows to Help Cut Afghan Civilian Deaths," NYT (5.20.09); King, "Afghan Deaths Still in Dispute," LAT (5.21.09); Schmitt & Shanker, "U.S. Report Finds Errors in Afghan Airstrikes," NYT (6.3.09); "Measuring Success in Afghanistan," NYT (6.8.09); DeYoung, "U.S. Troops Erred in Fight with Taliban," WP (6.9.09); Jawad, Letter to the Editor, NYT (6.11.09); Castle, "Gates Promises to Reduce Afghan Civilian Deaths," NYT (6.13.09); King, "U.S. General Faces Challenges in Afghanistan," LAT (6.16.09); Zucchino, "Civilian Deaths Weigh on Missions," LAT (6.19.09); Jaffe, "U.S. Troops Erred in Airstrikes on Civilians," WP (6.20.09); Shanker, "With Afghan People in Mind, a New Commander Rethinks How to Measure Success," NYT (6.20.09); Filkins, "U.S. Toughens Airstrike Policy in Afghanistan," NYT (6.21.09); Zucchino & King, "U.S. to Limit Airstrikes in Afghanistan to Help Reduce Civilian Deaths," LAT (6.23.09); Barnes, "U.S. Alters Policy on Death Toll Data," LAT (7.24.09); NATO/ISAF, "ISAF Tactical Directive" (July 2009); Open Society Institute and The Liaison Office (2010).

100 Shah & Gall, "U.S. Strike Kills 5 Civilians, Afghans Say," NYT (7.17.09); Filkins, "Road Bomb Kills Afghans: U.S. Airstrike Disputed," NYT (8.6.09); Filkins & Wafa, "5 Marines Die from Bombs as Afghans Alter Tactics," NYT (8.7.09); King, "New Tactics Cut Afghan Fatalities," LAT (8.28.09).

101 Farrell & Oppel, "NATO Strike Magnifies Divide on Afghan War," NYT (9.5.09); Chandrasekaran, "NATO Probing Deadly Airstrike," WP (9.5.09); Faiez & King, "A Setback to U.S. Efforts in Afghanistan," LAT (9.5.09); Faiez & King, "In Unusual Step, U.S. General Visits Site of Afghan Airstrike," LAT (9.6.09); "NATO Begins Investigation of Deadly

Airstrike on Fuel Tanks in Afghanistan," NYT (9.6.09); Chandrasekaran, "Sole Informant Guided Decision on Afghan Strike," WP (9.6.09); Connolly, "Afghanistan Tops Agenda in Germany," LAT (9.7.09); Kulish & Dempsey, "As Criticism Mounts, Germany Defends Decision on Afghan Airstrike," NYT (9.8.09); Constable, "Afghan Reaction to Strike Muted," WP (9.8.09); Whitlock, "In Germany, Political Turmoil over Ordering of Airstrike," WP (9.8.09); Kulish, "German Leader Warns Against Prematurely Judging Afghan Air Raid," NYT (9.9.09); "Afghan Official Says NATO Strike Killed 99," NYT (9.14.09); Kulish, "German General Quits over Airstrike," NYT (11.27.09); Kulish, "German Cabinet Minister Resigns over Afghan Raid That Killed Civilians," NYT (11.28.09); Connolly, "German Cabinet Official Resigns over Afghan Airstrike," LAT (11.28.09); "The Afghan Struggle: A Secret Archive," NYT (7.26.10); "German Court Sees Merit in Case Brought by Afghan Airstrike Victims, Asks for Video Evidence," WP (4.17.13).

102 Tyson, "Less Peril for Civilians, but More for Troops," WP (9.23.09).

103 Filkins, "His Long War," NYT Magazine (10.28.09).

104 Vaccaro, "The Next Surge: Counterbureaucracy," NYT (12.8.09).

105 Shah & Tavernise, "Afghans Say Airstrike Kills 8, Mostly Civilians," NYT (10.2.09); Rubin, "4 Afghans Killed as U.S. Convoy Fires at a Car," NYT (10.25.09); Rubin, "NATO Airstrike Killed 7 Afghan Soldiers, Officials Say," NYT (11.8.09); Oppel & Bumiller, "Afghanistan's President Says Army Will Need Allies' Help until 2024 or Longer," NYT (12.8.09); Bumiller, "Afghan Army Offers Raise, and Recruits Flock to Join," NYT (12.10.09); Rubin & Wafa, "Afghan Leader Says Attack Killed Civilians, but NATO Says the Victims were Taliban," NYT (12.29.09); King, "Afghan Panel Says U.S. Strike Killed 8 Schoolboys," LAT (12.30.09); Rubin & Rahimi, "Afghans Say Inquiry Shows Boys Were Killed in Allied Action," NYT (12.31.09); Warrick, "Suicide Bomber Attacks CIA Base in Afghanistan, Killing At Least 8 Americans," WP (12.31.09); Rubin, "Afghans Investigate Reports of More Civilian Deaths," NYT (1.1.10).

106 Rubin, "Afghans Investigate Reports of More Civilian Deaths," NYT (1.1.10); Rubin, "Deadly Explosion Arouses New Afghan Anger at U.S.," NYT (1.7.10); Filkins & Wafa, "Attack Leaves 10 Dead in Southeast Afghanistan," NYT (1.8.10); Filkins, "Eight Protesters Die in Afghan Unrest," NYT (1.13.10); Richburg & Partlow, "United Nations: In Deadliest Year for Afghan Civilians, Taliban Did Most Damage," WP (1.14.10); Filkins, "Loyalties of 4 Killed in Afghan Raid Remain Unclear," NYT (1.22.10); Partlow, "Killing of Cleric Prompts Outrage in Kabul and Apology from Coalition Forces," WP (1.29.10); King, "Afghan Cleric Killed by Western Troops, NATO Apologizes," LAT (1.29.10); Filkins, "4 Afghan Soldiers Are Killed by a Mistaken Airstrike," NYT (1.31.10); Cloud, "Anatomy of an Afghan War Tragedy," LAT (5.10.11).

107 Filkins, "09 Deadliest Year for Afghans, U.N. Says," NYT (1.14.10); Richburg & Partlow, "United Nations: In Deadliest Year for Afghan Civilians, Taliban Did Most Damage," WP (1.14.10).

108 Jaffe, "U.S. Commanders in Afghanistan Face Tougher Discipline for Battlefield Failures," WP (2.5.10); Shanker, "Afghan Battle Is Subject of Reproofs for 3 Officers," NYT (3.13.10); Jaffe, "Army Edits Its History of the Deadly Battle of Wanat," WP (12.29.10).
109 Perry & King, "Marines Focus on Civilian Safety in Afghanistan," LAT (2.9.10); Perry & King, "2 Afghans Killed in Errant Rocket Strike as U.S. Offensive Continues," LAT (2.15.10); Chivers & Nordland, "Errant Rocket Kills Civilians in Afghanistan," NYT (2.15.10); Perry & King, "Marines Inch Forward against Taliban," LAT (2.16.10); Chivers & Nordland, "Marines Join in Sorrow after Afghan Casualties," NYT (2.17.10).
110 Dadkhah, "Empty Skies over Afghanistan," NYT (2.17.10); Greenwald, "The New York Times's Mystery Op-Ed Writer," Salon.com (2.18.10) (citing Scott Horton).
111 Nordland, "Officials Fear 2 Dozen Afghan Police Officers Defected to Taliban," NYT (2.19.10); King, "Afghan Leader Urges Coalition Troops to Curb Civilian Deaths," LAT (2.21.10); King, "NATO Airstrike in Afghanistan Kills 27, Including Women and Children," LAT (2.23.10); Partlow & Chandrasekaran, "U.S. Airstrike Kills at least 27 Afghan Civilians," WP (23.23.10); Nordland, "NATO Airstrike Is Said to Have Killed 27 Civilians in Afghanistan," NYT (2.23.10); "Afghanistan: Report on Civilian Deaths," NYT (2.25.10); Shanker, "Joint Chiefs Chairman Readjusts Principles on Use of Force," NYT (3.4.10); "Afghanistan: NATO Cautions against Night Raids," NYT (3.6.10); Oppel & Nordland, "U.S. Is Reining in Special Forces in Afghanistan," NYT (3.16.10).
112 Filkins, "Military Report Faults Drone Operators in Deaths of 23 Afghan Civilians," NYT (5.30.10); Brulliard, "Drone Operators Blamed in Airstrike that Killed Afghan Civilians in February," WP (5.30.10); Drew, "Study Cites Drone Crew in Attack on Afghans," NYT (9.11.10); Cloud, "Anatomy of an Afghan War Tragedy," LAT (4.10.11); "Behind U.S. Condolence Payments for Afghan Civilians," LAT (4.13.11).
113 Oppel & Nordland, "U.S. Is Reining In Special Forces in Afghanistan," NYT (3.16.10); Starkey, "U.S.-led Forces in Afghanistan Are Committing Atrocities, Lying, and Getting Away With It," Nieman Watchdog (3.22.10); Oppel, "Military Admits a Role in Killings," NYT (4.5.10); Oppel & Wafa, "Afghan Investigators Say U.S. Troops Tried to Cover Up Evidence in Botched Raid," NYT (4.6.10); Starkey, "U.S. Special Forces 'Tried to Cover-Up' Botched Khataba Raid in Afghanistan," T (4.5.10); King, "Inquiry Puts Spotlight on U.S. Special Forces in Afghanistan," LAT (4.9.10); Woods (2015: 250–51); Scahill, "Special Ops Killing of Pregnant Afghan Women Was 'Appropriate' Use of Force," The Intercept (6.1.16).
114 Perry, "U.S. Air Support Troops Learn to Hold Back," LAT (3.22.10).
115 Oppel, "Tighter Rules Fail to Stem Deaths of Innocent Afghans at Checkpoints," NYT (3.27.10); Oppel & Shah, "Civilians Killed as U.S. Troops Hit Afghan Bus," NYT (4.13.10); Partlow, "Shooting by

U.S. Soldiers in Afghanistan Fuels Karzai's Anger," WP (4.13.10); King, "U.S. Troops Killed 4 on Passenger Bus in Afghanistan," LAT (4.13.10); Oppel & Sahak, "Dispute Flares after NATO Convoy Kills 4 in Afghanistan," NYT (4.21.10); King, "NATO Says 4 Killed in Afghanistan Were Civilians, Not 'Known Insurgents,'" LAT (4.21.10); Oppel, "NATO Apologizes for Killing Unarmed Afghans in Car," NYT (4.22.10).

116 Rubin, "Afghanistan Crowd Burns Trucks Carrying Fuel for a NATO Base," NYT (4.26.10); Partlow, "Afghans Burn NATO Trucks in Response to Killing of 3 Civilians," WP (4.26.10); Yaqubi, "Afghans Protest after Lawmaker's Relative Is Killed in Raid," LAT (4.29.10); Oppel & Sayre, "NATO Investigates 3 Afghan Civilian Deaths," NYT (5.1.10).

117 Oppel, "Shootings of Afghans on Rise at Checkpoints," NYT (5.8.10); Nordland, "Afghan Civilians Said to Be Killed in Airstrike," NYT (6.20.10).

118 Nordland, "Afghan Protests Turns Violent after Deadly U.S. Night Raid," NYT (5.15.10); Partlow, "NATO Says Night Raid Killed Afghan Insurgents; Residents Say It Killed Civilians," WP (5.18.10); King, "U.S. Night Raid in Afghanistan Elicits Outrage, Satisfaction," LAT (5.24.10).

119 Chivers, "Warriors Vexed by Rules for War," NYT (6.23.10); Londono, "U.S. Troops Express Mixed Views of Gen. McChrystal Controversy," WP (6.24.10); Bumiller, "Petraeus Says He'll Review Curbs on U.S. Strikes and Artillery in Afghanistan," NYT (6.30.10); McManus, "Petraeus Advisor Predicts Changes in Afghan Strategy," LAT (7.4.10).

120 Oppel & Wafa, "NATO Airstrike Accidentally Kills Afghan Troops," NYT (7.7.10); Oppel, "Airstrike Complicates Afghanistan Fight," NYT (7.7.10); "Afghanistan: 6 Civilians Die in Errant Artillery Strike," NYT (7.10.10); "NATO Takes Responsibility for Afghan Civilian Deaths," LAT (7.9.10); King, "Karzai Says 52 Afghan Civilians Killed in NATO Strike," LAT (7.27.10); Oppel & Shah, "Afghans Say Attack Killed 52 Civilians; NATO Differs," NYT (7.27.10); Oppel & Mashal, "66 Deaths of American Troops Set a Monthly Record for the Afghan War," NYT (7.31.10); Oppel & Mashal, "Afghan Police Clear U.S. in Crash that Led to Rioting," NYT (8.2.10); Partlow, "Afghans March in Kabul to Denounce NATO Strikes that Killed Civilians," WP (8.2.10).

121 Oppel & Nordland, "Petraeus to Expand Efforts to Protect Afghan Civilians," NYT (8.4.10); King, "Petraeus Establishes New Rules of Conduct for Western Forces in Afghanistan," LAT (8.5.10); Dilanian, "Study: Military Efforts to Prevent Afghan Civilian Casualties Help U.S. Troops Too," LAT (8.2.10); Nordland, "U.N. Blames Insurgents for Rising Share of Afghan Civilian Deaths," NYT (8.11.10); King, "Afghan Civilians Dying at a Faster Pace, U.N. Says," LAT (8.10.10); Nakamura, "Afghans Blame Civilian Deaths on U.S. Despite Spike from Insurgent Violence," WP (10.14.10).

122 "NATO Acknowledges Civilian Deaths in Afghan Airstrike," NYT (8.6.10); Filkins, "NATO Strike Cited in Afghan Civilian Deaths," NYT (8.15.10); Rubin, "In Afghanistan, More Attacks on Officials and a Protest over a Deadly NATO Raid," NYT (8.19.10); Nordland, "Taliban Intensify Attacks Against the Afghan Police," NYT (8.22.10); King, "21 Killed in Series of Afghanistan Attacks," LAT (8.21.10); "Afghans Say NATO Troops Killed 8 Civilians in Raid," LAT (8.21.10); Filkins, "Raid That Killed Civilians Prompts Inquiry," NYT (8.25.10); Nordland, "7 U.S. Soldiers Are Killed in Afghanistan Fighting," NYT (8.23.10).

123 Ellick & Rahimi, "Accounts Differ on Strike by NATO in Afghanistan," NYT (9.3.10); "Why Did Warnings about Murders by Soldiers in Afghanistan Go Unheeded?" WP (9.22.10); Nordland, "Dozens of Taliban Killed in 2 Airstrikes, NATO Says," NYT (9.26.10); Rubin, "U.S. Military Apologizes for Killing of Civilians," NYT (10.4.10); Rubin, "Mosque Bombing Kills Governor in Northern Afghanistan," NYT (10.9.10); "Kill/Capture," Frontline (5.10.11).

124 Burns, "U.S. Raid May Have Killed Briton Held by Taliban," NYT (10.12.10); Partlow & Faiola, "Rescue Attempt May Have Killed British Aid Worker in Afghanistan," WP (10.11.10); "Petraeus: Video Shows Grenade Use in Failed Rescue," NYT (10.16.10); Burns, "British Tell How Rescue by G.I.'s Broke Down," NYT (12.3.10).

125 Dunlap, "Could Airstrikes Save Lives in Afghanistan?" WP (10.22.10); Letter to the Editor, WP (10.28.10); Cloud, "Afghan Civilian Deaths Caused by Allied Forces Rise," LAT (11.1.10).

126 Partlow, "Karzai Wants U.S. to Reduce Military Operations in Afghanistan," WP (11.14.10); Partlow & DeYoung, "Petraeus Warns Afghans about Karzai's Criticism of U.S. War Strategy," WP (11.15.10); Nakamura, "Afghan Officials Dismiss Talk of Rift with U.S. after Karzai Criticism," WP (11.15.10); Nakamura, "Karzai Criticism 'Not Helpful,' NATO Envoy Says, Citing Progress in War," AP (11.17.10); Erlanger & Calmes, NATO Sees Long-Term Role after Afghan Combat," NYT (11.21.10); DeYoung, "NATO Adopts Transition Plan for Afghan War," WP (11.21.10).

127 Ignatius, "Afghans Want Their Country Back – and Americans Should Listen," WP (11.21.10); Partlow, "Refugees from Afghanistan's Helmand Province Disheartened at U.S. Presence," WP (11.22.10); Shah & Nordland, "NATO Is Razing Booby-trapped Afghan Homes," NYT (11.17.10); Shah & Nordland, "Afghan Panel and U.S. Dispute War's Toll on Property," NYT (1.14.11).

128 "NATO Forces Kill 3 Civilians," NYT (11.21.10); "Seven Afghans Killed in Paktia," NYT (12.12.10); Shah & Rubin, "Bomb Kills 2 Afghans in Attack in Kandahar," NYT (12.19.10); "Afghanistan: Civilian Deaths Examined," NYT (12.22.10); "Afghanistan: NATO Operation Leaves 2 Civilians Dead," NYT (12.24.10); Kamber & Sahak, "NATO Night Raid in Kabul Leaves Afghan Guards Dead," NYT (12.25.10); King, "Afghanistan Denounces Deadly NATO-led Raids," LAT (12.26.10); Londono & Constable, "NATO, Afghan Officials Offer Conflicting

Accounts of Deadly Raid in Kabul," WP (12.27.10); Kamber, "Car Bomb Kills 1 and Hurts 26 Near Afghan Police Station," NYT (12.28.10); Kamber, "Accounts Diverge Sharply in Night Raid Gone Wrong," NYT (12.29.10).

129 Chandrasekaran, "U.S.-led Afghan Reconstruction Projects to End because of Security Dispute," WP (10.22.10); Rubin, "Afghan Projects May Stop When Security Ban Begins," NYT (10.23.10); "Karzai May Compromise on Ban of Private Guards," NYT (10.25.10); Rubin, "Karzai Delays Order to Ban Private Security Companies," NYT (10.28.10); Partlow, "Karzai Gives Private Security Firms a Temporary Reprieve from Order to Disband," WP (10.28.10); Excerpts from Afghan President Hamid Karzai's Interview with the Washington Post, WP (11.14.10); Rubin, "Afghanistan Softens Ban on Private Security Firms," NYT (12.7.10); Chandrasekaran, "As U.S. Assesses Afghan War, Karzai a Question Mark," WP (12.13.10); Dempsey, "Karzai Seeks End to NATO Reconstruction Teams," NYT (2.7.11); Birnbaum, "Karzai Critical of Aid Bypassing Afghan Government," WP (2.7.11); Yaqoubi & King, "Afghan President Hamid Karzai Takes a Swipe at his Western Backers," LAT (2.9.11); Rivera, "Afghanistan Sets Timetable for Phasing Out Most Private Security Companies," NYT (3.17.11); Londono, "Afghanistan Cracks Down on Contractors," WP (12.30.11); Bowley & Sahak, "Two British Contractors Are Held on Weapons Charges in Kabul," NYT (1.5.12); Bowley, "Afghanistan Closes Firm Providing Security," NYT (1.6.12).

130 Rivera, "NATO Airstrike Kills 3 Police Officers," NYT (1.11.11); Rubin, "NATO Airstrike Is Said to Kill Afghan Civilians," NYT (2.21.11); Partlow & Zahon, "Afghan Officials Allege that 65 Civilians Were Killed in U.S. Military Operation," WP (2.21.11); Partlow, "Petraeus's Comments on Coalition Attack Reportedly Offend Karzai Government," WP (2.22.11); Rubin, "Afghan Team Says NATO Killed Civilians in Strikes," NYT (2.28.11).

131 Londono & Wilgoren, "Karzai Condemns NATO Airstrike that Reportedly Killed 9 Afghan Children," WP (3.2.11); King, "Gen. David Petraeus Apologizes for Deaths of 9 Afghan Children," LAT (3.2.11); Rubin & Rahimi, "NATO Helicopters Kill Nine Afghan Boys Collecting Firewood for their Families," NYT (3.3.11); "Obama Says He Deeply Regrets Civilian Deaths," NYT (3.4.11); Rubin, "Afghan Leader Calls Apology in Boys' Deaths Insufficient," NYT (3.7.11); Bumiller, "Gates Says U.S. Is in Position to Start Afghan Pullout," NYT (3.8.11); "Karzai Relative Killed in NATO Raid, Official Says," NYT (3.10.11); Londono & Hamdard, "NATO Troops Kill Karzai's Cousin, Afghans Say," WP (3.10.11); Rubin & Risen, "Cousin of Afghan President Is Killed in NATO Raid," NYT (3.11.11); Nordland, "Afghan Leader Questions U.S. Military Operations," NYT (3.13.11).

132 Rivera, "NATO Airstrike in Afghanistan Claims Civilians," NYT (3.26.11); Rivera, "NATO Airstrike in Afghanistan Kills 7 Civilians, Including 3 Children," NYT (3.27.11); Rubin, "Girl, 12, Killed in NATO Raid on Wrong Afghan Home," NYT (5.12.11); Rivera, "Taliban

Bomber Infiltrates Afghan–NATO Meeting, Killing Police Official and Others," NYT (5.29.11).

133 Rivera, "Civilians Are Killed in Airstrike by NATO," NYT (5.30.11); Rivera, "Karzai Gives 'Last' Warning to NATO on Airstrikes," NYT (6.1.11); King, "Afghan President Hamid Karzai Demands That NATO End Airstrikes on Houses," LAT (6.1.11); Shanker, "In Afghanistan, Gates Stresses U.S. Is Committed to the Fight," NYT (6.5.11); Gall, "Night Raids Curbing Taliban, but Afghans Cite Civilian Toll," NYT (7.9.11); Porter, "New Study Says U.S. Night Raids Aimed at Afghan Civilians," Inter Press Service (9.21.11).

134 Partlow & Salahuddin, "NATO Admits Civilian Deaths in Afghanistan," NYT (7.7.11); Rivera & Shah, "Airstrike Reportedly Kills Civilians in Southern Afghanistan," NYT (8.7.11); Rivera & Shah, "U.S. Troops Fire on Afghan Police, Survivors Say," NYT (8.12.11).

135 Open Society Institute and The Liaison Office (2011).

136 UNAMA & AIHRC, Annual Report on Protection of Civilians in Armed Conflict 2010 (March 2010).

137 Rubin, "Karzai Pushes Partnership with U.S. as Afghan Elders Convene," NYT (11.16.11); "Karzai Renews Calls for End to U.S. Night Raids against Taliban," LAT (11.16.11); Trofimov, "U.S. General Defends Afghanistan's Night Raids," WSJ (11.18.11); "Traditional Afghan Assembly Endorses President's Call for Security Pact with the United States," WP (11.19.11); Nordland, "Afghan Council Supports Karzai on U.S. Troop Presence," NYT (11.20.11).

138 Shah & Nordland, "Six Children Are Killed by NATO Airstrike in Afghanistan," NYT (11.25.11); "Afghan President Condemns Killing of 6 Children, 1 Man in Southern Afghanistan," WP (11.25.11); "Afghan President Says NATO Retraining Troops after Civilian Deaths during Military Operations," WP (11.29.11); King, "Postwar U.S.–Afghanistan Ties Are Expected to Remain Rocky," LAT (11.29.11).

139 Nordland, "For a Long-Term Afghan–American Accord, Night Raids Are a Sticking Point," NYT (12.4.11); "U.S. Commander Who Led bin Laden Operation Defends Unpopular Night Raids in Afghanistan," WP (12.12.11); Bowley & Sahak, "Karzai Honors Slain Officials in Speech," NYT (1.22.12).

140 Bowley & Rosenberg, "Video Inflames a Delicate Moment for U.S. in Afghanistan," NYT (1.12.12).

141 "Airstrike Killed Children, Karzai Says," NYT (2.10.12); Rubin & Sukhanyar, "Informer Misled NATO in Airstrike that Killed 9 Civilians Afghans Say," NYT (2.11.12); Rubin & Sahak, "Afghan Report Blames NATO for Airstrike That Killed Children," NYT (2.14.12); "NATO Expresses Regret for Airstrike That Killed 8 Young Afghan Civilians," WP (2.15.12); Rubin, "8 Young Afghans Killed in Strike, NATO Acknowledges," NYT (2.16.12).

142 Rubin, Sahak & Rahimi, "NATO Commander Apologizes for Koran Disposal in Afghanistan," NYT (2.21.12); Salahuddin & Sieff, "Huge

Crowd of Afghans Protests Reports of Burning of Koran at U.S. Base," WP (2.21.12); "Military Official: Islamic Books Burned at U.S. Base in Afghanistan Had Extremist Content," WP (2.21.12); Rubin, "Koran Burning in NATO Error Incites Afghans for 2nd Day," NYT (2.22.12); Sieff & Salahuddin, "Several Reported Killed in Second Day of Afghan Protests over Koran Burning," WP (2.22.12); "Afghan Interior Ministry Says 7 People Killed in Anti-US Demonstrations over Quran Burning," WP (2.22.12); Rubin & Bowley, "Obama Sends Apology as Afghan Koran Protests Rage," NYT (2.23.12); Rubin, Sahak & Sikhanyar, "Koran Protests Resume in Afghanistan Despite U.S. Apology," NYT (2.24.12); Sieff, "Seven Dead in Latest Afghan Violence over Koran Burning," WP (2.24.12); Sieff, "In Kabul, Afghan Police Sympathize with Protesters Angry over Koran Burning," WP (2.2412); "Gingrich: Obama Apology for Quran Burning in Afghanistan an 'Outrage' in Light of Deaths," WP (2.24.12); Rosenberg & Shanker, "Afghan Uproar Casts Shadows on U.S. Pullout," NYT (2.27.12); "Afghanistan on Edge," LAT (2.29.12); "Self-inflicted Wounds," NYT (2.24.12); Rubin & Sahak, "10 Afghans Killed in Protests as Anger Spreads over Burning of Korans," NYT (2.25.12); Bowley & Rubin, "Americans Slain: Advisers to Exit Kabul Ministries," NYT (2.26.12); Rubin & Bowley, "Blast Wounds Americans in Afghanistan," NYT (2.27.12); Rubin & Bowley, "Koran Burning in Afghanistan Prompts 3 Parallel Inquiries," NYT (2.29.12); Salahuddin, "Two U.S. Troops Gunned Down on NATO–Afghan Military Base," WP (3.1.12); Sieff, "U.S. Probe of Koran Burning Finds 5 Soldiers Responsible, Officials Say; Clerics Demand Trial," WP (3.2.12); Rubin, "Chain of Avoidable Errors Cited in Koran Burning," NYT (3.3.12); "Conflicting Accounts Emerge over Quran Burnings at Base in Afghanistan," WP (3.3.12); "Western Official: 5 US Troops May Face Review over Quran Burnings at US Base in Afghanistan," WP (3.3.12); Bowley, "No Sign of Progress in Afghanistan Talks Embittered by Koran Burnings," NYT (3.5.12); Rubin, "U.S.–Afghanistan Talks Falter Despite Leeway on Detention Facilities," NYT (3.5.12); Nordland, "In Reactions to Two Incidents, a U.S.–Afghan Disconnect," NYT (3.15.12); Nordland, Rubin & Rosenberg, "Gulf Widens between U.S. and a More Volatile Karzai," NYT (3.18.12).

143 DeYoung, "Afghan Officials Likely to Press for Veto Power over Night Raids in Formal Talks," WP (3.22.12); Rosenberg, "Deal Close on Night Raids, U.S. and Afghan Officials Say," NYT (4.4.12); Rubin, "U.S. Transfers Control of Night Raids to Afghanistan," NYT (4.9.12); "Afghans, U.S. Sign Deal on Night Raids, Clearing Way for Pact on Long-Term U.S. Presence," WP (4.8.12); Ackerman, "U.S. Commandos Can Raid Afghan Homes – and Ask Permission Later," Wired's Danger Room (4.10.12).

144 Zucchino, "U.S. Troops Posed with Body Parts of Afghan Bombers," LAT (4.18.12); Bowley & Rubin, "Photos Show U.S. Soldiers Posed with Afghan Body Parts," NYT (4.18.12); Sieff & Wilgoren, "Pentagon Condemns L.A. Times Photos of U.S. Troops Posing with Dead

Afghan Insurgents," WP (4.18.12); Shanker & Bowley, "Images of G.I.'s and Remains Fuel Fears of Ebbing Discipline," NYT (4.19.12); Muskal, "Times Explains Use of Photos of U.S. Soldiers, Body Parts," LAT (4.19.12); Whitlock, "Pentagon Condemns Photos of U.S. Troops Posing with Dead Afghan Insurgents," WP (4.19.12); "Afghan President Condemns Photos of U.S. Troops Posing with Corpses, Calls Them 'Disgusting,'" WP (4.19.12); King, "Afghanistan Leader Seeks Swifter Troop Pullout amid Photos Furor," LAT (4.20.12); Bacevich, "Why We Need More Accountability in Afghanistan," WP (4.21.12); Nordland & Shah, "3 Children Killed in Cross-Fire between Taliban and U.S.," NYT (5.1.12); Salahuddin, "Afghans Rally against U.S. over Children's Deaths," WP (5.1.12); Shanker, "Panetta Warns Military over Afghanistan Misconduct," NYT (5.5.12); Munoz, "Military Chiefs Consider Disciplinary Action for Quran Burnings in Afghanistan," *The Hill* (6.6.12).

145 Salahuddin, "NATO Airstrikes Said to Kill Civilians in Two Afghan Provinces," WP (5.7.12); Nordland, "U.S. Confirms Airstrike Wrongly Killed 6 in Afghan Family," NYT (5.8.12); Sieff, "Afghan Commanders Show New Defiance in Dealings with Americans," WP (5.11.12); "Afghan Officials Says NATO Airstrike Kills 8 Civilians; U.S.-led Coalition Probing Attack," WP (5.27.12); Rubin & Nordland, "Inquiry Ordered into Deaths of Afghan Family," NYT (5.28.12); "NATO Apologizes for Afghan Deaths in Airstrike," NYT (6.8.12); Partlow, "Gen. John Allen Apologizes for Civilians Killed in Airstrike in Afghanistan," WP (6.8.12); "Afghan President Calls US Airstrike 'One-Sided' Decision, Says Such Operations Violate Pact," WP (6.9.12); Rahimi & Rubin, "Afghan Official Rebukes NATO for Civilian Deaths," NYT (6.9.12); Schmitt, "Allies Restrict Airstrikes on Taliban in Civilian Homes," NYT (6.10.12); Partlow, "U.S. Military Restricts Airstrikes on Afghan Homes," WP (6.11.12); Rahimi & Rubin, "Days After an Order to Restrict Them, Afghanistan Calls for Airstrikes to End," NYT (6.12.12); Partlow, "Hamid Karzai Demands Halt to All Airstrikes on Afghan Homes," WP (6.12.12).

146 Bumiller, "U.S. Military Disciplines 9 over Video and Koran Burning," NYT (8.28.12); Whitlock, "U.S. Troops Tried to Burn 500 Copies of Koran, Investigation Says," WP (8.28.12); Cloud, "Pentagon Finds Soldiers Who Burned Korans Ignored Afghan Warnings," LAT (8.28.12); Bumiller, "Two Marines Face Charges," NYT (9.24.12); "Washington: Marine Sentenced in Taliban Urination Case," NYT (12.21.12); "North Carolina: Marine Admits He Desecrated Corpses," NYT (1.17.13); "U.S. Marine Pleads Guilty to Urinating on Corpse of Taliban Fighter in Afghanistan," G (1.16.13); "North Carolina: Case against Marines Widens," NYT (2.9.13); Hauser, "Marine Who Urinated on Taliban Corpses Says He Has No Regrets," NYT (7.18.13); "Panel: Discharge Marine Captain in Urination Case," AP (10.17.13); London & Nakashima, "Marine Corps Fight Escalates over Handling of Case Involving Troops Urinating on Corpses," WP (11.15.13);

Lamothe, "New Investigator Probes Alleged Marine Corps Cover-Up," FP (2.1.14); Savage, "Official Backs Marines' Move to Classify Photos of Forces with Taliban Bodies," NYT (6.11.14).

147 Oppel & Sukhanyar, "Bombers Strike Outside U.S. Military Base in Afghanistan," NYT (9.2.12); Rosenberg, "Karzai Denounces Coalition over Airstrikes," NYT (9.17.12); Rubin, "Questions Raised in Deaths of Afghan Children in Coalition Strike," NYT (10.17.12); Rubin, "4 Children Killed in Afghan Firefight," NYT (10.24.12).

148 UNAMA, Afghanistan: Annual Report 2012: Protection of Civilians in Armed Conflict (February 2013).

149 Constable and Whitlock, "Differing Afghan, U.S. Priorities Could Sabotage Proposed Security Agreement," WP (12.5.12); Kakar, "Karzai: US Troops Can have Immunity in Exchange for Sovereignty," *Stars and Stripes* (12.8.12); Behn, "Karzai Hints at Conditional Immunity for U.S. Personnel," Voice of America (12.8.12); Lee & Entous, "Obama to Speed Troop Exit," WSJ (1.12.13); Ahmed, "U.S. to Give Spy Drones to Afghans, Karzai Says," NYT (1.15.13).

150 "Airstrike Kills 9 Afghan Civilians in Province near Pakistani Border, Afghan Officials Say," WP (2.13.13); Rubin, "11 Afghans Killed in Military Actions near Pakistan Border," NYT (2.14.13); Rubin, "Karzai to Forbid Afghan Forces from Requesting Foreign Airstrikes," NYT (2.17.13); Leiby, "U.S., NATO Will Abide by Afghan President Karzai's Decree, Commander Says," WP (2.17.13); Nordland, "Two Afghan Boys Accidentally Killed by NATO Helicopter," NYT (3.3.13).

151 "Afghanistan's Karzai Says U.S. Special Forces Must Leave Wardak Province over Torture Allegations," Reuters (2.24.13); Rosenberg, "Afghanistan Bars Elite U.S. Troops from a Key Province," NYT (2.25.13); Leiby, "Karzai Aide Details Alleged Abuse by U.S. Special Forces," WP (2.25.13); "NATO Says There's No Evidence to Support Afghan Allegations of Misconduct by U.S. Special Forces," WP (2.25.13); Rosenberg, "Talk of Inquiry, but Not Much Is Sure after Afghan Ban on U.S. Troops," NYT (2.26.13); Dozier, "Karzai Calls on Afghan Troops to Clean Up Own Act," MH (3.5.13); Rubin & Shanker, "Afghan Leader Says U.S. Abets Taliban's Goal," NYT (3.11.13); Shah & Ahmed, "Afghan Says Force Backed by the C.I.A. Beat Him," NYT (3.11.13); Nordland, "Objections to U.S. Troops Intensify in Afghanistan," NYT (3.17.13); Ahmed, "Afghans Compromise on Special Forces Ban," NYT (3.20.13); Salahuddin, "U.S. Commandos Begin Pullout from Restive Afghan Province as Demanded by Karzai," WP (3.30.13).

152 Gannon, "Afghan Villagers Flee their Homes, Blame U.S. Drones," AP (3.28.13); Andalib, "NATO Strike Kills At Least One Child in Afghanistan," Reuters (3.30.13); "NATO Air Strike in Ghazni 'Kills Afghanistan Police,'" BBC News (4.4.13); "Afghanistan: Errant Airstrike Kills 6, Official Says," NYT (4.5.13); Ahmed, "Afghan Children Reported among Dead in U.S. Strike," NYT (4.7.13); "NATO Airstrike Said to Kill 10 Children in Afghanistan," LAT (4.7.13); "Afghan President Blames

Taliban and U.S. for Airstrike that Left 17 Dead, Including 12 Children," WP (4.13.13); Nordland, "After Airstrike, Afghan Points to C.I.A. and Secret Militias," NYT (4.20.13); Salarzaik, "Drone Strike Kills Children in Kunar," Pajhwok Afghan News (6.6.13); "Afghan Governor Says NATO; Airstrike Kills 3 in the East," WP (6.6.13); "NATO Denies UN Report Airstrike Killed 3 Children," WP (6.14.13); Welch & Sultan, "NATO to Investigate Drone Strike after Afghans Say Civilians Died," Reuters (9.19.13).

153 Sieff, "Afghan Officials Say Long-Term Security Agreement with the U.S. Is Still on Hold," NYT (10.3.13); Rosenberg, "Impasse with Afghanistan Raises Prospect of Total U.S. Withdrawal in 2014," NYT (10.5.13); Hakim, "Afghanistan's Hamid Karzai Says NATO Caused 'Great Suffering,'" BBC News (10.8.13); Rosenberg, "Talks Clear Path for U.S.–Afghan Deal on Troops," NYT (10.13.13); Nordland & Rosenberg, "Afghan Talks at Impasse before Vote, Officials Say," NYT (11.18.13); Nordland, "Afghans Demand that U.S. Admit Military Errors," NYT (11.20.13); DeYoung & Craig, "U.S. to Offer Afghans Assurances to Remove Hurdle in Post-2014 Deal," WP (11.20.13); Shanker & Nordland, "Pact May Extend U.S. Troops' Stay in Afghanistan," NYT (11.21.13); Craig, "Afghan President Hamid Karzai Outlines Plans for Post-2014 U.S. Mission," WP (11.21.13); Ahmed, "Karzai Says He'll Wait to Sign Security Pact with U.S. until Next Year," NYT (11.22.13); Nordland, "U.S. Upset by Karzai's Claim about Civilian Deaths," NYT (11.23.13); Craig & Salahuddin, "Karzai Rejects Call for Quick Decision on U.S. Troop Agreement," WP (11.23.13); Craig & DeYoung, "Afghan President Hamid Karzai Says He'll Delay Signing of U.S. Accord on Troops," WP (11.23.13); Craig & DeYoung, "Karzai Intends to Press Showdown with Obama over Security Pact, Aide Says," WP (11.24.13); Nordland, "Elders Back Security Pact that Karzai Won't Sign," NYT (11.25.13); Craig, "Afghan Elders Endorse U.S. Troops; Presence but President Karzai Still Refuses to Sign," WP (11.25.13); Nordland, "Obama's Visiting Security Adviser Tells Karzai to Sign Agreement," NYT (11.26.13); Craig & DeYoung, "Karzai Tells Susan Rice of More Demands for Accord Extending U.S. Troop Presence," WP (11.26.13); Nordland & Rubin, "Karzai's Bet: U.S. Is Bluffing in Warning on Security Pact," NYT (11.27.13); "Afghan President Softens Some Demands on U.S. Deal," WP (11.27.13).

154 Nordland, "U.S. General Apologizes after Afghan Drone Strike," NYT (11.29.13); Craig, "Karzai Says U.S. Drone Strike Killed Child," WP (11.29.13); Craig, "Coalition Apologizes for Killing Afghan Child," WP (11.29.13); Allen & O'Hanlon, "Ignore Karzai's Arrogant Insults," NYT (11.29.13); Podesta, Perriello & Wadhams, "Karzai Risks Much in His Latest Manufactured Crisis," WP (11.29.13); Nordland, "Afghans Assail Karzai's Disparate Views on Killings," NYT (12.1.13); Gearan, "U.S., NATO Warn Afghan Troop Plan Is in Peril," WP (12.4.13); Rubin, "NATO Cites Urgency in Reaching Pact between U.S. and Afghanistan," NYT (12.5.13); Gearan & Craig, "U.S. Looks for Work-around to

Afghan Security Impasse," WP (12.5.13); "U.S. Envoy: Afghan President Unchanged on Troop Deal," WP (12.5.13); Jha, "Top Democrat Chides Obama for Begging Karzai," Pajhwok Afghan News (12.6.13); Shanker & Ahmed, "In Afghanistan, Hagel Presses for Pact on Security, but Is Not Meeting Karzai," NYT (12.8.13); "Afghan President Lashes Out at U.S. 'Threats,'" WP (12.10.13); Ahmed, "Impasse over Security Deal Adds to Afghan Economy's Troubles," NYT (12.11.13); Quinn, "U.S. General: Afghan Pullout Could Reverse Gains," AP (12.11.13); "Karzai Rules Out to Be Intimidated on BSA," Pajhwok, Afghan News (12.13.13); "Karzai Hopes U.S. Will Reframe Security Agreement," WP (12.14.13); "Respect Jirga Decision on BSA, Senators Ask President," Pajhwok Afghan News (12.16.13); Ahmed, "A Top Iraqi Official's Advice to Karzai? Take America's Deal," NYT (12.18.13); Jha, "White House: Can No Longer Wait for BSA Signing," Pajhwok Afghan News (12.19.13); Woods (2015: 5–6).

155 Ahmed, "Tensions between Afghanistan and U.S. Increase as Airstrike Kills Civilians," NYT (1.16.14); Salahuddin & Craig, "U.S. Forces Killed 8 Civilians in Afghanistan, Mostly Children, in New Incident, Karzai Says," WP (1.16.14); Tanha, "Probe Team Finds 13 Civilians Killed in Parwan," Pajhwok Afghan News (1.17.14); Ahmed & Rosenberg, "Deadly Attack at Kabul Restaurant Hints at Changing Climate for Foreigners," NYT (1.19.14); "Hamid Karzai Pushes End to U.S. Raids," Politico (1.19.14); Rosenberg, "False Claims in Afghan Accusations on U.S. Add to Doubts on Karzai," NYT (1.26.14); Rosenberg, "Afghan Villagers Brought to Back Airstrike Report," NYT (1.27.14); Sieff, "Karzai Suspects U.S. Is Behind Insurgent-style Attacks, Afghan Officials Say," WP (1.28.14); "Afghan President Denies Blaming U.S. for 'Insurgent-style' Attacks," VOA (1.28.14); "President Karzai's Perfidies," NYT (1.30.14); Sief, "Interview: Karzai Says 12-year Afghanistan War Has Left Him Angry at U.S. Government," WP (3.3.14).

156 Cole, "UN: Civilian Drone Deaths Triple in Afghanistan," Informed Comment (2.13.14); Report of the Special Rapporteur on the Promotion and Protection of Human Rights and Fundamental Freedoms While Countering Terrorism, Ben Emmerson (2.28.14).

157 AI (2014a).

158 Nordland & Sukhanyar, "Afghan Broadcaster Says U.S. Soldiers Abused Him," NYT (3.2.14); Nordland, "U.S. Airstrike Kills 5 Afghan Soldiers," NYT (3.6.14); Sieff & Sharif, "NATO Airstrike Kills 5 Afghan Soldiers," WP (3.6.14); Ahmed, "Afghanistan Says NATO Airstrike in East Killed Civilians," NYT (4.16.14); Rosenberg & Shakib, "Afghan Civilians Killed in Airstrike by American-led Coalition," NYT (8.6.14); "Afghan Officials: 14 Killed in U.S. Airstrike," WP (9.10.14).

159 "Karzai Says Afghanistan Doesn't Need U.S. Troops," WP (3.14.14); Landler, "U.S. Troops to Leave Afghanistan by End of 2016," NYT (5.28.14); Walsh & Ahmed, "Mending Alliance, U.S. and Afghanistan Sign Long-Term Security Agreement," NYT (10.1.14); "Afghan Parliament Approves U.S. NATO Agreements," WP (11.23.14);

Nordland & Shah, "Afghanistan Quietly Lifts Ban on Nighttime Raids," NYT (11.24.14); Noori, "Afghan Security Officials Defend Drone Strategy as Necessary, Effective," Tolo News (2.23.15); Mashal, "Friendly Fire from U.S. Helicopters Kills Afghan Troops, Officials Say," NYT (7.20.15); Nordland & Mashal, "U.S. Denies an Airstrike Killed 11 Afghan Narcotics Officers," NYT (9.8.15).

160 Rubin, "Airstrike Hits Afghan Hospital, Killing At Least 9," NYT (10.3.15); Rubin, "Airstrike Hits Doctors Without Borders Hospital in Afghanistan," NYT (10.4.15); Rubin, "Doctors Without Borders Says It Is Leaving Kunduz after Strike on Hospital," NYT (10.5.15); Craig & Whitlock, "Afghan Response to Hospital Bombing Is Muted, Even Sympathetic," WP (10.5.15); Rosenberg, "U.S. General Says Afghans Requested Airstrike that Hit Kunduz Hospital," NYT (10.6.15); "The Aftermath of a Deadly Airstrike in Afghanistan," NYT (10.6.15); Gibbons-Neff, "U.S. Military Struggles to Explain How It Wound Up Bombing Doctors Without Borders Hospital," WP (10.6.15); Schmitt & Rosenberg, "General Is Said to Think Afghan Hospital Broke U.S. Rules," NYT (10.6.15); Lee & Schwartz, "Obama Apologizes for Airstrike on Afghan Hospital," WSJ (10.7.15); Shear & Sengupta, "Obama Issues Rare Apology over Bombing of Doctors Without Borders Hospital in Afghanistan," NYT (10.7.15); Nordland, "Death Toll in Airstrike on Doctors Without Borders Hospital May Rise, Group Says," NYT (10.8.15); Schreuer, "Inquiry into Kunduz Hospital Strike Awaits U.S. and Afghan Approval," NYT (10.14.15); Dilanian, "U.S. Analysts Knew Afghan Site Was Hospital," AP (10.15.15); Rahim & O'Donnell, "MSF Says Bombing of Afghan Hospital No Mistake," AP (10.18.15); O'Donnell, "Afghan Defense Minister Says Taliban Hid in Bombed Hospital," AP (10.19.15); Schmitt & Rosenberg, "Hospital Attack Fueled by Units New to Kunduz," NYT (10.20.15); Cone, "Doctors without Hospitals," NYT (10.23.15); Mashal, "General to Investigate U.S. Airstrike on Doctors Without Borders Hospital," NYT (10.24.15); "Hospital Charity Says Afghan Bombing Death Toll Rises to 30," *Marine Times* (10.25.15); Dilanian, "Troops Who Called In Afghan Strike Thought Hospital Was Overrun; MSF Says No," US News (10.26.15); Gibbons-Neff, "There Are Still a Lot of Questions around the U.S. Bombing of the MSF Hospital in Kunduz," WP (10.26.15); Aghavan, "U.S. Airstrikes in Kunduz Destroyed More Than a Hospital," WP (11.4.15); Goldstein, "Doctors Without Borders Says Clues Point to 'Illegal' U.S. Strike on Afghan Hospital," NYT (11.6.15); Lamothe, "Pentagon Faces Question: Should It Make Condolence Payments for Taliban Killed in Hospital Bombing?" WP (11.6.15); Salahuddin, Murphy & Lamothe, "Aid Group: U.S. Military Was Told of No Threats before Deadly Kunduz Airstrike," WP (11.6.15); Dilanian & O'Donnell, "U.S. Troops Didn't Have Eyes on Afghan Hospital before Attack," AP (11.11.15); Goldstein & Schmitt, "Human Error Cited in U.S. Strike on Kunduz Hospital," NYT (11.25.15); Nordland, "U.S. General Says Kunduz Hospital Strike Was 'Avoidable,'" NYT (11.26.15); Dilanian,

"Lawmaker: Were US Forces Manipulated into Striking Hospital?" AP (12.8.15); Gibbons-Neff, "Months after the Airstrike on MSF's Hospital in Kunduz, What Exactly Happened Is Still Unclear," WP (12.12.15); Nordland, "Doctors Without Borders Raises Death Toll in Kunduz Strike to 42," NYT (12.13.15); UNAMA and UN Office of the High Commissioner for Human Rights, Afghanistan: Human Rights and Protection of Civilians in Armed Conflict: Special Report on Kunduz Province (December 2015); Mcleary, "U.S. Military Readies Punishments for Botched Afghan Airstrike," FP (1.15.16); Centcom, Summary of the Airstrike on the MSF Trauma Center in Kunduz, Afghanistan on October 3, 2015; Investigation and Follow-On Actions (n.d.); Burns, "More Than 12 Punished for Mistaken Afghan Hospital Attack," AP (3.16.16); "No Charges in Afghan Hospital Bombing," Daily Beast (3.17.16); "U.S. Commander Apologizes for Hospital Bombing in Afghanistan," NYT (3.22.16); Fidell, "The Wrong Way to Handle the Kunduz Tragedy," NYT (5.2.16); "The Pentagon Insults Its Afghan Victims," NYT (4.21.16); McLary, "No Criminal Charges for U.S. Personnel Involved in Deadly Afghan Airstrike," FP (4.28.16); "U.S. Central Command Releases U.S. Forces–Afghanistan Investigation into Airstrike on Doctors Without Borders Trauma Center in Kunduz, Afghanistan" (4.29.16); Aisch, Keller & Pecanha, "How a Cascade of Errors Led to the U.S. Airstrike on an Afghan Hospital," NYT (4.30.16); Rosenberg, "Pentagon Details Chain of Errors in Strike on Afghan Hospital," NYT (4.30.16); Gibbons-Neff & Lamothe, "Pentagon: 2015 Strike on Doctors Without Borders Hospital in Afghanistan Was Not a War Crime," WP (4.30.16); Lamote, "Green Beret Officer Blames 'Moral Cowardice' for Doctors Without Borders Strike," WP (4.30.16); "A Moral Debt for Bombing the Doctors Without Borders Hospital," NYT (4.30.16); Rosenberg & Goldstein, "U.S. Role in Afghanistan Turns to Combat Again, with a Tragic Error," NYT (5.9.16); Smith, "Pentagon Report Reveals Confusion among U.S. Troops over Afghan Mission," Reuters (5.9.16); Gibbons-Neff, "Investigation Finds that Green Berets Fought in Afghan City without Proper Maps," WP (5.9.16).

161 Aikins, "Doctors with Enemies: Did Afghan Forces Target the M.S.F. Hospital?" NYT (5.17.16).

162 Mangal & Mashal, "At Least 17 Civilians Killed in U.S. Airstrikes, Afghan Officials Say," NYT (4.8.16); Qazi, "Families of Afghans Killed in U.S. Drone Raids Seek Probe," Al Jazeera (4.9.16).

163 Faiez, "Afghan Official: Airstrike Hits House, Killing 13 Civilians," WP (9.28.16); Alokozay & Nordland, "Airstrike in Eastern Afghanistan Kills At Least 13," NYT (9.29.16); Mashal, "'American Airstrike Killed Afghan Civilians,' U.N. Says," NYT (9.30.16).

164 "Airstrike in Afghanistan Causes Civilian Casualties," Reuters (10.28.16); Bearak, "NATO and Government Forces Are Increasingly Responsible for Afghan Civilian Deaths," WP (11.3.16); Rasmussen, "Thirty Civilians Die in Airstrike Called to Protect US and Afghan Troops," G (11.3.16); Constable, "Former Afghan President Hamid

Karzai Denounces Deadly NATO Airstrikes," WP (11.4.16); Constable & Salahuddin, "U.S. Military Acknowledges Anti-Taliban Airstrikes Killed Afghan Civilians," WP (11.5.16).

165 Mashal, "Kunduz Attack in November Killed 33 Civilians, U.S. Military Says," NYT (1.12.17); Salahuddin & Cunningham, "U.S. Military Says Battle with Taliban Killed 33 Civilians in Afghanistan," WP (1.12.17).

166 Mashal & Shah, "At Least 9 Civilians Killed as Coalition Strikes Taliban Arsenal, Officials Say," NYT (4.3.17); Cooper & Mashal, "U.S. Drops 'Mother of All Bombs' on ISIS Caves in Afghanistan," NYT (4.14.17); Mashal, "Calling Successor a 'Traitor,' Afghan Ex-Leader Denounces U.S. Bombing," NYT (4.15.17).

167 Mashal & Faizi, "Airstrikes in Afghanistan Kill More Than a Dozen Civilians," NYT (8.30.17); Abed, "At Least 11 Afghan Civilians Killed in American Airstrikes," NYT (8.30.17).

168 Mashal, Abed & Faizi, "Afghan Anger Simmers over U.S. Leaflets Seen as Insulting Islam," NYT (9.9.17).

169 William Shakespeare, *King Lear*, Act II, scene IV, lines 275–77.

170 Letter to the Editor, NYT (9.22.06); Herbert, "Due Process, Bulldozed," NYT (9.25.06); Quinn, "U.S. War Prisons Legal Vacuum for 14,000," LAT (9.18.06).

171 Oppel, "U.S. Seizes Son of a Top Shiite Stirring Uproar," NYT (2.24.07); Berthelsen, "Arrest Sparks Iraq Protest," LAT (2.25.07).

172 "Five Americans Held by U.S. Military in Iraq," NYT (7.6.05); "U.S. Detainees U.S. Navy Veteran in Iraq," NYT (7.6.05); Weinstein, "U.S. Holds Filmmaker in Iraq," LAT (7.6.05); "U.S. Says It Has Detained 5 American Suspects in Iraq," LAT (7.8.05); Golden, "U.S. Says It Will Release American Held in Iraq," NYT (7.10.05); Weinstein, "Filmmaker Held in Iraq to Be Freed," LAT (7.10.05); Daragahi & Paddock, "They Put Us in a Cell and Forgot Us," LAT (7.11.05); Golden, "American Filmmaker Held by the U.S. Military in Iraq for 7 Weeks Is Released," NYT (7.11.05); Golden, "How a Trip to Film in Iraq Ended in a Military Jail Cell," NYT (7.24.05); Weinstein, "Is This How You Treat One of Your Own?" LAT (7.24.05); "L.A. Man Detained in Iraq Sues U.S.," WP (7.9.06); Weinstein, "Filmmaker Sues U.S. over Iraq Detention," LAT (7.8.06).

173 Leonnig, "U.S. Resident Freed from Baghdad Prison," WP (9.7.05).

174 "U.S. Confirms Its Troops Killed Reuters Journalist in Iraq," NYT (9.1.05); Worth, "Detention of Iraqi Employees Angers Western News Media," NYT (9.15.05); Dreazen, "CBS Asks Why U.S. Imprisons Its Iraqi Hire," WSJ (9.15.05); Herbert, "Due Process, Bulldozed," NYT (9.25.06).

175 "U.S. Holds Photographer in Iraq," NYT (9.18.06); Letter to the Editor, NYT (9.22.06); Herbert, "Due Process, Bulldozed," NYT (9.25.06).

176 Sly, "Journalist Held in Iraq for Months," LAT (5.24.09); "U.S. Military Shuts Largest Detainee Camp in Iraq," NYT (9.17.09).

177 Murphy, "U.S. Forces Blamed in Death of British Journalist," LAT (10.14.06).

178 Dickinson (2011).
179 Finer, "Security Contractors in Iraq under Scrutiny after Shootings," WP (9.10.05); Miller, "Private Contractors Outnumber U.S. Troops in Iraq," LAT (7.4.07).
180 Susman & Berthelsen, "Private Security Guards Kill 2 in Iraq," LAT (10.10.07); Kramer & Glanz, "2 Iraqi Women Killed in Shooting by Security Convoy," NYT A1 (10.10.07); Partlow & Raghavan, "Guards Kill Two Women in Iraq," WP A1 (10.10.07); Berthelsen & Rifai, "The Brave Cabbie of Baghdad," LAT (10.11.07); Kramer, "At Home and Far Away, Grief for a Taxi Driver Killed in a Baghdad Shooting," NYT (10.11.07); Susman, "Iraqis Shot by Contractors Stymied in Search for Justice," LAT (10.16.07); Hennessy-Fiske, "A Death in Iraq, Grief in Glendale," LAT (10.17.07); Fainaru, "Iraqis Detail Shooting by Guard Firm," WP (11.26.07); Glanz, "Security Guard Kills Iraq Driver," NYT (11.12.07).
181 Broder, "Ex-Paratrooper Is Suspect in Drunken Killing of Iraqi," NYT (10.4.07); Broder, "State Department Plans Tighter Control of Security Firms," NYT (10.6.07); Spiegel, "U.S. Supervision Is Ordered for Convoys," LAT (10.6.07); DeYoung, "State Department Struggles to Oversee Private Army," WP (10.21.07); Glanz & Lehren, "Use of Contractors Added to War's Chaos in Iraq," NYT (10.24.10); Risen, "Efforts to Prosecute Blackwater Are Collapsing," NYT (10.21.10).
182 Partlow & Pincus, "Iraq Bans Security Contractor," WP (9.18.07); Parker, "U.S. Rushes to Smooth Iraq's Anger over Blackwater," LAT (9.18.07); Tavernise, "U.S. Contractor Banned by Iraq over Shootings," NYT (9.18.07); Parker, "U.S. Limits Diplomats' Travel in Iraq," LAT (9.19.07); Tavernise & Glanz, "Iraqi Report Says Guards for Blackwater Fired First," NYT (9.19.07); "Blackwater Down," LAT (9.19.07); Parker, "Maliki Insists U.S. Find New Guard Firm," LAT (9.20.07); Tavernise, "Maliki Alleges 7 Cases When Blackwater Killed Iraqis," NYT (9.20.07); Fainaru, "Where Military Rules Don't Apply," WP (9.20.07); Broder & Risen, "Armed Guards in Iraq Occupy a Legal Limbo," NYT (9.20.07); Parker & Salman, "Blackwater under Scrutiny in Iraq," LAT (9.21.07); Parker, "Blackwater Gets OK to Resume Iraq Duty," LAT (9.22.07); Partlow & Raghavan, "Iraq Probe of U.S. Security Firm Grows," WP (9.22.07); Kramer, "Blackwater Resumes Guarding U.S. Envoys in Iraq," NYT (9.22.07); Raghavan & Fainaru, "U.S. Repeatedly Rebuffed Iraq on Blackwater Complaints," WP (9.23.07); Spiegel, "State Dept. Intercedes in Blackwater Probe," LAT (9.26.07); Fainaru, "How Blackwater Sniper Fire Felled 3 Iraqi Guards," WP (11.8.07); Scahill (2007: Introduction).
183 Tavernise & Glanz, "Guards' Shots Not Provoked, Iraq Concludes," NYT (9.21.07); Glanz & Tavernise, "Security Firm Faces Criminal Charges in Iraq," NYT (9.23.07); Rubin & Kramer, "Iraqi Premier Says Blackwater Shootings Challenge His Nation's Supremacy," NYT (9.24.07); "Iraq Drafts Law on Security Companies," NYT (9.26.07); Risen, "House Panel and State Dept. Clash on Blackwater Inquiry," NYT (9.26.07); Raghavan & Ricks, "Private Security Puts Diplomats, Military

at Odds," WP (9.26.07); Broder & Risen, "Blackwater Tops All Firms in Iraq in Shooting Rate," NYT (9.27.07); Risen, "State Department Tallies 56 Shootings Involving Blackwater on Diplomatic Guard Duty," NYT (9.28.07); "Subcontracting the War," NYT (10.1.07); DeYoung, "Other Killings by Blackwater Staff Detailed," WP (10.2.07); Lardner, "Blackwater Portrayed as Out of Control," AP (10.1.07); Spiegel, "Blackwater Depicted as Aggressor," LAT (10.2.07); Broder, "Report Says Firm Tried Cover-Ups after Shootings," NYT (10.2.07); Schmitt, "Report Details Shooting by Drunken Blackwater Worker," NYT (10.2.07); "Blackwater Waves," WP (10.2.07); Spiegel, "Blackwater Gets a United Defense," LAT (10.3.07); DeYoung, "Blackwater Chief Defends Firm," WP (10.3.07); Broder, "Chief of Blackwater Defends His Employees," NYT (10.3.07).

184 Meyer & Barnes, "Congress Moves to Rein in Contractors," LAT (10.4.07); Hauser, "New Rules for Contractors Are Urged by Two Democrats," NYT (10.4.07); Herszenhorn, "House's Iraq Bill Applies U.S. Laws to Contractors," NYT (10.5.07); Weisman, "House Acts in Wake of Blackwater Incident," WP (10.5.07).

185 Broder, "State Department Plans Tighter Control of Security Firms," NYT (10.6.07); Spiegel, "U.S. Supervision Is Ordered for Convoys," LAT (10.6.07); Susman & Salman, "Iraqi Guard's Widow Reports No Compensation," LAT (10.8.07); Raghavan, "Iraqi Probe Faults Blackwater Guards," WP (10.8.07); Glanz & Rubin, "Blackwater Shootings 'Deliberate Murder,' Iraq Says," NYT (10.8.07); Zavis, "Blasts, Other Violence Kill 37 Iraqis," LAT (10.9.07); Susman & Berthelsen, "Private Security Guards Kill 2 in Iraq," LAT (10.10.07); "Accountability on the Battlefield," NYT (10.8.07); Rubin & von Zielbauer, "The Judgment Gap," NYT (10.11.07); Oppel & Gordon, "U.S. Military and Iraqis Say They Are Shut Out of Inquiry," NYT (10.11.07); Glanz, Oppel & Kamber, "New Evidence That Guards Took No Fire," NYT A1 (10.13.07); Raghavan & White, "Blackwater Guards Fired at Fleeing Cars, Soldiers Say," WP (10.12.07); Schmitt & Shankar, "Pentagon Sees One Authority over Guards," NYT (10.17.07); Spiegel, "Gates: Security Contractors Conflict with U.S. Mission in Iraq," LAT (10.19.07); Smith, "Iraqis Want Contractors Liable," LAT (10.25.07); Daragahi & Salman, "Grieving Iraqis Want Honor First, Not Money," LAT (5.4.08).

186 Neuman, "Rice Faces House's Questions about Iraq," LAT (10.26.07); DeYoung, "On Hill, Rice Talks about Blackwater," WP (10.26.07); Broder, "Rice Says 'Hole' in U.S. Law Shields Contractors in Iraq," NYT (10.26.07); DeYoung, "On Hill, Rice Talks about Blackwater," WP (10.26.07); Glanz & Kramer, "U.S. Envoy Presses Iraq to Act against Guerrillas," NYT (10.26.07); Hedgpeth, "Bill Calls for Contractors to Exit Iraq," WP (11.8.07); Glanz, "Iraq Plans to Confront Security Firms on Guns," NYT (11.8.07); "Blackwater Impunity," LAT (11.9.07); Johnston & Broderk, "F.B.I. Says Guards Killed 14 Iraqis without Cause," NYT (11.14.07).

187 Risen, "Iraq Contractor in Shooting Case Is Rehired by U.S.," NYT (5.10.08); "Blackwater's Impunity," NYT (5.16.08); Radia, "Govt Uses Contractors to Probe Iraq Contractors," ABC News (10.3.08); Pincus, "Private Iraq Investigators Out," WP (10.22.08); Risen, "End of Immunity Worries U.S. Contractors in Iraq," NYT (12.1.08); Londono & Mizher, "Iraq to Deny New License to Blackwater Security Firm," WP (1.29.09); Risen & Williams, "As Iraq Tries to Oust Blackwater, U.S. Lines up Other Security Options," NYT (1.30.09); Morin, "Iraq Rescinds License for Blackwater Security Firm," LAT (1.30.09); "No Pact for Blackwater," NYT (1.31.09); "Iraq: New U.S. Contractor," NYT (4.2.09); Nordland, "After Blackwater Loses Security Deal, Many Ex-Workers Will Return to Iraq Jobs," NYT (4.4.09); Landler, "Contractor to Continue Work in Iraq Temporarily," NYT (9.3.09); Mazzetti & Risen, "Blackwater Said to Pursue Bribes to Iraq after 17 Died," NYT (11.11.09); Risen, "Bribe Charges Prompt Iraqis to Look into Blackwater," NYT (11.12.09); Mazzetti & Risen, "Bribery at Issue as Inquiry Looks into Blackwater," NYT (2.1.10).

188 Schmidt & Schmitt, "Flexing Muscle, Baghdad Detains U.S. Contractors," NYT (1.16.12); Shanker, "U.S. Combat Commanders Should Handle War Zone Investigations, Panel Says," NYT (5.31.13).

189 Risen, "Before Shooting in Iraq, a Warning on Blackwater," NYT (6.30.14).

190 HRW (2005); Zagorin, "Pattern of Abuse," *Time* (9.23.05); Serrano, "Officer's Road Led Him outside Army," LAT (9.25.05); Schmitt, "3 in 82nd Airborne Say Beating Iraqi Prisoners Was Routine," NYT (9.24.05); "World Briefing," NYT (9.26.05); Serrano, "New Iraq Abuse Allegations Get McCain Moving," LAT (9.26.05); White, "Reservist Sentenced to 3 Years for Abu Ghraib Abuse," WP (9.28.05); Fishback letter, WP (9.28.05); Schmitt, "Officer Criticizes Detainee Abuse Inquiry," NYT (9.28.05); "Mr. Flanigan's Answers," WP (9.28.05); Schmitt, "Soldier Reports More Abuses to Senator," NYT (10.5.05); Fair, "An Iraq Interrogator's Nightmare," WP (2.9.07); Fair (2016).

191 "U.S. Troops in Iraq Held Insurgents' Wives to Get Husbands to Surrender," LAT (1.28.06); Youssef, "U.S. Has Detained Women in Iraq as Leverage," MH (1.28.06); Benjamin, "U.S. Accused of Kidnappings in Iraq," Salon (7.14.06).

192 Anderson, "Residents Say 17 Killed by U.S. Were Not Insurgents," WP (6.29.07); Salman & Parker, "U.S. Raid Provokes Iraqi Prime Minister," LAT (7.1.07); Rubin, "Accounts Differ Sharply on U.S. Attack in Iraq," NYT (10.6.07); Berthelsen, "Iraq Says Civilians Killed in U.S. Raid," LAT (10.22.07); "Iraq: U.S. Strikes Kill 11 Iraqis," LAT (10.23.07); Berthelsen, "Iraqis Weigh Limits on U.S. Military," LAT (10.23.07); Smith, "U.S. Airstrike Kills at Least 11 in Iraq," LAT (10.24.07); Kramer, "Helicopter Fire Kills Iraqis, Days after Sadr City Battle," NYT (10.24.07); Susman, "Conflicting Accounts of an Iraq Clash," LAT (11.17.07); Buckley, "Sunni Group Says U.S. Killed Its Members," NYT (11.17.07); Smith & Hameed, "Iraq Attacks Kill 20, Including 3 U.S.

Soldiers," LAT (11.19.07); Parker, "U.S. Troops Kill At Least 5 Iraqi Civilians," LAT (11.28.07); Cave, "35 Killed in Iraq, 5 by U.S. Troops," NYT (11.28.07); Susman, "Sunni Volunteers Angry over Civilian Deaths," LAT (2.18.08).

193 Kramer, "U.S. Regret at Koran's Desecration," NYT (5.19.08); Zavis, "U.S. Soldier Used Koran for Target Practice," LAT (5.19.08); Farrell, "Hussein Aide Faces Accusers in Trial on Mass Execution," NYT (5.21.08); "World Briefing," NYT (5.23.08); Oppel & Farrell, "Iraqis Angered by Marines Who Handed Out Coins with Bible Verse," NYT (5.30.08).

194 Londono, "4 U.S. Soldiers, Interpreter Killed in Iraq Fighting," WP (6.26.08); Oppel & Muhammed, "Civilians Killed in Day of Disputed Attacks, Iraq Says," NYT (6.26.08); Smith, "U.S. Troops Killed 9 Civilians, Local Authorities in Iraq Say," LAT (6.26.08); London & Sarhan, "Reported U.S. Raid Triggers Outrage," WP (6.29.08); Oppel & Hameed, "U.S. Forces Kill Relatives of Iraqi Governor," NYT (7.21.08); Raghavan & Mizher, "U.S. Says 3 Iraqis Killed in June Were Law-abiding," WP (7.28.08); Oppel, "U.S. Military Says Platoon of Soldiers Fired on Innocent Civilians in June, Killing 3," NYT (7.28.08); Hameed & Parker, "U.S. Says Iraqis Slain by Soldiers Not Armed," LAT (7.28.08); Myers & Tavernise, "Citing Stability in Iraq, Bush Sees Troop Cuts," NYT (8.1.08).

195 Graff, "U.S. Navy Charges Iraq Camp Guards with Abuse," WP (8.14.08); Susman & Parker, "Iraq Reports 7 Killed by U.S. Friendly Fire," LAT (9.4.08); Susman, "U.S. Says 3 Women Killed in Iraq Raid," LAT (9.20.08); Raghavan, "U.S. Assault Kills 8 Civilians, Iraq Asserts," WP (9.20.08); Farrell, "Iraqis Protest Deadly Raid by U.S. on Village in North," NYT (9.20.08); "Sunni Party Ends Contacts with U.S. over Raid in Anbar," LAT (10.26.08).

196 Robertson, "American Troops Wound Woman in Baghdad," NYT (1.4.09); Londono, "Iraqi Station Rebuts U.S. Account of Employees' Shooting," WP (1.4.09); Parker & Hameed, "Iraqi Couple Killed in U.S. Raid," LAT (1.25.09); Shahid & Mizher, "U.S. Forces Kill Couple in Raid on Iraqi House," WP (1.25.09); Santora, "Iraqis Say U.S. Patrol Killed Girl, 8, in Crowd," NYT (2.9.09); Myers, "After a U.S. Raid: 2 Iraqis Dead, Protests and Regrets," NYT (4.27.09); Dagher, "G.I. Kills Iraqi Driver Who Failed to Stop, U.S. Military Says," NYT (7.11.09); Londono, "After the Shooting, Another Showdown," WP (7.25.09); Parker & Redha, "U.S.-backed Forces Kill 2 in Iraqi Raid," LAT (9.10.09).

197 Bumiller, "Video Shows 2007 Air Attack in Baghdad That Killed Photographer," NYT (4.6.10); Cohen & Settler, "Airstrike Video Brings Notice to a Web Site," NYT (4.7.10); Carey, "Experts Cite Conditioning and Heat of Combat to Explain Iraq Airstrike Video," NYT (4.8.09); "Iraq War Video Raises More Than Just Ethical and Legal Questions," LAT (4.11.10).

198 Gordon, "New Iraqi Premier Backs U.S. Air Campaign, within Limits," NYT (9.26.14); "U.S. Troops Have Immunity in Iraq," WP (12.4.14);

Cooper, "Reports of Civilian Deaths Prompt Inquiry into Strikes against ISIS," NYT (1.7.15); Barnard, "Strikes on Syria Tied to Deaths of 52 Civilians," NYT (5.2.15); El Deeb, "Rights Group: 64 Civilians Killed in Syria Coalition Strike," WP (5.4.15); Youssef, "Pentagon Admits Anti-ISIS Strikes Killed Civilians," Daily Beast (5.4.15); Ryan & DeYoung, "U.S. Military Confirms Two Civilian Casualties in War against IS," WP (5.22.15); Weiss, "Did the U.S. Just Kill 5 Kids in Syria?" Daily Beast (8.12.15); Hubbard & Shoumali, "U.S.-led Air Campaign Is Linked to Civilian Deaths in Syria," NYT (8.15.15); Salama & Karam, "Report; US-led Strikes in Iraq, Syria Killed 459 Civilians," AP (8.3.15); Ross, "Civilian Deaths Claimed in 71 US-led Airstrikes on ISIS," G (9.3.15); Youssef, "U.S. to Admit Killing More Civilians in ISIS Strike," Daily Beast (9.4.15); Morris & Salim, "Iraqi Military Says Coalition Airstrike Hits Its Forces," WP (12.19.15); "Inquiry Is Promised about Airstrike in Iraq by Coalition Fighting ISIS," NYT (12.19.15); Lamothe, "U.S. Military Investigation: Civilians in Iraq Likely Killed in Airstrike," WP (11.21.15); "At Least 26 Syrian Civilians Killed in Suspected US-led Airstrike," G (12.7.15); Gordon, "U.S. Airstrike Killed Iraqis by Accident, Officials Say," NYT (12.20.16); DeYoung & Ryan, "As Bombing in Syria Intensifies, a Debate about the Rules of Engagement," WP (12.23.15); Gibbons-Neff, "For Third Time in War against the IS, Pentagon Admits to Killing Civilians," WP (1.16.16); Youssef, "U.S. Admits to Bombing 29 Civilians in ISIS War," Daily Beast (1.21.16); Lamothe, "U.S. Military Changes How it Discloses Civilian Casualties in Iraq and Syria," WP (1.27.16); "U.S.-led Strikes in Syria Kill 38 Civilians in Past Two Days: Monitor," Reuters (2.18.16); McLeary, "U.S. Hits al Qaeda in Syria for Second Time This Week," FP (4.6.16); Vanden Brook, "New Rules Allow More Civilian Casualties in Air War against ISIL," *USA Today* (4.19.16); Lamothe, "U.S. Military Doubles the Number of Civilians It Admits Killing in Anti-ISIS Fight," WP (4.23.16); Vanden Brook, "Civilian Casualties Mount in War on ISIL," *USA Today* (4.23.16); Jaffe & Morris, "A Desperate Woman's Email from Iraq Reveals the High Toll of Obama's Low-Cost Wars," WP (6.9.16); Jaffe, "U.S. Reopens Investigation into Bombing that Killed at Least 11 Iraqi Civilians," WP (6.27.16); "Airstrikes on ISIS-held Villages in Syria Kill 56, Activists Say," NYT (7.19.16); Woods, "Coalition-backed Manbij Assault Has Killed Hundreds of Civilians, Warn Locals," Airwars (7.19.16); Graham-Harrison & Ackerman, "U.S. Airstrikes Allegedly Kill At Least 73 Civilians in Northern Syria," G (7.20.16); "Investigation Begins into Allegations of Civilians Killed in Syria: U.S. Military Spokesman," Reuters (7.28.16); Ackerman, "US Military Says It May Have Killed More Civilians in Latest Airstrike in Syria," G (7.28.16); Woods, "Does the U.S. Ignore Its Civilian Casualties in Iraq and Syria?" NYT (8.18.16); "U.S. Says Strikes in Syria May Have Resulted in Civilian Casualties," Reuters (9.14.16); Barnard & Mazzetti, "U.S. Admits Airstrike in Syria, Meant to Hit ISIS, Killed Syrian Troops," NYT (9.17.16); Wong, "U.S. Reviewing Whether Strike Killed Syrian Forces," *The Hill* (9.19.16);

Ryan & Habib, "After an Apparently Errant Strike in Syria, Confusion and Competing Claims," WP (9.28.16).

199 "Syria Conflict: Coalition Strike 'Kills 20 Civilians near Raqqa,'" BBC News (11.9.16); Cooper, "U.S. Strike on Syria Mosque Complex Was Legal, Defense Dept. Says," NYT (6.8.17); Schmidt, "U.S. Says It Has Killed 119 Civilians in Iraq and Syria since 2014," NYT (11.10.16); Gibbons-Neff, "U.S.-led Coalition in Iraq and Syria Acknowledges 54 Civilians Killed in Airstrikes," WP (12.2.16).

200 Gordon & Saad, "U.S. Military Denies Reports It Bombed Mosque in Syria," NYT (3.17.17); Loveluck, "Mounting Claims of Civilian Deaths after U.S. Targets al-Qaeda in Syria," WP (3.17.17); Gordon & Saad, "Pentagon Releases Photo to Rebut Contention It Bombed a Mosque," NYT (3.18.17); Loveluck, Gibbons-Neff & Ryan, "Mounting Claims of Civilian Deaths after U.S. Targets al-Qaeda in Syria," WP (3.18.17); Barnard, "U.S. Airstrike in Syria Is Said to Kill Dozens of Civilians," NYT (3.22.17); Cooper, "U.S. Military Investigating Reports of Civilian Deaths in Syria Airstrike," NYT (3.22.17); Arango & Cooper, "U.S. Investigating Mosul Strikes Said to Have Killed up to 200 Civilians," NYT (3.25.17); Morris & Salim, "Mosul Residents Say U.S.-led Coalition Airstrikes Killed Scores of People," WP (3.25.17); Salaheddin, "Senior Statesmen in Iraq Decry Mosul Airstrike," WP (3.25.17); Gibbons-Neff, "Airstrike Monitoring Group Overwhelmed by Claims of U.S.-caused Civilian Casualties," WP (3.24.17); Schmidt & Arango, "U.S.-led Coalition Confirms Strikes Hit Mosul Site Where Civilians Died," NYT (3.26.17); Morris & Salim, "Rescue Workers Find 101 Bodies in Mosul Building, Destroyed in Alleged U.S.-led Strike," WP (3.27.17); Gordon, "U.S. Concedes It Played a Role in Iraqi Deaths," NYT (3.29.17); Gordon, "New ISIS Tactic in Iraq Fight: Gather Mosul Civilians, Then Lure an Airstrike," NYT (3.31.17); Kheel, "GOP Lawmakers Defend Trump Military Rules of Engagement," *The Hill* (3.28.17); Ryan, "In Letter to Mattis, Lawmaker and Former JAG Demands Answers on Civilian Casualties," WP (3.30.17); Cooper, "18 Syrian Fighters Allied with U.S. Are Killed in Coalition Airstrike," NYT (4.13.17); "Attack on the Omar Ibn al-Khatab Mosque," HRW (4.19.17); Jaffe, "U.S. Military Investigations Reveal Additional Civilian Deaths in Coalition Strikes," WP (5.2.17); Gibbons-Neff, "Pentagon Confirms Airstrike Killed More Than 100 Civilians in Mosul, Blames ISIS Explosives," WP (5.25.17); Szlanko & Abdul-Zahra, "Iraqis Demand Compensation after U.S. Probe into Mosul Strike," WP (5.26.17); Taylor, "Trump Said He Would 'Take Out' the Families of ISIS Fighters. Did an Airstrike in Syria Do Just That?" WP (5.27.17); Gibbons-Neff, "Pentagon Acknowledges More Civilian Deaths in U.S.-led Air Campaign Against Islamic State," WP (6.2.17); Cumming-Bruce, "U.S.-led Airstrikes in Syria Killed Hundreds of Civilians, U.N. Panel Says," NYT (6.15.17); Hubbard, "Airstrike on ISIS Prison in Syria Kills Dozens, Activists Say," NYT (6.27.17); "Syrian Observatory Says 30 Killed in East Syria Air Strike," Reuters (6.28.17).

201 Gupta, "Raqqa Faces Deadly 'Barrage' from US-led Coalition," Al Jazeera (9.20.17).
202 AI (2013b).
203 Mazzetti, "A Secret Deal on Drones, Sealed in Blood," NYT (4.7.13); Woods (2015: 108–09).
204 "U.S. Accused in Pakistan Deaths," NYT (9.3.08); Zaidi & King, "Pakistan Charges Cross-Border Troop Assault Left up to 20 Dead in Village," LAT (9.4.08); Rondeaux & DeYoung, "U.S. Troops Crossed Border, Pakistan Says," WP (9.4.08); Shah, Schmitt & Perlez, "American Forces Attack Militants on Pakistani Soil," NYT (9.4.08); Shah & Perlez, "U.S. Missiles Killed At Least Six People on Afghanistan–Pakistan Border, Residents Say," NYT (9.6.08); "Blasts Kill 9 in Pakistan Militant Stronghold," LAT (9.8.08); Ali & King, "Missile Strike in Pakistan Kills At Least 9," LAT (9.9.08); Hussain, "U.S. Missiles Said to Kill 20 in Pakistan near Afghan Border," WP (9.9.08); "Two Top al-Qaeda Operatives Killed in Pakistan," LAT (9.10.08); Schmitt & Mazzetti, "Bush Said to Give Orders Allowing Raids in Pakistan," NYT (9.11.08); Perlez, "Pakistan's Military Chief Criticizes U.S. over a Raid," NYT (9.11.08); DeYoung, "Pakistan Did Not Agree to New Rules, Officials Say," WP (9.12.08); Miller & Barnes, "Higher-tech Predators Targeting Pakistan," LAT (9.12.08); Rondeaux & Hussain, "Drone Attack Said to Kill 12 in Pakistan," WP (9.13.08); Shah & Masood, "U.S. Airstrike, Killing 12, Is Reported in Pakistan," NYT (9.13.08); "The War in Pakistan," WP (9.14.08); Alexander, "U.S. Military Chief Meets Pakistani Officials amid Rift over U.S. Incursions into Tribal Areas," LAT (9.17.08); Constable, "Mullen Visits Pakistan as U.S. Raids Stir Tensions," WP (9.17.08); Gall, "Pakistan's President Calls for End to Terrorism and Criticizes Intervention by U.S.," NYT (9.21.08); Shahzad, "Pakistanis Say Suspected U.S. Drone Shot Down," WP (9.24.08); Barnes, "U.S., Pakistan Troops Exchange Fire on Afghanistan Border," LAT (9.26.08); Schmitt, "U.S. and Pakistani Forces Clash at Volatile Border," NYT (9.26.08). For a history of drone strikes, see Coll (2014).
205 "U.S. Missile Strike Reported," NYT (10.1.08); Ali & King, "U.S. Missile Attack Reported in Pakistan; At Least 21 Killed," LAT (10.4.08); Hussain, "Pakistan Intelligence Says U.S. Strike Kills 21 Insurgents," WP (10.4.08); Hussain, "Suspected U.S. Missile Strike Kills At Least 10 in Pakistan," WP (10.23.08); Shah, "Airstrike Kills 8 Militants in Pakistan, Villagers Say," NYT (10.24.08); "Pakistan Tells U.S. to Stop Missile Strikes," LAT (10.29.08); "Pakistan: U.S. Envoy Hears Strikes Complaints," LAT (10.30.08); Perlez, "Pakistan Tells U.S. to Stop Airstrikes in Tribal Zone," NYT (10.30.08); Rondeaux, "U.S. Airstrikes Creating Tension, Pakistan Warns," WP (11.4.08); Perlez, "Petraeus, in Pakistan, Hears Complaints from All Sides about Missile Strikes," NYT (11.4.08); Ignatius, "A Quiet Deal with Pakistan," WP (11.4.08); "Airstrike Kills 13 in Pakistan," LAT (11.8.08); Shah & Cowell,

"American Missile Strike Kills At Least 10 in Pakistani Village," NYT (11.8.08); Perlez, "2 Journalists in Pakistan Are Wounded by Gunmen," NYT (11.15.08); Rondeaux, "Suspected U.S. Airstrike Kills 6 Fighters in Pakistan," WP (11.20.08); Graham, "Suspected U.S. Missile Strike Deep Inside Pakistan," WP (11.19.08); Perlez & Shah, "U.S. Strike Killed Five in Pakistan," NYT (11.20.08); "Top Al Qaeda Terrorist Abu Zubair al-Masri 'Was Missile Target in Bush Campaign or Favourable Legacy,'" T (11.24.08); "Immunity for Musharraf Likely after Zardari's Election as President," U.S. Embassy cable (8.23.08), leaked by WikiLeaks; Woodward (2010: 26).

206 "Nine Dead in Suspected U.S. Strikes in Pakistan," WP (1.23.09); Oppel, "Drone Attacks in Pakistan Continue into Obama's Term," NYT (1.23.09); King, "Missiles Kill 18 in West Pakistan," LAT (1.24.09); Perlez, "A Visit to a U.S. Ally, but an Increasingly Wary One," NYT (2.9.09); Perlez, "In Pakistan, Special Envoy from U.S. Finds Discontent," NYT (2.12.09); Miller, "Drones Based in Pakistan," LAT (2.13.09); Mazzetti & Sanger, "Obama Expands Missile Strikes Inside Pakistan," NYT (2.21.09); Schmitt & Perlez, "Secret U.S. Unit Trains Commandos in Pakistan," NYT (2.23.09); Miller, "CIA Begins Briefing Obama Daily on Economy," LAT (2.26.09); Landler, "U.S., Pakistan and Afghanistan to Hold Regular Talks," NYT (2.27.09); DeYoung & Warrick, "Drone Attacks Inside Pakistan Will Continue, CIA Chief Says," WP (2.26.09); Panetta, "Director's Remarks at the Pacific Council on International Policy" (5.18.09).

207 McManus, "U.S. Drone Attacks in Pakistan 'Backfiring,' Congress Told," LAT (5.3.09); Kilcullen & Exum, "Death from Above, Outrage Down Below," NYT (5.17.09).

208 Barnes & Miller, "Pakistanis Get a Say in Airstrikes," LAT (5.13.09); Barnes, "U.S. Acknowledges Joint Drone Program with Pakistan," LAT (5.14.09); Schmitt & Mazzetti, "In a First, U.S. Provides Pakistan with Drone Data," NYT (5.14.09); Bergen & Tiedemann, "Revenge of the Drones," New America Foundation (10.19.09); Shane, "C.I.A. Authorized to Expand Use of Drones in Pakistan," NYT (12.4.09); Miller & Barnes, "Drone Attacks May Be Expanded in Pakistan," LAT (12.14.09); Shah, "Strike Killed Hijacking Suspect, Pakistan Officials Say," NYT (1.16.10); Constable & Khan, "U.S. Drone Attack May Have Killed Pakistani Taliban Chief," WP (1.15.10); Mahsud & Dawar, "Alleged Hijacker Reportedly Killed in Pakistan Missile Strike," WP (1.16.10); Rodriguez & Ali, "U.S. Missile Strike Kills 16 in Pakistan," LAT (1.15.10); Shah, "Pakistani Officials Say Attack by U.S. Drones Killed up to 15," NYT (1.18.10); Shane, "C.I.A. Deaths Prompt Surge in Drone War," NYT (1.23.10); Warrick & Finn, "CIA Director Says Secret Attacks in Pakistan Have Hobbled al-Qaeda," WP (3.18.10); Sanger, "Drone Strike Said to Kill a Leader of al Qaeda," NYT (3.18.10); Rodriguez & Zucchino, "U.S. Drone Attacks in Pakistan Get Mixed Reception," LAT (5.2.10); Masood & Shah, "C.I.A. Drones Kill Civilians in Pakistan," NYT (3.18.11); Rodriguez, "Pakistan Denounces

U.S. Drone Strike," LAT (3.18.11). For an analysis of the experience of the victims, see Gaston & Wright (2009).

209 Warrick (2012).

210 Londano, "Rebuke from Islamabad after NATO Airstrikes Kill 55 on Pakistani Soil," WP (9.27.10); "Pakistan Protests NATO Helicopter Raid across Border," LAT (9.27.10); Rodriguez, "Pakistan Denounces NATO Airstrikes That Killed 50 Insurgents," LAT (9.27.10); Dozier & Brummitt, "Pakistan Warns against More NATO Raids," WP (9.28.10); Khan & Perlez, "Pakistan Halts NATO Supplies to Afghanistan after Attack," NYT (9.30.10); Brulliard, "Pakistan Blocks NATO's Afghanistan-bound Supply Trucks after Airstrike That Officials Say Killed 3 Soldiers," WP (9.30.10); Perlez & Cooper, "Signaling Tensions, Pakistan Shuts NATO Route," NYT (9.30.10); DeYoung & Brulliard, "U.S. Tense over Pakistan," WP (9.30.10); Cloud, Rodriguez & King, "Pakistan Closes Border Crossing, Says NATO Copters Killed 3 Soldiers," LAT (9.30.10); "Tankers for NATO Are Set on Fire in Pakistan," NYT (10.1.10); Brulliard & DeYoung, "NATO Fuel Tankers Are Torched in Pakistan," WP (10.1.10); Brulliard & Hussain, "Militants Set NATO Fuel Tankers Ablaze in Pakistan, Killing 3 as Key Border Pass Remains Closed," WP (10.4.10); "Trucks with Fuel for War Set Ablaze in Pakistan Again," NYT (10.4.10); Rodriguez, "3 Killed in Attack on NATO Fuel Trucks in Pakistan," LAT (10.5.10); Perlez & Gilani, "Gunmen Attack More NATO Supply Trucks in Pakistan," NYT (10.6.10); Cooper & Schmitt, "U.S. Tries to Calm Pakistan over Airstrike," NYT (10.7.10); DeYoung & Brulliard, "U.S. Apologizes for Fatal Airstrike in Pakistan," WP (10.6.10); Brulliard, "Pakistan Reopens Border to NATO Supply Trucks," WP (10.9.10); Gall, "Pakistan Will Reopen Route to Supplies for NATO," NYT (10.10.10); Baker, "President Will Travel to Pakistan Next Year," NYT (10.21.10).

211 Brulliard, "Pakistan Police: U.S. Shooter Committed 'Clear Murder,'" WP (2.11.11); Rodriguez, "American's Fatal Shooting of 2 Pakistanis Was Murder, Police Say," LAT (2.11.11); Brulliard & Sahi, "Pakistani Police Report Deems American Official 'Guilty' in Shootings," WP (2.13.11); Perlez, "Kerry Says U.S. Will Investigate Case of American Accused of Killing 2 Pakistanis," NYT (2.16.11); Miller, "U.S. Plans Own Criminal Investigation of U.S. Embassy Guard Held in Killings in Pakistan," WP (2.16.11); Brulliard & DeYoung, "Stakes Rise, Aid Cuts Mulled in Case of American Accused of Killing Pakistanis," WP (2.16.11); Brulliard & Sahi, "Court Gives Pakistan 3 Weeks to Decide American's Immunity," WP (2.17.11); Rodriguez, "In Pakistan, Rumbles of a Revolution over Raymond Davis," LAT (2.18.11); Brulliard, "In Aftermath of Shooting, Rising Skepticism about American Presence in Pakistan," WP (2.23.11); Rodriguez, "Pakistan Says Shooter Raymond Davis Is CIA Agent," LAT (2.21.11); Mazzetti, Parker, Perlez & Schmitt, "American Held in Pakistan Worked for CIA," NYT (2.22.11); Miller, "U.S. Officials: Raymond Davis, Accused in Pakistan Shootings, Worked for CIA," WP (2.22.11); Savage, "Pakistan Case Tests Laws on Diplomatic

Immunity," NYT (2.23.11); Perlez, "Pakistan Demands Data on C.I.A. Contractors," NYT (2.26.11); Horton, "Spy Games," *Harper's* (3.11.11); Miller & Constable, "CIA Contractor Raymond Davis Freed after 'Blood Money' Payment," WP (3.17.11); Gall & Mazzetti, "C.I.A. Security Officer Is Freed in Pakistan as Redress Is Paid," NYT A1 (3.17.11); Miller, "CIA Launches Review of Security Officers Stemming from Pakistan Case," WP (3.18.11); Constable, "Pakistan President, Opponents Mend Fences over CIA Contractor Case," WP (3.23.11); Perlez & Khan, "Pakistan Tells U.S. It Must Sharply Cut C.I.A. Activities," NYT A1 (4.12.11); Miller & DeYoung, "CIA, Pakistan Look to Repair Widening Rift," WP (4.13.11); DeYoung, "Pakistan Seeks an Update on Raymond Davis," WP (10.6.11); Brulliard, "In Raymond Davis Case, Justice for Some," WP (10.18.11); Davis & Reback (2017).

212 Miller, "Increased U.S. Drone Strikes in Pakistan Killing Few High-Value Militants," WP (2.21.11); Dilanian, "CIA Drones May Be Avoiding Pakistani Civilians," LAT (2.22.11); Masood & Shah, "C.I.A. Drones Kill Civilians in Pakistan," NYT (3.18.11); Rodriguez, "Pakistan Denounces U.S. Drone Strike," LAT (3.18.11); Rodriguez, "Pakistan Pulls Out of Talks with U.S. on Afghan War," LAT (3.20.11); Perlez & Khan, "Pakistan Tells U.S. It Must Sharply Cut C.I.A. Activities," NYT (4.12.11); Miller & DeYoung, "CIA, Pakistan Look to Repair Widening Rift," WP (4.13.11); Rodriguez, "Pakistan, U.S. Attempt to Rebuild Trust during Meetings in Washington," LAT (4.13.11); Perlez & Khan, "Drone Strikes Militants in Western Pakistan," NYT (4.22.11); Constable, "U.S., Pakistani Military Chiefs Trade Barbs," WP (4.21.11); Rodriguez, "U.S. Drone Attack Kills 25 in Pakistan," LAT (4.22.11); "Pakistanis Keep up Protest against U.S. Missiles as NATO Supply Trucks Halted," WP (4.24.11); Perlez & Schmitt, "Move to C.I.A. Puts Petraeus in Conflict with Pakistan," NYT (4.29.11); Entous, Gorman & Barnes, "U.S. Tightens Drone Rules," WSJ (11.4.11).

213 Mazzetti & Masood, "Pakistani Role Is Suspected in Revealing U.S. Spy's Name," NYT (11.18.10); Brulliard & Hussain, "Pakistani Man Threatens to Sue CIA If Not Compensated for Relatives' Deaths," WP (11.29.10); Miller & Brulliard, "Top CIA Spy in Pakistan Pulled amid Threats after Public Accusation over Attack," WP (12.18.10); Dilanian & Rodriguez, "CIA Recalls Pakistan Station Chief after His Name Becomes Public," LAT (12.18.10); Brulliard, "Pakistani Intelligence Official Denies Agency Role in Revealing Name of CIA Station Chief," WP (12.19.10); Rodriguez, "CIA Identity Breach Feeds Mistrust with Pakistani Agency," LAT (12.19.10); Leiby, "CIA Drone Strikes in Pakistan Lead to Lawsuits over Civilian Deaths," WP (5.14.12); Akbar, "Obama's Forgotten Victims," NYT (5.23.13); "UK Claims Possible Court Hearing into CIA Drone Strikes in Pakistan Would Risk Denting U.S. Ties," WP (10.26.12); Somaiya, "Drone Strike Prompts Suit, Raising Fears for U.S. Allies," NYT (1.30.13).

214 Dilanian, "In Finding OBL, CIA Soars from Distress to Success," LAT (5.8.11); Schmitt & Mazzetti, "Pakistan Arrests C.I.A. Informants in

Bin Laden Raid," NYT A1 (6.15.11); "Detainee Who Provided Key Information about bin Laden Courier Rejoins al-Qaida," WP (6.15.11); Rodriguez & Dilanian, "Pakistan's Arrest of CIA Informants Exposes bin Laden Raid Frustrations, Analysts Say," LAT (6.16.11); DeYoung & Witte, "Pakistan–U.S. Security Relationship at Lowest Point since 2001, Officials Say," WP (6.16.11); DeYoung, "CIA Idles Drone Flights from Base in Pakistan," WP (7.1.11); DeYoung, "U.S. Withholding Military Aid to Pakistan," WP (7.10.11); Mazzetti, "Vaccination Ruse Used in Pursuit of bin Laden," NYT (7.12.11); Ukman, "CIA Defends Running Vaccine Program to Find bin Laden," WP (7.14.11); Ignatius, "Renewed Cooperation between the U.S. and Pakistan," WP (7.18.11); Brulliard, "Pakistan Heightens Scrutiny of Foreigners, U.S. and Humanitarian Aid Officials Say," WP (7.25.11); Walsh, "Aid Agency Withdrew Pakistan Staff after CIA Fake Vaccination Scheme," G (9.28.11); "Pakistani Commission Says Doctor Who Helped CIA in bin Laden Operation Should Be Put on Trial," WP (10.7.11); Walsh, "Fury in Pakistan after U.S. Congressman Suggests That a Province Leave," NYT (2.22.12); Walsh, "Fallout of bin Laden Raid: Aid Groups in Pakistan Are Suspect," NYT (5.3.12); Leiby, "Pakistani Doctor Who Helped CIA Locate bin Laden Sentenced to Prison for Treason," WP (5.23.12); Khan, "Prison Term for Helping C.I.A. Find bin Laden," NYT (5.24.12); "Verdict against Pakistani Who Helped Track bin Laden: Guilty of Militancy, Not CIA Links," WP (5.30.12); Walsh & Khan, "New Details Emerge on Conviction of Pakistani Who Aided bin Laden Search," NYT (5.31.12); Masood, "Drone Strikes Continue in Pakistan as Tension Increases and Senate Panel Cuts Aid," NYT (5.25.12); Khan & Leiby, "U.S. Drone Strike in Pakistan Kills 10 Suspected Militants," WP (5.25.12); Leiby, "Brother of Pakistani Doctor Convicted of Treason Calls for U.S. Help," WP (5.28.12); "Family of Pakistani Doctor Who Helped U.S. Find bin Laden Blasts Trial, Says Will Appeal," WP (5.28.12); Leiby, "In Pakistan, A Legal System under Scrutiny," WP (5.29.12); Leiby, "Pakistan Spy Chief Puts Off Washington Visit amid Rift over Doctor's Treason Conviction," WP (5.29.12); Robillard, "Rand Paul to Leverage Pakistan Aid to Gain Doctor's Release," Politico (5.30.12); Imtiaz, "In Wake of Shakil Afridi's Hunger Strike, U.S. Reiterates Calls for His Release," *Express Tribune* (11.30.12); "Pakistan Official Orders Retrial of Doctor Who Helped CIA Find Osama bin Laden," WP (8.29.13); Masood & Walsh, "Pakistan Overturns Conviction of Doctor in bin Laden Hunt," NYT (8.30.13); Iqbal, "Sharif Agreed to Review Afridi Case," *Dawn* (10.28.13); "Pakistan Doctor Who Helped CIA Charged with Murder," WP (11.23.13); "No Chance of Shakil Afridi's Release over U.S. Pressure: Foreign Office," *Dawn* (1.23.14); Masood, "Sentence Cut for Bin Laden Figure," NYT (3.16.14); Kahn, "Lawyer Quits Case of Pakistan Doctor Who Aided CIA," AP (4.11.14); Mazzetti, "U.S. Cites End to C.I.A. Ruses Using Vaccines," NYT (5.20.14); Sun, "CIA: No More Vaccination Campaigns in Spy Operations," WP (5.20.14); "The C.I.A.'s Deadly Ruse in Pakistan," NYT (5.27.14); "Taliban Faction Kills

Lawyer," NYT (3.18.15); Noack, "Trump Promised to Free a Pakistan Surgeon Who Helped Find bin Laden. He's Still in Prison," WP (5.2.17).

215 Shah, "Drone Strike Said to Kill at Least 8 in Pakistan," NYT (5.7.11); Witte & DeYoung, "New Challenge for U.S.–Pakistan Ties," WP (6.11.11); Bumiller, "C.I.A. Director Warns Pakistan on Collusion with Militants," NYT (6.12.11); Perlez, "Pakistan's Chief of Army Fights to Keep His Job," NYT (6.16.11); DeYoung & Witte, "Pakistan–U.S. Security Relationship at Lowest Point since 2001, Officials Say," WP (6.16.11); Dilanian, "Obama Sees Precision Strikes as Key to al Qaeda Defeat," LAT (6.30.11); "Former Top Intelligence Official Calls Drone Strikes Counterproductive, War on Terror Too Expensive," WP (7.29.11); Schmitt & Sanger, "White House Adviser Says U.S. Has 6 months to 'Knock Out' Rattled Qaeda Leadership," NYT (7.30.11); Dilanian, "U.S. Is Refocused on Covert Strikes in Pakistan," LAT (7.30.11); Shane, "C.I.A. Is Disputed on Civilian Toll in Drone Strikes," NYT (8.12.11); "The C.I.A. and Drone Strikes," NYT (8.14.11); Blair, "Drones Alone Are Not the Answer," NYT (8.15.11); Bureau of Investigative Journalism, "Drone War Exposed – the Complete Picture of CIA Strikes in Pakistan" (8.10.11).

216 DeYoung, "Pakistan Backed Attacks on American Targets," WP (9.23.11); Bumiller & Perlez, "Pakistan's Spy Agency Is Tied to Attack on U.S. Embassy," NYT (9.23.11); Perlez, "Pakistan Scorns U.S. Scolding on Terrorism," NYT (9.24.11); Brulliard, "Pakistan Rejects U.S. Allegations about Aid to Insurgents," WP (9.24.11); "The Latest Ugly Truth about Pakistan," NYT (9.24.11); Masood, "In Pakistani Media, the U.S. Is a Target for Acrimony," NYT (9.28.11); Miller & DeYoung, "Adm. Mullen's Words on Pakistan Come under Scrutiny," WP (9.28.11); Schmitt, "U.S. Recalibrates Remarks about Pakistan," NYT (9.29.11); "America's Perceived Threat of Military Action Unites Pakistan's Right-Wing Media," WP (9.29.11); Masood, "Pakistani Politicians Reject Mullen's Charges," NYT (9.30.11); Rodriguez, "In Show of Unity, Top Pakistanis Meet and Denounce U.S. Charges," LAT (9.30.11); "Pakistan: U.S. Assures Ally, 'No Boots on the Ground,'" NYT (10.1.11); Zardari, "Talk to, Not at, Pakistan," WP (10.1.11).

217 Rodriguez & Yaqubi, "Pakistan Rejects Claim of ISI Role in Afghan's Assassination," LAT (10.3.11); Partlow, "Karzai Accuses Pakistan of Supporting Terrorists," WP (10.4.11); "Double Trouble in Afghanistan," WP (10.5.11); Healy & Rahimi, "Plot to Kill Afghan President Karzai Is Foiled," NYT (10.6.10); Gladstone, "Obama Warns Pakistanis on Militants," NYT (10.7.11); "U.S. Missiles Kill Haqqani 'Coordinator' in Pakistan, Upping Pressure on Afghan Militant Faction," WP (10.13.11); Shane, "Drone Attack Kills a Senior Militant Leader in Pakistan," NYT (10.14.11); DeYoung, "U.S. Goes after Haqqani Network," WP (10.15.11); "Pakistani Intelligence Officials Say U.S. Missiles Kill 6 in Drone Attack Spike," WP (10.15.11); "U.S. Drone Strike in Pakistan Kills 3 Egyptians Linked to Haqqani Militant Network," WP (10.16.11); Chivers, "Tensions Flare as G.I.'s Take Fire Out of Pakistan," NYT

(10.17.11); "Pakistan's Powerful Army Chief Advises U.S. to Focus on Afghanistan, not Pressure Islamabad," WP (10.19.11); Brulliard, "Pakistan Turns Tables on U.S. Accusations about Sheltering Militants," WP (10.20.11); "Clinton, in Afghanistan, Demands Pakistan Step Up Counterterrorism Effort," WP (10.20.11); Myers, "U.S. Officials Deliver Warning in Pakistan over Extremists," NYT (10.21.11); Warrick & Brulliard, "Clinton Warns Pakistan on Insurgent Havens," WP (10.21.11); Rodriguez & King, "U.S. Delivers Blunt Message to Pakistan on Haqqani Network," LAT (10.21.11); King, "Afghan Leader's Office Says Pakistan Remarks Misinterpreted," LAT (10.25.11); Rodriguez, "U.S. Changes Approach to Pressing Pakistan on Haqqani Network," LAT (10.22.11); Ukman, "Levin: U.S. Prepared to Walk Away from Pakistan," WP (10.22.11).

218 Masood, "Political Shift Seen in Rally in Pakistan," NYT (10.31.11); "U.S. Has No Permission for Drone Strikes: Gilani," *Dawn* (10.30.11); "Suspected U.S. Drone-fired Missiles Kill 2 Haqqani Militants in Pakistan, Officials Say," WP (11.3.11); Stafford-Smith, "For Our Allies, Death from Above," NYT (11.4.11); Dilanian, "U.S. Put New Restrictions on CIA Drone Strikes in Pakistan," LAT (11.8.11).

219 "Pakistan Reports Dozens of Deaths in NATO Attack," NYT (11.26.11); Brulliard & Khan, "Pakistani Officials Say NATO Attack Kills At Least 24," WP (11.26.11); Rodriguez, "Pakistan Accuses NATO of Cross-Border Attack That Kills At Least 20 Soldiers," LAT (11.26.11); Masood & Schmitt, "Tensions Flare between U.S. and Pakistan after Strike," NYT (11.27.11); "Drivers Carrying NATO Supplies through Pakistan Fear Attacks after Afghan Border Closed," WP (11.27.11); Rodriguez, "Alleged Strike in Pakistan Ratchets Up Tensions with U.S.," LAT (11.27.11); Myers, "In Fog of War, Rift Widens between U.S. and Pakistan," NYT (11.28.11); Rubin & Masood, "After Strike in Pakistan, Rage and Damage Control," NYT (11.28.11); "U.S. to Investigate Deadly NATO Airstrike in Pakistan, Lawmakers Call for Tough Diplomacy," WP (11.28.11); "Pakistan Says NATO Ignored Its Pleas to Hold Off during Attack That Killed 24 Soldiers," WP (11.28.11); "What Happened on the Border?" NYT (11.28.11); "Pakistan's Top Officials Continue to Express Anger Day after NATO Strike," WP (11.28.11); Masood & Schmidt, "Pakistan Rejects U.S. Account of NATO Strikes along Border," NYT (11.29.11); DeYoung & Partlow, "Afghans Say Commando Unit Was Attacked before Airstrike Was Called on Pakistan," WP (11.29.11); "Pakistan Calls Deadly NATO Raid an 'Act of Aggression,' Questions Point of U.S. Investigation," WP (11.29.11); Masood, "In Protest over NATO Strike, Pakistan Will Skip Afghan Conference," NYT (11.30.11); Zakaria & Hosenball, "U.S. Prepares to Vacate Pakistani Air Base," Reuters (11.30.11); Cooper & Mazzetti, "Obama Refrains from a Formal 'I'm Sorry' to Pakistan," NYT (12.1.11); Rodriguez, "Patching up Ties between Pakistan and U.S. Not a Given This Time," LAT (12.2.11); Rosenberg & Schmitt, "Pakistan Refuses to Help as U.S. Sorts Out a Fatal Attack," NYT (12.3.11); Cushman,

"Obama Offers 'Condolences' in Deaths of Pakistanis," NYT (12.5.11); DeYoung & Brulliard, "U.S. Breach with Pakistan Shows Imbalance between Diplomatic, Security Goals," WP (12.5.11); "Pakistan Prime Minister Says His Nation Committed to Ties with U.S., Hopes for Improvement despite NATO Raid," WP (12.5.11); "Pakistan Fans the Flames," NYT (12.6.11); "Pakistan: NATO Fuel Trucks Attacked," NYT (12.9.11); Masood, "C.I.A. Leaves Base in Pakistan Used for Drone Strikes," NYT (12.12.11); Whitlock, "U.S. Commander Reports 'Progress' in Repairing Ties with Pakistan," WP (12.14.11); Shah, "Pakistan to Tax U.S. Shipments to Afghanistan," *San Francisco Chronicle* (12.15.11); Constable, "At Pakistan Embassy, Officials Decry NATO Airstrike," WP (12.16.11); Dilanian, "Pakistan Says It Returned Fire in Deadly NATO Border Attack," LAT (12.16.11); Schmitt & Masood, "Pakistani Crisis Prompts Leader to Race Home," NYT (12.19.11); Rosenberg, "Afghanistan: Pakistani Liaison Officers Returning to Army Coordination Centers," NYT (12.20.11); "Official: Pakistan Sees Lull in US Drone Strikes," AP (12.20.11).

220 "Official: Pakistan Sees Lull in US Drone Strikes," AP (12.20.11); Schmitt & Rosenberg, "2 Sides Faulted in Deadly Strike," NYT (12.23.11); Dilanian, "CIA Has Suspended Drone Attacks in Pakistan, U.S. Officials Say," LAT (12.23.11); Cloud & King, "U.S. Acknowledges Mistakes, Doesn't Take Blame in Pakistan Strike," LAT (12.22.11); Rodriguez, "Pakistan Rejects U.S. Findings on Attack That Killed 24 Soldiers," LAT (12.23.11); Schmitt, "U.S. Report on Fatal Strike on Pakistani Soldiers Reveals Crucial NATO Delays," NYT (12.27.11); Schmitt, "Lull in Strikes by U.S. Drones Aids Militants in Pakistan," NYT (1.8.12); Schmitt, "3 Killed as Drone Strikes Resume in Pakistan," NYT (1.11.12); DeYoung & Brulliard, "As U.S.–Pakistani Relations Sink, Nations Try to Figure Out a 'New Normal,'" WP (1.17.12); Shane, "Drone Strike Kills Qaeda Operative in Pakistan, U.S. Says," NYT (1.20.12); Walsh, Schmitt & Mehsud, "Drones at Issue as U.S. Rebuilds Ties to Pakistan," NYT (3.19.12); Walsh, "Pakistani Parliament Demands End to U.S. Drone Strikes," NYT (3.20.12); Leiby & DeYoung, "Pakistan's Legislators Urged to Seek Halt to U.S. Drone Strikes," WP (3.20.12); "Officials: US and Pakistan Spy Chiefs Bargain over Future of CIA Drone Program," WP (3.27.12); Masood & Walsh, "Pakistan Gives U.S. a List of Demands, Including an End to C.I.A. Drone Strikes," NYT (4.13.12); Leiby, "Pakistan Calls for End to U.S. Drone Attacks," WP (4.13.12); Walsh, Schmitt & Myers, "United States Talks Fail as Pakistanis Seek Apology," NYT (4.27.12); Leiby & DeYoung, "U.S. Drone Strikes Resume in Pakistan: Action May Complicate Vital Negotiations," WP (4.30.12); Nazir, "PM Gilani Responds after Latest US Airstrike," AAJ News (5.1.12); "Officials: U.S. Drone Strike Kills 8 in Pakistan," NYT (5.5.12); Leiby, "CIA Drone Strikes in Pakistan Lead to Lawsuits over Civilian Deaths," WP (5.14.12); "Pakistan Says U.S. Drone Kills 10 Militants," AP/*USA Today* (5.24.12); Masood, "Drone Strikes Continue in Pakistan as Tension Increases and Senate

Panel Cuts Aid," NYT (5.25.12); Khan & Leiby, "U.S. Drone Strike Kills 10 Suspected Militants," WP (5.25.12); "Pakistan Officials: Missiles from US Drone Kill 4 Suspected Militants near Afghan Border," WP (5.27.12); Leiby, "Pakistan Spy Chief Puts Off Washington Visit amid Rift over Doctor's Treason Conviction," WP (5.29.12); Osborne, "It May Seem Painless, but Drone War in Afghanistan Is Destroying the West's Reputation," DT (5.30.12); Ignatius, "An Embassy Asks: Drones or Diplomacy?" WP (6.2.12).

221 Walsh, Schmitt & Mehsud, "Drones at Issue as U.S. Rebuilds Ties to Pakistan," NYT (3.19.12); Walsh, "Pakistani Parliament Demands End to U.S. Drone Strikes," NYT (3.20.12); Leiby & DeYoung, "Pakistan's Legislators Urged to Seek Halt to U.S. Drone Strikes," WP (3.20.12); "Taliban Threaten Pakistani Lawmakers Who Support Resumption of NATO Supplies to Afghanistan," WP (3.24.12); Schmitt, "U.S. Plans No Charges over Deadly Strike in Pakistan," NYT (3.24.12); Masood & Walsh, "U.S. and Pakistan Take Steps to Mend Relations," NYT (3.28.12); Bergen, "CIA Drone War in Pakistan in Sharp Decline," CNN (3.28.12); Walsh, "U.S. Offers $10 million Reward for Pakistani Militant," NYT (4.3.12); Masood, "Pakistani Lawmakers Criticize U.S. Reward for Militant Leader," NYT (3.6.12); Leiby, "Pakistani Militant Rallies Supporters, Defying U.S. Bounty," WP (4.6.12).

222 "Pakistani Foreign Minister Indicates Time Has Come to Reopen Afghan Border to NATO Supplies," WP (5.14.12); "NATO Invites Pakistani President to Summit after Foreign Minister Suggests Unblocking Afghan Supply Routes," WP (5.15.12); Leiby, "Many Will Profit If Pakistan Reopens NATO Supply Routes," WP (5.15.12); Leiby & DeYoung, "Pakistan Seeks $5,000 Transit Fee for Each NATO Container," WP (5.16.12); Cooper & Rosenberg, "Supply Lines Cast Shadow at NATO Meeting on Afghan War," NYT (5.20.12); Walsh, "Quiet Duo Forged Road Deal for U.S. and Pakistan," NYT (7.27.12).

223 "Pakistan Says U.S. Drone Kills 10 Militants," AP/*USA Today* (5.24.12); Masood, "Drone Strikes Continue in Pakistan as Tension Increases and Senate Panel Cuts Aid," NYT (5.25.12); Khan & Leiby, "U.S. Drone Strike in Pakistan Kills 10 Suspected Militants," WP (5.25.12); "Pakistan Officials: Missiles from U.S. Drone Kill 4 Suspected Militants near Afghan Border," WP (5.27.12); Schmitt, "U.S. Liaisons Are Restored to Outpost in Pakistan," NYT (6.1.12); "U.S. Drone Strike Kills 15 in Northwest Pakistan: Officials," Reuters (6.4.12); Walsh & Schmitt, "Qaeda Deputy Targeted in Drone Strike in Pakistan," NYT (6.4.12); "U.S. Drone Strike Kills 15 in Northwest Pakistan: Officials," Reuters (6.4.12); Walsh & Schmitt, "Qaeda Deputy Targeted in Drone Strike in Pakistan," NYT (6.4.12); "Drones Away," WSJ (6.5.12); "A Killer Killed," *New York Daily News* (6.6.12); Warrick & Miller, "Al-Qaeda's No. 2 Leader Killed in U.S. Airstrike," WP (6.5.12); "Drones Away," WSJ (6.7.12); Yoo, "Obama, Drones and Thomas Aquinas," WSJ (6.7.12); "Pakistan Summons Senior US Diplomat to Protest Recent Drone Strikes," WP (8.23.12); "Pakistan: US Drone-fired Missiles Slam into

Hideouts, Kill 18 Suspected Militants," WP (8.24.12); Entous, Gorman & Perez, "U.S. Unease over Drone Strikes," WSJ (9.27.12); "Pakistan Foreign Minister 'Embarrassed' by Riots, but Calls for Understanding," Asia Society (9.27.12); Haider & Iqbal, "Pakistan Endorses Drones, Rejects Method; Khar," *Dawn* (9.27.12); Leiby, "Pakistani Politician Plans Drone Protest in Off-Limits Tribal Area," WP (10.5.2); Temple-Raston, "U.S. Drones Navigate Murky Legal Path in Pakistan," NPR (10.6.12); Masood, "Americans Join Pakistan Convoy to Protest Drone Strikes," NYT (10.7.12); "Pakistani Military Blocks Convoy from Entering Tribal Region to Protest US Drone Strikes," WP (10.7.12); Masood, "In Pakistan, Drone Protest Takes Detour for Safety," NYT (10.8.12); Gul, "Pakistan Unhappy over Reports US Drone Strikes Will Continue," VOA (1.22.13).

224 Zenko, "How Many Civilians Are Killed by U.S. Drones?" CFR (6.4.12); Harris, "Drone Attacks Create Terrorist Safe Havens, Warns Former CIA Official," G (6.5.12); see generally Bergan & Tiedemann, "The Year of the Drone: An Analysis of U.S. Drone Strikes in Pakistan, 2004–2010," New America Foundation (2.24.10); "The Year of the Drone: An Analysis of U.S. Drone Strikes in Pakistan, 2004–2011," New American Foundation (2.22.11); "Drone Strikes: Pakistan" www.newamerica.org/in-depth/americas-counterterrorism-wars/pakistan/ (last accessed February 20, 2018).

225 "U.S. Defense Secretary Panetta Says U.S. 'Reaching the Limits of Our Patience' with Pakistan," WP (6.7.12); "Allies or Enemies? U.S.–Pakistan Relationship Becomes Increasingly Adversarial," WP (6.9.12); Walsh, "Notions of Honor Color High-Stakes Haggling over NATO Supply Routes," NYT (6.8.12); Schmitt & Walsh, "U.S. Takes Step toward Exit in Pakistan Talks," NYT (6.11.12); DeYoung, "Pakistan Border Closure Costs U.S. $100 Million a Month," WP (6.13.12); Ignatius, "An Embassy Asks: Drones or Diplomacy?" WP (6.21.12); Schmitt, "U.S. and Pakistan Hint at Deal to Reopen NATO Supply Routes," NYT (7.3.12); Schmitt, "Clinton's 'Sorry' to Pakistan Ends Barrier to NATO," NYT (7.4.12); DeYoung & Leiby, "Pakistan Agrees to Open Supply Lines after U.S. Apology," WP (7.4.12); Masood, "NATO Supply Trucks from Pakistan Resume Trek to Afghanistan," NYT (7.5.12); "Détente on Supply Routes," NYT (7.6.12); "Thousands of Hardline Islamists Stream to Pakistan's Capital to Protest NATO Supply Line," NYT (7.8.12); Munoz, "Pakistan Reopens Supply Routes after Rare Apology from Clinton for NATO Airstrike," *The Hill* (7.13.12); Walsh, "Quiet Duo Forged Road Deal for U.S. and Pakistan," NYT (7.27.12); Leiby, "U.S., Pakistan Sign Deal to Allow Supply Routes through 2015," WP (7.31.12).

226 Walsh & Khan, "Uzbek Group Says Drone Killed Leader," NYT (8.5.12); "Pakistan Summons Senior U.S. Diplomat to Protest Recent Drone Strikes," WP (8.23.12); "Pakistan: US Drone-fired Missiles Slam into Hideouts, Kill 18 Suspected Militants," WP (8.24.12); Entous, Gorman & Perez, "U.S. Unease over Drone Strikes," WSJ

(9.27.12); "Pakistan Foreign Minister Khar 'Embarrassed' by Riots, but Calls for Understanding," Asia Society (9.27.12); Haider & Iqbal, "Pakistan Endorses Drones, Rejects Method: Khar," *Dawn* (9.27.12); Leiby, "Pakistani Politician Plans Drone Protest in Off-Limits Tribal Area," WP (10.5.12); Boone, "U.S. Women May Stage Hunger Strike in Pakistan in Anti-drones Protest," G (10.3.12); Temple-Raston, "U.S. Drones Navigate Murky Legal Path in Pakistan," NPR (10.6.12); Masood, "Americans Join Pakistan Convoy to Protest Drone Strikes," NYT (10.7.12); "Pakistani Military Blocks Convoy from Entering Tribal Region to Protest Drone Strikes," WP (10.7.12); Masood, "In Pakistan, Drone Protest Takes Detour for Safety," NYT (10.8.12); International Human Rights and Conflict Resolution Clinic and Global Justice Clinic (2012).

227 "Drones Violate Sovereignty, Pakistan Tells UN," *Pakistan Tribune* (10.31.12); Walsh, "U.S. Disavows 2 Drone Strikes over Pakistan," NYT (3.5.13); Walsh, "Pakistan Rejects U.S. Disavowal of Drone Strikes," NYT (3.6.13); Khan & Walsh, "Drone Strike Reported in Pakistan," NYT (3.10.13); Landay, "U.S. Secret: CIA Collaborated with Pakistani Spy Agency in Drone War," McClatchy (4.9.13); Robertson & Botelho, "Ex-Pakistani President Musharraf Admits Secret Deal with U.S. on Drone Strikes," CNN (4.12.13).

228 "Drone Strikes Illegal, Whether Consented To or Not, Says Senior Pakistani Judge," Reprieve (4.11.13); Buncombe, "Pakistani Court Declares U.S. Drone Strikes in the Country's Tribal Belt Illegal," I (5.9.13); Akbar, "Obama's Forgotten Victims," NYT (5.23.13); AI (2013a).

229 Shane, "Debate Aside, Number of Drone Strikes Drops Sharply," NYT (5.22.13); Masood & Walsh, "Pakistan's New Prime Minister Calls for End to Drone Strikes," NYT (6.5.13); Craig, "Seven Killed in Suspected U.S. Drone Strike in Pakistan," WP (6.8.13); Masood, "U.S. Drone Strike Kills At Least 7 in Pakistan as New Prime Minister Announces Cabinet," NYT (6.8.13); Craig, "Seven Killed in Suspected U.S. Drone Strike in Pakistan," WP (6.8.13); Craig, "Pakistan Summons U.S. Embassy Officials over Drone Strikes," WP (6.9.13); "PTI Submits Anti-drone Resolution in Punjab Assembly," *Dawn* (6.10.13); Wasim, "PTI Wants Use of Force to End Drone Attacks," *Dawn* (6.11.13); Trofimov, "Karzai Condemns U.S. Drone Strikes in Pakistan," WSJ (6.16.13); Haider, "Pakistan Needs to Convince U.S. about Futility of Drone Attacks: Envoy," *Dawn* (7.20.13); Gordon, "Kerry in Pakistan, Expresses Optimism on Ending Drone Strikes Soon," NYT (9.2.13); Masood, "U.S. Drone Strike Kills 6 in Pakistan, Fueling Anger," NYT (9.6.13); Walsh & Khan, "U.S. Drone Strike Kills 6 in Pakistan, Fueling Anger," NYT (9.6.13); Khan & Masood, "A Deadly Week in Northwestern Pakistan Ends with a Car Bomb Blast," NYT (9.30.13); Mehsud, "Suspected Drone Strike Kills 4 in Pakistan," NYT (10.1.13); Rucker, "Malala Yousafzai Meets with the Obamas in the Oval Office," WP (10.12.13); Shanker, "Aid to Pakistan to Resume as Tension with U.S. Eases," NYT (10.19.13).

230 Miller & Woodward, "Secret Memos Reveal Explicit Nature of U.S., Pakistan Agreement on Drones," WP (10.23.13); Joint Statement by President Obama and Prime Minister Nawaz Sharif, White House (10.23.13); Craig, "Pakistan's Gilani Acknowledges Possibility of Contact with U.S. over Planned Drone Strikes," WP (10.24.13); "3 Dead in First U.S. Drone Strike in Pakistan since Leaders Met," CNN (10.31.13); Craig & Khan, "Pakistani Political Leader Says NATO Supply Routes Will Be Cut If U.S. Drone Strikes Continue," WP (11.1.13); Walsh, Mehsud & Khan, "Drone Strikes Are Said to Kill Taliban Chief," NYT (11.2.13); Craig, "Pakistani Officials Rebuke U.S. for Drone Strike," WP (11.13.13); Walsh, "In Pakistan, Drone Strike Turns a Villain into a Victim," NYT (11.4.13); "National Assembly Proceedings: PTI, JI Urge Government to Shoot Down Drones," *Express Tribune* (11.7.13); Iqbal, "Baitullah Targeted on Pakistan's Request: Husain Haqqani," *Dawn* (11.8.13); "No More Drone Strikes during Taliban Talks, U.S. Assures Pakistan," *Dawn* (11.20.13); "Khan & Masood, "Drone Strike Reported Outside Pakistan's Tribal Region," NYT (11.21.13); Khan & Craig, "Suspected U.S. Drone Hits Islamic Seminar in Pakistan, Killing Six," WP (11.21.13); "Pakistani Drone Protesters Block NATO Supplies," WP (11.23.13); "Pakistani Police Stop NATO Supply Truck Blockade," WP (11.25.13); Walsh, "Party Claims It Identified Top C.I.A. Spy in Pakistan," NYT (11.28.13); "Pakistan: U.S. Shuts Cargo Routes from Afghanistan over Drone Protests," NYT (12.4.13); Baloch, "NATO Containers Attacked in Balochistan," *Express Tribune* (12.8.13); "NATO Countries Request Reopening of Supply Routes, Imran Refuses," *Express Tribune* (12.9.13); Nabi, "U.S. Drone Targets Boat on Pakistan–Afghan Border, 7 Dead," *The Nation* (Pakistan) (12.15.13); "Pakistan Protests May Make U.Ss. Fly War Cargo Out," *Dawn* (12.19.13); Craig, "Imran Khan, a Pakistani Provincial Leader, Complicates NATO Plans for Afghanistan," WP (1.5.14); Craig, "Pakistan Party Drops Its Blockade of NATO Supply Routes," WP (2.27.14); DeYoung & Miller, "U.S. Said to Curtail Drone Strikes in Pakistan as Officials There Seek Peace Talks with Taliban," WP (2.5.14); Entous & Gorman, "U.S. to Curb Pakistan Drone Program," WSJ (2.5.14); "Pakistan Had Asked U.S. to Halt Drone Strikes, Foreign Office Says," *Express Tribune* (2.6.14).

231 Engel & Windrem, "CIA Didn't Always Know Who It Was Killing in Drone Strikes, Classified Documents Show," NBC News (6.6.13); Gordis, "Leaked Pakistani Document Exposes Civilian, Child Casualties of Drone War," Huffpost (7.23.13); Zaidi, "Drones Killed 67 Civilians in Five Years: Pakistan," *Dawn* (10.30.13); "The Numbers At Last: Drone Deaths," *Dawn* (11.1.13); Noorani, "Defence Ministry Admits Sending Wrong Drone Figures to Prime Minister," *The News* (11.6.13); "U.S. Drones Killed No More than Four Civilians in Pakistan in 2013: Study," Reuters (1.21.14); Ross, "Drone Strikes in Pakistan: Leaked Pakistan Document Contradicts U.S. Accounts of Drone Strikes," Bureau of

Investigative Journalism (1.31.14); Report of the Special Rapporteur on the Promotion and Protection of Human Rights and Fundamental Freedoms While Countering Terrorism, Ben Emmerson (2.28.14); Ross & Serie, "Drone Strike in Pakistan," Bureau of Investigative Journalism (5.23.14).

232 Sherazi, "Drone Kills Ten Suspected Militants on Pakistan–Afghan Border," *Dawn* (5.14.14); Khan & Walsh, "Missile Strike by C.I.A. Drone Kills At Least 4, Pakistan Reports," NYT (6.12.14); Sherazi, "Successive Drone Strikes Leave At Least 16 Dead in North Waziristan," *Dawn* (6.12.14); Haider, "Pakistan Condemns U.S. Drone Strikes in North Waziristan," *Dawn* (6.12.14); "Airstrikes in Northwest Pakistan Kill about 100 Militants," NYT (6.15.14); Khan & Walsh, "Drones Kill 5 as Pakistan and U.S. Target Tribal Belt," NYT (6.18.14); Khan, "15 Militants Are Reported Killed in U.S. Drone Strike in Pakistan," NYT (7.19.14); Hussain, "Pakistan, U.S. Appear Once Again to Be Cooperating on Drone Strikes," *Stars and Stripes* (10.14.14); Khan, "American Drone Strike Kills 6 in Pakistani Tribal Area," NYT (10.31.14); "Drone Kills Six Foreign Militants in North Waziristan," *Dawn* (11.12.14); Nasruminallah, "Drone Strike Leaves 7 Dead, Including Foreigners," *Express Tribune* (1.29.15); Masood, "Pakistani Court Orders Ex-C.I.A. Officials Charged over 2009 Drone Strike," NYT (4.8.15); "Pakistan Drops Case against Ex-CIA Chief, Agency's Lawyer," WP (4.30.15); Leopold, "Pakistan Is Investigating a CIA Official Accused of Murder after a U.S. Drone Strike," Vice News (4.30.15).

233 "Pakistan Says U.S. Drone Strike That Killed Taliban Leader Violated Its Sovereignty," G (5.22.16); Landler & Rosenberg, "U.S. Strike on Taliban Leader Is Seen as a Message to Pakistan," NYT (5.23.16); "What Happens after the Drone Strike?" NYT (5.25.16); Craig & Miller, "U.S. Airstrike against Taliban Leader Crossed a Pakistani 'Red Line,'" WP (5.23.16); Shah & Nauman, "Pakistan Says U.S. Airstrike Saturday Violated International Law," WSJ (5.24.16); Masood, "Pakistan Finally Confirms Taliban Leader's Death in U.S. Strike," NYT (5.26.16); Haider, "Future Drone Strikes Will Be Detrimental to Ties, Aziz Tells U.S. Delegation," *Dawn* (6.9.16).

234 For an understanding of how Yemeni politics shaped the response to drone strikes, see Johnsen (2013).

235 Meyer, "CIA Expands Use of Drones in Terror War," LAT A1 (1.29.06).

236 Ross, Esposito, Cole, Martinez & Radia, "Obama Ordered U.S. Military Strike on Yemen Terrorists, Administration Told," ABC News (12.18.09); Shanker & Landler, "U.S. Aids Yemen in Strikes on al Qaeda, Officials Say," NYT (12.19.09); Raghavan, "Yemeni Air Strike May Have Killed Cleric Linked to Ft Hood Attack," WP (12.24.09); Miller, "Yemen Airstrikes Hit Suspected al Qaeda Members," LAT (12.25.09); Healy & Shane, "Yemen Says It Attacked a Meeting of al Qaeda," NYT (12.25.09); Schmitt & Worth, "U.S. Widens Terror War to Yemen, al Qaeda Bastion," NYT (12.28.09); Raghavan, "al-Qaeda

Benefits from a Decade of Missteps to Become a Threat in Yemen," WP (1.3.10); Daragahi, "Yemen Dismisses al Qaeda Threat as 'Exaggerated,'" LAT (1.4.10); Raghavan, "Yemeni Officials, Fearing Backlash, Play Down Partnership with U.S.," WP (1.5.10); Shane, Mazzetti & Worth," A Secret Assault on Terror Widens on Two Continents," NYT (8.15.10); Cloud, "White House Considers Yemen Drone Strikes, Officials Say," LAT (11.8.10); Woods (2015: 195–97).

237 Shane, "Yemen Sets the Terms of a War on al Qaeda," NYT (12.4.10); Mazzetti, Savage & Shane, "How a U.S. Citizen Came to Be in America's Cross Hairs," NYT (3.10.13).

238 Raghavan, "In Yemen, U.S. Airstrikes Breed Anger, and Sympathy for al-Qaeda," WP (5.30.12); Mardell, "Is Obama's Drone Doctrine Counter-productive?" BBC News (5.30.12); Kelley, "Obama's Drone War in Yemen May Be al Qaeda's Best Recruitment Tool Ever," Business Insider (5.30.12); Miller, "U.S. Drone Targets in Yemen Raise Questions," WP (6.2.12); Harris, "Drone Attacks Create Terrorist Safe Havens, Warns Former CIA Official," G (6.5.12); Mothana, "How Drones Help al Qaeda," NYT (6.13.12); Morley, "Hatred: What the Drones Sow," Salon.com (6.12.12); Almasmari, "Suspected U.S. Drone Strike Kills Civilians in Yemen, Officials Say," CNN (9.3.12); Miller, "In Interview, Yemeni President Acknowledges Approving U.S. Drone Strikes," WP (9.29.12); Johnsen, "The Wrong Man for the C.I.A.," NYT (11.20.12); Raghavan, "When U.S. Drones Kill Civilians, Yemen's Government Tries to Conceal It," WP (12.15.12); Raghavan, "In Yemen, U.S. Airstrikes Breed Anger, and Sympathy for al-Qaeda," WP (5.30.12); McEvers, "Reporting from Yemen amid Ongoing Drone Attacks," NPR (7.9.12); Almasmari, "Suspected U.S. Drone Strike Kills Civilians in Yemen, Officials Say," CNN (9.3.12); Miller, "In Interview, Yemeni President Acknowledges Approving U.S. Drone Strikes," WP (9.29.12); Johnsen, "The Wrong Man for the C.I.A.," NYT (11.20.12); Raghavan, "When U.S. Drones Kill Civilians, Yemen's Government Tries to Conceal It," WP (12.15.12); Worth, Mazzetti & Shane, "Drone Strike's Dangers Get Rare Moment in the Public Eye," NYT (2.6.13); "U.S. Drone Strike Kills Two 'al-Qaeda Militants' in Yemen," al Arabiya (5.20.13); Shane, "Debate Aside, Number of Drone Strikes Drops Sharply," NYT (5.22.13).

239 Knuckey, "The U.S. Just Killed a Boy in Yemen: Will Obama Respond?" *Esquire* (6.22.13); "Every Yemen Drone Strike Creates 40 to 60 New Enemies, Former U.S. Official Says," Huffpost (10.24.13); HRW (2013); Isikoff & Sears, "Yemeni Tells White House of U.S. Drone Strike That He Says Killed Innocent Kin," NBC News (11.21.13); Worth & Shane, "Questions on Drone Find Only Silence," NYT (11.23.13); Hayoun, "U.S. Paid Family of Yemen Drone-Strike Victim $100,000, Rights Group Says," Al Jazeera America (11.11.14).

240 "U.S. Drone Strike Hits Convoy Headed To Wedding Party in Yemen, Killing At Least 13, Officials Say," G (12.12.13); Worth, "Drone Strike in Yemen Hits Wedding Convoy, Killing 11," NYT (12.12.13); "Yemen Says Airstrike Targeted al-Qaeda Militants," WP (12.14.13); Yemen

Parliament Bans Drone Attacks," AFP (12.15.13); Mazzetti & Worth, "Yemen Deaths Test Claims of New Drone Policy," NYT (12.21.13); Isikoff, "U.S. Investigates Yemenis' Charge That Drone Strike 'Turned Wedding into a Funeral,'" NBC News (1.7.14); Mashhour, "The United States' Bloody Messes in Yemen," WP (1.14.14); Miller, "Lawmakers Seek to Stymie Plan to Shift Control of Drone Campaign from CIA to Pentagon," WP (1.16.14); Dilanian, "Debate Grows over Proposal for CIA to Turn Over Drones to Pentagon," LAT (5.11.14); Miller, "Yemeni Victims of U.S. Military Drone Strike Get More than $1 Million in Compensation," WP (8.18.14); Woods (2015: 191–93); HRW (2014); Miller, "Deadly Drone Strike in Yemen Failed to Comply with Obama's Rules to Protect Civilians," WP (2.19.14); Al Batati & Kirkpatrick, "Qaeda Affiliate Steps Up Video Propaganda Push," NYT (5.13.14); "U.S. Drones Killed No More Than Four Civilians in Pakistan in 2013: Study," Reuters (1.21.14); Open Society Justice Institute (2015).

241 Almosawa & Nordland, "Renewed Fighting and Drone Strikes in Yemen Kill about 75," NYT (1.23.17); Schmitt, "U.S. Commando Killed in Yemen in Trump's First Counterterrorism Operation," NYT (1.30.17); Schmitt, "Women Killed in Yemen Raid Were Qaeda Fighters, Pentagon Says," NYT (1.31.17); Schmitt & Sanger, "Raid in Yemen: Risky from the Start and Costly in the End," NYT (2.2.17); Schmitt, "White House Defends Command Raid on Qaeda Branch in Yemen," NYT (2.3.17); Fordham & Bowman, "Yemen Aftermath: Trump's First Military Raid Continues to Raise Questions," NPR (2.2.17); "Yemen al Qaeda Leader Says U.S. Raid on Yemen a Blow to Trump," NYT (2.5.17); Sanger & Schmitt, "Yemen Withdraws Permission for U.S. Antiterror Ground Missions," NYT (2.8.17); Gibbons-Neff, "Yemen Reviews Deadly U.S. Raid on al-Qaeda but Stops Short of Issuing Ban," WP (2.8.17); Schmitt, "Yemen Backtracks on Suspending U.S. Raids after Civilian Casualties," NYT (2.9.17); "Rights Group Urges U.S. to Probe Civilian Deaths in Yemen Raid," WP (2.24.17); "Lingering Questions in the Yemen Raid," NYT (2.28.17); Savage & Schmitt, "Trump Administration Is Said to Be Working to Loosen Counterterrorism Rules," NYT (3.13.17).

242 See Grey (2007).

243 ECCHR (2009: 68–73).

244 Ibid. (75–79); Grey (2007: Chap. 3).

245 "Judge Says Agents of West Took Egyptian," LAT (5.20.05); Grey & Van Natta, "Thirteen with the C.I.A. Sought by Italy in a Kidnapping," NYT (6.25.05); Grey & Van Natta, "In Italy, Anger at U.S. Tactics Colors Spy Case," NYT (6.26.05); Whitlock, "Italians Detail Lavish CIA Operation," WP (6.26.05); Liptak, "Experts Doubt C.I.A. Operatives Will Stand Trial in Italy," NYT (6.26.05); Fisher, "Milan Mystery: Did Italy Have Role in Kidnapping Case?" NYT (6.29.05); Priest, "Italy Knew About Plan to Grab Suspect," WP (6.30.05); Wilkinson & Miller, "Italy Says It Didn't Know of CIA Plan," LAT (7.1.05); Fisher & Jehl, "Italy Denies Any Role in Seizure of Terror Suspect," NYT (7.1.05); Whitlock, "Italy Denies Complicity in Alleged CIA Action," WP (7.1.05); Povoledo, "Italian

Leader Chastises U.S. in Kidnapping Case in Milan," NYT (7.2.05); "Italy Prosecutor Seeks Arrest Warrants," NYT (7.20.05); Wilkinson, "Italians Issue Six New CIA Warrants," LAT (7.26.05); Wilkinson, "Italy Seeks Former U.S. Diplomat in Kidnapping," LAT (9.30.05); "Debating Rendition Tactics," PBS NewsHour (12.5.05); Whitlock, "CIA Ruse Is Said to Have Damaged Probe in Milan," WP (12.6.05); "EU Arrest Warrant Issued for 22 CIA Operatives," Reuters (12.23.05); Whitlock, "Italy's Pursuit of CIA Operatives Stalls," LAT (12.30.05); Olimpio (2005); ECCHR (2009: 80–86); Grey (2007: Chap. 9); Jenks & Jensen (2010).

246 Kleine-Brockhoff, "Die CIA hat das Recht, jades Gesetz zu brechen," *Die Zeit* (12.28.05) (trans. Ralf Kanitz).

247 Kiefer, "Italian Minister Declines to Seek Extradition of C.I.A. Operatives," NYT (4.13.06); Williams, "Italy Probes Agency's Link to CIA in Cleric's Abduction," WP (5.12.06); Whitlock, "Prosecutors: Italian Agency Helped CIA Seize Cleric," WP (7.6.06); "Italy Issues Arrest Warrants for 3 CIA Officers in 'Rendition' Case," LAT (7.6.06); Grey & Povoledo, "Italy Arrests 2 in Kidnapping of Imam in '03," NYT (7.6.06); Wilkinson, "Italian Probe Broadens Beyond Abduction," LAT (7.6.06); Grey & Povoledo, "Inquiry in 2003 Abduction Rivets Italy," NYT (7.8.06); "Intelligence Chief Questioned in Italy," LAT (7.16.06); "Italian Denies C.I.A. Link," NYT (8.7.06); Fisher & Povoledo, "Italy's Top Spy Is Expected to Be Indicted in Abduction Case," NYT (10.24.06); Povoledo, "Egyptian Says He Was Tortured after Being Kidnapped in Milan," NYT (11.1.06); "Italy: Top Intelligence Chiefs Removed," NYT (11.21.06); Wilkinson, "Italy's Spy Chief Ousted over CIA Kidnap Case," LAT (11.21.06); Fisher & Povoledo, "Italy Seeks Indictments of C.I.A. Operatives in Egyptian's Abduction," NYT (12.6.06); Crewdson, "Cleric's Story of Abduction and Torture," CT (1.7.07); Crewdson, "Wife: Cleric Offered $2 Million Deal," CT (1.7.07); "This Is How They Kidnapped Me from Italy," CT (1.7.07).

248 Whitlock, "Testimony Helps Detail CIA's Post-9/11 Reach," WP (12.16.06); Crewdson, "Italy Says CIA May Have Had Distorted View of Cleric," CT (1.7.07); Wilkinson, "Details Emerge in Cleric's Abduction," LAT (1.10.07); "Ex-Spy in Italy Denies Illegal Role," LAT (1.30.07); Fisher & Povoledo, "Italy Braces for Legal Fight over Secret C.I.A. Program," NYT (6.8.07).

249 Nasrawi, "Abducted Egyptian Cleric Released," CT (2.12.07); "Egypt Releases Cleric Allegedly Seized by CIA," LAT (2.12.07); Boustany, "Freed Cleric Is Planning Lawsuit," WP (2.13.07); Barry, "31 to Stand Trial in CIA Kidnapping Case," WP (2.16.07); Wilkinson & De Cristoforo, "Italy Indicts CIA Agents in Kidnapping," LAT (2.17.07); Fisher, "Italy Indicts 26, Many from C.I.A., in '03 Abduction," NYT (2.17.07); Delaney & Whitlock, "Milan Court Indicts 26 Americans in Abduction," WP (2.17.07); Whitlock, "U.S. Won't Send CIA. Defendants to Italy," WP (3.1.07); "Italy: U.S. Will Not Hand over C.I.A. Suspects," NYT (3.1.07).

250 Wilkinson, "In Italy, Trial of CIA Agents Begins," LAT (6.9.07); Fisher, "Italy Prosecutes C.I.A. Agents in Kidnapping," NYT (6.9.07); Povoledo, "Kidnapping Trial of C.I.A. Agents Is Suspended by Judge in Italy," NYT (6.19.07); Wilkinson, "CIA Agents' Rendition Trial on Hold," LAT (6.19.07); "Berlusconi to Testify in C.I.A. Case," AP (5.14.08); Rosenthal, "Italian Trial of C.I.A. Operatives Begins with Torture Testimony," NYT (5.15.08); Wilkinson, "Veiled Testimony at Trial," LAT (5.15.08); Wilkinson, "Italy Officer Tells of Spying on Spies in Cleric's Kidnapping," LAT (5.29.08); Povoledo, "Italian Investigator Says U.S. Agents Left Obvious Clues in Abduction Cases," NYT (5.29.08); Whitlock, "Computer Files Hold Key in CIA Case," WP (6.26.08); Donadio, "Italian Court Upends Trial Involving C.I.A. Links," NYT (3.12.09); Rotella & De Cristoforo, "Italian Court Rules against Prosecution in CIA Case," LAT (3.13.09).

251 Rotella, "Two Nations, 33 Spies and One Egyptian Extremist," LAT (5.20.09); "Italy: A Denial in C.I.A. Rendition Trial," NYT (5.28.09); Stewart, "U.S. Spy Says Just Followed Orders in Italy Kidnap," Reuters (6.30.09); "U.S. Spy in in Rendition Trial: 'I Followed Orders,'" AP (6.30.09).

252 Barry, "Prison Sought for 26 Americans in CIA Case," AP (9.30.09); Barry, "Cleric in CIA Kidnap Trial Seeks Millions," AP (10.6.09); Barry, "Lawyers in CIA Trial in Italy Argue for Diplomatic Immunity for U.S. Defendants," AP (10.15.09); Donadio, "Italy Convicts 23 Americans in C.I.A. Trials," NYT (11.5.09); De Cristofaro & Rotella, "Italy Judge Convicts 23 Americans in 2003 CIA Kidnapping of Egyptian Cleric," LAT (11.5.09); "Italy Got It Right: CIA Renditions Are Wrong," LAT (11.6.09); "A National Disgrace," NYT (11.11.09); AI (2010: 20).

253 Donadio, "Judge Links Italy Agency to Abduction of a Cleric," NYT (2.2.10); Bigo et al. (2015: 44–45).

254 Malkin, "Ex-Employee of C.I.A. Held in Abduction," NYT (7.19.13); Miller & DeYoung, "Panama Releases Former CIA Operative Wanted by Italy," WP (7.19.13); Shane, "Panama: Former Spy Returns to U.S.," NYT (7.20.13); "Ex-CIA Chief Seeks Italy Pardon for Egypt Rendition," BBC News (9.12.13).

255 Shapira, "Ex-CIA Officer Wanted in Italy Waits to Learn after Detention in Portugal," WP (10.8.15); Hatton, "Portuguese Court Rules to Extradite Ex-CIA Agent to Italy," AP (1.15.16); "Portuguese Court Rejects Ex-CIA Agent's Extradition Appeal," NYT (4.11.16); Minder, "Portuguese Supreme Court Upholds Extradition of C.I.A. Agent to Italy," NYT (4.11.16); "A Court Official Says a Former CIA Operative Has Lodged an Appeal at Portugal's Constitutional Court against Her Extradition to Italy," US News (4.11.16); Shapira, "Ex-CIA Officer Faces Extradition from Portugal to Italy for Alleged Role in Cleric's Rendition," WP (4.21.16); Povoledo, "Portugal Clears the Way for Extradition of Ex-C.I.A. Agent to Italy," NYT (4.23.16); "Ex-CIA Agent Appeal Fails, Faces Extradition to Italy," Reuters (6.8.16); Povoledo, "Italy

Reduces Sentence for Ex-C.I.A. Officer Sought in Rendition Case," NYT (2.28.17); Barry, "Former CIA Agent to Do Community Service for Cleric Kidnap," AP (11.7.17).

256 "Italy Reactivates Case against Kidnapped Imam," WP (11.23.13); "Milan Court Convicts Egyptian of Terror Charges," WP (12.6.13); "Court Tosses out Convictions of Five Italians in CIA Rendition Case," AP (2.24.14); "Italy Upholds Last U.S. Convictions in Rendition," WP (3.11.14); "European Court Condemns Italy for Role in 2003 Kidnap of Refugee Imam," Reuters (2.23.16).

257 Fleishman, "Man's Claim May Be a Look at Dark Side of War on Terror," LAT (4.12.05); Johnston, "Rice Ordered Release of German Sent to Afghan Prison in Error," NYT (4.23.05); "German Man to File Suit over U.S. 'Kidnapping,'" ABC News (11.9.05); Priest, "Wrongful Imprisonment: Anatomy of a CIA Mistake," WP (12.3.05); Shane, "German Held in Afghan Jail Files Lawsuit," NYT (12.7.05); Kessler, "Rice to Admit German's Abduction Was an Error," WP (12.7.05); Brinkley, "Rice Is Challenged in Europe over Secret Prisons," NYT (12.7.05); Mekhennet, "A German Man Held Captive in the CIA's Secret Prisons Gives First Interview in 8 Years," WP (9.16.15); ECCHR (2009: 107–13); Grey (2007: Chap. 4).

258 Van Natta, "Germany Weighs If It Played Role in Seizure by U.S.," NYT (2.21.06); "Germany: Spying Investigation Approved," NYT (4.8.06).

259 Mekhennet & Smith, "German Spy Agency Admits Mishandling Abduction Case," NYT (6.2.06); Fleishman, "Germany Is Urged to Ban CIA Agents Accused of Kidnapping," LAT (10.12.06); Fleishman & Goetz, "Germany May Indict U.S. Agents in Abduction," LAT (1.31.07); Landler, "German Court Challenges C.I.A. over Abduction," NYT (2.1.07); Fleishman, "Germany Seeks Arrest of U.S. Agents," LAT (2.1.07); Whitlock, "Germans Charge 13 Operatives," WP (2.1.07); "No More Renditions," OLAT (2.2.07); Whitlock, "In Another CIA Abduction, Germany Has an Uneasy Role," WP (2.5.07); Drogin & Goetz, "Pilots Traced to CIA Renditions," LAT (2.18.07).

260 Whitlock, "Germans Drop Bid for Extraditions in CIA Case," WP (9.24.07); "Lawsuit Demands German Government Pursue Extradition of CIA Agents," AP (6.9.08); OSI Press Release (10.14.10); Slackman, "Officials Pressed Germans on Kidnapping by C.I.A.," NYT (12.9.10); Gebauer & Goetz, "Cables Show Germany Caved to Pressure from Washington," *Der Spiegel* (12.9.10); "Germany: Court Rejects Lawsuit Related to a C.I.A. Kidnapping," NYT (12.11.10); Open Society Justice Initiative Press Release (2.7.12); "Court Rules German Citizen Was Victim of US Rendition, Torture," WP (12.13.12); Kulish, "Court Finds Rights Violations in C.I.A. Rendition Case," NYT (12.14.12).

261 *El-Masri* v. *Former Yugoslav Republic of Macedonia*, ECHR (12.13.12).

262 Dakwar, "New CIA Torture Documents Confirm Chilling Details of Khaled el-Masri's 'Kafka-esque' ordeal," ACLU (6.17.16); CHRGJ (2007).

263 Priest, "CIA Holds Terror Suspects in Secret Prisons," WP (11.2.05); Priest & White, "Policies on Terrorism Suspects Come under Fire," WP (11.3.05); Bush press conference (11.7.05) www.whitehouse.gov/news/releases/2005/11/20051107.html (last accessed December 1, 2005); Johnston & Hulse, "C.I.A. Asks Criminal Inquiry over Secret-Prison Article," NYT (11.9.05); Weisman, "GOP Leaders Urged Probe in Prisons Leak," WP (11.9.05); "Frist, Hastert Consider Prison Leak Probe," AP (11.9.05); "Senator Tells CNN He Believes Republican Leaked Info on CIA Jails," Raw Story (11.9.05); Weisman, "Senator Seeks to Defer Probe of CIA Prison Leak," WP (11.10.05); "Blaming the Messenger," NYT (11.10.05); BBC News (11.23.05); Ames, "E.U. May Suspend Nations with Secret Prisons," WP (11.28.05); Mascolo, Schlamp & Stark, "The Hunt for Hercules N8183J," *Der Spiegel* (11.29.05); Fisher, "Reports of Secret U.S. Prisons in Europe Draw Ire and Otherwise Red Faces," NYT (12.1.05); Brown & Buncombe, "Blair Faces Allegations of Complicity in Torture," I (12.2.05); Cobain, Gray & Norton-Taylor, "Britain's Role in War on Terror Revealed," G (12.6.05); Heritage, "European Watchdog Slams U.S. over CIA Secret Prisons," Reuters (12.13.05); Keaten, "Investigator: U.S. Shipped out Detainees," AP (12.13.05); Bennhold, "Kidnapping Study Tends to Fault U.S. Agents," NYT (12.14.05); Whitlock, "Investigator Sees Signs of CIA Role in Abductions," WP (12.14.05); "EU Lawmakers Agree [to] Set Up CIA Prisons Inquiry," NYT (12.15.05); "Switzerland: CIA Accused of Violating International Law," LAT (1.14.06); "Europe 'Complicit over CIA Jails," BBC News (1.14.06); Smith, "Europe's C.I.A. Inquiry Finds No Evidence of Secret Prisons," NYT (1.25.06); Rotella, "Covert Activity by U.S. Called No Big Secret," LAT (1.25.06); Council of Europe Parliamentary Assembly, Committee on Legal Affairs and Human Rights, Secret Detentions and Illegal Transfers of Detainees Involving Council of Europe Member States (Second Report) (6.11.07); TDIP, Report on the Alleged Use of European Countries by the CIA for the Transportation and Illegal Detention of Prisoners (6.20.07); AI (2010).

264 CE, "Alleged Secret Detentions and Unlawful Inter-state Transfers Involving Council of Europe Member States" (2006); CE, "Secret Detentions and Illegal Transfers of Detainees, Involving Council of Europe Member States (2007); CE, "Abuse of State Secrecy and National Security Obstacles to Parliamentary and Judicial Scrutiny of Human Rights Violations" (2011).

265 Harper, "Ghost Flights over Canada," *Toronto Star* (12.4.05); Cobain & Harding, "UK 'Breaking Law' over CIA Secret Flights," G (12.5.05); Ferguson, "UK 'Would Breach Law' if CIA Torture Flights Allowed to Land," *Scotsman* (12.5.05); AI, "USA: 800 Secret CIA Flights into and out of Europe" (12.5.05); "A German Hub for Secret Flights?" *Der Spiegel* (12.5.05); Cobain, Grey & Norton-Taylor, "Britain's Role in War on Terror Revealed," G (12.6.05); Brown, "US Planes Carrying Prisoners Were Allowed to Land in Britain, Says Straw," I (12.13.05); "Britain Says

U.S. Has Not Sought Permission to Use Base or Airspace for Prisoner Flights," NYT (12.13.05); AI, "UK: CIA Rendition Flights Used UK Airfields" (12.15.05); AI, Press Release (4.5.06).

266 Mutler, "Black Sea Base Used by U.S. Off-Limits to Romanians; May Have Been CIA Prison," AP (11.21.05); Fisher, "Reports of Secret U.S. Prisons in Europe Draw Ire and Otherwise Red Faces," NYT (12.1.05); Kessler, "Rice to Admit German's Abduction Was an Error," WP (12.7.05); Wood, "No C.I.A. Traces Seen in Romania in Amiable Hunt on Air Base," NYT (12.9.05); Bigo et al. (2015: 37).

267 See also "Debating Rendition Tactics," PBS's *NewsHour* (12.5.05); Ross & Esposito, "Sources Tell ABC News Top al Qaeda Figures Held in Secret CIA Prisons," ABC News (12.5.05); Kessler, "Rice Defends Tactics Used against Suspects," WP (12.6.05); Brinkley, "U.S. Interrogations Are Saving European Lives, Rice Says," NYT (12.6.05); "Secretary Rice's Rendition," NYT (12.7.05); Brinkley, "Rice Appears to Reassure Some Europeans on Treatment of Terror Detainees," NYT (12.9.05); Kessler, "Rice Wins Over E.U. Counterparts, Capping Months of Groundwork," WP (12.10.05); Bernstein, "Rice's Visit: Official Praise, Public Doubts," NYT (12.11.05); "Powell Raps Europe on CIA Flights," BBC News (12.17.05).

268 Lucas, "Poland Orders Probe into Alleged CIA Jails," AP (12.10.05); Bigo et al. (2015: 38).

269 Rennie, "Leaked Fax 'Shows Romania Helped CIA Interrogators,'" DT (1.10.06); Carvajal, "Swiss Investigate Leak to Paper on C.I.A. Prisons in Eastern Europe," NYT (1.12.06).

270 Walker & Baxter, "Revealed: the Terror Prison U.S. Is Helping to Build in Morocco," ST (2.12.06).

271 Bilefsky, "No Proof of Secret C.I.A. Prisons, European Antiterror Chief Says," NYT (4.21.06); Silva, "EU Official: No Evidence of Illegal CIA Actions," AP (4.21.06); "CIA Kidnapped Terrorism Suspects in EU: Lawmaker," NYT (4.26.06); "MEPs Reveal Extent of CIA Flights," BBC News (4.26.06); "Pattern of CIA Flights Is Cited," LAT (4.27.06); Bilefsky, "European Inquiry Says C.I.A. Flew 1,000 Flights in Secret," NYT (4.27.06); Brunnstrom, "CIA Row Hits US–Europe Intelligence Work: US," Reuters (5.4.06); DoS Press Conference (5.12.06); Miller, "Senators Want Details on Reported CIA Prisons," LAT (5.27.06); Whitlock, "European Probe Finds Signs of CI-run Secret Prisons," WP (6.8.06); Rotella, "14 Nations Aided CIA in Abductions, Report Says," LAT (6.8.06); Bilefsky, "Report Faults Europe in C.I.A. Detainee 'Web,'" NYT (6.8.06); TDIP, Working Document No. 7 on "Extraordinary Renditions," (11.16.06); TDIP, Working Document No. 8: on the Companies Linked to the CIA, Aircraft Used by the CIA and the European Countries in Which CIA Aircraft Have Made Stopovers (11.16.06); TDIP, Draft Report on the Alleged Use of European Countries by the CIA for the Transportation and Illegal Detention of Prisoners (11.24.06); Knowlton, "Report Rejects European Denial of C.I.A. Prisons," NYT (11.29.06); Whitlock, "European Report Details

Flights by CIA Aircraft," WP (11.29.06); "CIA Abuses: EU Report Condemns European Complicity," HRW (11.29.06); "Europe: EU Approves Report on CIA Flights," LAT (1.24.07); Walker, "EU States Urged to Investigate CIA Rendition Flights," G (1.23.07); "EU Endorses Damning Report on CIA," BBC News (2.14.07); Moore, "E.U. Report Faults 16 Nations in Probe of Secret CIA Flights," WP (2.15.07).

272 Stolberg, "President Moves 14 Held in Secret to Guantanamo: Seeks Tribunals," NYT (9.7.06); Anderson, "Confirmation of CIA Prisons Leaves Europeans Mistrustful," WP (9.8.06); Mazzetti, "Questions Raised about Bush's Primary Claims in Defense of Secret Detention System," NYT (9.8.06); "Romania's Effort Lax on CIA Jails, EU Says," *International Herald Tribune* (10.20.06); Mayer, "Outsourcing: The C.I.A.'s Travel Agent," *The New Yorker* (10.30.06).

273 Hundley, "Remote Polish Airstrip Holds Clues to Secret CIA Flights," CT (2.2.07); Alexandrovna & Dastych, "Soviet-Era Compound in Northern Poland Was Site of Secret CIA Interrogation," Raw Story (3.7.07).

274 Stein, "A CIA Man Speaks His Mind on Secret Abductions," CQ (4.20.07); Subcommittees on International Organizations, Human Rights and Oversight and on Europe, House Committee on Foreign Affairs, "Extraordinary Rendition in U.S. Counterterrorism Policy: The Impact on Transatlantic Relations" (4.17.07).

275 Shane, "Rights Groups Call for End to Secret Detentions," NYT (6.7.07); Grey, "Secret CIA Prisons Confirmed by Polish and Romanian Officials," G (6.7.07); Rotella, "Secret-Prison Inquiry Names Poland, Romania," LAT (6.9.07); Grey & Carvajal, "Secret Prisons in 2 Countries Held Qaeda Suspects, Report Says," NYT (6.8.07); Carvajal, "Rights Group Offers Grim View of C.I.A. Jails," NYT (6.9.07); Miller, "It Feels 'Like Sept. 10,' CIA Director Says," LAT (9.8.07).

276 Cobain & Norton-Taylor, "Claims of Secret CIA Jail for Terror Suspects on British Island to Be Investigated," G (10.19.07); Verkaik, "Government Blocks Access to Secret Military Papers on Diego Garcia," I (2.1.08); "UK Apology over Rendition Flights," BBC (2.21.08); Murphy, "Britain Says It Was Misled on CIA Flights," LAT (2.22.08); Burns, "C.I.A. Used a British Island to Transport Terrorism Suspects," NYT (2.22.08); "No Way to Treat a Friend," LAT (2.27.08); Stringer, "UK Lawmakers to Launch New Rendition Probe," WP (7.5.08); Zagorin, "Source: British Territory Used for US Terror Interrogation," *Time* (7.31.08).

277 Grey, "Flight Logs Reveal Secret Rendition," ST (11.25.07); Trevelyan, "Europe 'Fails to Act' on CIA Rendition Lessons," Reuters (1.17.08); Cole, "Romania Base Suspected CIA Prisoner Site," AP (2.24.08); Aremndariz & Palma, "Un Juez Critica del Archive del Caso por los Vuelos de la CIA," *Diario de Mallorca* (1.13.15).

278 Heckle, "Spanish Government to Probe Guantanamo Flights," AP (11.30.08).

279 Miller, "CIA Retains Power to Abduct," LAT (2.1.09); Savage, "Obama's War on Terror May Resemble Bush's in Some Areas," NYT (2.18.09); "Reassurance on the Economy and Addressing Afghanistan," NYT (3.8.09); Panetta, "Message from Director: Interrogation Policy and Contracts" (4.9.09); Shane, "C.I.A. to Close Secret Prisons, Scenes of Harsh Interrogations," NYT (4.10.09); Johnston, "Renditions to Continue, But with Better Oversight, U.S. Says," NYT (8.25.09); Mazzetti, "C.I.A. Resists Disclosure of Records on Detention," NYT (9.2.09); "Torture's Fallout," LAT (9.3.09).

280 Goetz & Sandberg, "New Evidence of a Torture Prison in Poland," *Der Spiegel* (4.27.09).

281 Johnston & Mazzetti, "A Window into C.I.A.'s Embrace of Secret Jails," NYT (8.13.09).

282 Cole, "Officials; Lithuania Hosted Secret Prison to Get 'Our Ear,'" ABC News (8.20.09); "Lithuania Must Probe CIA Jail Allegation: President," Reuters (10.20.09); Ross & Cole, "CIA Secret 'Torture' Prison Found at Fancy Horseback Riding Academy," ABC News (11.18.09); Whitlock, "Lithuania Investigates Facility That May Have Been CIA 'Black Site,'" WP (11.19.09); Whitlock, "CIA Detainees Again an Issue in Lithuania," WP (11.20.09); Seputyte, "Lithuania Let CIA Use Secret Prison for Interrogation," Bloomberg (12.22.09); "Lithuania Hosted Secret Prisons," BBC News (12.22.09); Dapkus, "Lithuanian Report Inconclusive on How Secret CIA Prisons Were Used," WP (12.23.09); Levy, "U.S. Puts Jails in Lithuania, Premier Says," NYT (12.23.09); AI (2010, 2011, 2014b).

283 Letter to the Editor, NYT (8.22.09); "Inside Romania's Secret Prison," AP (12.8.11); Goetz & Richter, "Geheimgefaengnis der CIA in Rumaenisch behorde entdeckt," *Süddeutsche Zeitung* (12.8.11).

284 Kulish & Shane, "Flight Logs Show That Planes for the C.I.A.'s Secret Detention Program Landed in Poland," NYT (2.23.10); "Documents Show CIA Prisoners Held in Poland," The News.Pl/International (7.30.10); Worthington, "New Evidence about Prisoners Held in Secret CIA Prisons in Poland and Romania," Truthout (8.3.10); "Europe: EU Approves Report on CIA Flights," LAT (1.24.07); Walker, "EU States Urged to Investigate CIA Rendition Flights," G (1.23.07); "EU Endorses Damning Report on CIA," BBC News (2.14.07); Moore, "E.U. Report Faults 16 Nations in Probe of Secret CIA Flights," WP (2.15.07); "Poland: Suspect Asks for Abuse Inquiry," NYT (12.17.10); "International Lawyers Launch Legal Action in Poland on Behalf of abu Zubaydah," Interights (12.20.10); Horton, "Justice Department Refuses Cooperation with Polish Prosecutors Investigating Torture at CIA Black Site," *Harper's* (December 2010); AI Press Release: "Rendition Victim Takes Case against Lithuania to European Court" (10.7.11); "Al Qaeda Terror Suspect at Guantanamo Bay Files Suit Alleging Torture at CIA-run Prison in Lithuania," Daily News (10.28.11); Leopold, "Department of Justice Balks at Turning over Guantanamo Detainee's 'Power-of-Attorney' Document to His Lawyers," Truthout (10.28.11).

285 "Former Polish Intelligence Chief Charged in CIA 'Black Sites' Case," News from Poland (3.17.12); Berenot & Kulish, "Polish Ex-Official Charged with Aiding CIA," NYT (3.28.12); Gera, "CIA Secret Prison: Polish Leaders Break Silence about Black Site," HuffPost (3.31.12); Gera, "Poles Talk about CIA Prison, Breaking Silence," AP (4.1.12); Williams, "Europe Takes Hard Look at Nations That Allowed U.S. Interrogations," LAT (5.1.12); Krzykowski & Czuchnowski, "The CIA Prison in Poland: Increasingly Less of a Question Mark" (4.17.12) (from Andy Worthington); Chu, "Poland Shaken by Case Alleging an Illicit CIA Prison There," LAT (6.22.12); Kublik, Czuchnowski & Krzykowski, "Mystery Unfolds of Poland's 'Extraterritorial' CIA Prison," *Gazeta Wyborcza* (6.21.12) (trans. Halszka Czarnocka); "Polish Prosecutors to Drop Charges in CIA Jail Inquiry – Report," Reuters (2.19.13).

286 "Poland Grants Victim Status to Guantanamo Detainee over Torture Allegations," AI (10.30.13).

287 Dapkus, "European Lawmakers Dismayed at CIA Prison Probe," BG (4.27.12); "CIA Flights: EU States Must Investigate Secret Detention Sites in Europe," European Parliament (7.10.12); "EU Parliament Raises Pressure for CIA Flights, Torture, Prisons Probe," AI Press Release (9.11.12); European Parliament, Report on Alleged Transportation and Illegal Detention of Prisoners in EU Countries by the CIA (8.2.12) (Flautre Report); European Parliament, Resolution 2013/2702 on Alleged Transportation and Illegal Detention of Prisoners in European Countries by the CIA.

288 Singh, "European Court Probes for Truth on CIA's Secret Prison in Poland," Open Society Justice Initiative (7.16.12); "Lowe, European Court to Hear New CIA Jail Case against Poland," Reuters (7.29.13); "Court: Poland Violated Human Rights in CIA Case," WP (7.24.14); Bilefsky, "Court Censures Poland over C.I.A. Renditions," NYT (7.25.14); Sierakowski, "Lessons from Poland's Past," NYT (7.31.14); Lyman, "Poland Appeals European Court of Human Rights Ruling on C.I.A. 'Black Site,'" NYT (10.25.14); Open Society Justice Institute, "European Court Rejects Poland's Bid to Challenge CIA Black Site Ruling" (2.17.15); "Poland to Pay $262,000 to Inmates Held at Secret CIA Prison," WP (2.18.15); Berendt, "Poland: Reparations Deadline to Be Met for 2 Terrorism Suspects Held by C.I.A.," NYT (5.16.15); "U.S. Refuses More Polish Requests for Assistance in CIA Case," NYT (9.22.15); *Case of Al Nashiri* v. *Poland*, ECHR Applic. No. 28761/11 (7.24.14).

289 AI, "Breaking the Conspiracy of Silence: USA's European 'Partners in Crime' Must Act after Senate Torture Report" (2015); "Ex-Leader: Poland Agreed to CIA Site, Not Torture," WP (12.10.14); Connolly, "Romanian Ex-Spy Chief Acknowledges CIA had 'Black Prisons' in Country," G (12.14.14); Ahmed, "From Blame Game to Half Confessions, How Global Leaders Are Reacting to Torture Report," Huffpost (12.15.14); Marinas & Lowe, "U.S. Torture Report Puts Romania's Role under

Scrutiny," Reuters (12.16.14); Sytas & Lowe, "Lithuanian Prosecutors Restart Investigation into CIA Jail," Reuters (4.2.15); "Former Romania President Admits Allowing CIA Site," Al Jazeera (4.27.15).

290 Somalia, Libya, and Syria are outside my scope.

291 Clark (2010); Johnsen (2013).

292 "Amnesty: All Sides Violated International Law in Mosul," Al Jazeera (7.11.17); Oakford, "Trump's Air War Has Already Killed More Than 2,000 Civilians," Daily Beast (7.17.17); Gibbons-Neff, "U.S. Airstrikes in Afghanistan Are at Levels Not Seen Since Obama Troop Surge," WP (7.17.17); Mashal & Shah, "American Airstrike Hits Afghan Security Forces," NYT (7.22.17); "'US-led Coalition' Air Raids Kill 29 Civilians in Raqqa," Al Jazeera (8.8.17); Alokozay & Abed, "Afghans Say U.S. Strike Hits Civilians," NYT (8.12.17); Loveluck, "U.S.-led Airstrikes Are Killing 100s of Civilians in the Battle for ISIS-held Raqqa This Summer," WP (8.23.17); "Children Are Among the Dead after a U.S.-backed Raid in Somalia," NYT (8.26.17); Shah & Mashal, "Afghan Forces, in Deadly Week, Killed by Airstrike," NYT (10.1.17); Davison, "Debris and Dust – Raqqa 'Sacrificed' to Defeat Islamic State," Reuters (10.6.17); Loveluck, "Civilian Casualties Spiral in Syria as Air Raids Target Areas Marked for Cease-Fire," WP (10.7.17); Bowcott, "Is the Targeting of ISIS Member Sally Jones Legally Justified?" G (10.12.17); Rahim & Mashal, "U.S. Strikes Caused At Least 13 Civilian Casualties, Afghans Say," NYT (11.5.17); Salahuddin, "Reports Suggest Dozens of Civilians Killed in U.S. Strikes in Afghanistan," WP (11.5.17); "U.S. Investigation Finds No Afghan Civilian Casualties in Kunduz Strike," Reuters (11.6.17); "U.N. Says Believes Afghanistan Air Strike Killed Civilians," Reuters (11.9.17); Rahim & Nordland, "Did Airstrikes in Afghanistan Last Week Kill Civilians? U.S. and U.N. Disagree," NYT (11.10.17).

CHAPTER 7 THE RESILIENCE OF THE RULE OF LAW

1 Sikkink (2008).

2 "The Must-Do List," NYT (3.4.07) exhorted the Bush administration (and the newly elected Democratic Congress) to address habeas corpus, electronic surveillance, torture, secret prisons and prisoners, extraordinary rendition, the definition of enemy combatants, CSRTs, military commissions and Guantanamo, and to apologize to Arar and el-Masri.

3 Kershner, "Israeli Soldier Who Shot Wounded Palestinian Assailant Is Convicted of Manslaughter," NYT (1.4.17); "The Latest: Israeli Minister: Pardon Convicted Soldier," NYT (1.4.17); "Israeli PM Netanyahu Backs Pardon for Manslaughter Soldier," BBC News (1.4.17).

4 Eggen & Kane, "Justice Dept. Would Have Kept 'Loyal Prosecutors: Aide Recommended Retaining Bushies' and Top Performers," WP (3.16.07).

5 Gonzales, "The Rule of Law and the Rules of War," NYT (5.15.04); Lewis, "Justice Memos Explained How to Skip Prisoner Rights," NYT (5.21.04); Edward J. Flynn, Letter to the Editor, NYT (5.22.04); New York City Bar (6.4.04); Priest & Smith, "Memo Offered Justification for the Use of Torture," WP (6.8.04); Bilder & Vagts (2004).
6 Letters to the Editor, NYT (6.9.04).
7 Bush Press Conference (6.10.04).
8 Ignatius, "Small Comfort," WP (6.15.04).
9 Clark & Mertus, "Torturing the Law," WP (6.20.04).
10 Locy & Biskupic, "Interrogation Memo to Be Replaced," *USA Today* (6.23.04); Allen & Schmidt, "Memo on Interrogation Tactics Is Disavowed," WP (6.23.04).
11 Priest, "CIA Puts Harsh Tactics on Hold," WP (6.27.04).
12 Wedgwood & Woolsey, "Law and Torture," WSJ (6.28.04).
13 "Torture and Democracy," *The Nation* (7.5.04).
14 Available at www.abanow.org/2004/08/aba-house-of-delegates-torture-resolution-2004/ (last accessed March 5, 2018).
15 Carroll (1865).
16 Müller (1991).
17 Priest, "Former CIA Spy Boss Made an Unhesitating Call to Destroy Interrogation Tapes," WP (4.24.12).
18 Shaw, "The Watchers: Assaults on Privacy in America," *Harvard Magazine* 56 (January–February 2017).
19 A sign on President Truman's desk.
20 Michaels, "Blood Oath: GOP Vowed to Block Obama from the First Day He Assumed Office," *District Chronicles* (9.16.12); Khan, "The Republicans' Plan for the New President," Frontline (1.15.13).
21 Grunwald, "The Party of No: New Details on the GOP Plot to Obstruct Obama," *Time* (8.23.12); Grunwald (2012).
22 William Blackstone, *Commentaries on the Laws of England* (1765).
23 When Sen. John Kerry was the Democratic candidate for president in 2004, Republicans made false allegations about his conduct as captain of a Swift boat in the Vietnam War.
24 Sikkink (2009: 192) notes that "no studies of human rights change in countries around the world have previously identified that military itself as a force for compliance with human rights law."
25 See Patten (2009).
26 Lyon & Olson (2012).
27 Janeway (1980); Scott (1985).
28 Mirsky, "How Tibet Is Being Crushed – While the Dalai Lama Survives," NYRB 95 (12.22.16).
29 Woeser (2016).
30 Huntington (1996).
31 Floor Statement by Senator John McCain on Senate Intelligence Committee Report on CIA Interrogation Methods (12.9.14) www.mccain.senate.gov/publc/index.cfm/2014/12/floor-rstatement (last accessed January 1, 2015).

32 Cardozo (1921).
33 "By the Numbers," MH (10.25.16); "Annual Determination of Average Cost of Incarceration" (3.9.15), 80 FR 12523.
34 Wellna, "Trump Has Vowed to Fill Guantánamo With 'Some Bad Dudes' – But Who?" NPR's *All Things Considered* (11.14.16).
35 "Trump Leads GOP Charge Embracing Torture: 'I'd Bring Back a Hell of a Lot Worse Than Waterboarding,'" Amy Goodman, *Democracy Now!* (2.8.16).
36 Johnston & Savage, "Obama Reluctant to Look into Bush Programs," NYT (1.11.09).
37 "Top Prosecutor Orders Probe into Interrogations; Obama Shifts Onus," CNN Politics (8.24.09); Shane, "No Charges Filed on Harsh Tactics Used by the C.I.A.," NYT (8.30.12).
38 Friedman, "A Torturous Compromise," NYT (4.28.09).
39 Hussain & Sarat (2010b); Herwitz (2010); Finkelstein (2010). For counter-arguments, see Holmes (2010); Horwitz (2010); Vladeck (2010).
40 Faulkner (1951).
41 Santayana (1905: 284).
42 Spitzer (1975).
43 McTaggart (1896); Stillman (1976).
44 Yoo, "Dianne Feinstein's Flawed Torture Report," LAT (12.13.14).
45 "Sen. Sessions Has the Experience to Be Attorney General, Gonzales Says," NPR Morning Edition (1.10.17).
46 *Korematsu* v. *U.S.*, 323 U.S. 214, 242 (1944).

REFERENCES

CHAPTERS 1 AND 7

Abel, Richard L. 1995. *Politics by Other Means: Law in the Struggle Against Apartheid, 1980–1994*. New York: Routledge.

Agamben, Giorgio. 2005. *State of Exception* (trans. Kevin Attell). Chicago: University of Chicago Press.

AI (Amnesty International). 2014c. *USA: Time for Truth and Justice*. London: AI.

Anderson, Carol. 2003. *Eyes Off the Prize: The United Nations and the African American Struggle for Human Rights, 1944–1955*. New York: Cambridge University Press.

Annan, Kofi. 1999. "Reflections by Nobel Laureates," in Y. Danieli et al. (eds.), *The Universal Declaration of Human Rights: Fifty Years and Beyond*. Amityville, NY: Baywood.

Aradau, Claudia. 2007. "Law Transformed: Guantánamo and the 'Other' Exception," 28 *Third World Quarterly* 489.

Armaline, William T., Davita Silfen Glasberg and Bandana Purkayastha (eds.). 2011. *Human Rights in Our Own Backyard: Injustice and Resistance in the United States*. Philadelphia: University of Pennsylvania Press.

Auerbach, Jerold. 1976. *Unequal Justice: Lawyers and Social Change in Modern America*. New York: Oxford University Press.

Baker, Peter. 2013. *Days of Fire: Bush and Cheney in the White House*. New York: Doubleday.

Ball, Howard. 2007. *Bush, the Detainees, and the Constitution: The Battle over Presidential Power in the War on Terror*. Lawrence: University Press of Kansas.

Banakar, Reza. 2010. "Introduction: Snapshots of the Rights Discourse," in Reza Banakar (ed.), *Rights in Context: Law and Justice in Late Modern Society*. Farnham: Ashgate.

Barkun, Michael. 1968. *Law without Sanctions*. New Haven: Yale University Press.

Barron, David J. 2016. *Waging War: The Clash Between Presidents and Congress, 1776 to ISIS*. New York: Simon & Schuster.

Becker, Jo. 2013. *Campaigning for Justice: Human Rights Advocacy in Practice*. Stanford: Stanford University Press.

Berlin, Isaiah. 1991. "European Unity and Its Vicissitudes," in *The Crooked Timber of Humanity*. London: Chatto & Windus.

Bilder, Richard B. and Detlev F. Vagts. 2004. "Speaking Law to Power: Lawyers and Torture," 98 *American Journal of International Law* 689.

Bin Abas, Mohamed Salleh, Tan Sri Dato Haji and K. Das. 1989. *May Day for Justice: The Lord President's Version*. Kuala Lumpur: Magnus Books.

Bingham, Tom. 2011. *The Rule of Law*. Harmondsworth: Penguin.

Blackstone, William. 1765. *Commentaries on the Laws of England*. Oxford: Clarendon Press.

Blum, Gabriella and Philip B. Heymann. 2010. *Laws, Outlaws, and Terrorists: Lessons from the War on Terrorism*. Cambridge, MA: MIT Press.

Böckenförde, Ernst-Wolfgang. 1991. *State, Society and Liberty: Studies in Political Theory and Constitutional Law* (trans. J. A. Underwood). Oxford: Berg.

Brooks, Rosa. 2016. *How Everything Became War and the Military Became Everything: Tales from the Pentagon*. New York: Simon & Schuster.

Brysk, Alison. 1994. *The Politics of Human Rights in Argentina: Protest, Change, and Democratization*. Stanford: Stanford University Press.

Cahn, Edmond N. 1949. *The Sense of Injustice: An Anthropocentric View of Law*. New York: New York University Press.

Call, Charles. 2007. "Introduction," to *Constructing Justice and Security after War*. Washington, D.C.: United States Institute of Peace Press.

Cardozo, Benjamin N. 1921. *The Nature of the Judicial Process*. New Haven: Yale University Press.

Carroll, Lewis (Charles Dodgson). 1865. *Alice's Adventures in Wonderland*. London: Macmillan.

Cass, Ronald. 2001. *The Rule of Law in America*. Baltimore: Johns Hopkins University Press.

Chafee, Zechariah. 1919. "Freedom of Speech in War Times," 32 *Harvard Law Review* 932.

1920. *Freedom of Speech*. New York: Harcourt, Brace and Howe.

Cheesman, Nick. 2015. *Opposing the Rule of Law: How Myanmar's Courts Make Law and Order*. New York: Cambridge University Press.

Cheney, Dick and Liz Cheney. 2011. *In My Time: A Personal and Political Memoir*. New York: Simon & Schuster.

Chertoff, Michael. 2009. *Homeland Security: Assessing the First Five Years*. Philadelphia: University of Pennsylvania Press.

Clark, Ann Marie. 2001a. "'A Calendar of Abuses': Amnesty International's Campaign on Guatemala," in Claude E. Welch, Jr. (ed.), *NGOs and Human Rights: Promise and Performance*. Philadelphia: University of Pennsylvania Press.

2001b. *Diplomacy of Conscience: Amnesty International and Changing Human Rights Norms*. Princeton: Princeton University Press.

2013. "The Normative Context of Human Rights Criticism: Treaty Ratification and UN Mechanisms," in Risse, Ropp & Sikkink, *The Power of Human Rights*.

Cohen, Stanley. 2001. *States of Denial: Knowing about Atrocities and Suffering*. Cambridge: Polity.

Cohn, Marjorie. 2007. *Cowboy Republic: Six Ways the Bush Gang Has Defied the Law*. Sausalito, CA: PoliPointPress.

Cole, David. 2016. *Engines of Liberty: The Power of Citizens to Make Constitutional Law*. New York: Basic Books.

Cooke, John Byrne. 2007. *Reporting the War: Freedom of the Press from the American Revolution to the War on Terrorism*. New York: Palgrave Macmillan.

Danner, Mark. 2016. *Spiral: Trapped in the Forever War*. New York: Simon & Schuster.

Dershowitz, Alan M. 2002a. *Shouting Fire: Civil Liberties in a Turbulent Age*. Boston, MA: Little, Brown.

2002b. *Why Terrorism Works: Understanding the Threat, Responding to the Challenge*. New Haven: Yale University Press.

Dicey, A. V. 1959. *Introduction to the Study of the Law of the Constitution* (first published 1885). London: Macmillan.

Donnelly, Jack. 2003. *Universal Human Rights in Theory and Practice*. Ithaca, NY: Cornell University Press.

Douglas, Lawrence, Austin Sarat and Martha Merrill Umphrey. 2014. "Law and War: An Introduction," in Austin Sarat, Lawrence Douglas and Martha Merrill Umphrey (eds.), *Law and War*. Stanford: Stanford University Press.

Downs, George W. and Michael A. Jones. 2002. "Reputation, Compliance, and International Law," 33 *Journal of Legal Studies* 295.

Draper, Robert. 2007. *Dead Certain: The Presidency of George W. Bush*. New York: Free Press.

Dudziak, Mary L. 2000. *Cold War Civil Rights: Race and the Image of American Democracy*. Princeton: Princeton University Press.

Dworkin, Ronald. 1977. *Taking Rights Seriously*. Cambridge, MA: Harvard University Press.

Dyzenhaus, David. 2008. "The Compulsion of Legality," in Victor V. Ramraj (ed.), *Emergencies and the Limits of Legality*. Cambridge: Cambridge University Press.

Edelson, Chris. 2016. *Power without Constraint: The Post-9/11 Presidency and the National Security*. Madison: University of Wisconsin Press.

European Commission for Democracy through Law (Venice Commission). 2011. *Report on the Rule of Law*. Brussels: Council of Europe.

Farrall, Jeremy Matam. 2007. *United Nations Sanctions and the Rule of Law*. New York: Cambridge University Press.

Fatovic, Clement. 2009. *Outside the Law: Emergency and Executive Power*. Baltimore: Johns Hopkins University Press.

Faulkner, William. 1951. *Requiem for a Nun*. New York: Random House.

Feingold, Russ. 2012. *While America Sleeps: A Wake-Up Call for the Post-9/11 Era*. New York: Crown Publishing.

Finan, Christopher M. 2007. *From the Palmer Raids to the Patriot Act: A History of the Fight for Free Speech in America*. Boston, MA: Beacon Press.

Fine, Bob. 1984. *Democracy and the Rule of Law: Liberal Ideals and Marxist Critiques*. London: Pluto Press.

Finkelstein, Claire. 2010. "Vindicating the Rule of Law: Prosecuting Free Riders on Human Rights," in Hussain & Sarat, *When Governments Break the Law*.

Finnemore, Martha. 1996. *National Interests in International Society*. Ithaca, NY: Cornell University Press.

Fisher, Louis. 2008. *The Constitution and 9/11: Recurring Threats to America's Freedoms*. Lawrence: University Press of Kansas.

Fiss, Owen and Judith Resnick. 1988. *Procedure*. Mineola, NY: Foundation Press.

Fitzpatrick, Peter and Richard Joyce. 2007. "The Normality of the Exception in Democracy's Empire," 34 *Journal of Law and Society* 65.

Fogelman, Eva. 1994. *Conscience and Courage: Rescuers of Jews During the Holocaust*. New York: Doubleday.

Forsythe, David P. 1977. *Humanitarian Politics: The International Committee of the Red Cross*. Baltimore: Johns Hopkins University Press.

Friedman, Lawrence. M. 2011. *The Human Rights Culture: A Study in History and Context*. New Orleans: Quid Pro Books.

Fuller, Lon. 1969. *The Morality of Law* (rev. edn.). New Haven: Yale University Press.

Gearty, Conor. 2007. *Civil Liberties*. Oxford: Oxford University Press.

Gellman, Barton. 2008. *Angler: The Cheney Vice Presidency*. New York: Penguin Press.

Gilligan, Michael J. and Nathaniel H. Nesbitt. 2009. "Do Norms Reduce Torture?" 38 *Journal of Legal Studies* 445.

Glaser, Barney G. and Anselm L. Strauss. 1967. *The Discovery of Grounded Theory: Strategies for Qualitative Research*. Chicago: Aldine.

Goldsmith, Jack and Stephen D. Krasner. 2003. "The Limits of Idealism," 132 *Daedalus* 47 (Winter).

Goldstein, Daniel M. 2001. "Human Rights As Culprit, Human Rights As Victim: Rights and Security in the State of Exception," in Daniel M. Goldstein, Jane K. Cowan, Marie-Benedicte Dembour and Richard A. Wilson (eds.), *Culture and Rights: Anthropological Perspectives*. New York: Cambridge University Press.

Goodman, Ryan and Derek Jinks. 2003. "Measuring the Effects of Human Rights Treaties," 14 *European Journal of International Law* 171.

Gordimer, Nadine. 1999. "Reflections by Nobel Laureates," in Y. Danieli et al. (eds.), *The Universal Declaration of Human Rights: Fifty Years and Beyond*. Amityville, New York: Baywood.

Gore, Al. 2007. *The Assault on Reason*. New York: Penguin Press.

Greenberg, Karen J. 2016. *Rogue Justice: The Making of the Security State*. New York: Crown Publishing.

Gross, Oren. 2008. "Extra-Legality and the Ethic of Political Responsibility," in Victor V. Ramraj (ed.), *Emergencies and the Limits of Legality*. Cambridge: Cambridge University Press.

Grunwald, Michael. 2012. *The New New Deal: The Hidden Story of Change in the Obama Era*. New York: Simon & Schuster.

Gutmann, Amy. 2001. "Introduction," in *Human Rights as Politics and Idolatry*. Princeton: Princeton University Press.

Hafner-Burton, Emilie M. and Kiyoteru Tsutsui. 2005. "Human Rights in a Globalizing World: The Paradox of Empty Promises," 110 *American Journal of Sociology* 1373.

Hafner-Burton, Emilie M., Kiyoteru Tsutsui and John Meyer. 2008. "International Human Rights Law and the Politics of Legitimation: Repressive States and Human Rights Treaties," 23 *International Sociology* 115.

Halliday, Terence C., Lucien Karpik and Malcolm Feeley. 2007. "The Legal Complex in Struggles for Political Liberalism," in Halliday, Karpik and Feeley (eds.), *Fighting for Political Freedom: Comparative Studies of the Legal Complex and Political Liberalism*. Oxford: Hart Publications.

Harding, Luke. 2014. *The Snowden Files: The Inside Story of the World's Most Wanted Man*. New York: Vintage Books.

Hathaway, Oona. 2002. "Do Human Rights Treaties Make a Difference?" 111 *Yale Law Journal* 1935.

Hayek, F. A. 1944. *The Road to Serfdom*. London: Routledge.

Healy, Thomas. 2013. *The Great Dissent: How Oliver Wendell Holmes Changed His Mind – and Changed the History of Free Speech in America*. New York: Picador.

Herman, Susan N. 2011. *Taking Liberties: The War on Terror and the Erosion of American Democracy*. New York: Oxford University Press.

Hertel, Shareen and Kathryn Libal. 2012. *Human Rights in the United States: Beyond Exceptionalism*. New York: Cambridge University Press.

Herwitz, Daniel. 2010. "Guantanamo in the Province of The Hague?" in Hussain & Sarat, *When Governments Break the Law*.

Holmes, Stephen. 2010. "The Spider's Web: How Government Lawbreakers Routinely Elude the Law," in Hussain & Sarat, *When Governments Break the Law*.

Honig, Bonnie. 2009. *Emergency Politics: Paradox, Law, Democracy*. Princeton: Princeton University Press.

Honigsberg, Peter Ian. 2009. *Our Nation Unhinged: The Human Consequences of the War on Terror*. Oakland: University of California Press.

Hope, D. 2004. "Torture," 53 *International and Comparative Law Quarterly* 807.

Hopgood, Stephen. 2006. *Keepers of the Flame: Understanding Amnesty International*. Ithaca, NY: Cornell University Press.

2013. *The Endtimes of Human Rights*. Ithaca, NY: Cornell University Press.

Horwitz, Paul. 2010. "Democracy as the Rule of Law," in Hussain & Sarat, *When Governments Break the Law*.

Huang, Margaret. 2008. "'Going Global': Appeals to International and Regional Human Rights Bodies," in Soohoo, Albisa & Davis, *Bringing Rights Home, Vol. 2: From Civil Rights to Human Rights*.

Hunt, Lynn. 2007. *Inventing Human Rights: A History*. New York: W. W. Norton.

Huntington, Samuel P. 1996. *The Clash of Civilizations and the Remaking of World Order*. New York: Simon & Schuster.

Hussain, Nasser. 2007. "Beyond Norm and Exception: Guantánamo," 33 *Critical Inquiry* 734.

Hussain, Nasser and Austin Sarat (eds.). 2010a. *When Governments Break the Law: The Rule of Law and the Prosecution of the Bush Administration*. New York: New York University Press.

2010b. "Introduction," in Hussain & Sarat, *When Governments Break the Law*.

Ignatieff, Michael. 2001a. "Human Rights as Idolatry," in Amy Gutmann (ed.), *Human Rights as Politics and Idolatry*. Princeton: Princeton University Press.

2001b. "Human Rights as Politics," in Amy Gutmann (ed.), *Human Rights as Politics and Idolatry*. Princeton: Princeton University Press.

Janeway, Elizabeth. 1980. *Powers of the Weak*. New York: Knopf.

Jetschke, Anja and Andrea Liese. 2013. "The Power of Human Rights a Decade After: From Euphoria to Contestation," in Risse, Ropp & Sikkink, *The Power of Human Rights*.

Johns, Fleur. 2005. "Guantánamo Bay and the Annihilation of the Exception," 16 *European Journal of International Law* 613.

Johnson, Paul. 1999. "Laying Down the Law: Britain and America Led the Way in Establishing Legal Regimes Based on Universal Principles," *Wall Street Journal* A22 (March 10).

Keck, Margaret E. and Kathryn Sikkink. 1998. *Activists beyond Borders: Advocacy Networks in International Politics*. Ithaca, NY: Cornell University Press.

Keith, Linda Camp. 1999. "The United Nations International Covenant on Civil and Political Rights: Does It Make a Difference in Human Rights Behavior?" 36 *Journal of Peace Research* 95.

2002. "Constitutional Provisions for Individual Human Rights (1977–1996): Are They More Than Mere 'Window Dressing'?" 55 *Political Research Quarterly* 111.

Keys, Barbara. 2014. *Reclaiming American Virtue: The Human Rights Revolution of the 1970s*. Cambridge, MA: Harvard University Press.

Kim, Hunjoon and Kathryn Sikkink. 2010. "Explaining the Deterrence Effect of Human Rights Prosecutions for Transitional Countries," 54 *International Studies Quarterly* 939.

Kirchheimer, Otto. 1967. "The Rechtsstaat as Magic Wall," in William E. Scheuerman (ed.), *The Rule of Law under Siege: Selected Essays of Franz L. Neumann and Otto Kirchheimer*. Berkeley: University of California Press.

Korey, William. 1998. *NGOs and the Universal Declaration of Human Rights: "A Curious Grapevine."* New York: St. Martin's Press.

Kratochwil, Friedrich V. 1989. *Rules, Norms, and Decisions: On the Conditions of Practical and Legal Reasoning in International Relations*. Cambridge: Cambridge University Press.

Krygier, Martin 2011. "Four Puzzles about the Rule of Law: Why, What, Where? And Who Cares?" in James E. Fleming (ed.), *Getting to the Rule of Law*. New York: New York University Press.

2012a. "Rule of Law," in Michel Rosenfeld and András Sajó (eds.), *The Oxford Handbook of Comparative Constitutional Law*. Oxford: Oxford University Press.

2012b. "Why the Rule of Law Is Too Important to Be Left to Lawyers," 2 *Prawo I Wiez* 30.

2013. "Still a Rule of Law Guy," 34 *Recht der Werkelijkheid* 47.

2014. "Rule of Law (and Rechtsstaat)," *International Encyclopedia of the Social and Behavioral Sciences* (2nd edn.). Amsterdam: Elsevier.

Landman, Todd. 2005. *Protecting Human Rights: A Comparative Study*. Washington, D.C.: Georgetown University Press.

Lawrence, Thomas A. 1974. "Eclipse of Liberty: Civil Liberties in the United States During the First World War," 21 *Wayne Law Review* 33.

Lazar, Nomi Claire. 2009. *States of Emergency in Liberal Democracies*. New Haven: Yale University Press.

Leone, Richard C. and Greg Anrig, Jr. (eds.). 2003. *The War on Our Freedoms: Civil Liberties in an Age of Terrorism*. New York: Public Affairs.

Levy, Leonard W. 1968. *Origins of the Fifth Amendment: The Right Against Self-Incrimination*. New York: Oxford University Press.

Lewis, Anthony. 2007. *Freedom for the Thought That We Hate: A Biography of the First Amendment*. New York: Basic Books.

Lichtblau, Eric. 2008. *Bush's Law: The Remaking of American Justice*. New York: Pantheon Books.

Luckham, Robin. 1981. "The Ghana Legal Profession: Natural History of a Research Project," in Robin Luckham (ed.), *Law and Social Enquiry: Case*

Studies of Research. Uppsala: Scandinavian Institute of African Studies and New York: International Center for Law in Development.

Lutz, Ellen L. and Caitlin Reiger (eds.). 2009. *Prosecuting Heads of State*. New York: Cambridge University Press.

Lyon, Arabella and Lester C. Olson (eds.). 2012. *Human Rights Rhetoric: Traditions of Testifying and Witnessing*. New York: Routledge.

MacCormick, Neil. 2005. *Rhetoric and the Rule of Law*. Oxford: Oxford University Press.

McTaggart, J. E. 1896. "Hegel's Theory of Punishment," 6 *International Journal of Ethics* 479–502.

Margulies, Joseph. 2013. *What Changed When Everything Changed: 9/11 and the Making of National Identity*. New Haven: Yale University Press.

Margulies, Peter. 2010. *Law's Detour: Justice Displaced in the Bush Administration*. New York: New York University Press.

Martinez, Jenny S. 2012. *The Slave Trade and the Origins of International Human Rights Law*. New York: Oxford University Press.

Marx, Karl. 1947. "Theses on Feuerbach," in Karl Marx and Friedrich Engels, *The German Ideology, Parts One and Two*. New York: International Publishers.

Medsger, Betty. 2014. *The Burglary: The Discovery of J. Edgar Hoover's Secret F.B.I.* New York: Knopf.

Moeckli, Daniel. 2010. "Human Rights Strategies in an Age of Counter-Terrorism," in Reza Banakar (ed.), *Rights in Context: Law and Justice in Late Modern Society*. Farnham: Ashgate.

Moeller, Susan. 1999. *Compassion Fatigue: How the Media Sell Disease, Famine, War, and Death*. New York: Routledge.

Morrell, Michael with Bill Harlow. 2015. *The Great War of Our Time: The CIA's Fight against Terrorism from al Qa'ida to ISIS*. New York: Twelve.

Müller, Ingo. 1991. *Hitler's Justice: The Courts of the Third Reich* (trans. Deborah Schneider). Cambridge, MA: Harvard University Press.

Murphy, Paul L. 1979. *World War I and the Origin of Civil Liberties in the United States*. New York: W. W. Norton.

Mutua, Makau. 2002. *Human Rights: A Political and Cultural Critique*. Philadelphia: University of Pennsylvania Press.

Neier, Aryeh. 2012. *The International Human Rights Movement: A History*. Princeton: Princeton University Press.

Neff, Stephen C. 2010. *Justice in Blue and Gray: A Legal History of the Civil War*. Cambridge, MA: Harvard University Press.

Neumann, Franz. 1942. *Behemoth: The Structure and Practice of National Socialism*. London: Victor Gollancz.

Norton, Mary Beth. 2002. *In the Devil's Snare: The Salem Witchcraft Crisis*. New York: Knopf.

Nozick, Robert. 1974. *Anarchy, State, and Utopia*. New York: Basic Books.
Oakeshott. Michael. 1991. *Rationalism in Politics and Other Essays*. Indianapolis: Liberty Press.
O'Donnell, Guillermo and Philippe C. Schmitter. 1986. *Transitions from Authoritarian Rule: Tentative Conclusions about Uncertain Democracies*. Baltimore: Johns Hopkins University Press.
Ohlin, Jens David. 2015. *The Assault on International Law*. New York: Oxford University Press.
Oliner, Samuel P. and Pearl M. Oliner. 1988. *The Altruistic Personality: Rescuers of Jews in Nazi Europe*. New York: Free Press.
Olsen, Tricia D., Leigh A. Payne and Andrew G. Reiter. 2010. *Transitional Justice in the Balance: Comparing Processes, Weighing Efficacy*. Washington, D.C.: USIP Press.
Palombella, Gianluigi. 2010. "The Rule of Law as an Institutional Ideal," in Leonardo Morlino and Gianluigi Palombella (eds.), *Rule of Law and Democracy: Inquiries into Internal and External Issues*. Leiden: Brill.
Patten, Wendy. 2009. "The Impact of September 11 and the Struggle against Terrorism on the U.S. Domestic Human Rights Movement," in Cynthia Soohoo, Catherine Albisa and Martha F. Davis (eds.), *Bringing Human Rights Home: A History of Human Rights in the United States*. New York: Prager.
Paust, Jordan J. 2007. *Beyond the Law: The Bush Administration's Unlawful Responses in the "War" on Terror*. New York: Cambridge University Press.
Peerenboom, Randall. 2004. *Asian Discourses of the Rule of Law*. London: Routledge.
Piccone, Ted. 2010. *Catalysts for Rights: The Unique Contribution of the UN's Independent Experts on Human Rights*. Washington, D.C.: Brookings Institution.
Posner, Eric and Adrian Vermeule. 2011. *The Executive Unbound: After the Madisonian Republic*. New York: Oxford University Press.
Power, Jonathan. 2001. *Like Water on Stone: The Story of Amnesty International*. London: Allen Lane.
Press, Eyal. 2012. *Beautiful Souls: Saying No, Breaking Ranks, and Heeding the Voice of Conscience in Dark Times*. New York: Farrar, Straus and Giroux.
Priest, Dana and William M. Arkin. 2011. *Top Secret America: The Rise of the New American Security State*. New York: Little Brown.
Prouvez, Nathalie and Nicholas M. L. Bovay. 2001. "The Role of the International Commission of Jurists," in Claude E. Welch, Jr. (ed.), *NGOs and Human Rights: Promise and Performance*. Philadelphia: University of Pennsylvania Press.
Quataert, Jean H. 2009. *Advocating Dignity: Human Rights Mobilizations in Global Politics*. Philadelphia: University of Pennsylvania Press.

Rajagopal, Balakrishnan. 2003. *International Law from Below: Development, Social Movements and Third World Resistance*. New York: Cambridge University Press.

Ramraj, Victor V. 2008. "No Doctrine More Pernicious: Emergencies and the Limits of Legality," in Victor V. Ramraj (ed.), *Emergencies and the Limits of Legality*. Cambridge: Cambridge University Press.

Raz, Joseph. 1979. "The Rule of Law and its Virtues," in *The Authority of Law: Essays on Law and Morality*. Oxford: Clarendon Press.

Rejali, Darius M. 2007. *Torture and Democracy*. Princeton: Princeton University Press.

Ricks, Thomas E. 2006. *Fiasco: The American Military Adventure in Iraq*. New York: Penguin Press.

Risen, James. 2006. *State of War: The Secret History of the CIA and the Bush Administration*. New York: Free Press.

2014. *Pay Any Price: Greed, Power, and Endless War*. Boston, MA: Houghton Mifflin Harcourt.

Risse, Thomas and Stephen C. Ropp. 1999. "International Human Rights Norms and Domestic Change: Conclusions," Risse, Ropp & Sikkink, *The Power of Human Rights*.

2013. "Introduction and Overview," in Risse, Ropp & Sikkink, *The Persistent Power of Human Rights*.

Risse, Thomas and Kathryn Sikkink. 1999. "The Socialization of International Human Rights Norms into Domestic Practices: Introduction," in Risse, Ropp & Sikkink, *The Power of Human Rights*.

2013. "Conclusions," in Risse, Ropp & Sikkink, *The Persistent Power of Human Rights*.

Risse, Thomas, Stephen C. Ropp and Kathryn Sikkink (eds.). 1999. *The Power of Human Rights: International Norms and Domestic Change*. New York: Cambridge University Press.

2013. *The Persistent Power of Human Rights: From Commitment to Compliance*. New York: Cambridge University Press.

Risse-Kappen, Thomas (ed.). 1995. *Bringing Transnational Relations Back In: Non-State Actors, Domestic Structures, and International Institutions*. Cambridge: Cambridge University Press.

Robben, Antonius. 2004. *Political Violence and Trauma in Argentina*. Philadelphia: University of Pennsylvania Press.

Rossiter, Clinton L. 1948. *Constitutional Dictatorships: Crisis Government in the Modern Democracies*. New York: Harcourt Brace.

Santayana. George. 1905. "Reason in Common Sense," in *The Life of Reason*, Vol. 1. New York: Charles Scribner's Sons.

Sarat, Austin and Thomas R. Kearns (eds.). 2011. *Human Rights: Concepts, Contests, Contingencies*. Ann Arbor: University of Michigan Press.

Savage, Charlie. 2007. *Takeover: The Return of the Imperial Presidency and the Subversion of American Democracy*. New York: Back Bay Books.

2015. *Power Wars: Inside Obama's Post-9/11 Presidency*. New York: Little, Brown & Co.

Scahill, Jeremy. 2013. *Dirty Wars: The World Is a Battlefield*. New York: Nation Books.

Schmitt, Carl. 2005. *Political Theology: Four Chapters on the Concept of Sovereignty* (trans. George Schwab). Chicago: University of Chicago Press.

Schmitt, Eric and Thom Shanker. 2011. *Counterstrike: The Untold Story of America's Secret Campaign against al Qaeda*. New York: Times Books.

Schwarz, Frederick A. O., Jr. and Aziz Z. Huq. 2008. *Unchecked and Unbalanced: Presidential Power in a Time of Terror*. New York: New Press.

Schrecker, Ellen W. 1998. *Many Are the Crimes: McCarthyism in America*. Boston, MA: Little Brown.

Scoble, Harry M. 1984. "Human Rights Non-Governmental Organizations in Black Africa: Their Problems and Prospects in the Wake of the Banjul Charter," in Claude E. Welch, Jr. and Ronald I. Meltzer (eds.), *Human Rights and Development in Africa*. Albany: SUNY Press.

Scoble, Harry M. and Laurie Eisenberg. 1976. "Human Rights NGOs: Notes toward Comparative Analysis," 9 *Human Rights* 611.

Scott, James. 1985. *Weapons of the Weak: Everyday Forms of Peasant Resistance*. New Haven: Yale University Press.

Scott, Katherine A. 2013. *Reining in the State: Civil Society and Congress in the Vietnam and Watergate Eras*. Lawrence: University Press of Kansas.

Selznick, Philip. 1959. "The Sociology of Law," in Robert K. Merton, Leonard Broom and Leonard S. Cottrell (eds.), *Sociology Today*. New York: Basic Books.

1968. "The Sociology of Law," 9 *International Encyclopedia of the Social Sciences* 52.

Seron, Carroll, Joseph Pereira and Jean Kovath. 2004. "Judging Police Misconduct: 'Street-Level' versus Professional Policing," 38 *Law & Society Review* 665.

Shane, Peter M. 2009. *Madison's Nightmare: How Executive Power Threatens American Democracy*. Chicago: University of Chicago Press.

Shipler, David K. 2012. *The Rights of the People: How Our Search for Safety Invades Our Liberties*. New York: Vintage Books.

Shklar, Judith. 1998. "The Liberalism of Fear," in Stanley Hoffman (ed.), *Political Thought and Political Thinkers*. Chicago: University of Chicago Press.

Shue, Henry. 1979. "Torture," 7 *Philosophy & Public Affairs* 124.

Sidel, Mark. 2004. *More Secure, Less Free? Antiterrorism Policy and Civil Liberties After September 11*. Ann Arbor: University of Michigan Press.

Sikkink, Kathryn. 1999. "The United States and Torture: Does the Spiral Model Work?" in Risse, Ropp & Sikkink, *The Power of Human Rights*.

2009. "Bush Administration Noncompliance with the Prohibition on Torture and Cruel and Degrading Treatment," in Soohoo, Albisa & Davis, *Bringing Rights Home, Vol. 2: From Civil Rights to Human Rights*.

2011. *The Justice Cascade: How Human Rights Prosecutions Are Changing World Politics*. New York: Norton.

Silkenat, James R. and Mark R. Shulman (eds). 2007. *The Imperial Presidency and the Consequences of 9/11: Lawyers React to the Global War on Terrorism* (2 vols.). Westport, CT: Prager Security International.

Simmons, Beth A. 2009. *Mobilizing for Human Rights: International Law in Domestic Politics*. New York: Cambridge University Press.

2013. "From Ratification to Compliance: Quantitative Evidence on the Spiral Model," in Risse, Ropp & Sikkink, *The Persistent Power of Human Rights*.

Snyder, Jack and Leslie Vinjamuri. 2004. "Advocacy and Scholarship in the Study of International War Crime Tribunals and Transitional Justice," 7 *Annual Review of Political Science* 345.

Soohoo, Cynthia. 2008. "Human Rights and the Transformation of the 'Civil Rights' and 'Civil Liberties' Lawyer," in Soohoo, Albisa & Davis, *Bringing Rights Home, Vol. 2: From Civil Rights to Human Rights*.

Soohoo, Cynthia, Catherine Albisa and Martha F. Davis (eds.). 2008. *Bringing Rights Home, Vol. 2: From Civil Rights to Human Rights*. Westport, CT: Praeger.

Spitzer, Steven. 1975. "Punishment and Social Organization: A Study of Durkheim's Theory of Penal Evolution," 9 *Law & Society Review* 613.

Steyn, Lord. 2004. "Deference: A Tangled Story" (2004 Judicial Studies Board Lecture: Belfast).

Stillman, Peter G. 1976. "Hegel's Idea of Punishment," 14 *Journal of the History of Philosophy* 169.

Stone, Deborah A. 1989. "Causal Stories and the Formation of Policy Agendas," 105 *Political Science Quarterly* 281.

Stone, Geoffrey R. 2004. *Perilous Times: Free Speech in Wartime from the Sedition Act of 1798 to the War on Terrorism*. New York: W. W. Norton.

Tamanaha, Brian Z. 2004. *On the Rule of Law: History, Politics, Theory*. New York: Cambridge University Press.

Thibaut, John and Laurens Walker. 1975. *Procedural Justice: A Psychological Analysis*. New York: John Wiley.

Thompson, E. P. 1975. *Whigs and Hunters: The Origin of the Black Act*. New York: Pantheon.

Tolley, Howard B., Jr. 1990–91. "Interest Group Litigation to Enforce Human Rights," 105 *Political Science Quarterly* 617.

1994. *The International Commission of Jurists: Global Advocates for Human Rights*. Philadelphia: University of Pennsylvania Press.

Tyler, Tom R. 1990. *Why People Obey the Law*. New Haven: Yale University Press.

Vladeck, Stephen. 2010. "Justice Jackson, the Memory of Internment, and the Rule of Law after the Bush Administration," in Hussain & Sarat, *When Governments Break the Law*.

Wade, A. L. 1967. *Administrative Law*. Oxford: Clarendon Press.

Waldron, Jeremy. 2010. *Torture, Terror, and Trade-Offs: Philosophy for the White House*. Oxford: Oxford University Press.

2011. "The Rule of Law and the Importance of Procedure," in James E. Fleming (ed.), *Getting to the Rule of Law (Nomos L)*. New York: New York University Press.

Walker, Samuel. 1990. *In Defense of American Liberties: A History of the ACLU*. New York: Oxford University Press.

2012. *Presidents and Civil Liberties from Wilson to Obama*. New York: Cambridge University Press.

Walsh, Lawrence E. 1997. *Firewall: The Iran–Contra Conspiracy and Cover-Up*. New York: Norton.

Waltz, Kenneth. 1979. *Theory of International Politics*. Reading, MA: Addison-Wesley Pub. Co.

Wechsler, Herbert. 1959. "Toward Neutral Principles of Constitutional Law," 73 *Harvard Law Review* 1.

Weiner, Tim. 2008. *Legacy of Ashes: The History of the CIA*. New York: Anchor Books.

2012. *Enemies: A History of the FBI*. New York: Random House.

Weingast, Barry R. 2010. "Why Developing Countries Prove so Resistant to the Rule of Law," in James J. Heckman, Robert L. Nelson and Lee Cabatingan (eds.), *Global Perspectives on the Rule of Law*. New York: Routledge.

Welch, Claude E., Jr. 2001a. "Introduction," to Claude E. Welch, Jr. (ed.), *NGOs and Human Rights: Promise and Performance*. Philadelphia: University of Pennsylvania Press.

2001b. "Amnesty International and Human Rights Watch: A Comparison," in Claude E. Welch, Jr. (ed.), *NGOs and Human Rights: Promise and Performance*. Philadelphia: University of Pennsylvania Press.

West, Robin. 2011. "The Limits of Process," in James E. Fleming (ed.), *Getting to the Rule of Law (Nomos L)*. New York: New York University Press.

Whitehead, Laurence. 1996. "Three International Dimensions of Democratization," in Laurence Whitehead (ed.), *The International Dimensions of Democratization: Europe and the Americas*. Oxford: Oxford University Press.

Wiesel, Elie. 1999. "A Tribute to Human Rights," in Y. Danieli et al. (eds.), *The Universal Declaration of Human Rights: Fifty Years and Beyond*. Amityville, NY: Baywood.

Williams, George. 2007. *A Charter of Rights for Australia*. Sydney: University of New South Wales Press.
Wilson, Richard and Richard D. Brown (eds.) 2009. *Humanitarianism and Suffering: The Mobilization of Empathy*. New York: Cambridge University Press.
Woeser, Tsering. 2016. *Tibet on Fire: Self-Immolation Against Chinese Rule* (trans. Kevin Carrico). New York: Verso.
Work, Clemens P. 2005. *Darkest before Dawn: Sedition and Free Speech in the American West*. Albuquerque: University of New Mexico Press.
Yoo, John. 2005. *The Powers of War and Peace: The Constitution and Foreign Affairs after 9/11*. Chicago: University of Chicago Press.
2006. *War by Other Means: An Insider's Account of the War on Terror*. New York: Atlantic Monthly Press.

CHAPTERS 2–6

ABA (American Bar Association) Task Force on Domestic Surveillance in the Fight against Terrorism; Association of the Bar of the City of New York, Sections on Criminal Justice, Individual Rights and Responsibilities, International Law, and Science and Technology; National Conference of Specialized Court Judges; and Beverly Hills Bar Association. 2006. *Resolution and Report*. ABA: Chicago.
ABCNY (Association of the Bar of the City of New York), Committee on Federal Courts. 2004. *The Indefinite Detention of "Enemy Combatants": Balancing Due Process and National Security in the Context of the War on Terror*. New York: ABCNY.
ABCNY (Association of the Bar of the City of New York) Task Force on National Security and the Rule of Law. 2008. *Reaffirming the U.S. Commitment to Common Article 3 of the Geneva Conventions (June)*. New York: ABCNY.
Ahmed, Akbar. 2013. *The Thistle and the Drone*. Washington, D.C.: Brookings Institution Press.
AI (Amnesty International). 2006. *Beyond Abu Graib: Detention and Torture in Iraq*. London: AI.
2007. *USA: Cruel and Inhuman: Conditions of Isolation for Detainees at Guantánamo Bay*. London: AI.
2010. *Open Secret: Mounting Evidence of Europe's Complicity in Rendition and Secret Detention*. London: AI.
2011. *Unlock the Truth in Lithuania: Investigate Secret Prisons Now*. London: AI.
2012. *United States of America: "Targeted Killing" Policies Violate the Right to Life*. London: AI.

2013a. *USA. The Devil in the (Still Undisclosed) Detail: Department of Justice "White Paper" on Use of Lethal Force against U.S. Citizens Made Public.* London: AI.

2013b. *"Will I Be Next?" US Drone Strikes in Pakistan*. London: AI.

2014a. *Left in the Dark: Failures of Accountability for Civilian Casualties Caused by International Military Operations in Afghanistan*. London: AI.

2014b. *Unlock the Truth in Lithuania: Investigate Secret Prisons Now.* London: AI.

2014c. *USA: Time for Truth and Justice*. London: AI.

2015. *USA Crimes and Impunity*. London: AI.

Alexander, Matthew, with John R. Brunning. 2008. *How to Break a Terrorist.* New York: Free Press.

Aid, Matthew M. 2009. *The Secret Sentry: The Untold History of the National Security Agency*. New York: Bloomsbury Press.

Allhoff, Fritz. 2012. *Terrorism, Ticking Time-Bombs, and Torture: A Philosophical Analysis*. Chicago: University of Chicago Press.

Alston, Philip. 2010. *Report of the Special Rapporteur on extrajudicial, summary or arbitrary executions: Study on targeted killings*. UN General Assembly Human Rights Council A/HRC/14/24/Add.6 (5.28.10).

2011. "The CIA and Targeted Killings beyond Borders," 2 *Harvard National Security Journal* 283.

Amman, Diane. 2004. "Guantanamo," 42 *Columbia Journal of Transnational Law* 263.

2005. "Abu Ghraib," 153 *University of Pennsylvania Law Review* 2085.

APT (Association for the Prevention of Torture). 2007. *Defusing the Ticking Bomb Scenario: Why We Must Say No to Torture, Always*. Geneva: APT.

Arsenault, Elizabeth Grimm. 2017. *How the Gloves Came Off: Lawyers, Policy Makers, and Norms in the Debate on Torture*. New York: Columbia University Press.

Baker, Stewart. 2010. *Skating on Stilts: Why We Aren't Stopping Tomorrow's Terrorism*. Stanford: Hoover Institution Press.

Bamford, James. 1983. *The Puzzle Palace: Inside the National Security Agency.* New York: Penguin.

2002. *Body of Secrets: Anatomy of the Ultra Secret National Security Agency.* New York: Anchor.

2008. *The Shadow Factory: The Ultra-Secret NSA from 9/11 to the Eavesdropping on America*. New York: Anchor Books.

2014. "Edward Snowden: The Untold Story," *Wired* (August).

Banham, Cynthia. 2017. *Liberal Democracies and the Torture of Their Citizens.* Oxford: Hart Publishers.

Bashir, Shahzad and Robert D. Crews (eds.). 2012. *Under the Drones: Modern Lives in the Afghanistan–Pakistan Borderlands*. Cambridge, MA: Harvard University Press.

Bazan, Elizabeth B. and Jennifer K. Elsea. 2006. *Presidential Authority to Conduct Warrantless Electronic Surveillance to Gather Foreign Intelligence Information*. Washington, D.C.: Congressional Research Service.

Begg, Moazzam with Victoria Brittain. 2006. *Enemy Combatant: My Imprisonment at Guantánamo, Bagram and Kandahar*. New York: New Press.

Bellavia, David with John R. Bruning. 2006. *House to House: An Epic Memoir of War*. New York: Free Press.

Benvenisti, Meron (ed.). 2004. *Abu Ghraib: The Politics of Torture*. Berkeley: North Atlantic Books.

Bergen, Peter L. and Daniel Rothenberg (eds.). 2014. *Drone Wars: Transforming Conflict, Law, and Policy*. New York: Cambridge University Press.

Bergen, Peter and Katherine Tiedemann. 2009. *Revenge of the Drones*. Washington, D.C.: New America Foundation.

Bigo, Dider, Sergio Carrera, Elspeth Guild and Raluca Radescu. 2015. *A Quest for Accountability? EU and Member State Inquiries into the CIA Rendition and Secret Detention Programme*. Brussels: EU Policy Department C.

Boumediene, Lakhdar and Mustafa Ait Idir. 2017. *Witnesses of the Unseen: Seven Years in Guantanamo*. Stanford: Stanford University Press.

Brecher, Bob. 2007. *Torture and the Ticking Bomb*. Oxford: Blackwell.

Brooks, Rosa. 2016. *How Everything Became War and the Military Became Everything: Tales from the Pentagon*. New York: Simon & Schuster.

Bruck, Connie. 2016. "Why Obama Has Failed to Close Guantánamo," *New Yorker* (August 1).

Burrows, Edwin G. 2010. *Forgotten Patriots: The Untold Story of American Prisoners during the Revolutionary War*. New York: Basic Books.

Bush, George W. 2010. *Decision Points*. New York: Crown.

Carle, Glenn L. 2011. *The Interrogator: An Education*. New York: Nation Books.

CCR (Center for Constitutional Rights). 2011. *Dealing with Torture in the United States: No Justice, No Accountability, No Remedy*. New York: CCR.

Chayes, Antonia. 2015. *Borderless Wars: Civil Military Disorder and Legal Uncertainty*. New York: Cambridge University Press.

Cheney, Richard B. and Liz Cheney. 2011. *In My Time: A Personal and Political Memoir*. New York: Threshold.

2015. *Exceptional*. New York: Simon & Schuster.

CHRGJ (Center for Human Rights and Global Justice) New York University. 2007. *Surviving the Darkness: Testimony from the U.S. "Black Sites."* New York: CHRGJ.

Clark, Victoria. 2010. *Yemen: Dancing on the Heads of Snakes*. New Haven: Yale University Press.

Cockburn, Andrew. 2007. *Rumsfeld: His Rise, Fall and Catastrophic Legacy*. New York: Scribner.

2015. *Kill Chain: The Rise of the High-Tech Assassin*. New York: Henry Holt.

Cohn, Marjorie (ed.). 2010. *The United States and Torture: Interrogation, Incarceration, and Abuse*. New York: New York University Press.
Cole, David (ed.). 2009. *The Torture Memos: Rationalizing the Unthinkable*. New York: New Press.
Coll, Steve. 2014. "The Unblinking Stare," *New Yorker* (November 24).
Columbia Law School Human Rights Clinic and Sana'a Center for Strategic Studies. 2017. *Out of the Shadows: Recommendations to Advance Transparency in the Use of Lethal Force*. New York: CLSHRC and Sana'a: SCSS.
Constitution Project. 2013. *The Report of the Constitution Project Task Force on Detainee Treatment*. Washington, D.C.: Constitution Project.
Cortwright, David, Rachel Fairhurst and Kristen Wall (eds.). 2015. *Drones and the Future of Armed Conflict: Ethical, Legal, and Strategic Implications*. Chicago: University of Chicago Press.
Danner, Mark. 2004. *Torture and Truth: America, Abu Ghraib, and the War on Terror*. New York: New York Review Books.
Davis, Raymond with Storms Reback. 2017. *The Contractor*. Dallas: BenBella Books, Inc.
Denbeaux, Mark P. 2007. *The 14 Myths of Guantánamo*. Newark, NJ: Seton Hall Law School Center for Policy and Research.
2009. *Death in Camp Delta*. Newark, NJ: Seton Hall Law School Center for Policy and Research.
Denbeaux, Mark P. and Joshua Denbeaux. 2006a. *No-Hearing Hearings: CSRT: The Modern Habeas Corpus?* Newark, NJ: Seton Hall Law School Center for Policy and Research.
2006b. *Report on Guantánamo Detainees*. Newark, NJ: Seton Hall Law School Center for Policy and Research.
2006c. *The Guantánamo Detainees during Detention*. Newark, NJ: Seton Hall Law School Center for Policy and Research.
2006d. *Second Report on the Guantánamo Detainees*. Newark, NJ: Seton Hall Law School Center for Policy and Research.
2006e. *June 10th Suicides at Guantánamo*. Newark, NJ: Seton Hall Law School Center for Policy and Research.
Denbeaux, Mark P. and Jonathan Hafetz (eds.). 2009. *The Guantánamo Lawyers: Inside a Prison Outside the Law*. NY: NYU Press.
Denbeaux, Mark P., Joshua Denbeaux and R. David Gratz. 2007. *The Meaning of "Battlefield."* Newark, NJ: Seton Hall Law School Center for Policy and Research.
2008a. *Profile of Released Guantánamo Detainees: The Government's Story Then and Now*. Newark, NJ: Seton Hall Law School Center for Policy and Research.
2008b. *Released Guantánamo Detainees and the Department of Defense: Propaganda by the Numbers*. Newark, NJ: Seton Hall Law School Center for Policy and Research.

2009. *Revisionist Recidivism: An Analysis of the Government's Representations of Alleged "Recidivism" of the Guantánamo Detainees*. Newark, NJ: Seton Hall Law School Center for Policy and Research.

Denbeaux, Mark P. et al. 2010. *Drug Abuse: An Exploration of the Government's Use of Mefloquine at Guantánamo*. Newark, NJ: Seton Hall Law School Center for Policy and Research.

2015. *Guantanamo: America's Battle Lab*. Newark, NJ: Seton Hall Law School Center for Policy and Research.

Dickinson, Laura. 2011. *Outsourcing War and Peace: Preserving Public Values in a World of Privatized Foreign Affairs*. New Haven: Yale University Press.

Dorison, Samuel H. 2011. *Counting the Days: Factors Influencing Length of Detention at Guantánamo Bay*. B.A. dissertation, Woodrow Wilson School of Public and International Affairs, Princeton University.

ECCHR (European Center for Constitutional and Human Rights). 2009. *CIA "Extraordinary Rendition": Flights, Torture and Accountability – A European Approach* (2nd edn.). Berlin: ECCHR.

Edmonds, Bill Russell. 2015. *God Is Not Here: A Soldier's Struggle with Torture, Trauma, and the Moral Injuries of War*. New York: Pegasus Books.

Elshtain, Jean Bethke. 2004. "Reflections on the Problem of 'Dirty Hands'," in Sanford Levinson (ed.), *Torture: A Collection*. New York: Oxford University Press.

Epstein, Edward J. 2016. *How America Lost Its Secrets: Edward Snowden, the Man and the Theft*. New York: Knopf.

Evangelista, Matthew and Henry Shue. 2014. *The American Way of Bombing: Changing Ethical and Legal Norms, from Flying Fortresses to Drones*. Ithaca, NY: Cornell University Press.

Fair, Eric. 2016. *Consequence: A Memoir*. New York: Henry Holt.

Fallon, Mark. 2017. *Unjustifiable Means*. New York: Reagan Arts.

Farah, Omar. 2016. "Nourishing Resistance: Tariq Ba Odah's Eight-Year Hunger Strike at Guantánamo Bay," in Hafetz, *Obama's Guantánamo*.

Felter, Joseph and Jarret Brachman. 2007a. *An Assessment of 516 Combatant Status Review Tribunal (CSRT) Unclassified Summaries*. West Point, NY: Combatting Terrorism Center.

2007b. *A Response to the Seton Hall Study*. West Point, NY: Combatting Terrorism Center.

Ferguson, Niall. 2012. *The War of the World: History's Age of Hatred*. New York: Penguin.

Fick, Nathaniel. 2005. *One Bullet Away: The Making of a Marine Officer*. New York: Mariner.

Finan, Christopher M. 2007. *From the Palmer Raids to the Patriot Act: A History of the Fight for Free Speech in America*. Boston, MA: Beacon Press.

Finkelstein, Claire, Jens David Ohlin and Andrew Altman. 2012. *Targeted Killings: Law and Morality in an Asymmetrical World.* New York: Oxford University Press.

Fisk, Kerstin and Jennifer M. Ramos. 2016. *Preventive Force: Drones, Targeted Killing, and the Transformation of Contemporary Warfare.* New York: New York University Press.

Fletcher, Laurel E. and Eric Stover. 2008. *Guantánamo and its Aftermath.* Berkeley: University of California, Berkeley Human Rights Center and International Human Rights Law Clinic.

2009. *The Guantánamo Effect: Exposing the Consequences of U.S. Detention and Interrogation Practices.* Berkeley: University of California Press.

Flynn, Michael and Fabiola Fernandez Salek (eds.). 2012. *Screening Torture: Media Representations of State Terror and Political Domination.* New York: Columbia University Press.

Fried, Charles and Gregory Fried. 2010. *Because It Is Wrong: Torture, Privacy, and Presidential Power in the Age of Terror.* New York: W. W. Norton & Co.

Gaston, E. L. and Rebecca Wright. 2009. *Losing the People: The Costs and Consequences of Civilian Suffering in Afghanistan.* Washington, D.C.: Campaign for Innocent Victims in Conflict.

Ginbar, Yuval. 2008. *Why Not Torture Terrorists? Moral, Practical and Legal Aspects of the "Ticking Bomb" Justification for Torture.* New York: Oxford University Press.

Goldsmith, Frank. 2016. "The 'Taliban Five' and the Prisoner Exchange," in Hafetz, *Obama's Guantánamo.*

Goldsmith, Jack. 2012. *Power and Constraint: The Accountable Presidency After 9/11.* New York: W. W. Norton & Co.

Gopal, Amand. 2014. *No Good Men among the Living: America, the Taliban, and the War through Afghan Eyes.* New York: Metropolitan Books.

Gordon, Michael R. and Bernard E. Trainor. 2006. *Cobra II: The Inside Story of the Invasion and Occupation of Iraq.* New York: Vintage.

Gordon, Rebecca. 2014. *Mainstreaming Torture: Ethical Approaches in the Post-9/11 United States.* New York: Oxford University Press.

Gotein, Elizabeth. 2016. *The New Era of Secret Law.* New York: Brennan Center.

Gourevitch, Philip and Errol Morris. 2008. *Standard Operating Procedure.* New York: Penguin Press.

Graham, Bradley. 2009. *By His Own Rules: The Ambitions, Successes, and Ultimate Failures of Donald Rumsfeld.* New York: PublicAffairs.

Granger, Montgomery J. 2010. *Saving Grace at Guantánamo Bay: A Memoir of a Citizen Warrior.* Houston: Strategic Book Publishing & Rights Agency.

Greenberg, Karen J. (ed.). 2006. *The Torture Debate in America.* New York: Cambridge University Press.

2010. *The Least Worst Place: Guantanamo's First 100 Days*. New York: Oxford University Press.

Greenberg, Karen J. and Joshua L. Dratel. 2005. *The Torture Papers: The Road to Abu Ghraib*. New York: Cambridge University Press.

Greenwald, Glenn. 2014. *No Place to Hide: Edward Snowden, the NSA, and the U.S. Surveillance State*. New York: Metropolitan Books.

Grey, Stephen. 2007. *Ghost Plane: The True Story of the CIA Rendition and Torture Program*. New York: St. Martin's Griffin.

Gronke, Paul and Darius Rejali. 2010. "U.S. Public Opinion on Torture, 2001–2009," 43 *PS* 437.

Gross, Michael L. 2009. *Moral Dilemmas of Modern War: Torture, Assassination and Blackmail in an Age of Asymmetric Conflict*. New York: Cambridge University Press.

Gurule, Jimmy. 2013. *Legitimate Target: A Criteria-Based Approach to Targeted Killing*. New York: Oxford University Press.

Gusterson, Hugh. 2016. *Drone: Remote Control Warfare*. Cambridge, MA: MIT Press.

Hafetz, Jonathan (ed.). 2016. *Obama's Guantánamo: Stories from an Enduring Prison*. New York: New York University Press.

Harbury, Jennifer. 2005. *Truth, Torture and the American Way: The History and Consequences of U.S. Involvement in Torture*. Boston, MA: Beacon Press.

Harding, Luke. 2014. *The Snowden Files: The Inside Story of the World's Most Wanted Man*. New York: Vintage.

Harlow, Bill (ed.). 2015. *Rebuttal: The CIA Responds to the Senate Intelligence Committee's Study of Its Detention and Interrogation Program*. Annapolis: Naval Institute Press.

Harris, Shane. 2010. *The Watchers: The Rise of America's Surveillance State*. New York: Penguin.

Hastings, Michael. 2012. *The Operators: The Wild and Terrifying Inside Story of America's War in Afghanistan*. New York: Blue Rider Press.

Hayden, Michael V. 2016. *Playing to the Edge: American Intelligence in the Age of Terror*. New York: Penguin Press.

Hersh, Seymour M. 2004. *Chain of Command: The Road from 9/11 to Abu Ghraib*. New York: HarperCollins.

2016. *The Killing of Osama bin Laden*. New York: Verso Books.

Hertsgaard, Mark. 2016. *Bravehearts: Whistle-Blowing in the Age of Snowden*. New York: Skyhorse Publishing.

Hickman, Joseph. 2015. *Murder at Camp Delta: A Staff Sergeant's Pursuit of the Truth about Guantánamo Bay*. New York: Simon & Schuster.

Hicks, David. 2010. *Guantánamo: My Journey*. North Sydney: Random House Australia.

Horton, Scott. 2015. *Lords of Secrecy: The National Security State and America's Stealth Warfare*. New York: Nation Books.

HRW (Human Rights Watch). 2004. *"Enduring Freedom": Abuses by U.S. Forces in Afghanistan*. New York: HRW.

2005. *Leadership Failure: Firsthand Accounts of Torture of Iraqi Detainees by the U.S. Army's 82nd Airborne Division*. New York: HRW.

2008. *"Troops in Contact": Airstrikes and Civilian Deaths in Afghanistan*. New York: HRW.

2011. *Getting Away with Torture: The Bush Administration and Mistreatment of Detainees*. New York: HRW.

2013. *"Between a Drone and al-Qaeda": The Civilian Cost of US Targeted Killing in Yemen* (October). New York: HRW.

2014. *A Wedding That Became a Funeral: US Drone Attack on Marriage Procession in Yemen* (February). New York: HRW.

Intelligence Science Board. 2006. *Educing Information: Interrogation: Science and Art. Foundations for the Future*. Washington, D.C.: National Defense Intelligence College.

International Human Rights and Conflict Resolution Clinic (Stanford Law School) and Global Justice Clinic (NYU Law School). 2012. *Living under Drones: Death, Injury, and Trauma to Civilians from US Drone Practices in Pakistan*. Stanford: IHRCR and NY: GJC.

Jaffer, Jameel and Amrit Singh. 2007. *Administration of Torture: A Documentary Record from Washington to Abu Ghraib and Beyond*. New York: Columbia University Press.

Jenks, Chris and Eric Talbot Jensen. 2010. "All Human Rights Are Equal, but Some Are More Equal Than Others: The Extraordinary Rendition of a Terror Suspect in Italy, the NATO SOFA, and Human Rights," 1 *Harvard National Security Journal* 171.

Johns, Fleur. 2013. *Non-Legality in International Law: Unruly Law*. New York: Cambridge University Press.

Johnsen, Gregory D. 2013. *The Last Refuge: Yemen, Al-Qaeda, and America's War in Arabia*. New York: W. W. Norton.

Johnson, Douglas A., Alberto Mora and Averell Schmidt. 2016. "The Strategic Costs of Torture: How 'Enhanced Interrogation' Hurt America," 95 *Foreign Affairs* 121.

Kaag, John and Sarah Kreps. 2014. *Drone Warfare*. Hoboken, NJ: John Wiley & Sons.

Karpinski, Janis with Steven Strasser. 2005. *One Woman's Army: The Commanding General of Abu Ghraib Tells Her Story*. New York: Hyperion.

Kelly, Tobias. 2011. *This Side of Silence: Human Rights, Torture, and the Recognition of Cruelty*. Philadelphia: University of Pennsylvania Press.

Khan, Mahvish Rukhsana. 2008. *My Guantánamo Diary: The Detainees and the Stories They Told Me*. New York: Public Affairs.

Kiriakou, John with Michael Ruby. 2012. *The Reluctant Spy: My Secret Life in the CIA's War on Terror*. New York: Skyhorse Publishing.

Klaidman, Daniel. 2012. *Kill or Capture: The War on Terror and the Soul of the Obama Presidency*. Boston, MA: Houghton-Mifflin Harcourt.

Krakauer, Jon. 2009. *Where Men Win Glory: The Odyssey of Pat Tilman*. New York: Doubleday.

Kreps, Sarah E. 2016. *Drones: What Everyone Needs to Know*. New York: Oxford University Press.

Kurnaz, Murat with Helmut Kuhn. 2008. *Five Years of My Life: An Innocent Man in Guantánamo* (trans. Jefferson Chase). New York: Palgrave Macmillan.

Lagouranis, Tony and Allen Mikaelian. 2007. *Fear Up Harsh: An Army Interrogator's Dark Journey through Iraq*. New York: New American Library.

Lokaneeta, Jinee. 2011. *Transnational Torture: Law, Violence, and State Power in the United States and India*. New York: New York University Press.

Luban, David. 2014. *Torture, Power, and Law*. New York: Cambridge University Press.

McChrystal, Stanley. 2013. *My Share of the Task: A Memoir*. New York: Penguin.

McKelvey, Tara. 2007. *Monstering: Inside America's Policy of Secret Interrogations and Torture in the Terror War*. New York: Carroll & Graf Publ.

Mackey, Chris and Greg Miller. 2004. *The Interrogators: Task Force 500 and America's Secret War against al Qaeda*. New York: Back Bay Books.

Margulies, Joseph. 2009. *Guantánamo and the Abuse of Presidential Power*. New York: Simon & Schuster.

Matthews, Richard. 2008. *The Absolute Violation: Why Torture Must Be Prohibited*. Montreal: McGill-Queen's University Press.

Mayer, Jane. 2008. *The Dark Side: The Inside Story of How the War on Terror Turned into a War on American Ideals*. New York: Random House.

Mazzetti. Mark. 2013. *The Way of the Knife: The CIA, a Secret Army, and a War at the Ends of the Earth*. New York: Penguin Press.

Meeropol, Rachel (ed.). 2005. *America's Disappeared: Secret Imprisonment, Detainees and the "War on Terror."* New York: Seven Stories Press.

Miller, Russell A. (ed.). 2016. *Privacy and Power: A Transatlantic Dialogue in the Shadow of the NSA-Affair*. New York: Cambridge University Press.

Mitchell, James E. and Bill Harlow. 2016. *Enhanced Interrogation: Inside the Minds and Motives of the Islamic Terrorists Trying to Destroy America*. New York: Crown.

Mitchell, W. J. T. 2011. *Cloning Terror: The War of Images, 9/11 to the Present*. Chicago: University of Chicago Press.

Olimpio, Guido. 2005. *Operazione Hotel California*. Milan: LaFeltrinelli.

O'Mara, Shane. 2015. *Why Torture Doesn't Work: The Neuroscience of Interrogation*. Cambridge, MA: Harvard University Press.

Open Society Institute (OSI) and The Liaison Office. 2010. *Strangers at the Door: Night Raids by International Forces Lose Hearts and Minds of Afghans* (February 23). New York: OSI.

2011. *The Cost of Kill/Capture: Impact of the Night Raid Surge on Afghan Civilians* (September 19). New York: OSI.
Open Society Justice Institute (OSJI). 2015. *Death by Drone: Civilian Harm Caused by U.S. Targeted Killings in Yemen*. New York: OSJI.
Otterman, Michael. 2007. *American Torture: From the Cold War to Abu Ghraib and Beyond*. Melbourne: Melbourne University Press.
Pallitto, Robert M. (ed.). 2011. *Torture and State Violence in the United States*. Baltimore: Johns Hopkins University Press.
Panetta, Leon. 2014. *Worthy Fights: A Memoir of Leadership in War and Peace*. New York: Penguin.
Parry, John T. 2010. *Understanding Torture: Law, Violence, and Political Identity*. Ann Arbor: University of Michigan Press.
PCLOB (Privacy and Civil Liberties Oversight Board). 2014a. *Report on the Telephone Records Program Conducted under Section 215 of the USA Patriot Act and on the Operations of the Foreign Intelligence Surveillance Court*. Washington, D.C.: PCLOB.
2014b. *Report on the Surveillance Program Operated Pursuant to Section 702 of the Foreign Intelligence Surveillance Act*. Washington, D.C.: PCLOB.
Perrow, Charles. 1999. *Normal Accidents: Living with High Risk Technologies*. Princeton: Princeton University Press.
Powell, H. Jefferson. 2016. *Targeting Americans: The Constitutionality of the US Drone War*. New York: Oxford University Press.
Prabhat, Devyani. 2016. *Unleashing the Force of Law: Legal Mobilization, National Security, and Basic Freedoms*. London: Palgrave.
Pradhan, Alka. 2016. "First, Do No Harm," in Hafetz, *Obama's Guantánamo*.
President's Commission on Care for America's Returning Wounded Warriors. 2007. *Report: Serve, Support, Simplify*. Washington, D.C.: Government Printing Office.
President's Review Group on Intelligence and Communications Technologies. 2013. *Liberty and Security in a Changing World*. Washington, D.C.: PRG on ICT.
Rejali, Darius. 2007. *Torture and Democracy*. Princeton: Princeton University Press.
Rieckhoff, Paul. 2006. *Chasing Ghosts: Failures and Facades in Iraq: A Soldier's Perspective*. New York: NAL Caliber.
Rizzo, John. 2014. *Company Man: Thirty Years of Controversy and Crisis in the CIA*. New York: Simon & Schuster.
Rodriguez, Jose, Jr. with Bill Harlow. 2012. *Hard Measures: How Aggressive C.I.A. Actions after 9/11 Saved American Lives*. New York: Threshold Editions.
Rose, David. 2004. *Guantánamo: The War on Human Rights*. New York: New Press.
Rumsfeld, Donald. 2011. *Known and Unknown: A Memoir*. New York: Sentinel.

Saar, Eric and Viveca Novak. 2005. *Inside the Wire: A Military Intelligence Soldier's Eyewitness Account of Life at Guantánamo*. New York: Penguin Press.
Sales, Leigh. 2007. *Detainee 002: The Case of David Hicks*. Melbourne: Melbourne University Press.
Sanchez, Ricardo S. and Donald T. Phillips. 2008. *Wiser in Battle: A Soldier's Story*. New York: HarperCollins.
Sands, Phillippe. 2005. *Lawless World: America and the Making and Breaking of Global Rules from F.D.R.'s Atlantic Charter to George W. Bush's Illegal War*. New York: Viking.
2008. *Torture Team: Rumsfeld's Memo and the Betrayal of American Values*. New York: Palgrave Macmillan.
Santayana, George. 1905. *The Life of Reason or the Phases of Human Progress*. New York: C. Scribner's Sons.
SASC (Senate Armed Services Committee). 2008. *Inquiry into the Treatment of Detainees in U.S. Custody*. Washington, D.C.: SASC.
Scahill, Jeremy. 2007. *Blackwater: The Rise of the World's Most Powerful Mercenary Army*. New York: Nation Books.
Scahill, Jeremy and the Staff of The Intercept. 2016. *The Assassination Complex: Inside the Government's Secret Drone Warfare Program*. New York: Simon & Schuster.
Schmidt, Mark and John Furlow. 2005. *CDR USSouthcom Directed AR 15–6 Investigation into Detainee-Abuse Allegations at Guantánamo Bay, Cuba*. Miami: US Southcom Command.
Schneier, Bruce. 2015. *Data and Goliath: The Hidden Battles to Collect Your Data and Control Your World*. New York: W. W. Norton.
Sentilles, Sarah. 2008. "'He Looked Like Jesus Christ': Crucifixion, Torture, and the Limits of Empathy as a Response to the Photographs from Abu Ghraib," 36(1) *Harvard Divinity Bulletin*.
Shane, Scott. 2015. *Objective Troy: A Terrorist, a President, and the Rise of the Drones*. New York: Tim Duggan Books.
Sharrock, Justine. 2010. *Tortured: When Good Soldiers Do Bad Things*. Hoboken, NJ: John Wiley & Sons.
Shipler, David K. 2012. *Rights at Risk: The Limits of Liberty in Modern America*. New York: Alfred A. Knopf.
Slahi, Mohamedou Ould. 2015. *Guantánamo Diary* (Larry Siems ed.). New York: Little Brown.
Smith, Brendan and Jeremy Brecher (eds.). 2005. *In the Name of Democracy: American War Crimes in Iraq and Beyond*. New York: Metropolitan/Holt.
Solis, Gary D. 2010. *The Law of Armed Conflict. International Humanitarian Law in War*. New York: Cambridge University Press.
Solove, Daniel J. 2011. *Nothing to Hide: The False Tradeoff between Privacy and Security*. New Haven: Yale University Press.

Soufan, Ali with Daniel Freedman. 2011. *The Black Banners: The Inside Story of 9/11 and the War Against al-Qaeda*. New York: W. W. Norton.

Springer, Paul J. 2010. *America's Captives: Treatment of POWs from the Revolutionary War to the War on Terror*. Lawrence: University Press of Kansas.

SSCI (Senate Select Committee on Intelligence). 2014. *Committee Study of the Central Intelligence Agency's Detention and Interrogation Program*. Washington, D.C.: SSCI.

Stafford Smith, Clive. 2007. *Eight O'Clock Ferry to the Windward Side: Seeking Justice in Guantánamo Bay*. New York: Nation Books.

Stimson Center. 2014. *Recommendations and Report of the Stimson Task Force on US Drone Policy*. Washington, D.C.: Stimson Center.

2016. *Grading Progress on U.S. Drone Policy: Report Card on the Recommendations of the Stimson Task Force on U.S. Drone Policy*. Washington, D.C.: Stimson Center.

Storm, Morton, with Paul Cruickshank and Tim Lister. 2014. *Agent Storm: My Life Inside Al-Qaeda and the CIA*. New York: Atlantic Monthly Press.

Strauss, David Levi, Charles Stein, Barbara Ehrenreich and John Gray. 2004. *Abu Ghraib: The Politics of Torture*. Berkeley: North Atlantic Books.

Strawser, Bradley Jay (ed.). 2013. *Killing by Remote Control: The Ethics of an Unmanned Military*. New York: Oxford University Press.

Stritzke, Werner G. K., Stephan Lewandowsky, David Denemark, Joseph Clare and Frank Morgan (eds.). 2009. *Terrorism and Torture: An Interdisciplinary Perspective*. New York: Cambridge University Press.

Suskind, Ron. 2006. *The One Percent Solution: Deep Inside America's Pursuit of Its Enemies Since 9/11*. New York: Simon & Schuster.

Tillman, Mary with Narda Zacchino. 2008. *Boots on the Ground by Dusk: My Tribute to Pat Tillman*. Athens: Modern Times.

Tirman, John. 2012. *The Deaths of Others: The Fate of Civilians in America's Wars*. New York: Oxford University Press.

Toh, Amos, Faiza Patel and Elizabeth Gotein. 2016. *Overseas Surveillance in an Interconnected World*. New York: Brennan Center for Justice.

Umansky, Eric. 2006. "Failures of Imagination," *Columbia Journalism Review* (September 5).

2014. "How American Journalists Covered Torture after 9/11," *Columbia Journalism Review* (August 8).

Warrick, Joby. 2012. *Triple Agent: The al-Qaeda Mole Who Infiltrated the CIA*. New York: Vintage Books.

Weiner, Tim. 2007. *Legacy of Ashes: The History of the CIA*. New York: Random House.

2012. *Enemies: A History of the FBI*. New York: Random House.

Willett, Sabin. 2016. "Twelve Years After," in Hafetz, *Obama's Guantánamo*.

Williams, Brian Glyn. 2013. *Predators: The C.I.A.'s Drone War on Al Qaeda.* Washington, D.C.: Potomac Books.
Williams, Kayla with Michael E. Staub. 2005. *Love My Rifle More Than You: Young and Female in the US Army*. New York: Norton.
Winkler, Gary S. 2009. *Tortured: Lynndie England, Abu Ghraib, and the Photographs that Shocked the World.* Keyser, WV: Bad Apple Books.
Wittes, Benjamin and Gabriella Blum. 2015. *The Future of Violence: Robots and Germans, Hackers and Drones: Confronting a New Age of Threat.* New York: Basic Books.
Woods, Chris. 2015. *Sudden Justice: America's Secret Drone Wars*. New York: Oxford University Press.
Woodward, Bob. 2010. *Obama's Wars: The Inside Story*. New York: Simon & Schuster.
Worthington, Andy. 2007. *The Guantanamo Files: The Stories of the 759 Detainees in America's Illegal Prison*. London: Pluto Press.
Wright, Evan. 2004. *Generation Kill: Devil Dogs, Iceman, Captain America, and the New Face of American War*. New York: Berkley Caliber.
Wypijewski, JoAnn. 2006. "Judgment Days: Lessons from the Abu Ghraib Courts-Martial," *Harpers* (February).
Yee, James. 2005. *For God and Country: Faith and Patriotism under Fire.* New York: PublicAffairs.
Zegart, Amy B. 2011. *Eyes on Spies: Congress and the United States Intelligence Community*. Stanford: Hoover Institution Press.
Zenko, Micah. 2013. *Reforming U.S. Drone Strike Policies* (Special Report 65). New York: Council on Foreign Relations.
Zimbardo, Philip. 2008. *The Lucifer Effect: Understanding How Good People Turn Evil.* New York: Random House.

INDEX

CAMBRIDGE STUDIES IN LAW AND SOCIETY

Books in the Series

Diseases of the Will: Alcohol and the Dilemmas of Freedom
Mariana Valverde

The Politics of Truth and Reconciliation in South Africa: Legitimizing the Post-Apartheid State
Richard A. Wilson

Modernism and the Grounds of Law
Peter Fitzpatrick

Unemployment and Government: Genealogies of the Social
William Walters

Autonomy and Ethnicity: Negotiating Competing Claims in Multi-Ethnic States
Yash Ghai

Constituting Democracy: Law, Globalism and South Africa's Political Reconstruction
Heinz Klug

The Ritual of Rights in Japan: Law, Society, and Health Policy
Eric A. Feldman

Governing Morals: A Social History of Moral Regulation
Alan Hunt

The Colonies of Law: Colonialism, Zionism and Law in Early Mandate Palestine
Ronen Shamir

Law and Nature
David Delaney

Social Citizenship and Workfare in the United States and Western Europe: The Paradox of Inclusion
Joel F. Handler

Law, Anthropology, and the Constitution of the Social: Making Persons and Things
Edited by Alain Pottage and Martha Mundy

Judicial Review and Bureaucratic Impact: International and Interdisciplinary Perspectives
Edited by Marc Hertogh and Simon Halliday

Immigrants at the Margins: Law, Race, and Exclusion in Southern Europe
Kitty Calavita

Lawyers and Regulation: The Politics of the Administrative Process
Patrick Schmidt

Law and Globalization from Below: Toward a Cosmopolitan Legality
Edited by Boaventura de Sousa Santos and Cesar A. Rodriguez-Garavito

Public Accountability: Designs, Dilemmas and Experiences
Edited by Michael W. Dowdle

Law, Violence and Sovereignty among West Bank Palestinians
Tobias Kelly

Legal Reform and Administrative Detention Powers in China
Sarah Biddulph

The Practice of Human Rights: Tracking Law between the Global and the Local
Edited by Mark Goodale and Sally Engle Merry

Judges beyond Politics in Democracy and Dictatorship: Lessons from Chile
Lisa Hilbink

Paths to International Justice: Social and Legal Perspectives
Edited by Marie-Bénédicte Dembour and Tobias Kelly

Law and Society in Vietnam: The Transition from Socialism in Comparative Perspective
Mark Sidel

Constitutionalizing Economic Globalization: Investment Rules and Democracy's Promise
David Schneiderman

The New World Trade Organization Knowledge Agreements: 2nd Edition
Christopher Arup

Justice and Reconciliation in Post-Apartheid South Africa
Edited by François du Bois and Antje du Bois-Pedain

Militarization and Violence against Women in Conflict Zones in the Middle East: A Palestinian Case-Study
Nadera Shalhoub-Kevorkian

Child Pornography and Sexual Grooming: Legal and Societal Responses
Suzanne Ost

Darfur and the Crime of Genocide
John Hagan and Wenona Rymond-Richmond

Fictions of Justice: The International Criminal Court and the Challenge of Legal Pluralism in Sub-Saharan Africa
Kamari Maxine Clarke

Conducting Law and Society Research: Reflections on Methods and Practices
Simon Halliday and Patrick Schmidt

Planted Flags: Trees, Land, and Law in Israel/Palestine
Irus Braverman

Culture under Cross-Examination: International Justice and the Special Court for Sierra Leone
Tim Kelsall

Cultures of Legality: Judicialization and Political Activism in Latin America
Javier Couso, Alexandra Huneeus, and Rachel Sieder

Courting Democracy in Bosnia and Herzegovina: The Hague Tribunal's Impact in a Postwar State
Lara J. Nettelfield

The Gacaca Courts, Post-Genocide Justice and Reconciliation in Rwanda: Justice without Lawyers
Phil Clark

Law, Society, and History: Themes in the Legal Sociology and Legal History of Lawrence M. Friedman
Edited by Robert W. Gordon and Morton J. Horwitz

After Abu Ghraib: Exploring Human Rights in America and the Middle East
Shadi Mokhtari

Adjudication in Religious Family Laws: Cultural Accommodation, Legal Pluralism, and Gender Equality in India
Gopika Solanki

Water on Tap: Rights and Regulation in the Transnational Governance of Urban Water Services
Bronwen Morgan

Elements of Moral Cognition: Rawls' Linguistic Analogy and the Cognitive Science of Moral and Legal Judgment
John Mikhail

Mitigation and Aggravation at Sentencing
Edited by Julian V. Roberts

Institutional Inequality and the Mobilization of the Family and Medical Leave Act: Rights on Leave
Catherine R. Albiston

Authoritarian Rule of Law: Legislation, Discourse and Legitimacy in Singapore
Jothie Rajah

Law and Development and the Global Discourses of Legal Transfers
Edited by John Gillespie and Pip Nicholson

Law against the State: Ethnographic Forays into Law's Transformations
Edited by Julia Eckert, Brian Donahoe, Christian Strümpell, and Zerrin Özlem Biner

Transnational Legal Ordering and State Change
Edited by Gregory C. Shaffer

Legal Mobilization under Authoritarianism: The Case of Post-Colonial Hong Kong
Edited by Waikeung Tam

Complementarity in the Line of Fire: The Catalyzing Effect of the International Criminal Court in Uganda and Sudan
Sarah M. H. Nouwen

Political and Legal Transformations of an Indonesian Polity: The Nagari from Colonisation to Decentralisation
Franz von Benda-Beckmann and Keebet von Benda-Beckmann

Pakistan's Experience with Formal Law: An Alien Justice
Osama Siddique

Human Rights under State-Enforced Religious Family Laws in Israel, Egypt, and India
Yüksel Sezgin

Why Prison?
Edited by David Scott

Law's Fragile State: Colonial, Authoritarian, and Humanitarian Legacies in Sudan
Mark Fathi Massoud

Rights for Others: The Slow Home-Coming of Human Rights in the Netherlands
Barbara Oomen

European States and Their Muslim Citizens: The Impact of Institutions on Perceptions and Boundaries
Edited by John R. Bowen, Christophe Bertossi, Jan Willem Duyvendak, and Mona Lena Krook

Environmental Litigation in China: A Study in Political Ambivalence
Rachel E. Stern

Indigeneity and Legal Pluralism in India: Claims, Histories, Meanings
Pooja Parmar

Paper Tiger: Law, Bureaucracy and the Developmental State in Himalayan India
Nayanika Mathur

Religion, Law and Society
Russell Sandberg

The Experiences of Face Veil Wearers in Europe and the Law
Edited by Eva Brems

The Contentious History of the International Bill of Human Rights
Christopher N. J. Roberts

Transnational Legal Orders
Edited by Terence C. Halliday and Gregory Shaffer

Lost in China? Law, Culture and Society in Post-1997 Hong Kong
Carol A. G. Jones

Security Theology, Surveillance and the Politics of Fear
Nadera Shalhoub-Kevorkian

Opposing the Rule of Law: How Myanmar's Courts Make Law and Order
Nick Cheesman

The Ironies of Colonial Governance: Law, Custom and Justice in Colonial India
James Jaffe

The Clinic and the Court: Law, Medicine and Anthropology
Edited by Ian Harper, Tobias Kelly, and Akshay Khanna

A World of Indicators: The Making of Government Knowledge through Quantification
Edited by Richard Rottenburg, Sally Engle Merry, Sung-Joon Park, and Johanna Mugler

Contesting Immigration Policy in Court: Legal Activism and Its Radiating Effects in the United States and France
Leila Kawar

The Quiet Power of Indicators: Measuring Governance, Corruption, and Rule of Law
Edited by Sally Engle Merry, Kevin Davis, and Benedict Kingsbury

Investing in Authoritarian Rule: Punishment and Patronage in Rwanda's Gacaca Courts for Genocide Crimes
Anuradha Chakravarty

Contractual Knowledge: One Hundred Years of Legal Experimentation in Global Markets
Edited by Grégoire Mallard and Jérôme Sgard

Iraq and the Crimes of Aggressive War: The Legal Cynicism of Criminal Militarism
John Hagan, Joshua Kaiser, and Anna Hanson

Culture in the Domains of Law
Edited by René Provost

China and Islam: The Prophet, the Party, and Law
Matthew S. Erie

Diversity in Practice: Race, Gender, and Class in Legal and Professional Careers
Edited by Spencer Headworth and Robert Nelson

A Sociology of Constitutions: Constitutions and State Legitimacy in Historical-Sociological Perspective
Chris Thornhill

A Sociology of Transnational Constitutions: Social Foundations of the Post-National Legal Structure
Chris Thornhill

Shifting Legal Visions: Judicial Change and Human Rights Trials in Latin America
Ezequiel A. González Ocantos

The Demographic Transformations of Citizenship
Heli Askola

Criminal Defense in China: The Politics of Lawyers at Work
Sida Liu and Terence C. Halliday

Contesting Economic and Social Rights in Ireland: Constitution, State and Society, 1848–2016
Thomas Murray

Buried in the Heart: Women, Complex Victimhood and the War in Northern Uganda
Erin Baines

Palaces of Hope: The Anthropology of Global Organizations
Edited by Ronald Niezen and Maria Sapignoli

The Politics of Bureaucratic Corruption in Post-Transitional Eastern Europe
Marina Zaloznaya

Revisiting the Law and Governance of Trafficking, Forced Labor and Modern Slavery
Edited by Prabha Kotiswaran

Incitement on Trial: Prosecuting International Speech Crimes
Richard Ashby Wilson

Criminalizing Children: Welfare and the State in Australia
David McCallum

Global Lawmakers: International Organizations in the Crafting of World Markets
Susan Block-Lieb and Terence C. Halliday

Duties to Care: Dementia, Relationality and Law
Rosie Harding

Insiders, Outsiders, Injuries, and Law: Revisiting "The Oven Bird's Song"
Mary Nell Trautner

Hunting Justice: Displacement, Law, and Activism in the Kalahari
Maria Sapignoli

Injury and Injustice: The Cultural Politics of Harm and Redress
Edited by Anne Bloom, David M. Engel, and Michael McCann

Ruling Before the Law: The Politics of Legal Regimes in China and Indonesia
William Hurst

The Powers of Law: A Comparative Analysis of Sociopolitical Legal Studies
Mauricio García-Villegas

A Sociology of Justice in Russia
Edited by Marina Kurkchiyan and Agnieszka Kubal

Constituting Religion: Islam, Liberal Rights, and the Malaysian State
Tamir Moustafa

The Invention of the Passport: Surveillance, Citizenship and the State, Second Edition
John C. Torpey

Law's Trials: The Performance of Legal Institutions in the US "War on Terror"
Richard L. Abel

Law's Wars: The Fate of the Rule of Law in the US "War on Terror"
Richard L. Abel

Transforming Gender Citizenship: The Irresistible Rise of Gender Quotas in Europe
Eléonore Lépinard and Ruth Rubio-Marín

Muslim Women's Quest for Justice: Gender, Law and Activism in India
Mengia Hong Tschalaer